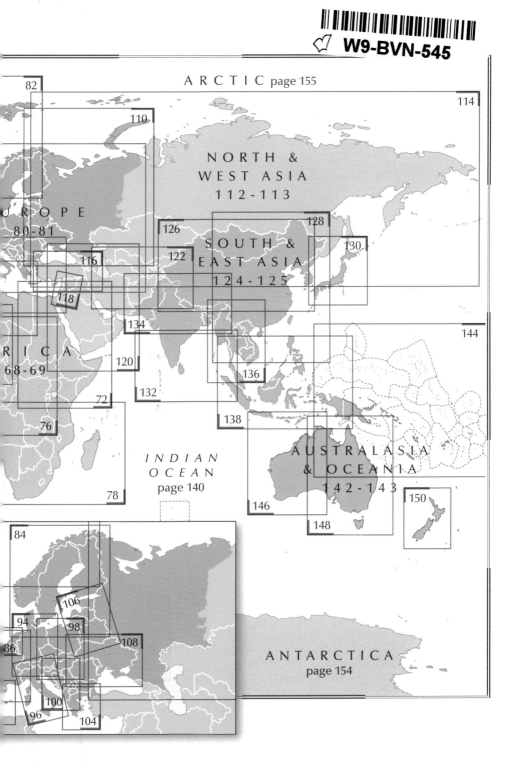

W9-BVN-545

ARCTIC page 155

82

114

110

NORTH &
WEST ASIA
112-113

EUROPE
80-81

126

128

116

122

130

SOUTH &
EAST ASIA
124-125

118

134

144

AFRICA
68-69

120

136

72

132

76

138

AUSTRALASIA
& OCEANIA
142-143

150

INDIAN
OCEAN
page 140

146

78

148

84

106

94

98

108

86

ANTARCTICA
page 154

100

96

104

ESSENTIAL
WORLD
ATLAS

Penguin
Random
House

TENTH EDITION

Senior Cartographic Editor Simon Mumford
Producer (Pre-Production) Andy Hilliard
Production Controller Mary Slater
Jacket Design Development Sophia MTT
Publisher Andrew Mcintyre
Associate Publishing Director Liz Wheeler
Art Director Karen Self
Publishing Director Jonathan Metcalf

FIRST EDITION

Project Cartography and Design Julia Lunn, Julie Turner
Cartographers James Anderson, Roger Bullen, Martin Darlison,
Simon Mumford, John Plumer, Peter Winfield
Design Katy Wall
Index-Gazetteer Natalie Clarkson, Ruth Duxbury,
Margaret Hynes, Margaret Stevenson
Art Direction Chez Picthall
Editorial Direction Andrew Heritage

This American Edition, 2019
First American edition, 1997
Published in the United States by DK Publishing
1450 Broadway, Suite 801, New York, NY 10018

A catalog record for this book is available from the Library of Congress.
ISBN 978-1-4654-8052-1

DK books are available at special discounts when purchased in bulk for
sales promotions, premiums, fund-raising, or educational use. For details, contact:
DK Publishing Special Markets, 1450 Broadway, Suite 801, New York, NY 10018
SpecialSales@dk.com

Printed and bound in Malaysia

A WORLD OF IDEAS:
SEE ALL THERE IS TO KNOW
www.dk.com

Key to map symbols

Physical features

Elevation

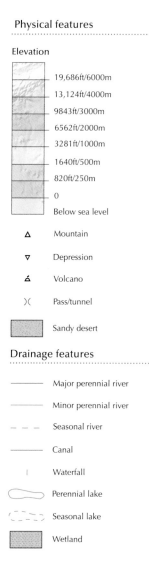

19,686ft/6000m

13,124ft/4000m

9843ft/3000m

6562ft/2000m

3281ft/1000m

1640ft/500m

820ft/250m

0

Below sea level

△ Mountain

▽ Depression

△ Volcano

)(Pass/tunnel

Sandy desert

Drainage features

——— Major perennial river

——— Minor perennial river

– – – Seasonal river

——— Canal

| Waterfall

⬭ Perennial lake

⟨ ⟩ Seasonal lake

Wetland

Ice features

Permanent ice cap/ice shelf

Winter limit of pack ice

Summer limit of pack ice

Borders

▬▬▬ Full international border

▬ ▬ ▬ Disputed de facto border

• • • • • Territorial claim border

✕–✕–✕ Cease-fire line

▬ ▬ ▪ Undefined boundary

——— Internal administrative boundary

Communications

——— Major road

——— Minor road

——— Railroad

✈ International airport

Settlements

⊡ Above 500,000

◉ 100,000 to 500,000

◎ 50,000 to 100,000

○ Below 50,000

● National capital

◉ Internal administrative capital

Miscellaneous features

+ Site of interest

ᨆᨆᨆ Ancient wall

Graticule features

——— Line of latitude/longitude/ Equator

– – – Tropic/Polar circle

25° Degrees of latitude/ longitude

Names

Physical features

Andes

Sahara | Landscape features

Ardennes

Land's End | Headland

Mont Blanc 4,807m | Elevation/volcano/pass

Blue Nile | River/canal/waterfall

Ross Ice Shelf | Ice feature

PACIFIC OCEAN

Sulu Sea | Sea features

Palk Strait

Chile Rise | Undersea feature

Regions

FRANCE | Country

BERMUDA (to UK) | Dependent territory

KANSAS | Administrative region

Dordogne | Cultural region

Settlements

PARIS | Capital city

SAN JUAN | Dependent territory capital city

Chicago

Kettering | Other settlements

Burke

Inset map symbols

Urban area

City

Park

▪ Place of interest

□ Suburb/district

Contents

The World Today

Flags of the World............................6-7
The Political World.........................8-9
The Physical World.......................10-11
Standard Time Zones...................12-13
Geology & Structure....................14-15
World Climate...............................16-17
Ocean Currents...........................18-19
Life Zones.....................................20-21
Population.....................................22-23
Languages.....................................24-25
Religion..26-27
The Global Economy....................28-29
Politics and Conflict.....................30-31

The World's Regions

North & Central America

North & Central America...............34-35
Western Canada & Alaska.............36-37
Eastern Canada............................38-39
USA: The Northeast......................40-41
USA: The Southeast......................42-43
  Bermuda
USA: Central States......................44-45
USA: The West..............................46-47
  Los Angeles & Hawaii

USA: The Southwest.....................48-49
Mexico...50-51
Central America............................52-53
The Caribbean..............................54-55
  Jamaica, St. Lucia, & Barbados

South America

South America...............................56-57
Northern South America...............58-59
Western South America................60-61
  Galápagos Islands
Brazil...62-63
Southern South America...............64-65
The Atlantic Ocean.......................66-67

Africa

Africa...68-69
Northwest Africa...........................70-71
Northeast Africa............................72-73
West Africa....................................74-75
Central Africa................................76-77
  Sao Tome & Principe
Southern Africa.............................78-79

Europe

Europe...80-81
The North Atlantic........................82-83
Scandinavia & Finland..................84-85
The Low Countries........................86-87
The British Isles............................88-89
  London

continued....

Europe continued

France, Andorra, & Monaco................90-91
  Paris, Andorra, & Monaco
Spain & Portugal.............................92-93
  Azores & Gibraltar
Germany & the Alpine States............94-95
  Liechtenstein
Italy..96-97
  San Marino & Vatican City
Central Europe.................................98-99
Southeast Europe.........................100-101
  Bosnia & Herzegovina
The Mediterranean.......................102-103
  Malta & Cyprus
Bulgaria & Greece........................104-105
The Baltic States & Belarus...........106-107
Ukraine, Moldova,
  & Romania.................................108-109
European Russia...........................110-111

North & West Asia

North & West Asia.........................112-113
Russia & Kazakhstan.....................114-115
Turkey & the Caucasus..................116-117
The Near East................................118-119
  West Bank
The Middle East............................120-121
Central Asia..................................122-123

South & East Asia

South & East Asia.........................124-125
Western China & Mongolia............126-127

Eastern China & Korea..................128-129
  Hong Kong
Japan...130-131
  Tokyo & Nansei-Shoto
South India & Sri Lanka................132-133
North India, Pakistan,
  & Bangladesh............................134-135
Mainland Southeast Asia...............136-137
Maritime Southeast Asia................138-139
  Singapore
The Indian Ocean.........................140-141

Australasia & Oceania

Australasia & Oceania....................142-143
The Southwest Pacific....................144-145
Western Australia..........................146-147
Eastern Australia...........................148-149
  Sydney
New Zealand.................................150-151
The Pacific Ocean.........................152-153
Antarctica...154
The Arctic Ocean...............................155

Index– Gazetteer

Overseas Territories
  & Dependencies.........................156-159
Glossary of Geographical
  Terms......................................160-161
Continental Factfiles......................162-163
Geographical Comparisons............164-166
Country Profiles............................167-179
Index-Gazetteer............................180-256

Flags of the World

NORTH & CENTRAL AMERICA

CANADA PAGES 36-39	UNITED STATES OF AMERICA PAGES 40-49	MEXICO PAGES 50-51	BELIZE PAGES 52-53	COSTA RICA PAGES 52-53	EL SALVADOR PAGES 52-53	GUATEMALA PAGES 52-53	HONDURAS PAGES 52-53

SOUTH AMERICA

GRENADA PAGES 54-55	HAITI PAGES 54-55	JAMAICA PAGES 54-55	ST KITTS & NEVIS PAGES 54-55	ST LUCIA PAGES 54-55	ST VINCENT & THE GRENADINES PAGES 54-55	TRINIDAD & TOBAGO PAGES 54-55	COLOMBIA PAGES 58-59

AFRICA

URUGUAY PAGES 64-65	CHILE PAGES 64-65	PARAGUAY PAGES 64-65	ALGERIA PAGES 70-71	LIBYA PAGES 70-71	MOROCCO PAGES 70-71	TUNISIA PAGES 70-71	BURUNDI PAGES 72-73
SUDAN PAGES 72-73	TANZANIA PAGES 72-73	UGANDA PAGES 72-73	BENIN PAGES 74-75	BURKINA FASO PAGES 74-75	CAPE VERDE PAGES 74-75	IVORY COAST (CÔTE D'IVOIRE) PAGES 74-75	THE GAMBIA PAGES 74-75	GHANA PAGES 74-75
SIERRA LEONE PAGES 74-75	TOGO PAGES 74-75	CAMEROON PAGES 76-77	CENTRAL AFRICAN REPUBLIC PAGES 76-77	CHAD PAGES 76-77	CONGO PAGES 76-77	DEM. REP. CONGO PAGES 76-77	EQUATORIAL GUINEA PAGES 76-77
MAURITIUS PAGES 78-79	MOZAMBIQUE PAGES 78-79	NAMIBIA PAGES 78-79	SEYCHELLES PAGES 78-79	SOUTH AFRICA PAGES 78-79	ESWATINI (SWAZILAND) PAGES 78-79	ZAMBIA PAGES 78-79	ZIMBABWE PAGES 78-79
UNITED KINGDOM PAGES 88-89	FRANCE PAGES 90-91	MONACO PAGES 90-91	ANDORRA PAGES 90-91	PORTUGAL PAGES 92-93	SPAIN PAGES 92-93	AUSTRIA PAGES 94-95	GERMANY PAGES 94-95
POLAND PAGES 98-99	SLOVAKIA PAGES 98-99	ALBANIA PAGES 100-101	BOSNIA & HERZEGOVINA PAGES 100-101	CROATIA PAGES 100-101	KOSOVO (disputed) PAGES 100-101	MACEDONIA PAGES 100-101	MONTENEGRO PAGES 100-101

ASIA

MOLDOVA PAGES 108-109	ROMANIA PAGES 108-109	UKRAINE PAGES 108-109	RUSSIA PAGES 110-115	KAZAKHSTAN PAGES 114-115	ARMENIA PAGES 116-117	AZERBAIJAN PAGES 116-117	GEORGIA PAGES 116-117
KUWAIT PAGES 120-121	OMAN PAGES 120-121	QATAR PAGES 120-121	SAUDI ARABIA PAGES 120-121	UNITED ARAB EMIRATES PAGES 120-121	YEMEN PAGES 120-121	AFGHANISTAN PAGES 122-123	KYRGYZSTAN PAGES 122-123
JAPAN PAGES 130-131	INDIA PAGES 132-135	SRI LANKA PAGES 132-133	MALDIVES PAGES 132-133	PAKISTAN PAGES 134-135	BANGLADESH PAGES 134-135	BHUTAN PAGES 134-135	NEPAL PAGES 134-135	CAMBODIA PAGES 136-137

AUSTRALASIA & OCEANIA

PHILIPPINES PAGES 138-139	SINGAPORE PAGES 138-139	FIJI PAGES 144-145	KIRIBATI PAGES 144-145	MARSHALL ISLANDS PAGES 144-145	MICRONESIA PAGES 144-145	NAURU PAGES 144-145	PALAU PAGES 144-145

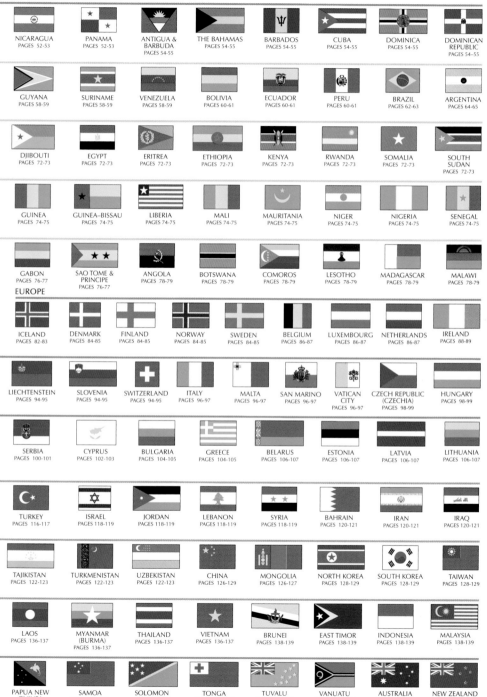

NICARAGUA
PAGES 52-53

PANAMA
PAGES 52-53

ANTIGUA &
BARBUDA
PAGES 54-55

THE BAHAMAS
PAGES 54-55

BARBADOS
PAGES 54-55

CUBA
PAGES 54-55

DOMINICA
PAGES 54-55

DOMINICAN
REPUBLIC
PAGES 54-55

GUYANA
PAGES 58-59

SURINAME
PAGES 58-59

VENEZUELA
PAGES 58-59

BOLIVIA
PAGES 60-61

ECUADOR
PAGES 60-61

PERU
PAGES 60-61

BRAZIL
PAGES 62-63

ARGENTINA
PAGES 64-65

DJIBOUTI
PAGES 72-73

EGYPT
PAGES 72-73

ERITREA
PAGES 72-73

ETHIOPIA
PAGES 72-73

KENYA
PAGES 72-73

RWANDA
PAGES 72-73

SOMALIA
PAGES 72-73

SOUTH
SUDAN
PAGES 72-73

GUINEA
PAGES 74-75

GUINEA–BISSAU
PAGES 74-75

LIBERIA
PAGES 74-75

MALI
PAGES 74-75

MAURITANIA
PAGES 74-75

NIGER
PAGES 74-75

NIGERIA
PAGES 74-75

SENEGAL
PAGES 74-75

GABON
PAGES 76-77

SAO TOME &
PRINCIPE
PAGES 76-77

ANGOLA
PAGES 78-79

BOTSWANA
PAGES 78-79

COMOROS
PAGES 78-79

LESOTHO
PAGES 78-79

MADAGASCAR
PAGES 78-79

MALAWI
PAGES 78-79

EUROPE

ICELAND
PAGES 82-83

DENMARK
PAGES 84-85

FINLAND
PAGES 84-85

NORWAY
PAGES 84-85

SWEDEN
PAGES 84-85

BELGIUM
PAGES 86-87

LUXEMBOURG
PAGES 86-87

NETHERLANDS
PAGES 86-87

IRELAND
PAGES 88-89

LIECHTENSTEIN
PAGES 94-95

SLOVENIA
PAGES 94-95

SWITZERLAND
PAGES 94-95

ITALY
PAGES 96-97

MALTA
PAGES 96-97

SAN MARINO
PAGES 96-97

VATICAN
CITY
PAGES 96-97

CZECH REPUBLIC
(CZECHIA)
PAGES 98-99

HUNGARY
PAGES 98-99

SERBIA
PAGES 100-101

CYPRUS
PAGES 102-103

BULGARIA
PAGES 104-105

GREECE
PAGES 104-105

BELARUS
PAGES 106-107

ESTONIA
PAGES 106-107

LATVIA
PAGES 106-107

LITHUANIA
PAGES 106-107

TURKEY
PAGES 116-117

ISRAEL
PAGES 118-119

JORDAN
PAGES 118-119

LEBANON
PAGES 118-119

SYRIA
PAGES 118-119

BAHRAIN
PAGES 120-121

IRAN
PAGES 120-121

IRAQ
PAGES 120-121

TAJIKISTAN
PAGES 122-123

TURKMENISTAN
PAGES 122-123

UZBEKISTAN
PAGES 122-123

CHINA
PAGES 126-129

MONGOLIA
PAGES 126-127

NORTH KOREA
PAGES 128-129

SOUTH KOREA
PAGES 128-129

TAIWAN
PAGES 128-129

LAOS
PAGES 136-137

MYANMAR
(BURMA)
PAGES 136-137

THAILAND
PAGES 136-137

VIETNAM
PAGES 136-137

BRUNEI
PAGES 138-139

EAST TIMOR
PAGES 138-139

INDONESIA
PAGES 138-139

MALAYSIA
PAGES 138-139

PAPUA NEW
GUINEA
PAGES 144-145

SAMOA
PAGES 144-145

SOLOMON
ISLANDS
PAGES 144-145

TONGA
PAGES 144-145

TUVALU
PAGES 144-145

VANUATU
PAGES 144-145

AUSTRALIA
PAGES 146-149

NEW ZEALAND
PAGES 150-151

The Political World

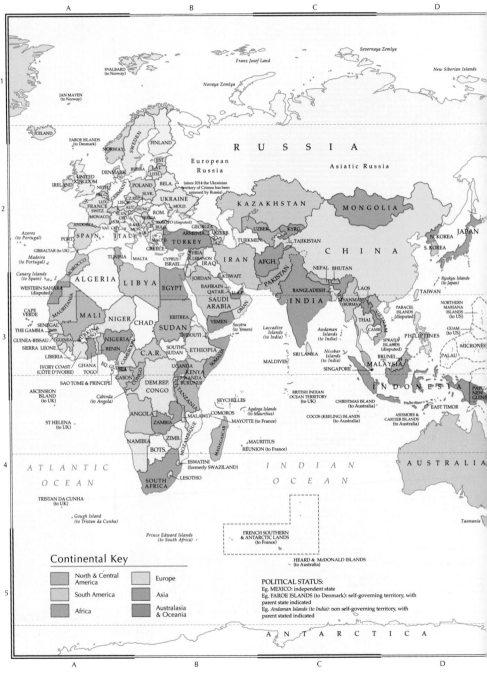

Continental Key

- North & Central America
- South America
- Africa
- Europe
- Asia
- Australasia & Oceania

POLITICAL STATUS:
Eg. MEXICO: independent state
Eg. FAROE ISLANDS (to Denmark): self-governing territory, with parent state indicated
Eg. *Andaman Islands (to India)*: non self-governing territory, with parent stated indicated

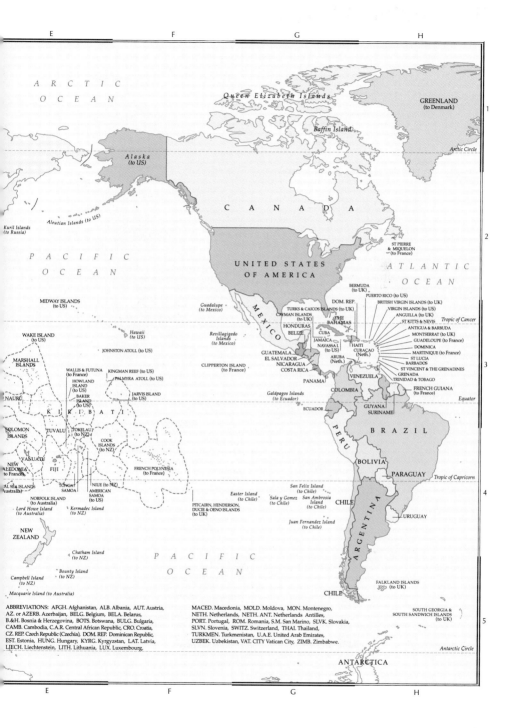

ABBREVIATIONS: AFGH. Afghanistan, ALB. Albania, AUT. Austria, AZ. or AZERB. Azerbaijan, BELG. Belgium, BELA. Belarus, B.&H. Bosnia & Herzegovina, BOTS. Botswana, BULG. Bulgaria, CAMB. Cambodia, C.A.R. Central African Republic, CRO. Croatia, CZ. REP. Czech Republic (Czechia), DOM. REP. Dominican Republic, EST. Estonia, HUNG. Hungary, KYRG. Kyrgyzstan, LAT. Latvia, LIECH. Liechtenstein, LITH. Lithuania, LUX. Luxembourg,

MACED. Macedonia, MOLD. Moldova, MON. Montenegro, NETH. Netherlands, NETH. ANT. Netherlands Antilles, PORT. Portugal, ROM. Romania, S.M. San Marino, SLVK. Slovakia, SLVN. Slovenia, SWITZ. Switzerland, THAI. Thailand, TURKMEN. Turkmenistan, U.A.E. United Arab Emirates, UZBEK. Uzbekistan, VAT. CITY Vatican City, ZIMB. Zimbabwe.

The Physical World

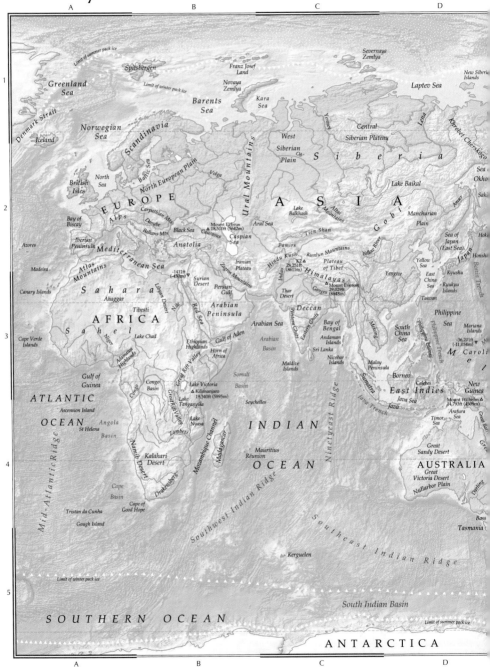

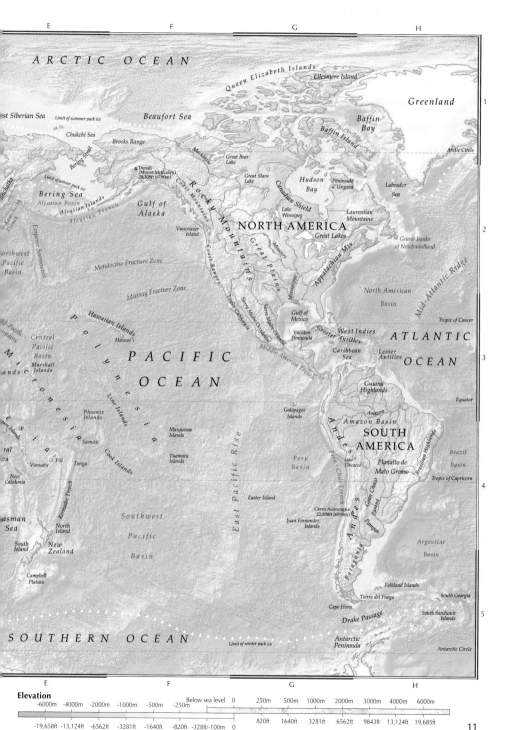

ARCTIC OCEAN

Queen Elizabeth Islands
Ellesmere Island

Greenland

st Siberian Sea
Limit of summer pack ice
Beaufort Sea

Baffin
Bay

Chukchi Sea
Brooks Range
Baffin Island

Arctic Circle

Bering Strait
Mackenzie
Great Bear
Lake

Labrador
Sea

△ Denali
(Mount McKinley)
20,308ft (6190m)
Great Slave
Lake

Hudson
Bay
Péninsule
d'Ungava

Limit of winter pack ice
Bering Sea
Aleutian Basin
Aleutian Islands
Aleutian Trench

Gulf of
Alaska

Vancouver
Island

Canadian Shield

Lake
Winnipeg

Laurentian
Mountains

i-Kamchatka Trench
Emperor Seamounts

orthwest
Pacific
Basin

Mendocino Fracture Zone

NORTH AMERICA

Great Lakes

North American
Basin

Grand Banks
of Newfoundland

Mid-Atlantic Ridge

Murray Fracture Zone

Missouri

Mississippi

Appalachian Mts

Tropic of Cancer

-Pacific
ntains

Central
Pacific
Basin

Marshall
Islands

Hawaiian Islands

Hawai'i

Gulf of
Mexico

Yucatán
Peninsula

Greater
Antilles

West Indies

Caribbean
Sea

Lesser
Antilles

ATLANTIC

OCEAN

Micronesia

nds

PACIFIC

OCEAN

Polynesia

Line Islands

Phoenix
Islands

Samoa

Marquesas
Islands

Galápagos
Islands

Guiana
Highlands

Amazon

Amazon Basin

Equator

Islands
ral
a

Vanuatu
Fiji
Tonga

Cook Islands

Tuamotu
Islands

Easter Island

Peru
Basin

Peru-Chile Trench

Lake
Titicaca

SOUTH
AMERICA

Planalto de
Mato Grosso

Andes

Brazilian Highlands

Brazil
Basin

Tropic of Capricorn

New
Caledonia

East Pacific Rise

Cerro Aconcagua
22,838ft (6959m)

Juan Fernández
Islands

Gran Chaco

Paraná

asman
Sea

North
Island

Southwest

Pacific

Pampas

Argentine
Basin

South
Island

New
Zealand

Basin

Patagonia

Falkland Islands

South Georgia

Campbell
Plateau

Kermadec Trench

Tierra del Fuego

Cape Horn

Drake Passage

South Sandwich
Islands

SOUTHERN OCEAN

Limit of winter pack ice

Antarctic
Peninsula

Antarctic Circle

Elevation

-6000m   -4000m   -2000m   -1000m   -500m   -250m   Below sea level   0   250m   500m   1000m   2000m   3000m   4000m   6000m

-19,658ft -13,124ft -6562ft -3281ft -1640ft -820ft -328ft/-100m   0   820ft   1640ft   3281ft   6562ft   9843ft   13,124ft   19,685ft

11

Standard Time Zones

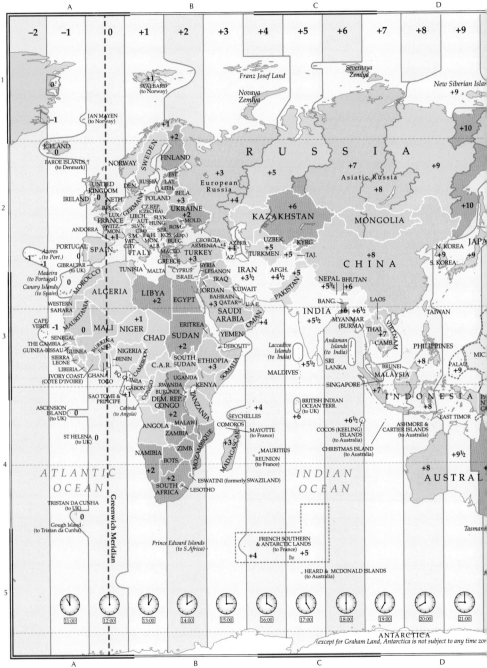

The numbers represented thus; +2/-2, indicate the number of hours each time zone is ahead or behind UCT (Coordinated Universal Time)

The clocks and 24-hour times given at the bottom of the map show time in each time zone when it is 12.00 hours noon UCT

Geology & Structure

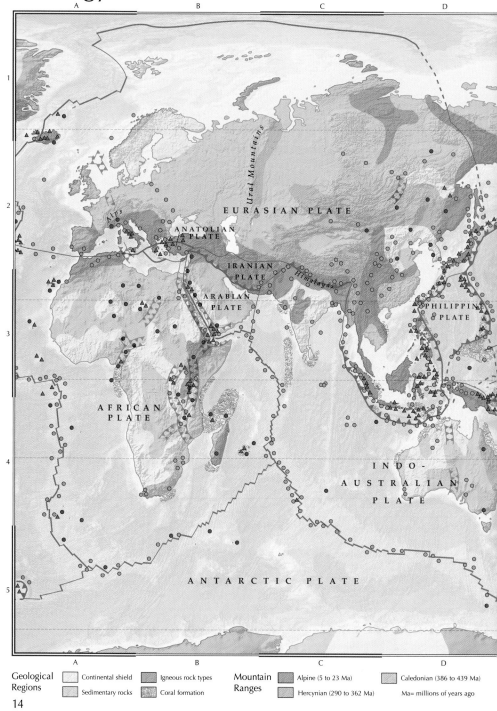

Ural Mountains

EURASIAN PLATE

Alps

ANATOLIAN PLATE

IRANIAN PLATE

Himalayas

ARABIAN PLATE

PHILIPPINE PLATE

AFRICAN PLATE

INDO-AUSTRALIAN PLATE

ANTARCTIC PLATE

Geological Regions			Mountain Ranges		
	Continental shield	Igneous rock types		Alpine (5 to 23 Ma)	Caledonian (386 to 439 Ma)
	Sedimentary rocks	Coral formation		Hercynian (290 to 362 Ma)	Ma= millions of years ago

14

World Climate

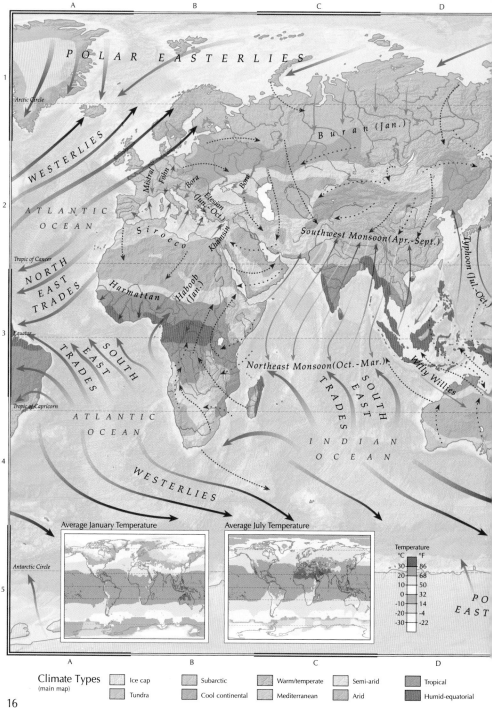

P O L A R   E A S T E R L I E S

Arctic Circle

WESTERLIES

B u r a n (Jan.)

ATLANTIC
OCEAN

Mistral
Föhn
Bora
Etesian
(Jun.-Oct.)
Bora

Southwest Monsoon (Apr.-Sept.)

Typhoon (Jul.-Oct.)

Tropic of Cancer

S i r o c c o

NORTH
EAST
TRADES

Khamsin

Harmattan

Haboob
(Jan.)

Equator

SOUTH
EAST
TRADES

Northeast Monsoon (Oct.-Mar.)

Willy Willies

Tropic of Capricorn

ATLANTIC
OCEAN

SOUTH
EAST
TRADES

I N D I A N
O C E A N

WESTERLIES

Average January Temperature

Average July Temperature

Antarctic Circle

Temperature
°C   °F
30   86
20   68
10   50
0   32
-10   14
-20   -4
-30   -22

P O
EAST

Climate Types
(main map)

Ice cap	Subarctic	Warm/temperate	Semi-arid	Tropical
Tundra	Cool continental	Mediterranean	Arid	Humid-equatorial

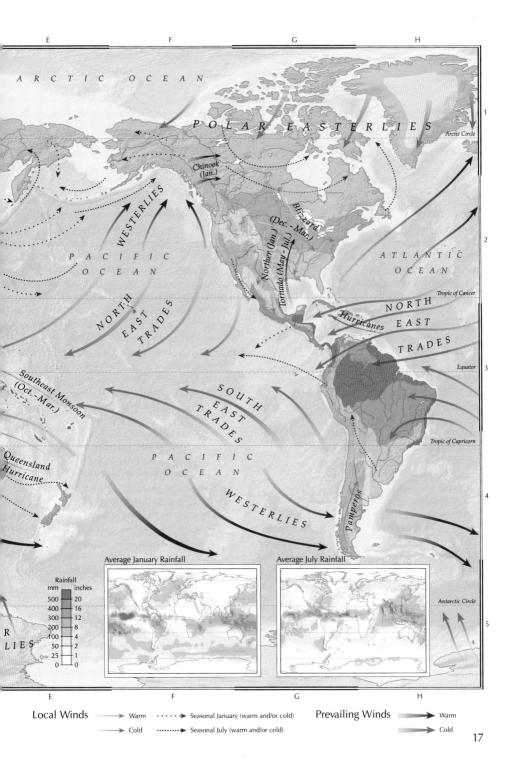

E   F   G   H

A R C T I C   O C E A N

1

Arctic Circle

P O L A R   E A S T E R L I E S

Chinook (Jan.)

Blizzard (Dec. - Mar.)

Norther (Jan.)

Tornado (May - Jul.)

WESTERLIES

P A C I F I C
O C E A N

A T L A N T I C
O C E A N

2

N O R T H   E A S T   T R A D E S

Tropic of Cancer

N O R T H   E A S T   T R A D E S

Hurricanes

Equator

3

Southeast Monsoon (Oct. - Mar.)

S O U T H   E A S T   T R A D E S

Tropic of Capricorn

Queensland Hurricane

P A C I F I C
O C E A N

4

W E S T E R L I E S

Pamperos

Average January Rainfall   Average July Rainfall

Rainfall
mm	inches
500	20
400	16
300	12
200	8
100	4
50	2
25	1
0	0

R
L I E S

Antarctic Circle

5

Local Winds   → Warm   ·····▷ Seasonal January (warm and/or cold)   Prevailing Winds   → Warm

→ Cold   ·······▷ Seasonal July (warm and/or cold)   → Cold

17

Ocean Currents

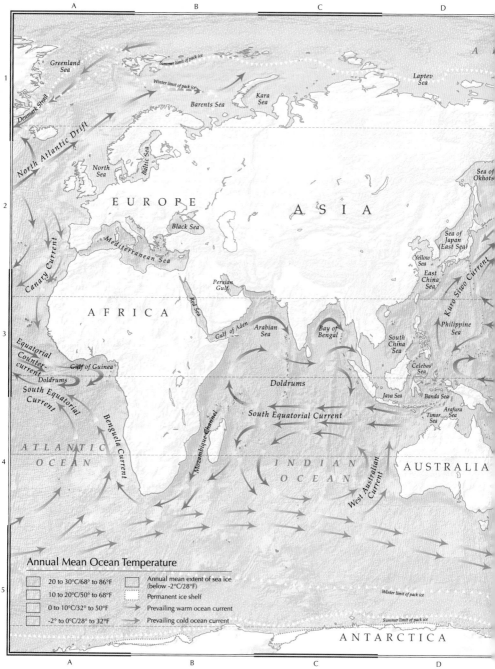

Annual Mean Ocean Temperature

- 20 to 30°C/68° to 86°F
- 10 to 20°C/50° to 68°F
- 0 to 10°C/32° to 50°F
- -2° to 0°C/28° to 32°F

- Annual mean extent of sea ice (below -2°C/28°F)
- Permanent ice shelf
- Prevailing warm ocean current
- Prevailing cold ocean current

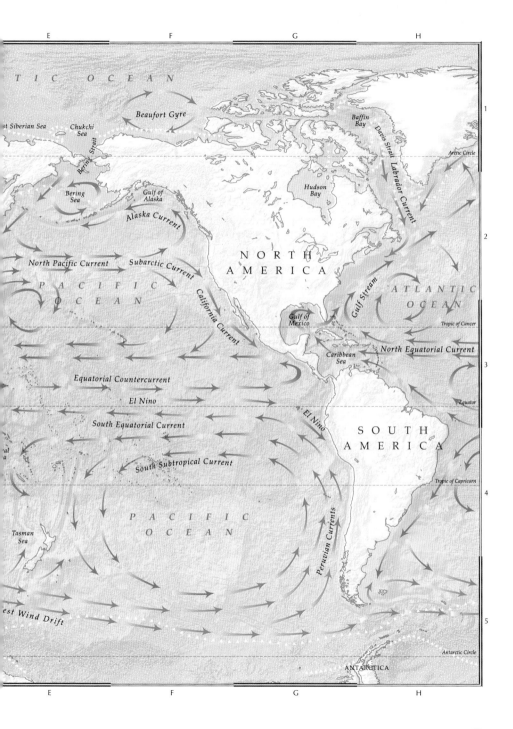

Life Zones

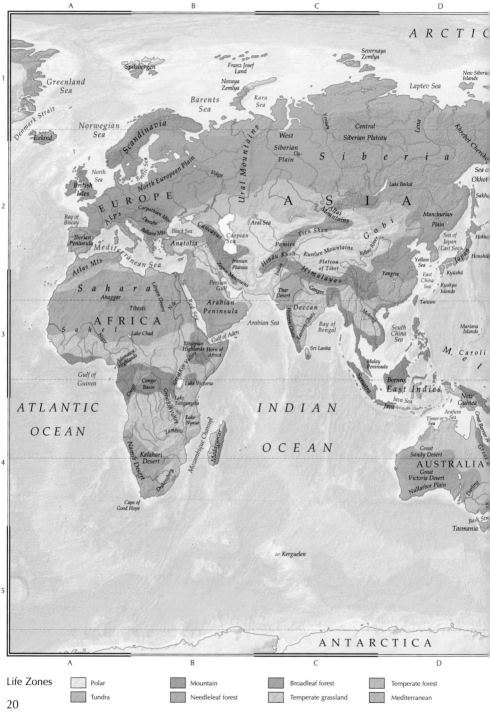

Life Zones

Polar	Mountain	Broadleaf forest	Temperate forest
Tundra	Needleleaf forest	Temperate grassland	Mediterranean

Dry woodland	Tropical rainforest
Tropical grassland	Hot desert
Cold desert	
Wetland	

21

Population

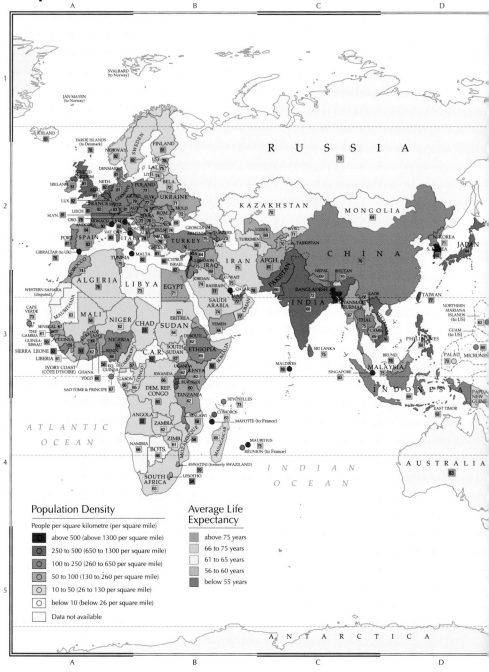

Population Density

People per square kilometre (per square mile)

- above 500 (above 1300 per square mile)
- 250 to 500 (650 to 1300 per square mile)
- 100 to 250 (260 to 650 per square mile)
- 50 to 100 (130 to 260 per square mile)
- 10 to 50 (26 to 130 per square mile)
- below 10 (below 26 per square mile)
- Data not available

Average Life Expectancy

- above 75 years
- 66 to 75 years
- 61 to 65 years
- 56 to 60 years
- below 55 years

ARCTIC OCEAN

GREENLAND
(to Denmark)
72

Arctic Circle

Alaska
(to US)

PACIFIC OCEAN

ATLANTIC OCEAN

CANADA
82

UNITED STATES
OF AMERICA
79

Tropic of Cancer

MEXICO
77

Hawaii
(to US)

PUERTO RICO (to US)
74

BERMUDA
(to UK)
75

CAYMAN ISLANDS
(to UK) 77

DOM. REP.
74

THE
BAHAMAS
76

ST KITTS & NEVIS
72

HONDURAS

CUBA
79

ANTIGUA & BARBUDA
76

BELIZE

JAMAICA
76

HAITI
63

GUADELOUPE (to France)
75

GUATEMALA 72

EL SALVADOR 73

CURAÇAO
(to Neth.)

DOMINICA
77

MARSHALL
ISLANDS
70

NICARAGUA 75

ARUBA
(to Neth.) 76

VENEZUELA
74

MARTINIQUE (to France)
76

ST LUCIA
75

BARBADOS
75

ST VINCENT &
THE GRENADINES
73

COSTA RICA 80

PANAMA 78

COLOMBIA
75

GRENADA
74

TRINIDAD & TOBAGO
71

FRENCH GUIANA
(to France)
75

NAURU
63

KIRIBATI

WALLIS & FUTUNA
(to France)

66

TUVALU

ECUADOR
76

GUYANA
56 72

SURINAME

Equator

SOLOMON
ISLANDS
69

66

TOKELAU
(to NZ)

COOK
ISLANDS
(to NZ)
74

PERU
75

BRAZIL
75

VANUATU
72

NEW
CALEDONIA
(to France)
74

FIJI
70

73

FRENCH POLYNESIA
(to France)
70

BOLIVIA
71

PARAGUAY
74

Tropic of Capricorn

TONGA

SAMOA

NIUE (to NZ)

AMERICAN
SAMOA
(to US)

PITCAIRN, HENDERSON,
DUCIE & OENO ISLANDS
(to UK)

CHILE
80

ARGENTINA
77

URUGUAY

NEW
ZEALAND
82

PACIFIC OCEAN

CHILE

FALKLAND ISLANDS
(to UK)

SOUTH GEORGIA &
SOUTH SANDWICH ISLANDS
(to UK)

Antarctic Circle

ANTARCTICA

23

Languages

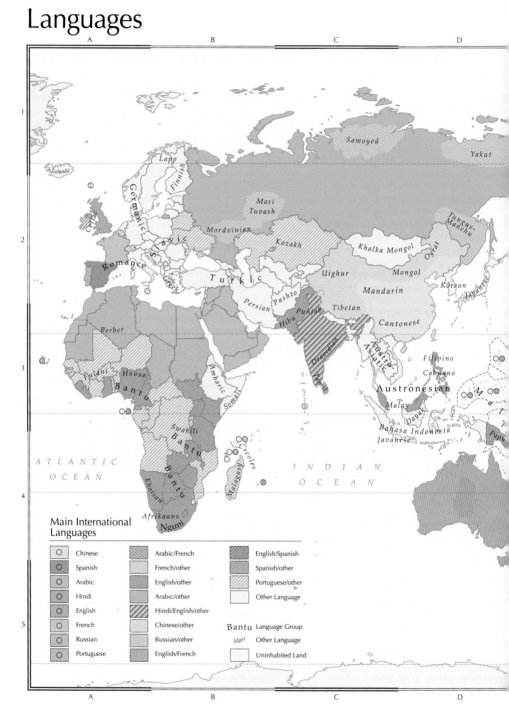

Main International Languages

○ Chinese	Arabic/French	English/Spanish
○ Spanish	French/other	Spanish/other
○ Arabic	English/other	Portuguese/other
○ Hindi	Arabic/other	Other Language
○ English	Hindi/English/other	
○ French	Chinese/other	**Bantu** Language Group
○ Russian	Russian/other	*Mari* Other Language
○ Portuguese	English/French	Uninhabited Land

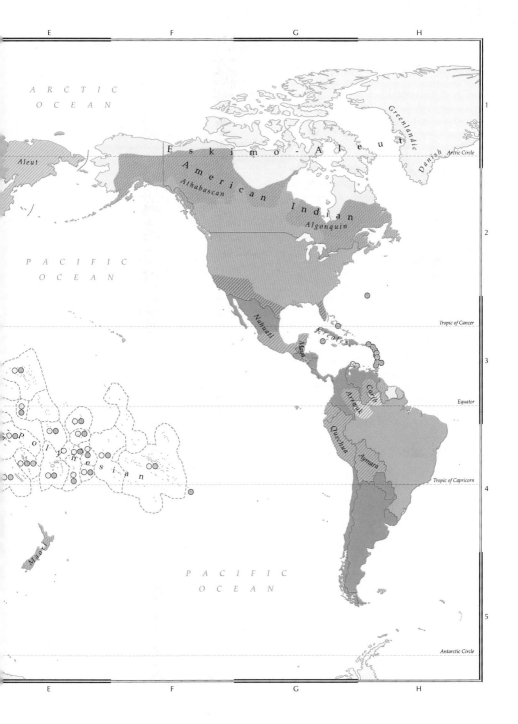

Religion

Majority Religions

- Protestant Christianity
- Catholic Christianity
- Orthodox Christianity
- Shi'a Islam
- Sunni Islam
- Hinduism
- Judaism
- Theravada Buddhism
- Mahayana Buddhism
- Tibetan Buddhism
- Traditional Chinese
- Other
- Marxism / Maoism

State Policy

- ▲ Secular ideologies governing
- ● Communist states during 20th century
- ■ Non-pluralist states

The Global Economy

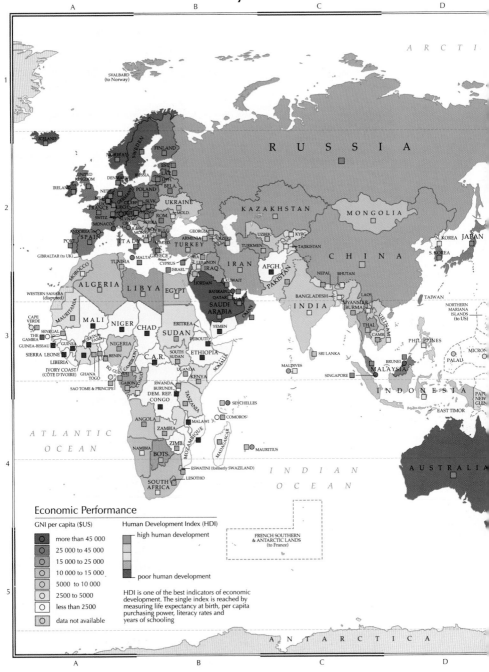

Economic Performance

GNI per capita ($US)

- more than 45 000
- 25 000 to 45 000
- 15 000 to 25 000
- 10 000 to 15 000
- 5000 to 10 000
- 2500 to 5000
- less than 2500
- data not available

Human Development Index (HDI)

- high human development
- poor human development

HDI is one of the best indicators of economic development. The single index is reached by measuring life expectancy at birth, per capita purchasing power, literacy rates and years of schooling

Politics and Conflict

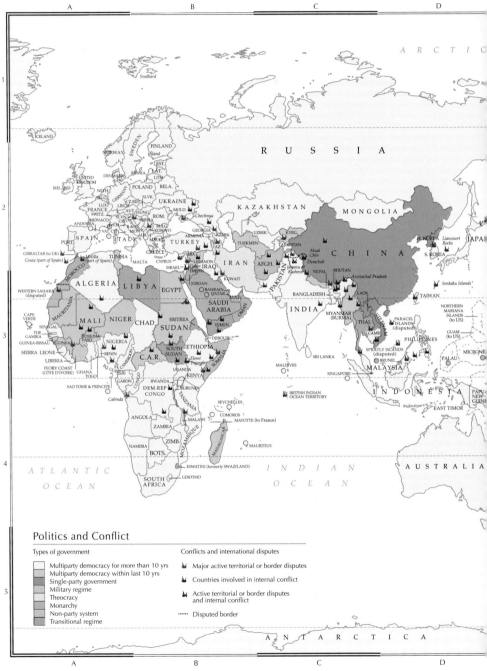

Politics and Conflict

Types of government

Multiparty democracy for more than 10 yrs
Multiparty democracy within last 10 yrs
Single-party government
Military regime
Theocracy
Monarchy
Non-party system
Transitional regime

Conflicts and international disputes

Major active territorial or border disputes

Countries involved in internal conflict

Active territorial or border disputes
and internal conflict

····· Disputed border

The —
WORLD'S
REGIONS

North & Central America

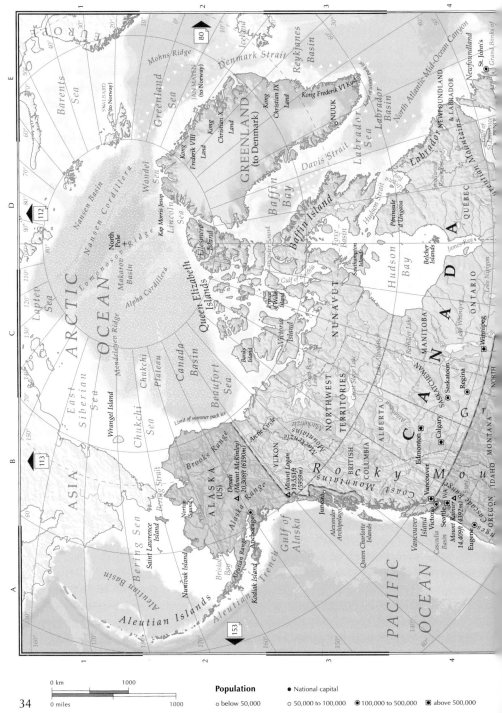

0 km   1000

0 miles   1000

Population

● National capital

○ below 50,000   ○ 50,000 to 100,000   ◉ 100,000 to 500,000   ■ above 500,000

ATLANTIC

OCEAN

(to France)

Halifax

Georges
Bank

Boston
Cape Cod

VT NH MAINE
NY Albany
MA
CT RI
New York
Philadelphia
Baltimore
WASHINGTON D.C.
Richmond
Raleigh

Sargasso Sea

BERMUDA
(to UK)

Nares Plain

Bermuda Rise

Hatteras Plain

Blake
Plateau

Straits of Florida

VIRGIN ISLANDS (to US)
BRITISH VIRGIN ISLANDS
(to UK) ANGUILLA (to UK)
ANTIGUA &
BARBUDA
GUADELOUPE
(to France)
DOMINICA
Lesser
Antilles
MARTINIQUE (to France)
ST LUCIA
ST VINCENT &
THE GRENADINES
BARBADOS
GRENADA

PUERTO
RICO
(to US)
ST KITTS & NEVIS
MONTSERRAT (to France)

TURKS & CAICOS
ISLANDS
(to UK)
Greater Antilles

DOMINICAN
REPUBLIC
SANTO
DOMINGO

ARUBA
(Neth)
CURAÇAO
(Neth)

PORT OF SPAIN

BONAIRE
(to Neth)

TRINIDAD
& TOBAGO

66

Equator

SOUTH

AMERICA

70°

Andes

56

THE
BAHAMAS

NASSAU

Cuba

HAITI
PORT-AU-PRINCE
JAMAICA
KINGSTON

HAVANA

Caribbean Sea

Colombian
Basin

PANAMA CITY

PANAMA

Panama
Basin

Jacksonville

FLORIDA

Miami

CAYMAN
ISLANDS
(to UK)

Guantánamo
Bay (to US)

Cocos Ridge

Galápagos Islands
(to Ecuador)

Colón Ridge

PACIFIC

OCEAN

East Pacific Rise

Tampa

New Orleans

Mississippi
Delta

Gulf of Mexico

Yucatán
Peninsula

BELMOPAN

BELIZE

GUATEMALA

GUATEMALA CITY

SAN SALVADOR
EL SALVADOR

HONDURAS
TEGUCIGALPA
NICARAGUA
MANAGUA
Lake Nicaragua
SAN JOSÉ
COSTA RICA

Guatemala
Basin

MEXICO CITY
Orizaba
Pico de Orizaba
18,491ft (5636m)

Acapulco

Middle America Trench

MEXICO

Sierra Madre Oriental

Sierra Madre Occidental

Revillagigedo Islands
(to Mexico)

CLIPPERTON
ISLAND
(to French Polynesia)

Tropic of Cancer

Clarion Fracture Zone

Equator

Gallego
Rise

153

153

UNITED STATES

OF AMERICA

MICHIGAN

Lake Superior
Lake Michigan
Lake Huron
Lake Erie
Lake Ontario
Niagara
Falls

OTTAWA
Montreal
TORONTO
Detroit
Cleveland
Buffalo
Pittsburgh

Niagara

Toronto

Milwaukee

Chicago

Madison

WISCONSIN

IOWA

Des Moines

Lincoln

NEBRASKA

Denver

COLORADO

Salt Lake City

UTAH

NEVADA

Mount Whitney
14,505ft (4421m)
Death Valley
-282ft (-86m)

CALIFORNIA

San Francisco
San Jose

Los Angeles
San Diego

Coast Ranges

ARIZONA

Phoenix

NEW
MEXICO

El Paso

Rio Grande

San Antonio

TEXAS

Dallas

Austin

Houston

Monterrey

Guadalajara

Gulf of California

Lower California

Columbus

Indianapolis

Nashville

Memphis

Jackson

Baton Rouge

Little Rock

Arkansas

Red River

OKLAHOMA

Oklahoma City

KANSAS

Kansas City

MISSOURI

Springfield

ILLINOIS

OHIO

IN

KY

TN

AL

GEORGIA

Atlanta

Montgomery

Columbia

SC

NC

VA

WV

MD
DE

Halifax

Niagara

Saint Paul

DAKOTA

MINNESOTA

Milwaukee

Grand Canyon

Colorado

N

153

153

56

66

ATLANTIC

Tropic of Cancer

50°

40°

30°

20°

10°

Equator

90°

80°

70°

110°

120°

130°

100°

E

D

C

B

A

5

6

7

8

5

7

8

6

35

Western Canada & Alaska

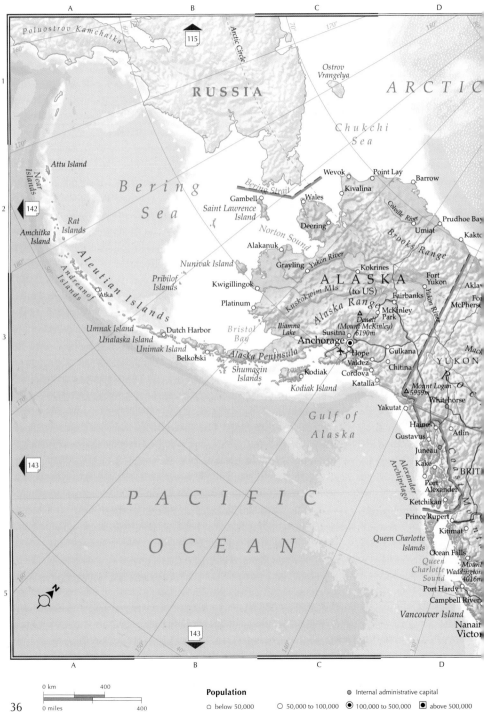

poluostrov Kamchatka

115

Arctic Circle

RUSSIA

ARCTIC

Ostrov Vrangelya

Chukchi Sea

Near Islands

Attu Island

142

Rat Islands

Amchitka Island

Bering Sea

Aleutian Islands

Andreanof Islands

Atka

Pribilof Islands

Saint Lawrence Island

Nunivak Island

Kwigillingok

Platinum

Gambell

Deering

Alakanuk

Grayling

Yukon River

Kuskokwim Mts

Wevok

Wales

Kivalina

Bering Strait

Point Lay

Barrow

Norton Sound

Kokrines

Brooks Range

Coville River

Prudhoe Bay

Umiat

Kakto

ALASKA
(to US)

Fort Yukon

Akla

Fairbanks

Yukon River

For
McPhers

Alaska Range

McKinley Park

Denali
(Mount McKinley)
6190m

Iliamna Lake

Susitna

Anchorage

Hope

Valdez

Gulkana

Chitina

YUKON

Mack

Bristol Bay

Umnak Island

Unalaska Island

Unimak Island

Dutch Harbor

Belkofski

Alaska Peninsula

Shumagin Islands

Kodiak

Cordova

Katalla

Kodiak Island

Mount Logan
5959m

Whitehorse

Yakutat

Gulf of Alaska

Haines

Gustavus

Atlin

143

Juneau

Kake

BRIT

Port Alexander

Alexander Archipelago

Coast Mou

Ketchikan

PACIFIC

Prince Rupert

Kitimat

Queen Charlotte Islands

Ocean Falls

Mount
Waddington
4016m

OCEAN

Queen Charlotte Sound

Port Hardy

Campbell River

Vancouver Island

Nanaim

Victor

143

0 km   400

0 miles   400

Population

○ below 50,000

○ 50,000 to 100,000

◉ 100,000 to 500,000

◉ Internal administrative capital

■ above 500,000

GREENLAND
(to Denmark)

OCEAN

Alert

Ellesmere Island

Knud Rasmussen Land

1

Axel Heiberg Island

Queen Elizabeth Islands

Ellef Ringnes Island
Isachsen

Amund Ringnes Island

Prince Patrick Island

Baffin Bay

Arctic Circle

Mould Bay

Devon Island

Bathurst Island *Cornwallis Island*

Melville Island

Resolute (Qausuittuq)

Lancaster Sound

Davis Strait

82

2

Beaufort Sea

Banks Island

Viscount Melville Sound

Somerset Island

M'Clintock Channel

Prince of Wales Island

Baffin Island

Sachs Harbour (Ikaahuk)

Boothia Peninsula

Gulf of Boothia

Cumberland Sound

Tuktoyaktuk
Amundsen Gulf
Holman

Igloolik

Nettilling Lake

Inuvik
Paulatuk

Victoria Island

King William Island
Kugaaruk (Pelly Bay)

Melville Peninsula

Foxe Basin

Amadjuak Lake

Iqaluit (Frobisher Bay)

Cambridge Bay (Ikaluktutiak)
Gjoa Haven (Uqsuqtuuq)

Kugluktuk (Coppermine)

Repulse Bay

Southampton Island

Hudson Strait

Fort Good Hope (Rádeyilikóé)

Burnside

NUNAVUT

Coral Harbour (Salliq)

Péninsule d'Ungava

3

Great Bear Lake
Echo Bay

Mackenzie Mountains

Back

Garry Lake

Baker Lake

Coats Island

Mansel Island

QUÉBEC

Tungsten

NORTHWEST TERRITORIES

Edzo *Yellowknife* *Reliance*

Rankin Inlet

Whale Cove (Tikiarjuaq)

Fort Simpson

Great Slave Lake
Lutselk'e (Snowdrift)

Dubawnt

Arviat

Hudson Bay

Fort Providence
Fort Liard

Hay River
Fort Smith

Belcher Islands

38

4

Fort Nelson

Lake Athabasca

Churchill

COLUMBIA

Ware

Fort Vermilion

Wollaston Lake

Reindeer Lake

Nelson

James Bay

Fort St. John

C   A   N   A   D   A

Fort McMurray
Buffalo Narrows

Lynn Lake

Southern Indian Lake

Prince George

ALBERTA

Grande Prairie

Athabasca
Athabasca

SASKATCHEWAN

Flin Flon

Thompson

ONTARIO

Edmonton

North Saskatchewan

Saskatchewan

The Pas
Lake Winnipeg

Mount Robson 3954m
Leduc

Prince Albert

MANITOBA

Red Deer

Saskatoon

5

Kamloops

Calgary
Kindersley
Yorkton

Lake Manitoba

Winnipeg

Lake Superior

Lake Huron

Kelowna
Cranbrook

Medicine Hat

Regina
Qu'Appelle

Brandon

Lake of the Woods

Lake Michigan

Vancouver
Lethbridge

Weyburn

Milk River

Estevan

Melita

45

U N I T E D   S T A T E S   O F   A M E R I C A

Elevation

-6000m	-4000m	-2000m	-1000m	-500m	-250m	Below sea level	0	250m	500m	1000m	2000m	3000m	4000m	6000m
-19,658ft	-13,124ft	-6562ft	-3281ft	-1640ft	-820ft	-328ft/-100m	0	820ft	1640ft	3281ft	6562ft	9843ft	13,124ft	19,685ft

Eastern Canada

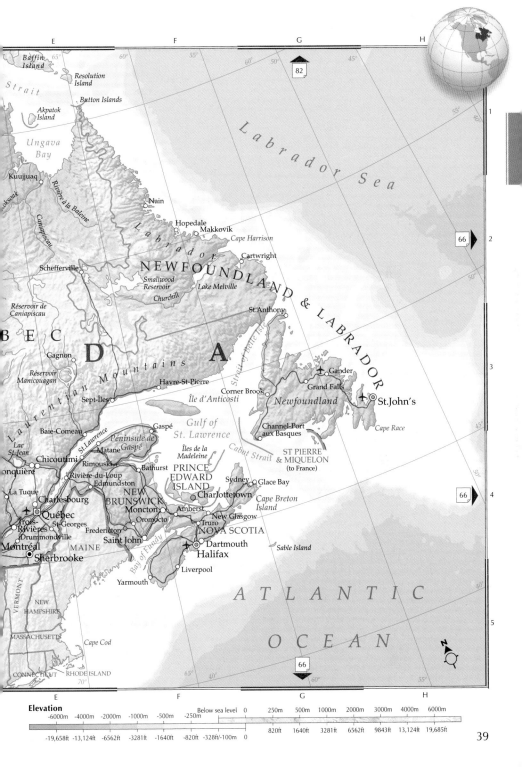

E   F   G   H

Baffin Island

Strait

Resolution Island

Akpatok Island

Button Islands

Ungava Bay

Kuujjuaq

Labrador Sea

82

Nain

Hopedale

Makkovik

Cape Harrison

Schefferville

NEWFOUNDLAND

Smallwood Reservoir

Churchill

Cartwright

Lake Melville

66

Réservoir de Caniapiscau

St.Anthony

&

L A B R A D O R

D   **A**

Gagnon

Laurentian Mountains

Havre-St-Pierre

Île d'Anticosti

Corner Brook

Straits of Belle Isle

Gander

Grand Falls

66

Réservoir Manicouagan

Sept-Îles

Newfoundland

St.John's

Cape Race

B E C

Baie-Comeau

St.Lawrence

Gulf of St. Lawrence

Gaspé

Péninsule de Gaspé

Channel-Port aux Basques

Lac St-Jean

Chicoutimi

Matane

Rimouski

Îles de la Madeleine

Cabot Strait

ST PIERRE & MIQUELON *(to France)*

onquière

Rivière-du-Loup

Bathurst

PRINCE EDWARD ISLAND

Sydney

Glace Bay

La Tuque

Edmundston

NEW

Sydney

Cape Breton Island

Charlesbourg

BRUNSWICK

Charlottetown

66

Québec

Moncton

Amherst

New Glasgow

Trois-Rivières

St-Georges

Oromocto

Truro

Drummondville

Fredericton

NOVA SCOTIA

Montréal

Saint John

Sable Island

MAINE

Dartmouth

Sherbrooke

Halifax

Bay of Fundy

Liverpool

VERMONT

NEW HAMPSHIRE

Yarmouth

A T L A N T I C

MASSACHUSETTS

Cape Cod

O C E A N

CONNECTICUT

RHODE ISLAND

66

N

E   F   G   H

Elevation

-6000m	-4000m	-2000m	-1000m	-500m	-250m	Below sea level 0	250m	500m	1000m	2000m	3000m	4000m	6000m
-19,658ft	-13,124ft	-6562ft	-3281ft	-1640ft	-820ft	-328ft/-100m 0	820ft	1640ft	3281ft	6562ft	9843ft	13,124ft	19,685ft

USA: The Northeast

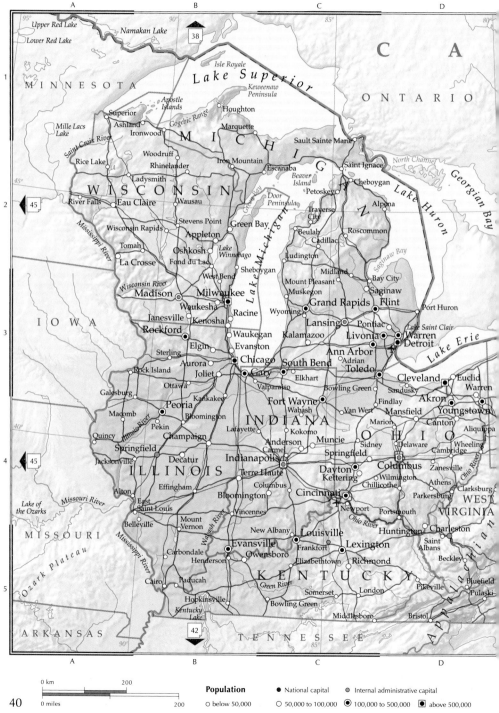

Upper Red Lake
Lower Red Lake
Namakan Lake
38
C A
ONTARIO
MINNESOTA
Isle Royale
Lake Superior
Keweenaw Peninsula
Apostle Islands
Houghton
North Channel
Superior
Ashland
Ironwood
Gogebic Range
Marquette
Sault Sainte Marie
Georgian Bay
Mille Lacs Lake
Woodruff
M I C H I G
Saint Ignace
Rice Lake
Rhinelander
Iron Mountain
Escanaba
Beaver Island
Cheboygan
Lake Huron
Saint Croix River
Ladysmith
Petoskey
Alpena
W I S C O N S I N
Wausau
Green Bay
Traverse City
Roscommon
River Falls
Eau Claire
Stevens Point
Beulah
45°
Wisconsin Rapids
Appleton
Cadillac
Door Peninsula
Tomah
Oshkosh
Lake Winnebago
Ludington
Midland
Bay City
Saginaw Bay
La Crosse
Fond du Lac
Sheboygan
Mount Pleasant
Saginaw
Wisconsin River
West Bend
Muskegon
Grand Rapids
Flint
Port Huron
Madison
Milwaukee
Waukesha
Racine
Wyoming
Lansing
Pontiac
Lake Saint Clair
Warren
I O W A
Janesville
Kenosha
Livonia
Detroit
Rockford
Waukegan
Kalamazoo
Ann Arbor
Lake Erie
Sterling
Elgin
Evanston
Lake Michigan
Aurora
Chicago
South Bend
Adrian
Toledo
Cleveland
Euclid
Rock Island
Joliet
Gary
Elkhart
Warren
Ottawa
Kankakee
Valparaiso
Bowling Green
Sandusky
Akron
Galesburg
Peoria
Fort Wayne
Findlay
Youngstown
Bloomington
Wabash
Van Wert
Mansfield
Canton
Macomb
Pekin
Lafayette
I N D I A N A
Kokomo
Marion
O H I O
Aliquippa
Quincy
Champaign
Anderson
Muncie
Sidney
Delaware
Wheeling
Springfield
Decatur
Carmel
Springfield
Cambridge
Jacksonville
Indianapolis
Columbus
Zanesville
Ohio River
I L L I N O I S
Terre Haute
Dayton
Athens
Clarksburg
Effingham
Columbus
Kettering
Wilmington
Chillicothe
Parkersburg
WEST
Alton
Bloomington
Cincinnati
Portsmouth
VIRGINIA
Lake of the Ozarks
East Saint Louis
Vincennes
Newport
Huntington
Charleston
Missouri River
Mount Vernon
New Albany
Louisville
Ohio River
Saint Albans
Belleville
Evansville
Owensboro
Frankfort
Lexington
Richmond
Beckley
M I S S O U R I
Carbondale
Henderson
Elizabethtown
Ozark Plateau
Mississippi River
Cairo
Paducah
Green River
K E N T U C K Y
Pikeville
Bluefield
Pulaski
Hopkinsville
Somerset
London
Mississippi River
Kentucky Lake
42
Bowling Green
Middlesboro
Bristol
Appalachian
A R K A N S A S
T E N N E S S E E

Population

- National capital
- Internal administrative capital
- below 50,000
- 50,000 to 100,000
- 100,000 to 500,000
- above 500,000

0 km — 200
0 miles — 200

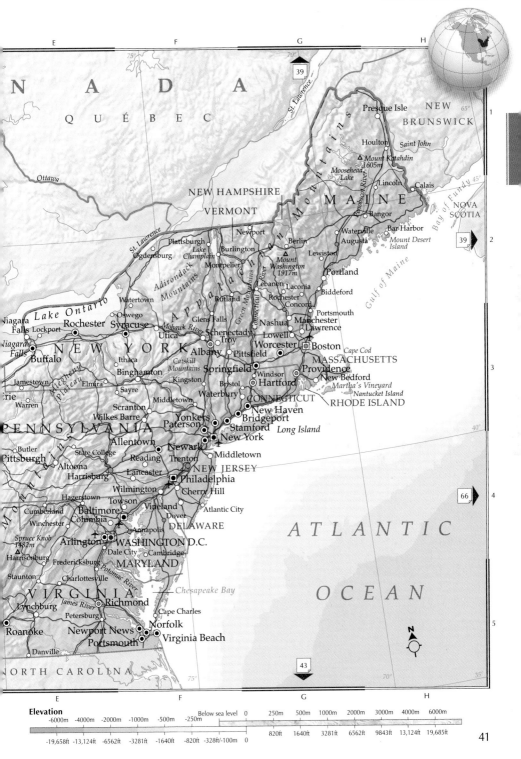

39
39
66
43

Elevation

-6000m	-4000m	-2000m	-1000m	-500m	-250m	Below sea level	0	250m	500m	1000m	2000m	3000m	4000m	6000m
-19,658ft	-13,124ft	-6562ft	-3281ft	-1640ft	-820ft/-100m	0		820ft	1640ft	3281ft	6562ft	9843ft	13,124ft	19,685ft

USA: The Southeast

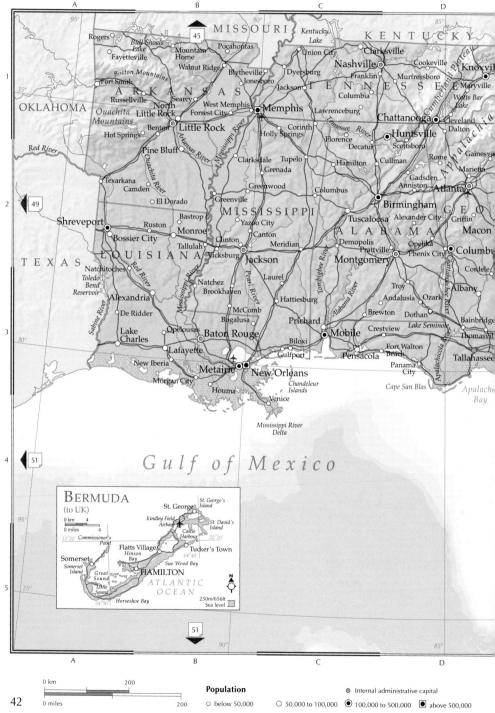

Population

○ below 50,000 ○ 50,000 to 100,000 ◉ 100,000 to 500,000 ■ above 500,000

◉ Internal administrative capital

0 km 200
0 miles 200

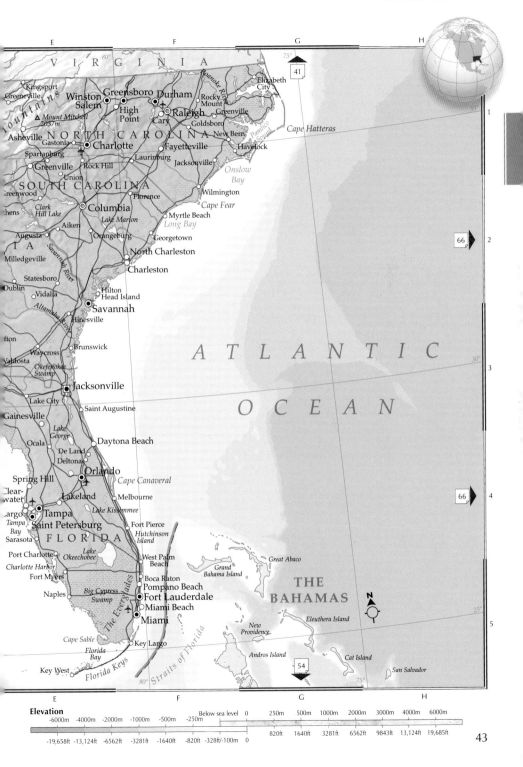

66

66

The map shows:

VIRGINIA

Kingsport
Greeneville
Winston Salem
Greensboro
Durham
Rocky Mount
Elizabeth City
High Point
Raleigh
Cary
Greenville
Asheville
Mount Mitchell 2037m
NORTH CAROLINA
New Bern
Cape Hatteras
Gastonia
Charlotte
Goldsboro
Spartanburg
Laurinburg
Fayetteville
Havelock
Greenville
Rock Hill
Jacksonville
SOUTH CAROLINA
Union
Onslow Bay
Greenwood
Florence
Wilmington
thens
Clark Hill Lake
Columbia
Cape Fear
Aiken
Lake Marion
Myrtle Beach
Long Bay
Augusta
Orangeburg
Georgetown
IA
Milledgeville
North Charleston
Statesboro
Charleston
Dublin
Vidalia
Hilton Head Island
fton
Savannah
Waycross
Hinesville
Valdosta
Brunswick
Okefenokee Swamp

ATLANTIC

Jacksonville
Lake City
Saint Augustine
Gainesville
Lake George
Ocala
Daytona Beach
De Land
Deltona
Orlando
Spring Hill
Cape Canaveral
Clearwater
Lakeland
Melbourne
Largo
Lake Kissimmee
Tampa
Saint Petersburg
Fort Pierce
Tampa Bay
Hutchinson Island
Sarasota
FLORIDA
Lake Okeechobee
Port Charlotte
West Palm Beach
Charlotte Harbor
Grand Bahama Island
Great Abaco
Fort Myers
Boca Raton
Naples
Big Cypress Swamp
Pompano Beach
Fort Lauderdale
THE BAHAMAS
Miami Beach
Miami
New Providence
Eleuthera Island
Cape Sable
Key Largo
Florida Bay
Andros Island
Cat Island
Key West
Florida Keys
Straits of Florida
San Salvador

OCEAN

54

Elevation

-6000m	-4000m	-2000m	-1000m	-500m	Below sea level	0	250m	500m	1000m	2000m	3000m	4000m	6000m
-19,658ft	-13,124ft	-6562ft	-3281ft	-1640ft	-250m								
					-820ft	-328ft/-100m	0	820ft	1640ft	3281ft	6562ft	9843ft	13,124ft	19,685ft

43

USA: Central States

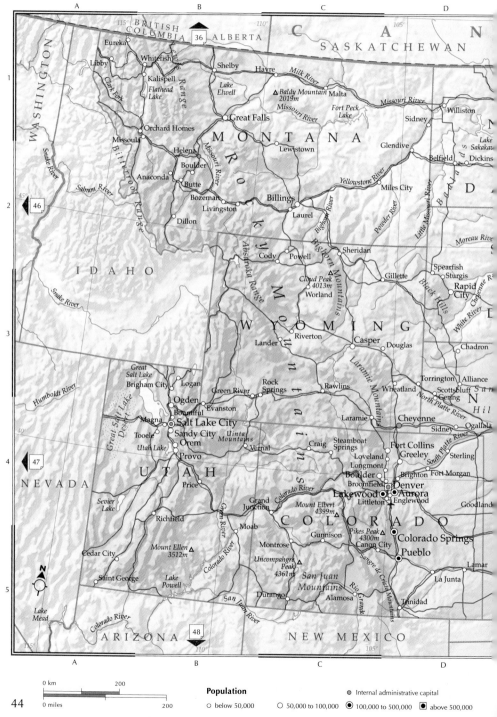

Population

○ below 50,000   ○ 50,000 to 100,000   ◉ 100,000 to 500,000   ■ above 500,000

◉ Internal administrative capital

0 km   200

0 miles   200

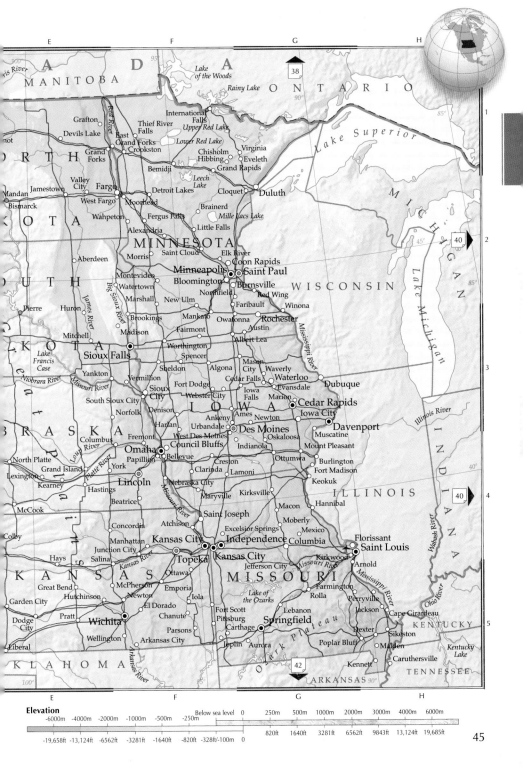

Elevation

						Below sea level							
-6000m	-4000m	-2000m	-1000m	-500m	-250m	0	250m	500m	1000m	2000m	3000m	4000m	6000m
-19,658ft	-13,124ft	-6562ft	-3281ft	-1640ft	-820ft	-328ft/-100m	0	820ft	1640ft	3281ft	6562ft	9843ft	13,124ft	19,685ft

45

USA: The West

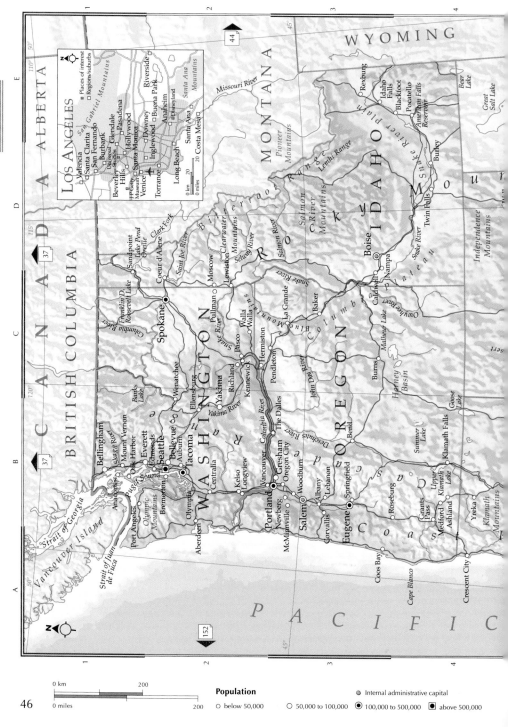

LOS ANGELES
- Places of interest
- Regions/suburbs

San Gabriel Mountains
Santa Ana Mountains

Valencia
Santa Clarita
San Fernando
Riverside
Pasadena
Burbank
Glendale
Buena Park
Universal Studios
Hollywood
Disneyland
Beverley Hills
Santa Monica
Inglewood
Anaheim
Venice
Downey
Santa Ana
Museum
Torrance
Long Beach
Costa Mesa

0 km   20
0 miles   20

Population

○ below 50,000
○ 50,000 to 100,000
◉ 100,000 to 500,000
■ above 500,000

◉ Internal administrative capital

0 km   200
0 miles   200

46

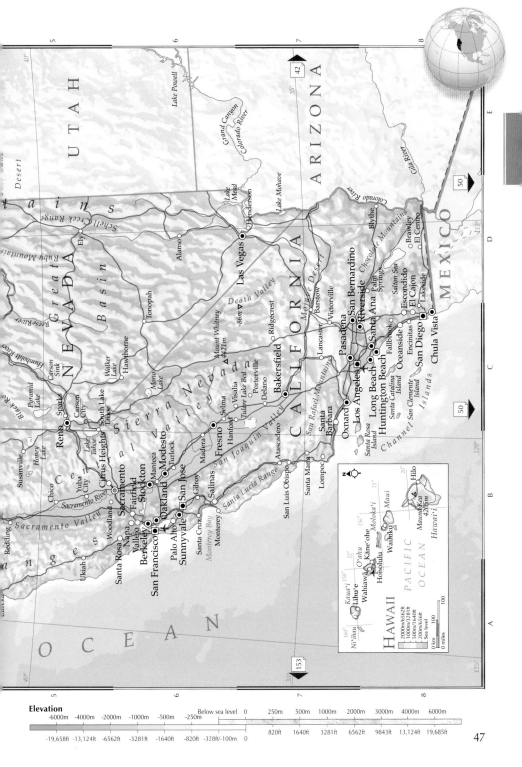

Elevation

-6000m	-4000m	-2000m	-1000m	-500m	-250m	Below sea level	0	250m	500m	1000m	2000m	3000m	4000m	6000m

| -19,658ft | -13,124ft | -6562ft | -3281ft | -1640ft | -820ft | -328ft/-100m | 0 | 820ft | 1640ft | 3281ft | 6562ft | 9843ft | 13,124ft | 19,685ft |

USA: The Southwest

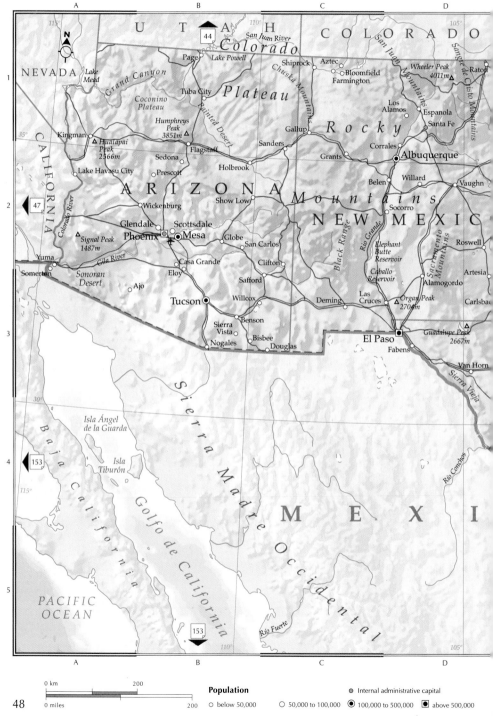

Population

- Internal administrative capital
- ○ below 50,000
- ○ 50,000 to 100,000
- ◉ 100,000 to 500,000
- ■ above 500,000

0 km   200

0 miles   200

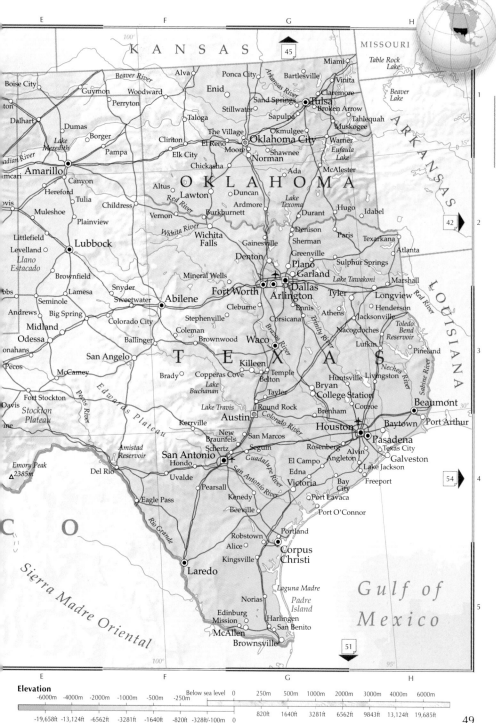

E   F   G   H

KANSAS

MISSOURI

Table Rock Lake

Miami

Boise City

Alva

Ponca City

Bartlesville

Vinita

Beaver River

Guymon

Woodward

Enid

Sand Springs

Tulsa

Claremore

Beaver Lake

ton

Perryton

Stillwater

Sapulpa

Broken Arrow

Dalhart

Taloga

Okmulgee

Tahlequah

Dumas

Clinton

The Village

Muskogee

Borger

El Reno

Oklahoma City

Warner

Lake Meredith

Pampa

Elk City

Moore

Shawnee

Eufaula Lake

adian River

Amarillo

Chickasha

Norman

Ada

McAlester

mcari

Canyon

OKLAHOMA

Hereford

Altus

Lawton

Duncan

Lake Texoma

Hugo

Idabel

Tulia

Childress

Ardmore

Durant

ovis

Muleshoe

Vernon

Burkburnett

Red River

Plainview

Wichita River

Denison

Paris

Texarkana

Littlefield

Lubbock

Wichita Falls

Gainesville

Sherman

Atlanta

Levelland

Denton

Greenville

Sulphur Springs

Llano Estacado

Brownfield

Mineral Wells

Plano

Garland

Lake Tawakoni

Marshall

Lamesa

Snyder

Fort Worth

Dallas

bbs

Seminole

Sweetwater

Abilene

Arlington

Tyler

Longview

Andrews

Big Spring

Colorado City

Cleburne

Athens

Henderson

Midland

Stephenville

Corsicana

Jacksonville

Toledo Bend Reservoir

Odessa

Ballinger

Coleman

Ennis

Nacogdoches

onahans

San Angelo

Brownwood

Waco

Lufkin

Pineland

Pecos

McCamey

TEXAS

Brazos River

Trinity River

Neches River

Sabine River

Fort Stockton

Brady

Copperas Cove

Killeen

Temple

Huntsville

Livingston

Davis

Stockton Plateau

Lake Buchanan

Belton

Bryan

ine

Edwards Plateau

Pecos River

Lake Travis

Tayler

College Station

Conroe

Beaumont

Kerrville

Round Rock

Brenham

Houston

Baytown

Port Arthur

Austin

Colorado River

Pasadena

New Braunfels

San Marcos

Rosenberg

Alvin

Texas City

Amistad Reservoir

Schertz

Seguin

El Campo

Angleton

Galveston

Emory Peak
△2385m

San Antonio

Hondo

Guadalupe River

Edna

Victoria

Lake Jackson

Freeport

Del Rio

Uvalde

San Antonio River

Bay City

Pearsall

Kenedy

Port Lavaca

Eagle Pass

Beeville

Port O'Connor

Rio Grande

Portland

Robstown

Alice

Corpus Christi

Kingsville

Laredo

Laguna Madre

Padre Island

Norias

Gulf of Mexico

Edinburg

Mission

Harlingen

San Benito

McAllen

Brownsville

Sierra Madre Oriental

Elevation

| -6000m | -4000m | -2000m | -1000m | -500m | -250m | Below sea level | 0 | 250m | 500m | 1000m | 2000m | 3000m | 4000m | 6000m |

| -19,658ft | -13,124ft | -6562ft | -3281ft | -1640ft | -820ft | -328ft/-100m | 0 | 820ft | 1640ft | 3281ft | 6562ft | 9843ft | 13,124ft | 19,685ft |

E   F   G   H

49

Mexico

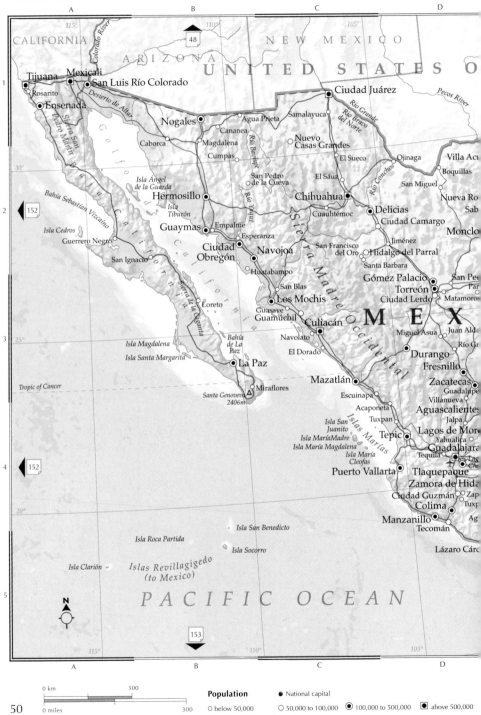

A   B   C   D

115°

CALIFORNIA

110°

48

NEW MEXICO

105°

ARIZONA

UNITED STATES O

Colorado River

Tijuana Mexicali

San Luis Río Colorado

Ciudad Juárez

Pecos River

Rosarito

Ensenada

Desierto de Altar

Río Grande
del Norte

Nogales

Agua Prieta Samalayuca

Río Bravo
del Norte

Sierra San
Pedro Mártir

Golfo

Caborca

Cananea

Magdalena

Cumpas

Nuevo
Casas Grandes

El Sueco

Ojinaga

Villa Acu

30°

Isla Ángel
de la Guarda

San Pedro
de la Cueva

El Sáuz

San Miguel

Boquillas

Bahía Sebastián Vizcaíno

Hermosillo

Río Yaqui

Chihuahua

Nueva Ro

152

Isla
Tiburón

Cuauhtémoc

Delicias

Río Conchos

Sab

Isla Cedros

Guaymas

Empalme

Ciudad Camargo

Moncl

Guerrero Negro

Esperanza

San Francisco
del Oro

Jiménez

San Ignacio

Ciudad
Obregón

Navojoa

Hidalgo del Parral

Santa Barbara

de California

Huatabampo

Gómez Palacio

San Pe

Sierra de la Giganta

San Blas

Torreón

Par

Loreto

Los Mochis

Ciudad Lerdo

Matamoros

Guasave

Guamúchil

M E X

Isla Magdalena

Bahía
de La
Paz

Navolato

Culiacán

Miguel Asua

Juan Alda

25°

Isla Santa Margarita

El Dorado

Río Gr

La Paz

Durango

Tropic of Cancer

Mazatlán

Fresnillo

Santa Genoveva

Miraflores

Zacatecas

2406m

Escuinapa

Guadalupe

Acaponeta

Villanueva

Isla San
Juanito

Tuxpan

Aguascalientes

Islas Marías

Isla MaríaMadre

Tepic

Lagos de Mor

Jalpa

Isla María Magdalena

Yahualica

Isla María
Cleofas

Tequila

Guadalajara

152

Puerto Vallarta

Tlaquepaque

Lag
Ch

Zamora de Hida

20°

Ciudad Guzmán

Zap

Colima

Tux

Manzanillo

Ag

Tecomán

Isla San Benedicto

Isla Roca Partida

Lázaro Cárc

Isla Socorro

Islas Revillagigedo
(to Mexico)

Isla Clarión

P A C I F I C O C E A N

N

153

115°   110°   105°

A   B   C   D

0 km   300

Population   ● National capital

0 miles   300   ○ below 50,000 ○ 50,000 to 100,000 ◉ 100,000 to 500,000 ▣ above 500,000

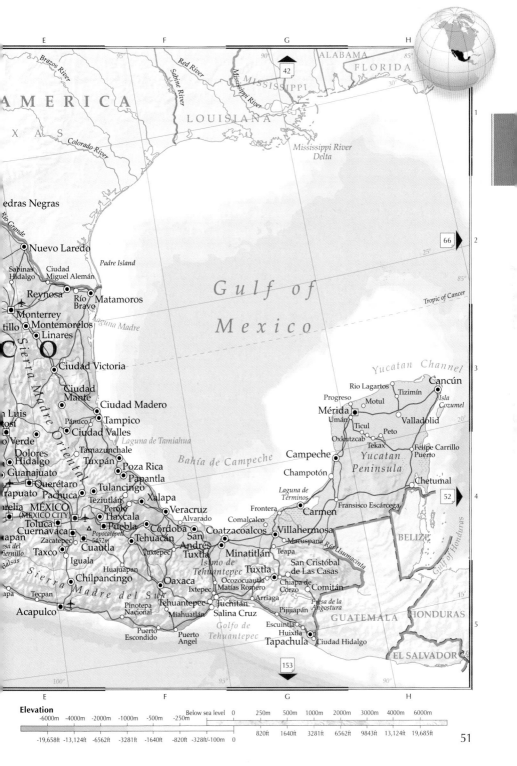

E   F   G   H

Brazos River   95°   Red River   90°   ALABAMA   85°

Sabine River   Mississippi   FLORIDA

Mississippi River   42   30°

AMERICA   LOUISIANA

Colorado River   Mississippi River
Delta

X A S

edras Negras

Río Grande

Nuevo Laredo   25°   66   2

Sabinas
Hidalgo   Ciudad
Miguel Alemán   Padre Island   85°

Reynosa   Río
Bravo   Matamoros   Gulf of   Tropic of Cancer

Monterrey   Laguna Madre   Mexico

tillo   Montemorelos
Linares

C O   Sierra Madre Oriental

Ciudad Victoria   Yucatan Channel   3

Ciudad
Mante   Río Lagartos   Cancún

Luis   Ciudad Madero   Progreso   Tizimín   Isla
Cozumel

osí   Pánuco   Tampico   Mérida   Motul

Verde   Ciudad Valles   Umán   Valladolid   20°

Dolores   Laguna de Tamiahua   Ticul   Peto

Hidalgo   Tamazunchale   Oxkutzcab   Tekax   Felipe Carrillo
Puerto

Guanajuato   Tuxpán   Bahía de Campeche   Campeche   Yucatan
Peninsula

rapuato   Querétaro   Poza Rica   Champotón   Chetumal

Pachuca   Papantla

relia   Tulancingo   Laguna de
Términos   52   4

MÉXICO   Teziutlán   Xalapa   Frontera   Francisco Escárcega

(MEXICO CITY)   Perote   Veracruz   Carmen

Toluca   Tlaxcala   Alvarado   Comalcalco   BELIZE

apan   Cuernavaca   Puebla   Córdoba   San   Coatzacoalcos   Villahermosa

sa del   Zacatepec   Popocatépetl   Tehuacán   Andrés   Macuspana   Río Usumacinta

iernillo   Taxco   Cuautla   5452m   Tuxtla   Minatitlán   Teapa

alsas   Iguala   Tuxtepec   Istmo de   Tuxtla   San Cristóbal
de Las Casas

Sierra   Chilpancingo   Huajuapan   Tehuantepec   Ocozocuautla   Chiapa de
Corzo   Comitán

Madre del Sur   Oaxaca   Ixtepec   Matías Romero   Arriaga   15°

Tecpan   Pinotepa   Tehuantepec   Juchitán   Pijijiapán   Presa de la
Angostura

apa   Acapulco   Nacional   Miahuatlán   Salina Cruz   GUATEMALA   HONDURAS

Puerto   Puerto   Golfo de   Escuintla

Escondido   Angel   Tehuantepec   Huixtla

Tapachula   Ciudad Hidalgo

153   EL SALVADOR

100°   95°   90°

E   F   G   H

Elevation

-6000m -4000m -2000m -1000m -500m -250m   Below sea level 0   250m 500m 1000m 2000m 3000m 4000m 6000m

-19,658ft -13,124ft -6562ft -3281ft -1640ft -820ft -328ft/-100m 0   820ft 1640ft 3281ft 6562ft 9843ft 13,124ft 19,685ft

Central America

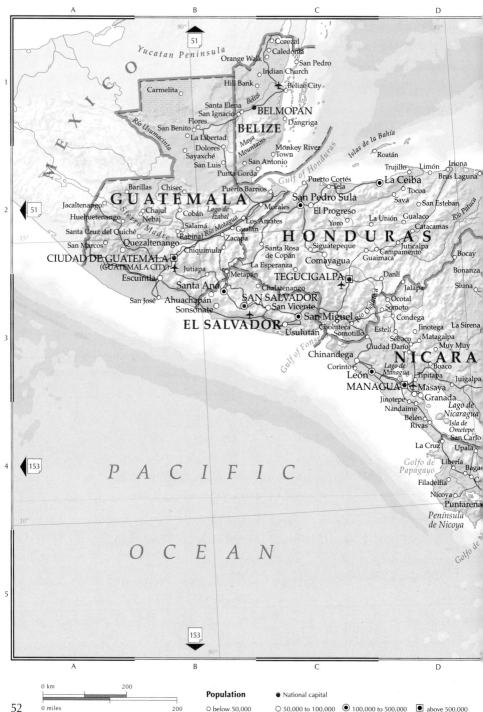

Population

● National capital

O below 50,000   O 50,000 to 100,000   ◉ 100,000 to 500,000   ■ above 500,000

0 km   200

0 miles   200

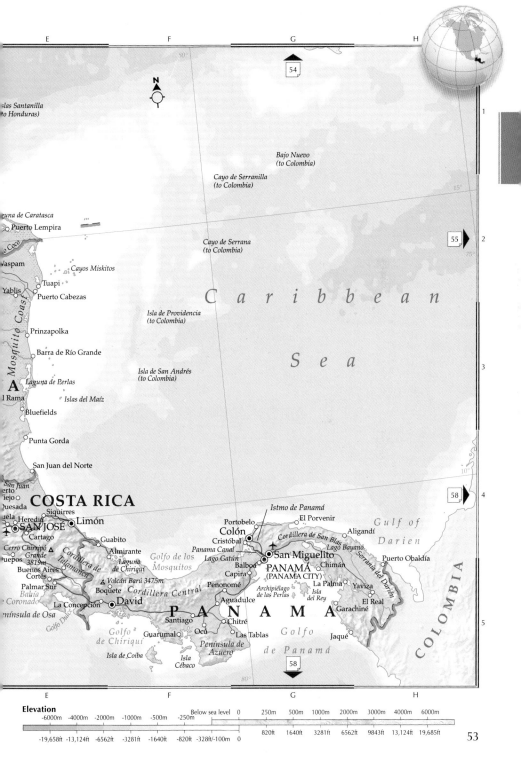

Bajo Nuevo
(to Colombia)

Cayo de Serranilla
(to Colombia)

una de Caratasca

Puerto Lempira

o Coco

Cayo de Serrana
(to Colombia)

Vaspam

Cayos Miskitos

Tuapi

Yablis

Puerto Cabezas

C a r i b b e a n

Prinzapolka

Isla de Providencia
(to Colombia)

Barra de Río Grande

S e a

A

Laguna de Perlas

Isla de San Andrés
(to Colombia)

l Rama

Islas del Maíz

Bluefields

Punta Gorda

San Juan del Norte

San Juan
erto
iejo

uesada

COSTA RICA

Istmo de Panamá

El Porvenir

Gulf of

uela

Heredi

Siquirres

Portobelo

Aligandí

Darien

SAN JOSE

Limón

Colón

Cordillera de San Blas

Cerro Chirripó
Grande
3819m

Guabito

Cristóbal

Lago Bayano

Puerto Obaldía

uepos

Almirante

Panama Canal

Balboa

Chimán

Buenos Aires
Cortés

Laguna
de Chiriquí

Golfo de los
Mosquitos

Lago Gatún

San Miguelito

Capira

PANAMÁ
(PANAMA CITY)

Palmar Sur

Volcán Barú 3475m

Penonomé

La Palma

Yaviza

Bahía
Coronado

Boquete

La Concepción

David

Cordillera Central

P A N A M A

Aguadulce

Archipiélago
de las Perlas

Isla
del Rey

El Real

Garachiné

enínsula de Osa

Golfo Dulce

Santiago

Chitré

Guarumal

Ocú

Las Tablas

Golfo

Jaqué

Golfo
de Chiriquí

Península de
Azuero

de Panamá

Isla de Coiba

Isla
Cébaco

Elevation

-6000m	-4000m	-2000m	-1000m	-500m	-250m	Below sea level	0	250m	500m	1000m	2000m	3000m	4000m	6000m
-19,658ft	-13,124ft	-6562ft	-3281ft	-1640ft	-820ft	-328ft/-100m	0	820ft	1640ft	3281ft	6562ft	9843ft	13,124ft	19,685ft

The Caribbean

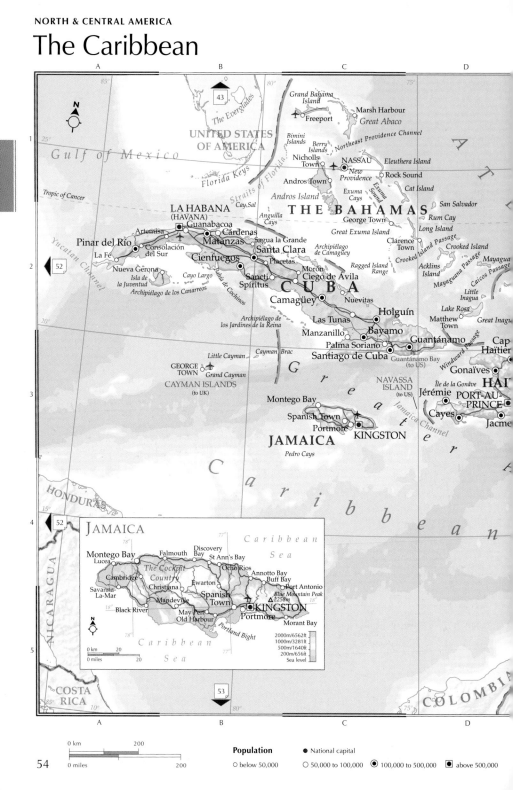

Population ● National capital

○ below 50,000 ⦾ 50,000 to 100,000 ◉ 100,000 to 500,000 ◼ above 500,000

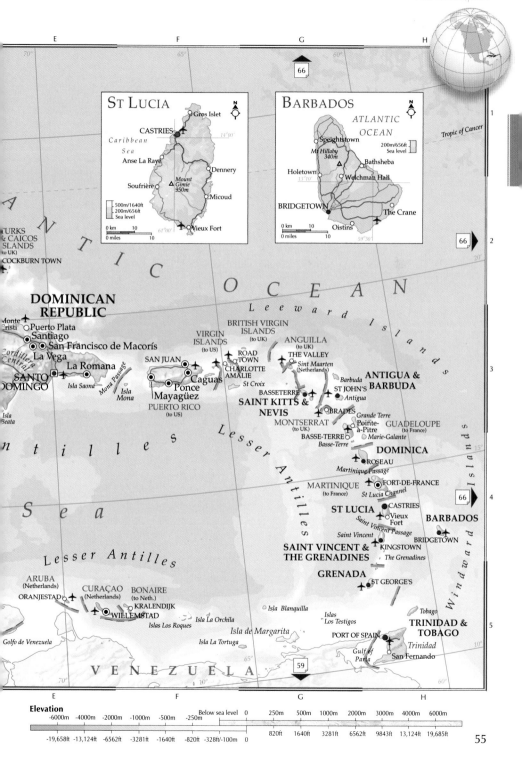

St Lucia

- Gros Islet
- CASTRIES
- Caribbean Sea
- Anse La Raye
- Dennery
- Soufrière
- Mount Gimie 950m
- Micoud
- Vieux Fort

14°00'
61°00'

500m/1640ft
200m/656ft
Sea level

0 km 10
0 miles 10

N

Barbados

ATLANTIC OCEAN

- Speightstown
- Mt Hillaby 340m
- Holetown
- Bathsheba
- Welchman Hall
- BRIDGETOWN
- The Crane
- Oistins

13°10'
59°30'

200m/656ft
Sea level

0 km 10
0 miles 10

N

66

66

66

Tropic of Cancer

ATLANTIC OCEAN

TURKS & CAICOS ISLANDS (to UK)
COCKBURN TOWN

DOMINICAN REPUBLIC

Leeward Islands

Monte Cristi
Puerto Plata
Santiago
San Francisco de Macorís
La Vega
La Romana
SANTO DOMINGO
Isla Saona
Mona Passage
Isla Mona
Isla Beata

VIRGIN ISLANDS (to US)
SAN JUAN
Caguas
Ponce
Mayagüez
PUERTO RICO (to US)

BRITISH VIRGIN ISLANDS (to UK)
ROAD TOWN
CHARLOTTE AMALIE
St Croix

ANGUILLA (to UK)
THE VALLEY
Sint Maarten (Netherlands)

Barbuda
ANTIGUA & BARBUDA
ST JOHN'S
Antigua
BASSETERRE
SAINT KITTS & NEVIS
BRADES
MONTSERRAT (to UK)
Grande Terre
Pointe-à-Pitre
GUADELOUPE (to France)
BASSE-TERRE
Basse-Terre
Marie-Galante

DOMINICA
ROSEAU
Martinique Passage

MARTINIQUE (to France)
FORT-DE-FRANCE
St Lucia Channel

ST LUCIA
CASTRIES
Vieux Fort
Saint Vincent Passage
Saint Vincent
SAINT VINCENT & THE GRENADINES
KINGSTOWN
The Grenadines

GRENADA
ST GEORGE'S

BARBADOS
BRIDGETOWN

Windward Islands

Windward Islands

n t i l l e s
Lesser Antilles

Sea

Lesser Antilles

ARUBA (Netherlands)
ORANJESTAD
CURAÇAO (Netherlands)
BONAIRE (to Neth.)
KRALENDIJK
WILLEMSTAD
Islas Los Roques
Isla La Orchila

Isla Blanquilla

Islas Los Testigos
Isla de Margarita
Isla La Tortuga

Tobago
TRINIDAD & TOBAGO
PORT OF SPAIN
Trinidad
San Fernando
Gulf of Paria

Golfo de Venezuela
VENEZUELA

59

Elevation

-6000m	-4000m	-2000m	-1000m	-500m	-250m	Below sea level 0	250m	500m	1000m	2000m	3000m	4000m	6000m
-19,658ft	-13,124ft	-6562ft	-3281ft	-1640ft	-820ft	-328ft/-100m 0	820ft	1640ft	3281ft	6562ft	9843ft	13,124ft	19,685ft

South America

ATLANTIC OCEAN

Mid-Atlantic Ridge

Equator

66

67

35

35

Demerara Plain

Ceará Plain

Amazon Fan

Puerto Rico Trench

Lesser Antilles

Greater Antilles

Hispaniola

Jamaica

Caribbean Sea

Colombian Basin

Venezuelan Basin

Panama Basin

Isthmus of Panama

Trinidad

Cumaná

CARACAS

Valencia

Maracay

Maracaibo

Barquisimeto

Santa Marta

Barranquilla

Cartagena

Montería

Medellín

Manizales

Pereira

Cali

Pasto

Esmeraldas

Portoviejo

Chimborazo △ 20,564ft (6268m)

Guayaquil

Gulf of Guayaquil

Machala

Cuenca

Riobamba

QUITO

ECUADOR

Piura

Chiclayo

Trujillo

Chimbote

Callao

LIMA

Cusco

Arequipa

Tacna

Arica

Iquique

PERU

P E R U

Peru-Chile Trench

Peru Basin

Andes

Altiplano

LA PAZ

Oruro

Cochabamba

SUCRE

Santa Cruz

BOLIVIA

B O L I V I A

Lake Titicaca

Río Branco

Porto Velho

Cuiabá

Chapada dos Parecis

Pantanal

Mato Grosso

Goiânia

Planalto de Mato Grosso

Serra do Roncador

BRASÍLIA

Brazilian Highlands

Belo Horizonte

Salvador

Aracaju

Maceió

Recife

João Pessoa

Natal

Mossoró

Fortaleza

Teresina

São Luís

Belém

Santarém

Manaus

Represa Balbina

Represa de Sobradinho

São Francisco

Planalto da Borborema

Abrolhos Bank

Serra da Capivara

Tocantins

Araguaia

Xingu

Tapajós

Amazon

Madeira

Purús

Juruá

Serra do Cachimbo

Serra Formosa

B R A Z I L

Brasil

Amazon Basin

Negro

Branco

Iça

Putumayo

Napo

Marañón

Ucayali

Madre de Dios

Beni

Mamoré

Río Negro

VENEZUELA

COLOMBIA

Cúcuta

Bucaramanga

San Cristóbal

Barinas

BOGOTÁ

Ibagué

Orinoco

Apure

Meta

Guaviare

Caquetá

Caroní

Guiana Highlands

GUYANA

GEORGETOWN

Linden

Essequibo

(claimed by Venezuela)

PARAMARIBO

SURINAME

CAYENNE

FRENCH GUIANA (to France)

(claimed by Suriname)

0 km 500

0 miles 500

Population

● National capital

○ below 50,000   ◌ 50,000 to 100,000   ◉ 100,000 to 500,000   ■ above 500,000

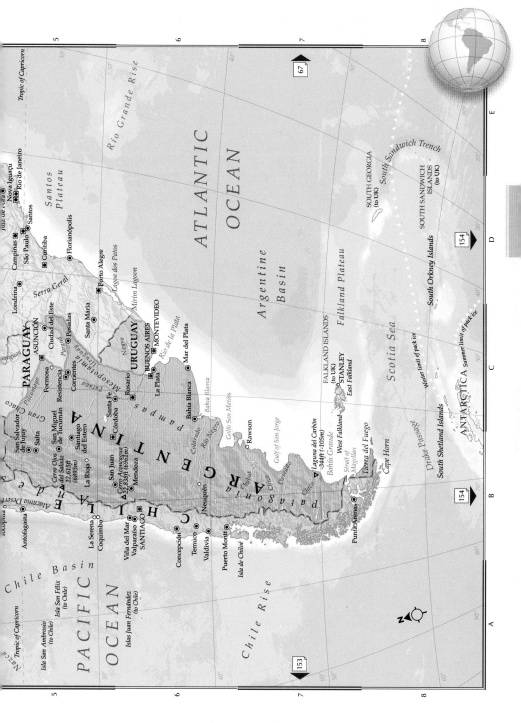

ATLANTIC

OCEAN

PACIFIC

OCEAN

Tropic of Capricorn

Nazca

Chile Basin

Isla San Ambrosio
(to Chile)

Isla San Félix
(to Chile)

Islas Juan Fernández
(to Chile)

Antofagasta

Tropic of Capricorn

Juiz de Fora
Nova Iguaçu
Rio de Janeiro
São Paulo
Campinas
Santos

Santos
Plateau

Curitiba

Florianópolis

Londrina

Serra Geral

Porto Alegre

Lagoa dos Patos

Rio Grande Rise

Santa Maria

Ciudad del Este

Posadas

Mirim Lagoon

PARAGUAY

ASUNCIÓN

URUGUAY

MONTEVIDEO

BUENOS AIRES
La Plata

Mar del Plata

Rio de la Plata

Gran Chaco

Formosa

Resistencia
Corrientes

Santa Fe

Córdoba
Rosario

Bahía Blanca

Bahía Blanca

Argentine

Basin

Salta
San Salvador
de Jujuy

San Miguel
de Tucumán

Cerro Ojos
del Salado
22.615ft
(6893m)

Santiago
del Estero

La Rioja

San Juan

Cerro Aconcagua
22.831ft (6961m)
Mendoza

A N D E S

P A M P A S

Atacama Desert

Cerro Ojos

La Serena
Coquimbo

Viña del Mar
Valparaíso
SANTIAGO

Concepción

Temuco

Valdivia

Puerto Montt

Isla de Chiloé

Chile Rise

C H I L E

A R G E N T I N A

Neuquén

Colorado

Río Negro

P A T A G O N I A

Chubut

Chico

Desaado

Rawson

Golfo San Jorge

Gulf of San Matías

Río Negro

Laguna del Carbón
-344ft (-105m)

Bahía Grande

West Falkland

East Falkland

FALKLAND ISLANDS
(to UK)
STANLEY

Falkland Plateau

Scotia Sea

SOUTH GEORGIA
(to UK)

South Sandwich Trench

SOUTH SANDWICH
ISLANDS
(to UK)

South Orkney Islands

Winter limit of pack ice

Summer limit of pack ice

ANTARCTICA

South Shetland Islands

Drake Passage

Cape Horn

Tierra del Fuego

Strait of
Magellan

Punta Arenas

67

154

154

153

57

Northern South America

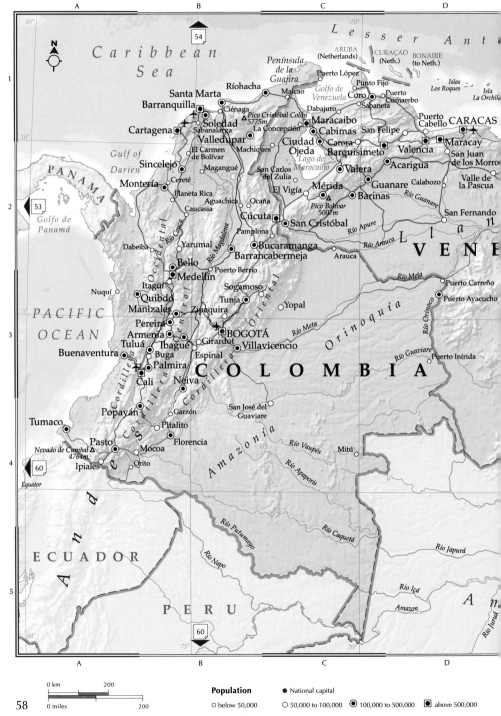

54

N

Caribbean Sea

L e s s e r   A n t

ARUBA (Netherlands)
CURAÇAO (Neth.)
BONAIRE (to Neth.)

Península de la Guajira

Puerto López

Islas Los Roques

Isla La Orchíl

Ríohacha
Maicao
Golfo de Venezuela
Punto Fijo
Coro
Puerto Cumarebo

Santa Marta
Ciénaga
Dabajuro
Sabaneta

Barranquilla
Pico Cristóbal Colón 5775m
Maracaibo

Puerto Cabello
CARACAS

Soledad
Sabanalarga
La Concepción
Cabimas
San Felipe
Maracay

Cartagena
El Carmen de Bolívar
Machiques
Ciudad Ojeda
Carora
Barquisimeto
Valencia
San Juan de los Morro

Valledupar
Magangué
San Carlos del Zulia
Valera
Acarigua

Sincelejo
Lago de Maracaibo
Guanare
Calabozo
Valle de la Pascua

Montería
Cereté
El Vigía
Mérida
Barinas

Gulf of Darien

P A N A M A

Planeta Rica
Aguachica
Ocaña
Pico Bolívar 5007m

San Fernando

53

Golfo de Panamá

Caucasia
Cúcuta
San Cristóbal
Río Apure

L
a
n
V E N E

Dabeiba
Yarumal
Pamplona
Bucaramanga
Río Arauca

Bello
Barrancabermeja
Arauca

Río Cauca
Río Magdalena

Medellín
Puerto Berrío

Itagüí
Sogamoso
Río Meta
Puerto Carreño

Nuquí
Quibdó
Tunja
Puerto Ayacucho

P A C I F I C
O C E A N

Manizales
Zipaquira
Yopal

Río Orinoco

Pereira
Armenia
BOGOTÁ

Orinoquía

Tuluá
Ibagué
Girardot
Villavicencio

Buenaventura
Buga
Espinal
Río Meta

Palmira
Río Guaviare
Puerto Inírida

Cali
Neiva

C O L O M B I A

Popayán
Garzón
San José del Guaviare

Pitalito

Tumaco
Florencia
Mitú

Pasto
Mocoa
Río Vaupés
Río Apaporis

Nevado de Cumbal 4764m

60

Ipiales
Orito

A m a z o n i a

Equator

Río Putumayo
Río Caquetá
Río Japurá

E C U A D O R

Río Napo

Río Içá

A m

Río Juruá

5

P E R U

Amazon

60

0 km   200
0 miles   200

Population   ● National capital

○ below 50,000   ◎ 50,000 to 100,000   ◉ 100,000 to 500,000   ◼ above 500,000

ATLANTIC

OCEAN

SAINT VINCENT & THE GRENADINES

BARBADOS

GRENADA

Tobago

TRINIDAD & TOBAGO

Isla Blanquilla

Isla de Margarita

Islas Los Testigos

Isla La Tortuga

La Asunción

Porlamar

Cumaná

Carúpano

Güiria

Gulf of Paria

Cariaco

Puerto La Cruz

Trinidad

Barcelona

San Mateo

Maturín

Anaco

Cantaura

Zaraza

El Tigre

Tucupita

Río Orinoco

Ciudad Guayana

Ciudad Bolívar

Upata

Embalse de Guri

Matthews Ridge

Charity

El Callao

Spring Garden

GEORGETOWN

El Dorado

Parika

Aurora

New Amsterdam

Peters Mine

Bartica

Totness

PARAMARIBO

Nieuw Amsterdam

Salto Angel

Rockstone

Linden

St-Laurent-du-Maroni

Sinnamary

Kamarang

Nieuw Nickerie

Kaaimanston

Kourou

Mount Roraima 2810m

Orealla

Apoera

W. J. van Blommesteinmeer

CAYENNE

Ouanary

GUYANA

Pakaraima Mountains

SURINAME

Grand Santi

FRENCH GUIANA (to France)

St-Georges

Kurupukari

Juliana Top 1230m

Camopi

(Venezuela claims all of Guyana west of Essequibo River)

Lethem

Acarai Mountains

Tumuc-Humac Mountains

(claimed by Suriname)

Equator

(claimed by Suriname)

Río Negro

B R A Z I L

Río Orinoco

Amazon

Río Caura

Río Caroní

Río Paragua

G u i a n a H i g h l a n d s

Amazon

Z U E L A

O

S

Cuyuni River

Essequibo River

Courantyne River

Maroni River

Montagnes de la Trinité

Montagne Tortue

The Serpent's Mouth

The Serpent's Mouth

A m a z o n B a s i n

Amazon

Río Purús

Río Tapajós

55

67

5

62

62

55

60°

55°

55°

60°

65°

60°

E   F   G   H

1

2

3

4

5

Elevation

-6000m -4000m -2000m -1000m -500m -250m Below sea level 0 250m 500m 1000m 2000m 3000m 4000m 6000m

-19,658ft -13,124ft -6562ft -3281ft -1640ft -820ft -328ft/-100m 0 820ft 1640ft 3281ft 6562ft 9843ft 13,124ft 19,685ft

Western South America

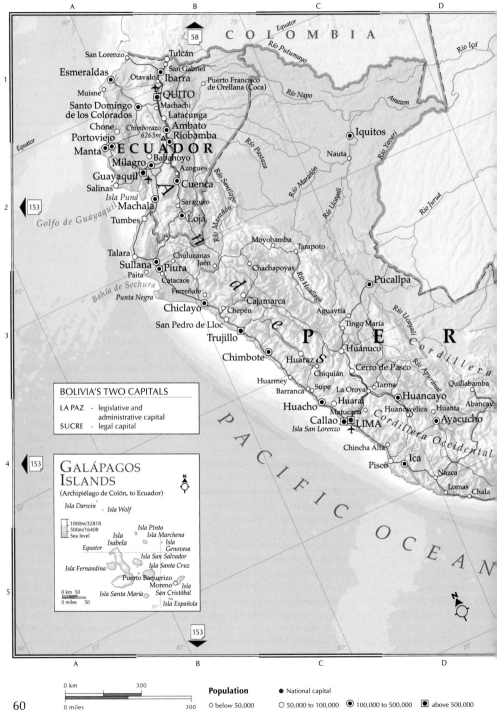

BOLIVIA'S TWO CAPITALS

LA PAZ - legislative and
administrative capital

SUCRE - legal capital

GALÁPAGOS ISLANDS
(Archipiélago de Colón, to Ecuador)

Isla Darwin   Isla Wolf

1000m/3281ft
500m/1640ft
Sea level

Isla Pinta   Isla Marchena
Isla
Isabela   Isla
Genovesa

Equator

Isla San Salvador
Isla Fernandina   Isla Santa Cruz
Puerto Baquerizo
Moreno   Isla
San Cristóbal
Isla Santa María   Isla Española

0 km   50
0 miles   50

Population   ● National capital

○ below 50,000   ○ 50,000 to 100,000   ◉ 100,000 to 500,000   ▣ above 500,000

0 km   300
0 miles   300

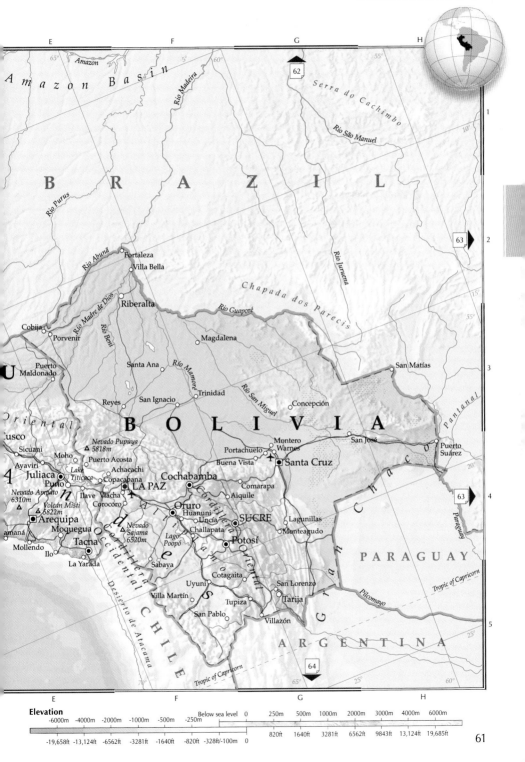

E   F   G   H

Amazon

62

A m a z o n B a s i n

Rio Madeira

Serra do Cachimbo

Rio São Manuel

Rio Purus

B   R   A   Z   I   L

63

Rio Abuná   Portaleza

Villa Bella

Rio Ituriena

Rio Madre de Dios

Chapada dos Parecis

Riberalta

Rio Guaporé

Cobija

Porvenir

Río Beni

Magdalena

U

Puerto
Maldonado

Santa Ana

Río Mamoré

San Matías

Oriental

Reyes   San Ignacio   Trinidad

Río San Miguel

Pantanal

usco

Concepción

Sicuani

Nevado Pupuya
△5818m

Montero
Warnes

San José

Puerto
Suárez

Ayaviri

Moho

Puerto Acosta

Achacachi

Portachuelo

Buena Vista

4   Juliaca

Puno

Lake
Titicaca

Copacabana

Cochabamba

Santa Cruz

Nevado Ampato
6310m
△

Ilave   Viacha

LA PAZ

Comarapa

Volcán Misti
△5822m

Corocoro

Oruro

Aiquile

Arequipa

Moquegua

Huanuni

Uncía

SUCRE

Lagunillas

amaná

Nevado
Sajama
6520m

Challapata

Monteagudo

Mollendo

Ilo

Tacna

Lago
Poopó

Potosí

Cordillera Oriental

La Yarada

Sabaya

PARAGUAY

Uyuni

Cotagaita

Gran Chaco

Villa Martín

San Lorenzo

Tupiza

Tarija

Pilcomayo

Tropic of Capricorn

San Pablo

Villazón

Cordillera Occidental

Desierto de Atacama

CHILE

64

Tropic of Capricorn

A   R   G   E   N   T   I   N   A

B   O   L   I   V   I   A

E   F   G   H

Elevation

| -6000m | -4000m | -2000m | -1000m | -500m | -250m | Below sea level | 0 | 250m | 500m | 1000m | 2000m | 3000m | 4000m | 6000m |

-19,658ft   -13,124ft   -6562ft   -3281ft   -1640ft   -820ft/-100m   0   820ft   1640ft   3281ft   6562ft   9843ft   13,124ft   19,685ft

Brazil

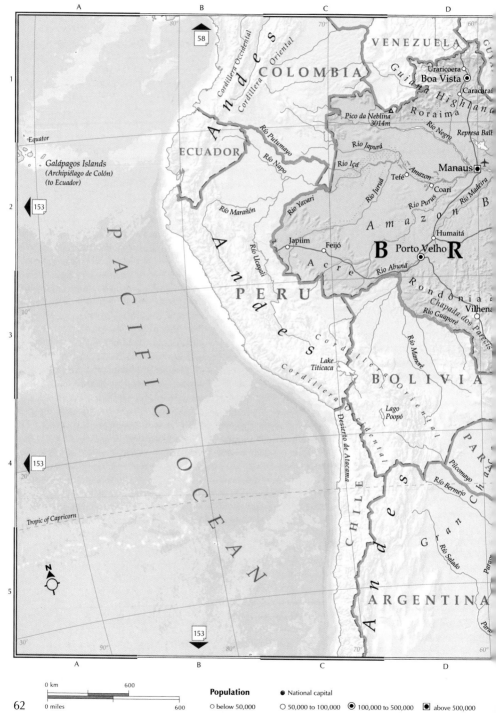

Galápagos Islands
(Archipiélago de Colón)
(to Ecuador)

Population
○ below 50,000
◉ National capital
○ 50,000 to 100,000
◉ 100,000 to 500,000
▣ above 500,000

SURINAME

FRENCH GUIANA
(to France)

Tumuc-Humac Mountains

Mouths of the Amazon

A T L A N T I C

O C E A N

Equator

Amapá

Macapá

Ilha Caviana de Fora

Ilha de Marajó

Baía de Marajó

Belém

Baía de São Marcos

São Luís

Parnaíba

Camocim

Atol das Rocas

San Fernando de Noronha
(to Brazil)

lenquer

Amazon

Santarém

Altamira

Bacabal

Piripiri

Fortaleza

Mossoró

Cabo de São Roque

Itaituba

Represa de Tucuruí

Teresina

Ceará

Assu

Natal

Marabá

Imperatriz

Maranhão

Floriano

Rio Grande do Norte

Juazeiro do Norte

João Pessoa

Carolina

Picos

Paraíba

Campina Grande

Pará

Balsas

Piauí

Pernambuco

Recife

Serra do Cachimbo

B   A   Z   I   L

Represa de Sobradinho

Juazeiro

Alagoas

Maceió

Serra Formosa

Palmas do Tocantins

Chapada Diamantina

Aracaju

Estância

Mato

Serra dos Gradaús

Tocantins

Rio Tocantins

Rio São Francisco

Feira de Santana

Salvador

Rio Xingu

Taguatinga

Bahia

Baía de Todos os Santos

Grosso

Rio Araguaia

Goiás

Planalto

Itabuna

Cuiabá

Anápolis

BRASÍLIA

Central

Janaúba

Vitória da Conquista

ndonópolis

Goiânia

Jataí

Minas

Montes Claros

Canavieiras

Mato Grosso do Sul

Araguari

Gerais

Araçuai

anal

Uberlândia

Uberaba

Governador Valadares

Campo Grande

Espírito Santo

quidauana

Ribeirão Preto

Belo Horizonte

Vitória

sidente Prudente

Marília

Divinópolis

Juiz de Fora

Campos dos Goytacazes

Londrina

Campinas

Maringá

São Paulo

Nova Iguaçu

Rio de Janeiro

AY

Paraná

Santos

Tropic of Capricorn

Represa de Itaipu

Ponta Grossa

Curitiba

Saltos do Rio Iguaçu

Joinville

Paraná

Santa Catarina

Blumenau

Florianópolis

Passo Fundo

Rio Grande

ta Maria

Canoas

do Sul

Porto Alegre

Bagé

Lagoa dos Patos

Rio Negro

Rio Grande

Mirim Lagoon

URUGUAY

A T L A N T I C   O C E A N

Elevation

| -6000m | -4000m | -2000m | -1000m | -500m | -250m | Below sea level 0 | 250m | 500m | 1000m | 2000m | 3000m | 4000m | 6000m |

-19,658ft -13,124ft -6562ft -3281ft -1640ft -820ft -328ft/-100m 0   820ft 1640ft 3281ft 6562ft 9843ft 13,124ft 19,685ft

Southern South America

0 km 200

0 miles 200

Population

● National capital

○ below 50,000   ◉ 50,000 to 100,000   ◉ 100,000 to 500,000   ■ above 500,000

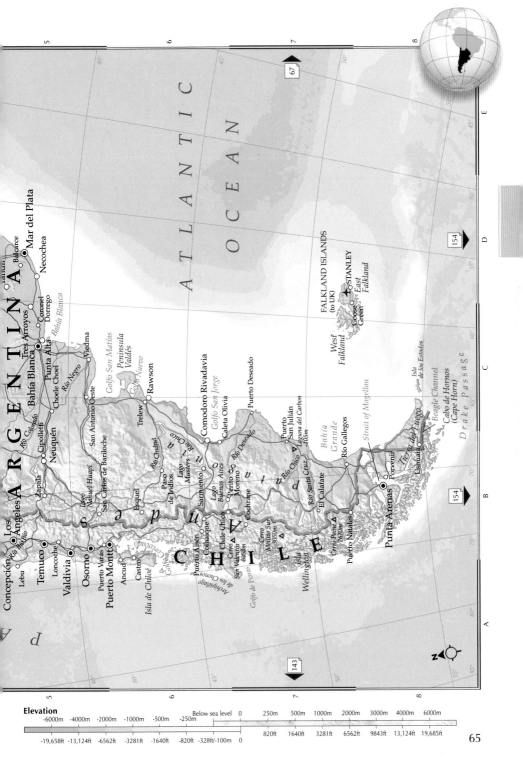

Elevation

| -6000m | -4000m | -2000m | -1000m | -500m | Below sea level 0 | 250m | 500m | 1000m | 2000m | 3000m | 4000m | 6000m |
| | | | | -250m | | | | | | | | |

| -19,658ft | -13,124ft | -6562ft | -3281ft | -1640ft | -820ft -328ft/-100m 0 | 820ft | 1640ft | 3281ft | 6562ft | 9843ft | 13,124ft | 19,685ft |

The Atlantic Ocean

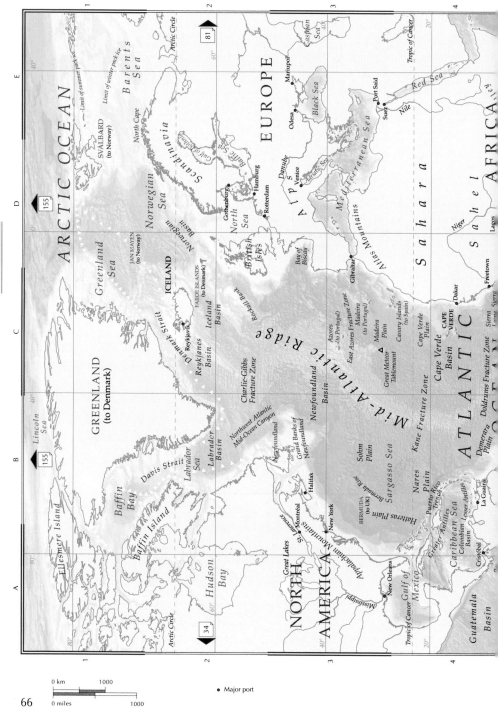

0 km   1000

0 miles   1000

● Major port

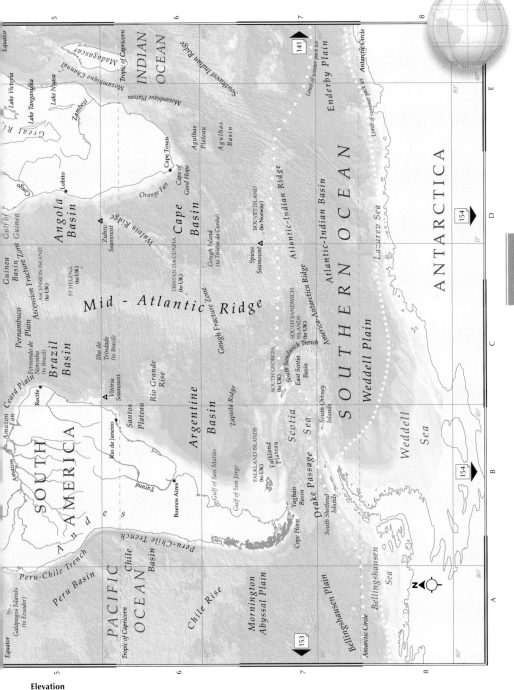

Equator

INDIAN OCEAN

Madagascar

Mozambique Channel

Mozambique Plateau

Lake Victoria
Lake Tanganyika
Lake Nyasa
Zambezi
Great Ri

Tropic of Capricorn

Southwest Indian Ridge

141

Limit of winter pack ice
Limit of summer pack ice

Antarctic Circle

Enderby Plain

Agulhas
Plateau

Agulhas
Basin

Cape Town

Cape of
Good Hope

Orange Fan

Gulf of
Guinea

Guinea
Basin Fracture Zone

Congo

Lobito

Angola
Basin

Walvis Ridge

Zaire
Seamount

**Cape
Basin**

Atlantic–Indian Ridge

154

BOUVET ISLAND
(to Norway)

Lazarev Sea

Atlantic–Indian Basin

Ascension Fracture Zone

ASCENSION ISLAND
(to UK)

ST HELENA
(to UK)

Gough Island
(to Tristan da Cunha)

TRISTAN DA CUNHA
(to UK)

Spiess
Seamount

SOUTHERN OCEAN

ANTARCTICA

Pernambuco
Plain

Mid - Atlantic Ridge

Gough Fracture Zone

America–Antarctica Ridge

Weddell Plain

Ceará Plain

Fernando de
Noronha
(to Brazil)

**Brazil
Basin**

Ilha da
Trindade
(to Brazil)

Recife

Vitória
Seamount

Rio Grande
Rise

SOUTH GEORGIA
(to UK)

SOUTH SANDWICH
ISLANDS
(to UK)

South Sandwich Trench

East Scotia
Basin

Amazon
Fan

**SOUTH
AMERICA**

Rio de Janeiro

Santos
Plateau

Zapiola Ridge

**Argentine
Basin**

Scotia
Sea

South Orkney
Islands

Weddell
Sea

Amazon

A
n
d
e
s

Paraná

Buenos Aires

Gulf of San Matías

Gulf of San Jorge

FALKLAND ISLANDS
(to UK)

Falkland
Plateau

Drake Passage

Yaghan
Basin

South Shetland
Islands

Weddell
Sea

Peru-Chile Trench

Peru Basin

Chile
Basin

Peru-Chile Trench

**PACIFIC
OCEAN**

Chile Rise

Mornington
Abyssal Plain

Cape Horn

Bellingshausen Plain

Antarctic Circle

Bellingshausen
Sea

153

Galápagos Islands
(to Ecuador)

Equator
Tropic of Capricorn

N

Elevation

-6000m	-4000m	-2000m	-1000m	-250m	0
-19,658ft	-13,124ft	-6562ft	-3281ft	-820ft	0

67

Africa

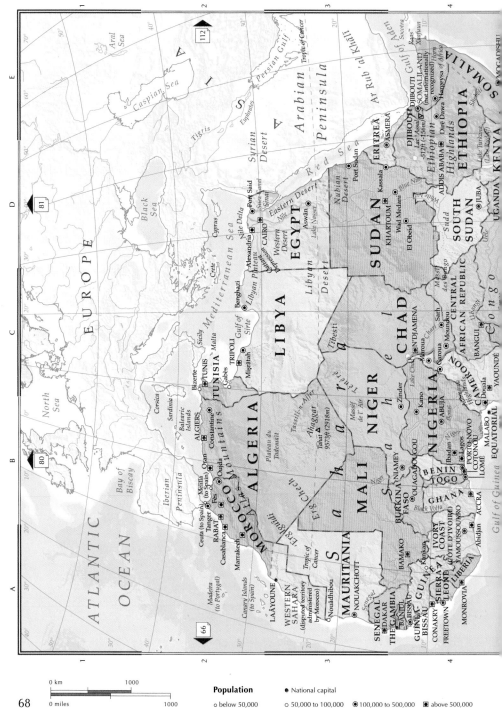

Population

● National capital

o below 50,000　　o 50,000 to 100,000　　◉ 100,000 to 500,000　　■ above 500,000

0 km　　　　1000

0 miles　　　　1000

Northwest Africa

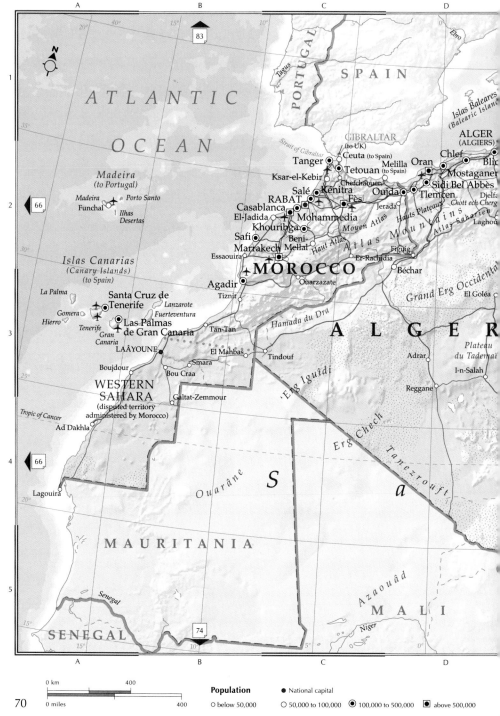

0 km   400

0 miles   400

Population
- ● National capital
- ○ below 50,000
- ◎ 50,000 to 100,000
- ◉ 100,000 to 500,000
- ▣ above 500,000

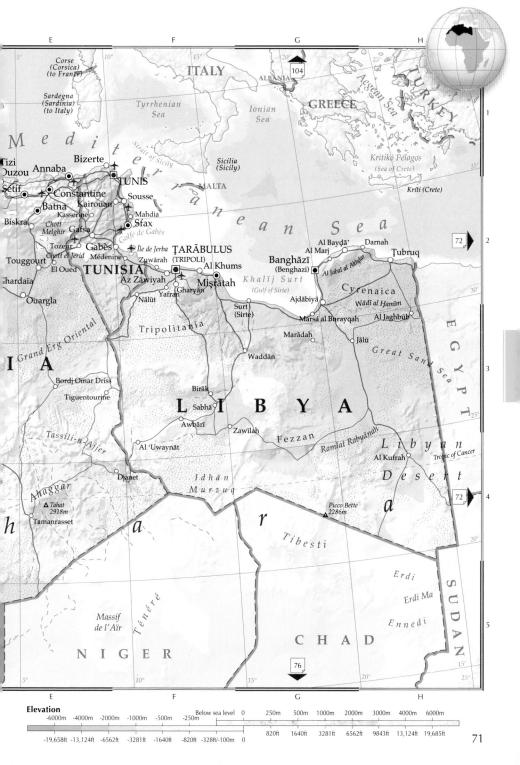

Elevation

-6000m	-4000m	-2000m	-1000m	-500m	-250m	Below sea level	0	250m	500m	1000m	2000m	3000m	4000m	6000m

| -19,658ft | -13,124ft | -6562ft | -3281ft | -1640ft | -820ft | -328ft/-100m | 0 | 820ft | 1640ft | 3281ft | 6562ft | 9843ft | 13,124ft | 19,685ft |

Northeast Africa

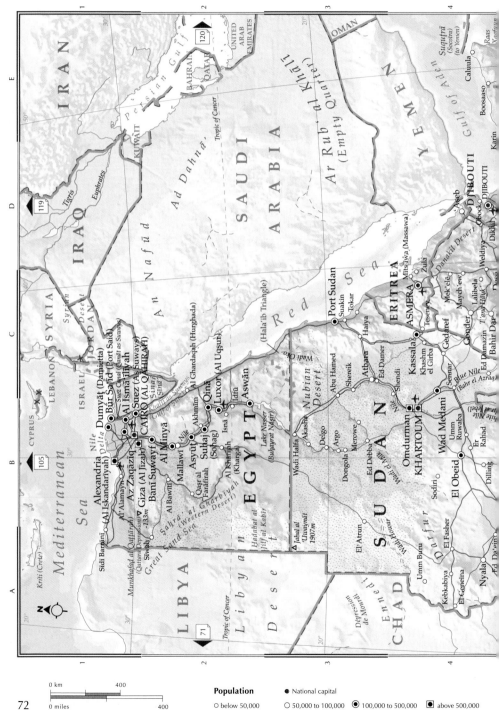

Population

- National capital

○ below 50,000   ○ 50,000 to 100,000   ◉ 100,000 to 500,000   ◼ above 500,000

0 km   400

0 miles   400

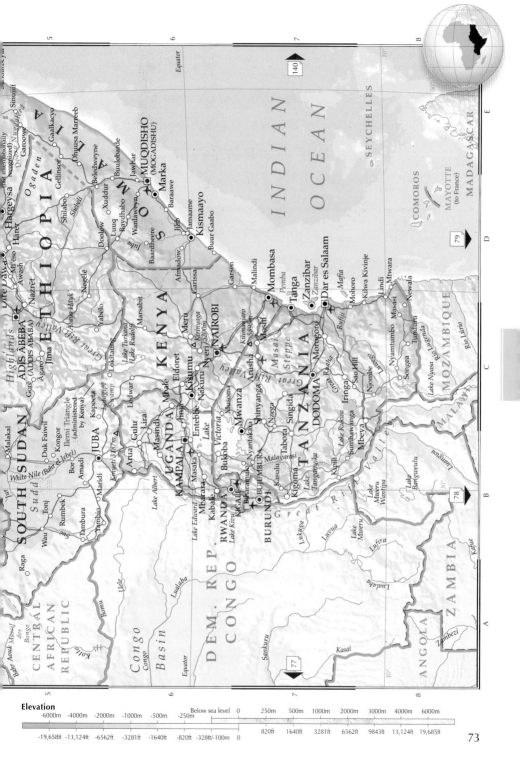

West Africa

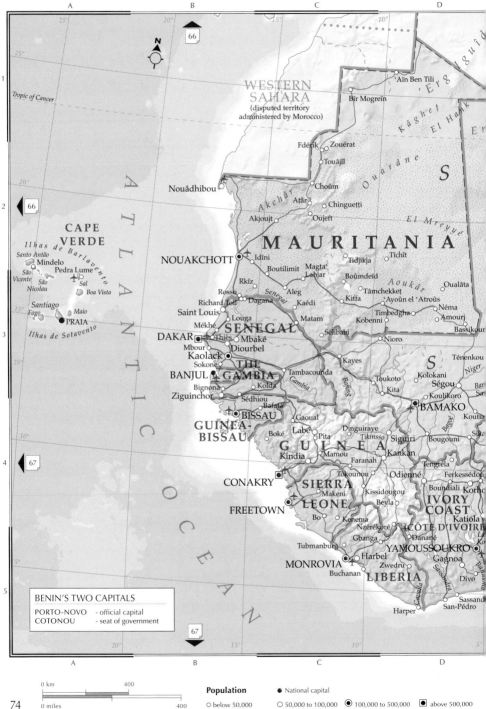

WESTERN SAHARA
(disputed territory
administered by Morocco)

MAURITANIA

CAPE VERDE
Ilhas de Barlavento
Santo Antão
Mindelo
São Vicente
Pedra Lume
São Nicolau
Sal
Boa Vista
Santiago
Fogo
Maio
PRAIA
Ilhas de Sotavento

'Aïn Ben Tili
Bîr Mogreïn
Fdérik
Zouérat
Touâjil
Nouâdhibou
Choûm
Atâr
Chinguetti
Akjoujt
Oujeft
El Mreyyé
NOUAKCHOTT
Idîni
Tidjikja
Tîchît
Boutilimit
Magta'
Lahjar
Boûmdeïd
Aoukâr
Oualâta
Rkîz
Aleg
Tâmchekket
Ayoûn el 'Atroûs
Néma
Rosso
Richard Toll
Dagana
Kaédi
Kiffa
Timbedgha
Amourj
Saint Louis
Matam
Kobenni
Bassikour
Louga
Sélibabi
Mékhé
Nioro
Ténenkou
DAKAR
Thiès
Mbaké
Kayes
SENEGAL
Mbour
Diourbel
Kaolack
Sokone
Toukoto
Kolokani
Ségou
BANJUL
THE GAMBIA
Tambacounda
Kita
Koulikoro
Bignona
Kolda
BAMAKO
Ziguinchor
Sédhiou
Koutia
BISSAU
Bafata
Gaoual
GUINEA-BISSAU
Labé
Dinguiraye
Tikinsso
Siguiri
Bougouni
Sika
Boké
Pita
GUINEA
Kindia
Mamou
Kankan
Tengréla
CONAKRY
Tokounou
Odienné
Ferkessédou
SIERRA LEONE
Makeni
Kissidougou
Boundiali
Korh
Beyla
IVORY COAST
FREETOWN
Bo
Kenema
Katiola
Nzérékoré
CÔTE D'IVOIRE
Tubmanburg
Gbanga
Danané
YAMOUSSOUKRO
MONROVIA
Harbel
Gagnoa
Buchanan
Zwedru
Divo
LIBERIA
Sassand
Harper
San-Pédro

ATLANTIC OCEAN

Tropic of Cancer

BENIN'S TWO CAPITALS

PORTO-NOVO - official capital
COTONOU - seat of government

0 km   400
0 miles   400

Population   • National capital
○ below 50,000   ◎ 50,000 to 100,000   ◉ 100,000 to 500,000   ▣ above 500,000

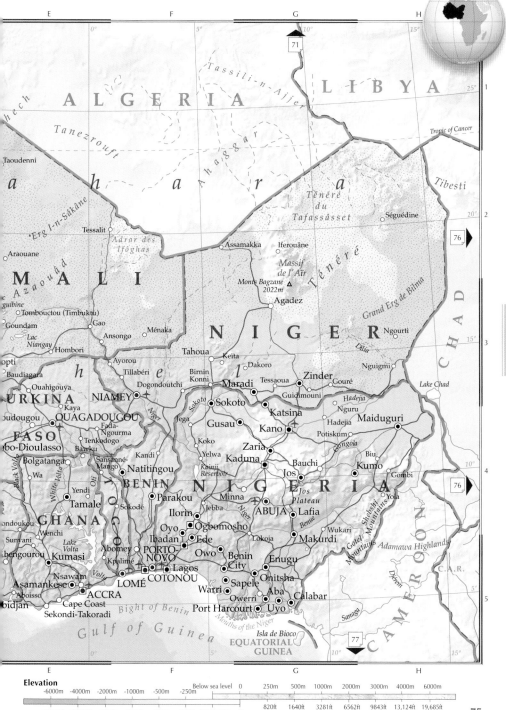

Elevation

					Below sea level	0	250m	500m	1000m	2000m	3000m	4000m	6000m
-6000m	-4000m	-2000m	-1000m	-500m	-250m								
-19,658ft	-13,124ft	-6562ft	-3281ft	-1640ft	-820ft	-328ft/-100m	0	820ft	1640ft	3281ft	6562ft	9843ft	13,124ft	19,685ft

Central Africa

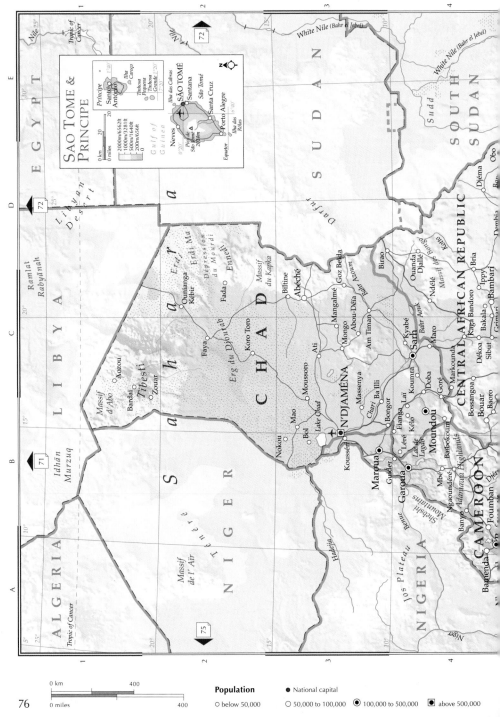

SÃO TOMÉ & PRÍNCIPE

Príncipe
Santo
António
Ilha
Caroço
Timbosa
Pequena
Timbosa
Grande
Ilha das Cabras
SÃO TOMÉ
Santana
São Tomé
Pico de
São Tomé
2024m
Santa Cruz
Neves
Porto Alegre
Equator
Ilha das
Rôlas

Gulf of
Guinea

2000m/6562ft
1000m/3281ft
500m/1640ft
200m/656ft
0

0 km   20
0 miles   20

Population

National capital

○ below 50,000   ○ 50,000 to 100,000   ◉ 100,000 to 500,000   ◼ above 500,000

0 km   400
0 miles   400

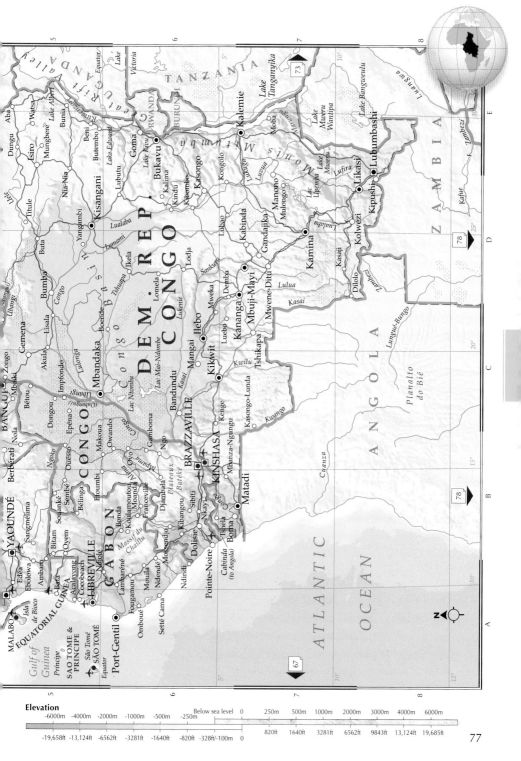

Elevation

-6000m	-4000m	-2000m	-1000m	-500m	-250m	Below sea level 0	250m	500m	1000m	2000m	3000m	4000m	6000m
-19,658ft	-13,124ft	-6562ft	-3281ft	-1640ft	-820ft	-328ft/-100m 0	820ft	1640ft	3281ft	6562ft	9843ft	13,124ft	19,685ft

Southern Africa

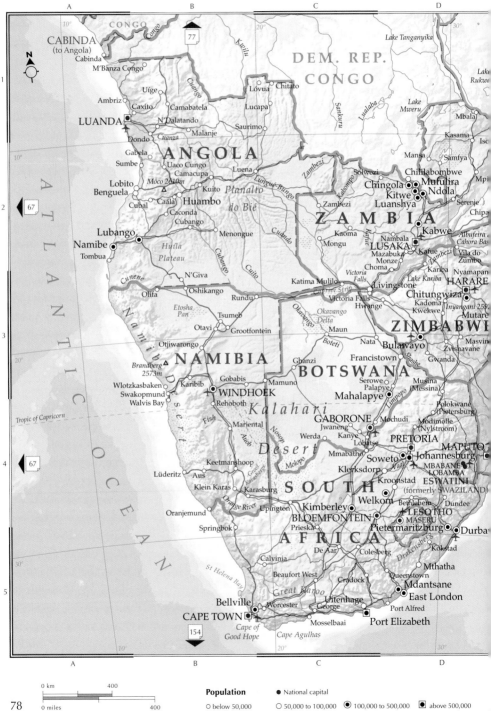

CONGO

Congo

CABINDA
(to Angola)
Cabinda
M'Banza Congo

DEM. REP.
CONGO

Lake Tanganyika

Lake
Rukwe

Uíge
Lóvua
Chitato
Lucapa
Ambriz
Caxito
Camabatela
N'Dalatando
Saurimo

Lake
Mweru

Mbala
LUANDA
Dondo
Malanje
Kasama
Isc

Cuanza

Gabela
Sumbe
Uaco Cungo
Camacupa
Luena
Zambezi
Mansa
Samfya

ANGOLA

Solwezi
Chililabombwe
Mp
Lobito
Benguela
Môco 2610m
Kuito
Planalto
Chingola
Mufulira
Kitwe
Ndola
Cubal
Caála
Huambo
do Bié
Zambezi
Luanshya
Serenje
Chipa
Caconda
Cubango

ZAMBIA

Lubango
Menongue
Kaoma
Nambala
Kabwe
Albufeira
Cahora Bas
Namibe
Mongu
LUSAKA
Tombua
N'Giva
Mazabuka
Monze
Kafue
Vila do
Zumbo

Huíla
Plateau

Cunene

Cuando

Cuito

Choma
Kariba
Nyamapan
Livingstone
HARARE
Olita
Oshikango
Rundu
Victoria
Falls
Lake Kariba
Kadoma
Kwekwe
Chitungwiza

Etosha
Pan

Caprivi Strip
Victoria Falls
Hwange
Inyangani 259.
Mutare

Tsumeb

Okavango

Kadoma
Kwekwe

ZIMBABWE

Otavi
Grootfontein
Okavango
Delta
Maun
Nata
Bulawayo
Masvin

Otjiwarongo
Boteti
Zvishavane

NAMIBIA
Ghanzi
Francistown
Gwanda

Brandberg
2573m
BOTSWANA
Shashe
Karibib
Gobabis
Mamuno
Serowe
Palapye
Musina
(Messina)
Wlotzkasbaken
Swakopmund
Walvis Bay
WINDHOEK
Rehoboth
Mahalapye
Limpopo
Polokwane
(Pietersburg)

Tropic of Capricorn
Kalahari
GABORONE
Mochudi
Modimolle
(Nylstroom)
Mariental
Jwaneng
Kanye
PRETORIA
Werda
Lobatse
MAPUTO

Desert
Mmabatho
Soweto
Johannesburg
MBABANE
LOBAMBA

Keetmanshoop
Klerksdorp
ESWATINI
(formerly SWAZILAND)

Lüderitz
Aus
Karasburg
Kroonstad
Vaal

SOUTH

Klein Karas
Welkom
Bethlehem
Dundee

Oranjemund
Upington
Kimberley
LESOTHO
Prieska
BLOEMFONTEIN
MASERU
Pietermaritzburg
Durba

Springbok

AFRICA
De Aar
Colesberg
Kokstad

Calvinia
Mthatha

St Helena Bay
Beaufort West
Cradock
Queenstown
Mdantsane
East London

Great Karoo
Uitenhage
Port Alfred

Bellville
Worcester
George

CAPE TOWN
Mosselbaai
Port Elizabeth

Cape of
Good Hope
Cape Agulhas

ATLANTIC OCEAN

Namib Desert

0 km   400

0 miles   400

Population   ● National capital

○ below 50,000   ○ 50,000 to 100,000   ◎ 100,000 to 500,000   ■ above 500,000

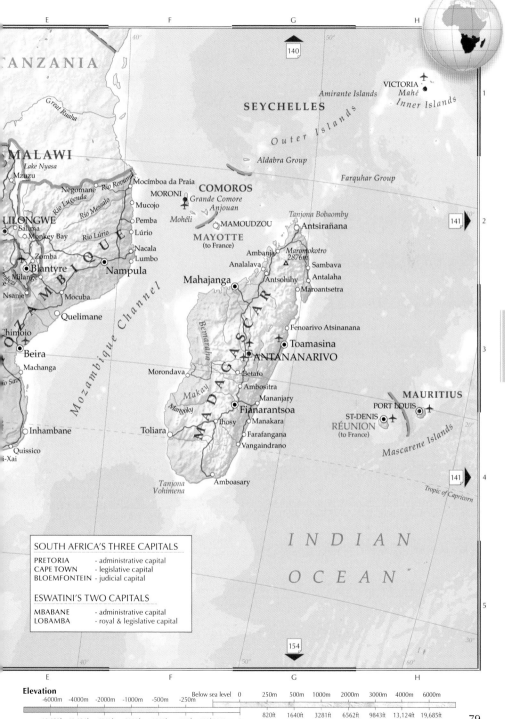

E   F   G   H

140

TANZANIA

40°

50°

VICTORIA
Amirante Islands   *Mahé*
Inner Islands

SEYCHELLES

1

Outer Islands

MALAWI

Great Ruaha

Mzuzu

Lake Nyasa

Aldabra Group

Farquhar Group

Negomane   *Rio Rovuma*
Rio Lugenda

Mocímboa da Praia

MORONI
Rio Messalo

COMOROS

141

2

LILONGWE   Mucojo
Salima
Monkey Bay   *Rio Lúrio*   Pemba
Zomba   Nacala

Grande Comore
Anjouan

Mohéli

MAMOUDZOU

MAYOTTE
(to France)

Antsirañana

Maromokotro
2876m

Ambanja

Analalava

Sambava

Blantyre   Lumbo
Milange
Nsanje

Nampula

Antsohihy

Antalaha

Maroantsetra

Mocuba

Mahajanga

Quelimane

MADAGASCAR

Fenoarivo Atsinanana

3

Chimoio

Mozambique Channel

Toamasina

ANTANANARIVO

Beira
Machanga

Morondava

Bemaraha

Betafo

Ambositra

MAURITIUS

PORT LOUIS

o Save

Inhambane

Makay

Mangoky

Mananjary

Fianarantsoa

Ihosy

Manakara

ST-DENIS

RÉUNION
(to France)

20°

Mascarene Islands

Quissico

-Xai

Farafangana

Vangaindrano

4

*Tanjona
Vohimena*

Amboasary

141

Tropic of Capricorn

INDIAN

SOUTH AFRICA'S THREE CAPITALS

PRETORIA   - administrative capital
CAPE TOWN   - legislative capital
BLOEMFONTEIN - judicial capital

OCEAN

ESWATINI'S TWO CAPITALS

MBABANE   - administrative capital
LOBAMBA   - royal & legislative capital

5

154

40°

50°

60°

30°

E   F   G   H

Elevation

| -6000m | -4000m | -2000m | -1000m | -500m | -250m | Below sea level | 0 | 250m | 500m | 1000m | 2000m | 3000m | 4000m | 6000m |

| -19,658ft | -13,124ft | -6562ft | -3281ft | -1640ft | -820ft | -328ft/-100m | 0 | 820ft | 1640ft | 3281ft | 6562ft | 9843ft | 13,124ft | 19,685ft |

Europe

155

66

66

68

REYKJAVÍK
ICELAND
Vatnajökull
Arctic Circle
Limit of winter pack ice

Reykjanes Ridge

Iceland Basin

Hatton Ridge

FAROE ISLANDS
(to Denmark)

Faroe-Iceland Ridge

Faroe-Shetland Trough

Trondheim

Bergen
OSLO
Stavanger

N O R W A Y

Norwegian Basin

Norwegian Sea

Lofo

Charlie - Gibbs Fracture Zone

Mid - Atlantic Ridge

Rockall Bank
Rockall Trough

Porcupine Plain

Shetland Islands
Orkney Islands
Outer Hebrides

British Isles

Ireland
Glasgow
Edinburgh
Belfast
Isle of Man

North Sea

Gothenburg
Aalborg
Odense

Jönköping
Vätter

Jutland

IRELAND
DUBLIN

UNITED KINGDOM

Liverpool Manchester
Britain

DENMARK
COPENHAG
Malmö

ATLANTIC

OCEAN

Azores-Biscay Rise
Charcot Seamounts

Biscay Plain

Iberian Plain

Galicia Bank

Cardiff
Birmingham
LONDON

Celtic Sea
Celtic Shelf
English Channel
Channel Is.
Channel Islands
le Havre

Rennes
Nantes
PARIS

Orléans
Seine
Loire

NETHERLANDS
THE HAGUE
AMSTERDAM
Rotterdam
BELGIUM
BRUSSELS
Liège
LUXEMBOURG
LUXEMBOURG

Hamburg
Hanover
Düsseldorf
Bonn
Frankfurt am Main
Stuttgart
Strasbourg

BERLIN
GERMANY
PRAGUE
CZECH REPUBLI
(CZECHIA)

Elbe
N O
Pozn
Wroclaw
Odr

Bay of Biscay
Bordeaux
Bilbao
Garonne

A Coruña
Cordillera Cantábrica

Porto
PORTUGAL

Duero

Tagus Plain
LISBON

Iberian
Peninsula
SPAIN

MADRID
Zaragoza
Ebro
Tagus

Seville
Guadalquivir

Barcelona
Valencia

Palma
Balearic Islands

Málaga
GIBRALTAR (to UK)
Ceuta (to Spain)
Melilla (to Spain)

Madeira
(to Portugal)

Horseshoe Seamounts

Canary Islands
(to Spain)

Strait of Gibraltar

Toulouse
Pyrenees
ANDORRA
Marseille

FRANCE

Massif Central

Lyon
BERN
SWITZERLAND

Mont Blanc
15,774ft
(4808m)
Nice
MONACO

Zurich
Munich
LIECH
VIENNA
Salzburg
AUSTRIA
Innsbruck

Milan
Turin
Venice
Pisa
Bologna

BRATISL
SLOVENIA
LJUBLJANA
ZAGR
Trieste
CROAT
SAN MARINO
BOSN & HE
SARAJE
Mosta

Corsica

I T A L Y
Apennines

VATICAN CITY
ROME

Adriatic Sea

Sardinia
Algerian Basin
Cagliari
Tyrrhenian Sea

Naples
Bari

Cosenza
Palermo
Mount Etna
10,922ft
(3329m)
Sicily
Catania

Ioni
Se
Ioni
Bas

MALTA
VALLETTA

Atlas Mountains

M o u n t a i n s

AFRICA

M e d i t e r r a n e a n

Population
- National capital

o below 50,000   o 50,000 to 100,000   ◉ 100,000 to 500,000   ▣ above 500,000

0 km   500
0 miles   500

The North Atlantic

ATLANTIC OCEAN

Population ● National capital

○ below 50,000 ○ 50,000 to 100,000 ◉ 100,000 to 500,000 ■ above 500,000

0 km   400
0 miles   400

E   F   G   H

Lincoln Sea

ARCTIC OCEAN

Kap Morris Jesup

Wandel Sea

Zemlya Frantsa-Iosifa

Independence Fjord

Kvitøya

Nord

SVALBARD
(to Norway)

Novaya Zemlya

Nordaustlandet

Kong Karls Land

Kong Frederik VIII Land

Spitsbergen

Barentsøya

Barents Sea

LONGYEARBYEN
Barentsburg

Edgeøya

155

110

Greenland Sea

Storfjorden

Limit of winter pack ice

Bjørnøya
(to Norway)

Kong Christian X Land

Daneborg

Nordkapp
(North Cape)

△ Petermann Bjerg
2940m

Limit of summer pack ice

FINLAND

Kong Oscar Fjord

Mohns Ridge

Arctic Circle

Ittoqqortoormiit
Kangertittivaq
Kangikajik

JAN MAYEN
(to Norway)

S W E D E N

Norwegian Sea

84

trait

ICELAND

Norwegian Basin

Vestfjorden

Bolungarvík
Siglufjörður Raufarhöfn
saförður
    Húsavík
  Akureyri
Stykkishólmur Seyðisfjörður
REYKJAVÍK Neskaupstaður
  Selfoss Vatnajökull △
Thorlákshöfn Djúpivogur
Surtsey Hvannadalshnúkur
  Vestmannaeyjar 2119m

Gulf of Bothnia

N O R W A Y

N
↑

FAROE ISLANDS
(to Denmark)

TÓRSHAVN

85

Shetland Islands

E   F   G   H

Elevation

| -6000m | -4000m | -2000m | -1000m | -500m | -250m | Below sea level 0 | 250m | 500m | 1000m | 2000m | 3000m | 4000m | 6000m |

| -19,658ft | -13,124ft | -6562ft | -3281ft | -1640ft | -820ft | -328ft/-100m | 0 | 820ft | 1640ft | 3281ft | 6562ft | 9843ft | 13,124ft | 19,685ft |

Scandinavia & Finland

Population

- National capital
- ○ below 50,000
- ○ 50,000 to 100,000
- ◎ 100,000 to 500,000
- ▣ above 500,000

0 km   200

0 miles   200

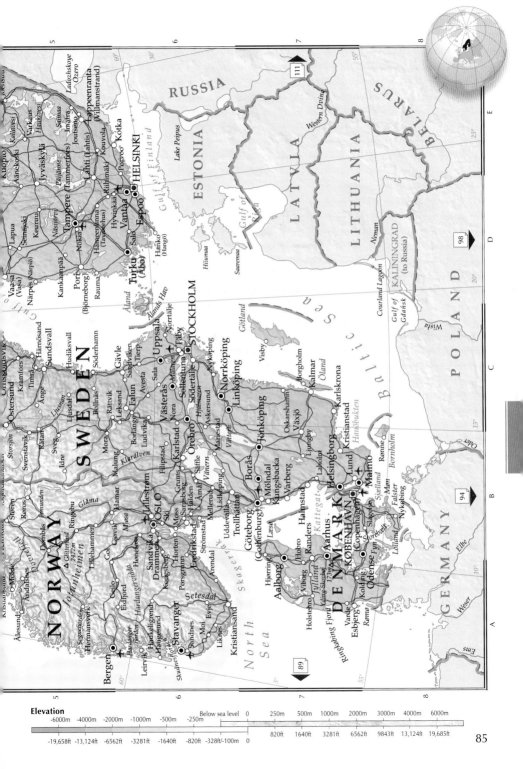

RUSSIA

111

Ladozhskoye
Ozero

Kallavesi
Varkaus
Iisalmi
Kuopio

Äänekoski
Savonlinna
Imatra
Lappeenranta
(Villmanstrand)

Jyväskylä
Hankesi
Joutseno
Kuovola
Kotka

Päijänne
Lahti (Lahtis)

Jämsä
(Tammerfors)

Keuruu
Näsijärvi
Tampere
Nokia
Hyvinkää
Porvoo

Lapua
Seinäjoki
Hämeenlinna
(Tavastehus)
Vantaa
HELSINKI
ESPOO

Vaasa
(Vasa)
Kankaanpää
Pori
(Björneborg)
Rauma
Salo
Turku
(Åbo)

Närpes (Närpio)

Lake Peipus

ESTONIA

Gulf of Finland

Hanko
(Hango)

Hiiumaa

Gulf of
Riga

Saaremaa

LATVIA

Western Drina

LITHUANIA

Neman

Courland Lagoon

Gulf of
Gdansk

KALININGRAD
(to Russia)

98

BELARUS

POLAND

Wisła

Åland
Ålands Hav

Gulf of Bothnia

STOCKHOLM

Uppsala
Norrtälje
Täby

Gävle
Sandviken
Tierp

Sundsvall
Hudiksvall
Söderhamn

Harnösand

Ljusdal

Östersund
Krokom
Timrå
Ånge

Storsjön
Svenstavik
Rätvik
Leksand
Falun
Borlänge
Avesta
Sala
Mälaren
Solna
Södertälje
Nyköping

Norrköping
Linköping

Gotland

Visby

Borgholm
Kalmar
Öland

Karlskrona
Kristianstad

Baltic Sea

Bornholm
Rønne

Härsida
Idre
Sveg
Mora
Malung
Ludvika
Nora
Västerås

Örebro
Askersund
Motala
Vättern

Jönköping

Oskarshamn
Växjö

Ljungby

Hälsingborg
Lund
Malmö

Helsingør

Møn
Falster
Nykøbing

Slagelse
Storebælt
Lolland

Odense

KØBENHAVN
Copenhagen
Sjælland

DENMARK

Aarhus
Randers
Hobro
Viborg
Jylland

Aalborg
Hjørring
Holstebro
Ringkøbing Fjord
Varde
Esbjerg
Rømø
Kolding

Hanöbukten

GERMANY

Oder

Elbe

Weser

Ems

94

NORWAY
SWEDEN

Glitterind
2472m
Jotunheimen

Storen
Røros
Femunden
Dombås
Ringbu
Lillehammer

Hamar
Gjøvik
Mjøsa
Lillestrøm
OSLO
Ski
Drammen
Moss
Sarpsborg
Halden
Fredrikstad
Strömstad
Uddevalla
Trollhättan
Göteborg
(Gothenburg)
Läsö
Mölndal
Kungsbacka
Varberg
Halmstad
Laholm
Falkenberg
Borås

Vänern
Mariestad
Lidköping
Skövde
Amål
Grums
Karlstad
Filipstad
Ludvika
Klarälven

Andalsnes
Molde
Andalshes
Ålesund

Bergen

Leirvik
Stord
Haugesund
Hardanger
Hardangervidda
Eidfjord
Geilo
Gol
Hønefoss
Sandvika
Horten
Sandefjord
Larvik
Porsgrunn
Skien
Kongsberg

Setesdal

Kristiansand
Liknes
Mandal
Moi
Evje
Flekkefjord
Sandnes
Stavanger

North
Sea

Skagerrak

Kattegat

89

Elevation

| -6000m | -4000m | -2000m | -1000m | -500m | -250m | Below sea level | 0 | 250m | 500m | 1000m | 2000m | 3000m | 4000m | 6000m |

| -19,658ft | -13,124ft | -6562ft | -3281ft | -1640ft | -820ft | -328ft/-100m | 0 | 820ft | 1640ft | 3281ft | 6562ft | 9843ft | 13,124ft | 19,685ft |

The Low Countries

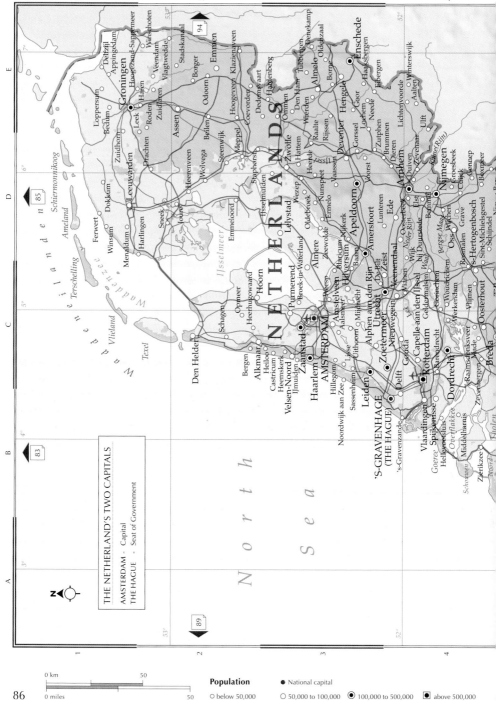

THE NETHERLAND'S TWO CAPITALS

AMSTERDAM - Capital
THE HAGUE - Seat of Government

Population

○ below 50,000   ○ 50,000 to 100,000   ◉ 100,000 to 500,000   ■ above 500,000

● National capital

0 km   50
0 miles   50

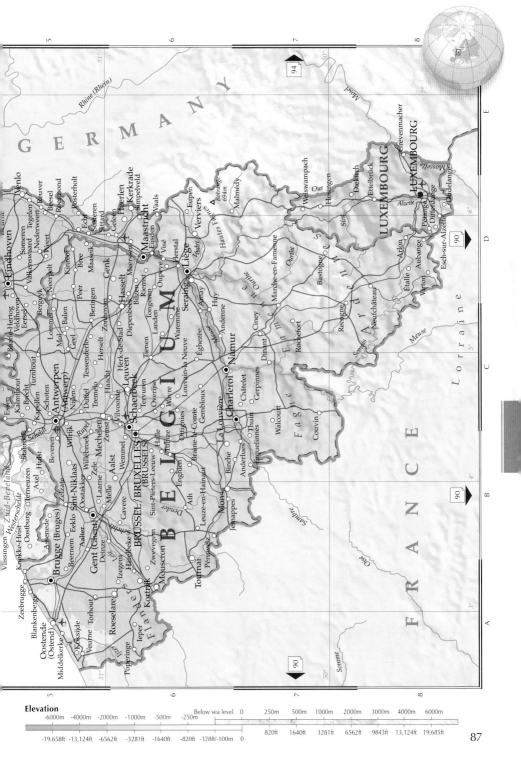

Elevation

-6000m	-4000m	-2000m	-1000m	-500m	-250m	Below sea level	0	250m	500m	1000m	2000m	3000m	4000m	6000m
-19,658ft	-13,124ft	-6562ft	-3281ft	-1640ft	-820ft	-328ft/-100m	0	820ft	1640ft	3281ft	6562ft	9843ft	13,124ft	19,685ft

The British Isles

0 km — 100

0 miles — 100

Population

● National capital
◉ Internal administrative capital

○ below 50,000
○ 50,000 to 100,000
◉ 100,000 to 500,000
■ above 500,000

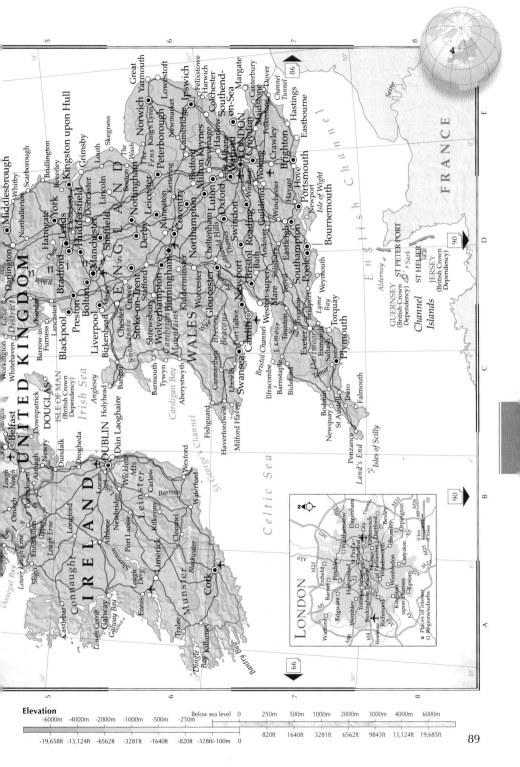

LONDON

Places of interest
Regions/suburbs

Elevation

-6000m	-4000m	-2000m	-1000m	-500m	-250m	Below sea level	0	250m	500m	1000m	2000m	3000m	4000m	6000m
-19,658ft	-13,124ft	-6562ft	-3281ft	-1640ft	-820ft	-328ft/-100m	0	820ft	1640ft	3281ft	6562ft	9843ft	13,124ft	19,685ft

France, Andorra & Monaco

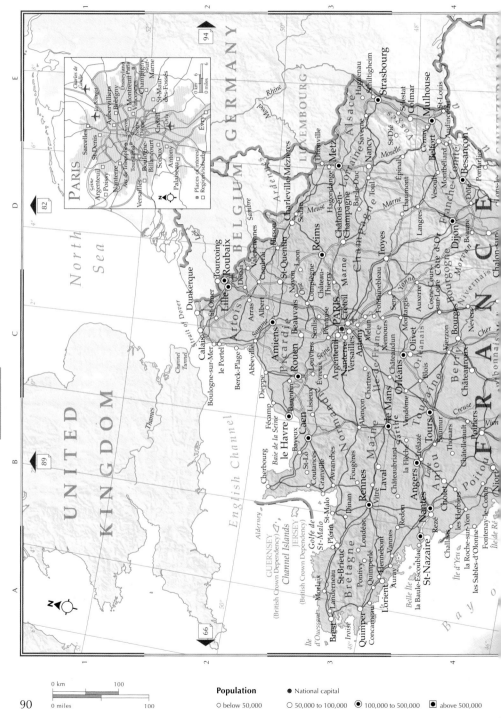

PARIS

Charles de
Gaulle

Sarcelles
St-Denis
Argenteuil
Poissy
Bezons
BZy
Nanterre
Aubervilliers
Bobigny
Disneyland
Paris
Montreuil
Champs-sur-
Marne
Vincennes
St-Maur-
des-Fossés
Evry
Arc de Triomphe
Tour Eiffel
Louvre
Boulogne-
Billancourt
Créteil
Orly
Versailles
Sceaux
Antony
Palaiseau

0 km 6
0 miles 6

□ Places of interest
□ Regions/suburbs

Population

● National capital

○ below 50,000   ○ 50,000 to 100,000   ◉ 100,000 to 500,000   ■ above 500,000

0 km 100
0 miles 100

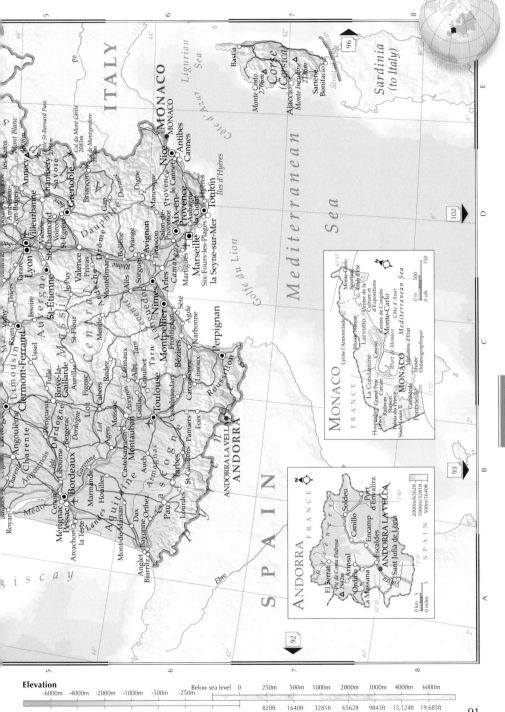

Elevation

-6000m	-4000m	-2000m	-1000m	-500m	Below sea level	0	250m	500m	1000m	2000m	3000m	4000m	6000m
				-250m									

| -19,658ft | -13,124ft | -6562ft | -3281ft | -1640ft | -820ft | -328ft/-100m | 0 | 820ft | 1640ft | 3281ft | 6562ft | 9843ft | 13,124ft | 19,685ft |

Spain & Portugal

Population   ● National capital

○ below 50,000   ○ 50,000 to 100,000   ◉ 100,000 to 500,000   ■ above 500,000

E F G H

Bay of
Biscay

do Bermeo
Zarautz
Eibar
Donostia/San Sebastián
Irun
F R A N C E
bao
Tolosa
Bergara
País Vasco
itoria-Gasteiz
Pamplona
Miranda
de Ebro
Estella
Jaca
ogroño
Navarra
Arnedo
Calahorra
La Rioja
Tudela
Tarazona
Soria
Pyrenees
Monte Perdido
3348m
La Seu d'Urgell
Huesca
Barbastro
Monzón
Balaguer
Cervera
Ejea de
los Caballeros
ANDORRA
Ripoll
Berga
Manlleu
Cataluña
Vic
Figueres
Banyoles
Girona
Palafrugell
Palamós
Blanes
Arenys de Mar
Golfe du Lion

42°

96

Burgo
e Osma
Medinaceli
Calatayud
Aragón
Daroca
Alcañiz
Zaragoza
Lleida
(Lérida)
Tàrrega
Fraga
Sabadell
Terrassa
Mataró
Barcelona
L'Hospitalet de Llobregat
Costa Brava

I N
Guadalajara
lcalá de Henares
rejón de Ardoz
Teruel
Tortosa
Amposta
Sant Carles de la Ràpita
Vinaròs
Vilafranca del Penedès
Valls
Reus
Sitges
El Vendrell
Tarragona

Tagus
Tarancón
Cuenca
Javalambre
2020m
Onda
Castellón de la Plana/
Castelló de la Plana
País Valenciana

40°

97

astilla-La Mancha
Mota del Cuervo
Campo de Criptana
Socuéllamos
Tomelloso
La Roda
anzanares
La Solana
depeñas
Villanueva de los Infantes
Albacete
Almansa
Vall d'Uxó/La Vall d'Uxó
Burjassot
Borriana/Burriana
Sagunto/Sagunt
Valencia
Catarroja
Sueca
Cullera
Gandia
Oliva
Xàtiva
Torrent
Algemesí
Júcar
Costa del
Azahar
Golfo de
Valencia
Ibiza
Eivissa (Ibiza)
Formentera
Menorca
(Minorca)
Ciutadella
Maó-Mahón
Pollença
Sa Pobla
Palma
Llucmajor
Manacor
Felanitx
Illa de
Cabrera
Mallorca
(Majorca)
Islas Baleares
(Balearic Islands)

Beas de Segura
Hellín
Segura
Jumilla
Ontinyent
Villena
Alcoy
Monóvar
Elda
Benidorm
Villajoyosa/La Vila Joiosa
Dénia
Sant Joan d'Alacant
Alicante/Alacant
Elche/
Elx
Callosa de Segura
Orihuela
Murcia
Moratalla
Cieza
Mula
Murcia
Huéscar
Totana
La Unión
Lorca
Cartagena
Baza
Aguilas
Guadix
Mulhacén
3481m
Mojácar
evada
Berja
Almería
Adra
Costa Blanca
Mediterranean Sea

ALGERIA

GIBRALTAR (to UK)

N
SPAIN
Gibraltar
Airport
North Mole
Gibraltar
Harbour
Catalan Bay
Catalan
Bay
Bay of Gibraltar
The Rock
Sandy
Bay
Rosia
Summit
426m
Rosia
Bay
Little
Bay
Buena Vista
Europa Point
Strait of Gibraltar

200m/656ft
Sea level

0 km   1
0 mile   1

E F G H

Germany & the Alpine States

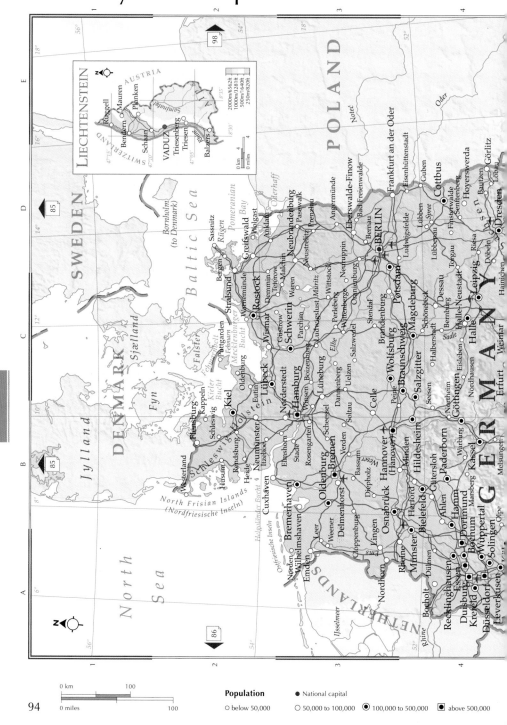

Population

○ below 50,000 ○ 50,000 to 100,000 ◉ 100,000 to 500,000 ◼ above 500,000

● National capital

0 km   100

0 miles   100

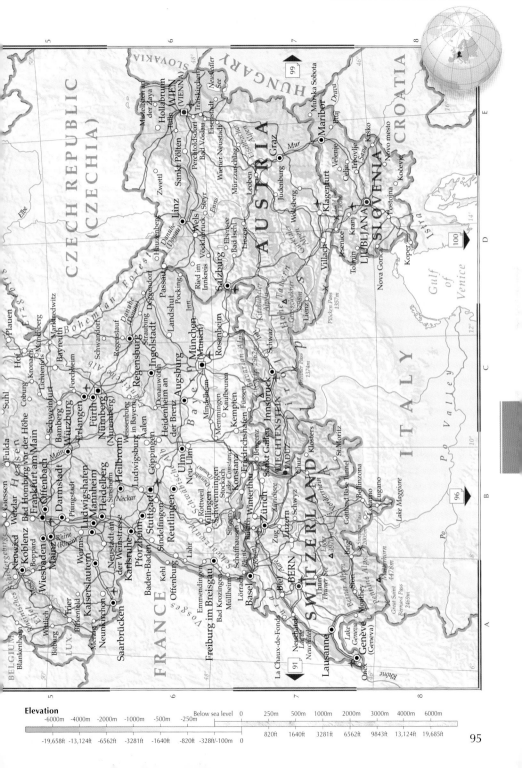

Elevation

						Below sea level	0	250m	500m	1000m	2000m	3000m	4000m	6000m
-6000m	-4000m	-2000m	-1000m	-500m	-250m									
-19,658ft	-13,124ft	-6562ft	-3281ft	-1640ft	-820ft	-328ft/-100m	0	820ft	1640ft	3281ft	6562ft	9843ft	13,124ft	19,685ft

Population
- ○ below 50,000
- ○ 50,000 to 100,000
- ◉ 100,000 to 500,000
- ■ above 500,000
- ● National capital

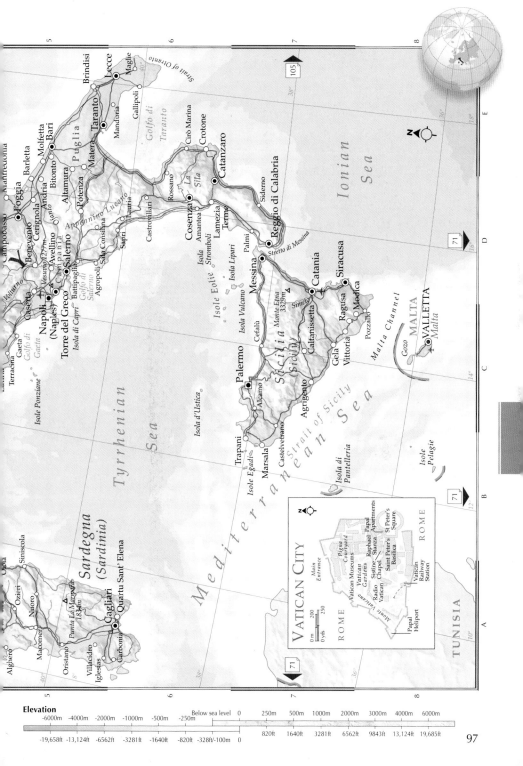

E

71

D

71

B

71

Ionian Sea

Strait of Otranto

Golfo di Taranto

Brindisi
Lecce
Maglie
Taranto
Manduria
Gallipoli
Bari
Molfetta
Bitonto
Barletta
Andria
Cerignola
Foggia
Manfredonia
Benevento
Avellino
Campobasso
Potenza
Altamura
Matera
Sala Consilina
Sapri
Castrovillari
Rossano
Cirò Marina
Crotone
Catanzaro
Siderno
Reggio di Calabria

Puglia

Appennino Lucano

La Sila

Campania

Vesuvio 1277m

Napoli (Naples)
Caserta
Gaeta
Terracina
Torre del Greco
Battipaglia
Agropoli
Salerno
Lauria
Cosenza
Amantea
Lamezia Terme
Palmi
Stretto di Messina

Golfo di Salerno

Golfo di Gaeta

Isola di Capri
Isole Ponziane

Volturno

Tyrrhenian Sea

Isola d'Ustica

Isole Eolie
Isola Stromboli
Isola Lipari
Isola Vulcano

Messina
Cefalù
Palermo
Alcamo
Trapani
Isole Egadi
Marsala
Castelvetrano
Agrigento
Caltanissetta
Gela
Vittoria
Ragusa
Modica
Pozzallo
Catania
Siracusa
Monte Etna 3329m
Simeto

Sicilia (Sicily)

Strait of Sicily

Mediterranean Sea

Isola di Pantelleria

Isole Pelagie

Malta Channel

Gozo
MALTA
VALLETTA
Malta

TUNISIA

Sardegna (Sardinia)

Siniscola
Ozieri
Nuoro
Olbia
Macomer
Oristano
Alghero
Iglesias
Villacidro
Carbonia
Cagliari
Quartu Sant'Elena
Quartu Sant' Elena
Punta La Marmora 1834m

N◄○

VATICAN CITY

ROME

Main Entrance
Vatican Museums
Pigna Courtyard
Raphael Stanza
Sistine Chapel
Radio Vatican
Vatican Gardens
Papal Apartments
Saint Peter's Basilica
St Peter's Square
Vatican Railway Station
Papal Heliport
Monte Vaticano

ROME

0 m   200   250
0 yds   250

Elevation

-6000m	-4000m	-2000m	-1000m	-500m	-250m	Below sea level 0	250m	500m	1000m	2000m	3000m	4000m	6000m
-19,658ft	-13,124ft	-6562ft	-3281ft	-1640ft	-820ft	-328ft/-100m 0	820ft	1640ft	3281ft	6562ft	9843ft	13,124ft	19,685ft

97

Central Europe

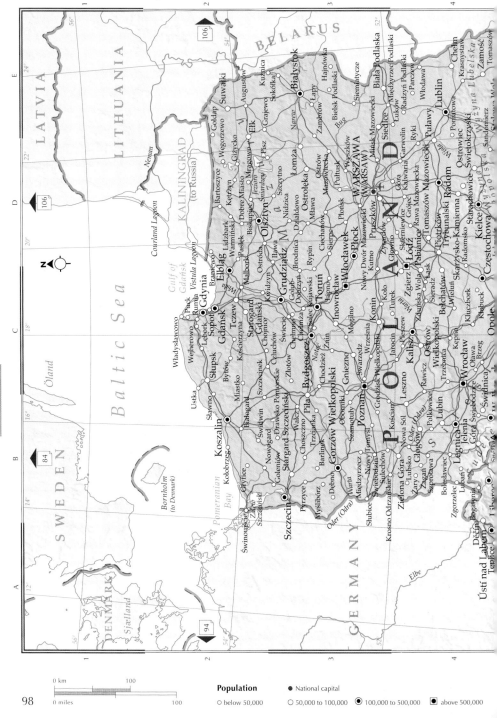

0 km 100

0 miles 100

Population ● National capital

○ below 50,000 ○ 50,000 to 100,000 ◉ 100,000 to 500,000 ◼ above 500,000

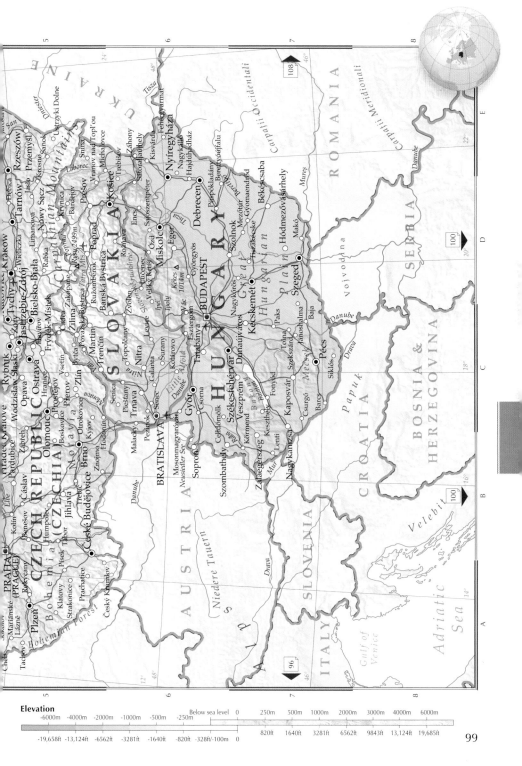

Elevation

-6000m	-4000m	-2000m	-1000m	-500m	-250m	Below sea level	0	250m	500m	1000m	2000m	3000m	4000m	6000m
-19,658ft	-13,124ft	-6562ft	-3281ft	-1640ft	-820ft	-328ft/-100m	0	820ft	1640ft	3281ft	6562ft	9843ft	13,124ft	19,685ft

99

Southeast Europe

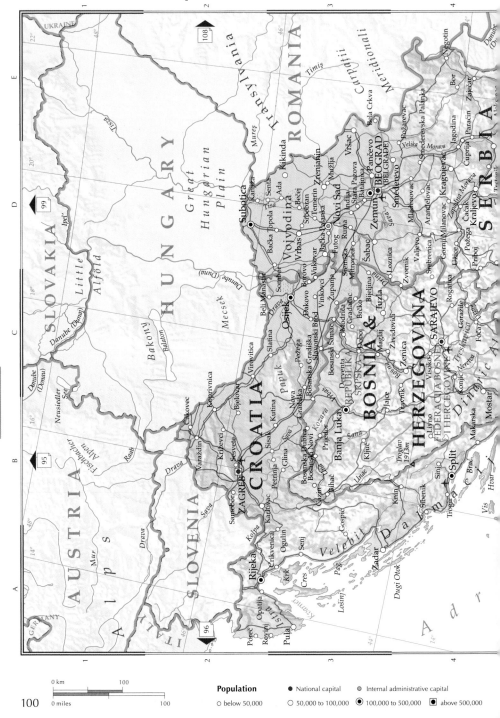

Population

0 km   100
0 miles   100

● National capital   ◎ Internal administrative capital

○ below 50,000   ◯ 50,000 to 100,000   ◉ 100,000 to 500,000   ◼ above 500,000

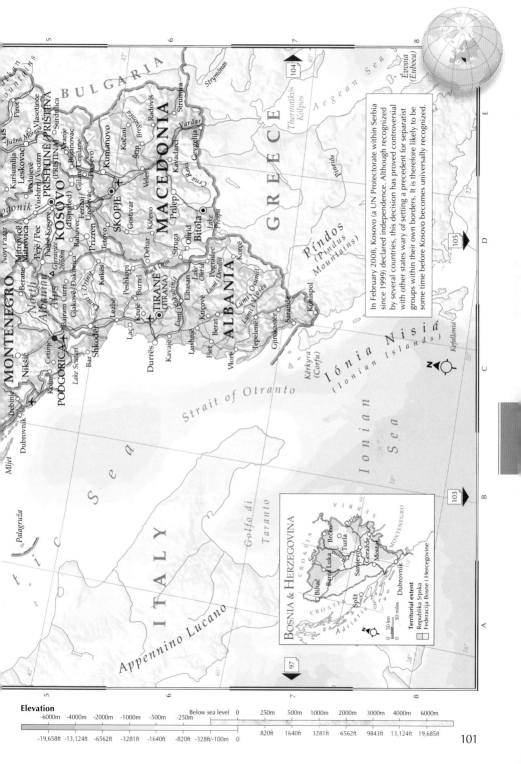

The Mediterranean

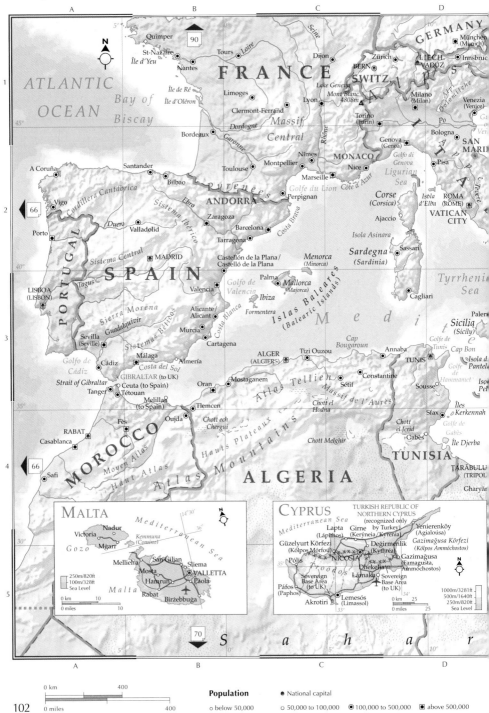

ATLANTIC OCEAN

Bay of Biscay

90

N

Quimper
St-Nazaire
Île d'Yeu
Nantes
Tours
Dijon
Zürich
BERN
SWITZ
München (Munich)
GERMANY
LIECH. VADUZ
Innsbruc

FRANCE

Île de Ré
Île d'Oléron
Limoges
Lake Geneva
Mont Blanc 4808m
Lyon
Milano (Milan)
Venezia (Venice)

45°

Clermont-Ferrand
Dordogne
Massif
Torino (Turin)
Po
Gé
Ver

Bordeaux
Garonne
Central
Genova (Genoa)
Bologna
SAN MARI

A Coruña
Santander
Bilbao
Pyrenees
Toulouse
Montpellier
Nîmes
MONACO
Nice
Côte d'Azur
Golfo di Genova
Pisa

66

Vigo
Cordillera Cantábrica
Sistema Ibérico
ANDORRA
Perpignan
Marseille
Golfe du Lion
Ligurian Sea
Corse (Corsica)
Isola d'Elba
ROMA (ROME)
VATICAN CITY

Ebro
Zaragoza
Barcelona
Costa Brava
Ajaccio

Porto
Duero
Valladolid
Tarragona
Isola Asinara
Sassari

40°

SPAIN
Sistema Central
MADRID
Castellón de la Plana/ Castelló de la Plana
Menorca (Minorca)
Sardegna (Sardinia)
Tyrrheni Sea

LISBOA (LISBON)
Tagus
Valencia
Golfo de Valencia
Palma
Mallorca (Majorca)
Cagliari

Sierra Morena
Sevilla (Seville)
Guadalquivir
Málaga
Alicante/ Alicant
Ibiza
Formentera
Islas Baleares (Balearic Islands)
M e d i
Paler

Cartagena
Costa Blanca
Murcia
Cap Bougaroun
Golfo di Tunis
Cap Bon
Sicilia (Sicily)

Golfo de Cádiz
Cádiz
Costa del Sol
Almería
ALGER (ALGIERS)
Tizi Ouzou
Annaba
TUNIS
Isola di Pantel

35°

GIBRALTAR (to UK)
Ceuta (to Spain)
Tétouan
Tanger
Oran
Mostaganem
Sétif
Constantine
Sousse
Iso Pel

Strait of Gibraltar
Melilla (to Spain)
Tlemcen
Atlas Tellien
Massif de l'Aurès
Sfax
Îles Kerkennah

RABAT
Fes
Oujda
Chott ech Chergui
Chott el Hodna
Chott el Jerid
Gabès
Golfe de Gabès
Île Djerba

Casablanca
MOROCCO
Moyen Atlas
Hauts Plateaux
Chott Melghir
TUNISIA
TARÁBULU (TRIPOL

66

Safi
Haut Atlas
Atlas Mountains
ALGERIA
Gharyár

MALTA

Mediterranean Sea
N

Victoria
Nadur
Kemmuna (Comino)
Gozo
Mgarr
Mellieha
San Giljan
Sliema
Mosta
VALLETTA
Hamrun
Paola
Rabat
Birzebbuga
Malta

250m/820ft
100m/328ft
Sea Level
0 km 10
0 miles 10

CYPRUS

TURKISH REPUBLIC OF NORTHERN CYPRUS (recognized only by Turkey)

Mediterranean Sea
Lapta (Lápithos)
Girne (Kerýneia/Kyrenia)
Yenierenköy (Agialoúsa)
Gazimağusa Körfezi (Kólpos Ammóchostos)

Güzelyurt Körfezi (Kólpos Mórfou)
Değirmenlik (Kythréa)
Pólis
NICOSIA
Gazimağusa (Famagusta, Ammóchostos)
Dhekelia
Tróodos
Lárnaka
N

Páfos (Paphos)
Sovereign Base Area (to UK)
Sovereign Base Area (to UK)
Akrotiri
Lemesós (Limassol)

1000m/3281ft
500m/1640ft
250m/820ft
Sea Level
0 km 25
0 miles 25

70

N

S a h a r

---

0 km 400
Population
• National capital

0 miles 400

○ below 50,000   ○ 50,000 to 100,000   ● 100,000 to 500,000   ■ above 500,000

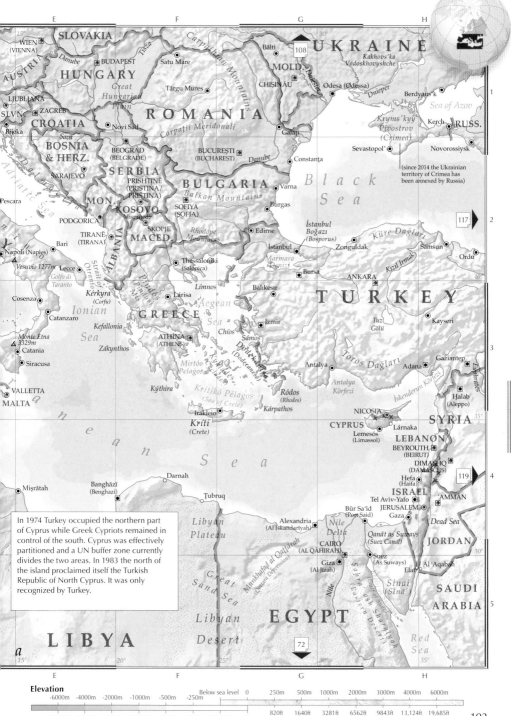

In 1974 Turkey occupied the northern part of Cyprus while Greek Cypriots remained in control of the south. Cyprus was effectively partitioned and a UN buffer zone currently divides the two areas. In 1983 the north of the island proclaimed itself the Turkish Republic of North Cyprus. It was only recognized by Turkey.

(since 2014 the Ukrainian territory of Crimea has been annexed by Russia)

Elevation

						Below sea level	0	250m	500m	1000m	2000m	3000m	4000m	6000m
-6000m	-4000m	-2000m	-1000m	-500m	-250m									
-19,658ft	-13,124ft	-6562ft	-3281ft	-1640ft	-820ft	-328ft/-100m	0	820ft	1640ft	3281ft	6562ft	9843ft	13,124ft	19,685ft

Bulgaria & Greece

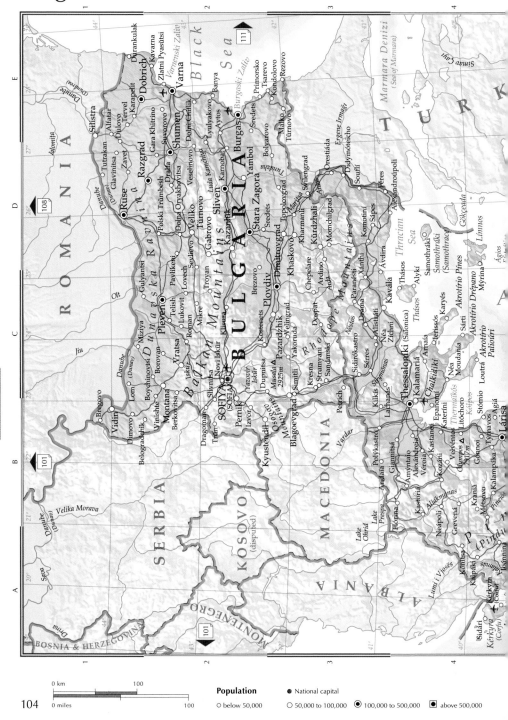

0 km　　　　100

0 miles　　　　100

Population　　● National capital

○ below 50,000　　○ 50,000 to 100,000　　◎ 100,000 to 500,000　　■ above 500,000

MYTILINI
Kalloní
Antíssa
Lésvos
(Lesbos)
Plomári
Chíos
Antípsara
Psará
Chíos

A e g e a n   S e a

Sámos
Sámos
Ikaría
Ikaría

Thérma

Arkoí
Agathonísi
Patmos
Léros
Lípsi

Dodekánisa (Dodecanese)

Agía
Martína
Kálymnos
Kos
Kos
Kastellórizo
Astypálaia

Nísyros
Tílos
Chálki
Ródos
(Rhodes)
Líndos

Ródos
(Rhodes)
Kattaviá

Kárpathos
Kárpathos

Sýrna

Saría

Kásos

Anáfi

Sýros
Ermoúpoli
Mýkonos
Délos
Náxos
Páros
Páros
Kástro
Amorgós
Amorgós
Akrotírio Flouda

Kykládes (Cyclades)

Sýros
Kýthnos
Kéa
(Tzía)
Ioulída
Tínos
Tínos
Ándros
Ándros

Skýros
Skýros
Kými
Évvoia
(Euboea)

Sporádes
Kyra Panagía
Alónnisos
Skópelos
Skiáthos

Vólos
Argalastí
Soúrpi

Almyrós
Livanátes
Chalkída
Aliartos
Álva
Maroússi

ATHÍNA
(ATHENS)
Keratéa
Kýthnos

Sérifos
Sífnos
Sérifos

Ermoúpoli
Chóra
íos

Santoríni
(Thíra)
Thíra
Thíra
Folégandros

Milos
Páka
Sífnos

Kritikó Pélagos
(Sea of Crete)

Chaniá
Kíssamos
Kántanos

Lefká Óri
Spíli
Chóra Stakíon
Ág.
Nikóla

Panormos

Kríti (Crete)
Irákleio
Zarós
Tympáki

Néapoli
Sitía
Ágios Nikólaos
Diktí
Myrtos
Ierápetra

G R E E C E

Kardítsa
Lamía
Karpenísi
Rentína
Thérmo
Náfpaktos

Vólos
Argalastí
Domokós
Agrínio
Agrýovo

Lártos
Livadeiá
Thíva
Chalkída

Maroússi
Megara
Aígina
Póros
Ermióni
Ýdra

Léa
Palaiá Epídavros

Peiraiás
(Piraeus)

Korinthou

Áfýo
Kiáto
Korinthos
Xylókastro
Nemea
Árgos
Trípoli
Spárti

Pátra
Kalávryta
Korinthos
Aigío

Peloponnísos
(Peloponnese)

Lámpeia
Pýrgos
Olympía
Zacháro
Kyparissía
Pýlos

Messíni
Kalamáta
Koróni
Geroliménas

Leonídio
Néapoli
Karavás
Kýthira
Areópoli
Gytheio
Geráki
Lakonikós Kólpos

Antikýthira
Potamós
Kýthira

Mírtóo Pélagos
(Myrtoan Sea)

Lefkáda
Vasilikí
Argostóli
Kefalloniá
Lixoúri

Neochóri
Póros
Lechainá
Gastoúni
Keri
Zákynthos
(Zante)

Préveza
Arta
Katoúna
Amfilochía

Rentína

Ióni a   N i s i á
(Ionian Islands)

I o n i a n   S e a

M e d i t e r r a n e a n   S e a

N

Elevation

						Below sea level								
-6000m	-4000m	-2000m	-1000m	-500m	-250m	0	250m	500m	1000m	2000m	3000m	4000m	6000m
-19,658ft	-13,124ft	-6562ft	-3281ft	-1640ft	-820ft	-328ft/-100m	0	820ft	1640ft	3281ft	6562ft	9843ft	13,124ft	19,685ft

The Baltic States & Belarus

0 km 100
0 miles 100

Population

● National capital

○ below 50,000   ○ 50,000 to 100,000   ◉ 100,000 to 500,000   ▣ above 500,000

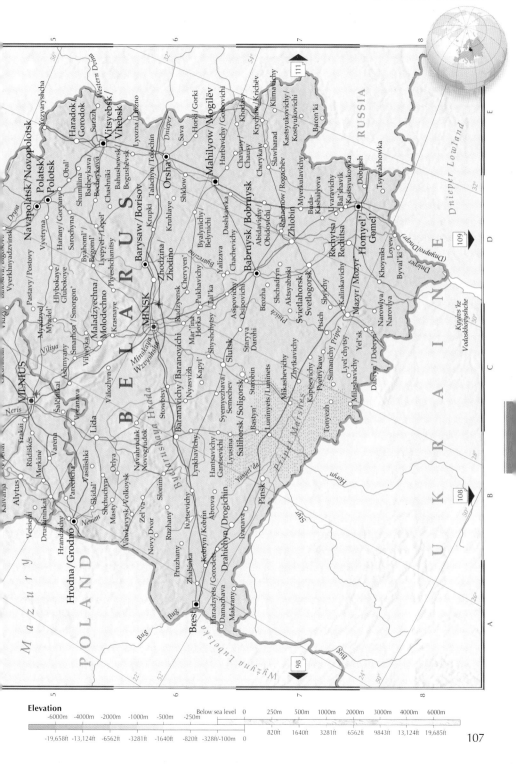

Elevation

-6000m	-4000m	-2000m	-1000m	-500m	-250m	Below sea level	0	250m	500m	1000m	2000m	3000m	4000m	6000m
-19,658ft	-13,124ft	-6562ft	-3281ft	-1640ft	-820ft	-328ft/-100m	0	820ft	1640ft	3281ft	6562ft	9843ft	13,124ft	19,685ft

Ukraine, Moldova & Romania

Population

○ below 50,000   ○ 50,000 to 100,000   ◉ 100,000 to 500,000   ■ above 500,000

● National capital

RUSSIA

Sredne-russkaya Vozvyshennost'

Horodnya
Snovs'k (Shchors)
Shostka
Hlukhiv
Chernihiv
Krolevets'
Konotop
Nizhyn
Bakhmach
Sumy
Nosivka
Romny
Oster
Brovary
Pryluky
Yahotyn
Pyryatyn
Lebedyn
Okhtyrka
Zolochiv
Derhachi
Vasyl'kiv
Hrebinka
Lubny
Myrhorod
Lyubotyn
Kharkiv
Bila Tserkva
Kaniv
Zolotonosha
Merefa
Kup"yans'k
Bohuslav
Horodyshche
Cherkasy
Hlobyne
Poltava
Donets
Starobil's'k
Smila
Izyum
Shpola
Chyhyryn
Svitlovods'k
Kremenchuk
Slov"yans'k
Kreminna
Rubizhne
Oleksandrivka
Syeverodonets'k
Znam"yanka
Kramators'k
Zolote
Lysychans'k
Oleksandriya
Zhovti Vody
Kam"yans'ke
Novomoskovs'k
Luhans'k
Kropyvnyts'kyy
P"yatykhatky
Kostyantynivka
Sorokyne
(Kirovohrad)
Dnipro
Pavlohrad
Horlivka
Kadiyivka
(Krasnodon)
Dolyns'ka
Synel'nykove
Yenakiyeve
(Stakhanov)
Pervomays'k
Bobrynets'
Kryvyy Rih
Pokrovs'ke
Makiyivka
Khrustal'nyy
(Krasnyy Luch)
Arbuzynka
Inhulets'
Pokrov
Nikopol'
Zaporizhzhya
Donets'k
Chystyakove
(Torez)
Novyy Buh
(Ordzhonikidze)
Marhanets'
Orikhiv
Amvrosiyivka
Voznesens'k
Kam"yanka-Dniprovs'ka
Dniprorudne
Volnovakha
Dokuchayevs'k
Novoazovs'k
Polohy
Mykolayiv
Kakhovs'ka Vodoskhovyshche
Tokmak
Mariupol'
Zhovtneve
Kakhovka
Molochans'k
Melitopol'
Gulf of Taganrog
Yeya
Kherson
Oleshky (Tsyurupyns'k)
Yakymivka
Prymors'k
Berdyans'k
Ochakiv
Hola Prystan'
Chaplynka
Novotroyits'ke
Chornomors'k
(Illichivs'k)
Kalanchak
Armyans'k
Heniches'k
Odesa
(Odessa)
Sea of Azov
RUSSIA
Kerch Strait
Yany Kapu
(Krasnoperekops'k)
Rozdol'ne
Dzhankoy
Nyzhn'ohirs'kyy
Zatoka Syvash
Chornomors'ke
Krasnohvardiys'ke
Kerch
Kuban'
Yevpatoriya
Kryms'kyy Pivostriv (Crimea)
Lenine
Simferopol'
Saky
Feodosiya
Bakhchysaray
Krym'ski Hory
Alushta
(since 2014 the Ukrainian territory of Crimea has been annexed by Russia)
Sevastopol'
Yalta
Alupka

Black Sea

Elevation

-6000m	-4000m	-2000m	-1000m	-500m	-250m	Below sea level 0	250m	500m	1000m	2000m	3000m	4000m	6000m
-19,658ft	-13,124ft	-6562ft	-3281ft	-1640ft	-820ft	-328ft/-100m 0	820ft	1640ft	3281ft	6562ft	9843ft	13,124ft	19,685ft

North & West Asia

A   B   C   D

155

Franz Josef Land   A R C T I C

20°   40°   60°   80°   100°

Ostrov Komsomolets   *Severnaya Ze...*

Ostrov Oktyabr'skoy Revolyutsii
Ostrov Bol'shevik   *Poluostrov Taymyr*

1

80°   *Summer limit of pack ice*   *Kara Sea*   *East Novaya Zemlya Trench*   *Poluostrov Yamal*   *North Siber...*
Kheta

70°   *Winter limit of pack ice*   *Barents Sea*   *Ostrov Kolguyev*   ● Noril'sk   *Central Siberian Plateau*

Norwegian Sea   *North Cape*   ● Murmansk   *Kola Peninsula*   *White Sea*   R U S   *Kureyka*

2   Arctic Circle   81   ● Archangel   *Northern Dvina*   *Ob'*   *West Siberian Plain*   S i   *Lower Tunguska*   *Stony Tunguska*

60°   *Gulf of Bothnia*   *Lake Onega*   *Lake Ladoga*   ● Vologda   ● Perm'   *Ural Mountains*   *Ob'*   *Irtysh*   *Chulym*   *Angara*

● Saint Petersburg   ● Yaroslavl'   ● Nizhniy Novgorod   ● Yekaterinburg   ● Tomsk   ● Krasnoyarsk

Baltic Sea   MOSCOW   ● Kazan'   *Volga*   ● Chelyabinsk   ● Omsk   ● Novosibirsk   *Yenisey*

■ Kaliningrad   *Central Russian Upland*   ● Ul'yanovsk   ● Ufa   ● Novokuznetsk   *Sayanskiy Khrebet*

KALININGRAD (to Russia)   ● Samara   *Ishim*   ● ASTANA   A   *Irkut...*

3   50°   E U R O P E   ● Voronezh   ● Saratov   ● Orenburg   *Kirghiz Steppe*   ● Karagandy   ● Semipalatinsk   S

(since 2014 the Ukrainian territory of Crimea has been annexed by Russia)   ● Volgograd   *Ural*   *Kazakh Uplands*   *Altai Mountains*   G

● Rostov-na-Donu   Aral'sk ●   KAZAKHSTAN   *Ozero Zaysan*

Danube   ● Stavropol'   ● Astrakhan'   *Syr Darya*   *Lake Balkhash*

Black Sea   El'brus 18,510ft (5642m)▲   ● Aktau   *Ustyurt Plateau*   *Aral Sea*   *Kyzyl Kum*   ● Kyzylorda   ● Taraz   ● Almaty   *Shan*

● Istanbul   *Küre Dağları*   *Caucasus*   *Caspian Sea*   ● Dasoguz   UZBEKISTAN   ● BISHKEK   ▲ Jengish Chokusu/Tömür Feng 24,406ft (7439m)

4   ANKARA ■   GEORGIA   TBILISI ●   BAKU ●   TURKMENISTAN   ● TASHKENT   KYRGYZSTAN

ARMENIA   ● YEREVAN   AZERB.   *Garagum*   ● DUSHANBE   TAJIKISTAN

TURKEY   ● Tabriz   ● ASHGABAT

● Adana   ● Gaziantep   QOM ●   ● TEHRAN   ● KABUL   *Hindu Kush*   *Kunlun Mountains*   *Jalalabad*

CYPRUS   SYRIA   IRAQ   ● Isfahan   IRAN   ● Herat   AFGHANISTAN   *Khyber Pass*   *Himalayas*

● Aleppo   ● Mosul   *Iranian Plateau*   *Zagros Mountains*   *Thar Desert*

BEIRUT   ● DAMASCUS   ● BAGHDAD   *Syrian Desert*   ● Basra   ● Shiraz   ● Zahedan   *Indus Fan*

LEBANON   ISRAEL   ● AMMAN   *Euphrates*   ● KUWAIT   KUWAIT   ● Bandar-e 'Abbas   *Ganges*

JERUSALEM ●   JORDAN   *Dead Sea -1411ft (-430m)*   *An Nafud*   MANAMA ●   ● Dubai   *Gulf of Oman*   ● MUSCAT   *Ganges Fan*

SAUDI ARABIA   BAHRAIN   DOHA ●   U.A.E.   ● Sur   *Murray Ridge*

● RIYADH   QATAR   ABU DHABI ●   OMAN

Tropic of Cancer   ● Jedda   *Arabian Peninsula*   *Bay of Bengal*

20°   ● At Ta'if   *Ar Rub' al Khali*   *Arabian Sea*

AFRICA   *Red Sea*

5   10°   ● SANAA   YEMEN   *Socotra (to Yemen)*   *Arabian Sea*

● Ta'izz   ▲ Aden   *Gulf of Aden*   69

N

20°   40°   60°   100°

A   B   C   D

0 km   800
0 miles   800

Population   ● National capital

○ below 50,000
○ 50,000 to 100,000
◉ 100,000 to 500,000
■ above 500,000

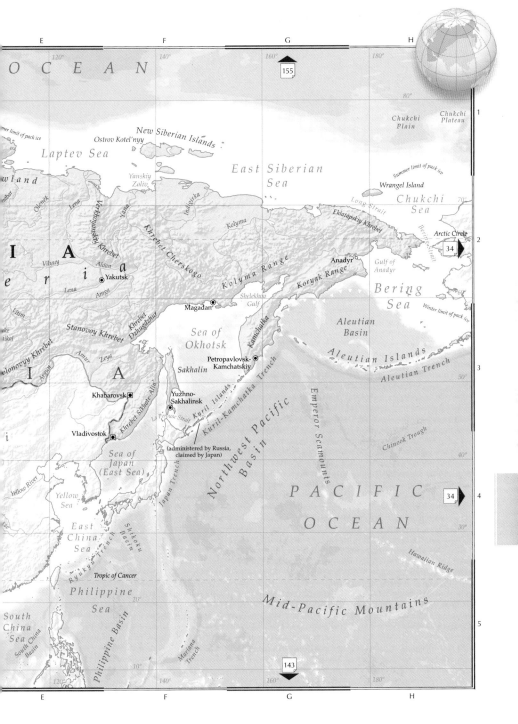

O C E A N

E   F   G   H

120°   140°   160°   180°

155

80°

1

Chukchi   Chukchi
Plain   Plateau

New Siberian Islands
Ostrov Kotel'nyy

Laptev Sea

East Siberian
Sea

Summer limit of pack ice

Summer limit of pack ice

Wrangel Island

Yanskiy
Zaliv

Chukchi
Sea

Long Strait   70°

Verkhoyanskiy Khrebet

Yana

Indigirka

Ekiatapskiy Khrebet

2

Olenek

Lena

Khrebet Cherskogo

Kolyma

Kolyma Range

Anadyr

Gulf of
Anadyr

Bering Strait

Arctic Circle

34

I   A

a

Vilyuy

Aldan

Yakutsk

Koryak Range

Bering

r   i

Lena   Amga

Shelekhov
Gulf

Sea   Winter limit of pack ice

e   Magadan   Kamchatka

Aleutian
Basin

Stanovoy Khrebet

Khrebet
Dzhugdzhur

Sea of
Okhotsk

Aleutian Islands

Aleutian Trench   50°   3

Yablonovyy Khrebet

Amur

Zeya

Petropavlovsk-
Kamchatskiy

Sakhalin

Emperor Seamounts

Chinook Trough

I   A

Khabarovsk

Yuzhno-
Sakhalinsk

Kuril Islands

Kuril-Kamchatka Trench

Northwest Pacific

40°

Khrebet Sikhote-Alin'

Vladivostok

La Perouse Strait

(administered by Russia,
claimed by Japan)

Basin

P A C I F I C

34   4

Sea of
Japan
(East Sea)

Japan Trench

30°

Yellow River

Yellow
Sea

O C E A N

Hawaiian Ridge

East
China
Sea

Shikoku
Basin

Ryukyu Trench

Tropic of Cancer

20°

Philippine

Sea

Mid-Pacific Mountains

5

South
China
Sea

South China
Basin

Philippine Basin

Mariana Trench

143

10°

120°   140°   160°   180°

E   F   G   H

113

Russia & Kazakhstan

Population

● National capital
○ below 50,000
○ 50,000 to 100,000
◉ 100,000 to 500,000
■ above 500,000

0 km 600

0 miles 600

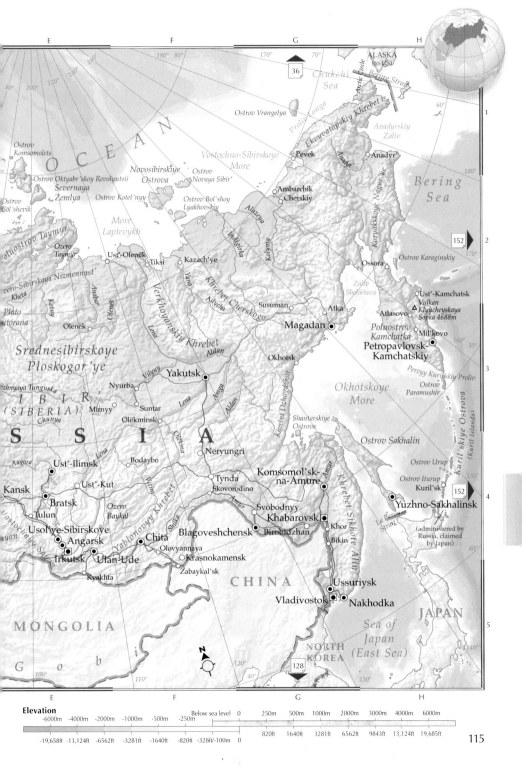

Turkey & the Caucasus

ROMANIA

UKRAINE
Kryms'kyy
Pivostriv
(Crimea)
(since 2014 the Ukrainian territory of Crimea has been annexed by Russia)

Dacul Sinoie

108

Danube

BULGARIA

Varnenski
Zaliv

Burgaski
Zaliv

Black Sea

Maritsa

104

Kırklareli
Edirne

Çorlu

Ergene Çayı

Tekirdağ

İstanbul Boğazı
(Bosporus)

Zonguldak

Devrek

Cide

Bartın

İnebolu

Küre Dağları

Sinop

Gerze

Kastamonu

Kargı

Bafra

Samsun

Ünye

Ordu

Karabük

Marmara Denizi
(Sea of Marmara)

İstanbul

İzmit

Adapazarı

Çerkeş

İznik Gölü

Çanakkale

Bandırma

Yalova

Bursa

Bilecik

Gerede

Bolu

Çankırı

Kızıl Irmak

Merzifon

Çorum

Tokat

Canik Dağları

Çanakkale Boğazı
(Dardanelles)

Balıkesir

Bozüyük

Eskişehir

ANKARA

Kalecik

Alaca

Yıldızeli

Za

Edremit
Ayvalık

Kütahya

Polatlı

Kırıkkale

Sorgun

Şarkışla

Sivas

K

GREECE

Lésvos

Akhisar

Simav

Gediz

Afyon

Kulu

Hirfanlı
Barajı

Tuz Gölü

Boğazlıyan

Bünyan

Gürün

Günn

G

Chíos

Manisa

Uşak

T U R K

Menemen

Gediz Nehri

İzmir

Ödemiş

Alaşehir

Cihanbeyli

Akşehir

Nevşehir

İncesu

Kayseri

Sámos

Aydın

Nazilli

Büyükmenderes Nehri

Dinar

Denizli

Beyşehir
Gölü

Aksaray

Niğde

Göksun

Kahramanmaras

Söke

Tavas

Burdur

Isparta

Konya

Ereğli

Milas

Muğla

Burdur
Gölü

Karaman

Toros Dağları

Tarsus

Ceyhan

Gaziant

Bodrum

105

Marmaris

Dalaman

Antalya

Manavgat

Suğla Gölü

Mersin (İçel)

Adana

Osmaniye

İskenderun

Kilis

Fethiye

Kaş

Finike

Alanya

Mut

Silifke

Antakya

Kırıkhan

Dodekánisa
(Dodecanese)

Ródos
(Rhodes)

Antalya
Körfezi

Anamur

Orantes

Kárpathos

CYPRUS

TURKISH REPUBLIC OF
NORTHERN CYPRUS
(recognized only by Turkey)

LEBANON

72

Mediterranean
Sea

Population

- National capital
- ○ below 50,000
- ○ 50,000 to 100,000
- ◉ 100,000 to 500,000
- ■ above 500,000

0 km   200

0 miles   200

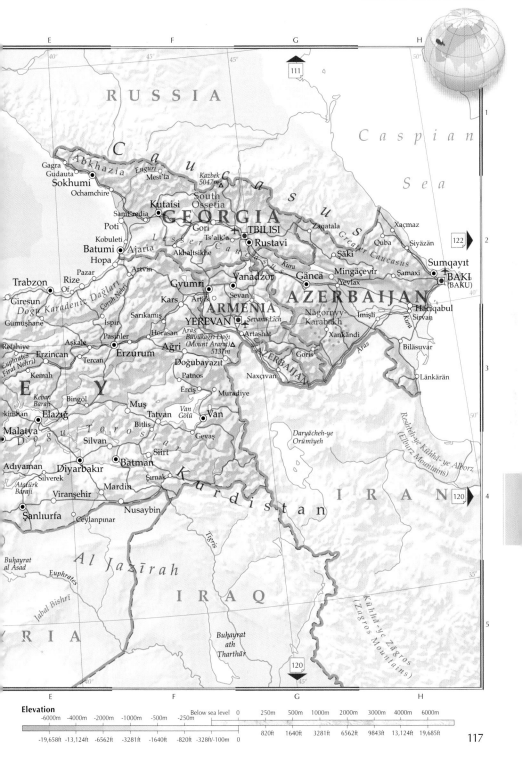

RUSSIA

Caspian Sea

Gagra
Gudauta
Sokhumi
Ochamchire
Abkhazia
Enguri
Mest'ia
Kazbek 5047m

GEORGIA
South Ossetia
Kutaisi
Samtredia
Poti
Kobuleti
Gori
Ts'alk'a
TBILISI
Rustavi
Zaqatala
Xaçmaz
Quba
Siyäzän

Batumi
Ajaria
Akhaltsikhe
Säki
Samaxi
Mingäçevir
Sumqayıt
BAKI
(BAKU)

Hopa
Pazar
Artvin
Gyumri
Vanadzor
Gäncä
Yevlax
Trabzon
Rize
Of
Kars
Sevan
AZERBAIJAN
Hacıqabul

Giresun
Doğu Karadeniz Dağları
Çoruh Nehri
Artik
Sevana Lich
Nagornyy-Karabakh
Imişli
Sirvan
Gümüşhane
İspir
ARMENIA
YEREVAN
Xankändi
Biläsuvar

Refahiye
Erzincan
Aşkale
Pasinler
Horasan
Ağrı
Artashat
Büyükağrı Dağı
(Mount Ararat) 5137m
Goris
Aras

Kemah
Tercan
Erzurum
Doğubayazıt
Naxçıvan
Länkärän

Keban Barajı
Bingöl
Patnos
Erciş
Muradiye
Daryācheh-ye Orūmīyeh
Reshteh-ye Kühhā-ye Alborz (Elburz Mountains)

Malatya
Elazığ
Muş
Tatvan
Van Gölü
Van

Adıyaman
Silvan
Bitlis
Gevaş
Diyarbakır
Siirt
Batman
Atatürk Barajı
Silverek
Mardin
Şırnak
IRAN

Şanlıurfa
Viranşehir
Nusaybin
Kurdistan

Buhayrat al Asad
Al Jazīrah
Euphrates
Jabal Bishrī
Tigris

IRAQ
Buhayrat ath Tharthār
Kühhā-ye Zāgros (Zagros Mountains)

RIA

Elevation

-6000m	-4000m	-2000m	-1000m	-500m	-250m	Below sea level 0	250m	500m	1000m	2000m	3000m	4000m	6000m
-19,658ft	-13,124ft	-6562ft	-3281ft	-1640ft	-820ft	-328ft/-100m 0	820ft	1640ft	3281ft	6562ft	9843ft	13,124ft	19,685ft

The Near East

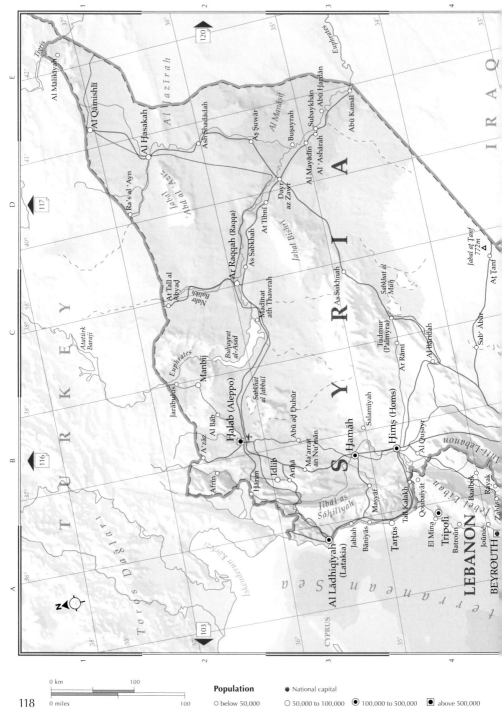

Population   • National capital

○ below 50,000   ○ 50,000 to 100,000   ◉ 100,000 to 500,000   ▣ above 500,000

0 km   100

0 miles   100

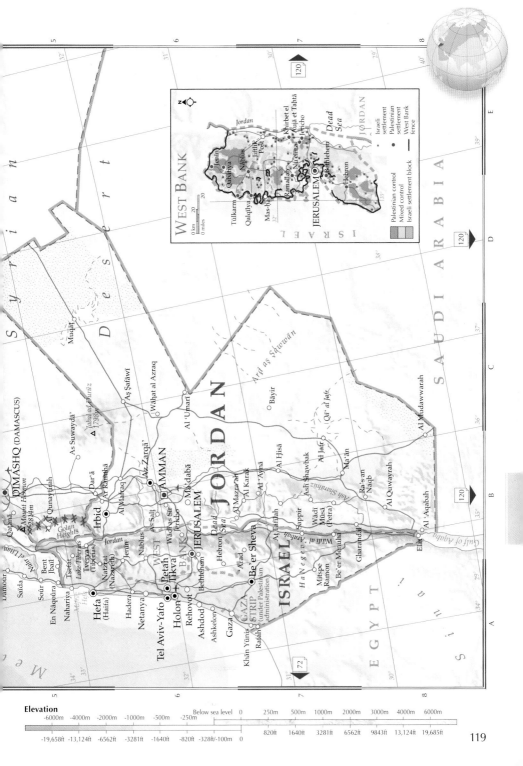

The Middle East

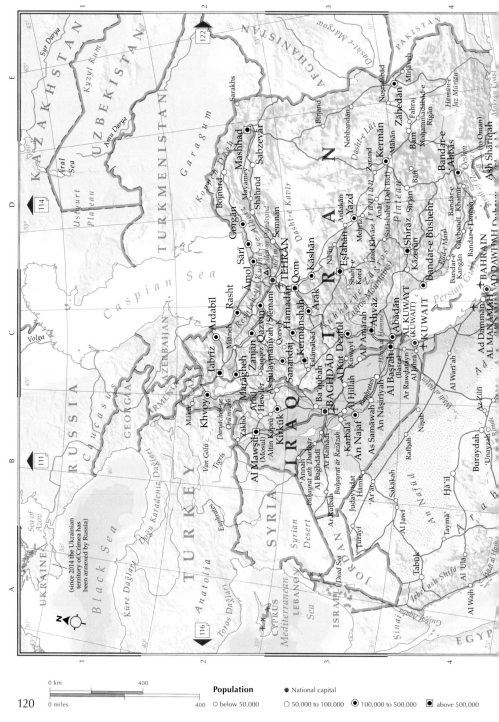

Population

● National capital

○ below 50,000   ○ 50,000 to 100,000   ◉ 100,000 to 500,000   ■ above 500,000

0 km   400

0 miles   400

(since 2014 the Ukrainian territory of Crimea has been annexed by Russia)

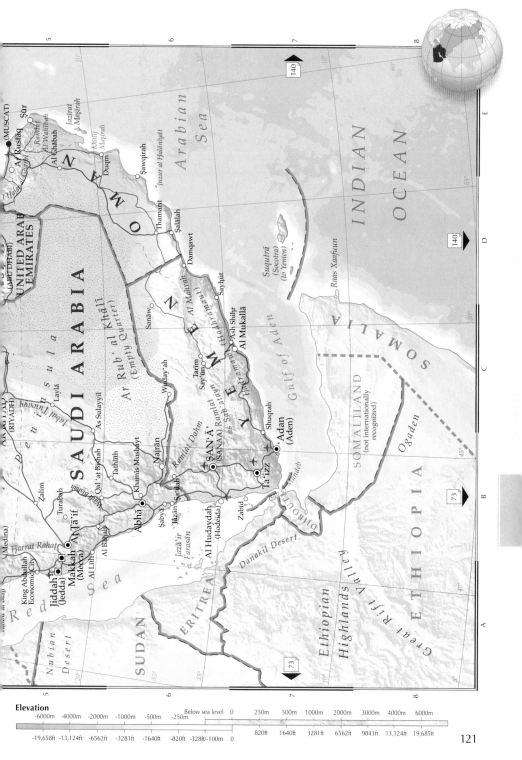

A r a b i a n   S e a

INDIAN   OCEAN

(MUSCAT)
Sūr
Ra's al Ḥadd
Al Wāḥibah
Jazīrat Maṣīrah

O M A N

UNITED ARAB EMIRATES
(ABU DHABI)

Al Ghābah
Duqm
Ramlat Al Wāḥibah
Khalīj Maṣīrah
Jazīrat Maṣīrah

Sawqirah

Thamarīt
Ṣalālah

Jazīrat al Ḥalānīyāt

Damqawt

Suquṭrā
(Socotra)
(to Yemen)

Raas Xaafuun

Y E M E N
Al Mahrah (Hadramaut)

SAUDI ARABIA

Jabal Tuwayq
(RIYADH)

Layla
As Sulayyil

Sanaw
Wudayʿah

Sayhūt
Ash Shiḥr
Al Mukallā

Tarīm
Sayʾūn
Ḥadramawt

S O M A L I A

Ramlat as Sabʿatayn
Ramlat Dahm

SOMALILAND
(not internationally recognized)

Gulf of Aden

Ogaden

Najrān
Khamīs Mushayt

Shuqrah
Adan
(Aden)

Tafhlīt
SANʿAʾ
(SANA)
Saʿdah

ETHIOPIA

Taʿizz

Abhā
Sabyā
Jāzān

Turabah
At Tāʾif
Al Bāḥah
Al Lith

Ṣābʿir Farasān
Al Hudaydah
(Hodeida)
Zabīd

Qalim

Khamīs Mushayt
Qalʿat Bīshah

Djibouti
Bab el Mandeb

Danakil Desert

Great Rift Valley

Ethiopian Highlands

Medina
Harrat Rahat
King Abdullah Economic City
Jiddah
(Jedda)
Makkah
(Mecca)

ERITREA

SUDAN

R e d   S e a

Nubian Desert

Elevation

| -6000m | -4000m | -2000m | -1000m | -500m | -250m | Below sea level | 0 | 250m | 500m | 1000m | 2000m | 3000m | 4000m | 6000m |

| -19,658ft | -13,124ft | -6562ft | -3281ft | -1640ft | -820ft | -328ft/-100m | 0 | 820ft | 1640ft | 3281ft | 6562ft | 9843ft | 13,124ft | 19,685ft |

121

Central Asia

RUSSIA

GEORGIA

AZERBAIJAN

Caspian Sea

Ustyurt Plateau

Aral Sea

Mo'ynoq

Chimboy
Taxtako'pir

Köneürgenç
Gurbansoltan Eje
Daşoguz

Nukus
Taxiatosh
Gubadag

Kyzy

Uchquduq

Urganch
To'rtko'l

UZBEKI

Garabogaz Aylagy

Türkmenbaşy

Türkmenbaşy Aylagy
Hazar

Türkmen Aylagy

Balkanabat

Bereket

Serdar

Magtymguly

Esenguly

Köpetdag Gershi

 Üstyurt Plateau

Üçtagan Gumy

Çaplangyr Platosy

Turan Lowland

Xiva
Gazojak

Lebap

Zarafshon

Üngüz
Angyrsyndaky Garagum

Derweze

TURKMENISTAN

Garagum

Gazli
G'ijdu
Buxoro

Amu Darýa

Seýdi
Galkynyş

Türkmenabat

Koş
Saýat

Reshteh-ye Kūhhā-ye Alborz

Baharly

Gökdepe
Gora Chapan
2889m

Abadan
AŞGABAT
(ASHKHABAD)

Tejen

Kaka

Mary
Murgap

Sarahs

Bäýramaly

Kel
Garagum Ka
U'zb

Andkh
Garabil

Belentligi

Maýmana

Darýaý-ye Mur

IRAN

Kūhhā-ye Zāgros

Iranian Plateau

Bālā Murghāb

Serhetabat
Towraghoudī

Selseleh-ye Sefid Kūh

Ghōriān
Herāt

AFGHAN

Shīndand

Farāh Rūd
Farāh
Dilārām

Geres

Dasht-e Khāsh

Hāmūn-e Şāberī
Zaranj

Dasht-e Mārgo

Lashkar Gāh
Chakhānsūr

Kūchna Darwēs

Dishū

Darýā-ye Helmand

Rēges

Chāgai Hills

Population

● National capital

○ below 50,000

◉ 50,000 to 100,000

◉ 100,000 to 500,000

■ above 500,000

0 km   200
0 miles   200

122

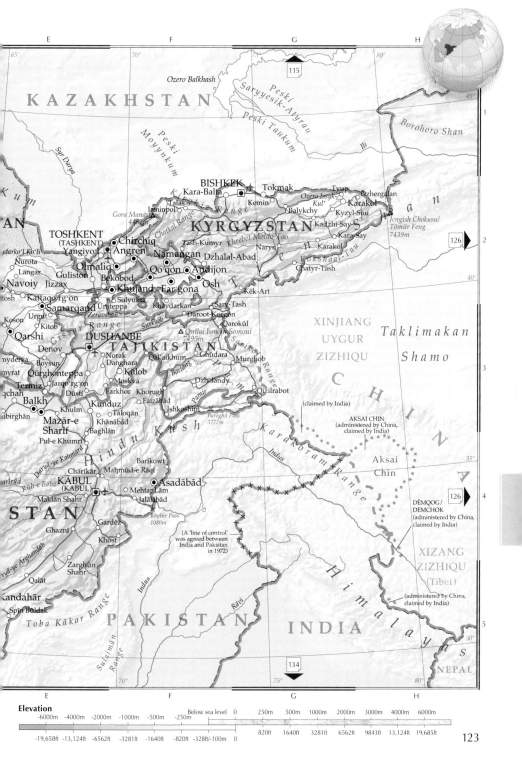

E   F   G   H

65°   70°   75°   80°

45°

115

Ozero Balkhash

K A Z A K H S T A N

Peski Saryyesik-Atyrau

Peski Taukum

Ili

Borohoro Shan

1

Syr Darya

Peski Moyynkum

Kum

Kirghiz Range

BISHKEK   Tokmak

Kara-Balta

Ireninpol   Kemin

Ozero Issyk Kul'   Dzhergalan

Talas   Balykchy   Karakol

Kyzyl-Suu

Gora Manas   Kadzhi-Say   *Jengish Chokusu/*

4482m   **K Y R G Y Z S T A N**   Kara-Say   *Tömür Feng*

Chatkal Range   Tash-Kumyr   *Khrebet Moldo-Too*   7439m

TOSHKENT   Chirchiq   Namangan   Naryn   Karakol

(TASHKENT)   Yangiyo'   Angren   Dzhalal-Abad   *Kokshaal-Tau*

darko'l Ko'li   Olmaliq   Qo'qon   Andijon   Chatyr-Tash

Nurota   Guliston   Bekobod   Osh

Langar   Khujand   Farg'ona   Kök-Art

Navoiy   Jizzax

tosh   Kattaqo'rg'on   Sulyukta

Koson   Samarqand   Uroteppa   Khaydarkan   Sary-Tash

Urgut   *Zeravshan*   Daroot-Korgon

Kitob   *Range*   *Surkhob*   Qarokül

Qarshi   **X I N J I A N G**

DUSHANBE   △ *Qullai Ismoil Somoni*   **U Y G U R**

Denov   7495m   **Z I Z H I Q U**   *T a k l i m a k a n*

nyderya   Norak   Qal'aikhum   Ghŭdara   Murghob   *S h a m o*

Boysun   Danghara   *Bartang*

myrat   **T A J I K I S T A N**   Dzhelandy

Qŭrghonteppa   Jarqo'rg'on   Moskva   *Pamir*   Qizilrabot   **C H I N A**

chah   Termiz   Dŭsti   Farkhor   Khorugh

Balkh   Khulm   Kunduz   Faizabad   Ishkoshim   *(claimed by India)*

ibirghān   Mazār-e   Tāloqān   *Baroghil Pass*

Sharif   Khānābād   3777m   AKSAI CHIN

Pul-e Khumrī   Baghlān   *Karakoram Range*   (administered by China, claimed by India)

Daryā-ye Kohmard   *Indus*   **Aksai**

Kuh-e Bābā   Barīkowt   **Chin**

arirūd   Chārīkār   Mahmūd-e Rāqī

KABUL   Asadābād   DÊMQOG/

(KABUL)   Mehtap Lām   DEMCHOK

Maīdān Shahr   Jalālābād   (administered by China, claimed by India)

126

S T A N   Gardēz   *Khyber Pass*   4

Ghaznī   1080m   **X I Z A N G**

Khōst   (A 'line of control'   **Z I Z H I Q U**

was agreed between   **(Tibet)**

Zarghūn   India and Pakistan

Shahr   in 1972)   (administered by China, claimed by India)

Qalāt

ryā-ye Arghandāb

Kandahār   *Indus*

Spīn Būldak   *Ravi*

Toba Kākar Range   *Sulaimān Range*

P A K I S T A N   **I N D I A**   *Himalayas*   5

30°

NEPAL

134

70°   75°   80°

E   F   G   H

Elevation

-6000m   -4000m   -2000m   -1000m   -500m   -250m   Below sea level   0   250m   500m   1000m   2000m   3000m   4000m   6000m

-19,658ft   -13,124ft   -6562ft   -3281ft   -1640ft   -820ft   -328ft/-100m   0   820ft   1640ft   3281ft   6562ft   9843ft   13,124ft   19,685ft

South & East Asia

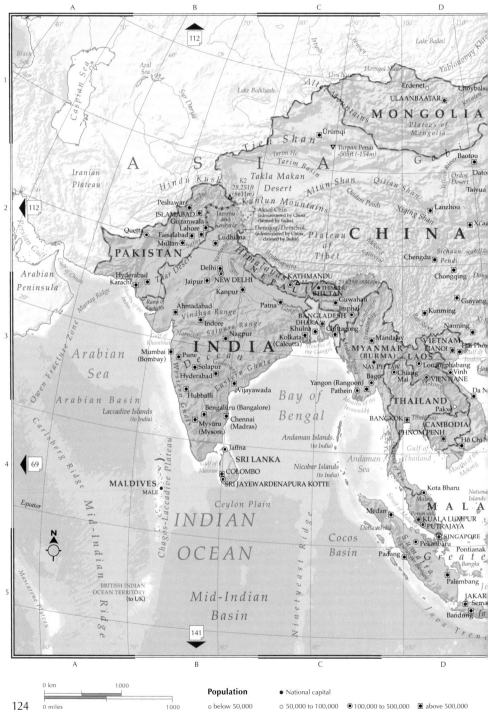

Population • National capital

o below 50,000   ⊙ 50,000 to 100,000   ◉ 100,000 to 500,000   ■ above 500,000

E   F   G   H

113

152

152

142

Qiqihar

Manchuria
Plain — Harbin   *Lake Khanka*

Changchun

Shenyang

BEIJING

Tianjin   Dalian

Shijiazhuang

Jinan

Qingdao

Nanjing

Wuhan   Shanghai

Hangzhou

Nanchang

Fuzhou

Guangzhou

Hong Kong (S.A.R.)

Macao (S.A.R.)

South China Basin

Sea

Sakhalin

Kuril Islands

Kuril-Kamchatka Trench

Hokkaido

Sapporo

JAPAN

NORTH
KOREA
PYONGYANG

SOUTH
KOREA
SEOUL
SEJONG
CITY

*Sea of
Japan
(East Sea)*

Sendai

Nagoya   TOKYO
Kyoto   Yokohama
Osaka △ *Fuji-san*
12,389ft (3776m)

Hiroshima

Kitakyushu

Kyushu

Shikoku

Yellow
Sea

*East China
Sea*

Ryukyu Islands

TAIPEI

TAIWAN

Kaohsiung

Luzon Strait

Philippine Sea

Luzon

Baguio

MANILA

Mindoro

PHILIPPINES

SPRATLY ISLANDS
(disputed)

Bacolod   Cebu

Negros

Panay   Samar

Palawan

Sulu
Sea

Zamboanga

Mindanao

Davao

BANDAR
SERI BEGAWAN

Celebes
Sea

Manado

Borneo

Balikpapan

Banjarmasin

Makassar

Celebes

Surabaya

Malang

Flores
Sea

Bali

Sumba

Lesser Sunda Islands

Flores

Timor

DILI

EAST TIMOR

Timor
Sea

Halmahera

Moluccas

Serami

Buru

Ambon

Banda Sea

Arafura
Sea

Jayapura

New Guinea

Pegunungan Maoke

Bismarck Archipelago

Solomon
Islands

Solomon
Sea

Coral
Sea

AUSTRALIA

*Northwest
Pacific
Basin*

Shatskiy Rise

Marcus-Necker Ridge Seamounts

Mid-Pacific Mountains

PACIFIC

OCEAN

East
Mariana
Basin

Melanesian
Basin

Micronesia

West
Mariana
Basin

Mariana
Trench

Palau Ridge

Yap Trench

Eauripik Rise

Ontong
Java
Rise

Melanesia

Equator

Japan Trench

Izu Trench

Kyushu-Palau Ridge

Shikoku Basin

Philippine Basin

125

Western China & Mongolia

Population

● National capital   ◎ Internal administrative capital

○ below 50,000   ○ 50,000 to 100,000   ◉ 100,000 to 500,000   ■ above 500,000

0 km   400

0 miles   400

Elevation

-6000m	-4000m	-2000m	-1000m	-500m	-250m	Below sea level	0	250m	500m	1000m	2000m	3000m	4000m	6000m
-19,658ft	-13,124ft	-6562ft	-3281ft	-1640ft	-820ft	-328ft/-100m	0	820ft	1640ft	3281ft	6562ft	9843ft	13,124ft	19,685ft

Eastern China & Korea

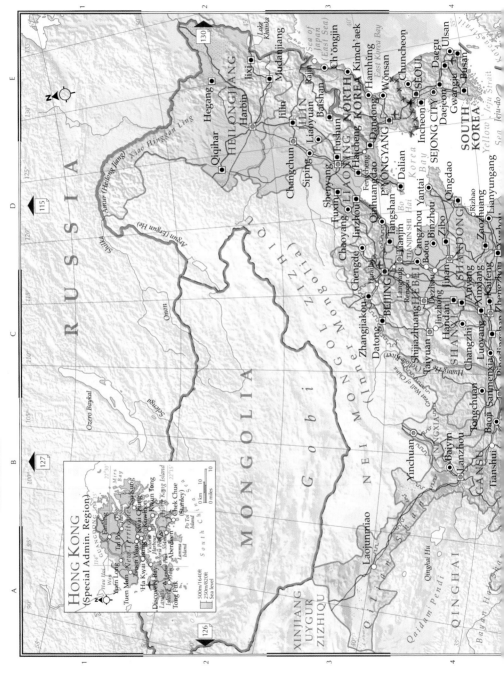

Population

● National capital   ◉ Internal administrative capital

○ below 50,000   ○ 50,000 to 100,000   ◉ 100,000 to 500,000   ■ above 500,000

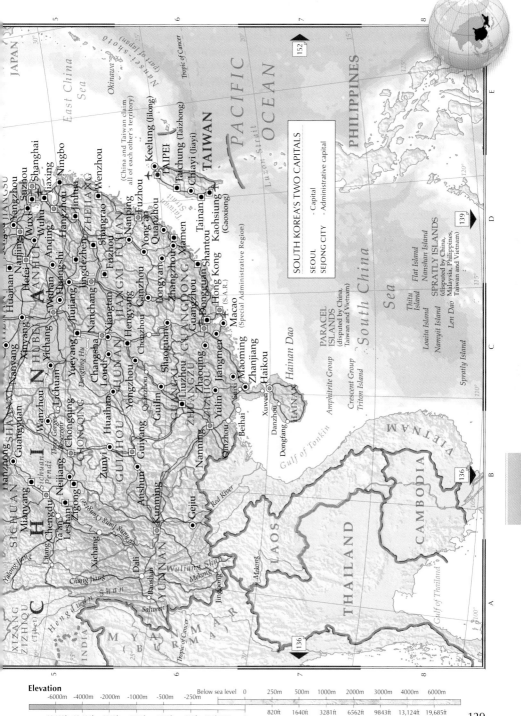

SOUTH KOREA'S TWO CAPITALS

SEOUL - Capital
SEJONG CITY - Administrative capital

JAPAN

East China Sea

Okinawa

Tropic of Cancer

Keelung (Jilong)

Taichung (Taizhong)

Chiayi (Jiayi)

TAIPEI

TAIWAN

(China and Taiwan claim
all of each other's territory)

PACIFIC

OCEAN

PHILIPPINES

Luzon Strait

Tainan

Kaohsiung
(Gaoxiong)

SHANDONG

JIANGSU

Qingdao

Nanjing

Suzhou

Wuxi

Shanghai

Hefei

Jiaxing

Huainan

Anqing

Hangzhou

Ningbo

SHAANXI

ANHUI

ZHEJIANG

Jinhua

Wenzhou

Nanyang

Xinyang

Wuhan

Huangshi

Shangrao

Fuzhou

Shaoxing

Xiangyang

HUBEI

Jiujiang

Jingdezhen

Lichuan

Yichang

Nanchang

Fuzhou

FUJIAN

Yueyang

Changsha

Loudi

Xiangtan

Yong'an

Quanzhou

Chongqing

HUNAN

Hengyang

Chenzhou

Ganzhou

Longyan

Zhangzhou

Xiamen

Huaihua

JIANGXI

Zunyi

GUIZHOU

Shaoguan

GUANGDONG

Dongguan

Shantou

Guiyang

Liuzhou

Zhaoqing

Guangzhou

Shenzhen

Anshun

Guilin

Jiangmen

Hong Kong
(S.A.R.)

Xichang

GUANGXI
ZHUANGZU

Yulin

Zhaoqing

Macao
(Special Administrative Region)

YUNNAN

Nanning

Quzhou

Maoming

Zhanjiang

Gejiu

Beihai

Xuwen

Haikou

Danzhou

HAINAN

Hainan Dao

Dongfang

Gulf of Tonkin

South China

Sea

PARACEL
ISLANDS
(disputed by China,
Taiwan and Vietnam)

Amphitrite Group

Crescent Group
Triton Island

Thitu
Island

Loaita Island

Namyit Island

Flat Island

Nanshan Island

SPRATLY ISLANDS
(disputed by China,
Malaysia, Philippines,
Taiwan and Vietnam)

Len Dao

Spratly Island

VIETNAM

LAOS

THAILAND

CAMBODIA

Gulf of Thailand

Red River

Mekong

SICHUAN

Sichuan
Pendi

Chengdu

Neijiang

Leshan

Zigong

Mianyang

MYANMAR
(BURMA)

INDIA

Hengduan Shan

Dali

Baoshan

Salween

Wuliang Shan

Jinsha Jiang

Tropic of Cancer

CHINA

XIZANG
ZIZHIQU
(Tibet)

Yangtze

Elevation

-6000m	-4000m	-2000m	-1000m	-500m	-250m	Below sea level 0	250m	500m	1000m	2000m	3000m	4000m	6000m
-19,658ft	-13,124ft	-6562ft	-3281ft	-1640ft	-820ft	-328ft/-100m 0	820ft	1640ft	3281ft	6562ft	9843ft	13,124ft	19,685ft

Japan

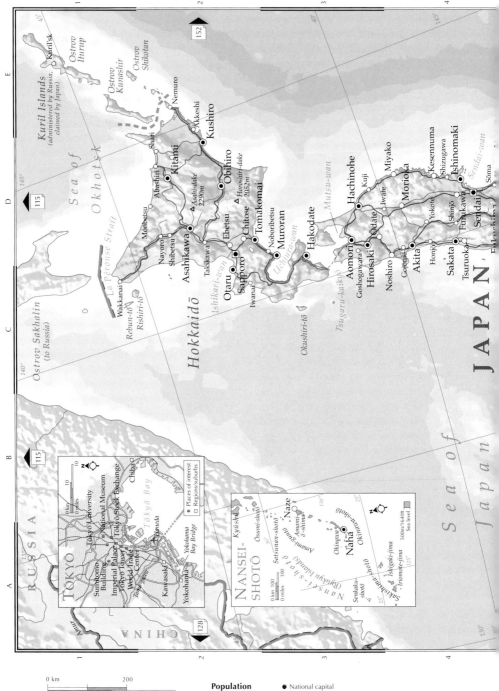

SOUTH & EAST ASIA

Kuril'sk
Ostrov Iturup
Ostrov Shikotan
Ostrov Kunashir

Kuril Islands
(administered by Russia,
claimed by Japan)

Nemuro
Shari
Akkeshi
Kushiro

Sea of Okhotsk

Kitami
Abashiri
Monbetsu
Obihiro
△ Asahi-dake 2290m
△ Horoshiri-dake 2052m

Wakkanai
Nayoro
Shibetsu
Asahikawa
Takikawa
Ishikari-wan
Ebetsu
Chitose
Tomakomai
Noboribetsu
Muroran
Uchiura-wan

Rebun-tō
Rishiri-tō
Otaru
Sapporo
Iwanai

Hokkaidō

La Pérouse Strait

Ostrov Sakhalin
(to Russia)

Okushiri-tō

Hakodate

Tsugaru-kaikyō

Odate
Aomori
Hirosaki
Goshogawara
Noshiro

Kesennuma
Shizugawa
Ishinomaki
Miyako
Kuji
Iwate
Morioka
Yokote
Shinjō
Funakawa
Sendai
Sōma
Sendai-wan

Hachinohe
Akita
Honjō
Sakata
Tsuruoka

JAPAN

Mutsu-wan

Sea of Japan

RUSSIA

Amur

CHINA

TOKYO

Chiba
Tokyo University
National Museum
Tokyo Stock Exchange
Haneda
Tōkyō Bay
Sumitomo Building
Tokyo Tower
Imperial Palace
World Trade Center
Yokohama Bay Bridge
Kawasaki
Yokohama

NANSEI-SHOTŌ

Kyūshū
Ōsumi-shotō
Satsunan-shotō
Naze
Amami-ō-shima
Amami-guntō

Tokunoshima
Okinawa
Naha
Okinawa-shotō
Sakishima-shotō
Ishigaki-jima
Iriomote-jima
Senkaku-shotō

Nansei-shotō (Ryūkyū Islands)

500m/1640ft
Sea level

0 km 200
0 miles 200

Population
● National capital
○ below 50,000
○ 50,000 to 100,000
◉ 100,000 to 500,000
◼ above 500,000

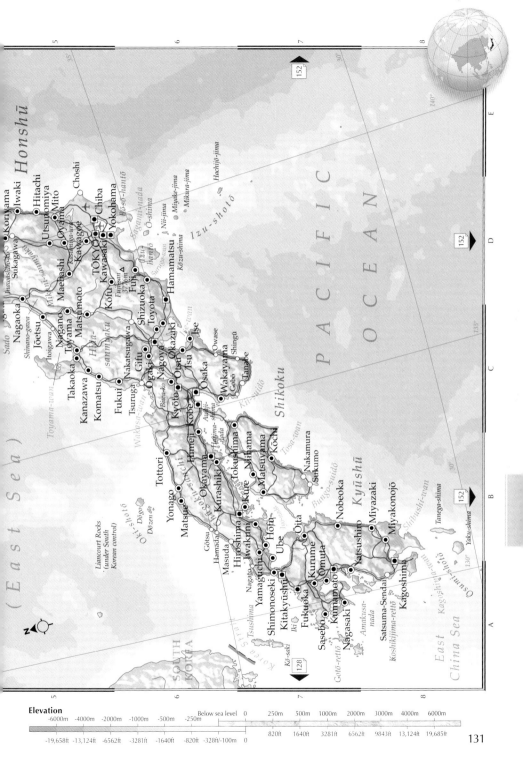

Elevation

-6000m	-4000m	-2000m	-1000m	-500m	-250m	Below sea level	0	250m	500m	1000m	2000m	3000m	4000m	6000m
-19,658ft	-13,124ft	-6562ft	-3281ft	-1640ft	-820ft	-328ft/-100m	0	820ft	1640ft	3281ft	6562ft	9843ft	13,124ft	19,685ft

Southern India & Sri Lanka

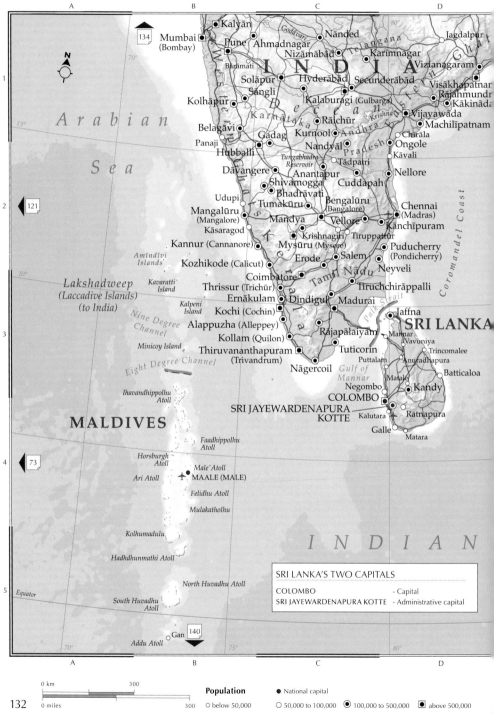

Kalyān
Mumbai (Bombay)
Pune
Ahmadnagar
Nānded
Jagdalpur
134
Godāvari
Nizāmābād
Telangana
Karimnagar
Bārāmati
Solāpur
Hyderābād
Secunderābād
Vizianagaram
Sāngli
Kalaburāgi (Gulbarga)
Visākhapatnam
Kolhāpur
Rājahmundry
Kākināda
Karnātaka
Rāichūr
Krishna
Vijayawāda
Machilīpatnam
Belagāvi
Kurnool
Andhra
Chīrāla
Panaji
Gadag
Nandyāl
Pradesh
Ongole
Hubballi
Tungabhadra Reservoir
Tādpatri
Kāvali
Dāvangere
Anantapur
Nellore
Shivamogga
Cuddapah
Udupi
Bhadrāvati
Bengaluru (Bangalore)
Chennai (Madras)
Mangalūru (Mangalore)
Tumakūru
Mandya
Vellore
Kānchīpuram
Kāsaragod
Krishnagiri
Tiruppattūr
Kannur (Cannanore)
Mysūru (Mysore)
Puducherry (Pondicherry)
Kozhikode (Calicut)
Erode
Salem
Neyveli
Coimbatore
Tamil Nādu
Thrissur (Trichūr)
Tiruchchirāppalli
Ernākulam
Dindigul
Madurai
Kochi (Cochin)
Park Strait
Jaffna
Alappuzha (Alleppey)
Rājapālaiyam
Mannar
SRI LANKA
Kollam (Quilon)
Vavuniya
Thiruvananthapuram (Trivandrum)
Tuticorin
Trincomalee
Puttalam
Anurādhapura
Nāgercoil
Gulf of Mannar
Batticaloa
Matale
Negombo
Kandy
COLOMBO
SRI JAYEWARDENAPURA KOTTE
Kalutara
Ratnapura
Galle
Matara

A r a b i a n

S e a

Lakshadweep
(Laccadive Islands)
(to India)

Amīndīvi Islands
Kavaratti Island
Kalpeni Island

Nine Degree Channel

Minicoy Island

Eight Degree Channel

Ihavandhippolhu Atoll

MALDIVES

Faadhippolhu Atoll

Horsburgh Atoll
Ari Atoll
Male'Atoll
MAALE (MALE)

Felidhu Atoll

Mulakatholhu

Kolhumadulu

Hadhdhunmathi Atoll

North Huvadhu Atoll

Equator

South Huvadhu Atoll

Gan
140

Addu Atoll

I N D I A

Deccan

Coromandel Coast

I N D I A N

121

73

SRI LANKA'S TWO CAPITALS	
COLOMBO	- Capital
SRI JAYEWARDENAPURA KOTTE	- Administrative capital

0 km   300
0 miles   300

Population
○ below 50,000
○ 50,000 to 100,000
◉ 100,000 to 500,000
■ above 500,000

● National capital

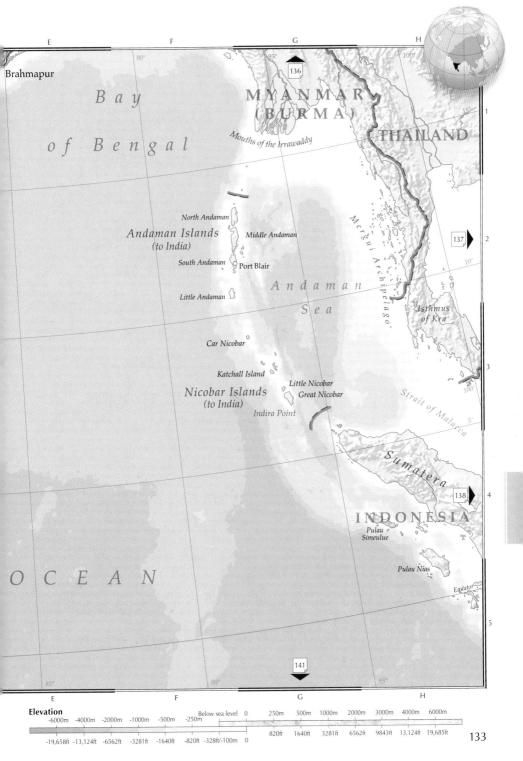

Brahmapur

B a y

o f   B e n g a l

MYANMAR
(BURMA)

Mouths of the Irrawaddy

THAILAND

North Andaman

Andaman Islands
(to India)

Middle Andaman

South Andaman   Port Blair

Little Andaman

A n d a m a n

S e a

Mergui Archipelago

*Isthmus
of Kra*

Car Nicobar

Katchall Island

Nicobar Islands
(to India)

Little Nicobar
Great Nicobar

Indira Point

Strait of Malacca

S u m a t e r a

INDONESIA
Pulau
Simeulue

O C E A N

Pulau Nias

Equator

Elevation

-6000m	-4000m	-2000m	-1000m	-500m	-250m	Below sea level 0	250m	500m	1000m	2000m	3000m	4000m	6000m

820ft 1640ft 3281ft 6562ft 9843ft 13,124ft 19,685ft

-19,658ft -13,124ft -6562ft -3281ft -1640ft -820ft -328ft/-100m 0

133

Northern India, Pakistan & Bangladesh

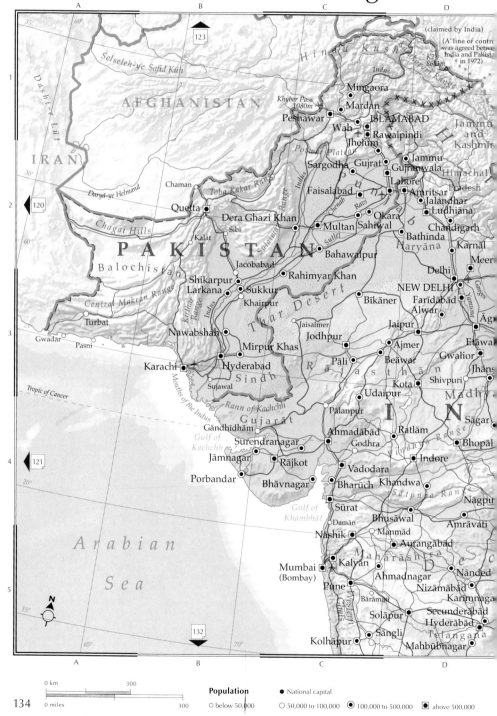

123

(claimed by India)
(A"line of contro
was agreed betwe
India and Pakista
in 1972)

Selseleh-ye Safid Kuh

Hindu Kush

Indus

Karakoram Range

K2
8611m

AFGHANISTAN

Mingaora
Mardan
Khyber Pass
1080m
Peshawar
Wah
Jhelum
Rawalpindi
ISLAMABAD

Jammu
and
Kashmir

Dasht-e Lut

IRAN

Daryā-ye Helmand

Chaman

Toba Kakar Range

Quetta

Potwar Plateau

Sargodha
Gujrat
Jammu

Gujranwala
Lahore

Himachal
Pradesh

Faisalabad
Amritsar
Jalandhar
Ludhiāna

Chagai Hills

Sibi

Kalat

P A K I S T A N

Sulaiman Range

Indus

Chenab
Ravi
Okara
Sahiwal

Multan

Sutlej

Bahawalpur

Chandīgarh

Bathinda
Karnāl
Haryāna

Meer

Delhi

Balochistan

Central Makran Range

Kirthar Range

Jacobabad

Shikarpur
Larkana
Sukkur

Rahimyar Khan

NEW DELHI

Bīkāner
Farīdābād
Alwar

Agr

Turbat

Gwadar

Pasni

Khairpur

Indus

Nawabshah

Mirpur Khas

Jaisalmer

Jodhpur

Thar Desert

Jaipur

Rājasthān

Ajmer
Beāwar

Etawa

Gwalior

Karachi

Hyderabad

Sind

Sujawal

Pāli

Kota

Shivpuri

Jhāns

Udaipur

Madhy

Tropic of Cancer

Mouths of the Indus

Rann of Kachchh

Pālanpur

I N

Gāndhīdhām

Gujarāt

Ahmadābād
Godhra

Ratlām

Sāgar

Gulf of
Kachchh

Surendranagar

Narmada Range

Bhopāl

Jāmnagar
Rājkot

Vadodara

Indore

Porbandar

Bhāvnagar

Bharūch

Khandwa

Satpura Range

Nagpu

Surat

Gulf of
Khambhāt

Daman

Bhusāwal

Amrāvati

Nāshik

Manmād
Aurangābād

A r a b i a n

Mumbai
(Bombay)

Kalyan

Maharashtra

Deca

Nānded

Ahmadnagar

Nizāmābād
Karīmnaga

Pune

S e a

Bārāmati

Solāpur
Sangli

Western Ghats

Secunderābād
Hyderābād

Telangana

Mahbūbnagar

132

Kolhāpur

A   B   C   D

0 km   300
0 miles   300

Population   ● National capital
○ below 50,000   ○ 50,000 to 100,000   ◉ 100,000 to 500,000   ■ above 500,000

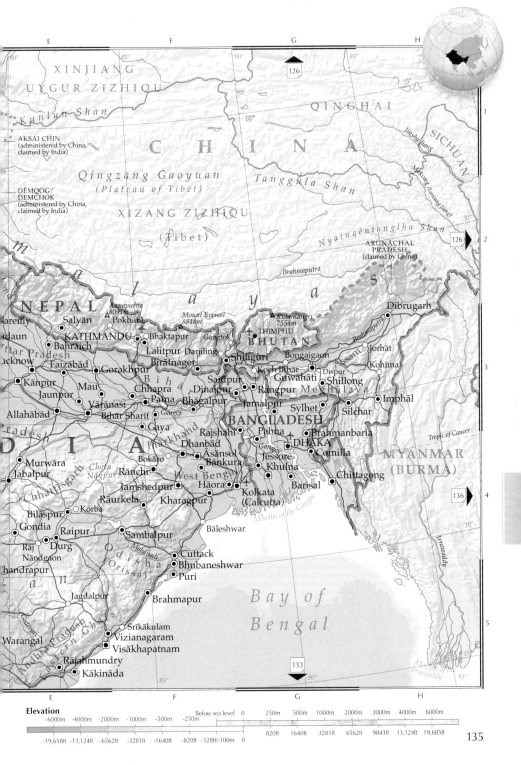

XINJIANG

UYGUR ZIZHIQU

Kunlun Shan

QINGHAI

SICHUAN

AKSAI CHIN
(administered by China,
claimed by India)

C H I N A

Qingzang Gaoyuan
(Plateau of Tibet)

Tanggula Shan

Jinsha Jiang

Mekong (Lancang Jiang)

DÊMQOG/
DEMCHOK
(administered by China,
claimed by India)

XIZANG ZIZHIQU

(Tibet)

Nyainqêntanglha Shan

ARUNĀCHAL
PRADESH
(claimed by China)

Brahmaputra

H i m a l a y a s

NEPAL
Annapurna
8091m ▲
Pokhatā

Mount Everest
8848m ▲

△ Kula Kangri
7554m

Dibrugarh

Salyān

Bhaktapur

Gangtok

THIMPHU

Jorhāt

areilly
Bahraich

KATHMANDU

Lalitpur Darjiling

BHUTAN

Assam

Kohīma

idaun

Faizābād

Gorakhpur

Birātnagar

Shiliguri

Bongaigaon

Koch Bihār

Guwāhāti

Dispur

Shillong

Meghalaya

Imphāl

cknow

Kānpur

Jaunpur

Mau

B i h a r

Chhapra

Saidpur

Dinajpur

Rangpur

Uttar Pradesh

Vāranāsi

Patna

Bhāgalpur

Jamalpur

Sylhet

Silchar

Allahābād

Bihar Sharif

Ganges

Gaya

Jharkhand

Rajshāhi

Pabna

BANGLADESH

Brahmanbaria

Tropic of Cancer

Pradesh

Murwāra

Jabalpur

Bokāro

Dhanbād

Āsānsol

DHAKA

Comilla

MYANMAR
(BURMA)

I N D I A

 Chota
Nāgpur

Rānchi

Bānkura

Jessore

Khulna

Chittagong

Bilāspur

Korba

Jamshedpur

Rāurkela

Kharagpur

West Bengal

Hāora

Kolkata
(Calcutta)

Barisal

Gondia

Raipur

Sambalpur

Bāleshwar

Mouths of the Ganges

Irawaddy

Raj
Nāndgaon

Durg

Mahānadi

Cuttack

Odisha
(Orissa)

Bhubaneshwar

Puri

handrapur

B a y o f

B e n g a l

Warangal

Jagdalpur

Brahmapur

Srīkākulam

Vizianagaram

Visākhapatnam

Eastern Ghats

Rājahmundry

Kākināda

Andhra Pradesh

Godāvari

Chhattisgarh

Elevation

-6000m	-4000m	-2000m	-1000m	-500m	-250m	Below sea level	0	250m	500m	1000m	2000m	3000m	4000m	6000m
-19,658ft	-13,124ft	-6562ft	-3281ft	-1640ft	-820ft	-328ft/-100m	0	820ft	1640ft	3281ft	6562ft	9843ft	13,124ft	19,685ft

Mainland Southeast Asia

0 km   200

0 miles   200

Population   ● National capital

○ below 50,000   ○ 50,000 to 100,000   ◉ 100,000 to 500,000   ◼ above 500,000

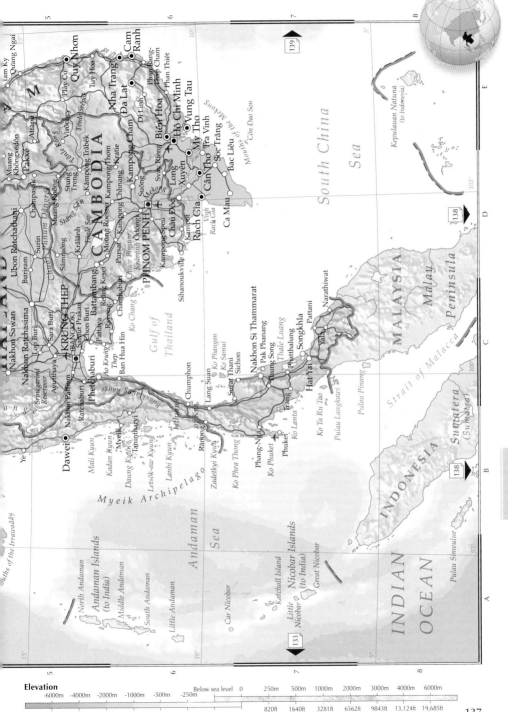

Elevation

Below sea level													
-6000m	-4000m	-2000m	-1000m	-500m	-250m	0	250m	500m	1000m	2000m	3000m	4000m	6000m
-19,658ft	-13,124ft	-6562ft	-3281ft	-1640ft	-820ft	-328ft/-100m	0	820ft	1640ft	3281ft	6562ft	9843ft	13,124ft	19,685ft

Maritime Southeast Asia

SINGAPORE

MALAYSIA

0 km 10
0 miles 10

Johore Strait
Causeway
Pulau Ubin
Pulau Tekong
Lim Chu Kang
Bukit Panjang
Hougang
New Town
Changi
Choa Chu Kang
Bukit Timah
New Town
Jurong Industrial Estate
Queenstown
City
Bedok
New Town
Telok Blangah
Sentosa
Selat Pandan
Pulau Sudong
Pulau Pawai
Strait of Singapore

Urban areas
Open areas
Nature reserves

MYANMAR (BURMA)
LAOS
THAILAND
VIETNAM
Gulf of Tonkin
Hainan Dao (to China)
CAMBODIA
Mekong
Mouths of the Mekong

South China Sea

PARACEL ISLANDS
(disputed by China, Taiwan and Vietnam)

SPRATLY ISLANDS
(disputed by China, Malaysia, Philippines, Taiwan and Vietnam)

Andaman Sea
Nicobar Islands (to India)
Gulf of Thailand
Isthmus of Kra

Banda Aceh
Sigli
George Town
Butterworth
Kota Bharu
Langsa
Pulau Pinang
Taiping
Kuala Terengganu
Meulaboh
Ipoh
Dungun
Cukai
Medan
Kuantan
Pematangsiantar
Tebingtinggi
Klang
KUALA LUMPUR
Kepulauan Natuna
Pulau Simeulue
PUTRAJAYA
Danau Toba
Melaka
Kepulauan Banyak
Sibolga
Muar
Kluang
Johor Bahru
Kuching
Pulau Nias
Batu Pahat
SINGAPORE
Selat Serasan
Sri Aman
Batang Rajang
Sibu
Sarawak
Equator
Pekanbaru
Singkawang
Sidas
Sungai Kapuas
Solok
Rengat
Pontianak
Borneo
Padang
Kepulauan Lingga
Pulau Siberut
Batang Hari
Kualatungkal
Samarinda
Kepulauan Mentawai
Jambi
Bangka
Balikpapan
Sungaipenuh
Pangkalpinang
Kalimantan
Bengkulu
Palembang
Sampit
Amuntai
Kandangan
Lahat
Pulau Belitung
I   N   D
Banjarmasin
Sumatera (Sumatra)
Kotabumi
Pulau Laut
Bandar Lampung
Cirebon
Tegal
Java Sea
INDIAN
Serang
JAKARTA
Pekalongan
Semarang
Pulau Madura
OCEAN
Bogor
Kudus
Sukabumi
Bandung
Surabaya
Jawa (Java)
Tasikmalaya
Probolinggo
Cilacap
Magelang
Kediri
Malang
Jember
Matara
Yogyakarta
Madiun
Bali
Denpasar
Surakarta
Pulau Lombok

BRUNEI
BANDAR SERI BEGAWAN
Miri
Taw
Bintulu
Gunung Kinabalu
4101m
Kota Kinabalu
Balabac
Pulau

MALAYSIA'S TWO CAPITALS

KUALA LUMPUR - Capital
PUTRAJAYA - Administrative capital

0 km 200
0 miles 200

Population   ● National capital

○ below 50,000   ○ 50,000 to 100,000   ◉ 100,000 to 500,000   ▣ above 500,000

Luzon Strait
Babuyan Island
Babuyan Channel
120°
130°
131
1
Cordillera
Tuguegarao
Ilagan
aguio
Baguio
Luzon
ngeles
Dagupan
Cabanatuan
ANILA
Lucena
atangas
Naga
Mindoro
Legazpi City
Mindoro Strait
Calbayog
Sibuyan
Samar
Roxas City
Panay
Cadiz
Tacloban
Island
Leyte
Iloilo
Bacolod
City
Cebu
Palawan
Bohol Sea
Butuan
Puerto
Princesa
Negros
Iligan
Cagayan de Oro
Bislig
Sulu Sea
Mindanao
Zamboanga
Moro
Davao
Gulf
Basilan
Davao Gulf
adakan
Lebak
General
Santos
Sulu Archipelago
Kepulauan Sangir

PHILIPPINES

Philippine
Sea

NORTHERN
MARIANA
ISLANDS
(to US)

GUAM
(to US)

10°

144
2

Yap
MICRONESIA

P A C I F I C

Babeldaob

P A L A U

O C E A N

Equator

144
4

Kepulauan
Talaud

Celebes Sea

Manado
Bitung
Gorontalo
alu
Tomini
Teluk

Kepulauan
Banggai
Sulawesi
(Celebes)
Kepulauan
Sula
Danau
Towuti
repare
N E
Kendari
ngkang
Kolaka
Pulau
Buton
Watampone
Makassar
Bulukumba

Pulau Morotai
Pulau
Halmahera

Pulau Waigeo
Sorong
Jazirah
Doberai
Manokwari
Pulau
Biak
Pulau
Yapen
Jayapura

Halmahera
Maluku (Moluccas)
Laut Seram
Wahai
Waflia
Tifu
Ambon
Pulau
Buru
Pulau
Seram

S I
Pulau
Misool

A
Puncak Jaya
5030m

Teluk
Berau
Teluk
Cenderawasih

Sungai Mamberamo

Pegunungan
Maoke
Papua
(Irian Jaya)

New Guinea

PAPUA

NEW
GUINEA

Kepulauan
Kai
Kepulauan
Aru

Sungai Digul

Banda Sea

Kepulauan
Tanimbar
Pulau Yamdena

Flores
Sea
a
T e n g g a r a
Flores
Pulau
Alor
Pulau
Wetar
DILI
Kepulauan Leti

EAST TIMOR

lat Sumba
Savu Sea
Timor
Nikiniki
Pulau
Sumba
Kupang

120°
Timor Sea
130°
148
Arafura Sea
10°
5

Torres Strait
A U S T R A L I A
140°

E   F   G   H

Elevation

| -6000m | -4000m | -2000m | -1000m | -500m | -250m | Below sea level 0 | 250m | 500m | 1000m | 2000m | 3000m | 4000m | 6000m |

| -19,658ft | -13,124ft | -6562ft | -3281ft | -1640ft | -820ft | -328ft/-100m | 0 | 820ft | 1640ft | 3281ft | 6562ft | 9843ft | 13,124ft | 19,685ft |

The Indian Ocean

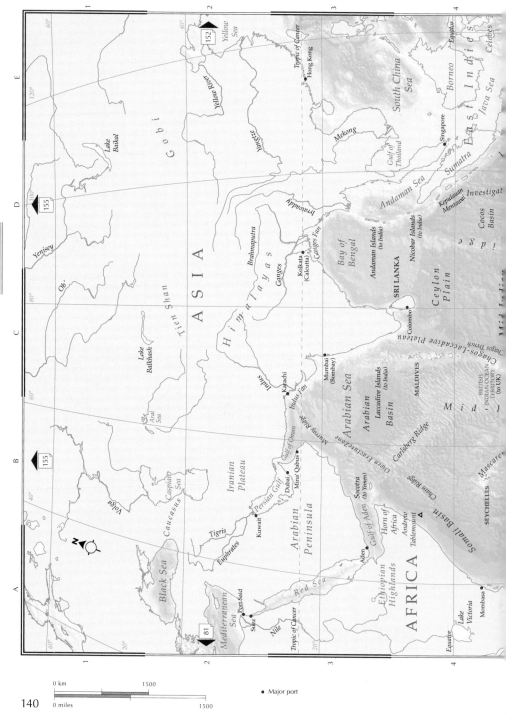

	1	2	3	4

E

152

120°

Yellow Sea

Yellow River

Tropic of Cancer

Hong Kong

South China Sea

Borneo

Equator

Celebes

155

100°

Lake Baikal

G o b i

Yangtze

Mekong

Sumatra

Java Sea

D

Yenisey

Ob'

Brahmaputra

Irrawaddy

Gulf of Thailand

Andaman Sea

Singapore

E a s t   I n d i e s

Kepulauan Mentawai

Investigat

Cocos Basin

80°

A S I A

Ganges Fan

Kolkata (Calcutta)

Bay of Bengal

Andaman Islands (to India)

Nicobar Islands (to India)

Ceylon Plain

Mid Indian

C

Tien Shan

H i m a l a y a s

Ganges

SRI LANKA

Colombo

60°

Lake Balkhash

Aral Sea

Indus

Karachi

Indus Fan

Mumbai (Bombay)

Arabian Sea

Laccadive Islands (to India)

Arabian Basin

MALDIVES

Chagos-Laccadive Plateau

Chagos Trench

BRITISH INDIAN OCEAN TERRITORY (to UK)

M i d l

B

155

Volga

Caspian Sea

Iranian Plateau

Persian Gulf

Gulf of Oman

Dubai

Mina' Qabus

Murray Ridge

Owen Fracture Zone

Carlsberg Ridge

Chain Ridge

Mascare

40°

Caucasus Mts

Tigris

Kuwait

Arabian Peninsula

Socotra (to Yemen)

Horn of Africa

Andryta

Tablemount

Somali Basin

SEYCHELLES

A

N

Black Sea

Euphrates

Red Sea

Aden

Gulf of Aden

Ethiopian Highlands

A F R I C A

Equator

Lake Victoria

Mombasa

81

20°

Mediterranean Sea

Port Said

Suez

Nile

Tropic of Cancer

0 km   1500

0 miles   1500

● Major port

North Australian Basin

Exmouth Plateau

Tropic of Capricorn

AUSTRALIA

Fremantle

Cuvier Plateau

Perth Basin

Naturaliste Plateau

Wharton Basin

Diamantina Fracture Zone

East Indian Ridge

Broken Ridge

COCOS ISLANDS (to Australia)

Ridge

Osborn Plateau

N i n e t y e a s t

I N D I A N

O C E A N

Amsterdam Island

St-Paul Island

FRENCH SOUTHERN & ANTARCTIC LANDS (to France)

Kerguelen Plateau

Kerguelen

HEARD & McDONALD ISLANDS (to Australia)

S o u t h e a s t   I n d i a n   R i d g e

South Indian Basin

SOUTHERN OCEAN

ANTARCTICA

Limit of winter pack ice

Limit of summer pack ice

Antarctic Circle

Crozet Basin

Banzare Seamounts

Crozet Islands

Crozet Plateau

△ Lena Tablemount

Ob' Tablemount △

E n d e r b y   P l a i n

Indomed Fracture Zone

S o u t h w e s t   I n d i a n   R i d g e

MAURITIUS

RÉUNION (to France)

Egeria Fracture Zone

Réunion Fracture Zone

Argo Fracture Zone

Mascarene Basin

Plateau

R i d g e

Mascarene Plain

Farafangana

MADAGASCAR

Madagascar Basin

Madagascar Plateau

COMOROS

MAYOTTE (to France)

Davie Ridge

Mozambique Channel

Lake Nyasa

Zambezi

Tropic of Capricorn

Durban

Mozambique Plateau

Natal Basin

Africana Seamount △

Agulhas

Agulhas Plateau

Agulhas Basin

Prince Edward Islands (to South Africa)

Atlantic-Indian Basin

Antarctic Circle

152

154

154

67

Elevation

-6000m -4000m -2000m -1000m -250m 0

-19,658ft -13,124ft -6562ft -3281ft -820ft 0

141

Australasia & Oceania

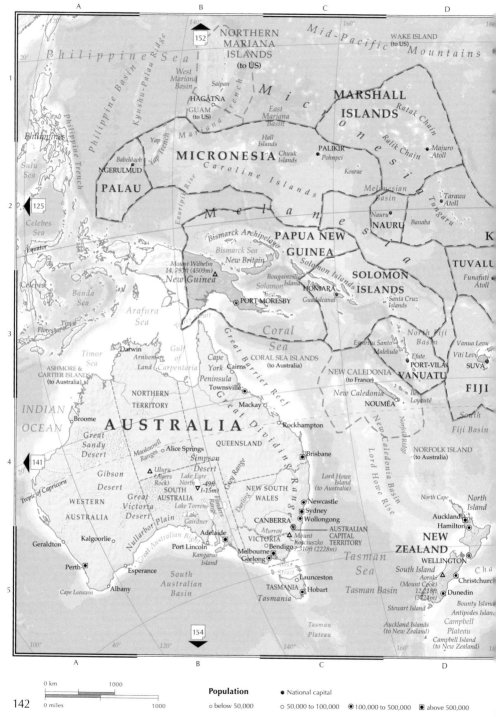

Population

● National capital

○ below 50,000 ○ 50,000 to 100,000 ◉ 100,000 to 500,000 ◼ above 500,000

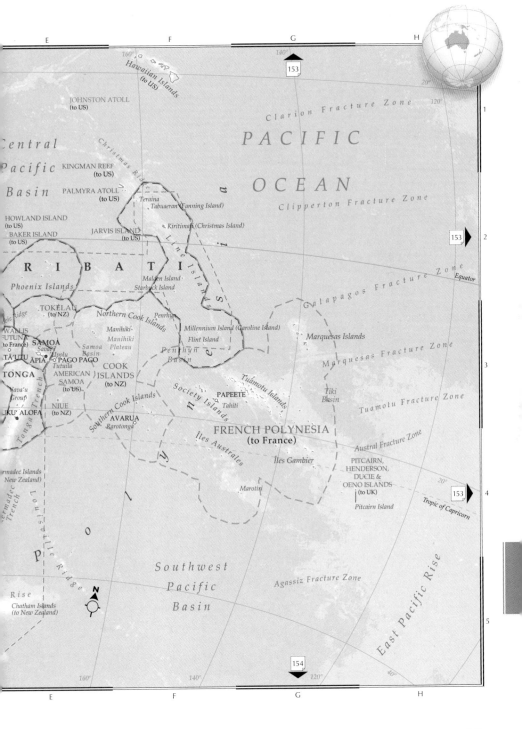

Central
Pacific
Basin

HOWLAND ISLAND
(to US)
BAKER ISLAND
(to US)

JOHNSTON ATOLL
(to US)

KINGMAN REEF
(to US)

PALMYRA ATOLL
(to US)

JARVIS ISLAND
(to US)

K I R I B A T I

Phoenix Islands

TOKELAU
(to NZ)

WALLIS
-FUTUNA
to France)

TĀʻŪTU
SAMOA
Savaiʻi Upolu
APIA PAGO PAGO
Tutuila
AMERICAN
SAMOA
(to US)

TONGA

Vavaʻu
Group

NIUE
(to NZ)

KUʻALOFA

AVARUA
Rarotonga

COOK
ISLANDS
(to NZ)

Northern Cook Islands

Manihiki
Manihiki
Plateau

Penrhyn

Penrhyn
Basin

Southern Cook Islands

Christmas Ridge

Teraina
Tabuaeran (Fanning Island)

Kiritimati (Christmas Island)

Malden Island
Starbuck Island

Millennium Island (Caroline Island)
Flint Island

Line Islands

Society Islands

PAPEETE
Tahiti

Tuamotu Islands

FRENCH POLYNESIA
(to France)

Îles Australes

Marotiri

Îles Gambier

PITCAIRN,
HENDERSON,
DUCIE &
OENO ISLANDS
(to UK)

Pitcairn Island

Hawaiian Islands
(to US)

P A C I F I C

O C E A N

Clarion Fracture Zone

Clipperton Fracture Zone

Galapagos Fracture Zone
Equator

Marquesas Islands

Marquesas Fracture Zone

Tiki
Basin

Tuamotu Fracture Zone

Austral Fracture Zone

Tropic of Capricorn

Southwest
Pacific
Basin

Agassiz Fracture Zone

East Pacific Rise

Kermadec Islands
New Zealand)

Kermadec
Trench

Tonga Trench

Louisville Ridge

Rise

Chatham Islands
(to New Zealand)

N

153

153

153

153

154

143

The Southwest Pacific

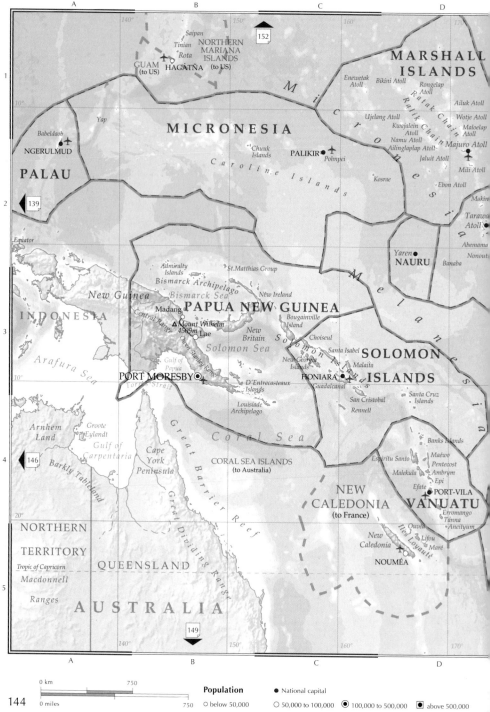

Population

● National capital

○ below 50,000 ○ 50,000 to 100,000 ◉ 100,000 to 500,000 ⬛ above 500,000

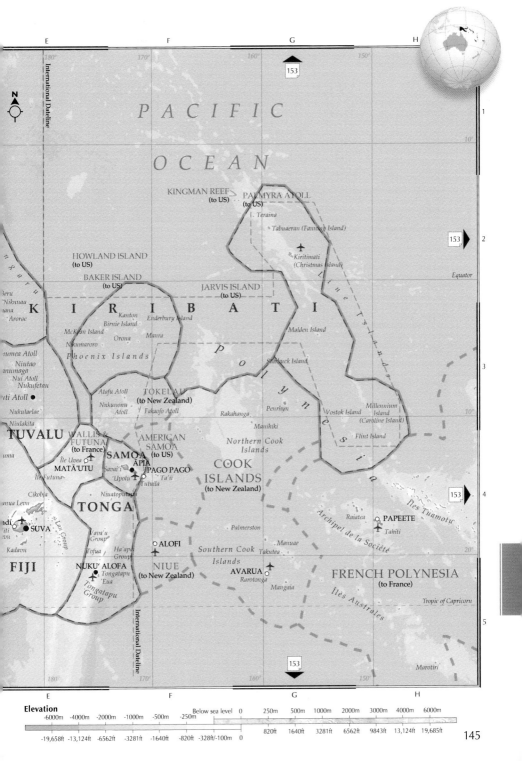

The Southwest Pacific

E   F   G   H

153

N

International Dateline

1

P A C I F I C

O C E A N

KINGMAN REEF
(to US)   PALMYRA ATOLL
(to US)

I. Teraina

153

2

Tabuaeran (Fanning Island)

HOWLAND ISLAND
(to US)

Kiritimati
(Christmas Island)

BAKER ISLAND
(to US)   JARVIS ISLAND
(to US)

Equator

K   I   R   I   B   A   T   I

Beru   *Nikunau*   *uma*   *Arorae*   Kanton   Enderbury Island   Malden Island

McKean Island   Birnie Island

numea Atoll   *Niutao*   Nikumaroro   Orona   Maura

munaga   Nui Atoll   Nukufetau   *Phoenix Islands*   *P*

ti Atoll   *Nukulaelae*   Atafu Atoll   Starbuck Island   *o*   *l*   Vostok Island   Millennium
Island
(Caroline Island)

3

Niulakita   Nukunonu
Atoll   TOKELAU
(to New Zealand)   *y*   *n*

Fakaofo Atoll   Rakahanga   Penrhyn   *e*   Flint Island

TUVALU   WALLIS &
FUTUNA
(to France)   AMERICAN
SAMOA
(to US)   Manihiki   *s*   *i*

Ile Uvea   **SAMOA**   Northern Cook
Islands   *a*

una   MATĀ'UTU   ÁPIA

Ile Futuna   Savai'i   PAGO PAGO

Cikobia   'Upolu   Ta'ti
Tutuila   **COOK**

anua Levu   Niuatoputapu   **ISLANDS**
(to New Zealand)

di   **TONGA**   Raiatea   PAPEETE   4

SUVA   Lau Group   Palmerston   Archipel de la Société   Tahiti   153

vu   Vava'u
Group   Manuae   Îles Tuamotu

Kadavu   ALOFI   Mauae   Takutea

FIJI   Tofua   Ha'apai
Group   Southern Cook
Islands

NUKU'ALOFA   NIUE
(to New Zealand)   AVARUA   **FRENCH POLYNESIA**
(to France)

'Eua   Rarotonga
Tongatapu   Mangaia

Tongatapu
Group   *Îles Australes*

Tropic of Capricorn

International Dateline

5

153   Marotiri

E   F   G   H

Elevation

| -6000m | -4000m | -2000m | -1000m | -500m | -250m | Below sea level | 0 | 250m | 500m | 1000m | 2000m | 3000m | 4000m | 6000m |

| -19,658ft | -13,124ft | -6562ft | -3281ft | -1640ft | -820ft | -328ft/-100m | 0 | 820ft | 1640ft | 3281ft | 6562ft | 9843ft | 13,124ft | 19,685ft |

Western Australia

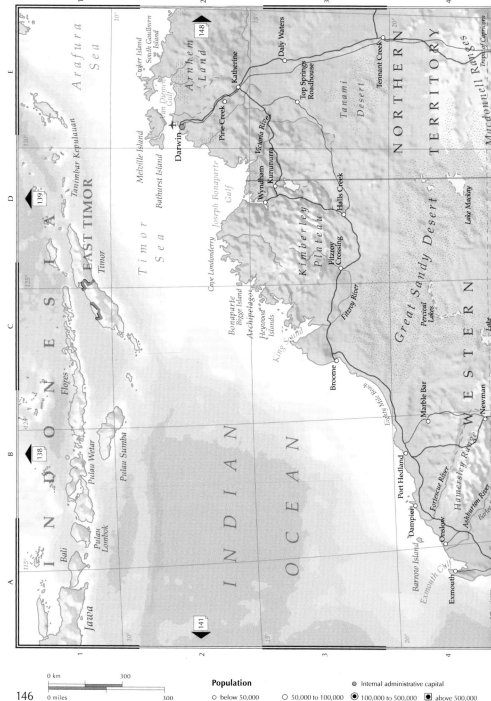

Arafura Sea

Tanimbar Kepulauan

EAST TIMOR

Timor

INDONESIA

Flores

Pulau Wetar

Bali

Pulau Lombok

Pulau Sumba

Jawa

INDIAN

OCEAN

Melville Island

Bathurst Island

Timor Sea

Coker Island

South Goulburn Island

Van Diemen Gulf

Darwin

Pine Creek

Katherine

Daly Waters

Arnhem Land

Top Springs Roadhouse

Tanami Desert

Tennant Creek

NORTHERN TERRITORY

Macdonnell Ranges

Tropic of Capricorn

Joseph Bonaparte Gulf

Cape Londonderry

Wyndham

Kununurra

Victoria River

Halls Creek

Kimberley Plateau

Fitzroy Crossing

Lake Mackay

Bonaparte Archipelago

Bigge Island

Heywood Islands

King Sound

Fitzroy River

Great Sandy Desert

Percival Lakes

Lake

Broome

Eighty Mile Beach

Marble Bar

Newman

Port Hedland

Hamersley Range

WESTERN

Dampier

Onslow

Fortescue River

Ashburton River

Barlee

Barrow Island

Exmouth Gulf

Exmouth

Population

⊙ Internal administrative capital

○ below 50,000   ○ 50,000 to 100,000   ◉ 100,000 to 500,000   ■ above 500,000

0 km   300
0 miles   300

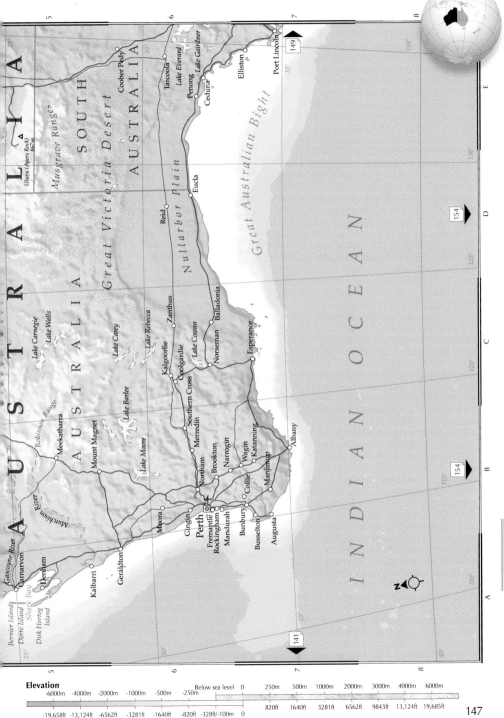

AUSTRALIA

SOUTH AUSTRALIA

Uluru (Ayers Rock) 867m

Musgrave Ranges

Great Victoria Desert

Coober Pedy

Tarcoola

Lake Everard

Penong

Lake Gairdner

Ceduna

Elliston

Port Lincoln

149

Reid

Nullarbor Plain

Eucla

Great Australian Bight

INDIAN OCEAN

154

Lake Carnegie

Lake Wells

Lake Carey

Lake Rebecca

Zanthus

Kalgoorlie

Coolgardie

Lake Cowan

Balladonia

Norseman

Esperance

Lake Barlee

Robinson Range

Southern Cross

Merredin

Brookton

Narrogin

Wagin

Katanning

Albany

Meekatharra

Mount Magnet

Lake Moore

Northam

Collie

Manjimup

Moora

Gingin

Perth

Fremantle

Rockingham

Mandurah

Bunbury

Busselton

Augusta

154

Gascoyne River

Carnarvon

Denham

Shark Bay

Murchison River

Kalbarri

Geraldton

Bernier Island

Dorre Island

Dirk Hartog Island

141

N

Elevation

Below sea level													
-6000m	-4000m	-2000m	-1000m	-500m	-250m	0	250m	500m	1000m	2000m	3000m	4000m	6000m
-19,658ft	-13,124ft	-6562ft	-3281ft	-1640ft	-820ft	-328ft/-100m 0		820ft	1640ft	3281ft	6562ft	9843ft	13,124ft	19,685ft

147

Eastern Australia

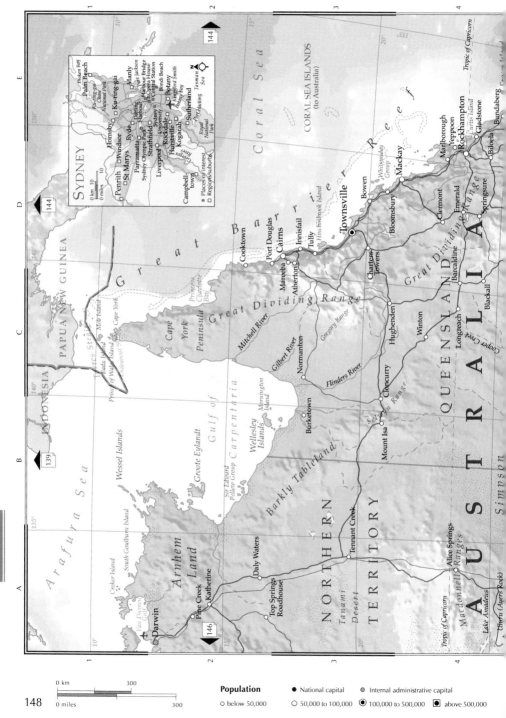

SYDNEY

Broken Bay
Palm Beach
Ku-ring-gai Chase National Park
Manly
Port Jackson
Harbour Bridge
Opera House
Central Station
Botany
Bondi Beach
Botany Bay
Kurnell
Kingsford Smith
Hornsby
Windsor
Ryde
Parramatta
Darling
Bathurst
Sydney
Sydney Olympic Park
Strathfield
University
Penrith
St Marys
Liverpool
Rockdale
Hurstville
Kogarah
Sutherland
Port Hacking
Royal National Park
Campbell town

0 km 10
0 miles 10

Tasman Sea

□ Places of interest
■ Regions/suburbs

Coral Sea

CORAL SEA ISLANDS (to Australia)

PAPUA NEW GUINEA

INDONESIA

Arafura Sea

Wessel Islands

Croker Island
South Goulburn Island

Van Diemen Gulf

Darwin
Pine Creek
Katherine
Top Springs Roadhouse
Daly Waters

Arnhem Land

Groote Eylandt

Sir Edward Pellew Group

Wellesley Islands
Mornington Island

Gulf of Carpentaria

Torres Strait
Badu Island
Moa Island
Prince of Wales Island
Deliverance Island
Cape York

Cape York Peninsula

Princess Charlotte Bay

Great Barrier Reef

Cooktown
Port Douglas
Mareeba
Cairns
Atherton
Innisfail
Tully
Hinchinbrook Island

Mitchell River
Gilbert River
Normanton
Flinders River
Burketown

Barkly Tableland

Tanami Desert

NORTHERN TERRITORY

Tennant Creek
Alice Springs
Macdonnell Ranges
Uluru (Ayers Rock)
Lake Amadeus

Mount Isa
Cloncurry
Selwyn Range
Winton
Longreach
Cooper Creek

QUEENSLAND

AUSTRALIA

Simpson

Blackall
Barcaldine
Emerald
Springsure
Clermont
Bloomsbury
Whitsunday Group
Mackay

Marlborough
Yeppoon
Rockhampton
Gladstone
Curtis Island
Biloela
Bundaberg

Bowen
Townsville
Charters Towers
Hughenden

Great Dividing Range

Tropic of Capricorn

10°

15°

20°

135°
140°
145°
150°
155°

0 km 300
0 miles 300

Population

● National capital
◉ Internal administrative capital
○ below 50,000
○ 50,000 to 100,000
◉ 100,000 to 500,000
■ above 500,000

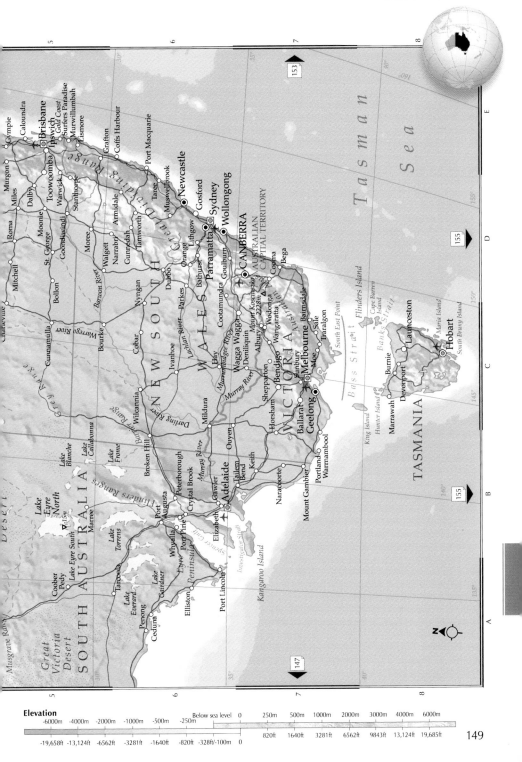

Elevation

-6000m	-4000m	-2000m	-1000m	-500m	-250m	Below sea level	0	250m	500m	1000m	2000m	3000m	4000m	6000m
-19,658ft	-13,124ft	-6562ft	-3281ft	-1640ft	-820ft	-328ft/-100m	0	820ft	1640ft	3281ft	6562ft	9843ft	13,124ft	19,685ft

New Zealand

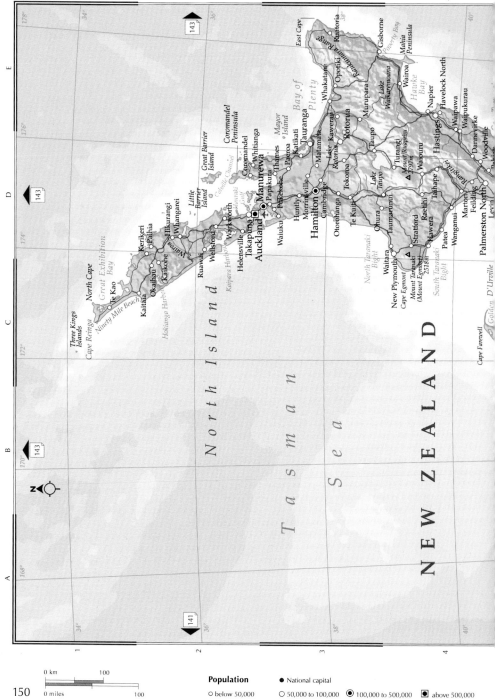

Population   ● National capital

○ below 50,000   ○ 50,000 to 100,000   ◉ 100,000 to 500,000   ■ above 500,000

0 km   100
0 miles   100

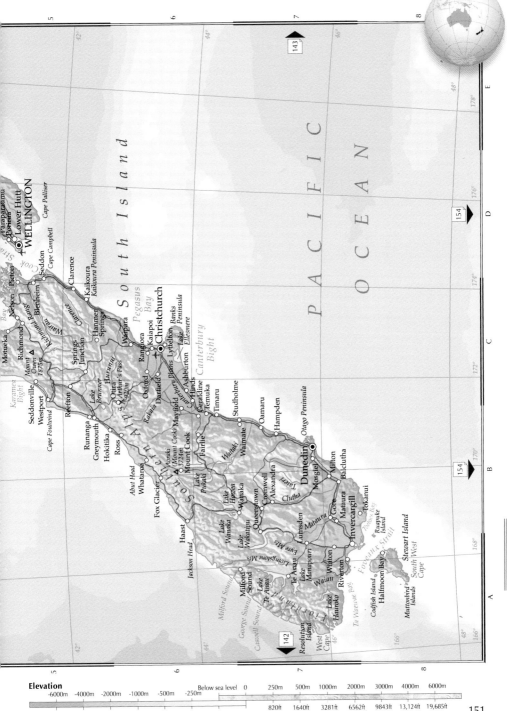

143

154

154

South Island

PACIFIC

OCEAN

Harapaaatumu
Porirua
Lower Hutt
WELLINGTON
Cape Palliser
Cape Campbell
Picton
Seddon
Clarence
Cape Campbell
Blenheim
Kaikoura
Kaikoura Peninsula
Nelson
Motueka
Richmond
Mount
Owen
1875m
Springs
Junction
Hanmer
Springs
Waiparu
Pegasus
Bay
Seddonville
Westport
Cape Foulwind
Reefton
Lake
Brunner
Harihari
Otira
Arthur's Pass
920m
Oxford
Darfield
Rangiora
Kaiapoi
Christchurch
Lyttelton
Banks
Peninsula
Lake
Ellesmere
Canterbury
Bight

Karamea
Bight

Runanga
Greymouth
Hokitika
Ross
Mayfield
Ashburton
Hinds
Geraldine
Temuka
Timaru

Abut Head
Whataroa
Aoraki
(Mount Cook)
3724m
Mount Cook
Fairlie
Waitaki
Waimate
Studholme
Oamaru
Hampden
Otago Peninsula

Fox Glacier

Haast
Jackson Head

Lake
Pukaki
Lake
Hawea
Wanaka
Cromwell
Alexandra
Lunsden
Cluthu
Dunedin
Mosgiel
Milton
Balclutha

Lake
Wanaka
Lake
Wakatipu
Queenstown
Mataura
Gore
Mataura
Tokanui

Milford Sound
Te Anau
Lake
Te Anau
Lake
Manapouri
Waiau
Winton
Riverton
Invercargill

Halfmoon Bay
Ruapuke
Island
Stewart Island
South West
Cape

Milford Sound
George Sound
Caswell Sound

Resolution
Island
West
Cape

142

Codfish Island
Muttonbird
Islands

Elevation

Below sea level	0						
-6000m	-4000m	-2000m	-1000m	-500m	-250m	250m	500m	1000m	2000m	3000m	4000m	6000m

-19,658ft -13,124ft -6562ft -3281ft -1640ft -820ft -328ft/-100m 0   820ft 1640ft 3281ft 6562ft 9843ft 13,124ft 19,685ft

The Pacific Ocean

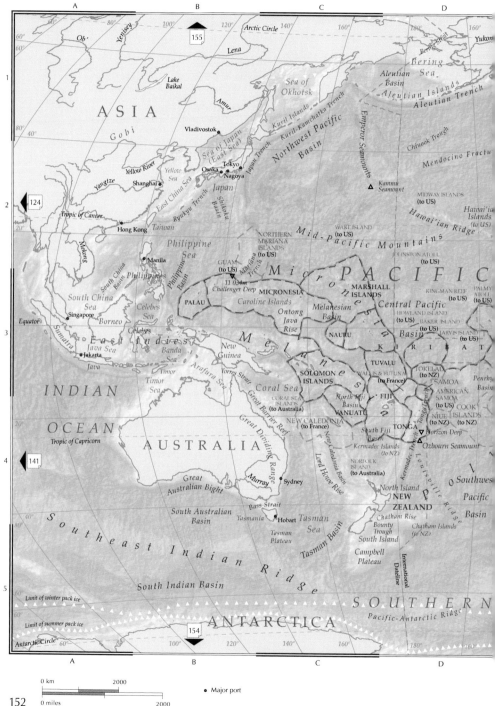

0 km 2000

0 miles 2000

• Major port

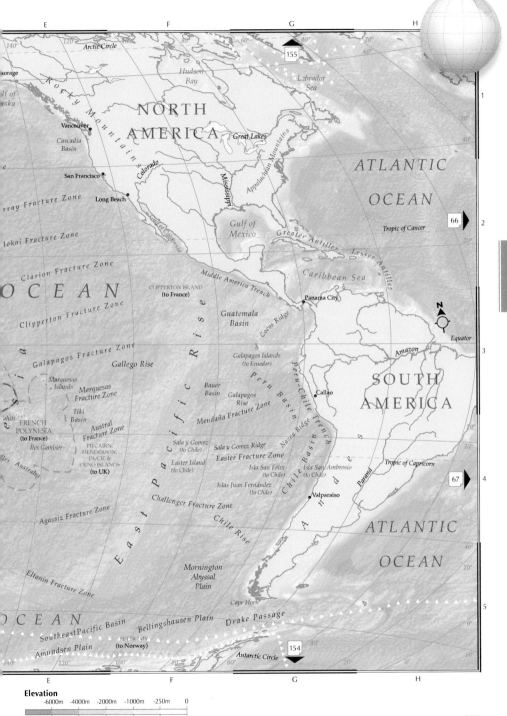

E **F** **G** **H**

140° 120° 100° 80° 60° 40° 20°

Arctic Circle

orage Rocky Mountains Hudson Bay Labrador Sea 155 60°

1

lf of *ska* NORTH AMERICA 40°

Vancouver

Cascadia Basin Great Lakes ATLANTIC

c Colorado Appalachian Mountains OCEAN 66

San Francisco Mississippi

rray Fracture Zone Long Beach Tropic of Cancer **2**

Gulf of Mexico Greater Antilles 20°

lokai Fracture Zone Gulf of California Lesser Antilles

Clarion Fracture Zone Middle America Trench Caribbean Sea

O C E A N CLIPPERTON ISLAND (to France) Panama City N

Clipperton Fracture Zone Guatemala Basin Cocos Ridge Equator

Galapagos Fracture Zone Gallego Rise Galápagos Islands (to Ecuador) Amazon **3**

a East Pacific Rise Peru Basin SOUTH

Marquesas Islands Marquesas Fracture Zone Bauer Basin Galapagos Rise Callao AMERICA

hiti Tiki Basin Mendaña Fracture Zone 10°

FRENCH POLYNESIA (to France) Austral Fracture Zone Nazca Ridge 20°

Îles Gambier PITCAIRN, HENDERSON, DUCIE & OENO ISLANDS (to UK) Sala y Gomez (to Chile) Sala y Gomez Ridge Easter Fracture Zone Chile Basin Tropic of Capricorn

es Australes Easter Island (to Chile) Isla San Félix (to Chile) Isla San Ambrosio (to Chile) 67 **4**

Islas Juan Fernández (to Chile) Valparaíso Paraná

Challenger Fracture Zone Chile Rise Andes

Agassiz Fracture Zone ATLANTIC

Eltanin Fracture Zone Mornington Abyssal Plain OCEAN 20°

Cape Horn

O C E A N Southeast Pacific Basin Bellingshausen Plain Drake Passage **5**

Amundsen Plain PETER I ØY (to Norway) Antarctic Circle 154 60°

140° 120° 100° 80° 60° 40° 20°

E **F** **G** **H**

Elevation

-6000m -4000m -2000m -1000m -250m 0

-19,658ft -13,124ft -6562ft -3281ft -820ft 0

Antarctica

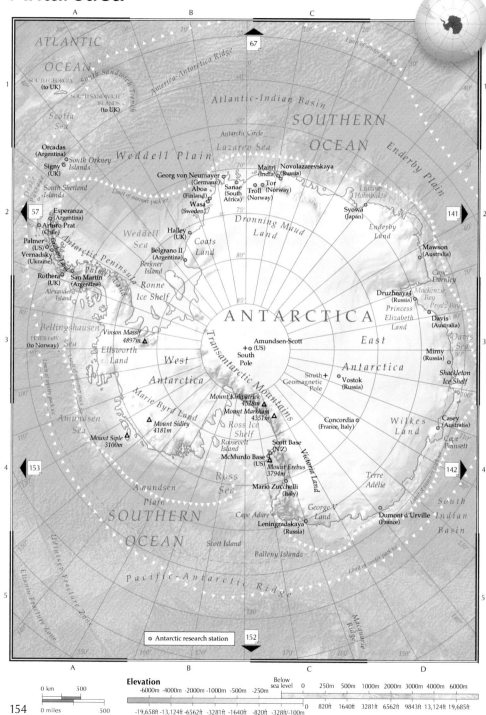

ATLANTIC OCEAN

SOUTH GEORGIA (to UK)

South Sandwich Trench

America-Antarctica Ridge

Atlantic-Indian Basin

SOUTHERN OCEAN

SOUTH SANDWICH ISLANDS (to UK)

Scotia Sea

Antarctic Circle

Lazarev Sea

Enderby Plain

Orcadas (Argentina)

South Orkney Islands

Weddell Plain

Signy (UK)

Maitri (India)

Novolazarevskaya (Russia)

Georg von Neumayer (Germany)

Sanae (South Africa)

Tor (Norway)

Lützow-Holmbukta

South Shetland Islands

Limit of summer pack ice

Aboa (Finland)

Troll (Norway)

Wasa (Sweden)

Dronning Maud Land

Syowa (Japan)

Esperanza (Argentina)

Arturo Prat (Chile)

Weddell Sea

Halley (UK)

Coats Land

Enderby Land

Mawson (Australia)

Palmer (US)

Belgrano II (Argentina)

Vernadsky (Ukraine)

Berkner Island

Cape Darnley

Rothera (UK)

San Martín (Argentina)

Ronne Ice Shelf

Druzhnaya (Russia)

Mackenzie Bay

Prydz Bay

Alexander Island

Princess Elizabeth Land

Davis (Australia)

Bellingshausen Sea

PETER I ØY (to Norway)

Vinson Massif 4897m

A N T A R C T I C A

East Antarctica

Davis Sea

Ellsworth Land

Amundsen-Scott (US) South Pole

Transantarctic Mountains

South Geomagnetic Pole

Mirny (Russia)

Amundsen Sea

West Antarctica

Vostok (Russia)

Shackleton Ice Shelf

Marie Byrd Land

Mount Kirkpatrick 4528m

Mount Sidley 4181m

Mount Markham 4351m

Concordia (France, Italy)

Wilkes Land

Casey (Australia)

Mount Siple 3100m

Ross Ice Shelf

Roosevelt Island

Scott Base (N.Z.)

Cape Poinsett

McMurdo Base (US)

Mount Erebus 3794m

Victoria Land

Terre Adélie

Amundsen Plain

Ross Sea

Mario Zucchelli (Italy)

George V Land

SOUTHERN OCEAN

Cape Adare

Dumont d'Urville (France)

South Indian Basin

Leningradskaya (Russia)

Scott Island

Balleny Islands

Macquarie Ridge

Pacific-Antarctic Ridge

Udintsev Fracture Zone

Eltanin Fracture Zone

o Antarctic research station

0 km 500
0 miles 500

Elevation

Below sea level											
-6000m	-4000m	-2000m	-1000m	-500m	-250m	0	250m	500m	1000m	2000m	3000m	4000m	6000m
-19,658ft	-13,124ft	-6562ft	-3281ft	-1640ft	-820ft	-328ft/-100m	0	820ft	1640ft	3281ft	6562ft	9843ft	13,124ft	19,685ft

Arctic Ocean

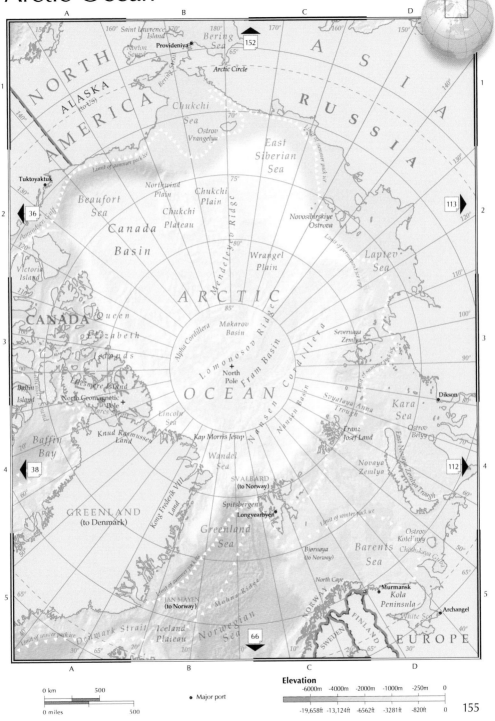

NORTH AMERICA

ALASKA (to US)

Saint Lawrence Island

Norton Sound

Provid>eniya

Bering Strait

Bering Sea

Arctic Circle

Chukchi Sea

Ostrov Vrangelya

ASIA

RUSSIA

East Siberian Sea

152

Tuktoyaktuk

Northwind Plain

Chukchi Plain

Chukchi Plateau

Beaufort Sea

Canada Basin

Amundsen Gulf

Victoria Island

CANADA

Queen

Elizabeth

Islands

Baffin Island

Ellesmere Island

Nares Strait

Baffin Bay

Knud Rasmussen Land

Lincoln Sea

North Geomagnetic Pole

Limit of summer pack ice

Mendeleyev Ridge

Wrangel Plain

ARCTIC

Makarov Basin

Alpha Cordillera

Lomonosov Ridge

North Pole

Fram Basin

OCEAN

Novosibirskiye Ostrova

Laptev Sea

Limit of permanent ice cap

Severnaya Zemlya

Nansen Cordillera

Nansen Basin

Svyataya Anna Trough

Franz Josef Land

Kara Sea

Dikson

Ostrov Belyy

36

113

112

Kap Morris Jesup

Wandel Sea

SVALBARD (to Norway)

Spitsbergen

Longyearbyen

Kong Frederik VIII Land

GREENLAND (to Denmark)

Greenland Sea

Novaya Zemlya

East Novaya Zemlya Trough

Ostrov Kotel'nyy

Cheshskaya Guba

Barents Sea

38

JAN MAYEN (to Norway)

Bjørnøya (to Norway)

North Cape

Mohns Ridge

Iceland Plateau

Norwegian Sea

Denmark Strait

Limit of winter pack ice

NORWAY

SWEDEN

FINLAND

North Cape

Murmansk

Kola Peninsula

White Sea

Archangel

EUROPE

66

Elevation

| -6000m | -4000m | -2000m | -1000m | -250m | 0 |

| -19,658ft | -13,124ft | -6562ft | -3281ft | -820ft | 0 |

0 km — 500

0 miles — 500

● Major port

155

Overseas territories & dependencies

Despite the rapid process of global decolonization since the Second World War, around 8 million people in more than 50 territories around the world continue to live under the protection of France, Australia, the Netherlands, Denmark, Norway, New Zealand, the UK, or the USA. These remnants of former colonial empires may have persisted for economic, strategic or political reasons and are administered in a variety of ways.

AUSTRALIA

Australia's overseas territories have not been an issue since Papua New Guinea became independent in 1975. Consequently there is no overriding policy toward them. Norfolk Island is inhabited by descendants of the H.M.S Bounty mutineers and more recent Australian migrants.

Ashmore & Cartier Islands
Indian Ocean
Status: External territory
Claimed: 1931
Capital: Not applicable
Population: None
Area: 2 sq miles
(5.2 sq km)

Christmas Island
Indian Ocean
Status: External territory
Claimed: 1958
Capital: The Settlement
Population: 2205
Area: 52 sq miles
(135 sq km)

Cocos Islands
Indian Ocean
Status: External territory
Claimed: 1955
Capital: West Island
Population: 596
Area: 5.5 sq miles
(14 sq km)

Coral Sea Islands
South Pacific
Status: External territory
Claimed: 1969
Capital: None
Population: below 10 (scientists)
Area: Less than 1.2 sq miles
(3 sq km)

Heard & McDonald Is.
Indian Ocean
Status: External territory
Claimed: 1947
Capital: Not applicable
Population: None
Area: 161 sq miles
(417 sq km)

Norfolk Island
South Pacific
Status: External territory
Claimed: 1774
Capital: Kingston
Population: 1748
Area: 13 sq miles (34 sq km)

DENMARK

The Faroe Islands have been under Danish administration since Queen Margreth I of Denmark inherited Norway in 1380. The Home Rule Act of 1948 gave the Faroese control over all their internal affairs. Greenland first came under Danish rule in 1380. Today, Denmark is responsible for the island's foreign affairs and defense.

Faroe Islands
North Atlantic
Status: Self-governing territory of Denmark
Claimed: 1380
Capital: Tórshavn
Population: 49,117
Area: 540 sq miles
(1399 sq km)

Greenland
North Atlantic
Status: Self-governing territory of Denmark
Claimed: 1380
Capital: Nuuk
Population: 56,190
Area: 836,109 sq miles
(2,166,086 sq km)

FRANCE

France has developed economic ties with its *Territoires d'Outre-Mer*, thereby stressing interdependence over independence. Overseas *départements*, officially part of France, have their own governments. Territorial *collectivités* and overseas *territoires* have varying degrees of autonomy.

Clipperton Island
East Pacific
Status: Dependency of French Polynesia
Claimed: 1935
Capital: Not applicable
Population: None
Area: 2.7 sq miles
(7 sq km)

French Guiana
South America
Status: Overseas department
Claimed: 1817
Capital: Cayenne
Population: 276,000
Area: 35,135 sq miles
(91,000 sq km)

French Polynesia
South Pacific
Status: Overseas collectivity
Claimed: 1843
Capital: Papeete
Population: 280,210
Area: 1608 sq miles
(4165 sq km)

Guadeloupe
West Indies
Status: Overseas department
Claimed: 1635
Capital: Basse-Terre
Population: 400,187
Area: 629 sq miles
(1628 sq km)

Martinique
West Indies
Status: Overseas department
Claimed: 1635
Capital: Fort-de-France
Population: 396,000
Area: 425 sq miles (1100 sq km)

Mayotte
Indian Ocean
Status: Overseas department
Claimed: 1843
Capital: Mamoudzou
Population: 212,645
Area: 144 sq miles (374 sq km)

New Caledonia
South Pacific
Status: Self-governing territory
Claimed: 1853
Capital: Nouméa
Population: 278,000
Area: 7347 sq miles (19,100 sq km)

Réunion
Indian Ocean
Status: Overseas department
Claimed: 1638
Capital: Saint-Denis
Population: 867,000
Area: 970 sq miles (2500 sq km)

St. Pierre & Miquelon
North America
Status: Overseas collectivity
Claimed: 1604
Capital: Saint-Pierre
Population: 5533
Area: 93 sq miles (242 sq km)

Wallis & Futuna
South Pacific
Status: Overseas collectivity
Claimed: 1842
Capital: Matá'Utu
Population: 15,714
Area: 106 sq miles (274 sq km)

NETHERLANDS

The country's remaining overseas territories were formerly part of the Dutch West Indies. The Netherlands Antilles dissolved in 2010 leaving the constituent islands with varying degrees of autonomy, but the Netherlands remains responsible for their security.

Aruba
West Indies
Status: Self-governing country of the Netherlands
Claimed: 1643
Capital: Oranjestad
Population: 104,882
Area: 75 sq miles (194 sq km)

Bonaire
West Indies
Status: Special municipality of the Netherlands
Claimed: 1816
Capital: Kralendijk
Population: 19,400
Area: 113 sq miles (294 sq km)

Curaçao
West Indies
Status: Self-governing country of the Netherlands
Claimed: 1816
Capital: Willemstad
Population: 160,000
Area: 171 sq miles (444 sq km)

Sint Maarten
West Indies
Status: Constituent country of the Netherlands
Claimed: 1648
Capital: Philipsburg
Population: 39,689
Area: 13 sq miles (34 sq km)

NEW ZEALAND

New Zealand's government has no desire to retain any overseas territories. However, the economic weakness of its dependent territory Tokelau and its freely associated states, Niue and the Cook Islands, has forced New Zealand to remain responsible for their foreign policy and defense.

Cook Islands
South Pacific
Status: Associated territory
Claimed: 1901
Capital: Avarua
Population: 11,700
Area: 91 sq miles (235 sq km)

Niue
South Pacific
Status: Associated territory
Claimed: 1901
Capital: Alofi
Population: 1618
Area: 102 sq miles (264 sq km)

Tokelau
South Pacific
Status: Dependent territory
Claimed: 1926
Capital: Not applicable
Population: 1337
Area: 4 sq miles (10 sq km)

NORWAY

In 1920, 41 nations signed the Spits-bergen Treaty recognizing Norwegian sovereignty over Svalbard. There is a NATO base on Jan Mayen. Bouvet Island is a nature reserve.

Bouvet Island
South Atlantic
Status: Dependency
Claimed: 1928
Capital: Not applicable
Population: None
Area: 22 sq miles (58 sq km)

Jan Mayen
North Atlantic
Status: Dependency
Claimed: 1929
Capital: Not applicable
Population: 18 (meteorologists)
Area: 147 sq miles (381 sq km)

Continued on page158

Overseas territories & dependencies

Peter I. Island
Southern Ocean
Status: Dependency
Claimed: 1931
Capital: Not applicable
Population: None
Area: 69 sq miles (180 sq km)

Svalbard
Arctic Ocean
Status: Dependency
Claimed: 1920
Capital: Longyearbyen
Population: 2752
Area: 24,289 sq miles
(62,906 sq km)

UNITED KINGDOM

The UK still has the largest number
of overseas territories. These are
locally-governed by a mixture
of elected representatives and
appointed officials, and they
all enjoy a large measure of internal
self-government, but certain powers,
such as foreign affairs and defense,
are reserved for Governors
of the British Crown.

Anguilla
West Indies
Status: Overseas
Territory
Claimed: 1650
Capital: The Valley
Population: 17,087
Area: 37 sq miles
(96 sq km)

Ascension Island
South Atlantic
Status: Overseas Territory
Claimed: 1673
Capital: Georgetown
Population: 806
Area: 34 sq miles
(88 sq km)

Bermuda
North Atlantic
Status: Overseas Territory
Claimed: 1612
Capital: Hamilton
Population: 65,331
Area: 20 sq miles (53 sq km)

British Indian Ocean Territory
Status: Overseas
Territory
Claimed: 1814
Capital: Diego Garcia
Population: 4200
Area: 23 sq miles
(60 sq km)

British Virgin Islands
West Indies
Status: Overseas Territory
Claimed: 1672
Capital: Road Town
Population: 30,661
Area: 59 sq miles
(153 sq km)

Cayman Islands
West Indies
Status: Overseas Territory
Claimed: 1670
Capital: George Town
Population: 60,765
Area: 100 sq miles (259 sq km)

Falkland Islands
South Atlantic
Status: Overseas Territory
Claimed: 1832
Capital: Stanley
Population: 3198
Area: 4699 sq miles
(12,173 sq km)

Gibraltar
Southwest Europe
Status: Overseas Territory
Claimed: 1713
Capital: Gibraltar
Population: 34,410
Area: 2.5 sq miles (6.5 sq km)

Guernsey
Channel Islands
Status: Crown Dependency
Claimed: 1066
Capital: St. Peter Port
Population: 66,502
Area: 25 sq miles (65 sq km)

Isle of Man
British Isles
Status: Crown Dependency
Claimed: 1765
Capital: Douglas
Population: 83,740
Area: 221 sq miles (572 sq km)

Jersey
Channel Islands
Status: Crown Dependency
Claimed: 1066
Capital: St. Helier
Population: 98,840
Area: 45 sq miles (116 sq km)

Montserrat
West Indies
Status: Overseas Territory
Claimed: 1632
Capital: Plymouth *(de jure)*,
Brades *(de facto)*
Population: 5292
Area: 40 sq miles (102 sq km)

Pitcairn Group of Islands
South Pacific
Status: Overseas Territory
Claimed: 1887
Capital: Adamstown
Population: 54
Area: 18 sq miles (47 sq km)

St. Helena
South Atlantic
Status: Overseas Territory
Claimed: 1673
Capital: Jamestown
Population: 4800
Area: 47 sq miles (122 sq km)

South Georgia & The South Sandwich Islands
South Atlantic
Status: Overseas Territory
Claimed: 1775
Capital: Not applicable
Population: No permanent
residents
Area: 1387 sq miles
(3592 sq km)

Tristan da Cunha
South Atlantic
Status: Overseas
territory
Claimed: 1612
Capital: Edinburgh
Population: 293
Area: 38 sq miles (98 sq km)

Turks & Caicos Islands
West Indies
Status: Overseas territory
Claimed: 1766
Capital: Cockburn Town
Population: 34,900
Area: 166 sq miles
(430 sq km)

UNITED STATES OF AMERICA

America's overseas territories
have been seen as strategically
useful, if expensive, links with its
"backyards." The US has, in most
cases, given the local population a
say in deciding their own status.
A US Commonwealth territory, such
as Puerto Rico, has a greater level
of independence than that of a US
unincorporated territory.

American Samoa
South Pacific
Status: Unincorporated
territory
Claimed: 1900
Capital: Pago Pago
Population: 55,600
Area: 75 sq miles (195 sq km)

Baker & Howland Islands
South Pacific
Status: Unincorporated
territory
Claimed: 1856
Capital: Not applicable
Population: None
Area: 0.5 sq miles (1.4 sq km)

Guam
West Pacific
Status: Unincorporated
territory
Claimed: 1898
Capital: Hagåtña
Population: 162,900
Area: 212 sq miles
(549 sq km)

Jarvis Island
South Pacific
Status: Unincorporated territory
Claimed: 1856
Capital: Not applicable
Population: None
Area: 1.7 sq miles (4.5 sq km)

Johnston Atoll
Central Pacific
Status: Unincorporated
territory
Claimed: 1858
Capital: Not applicable
Population: Not applicable
Area: 1 sq mile (2.8 sq km)

Kingman Reef
Central Pacific
Status: Unincorporated territory
Claimed: 1856
Capital: Not applicable
Population: None
Area: 0.4 sq mile
(1 sq km)

Midway Islands
Central Pacific
Status: Unincorporated
territory
Claimed: 1867
Capital: Not applicable
Population: 40
Area: 2 sq miles
(5.2 sq km)

Navassa Island
West Indies
Status: Unincorporated
territory
Claimed: 1856
Capital: Not applicable
Population: None
Area: 2 sq miles (5.2 sq km)

Northern Mariana Islands
West Pacific
Status: Commonwealth
territory
Claimed: 1947
Capital: Saipan
Population: 55,020
Area: 177 sq miles (457 sq km)

Palmyra Atoll
Central Pacific
Status: Incorporated
territory
Claimed: 1898
Capital: Not applicable
Population: None
Area: 5 sq miles (12 sq km)

Puerto Rico
West Indies
Status: Commonwealth
territory
Claimed: 1898
Capital: San Juan
Population: 3.7 million
Area: 3515 sq miles
(9104 sq km)

Virgin Islands
West Indies
Status: Unincorporated
territory
Claimed: 1917
Capital: Charlotte Amalie
Population: 102,950
Area: 137 sq miles
(355 sq km)

Wake Island
Central Pacific
Status: Unincorporated
territory
Claimed: 1898
Capital: Not applicable
Population: 150 (US air base)
Area: 2.5 sq miles
(6.5 sq km)

Glossary of geographical terms

The following glossary lists all geographical terms occuring on the maps and in the main-entry names in the Index–Gazetteer. These terms may precede, follow or be run together with the proper elements of the name; where they precede it the term is reversed for indexing purposes – thus Poluostov Yamal is indexed as Yamal, Poluostrov.

A
Å *Danish, Norwegian,* River
Alpen *German,* Alps
Altiplanicie *Spanish,* Plateau
Älv(en) *Swedish,* River
Anse *French,* Bay
Archipiélago *Spanish,* Archipelago
Arcipelago *Italian,* Archipelago
Arquipélago *Portuguese,* Archipelago
Aukštuma *Lithuanian,* Upland

B
Bahía *Spanish,* Bay
Baía *Portuguese,* Bay
Baḩr *Arabic,* River
Baie *French,* Bay
Bandao *Chinese,* Peninsula
Banjaran *Malay,* Mountain range
Batang *Malay,* Stream
-berg *Afrikaans, Norwegian,* Mountain
Birket *Arabic,* Lake
Boğazı *Turkish,* Strait
Bucht *German,* Bay
Bugten *Danish,* Bay
Buḩayrat *Arabic,* Lake, reservoir
Buḩeiret *Arabic,* Lake
Bukit *Malay,* Mountain
-bukta *Norwegian,* Bay
bukten *Swedish,* Bay
Burnu *Turkish,* Cape, point
Buuraha *Somali,* Mountains

C
Cabo *Portuguese,* Cape
Cap *French,* Cape
Cascada *Portuguese,* Waterfall
Cerro *Spanish,* Hill
Chaîne *French,* Mountain range
Chau *Cantonese,* Island
Cháy *Turkish,* Stream
Chhâk *Cambodian,* Bay
Chhu *Tibetan,* River
-chôsuji *Korean,* Reservoir

Chott *Arabic,* Salt lake, depression
Ch'ün-tao *Chinese,* Island group
**Cambodian,* Mountains
Cordillera *Spanish,* Mountain range
Costa *Spanish,* Coast
Côte *French,* Coast
Cuchilla *Spanish,* Mountains

D
Dağı *Azerbaijani, Turkish,* Mountain
Dağları *Azerbaijani, Turkish,* Mountains
-dake *Japanese,* Peak
Danau *Indonesian,* Lake
Đao *Vietnamese,* Island
Daryá *Persian,* River
Daryácheh *Persian,* Lake
Dasht *Persian,* Plain, desert
Dawḩat *Arabic,* Bay
Dere *Turkish,* Stream
Dili *Azerbaijani,* Spit
-do *Korean,* Island
Dooxo *Somali,* Valley
Düzü *Azerbaijani,* Steppe
-dwíp *Bengali,* Island

E
Embalse *Spanish,* Reservoir
Erg *Arabic,* Dunes
Estany *Catalan,* Lake
Estrecho *Spanish,* Strait
-ey *Icelandic,* Island
Ezero *Bulgarian, Macedonian,* Lake

F
Fjord *Danish,* Fjord
-fjorden *Norwegian,* Fjord
-fjørdhur *Faeroese,* Fjord
Fleuve *French,* River
Fliegu *Maltese,* Channel
-fljór *Icelandic,* River

G
-gang *Korean,* River
Ganga *Nepali, Sinhala,* River
Gaoyuan *Chinese,* Plateau
-gawa *Japanese,* River

Gebel *Arabic,* Mountain
-gebirge *German,* Mountains
Ghubbat *Arabic,* Bay
Gjiri *Albanian,* Bay
Gol *Mongolian,* River
Golfe *French,* Gulf
Golfo *Italian, Spanish,* Gulf
Gora *Russian, Serbian,* Mountain
Gory *Russian,* Mountains
Guba *Russian,* Bay
Gunung *Malay,* Mountain

H
Ḩadd *Arabic,* Spit
-haehyôp *Korean,* Strait
Haff *German,* Lagoon
Hai *Chinese,* Sea, bay
Ḩammádat *Arabic,* Plateau
Hámún *Persian,* Lake
Hawr *Arabic,* Lake
Háyk' *Amharic,* Lake
He *Chinese,* River
Helodrano *Malagasy,* Bay
-hegység *Hungarian,* Mountain range
Hka *Burmese,* River
-ho *Korean,* Lake
Hô *Korean,* Reservoir
/olot *Hebrew,* Dunes
Hora *Belorussian,* Mountain
Hrada *Belorussian,* Mountains, ridge
Hsi *Chinese,* River
Hu *Chinese,* Lake

I
Île(s) *French,* Island(s)
Ilha(s) *Portuguese,* Island(s)
Ilhéu(s) *Portuguese,* Islet(s)
Irmak *Turkish,* River
Isla(s) *Spanish,* Island(s)
Isola (Isole) *Italian,* Island(s)

J
Jabal *Arabic,* Mountain
Jál *Arabic,* Ridge
-järvi *Finnish,* Lake
Jazírat *Arabic,* Island
Jazíreh *Persian,* Island

Jebel *Arabic,* Mountain
Jezero *Serbian/Croatian,* Lake
Jiang *Chinese,* River
-joki *Finnish,* River
-jökull *Icelandic,* Glacier
Juzur *Arabic,* Islands

K
Kaikyó *Japanese,* Strait
-kaise *Lappish,* Mountain
Kali *Nepali,* River
Kalnas *Lithuanian,* Mountain
Kalns *Latvian,* Mountain
Kang *Chinese,* Harbor
Kangri *Tibetan,* Mountain(s)
Kaôh *Cambodian,* Island
Kapp *Norwegian,* Cape
Kavír *Persian,* Desert
K'edi *Georgian,* Mountain range
Kediet *Arabic,* Mountain
Kepulauan *Indonesian, Malay,* Island group
Khalíj, Khalíj *Arabic,* Gulf
Khawr *Arabic,* Inlet
Khola *Nepali,* River
Khrebet *Russian,* Mountain range
Ko *Thai,* Island
Kolpos *Greek,* Bay
-kopf *German,* Peak
Körfäzi *Azerbaijani,* Bay
Körfezi *Turkish,* Bay
Kõrgustik *Estonian,* Upland
Koshi *Nepali,* River
Kowtal *Persian,* Pass
Kúh(há) *Persian,* Mountain(s)
-kundo *Korean,* Island group
-kysten *Norwegian,* Coast
Kyun *Burmese,* Island

L
Laaq *Somali,* Watercourse
Lac *French,* Lake
Lacul *Romanian,* Lake
Lago *Italian, Portuguese, Spanish,* Lake
Laguna *Spanish,*

Lagoon, Lake
Laht *Estonian*, Bay
Laut *Indonesian*, Sea
Lembalemba *Malagasy*, Plateau
Lerr *Armenian*, Mountain
Lermashght'a *Armenian*, Mountain range
Les *Czech*, Forest
Lich *Armenian*, Lake
Liqeni *Albanian*, Lake
Lumi *Albanian*, River
Lyman *Ukrainian*, Estuary

M

Mae Nam *Thai*, River
-mägi *Estonian*, Hill
Maja *Albanian*, Mountain
-man *Korean*, Bay
Marios *Lithuanian*, Lake
-meer *Dutch*, Lake
Melkosopochnik *Russian*, Plain
-meri *Estonian*, Sea
Mifraz *Hebrew*, Bay
Monkhafad *Arabic*, Depression
Mont(s) *French*, Mountain(s)
Monte *Italian*, Portuguese, Mountain
More *Russian*, Sea
Mörön *Mongolian*, River

N

Nagor'ye *Russian*, Upland
Naḥal *Hebrew*, River
Nahr *Arabic*, River
Nam *Laotian*, River
Nehri *Turkish*, River
Nevado *Spanish*, Mountain (snow-capped)
Nisoi *Greek*, Islands
Nizmennost' *Russian*, Lowland, plain
Nosy *Malagasy*, Island
Nur *Mongolian*, Lake
Nuruu *Mongolian*, Mountains
Nuur *Mongolian*, Lake
Nyzovyna *Ukrainian*, Lowland, plain

O

Ostrov(a) *Russian*, Island(s)
Oued *Arabic*, Watercourse
-oy *Faeroese*, Island
-øy(a) *Norwegian*, Island
Oya *Sinhala*, River
Ozero *Russian*, Ukrainian, Lake

P

Passo *Italian*, Pass
Pegunungan *Indonesian, Malay*, Mountain range
Pelagos *Greek*, Sea
Penisola *Italian*, Peninsula
Peski *Russian*, Sands
Phanom *Thai*, Mountain
Phou *Laotian*, Mountain
Pic *Catalan*, Peak
Pico *Portuguese, Spanish*, Peak
Pik *Russian*, Peak
Planalto *Portuguese*, Plateau
Planina, Planini *Bulgarian, Macedonian, Serbian, Croatian*, Mountain range
Ploskogor'ye *Russian*, Upland
Poluostrov *Russian*, Peninsula
Potamos *Greek*, River
Proliv *Russian*, Strait
Pulau *Indonesian, Malay*, Island
Pulu *Malay*, Island
Punta *Portuguese, Spanish*, Point

Q

Qá' *Arabic*, Depression
Qolleh *Persian*, Mountain

R

Raas *Somali*, Cape
-rags *Latvian*, Cape
Ramlat *Arabic*, Sands
Ra's *Arabic*, Cape, point, headland
Ravnina *Bulgarian, Russian*, Plain
Récif *French*, Reef
Represa (Rep.) *Spanish, Portuguese*, Reservoir
-rettó *Japanese*, Island chain
Riacho *Spanish*, Stream
Riban' *Malagasy*, Mountains
Rio *Portuguese*, River
Río *Spanish*, River
Riu *Catalan*, River
Rivier *Dutch*, River
Rivière *French*, River
Rowd *Pashtu*, River
Rúd *Persian*, River
Rudohorie *Slovak*, Mountains
Ruisseau *French*, Stream

S

Sabkhat *Arabic*, Salt marsh
Şaḥrá' *Arabic*, Desert
Samudra *Sinhala*, Reservoir
-san *Japanese, Korean*, Mountain
-sanchi *Japanese*, Mountains
-sanmaek *Korean*, Mountain range
Sarír *Arabic*, Desert
Sebkha, Sebkhet *Arabic*, Salt marsh, depression
See *German*, Lake
Selat *Indonesian*, Strait
-selkä *Finnish*, Ridge
Selseleh *Persian*, Mountain range
Serra *Portuguese*, Mountain
Serranía *Spanish*, Mountain
Sha'íb *Arabic*, Watercourse
Shamo *Chinese*, Desert
Shan *Chinese*, Mountain(s)
Shan-mo *Chinese*, Mountain range
Shaṭṭ *Arabic*, Distributary
-shima *Japanese*, Island
Shui-tao *Chinese*, Channel
Sierra *Spanish*, Mountains
Sòn *Vietnamese*, Mountain
Sông *Vietnamese*, River
-spitze *German*, Peak
Štít *Slovak*, Peak
Stoeng *Cambodian*, River
Stretto *Italian*, Strait
Su Anbarı *Azerbaijani*, Reservoir
Sungai *Indonesian, Malay*, River
Suu *Turkish*, River

T

Tal *Mongolian*, Plain
Tandavan' *Malagasy*, Mountain range
Tangorombohitr' *Malagasy*, Mountain massif
Tao *Chinese*, Island
Tassili *Berber*, Plateau, mountain
Tau *Russian*, Mountain(s)
Taungdan *Burmese*, Mountain range

Teluk *Indonesian, Malay*, Bay
Terara *Amharic*, Mountain
Tog *Somali*, Valley
Tônlé *Cambodian*, Lake
Top *Dutch*, Peak
-tunturi *Finnish*, Mountain
Tur'at *Arabic*, Channel

V

Väin *Estonian*, Strait
-vatn *Icelandic*, Lake
-vesi *Finnish*, Lake
Vinh *Vietnamese*, Bay
Vodokhranilishche (Vdkhr.) *Russian*, Reservoir
Vodoskhovyshche (Vdskh.) *Ukrainian*, Reservoir
Volcán *Spanish*, Volcano
Vozvyshennost' *Russian*, Upland, plateau
Vrh *Macedonian*, Peak
Vysochyna *Ukrainian*, Upland
Vysočina *Czech*, Upland

W

Waadi *Somali*, Watercourse
Wádí *Arabic*, Watercourse
Wáḥat, Wâhat *Arabic*, Oasis
Wald *German*, Forest
Wan *Chinese*, Bay
Wyżyna *Polish*, Upland

X

Xé *Laotian*, River

Y

Yarımadası *Azerbaijani*, Peninsula
Yazovir *Bulgarian*, Reservoir
Yoma *Burmese*, Mountains
Yu *Chinese*, Islet

Z

Zaliv *Bulgarian, Russian*, Bay
Zatoka *Ukrainian*, Bay
Zemlya *Russian*, Land

Continental factfile

North & Central America

Total area:
8,116,571 sq miles
(21,021,940 sq km)

Total number of countries: 23

Total population:
583 million

Largest city with population: Mexico City, Mexico 22.6 million

Country with highest population density: Barbados 1723 people per sq mile (665 people per sq km)

Largest country:
Canada 3,560,217 sq miles
(9,220,970 sq km)

Smallest country:
Grenada 131 sq miles
(340 sq km)

Largest lake: Lake Superior, Canada/ USA 32,151 sq miles (83,270 sq km)

Longest river: Mississippi-Missouri, USA 3710 miles (5969 km)

Highest point: Denali (Mt. McKinley), Alaska, USA 20,310 ft (6190 m)

Lowest point: Death Valley, California, USA -282 ft (-86 m) below sea level

South America

Total area:
6,731,428 sq miles
(17,434,410 sq km)

Total number of countries: 12

Total population:
428 million

Largest city with population: São Paulo, Brazil 22.1 million

Country with highest population density: Ecuador 158 people per sq mile (61 people per sq km)

Largest country:
Brazil 3,265,059 sq miles
(8,456,510 sq km)

Smallest country:
Suriname 62,344 sq miles
(161,470 sq km)

Largest lake: Lake Titicaca, Bolivia/Peru 3220 sq miles (8340 sq km)

Longest river: Amazon, Brazil 4049 miles (6516 km)

Highest point: Cerro Aconcagua, Argentina 22,838 ft (6961 m)

Lowest point: Laguna del Carbón, Argentina -344 ft (-105 m) below sea level

Africa

Total area:
11,437,865 sq miles
(29,624,100 sq km)

Total number of countries: 54

Total population:
1287 million

Largest city with population: Cairo, Egypt/ Lagos, Nigeria 18.2 million

Country with highest population density: Mauritius 1811 people per sq mile (699 people per sq km)

Largest country:
Algeria 919,590 sq miles
(2,381,740 sq km)

Smallest country:
Seychelles 104 sq miles
(270 sq km)

Largest lake: Lake Victoria, Uganda, Kenya, Tanzania 26,828 sq miles (69,484 sq km)

Longest river: Nile, Uganda/Sudan/Egypt 4160 miles (6695 km)

Highest point: Kilimanjaro, Tanzania 19,340 ft (5895 m)

Lowest point: Lac', Assal, Djibouti -512 ft (-156 m) below sea level

Europe

Total area:
3,743,246 sq miles
(9,694,996 sq km)

Total number of countries: 47

Total population:
730 million

Largest city with population: Moscow, European Russia 17 million

Country with highest population density: Monaco 52,000 people per sq mile (20,000 people per sq km)

Largest country: European Russia 1,527,341 sq miles (3,955,818 sq km)

Smallest country:
Vatican City, Italy 0.17 sq miles
(0.44 sq km)

Largest lake: Ladoga, European Russia 7100 sq miles (18,390 sq km)

Longest river: Volga, European Russia 2290 miles (3688 km)

Highest point: El'brus, Caucasus Mts, European Russia 18,511 ft (5642 m)

Lowest point: Volga Delta, Caspian Sea, European Russia -92 ft (-28 m) below sea level

North & West Asia

Total area:
9,032,428 sq miles
(23,393,973 sq km)

Total number of countries: 23

Total population:
436 million

Largest city with population: Istanbul, Turkey 14.8 million

Country with highest population density: Bahrain 5861 people per sq mile (2266 people per sq km)

Largest country: Asiatic Russia 5,052,817 sq miles (13,086,766 sq km)

Smallest country: Bahrain 273 sq miles (706 sq km)

Largest lake:
Caspian Sea 142,243 sq miles (371,000 sq km)

Longest river: Ob'-Irtysh, Asiatic Russia 3461 miles (5570 km)

Highest point: Pik Pobedy, Kyrgyzstan/China 24,406 ft (7439 m)

Lowest point: Dead Sea, Israel/Jordan -1411 ft (-430 m) below sea level

South & East Asia

Total area:
7,970,358 sq miles
(20,643,259 sq km)

Total number of countries: 25

Total population:
4111 million

Largest city with population: Guangzhou, China 46.5 million

Country with highest population density: Singapore 24,576 people per sq mile (9508 people per sq km)

Largest country:
China 3,600,927 sq miles (9,326,410 sq km)

Smallest country:
Maldives 116 sq miles (300 sq km)

Largest lake: Tonle Sap, Cambodia 1000 sq miles (2850 sq km)

Longest river: Chang Jiang (Yangtze) 3965 miles (6380 km)

Highest point:
Mount Everest, Nepal 29,029 ft (8848 m)

Lowest point: Turpan Hami, (Turfan basin), China -505 ft (-154 m) below sea level

Australasia & Oceania

Total area:
3,244,632 sq miles
(8,403,608 sq km)

Total number of countries: 14

Total population:
40.3 million

Largest city with population: Sydney, Australia 5 million

Country with highest population density: Nauru 1358 people per sq mile (524 people per sq km)

Largest country:
Australia 2,941,283 sq miles (7,617,930 sq km)

Smallest country:
Nauru 8 sq miles (21 sq km)

Largest lake: Lake Eyre, Australia 3700 sq miles (9583 sq km)

Longest river: Murray-Darling, Australia 2330 miles (3750 km)

Highest point: Mt. Wilhelm, Papua New Guinea 14,795 ft (4509 m)

Lowest point: Lake Eyre, Australia -49 ft (-15 m) below sea level

Antarctica

Total area: 5,450,500 sq miles (14,000,000 sq km) of which approx. 324,300 sq miles (840,000 sq km) is ice-free.

Total number of countries: The Antarctic Treaty has 29 participating nations and 24 with observer status. Claims by Australia, France, New Zealand, Norway, Argentina, Chile, and the UK are not recognized by other member states.

Total Population: No indigenous population. 92 research stations, (43 are staffed all year-round). Population varies between about 1000 (winter) and 4000 (summer).

Total volume of ice:
7,200,000 cu miles (30,000,000 cu km): contains 90% of Earth's fresh water

Sea ice: 1,158,300 sq miles (3,000,000 sq km) in February. 7,722,000 sq miles (20,000,000 sq km) in October

Lowest temperature: Vostok station -89.5°C (-129°F)

Highest point: Vinson Massif 16,072 ft (4897 m)

Lowest Point: Coastline 0ft/m

Geographical comparisons

Largest countries

Russia	6,592,735 sq miles	(17,075,200 sq km)
Canada	3,855,171 sq miles	(9,984,670 sq km)
USA	3,717,792 sq miles	(9,626,091 sq km)
China	3,705,386 sq miles	(9,596,960 sq km)
Brazil	3,286,470 sq miles	(8,511,965 sq km)
Australia	2,967,893 sq miles	(7,686,850 sq km)
India	1,269,338 sq miles	(3,287,590 sq km)
Argentina	1,068,296 sq miles	(2,766,890 sq km)
Kazakhstan	1,049,150 sq miles	(2,717,300 sq km)
Algeria	919,590 sq miles	(2,381,740 sq km)

Smallest countries

Vatican City	0.17 sq miles	(0.44 sq km)
Monaco	0.75 sq miles	(1.95 sq km)
Nauru	8 sq miles	(21 sq km)
Tuvalu	10 sq miles	(26 sq km)
San Marino	24 sq miles	(61 sq km)
Liechtenstein	62 sq miles	(160 sq km)
Marshall Islands	70 sq miles	(181 sq km)
St. Kitts & Nevis	101 sq miles	(261 sq km)
Maldives	116 sq miles	(300 sq km)
Malta	122 sq miles	(316 sq km)

Largest islands

Greenland	840,000 sq miles (2,175,600 sq km)
New Guinea	312,000 sq miles (808,000 sq km)
Borneo	292,222 sq miles (757,050 sq km)
Madagascar	226,656 sq miles (587,040 sq km)
Sumatra	202,300 sq miles (524,000 sq km)
Baffin Island	183,800 sq miles (476,000 sq km)
Honshu	88,800 sq miles (230,000 sq km)
Britain	88,700 sq miles (229,800 sq km)
Victoria Island	81,900 sq miles (212,000 sq km)
Ellesmere Island	75,700 sq miles (196,000 sq km)

Richest countries (GNI per capita, in US$)

Monaco	168,004
Liechtenstein	134,660
Switzerland	80,560
Norway	75,990
Luxembourg	70,260
Qatar	61,070
Iceland	60,830
USA	58,270
Ireland	55,290
Denmark	55,220

Poorest countries (GNI per capita, in US$)

Somalia	88
Burundi	290
Malawi	320
Niger	360
Liberia	380
Central African Republic	390
Madagascar	400
Mozambique	420
Gambia, The	450
Congo, Democratic Republic	450

Most populous countries

China	1.415 billion
India	1.354 billion
USA	327 million
Indonesia	267 million
Brazil	211 million
Pakistan	201 million
Nigeria	196 million
Bangladesh	166 million
Russia	144 million
Mexico	131 million

Least populous countries

Vatican City	800
Nauru	11,000
Tuvalu	11,000
Palau	22,000
San Marino	34,000
Liechtenstein	38,000
Monaco	39,000
Marshall Islands	53,000
St. Kitts & Nevis	56,000
Dominica	74,000

Most densely populated countries

Monaco	52,000 people per sq mile (20,000 per sq km)
Singapore	24,576 people per sq mile (9508 per sq km)
Bahrain	5861 people per sq mile (2266 per sq km)
Vatican City	4706 people per sq mile (1818 per sq km)
Maldives	3828 people per sq mile (1480 per sq km)
Malta	3484 people per sq mile (1350 per sq km)
Bangladesh	3218 people per sq mile (1243 per sq km)
Taiwan	1895 people per sq mile (732 per sq km)
Mauritius	1811 people per sq mile (699 per sq km)
Barbados	1723 people per sq mile (665 per sq km)

Most sparsely populated countries

Mongolia .... 5 people per sq mile .... (2 per sq km)
Namibia .... 8 people per sq mile .... (3 per sq km)
Australia .... 8 people per sq mile .... (3 per sq km)
Iceland .... 9 people per sq mile .... (3 per sq km)
Suriname .... 9 people per sq mile .... (4 per sq km)
Canada .... 10 people per sq mile .... (4 per sq km)
Libya .... 10 people per sq mile .... (4 per sq km)
Guyana .... 10 people per sq mile .... (4 per sq km)
Mauritania ..... 11 people per sq mile .... (4 per sq km)
Botswana .... 11 people per sq mile .... (4 per sq km)

Most widely spoken languages

1. Chinese (Mandarin)
2. Spanish
3. English
4. Arabic
5. Hindi
6. Bengali
7. Portuguese
8. Russian
9. Japanese
10. Lahnda/Punjabi

Largest conurbations

Guangzhou (China) 45,600,000
Tokyo (Japan) 39,900,000
Jakarta (Indonesia) 30,300,000
Shanghai (China) 29,500,000
Delhi (India) 28,400,000
Manila (Philippines) 24,600,000
Seoul (South Korea) 24,600,000
Mumbai (India) 24,200,000
Mexico City (Mexico) 22,600,000
New York (USA) 22,200,000
São Paulo (Brazil) 22,100,000
Beijing (China) 20,000,000
Dhaka (Bangladesh) 18,800,000
Bangkok (Thailand) 18,400,000
Lagos (Nigeria) 18,200,000
Cairo (Egypt) 18,200,000
Los Angeles (USA) 17,700,000
Osaka (Japan) 17,700,000
Moscow (Russia) 17,000,000
Karachi (Pakistan) 16,900,000
Kolkata (India) 16,400,000
Buenos Aires (Argentina) 16,100,000
Istanbul (Turkey) 14,800,000
Tehran (Iran) 14,700,000
London (UK) 14,600,000

Longest rivers

Nile (Northeast Africa) .... 4160 miles ...... (6695 km)
Amazon (South America) .... 4049 miles ...... (6516 km)
Yangtze (China) .... 3915 miles ...... (6299 km)
Mississippi/Missouri (USA) .... 3710 miles ...... (5969 km)
Ob'-Irtysh (Russia) .... 3461 miles ...... (5570 km)
Yellow River (China) .... 3395 miles ...... (5464 km)
Congo (Central Africa) .... 2900 miles ...... (4667 km)
Mekong (Southeast Asia) .... 2749 miles ...... (4425 km)
Lena (Russia) .... 2734 miles ...... (4400 km)
Mackenzie (Canada) .... 2640 miles ...... (4250 km)
Yenisey (Russia) .... 2541 miles ...... (4090 km)

Highest mountains   (Height above sea level)

Everest .... 29,029 ft .... (8848 m)
K2 .... 28,253 ft ...... (8611 m)
Kanchenjunga I .... 28,210 ft ...... (8598 m)
Makalu I .... 27,767 ft ...... (8463 m)
Cho Oyu .... 26,907 ft ...... (8201 m)
Dhaulagiri I .... 26,796 ft ...... (8167 m)
Manaslu I .... 26,783 ft ...... (8163 m)
Nanga Parbat I .... 26,661 ft ...... (8126 m)
Annapurna I .... 26,547 ft ...... (8091 m)
Gasherbrum I .... 26,471 ft .... (8068 m)

Largest bodies of inland water (Area & depth)

Caspian Sea
143,243 sq miles (371,000 sq km) .... 3215 ft (980 m)
Lake Superior
32,151 sq miles (83,270 sq km) .... 1289 ft (393 m)
Lake Victoria
26,560 sq miles (68,880 sq km) .... 328 ft (100 m)
Lake Huron
23,436 sq miles (60,700 sq km) .... 751 ft (229 m)
Lake Michigan
22,402 sq miles (58,020 sq km) .... 922 ft (281 m)
Lake Tanganyika
12,915 sq miles (32,900 sq km) .... 4700 ft (1435 m)
Great Bear Lake
12,274 sq miles (31,790 sq km) ...... 1047 ft (319 m)
Lake Baikal
11,776 sq miles (30,500 sq km) .... 5712 ft (1741 m)
Great Slave Lake
10,981 sq miles (28,440 sq km) .... 459 ft (140 m)
Lake Erie
9915 sq miles (25,680 sq km) .... 197 ft (60 m)

......continued on page 166

Geographical comparisons continued

Deepest ocean features

Challenger Deep, Mariana Trench (Pacific)
36,201 ft .... (11,034 m)
Vityaz III Depth, Tonga Trench (Pacific)
35,704 ft .... (10,882 m)
Vityaz Depth, Kurile-Kamchatka Trench (Pacific)
34,588 ft .... (10,542 m)
Cape Johnson Deep, Philippine Trench (Pacific)
34,441 ft .... (10,497 m)
Kermadec Trench (Pacific)
32,964 ft .... (10,047 m)
Ramapo Deep, Japan Trench (Pacific)
32,758 ft .... (9984 m)
Milwaukee Deep, Puerto Rico Trench (Atlantic)
30,185 ft .... (9200 m)
Argo Deep, Torres Trench (Pacific)
30,070 ft .... (9165 m)
Meteor Depth, South Sandwich Trench (Atlantic)
30,000 ft .... (9144 m)
Planet Deep, New Britain Trench (Pacific)
29,988 ft .... (9140 m)

Greatest waterfalls   (Mean flow of water)

Boyoma (D.R. Congo)..... 600,400 cu. ft/sec (17,000 cu.m/sec)
Khône (Laos/Cambodia) ... 410,000 cu. ft/sec (11,600 cu.m/sec)
Niagara (USA/Canada).......... 195,000 cu. ft/sec (5500 cu.m/sec)
Salto Grande (Uruguay)...... 160,000 cu. ft/sec (4500 cu.m/sec)
Paulo Afonso (Brazil)............ 100,000 cu. ft/sec (2800 cu.m/sec)
Urubupungá (Brazil)............97,000 cu. ft/sec (2750 cu.m/sec)
Iguaçu (Argentina/Brazil).........62,000 cu. ft/sec (1700 cu.m/sec)
Maribondo (Brazil)................53,000 cu. ft/sec (1500 cu.m/sec)
Victoria (Zimbabwe)...............39,000 cu. ft/sec (1100 cu.m/sec)
Murchison Falls (Uganda).....42,000 cu. ft/sec (1200 cu.m/sec)
Churchill (Canada)..................35,000 cu. ft/sec (1000 cu.m/sec)
Kaveri Falls (India).....................33,000 cu. ft/sec (900 cu.m/sec)

Highest waterfalls

Angel (Venezuela) ....3212 ft............. (979 m)
Tugela (South Africa) ....3110 ft............. (948 m)
Utigard (Norway)............................2625 ft............. (800 m)
Mongefossen (Norway) ....2539 ft............. (774 m)
Mtarazi (Zimbabwe) ....2500 ft............. (762 m)
Yosemite (USA) ....2425 ft............. (739 m)
Ostre Mardola Foss (Norway) .....2156 ft .... (657 m)
Tyssestrengane (Norway)............2119 ft............. (646 m)
*Cuquenan (Venezuela)...............2001 ft............. (610 m)
Sutherland (New Zealand).............1903 ft............. (580 m)
*Kjellfossen (Norway) ....1841 ft............(561 m)

* indicates that the total height is a single leap

Largest deserts

Sahara................3,450,000 sq miles (9,065,000 sq km)
Gobi............. 500,000 sq miles (1,295,000 sq km)
Ar Rub al Khali ...... 289,600 sq miles (750,000 sq km)
Great Victorian ..... 249,800 sq miles (647,000 sq km)
Sonoran .... 120,000 sq miles (311,000 sq km)
Kalahari .... 120,000 sq miles (310,800 sq km)
Kara Kum............... 115,800 sq miles (300,000 sq km)
Takla Makan .... 100,400 sq miles (260,000 sq km)
Namib.....................52,100 sq miles (135,000 sq km)
Thar.....................33,670 sq miles (130,000 sq km)

NB – Most of Antarctica is a polar desert, with only
2 inches (50 mm) of precipitation annually

Hottest inhabited places

Djibouti (Djibouti) .... 86.0°F .... (30.0°C)
Tombouctou (Mali) .... 84.7°F .... (29.3°C)
Tirunelveli (India)....................... 84.7°F .... (29.3°C)
Tuticorin (India)........................... 84.7°F .... (29.3°C)
Nellore (India)............................. 84.5°F .... (29.2°C)
Santa Marta (Colombia) .... 84.5°F .... (29.2°C)
Aden (Yemen) .... 84.0°F .... (29.0°C)
Madurai (India)........................... 84.0°F .... (29.0°C)
Niamey (Niger)............................ 84.0°F .... (29.0°C)

Driest inhabited places

Aswân (Egypt)................................0.02 in ....(0.5 mm)
Luxor (Egypt)...................................0.03 in ....(0.7 mm)
Arica (Chile)....................................0.04 in ....(1.1 mm)
Ica (Peru)..0.10 in ....(2.3 mm)
Antofagasta (Chile).........................0.20 in ....(4.9 mm)
El Minya (Egypt) ....0.20 in ....(5.1 mm)
Asyut (Egypt)..................................0.20 in ....(5.2 mm)
Callao (Peru)...................................0.50 in .....(12.0 mm)
Trujillo (Peru)...................................0.55 in .....(14.0 mm)
Al Fayyum (Egypt)...........................0.80 in .....(19.0 mm)

Wettest inhabited places

Mawsynram (India) .... 467 in ..(11,862 mm)
Mt Waialeale (Hawaii, USA)....... 460 in ..(11,684 mm)
Cherrapunji (India) .... 450 in ..(11,430 mm)
Cape Debundsha (Cameroon) ... 405 in ..(10,290 mm)
Quibdo (Colombia).................... 354 in ...(8892 mm)
Buenaventura (Colombia) .... 265 in ...(6743 mm)
Monrovia (Liberia) .... 202 in ...(5131 mm)
Pago Pago (American Samoa)..... 196 in ....(4990 mm)
Moulmein (Myanmar) .... 191 in ....(4852 mm)
Lae (Papua New Guinea)............ 183 in ....(4645 mm)

Country profiles

These country profiles are intended as a guide to a world that is continually changing. All the data has been researched from the most up-to-date and authoritative sources to give an overview of the geographical, political, and social characteristics that make each country so unique.

There are currently 196 independent countries in the world - more than at any previous time - and over 50 dependencies. Antarctica is the only land area on Earth that is not officially part of, and does not belong to, any single country.

Country profile key

Formation Date of formation denotes the date of political origin or independence of a state, i.e. its emergence as a recognizable entity in the modern political world / date current borders were established

Population Total population / population density – based on total *land* area

Languages An asterisk (*) denotes the official language(s)

Calorie consumption Average number of kilocalories consumed daily per person

---

AFGHANISTAN
Central Asia

Official name Islamic Republic of Afghanistan
Formation 1919 / 1919
Capital Kabul
Population 36.4 million / 145 people per sq mile (56 people per sq km)
Total area 250,000 sq. miles (647,500 sq. km)
Languages Pashtu*, Tajik, Dari*, Farsi, Uzbek, Turkmen
Religions Sunni Muslim 80%, Shi'a Muslim 19%, Other 1%
Ethnic mix Pashtun 38%, Tajik 25%, Hazara 19%, Uzbek and Turkmen 15%, Other 3%
Government Nonparty system
Currency Afghani = 100 puls
Literacy rate 32%
Calorie consumption 2090 kilocalories

ANDORRA
Southwest Europe

Official name Principality of Andorra
Formation 1278 / 1278
Capital Andorra la Vella
Population 77,000 / 428 people per sq mile (166 people per sq km)
Total area 181 sq. miles (468 sq. km)
Languages Spanish, Catalan*, French, Portuguese
Religions Roman Catholic 94%, Other 6%
Ethnic mix Spanish 46%, Andorran 28%, Other 18%, French 8%
Government Parliamentary system
Currency Euro = 100 cents
Calorie consumption Not available

ARGENTINA
South America

Official name Republic of Argentina
Formation 1816 / 1816
Capital Buenos Aires
Population 44.7 million / 42 people per sq mile (16 people per sq km)
Total area 1,068,296 sq. miles (2,766,890 sq. km)
Languages Spanish*, Italian, Amerindian languages
Religions Roman Catholic 71%, Protestant 15%, Nonreligious 11%, Other 3%
Ethnic mix Indo-European 97%, Mestizo 2%, Amerindian 1%
Government Presidential system
Currency Argentine peso = 100 centavos
Literacy rate 99%
Calorie consumption 3229 kilocalories

AUSTRIA
Central Europe

Official name Republic of Austria
Formation 1918 / 1919
Capital Vienna
Population 8.8 million / 275 people per sq mile (106 people per sq km)
Total area 32,378 sq. miles (83,858 sq. km)
Languages German*, Croatian, Slovenian, Hungarian (Magyar)
Religions Roman Catholic 75%, Nonreligious 12%, Other Christian 8%, Muslim 4%, Other 1%
Ethnic mix Austrian 93%, Croat, Slovene, and Hungarian 6%, Other 1%
Government Parliamentary system
Currency Euro = 100 cents
Literacy rate 99%
Calorie consumption 3768 kilocalories

ALBANIA
Southeast Europe

Official name Republic of Albania
Formation 1912 / 1921
Capital Tirana
Population 2.9 million / 274 people per sq mile (106 people per sq km)
Total area 11,100 sq. miles (28,748 sq. km)
Languages Albanian*, Greek
Religions Muslim 68%, Roman Catholic 12%, Albanian Orthodox 8%, Other 12%
Ethnic mix Albanian 98%, Greek 1%, Other 1%
Government Parliamentary system
Currency Lek = 100 qindarka (qintars)
Literacy rate 97%
Calorie consumption 3193 kilocalories

ANGOLA
Southern Africa

Official name Republic of Angola
Formation 1975 / 1975
Capital Luanda
Population 30.8 million / 64 people per sq mile (25 people per sq km)
Total area 481,351 sq. miles (1,246,700 sq. km)
Languages Portuguese*, Umbundu, Kimbundu, Kikongo
Religions Roman Catholic 40%, Protestant 38%, Nonreligious 12%
Ethnic mix Ovimbundu 37%, Other 25%, Ambundu 25%, Bakongo 13%
Government Presidential system
Currency Readjusted kwanza = 100 lwei
Literacy rate 66%
Calorie consumption 2473 kilocalories

ARMENIA
Southwest Asia

Official name Republic of Armenia
Formation 1991 / 1991
Capital Yerevan
Population 2.9 million / 252 people per sq mile (97 people per sq km)
Total area 11,506 sq. miles (29,800 sq. km)
Languages Armenian*, Azeri, Russian
Religions Orthodox Christian 89%, Other 8%, Nonreligious 2%, Armenian Catholic Church 1%
Ethnic mix Armenian 98%, Other 1%, Yezidi 1%
Government Parliamentary system
Currency Dram = 100 luma
Literacy rate 99%
Calorie consumption 2928 kilocalories

AZERBAIJAN
Southwest Asia

Official name Republic of Azerbaijan
Formation 1991 / 1991
Capital Baku
Population 9.9 million / 296 people per sq mile (114 people per sq km)
Total area 33,436 sq. miles (86,600 sq. km)
Languages Azeri*, Russian
Religions Shi'a Muslim 68%, Sunni Muslim 26%, Russian Orthodox 3%, Armenian Apostolic Church (Orthodox) 2%, Other 1%
Ethnic mix Azeri 91%, Other 3%, Lazs 2%, Armenian 2%, Russian 2%
Government Presidential system
Currency New manat = 100 gopik
Literacy rate 99%
Calorie consumption 3118 kilocalories

ALGERIA
North Africa

Official name People's Democratic Republic of Algeria
Formation 1962 / 1962
Capital Algiers
Population 42 million / 46 people per sq mile (18 people per sq km)
Total area 919,590 sq. miles (2,381,740 sq. km)
Languages Arabic*, Tamazight* (Kabyle, Shawia, Tamashek), French
Religions Sunni Muslim 99%, Christian and Jewish 1%
Ethnic mix Arab 75%, Berber 24%, European and Jewish 1%
Government Presidential system
Currency Algerian dinar = 100 centimes
Literacy rate 75%
Calorie consumption 3296 kilocalories

ANTIGUA & BARBUDA
West Indies

Official name Antigua and Barbuda
Formation 1981 / 1981
Capital St. John's
Population 103,000 / 606 people per sq mile (234 people per sq km)
Total area 170 sq. miles (442 sq. km)
Languages English*, English patois
Religions Anglican 19%, Seventh-day Adventist 13%, Other Christian 49%, Other 19%
Ethnic mix Black African 87%, Mixed race 5%, Hispanic 3%, Other 5%
Government Parliamentary system
Currency E. Caribbean dollar = 100 cents
Literacy rate 99%
Calorie consumption 2417 kilocalories

AUSTRALIA
Australasia & Oceania

Official name Commonwealth of Australia
Formation 1901 / 1901
Capital Canberra
Population 24.8 million / 8 people per sq mile (3 people per sq km)
Total area 2,967,893 sq. miles (7,686,850 sq. km)
Languages English*, Italian, Cantonese, Greek, Arabic, Vietnamese, Aboriginal
Religions Roman Catholic 28%, Nonreligious 24%, Anglican 19%, Other Christian 20%, Other 9%
Ethnic mix British 34%, Australian 27%, Other 27%, Irish 8%, Italian 4%
Government Parliamentary system
Currency Australian dollar = 100 cents
Literacy rate 99%
Calorie consumption 3276 kilocalories

BAHAMAS, THE
West Indies

Official name Commonwealth of the Bahamas
Formation 1973 / 1973
Capital Nassau
Population 399,000 / 103 people per sq mile (40 people per sq km)
Total area 5382 sq. miles (13,940 sq. km)
Languages English*, English Creole, French Creole
Religions Baptist 36%, Anglican 14%, Roman Catholic 12%, Pentecostal 9%, Seventh-day Adventist 5%, Other 24%
Ethnic mix Black African 85%, Other 15%
Government Parliamentary system
Currency Bahamian dollar = 100 cents
Literacy rate 96%
Calorie consumption 2670 kilocalories

BAHRAIN
Southwest Asia

Official name Kingdom of Bahrain
Formation 1971 / 1971
Capital Manama
Population 1.6 million / 5861 people per sq mile (2266 people per sq km)
Total area 239 sq. miles (620 sq. km)
Languages Arabic*
Religions Muslim (mainly Shi'a) 70%, Other 30%
Ethnic mix Bahraini 46%, Asian 46%, Other Arab 5%, Other 3%
Government Monarchical / parliamentary system
Currency Bahraini dinar = 1000 fils
Literacy rate 95%
Calorie consumption Not available

BELGIUM
Northwest Europe

Official name Kingdom of Belgium
Formation 1830 / 1919
Capital Brussels
Population 11.5 million / 908 people per sq mile (350 people per sq km)
Total area 11,780 sq. miles (30,510 sq. km)
Languages Dutch*, French*, German*
Religions Roman Catholic 88%, Other 10%, Muslim 2%
Ethnic mix Fleming 58%, Walloon 33%, Other 6%, Italian 2%, Moroccan 1%
Government Parliamentary system
Currency Euro = 100 cents
Literacy rate 99%
Calorie consumption 3733 kilocalories

BOLIVIA
South America

Official name Plurinational State of Bolivia
Formation 1825 / 1938
Capital La Paz (administrative); Sucre (legal)
Population 11.2 million / 27 people per sq mile (10 people per sq km)
Total area 424,162 sq. miles (1,098,580 sq. km)
Languages Aymara*, Quechua*, Spanish*
Religions Roman Catholic 77%, Protestant 16%, Other 7%
Ethnic mix Quechua 37%, Aymara 32%, Mixed race 13%, European 10%, Other 8%
Government Presidential system
Currency Boliviano = 100 centavos
Literacy rate 92%
Calorie consumption 2256 kilocalories

BRUNEI
Southeast Asia

Official name Brunei Darussalam
Formation 1984 / 1984
Capital Bandar Seri Begawan
Population 434,000 / 213 people per sq mile (82 people per sq km)
Total area 2228 sq. miles (5770 sq. km)
Languages Malay*, English, Chinese
Religions Muslim (mainly Sunni) 79%, Christian 9%, Buddhist 8%, Other 4%
Ethnic mix Malay 66%, Other 21%, Chinese 10%, Indigenous 3%
Government Monarchy
Currency Brunei dollar = 100 cents
Literacy rate 95%
Calorie consumption 2985 kilocalories

BANGLADESH
South Asia

Official name People's Republic of Bangladesh
Formation 1971 / 1971
Capital Dhaka
Population 166 million / 3218 people per sq mile (1243 people per sq km)
Total area 55,598 sq. miles (144,000 sq. km)
Languages Bengali*, Urdu, Chakma, Marma (Magh), Garo, Khasi, Santhali, Tripuri, Mro
Religions Muslim (mainly Sunni) 90%, Hindu 9%, Other 1%
Ethnic mix Bengali 98%, Other 2%
Government Parliamentary system
Currency Taka = 100 poisha
Literacy rate 73%
Calorie consumption 2450 kilocalories

BELIZE
Central America

Official name Belize
Formation 1981 / 1981
Capital Belmopan
Population 382,000 / 43 people per sq mile (17 people per sq km)
Total area 8867 sq. miles (22,966 sq. km)
Languages English*, English Creole, Spanish, Mayan, Garifuna (Carib)
Religions Roman Catholic 40%, Other Christian 34%, Nonreligious 16%, Other 10%
Ethnic mix Mestizo 49%, Creole 24%, Maya 10%, Other 7%, Garifuna 6%, Asian Indian 4%
Government Parliamentary system
Currency Belizean dollar = 100 cents
Literacy rate 75%
Calorie consumption 2751 kilocalories

BOSNIA & HERZEGOVINA
Southeast Europe

Official name Bosnia and Herzegovina
Formation 1992 / 1992
Capital Sarajevo
Population 3.5 million / 177 people per sq mile (68 people per sq km)
Total area 19,741 sq. miles (51,129 sq. km)
Languages Bosnian*, Serbian*, Croatian*
Religions Muslim (mainly Sunni) 53%, Orthodox Christian 35%, Roman Catholic 8%, Nonreligious 3%, Other 1%
Ethnic mix Bosniak 48%, Serb 34%, Croat 16%, Other 2%
Government Parliamentary system
Currency Marka = 100 pfeninga
Literacy rate 97%
Calorie consumption 3154 kilocalories

BULGARIA
Southeast Europe

Official name Republic of Bulgaria
Formation 1908 / 1947
Capital Sofia
Population 7 million / 164 people per sq mile (63 people per sq km)
Total area 42,822 sq. miles (110,910 sq. km)
Languages Bulgarian*, Turkish, Romani
Religions Orthodox Christian 75%, Muslim 15%, Nonreligious 5%, Other 3%, Protestant 1%, Roman Catholic 1%
Ethnic mix Bulgarian 85%, Turkish 9%, Roma 5%, Other 1%
Government Parliamentary system
Currency Lev = 100 stotinki
Literacy rate 98%
Calorie consumption 2829 kilocalories

BARBADOS
West Indies

Official name Barbados
Formation 1966 / 1966
Capital Bridgetown
Population 286,000 / 1723 people per sq mile (665 people per sq km)
Total area 166 sq. miles (430 sq. km)
Languages Bajan (Barbadian English), English*
Religions Anglican 24%, Nonreligious 21%, Pentecostal 20%, Seventh-day Adventist 6%, Methodist 4%, Other 25%
Ethnic mix Black 93%, Mixed race 3%, White 3%, Other 1%
Government Parliamentary system
Currency Barbados dollar = 100 cents
Literacy rate 99%
Calorie consumption 2937 kilocalories

BENIN
West Africa

Official name Republic of Benin
Formation 1960 / 1960
Capital Porto-Novo, Cotonou (seat of government)
Population 11.5 million / 269 people per sq mile (104 people per sq km)
Total area 43,483 sq. miles (112,620 sq. km)
Languages Fon, Bariba, Yoruba, Adja, Houeda, Somba, French*
Religions Indigenous beliefs and Voodoo 50%, Christian 30%, Muslim 20%
Ethnic mix Fon 41%, Other 21%, Adja 16%, Yoruba 12%, Bariba 10%
Government Presidential system
Currency CFA franc = 100 centimes
Literacy rate 33%
Calorie consumption 2619 kilocalories

BOTSWANA
Southern Africa

Official name Republic of Botswana
Formation 1966 / 1966
Capital Gaborone
Population 2.3 million / 11 people per sq mile (4 people per sq km)
Total area 231,803 sq. miles (600,370 sq. km)
Languages Setswana, English*, Shona, San, Khoikhoi, isiNdebele
Religions Christian 80%, Nonreligious 15%, Traditional beliefs 4%, Other 1%
Ethnic mix Tswana 79%, Kalanga 11%, Other 10%
Government Presidential system
Currency Pula = 100 thebe
Literacy rate 88%
Calorie consumption 2326 kilocalories

BURKINA FASO
West Africa

Official name Burkina Faso
Formation 1960 / 1960
Capital Ouagadougou
Population 19.8 million / 187 people per sq mile (72 people per sq km)
Total area 105,869 sq. miles (274,200 sq. km)
Languages Mossi, Fulani, French*, Tuareg, Dyula, Songhai
Religions Muslim 61%, Roman Catholic 19%, Traditional beliefs 15%, Protestant 4%, Other and nonreligious 1%
Ethnic mix Mossi 48%, Other 21%, Peul 10%, Lobi 7%, Bobo 7%, Mandé 7%
Government Presidential system
Currency CFA franc = 100 centimes
Literacy rate 35%
Calorie consumption 2720 kilocalories

BELARUS
Eastern Europe

Official name Republic of Belarus
Formation 1991 / 1991
Capital Minsk
Population 9.5 million / 119 people per sq mile (46 people per sq km)
Total area 80,154 sq. miles (207,600 sq. km)
Languages Belarussian*, Russian*
Religions Orthodox Christian 73%, Roman Catholic 12%, Other 15%
Ethnic mix Belarussian 86%, Russian 8%, Polish 3%, Other 2%, Ukrainian 1%
Government Presidential system
Currency Belarussian rouble = 100 kopeks
Literacy rate 99%
Calorie consumption 3250 kilocalories

BHUTAN
South Asia

Official name Kingdom of Bhutan
Formation 1656 / 1865
Capital Thimphu
Population 817,000 / 45 people per sq mile (17 people per sq km)
Total area 18,147 sq. miles (47,000 sq. km)
Languages Dzongkha*, Nepali, Assamese
Religions Mahayana Buddhist 75%, Hindu 25%
Ethnic mix Drukpa (Bhutanese) 50%, Nepalese 35%, Other 15%
Government Monarchical / parliamentary system
Currency Ngultrum = 100 chetrum
Literacy rate 57%
Calorie consumption Not available

BRAZIL
South America

Official name Federative Republic of Brazil
Formation 1822 / 1828
Capital Brasilia
Population 211 million / 65 people per sq mile (25 people per sq km)
Total area 3,286,470 sq. miles (8,511,965 sq. km)
Languages Portuguese*, German, Italian, Spanish, Polish, Japanese, Amerindian languages
Religions Roman Catholic 61%, Protestant 26%, Nonreligious 8%, Other 5%
Ethnic mix White 48%, Mixed race 43%, Black 8%, Other 1%
Government Presidential system
Currency Real = 100 centavos
Literacy rate 92%
Calorie consumption 3263 kilocalories

BURUNDI
Central Africa

Official name Republic of Burundi
Formation 1962 / 1962
Capital Bujumbura
Population 11.2 million / 1131 people per sq mile (437 people per sq km)
Total area 10,745 sq. miles (27,830 sq. km)
Languages Kirundi*, French*, Kiswahili
Religions Roman Catholic 65%, Protestant 23%, Other 7%, Muslim 3%, Seventh-day Adventist 2%
Ethnic mix Hutu 85%, Tutsi 14%, Twa 1%
Government Presidential system
Currency Burundian franc = 100 centimes
Literacy rate 62%
Calorie consumption 1604 kilocalories

CAMBODIA
Southeast Asia

Official name Kingdom of Cambodia
Formation 1953 / 1953
Capital Phnom Penh
Population 16.2 million / 238 people per sq mile (92 people per sq km)
Total area 69,900 sq. miles (181,040 sq. km)
Languages Khmer*, French, Chinese, Vietnamese, Cham
Religions Buddhist 97%, Muslim 2%, Other (mostly Christian) 1%
Ethnic mix Khmer 90%, Vietnamese 5%, Other 4%, Chinese 1%
Government Parliamentary system
Currency Riel = 100 sen
Literacy rate 81%
Calorie consumption 2477 kilocalories

CENTRAL AFRICAN REPUBLIC
Central Africa

Official name Central African Republic
Formation 1960 / 1960
Capital Bangui
Population 4.7 million / 20 people per sq mile (8 people per sq km)
Total area 240,534 sq. miles (622,984 sq. km)
Languages Sango, Banda, Gbaya, French*
Religions Traditional beliefs 35%, Roman Catholic 25%, Protestant 25%, Muslim 15%
Ethnic mix Baya 33%, Banda 27%, Other 17%, Mandjia 13%, Sara 10%,
Government Presidential system
Currency CFA franc = 100 centimes
Literacy rate 37%
Calorie consumption 1879 kilocalories

COLOMBIA
South America

Official name Republic of Colombia
Formation 1819 / 1903
Capital Bogotá
Population 49.5 million / 123 people per sq mile (48 people per sq km)
Total area 439,733 sq. miles (1,138,910 sq. km)
Languages Spanish*, Wayuu, Páez, other Amerindian languages
Religions Roman Catholic 79%, Other 21%
Ethnic mix Mestizo 58%, White 20%, European–African 14%, African 4%, African–Amerindian 3%, Amerindian 1%
Government Presidential system
Currency Colombian peso = 100 centavos
Literacy rate 95%
Calorie consumption 2804 kilocalories

COSTA RICA
Central America

Official name Republic of Costa Rica
Formation 1838 / 1838
Capital San José
Population 5 million / 254 people per sq mile (98 people per sq km)
Total area 19,730 sq. miles (51,100 sq. km)
Languages Spanish*, English Creole, Bribri, Cabecar
Religions Roman Catholic 62%, Protestant 25%, Nonreligious 9%, Other 4%
Ethnic mix Mestizo and European 96%, Amerindian 3%, Black 1%
Government Presidential system
Currency Costa Rican colón = 100 céntimos
Literacy rate 97%
Calorie consumption 2848 kilocalories

CAMEROON
Central Africa

Official name Republic of Cameroon
Formation 1960 / 1961
Capital Yaoundé
Population 24.7 million / 137 people per sq mile (53 people per sq km)
Total area 183,567 sq. miles (475,400 sq. km)
Languages Bamileke, Fang, Fulani, French*, English*
Religions Roman Catholic 35%, Traditional beliefs 25%, Muslim 22%, Protestant 18%
Ethnic mix Cameroon highlanders 31%, Other 21%, Equatorial Bantu 19%, Kirdi 11%, Fulani 10%, Northwestern Bantu 8%
Government Presidential system
Currency CFA franc = 100 centimes
Literacy rate 71%
Calorie consumption 2671 kilocalories

CHAD
Central Africa

Official name Republic of Chad
Formation 1960 / 1960
Capital N'Djaména
Population 15.4 million / 32 people per sq mile (12 people per sq km)
Total area 495,752 sq. miles (1,284,000 sq. km)
Languages French*, Sara, Arabic*, Maba
Religions Muslim 51%, Christian 35%, Animist 7%, Traditional beliefs 7%
Ethnic mix Other 30%, Sara 28%, Mayo-Kebbi 12%, Arab 12%, Ouaddai 9%, Kanem-Bornou 9%
Government Presidential system
Currency CFA franc = 100 centimes
Literacy rate 22%
Calorie consumption 2110 kilocalories

COMOROS
Indian Ocean

Official name Union of the Comoros
Formation 1975 / 1975
Capital Moroni
Population 832,000 / 966 people per sq mile (373 people per sq km)
Total area 838 sq. miles (2170 sq. km)
Languages Arabic*, Comoran*, French*
Religions Muslim (mainly Sunni) 98%, Other 1%, Roman Catholic 1%
Ethnic mix Comoran 97%, Other 3%
Government Presidential system
Currency Comoros franc = 100 centimes
Literacy rate 49%
Calorie consumption 2139 kilocalories

CROATIA
Southeast Europe

Official name Republic of Croatia
Formation 1991 / 1991
Capital Zagreb
Population 4.2 million / 192 people per sq mile (74 people per sq km)
Total area 21,831 sq. miles (56,542 sq. km)
Languages Croatian*
Religions Roman Catholic 84%, Nonreligious 7%, Orthodox Christian 4%, Other 3%, Muslim 2%
Ethnic mix Croat 92%, Serb 4%, Other 3%, Bosniak 1%
Government Parliamentary system
Currency Kuna = 100 lipa
Literacy rate 99%
Calorie consumption 3059 kilocalories

CANADA
North America

Official name Canada
Formation 1867 / 1949
Capital Ottawa
Population 37 million / 10 people per sq mile (4 people per sq km)
Total area 3,855,171 sq. miles (9,984,670 sq. km)
Languages English*, French*, Chinese, Italian, German, Ukrainian, Portuguese, Inuktitut, Cree
Religions Roman Catholic 39%, Other Christian 28%, Nonreligious 24%, Other 6%, Muslim 3%
Ethnic mix European origin 80%, Asian 15%, First Nations and Métis 5%
Government Parliamentary system
Currency Canadian dollar = 100 cents
Literacy rate 99%
Calorie consumption 3494 kilocalories

CHILE
South America

Official name Republic of Chile
Formation 1818 / 1883
Capital Santiago
Population 18.2 million / 63 people per sq mile (24 people per sq km)
Total area 292,258 sq. miles (756,950 sq. km)
Languages Spanish*, Amerindian languages
Religions Roman Catholic 64%, Protestant 17%, Nonreligious 16%, Other 3%
Ethnic mix Mestizo and European 95%, Mapuche 4%, Other Amerindian 1%
Government Presidential system
Currency Chilean peso = 100 centavos
Literacy rate 97%
Calorie consumption 2979 kilocalories

CONGO
Central Africa

Official name Republic of the Congo
Formation 1960 / 1960
Capital Brazzaville
Population 5.4 million / 41 people per sq mile (16 people per sq km)
Total area 132,046 sq. miles (342,000 sq. km)
Languages Kongo, Teke, Lingala, French*
Religions Traditional beliefs 50%, Roman Catholic 35%, Protestant 13%, Muslim 2% Other 16%, Mbochi 11%, Mbédé 5%
Ethnic mix Bakongo 51%, Teke 17%, Other 16%, Mbochi 11%, Mbédé 5%
Government Presidential system
Currency CFA franc = 100 centimes
Literacy rate 79%
Calorie consumption 2208 kilocalories

CUBA
West Indies

Official name Republic of Cuba
Formation 1902 / 1902
Capital Havana
Population 11.5 million / 269 people per sq mile (104 people per sq km) / 76%
Total area 42,803 sq. miles (110,860 sq. km)
Languages Spanish*
Religions Nonreligious 49%, Roman Catholic 40%, Atheist 6%, Other 4%, Protestant 1%
Ethnic mix White 65%, Mulatto (mixed race) 25%, Black 10%
Government One-party state
Currency Cuban peso = 100 centavos
Literacy rate 99%
Calorie consumption 3409 kilocalories

CAPE VERDE
Atlantic Ocean

Official name Republic of Cape Verde
Formation 1975 / 1975
Capital Praia
Population 553,000 / 355 people per sq mile (137 people per sq km)
Total area 1557 sq. miles (4033 sq. km)
Languages Portuguese Creole, Portuguese*
Religions Roman Catholic 97%, Other 2%, Protestant (Church of the Nazarene) 1%
Ethnic mix Mestiço 71%, African 28%, European 1%
Government Presidential / parliamentary system
Currency Cape Verde escudo = 100 centavos
Literacy rate 87%
Calorie consumption 2609 kilocalories

CHINA
East Asia

Official name People's Republic of China
Formation 960 / 1999
Capital Beijing
Population 1.42 billion / 393 people per sq mile (152 people per sq km)
Total area 3,705,386 sq. miles (9,596,960 sq. km)
Languages Mandarin*, Wu, Cantonese, Hsiang, Min, Hakka, Kan
Religions Nonreligious or traditional beliefs 73%, Buddhist 16%, Other 7%, Christian 3%, Muslim 1%
Ethnic mix Han 92%, Zhuang 1%, Hui 1%, Manchu 1%, Uighur 1%, Other 4%
Government One-party state
Currency Renminbi (known as yuan) = 10 jiao = 100 fen
Literacy rate 95%
Calorie consumption 3108 kilocalories

CONGO, DEM. REP.
Central Africa

Official name Democratic Republic of the Congo
Formation 1960 / 1960
Capital Kinshasa
Population 84 million / 96 people per sq mile (37 people per sq km)
Total area 905,563 sq. miles (2,345,410 sq. km)
Languages Kiswahili, Tshiluba, Kikongo, Lingala, French*
Religions Roman Catholic 50%, Protestant 20%, Traditional beliefs and other 10%, Muslim 10%, Kimbanguist 10%
Ethnic mix Other 55%, Mongo, Luba, Kongo, and Mangbetu-Azande 45%
Government Presidential system
Currency Congolese franc = 100 centimes
Literacy rate 77%
Calorie consumption 1585 kilocalories

CYPRUS
Southeast Europe

Official name Republic of Cyprus
Formation 1960 / 1960
Capital Nicosia
Population 1.2 million / 336 people per sq mile (130 people per sq km)
Total area 3571 sq. miles (9250 sq. km)
Languages Greek*, Turkish*
Religions Orthodox Christian 78%, Muslim 18%, Other 4%
Ethnic mix Greek 81%, Turkish 11%, Other 8%
Government Presidential system
Currency Euro = 100 cents (In TRNC, Turkish lira = 100 kurus)
Literacy rate 99%
Calorie consumption 2649 kilocalories

CZECH REPUBLIC (CZECHIA)
Central Europe

Official name Czech Republic
Formation 1993 / 1993
Capital Prague
Population 10.6 million / 348 people per sq mile (134 people per sq km)
Total area 30,450 sq. miles (78,866 sq. km)
Languages Czech*, Slovak, Hungarian (Magyar)
Religions Nonreligious 72%, Roman Catholic 21%, Other 6%, Orthodox Christian 1%
Ethnic mix Czech 86%, Moravian 7%, Other 5%, Slovak 2%
Government Parliamentary system
Currency Czech koruna = 100 haleru
Literacy rate 99%
Calorie consumption 3256 kilocalories

DOMINICAN REPUBLIC
West Indies

Official name Dominican Republic
Formation 1865 / 1865
Capital Santo Domingo
Population 10.9 million / 584 people per sq mile (225 people per sq km)
Total area 18,679 sq. miles (48,380 sq. km)
Languages Spanish*, French Creole
Religions Roman Catholic 57%, Protestant 23%, Nonreligious 18%, Other 2%
Ethnic mix Mixed race 73%, European 16%, Black African 11%
Government Presidential system
Currency Dominican Republic peso = 100 centavos
Literacy rate 94%
Calorie consumption 2614 kilocalories

EL SALVADOR
Central America

Official name Republic of El Salvador
Formation 1841 / 1841
Capital San Salvador
Population 6.4 million / 800 people per sq mile (309 people per sq km)
Total area 8124 sq. miles (21,040 sq. km)
Languages Spanish*
Religions Roman Catholic 50%, Protestant 36%, Nonreligious 12%, Other 2%
Ethnic mix Mestizo 86%, White 13%, Other and Amerindian 1%
Government Presidential system
Currency Salvadorean colón = 100 centavos; US dollar = 100 cents
Literacy rate 88%
Calorie consumption 2577 kilocalories

ESWATINI (formerly Swaziland)
Southern Africa

Official name Kingdom of eSwatini
Formation 1968 / 1968
Capital Mbabane (administrative); Lobamba (royal & legislative)
Population 1.4 million / 211 people per sq mile (81 people per sq km)
Total area 6704 sq. miles (17,363 sq. km)
Languages English*, siSwati*, isiZulu, Xitsonga
Religions Traditional beliefs 40%, Other 30%, Roman Catholic 20%, Muslim 10%
Ethnic mix Swazi 97%, Other 3%
Government Monarchy
Currency Lilangeni = 100 cents
Literacy rate 83%
Calorie consumption 2329 kilocalories

DENMARK
Northern Europe

Official name Kingdom of Denmark
Formation 950 / 1944
Capital Copenhagen
Population 5.8 million / 355 people per sq mile (137 people per sq km)
Total area 16,639 sq. miles (43,094 sq. km)
Languages Danish*
Religions Evangelical Lutheran 95%, Roman Catholic 3%, Muslim 2%
Ethnic mix Danish 96%, Other (including Scandinavian and Turkish) 3%, Faroese and Inuit 1%
Government Parliamentary system
Currency Danish krone = 100 øre
Literacy rate 99%
Calorie consumption 3367 kilocalories

EAST TIMOR
Southeast Asia

Official name Democratic Republic of Timor-Leste
Formation 2002 / 2002
Capital Dili
Population 1.3 million / 230 people per sq mile (89 people per sq km)
Total area 5756 sq. miles (14,874 sq. km)
Languages Tetum* (Portuguese/ Austronesian), Bahasa Indonesia, Portuguese*
Religions Roman Catholic 96%, Protestant 2%, Other 2%
Ethnic mix Papuan groups approx. 85%, Indonesian groups approx. 13%, Chinese 2%
Government Parliamentary system
Currency US dollar = 100 cents
Literacy rate 58%
Calorie consumption 2131 kilocalories

EQUATORIAL GUINEA
Central Africa

Official name Republic of Equatorial Guinea
Formation 1968 / 1968
Capital Malabo
Population 1.3 million / 120 people per sq mile (46 people per sq km)
Total area 10,830 sq. miles (28,051 sq. km)
Languages Spanish*, Fang, Bubi, French*
Religions Roman Catholic 90%, Other 10%
Ethnic mix Fang 85%, Other 11%, Bubi 4%
Government Presidential system
Currency CFA franc = 100 centimes
Literacy rate 95%
Calorie consumption Not available

ETHIOPIA
East Africa

Official name Federal Democratic Republic of Ethiopia
Formation 1896 / 2002
Capital Addis Ababa
Population 108 million / 251 people per sq mile (97 people per sq km)
Total area 435,184 sq. miles (1,127,127 sq. km)
Languages Amharic*, Tigrinya, Galla, Sidamo, Somali, English, Arabic
Religions Orthodox Christian 44%, Muslim 34%, Protestant 18%, Traditional beliefs 3%, Other 1%
Ethnic mix Oromo 34%, Amhara 27%, Other 23%, Somali 6%, Tigray 6%, Sidama 4%
Government Parliamentary system
Currency Birr = 100 cents
Literacy rate 39%
Calorie consumption 2131 kilocalories

DJIBOUTI
East Africa

Official name Republic of Djibouti
Formation 1977 / 1977
Capital Djibouti
Population 971,000 / 108 people per sq mile (42 people per sq km)
Total area 8494 sq. miles (22,000 sq. km)
Languages Somali, Afar, French*, Arabic*
Religions Muslim (mainly Sunni) 94%, Christian 6%
Ethnic mix Issa 60%, Afar 35%, Other 5%
Government Presidential system
Currency Djibouti franc = 100 centimes
Literacy rate 70%
Calorie consumption 2607 kilocalories

ECUADOR
South America

Official name Republic of Ecuador
Formation 1830 / 1942
Capital Quito
Population 16.9 million / 158 people per sq mile (61 people per sq km)
Total area 109,483 sq. miles (283,560 sq. km)
Languages Spanish*, Quechua, other Amerindian languages
Religions Roman Catholic 79%, Protestant 13%, Nonreligious 5%, Other 3%
Ethnic mix Mestizo 79%, Black African 7%, Amerindian 7%, White 6%, Other 1%
Government Presidential system
Currency US dollar = 100 cents
Literacy rate 94%
Calorie consumption 2344 kilocalories

ERITREA
East Africa

Official name State of Eritrea
Formation 1993 / 2002
Capital Asmara
Population 5.2 million / 115 people per sq mile (44 people per sq km)
Total area 46,842 sq. miles (121,320 sq. km)
Languages Tigrinya*, English*, Tigre, Afar, Arabic*, Saho, Bilen, Kunama, Nara, Hadareb
Religions Christian 50%, Muslim 48%, Other 2%
Ethnic mix Tigray 50%, Tigre 31%, Other 9%, Afar 5%, Saho 5%
Government Presidential system
Currency Nakfa = 100 cents
Literacy rate 70%
Calorie consumption 1640 kilocalories

FIJI
Australasia & Oceania

Official name Republic of Fiji
Formation 1970 / 1970
Capital Suva
Population 912,000 / 129 people per sq mile (50 people per sq km)
Total area 7054 sq. miles (18,270 sq. km)
Languages Fijian*, English*, Hindi*, Urdu, Tamil, Telugu
Religions Methodist 35%, Hindu 28%, Other Christian 21%, Roman Catholic 9%, Muslim 6%, Other / nonreligious 1%
Ethnic mix Melanesian 57%, Indian 38%, Other 5%
Government Parliamentary system
Currency Fiji dollar = 100 cents
Literacy rate 94%
Calorie consumption 2943 kilocalories

DOMINICA
West Indies

Official name Commonwealth of Dominica
Formation 1978 / 1978
Capital Roseau
Population 74,000 / 255 people per sq mile (99 people per sq km)
Total area 291 sq. miles (754 sq. km)
Languages French Creole, English*
Religions Roman Catholic 62%, Protestant 30%, Nonreligious 6%, Other 2%
Ethnic mix Black 87%, Mixed race 9%, Carib 3%, Other 1%
Government Parliamentary system
Currency East Caribbean dollar = 100 cents
Literacy rate 88%
Calorie consumption 2931 kilocalories

EGYPT
North Africa

Official name Arab Republic of Egypt
Formation 1936 / 1982
Capital Cairo
Population 99.4 million / 259 people per sq mile (100 people per sq km)
Total area 386,660 sq. miles (1,001,450 sq. km)
Languages Arabic*, French, English, Berber
Religions Muslim (mainly Sunni) 90%, Coptic Christian and other 10%
Ethnic mix Egyptian 99%, Other (including Nubian) 1%
Government Presidential system
Currency Egyptian pound = 100 piastres
Literacy rate 81%
Calorie consumption 3522 kilocalories

ESTONIA
Northeast Europe

Official name Republic of Estonia
Formation 1991 / 1991
Capital Tallinn
Population 1.3 million / 75 people per sq mile (29 people per sq km)
Total area 17,462 sq. miles (45,226 sq. km)
Languages Estonian*, Russian
Religions Nonreligious 45%, Orthodox Christian 25%, Lutheran 20%, Other 10%
Ethnic mix Estonian 70%, Russian 25%, Other 2%, Ukrainian 2%, Belarussian 1%
Government Parliamentary system
Currency Euro = 100 cents
Literacy rate 99%
Calorie consumption 3253 kilocalories

FINLAND
Northern Europe

Official name Republic of Finland
Formation 1917 / 1947
Capital Helsinki
Population 5.5 million / 47 people per sq mile (18 people per sq km)
Total area 130,127 sq. miles (337,030 sq. km)
Languages Finnish*, Swedish*, Sámi
Religions Evangelical Lutheran 78%, Nonreligious 19%, Other 2%, Orthodox Christian 1%
Ethnic mix Finnish 93%, Other (including Sámi) 7%
Government Parliamentary system
Currency Euro = 100 cents
Literacy rate 99%
Calorie consumption 3368 kilocalories

FRANCE
Western Europe

Official name French Republic
Formation 987 / 1919
Capital Paris
Population 65.2 million / 307 people per sq mile (119 people per sq km)
Total area 211,208 sq. miles (547,030 sq. km)
Languages French*, Provençal, German, Breton, Catalan, Basque
Religions Christian 51%, Nonreligious 40%, Muslim 6%, Other 2%, Jewish 1%
Ethnic mix French 86%, Black 5%, North African 5%, German (Alsace) 2%, Breton 1%, Other 1%
Government Presidential / parliamentary system
Currency Euro = 100 cents
Literacy rate 99%
Calorie consumption 3482 kilocalories

GERMANY
Northern Europe

Official name Federal Republic of Germany
Formation 1871 / 1990
Capital Berlin
Population 82.3 million / 610 people per sq mile (235 people per sq km)
Total area 137,846 sq. miles (357,021 sq. km)
Languages German*, Turkish
Religions Nonreligious 36%, Catholic 29%, Protestant 26%, Muslim 5%, Other 4%
Ethnic mix German 81%, Other European 10%, Other 6%, Turkish 3%
Government Parliamentary system
Currency Euro = 100 cents
Literacy rate 99%
Calorie consumption 3499 kilocalories

GUATEMALA
Central America

Official name Republic of Guatemala
Formation 1838 / 1838
Capital Guatemala City
Population 17.2 million / 411 people per sq mile (159 people per sq km)
Total area 42,042 sq. miles (108,890 sq. km)
Languages Quiché, Mam, Cakchiquel, Kekchí, Spanish*
Religions Roman Catholic 50%, Protestant 41%, Nonreligious 6%, Other 3%
Ethnic mix Amerindian 60%, Mestizo 30%, Other 10%
Government Presidential system
Currency Quetzal = 100 centavos
Literacy rate 81%
Calorie consumption 2419 kilocalories

HAITI
West Indies

Official name Republic of Haiti
Formation 1804 / 1844
Capital Port-au-Prince
Population 11.1 million / 1043 people per sq mile (403 people per sq km)
Total area 10,714 sq. miles (27,750 sq. km)
Languages French Creole*, French*
Religions Roman Catholic 55%, Protestant 28%, Other (including Voodoo) 16%, Nonreligious 1%
Ethnic mix Black African 95%, Mulatto (mixed race) and European 5%
Government Presidential system
Currency Gourde = 100 centimes
Literacy rate 49%
Calorie consumption 2091 kilocalories

GABON
Central Africa

Official name Gabonese Republic
Formation 1960 / 1960
Capital Libreville
Population 2.1 million / 21 people per sq mile (8 people per sq km)
Total area 103,346 sq. miles (267,667 sq. km)
Languages Fang, French*, Punu, Sira, Nzebi, Mpongwe
Religions Christian (mainly Roman Catholic) 55%, Traditional beliefs 40%, Other 4%, Muslim 1%
Ethnic mix Fang 26%, Shira-punu 24%, Other 16%, Foreign residents 15%, Nzabi-duma 11%, Mbédé-Teke 8%
Government Presidential system
Currency CFA franc = 100 centimes
Literacy rate 82%
Calorie consumption 2830 kilocalories

GHANA
West Africa

Official name Republic of Ghana
Formation 1957 / 1957
Capital Accra
Population 29.5 million / 332 people per sq mile (128 people per sq km)
Total area 92,100 sq. miles (238,540 sq. km)
Languages Twi, Fanti, Ewe, Ga, Adangbe, Gurma, Dagomba (Dagbani), English*
Religions Christian 71%, Muslim 18%, Traditional beliefs 5%, Other 6%
Ethnic mix Akan 47%, Gurma 17%, Ga-Dangme 14%, Other 9%, Ewe 7%, Guan 6%
Government Presidential system
Currency Cedi = 100 pesewas
Literacy rate 72%
Calorie consumption 3016 kilocalories

GUINEA
West Africa

Official name Republic of Guinea
Formation 1958 / 1958
Capital Conakry
Population 13.1 million / 138 people per sq mile (53 people per sq km)
Total area 94,925 sq. miles (245,857 sq. km)
Languages Pulaar, Malinké, Soussou, French*
Religions Muslim 89%, Christian 7%, Traditional beliefs 2%, Other 2%
Ethnic mix Peul 40%, Malinké 30%, Soussou 20%, Other 10%
Government Presidential system
Currency Guinea franc = 100 centimes
Literacy rate 32%
Calorie consumption 2566 kilocalories

HONDURAS
Central America

Official name Republic of Honduras
Formation 1838 / 1838
Capital Tegucigalpa
Population 9.4 million / 218 people per sq mile (84 people per sq km)
Total area 43,278 sq. miles (112,090 sq. km)
Languages Spanish*, Garifuna (Carib), English Creole
Religions Roman Catholic 46%, Protestant 41%, Nonreligious 10%, Other 3%
Ethnic mix Mestizo 90%, Black African 5%, Amerindian 4%, White 1%
Government Presidential system
Currency Lempira = 100 centavos
Literacy rate 89%
Calorie consumption 2641 kilocalories

GAMBIA, THE
West Africa

Official name Republic of the Gambia
Formation 1965 / 1965
Capital Banjul
Population 2.2 million / 570 people per sq mile (220 people per sq km)
Total area 4363 sq. miles (11,300 sq. km)
Languages Mandinka, Fulani, Wolof, Jola, Soninke, English*
Religions Sunni Muslim 90%, Christian 8%, Traditional beliefs 2%
Ethnic mix Mandinka 42%, Fulani 18%, Wolof 16%, Jola 10%, Serahuli 9%, Other 5%
Government Presidential system
Currency Dalasi = 100 butut
Literacy rate 42%
Calorie consumption 2628 kilocalories

GREECE
Southeast Europe

Official name Hellenic Republic
Formation 1829 / 1947
Capital Athens
Population 11.1 million / 220 people per sq mile (85 people per sq km)
Total area 50,942 sq. miles (131,940 sq. km)
Languages Greek*, Turkish, Macedonian, Albanian
Religions Orthodox Christian 90%, Nonreligious 4%, Other 4%, Muslim 2%
Ethnic mix Greek 98%, Other 2%
Government Parliamentary system
Currency Euro = 100 cents
Literacy rate 97%
Calorie consumption 3400 kilocalories

GUINEA-BISSAU
West Africa

Official name Republic of Guinea-Bissau
Formation 1974 / 1974
Capital Bissau
Population 1.9 million / 175 people per sq mile (68 people per sq km)
Total area 13,946 sq. miles (36,120 sq. km)
Languages Portuguese Creole, Balante, Fulani, Malinké, Portuguese*
Religions Muslim 54%, Christian 26%, Traditional beliefs 18%, Nonreligious 2%
Ethnic mix Balante 30%, Fulani 20%, Other 16%, Mandyako 14%, Mandinka 13%, Papel 7%
Government Presidential system
Currency CFA franc = 100 centimes
Literacy rate 46%
Calorie consumption 2292 kilocalories

HUNGARY
Central Europe

Official name Republic of Hungary
Formation 1918 / 1947
Capital Budapest
Population 9.7 million / 272 people per sq mile (105 people per sq km)
Total area 35,919 sq. miles (93,030 sq. km)
Languages Hungarian* (Magyar)
Religions Roman Catholic 56%, Nonreligious 21%, Presbyterian 13%, Other (mostly Protestant) 10%
Ethnic mix Magyar 92%, Roma 3%, Other 3%, German 2%
Government Parliamentary system
Currency Forint = 100 fillér
Literacy rate 99%
Calorie consumption 3037 kilocalories

GEORGIA
Southwest Asia

Official name Georgia
Formation 1991 / 1991
Capital Tbilisi
Population 3.9 million / 145 people per sq mile (56 people per sq km)
Total area 26,911 sq. miles (69,700 sq.km)
Languages Georgian*, Russian, Azeri, Armenian, Mingrelian, Ossetian, Abkhazian* *(in Abkhazia)*
Religions Orthodox Christian 89%, Muslim 9%, Roman Catholic 1%, Other 1%
Ethnic mix Georgian 87%, Azeri 6%, Armenian 4%, Other 2%, Russian 1%
Government Parliamentary system
Currency Lari = 100 tetri
Literacy rate 99%
Calorie consumption 2905 kilocalories

GRENADA
West Indies

Official name Grenada
Formation 1974 / 1974
Capital St. George's
Population 108,000 / 824 people per sq mile (318 people per sq km)
Total area 131 sq. miles (340 sq. km)
Languages English*, English Creole
Religions Roman Catholic 68%, Anglican 17%, Other 15%
Ethnic mix Black African 82%, Mulatto (mixed race) 13%, East Indian 3%, Other 2%
Government Parliamentary system
Currency East Caribbean dollar = 100 cents
Literacy rate 99%
Calorie consumption 2447 kilocalories

GUYANA
South America

Official name Cooperative Republic of Guyana
Formation 1966 / 1966
Capital Georgetown
Population 782,000 / 10 people per sq mile (4 people per sq km)
Total area 83,000 sq. miles (214,970 sq. km)
Languages English Creole, Hindi, Tamil, Amerindian languages, English*
Religions Christian 57%, Hindu 28%, Muslim 10%, Other 5%
Ethnic mix East Indian 43%, Black African 30%, Mixed race 17%, Amerindian 9%, Other 1%
Government Presidential system
Currency Guyanese dollar = 100 cents
Literacy rate 86%
Calorie consumption 2764 kilocalories

ICELAND
Northwest Europe

Official name Republic of Iceland
Formation 1944 / 1944
Capital Reykjavík
Population 338,000 / 9 people per sq mile (3 people per sq km)
Total area 39,768 sq. miles (103,000 sq. km)
Languages Icelandic*
Religions Evangelical Lutheran 70%, Other (mostly Christian) 20%, Nonreligious 6%, Roman Catholic 4%
Ethnic mix Icelandic 89%, Other 7%, Polish 3%, Danish 1%
Government Parliamentary system
Currency Icelandic króna = 100 aurar
Literacy rate 99%
Calorie consumption 3380 kilocalories

INDIA
South Asia

Official name Republic of India
Formation 1947 / 1947
Capital New Delhi
Population 1.35 billion / 1180 people per sq mile (455 people per sq km)
Total area 1,269,338 sq. miles (3,287,590 sq. km)
Languages Hindi*, English*, Urdu, Bengali, Marathi, Telugu, Tamil, Bihari, Gujarati, Kanarese
Religions Hindu 81%, Muslim 13%, Christian 2%, Sikh 2%, Buddhist 1%, Other 1%
Ethnic mix Indo-Aryan 72%, Dravidian 25%, Mongoloid and other 3%
Government Parliamentary system
Currency Indian rupee = 100 paise
Literacy rate 69%
Calorie consumption 2459 kilocalories

INDONESIA
Southeast Asia

Official name Republic of Indonesia
Formation 1949 / 1999
Capital Jakarta
Population 267 million / 385 people per sq mile (148 people per sq km)
Total area 741,096 sq. miles (1,919,440 sq. km)
Languages Javanese, Sundanese, Madurese, Bahasa Indonesia*, Dutch
Religions Sunni Muslim 87%, Protestant 7%, Roman Catholic 3%, Hindu 2%, Buddhist 1%
Ethnic mix Javanese 40%, Other 27%, Sundanese 16%, Coastal Malays 14%, Madurese 3%
Government Presidential system
Currency Rupiah = 100 sen
Literacy rate 95%
Calorie consumption 2777 kilocalories

IRAN
Southwest Asia

Official name Islamic Republic of Iran
Formation 1502 / 1990
Capital Tehran
Population 82 million / 130 people per sq mile (50 people per sq km)
Total area 636,293 sq. miles (1,648,000 sq. km)
Languages Farsi*, Azeri, Luri, Gilaki, Mazanderani, Kurdish, Turkmen, Arabic, Baluchi
Religions Shi'a Muslim 90%, Sunni Muslim 9%, Other 1%
Ethnic mix Persian 51%, Azari 24%, Other 10%, Lur and Bakhtiari 8%, Kurdish 7%
Government Islamic theocracy
Currency Iranian rial = 100 dinars
Literacy rate 86%
Calorie consumption 3094 kilocalories

IRAQ
Southwest Asia

Official name Republic of Iraq
Formation 1932 / 1990
Capital Baghdad
Population 39.3 million / 233 people per sq mile (90 people per sq km)
Total area 168,753 sq. miles (437,072 sq. km)
Languages Arabic*, Kurdish*, Turkic languages, Armenian, Assyrian
Religions Shi'a Muslim 60%, Sunni Muslim 35%, Other (including Christian) 5%
Ethnic mix Arab 80%, Kurdish 15%, Turkmen 3%, Other 2%
Government Parliamentary system
Currency New Iraqi dinar = 1000 fils
Literacy rate 44%
Calorie consumption 2545 kilocalories

IRELAND
Northwest Europe

Official name Ireland
Formation 1922 / 1922
Capital Dublin
Population 4.8 million / 180 people per sq mile (70 people per sq km)
Total area 27,135 sq. miles (70,280 sq. km)
Languages English*, Irish*
Religions Roman Catholic 86%, Other 14%
Ethnic mix Irish 86%, Other White 9%, Asian 2%, Other 2%, Black 1%
Government Parliamentary system
Currency Euro = 100 cents
Literacy rate 99%
Calorie consumption 3600 kilocalories

ISRAEL
Southwest Asia

Official name State of Israel
Formation 1948 / 1994
Capital Jerusalem (not internationally recognized)
Population 8.5 million / 1083 people per sq mile (418 people per sq km)
Total area 8019 sq. miles (20,770 sq. km)
Languages Hebrew*, Arabic*, Yiddish, German, Russian, Polish, Romanian, Persian
Religions Jewish 81%, Muslim (mainly Sunni) 14%, Druze 2%, Christian 2%, Other and nonreligious 1%
Ethnic mix Jewish 81%, Arab 18%, Other 1%
Government Parliamentary system
Currency Shekel = 100 agorot
Literacy rate 98%
Calorie consumption 3610 kilocalories

ITALY
Southern Europe

Official name Italian Republic
Formation 1861 / 1947
Capital Rome
Population 59.3 million / 522 people per sq mile (202 people per sq km)
Total area 116,305 sq. miles (301,230 sq. km)
Languages Italian*, German, French, Rhaeto-Romanic, Sardinian
Religions Roman Catholic 90%, Nonreligious 6%, Muslim 2%, Other 2%
Ethnic mix Italian 92%, Other European 5%, Other 2%, North African 1%
Government Parliamentary system
Currency Euro = 100 cents
Literacy rate 99%
Calorie consumption 3579 kilocalories

IVORY COAST (CÔTE D'IVOIRE)
West Africa

Official name Republic of Côte d'Ivoire
Formation 1960 / 1960
Capital Yamoussoukro
Population 24.9 million / 203 people per sq mile (79 people per sq km)
Total area 124,502 sq. miles (322,460 sq. km)
Languages Akan, French*, Krou, Voltaique
Religions Muslim 43%, Nonreligious or traditional beliefs 23%, Roman Catholic 17%, Evangelical 12%, Other 5%
Ethnic mix Akan 42%, Voltaique 18%, Mandé du Nord 17%, Krou 11%, Mandé du Sud 10%, Other 2%
Government Presidential system
Currency CFA franc = 100 centimes
Literacy rate 44%
Calorie consumption 2799 calories

JAMAICA
West Indies

Official name Jamaica
Formation 1962 / 1962
Capital Kingston
Population 2.9 million / 694 people per sq mile (268 people per sq km)
Total area 4243 sq. miles (10,990 sq. km)
Languages English Creole, English*
Religions Other Christian 32%, Church of God 26%, Nonreligious 22%, Seventh-day Adventist 12%, Other 8%
Ethnic mix Black African 92%, Mulatto (mixed race) 6%, East Indian 1%, Other 1%
Government Parliamentary system
Currency Jamaican dollar = 100 cents
Literacy rate 88%
Calorie consumption 2746 kilocalories

JAPAN
East Asia

Official name Japan
Formation 1590 / 1972
Capital Tokyo
Population 127 million / 875 people per sq mile (338 people per sq km)
Total area 145,882 sq. miles (377,835 sq. km)
Languages Japanese*, Korean, Chinese
Religions Buddhist 50%, Nonreligious 23%, Shinto 16%, Christian 10%, Muslim 1%
Ethnic mix Japanese 99%, Other (mainly Korean) 1%
Government Parliamentary system
Currency Yen = 100 sen
Literacy rate 99%
Calorie consumption 2726 kilocalories

JORDAN
Southwest Asia

Official name Hashemite Kingdom of Jordan
Formation 1946 / 1967
Capital Amman
Population 9.9 million / 288 people per sq mile (111 people per sq km)
Total area 35,637 sq. miles (92,300 sq. km)
Languages Arabic*
Religions Sunni Muslim 92%, Christian 6%, Other 2%
Ethnic mix Arab 98%, Circassian 1%, Armenian 1%
Government Monarchy
Currency Jordanian dinar = 1000 fils
Literacy rate 98%
Calorie consumption 3100 kilocalories

KAZAKHSTAN
Central Asia

Official name Republic of Kazakhstan
Formation 1991 / 1991
Capital Astana
Population 18.4 million / 18 people per sq mile (7 people per sq km)
Total area 1,049,150 sq. miles (2,717,300 sq. km)
Languages Kazakh*, Russian, Ukrainian, German, Uzbek, Tatar, Uighur
Religions Muslim (mainly Sunni) 71%, Christian 26%, Nonreligious 3%
Ethnic mix Kazakh 63%, Russian 24%, Other 5%, Uzbek 3%, Ukrainian 2%, Uighur 1%, Tatar 1%, German 1%
Government Presidential system
Currency Tenge = 100 tiyn
Literacy rate 99%
Calorie consumption 3264 kilocalories

KENYA
East Africa

Official name Republic of Kenya
Formation 1963 / 1963
Capital Nairobi
Population 51 million / 233 people per sq mile (90 people per sq km)
Total area 224,961 sq. miles (582,650 sq. km)
Languages Kiswahili*, English*, Kikuyu, Luo, Kalenjin, Kamba
Religions Other Christian 60%, Roman Catholic 23%, Muslim 11%, Other 6%
Ethnic mix Other 35%, Kikuyu 17%, Luhya 14%, Kalenjin 13%, Luo 11%, Kamba 10%
Government Presidential system
Currency Kenya shilling = 100 cents
Literacy rate 79%
Calorie consumption 2206 kilocalories

KIRIBATI
Australasia & Oceania

Official name Republic of Kiribati
Formation 1979 / 1979
Capital Tarawa Atoll
Population 118,000 / 431 people per sq mile (166 people per sq km)
Total area 277 sq. miles (717 sq. km)
Languages English*, Kiribati
Religions Roman Catholic 56%, Kiribati Protestant 34%, Mormon 5%, Other 5%
Ethnic mix Micronesian 99%, Other 1%
Government Presidential system
Currency Australian dollar = 100 cents
Literacy rate 99%
Calorie consumption 3040 kilocalories

KOSOVO (not fully recognized)
Southeast Europe

Official name Republic of Kosovo
Formation 2008 / 2008
Capital Pristina
Population 1.8 million / 427 people per sq mile (165 people per sq km)
Total area 4212 sq. miles (10,908 sq km)
Languages Albanian*, Serbian*, Bosniak, Gorani, Roma, Turkish
Religions Muslim 92%, Roman Catholic 4%, Orthodox Christian 4%
Ethnic mix Albanian 92%, Serb 4%, Bosniak and Gorani 2%, Turkish 1%, Roma 1%
Government Parliamentary system
Currency Euro = 100 cents
Literacy rate 94%
Calorie consumption Not available

KUWAIT
Southwest Asia

Official name State of Kuwait
Formation 1961 / 1961
Capital Kuwait City
Population 4.2 million / 610 people per sq mile (236 people per sq km)
Total area 6880 sq. miles (17,820 sq. km)
Languages Arabic*, English
Religions Sunni Muslim 45%, Shi'a Muslim 40%, Christian, Hindu, and other 15%
Ethnic mix Asian 39%, Kuwaiti 37%, Other Arab 21%, African 2%, Other 1%
Government Monarchy
Currency Kuwaiti dinar = 1000 fils
Literacy rate 96%
Calorie consumption 3501 kilocalories

KYRGYZSTAN
Central Asia

Official name Kyrgyz Republic
Formation 1991 / 1991
Capital Bishkek
Population 6.1 million / 80 people per sq mile (31 people per sq km)
Total area 76,641 sq. miles (198,500 sq. km)
Languages Kyrgyz*, Russian*, Uzbek, Tatar, Ukrainian
Religions Muslim (mainly Sunni) 70%, Orthodox Christian 30%
Ethnic mix Kyrgyz 71%, Uzbek 14%, Russian 8%, Other 6%, Dungan 1%
Government Presidential / parliamentary system
Currency Som = 100 tyiyn
Literacy rate 99%
Calorie consumption 2817 kilocalories

LAOS
Southeast Asia

Official name Lao People's Democratic Republic
Formation 1953 / 1953
Capital Vientiane
Population 7 million / 79 people per sq mile (30 people per sq km)
Total area 91,428 sq. miles (236,800 sq. km)
Languages Lao*, Mon-Khmer, Yao, Vietnamese, Chinese, French
Religions Buddhist 67%, Other 31%, Christian 2%
Ethnic mix Lao Loum 66%, Lao Theung 30%, Lao Soung 2%, Other 2%
Government One-party state
Currency Kip = 100 at
Literacy rate 85%
Calorie consumption 2451 kilocalories

LATVIA
Northeast Europe

Official name Republic of Latvia
Formation 1991 / 1991
Capital Riga
Population 1.9 million / 76 people per sq mile (29 people per sq km)
Total area 24,938 sq. miles (64,589 sq. km)
Languages Latvian*, Russian
Religions Orthodox Christian 31%, Roman Catholic 23%, Nonreligious 21%, Lutheran 19%, Other 6%
Ethnic mix Latvian 62%, Russian 27%, Belarussian 3%, Other 3%, Polish 2%, Ukrainian 2%, Lithuanian 1%
Government Parliamentary system
Currency Euro = 100 cents
Literacy rate 99%
Calorie consumption 3174 kilocalories

LEBANON
Southwest Asia

Official name Republic of Lebanon
Formation 1941 / 1941
Capital Beirut
Population 6.1 million / 1544 people per sq mile (596 people per sq km)
Total area 4015 sq. miles (10,400 sq. km)
Languages Arabic*, French, Armenian, Assyrian
Religions Muslim 60%, Christian 39%, Other 1%
Ethnic mix Arab 95%, Armenian 4%, Other 1%
Government Parliamentary system
Currency Lebanese pound = 100 piastres
Literacy rate 91%
Calorie consumption 3066 kilocalories

LESOTHO
Southern Africa

Official name Kingdom of Lesotho
Formation 1966 / 1966
Capital Maseru
Population 2.3 million / 196 people per sq mile (76 people per sq km)
Total area 11,720 sq. miles (30,355 sq. km)
Languages English*, Sesotho*, isiZulu
Religions Christian 90%, Traditional beliefs 10%
Ethnic mix Sotho 99%, European and Asian 1%
Government Parliamentary system
Currency Loti = 100 lisente; South African rand = 100 cents
Literacy rate 77%
Calorie consumption 2529 kilocalories

LIBERIA
West Africa

Official name Republic of Liberia
Formation 1847 / 1847
Capital Monrovia
Population 4.9 million / 132 people per sq mile (51 people per sq km)
Total area 43,000 sq. miles (111,370 sq. km)
Languages Kpelle, Vai, Bassa, Kru, Grebo, Kissi, Gola, Loma, English*
Religions Christian 86%, Muslim 12%, Nonreligious 1%, Other 1%
Ethnic mix Indigenous tribes (12 groups) 50%, Kpellé 20%, Bassa 14%, Gio 8%, Krou 6%, Other 2%
Government Presidential system
Currency Liberian dollar = 100 cents
Literacy rate 43%
Calorie consumption 2204 kilocalories

LIBYA
North Africa

Official name State of Libya
Formation 1951 / 1951
Capital Tripoli
Population 6.5 million / 10 people per sq mile (4 people per sq km)
Total area 679,358 sq. miles (1,759,540 sq. km)
Languages Arabic*, Tuareg
Religions Muslim (mainly Sunni) 97%, Other 3%
Ethnic mix Arab and Berber 97%, Other 3%
Government Transitional regime
Currency Libyan dinar = 1000 dirhams
Literacy rate 90%
Calorie consumption 3211 kilocalories

LIECHTENSTEIN
Central Europe

Official name Principality of Liechtenstein
Formation 1719 / 1719
Capital Vaduz
Population 38,000 / 613 people per sq mile (238 people per sq km)
Total area 62 sq. miles (160 sq. km)
Languages German*, Alemannish dialect, Italian
Religions Roman Catholic 78%, Protestant 9%, Muslim 6%, Other 7%
Ethnic mix Liechtensteiner 66%, Other 12%, Swiss 10%, Austrian 6%, German 3%, Italian 3%
Government Parliamentary system
Currency Swiss franc = 100 rappen/centimes
Literacy rate 99%
Calorie consumption Not available

LITHUANIA
Northeast Europe

Official name Republic of Lithuania
Formation 1991 / 1991
Capital Vilnius
Population 2.9 million / 115 people per sq mile (44 people per sq km)
Total area 25,174 sq. miles (65,200 sq. km)
Languages Lithuanian*, Russian
Religions Roman Catholic 75%, Christian 14%, Nonreligious 6%, Orthodox Christian 3%, Other 2%
Ethnic mix Lithuanian 85%, Polish 7%, Russian 6%, Belarussian 1%, Other 1%
Government Parliamentary system
Currency Euro = 100 cents
Literacy rate 99%
Calorie consumption 3417 kilocalories

LUXEMBOURG
Northwest Europe

Official name Grand Duchy of Luxembourg
Formation 1867 / 1867
Capital Luxembourg
Population 590,000 / 591 people per sq mile (228 people per sq km)
Total area 998 sq. miles (2586 sq. km)
Languages Luxembourgish*, German*, French*
Religions Roman Catholic 97%, Protestant, Orthodox Christian, and Jewish 3%
Ethnic mix Luxembourger 62%, Foreign residents 38%
Government Parliamentary system
Currency Euro = 100 cents
Literacy rate 99%
Calorie consumption 3539 kilocalories

MACEDONIA
Southeast Europe

Official name Republic of Macedonia
Formation 1991 / 1991
Capital Skopje
Population 2.1 million / 212 people per sq mile (82 people per sq km)
Total area 9781 sq. miles (25,333 sq. km)
Languages Macedonian*, Albanian*, Turkish, Romani, Serbian
Religions Orthodox Christian 65%, Muslim 33%, Other 2%
Ethnic mix Macedonian 64%, Albanian 25%, Turkish 4%, Roma 3%, Serb 2%, Other 2%
Government Presidential / parliamentary system
Currency Macedonian denar = 100 deni
Literacy rate 98%
Calorie consumption 2949 kilocalories

MADAGASCAR
Indian Ocean

Official name Republic of Madagascar
Formation 1960 / 1960
Capital Antananarivo
Population 26.3 million / 117 people per sq mile (45 people per sq km)
Total area 226,656 sq. miles (587,040 sq. km)
Languages Malagasy*, French*, English
Religions Traditional beliefs 52%, Christian (mainly Roman Catholic) 41%, Muslim 7%
Ethnic mix Other Malay 46%, Merina 26%, Betsimisaraka 15%, Betsileo 12%, Other 1%
Government Presidential / parliamentary system
Currency Ariary = 5 iraimbilanja
Literacy rate 72%
Calorie consumption 2052 kilocalories

MALAWI
Southern Africa

Official name Republic of Malawi
Formation 1964 / 1964
Capital Lilongwe
Population 19.2 million / 529 people per sq mile (204 people per sq km)
Total area 45,745 sq. miles (118,480 sq. km)
Languages Chewa, Lomwe, Yao, Ngoni, English*
Religions Christian (mainly Protestant) 83%, Muslim 13%, Nonreligious 2%, Other 2%
Ethnic mix Bantu 99%, Other 1%
Government Presidential system
Currency Malawi kwacha = 100 tambala
Literacy rate 62%
Calorie consumption 2367 kilocalories

MALAYSIA
Southeast Asia

Official name Malaysia
Formation 1963 / 1965
Capital Kuala Lumpur; Putrajaya (administrative)
Population 32 million / 252 people per sq mile (97 people per sq km)
Total area 127,316 sq. miles (329,750 sq. km)
Languages Bahasa Malaysia*, Malay, Chinese, Tamil, English
Religions Muslim (mainly Sunni) 62%, Buddhist 20%, Christian 9%, Hindu 6%, Other and nonreligious 3%
Ethnic mix Malay 50%, Chinese 22%, Indigenous tribes 12%, Other 9%, Indian 7%
Government Parliamentary system
Currency Ringgit = 100 sen
Literacy rate 93%
Calorie consumption 2916 kilocalories

MALDIVES
Indian Ocean

Official name Republic of Maldives
Formation 1965 / 1965
Capital Male
Population 444,000 / 3828 people per sq mile (1480 people per sq km)
Total area 116 sq. miles (300 sq. km)
Languages Dhivehi* (Maldivian), Sinhala, Tamil, Arabic
Religions Sunni Muslim 94%, Other 6%
Ethnic mix Arab–Sinhalese–Malay 100%
Government Presidential system
Currency Rufiyaa = 100 laari
Literacy rate 99%
Calorie consumption 2732 kilocalories

MALI
West Africa

Official name Republic of Mali
Formation 1960 / 1960
Capital Bamako
Population 19.1 million / 41 people per sq mile (16 people per sq km)
Total area 478,764 sq. miles (1,240,000 sq. km)
Languages Bambara, Fulani, Senufo, Soninke, French*
Religions Muslim (mainly Sunni) 90%, Traditional beliefs 6%, Christian 4%
Ethnic mix Bambara 52%, Other 14%, Fulani 11%, Saracolé 7%, Soninka 7%, Tuareg 5%, Mianka 4%
Government Presidential system
Currency CFA franc = 100 centimes
Literacy rate 33%
Calorie consumption 2890 kilocalories

MALTA
Southern Europe

Official name Republic of Malta
Formation 1964 / 1964
Capital Valletta
Population 432,000 / 3484 people per sq mile (1350 people per sq km)
Total area 122 sq. miles (316 sq. km)
Languages Maltese*, English*
Religions Roman Catholic 98%, Other and nonreligious 2%
Ethnic mix Maltese 96%, Other 4%
Government Parliamentary system
Currency Euro = 100 cents
Literacy rate 93%
Calorie consumption 3378 kilocalories

MEXICO
North America

Official name United Mexican States
Formation 1836 / 1848
Capital Mexico City
Population 131 million / 177 people per sq mile (69 people per sq km)
Total area 761,602 sq. miles (1,972,550 sq. km)
Languages Spanish*, Nahuatl, Mayan, Zapotec, Mixtec, Otomi, Totonac, Tzotzil, Tzeltal
Religions Roman Catholic 81%, Protestant 9%, Nonreligious 7%, Other 3%
Ethnic mix Mestizo 60%, Amerindian 30%, European 9%, Other 1%
Government Presidential system
Currency Mexican peso = 100 centavos
Literacy rate 95%
Calorie consumption 3072 kilocalories

MONGOLIA
East Asia

Official name Mongolia
Formation 1924 / 1924
Capital Ulaanbaatar
Population 3.1 million / 5 people per sq mile (2 people per sq km)
Total area 604,247 sq. miles (1,565,000 sq. km)
Languages Khalkha Mongolian*, Kazakh, Chinese, Russian
Religions Tibetan Buddhist 53%, Nonreligious 38%, Muslim 3%, Shamanist 3%, Christian 2%, Other 1%
Ethnic mix Khalkh 82%, Other 9%, Kazakh 4%, Dorvod 3%, Bayad 2%
Government Presidential / parliamentary system
Currency Tugrik (tögrög) = 100 möngö
Literacy rate 98%
Calorie consumption 2510 kilocalories

MYANMAR (BURMA)
Southeast Asia

Official name Republic of the Union of Myanmar
Formation 1948 / 1948
Capital Nay Pyi Taw
Population 53.9 million / 212 people per sq mile (82 people per sq km)
Total area 261,969 sq. miles (678,500 sq. km)
Languages Myanmar* (Burmese), Shan, Karen, Rakhine, Chin, Yangbye, Kachin, Mon
Religions Buddhist 88%, Christian 6%, Muslim 4%, Animist 1%, Other 1%
Ethnic mix Burman (Bamah) 68%, Other 12%, Shan 9%, Karen 7%, Rakhine 4%
Government Presidential system
Currency Kyat = 100 pyas
Literacy rate 76%
Calorie consumption 2571 kilocalories

MARSHALL ISLANDS
Australasia & Oceania

Official name Republic of the Marshall Islands
Formation 1986 / 1986
Capital Majuro Atoll
Population 53,000 / 757 people per sq mile (293 people per sq km)
Total area 70 sq. miles (181 sq. km)
Languages Marshallese*, English*, Japanese, German
Religions Protestant 81%, Other 11%, Roman Catholic 8%
Ethnic mix Micronesian 90%, Other 10%
Government Presidential system
Currency US dollar = 100 cents
Literacy rate 98%
Calorie consumption Not available

MICRONESIA
Australasia & Oceania

Official name Federated States of Micronesia
Formation 1986 / 1986
Capital Palikir (Pohnpei Island)
Population 106,000 / 391 people per sq mile (151 people per sq km)
Total area 271 sq. miles (702 sq. km)
Languages Trukese, Pohnpeian, Kosraean, Yapese, English*
Religions Roman Catholic 53%, Protestant 43%, Other 3%, Nonreligious 1%
Ethnic mix Chuukese 49%, Pohnpeian 24%, Other 14%, Kosraean 6%, Yapese 5%, Asian 2%
Government Nonparty system
Currency US dollar = 100 cents
Literacy rate 81%
Calorie consumption Not available

MONTENEGRO
Southeast Europe

Official name Montenegro
Formation 2006 / 2006
Capital Podgorica
Population 629,000 / 118 people per sq mile (46 people per sq km)
Total area 5332 sq. miles (13,812 sq. km)
Languages Montenegrin*, Serbian, Albanian, Bosniak, Croatian
Religions Orthodox Christian 74%, Muslim 20%, Roman Catholic 4%, Nonreligious 1%, Other 1%
Ethnic mix Montenegrin 43%, Serb 32%, Other 12%, Bosniak 8%, Albanian 5%
Government Parliamentary system
Currency Euro = 100 cents
Literacy rate 98%
Calorie consumption 3491 kilocalories

NAMIBIA
Southern Africa

Official name Republic of Namibia
Formation 1990 / 1994
Capital Windhoek
Population 2.6 million / 8 people per sq mile (3 people per sq km)
Total area 318,694 sq. miles (825,418 sq. km)
Languages Ovambo, Kavango, English*, Bergdama, German, Afrikaans
Religions Christian 90%, Traditional beliefs 10%
Ethnic mix Ovambo 50%, Other tribes 22%, Kavango 9%, Damara 7%, Herero 7%, Other 5%
Government Presidential system
Currency Namibian dollar = 100 cents; South African rand = 100 cents
Literacy rate 88%
Calorie consumption 2171 kilocalories

MAURITANIA
West Africa

Official name Islamic Republic of Mauritania
Formation 1960 / 1960
Capital Nouakchott
Population 4.5 million / 11 people per sq mile (4 people per sq km)
Total area 397,953 sq. miles (1,030,700 sq. km)
Languages Arabic*, Hassaniyah Arabic, Wolof, French
Religions Sunni Muslim 100%
Ethnic mix Maure 81%, Wolof 7%, Tukolor 5%, Other 4%, Soninka 3%
Government Presidential system
Currency Ouguiya = 5 khoums
Literacy rate 46%
Calorie consumption 2876 kilocalories

MOLDOVA
Southeast Europe

Official name Republic of Moldova
Formation 1991 / 1991
Capital Chisinau
Population 4 million / 307 people per sq mile (119 people per sq km)
Total area 13,067 sq. miles (33,843 sq. km)
Languages Moldovan*, Ukrainian, Russian
Religions Orthodox Christian 92%, Other 6%, Nonreligious 2%
Ethnic mix Moldovan 76%, Ukrainian 9%, Russian 6%, Gagauz 4%, Romanian 2%, Bulgarian 2%, Other 1%
Government Parliamentary system
Currency Moldovan leu = 100 bani
Literacy rate 99%
Calorie consumption 2714 kilocalories

MOROCCO
North Africa

Official name Kingdom of Morocco
Formation 1956 / 1969
Capital Rabat
Population 36.2 million / 210 people per sq mile (81 people per sq km)
Total area 172,316 sq. miles (446,300 sq. km)
Languages Arabic*, Tamazight* (Berber), French, Spanish
Religions Muslim (mainly Sunni) 99%, Other (mostly Christian) 1%
Ethnic mix Arab 70%, Berber 29%, European 1%
Government Monarchical / parliamentary system
Currency Moroccan dirham = 100 centimes
Literacy rate 69%
Calorie consumption 3403 kilocalories

NAURU
Australasia & Oceania

Official name Republic of Nauru
Formation 1968 / 1968
Capital None (Yaren District *de facto*)
Population 11,000 / 1358 people per sq mile (524 people per sq km)
Total area 8.1 sq. miles (21 sq. km)
Languages Nauruan*, Kiribati, Chinese, Tuvaluan, English
Religions Nauruan Congregational Church 60%, Roman Catholic 35%, Other 5%
Ethnic mix Nauruan 93%, Chinese 5%, European 1%, Other Pacific islanders 1%
Government Nonparty system
Currency Australian dollar = 100 cents
Literacy rate 95%
Calorie consumption Not available

MAURITIUS
Indian Ocean

Official name Republic of Mauritius
Formation 1968 / 1968
Capital Port Louis
Population 1.3 million / 1811 people per sq mile (699 people per sq km)
Total area 718 sq. miles (1860 sq. km)
Languages French Creole, Hindi, Urdu, Tamil, Chinese, English*, French
Religions Hindu 48%, Roman Catholic 26%, Muslim 17%, Other Christian 7%, Other 2%
Ethnic mix Indo-Mauritian 68%, Creole 27%, Sino-Mauritian 3%, Franco-Mauritian 2%
Government Parliamentary system
Currency Mauritian rupee = 100 cents
Literacy rate 93%
Calorie consumption 3065 kilocalories

MONACO
Southern Europe

Official name Principality of Monaco
Formation 1861 / 1861
Capital Monaco
Population 39,000 / 52,000 people per sq mile (20,000 people per sq km)
Total area 0.75 sq. miles (1.95 sq. km)
Languages French*, Italian, Monégasque, English
Religions Roman Catholic 89%, Protestant 6%, Other 5%
Ethnic mix French 47%, Other 21%, Italian 16%, Monégasque 16%
Government Monarchical / parliamentary system
Currency Euro = 100 cents
Literacy rate 99%
Calorie consumption Not available

MOZAMBIQUE
Southern Africa

Official name Republic of Mozambique
Formation 1975 / 1975
Capital Maputo
Population 30.5 million / 101 people per sq mile (39 people per sq km)
Total area 309,494 sq. miles (801,590 sq. km)
Languages Makua, Xitsonga, Sena, Lomwe, Portuguese*
Religions Roman Catholic 28%, Nonreligious 19%, Muslim 18%, Traditional beliefs 16%, Other 19%
Ethnic mix Makua Lomwe 47%, Tsonga 23%, Malawi 12%, Shona 11%, Yao 4%, Other 3%
Government Presidential system
Currency New metical = 100 centavos
Literacy rate 56%
Calorie consumption 2283 kilocalories

NEPAL
South Asia

Official name Federal Democratic Republic of Nepal
Formation 1769 / 1769
Capital Kathmandu
Population 29.6 million / 560 people per sq mile (216 people per sq km)
Total area 54,363 sq. miles (140,800 sq. km)
Languages Nepali*, Maithili, Bhojpuri
Religions Hindu 82%, Buddhist 9%, Other 5%, Muslim 4%
Ethnic mix Other 57%, Chhetri 17%, Hill Brahman 12%, Magar 7%, Tharu 7%
Government Parliamentary system
Currency Nepalese rupee = 100 paisa
Literacy rate 60%
Calorie consumption 2673 kilocalories

NETHERLANDS
Northwest Europe

Official name Kingdom of the Netherlands
Formation 1648 / 1839
Capital Amsterdam; The Hague (administrative)
Population 17.1 million / 1306 people per sq mile (504 people per sq km)
Total area 16,033 sq. miles (41,526 sq. km)
Languages Dutch*, Frisian
Religions Roman Catholic 36%, Other 34%, Protestant 27%, Muslim 3%
Ethnic mix Dutch 82%, Other 12%, Surinamese 2%, Turkish 2%, Moroccan 2%
Government Parliamentary system
Currency Euro = 100 cents
Literacy rate 99%
Calorie consumption 3228 kilocalories

NEW ZEALAND
Australasia & Oceania

Official name New Zealand
Formation 1947 / 1947
Capital Wellington
Population 4.7 million / 45 people per sq mile (17 people per sq km)
Total area 103,737 sq. miles (268,680 sq. km)
Languages English*, Maori*
Religions Nonreligious 36%, Anglican 15%, Roman Catholic 14%, Presbyterian 11%, Other Christian 16%, Other 8%
Ethnic mix European 60%, Other 19%, Maori 14%, Chinese 4%, Samoan 3%
Government Parliamentary system
Currency New Zealand dollar = 100 cents
Literacy rate 99%
Calorie consumption 3137 kilocalories

NICARAGUA
Central America

Official name Republic of Nicaragua
Formation 1838 / 1838
Capital Managua
Population 6.3 million / 137 people per sq mile (53 people per sq km)
Total area 49,998 sq. miles (129,494 sq. km)
Languages Spanish*, English Creole, Miskito
Religions Roman Catholic 50%, Protestant 40%, Nonreligious 7%, Other 3%
Ethnic mix Mestizo 69%, White 17%, Black 9%, Amerindian 5%
Government Presidential system
Currency Córdoba oro = 100 centavos
Literacy rate 78%
Calorie consumption 2638 kilocalories

NIGER
West Africa

Official name Republic of Niger
Formation 1960 / 1960
Capital Niamey
Population 22.3 million / 46 people per sq mile (18 people per sq km)
Total area 489,188 sq. miles (1,267,000 sq. km)
Languages Hausa, Djerma, Fulani, Tuareg, Teda, French*
Religions Muslim 99%, Other (including Christian) 1%
Ethnic mix Hausa 55%, Djerma and Songhai 21%, Tuareg 9%, Peul 9%, Kanuri 5%, Other 1%
Government Presidential system
Currency CFA franc = 100 centimes
Literacy rate 31%
Calorie consumption 2547 kilocalories

NIGERIA
West Africa

Official name Federal Republic of Nigeria
Formation 1960 / 1961
Capital Abuja
Population 196 million / 557 people per sq mile (215 people per sq km)
Total area 356,667 sq. miles (923,768 sq. km)
Languages Hausa, English*, Yoruba, Ibo
Religions Muslim 50%, Christian 40%, Traditional beliefs 10%
Ethnic mix Other 29%, Hausa 21%, Yoruba 21%, Ibo 18%, Fulani 11%
Government Presidential system
Currency Naira = 100 kobo
Literacy rate 51%
Calorie consumption 2700 kilocalories

NORTH KOREA
East Asia

Official name Democratic People's Republic of Korea
Formation 1948 / 1953
Capital Pyongyang
Population 25.6 million / 551 people per sq mile (213 people per sq km)
Total area 46,540 sq. miles (120,540 sq. km)
Languages Korean*
Religions Atheist 100%
Ethnic mix Korean 100%
Government One-party state
Currency North Korean won = 100 chon
Literacy rate 99%
Calorie consumption 2094 kilocalories

NORWAY
Northern Europe

Official name Kingdom of Norway
Formation 1905 / 1905
Capital Oslo
Population 5.4 million / 46 people per sq mile (18 people per sq km)
Total area 125,181 sq. miles (324,220 sq. km)
Languages Norwegian* (Bokmål "book language" and Nynorsk "new Norsk"), Sámi
Religions Evangelical Lutheran 88%, Other and nonreligious 8%, Muslim 2%, Pentecostal 1%, Roman Catholic 1%
Ethnic mix Norwegian 93%, Other 6%, Sámi 1%
Government Parliamentary system
Currency Norwegian krone = 100 øre
Literacy rate 99%
Calorie consumption 3485 kilocalories

OMAN
Southwest Asia

Official name Sultanate of Oman
Formation 1951 / 1951
Capital Muscat
Population 4.8 million / 59 people per sq mile (23 people per sq km)
Total area 82,031 sq. miles (212,460 sq. km)
Languages Arabic*, Baluchi, Farsi, Hindi, Punjabi
Religions Other Muslim 50%, Ibadi Muslim 25%, Hindu 17%, other 8%
Ethnic mix Arab 54%, Bangladeshi 15%, Indian 15%, African and other 11%, Pakistani 5%
Government Monarchy
Currency Omani rial = 1000 baisa
Literacy rate 96%
Calorie consumption 3143 kilocalories

PAKISTAN
South Asia

Official name Islamic Republic of Pakistan
Formation 1947 / 1971
Capital Islamabad
Population 201 million / 675 people per sq mile (260 people per sq km)
Total area 310,401 sq. miles (803,940 sq. km)
Languages Punjabi, Sindhi, Pashtu, Urdu*, Baluchi, Brahui
Religions Sunni Muslim 77%, Shi'a Muslim 20%, Hindu 2%, Christian 1%
Ethnic mix Punjabi 56%, Pathan (Pashtun) 15%, Sindhi 14%, Mohajir 7%, Baluchi 4%, Other 4%
Government Parliamentary system
Currency Pakistani rupee = 100 paisa
Literacy rate 57%
Calorie consumption 2440 kilocalories

PALAU
Australasia & Oceania

Official name Republic of Palau
Formation 1994 / 1994
Capital Ngerulmud
Population 22,000 / 112 people per sq mile (43 people per sq km)
Total area 177 sq. miles (458 sq. km)
Languages Palauan*, English*, Japanese
Religions Roman Catholic 49%, Protestant 33%, Modekngei 9%, Other 9%
Ethnic mix Palauan 73%, Filipino 16%, Other Asian 7%, Other 4%
Government Nonparty system
Currency US dollar = 100 cents
Literacy rate 97%
Calorie consumption Not available

PANAMA
Central America

Official name Republic of Panama
Formation 1903 / 1903
Capital Panama City
Population 4.2 million / 143 people per sq mile (55 people per sq km)
Total area 30,193 sq. miles (78,200 sq. km)
Languages English Creole, Spanish*, Amerindian languages, Chibchan languages
Religions Roman Catholic 70%, Protestant 19%, Nonreligious 7%, Other 4%
Ethnic mix Mestizo 70%, Black 14%, White 10%, Amerindian 6%
Government Presidential system
Currency Balboa = 100 centésimos; US dollar = 100 cents
Literacy rate 94%
Calorie consumption 2733 kilocalories

PAPUA NEW GUINEA
Australasia & Oceania

Official name Independent State of Papua New Guinea
Formation 1975 / 1975
Capital Port Moresby
Population 8.4 million / 48 people per sq mile (19 people per sq km)
Total area 178,703 sq. miles (462,840 sq. km)
Languages Pidgin English* (Tok Pisin), Papuan, English*, Hiri Motu*, 800 (est.) native languages
Religions Protestant 60%, Roman Catholic 37%, Other 3%
Ethnic mix Melanesian / mixed race 100%
Government Parliamentary system
Currency Kina = 100 toea
Literacy rate 63%
Calorie consumption 2193 kilocalories

PARAGUAY
South America

Official name Republic of Paraguay
Formation 1811 / 1938
Capital Asunción
Population 6.9 million / 45 people per sq mile (17 people per sq km)
Total area 157,046 sq. miles (406,750 sq. km)
Languages Guaraní*, Spanish*, German
Religions Roman Catholic 89%, Protestant (including Mennonite) 7%, Other 4%
Ethnic mix Mestizo 91%, Other 7%, Amerindian 2%
Government Presidential system
Currency Guaraní = 100 céntimos
Literacy rate 95%
Calorie consumption 2589 kilocalories

PERU
South America

Official name Republic of Peru
Formation 1824 / 1941
Capital Lima
Population 32.6 million / 66 people per sq mile (25 people per sq km)
Total area 496,223 sq. miles (1,285,200 sq. km)
Languages Spanish*, Quechua*, Aymara*
Religions Roman Catholic 76%, Protestant 17%, Nonreligious 4%, Other 3%
Ethnic mix Amerindian 45%, Mestizo 37%, White 15%, Other 3%
Government Presidential system
Currency New sol = 100 céntimos
Literacy rate 94%
Calorie consumption 2700 kilocalories

PHILIPPINES
Southeast Asia

Official name Republic of the Philippines
Formation 1946 / 1946
Capital Manila
Population 106 million / 925 people per sq mile (357 people per sq km)
Total area 115,830 sq. miles (300,000 sq. km)
Languages Filipino*, English*, Tagalog, Cebuano, Ilocano, Hiligaynon, many other local languages
Religions Roman Catholic 81%, Other Christian 11%, Muslim 5%, Other 3%
Ethnic mix Other 34%, Tagalog 28%, Cebuano 13%, Ilocano 9%, Hiligaynon 8%, Bisaya 8%
Government Presidential system
Currency Philippine peso = 100 centavos
Literacy rate 96%
Calorie consumption 2570 kilocalories

POLAND
Northern Europe

Official name Republic of Poland
Formation 1918 / 1945
Capital Warsaw
Population 38.1 million / 324 people per sq mile (125 people per sq km)
Total area 120,728 sq. miles (312,685 sq. km)
Languages Polish*
Religions Roman Catholic 87%, Nonreligious 7%, Other 6%
Ethnic mix Polish 97%, Silesian 2%, Other 1%
Government Parliamentary system
Currency Zloty = 100 groszy
Literacy rate 99%
Calorie consumption 3451 kilocalories

PORTUGAL
Southwest Europe

Official name Portuguese Republic
Formation 1139 / 1640
Capital Lisbon
Population 10.3 million / 290 people
per sq mile (112 people per sq km)
Total area 35,672 sq. miles (92,391 sq. km)
Languages Portuguese*
Religions Roman Catholic 88%,
Nonreligious 7%, Other 5%
Ethnic mix Portuguese 98%,
African and other 2%
Government Parliamentary system
Currency Euro = 100 cents
Literacy rate 94%
Calorie consumption 3477 kilocalories

RWANDA
Central Africa

Official name Republic of Rwanda
Formation 1962 / 1962
Capital Kigali
Population 12.5 million / 1298 people
per sq mile (501 people per sq km)
Total area 10,169 sq. miles (26,338 sq. km)
Languages Kinyarwanda*, French*,
Kiswahili, English*
Religions Roman Catholic 44%, Protestant
38%, Other and nonreligious 18%
Ethnic mix Hutu 85%, Tutsi 14%,
Other (including Twa) 1%
Government Presidential system
Currency Rwanda franc = 100 centimes
Literacy rate 71%
Calorie consumption 2228 kilocalories

SAMOA
Australasia & Oceania

Official name Independent State of Samoa
Formation 1962 / 1962
Capital Apia
Population 198,000 / 181 people
per sq mile (70 people per sq km)
Total area 1104 sq. miles (2860 sq. km)
Languages Samoan*, English*
Religions Other Christian 78%, Roman
Catholic 20%, Other 2%
Ethnic mix Polynesian 91%,
Euronesian 7%, Other 2%
Government Parliamentary system
Currency Tala = 100 sene
Literacy rate 99%
Calorie consumption 2960 kilocalories

SENEGAL
West Africa

Official name Republic of Senegal
Formation 1960 / 1960
Capital Dakar
Population 16.3 million / 219 people
per sq mile (85 people per sq km)
Total area 75,749 sq. miles (196,190 sq. km)
Languages Wolof, Pulaar, Serer, Diola,
Mandinka, Malinké, Soninké, French*
Religions Sunni Muslim 95%, Christian
(mainly Roman Catholic) 4%, Traditional
beliefs 1%
Ethnic mix Wolof 43%, Serer 15%,
Peul 14%, Other 14%, Toucouleur 9%,
Diola 5%
Government Presidential system
Currency CFA franc = 100 centimes
Literacy rate 52%
Calorie consumption 2456 kilocalories

QATAR
Southwest Asia

Official name State of Qatar
Formation 1971 / 1971
Capital Doha
Population 2.7 million / 636 people
per sq mile (245 people per sq km)
Total area 4416 sq. miles (11,437 sq. km)
Languages Arabic*
Religions Muslim (mainly Sunni) 78%,
Other 14%, Christian 8%
Ethnic mix Qatari 20%, Indian 20%,
Other Arab 20%, Nepalese 13%,
Filipino 10%, Other 10%, Pakistani 7%
Government Monarchy
Currency Qatar riyal = 100 dirhams
Literacy rate 98%
Calorie consumption Not available

SAINT KITTS & NEVIS
West Indies

Official name Federation of Saint
Christopher and Nevis
Formation 1983 / 1983
Capital Basseterre
Population 56,000 / 403 people
per sq mile (156 people per sq km)
Total area 101 sq. miles (261 sq. km)
Languages English*, English Creole
Religions Anglican 33%, Methodist 29%,
Other 22%, Moravian 9%, Roman
Catholic 7%
Ethnic mix Black 95%, Mixed race 3%,
White 1%, Other and Amerindian 1%
Government Parliamentary system
Currency East Caribbean dollar
= 100 cents
Literacy rate 98%
Calorie consumption 2492 kilocalories

SAN MARINO
Southern Europe

Official name Republic of San Marino
Formation 1631 / 1631
Capital San Marino
Population 34,000 / 1417 people
per sq mile (557 people per sq km)
Total area 23.6 sq. miles (61 sq. km)
Languages Italian*
Religions Roman Catholic 93%,
Other and nonreligious 7%
Ethnic mix Sammarinese 88%,
Italian 10%, Other 2%
Government Parliamentary system
Currency Euro = 100 cents
Literacy rate 99%
Calorie consumption Not available

SERBIA
Southeast Europe

Official name Republic of Serbia
Formation 2006 / 2008
Capital Belgrade
Population 8.8 million / 294 people
per sq mile (114 people per sq km)
Total area 29,905 sq. miles (77,453 sq km)
Languages Serbian*, Hungarian (Magyar)
Religions Orthodox Christian 88%,
Roman Catholic 4%, Nonreligious 4%,
Muslim 2%, Other 2%
Ethnic mix Serb 87%, Magyar 4%, Other
4%, Roma 2%, Bosniak 2%, Croat 1%
Government Parliamentary system
Currency Serbian dinar = 100 para
Literacy rate 99%
Calorie consumption 2728 kilocalories

ROMANIA
Southeast Europe

Official name Romania
Formation 1878 / 1947
Capital Bucharest
Population 19.6 million / 220 people
per sq mile (85 people per sq km)
Total area 91,699 sq. miles (237,500 sq. km)
Languages Romanian*, Hungarian
(Magyar), Romani, German
Religions Orthodox Christian 86%,
Other 8%, Roman Catholic 5%,
Nonreligious 1%
Ethnic mix Romanian 89%, Magyar 7%,
Roma 2%, Other 2%
Government Presidential / parliamentary
system
Currency New Romanian leu = 100 bani
Literacy rate 99%
Calorie consumption 3358 kilocalories

SAINT LUCIA
West Indies

Official name Saint Lucia
Formation 1979 / 1979
Capital Castries
Population 180,000 / 763 people
per sq mile (295 people per sq km)
Total area 239 sq. miles (620 sq. km)
Languages English*, French Creole
Religions Roman Catholic 68%,
Seventh-day Adventist 9%, Other
Christian 15%, Rastafarian 2%, Other 6%
Ethnic mix Black 84%, Mulatto (mixed
race) 12%, Asian 3%, Other 1%
Government Parliamentary system
Currency E. Caribbean dollar = 100 cents
Literacy rate 95%
Calorie consumption 2595 kilocalories

SÃO TOMÉ & PRÍNCIPE
West Africa

Official name Democratic Republic
of São Tomé and Príncipe
Formation 1975 / 1975
Capital São Tomé
Population 209,000 / 563 people
per sq mile (218 people per sq km)
Total area 386 sq. miles (1001 sq. km)
Languages Portuguese Creole, Portuguese*
Religions Roman Catholic 56%,
Nonreligious 17%, Other 27%
Ethnic mix Black 90%, Creole / Other 10%
Government Presidential / parliamentary
system
Currency Dobra = 100 céntimos
Literacy rate 90%
Calorie consumption 2400 kilocalories

SEYCHELLES
Indian Ocean

Official name Republic of Seychelles
Formation 1976 / 1976
Capital Victoria
Population 95,000 / 913 people
per sq mile (352 people per sq km)
Total area 176 sq. miles (455 sq. km)
Languages French Creole*,
English*, French*
Religions Roman Catholic 84%,
Anglican 6%, Other Christian 5%,
Hindu 2%, Other and nonreligious 2%,
Muslim 1%
Ethnic mix Creole 89%, Indian 5%,
Other 4%, Chinese 2%
Government Presidential system
Currency Seychelles rupee = 100 cents
Literacy rate 92%
Calorie consumption 2426 kilocalories

RUSSIA
Europe / Asia

Official name Russian Federation
Formation 1480 / 1991
Capital Moscow
Population 144 million / 22 people
per sq mile (8 people per sq km)
Total area 6,592,735 sq. miles
(17,075,200 sq. km)
Languages Russian*, Tatar, Ukrainian,
Chavash, various other national languages
Religions Orthodox Christian 71%,
Nonreligious 15%, Muslim 11%, Other 3%
Ethnic mix Russian 80%, Other 11%,
Tatar 4%, Ukrainian 1%, Bashkir 1%,
Chavash 1%, Chechen 1%
Government Presidential /
parliamentary system
Currency Russian rouble = 100 kopeks
Literacy rate 99%
Calorie consumption 3361 kilocalories

SAINT VINCENT &
THE GRENADINES
West Indies

Official name Saint Vincent
and the Grenadines
Formation 1979 / 1979
Capital Kingstown
Population 110,000 / 840 people
per sq mile (324 people per sq km)
Total area 150 sq. miles (389 sq. km)
Languages English*, English Creole
Religions Anglican 18%, Pentecostal 18%,
Methodist 11%, Other Christian 37%,
Nonreligious 9%, Other 7%
Ethnic mix Black 73%, Mulatto (mixed
race) 20%, Carib 4%, Asian 2%, Other 1%
Government Parliamentary system
Currency E. Caribbean dollar = 100 cents
Literacy rate 88%
Calorie consumption 2968 kilocalories

SAUDI ARABIA
Southwest Asia

Official name Kingdom of Saudi Arabia
Formation 1932 / 1932
Capital Riyadh
Population 33.6 million / 41 people
per sq mile (16 people per sq km)
Total area 756,981 sq. miles
(1,960,582 sq. km)
Languages Arabic*
Religions Sunni Muslim 85%,
Shi'a Muslim 15%
Ethnic mix Arab 72%, Foreign residents
(mostly south and southeast Asian) 20%,
Afro-Asian 8%
Government Monarchy
Currency Saudi riyal = 100 halalat
Literacy rate 94%
Calorie consumption 3255 kilocalories

SIERRA LEONE
West Africa

Official name Republic of Sierra Leone
Formation 1961 / 1961
Capital Freetown
Population 7.7 million / 278 people
per sq mile (108 people per sq km)
Total area 27,698 sq. miles (71,740 sq. km)
Languages Mende, Temne, Krio, English*
Religions Muslim 60%, Christian 30%,
Traditional beliefs 10%
Ethnic mix Mende 35%, Temne 32%,
Other 21%, Limba 8%, Kuranko 4%
Government Presidential system
Currency Leone = 100 cents
Literacy rate 32%
Calorie consumption 2404 kilocalories

SINGAPORE
Southeast Asia

Official name Republic of Singapore
Formation 1965 / 1965
Capital Singapore
Population 5.8 million / 24,576 people per sq mile (9508 people per sq km)
Total area 250 sq. miles (648 sq. km)
Languages Mandarin*, Malay*, Tamil*, English*
Religions Christian 31%, Buddhist 28%, Nonreligious 14%, Muslim 13%, Other 14%
Ethnic mix Chinese 74%, Malay 14%, Indian 9%, Other 3%
Government Parliamentary system
Currency Singapore dollar = 100 cents
Literacy rate 97%
Calorie consumption Not available

SOMALIA
East Africa

Official name Federal Republic of Somalia
Formation 1960 / 1960
Capital Mogadishu
Population 15.2 million / 63 people per sq mile (24 people per sq km)
Total area 246,199 sq. miles (637,657 sq. km)
Languages Somali*, Arabic*, English, Italian
Religions Sunni Muslim 99%, Christian 1%
Ethnic mix Somali 85%, Other 15%
Government Nonparty system
Currency Somali shilin = 100 senti
Literacy rate 24%
Calorie consumption 1696 kilocalories

SPAIN
Southwest Europe

Official name Kingdom of Spain
Formation 1492 / 1713
Capital Madrid
Population 46.4 million / 241 people per sq mile (93 people per sq km)
Total area 194,896 sq. miles (504,782 sq. km)
Languages Spanish*, Catalan*, Galician*, Basque*
Religions Roman Catholic 71%, Nonreligious 26%, Other 3%
Ethnic mix Castilian Spanish 72%, Catalan 17%, Galician 6%, Basque 2%, Other 2%, Roma 1%
Government Parliamentary system
Currency Euro = 100 cents
Literacy rate 98%
Calorie consumption 3174 kilocalories

SWEDEN
Northern Europe

Official name Kingdom of Sweden
Formation 1523 / 1921
Capital Stockholm
Population 10 million / 63 people per sq mile (24 people per sq km)
Total area 173,731 sq. miles (449,964 sq. km)
Languages Swedish*, Finnish, Sámi
Religions Evangelical Lutheran 75%, Other 13%, Muslim 5%, Other Protestant 5%, Roman Catholic 2%
Ethnic mix Swedish 86%, Foreign-born or first-generation immigrant 12%, Finnish and Sámi 2%
Government Parliamentary system
Currency Swedish krona = 100 öre
Literacy rate 99%
Calorie consumption 3179 kilocalories

SLOVAKIA
Central Europe

Official name Slovak Republic
Formation 1993 / 1993
Capital Bratislava
Population 5.4 million / 285 people per sq mile (110 people per sq km)
Total area 18,859 sq. miles (48,845 sq. km)
Languages Slovak*, Hungarian (Magyar), Czech
Religions Roman Catholic 69%, Nonreligious 15%, Other Christian 11%, Greek Catholic (Uniate) 4%, Other 1%
Ethnic mix Slovak 87%, Magyar 9%, Roma 2%, Other 1%, Czech 1%
Government Parliamentary system
Currency Euro = 100 cents
Literacy rate 99%
Calorie consumption 2944 kilocalories

SOUTH AFRICA
Southern Africa

Official name Republic of South Africa
Formation 1934 / 1994
Capital Pretoria; Cape Town; Bloemfontein
Population 57.4 million / 122 people per sq mile (47 people per sq km)
Total area 471,008 sq. miles (1,219,912 sq. km)
Languages English*, isiZulu*, isiXhosa*, Afrikaans*, Sepedi*, Setswana*, Sesotho*, Xitsonga*, siSwati*, Tshivenda*, isiNdebele*
Religions Christian 81%, Nonreligious 15%, Muslim 2%, Hindu 1%, Other 1%
Ethnic mix Black 80%, Colored 9%, White 9%, Asian 2%
Government Presidential system
Currency Rand = 100 cents
Literacy rate 94%
Calorie consumption 3022 kilocalories

SRI LANKA
South Asia

Official name Democratic Socialist Republic of Sri Lanka
Formation 1948 / 1948
Capital Colombo; Sri Jayewardenapura Kotte (admin.)
Population 21 million / 840 people per sq mile (324 people per sq km)
Total area 25,332 sq. miles (65,610 sq. km)
Languages Sinhala*, Tamil*, Sinhala-Tamil, English
Religions Buddhist 70%, Hindu 13%, Muslim 10%, Christian 7%
Ethnic mix Sinhalese 75%, Tamil 15%, Moor 9%, Other 1%
Government Presidential / parliamentary system
Currency Sri Lanka rupee = 100 cents
Literacy rate 92%
Calorie consumption 2539 kilocalories

SWITZERLAND
Central Europe

Official name Swiss Confederation
Formation 1291 / 1857
Capital Bern
Population 8.5 million / 554 people per sq mile (214 people per sq km)
Total area 15,942 sq. miles (41,290 sq. km)
Languages German*, Swiss-German, French*, Italian*, Romansh
Religions Roman Catholic 39%, Other Christian 34%, Nonreligious 21%, Muslim 5%, Other 1%
Ethnic mix German 64%, French 20%, Other 9.5%, Italian 6%, Romansch 0.5%
Government Parliamentary system
Currency Swiss franc = 100 rappen/centimes
Literacy rate 99%
Calorie consumption 3391 kilocalories

SLOVENIA
Central Europe

Official name Republic of Slovenia
Formation 1991 / 1991
Capital Ljubljana
Population 2.1 million / 269 people per sq mile (104 people per sq km)
Total area 7820 sq. miles (20,253 sq. km)
Languages Slovenian*
Religions Roman Catholic 75%, Nonreligious 18%, Muslim 3%, Orthodox Christian 3%, Other 1%
Ethnic mix Slovene 92%, Other 3%, Serb 2%, Croat 2%, Bosniak 1%
Government Parliamentary system
Currency Euro = 100 cents
Literacy rate 99%
Calorie consumption 3168 kilocalories

SOUTH KOREA
East Asia

Official name Republic of Korea
Formation 1948 / 1953
Capital Seoul; Sejong City (admin.)
Population 51.2 million / 1343 people per sq mile (519 people per sq km)
Total area 38,023 sq. miles (98,480 sq. km)
Languages Korean*
Religions Nonreligious 47%, Mahayana Buddhist 23%, Other Christian 18%, Roman Catholic 11%, Other 1%
Ethnic mix Korean 100%
Government Presidential system
Currency South Korean won = 100 chon
Literacy rate 99%
Calorie consumption 3334 kilocalories

SUDAN
East Africa

Official name Republic of the Sudan
Formation 1956 / 2011
Capital Khartoum
Population 41.5 million / 58 people per sq mile (22 people per sq km)
Total area 718,722 sq. miles (1,861,481 sq. km)
Languages Arabic*, Nubian, Beja, Fur, English*
Religions Nearly the whole population is Muslim (mainly Sunni)
Ethnic mix Arab 60%, Other 18%, Nubian 10%, Beja 8%, Fur 3%, Zaghawa 1%
Government Presidential system
Currency New Sudanese pound = 100 piastres
Literacy rate 73%
Calorie consumption 2336 kilocalories

SYRIA
Southwest Asia

Official name Syrian Arab Republic
Formation 1941 / 1967
Capital Damascus
Population 18.3 million / 258 people per sq mile (99 people per sq km)
Total area 71,498 sq. miles (184,180 sq. km)
Languages Arabic*, French, Kurdish, Armenian, Circassian, Turkic languages, Assyrian, Aramaic
Religions Sunni Muslim 74%, Alawi 12%, Christian 10%, Druze 3%, Other 1%
Ethnic mix Arab 90%, Kurdish 9%, Armenian, Turkmen, and Circassian 1%
Government Presidential system
Currency Syrian pound = 100 piastres
Literacy rate 85%
Calorie consumption 3106 kilocalories

SOLOMON ISLANDS
Australasia & Oceania

Official name Solomon Islands
Formation 1978 / 1978
Capital Honiara
Population 623,000 / 58 people per sq mile (22 people per sq km)
Total area 10,985 sq. miles (28,450 sq. km)
Languages English*, Pidgin English, Melanesian Pidgin, around 120 native languages
Religions Church of Melanesia 34%, Roman Catholic 19%, South Seas Evangelical Church 17%, Seventh-day Adventist 10%, Other 9%
Ethnic mix Melanesian 93%, Polynesian 4%, Micronesian 2%, Other 1%
Government Parliamentary system
Currency Solomon Is. dollar = 100 cents
Literacy rate 77%
Calorie consumption 2391 kilocalories

SOUTH SUDAN
East Africa

Official name Republic of South Sudan
Formation 2011 / 2011
Capital Juba
Population 12.9 million / 52 people per sq mile (20 people per sq km)
Total area 248,777 sq. miles (644,329 sq. km)
Languages Arabic, Dinka, Nuer, Zande, Bari, Shilluk, Lotuko, English*
Religions Over 50% Christian beliefs
Ethnic mix Dinka 36%, Nuer 15%, Bari 10%, Shilluk/Anwak 10%, Azande 10%, Arab 10%, Other 5%
Government Transitional regime
Currency South Sudan pound = 100 piastres
Literacy rate 37%
Calorie consumption Not available

SURINAME
South America

Official name Republic of Suriname
Formation 1975 / 1975
Capital Paramaribo
Population 568,000 / 9 people per sq mile (4 people per sq km)
Total area 63,039 sq. miles (163,270 sq. km)
Languages Sranan (Creole), Dutch*, Javanese, Sarnami Hindi, Saramaccan, Chinese, Carib
Religions Christian 50%, Hindu 23%, Muslim 14%, Other 13%
Ethnic mix East Indian 27%, Creole 18%, Black 15%, Javanese 15%, Mixed race 13%, Other 6%, Amerindian 4%, Chinese 2%
Government Presidential / parliamentary system
Currency Surinamese dollar = 100 cents
Literacy rate 93%
Calorie consumption 2753 kilocalories

TAIWAN
East Asia

Official name Republic of China (ROC)
Formation 1949 / 1949
Capital Taipei
Population 23.6 million / 1895 people per sq mile (732 people per sq km)
Total area 13,892 sq. miles (35,980 sq. km)
Languages Amoy Chinese, Mandarin Chinese*, Hakka Chinese
Religions Buddhist, Confucianist, and Taoist 93%, Christian 5%, Other 2%
Ethnic mix Han (pre-20th-century migration) 84%, Han (20th-century migration) 14%, Aboriginal 2%
Government Presidential system
Currency Taiwan dollar = 100 cents
Literacy rate 99%
Calorie consumption 2997 kilocalories

TAJIKISTAN
Central Asia

Official name Republic of Tajikistan
Formation 1991 / 1991
Capital Dushanbe
Population 9.1 million / 165 people
per sq mile (64 people per sq km)
Total area 55,251 sq. miles (143,100 sq. km)
Languages Tajik*, Uzbek, Russian
Religions Sunni Muslim 95%,
Shi'a Muslim 3%, Other 2%
Ethnic mix Tajik 84%, Uzbek 12%,
Other 2%, Kyrgyz 1%, Russian 1%
Government Presidential system
Currency Somoni = 100 diram
Literacy rate 99%
Calorie consumption 2201 kilocalories

TONGA
Australasia & Oceania

Official name Kingdom of Tonga
Formation 1970 / 1970
Capital Nuku'alofa
Population 109,000 / 392 people
per sq mile (151 people per sq km)
Total area 289 sq. miles (748 sq. km)
Languages English*, Tongan*
Religions Free Wesleyan 38%, Church
of Jesus Christ of Latter-day Saints 17%,
Roman Catholic 16%, Other Christian 16%,
Free Church of Tonga 12%, Other 1%
Ethnic mix Tongan 98%, Other 2%
Government Monarchy
Currency Pa'anga (Tongan dollar)
= 100 seniti
Literacy rate 99%
Calorie consumption Not available

TURKMENISTAN
Central Asia

Official name Turkmenistan
Formation 1991 / 1991
Capital Ashgabat
Population 5.9 million / 31 people
per sq mile (12 people per sq km)
Total area 188,455 sq. miles
(488,100 sq. km)
Languages Turkmen*, Uzbek, Russian,
Kazakh, Tatar
Religions Sunni Muslim 89%,
Orthodox Christian 9%, Other 2%
Ethnic mix Turkmen 85%, Other 6%,
Uzbek 5%, Russian 4%
Government Presidential system
Currency New Manat = 100 tenge
Literacy rate 99%
Calorie consumption 2840 kilocalories

UNITED ARAB EMIRATES
Southwest Asia

Official name United Arab Emirates
Formation 1971 / 1972
Capital Abu Dhabi
Population 9.5 million / 294 people
per sq mile (114 people per sq km)
Total area 32,000 sq. miles (82,880 sq. km)
Languages Arabic*, Farsi, Indian and
Pakistani languages, English
Religions Muslim (mainly Sunni) 96%,
Christian, Hindu, and other 4%
Ethnic mix Asian 60%, Emirian 25%,
Other Arab 12%, European 3%
Government Monarchy
Currency UAE dirham = 100 fils
Literacy rate 90%
Calorie consumption 3280 kilocalories

TANZANIA
East Africa

Official name United Republic
of Tanzania
Formation 1964 / 1964
Capital Dodoma
Population 59.1 million / 173 people
per sq mile (67 people per sq km)
Total area 364,898 sq. miles
(945,087 sq. km)
Languages Kiswahili*, Sukuma, Chagga,
Nyamwezi, Hehe, Makonde, Yao,
Sandawe, English*
Religions Christian 63%, Muslim 35%,
Other 2%
Ethnic mix Native African (over 120
tribes) 99%, European, Asian, and Arab 1%
Government Presidential system
Currency Tanzanian shilling = 100 cents
Literacy rate 78%
Calorie consumption 2208 kilocalories

TRINIDAD & TOBAGO
West Indies

Official name Republic of Trinidad and
Tobago
Formation 1962 / 1962
Capital Port of Spain
Population 1.4 million / 707 people
per sq mile (273 people per sq km)
Total area 1980 sq. miles (5128 sq. km)
Languages English Creole, English*, Hindi,
French, Spanish
Religions Protestant 38%,
Roman Catholic 24%, Hindu 20%,
Other 9%, Muslim 6%, Nonreligious 3%
Ethnic mix East Indian 38%,
Black 36%, Mixed race 24%,
White and Chinese 1%, Other 1%
Government Parliamentary system
Currency Trinidad & Tobago dollar = 100 cents
Literacy rate 99%
Calorie consumption 3052 kilocalories

TUVALU
Australasia & Oceania

Official name Tuvalu
Formation 1978 / 1978
Capital Funafuti Atoll
Population 11,000 / 1100 people
per sq mile (423 people per sq km)
Total area 10 sq. miles (26 sq. km)
Languages Tuvaluan*, Kiribati, English*
Religions Church of Tuvalu 91%,
Other (mostly Protestant) 5%,
Seventh-day Adventist 2%, Baha'i 2%
Ethnic mix Polynesian 96%,
Micronesian 4%
Government Nonparty system
Currency Australian dollar = 100 cents;
Tuvaluan dollar = 100 cents
Literacy rate 95%
Calorie consumption Not available

UNITED KINGDOM
Northwest Europe

Official name United Kingdom of Great
Britain and Northern Ireland
Formation 1707 / 1922
Capital London
Population 66.6 million / 714 people
per sq mile (276 people per sq km)
Total area 94,525 sq. miles
(244,820 sq. km)
Languages English*, Welsh* (in Wales),
Scottish Gaelic, Irish
Religions Christian 64%, Nonreligious
28%, Muslim 5%, Other 2%, Hindu 1%
Ethnic mix White 87%,
Indian and Pakistani 4%, Black 3%, Bengali
1%, Chinese 1%, Other Asian 1%, Other 3%
Government Parliamentary system
Currency Pound sterling = 100 pence
Literacy rate 99%
Calorie consumption 3424 kilocalories

THAILAND
Southeast Asia

Official name Kingdom of Thailand
Formation 1238 / 1907
Capital Bangkok
Population 69.2 million / 351 people
per sq mile (135 people per sq km)
Total area 198,455 sq. miles
(514,000 sq. km)
Languages Thai*, Chinese, Malay, Khmer,
Mon, Karen, Miao
Religions Buddhist 94%, Muslim 5%,
Other (including Christian) 1%
Ethnic mix Thai 83%, Chinese 12%,
Malay 3%, Khmer and Other 2%
Government Transitional regime
Currency Baht = 100 satang
Literacy rate 93%
Calorie consumption 2784 kilocalories

TUNISIA
North Africa

Official name Republic of Tunisia
Formation 1956 / 1956
Capital Tunis
Population 11.7 million / 195 people per sq
mile (75 people per sq km)
Total area 63,169 sq. miles (163,610 sq. km)
Languages Arabic*, French
Religions Muslim (mainly Sunni) 98%,
Christian 1%, Jewish 1%
Ethnic mix Arab and Berber 98%, Other 2%
Government Presidential / parliamentary
system
Currency Tunisian dinar = 1000 millimes
Literacy rate 79%
Calorie consumption 3349 kilocalories

UGANDA
East Africa

Official name Republic of Uganda
Formation 1962 / 1962
Capital Kampala
Population 44.3 million / 575 people
per sq mile (222 people per sq km)
Total area 91,135 sq. miles (236,040 sq. km)
Languages Luganda, Nkole, Chiga, Lango,
Acholi, Teso, Lugbara, English*
Religions Roman Catholic 42%, Protestant
42%, Muslim (mainly Sunni) 12%, Other 4%
Ethnic mix Other 50%, Baganda 17%,
Banyakole 10%, Basoga 9%, Iteso 7%,
Bakiga 7%
Government Presidential system
Currency Uganda shilling = 100 cents
Literacy rate 70%
Calorie consumption 2130 kilocalories

UNITED STATES
North America

Official name United States of America
Formation 1776 / 1959
Capital Washington D.C.
Population 327 million / 92 people
per sq mile (36 people per sq km)
Total area 3,717,792 sq. miles (9,626,091 sq. km)
Languages English*, Spanish, Chinese,
French, German, Tagalog, Vietnamese,
Italian, Korean, Russian, Polish
Religions Protestant 47%, Nonreligious
23%, Roman Catholic 21%, Other 6%,
Jewish 2%, Muslim 1%
Ethnic mix White 60%, Hispanic 17%,
Black American/African 14%,
Asian 6%, Native Peoples 3%
Government Presidential system
Currency US dollar = 100 cents
Literacy rate 99%
Calorie consumption 3682 kilocalories

TOGO
West Africa

Official name Republic of Togo
Formation 1960 / 1960
Capital Lomé
Population 8 million / 381 people
per sq mile (147 people per sq km)
Total area 21,924 sq. miles (56,785 sq. km)
Languages Ewe, Kabye, Gurma, French*
Religions Christian 47%, Traditional
beliefs 33%, Muslim 14%, Other 6%
Ethnic mix Ewe 46%, Other African 41%,
Kabye 12%, European 1%
Government Presidential system
Currency CFA franc = 100 centimes
Literacy rate 64%
Calorie consumption 2454 kilocalories

TURKEY
Asia / Europe

Official name Republic of Turkey
Formation 1923 / 1939
Capital Ankara
Population 81.9 million / 276 people
per sq mile (106 people per sq km)
Total area 301,382 sq. miles
(780,580 sq. km)
Languages Turkish*, Kurdish,
Arabic, Circassian, Armenian, Greek,
Georgian, Ladino
Religions Muslim (mainly Sunni) 99%,
Other 1%
Ethnic mix Turkish 70%, Kurdish 20%,
Other 8%, Arab 2%
Government Presidential system
Currency Turkish lira = 100 kurus
Literacy rate 96%
Calorie consumption 3706 kilocalories

UKRAINE
Eastern Europe

Official name Ukraine
Formation 1991 / 1991
Capital Kyiv
Population 44 million / 189 people
per sq mile (73 people per sq km)
Total area 233,089 sq. miles (603,700 sq. km)
Languages Ukrainian*, Russian, Tatar
Religions Orthodox Christian 78%, Roman
Catholic 10%, Nonreligious 7%, Other 5%
Ethnic mix Ukrainian 78%, Russian 17%,
Other 4%, Belarussian 1%
Government Presidential / parliamentary
system
Currency Hryvna = 100 kopiykas
Literacy rate 99%
Calorie consumption 3138 kilocalories

URUGUAY
South America

Official name Eastern Republic
of Uruguay
Formation 1828 / 1828
Capital Montevideo
Population 3.5 million / 52 people
per sq mile (20 people per sq km)
Total area 68,039 sq. miles (176,220 sq. km)
Languages Spanish*
Religions Roman Catholic 42%,
Protestant 15%, Nonreligious 37%,
Other 6%
Ethnic mix White 87%, Black 7%,
Mestizo 5%, Other 1%
Government Presidential system
Currency Uruguayan peso
= 100 centésimos
Literacy rate 99%
Calorie consumption 3050 kilocalories

UZBEKISTAN
Central Asia

Official name Republic of Uzbekistan
Formation 1991 / 1991
Capital Tashkent
Population 32.4 million / 188 people per sq mile (72 people per sq km)
Total area 172,741 sq. miles (447,400 sq. km)
Languages Uzbek*, Russian, Tajik, Kazakh
Religions Sunni Muslim 88%, Orthodox Christian 9%, Other 3%
Ethnic mix Uzbek 80%, Russian 6%, Other 6%, Tajik 5%, Kazakh 3%
Government Presidential system
Currency Som = 100 tiyin
Literacy rate 99%
Calorie consumption 2760 kilocalories

VANUATU
Australasia & Oceania

Official name Republic of Vanuatu
Formation 1980 / 1980
Capital Port Vila
Population 282,000 / 60 people per sq mile (23 people per sq km)
Total area 4710 sq. miles (12,200 sq. km)
Languages Bislama* (Melanesian pidgin), English*, French*, other indigenous languages
Religions Other 33%, Presbyterian 28%, Anglican 15%, Seventh-day Adventist 12%, Roman Catholic 12%
Ethnic mix ni-Vanuatu 99%, Other 1%
Government Parliamentary system
Currency Vatu = 100 centimes
Literacy rate 85%
Calorie consumption 2836 kilocalories

VATICAN CITY
Southern Europe

Official name State of the Vatican City
Formation 1929 / 1929
Capital Vatican City
Population 800 / 4706 people per sq mile (1818 people per sq km)
Total area 0.17 sq. miles (0.44 sq. km)
Languages Italian*, Latin*
Religions Roman Catholic 100%
Ethnic mix Most resident lay persons are Italian
Government Papal state
Currency Euro = 100 cents
Literacy rate 99%
Calorie consumption Not available

VENEZUELA
South America

Official name Bolivarian Republic of Venezuela
Formation 1830 / 1830
Capital Caracas
Population 32.4 million / 95 people per sq mile (37 people per sq km)
Total area 352,143 sq. miles (912,050 sq. km)
Languages Spanish*, Amerindian languages
Religions Roman Catholic 73%, Protestant 17%, Nonreligious 7%, Other 3%
Ethnic mix Mestizo 69%, White 20%, Black 9%, Amerindian 2%
Government Presidential system
Currency Bolívar fuerte = 100 céntimos
Literacy rate 97%
Calorie consumption 2631 kilocalories

VIETNAM
Southeast Asia

Official name Socialist Republic of Vietnam
Formation 1976 / 1976
Capital Hanoi
Population 96.5 million / 768 people per sq mile (297 people per sq km)
Total area 127,243 sq. miles (329,560 sq. km)
Languages Vietnamese*, Chinese, Thai, Khmer, Muong, Nung, Miao, Yao, Jarai
Religions Nonreligious 81%, Buddhist 9%, Roman Catholic 7%, Hoa Hao 1%, Cao Dai 1%, Other 1%
Ethnic mix Vietnamese 86%, Other 8%, Tay 2%, Thai 2%, Muong 1%, Khome 1%
Government One-party state
Currency Dông = 10 hao = 100 xu
Literacy rate 94%
Calorie consumption 2745 kilocalories

YEMEN
Southwest Asia

Official name Republic of Yemen
Formation 1990 / 1990
Capital Saana
Population 28.9 million / 133 people per sq mile (51 people per sq km)
Total area 203,849 sq. miles (527,970 sq. km)
Languages Arabic*
Religions Sunni Muslim 55%, Shi'a Muslim 42%, Christian, Hindu, and Jewish 3%
Ethnic mix Arab 99%, Afro-Arab, Indian, Somali, and European 1%
Government Transitional regime
Currency Yemeni rial = 100 fils
Literacy rate 66%
Calorie consumption 2223 kilocalories

ZAMBIA
Southern Africa

Official name Republic of Zambia
Formation 1964 / 1964
Capital Lusaka
Population 17.6 million / 62 people per sq mile (24 people per sq km)
Total area 290,584 sq. miles (752,614 sq. km)
Languages Bemba, Tonga, Nyanja, Lozi, Lala-Bisa, Nsenga, English*
Religions Protestant 75%, Roman Catholic 20%, Other 3%, Nonreligious 2%
Ethnic mix Bemba 34%, Other African 26%, Tonga 16%, Nyanja 14%, Lozi 9%, European 1%
Government Presidential system
Currency New Zambian kwacha = 100 ngwee
Literacy rate 83%
Calorie consumption 1930 kilocalories

ZIMBABWE
Southern Africa

Official name Republic of Zimbabwe
Formation 1980 / 1980
Capital Harare
Population 16.9 million / 113 people per sq mile (44 people per sq km)
Total area 150,803 sq. miles (390,580 sq. km)
Languages Shona, isiNdebele, English*
Religions Syncretic (Christian/traditional beliefs) 50%, Christian 25%, Traditional beliefs 24%, Other 1%
Ethnic mix Shona 71%, Ndebele 16%, Other African 11%, White 1%, Asian 1%
Government Presidential system
Currency Zimbabwe dollar suspended in 2009; nine other currencies are legal tender
Literacy rate 89%
Calorie consumption 2110 kilocalories

GLOSSARY OF ABBREVIATIONS

This Glossary provides a comprehensive guide to the abbreviations used in this Atlas, and in the Index.

A
abbrev. abbreviated
admin. administrative
Afr. Afrikaans
Alb. Albanian
Amh. Amharic
anc. ancient
Ar. Arabic
Arm. Armenian
Az. Azerbaijani

B
Basq. Basque
Bel. Belorussian
Ben. Bengali
Bibl. Biblical
Bret. Breton
Bul. Bulgarian
Bur. Burmese

C
Cam. Cambodian
Cant. Cantonese
Cast. Castilian
Cat. Catalan
Chin. Chinese
Cro. Croat
Cz. Czech

D
Dan. Danish
Dut. Dutch

E
E. East
Eng. English
Est. Estonian
est. estimated

F
Faer. Faeroese
Fij. Fijian
Fin. Finnish
Flem. Flemish
Fr. French
Fris. Frisian

G
Geor. Georgian
Ger. German
Gk. Greek
Guj. Gujarati

H
Haw. Hawaiian
Heb. Hebrew
Hind. Hindi
hist. historical
Hung. Hungarian

I
Icel. Icelandic
Ind. Indonesian
In. Inuit
Ir. Irish
It. Italian

J
Jap. Japanese

K
Kaz. Kazakh
Kir. Kirghiz
Kor. Korean
Kurd. Kurdish

L
Lao. Laotian
Lapp. Lappish
Lat. Latin
Latv. Latvian
Lith. Lithuanian
Lus. Lusatian

M
Mac. Macedonian
Mal. Malay
Malg. Malagasy
Malt. Maltese
Mon. Montenegro
Mong. Mongolian

N
Nepali. Nepali
Nor. Norwegian

O
off. officially

P
Pash. Pashtu
Per. Persian
Pol. Polish
Port. Portuguese
prev. previously

R
Rmsch. Romansh
Roman. Romanian
Rus. Russian

S
SCr. Serbo - Croatian
Serb. Serbian
Slvk. Slovak
Slvn. Slovene
Som. Somali
Sp. Spanish
Swa. Swahili
Swe. Swedish

T
Taj. Tajik
Th. Thai
Tib. Tibetan
Turk. Turkish
Turkm. Turkmenistan

U
Uigh. Uighur
Ukr. Ukrainian
Uzb. Uzbek

V
var. variant
Vtn. Vietnamese

W
Wel. Welsh

X
Xh. Xhosa

A

Aa see Gauja
Aachen *94 A4 Dut.* Aken, *Fr.*
   Aix-la-Chapelle; *anc.* Aquae Grani,
   Aquisgranum. Nordrhein-Westfalen,
   W Germany
Aaiún see Laâyoune
Aalborg *85 B7 var.* Ålborg,
   Ålborg-Nørresundby; *anc.* Alburgum.
   Nordjylland, N Denmark
Aalen *95 B6* Baden-Württemberg,
   S Germany
Aalsmeer *86 C3* Noord-Holland,
   C Netherlands
Aalst *87 B6* Oost-Vlaanderen, C Belgium
Aalten *86 E4* Gelderland, E Netherlands
Aalter *87 B5* Oost-Vlaanderen,
   NW Belgium
Aanaarjävri see Inarijärvi
Äänekoski *85 D5* Keski-Suomi,
   W Finland
Aar see Aare
Aare *95 A7 var.* Aar. *river* W Switzerland
Aarhus *85 B7 var.* Århus, C Denmark
Aarlen see Arlon
Aat see Ath
Aba *77 E5* Orientale, NE Dem. Rep.
   Congo
Aba *75 G5* Abia, S Nigeria
Abā as Su'ûd see Najrān
Abaco Island see Great Abaco, N The
   Bahamas
Ābādān *120 C4* Khūzestān, SW Iran
Abadan *122 C3 prev.* Bezmein,
   Büzmeýin, *Rus.* Byuzmeyin. Ahal
   Welaýaty, C Turkmenistan
Abai see Blue Nile
Abakan *114 D4* Respublika Khakasiya,
   S Russia
Abancay *60 D4* Apurímac, SE Peru
Abariringa see Kanton
Abashiri *130 D2 var.* Abasiri. Hokkaidō,
   NE Japan
Abasiri see Abashiri
Äbay Wenz see Blue Nile
Abbaia see Äbaya Häyk'
Abbatis Villa see Abbeville
Abbazia see Opatija
Abbeville *90 C2 anc.* Abbatis Villa.
   Somme, N France
'Abd al 'Azīz, Jabal *118 D2 mountain*
   range NE Syria
Abéché *76 C4 var.* Abécher, Abeshr.
   Ouaddaï, SE Chad
Abécher see Abéché
Abela see Ávila
Abellinum see Avellino
Abemama *144 D2 var.* Apamama; *prev.*
   Roger Simpson Island. *atoll* Tungaru,
   W Kiribati
Abengourou *75 E5* E Ivory Coast
Aberbrothock see Arbroath
Abercorn see Mbala
Aberdeen *88 D3 anc.* Devana.
   NE Scotland, United Kingdom
Aberdeen *45 E2* South Dakota, N USA
Aberdeen *46 B2* Washington, NW USA
Abergwaun see Fishguard
Abertawe see Swansea
Aberystwyth *89 C6* W Wales, United
   Kingdom
Abeshr see Abéché
Abhā *121 B6* 'Asīr, SW Saudi Arabia
Abidavichy *107 D7 Rus.* Obidovichi.
   Mahilyowskaya Voblasts', E Belarus
Abidjan *75 E5* S Ivory Coast
Abilene *49 F3* Texas, SW USA
Abingdon see Pinta, Isla
Abkhazia *117 E1 var.* Apkhazeti,
   Ap'khazet'i. *autonomous republic*
   NW Georgia
Åbo see Turku
Aboa *154 B2* Finnish research station
   Antarctica
Aboisso *75 E5* SE Ivory Coast
Abo, Massif d' *76 B1 mountain range*
   NW Chad
Abomey *75 F5* S Benin
Abou-Déïa *76 C3* Salamat, SE Chad
Aboudouhour see Abū aḍ Ḍuhūr
Abou Kémal see Abū Kamāl
Abrantes *92 B3 var.* Abrántes. Santarém,
   C Portugal
Abrashlare see Brezovo
Abrolhos Bank *56 E4 undersea bank*
   W Atlantic Ocean
Abrova *107 B6 Rus.* Obrovo. Brestskaya
   Voblasts', SW Belarus

Abrud *108 B4 Ger.* Gross-Schlatten,
   Hung. Abrudbánya. Alba, SW Romania
Abrudbánya see Abrud
Abruzzese, Appennino *96 C4 mountain*
   range C Italy
Absaroka Range *44 B2 mountain range*
   Montana/Wyoming, NW USA
Abū aḍ Ḍuhūr *118 B3 Fr.* Aboudouhour.
   Idlib, NW Syria
Abu Dhabi see Abū Ẓabī
Abu Hamed *72 C3* River Nile, N Sudan
Abū Ḥardān *118 E3 var.* Hajîne. Dayr az
   Zawr, E Syria
Abuja *75 G4 country capital* (Nigeria)
   Federal Capital District, C Nigeria
Abula see Ávila
Abunã, Rio *62 C2 var.* Río Abuná. *river*
   Bolivia/Brazil
Abut Head *151 B6 headland* South
   Island, New Zealand
Abuye Meda *72 D4 mountain*
   C Ethiopia
Abū Ẓabī *121 C5 var.* Abū Ẓaby, *Eng.*
   Abu Dhabi. *country capital* (United
   Arab Emirates) Abū Ẓaby, C United
   Arab Emirates
Abū Ẓaby see Abū Ẓabī
Abyaḍ, Al Baḥr al see White Nile
Abyei Area *73 B5 disputed region*
   Southern Kordofan, S Sudan
Abyla see Ávila
Abyssinia see Ethiopia
Acalayong *77 A5* SW Equatorial Guinea
Acaponeta *50 D4* Nayarit, C Mexico
Acapulco *51 E5 var.* Acapulco de Juárez.
   Guerrero, S Mexico
Acapulco de Juárez see Acapulco
Acaraí Mountains *59 F4 Sp.* Serra
   Acaraí. *mountain range* Brazil/Guyana
Acaraí, Serra see Acaraí Mountains
Acarigua *58 D2* Portuguesa, N Venezuela
Accra *75 E5 country capital* (Ghana)
   SE Ghana
Achacachi *61 E4* La Paz, W Bolivia
Ach'ara see Ajaria
Achara see Ajaria
Acklins Island *54 C2 island* SE The
   Bahamas
Aconcagua, Cerro *64 B4 mountain*
   W Argentina
Açores/Açores, Arquipélago dos/
   Açores, Ilhas dos see Azores
A Coruña *92 B1 Cast.* La Coruña, *Eng.*
   Corunna; *anc.* Caronium. Galicia,
   NW Spain
Acre *62 C2 off.* Estado do Acre. *state/*
   region W Brazil
Açu see Assu
Acunum Acusio see Montélimar
Ada *100 D3* Vojvodina, N Serbia
Ada *49 G2* Oklahoma, C USA
Ada Bazar see Adapazarı
Adalia see Antalya
Adalia, Gulf of see Antalya Körfezi
Adama see Nazrēt
'Adan *121 C7 Eng.* Aden. SW Yemen
Adana *116 D4 var.* Seyhan. Adana,
   S Turkey
Adâncata see Horlivka
Adapazarı *116 B2 prev.* Ada Bazar.
   Sakarya, NW Turkey
Adare, Cape *154 B4 cape* Antarctica
Ad Dahna *120 C4 desert* E Saudi Arabia
Ad Dakhla *70 A4 var.* Dakhla.
   SW Western Sahara
Ad Dalanj see Dilling
Ad Damar see Ed Damer
Ad Damazīn see Ed Damazin
Ad Dāmir see Ed Damer
Ad Dammām *120 C4 var.* Dammām.
   Ash Sharqīyah, NE Saudi Arabia
Ad Dāmūr see Damoûr
Ad Dawḥah *120 D4 Eng.* Doha. *country*
   capital (Qatar) C Qatar
Ad Diffah see Libyan Plateau
Addis Ababa see Ādīs Ābeba
Addoo Atoll see Addu Atoll
Addu Atoll *132 A5 var.* Addoo Atoll,
   Seenu Atoll. *atoll* S Maldives
Adelaide *149 B6 state capital* South
   Australia
Adelsberg see Postojna
Aden see 'Adan
Aden, Gulf of *121 C7 gulf*
   SW Arabian Sea
Adige *96 C2 Ger.* Etsch. *river* N Italy
Adirondack Mountains *41 F2 mountain*
   range New York, NE USA

Ādīs Ābeba *73 C5 Eng.* Addis Ababa.
   country capital (Ethiopia) Ādīs Ābeba,
   C Ethiopia
Adıyaman *117 E4* Adıyaman,
   SE Turkey
Adjud *108 C4* Vrancea, E Romania
Admiralty Islands *144 B3 island group*
   N Papua New Guinea
Adra *93 E5* Andalucía, S Spain
Adrar *70 D3* C Algeria
Adrian *40 C3* Michigan, N USA
Adrianople/Adrianopolis see Edirne
Adriatico, Mare see Adriatic Sea
Adriatic Sea *103 E2 Alb.* Deti Adriatik,
   It. Mare Adriatico, *SCr.* Jadransko
   More, *Slvn.* Jadransko Morje. *sea*
   N Mediterranean Sea
Adriatik, Deti see Adriatic Sea
Adycha *117 F2 river* NE Russia
Aegean Sea *105 C5 Gk.* Aigaíon Pelagos,
   Aigaío Pélagos, *Turk.* Ege Denizi. *sea*
   NE Mediterranean Sea
Aegviidu *106 D2 Ger.* Charlottenhof.
   Harjumaa, NW Estonia
Aegyptus see Egypt
Aelana see Al 'Aqabah
Aelok see Ailuk Atoll
Aelönlaplap see Ailinglaplap Atoll
Aemona see Ljubljana
Aeolian Islands *97 C6 var.* Isole Lipari,
   Eng. Aeolian Islands, Lipari Islands.
   island group S Italy
Aeolian Islands see Eolie, Isole
Æsernia see Isernia
Afar Depression see Danakil Desert
Afars et des Issas, Territoire Français
   des see Djibouti
Afghānestān, Dowlat-e Eslāmī-ye see
   Afghanistan
Afghanistan *122 C4 off.* Islamic Republic
   of Afghanistan, *Per.* Dowlat-e Eslāmī-ye
   Afghānestān; *prev.* Republic of
   Afghanistan. *country* C Asia
Afmadow *73 D6* Jubbada Hoose,
   S Somalia
Africa *68 continent*
Africa, Horn of *68 E4 physical region*
   Ethiopia/Somalia
Africana Seamount *141 A6 seamount*
   SW Indian Ocean
'Afrīn *118 B2* Ḥalab, N Syria
Afyon *116 B3 prev.* Afyonkarahisar.
   Afyon, W Turkey
Agadès see Agadez
Agadez *75 G3 prev.* Agadès. Agadez,
   C Niger
Agadir *70 B3* SW Morocco
Agana/Agaña see Hagåtña
Ägaro *73 C5* Oromīya, C Ethiopia
Agassiz Fracture Zone *143 G5 fracture*
   zone S Pacific Ocean
Agatha see Agde
Agathónisi *105 D6 island* Dodekánisa,
   Greece, Aegean Sea
Agde *91 C6 anc.* Agatha. Hérault,
   S France
Agedabia see Ajdābiyā
Agen *91 B5 anc.* Aginnum.
   Lot-et-Garonne, SW France
Agendicum see Sens
Aghri Dagh see Büyükağrı Dağı
Agia *104 B4 var.* Ayiá. Thessalía,
   C Greece
Agialoúsa see Yenierenköy
Agía Marína *105 E6* Léros, Dodekánisa,
   Greece, Aegean Sea
Aginnum see Agen
Ágios Efstrátios *104 D4 var.* Áyios
   Evstrátios, Hagios Evstrátios. *island*
   E Greece
Ágios Nikólaos *105 D8 var.* Áyios
   Nikólaos. Kríti, Greece,
   E Mediterranean Sea
Āgra *134 D3* Uttar Pradesh, N India
Agra and Oudh, United Provinces of see
   Uttar Pradesh
Agram see Zagreb
Ağrı *117 F3 var.* Karaköse; *prev.*
   Karakilisse. Ağrı, NE Turkey
Agri Dagi see Büyükağrı Dağı
Agrigento *97 C7 Gk.* Akragas; *prev.*
   Girgenti. Sicilia, Italy,
   C Mediterranean Sea
Agriovótano *105 C5* Évvoia,
   C Greece
Agropoli *97 D5* Campania, S Italy
Aguachica *58 B2* Cesar, N Colombia
Aguadulce *53 F5* Coclé, S Panama
Agua Prieta *50 B1* Sonora,
   NW Mexico

Aguascalientes *50 D4* Aguascalientes,
   C Mexico
Aguaytía *60 C3* Ucayali, C Peru
Aguilas *93 E4* Murcia, SE Spain
Aguililla *50 D4* Michoacán,
   SW Mexico
Agulhas Basin *69 D8 undersea basin*
   SW Indian Ocean
Agulhas, Cape *78 C5 headland*
   SW South Africa
Agulhas Plateau *67 D6 undersea plateau*
   SW Indian Ocean
Ahaggar *75 F2 high plateau region*
   SE Algeria
Ahlen *94 B4* Nordrhein-Westfalen,
   W Germany
Ahmadābād *134 C4 var.* Ahmedabad.
   Gujarāt, W India
Ahmadnagar *134 C5 var.* Ahmednagar.
   Mahārāshtra, W India
Ahmedabad see Ahmadābād
Ahmednagar see Ahmadnagar
Ahuachapán *52 B3* Ahuachapán,
   W El Salvador
Ahvāz *120 C3 var.* Ahwāz; *prev.* Nāsiri.
   Khūzestān, SW Iran
Ahvenanmaa see Åland
Ahwāz see Ahvāz
Aigaíon Pelagos/Aigaío Pélagos see
   Aegean Sea
Aígina *105 C6 var.* Aíyina, Egina.
   Aígina, C Greece
Aígio *105 B5 var.* Egio; *prev.* Aíyion.
   Dytikí Elláda, S Greece
Aiken *43 E2* South Carolina, SE USA
Ailinglaplap Atoll *144 D2 var.*
   Aelönlaplap. *atoll* Ralik Chain,
   S Marshall Islands
Ailuk Atoll *144 D1 var.* Aelok. *atoll*
   Ratak Chain, NE Marshall Islands
Ainaži *106 D3 Est.* Heinaste, *Ger.*
   Hainasch. N Latvia
'Aïn Ben Tili *74 D1* Tiris Zemmour,
   N Mauritania
Aintab see Gaziantep
Aïoun el Atrous/Aïoun el Atroûss see
   'Ayoûn el 'Atroûs
Aiquile *61 F4* Cochabamba, C Bolivia
Aïr see Aïr, Massif de l'
Air du Azbine see Aïr, Massif de l'
Aïr, Massif de l' *75 G2 var.* Aïr, Air du
   Azbine, Asben. *mountain range*
   NC Niger
Aiud *108 B4 Ger.* Strassburg, *Hung.*
   Nagyenyed; *prev.* Engeten. Alba,
   SW Romania
Aix see Aix-en-Provence
Aix-en-Provence *91 D6 var.* Aix; *anc.*
   Aquae Sextiae. Bouches-du-Rhône,
   SE France
Aix-la-Chapelle see Aachen
Aíyina see Aígina
Aíyion see Aígio
Aizkraukle *106 C4* S Latvia
Ajaccio *91 E7* Corse, France,
   C Mediterranean Sea
Ajaria *117 F2 prev.* Achara, Ach'ara.
   autonomous republic SW Georgia
Ajastan see Armenia
Aj Bogd Uul *126 D2 mountain*
   SW Mongolia
Ajdābiyā *71 G2 var.* Agedabia,
   Ajdâbiyah. NE Libya
Ajdâbiyah see Ajdābiyā
Ajjinena see El Geneina
Ajmer *134 D3 var.* Ajmere. Rājasthān,
   N India
Ajmere see Ajmer
Ajo *48 A3* Arizona, SW USA
Akaba see Al 'Aqabah
Akamagaseki see Shimonoseki
Akasha *72 B3* Northern, N Sudan
Akchâr *74 C2 desert* W Mauritania
Aken see Aachen
Akermanceaster see Bath
Akhaltsikhe *117 F2 prev.* Akhalts'ikhe.
   SW Georgia
Akhalts'ikhe see Akhaltsikhe
Akhisar *116 A3* Manisa, W Turkey
Akhmîm *72 B2 var.* Akhmîm; *anc.*
   Panopolis. C Egypt
Akhtubinsk *111 C7* Astrakhanskaya
   Oblast', SW Russia
Akhtyrka see Okhtyrka
Akimiski Island *38 C3 island* Nunavut,
   C Canada
Akinovka *109 F4* Zaporiz'ka Oblast',
   S Ukraine
Akita *130 D4* Akita, Honshū, C Japan
Akjoujt *74 C2 prev.* Fort-Repoux.
   Inchiri, W Mauritania

Akkeshi 130 E2 Hokkaidō, NE Japan
Aklavik 36 D3 Northwest Territories, NW Canada
Akmola see Astana
Akmolinsk see Astana
Aknavásár see Târgu Ocna
Akpatok Island 39 E1 island Nunavut, E Canada
Akragas see Agrigento
Akron 40 D4 Ohio, N USA
Akrotiri see Akrotírion
Akrotírion 102 C5 var. Akrotiri. UK air base S Cyprus
Aksai Chin 124 B2 Chin. Aksayqin. disputed region China/India
Aksaray 116 C4 Aksaray, C Turkey
Aksayqin see Aksai Chin
Akşehir 116 B4 Konya, W Turkey
Aktash see Oqtosh
Aktau 114 A4 Kaz. Aqtaū; prev. Shevchenko. Mangistau, W Kazakhstan
Aktjubinsk/Aktyubinsk see Aktobe
Aktobe 114 B4 Kaz. Aqtöbe; prev. Aktjubinsk, Aktyubinsk. Aktyubinsk, NW Kazakhstan
Aktsyabrski 107 C7 Rus. Oktyabr'skiy; prev. Karpilovka. Homyel'skaya Voblasts', SE Belarus
Aktyubinsk see Aktobe
Akula 77 C5 Equateur, NW Dem. Rep. Congo
Akureyri 83 E4 Nordhurland Eystra, N Iceland
Akyab see Sittwe
Alabama 42 C2 off. State of Alabama, also known as Camellia State, Heart of Dixie, The Cotton State, Yellowhammer State. state S USA
Alabama River 42 C3 river Alabama, S USA
Alaca 116 C3 Çorum, N Turkey
Alacant see Alicante
Alagoas 63 G2 off. Estado de Alagoas. state/region E Brazil
Alais see Alès
Alajuela 53 E4 Alajuela, C Costa Rica
Alakanuk 36 C2 Alaska, USA
Al 'Alamayn 72 B1 var. El 'Alamein. N Egypt
Al 'Amārah 120 C4 var. Amara. Maysān, E Iraq
Alamo 47 D6 Nevada, W USA
Alamogordo 48 D3 New Mexico, SW USA
Alamosa 44 C5 Colorado, C USA
Åland Islands 85 C6 var. Åland Islands, Fin. Ahvenanmaa. island group SW Finland
Aland Islands see Åland
Åland Sea 85 C6 var. Åland Sea. strait Baltic Sea/Gulf of Bothnia
Aland Sea see Ålands Hav
Alanya 116 C4 Antalya, S Turkey
Alappuzha 132 C3 var. Alleppey. Kerala, SW India
Al 'Aqabah 119 B8 var. Akaba, Aqaba, 'Aqaba; anc. Aelana, Elath. Al 'Aqabah, SW Jordan
Alasca, Golfo de see Alaska, Gulf of
Alaşehir 116 A4 Manisa, W Turkey
Al 'Ashārah 118 E3 var. Ashara. Dayr az Zawr, E Syria
Alaska 36 C3 off. State of Alaska, also known as Land of the Midnight Sun, The Last Frontier, Seward's Folly; prev. Russian America. state NW USA
Alaska, Gulf of 36 C4 var. Golfo de Alasca. gulf Canada/USA
Alaska Peninsula 36 C3 peninsula Alaska, USA
Alaska Range 34 B2 mountain range Alaska, USA
Al-Asnam see Chlef
Alattio see Alta
Al Awaynāt see Al 'Uwaynāt
Alaykel'/Alay-Kuu see Kök-Art
Al 'Aynā 119 B7 Al Karak, W Jordan
Alazeya 115 G2 river NE Russia
Al Bāb 118 B2 Ḥalab, N Syria
Albacete 93 E3 Castilla-La Mancha, C Spain
Al Baghdādī 120 B3 var. Khan al Baghdādī. Al Anbār, SW Iraq
Al Bāha see Al Bāha
Al Bāḥah 121 B5 var. Al Bāha. Al Bāḥaḥ, SW Saudi Arabia
Al Baḥrayn see Bahrain

Alba Iulia 108 B4 Ger. Weissenburg, Hung. Gyulafehérvár; prev. Bálgrad, Karlsburg, Károly-Fehérvár. Alba, W Romania
Albania 101 C7 off. Republic of Albania, Alb. Republika e Shqipërisë, Shqipëria; prev. People's Socialist Republic of Albania. country SE Europe
Albania see Aubagne
Albany 147 B7 Western Australia
Albany 41 F3 state capital New York, NE USA
Albany 46 B3 Oregon, NW USA
Albany 38 C3 river Ontario, S Canada
Alba Regia see Székesfehérvár
Al Bāridah 118 C4 var. Bāridah. C Syria
Al Başrah 120 C3 Eng. Basra, hist. Busra, Bussora. Al Başrah, SE Iraq
Al Batrūn see Batroûn
Al Bawiti 72 B2 var. Bawiti, Bawiṭi. C Egypt
Al Bayḍā' 71 G2 var. Beida. NE Libya
Albemarle Island see Isabela, Isla
Albemarle Sound 43 G1 inlet W Atlantic Ocean
Albergaria-a-Velha 92 B2 Aveiro, N Portugal
Albert 90 C3 Somme, N France
Alberta 37 E4 province SW Canada
Albert Edward Nyanza see Edward, Lake
Albert, Lake 73 B6 var. Albert Nyanza, Lac Mobutu Sese Seko. lake Uganda/Dem. Rep. Congo
Albert Lea 45 F3 Minnesota, N USA
Albert Nyanza see Albert, Lake
Albertville see Kalemie
Albi 91 C6 anc. Albiga. Tarn, S France
Albiga see Albi
Ålborg see Aalborg
Ålborg-Nørresundby see Aalborg
Albuquerque 48 D2 New Mexico, SW USA
Al Burayqah see Marsá al Burayqah
Alburgum see Aalborg
Albury 149 C7 New South Wales, SE Australia
Alcácer do Sal 92 B4 Setúbal, W Portugal
Alcalá de Henares 93 E3 Ar. Alkal'a; anc. Complutum. Madrid, C Spain
Alcamo 97 C7 Sicilia, Italy, C Mediterranean Sea
Alcañiz 93 F2 Aragón, NE Spain
Alcántara, Embalse de 92 C3 reservoir W Spain
Alcaudete 92 D4 Andalucía, S Spain
Alcázar see Ksar-el-Kebir
Alcazarquivir see Ksar-el-Kebir
Alcoi see Alcoy
Alcoy 93 F4 Cat. Alcoi. Valenciana, E Spain
Aldabra Group 79 G2 island group SW Seychelles
Aldan 115 F3 river NE Russia
al Dar al Baida see Rabat
Alderney 90 A2 island Channel Islands
Aleg 74 C3 Brakna, SW Mauritania
Aleksandriya see Aliákmonas
Aleksandropol' see Gyumri
Aleksandrovsk see Oleksandriva
Aleksandrovsk see Zaporizhzhya
Aleksin 111 B5 Tul'skaya Oblast', W Russia
Aleksinac 100 E4 Serbia, SE Serbia
Alençon 90 B3 Orne, N France
Alenquer 63 E2 Pará, NE Brazil
Alep/Aleppo see Ḥalab
Alert 37 F1 Ellesmere Island, Nunavut, N Canada
Alès 91 C6 prev. Alais. Gard, S France
Aleşd 108 B3 Hung. Élesd. Bihor, SW Romania
Alessandria 96 B2 Fr. Alexandrie. Piemonte, N Italy
Ålesund 85 A5 Møre og Romsdal, S Norway
Aleutian Basin 113 G3 undersea basin Bering Sea
Aleutian Islands 36 A3 island group Alaska, USA
Aleutian Range 34 A2 mountain range Alaska, USA
Aleutian Trench 113 H3 trench S Bering Sea
Alexander Archipelago 36 D4 island group Alaska, USA
Alexander City 42 D2 Alabama, S USA

Alexander Island 154 A3 island Antarctica
Alexander Range see Kirghiz Range
Alexandra 151 B7 Otago, South Island, New Zealand
Alexándreia 104 B4 var. Alexándria. Kentrikí Makedonía, N Greece
Alexandretta see İskenderun
Alexandretta, Gulf of see İskenderun Körfezi
Alexandria 72 B1 Ar. Al Iskandarīyah. N Egypt
Alexandria 108 C5 Teleorman, S Romania
Alexandria 42 B3 Louisiana, S USA
Alexandria 45 F2 Minnesota, N USA
Alexándria see Alexándreia
Alexandrie see Alessandria
Alexandroúpoli 104 D4 var. Alexandroúpolis, Turk. Dedeagaç, Dedeagach. Anatolikí Makedonía kai Thráki, NE Greece
Alexandroúpolis see Alexandroúpoli
Al Fāshir see El Fasher
Alfatar 104 D1 Silistra, NE Bulgaria
Alfeiós 105 B6 prev. Alfiós; anc. Alpheius, Alpheus. river S Greece
Alfiós see Alfeiós
Alföld see Great Hungarian Plain
Al-Furāt see Euphrates
Alga 114 B4 Kaz. Algha. Aktyubinsk, NW Kazakhstan
Algarve 92 B4 cultural region S Portugal
Algeciras 92 C5 Andalucía, SW Spain
Algemesí 93 F3 Valenciana, E Spain
Al-Genain see El Geneina
Alger 71 E1 var. Algiers, El Djazaïr, Al Jazair. country capital (Algeria) N Algeria
Algeria 70 C3 off. Democratic and Popular Republic of Algeria. country N Africa
Algeria, Democratic and Popular Republic of see Algeria
Algerian Basin 80 C5 var. Balearic Plain. undersea basin W Mediterranean Sea
Algha see Alga
Al Ghābah 121 E5 var. Ghaba. C Oman
Al Ghardaqah 72 C2 var. Hurghada, Ghurdaqah. E Egypt
Alghero 97 A5 Sardegna, Italy, C Mediterranean Sea
Algiers see Alger
Al Golea see El Goléa
Algona 45 F3 Iowa, C USA
Al Hajar al Gharbi 121 D5 mountain range N Oman
Al Hamad see Syrian Desert
Al Ḥasakah 118 E2 var. Al Hasijah, El Haseke, Fr. Hassetché. Al Ḥasakah, NE Syria
Al Hasijah see Al Ḥasakah
Al Ḥillah 120 B3 var. Hilla. Bābil, C Iraq
Al Ḥişā 119 B7 Aṭ Ṭafīlah, W Jordan
Al Ḥudaydah 121 B6 Eng. Hodeida. W Yemen
Al Hufūf 120 C4 var. Hofuf. Ash Sharqīyah, NE Saudi Arabia
Aliákmon see Aliákmonas
Aliákmonas 104 B4 prev. Aliákmon; anc. Haliacmon. river N Greece
Aliartos 105 C5 Stereá Elláda, C Greece
Alicante 93 F4 Cat. Alacant, Lat. Lucentum. Valenciana, SE Spain
Alice 49 G5 Texas, SW USA
Alice Springs 148 A4 Northern Territory, C Australia
Alifu Atoll see Ari Atoll
Aligandi 53 G4 Kuna Yala, NE Panama
Aliki see Alykí
Alima 77 B6 river C Congo
Al Imārāt al 'Arabīyah al Muttaḥidah see United Arab Emirates
Alindao 76 C4 Basse-Kotto, S Central African Republic
Aliquippa 40 D4 Pennsylvania, NE USA
Al Iskandarīyah see Alexandria
Al Ismā'īlīya 72 B1 var. Ismailia, Ismâ'ilîya. N Egypt
Alistráti 104 C3 Kentrikí Makedonía, NE Greece
Alivéri 105 C5 var. Alivérion. Évvoia, C Greece
Alivérion see Alivéri
Al Jabal al Akhḍar 71 G2 mountain range NE Libya

Al Jaghbūb 71 H3 NE Libya
Al Jahrā' 120 C4 var. Al Jahrah, Jahra. C Kuwait
Al Jahrah see Al Jahrā'
Al Jamāhīrīyah al 'Arabīyah al Lībīyah ash Sha'bīyah al Ishtirākīy see Libya
Al Jawf 120 B4 off. Jauf. Al Jawf, NW Saudi Arabia
Al Jawlān see Golan Heights
Al Jazair see Alger
Al Jazīrah 118 E2 physical region Iraq/Syria
Al Jīzah see Giza
Al Junaynah see El Geneina
Alkal'a see Alcalá de Henares
Al Karak 119 B7 var. El Kerak, Karak, Kerak; anc. Kir Moab, Kir of Moab. Al Karak, W Jordan
Al-Kasr al-Kebir see Ksar-el-Kebir
Al Khalil see Hebron
Al Khārijah 72 B2 var. El Khârga, Kharga. C Egypt
Al Khums 71 F2 var. Homs, Khoms, Khums. NW Libya
Alkmaar 86 C2 Noord-Holland, NW Netherlands
Al Kufrah 71 H4 SE Libya
Al Kūt 120 C3 var. Kūt al 'Amārah, Kut al Imara. Wāsiṭ, E Iraq
Al-Kuwait see Al Kuwayt
Al Kuwayt 120 C4 var. Al-Kuwait, Eng. Kuwait, Kuwait City; prev. Qurein. country capital (Kuwait) E Kuwait
Al Lādhiqīyah 118 A3 Eng. Latakia, Fr. Lattaquié; anc. Ladicea, Laodicea ad Mare. Al Lādhiqīyah, W Syria
Allahābād 135 E3 Uttar Pradesh, N India
Allanmyo see Aunglan
Allegheny Plateau 41 E3 mountain range New York/Pennsylvania, NE USA
Allenstein see Olsztyn
Allentown 41 F4 Pennsylvania, NE USA
Alleppey see Alappuzha
Alliance 44 D3 Nebraska, C USA
Al Līth 121 B5 Makkah, SW Saudi Arabia
Al Lubnān see Lebanon
Alma-Ata see Almaty
Almada 92 B4 Setúbal, W Portugal
Al Madīnah 121 A5 Eng. Medina. Al Madīnah, W Saudi Arabia
Al Mafraq 119 B6 var. Mafraq. N Jordan
Al Mahdīyah see Mahdia
Al Mahrah 121 C6 mountain range E Yemen
Al Majma'ah 120 B4 Ar Riyāḍ, C Saudi Arabia
Al Mālikīyah 118 E1 var. Malkiye. Al Ḥasakah, N Syria
Almalyk see Olmaliq
Al Mamlakah see Morocco
Al Mamlaka al Urdunīya al Hashemīyah see Jordan
Al Manāmah 120 C4 Eng. Manama. country capital (Bahrain) N Bahrain
Al Manāşif 118 E3 mountain range E Syria
Almansa 93 F4 Castilla-La Mancha, C Spain
Al-Mariyya see Almería
Al Marj 71 G2 var. Barka, It. Barce. NE Libya
Almaty 114 C5 var. Alma-Ata. Almaty, SE Kazakhstan
Al Mawşil 120 B2 Eng. Mosul. Nīnawá, N Iraq
Al Mayādīn 118 D3 var. Mayadin, Fr. Meyadine. Dayr az Zawr, E Syria
Al Mazra' see Al Mazra'ah
Al Mazra'ah 119 B6 var. Al Mazra', Al Mazra'. Al Karak, W Jordan
Almelo 86 E3 Overijssel, E Netherlands
Almendra, Embalse de 92 C2 reservoir Castilla y León, NW Spain
Almendralejo 92 C4 Extremadura, W Spain
Almere 86 D3 var. Almere-stad. Flevoland, C Netherlands
Almere-stad see Almere
Almería 93 E5 Ar. Al-Mariyya; anc. Unci, Lat. Portus Magnus. Andalucía, S Spain
Al'met'yevsk 111 D5 Respublika Tatarstan, W Russia
Al Mīnā' see El Mina
Al Minyā 72 B2 var. El Minya, Minya. C Egypt
Almirante 53 E4 Bocas del Toro, NW Panama

Al Mudawwarah 119 B8 Ma'ān, SW Jordan
Al Mukallā 121 C6 var. Mukalla. SE Yemen
Al Obayyid see El Obeid
Alofi 145 F4 dependent territory capital (Niue) W Niue
Aloha State see Hawaii
Aloja 106 D3 N Latvia
Alónnisos 105 C5 island Vóreies Sporádes, Greece, Aegean Sea
Álora 92 D5 Andalucía, S Spain
Alor, Kepulauan 139 E5 island group E Indonesia
Al Oued see El Oued
Alpen see Alps
Alpena 40 D2 Michigan, N USA
Alpes see Alps
Alpha Cordillera 155 B3 var. Alpha Ridge. seamount range Arctic Ocean
Alpha Ridge see Alpha Cordillera
Alpheius see Alfeiós
Alphen see Alphen aan den Rijn
Alphen aan den Rijn 86 C3 var. Alphen. Zuid-Holland, C Netherlands
Alpheus see Alfeiós
Alpi see Alps
Alpine 49 E4 Texas, SW USA
Alps 102 C1 Fr. Alpes, Ger. Alpen, It. Alpi. mountain range C Europe
Al Qaḍārif see Gedaref
Al Qāhirah see Cairo
Al Qāmishlī 118 E1 var. Kamishli, Qamishly. Al Ḥasakah, NE Syria
Al Qaṣrayn see Kasserine
Al Qayrawān see Kairouan
Al-Qsar al-Kbir see Ksar-el-Kebir
Al Qubayyāt see Qoubaïyât
Al Quds/Al Quds ash Sharīf see Jerusalem
Alqueva, Barragem do 92 C4 reservoir Portugal/Spain
Al Qunayṭirah 119 B5 var. El Kuneitra, El Quneitra, Kuneitra, Qunaytra. Al Qunayṭirah, SW Syria
Al Quṣayr 118 B4 var. El Quseir, Quṣayr, Fr. Kousseir. Ḥimṣ, W Syria
Al Quwayrah 119 B8 var. El Quweira. Al 'Aqabah, SW Jordan
Alsace 90 E4 Ger. Elsass; anc. Alsatia. cultural region NE France
Alsatia see Alsace
Alsdorf 94 A4 Nordrhein-Westfalen, W Germany
Alt see Olt
Alta 84 D2 Fin. Alattio. Finnmark, N Norway
Altai see Altai Mountains
Altai Mountains 126 C2 var. Altai, Chin. Altay Shan, Rus. Altay. mountain range Asia/Europe
Altamaha River 43 E3 river Georgia, SE USA
Altamira 63 E2 Pará, NE Brazil
Altamura 97 E5 anc. Lupatia. Puglia, SE Italy
Altar, Desierto de 50 A1 var. Sonoran Desert. desert Mexico/USA
Altar, Desierto de see Sonoran Desert
Altay 126 C2 Xinjiang Uygur Zizhiqu, NW China
Altay 126 D2 prev. Yösönbulag. Govĭ-Altay, W Mongolia
Altay Altai Mountains, Asia/Europe
Altay Shan see Altai Mountains
Altbetsche see Bečej
Altenburg 94 D4 Bucureşti, Romania
Altın Köprü see Altûn Kûbrî
Altiplano 61 F4 physical region W South America
Altkanischa see Kanjiža
Alton 40 B5 Illinois, N USA
Altoona 41 E4 Pennsylvania, NE USA
Alto Paraná see Paraná
Altpasua see Stara Pazova
Alt-Schwanenburg see Gulbene
Altsohl see Zvolen
Altûn Kûbrî see Altûn Köprü. At Ta'mím, N Iraq
Altun Shan 126 C3 var. Altyn Tagh. mountain range NW China
Altus 49 F2 Oklahoma, C USA
Altyn Tagh see Altun Shan
Al Ubayyiḍ see El Obeid
Alūksne 106 D3 Ger. Marienburg. NE Latvia
Al 'Ulā 120 A4 Al Madīnah, NW Saudi Arabia
Al 'Umarī 119 C6 'Ammān, E Jordan

Alupka 109 F5 Avtonomna Respublika Krym, S Ukraine
Al Uqsur see Luxor
Al Urdunn see Jordan
Alushta 109 F5 Avtonomna Respublika Krym, S Ukraine
Al 'Uwaynāt 71 F4 var. Al Awaynāt. SW Libya
Alva 49 F1 Oklahoma, C USA
Alvarado 51 F4 Veracruz-Llave, E Mexico
Alvin 49 H4 Texas, SW USA
Al Wajh 120 A4 Tabūk, NW Saudi Arabia
Alwar 134 D3 Rājasthān, N India
Al Warī'ah 120 C4 Ash Sharqīyah, N Saudi Arabia
Al Yaman see Yemen
Alykí 104 C4 var. Aliki. Thásos, N Greece
Alytus 107 B5 Pol. Olita. Alytus, S Lithuania
Alzette 87 D8 river S Luxembourg
Amadeus, Lake 147 D5 seasonal lake Northern Territory, C Australia
Amadi 73 B5 Western Equatoria, SW South Sudan
Amadjuak Lake 37 G3 lake Baffin Island, Nunavut, N Canada
Amakusa-nada 131 A2 gulf SW Japan
Åmål 85 B6 Västra Götaland, S Sweden
Amami-gunto 130 A3 island group SW Japan
Amami-o-shim 130 A3 island S Japan
Amantea 97 D6 Calabria, SW Italy
Amapá 63 E1 off. Estado de Amapá; prev. Território de Amapá. state/region NE Brazil
Amapá, Estado de see Amapá
Amapá, Território de see Amapá
Amara see Al 'Amārah
Amarapura 136 B3 Mandalay, C Myanmar (Burma)
Amarillo 49 E2 Texas, SW USA
Amay 87 C6 Liège, E Belgium
Amazon 63 E1 Sp. Amazonas. river Brazil/Peru
Amazonas see Amazon
Amazon Basin 62 D2 basin N South America
Amazonia 36 B4 region S Colombia
Amazon, Mouths of the 63 F1 delta NE Brazil
Ambam 77 B5 Sud, S Cameroon
Ambanja 79 G2 Antsiraňana, N Madagascar
Ambarchik 115 G2 Respublika Sakha (Yakutiya), NE Russia
Ambato 60 B1 Tungurahua, C Ecuador
Ambérieu-en-Bugey 91 D5 Ain, E France
Ambianum see Amiens
Amboasary 79 F4 Toliara, S Madagascar
Amboina see Ambon
Ambon 139 F4 prev. Amboina, Amboyna. Pulau Ambon, E Indonesia
Ambositra 79 G3 Fianarantsoa, SE Madagascar
Amboyna see Ambon
Ambracia see Árta
Ambre, Cap d' see Bobaomby, Tanjona
Ambrim see Ambrym
Ambriz 78 A1 Bengo, NW Angola
Ambrym 144 D4 var. Ambrim. island C Vanuatu
Amchitka Island 36 A2 island Aleutian Islands, Alaska, USA
Amdo 126 C5 Xizang Zizhiqu, W China
Ameland 86 D1 Fris. It Amelân. island Waddeneilanden, N Netherlands
Amelàn, It see Ameland
America see United States of America
America-Antarctica Ridge 67 C7 undersea ridge S Atlantic Ocean
America in Miniature see Maryland
American Falls Reservoir 46 E4 reservoir Idaho, NW USA
American Samoa 145 F4 US unincorporated territory W Polynesia
Amersfoort 86 D3 Utrecht, C Netherlands
Ames 45 F3 Iowa, C USA
Amfilochía 105 A5 var. Amfilokhía. Dytikí Elláda, C Greece
Amfilokhía see Amfilochía
Amga 115 F3 river NE Russia
Amherst 39 F4 Nova Scotia, SE Canada
Amherst see Kyaikkami
Amida see Diyarbakır

Amiens 90 C3 anc. Ambianum, Samarobriva. Somme, N France
Amíndaion/Amindeo see Amýntaio
Amindivi Islands 132 A2 island group Lakshadweep, India, N Indian Ocean
Amirante Islands 79 G1 var. Amirantes Group. island group C Seychelles
Amirantes Group see Amirante Islands
Amistad, Presa de la see Amistad Reservoir
Amistad Reservoir 49 F4 var. Presa de la Amistad. reservoir Mexico/USA
Amisus see Samsun
Ammaia see Portalegre
'Amman 119 B6 anc. Philadelphia, Bibl. Rabbah Ammon, Rabbath Ammon. country capital (Jordan) 'Ammān, NW Jordan
Ammassalik 82 D4 var. Angmagssalik. Tunu, S Greenland
Ammóchostos see Gazimağusa
Ammóchostos, Kólpos see Gazimağusa Körfezi
Amnok-kang see Yalu
Amoea see Portalegre
Amoentai see Amuntai
Āmol 120 D2 var. Amul. Māzandarān, N Iran
Amorgós 105 D6 Amorgós, Kykládes, Greece, Aegean Sea
Amorgós 105 D6 island Kykládes, Greece, Aegean Sea
Amos 38 D4 Québec, SE Canada
Amourj 74 D3 Hodh ech Chargui, SE Mauritania
Amoy see Xiamen
Ampato, Nevado 61 E4 mountain S Peru
Amposta 93 F2 Cataluña, NE Spain
Amraoti see Amrāvati
Amrāvati 134 D4 prev. Amraoti. Mahārāshtra, C India
Amritsar 134 D2 Punjab, N India
Amstelveen 86 C3 Noord-Holland, C Netherlands
Amsterdam 86 C3 country capital (Netherlands) Noord-Holland, C Netherlands
Amsterdam Island 141 C6 island NE French Southern and Antarctic Lands
Am Timan 76 C3 Salamat, SE Chad
Amu Darya 122 D2 Rus. Amudar'ya, Taj. Dar''yoi Amu, Turkm. Amyderya, Uzb. Amudaryo; anc. Oxus. river C Asia
Amu-Dar'yk see Amyderya
Amudar'ya/Amudaryo/Amu, Dar''yoi see Amu Darya
Amul see Āmol
Amund Ringnes Island 37 F2 island Nunavut, N Canada
Amundsen Basin 155 C3 prev. Fram Basin. undersea basin Arctic Ocean
Amundsen Plain 154 A4 abyssal plain S Pacific Ocean
Amundsen-Scott 154 B3 US research station Antarctica
Amundsen Sea 154 A4 sea S Pacific Ocean
Amuntai 138 D4 prev. Amoentai. Borneo, C Indonesia
Amur 115 G4 Chin. Heilong Jiang. river China/Russia
Amvrosiyevka see Amvrosiyivka
Amvrosiyivka 109 H3 Rus. Amvrosiyevka. Donets'ka Oblast', SE Ukraine
Amyderya 122 D3 Rus. Amu-Dar'ya. Lebap Welaýaty, NE Turkmenistan
Amyderya see Amu Darya
Amýntaio 104 B4 var. Amíndeo; prev. Amíndaion. Dytikí Makedonía, N Greece
Anabar 115 E2 river NE Russia
An Abhainn Mhór see Blackwater
Anaco 59 E2 Anzoátegui, NE Venezuela
Anaconda 44 B2 Montana, NW USA
Anacortes 46 B1 Washington, NW USA
Anadolu Dağları see Doğu Karadeniz Dağları
Anadyr' 115 H1 Chukotskiy Avtonomnyy Okrug, NE Russia
Anadyr' 115 G1 river NE Russia
Anadyr, Gulf of 115 H1 Eng. Gulf of Anadyr. gulf NE Russia
Anadyr, Gulf of see Anadyrskiy Zaliv
Anáfi 105 D7 anc. Anaphe. island Kykládes, Greece, Aegean Sea

'Ānah see 'Annah
Anaheim 46 E2 California, W USA
Anaiza see 'Unayzah
Analalava 79 G2 Mahajanga, NW Madagascar
Anamur 116 C5 İçel, S Turkey
Anantapur 132 C2 Andhra Pradesh, S India
Anaphe see Anáfi
Anápolis 63 F3 Goiás, C Brazil
Anār 120 D3 Kermān, C Iran
Anatolia 116 C4 plateau C Turkey
Anatom see Aneityum
Añatuya 64 C3 Santiago del Estero, N Argentina
An Bhearú see Barrow
Anchorage 36 C3 Alaska, USA
Ancona 96 C3 Marche, C Italy
Ancud 65 B6 prev. San Carlos de Ancud. Los Lagos, S Chile
Ancyra see Ankara
Åndalsnes 85 A5 Møre og Romsdal, S Norway
Andalucía 92 D4 cultural region S Spain
Andalusia 42 C3 Alabama, S USA
Andaman Islands 124 B4 island group India, NE Indian Ocean
Andaman Sea 124 C4 sea NE Indian Ocean
Andenne 87 C6 Namur, SE Belgium
Anderlues 87 B7 Hainaut, S Belgium
Anderson 40 C4 Indiana, N USA
Andes 64 B3 mountain range W South America
Andhra Pradesh 135 E5 cultural region E India
Andijon 123 F2 Rus. Andizhan. Andijon Viloyati, E Uzbekistan
Andikíthira see Antikýthira
Andipaxoí see Antípaxoi
Andípsara see Antípsara
Andíssa see Ántissa
Andizhan see Andijon
Andkhvóy 122 D3 prev. Andkhvoy. Fāryāb, N Afghanistan
Andorra 91 A7 off. Principality of Andorra, Cat. Valls d'Andorra, Fr. Vallée d'Andorre. country SW Europe
Andorra la Vella 91 A8 var. Andorra, Fr. Andorre la Vielle, Sp. Andorra la Vieja. country capital (Andorra) C Andorra
Andorra la Vieja see Andorra la Vella
Andorra, Principality of see Andorra
Andorra, Valls d'/Andorra, Vallée d' see Andorra
Andorre la Vielle see Andorra la Vella
Andover 89 D7 S England, United Kingdom
Andoya 84 C2 island C Norway
Andreanof Islands 36 A3 island group Aleutian Islands, Alaska, USA
Andrews 49 E3 Texas, SW USA
Andrew Tablemount 140 E4 var. Gora Andryu. seamount W Indian Ocean
Andria 97 D5 Puglia, SE Italy
An Droichead Nua see Newbridge
Andropov see Rybinsk
Ándros 105 D6 Ándros, Kykládes, Greece, Aegean Sea
Ándros 105 C6 island Kykládes, Greece, Aegean Sea
Andros Island 54 B2 island NW The Bahamas
Andros Town 54 C1 Andros Island, NW The Bahamas
Andryu, Gora see Andrew Tablemount
Aneityum 144 D5 var. Anatom; prev. Kéamu. island S Vanuatu
Ånewetak see Enewetak Atoll
Angara 115 E4 river C Russia
Angarsk 115 E4 Irkutskaya Oblast', S Russia
Ånge 85 C5 Västernorrland, C Sweden
Ángel de la Guarda, Isla 50 B2 island NW Mexico
Angeles 139 E1 off. Angeles City. N Philippines
Angeles City see Angeles
Angel Falls 59 E3 Eng. Angel Falls. waterfall E Venezuela
Angel Falls see Ángel, Salto
Angerburg see Węgorzewo
Ångermanälven 84 C4 river N Sweden
Angermünde 94 D3 Brandenburg, NE Germany
Angers 90 B4 anc. Juliomagus. Maine-et-Loire, NW France

Anglesey 89 C5 *island* NW Wales, United Kingdom
Anglet 91 A6 Pyrénées-Atlantiques, SW France
Angleton 49 H4 Texas, SW USA
Anglia *see* England
Anglo-Egyptian Sudan *see* Sudan
Angmagssalik *see* Ammassalik
Ang Nam Ngum 136 C4 *lake* C Laos
Angola 78 B2 *off.* Republic of Angola; *prev.* People's Republic of Angola, Portuguese West Africa. *country* SW Africa
Angola Basin 69 B5 *undersea basin* E Atlantic Ocean
Angola, People's Republic of *see* Angola
Angola, Republic of *see* Angola
Angora *see* Ankara
Angostura *see* Ciudad Bolívar
Angostura, Presa de la 51 G5 *reservoir* SE Mexico
Angoulême 91 B5 *anc.* Iculisma. Charente, W France
Angoumois 91 B5 *cultural region* W France
Angra Pequena *see* Lüderitz
Angren 123 F2 Toshkent Viloyati, E Uzbekistan
Anguilla 55 G3 *UK Overseas Territory* E West Indies
Anguilla Cays 54 B2 *islets* SW The Bahamas
Anhui 128 C5 *var.* Anhui Sheng, Anhwei, Wan. *province* E China
AnhuiSheng/Anhwei Wan *see* Anhui
Anicium *see* le Puy
Anina 108 A4 *Ger.* Steierdorf, *Hung.* Stájerlakanina; *prev.* Ştaierdorf-Anina, Steierdorf-Anina, Steyerlak-Anina. Caraş-Severin, SW Romania
Anjou 90 B4 *cultural region* NW France
Anjouan *see* Nzwani
Ankara 116 C3 *prev.* Angora; *anc.* Ancyra. *country capital (Turkey)* Ankara, C Turkey
Ankeny 45 F3 Iowa, C USA
Anklam 94 D2 Mecklenburg-Vorpommern, NE Germany
An Mhuir Cheilteach *see* Celtic Sea
Annaba 71 E1 *prev.* Bône. NE Algeria
An Nafud 120 B4 *desert* NW Saudi Arabia
'Annah 120 B3 *var.* 'Ānah. Al Anbār, NW Iraq
An Najaf 120 B3 *var.* Najaf. An Najaf, S Iraq
Annamite Mountains 136 D4 *Fr.* Annamitique, Chaîne. *mountain range* C Laos
Annamitique, Chaîne *see* Annamite Mountains
Annamses Cordillera *see* Annamite Mountains
Annapolis 41 F4 *state capital* Maryland, NE USA
Annapurna 135 E3 *mountain* C Nepal
An Nâqûrah *see* En Nâqoûra
Ann Arbor 40 C3 Michigan, N USA
An Năşiriyah 120 C3 *var.* Nasiriya. Dhi Qâr, SE Iraq
Anneciacum *see* Annecy
Annecy 91 D5 *anc.* Anneciacum. Haute-Savoie, E France
An Nil al Abyad *see* White Nile
An Nil al Azraq *see* Blue Nile
Anniston 42 D2 Alabama, S USA
Annotto Bay 54 B4 C Jamaica
An Ómaigh *see* Omagh
Anqing 128 D5 Anhui, E China
Anse La Raye 55 F1 NW Saint Lucia
Anshun 128 B6 Guizhou, S China
Ansongo 75 E3 Gao, E Mali
An Srath Bán *see* Strabane
Antakya 116 D4 *anc.* Antioch, Antiochia. Hatay, S Turkey
Antalaha 79 G2 Antsirañana, NE Madagascar
Antalya 116 B4 *prev.* Adalia; *anc.* Attaleia, *Bibl.* Attalia. Antalya, SW Turkey
Antalya, Gulf of *see* Antalya Körfezi
Antalya, Gulf of 116 B4 *var.* Gulf of Adalia, *Eng.* Gulf of Antalya. *gulf* SW Turkey
Antananarivo 79 G3 *prev.* Tananarive. *country capital (Madagascar)* Antananarivo, C Madagascar
Antarctica 154 B3 *continent*

Antarctic Peninsula 154 A2 *peninsula* Antarctica
Antep *see* Gaziantep
Antequera 92 D5 *anc.* Anticaria, Antiquaria. Andalucía, S Spain
Antequera *see* Oaxaca
Antibes 91 D6 *anc.* Antipolis. Alpes-Maritimes, SE France
Anticaria *see* Antequera
Anticosti, Île d' 39 F3 *Eng.* Anticosti Island. *island* Québec, E Canada
Anticosti Island *see* Anticosti, Île d'
Antigua 55 G3 *island* S Antigua and Barbuda, Leeward Islands
Antigua and Barbuda 55 G3 *country* E West Indies
Antikythira 105 B7 *var.* Andikíthira. *island* S Greece
Anti-Lebanon 118 B4 *var.* Jebel esh Sharqi, *Ar.* Al Jabal ash Sharqi, *Fr.* Anti-Liban. *mountain range* Lebanon/Syria
Anti-Liban *see* Anti-Lebanon
Antioch *see* Antakya
Antiochia *see* Antakya
Antípaxoi 105 A5 *var.* Andipaxi. *island* Iónia Nísiá, Greece, C Mediterranean Sea
Antipodes Islands 142 D5 *island group* S New Zealand
Antipolis *see* Antibes
Antípsara 105 D5 *var.* Andípsara. *island* E Greece
Antiquaria *see* Antequera
Ántissa 105 D5 *var.* Ándissa. Lésvos, E Greece
An tIúr *see* Newry
Antivari *see* Bar
Antofagasta 64 B2 Antofagasta, N Chile
Antony 90 E2 Hauts-de-Seine, N France
An tSionainn *see* Shannon
Antsirañana 79 G2 *province* N Madagascar
Antsohihy 79 G2 Mahajanga, NW Madagascar
An-tung *see* Dandong
Antwerpen 87 C5 *Eng.* Antwerp, *Fr.* Anvers. Antwerpen, N Belgium
Anuradhapura 132 D3 North Central Province, C Sri Lanka
Anvers *see* Antwerpen
Anyang 128 C4 Henan, C China
A'nyêmaqên Shan 126 D4 *mountain range* C China
Anykščiai 106 C4 Utena, E Lithuania
Anzio 97 C5 Lazio, C Italy
Ao Krung Thep 137 C5 *var.* Krung Thep Mahanakhon, *Eng.* Bangkok. *country capital (Thailand)* Bangkok, C Thailand
Aomori 130 D3 Aomori, Honshū, C Japan
Aóos *see* Vjosës, Lumi i
Aoraki 151 B6 *prev.* Aorangi, Mount Cook. *mountain* South Island, New Zealand
Aorangi *see* Aoraki
Aosta 96 A1 *anc.* Augusta Praetoria. Valle d'Aosta, NW Italy
Aoukâr 74 D3 *var.* Aouker. *plateau* C Mauritania
Aouk, Bahr 76 C4 *river* Central African Republic/Chad
Aouker *see* Aoukâr
Aozou 76 C1 Borkou-Ennedi-Tibesti, N Chad
Apalachee Bay 42 D3 *bay* Florida, SE USA
Apalachicola River 42 D3 *river* Florida, SE USA
Apamama *see* Abemama
Apaporis, Río 58 C4 *river* Brazil/Colombia
Apatity 110 C2 Murmanskaya Oblast', NW Russia
Ape 106 D3 NE Latvia
Apeldoorn 86 D3 Gelderland, E Netherlands
Apennines 96 C2 *Eng.* Apennines. *mountain range* Italy/San Marino
Apennines *see* Appennino
Äpia 145 F4 *country capital (Samoa)* Upolu, SE Samoa
Apkhazeti *see* Abkhazia
Ap'khazet'i *see* Abkhazia
Apoera 59 G3 Sipaliwini, NW Suriname
Apostle Islands 40 B1 *island group* Wisconsin, N USA

Appalachian Mountains 35 D5 *mountain range* E USA
Appingedam 86 E1 Groningen, NE Netherlands
Appleton 40 B2 Wisconsin, N USA
Apulia *see* Puglia
Apure, Río 58 C2 *river* W Venezuela
Apurímac, Río 60 D3 *river* S Peru
Aqaba/'Aqaba *see* Al 'Aqabah
Aqaba, Gulf of 120 A4 *var.* Gulf of Elat, *Ar.* Khalīj al 'Aqabah; *anc.* Sinus Aelaniticus. *gulf* NE Red Sea
'Aqabah, Khalīj al *see* Aqaba, Gulf of
Äqchah 123 E3 *var.* Āqcheh. Jowzjān, N Afghanistan
Āqcheh *see* Äqchah
Aqmola *see* Astana
Aqtöbe *see* Aktobe
Aquae Augustae *see* Dax
Aquae Calidae *see* Bath
Aquae Flaviae *see* Chaves
Aquae Grani *see* Aachen
Aquae Sextiae *see* Aix-en-Provence
Aquae Solis *see* Bath
Aquae Tarbelicae *see* Dax
Aquidauana 63 E4 Mato Grosso do Sul, S Brazil
Aquila/Aquila degli Abruzzi *see* L'Aquila
Aquisgranum *see* Aachen
Aquitaine 91 B6 *cultural region* SW France
'Arabah, Wadi al 119 B7 *Heb.* Ha'Arava. *dry watercourse* Israel/Jordan
Arabian Basin 124 A4 *undersea basin* N Arabian Sea
Arabian Desert *see* Şaḥrā' ash Sharqīyah
Arabian Peninsula 121 B5 *peninsula* SW Asia
Arabian Sea 124 A3 *sea* NW Indian Ocean
Arabicus, Sinus *see* Red Sea
'Arabī, Khalīj al *see* Persian Gulf
'Arabīyah as Su'ūdīyah, Al Mamlakah al *see* Saudi Arabia
'Arabīyah Jumhūrīyah, Mişr al *see* Egypt
Arab Republic of Egypt *see* Egypt
Aracaju 63 G3 *state capital* Sergipe, E Brazil
Araçuai 63 F3 Minas Gerais, SE Brazil
Arad 108 A4 Arad, W Romania
Arafura Sea 142 A3 *Ind.* Laut Arafuru. *sea* W Pacific Ocean
Arafuru, Laut *see* Arafura Sea
Aragón 93 E2 *autonomous community* E Spain
Araguaia, Río 63 E3 *var.* Araguaya. *river* C Brazil
Araguaí 63 F3 Minas Gerais, SE Brazil
Araguaya *see* Araguaia, Río
Ara Jovis *see* Aranjuez
Arāk 120 C3 *prev.* Sultānābād. Markazī, W Iran
Arakan Yoma 136 A3 *mountain range* W Myanmar (Burma)
Araks/Arak's *see* Aras
Aral *see* Aralsk, Kazakhstan
Aral Sea 122 C1 *Kaz.* Aral Tengizi, *Rus.* Aral'skoye More, *Uzb.* Orol Dengizi. *inland sea* Kazakhstan/Uzbekistan
Aral'sk 114 B4 *Kaz.* Aral. Kyzylorda, SW Kazakhstan
Aral'skoye More/Aral Tengizi *see* Aral Sea
Aranda de Duero 92 D2 Castilla y León, N Spain
Arandelovac 100 D4 *prev.* Arandjelovac. Serbia, C Serbia
Arandjelovac *see* Arandelovac
Aranjuez 92 D3 *anc.* Ara Jovis. Madrid, C Spain
Araouane 75 E2 Tombouctou, N Mali
'Ar'ar 120 B3 Al Ḩudūd ash Shamālīyah, NW Saudi Arabia
Mount Ararat 117 F3 *var.* Aghri Dagh, Agri Dagi, Koh I Noh, Masis, *Eng.* Great Ararat, Mount Ararat. *mountain* E Turkey
Ararat, Mount *see* Büyükağrı Dağı
Aras 117 G3 *Arm.* Arak's, *Az.* Araz Nehri, *Per.* Rūd-e Aras, *Rus.* Araks; *prev.* Araxes. *river* SW Asia
Aras, Rūd-e *see* Aras
Arauca 58 C2 Arauca, NE Colombia
Arauca, Río 58 C2 *river* Colombia/Venezuela
Arausio *see* Orange

Araxes *see* Aras
Araz Nehri *see* Aras
Arbela *see* Arbil
Arbil 120 B2 *var.* Erbil, Irbīl, *Kurd.* Hewlêr; *anc.* Arbela. Arbil, N Iraq
Arbroath 88 D3 *anc.* Aberbrothock. E Scotland, United Kingdom
Arbuzinka *see* Arbuzynka
Arbuzynka 109 E3 *Rus.* Arbuzinka. Mykolayivs'ka Oblast', S Ukraine
Arcachon 91 B5 Gironde, SW France
Arcae Remorum *see* Châlons-en-Champagne
Arcata 46 A4 California, W USA
Archangel *see* Arkhangel'sk
Archangel Bay *see* Chëshskaya Guba
Archidona 92 D5 Andalucía, S Spain
Arco 96 C2 Trentino-Alto Adige, N Italy
Arctic Mid Oceanic Ridge *see* Gakkel Ridge
Arctic Ocean 155 B3 *ocean*
Arda 104 C3 *var.* Ardhas, *Gk.* Ardas. *river* Bulgaria/Greece
Ardabīl 120 C2 *var.* Ardebil. Ardabīl, NW Iran
Ardakān 120 D3 Yazd, C Iran
Ardas 104 D3 *var.* Ardhas, *Bul.* Arda. *river* Bulgaria/Greece
Arḍ aş Şawwān 119 C7 *var.* Ardh es Suwwân. *plain* S Jordan
Ardeal *see* Transylvania
Ardebil *see* Ardabīl
Ardèche 91 C5 *cultural region* E France
Ardennes 87 C8 *physical region* Belgium/France
Ardhas *see* Arda/Ardas
Ardh es Suwwân *see* Arḍ aş Şawwān
Ardino 104 D3 Kŭrdzhali, S Bulgaria
Ard Mhacha *see* Armagh
Ardmore 49 G2 Oklahoma, C USA
Arel *see* Arlon
Arelas/Arelate *see* Arles
Arendal 85 A6 Aust-Agder, S Norway
Arensburg *see* Kuressaare
Arenys de Mar 93 G2 Cataluña, NE Spain
Areópoli 105 B7 *prev.* Areópolis. Pelopónnisos, S Greece
Areópolis *see* Areópoli
Arequipa 61 E4 Arequipa, SE Peru
Arezzo 96 C3 *anc.* Arretium. Toscana, C Italy
Argalastí 105 C5 Thessalía, C Greece
Argenteuil 90 D1 Val-d'Oise, N France
Argentina 65 B5 *off.* Argentine Republic. *country* S South America
Argentina Basin *see* Argentine Basin
Argentine Basin 57 C7 *var.* Argentina Basin. *undersea basin* SW Atlantic Ocean
Argentine Republic *see* Argentina
Argentine Rise *see* Falkland Plateau
Argentoratum *see* Strasbourg
Darya-ye Arghandab 123 E5 *river* SE Afghanistan
Argirocastro *see* Gjirokastër
Argo 72 B3 Northern, N Sudan
Argo Fracture Zone 141 C5 *tectonic feature* C Indian Ocean
Árgos 105 B6 Pelopónnisos, S Greece
Argostóli 105 A5 *var.* Argostólion. Kefallonía, Iónia Nísiá, Greece, C Mediterranean Sea
Argostólion *see* Argostóli
Argun 125 E1 *Chin.* Ergun He, *Rus.* Argun'. *river* China/Russia
Argyrokastron *see* Gjirokastër
Århus *see* Aarhus
Aria *see* Herāt
Ari Atoll 132 A4 *var.* Alifu Atoll. *atoll* C Maldives
Arica 64 B1 *hist.* San Marcos de Arica. Arica y Parinacota, N Chile
Aridaía 104 B3 *var.* Aridea, Aridhaía. Dytikí Makedonía, N Greece
Aridea *see* Aridaía
Aridhaía *see* Aridaía
Arīhā 118 B3 Al Karak, W Jordan
Arīḩā *see* Jericho
Ariminum *see* Rimini
Arinsal 91 A7 NW Andorra Europe
Arizona 48 A2 *off.* State of Arizona, *also known as* Copper State, Grand Canyon State. *state* SW USA
Arkansas 42 A1 *off.* State of Arkansas, *also known as* The Land of Opportunity. *state* S USA

Arkansas City *45 F5* Kansas, C USA
Arkansas River *49 G1* river C USA
Arkhangel'sk *114 B2* Eng. Archangel.
  Arkhangel'skaya Oblast', NW Russia
Arkoí *105 E6* island Dodekánisa, Greece,
  Aegean Sea
Arles *91 D6* var. Arles-sur-Rhône; anc.
  Arelas, Arelate. Bouches-du-Rhône,
  SE France
Arles-sur-Rhône see Arles
Arlington *49 G2* Texas, SW USA
Arlington *41 E4* Virginia, NE USA
Arlon *87 D8* Dut. Aarlen, Ger. Arel,
  Lat. Orolaunum. Luxembourg,
  SE Belgium
Armagh *89 B5* Ir. Ard Mhacha.
  S Northern Ireland, United Kingdom
Armagnac *91 B6* cultural region
  S France
Armenia *58 B3* Quindío, W Colombia
Armenia *117 F3* off. Republic of
  Armenia, var. Ajastan, Arm. Hayastani
  Hanrapetut'yun; prev. Armenian Soviet
  Socialist Republic. country SW Asia
Armenian Soviet Socialist Republic see
  Armenia
Armenia, Republic of see Armenia
Armidale *149 D6* New South Wales,
  SE Australia
Armstrong *38 B3* Ontario, S Canada
Armyans'k *109 F4* Rus. Armyansk.
  Avtonomna Respublika Krym,
  S Ukraine
Arnaia *104 C4* Cont. Arnea. Kentrikí
  Makedonía, N Greece
Arnaud *82 A3* river Québec, E Canada
Arnea see Arnaía
Arnedo *93 E2* La Rioja, N Spain
Arnhem *86 D4* Gelderland,
  SE Netherlands
Arnhem Land *148 A2* physical region
  Northern Territory, N Australia
Arno *96 B3* river C Italy
Arnold *45 G4* Missouri, C USA
Arnswalde see Choszczno
Aroe Islands see Aru, Kepulauan
Arorae *145 E3* atoll Tungaru, W Kiribati
Arrabona see Győr
Ar Rahad see Er Rahad
Ar Ramādī *120 B3* var. Ramadi,
  Rumadiya. Al Anbār, SW Iraq
Ar Rāmī *118 C4* Hïms, C Syria
Ar Ramthā *119 B5* var. Ramtha. Irbid,
  N Jordan
Arran, Isle of *88 C4* island SW Scotland,
  United Kingdom
Ar Raqqah *118 C2* var. Rakka, Raqqa;
  anc. Nicephorium. Ar Raqqah,
  N Syria
Arras *90 C2* anc. Nemetocenna.
  Pas-de-Calais, N France
Ar Rawdatayn *120 C4* var. Raudhatain.
  N Kuwait
Arretium see Arezzo
Arriaca see Guadalajara
Arriaga *51 G5* Chiapas, SE Mexico
Ar Riyād *121 C5* Eng. Riyadh. country
  capital (Saudi Arabia) Ar Riyād,
  C Saudi Arabia
Ar Rub 'al Khali *121 C6* Eng. Empty
  Quarter, Great Sandy Desert. desert
  SW Asia
Ar Rustāq *121 E5* var. Rostak, Rustaq.
  N Oman
Ar Rutbah *120 B3* var. Rutba. Al Anbār,
  SW Iraq
Árta *105 A5* anc. Ambracia. Ípeiros,
  W Greece
Artashat *117 F3* S Armenia
Artemisa *54 B2* La Habana, W Cuba
Artesia *48 D3* New Mexico, SW USA
Arthur's Pass *151 C6* pass South Island,
  New Zealand
Artigas *64 D3* prev. San Eugenio, San
  Eugenio del Cuareim. Artigas,
  N Uruguay
Art'ik *117 F2* W Armenia
Artois *90 C2* cultural region N France
Artsiz see Artsyz
Artsyz *108 D4* Rus. Artsiz. Odes'ka
  Oblast', SW Ukraine
Arturo Prat *154 A2* Chilean research
  station South Shetland Islands,
  Antarctica
Artvin *117 F2* Artvin, NE Turkey
Arua *73 B6* NW Uganda
Aruba *58 C1* var. Oruba. Self-governing
  country of the Netherlands
  S West Indies
Aru Islands see Aru, Kepulauan

Aru, Kepulauan *139 G4* Eng. Aru
  Islands; prev. Aroe Islands. island
  group E Indonesia
Arunāchal Pradesh *135 G3* prev. North
  East Frontier Agency, North East
  Frontier Agency of Assam. cultural
  region NE India
Arusha *73 C7* Arusha, N Tanzania
Arviat *37 G4* prev. Eskimo Point.
  Nunavut, C Canada
Arvidsjaur *84 C4* Norrbotten, N Sweden
'Arys' *114 B5* prev. Arys'. Yuzhnyy
  Kazakhstan, S Kazakhstan
Arys' see 'Arys'
Asadābād *123 F4* var. Asadābād; prev.
  Chaghasarāy. Kunar, E Afghanistan
Asadābād see Asadābād
Asahi-dake *130 D2* mountain Hokkaidō,
  N Japan
Asahikawa *130 D2* Hokkaidō, N Japan
Asamankese *75 E5* SE Ghana
Āsānsol *135 F4* West Bengal, NE India
Asben see Aïr, Massif de l'
Ascension Fracture Zone *69 A5* tectonic
  Feature C Atlantic Ocean
Ascension Island see St Helena,
  Ascension and Tristan da Cunha
Ascoli Piceno *96 C4* anc. Asculum
  Picenum. Marche, C Italy
Asculum Picenum see Ascoli Piceno
'Aseb *72 D4* var. Assab, Amh. Āseb.
  SE Eritrea
Assen *86 E2* Drenthe, NE Netherlands
A Serra de Outes *92 B1* Galicia,
  NW Spain
Aşgabat *122 C3* prev. Ashgabat,
  Ashkhabad, Poltoratsk. country capital
  (Turkmenistan) Ahal Welaýaty,
  C Turkmenistan
Ashara see Al 'Ashārah
Ashburton *151 C6* Canterbury, South
  Island, New Zealand
Ashburton River *146 A4* river
  Western Australia
Ashdod *119 A6* anc. Azotos, Lat. Azotus.
  Central, W Israel
Asheville *43 E1* North Carolina, SE USA
Ashgabat see Aşgabat
Ashkelon *119 A6* prev. Ashqelon.
  Southern, C Israel
Ashkhabad see Aşgabat
Ashland *46 B4* Oregon, NW USA
Ashland *40 B1* Wisconsin, N USA
Ashmore and Cartier Islands *142 A3*
  Australian external territory E
  Indian Ocean
Ashmyany *107 C5* Rus. Oshmyany.
  Hrodzyenskaya Voblasts', W Belarus
Ashqelon see Ashkelon
Ash Shaddādah *118 D2* var. Ash
  Shaddādah, Jisr ash Shadadi, Shaddādī,
  Shedadi, Tell Shedadi. Al Ḥasakah,
  NE Syria
Ash Shaddādah see Ash Shadādah
Ash Sharah *119 B7* var. Esh Sharā.
  mountain range W Jordan
Ash Shāriqah *120 D4* Eng. Sharjah. Ash
  Shāriqah, NE United Arab Emirates
Ash Shawbak *119 B7* Ma'ān, W Jordan
Ash Shiḩr *121 C6* SE Yemen
Asia *112* continent
Asinara *96 A4* island W Italy
Asipovichy *107 D6* Rus. Osipovichi.
  Mahilyowskaya Voblasts', C Belarus
Aşkale *117 E3* Erzurum, NE Turkey
Askersund *85 C6* Örebro, C Sweden
Asmara see Asmera
Asmera *72 C4* var. Asmara. country
  capital (Eritrea) C Eritrea
Aspadana see Eşfahān
Asphaltites, Lacus see Dead Sea
Aspinwall see Colón
Assab see 'Aseb
As Sabkhah *118 D2* var. Sabkha. Ar
  Raqqah, NE Syria
Assad, Lake *118 C2* Eng. Lake Assad.
  lake N Syria
Aş Şafāwī *119 C6* Al Mafraq, N Jordan
Aş Şaḥrā' ash Sharqīyah see
  Sahara el Sharqīya
As Salamīyah see Salamīyah
'Assal, Lac *68 E4* lake C Djibouti
As Salṭ *119 B6* var. Salt. Al Balqā',
  NW Jordan
Assamaka see Assamakka
Assamakka *75 F2* var. Assamaka.
  Agadez, NW Niger
As Samāwah *120 B3* var. Samawa. Al
  Muthanná, S Iraq

Assenede *87 B5* Oost-Vlaanderen,
  NW Belgium
Assiout see Asyūṭ
Assiut see Asyūṭ
Assling see Jesenice
Assouan see Aswān
Assu *63 G2* var. Açu. Rio Grande do
  Norte, E Brazil
Assuan see Aswān
As Sukhnah *118 C3* var. Sukhne, Fr.
  Soukhné. Ḥimṣ, C Syria
As Sulaymāniyah *120 C3* var.
  Sulaimaniya, Kurd. Slēmānī. As
  Sulaymāniyah, NE Iraq
As Sulayyil *121 B5* Ar Riyāḍ,
  S Saudi Arabia
As Suwaydā' *119 B5* var. El Suweida, Es
  Suweida, Suweida, Fr. Soueida. As
  Suwaydā', SW Syria
As Suways see Suez
Asta Colonia see Asti
Astacus see İzmit
Astana *114 C4* prev. Akmola,
  Akmolinsk, Tselinograd, Aqmola.
  country capital (Kazakhstan) Akmola,
  N Kazakhstan
Asta Pompeia see Asti
Astarabad see Gorgān
Asterābād see Gorgān
Asti *96 A2* anc. Asta Colonia, Asta
  Pompeia, Hasta Colonia, Hasta
  Pompeia. Piemonte, NW Italy
Astigi see Ecija
Astipálaia see Astypálaia
Astorga *92 C1* anc. Asturica Augusta.
  Castilla y León, N Spain
Astrabad see Gorgān
Astrakhan' *111 C7* Astrakhanskaya
  Oblast', SW Russia
Asturias *92 C1* autonomous community
  NW Spain
Asturias see Oviedo
Asturica Augusta see Astorga
Astypálaia *105 D7* var. Astipálaia, It.
  Stampalia. island Kykládes, Greece,
  Aegean Sea
Asunción *64 D2* country capital
  (Paraguay) Central, S Paraguay
Aswān *72 B2* var. Assouan, Assuan,
  Aswān; anc. Syene. SE Egypt
Aswān see Aswān
Asyūṭ *72 B2* var. Assiout, Assiut, Asyūt,
  Siut; anc. Lycopolis. C Egypt
Asyūt see Asyūṭ
Atacama Desert *64 B2* Eng. Atacama
  Desert. desert N Chile
Atacama Desert see Atacama, Desierto de
Atafu Atoll *145 E3* island N Tokelau
Atamyrat *122 D3* prev. Kerki. Lebap
  Welaýaty, E Turkmenistan
Atâr *74 C2* Adrar, W Mauritania
Atas Bogd *126 D3* mountain
  SW Mongolia
Atatürk Baraji *117 F4* reservoir
  S Turkey
Atbara *72 C3* var. 'Aṭbārah. River Nile,
  NE Sudan
Atbasar *114 C4* Akmola,
  N Kazakhstan
Atchison *45 F4* Kansas, C USA
Aternum see Pescara
Ath *87 B6* var. Aat. Hainaut, SW Belgium
Athabasca *37 E5* Alberta, SW Canada
Athabasca *37 E5* var. Athabaska. river
  Alberta, SW Canada
Athabasca, Lake *37 F4* lake Alberta/
  Saskatchewan, SW Canada
Athabaska see Athabasca
Athenae see Athína
Athens *43 E2* Georgia, SE USA
Athens *40 D4* Ohio, N USA
Athens *49 G3* Texas, SW USA
Athens see Athína
Atherton *148 D3* Queensland,
  NE Australia
Athina *105 C6* Eng. Athens, prev.
  Athínai; anc. Athenae. country capital
  (Greece) Attikí, C Greece
Athínai see Athína
Athlone *89 B5* Ir. Baile Átha Luain.
  C Ireland
Ath Thawrah see Madīnat ath Thawrah
Ati *76 C3* Batha, C Chad
Atikokan *38 B4* Ontario, S Canada
Atka *115 G3* Magadanskaya Oblast',
  E Russia

Atka *36 A3* Atka Island, Alaska, USA
Atlanta *42 D2* state capital Georgia,
  SE USA
Atlanta *49 H2* Texas, SW USA
Atlantic City *41 F4* New Jersey, NE USA
Atlantic-Indian Basin *67 D7* undersea
  basin SW Indian Ocean
Atlantic-Indian Ridge *69 B8* undersea
  ridge SW Indian Ocean
Atlantic Ocean *66 B4* ocean
Atlas Mountains *70 C2* mountain range
  NW Africa
Atlasovo *115 H3* Kamchatskiy Kray,
  E Russia
Atlas, Tell *102 C3* Eng. Tell Atlas.
  mountain range N Algeria
Atlas, Tell see Atlas Tellien
Atlin *36 D4* British Columbia, W Canada
Aṭ Ṭafīlah *119 B7* var. Et Tafila, Tafila.
  Aṭ Ṭafīlah, W Jordan
Aṭ Ṭā'if *121 B5* Makkah, W Saudi Arabia
Attaleia/Attalia see Antalya
At Tall al Abyaḍ *118 C2* var. Tall al
  Abyaḍ, Tell Abyad, Fr. Tell Abiad. Ar
  Raqqah, N Syria
Aṭ Ṭanf *118 D4* Ḥimṣ, S Syria
Attapu *137 E5* var. Samakhixai, Attopeu.
  Attapu, S Laos
Attawapiskat *38 C3* Ontario, C Canada
Attawapiskat *38 C3* river Ontario,
  S Canada
At Tibnī *118 D2* var. Tibnī. Dayr az
  Zawr, NE Syria
Attopeu see Attapu
Attu Island *36 A2* island Aleutian
  Islands, Alaska, USA
Atyrau *114 B4* prev. Gur'yev. Atyrau,
  W Kazakhstan
Aubagne *91 D6* anc. Albania.
  Bouches-du-Rhône, SE France
Aubange *87 D8* Luxembourg,
  SE Belgium
Aubervilliers *90 E1* Seine-St-Denis,
  Île-de-France, N France Europe
Auburn *42 B2* Washington, NW USA
Auch *91 B6* Lat. Augusta Auscorum,
  Elimberrum. Gers, S France
Auckland *150 D2* Auckland, North
  Island, New Zealand
Auckland Islands *142 C5* island group
  S New Zealand
Audern see Audru
Audincourt *90 E4* Doubs, E France
Audru *106 D2* Ger. Audern. Pärnumaa,
  SW Estonia
Augathella *149 D5* Queensland,
  E Australia
Augsbourg see Augsburg
Augsburg *95 C6* Fr. Augsbourg; anc.
  Augusta Vindelicorum. Bayern,
  S Germany
Augusta *147 A7* Western Australia
Augusta *43 E2* Georgia, SE USA
Augusta *41 G2* state capital Maine,
  NE USA
Augusta see London
Augusta Auscorum see Auch
Augusta Emerita see Mérida
Augusta Praetoria see Aosta
Augusta Trajana see Stara Zagora
Augusta Treverorum see Trier
Augusta Vangionum see Worms
Augusta Vindelicorum see Augsburg
Augustobona Tricassium see Troyes
Augustodurum see Bayeux
Augustoritum Lemovicensium see
  Limoges
Augustów *98 E2* Rus. Avgustov.
  Podlaskie, NE Poland
Aulie Ata/Auliye-Ata see Taraz
Aunglan *136 B4* var. Allanmyo, Myaydo.
  Magway, C Myanmar (Burma)
Auob *78 B4* var. Oup. river Namibia/
  South Africa
Aurangābād *134 D5* Mahārāshtra,
  C India
Auray *90 A3* Morbihan, NW France
Aurelia Aquensis see Baden-Baden
Aurelianum see Orléans
Aurès, Massif de l' *102 C4* mountain
  range NE Algeria
Aurillac *91 C5* Cantal, C France
Aurium see Ourense
Aurora *59 F3* NE Guyana
Aurora *44 D4* Colorado, C USA
Aurora *40 B3* Illinois, N USA
Aurora *45 G5* Missouri, C USA
Aurora see Maéwo, Vanuatu
Aus *78 B4* Karas, SW Namibia
Ausa see Vic

Aussig *see* Ústí nad Labem
Austin 45 G3 Minnesota, N USA
Austin 49 G3 *state capital* Texas, SW USA
Australes, Archipel des *see* Australes, Îles
Australes et Antarctiques Françaises, Terres *see* French Southern and Antarctic Lands
Australes, Îles 143 F4 *var.* Archipel des Australes, Îles Tubuai, Tubuai Islands, *Eng.* Austral Islands. *island group* SW French Polynesia
Austral Fracture Zone 143 H4 *tectonic feature* S Pacific Ocean
Australia 142 A4 *off.* Commonwealth of Australia. *country*
Australia, Commonwealth of *see* Australia
Australian Alps 149 C7 *mountain range* SE Australia
Australian Capital Territory 149 D7 *prev.* Federal Capital Territory. *territory* SE Australia
Australie, Bassin Nord de l' *see* North Australian Basin
Austral Islands *see* Australes, Îles
Austrava *see* Ostrov
Austria 95 D7 *off.* Republic of Austria, *Ger.* Österreich. *country* C Europe
Austria, Republic of *see* Austria
Autesiodorum *see* Auxerre
Autissiodorum *see* Auxerre
Autricum *see* Chartres
Auvergne 91 C5 *cultural region* C France
Auxerre 90 C4 *anc.* Autesiodorum, Autissiodorum. Yonne, C France
Avaricum *see* Bourges
Avarua 145 G5 *dependent territory capital* (Cook Islands) Rarotonga, S Cook Islands
Avasfelsőfalu *see* Negreşti-Oaş
Ávdira 104 C3 Anatolikí Makedonía kai Thráki, NE Greece
Aveiro 92 B2 *anc.* Talabriga. Aveiro, W Portugal
Avela *see* Ávila
Avellino 97 D5 *anc.* Abellinum. Campania, S Italy
Avenio *see* Avignon
Avesta 85 C6 Dalarna, C Sweden
Aveyron 91 C6 *river* S France
Avezzano 96 C4 Abruzzo, C Italy
Avgustov *see* Augustów
Aviemore 88 C3 N Scotland, United Kingdom
Avignon 91 D6 *anc.* Avenio. Vaucluse, SE France
Ávila 92 D3 *var.* Avila; *anc.* Abela, Abula, Abyla, Avela. Castilla y León, C Spain
Avilés 92 C1 Asturias, NW Spain
Avranches 90 B3 Manche, N France
Avveel *see* Ivalo, Finland
Avvil *see* Ivalo
Awaji-shima 131 C6 *island* SW Japan
Āwash 73 D5 Āfar, NE Ethiopia
Awbārī 71 F3 SW Libya
Ax *see* Dax
Axel 87 B5 Zeeland, SW Netherlands
Axel Heiberg Island 37 E1 *var.* Axel Heiburg. *island* Nunavut, N Canada
Axel Heiburg *see* Axel Heiberg Island
Axiós *see* Vardar
Ayacucho 60 D4 Ayacucho, S Peru
Ayagoz 114 C5 *var.* Ayaguz, *Kaz.* Ayakoz. *river* E Kazakhstan
Ayamonte 92 C4 Andalucía, S Spain
Ayaviri 61 E4 Puno, S Peru
Aydarko'l Ko'li 123 E2 *Rus.* Ozero Aydarkul'. *lake* C Uzbekistan
Aydarkul', Ozero *see* Aydarko'l Ko'li
Aydın 116 A4 *var.* Aidin; *anc.* Tralles Aydin. Aydın, SW Turkey
Ayers Rock *see* Uluru
Ayeyarwady *see* Irrawaddy
Ayiá *see* Agiá
Áyios Evstrátios *see* Ágios Efstrátios
Áyios Nikólaos *see* Ágios Nikólaos
Ayorou 75 E3 Tillabéri, W Niger
'Ayoûn el 'Atroûs 74 D3 *var.* Aïoun el Atrous, Aïoun el Atroûss. Hodh el Gharbi, SE Mauritania
Ayr 88 C4 W Scotland, United Kingdom
Ayteke Bi 114 B4 *Kaz.* Zhangaqazaly; *prev.* Novokazalinsk. Kzylorda, SW Kazakhstan
Aytos 100 E2 Burgas, E Bulgaria
Ayutthaya 137 C5 *var.* Phra Nakhon Si Ayutthaya. Phra Nakhon Si Ayutthaya, C Thailand

Ayvalık 116 A3 Balıkesir, W Turkey
Azahar, Costa del 93 F3 *coastal region* E Spain
Azaouâd 75 E3 *desert* C Mali
Azärbaycan/Azärbaycan Respublikasï *see* Azerbaijan
A'zāz 118 B2 Ḥalab, NW Syria
Azerbaijan 117 G2 *off.* Azerbaijani Republic, *Az.* Azärbaycan, Azärbaycan Respublikasï; *prev.* Azerbaijan SSR. *country* SE Asia
Azerbaijani Republic *see* Azerbaijan
Azerbaijan SSR *see* Azerbaijan
Azimabad *see* Patna
Azizie *see* Telish
Azogues 60 B2 Cañar, S Ecuador
Azores 92 A4 *var.* Açores, Ilhas dos Açores, *Port.* Arquipélago dos Açores. *island group* Portugal, NE Atlantic Ocean
Azores-Biscay Rise 80 A3 *undersea rise* E Atlantic Ocean
Azotos/Azotus *see* Ashdod
Azoum, Bahr 76 C3 *seasonal river* SE Chad
Azov, Sea of 103 H1 *Rus.* Azovskoye More, *Ukr.* Azovs'ke More. *sea* NE Black Sea
Azovs'ke More/Azovskoye More *see* Azov, Sea of
Azraq, Wāḥat al 119 C6 *oasis* N Jordan
Aztec 48 C1 New Mexico, SW USA
Azuaga 92 C4 Extremadura, W Spain
Azuero, Península de 53 F5 *peninsula* S Panama
Azul 65 D5 Buenos Aires, E Argentina
Azur, Côte d' 91 E6 *coastal region* SE France
'Azza *see* Gaza
Az Zaqāziq 72 B1 *var.* Zagazig. N Egypt
Az Zarqā' 119 B6 *var.* Zarqa. Az Zarqā', NW Jordan
Az Zāwiyah 71 F2 *var.* Zawia. NW Libya
Az Zilfī 120 B4 Ar Riyāḍ, N Saudi Arabia

B

Baalbek 118 B4 *var.* Ba'labakk; *anc.* Heliopolis. E Lebanon
Baardheere 73 D6 *var.* Bardere, *It.* Bardera. Gedo, SW Somalia
Baarle-Hertog 87 C5 Antwerpen, N Belgium
Baarn 86 C3 Utrecht, C Netherlands
Babadag 108 E1 Tulcea, SE Romania
Babahoyo 60 B2 *prev.* Bodegas. Los Ríos, C Ecuador
Bābā, Kūh-e 123 E4 *mountain range* C Afghanistan
Babayevo 110 B4 Vologodskaya Oblast', NW Russia
Babeldaob 144 A1 *var.* Babeldaop, Babelthuap. *island* N Palau
Babeldaop *see* Babeldaob
Bab el Mandeb 121 B7 *strait* Gulf of Aden/Red Sea
Babelthuap *see* Babeldaob
Babian Jiang *see* Black River
Babruysk 107 D7 *Rus.* Bobruysk. Mahilyowskaya Voblasts', E Belarus
Babuyan Channel 139 E1 *channel* N Philippines
Babuyan Islands 139 E1 *island group* N Philippines
Bacabal 63 F2 Maranhão, E Brazil
Bacău 108 C4 Hung. Bákó. Bacău, NE Romania
Băc Bộ, Vinh *see* Tonkin, Gulf of
Băc Giang 136 D3 Ha Băc, N Vietnam
Bachevskaya 107 D5 *Rus.* Bocheykovo. Vitsyebskaya Voblasts', N Belarus
Back 37 F3 *river* Nunavut, N Canada
Bačka Palanka 100 D3 *prev.* Palanka. Serbia, NW Serbia
Bačka Topola 100 D3 *Hung.* Topolya; *prev.* Hung. Bácstopolya. Vojvodina, N Serbia
Bac Liêu 137 D6 *var.* Vinh Loi. Minh Hai, S Vietnam
Bacolod 125 E4 *off.* Bacolod City. Negros, C Philippines
Bacolod City *see* Bacolod
Bácsszenttamás *see* Srbobran
Bácstopolya *see* Bačka Topola
Bactra *see* Balkh
Badajoz 92 C4 *anc.* Pax Augusta. Extremadura, W Spain

Baden-Baden 95 B6 *anc.* Aurelia Aquensis. Baden-Württemberg, SW Germany
Badger State *see* Wisconsin
Bad Freienwalde 94 D3 Brandenburg, NE Germany
Bad Hersfeld 94 B4 Hessen, C Germany
Bad Homburg *see* Bad Homburg vor der Höhe
Bad Homburg vor der Höhe 95 B5 *var.* Bad Homburg. Hessen, W Germany
Bad Ischl 95 D7 Oberösterreich, N Austria
Bad Krozingen 95 A6 Baden-Württemberg, SW Germany
Badlands 44 D2 *physical region* North Dakota/South Dakota, N USA
Badu Island 148 C1 *island* Queensland, NE Australia
Bad Vöslau 95 E6 Niederösterreich, NE Austria
Baeterrae/Baeterrae Septimanorum *see* Béziers
Baetic Cordillera/Baetic Mountains *see* Béticos, Sistemas
Bafatá 74 C4 C Guinea-Bissau
Baffin Bay 37 G2 *bay* Canada/Greenland
Baffin Island 37 G2 *island* Nunavut, NE Canada
Bafing 74 C3 *river* W Africa
Bafoussam 76 A4 Ouest, W Cameroon
Bafra 116 D2 Samsun, N Turkey
Bāft 120 D4 Kermān, S Iran
Bagaces 52 D4 Guanacaste, NW Costa Rica
Bagdad *see* Baghdād
Bagé 63 E5 Rio Grande do Sul, S Brazil
Baghdād 120 B3 *var.* Bagdad, *Eng.* Baghdad (Iraq) Baghdād, C Iraq
Baghlān 123 E3 Baghlān, NE Afghanistan
Bago 136 B4 *var.* Pegu. Bago, SW Myanmar (Burma)
Bagoé 74 D4 *river* Ivory Coast/Mali
Bagrationovsk 106 A4 *Ger.* Preussisch Eylau. Kaliningradskaya Oblast', W Russia
Bagrax Hu *see* Bosten Hu
Baguio 139 E1 *off.* Baguio City. Luzon, N Philippines
Baguio City *see* Baguio
Bagzane, Monts 75 F3 *mountain* N Niger
Bahama Islands *see* Bahamas, The
Bahamas, The 54 C2 *off.* Commonwealth of The Bahamas. *country* N West Indies
Bahamas, Commonwealth of The *see* Bahamas, The
Baharly 122 C3 *var.* Bäherden, *Rus.* Bakharden; *prev.* Bakherden. Ahal Welaýaty, C Turkmenistan
Bahawalpur 134 C2 Punjab, E Pakistan
Bäherden *see* Baharly
Bahia 63 F3 *off.* Estado da Bahia. *state/region* E Brazil
Bahía Blanca 65 C5 Buenos Aires, E Argentina
Bahia, Estado da *see* Bahia
Bahir Dar 72 C4 *var.* Bahr Dar, Bahrdar Giyorgis. Āmara, N Ethiopia
Bahraich 135 E3 Uttar Pradesh, N India
Bahrain 120 C4 *off.* State of Bahrain, Dawlat al Bahrayn, *Ar.* Al Baḥrayn; *prev.* Bahrein; *anc.* Tylos, Tyros. *country* SW Asia
Bahrain, State of *see* Bahrain
Bahrayn, Dawlat al *see* Bahrain
Bahr el, Azraq *see* Blue Nile
Bahr Tabariya, Sea of *see* Tiberias, Lake
Bahushewsk 107 E6 *Rus.* Bogushëvsk. Vitsyebskaya Voblasts', NE Belarus
Baia Mare 108 B3 *Ger.* Frauenbach, *Hung.* Nagybánya; *prev.* Neustadt. Maramureş, NW Romania
Baia Sprie 108 B3 *Ger.* Mittelstadt, *Hung.* Felsőbánya. Maramureş, NW Romania
Baïbokoum 76 B4 Logone-Oriental, SW Chad
Baidoa *see* Baydhabo
Baie-Comeau 39 E3 Québec, SE Canada
Baikal, Lake *see* Baykal, Ozero
Baile Átha Cliath *see* Dublin
Baile Átha Luain *see* Athlone
Bailén 92 D4 Andalucía, S Spain
Baile na Mainistreach *see* Newtownabbey
Băileşti 108 B5 Dolj, SW Romania
Ba Illi 76 B3 Chari-Baguirmi, SW Chad

Bainbridge 42 D3 Georgia, SE USA
Bã'ir *see* Bāyir
Baireuth *see* Bayreuth
Bairnsdale 149 C7 Victoria, SE Australia
Baishan 129 E3 *prev.* Hunjiang. Jilin, NE China
Baiyin 128 B4 Gansu, C China
Baja 99 C7 Bács-Kiskun, S Hungary
Baja California Norte 50 B2 *state* NW Mexico
Bajo Boquete *see* Boquete
Bajram Curri 101 D5 Kukës, N Albania
Bakala 76 C4 Ouaka, C Central African Republic
Bakan *see* Shimonoseki
Baker 46 C3 Oregon, NW USA
Baker Island 145 E2 US *unincorporated territory* W Polynesia
Baker Lake 37 F3 *var.* Qamanittuaq. Nunavut, N Canada
Bakersfield 47 C7 California, W USA
Bakharden *see* Baharly
Bakhchisaray *see* Bakhchysaray
Bakhchysaray 109 F5 *Rus.* Bakhchisaray. Avtonomna Respublika Krym, S Ukraine
Bakherden *see* Baharly
Bakhmach 109 F1 Chernihivs'ka Oblast', N Ukraine
Bäkhtarãn *see* Kermānshāh
Bakı 117 H2 *Eng.* Baku. *country capital* (Azerbaijan) E Azerbaijan
Bäkó *see* Bacău
Bakony 99 C7 *Eng.* Bakony Mountains, *Ger.* Bakonywald. *mountain range* W Hungary
Bakony Mountains/Bakonywald *see* Bakony
Baku *see* Bakı
Bakwanga *see* Mbuji-Mayi
Balabac Island 129 C8 *island* W Philippines
Balabac, Selat *see* Balabac Strait
Balabac Strait 138 D2 *var.* Selat Balabac. *strait* Malaysia/Philippines
Ba'labakk *see* Baalbek
Balaguer 93 F2 Cataluña, NE Spain
Balakovo 111 C6 Saratovskaya Oblast', W Russia
Bālā Morghāb *see* Bālā Murghāb
Bālā Murghāb 122 D4 *prev.* Bālā Morghāb. Laghmān, NW Afghanistan
Balashov 111 B6 Saratovskaya Oblast', W Russia
Balasore *see* Bāleshwar
Balaton, Lake 99 C7 *var.* Lake Balaton, *Ger.* Plattensee. *lake* W Hungary
Balaton, Lake *see* Balaton
Balbina, Represa 62 D1 *reservoir* NW Brazil
Balboa 53 G4 Panamá, C Panama
Balcarce 65 D5 Buenos Aires, E Argentina
Balclutha 151 B7 Otago, South Island, New Zealand
Baldy Mountain 44 C1 *mountain* Montana, NW USA
Bâle *see* Basel
Balearic Plain *see* Algerian Basin
Baleares Major *see* Mallorca
Balearic Islands 93 G3 *Eng.* Balearic Islands. *island group* Spain, W Mediterranean Sea
Balearides, Insulae *see* Balearic Islands
Balearis Minor *see* Menorca
Baleine, Rivière à la 39 E2 *river* Québec, E Canada
Balen 87 C5 Antwerpen, N Belgium
Bāleshwar 135 F4 *prev.* Balasore. Odisha, E India
Bålgrad *see* Alba Iulia
Bali 138 D5 *island* C Indonesia
Balıkesir 116 A3 Balıkesir, W Turkey
Balikh, Nahr 118 C2 *river* N Syria
Balikpapan 138 D4 Borneo, C Indonesia
Balkanabat 122 B2 *Rus.* Nebitdag. Balkan Welaýaty, W Turkmenistan
Balkan Mountains 104 C2 Bul./SCr. Stara Planina. *mountain range* Bulgaria/Serbia
Balkash *see* Balkhash
Balkash, Ozero *see* Balkhash, Ozero
Balkh 123 E3 *anc.* Bactra. Balkh, N Afghanistan
Balkhash 114 C5 *Kaz.* Balqash; *var.* Balkash. Karagandy, SE Kazakhstan
Balkhash, Ozero *see* Balkhash

Balkhash, Lake see Balkhash, Ozero
Balkhash, Ozero 114 C5 *Eng.* Lake
  Balkhash, *Kaz.* Balqash; *var.* Ozero
  Balkash. *lake* SE Kazakhstan
Balladonia 147 C6 Western Australia
Ballarat 149 C7 Victoria, SE Australia
Balleny Islands 154 B5 *island group*
  Antarctica
Ballinger 49 F3 Texas, SW USA
Balochistan 134 B3 *prev.* Baluchistan,
  Beluchistan. *province* SW Pakistan
Balqash see Balkhash/Balkhash, Ozero
Balş 108 B5 Olt, S Romania
Balsas 63 F2 Maranhão, E Brazil
Balsas, Río 10 E5 *var.* Río Mexcala.
  river S Mexico
Bal'shavik 107 D7 *Rus.* Bol'shevik.
  Homyel'skaya Voblasts', SE Belarus
Balta 108 D3 Odes'ka Oblast',
  SW Ukraine
Bălţi 108 D3 *Rus.* Bel'tsy. N Moldova
Baltic Port see Paldiski
Baltic Sea 85 C7 *Ger.* Ostee, *Rus.*
  Baltiskoye More. *sea* N Europe
Baltimore 41 F4 Maryland, NE USA
Baltischport/Baltiski see Paldiski
Baltiskoye More see Baltic Sea
Baltkrievija see Belarus
Baluchistan see Balochistan
Balvi 106 D4 NE Latvia
Balykchy 123 G2 *Kir.* Ysyk-Köl; *prev.*
  Issyk-Kul', Rybach'ye. Issyk-Kul'skaya
  Oblast', E Kyrgyzstan
Balzers 94 E2 S Liechtenstein
Bam 120 E4 Kermān, SE Iran
Bamako 74 D4 *country capital* (Mali)
  Capital District, SW Mali
Bambari 76 C4 Ouaka, C Central African
  Republic
Bamberg 95 C5 Bayern, SE Germany
Bamenda 76 A4 Nord-Ouest,
  W Cameroon
Banaba 144 D2 *var.* Ocean Island.
  island Tungaru, W Kiribati
Banaras see Vārānasi
Banda Aceh 138 A3 *var.* Banda Atjeh;
  prev. Koetaradja, Kutaradja, Kutaraja.
  Sumatera, W Indonesia
Banda Atjeh see Banda Aceh
Banda, Laut see Banda Sea
Bandama 74 D5 *var.* Bandama Fleuve.
  river S Ivory Coast
Bandama Fleuve see Bandama
Bandar 'Abbās see Bandar-e 'Abbās
Bandarbeyla 73 E5 *var.* Bender Beila,
  Bender Beyla. Bari, NE Somalia
Bandar-e 'Abbās 120 D4 *var.* Bandar
  'Abbās; *prev.* Gombroon. Hormozgān,
  S Iran
Bandar-e Būshehr 120 C4 *var.* Būshehr,
  Eng. Bushire. Būshehr, S Iran
Bandar-e Kangān 120 D4 *var.* Kangān.
  Būshehr, S Iran
Bandar-e Khamīr 120 D4 Hormozgān,
  S Iran
Bandar-e Langeh see Bandar-e Lengeh
Bandar-e Lengeh 120 D4 *var.* Bandar-e
  Langeh, Lingeh. Hormozgān, S Iran
Bandar Kassim see Boosaaso
Bandar Lampung 138 C4 *var.*
  Bandarlampung, Tanjungkarang-
  Telukbetung; *prev.* Tandjoengkarang,
  Tanjungkarang, Teloekbetoeng,
  Telukbetung. Sumatera, W Indonesia
Bandarlampung see Bandar Lampung
Bandar Maharani see Muar
Bandar Masulipatnam see
  Machilipatnam
Bandar Penggaram see Batu Pahat
Bandar Seri Begawan 138 D3 *prev.*
  Brunei Town. *country capital* (Brunei)
  N Brunei
Banda Sea 139 F5 *var.* Laut Banda. *sea*
  E Indonesia
Bandiagara 75 E3 Mopti, C Mali
Bandırma 116 A3 *var.* Penderma.
  Balıkesir, NW Turkey
Bandjarmasin see Banjarmasin
Bandoeng see Bandung
Bandundu 77 C6 *prev.* Banningville.
  Bandundu, W Dem. Rep. Congo
Bandung 138 C5 *prev.* Bandoeng. Jawa,
  C Indonesia
Bangalore see Bengalūru
Bangassou 76 D4 Mbomou, SE Central
  African Republic
Banggai, Kepulauan 139 E4 *island
  group* C Indonesia
Banghāzī 71 G2 *Eng.* Bengazi, Benghazi,
  It. Bengasi. NE Libya

Bangka, Pulau 138 C4 *island*
  W Indonesia
Bangkok see Ao Krung Thep
Bangkok, Bight of see Krung Thep, Ao
Bangladesh 135 G3 *off.* People's
  Republic of Bangladesh; *prev.* East
  Pakistan. *country* S Asia
Bangladesh, People's Republic of see
  Bangladesh
Ba Ngoi see Cam Ranh
Bangor 89 C6 NW Wales, United
  Kingdom
Bangor 89 B5 *Ir.* Beannchar. E Northern
  Ireland, United Kingdom
Bangor 41 G2 Maine, NE USA
Bang Pla Soi see Chon Buri
Bangui 77 B5 *country capital*
  (Central African Republic)
  Ombella-Mpoko,
  SW Central African Republic
Bangweulu, Lake 73 B8 *var.* Lake
  Bengweulu. *lake* N Zambia
Ban Hat Yai see Hat Yai
Ban Hin Heup 136 C4 Viangchan,
  C Laos
Ban Houayxay/Ban Houei Sai see
  Houayxay
Ban Hua Hin 137 C6 *var.* Hua Hin.
  Prachuap Khiri Khan, SW Thailand
Bani 74 D3 *river* S Mali
Banias see Bāniyās
Banijska Palanka see Glina
Banī Suwayf 72 B2 *var.* Beni Suef.
  N Egypt
Bāniyās 118 B3 *var.* Banias, Baniyas,
  Paneas. Ṭarṭūs, W Syria
Banjak, Kepulauan see Banyak,
  Kepulauan
Banja Luka 100 B3 Republika Srpska,
  NW Bosnia and Herzegovina
Banjarmasin 138 D4 *prev.*
  Bandjarmasin. Borneo, C Indonesia
Banjul 74 B3 *prev.* Bathurst. *country
  capital* (The Gambia) W The Gambia
Banks, Îles see Banks Islands
Banks Island 37 E2 *island* Northwest
  Territories, NW Canada
Banks Islands 144 D4 *Fr.* Îles Banks.
  island group N Vanuatu
Banks Lake 46 B1 *reservoir* Washington,
  NW USA
Banks Peninsula 151 C6 *peninsula*
  South Island, New Zealand
Banks Strait 149 C8 *strait*
  SW Tasman Sea
Bānkura 135 F4 West Bengal, NE India
Ban Mak Khaeng see Udon Thani
Banmo see Bhamo
Banningville see Bandundu
Bañolas see Banyoles
Ban Pak Phanang see Pak Phanang
Ban Sichon see Sichon
Banská Bystrica 99 C6 *Ger.* Neusohl,
  Hung. Besztercebánya.
  Banskobystrický Kraj, C Slovakia
Bantry Bay 89 A7 *Ir.* Bá Bheanntraí.
  bay SW Ireland
Banya 104 E2 Burgas, E Bulgaria
Banyak, Kepulauan 138 A3 *prev.*
  Kepulauan Banjak. *island group*
  NW Indonesia
Banyo 76 B4 Adamaoua, NW Cameroon
Banyoles 93 G2 *var.* Bañolas. Cataluña,
  NE Spain
Banzare Seamounts 141 C7
  seamount range S Indian Ocean
Banzart see Bizerte
Baoji 128 B4 *var.* Pao-chi, Paoki.
  Shaanxi, C China
Baoro 76 B4 Nana-Mambéré,
  W Central African Republic
Baoshan 128 A6 *var.* Pao-shan. Yunnan,
  SW China
Baotou 127 F3 *var.* Pao-t'ou, Paotow.
  Nei Mongol Zizhiqu, N China
Ba'qūbah 120 B3 *var.* Qubba. Diyālá,
  C Iraq
Baquerizo Moreno see
  Puerto Baquerizo Moreno
Bar 101 C5 *It.* Antivari. S Montenegro
Baraawe 73 D6 *It.* Brava. Shabeellaha
  Hoose, S Somalia
Bārāmati 134 C5 Mahārāshtra, W India
Baranavichy 107 B6 *Pol.* Baranowicze,
  Rus. Baranovichi. Brestskaya Voblasts',
  SW Belarus
Baranovichi/Baranowicze see
  Baranavichy
Barbados 55 G1 *country* SE West Indies
Barbastro 93 F2 Aragón, NE Spain

Barbate de Franco 92 C5 Andalucía,
  S Spain
Barbuda 55 G3 *island* N Antigua and
  Barbuda
Barcaldine 148 C4 Queensland,
  Australia
Barcarozsnyó see Râşnov
Barcău see Berettyó
Barce see Al Marj
Barcelona 93 G2 *anc.* Barcino,
  Barcinona. Cataluña, E Spain
Barcelona 59 E2 Anzoátegui,
  NE Venezuela
Barcino/Barcinona see Barcelona
Barcoo see Cooper Creek
Barcs 99 C7 Somogy, SW Hungary
Bardaï 76 C1 Borkou-Ennedi-Tibesti,
  N Chad
Bardejov 99 D5 *Ger.* Bartfeld, *Hung.*
  Bártfa. Prešovský Kraj, E Slovakia
Bardera/Bardere see Baardheere
Barduli see Barletta
Bareilly 135 E3 *var.* Bareli. Uttar
  Pradesh, N India
Bareli see Bareilly
Barendrecht 86 C4 Zuid-Holland,
  SW Netherlands
Barentin 90 C3 Seine-Maritime,
  N France
Barentsburg 83 G2 Spitsbergen,
  W Svalbard
Barentsevo More/Barents Havet see
  Barents Sea
Barentsøya 83 G2 *island* E Svalbard
Barents Sea 110 C2 *Nor.* Barents Havet,
  Rus. Barentsevo More.
  sea Arctic Ocean
Bar Harbor 41 H2 Mount Desert Island,
  Maine, NE USA
Bari 97 E5 *var.* Bari delle Puglie; *anc.*
  Barium. Puglia, SE Italy
Bari delle Puglie see Bari
Barikot see Barīkowţ
Barīkowţ 123 F4 *var.* Barikot. Kunar,
  NE Afghanistan
Barillas 52 A2 *var.* Santa Cruz Barillas.
  Huehuetenango, NW Guatemala
Barinas 58 C2 Barinas, W Venezuela
Barisal 135 G4 Barisal, S Bangladesh
Barisan, Pegunungan 138 B4
  mountain range Sumatera,
  W Indonesia
Barito, Sungai 138 D4 *river* Borneo,
  C Indonesia
Barium see Bari
Barka see Al Marj
Barkly Tableland 148 B3 *plateau*
  Northern Territory/Queensland,
  N Australia
Bârlad 108 D4 *prev.* Bîrlad. Vaslui,
  E Romania
Barlavento, Ilhas de 74 A2 *var.*
  Windward Islands. *island group*
  N Cape Verde
Bar-le-Duc 90 D3 *var.* Bar-sur-Ornain.
  Meuse, NE France
Barlee, Lake 147 B6 *lake* Western
  Australia
Barlee Range 146 A4 *mountain range*
  Western Australia
Barletta 97 D5 *anc.* Barduli. Puglia,
  SE Italy
Barlinek 98 B3 *Ger.* Berlinchen.
  Zachodnio-pomorskie, NW Poland
Barmen-Elberfeld see Wuppertal
Barmouth 89 C6 NW Wales, United
  Kingdom
Barnaul 114 D4 Altayskiy Kray, C Russia
Barnet 89 A7 United Kingdom
Barnstaple 89 C7 SW England, United
  Kingdom
Baroda see Vadodara
Baroghil Pass 123 F3 *var.* Kowtal-e
  Barowghīl. *pass* Afghanistan/Pakistan
Baron'ki 107 E7 *Rus.* Boron'ki.
  Mahilyowskaya Voblasts', E Belarus
Barowghil, Kowtal-e see Baroghil Pass
Barquisimeto 58 C2 Lara,
  NW Venezuela
Barra 88 B3 *island* NW Scotland, United
  Kingdom
Barra de Río Grande 53 E3 Región
  Autónoma Atlántico Sur, E Nicaragua
Barranca 60 C3 Lima, W Peru
Barrancabermeja 58 B2 Santander,
  N Colombia
Barranquilla 58 B1 Atlántico,
  N Colombia
Barreiro 92 B4 Setúbal, W Portugal

Barrier Range 149 C6 *hill range*
  New South Wales, SE Australia
Barrow 36 D2 Alaska, USA
Barrow 89 B6 *Ir.* An Bhearú. *river*
  SE Ireland
Barrow-in-Furness 89 C5 NW England,
  United Kingdom
Barrow Island 146 A4 *island*
  Western Australia
Barstow 47 C7 California, W USA
Bar-sur-Ornain see Bar-le-Duc
Bartang 123 F3 *river* SE Tajikistan
Bartenstein see Bartoszyce
Bártfa/Bartfeld see Bardejov
Bartica 59 F3 N Guyana
Bartın 116 C2 Bartın, N Turkey
Bartlesville 49 G1 Oklahoma, C USA
Bartoszyce 98 D2 *Ger.* Bartenstein.
  Warmińsko-mazurskie, NE Poland
Baruun-Urt 127 F2 Sühbaatar,
  E Mongolia
Barú, Volcán 53 E5 *var.* Volcán de
  Chiriquí. *volcano* W Panama
Barwon River 149 D5 *river* New South
  Wales, SE Australia
Barysaw 107 D6 *Rus.* Borisov. Minskaya
  Voblasts', NE Belarus
Basarabeasca 108 D4 *Rus.* Bessarabka.
  SE Moldova
Basel 95 A7 *Eng.* Basle, *Fr.* Bâle. Basel
  Stadt, NW Switzerland
Basilan 139 E3 *island* Sulu Archipelago,
  SW Philippines
Basle see Basel
Basra see Al Başrah
Bassano del Grappa 96 C2 Veneto,
  NE Italy
Bassein see Pathein
Basseterre 55 G4 *country capital*
  (Saint Kitts and Nevis) Saint Kitts,
  Saint Kitts and Nevis
Basse-Terre 55 G3 *dependent territory
  capital* (Guadeloupe) Basse Terre,
  SW Guadeloupe
Basse Terre 55 G4 *island* W Guadeloupe
Bassikounou 74 D3 Hodh ech Chargui,
  SE Mauritania
Bass, Îlots de see Marotiri
Bass Strait 149 C7 *strait* SE Australia
Bassum 94 B3 Niedersachsen,
  NW Germany
Bastia 91 E7 Corse, France,
  C Mediterranean Sea
Bastogne 87 D7 Luxembourg,
  SE Belgium
Bastrop 42 B2 Louisiana, S USA
Bastyn' 107 B7 *Rus.* Bostyn'. Brestskaya
  Voblasts', SW Belarus
Basuo see Dongfang
Basutoland see Lesotho
Bata 77 A5 NW Equatorial Guinea
Batae Coritanorum see Leicester
Batajnica 100 D3 Vojvodina, N Serbia
Batangas 139 E2 *off.* Batangas City.
  Luzon, N Philippines
Batangas City see Batangas
Batavia see Jakarta
Bătdâmbâng see Bătdâmbâng
Batéké, Plateaux 77 B6 *plateau* S Congo
Bath 89 D7 *hist.* Akermancester; *anc.*
  Aquae Calidae, Aquae Solis.
  SW England, United Kingdom
Bathinda 134 D2 Punjab, NW India
Bathsheba 55 G1 E Barbados
Bathurst 149 D6 New South Wales,
  SE Australia
Bathurst 39 F4 New Brunswick,
  SE Canada
Bathurst see Banjul
Bathurst Island 146 D2 *island* Northern
  Territory, N Australia
Bathurst Island 37 F2 *island* Parry
  Islands, Nunavut, N Canada
Wadi al Batin 120 C4 *dry watercourse*
  SW Asia
Batman 117 E4 *var.* Iluh. Batman,
  SE Turkey
Batna 71 E2 NE Algeria
Baton Rouge 42 B3 *state capital*
  Louisiana, S USA
Batroûn 118 A4 *var.* Al Batrun.
  N Lebanon
Battambang 137 C5 *var.* Bătdâmbâng.
  Bătdâmbâng, NW Cambodia
Batticaloa 132 D3 Eastern Province,
  E Sri Lanka
Battipaglia 97 D5 Campania, S Italy
Battle Born State see Nevada
Batumi 117 F2 *prev.* Bat'umi. W Georgia
Bat'umi see Batumi

Batu Pahat *138 B3 prev.* Bandar
  Penggaram. Johor, Peninsular Malaysia
Bauchi *75 G4* Bauchi, NE Nigeria
Bauer Basin *153 F3 undersea basin*
  E Pacific Ocean
Bauska *106 C3* Ger. Bauske. S Latvia
Bauske *see* Bauska
Bautzen *94 D4 Lus.* Budyšin. Sachsen,
  E Germany
Bauzanum *see* Bolzano
Bavaria *see* Bayern
Bavarian Alps *95 C7 Ger.* Bayrische
  Alpen. *mountain range* Austria/
  Germany
Bavière *see* Bayern
Bavispe, Río *50 C2 river* NW Mexico
Bawīṭī *see* Al Bawīṭī
Bawku *75 E4* N Ghana
Bayamo *54 C3* Granma, E Cuba
Bayan Har Shan *126 D4 var.* Bayan
  Khar. *mountain range* C China
Bayanhongor *126 D2* Bayanhongor,
  C Mongolia
Bayan Khar *see* Bayan Har Shan
Bayano, Lago *53 G4 lake* E Panama
Bay City *40 C3* Michigan, N USA
Bay City *49 G4* Texas, SW USA
Baydhabo *73 D6 var.* Baydhowa, Isha
  Baydhabo, *It.* Baidoa. Bay, SW Somalia
Baydhowa *see* Baydhabo
Bayern *95 C6 Eng.* Bavaria, *Fr.* Bavière.
  state SE Germany
Bayeux *90 B3 anc.* Augustodurum.
  Calvados, N France
Bāyir *119 C7 var.* Bā'ir. Ma'ān, S Jordan
Bay Islands *52 C1 Eng.* Bay Islands.
  island group N Honduras
Bay Islands *see* Bahía, Islas de la
Baykal, Ozero *115 E4 Eng.* Lake Baikal.
  lake S Russia
Baymak *111 D6* Respublika
  Bashkortostan, W Russia
Bayonne *91 A6 anc.* Lapurdum.
  Pyrénées-Atlantiques, SW France
Bayou State *see* Mississippi
Bayram-Ali *see* Baýramaly
Baýramaly *122 D3 var.* Bayramaly; *prev.*
  Bayram-Ali. Mary Welaýaty,
  S Turkmenistan
Bayreuth *95 C5 var.* Baireuth. Bayern,
  SE Germany
Bayrische Alpen *see* Bavarian Alps
Bayrūt *see* Beyrouth
Bay State *see* Massachusetts
Baysun *see* Boysun
Bayt Laḥm *see* Bethlehem
Baytown *49 H4* Texas, SW USA
Baza *93 E4* Andalucía, S Spain
Bazargic *see* Dobrich
Bazin *see* Pezinok
Beagle Channel *65 C8 channel*
  Argentina/Chile
Béal Feirste *see* Belfast
Beannchar *see* Bangor, Northern Ireland,
  UK
Bear Island *see* Bjørnøya
Beas de Segura *93 E4* Andalucía, S Spain
Beata, Isla *55 E3 island* SW Dominican
  Republic
Beatrice *45 F4* Nebraska, C USA
Beaufort Sea *36 D2 sea* Arctic Ocean
Beaufort-Wes *see* Beaufort West
Beaufort West *78 C5 Afr.* Beaufort-Wes.
  Western Cape, SW South Africa
Beaumont *49 H3* Texas, SW USA
Beaune *90 D4* Côte d'Or, C France
Beauvais *90 C3 anc.* Bellovacum,
  Caesaromagus. Oise, N France
Beaver Island *40 C2 island* Michigan,
  N USA
Beaver Lake *49 H1 reservoir* Arkansas,
  C USA
Beaver River *49 F1 river* Oklahoma,
  C USA
Beaver State *see* Oregon
Beāwar *134 C3* Rājasthān, N India
Bečej *100 D3 Ger.* Altbetsche, *Hung.*
  Óbecse, Rácz-Becse; *prev.*
  Magyar-Becse, Stari Bečej. Vojvodina,
  N Serbia
Béchar *70 D2 prev.* Colomb-Béchar.
  W Algeria
Beckley *40 D5* West Virginia, NE USA
Bécs *see* Wien
Bedford *89 D6* E England, United
  Kingdom
Bedum *86 E1* Groningen,
  NE Netherlands

Beehive State *see* Utah
Be'er Menuha *119 B7 prev.* Be'ér
  Menuḥa. Southern, S Israel
Be'ér Menuḥa *see* Be'er Menuha
Beernem *87 A5* West-Vlaanderen,
  NW Belgium
Beersheba *see* Be'er Sheva
Be'er Sheva *119 A7 var.* Beersheba, *Ar.*
  Bir es Saba; *prev.* Be'ér Sheva'.
  Southern, S Israel
Be'ér Sheva' *see* Be'er Sheva
Beesel *87 D5* Limburg, SE Netherlands
Beeville *49 G4* Texas, SW USA
Bega *149 D7* New South Wales,
  SE Australia
Begoml' *see* Byahoml'
Begovat *see* Bekobod
Behagle *see* Laï
Behar *see* Bihār
Beibu Wan *see* Tonkin, Gulf of
Beida *see* Al Bayḍā'
Beihai *128 B6* Guangxi Zhuangzu
  Zizhiqu, S China
Beijing *128 C3 var.* Pei-ching, Peking;
  prev. Pei-p'ing. *country capital* (China)
  Beijing Shi, E China
Beilen *86 E2* Drenthe, NE Netherlands
Beira *79 E3* Sofala, C Mozambique
Beirut *see* Beyrouth
Beit Lekhem *see* Bethlehem
Beiuş *108 B3 Hung.* Belényes. Bihor,
  NW Romania
Beja *92 B4 anc.* Pax Julia. Beja,
  SE Portugal
Béja *92 C3* Castilla y León, N Spain
Bejraburi *see* Phetchaburi
Bekabad *see* Bekobod
Békás *see* Bicaz
Bek-Budi *see* Qarshi
Békéscsaba *99 D7 Rom.* Bichiş-Ciaba.
  Békés, SE Hungary
Bekobod *123 E2 Rus.* Bekabad; *prev.*
  Begovat. Toshkent Viloyati,
  E Uzbekistan
Bela Crkva *100 E3 Ger.* Weisskirchen,
  Hung. Fehértemplom. Vojvodina,
  W Serbia
Belāgavi *132 B1 prev.* Belgaum.
  Karnātaka, W India
Belarus *107 B6 off.* Republic of Belarus,
  var. Belorussia, *Latv.* Baltkrievija;
  prev. Belorussian SSR, *Rus.*
  Belorusskaya SSR. *country* E Europe
Belarus, Republic of *see* Belarus
Belau *see* Palau
Belaya Tserkov' *see* Bila Tserkva
Bełchatów *98 C4 var.* Belchatow.
  Łódzki, C Poland
Belchatow *see* Bełchatów
Belcher, Îles *see* Belcher Islands
Belcher Islands *38 C2 Fr.* Îles Belcher.
  island group Nunavut, SE Canada
Beledweyne *73 D6 var.* Belet Huen,
  It. Belet Uen. Hiiraan, C Somalia
Belém *63 F1 var.* Pará. *state capital* Pará,
  N Brazil
Belén *52 D4* Rivas, SW Nicaragua
Belen *48 D2* New Mexico, SW USA
Belényes *see* Beiuş
Belet Huen/Belet Uen *see* Beledweyne
Belfast *89 B5 Ir.* Béal Feirste.
  national capital E Northern Ireland,
  United Kingdom
Belfield *44 D2* North Dakota, N USA
Belfort *90 E4* Territoire-de-Belfort,
  E France
Belgard *see* Białogard
Belgaum *see* Belāgavi
Belgian Congo *see*
  Congo (Democratic Republic of)
België/Belgique *see* Belgium
Belgium *87 B6 off.* Kingdom of Belgium,
  Dut. België, *Fr.* Belgique. *country*
  NW Europe
Belgium, Kingdom of *see* Belgium
Belgorod *111 A6* Belgorodskaya Oblast',
  W Russia
Belgrano II *154 A2* Argentinian research
  station Antarctica
Belice *see* Belize/Belize City
Beligrad *see* Berat
Beli Manastir *100 C3 Hung.*
  Pélmonostor; *prev.* Monostor.
  Osijek-Baranja, NE Croatia
Belinga *77 B5* Ogooué-Ivindo, NE Gabon
Belitung, Pulau *138 C4 island*
  W Indonesia
Belize *52 B1 Sp.* Belice; *prev.* British
  Honduras, Colony of Belize. *country*
  Central America

Belize *52 B1 river* Belize/Guatemala
Belize *see* Belize City
Belize City *52 C1 var.* Belize, *Sp.* Belice.
  Belize, NE Belize
Belize, Colony of *see* Belize
Beljak *see* Villach
Belkofski *36 B3* Alaska, USA
Belle Île *90 A4 island* NW France
Belle Isle, Strait of *39 G3 strait*
  Newfoundland and Labrador, E Canada
Bellenz *see* Bellinzona
Belleville *40 B4* Illinois, N USA
Bellevue *45 F4* Iowa, C USA
Bellevue *46 B2* Washington, NW USA
Bellingham *46 B1* Washington, NW USA
Belling Hausen Mulde *see* Southeast
  Pacific Basin
Bellingshausen Abyssal Plain *see*
  Bellingshausen Plain
Bellingshausen Plain *153 F5 var.*
  Bellingshausen Abyssal Plain. *abyssal*
  plain SE Pacific Ocean
Bellingshausen Sea *154 A3 sea*
  Antarctica
Bellinzona *95 B8 Ger.* Bellenz. Ticino,
  S Switzerland
Bello *58 B2* Antioquia, W Colombia
Bello Horizonte *see* Belo Horizonte
Bellovacum *see* Beauvais
Bellville *78 B5* Western Cape, SW South
  Africa
Belmopan *52 C1 country capital* (Belize)
  Cayo, C Belize
Belogradchik *104 B1* Vidin,
  NW Bulgaria
Belo Horizonte *63 F4 prev.* Bello
  Horizonte. *state capital* Minas Gerais,
  SE Brazil
Belomorsk *110 B3* Respublika Kareliya,
  NW Russia
Beloretsk *111 D6* Respublika
  Bashkortostan, W Russia
Belorussia/Belorussian SSR
  see Belarus
Belorusskaya Gryada *see* Byelaruskaya
  Hrada
Belorusskaya SSR *see* Belarus
Beloshchel'ye *see* Nar'yan-Mar
Belostok *see* Białystok
Belovár *see* Bjelovar
Beloye More *110 C3 Eng.* White Sea. *sea*
  NW Russia
Belozërsk *110 B4* Vologodskaya Oblast',
  NW Russia
Belton *49 G3* Texas, SW USA
Bel'tsy *see* Bălţi
Beluchistan *see* Balochistan
Belukha, Gora *114 D5 mountain*
  Kazakhstan/Russia
Belynichi *see* Byalynichy
Belyy, Ostrov *114 D2 island* N Russia
Bemaraha *79 F3 var.* Plateau du
  Bemaraha. *mountain range*
  W Madagascar
Bemaraha, Plateau du *see* Bemaraha
Bemidji *45 F1* Minnesota, N USA
Bemmel *86 D4* Gelderland,
  SE Netherlands
Benaco *see* Garda, Lago di
Benares *see* Vārānasi
Benavente *92 D2* Castilla y León,
  N Spain
Bend *46 B3* Oregon, NW USA
Bender *see* Tighina
Bender Beila/Bender Beyla *see*
  Bandarbeyla
Bender Cassim/Bender Qaasim *see*
  Boosaaso
Bendern *94 E1* NW Liechtenstein Europe
Bendigo *149 C7* Victoria, SE Australia
Bendor *see* Tighina
Beneschau *see* Benešov
Beneški Zaliv *see* Venice, Gulf of
Benešov *99 B5 Ger.* Beneschau.
  Středočeský Kraj, W Czech Republic
  (Czechia)
Benevento *97 D5 anc.* Beneventum,
  Malventum. Campania, S Italy
Beneventum *see* Benevento
Bengal, Bay of *124 C4 bay* N Indian
  Ocean
Bengalooru *see* Bengalūru
Bengaluru *132 C2 var.* Bengalooru,
  Bangalore. *state capital* Karnātaka,
  S India
Bengasi *see* Banghāzī
Bengazi *see* Banghāzī
Bengbu *128 D5 var.* Peng-pu. Anhui,
  E China
Benghazi *see* Banghāzī

Bengkulu *138 B4 prev.* Bengkoeloe,
  Benkoelen, Benkulen. Sumatera,
  W Indonesia
Benguela *78 A2 var.* Benguella.
  Benguela, W Angola
Benguella *see* Benguela
Bengweulu, Lake *see* Bangweulu, Lake
Ben Hope *88 B2 mountain* N Scotland,
  United Kingdom
Beni *77 E5* Nord-Kivu, NE Dem. Rep.
  Congo
Benidorm *93 F4* Valenciana, SE Spain
Beni-Mellal *70 C2* C Morocco
Benin *75 F4 off.* Republic of Benin; *prev.*
  Dahomey. *country* W Africa
Benin, Bight of *75 F5 gulf* W Africa
Benin City *75 F5* Edo, SW Nigeria
Benin, Republic of *see* Benin
Beni, Río *61 E3 river* N Bolivia
Beni Suef *see* Banī Suwayf
Ben Nevis *88 C3 mountain* N Scotland,
  United Kingdom
Bénoué *see* Benue
Benson *48 B3* Arizona, SW USA
Bent Jbaïl *119 A5 var.* Bint Jubayl.
  S Lebanon
Benton *42 B1* Arkansas, C USA
Benue *76 B4 Fr.* Bénoué. *river*
  Cameroon/Nigeria
Berane *101 D5 prev.* Ivangrad.
  E Montenegro
Berat *101 C6 var.* Berati, *SCr.* Beligrad.
  Berat, C Albania
Berati *see* Berat
Berätäu *see* Berettyó
Berau, Teluk *139 G4 var.* MacCluer
  Gulf. *bay* Papua, E Indonesia
Berbera *72 D4* Woqooyi Galbeed,
  NW Somalia
Berbérati *77 B5* Mambéré-Kadéï,
  SW Central African Republic
Berck-Plage *90 C2* Pas-de-Calais,
  N France
Berdichev *see* Berdychiv
Berdyans'k *109 G4 Rus.* Berdyansk; *prev.*
  Osipenko. Zaporiz'ka Oblast',
  SE Ukraine
Berdychiv *108 D2 Rus.* Berdichev.
  Zhytomyrs'ka Oblast', N Ukraine
Berehove *108 B3 Cz.* Berehovo, *Hung.*
  Beregszász, *Rus.* Beregovo.
  Zakarpats'ka Oblast', W Ukraine
Berehovo *see* Berehove
Bereket *122 B2 prev.* Rus. Gazandzhyk,
  Kazandzhik, *Turkm.* Gazanjyk. Balkan
  Welaýaty, W Turkmenistan
Berettäu *see* Berettyó
Berettyó *99 D7 Rom.* Barcău; *prev.*
  Berätäu, Berettäu. *river* Hungary/
  Romania
Berettyóújfalu *99 D6* Hajdú-Bihar,
  E Hungary
Berezhany *108 C2 Pol.* Brzeżany.
  Ternopil's'ka Oblast', W Ukraine
Berezina *see* Byarezina
Bereznik *111 D5* Permskiy Kray,
  NW Russia
Berga *93 G2* Cataluña, NE Spain
Bergamo *96 B2 anc.* Bergomum.
  Lombardia, N Italy
Bergara *93 E1* País Vasco, N Spain
Bergen *94 D2* Mecklenburg-
  Vorpommern, NE Germany
Bergen *85 A5* Noord-Holland,
  NW Netherlands
Bergen *85 A5* Hordaland, S Norway
Bergen *see* Mons
Bergerac *91 B5* Dordogne, SW France
Bergeyk *87 C5* Noord-Brabant,
  S Netherlands
Bergomum *see* Bergamo
Bergse Maas *86 C4 river* S Netherlands
Beringen *87 C5* Limburg, NE Belgium
Beringov Proliv *see* Bering Strait
Bering Sea *36 A2 sea* N Pacific Ocean
Bering Strait *34 C2 Rus.* Beringov Proliv.
  strait Bering Sea/Chukchi Sea
Berja *93 E5* Andalucía, S Spain
Berkeley *47 B6* California, W USA
Berkner Island *154 A2 island* Antarctica
Berkovitsa *104 C2* Montana,
  NW Bulgaria
Berlin *94 D3 country capital* (Germany)
  Berlin, NE Germany
Berlin *41 G2* New Hampshire, NE USA
Berlinchen *see* Barlinek
Bermejo, Río *64 C2 river* N Argentina

Bermeo 93 E1 País Vasco, N Spain
Bermuda 35 D6 var. Bermuda Islands, Bermudas; prev. Somers Islands. UK crown colony NW Atlantic Ocean
Bermuda Islands see Bermuda
Bermuda Rise 35 E6 undersea rise C Sargasso Sea
Bermudas see Bermuda
Bern 95 A7 Fr. Berne. country capital (Switzerland) Bern, W Switzerland
Bernau 94 D3 Brandenburg, NE Germany
Bernburg 94 C4 Sachsen-Anhalt, C Germany
Berne see Bern
Berner Alpen 95 A7 var. Berner Oberland, Eng. Bernese Oberland. mountain range SW Switzerland
Berner Oberland/Bernese Oberland see Berner Alpen
Bernier Island 147 A5 island Western Australia
Beroea see Ḩalab
Berry 90 C4 cultural region C France
Berry Islands 54 C1 island group N The Bahamas
Bertoua 77 B5 Est, E Cameroon
Beru 145 E2 var. Peru. atoll Tungaru, W Kiribati
Berwick-upon-Tweed 88 D4 N England, United Kingdom
Berytus see Beyrouth
Besançon 90 D4 anc. Besontium, Vesontio. Doubs, E France
Beskra see Biskra
Besontium see Besançon
Bessarabka see Basarabeasca
Besztercebánya see Banská Bystrica
Betafo 79 G3 Antananarivo, C Madagascar
Betanzos 92 B1 Galicia, NW Spain
Bethlehem 78 D4 Free State, C South Africa
Bethlehem 119 B6 var. Beit Lekhem, Ar. Bayt Laḥm, Heb. Bet Leḥem. C West Bank
Béticos, Sistemas 92 D4 var. Sistema Penibético, Eng. Baetic Cordillera, Baetic Mountains. mountain range S Spain
Bet Leḥem see Bethlehem
Bétou 77 C5 Likouala, N Congo
Bette, Pic see Bette, Picco
Bette, Picco 71 G4 var. Bikkū Bīttī, Pic Bette. mountain S Libya
Beulah 40 C2 Michigan, N USA
Beuthen see Bytom
Beveren 87 B5 Oost-Vlaanderen, N Belgium
Beverley 89 D5 E England, United Kingdom
Bexley 89 B8 Bexley, SE England, United Kingdom
Beyla 74 D4 SE Guinea
Beyrouth 118 A4 var. Bayrūt, Eng. Beirut; anc. Berytus. country capital (Lebanon) W Lebanon
Beyşehir 116 B4 Konya, SW Turkey
Beyşehir Gölü 116 B4 lake C Turkey
Béziers 91 C6 anc. Baeterrae, Baeterrae Septimanorum, Julia Beterrae. Hérault, S France
Bezmein see Abadan
Bezwada see Vijayawāda
Bhadrāvati 132 C2 Karnātaka, SW India
Bhāgalpur 135 F3 Bihār, NE India
Bhaktapur 135 F3 Central, C Nepal
Bhamo 136 B2 var. Banmo. Kachin State, N Myanmar (Burma)
Bhārat see Abadan
Bharūch 134 C4 Gujarāt, W India
Bhaunagar see Bhāvnagar
Bhāvnagar 134 C4 prev. Bhaunagar. Gujarāt, W India
Bheanntraí, Bá see Bantry Bay
Bhopāl 134 D4 state capital Madhya Pradesh, C India
Bhubaneshwar 135 F5 prev. Bhubaneswar, Bhuvaneshwar. state capital Odisha, E India
Bhubaneswar see Bhubaneshwar
Bhuket see Phuket
Bhusawal see Bhusāwal
Bhusāwal 134 D4 prev. Bhusaval. Mahārāshtra, C India
Bhutan 135 G3 off. Kingdom of Bhutan, var. Druk-yul. country S Asia
Bhutan, Kingdom of see Bhutan
Bhuvaneshwar see Bhubaneshwar

Biak, Pulau 139 G4 island E Indonesia
Biała Podlaska 98 E3 Lubelskie, E Poland
Białogard 98 B2 Ger. Belgard. Zachodnio-pomorskie, NW Poland
Białystok 98 E3 Rus. Belostok, Bielostok. Podlaskie, NE Poland
Bianco, Monte see Blanc, Mont
Biarritz 91 A6 Pyrénées-Atlantiques, SW France
Bicaz 108 C3 Hung. Békás. Neamţ, NE Romania
Bichiş-Ciaba see Békéscsaba
Biddeford 41 G2 Maine, NE USA
Bideford 89 C7 SW England, United Kingdom
Biel 95 A7 Fr. Bienne. Bern, W Switzerland
Bielefeld 94 B4 Nordrhein-Westfalen, NW Germany
Bielitz/Bielitz-Biala see Bielsko-Biała
Bielostok see Białystok
Bielsko-Biała 99 C5 Ger. Bielitz, Bielitz-Biala. Śląskie, S Poland
Bielsk Podlaski 98 E3 Białystok, E Poland
Bien Bien see Điện Biên Phu
Biên Đông see China Sea
Biên Hoa 137 E6 Đông Nai, S Vietnam
Bienne see Biel
Bienville, Lac 38 D2 lake Québec, C Canada
Bié Plateau 78 B2 var. Bié Plateau. plateau C Angola
Bié Plateau see Bié, Planalto do
Big Cypress Swamp 43 E5 wetland Florida, SE USA
Bigge Island 146 C2 island Western Australia
Bighorn Mountains 44 C2 mountain range Wyoming, C USA
Bighorn River 44 C2 river Montana/ Wyoming, NW USA
Bignona 74 B3 SW Senegal
Bigorra see Tarbes
Bigosovo see Bihosava
Big Sioux River 45 E2 river Iowa/South Dakota, N USA
Big Spring 49 E3 Texas, SW USA
Bihać 100 B3 Federacija Bosne I Hercegovine, NW Bosnia and Herzegovina
Bihār 135 F3 prev. Behar. cultural region N India
Bihār see Bihār Sharīf
Biharamulo 73 B7 Kagera, NW Tanzania
Bihār Sharīf 135 F3 var. Bihār. Bihār, N India
Bihosava 107 D5 Rus. Bigosovo. Vitsyebskaya Voblasts', NW Belarus
Bijeljina 100 C3 Republika Srpska, NE Bosnia and Herzegovina
Bijelo Polje 101 D5 E Montenegro
Bīkāner 134 C3 Rājasthān, NW India
Bikin 115 G4 Khabarovskiy Kray, SE Russia
Bikini Atoll 144 C1 var. Pikinni. atoll Ralik Chain, NW Marshall Islands
Bīkkū Bīttī see Bette, Picco
Bilāspur 135 E4 Chhattīsgarh, C India
Bilāsuvar 117 H3 Rus. Bilyasuvar; prev. Pushkino. SE Azerbaijan
Bila Tserkva 109 E2 Rus. Belaya Tserkov'. Kyyivs'ka Oblast', N Ukraine
Bilauktaung Range 137 C6 var. Thaninthari Taungdan. mountain range Myanmar (Burma)/Thailand
Bilbao 93 E1 Basq. Bilbo. País Vasco, N Spain
Bilbo see Bilbao
Bilecik 116 B3 Bilecik, NW Turkey
Billings 44 C2 Montana, NW USA
Bilma, Grand Erg de 75 H3 desert NE Niger
Biloela 148 D4 Queensland, E Australia
Biloxi 42 C3 Mississippi, S USA
Biltine 76 C3 Biltine, E Chad
Bilwi see Puerto Cabezas
Bilyasuvar see Bilāsuvar
Bilzen 87 D6 Limburg, NE Belgium
Bimini Islands 54 C1 island group W The Bahamas
Binche 87 B7 Hainaut, S Belgium
Bindloe Island see Marchena, Isla
Bin Ghalfān, Jazā'ir see Ḩalāniyāt, Juzur al
Binghamton 41 F3 New York, NE USA
Bingöl 117 F3 Bingöl, E Turkey
Bint Jubayl see Bent Jbaïl
Bintulu 138 D3 Sarawak, East Malaysia

Binzhou 128 D4 Shandong, E China
Bío Bío, Río 65 B5 river C Chile
Bioco, Isla de 77 A5 var. Bioko, Eng. Fernando Po, Sp. Fernando Póo; prev. Macías Nguema Biyogo. island NW Equatorial Guinea
Bioko see Bioco, Isla de
Birāk 71 F3 var. Brak. C Libya
Birao 76 D3 Vakaga, NE Central African Republic
Birātnagar 135 F3 Eastern, SE Nepal
Bir es Saba see Be'er Sheva
Birjand 120 E3 Khorāsān-e Janūbī, E Iran
Birkenfeld 95 A5 Rheinland-Pfalz, SW Germany
Birkenhead 89 C5 NW England, United Kingdom
Birlad see Bârlad
Birmingham 89 C6 C England, United Kingdom
Birmingham 42 C2 Alabama, S USA
Bir Moghrein see Bîr Mogreïn
Bîr Mogreïn 74 C1 var. Bir Moghrein; prev. Fort-Trinquet. Tiris Zemmour, N Mauritania
Birnie Island 145 E3 atoll Phoenix Islands, C Kiribati
Birnin Konni 75 F3 var. Birni-Nkonni. Tahoua, SW Niger
Birni-Nkonni see Birnin Konni
Birobidzhan 115 G4 Yevreyskaya Avtonomnaya Oblast', SE Russia
Birsen see Biržai
Birsk 111 D5 Respublika Bashkortostan, W Russia
Biržai 106 C4 Ger. Birsen. Panevėžys, NE Lithuania
Birżebbuġa 102 B5 SE Malta
Bisanthe see Tekirdağ
Bisbee 48 B3 Arizona, SW USA
Biscaia, Baía de see Biscay, Bay of
Biscay, Bay of 80 B4 Sp. Golfo de Vizcaya, Port. Baía de Biscaia. bay France/Spain
Biscay Plain 80 B3 abyssal plain SE Bay of Biscay
Bischofsburg see Biskupiec
Bishah, Wadi 121 B5 dry watercourse C Saudi Arabia
Bishkek 123 G2 var. Pishpek; prev. Frunze. country capital (Kyrgyzstan) Chuyskaya Oblast', N Kyrgyzstan
Bishop's Lynn see King's Lynn
Bishrī, Jabal 118 D3 mountain range E Syria
Biskara see Biskra
Biskra 71 E2 var. Beskra, Biskara. NE Algeria
Biskupiec 98 D2 Ger. Bischofsburg. Warmińsko-Mazurskie, NE Poland
Bislig 139 F2 Mindanao, S Philippines
Bismarck 45 E2 state capital North Dakota, N USA
Bismarck Archipelago 144 B3 island group NE Papua New Guinea
Bismarck Sea 144 B3 sea W Pacific Ocean
Bisnulok see Phitsanulok
Bissau 74 B4 country capital (Guinea-Bissau) W Guinea-Bissau
Bistrița 108 B3 Ger. Bistritz, Hung. Besztercze; prev. Nösen. Bistrița-Năsăud, N Romania
Bistritz see Bistrița
Bitam 77 B5 Woleu-Ntem, N Gabon
Bitburg 95 A5 Rheinland-Pfalz, SW Germany
Bitlis 117 F3 Bitlis, SE Turkey
Bitoeng see Bitung
Bitola 101 D6 Turk. Monastir; prev. Bitolj. S Macedonia
Bitolj see Bitola
Bitonto 97 D5 anc. Butuntum. Puglia, SE Italy
Bitterroot Range 46 D2 mountain range Idaho/Montana, NW USA
Bitung 139 F3 prev. Bitoeng. Sulawesi, C Indonesia
Biu 75 H4 Borno, E Nigeria
Biwa-ko 131 C6 lake Honshū, SW Japan
Bizerta see Bizerte
Bizerte 71 E1 Ar. Banzart, Eng. Bizerta. N Tunisia
Bjelovar 100 B2 Hung. Belovár. Bjelovar-Bilogora, N Croatia
Bjeshkët e Namuna see North Albanian Alps
Björneborg see Pori

Bjørnøya 83 F3 Eng. Bear Island. island N Norway
Blackall 148 C4 Queensland, E Australia
Black Drin 101 D6 Alb. Lumi i Drinit të Zi, SCr. Crni Drim. river Albania/Macedonia
Blackfoot 46 E4 Idaho, NW USA
Black Forest 95 B6 Eng. Black Forest. mountain range SW Germany
Black Forest see Schwarzwald
Black Hills 44 D3 mountain range South Dakota/Wyoming, N USA
Blackpool 89 C5 NW England, United Kingdom
Black Range 48 C2 mountain range New Mexico, SW USA
Black River 54 A5 W Jamaica
Black River 136 C3 Chin. Babian Jiang, Lixian Jiang, Fr. Rivière Noire, Vtn. Sông Đa. river China/Vietnam
Black Rock Desert 47 C5 desert Nevada, W USA
Black Sand Desert see Garagum
Black Sea 116 D3 Rom. Marea Neagrǎ, Rus. Chernoye More, Turk. Karadeniz, Ukr. Chorne More. sea Asia/Europe
Black Sea Lowland 109 E4 Ukr. Prychornomor'ska Nyzovyna. depression SE Europe
Black Volta 75 E4 var. Borongo, Mouhoun, Moun Hou, Fr. Volta Noire. river W Africa
Blackwater 89 A6 Ir. An Abhainn Mhór. river S Ireland
Blackwater State see Nebraska
Blagoevgrad 104 C3 prev. Gorna Dzhumaya. Blagoevgrad, W Bulgaria
Blagoveshchensk 115 G4 Amurskaya Oblast', SE Russia
Blahovishchens'ke 109 E3 Rus. Ulyanovka. Kirovohrads'ka Oblast', C Ukraine
Blake Plateau 33 D6 var. Blake Terrace. undersea plateau W Atlantic Ocean
Blake Terrace see Blake Plateau
Blanca, Bahía 65 C5 bay E Argentina
Blanca, Costa 93 F4 physical region SE Spain
Blanche, Lake 149 B5 lake South Australia
Blanc, Mont 91 D5 It. Monte Bianco. mountain France/Italy
Blanco, Cape 46 A4 headland Oregon, NW USA
Blanes 93 G2 Cataluña, NE Spain
Blankenberge 87 A5 West-Vlaanderen, NW Belgium
Blankenheim 95 A5 Nordrhein-Westfalen, W Germany
Blanquilla, Isla 59 E1 var. La Blanquilla. island N Venezuela
Blanquilla, La see Blanquilla, Isla
Blantyre 79 E2 var. Blantyre-Limbe. Southern, S Malawi
Blantyre-Limbe see Blantyre
Blaricum 86 C3 Noord-Holland, C Netherlands
Blatnitsa see Durankulak
Blenheim 151 C5 Marlborough, South Island, New Zealand
Blesae see Blois
Blida 70 D2 var. El Boulaida, El Boulaïda. N Algeria
Bloemfontein 78 C4 var. Mangaung. country capital (South Africa-judicial capital) Free State, C South Africa
Blois 90 C4 anc. Blesae. Loir-et-Cher, C France
Bloomfield 48 C1 New Mexico, SW USA
Bloomington 40 B4 Illinois, N USA
Bloomington 40 C4 Indiana, N USA
Bloomington 45 F2 Minnesota, N USA
Bloomsbury 148 D3 Queensland, NE Australia
Bluefield 40 D5 West Virginia, NE USA
Bluefields 53 E3 Región Autónoma Atlántico Sur, SE Nicaragua
Bluegrass State see Kentucky
Blue Hen State see Delaware
Blue Law State see Connecticut
Blue Mountain Peak 54 B5 mountain E Jamaica
Blue Mountains 46 C3 mountain range Oregon/Washington, NW USA
Blue Nile 72 C4 var. Abai, Bahr el, Azraq, Amh. Ābay Wenz, Ar. An Nil al Azraq. river Ethiopia/Sudan
Blumenau 63 E5 Santa Catarina, S Brazil

Blythe *47 D8* California, W USA
Blytheville *42 C1* Arkansas, C USA
Bo *74 C4* S Sierra Leone
Boaco *52 D3* Boaco, S Nicaragua
Boa Vista *62 D1 state capital* Roraima,
NW Brazil
Boa Vista *74 A3 island* Ilhas de
Barlavento, E Cape Verde
Bobaomby, Tanjona *79 G2 Fr.* Cap
d'Ambre. *headland* N Madagascar
Bobigny *90 E1* Seine-St-Denis, N France
Bobo-Dioulasso *74 D4* SW Burkina Faso
Bobrinets *see* Bobrynets'
Bobruysk *see* Babruysk
Bobrynets' *109 E3 Rus.* Bobrinets.
Kirovohrads'ka Oblast', C Ukraine
Boca Raton *43 F5* Florida, SE USA
Bocay *52 D2* Jinotega, N Nicaragua
Bocheykovo *see* Bacheykava
Bocholt *94 A4* Nordrhein-Westfalen,
W Germany
Bochum *94 A4* Nordrhein-Westfalen,
W Germany
Bocşa *108 A4 Ger.* Bokschen, *Hung.*
Boksánbánya. Caraş-Severin,
SW Romania
Bodaybo *115 F4* Irkutskaya Oblast',
E Russia
Bodegas *see* Babahoyo
Boden *84 D4* Norrbotten, N Sweden
Bodensee *see* Constance, Lake,
C Europe
Bodmin *89 C7* SW England, United
Kingdom
Bodø *84 C3* Nordland, C Norway
Bodrum *116 A4* Muğla, SW Turkey
Boeloekoemba *see* Bulukumba
Boende *77 C5* Equateur, C Dem. Rep.
Congo
Boeroe *see* Buru, Pulau
Boetoeng *see* Buton, Pulau
Bogale *136 B4* Ayeyarwady,
SW Myanmar (Burma)
Bogalusa *42 B3* Louisiana, S USA
Bogatynia *98 B4 Ger.* Reichenau.
Dolnosląskie, SW Poland
Bo Hai *128 D4 var.* Gulf of Chihli. *gulf*
NE China
Bohemia *99 A5 Cz.* Čechy, *Ger.* Böhmen.
W Czech Republic (Czechia)
Bohemian Forest *95 C5 Cz.* Český Les,
Šumava, *Ger.* Böhmerwald. *mountain*
range C Europe
Böhmen *see* Bohemia
Böhmerwald *see* Bohemian Forest
Böhmisch-Krumau *see* Český Krumlov
Bohol Sea *139 E2 var.* Mindanao Sea. *sea*
S Philippines
Bohuslav *109 E2 Rus.* Boguslav.
Kyyivs'ka Oblast', N Ukraine
Boise *46 D3 var.* Boise City. *state capital*
Idaho, NW USA
Boise City *49 E1* Oklahoma, C USA
Boise City *see* Boise
Bois, Lac des *see* Woods, Lake of the
Bois-le-Duc *see* 's-Hertogenbosch
Boizenburg *94 C3* Mecklenburg-
Vorpommern, N Germany
Bojador *see* Boujdour
Bojnūrd *120 D2 var.* Bujnurd.
Khorāsān-e Shemālī, N Iran
Bokāro *135 F4* Jhārkhand, N India
Boké *74 C4* W Guinea
Bokhara *see* Buxoro
Boksánbánya/Bockschen *see* Bocşa
Bol *76 B3 Lac* N Chad
Bolgatanga *75 E4* N Ghana
Bolgrad *see* Bolhrad
Bolhrad *108 D4 Rus.* Bolgrad. Odes'ka
Oblast', SW Ukraine
Bolívar, Pico *58 C2 mountain*
W Venezuela
Bolivia *61 F3 off.* Republic of Bolivia.
country W South America
Bolivia, Republic of *see* Bolivia
Bollène *91 D6* Vaucluse, SE France
Bollnäs *85 C5* Gävleborg, C Sweden
Bollon *149 D5* Queensland, C Australia
Bologna *96 C3* Emilia-Romagna,
N Italy
Bol'shevik *see* Bal'shavik

Bol'shevik, Ostrov *115 E2 island*
Severnaya Zemlya, Russia
Bol'shezemel'skaya Tundra *110 E3*
physical region NW Russia
Bol'shoy Lyakhovskiy, Ostrov *115 F2*
island NE Russia
Bolton *89 D5 prev.* Bolton-le-Moors.
NW England, United Kingdom
Bolton-le-Moors *see* Bolton
Bolu *116 B3* Bolu, NW Turkey
Bolungarvík *83 E4* Vestfirðhir,
NW Iceland
Bolyarovo *104 D3 prev.* Pashkeni.
Yambol, E Bulgaria
Bolzano *96 C1 Ger.* Bozen, *anc.*
Bauzanum. Trentino-Alto Adige,
N Italy
Boma *77 B6* Bas-Congo, W Dem. Rep.
Congo
Bombay *see* Mumbai
Bomu *76 D4 var.* Mbomou, Mbomu,
M'Bomu. *river* Central African
Republic/Dem. Rep. Congo
Bonaire *55 F5 Special municipality of the*
Netherlands S West Indies
Bonanza *52 D2* Región Autónoma
Atlántico Norte, NE Nicaragua
Bonaparte Archipelago *146 C2 island*
group Western Australia
Bon, Cap *102 D3 headland* N Tunisia
Bonda *77 B6* Ogooué-Lolo, C Gabon
Bondoukou *75 E4* E Ivory Coast
Bône *see* Annaba, Algeria
Bone *see* Watampone, Indonesia
Bone, Teluk *139 E4 bay* Sulawesi,
C Indonesia
Bongaigaon *135 G3* Assam, NE India
Bongo, Massif des *76 D4 var.* Chaîne des
Mongos. *mountain range* NE Central
African Republic
Bongor *76 B3* Mayo-Kébbi, SW Chad
Bonifacio *91 E7* Corse, France,
C Mediterranean Sea
Bonifacio, Bocche de/Bonifacio,
Bouches de *see* Bonifacio, Strait of
Bonifacio, Strait of *96 A4 Fr.* Bouches
de Bonifacio, *It.* Bocche di Bonifacio.
strait C Mediterranean Sea
Bonn *95 A5* Nordrhein-Westfalen,
W Germany
Bononia *see* Vidin, Bulgaria
Bononia *see* Boulogne-sur-Mer, France
Boosaaso *72 E4 var.* Bandar Kassim,
Bender Qaasim, Bosaso, *It.* Bender
Cassim. Bari, N Somalia
Boothia Felix *see* Boothia Peninsula
Boothia, Gulf of *37 F2 gulf* Nunavut,
NE Canada
Boothia Peninsula *37 F2 prev.* Boothia
Felix. *peninsula* Nunavut, NE Canada
Boppard *95 A5* Rheinland-Pfalz,
W Germany
Boquete *53 E5 var.* Bajo Boquete.
Chiriquí, W Panama
Boquillas *50 D2 var.* Boquillas del
Carmen. Coahuila, NE Mexico
Boquillas del Carmen *see* Boquillas
Bor *100 E4* Serbia, E Serbia
Bor *73 B5* Jonglei, E South Sudan
Borås *85 B7* Västra Götaland,
S Sweden
Borbetomagus *see* Worms
Borborema, Planalto da *56 E3 plateau*
NE Brazil
Bordeaux *91 B5 anc.* Burdigala.
Gironde, SW France
Bordj Omar Driss *71 E3* E Algeria
Borgå *see* Porvoo
Børgefjell *84 C4 mountain range*
C Norway
Borger *86 E2* Drenthe, NE Netherlands
Borger *49 E1* Texas, SW USA
Borgholm *85 C7* Kalmar, S Sweden
Borgo Maggiore *96 E1* NW San Marino
Borislav *see* Boryslav
Borisoglebsk *111 B6* Voronezhskaya
Oblast', W Russia
Borisov *see* Barysaw
Borlänge *85 C6* Dalarna, C Sweden
Borne *86 E3* Overijssel, E Netherlands
Borneo *138 C4 island* Brunei/Indonesia/
Malaysia
Bornholm *85 B8 island* E Denmark
Borohoro Shan *126 B2 mountain range*
NW China
Borongo *see* Black Volta
Boron'ki *see* Baron'ki
Borosjenő *see* Ineu
Borovan *104 C2* Vratsa, NW Bulgaria
Borovichi *110 B4* Novgorodskaya
Oblast', W Russia

Borovo *100 C3* Vukovar-Srijem,
NE Croatia
Borriana *93 F3 var.* Burriana.
País Valenciana, E Spain
Borşa *108 C3 Hung.* Borsa.
N Romania
Boryslav *108 B2 Pol.* Borysław, *Rus.*
Borislav. L'vivs'ka Oblast', NW Ukraine
Borysław *see* Boryslav
Bosanska Dubica *100 B3 var.* Kozarska
Dubica. Republika Srpska, NW Bosnia
and Herzegovina
Bosanska Gradiška *100 B3 var.*
Gradiška. Republika Srpska, N Bosnia
and Herzegovina
Bosanski Novi *100 B3 var.* Novi Grad.
Republika Srpska, NW Bosnia and
Herzegovina
Bosanski Šamac *100 C3 var.* Šamac.
Republika Srpska, N Bosnia and
Herzegovina
Bosaso *see* Boosaaso
Bösing *see* Pezinok
Boskovice *99 B5 Ger.* Boskowitz.
Jihomoravský Kraj, SE Czech Republic
(Czechia)
Boskowitz *see* Boskovice
Bosna *100 C4 river* N Bosnia and
Herzegovina
Bosne I Hercegovina, Federacija *100 B3*
republic Bosnia and Herzegovina
Bosnia and Herzegovina *100 B3 off.*
Republic of Bosnia and Herzegovina.
country SE Europe
Bosnia and Herzegovina, Republic of
see Bosnia and Herzegovina
Boso-hanto *131 D6 peninsula* Honshū,
S Japan
Bosphorus/Bosporus *see* İstanbul Boğazı
Bosporus *see* İstanbul Boğazı
Bosporus Cimmerius *see* Kerch Strait
Bosporus Thracius *see* İstanbul Boğazı
Bossangoa *76 C4* Ouham, C Central
African Republic
Bossembélé *76 C4* Ombella-Mpoko,
C Central African Republic
Bossier City *42 A2* Louisiana, S USA
Bosten Hu *126 C3 var.* Bagrax Hu. *lake*
NW China
Boston *89 E6 prev.* St.Botolph's Town.
E England, United Kingdom
Boston *41 G3 state capital* Massachusetts,
NE USA
Boston Mountains *42 B1 mountain*
range Arkansas, C USA
Bostyn' *see* Bastyn'
Botany *148 E2* New South Wales,
E Australia
Botany Bay *148 E2 inlet* New South
Wales, SE Australia
Boteti *78 C3 var.* Botletle. *river*
N Botswana
Bothnia, Gulf of *85 D5 Fin.* Pohjanlahti,
Swe. Bottniska Viken. *gulf* N Baltic Sea
Botletle *see* Boteti
Botoşani *108 C3 Hung.* Botosány.
Botoşani, NE Romania
Botosány *see* Botoşani
Botou *128 C4 prev.* Bozhen. Hebei,
E China
Botrange *87 D6 mountain* E Belgium
Botswana *78 C3 off.* Republic of
Botswana. *country* S Africa
Botswana, Republic of *see* Botswana
Bottniska Viken *see* Bothnia, Gulf of
Bouar *76 B4* Nana-Mambéré, W Central
African Republic
Bou Craa *70 B3 var.* Bu Craa.
NW Western Sahara
Bougainville Island *142 B3 island*
NE Papua New Guinea
Bougaroun, Cap *102 C3 headland*
NE Algeria
Bougouni *74 D4* Sikasso, SW Mali
Boujdour *70 A3 var.* Bojador.
W Western Sahara
Boulder *44 C4* Colorado, C USA
Boulder *44 B2* Montana, NW USA
Boulogne *see* Boulogne-sur-Mer
Boulogne-Billancourt *90 E2* Boulogne;
anc. Bononia, Gesoriacum,
Gessoriacum. Pas-de-Calais,
N France
Boûmdeïd *74 C3 var.* Boumdeït. Assaba,
S Mauritania
Boumdeït *see* Boûmdeïd
Boundiali *74 D4* N Ivory Coast
Bountiful *44 B4* Utah, W USA
Bounty Basin *see* Bounty Trough

Bounty Islands *142 D5 island group*
S New Zealand
Bounty Trough *152 C5 var.* Bounty
Basin. *trough* S Pacific Ocean
Bourbonnais *90 C4 cultural region*
C France
Bourbon Vendée *see* la Roche-sur-Yon
Bourg *see* Bourg-en-Bresse
Bourgas *see* Burgas
Bourge-en-Bresse *see* Bourg-en-Bresse
Bourg-en-Bresse *91 D5 var.* Bourg,
Bourge-en-Bresse. Ain, E France
Bourges *90 C4 anc.* Avaricum. Cher,
C France
Bourgogne *90 C4 Eng.* Burgundy.
cultural region E France
Bourke *149 C5* New South Wales,
SE Australia
Bournemouth *89 D7* S England, United
Kingdom
Boutilimit *74 C3* Trarza, SW Mauritania
Bouvet Island *67 D7 Norwegian*
dependency S Atlantic Ocean
Bowen *148 D3* Queensland, NE Australia
Bowling Green *40 B5* Kentucky, S USA
Bowling Green *40 C3* Ohio, N USA
Boxmeer *86 D4* Noord-Brabant,
SE Netherlands
Boyarka *109 E2* Kyyivs'ka Oblast',
N Ukraine
Boychinovtsi *104 C2 prev.* Lekhchevo.
Montana, NW Bulgaria
Boysun *123 E3 Rus.* Baysun.
Surkhondaryo Viloyati, S Uzbekistan
Bozeman *44 B2* Montana, NW USA
Bozen *see* Bolzano
Bozhen *see* Botou
Bozüyük *116 B3* Bilecik, NW Turkey
Brač *100 B4 var.* Brach, *It.* Brazza; *anc.*
Brattia. *island* S Croatia
Bracara Augusta *see* Braga
Brach *see* Brač
Brades *55 G3 de facto dependent territory*
capital, de jure capital, Plymouth,
destroyed by volcano in 1995
(Montserrat) SW Montserrat
Bradford *89 D5* N England, United
Kingdom
Brady *49 F3* Texas, SW USA
Braga *92 B2 anc.* Bracara Augusta.
Braga, NW Portugal
Bragança *92 C2 Eng.* Braganza; *anc.* Julio
Briga. Bragança, NE Portugal
Braganza *see* Bragança
Braganza *see* Bragança
Brahestad *see* Raahe
Brahmanbaria *135 G4* Chittagong,
E Bangladesh
Brahmapur *135 F5* Odisha, E India
Brahmaputra *135 H3 var.* Padma,
Tsangpo, *Ben.* Jamuna, *Chin.* Yarlung
Zangbo Jiang, *Ind.* Brahmaputra,
Dihang, Siang. *river* S Asia
Brăila *108 D4* Brăila, E Romania
Braine-le-Comte *87 B6* Hainaut,
SW Belgium
Brainerd *45 F2* Minnesota,
N USA
Brak *see* Birāk
Bramaputra *see* Brahmaputra
Brampton *38 D5* Ontario, S Canada
Branco, Rio *56 C3 river* N Brazil
Brandberg *78 A3 mountain*
NW Namibia
Brandenburg *94 C3 var.* Brandenburg
an der Havel. Brandenburg,
NE Germany
Brandenburg an der Havel *see*
Brandenburg
Brandon *37 F5* Manitoba, S Canada
Braniewo *98 D2 Ger.* Braunsberg.
Warmińsko-mazurskie, N Poland
Brasil *see* Brazil
Brasília *63 F3 country capital* (Brazil)
Distrito Federal, C Brazil
Brasil, República Federativa do *see*
Brazil
Braşov *108 C4 Ger.* Kronstadt, *Hung.*
Brassó; *prev.* Oraşul Stalin. Braşov,
C Romania
Brassó *see* Braşov
Bratislava *99 C6 Ger.* Pressburg, *Hung.*
Pozsony. *country capital* (Slovakia)
Bratislavský Kraj, W Slovakia
Bratsk *115 E4* Irkutskaya Oblast',
C Russia
Brattia *see* Brač
Braunsberg *see* Braniewo
Braunschweig *94 C4 Eng./Fr.*
Brunswick. Niedersachsen, N Germany

Brava *see* Baraawe

189

Brava, Costa *93 H2 coastal region* NE Spain
Bravo del Norte, Río/Bravo, Río *see* Grande, Río
Bravo, Río *50 C1 river* Mexico/USA North America
Brawley *47 D8* California, W USA
Brazil *62 C2 off.* Federative Republic of Brazil, *Port.* República Federativa do Brasil, *Sp.* Brasil; *prev.* United States of Brazil. *country* South America
Brazil Basin *67 C5 var.* Brazilian Basin, Brazil'skaya Kotlovina. *undersea basin* W Atlantic Ocean
Brazil, Federative Republic of *see* Brazil
Brazilian Basin *see* Brazil Basin
Brazilian Highlands *63 F3 var.* Brazilian Highlands. *mountain range* E Brazil
Brazilian Highlands *see* Central, Planalto
Brazil'skaya Kotlovina *see* Brazil Basin
Brazil, United States of *see* Brazil
Brazos River *49 G3 river* Texas, SW USA
Brazza *see* Brač
Brazzaville *77 B6 country capital* (Congo) Capital District, S Congo
Brčko *100 C3* Brčko Distrikt, NE Bosnia and Herzegovina
Brčko Distrikt *100 B3 autonomous district* Bosnia and Herzegovina
Brecht *87 C5* Antwerpen, N Belgium
Brecon Beacons *89 C6 mountain range* S Wales, United Kingdom
Breda *86 C4* Noord-Brabant, S Netherlands
Bree *87 D5* Limburg, NE Belgium
Bregalnica *101 E6 river* E Macedonia
Bregenz *57 B7 anc.* Brigantium. Vorarlberg, W Austria
Bregovo *104 B1* Vidin, NW Bulgaria
Bremen *94 B3 Fr.* Brême. Bremen, NW Germany
Bremerhaven *94 B3* Bremen, NW Germany
Bremerton *46 B2* Washington, NW USA
Brenham *49 G3* Texas, SW USA
Brenner, Col du/Brennero, Passo del *see* Brenner Pass
Brenner Pass *96 C1 var.* Brenner Sattel, *Fr.* Col du Brenner, *Ger.* Brennerpass, *It.* Passo del Brennero. *pass* Austria/ Italy
Brennerpass *see* Brenner Pass
Brenner Sattel *see* Brenner Pass
Brescia *96 B2 anc.* Brixia. Lombardia, N Italy
Breslau *see* Wrocław
Bressanone *96 C1 Ger.* Brixen. Trentino-Alto Adige, N Italy
Brest *107 A6 Pol.* Brześć nad Bugiem, *Rus.* Brest-Litovsk; *prev.* Brześć Litewski. Brestskaya Voblasts', SW Belarus
Brest *90 A3* Finistère, NW France
Brest-Litovsk *see* Brest
Bretagne *90 A3 Eng.* Brittany, *Lat.* Britannia Minor. *cultural region* NW France
Brewster, Kap *see* Kangikajik
Brewton *42 C3* Alabama, S USA
Brezhnev *see* Naberezhnyye Chelny
Brezovo *104 D2 prev.* Abrashlare. Plovdiv, C Bulgaria
Bria *76 D4* Haute-Kotto, C Central African Republic
Briançon *91 D5 anc.* Brigantio. Hautes-Alpes, SE France
Bricgstow *see* Bristol
Bridgeport *41 F3* Connecticut, NE USA
Bridgetown *55 G2 country capital* (Barbados) SW Barbados
Bridlington *89 D5* E England, United Kingdom
Bridport *89 D7* S England, United Kingdom
Brieg *see* Brzeg
Brig *95 A7 Fr.* Brigue, *It.* Briga. Valais, SW Switzerland
Briga *see* Brig
Brigantio *see* Briançon
Brigantium *see* Bregenz
Brigham City *44 B3* Utah, W USA
Brighton *89 E7* SE England, United Kingdom
Brighton *44 D4* Colorado, C USA
Brigue *see* Brig
Brindisi *97 E5 anc.* Brundisium, Brundusium. Puglia, SE Italy
Briovera *see* St-Lô
Brisbane *149 E5 state capital* Queensland, E Australia

Bristol *89 D7 anc.* Bricgstow. SW England, United Kingdom
Bristol *41 F3* Connecticut, NE USA
Bristol *40 D5* Tennessee, S USA
Bristol Bay *36 B3 bay* Alaska, USA
Bristol Channel *89 C7 inlet* England/ Wales, United Kingdom
Britain *80 C3 var.* Great Britain. *island* United Kingdom
Britannia Minor *see* Bretagne
British Columbia *36 D4 Fr.* Colombie-Britannique. *province* SW Canada
British Guiana *see* Guyana
British Honduras *see* Belize
British Indian Ocean Territory *141 B5 UK dependent territory* C Indian Ocean
British Isles *89 island group* NW Europe
British North Borneo *see* Sabah
British Solomon Islands Protectorate *see* Solomon Islands
British Virgin Islands *55 F3 var.* Virgin Islands. *UK Overseas Territory* E West Indies
Brittany *see* Bretagne
Briva Curretia *see* Brive-la-Gaillarde
Briva Isarae *see* Pontoise
Brive *see* Brive-la-Gaillarde
Brive-la-Gaillarde *91 C5 prev.* Brive; *anc.* Briva Curretia. Corrèze, C France
Brixen *see* Bressanone
Brixia *see* Brescia
Brno *99 B5 Ger.* Brünn. Jihomoravský Kraj, SE Czech Republic (Czechia)
Bročeni *106 B3* SW Latvia
Brod/Bród *see* Slavonski Brod
Brodeur Peninsula *37 F2 peninsula* Baffin Island, Nunavut, NE Canada
Brod na Savi *see* Slavonski Brod
Brodnica *98 C3 Ger.* Buddenbrock. Kujawski-pomorskie, C Poland
Broek-in-Waterland *86 C3* Noord-Holland, C Netherlands
Broken Arrow *49 G1* Oklahoma, C USA
Broken Bay *148 E1 bay* New South Wales, SE Australia
Broken Hill *149 B6* New South Wales, SE Australia
Broken Ridge *141 D6 undersea plateau* S Indian Ocean
Bromberg *see* Bydgoszcz
Bromley *89 B8* United Kingdom
Brookhaven *42 B3* Mississippi, S USA
Brookings *45 F3* South Dakota, N USA
Brooks Range *36 D2 mountain range* Alaska, USA
Brookton *147 B6* Western Australia
Broome *146 B3* Western Australia
Broomfield *44 D4* Colorado, C USA
Broucsella *see* Brussel/Bruxelles
Brovary *109 E2* Kyyivs'ka Oblast', N Ukraine
Brownfield *49 E2* Texas, SW USA
Brownsville *49 G5* Texas, SW USA
Brownwood *49 F3* Texas, SW USA
Brozha *107 D7* Mahilyowskaya Voblasts', E Belarus
Bruges *see* Brugge
Brugge *87 A5 Fr.* Bruges. West-Vlaanderen, NW Belgium
Brummen *86 D3* Gelderland, E Netherlands
Brundisium/Brundusium *see* Brindisi
Brunei *138 D3 off.* Brunei Darussalam, *Mal.* Negara Brunei Darussalam. *country* SE Asia
Brunei Darussalam *see* Brunei
Brunei Town *see* Bandar Seri Begawan
Brünn *see* Brno
Brunner, Lake *151 C5 lake* South Island, New Zealand
Brunswick *43 E3* Georgia, SE USA
Brunswick *see* Braunschweig
Brusa *see* Bursa
Brus Laguna *52 D2* Gracias a Dios, E Honduras
Brussa *see* Bursa
Brussel *87 C6 var.* Brussels, *Fr.* Bruxelles, *Ger.* Brüssel; *anc.* Broucsella. *country capital* (Belgium) Brussels, C Belgium
Brüssel/Brussels *see* Brussel/Bruxelles
Brüx *see* Most
Bruxelles *see* Brussel
Bryan *49 G3* Texas, SW USA
Bryansk *111 A5* Bryanskaya Oblast', W Russia
Brzeg *98 C4 Ger.* Brieg; *anc.* Civitas Altae Ripae. Opolskie, S Poland

Brześć Litewski/Brześć nad Bugiem *see* Brest
Brzeżany *see* Berezhany
Bucaramanga *58 B2* Santander, N Colombia
Buchanan *74 C5 prev.* Grand Bassa. SW Liberia
Buchanan, Lake *49 F3 reservoir* Texas, SW USA
Bucharest *see* București
Buckeye State *see* Ohio
Bu Craa *see* Bou Craa
București *108 C5 Eng.* Bucharest, *Ger.* Bukarest, *prev.* Altenburg; *anc.* Cetatea Damboviței. *country capital* (Romania) București, S Romania
Buda-Koshelyovo *107 D7 Rus.* Buda-Koshelëvo. Homyel'skaya Voblasts', SE Belarus
Buda-Koshelëvo *see* Buda-Koshelyovo
Budapest *99 C6 off.* Budapest Főváros, *SCr.* Budimpešta. *country capital* (Hungary) Pest, N Hungary
Budapest Főváros *see* Budapest
Budaun *134 D3* Uttar Pradesh, N India
Buddenbrock *see* Brodnica
Budimpešta *see* Budapest
Budweis *see* České Budějovice
Budyšin *see* Bautzen
Buena Park *46 E2* California, W USA North America
Buenaventura *58 A3* Valle del Cauca, W Colombia
Buena Vista *61 G4* Santa Cruz, C Bolivia
Buena Vista *93 H5* S Gibraltar Europe
Buenavista *93 H5* Baja California Sur, NW Mexico
Buenaventura *93 H5* Sonora, NW Mexico
Buena Vista *93 H5* Colorado, C USA
Buena Vista *93 H5* Georgia, SE USA
Buena Vista *93 H5* Virginia, NE USA
Buenos Aires *64 D4 hist.* Santa Maria del Buen Aire. *country capital* (Argentina) Buenos Aires, E Argentina
Buenos Aires *53 E5* Puntarenas, SE Costa Rica
Buenos Aires, Lago *65 B6 var.* Lago General Carrera. *lake* Argentina/Chile
Buffalo *41 E3* New York, NE USA
Buffalo Narrows *37 F4* Saskatchewan, C Canada
Buff Bay *54 B5* E Jamaica
Buftea *108 C5* Ilfov, S Romania
Bug *81 E3 Bel.* Zakhodni Buh, *Eng.* Western Bug, *Rus.* Zapadnyy Bug, *Ukr.* Zakhidnyy Buh. *river* E Europe
Buga *58 B3* Valle del Cauca, W Colombia
Bughotu *see* Santa Isabel
Buguruslan *111 D6* Orenburgskaya Oblast', W Russia
Buitenzorg *see* Bogor
Bujalance *92 D4* Andalucía, S Spain
Bujanovac *101 E5* S Serbia
Bujnurd *see* Bojnūrd
Bujumbura *73 B7 prev.* Usumbura. *country capital* (Burundi) W Burundi
Bukarest *see* București
Bukavu *77 E6 prev.* Costermansville. Sud-Kivu, E Dem. Rep. Congo
Bukhara *see* Buxoro
Bukoba *73 B6* Kagera, NW Tanzania
Bülach *95 B7* Zürich, NW Switzerland
Bulawayo *78 D3* Matabeleland North, SW Zimbabwe
Bulgan *127 E2* Bulgan, N Mongolia
Bulgaria *104 C2 off.* Republic of Bulgaria, *Bul.* Bŭlgariya; *prev.* People's Republic of Bulgaria. *country* SE Europe
Bulgaria, People's Republic of *see* Bulgaria
Bulgaria, Republic of *see* Bulgaria
Bŭlgariya *see* Bulgaria
Bullion State *see* Missouri
Bull Shoals Lake *42 B1 reservoir* Arkansas/Missouri, C USA
Bulukumba *139 E4 prev.* Boeloekoemba. Sulawesi, C Indonesia
Bumba *77 D5* Équateur, N Dem. Rep. Congo
Bunbury *147 A7* Western Australia
Bundaberg *148 E4* Queensland, E Australia
Bungo-suido *131 B7 strait* SW Japan
Bunia *77 E5* Orientale, NE Dem. Rep. Congo
Bünyan *116 D3* Kayseri, C Turkey
Buraida *see* Buraydah

Buraydah *120 B4 var.* Buraida. Al Qaşīm, N Saudi Arabia
Burdigala *see* Bordeaux
Burdur *116 B4 var.* Buldur. Burdur, SW Turkey
Burdur Gölü *116 B4 salt lake* SW Turkey
Burē *72 C4* Āmara, N Ethiopia
Burgas *104 E2 var.* Bourgas. Burgas, E Bulgaria
Burgaski Zaliv *104 E2 gulf* E Bulgaria
Burgos *92 D2* Castilla y León, N Spain
Burgundy *see* Bourgogne
Burhan Budai Shan *126 D4 mountain range* C China
Buriram *137 D5 var.* Buri Ram, Puriramya. Buri Ram, E Thailand
Buri Ram *see* Buriram
Burjassot *93 F3* Valenciana, E Spain
Burkburnett *49 F2* Texas, SW USA
Burketown *148 B3* Queensland, NE Australia
Burkina *see* Burkina Faso
Burkina Faso *75 E4 off.* Burkina Faso; *var.* Burkina, *prev.* Upper Volta. *country* W Africa
Burley *46 D4* Idaho, NW USA
Burlington *45 G4* Iowa, C USA
Burlington *41 F2* Vermont, NE USA
Burma *136 A3 off.* Union of Myanmar. *country* SE Asia *see also* Myanmar
Burnie *149 C8* Tasmania, SE Australia
Burns *46 C3* Oregon, NW USA
Burnside *37 F3 river* Nunavut, NW Canada
Burnsville *45 F2* Minnesota, N USA
Burrel *101 D6 var.* Burreli. Dibër, C Albania
Burreli *see* Burrel
Burriana *see* Borriana
Bursa *116 B3 var.* Brussa, *prev.* Brusa; *anc.* Prusa. Bursa, NW Turkey
Bür Sa'īd *72 B1 var.* Port Said. N Egypt
Burtnieks *106 C3 var.* Burtnieks Ezers. *lake* N Latvia
Burtnieks Ezers *see* Burtnieks
Burundi *73 B7 off.* Republic of Burundi; *prev.* Kingdom of Burundi, Urundi. *country* C Africa
Burundi, Kingdom of *see* Burundi
Burundi, Republic of *see* Burundi
Buru, Pulau *139 F4 prev.* Boeroe. *island* E Indonesia
Busan *129 E4 off.* Busan Gwang-yeoksi, *prev.* Pusan, *Jap.* Fusan. SE South Korea
Busan Gwang-yeoksi *see* Busan
Buşayrah *118 D3* Dayr az Zawr, E Syria
Büsheh/Bushire *see* Bandar-e Büshehr
Busra *see* Al Başrah, Iraq
Busselton *147 A7* Western Australia
Bussora *see* Al Başrah
Buta *77 D5* Orientale, N Dem. Rep. Congo
Butembo *77 E5* Nord-Kivu, NE Dem. Rep. Congo
Butler *41 E4* Pennsylvania, NE USA
Buton, Pulau *139 E4 var.* Pulau Butung; *prev.* Boetoeng. *island* C Indonesia
Bütow *see* Bytów
Butte *44 B2* Montana, NW USA
Butterworth *138 B3* Pinang, Peninsular Malaysia
Button Islands *39 E1 island group* Nunavut, NE Canada
Butuan *139 F2 off.* Butuan City. Mindanao, S Philippines
Butuan City *see* Butuan
Butung, Pulau *see* Buton, Pulau
Butuntum *see* Bitonto
Buulobarde *73 D5 var.* Buulo Berde. Hiiraan, C Somalia
Buulo Berde *see* Buulobarde
Buur Gaabo *73 D6* Jubbada Hoose, S Somalia
Buxoro *122 D2 var.* Bokhara, *Rus.* Bukhara. Buxoro Viloyati, C Uzbekistan
Buynaksk *111 B8* Respublika Dagestan, SW Russia
Büyükmenderes Nehri *116 A4 river* SW Turkey
Büzmeýin *see* Abadan
Buzău *108 C4* Buzău, SE Romania
Buzuluk *111 D6* Orenburgskaya Oblast', W Russia
Byahoml' *107 D5 Rus.* Begoml'. Vitsyebskaya Voblasts', N Belarus
Byalynichy *107 D6 Rus.* Belynichi. Mahilyowskaya Voblasts', E Belarus
Byan Tumen *see* Choybalsan

Byarezina 107 D6 prev. Byerezino, *Rus.* Berezina. *river* C Belarus
Bydgoszcz 98 C3 *Ger.* Bromberg. Kujawski-pomorskie, C Poland
Byelaruskaya Hrada 107 B6 *Rus.* Belorusskaya Gryada. *ridge* N Belarus
Byerezino *see* Byarezina
Byron Island *see* Nikunau
Bystrovka *see* Kemin
Bytča 99 C5 Žilinský Kraj, N Slovakia
Bytom 99 C5 *Ger.* Beuthen. Śląskie, S Poland
Bytów 98 C2 *Ger.* Bütow. Pomorskie, N Poland
Byuzmeyin *see* Abadan
Byval'ki 107 D8 Homyel'skaya Voblasts', SE Belarus
Byzantium *see* İstanbul

C

Caála 78 B2 *var.* Kaala, Robert Williams, *Port.* Vila Robert Williams. Huambo, C Angola
Caazapá 64 D3 Caazapá, S Paraguay
Caballo Reservoir 48 C3 *reservoir* New Mexico, SW USA
Cabanaquinta 92 D1 *var.* Cabañaquinta. Asturias, N Spain
Cabañaquinta *see* Cabanaquinta
Cabanatuan 139 E1 *off.* Cabanatuan City. Luzon, N Philippines
Cabanatuan City *see* Cabanatuan
Cabillonum *see* Chalon-sur-Saône
Cabimas 58 C1 Zulia, NW Venezuela
Cabinda 78 A1 *var.* Kabinda. Cabinda, NW Angola
Cabinda 78 A1 *var.* Kabinda. *province* NW Angola
Cabora Bassa, Lake 78 D2 *var.* Lake Cabora Bassa. *reservoir* NW Mozambique
Cabora Bassa, Lake *see* Cahora Bassa, Albufeira de
Caborca 50 B1 Sonora, NW Mexico
Cabot Strait 39 G4 *strait* E Canada
Cabo Verde *see* Cape Verde
Cabo Verde, Republic of *see* Cape Verde
Cabo Verde, Ilhas do *see* Cape Verde
Cabras, Ilha das 76 E2 *island* S Sao Tome and Principe, Africa, E Atlantic Ocean
Cabrera, Illa de 93 G3 *island* E Spain
Cáceres 92 C3 *Ar.* Qazris. Extremadura, W Spain
Cachimbo, Serra do 63 E2 *mountain range* C Brazil
Caconda 78 B2 Huíla, C Angola
Čadca 99 C5 Hung. Csaca. Žilinský Kraj, N Slovakia
Cadillac 40 C2 Michigan, N USA
Cadiz 139 E2 *off.* Cadiz City. Negros, C Philippines
Cádiz 92 C5 *anc.* Gades, Gadier, Gadir, Gadire. Andalucía, SW Spain
Cadiz City *see* Cadiz
Gulf of Cadiz 92 B5 *Eng.* Gulf of Cadiz. *gulf* Portugal/Spain
Cadiz, Gulf of *see* Cádiz, Golfo de
Cadurcum *see* Cahors
Caen 90 B3 Calvados, N France
Caene/Caenepolis *see* Qinā
Caerdydd *see* Cardiff
Caer Glou *see* Gloucester
Caer Gybi *see* Holyhead
Caerleon *see* Chester
Caer Luel *see* Carlisle
Caesaraugusta *see* Zaragoza
Caesarea Mazaca *see* Kayseri
Caesarobriga *see* Talavera de la Reina
Caesarodunum *see* Tours
Caesaromagus *see* Beauvais
Caesena *see* Cesena
Cafayate 64 C2 Salta, N Argentina
Cagayan de Oro 139 E2 *off.* Cagayan de Oro City. Mindanao, S Philippines
Cagayan de Oro City *see* Cagayan de Oro
Cagliari 97 A6 *anc.* Caralis. Sardegna, Italy, C Mediterranean Sea
Caguas 55 F3 E Puerto Rico
Cahors 91 B5 *anc.* Cadurcum. Lot, S France
Cahul 108 D4 *Rus.* Kagul. S Moldova
Caicos Passage 54 D2 *strait* The Bahamas/Turks and Caicos Islands
Caiffa *see* Hefa
Cailungo 96 E1 N San Marino
Caiphas *see* Hefa

Cairns 148 D3 Queensland, NE Australia
Cairo 72 B2 *var.* El Qâhira, *Ar.* Al Qâhirah. *country capital* (Egypt) N Egypt
Cairo 40 B5 Illinois, N USA
Caisleán an Bharraigh *see* Castlebar
Cajamarca 60 B3 *prev.* Caxamarca. Cajamarca, NW Peru
Čakovec 100 B2 *Ger.* Csakathurn, *Hung.* Csáktornya; *prev. Ger.* Tschakathurn. Medimurje, N Croatia
Calabar 75 G5 Cross River, S Nigeria
Calabozo 58 D2 Guárico, C Venezuela
Calafat 108 B5 Dolj, SW Romania
Calafate *see* El Calafate
Calahorra 93 E2 La Rioja, N Spain
Calais 90 C2 Pas-de-Calais, N France
Calais 41 H2 Maine, NE USA
Calais, Pas de *see* Dover, Strait of
Calama 64 B2 Antofagasta, N Chile
Călăras *see* Călăraşi
Călăraşi 108 D3 *var.* Călăras, *Rus.* Kalarash. C Moldova
Călăraşi 108 C5 Călăraşi, SE Romania
Calatayud 93 E2 Aragón, NE Spain
Calbayog 139 E2 *off.* Calbayog City. Samar, C Philippines
Calbayog City *see* Calbayog
Calcutta *see* Kolkata
Caldas da Rainha 92 B3 Leiria, W Portugal
Caldera 64 B3 Atacama, N Chile
Caldwell 46 C3 Idaho, NW USA
Caledonia 52 C1 Corozal, N Belize
Caleta Olivia 65 B6 Santa Cruz, SE Argentina
Calgary 37 E5 Alberta, SW Canada
Cali 58 B3 Valle del Cauca, W Colombia
Calicut *see* Kozhikode
California 47 B7 *off.* State of California, *also known as* El Dorado, The Golden State. *state* W USA
Gulf of California 50 B2 *Eng.* Gulf of California; *prev.* Sea of Cortez. *gulf* W Mexico
California, Gulf of *see* California, Golfo de
Călimăneşti 108 B4 Vâlcea, SW Romania
Calisia *see* Kalisz
Callabonna, Lake 149 B5 *lake* South Australia
Callao 60 C4 Callao, W Peru
Callatis *see* Mangalia
Callosa de Segura 93 F4 Valenciana, E Spain
Calmar *see* Kalmar
Caloundra 149 E5 Queensland, E Australia
Caltanissetta 97 C7 Sicilia, Italy, C Mediterranean Sea
Caluula 72 E4 Bari, NE Somalia
Calvinia 78 C5 W South Africa
Camabatela 78 B1 Cuanza Norte, NW Angola
Camacupa 78 B2 *var.* General Machado, *Port.* Vila General Machado. Bié, C Angola
Camagüey 54 C2 *prev.* Puerto Príncipe. Camagüey, C Cuba
Camagüey, Archipiélago de 54 C2 *island group* C Cuba
Camana 61 E4 *var.* Camaná. Arequipa, SW Peru
Camargue 91 D6 *physical region* SE France
Ca Mau 137 D6 *var.* Quan Long. Minh Hai, S Vietnam
Cambay, Gulf of *see* Khambhât, Gulf of
Camberia *see* Chambéry
Cambodia 137 D5 *off.* Kingdom of Cambodia, *var.* Democratic Kampuchea, Roat Kampuchea, *Cam.* Kampuchea; *prev.* People's Democratic Republic of Kampuchea. *country* SE Asia
Cambodia, Kingdom of *see* Cambodia
Cambrai 90 C2 *Flem.* Kambryk, *prev.* Cameracum. Nord, N France
Cambray *see* Cambrai
Cambrian Mountains 89 C6 *mountain range* C Wales, United Kingdom
Cambridge 88 A4 W Jamaica
Cambridge 150 D3 Waikato, North Island, New Zealand
Cambridge 89 E6 *Lat.* Cantabrigia. E England, United Kingdom
Cambridge 41 F4 Maryland, NE USA
Cambridge 40 D4 Ohio, NE USA

Cambridge Bay 37 F3 *var.* Ikaluktutiak. Victoria Island, Nunavut, NW Canada
Camden 42 B2 Arkansas, C USA
Camellia State *see* Alabama
Cameracum *see* Cambrai
Cameroon 76 A4 *off.* Republic of Cameroon, *Fr.* Cameroun. *country* W Africa
Cameroon, Republic of *see* Cameroon
Cameroun *see* Cameroon
Camocim 63 F2 Ceará, E Brazil
Camopi 59 H3 E French Guiana
Campamento 52 C2 Olancho, C Honduras
Campania 97 D5 *Eng.* Champagne. *region* S Italy
Campbell, Cape 151 D5 *headland* South Island, New Zealand
Campbell Island 142 D5 *island* S New Zealand
Campbell Plateau 142 D5 *undersea plateau* SW Pacific Ocean
Campbell River 36 D5 Vancouver Island, British Columbia, SW Canada
Campeche 51 G4 Campeche, SE Mexico
Bay of Campeche 51 F4 *Eng.* Bay of Campeche. *bay* E Mexico
Campeche, Bay of *see* Campeche, Bahía de
Câm Pha 136 E3 Quang Ninh, N Vietnam
Câmpina 108 C4 *prev.* Cîmpina. Prahova, SE Romania
Campina Grande 63 G2 Paraíba, E Brazil
Campinas 63 F4 São Paulo, S Brazil
Campobasso 97 D5 Molise, C Italy
Campo Criptana *see* Campo de Criptana
Campo de Criptana 93 E3 *var.* Campo Criptana. Castilla-La Mancha, C Spain
Campo Grande 63 E4 *state capital* Mato Grosso do Sul, SW Brazil
Campos dos Goytacazes 63 F4 Rio de Janeiro, SE Brazil
Câmpulung 108 B4 *prev.* Câmpulung-Muşcel, Cîmpulung. Argeş, S Romania
Câmpulung-Muşcel *see* Câmpulung
Campus Stellae *see* Santiago de Compostela
Cam Ranh 137 E6 *prev.* Ba Ngoi. Khanh Hoa, S Vietnam
Canada 34 B4 *country* N North America
Canada Basin 34 C2 *undersea basin* Arctic Ocean
Canadian River 49 E2 *river* SW USA
Çanakkale 116 A3 *var.* Dardanelli; *prev.* Chanak, Kale Sultanie. Çanakkale, W Turkey
Cananea 50 B1 Sonora, NW Mexico
Canarreos, Archipiélago de los 54 B2 *island group* W Cuba
Canary Islands 70 A2 *Eng.* Canary Islands. *island group* Spain, NE Atlantic Ocean
Canary Islands *see* Canarias, Islas
Cañas 52 D4 Guanacaste, NW Costa Rica
Canaveral, Cape 43 E4 *headland* Florida, SE USA
Canavieiras 63 G3 Bahia, E Brazil
Canberra 142 C4 *country capital* (Australia) Australian Capital Territory, SE Australia
Cancún 51 H3 Quintana Roo, SE Mexico
Candia *see* Irákleio
Canea *see* Chaniá
Cangzhou 128 C4 Hebei, E China
Caniapiscau 39 E2 *river* Québec, E Canada
Caniapiscau, Réservoir de 38 D3 *reservoir* Québec, C Canada
Canik Dağları 116 D2 *mountain range* N Turkey
Canillo 91 A7 Canillo, C Andorra Europe
Çankırı 116 C3 *var.* Chankiri; *anc.* Gangra, Germanicopolis. Çankırı, N Turkey
Cannanore *see* Kannur
Cannes 91 D6 Alpes-Maritimes, SE France
Canoas 63 E5 Rio Grande do Sul, S Brazil
Canon City 44 C5 Colorado, C USA
Cantabria 92 D1 *autonomous community* N Spain
Cantábrica, Cordillera 92 C1 *mountain range* N Spain
Cantabrigia *see* Cambridge
Cantaura 59 E2 Anzoátegui, NE Venezuela
Canterbury 89 E7 *hist.* Cantwaraburh; *anc.* Durovernum, *Lat.* Cantuaria. SE England, United Kingdom

Canterbury Bight 151 C6 *bight* South Island, New Zealand
Canterbury Plains 151 C6 *plain* South Island, New Zealand
Cân Thơ 137 E6 Cân Thơ, S Vietnam
Canton 42 B2 Mississippi, S USA
Canton 40 D4 Ohio, N USA
Canton *see* Guangzhou
Canton Island *see* Kanton
Cantuaria/Cantwaraburh *see* Canterbury
Canyon 49 E2 Texas, SW USA
Cao Băng 136 D3 *var.* Caobang. Cao Băng, N Vietnam
Caobang *see* Cao Băng
Cap-Breton, Île du *see* Cape Breton Island
Cape Barren Island 149 C8 *island* Furneaux Group, Tasmania, SE Australia
Cape Basin 69 B7 *undersea basin* S Atlantic Ocean
Cape Breton Island 39 G4 *Fr.* Île du Cap-Breton. *island* Nova Scotia, SE Canada
Cape Charles 41 F5 Virginia, NE USA
Cape Coast 75 E5 *prev.* Cape Coast Castle. S Ghana
Cape Coast Castle *see* Cape Coast
Cape Girardeau 45 H5 Missouri, C USA
Capelle aan den IJssel 86 C4 Zuid-Holland, SW Netherlands
Cape Palmas *see* Harper
Cape Saint Jacques *see* Vung Tau
Cape Town 78 B5 *var.* Ekapa, *Afr.* Kaapstad, Kapstad. *country capital* (South Africa-legislative capital) Western Cape, SW South Africa
Cape Verde 74 A2 *off.* Republic of Cabo Verde, *Port.* Cabo Verde, Ilhas do Cabo Verde. *country* E Atlantic Ocean
Cape Verde Basin 66 C4 *undersea basin* E Atlantic Ocean
Cape Verde Plain 66 C4 *abyssal plain* E Atlantic Ocean
Cape York Peninsula 148 C2 *peninsula* Queensland, N Australia
Cap-Haïtien 54 D3 *var.* Le Cap. N Haiti
Capira 53 G5 Panamá, C Panama
Capitán Pablo Lagerenza 64 D1 *var.* Mayor Pablo Lagerenza. Chaco, N Paraguay
Capodistria *see* Koper
Capri 97 C5 *island* S Italy
Caprivi Concession *see* Caprivi Strip
Caprivi Strip 78 C3 *Ger.* Caprivizipfel; *prev.* Caprivi Concession. *cultural region* NE Namibia
Caprivizipfel *see* Caprivi Strip
Cap Saint-Jacques *see* Vung Tau
Caquetá, Río 58 C5 *var.* Río Japurá, Yapurá. *river* Brazil/Colombia
Caquetá, Río *see* Japurá, Rio
CAR *see* Central African Republic
Caracal 108 B5 Olt, S Romania
Caracaraí 62 D1 Rondônia, W Brazil
Caracas 58 D1 *country capital* (Venezuela) Distrito Federal, N Venezuela
Caralis *see* Cagliari
Carataska, Laguna de 53 E2 *lagoon* NE Honduras
Carballiño *see* O Carballiño
Carbón, Laguna del 64 B7 *physical feature* SE Argentina
Carbondale 40 B5 Illinois, N USA
Carbonia 97 A6 *var.* Carbonia Centro. Sardegna, Italy, C Mediterranean Sea
Carbonia Centro *see* Carbonia
Carcaso *see* Carcassonne
Carcassonne 91 C6 *anc.* Carcaso. Aude, S France
Cardamomes, Chaîne des *see* Krâvanh, Chuŏr Phnum
Cardamom Mountains *see* Krâvanh, Chuŏr Phnum
Cárdenas 54 B2 Matanzas, W Cuba
Cardiff 89 C7 *Wel.* Caerdydd. *national capital* S Wales, United Kingdom
Cardigan Bay 89 C6 *bay* W Wales, United Kingdom
Carei 108 B3 *Ger.* Gross-Karol, Karol, *Hung.* Nagykároly; *prev.* Careii-Mari. Satu Mare, NW Romania
Careii-Mari *see* Carei
Carey, Lake 147 B6 *lake* Western Australia
Cariaco 59 E1 Sucre, NE Venezuela

Caribbean Sea 54 C4 *sea* W Atlantic Ocean
Caribrod *see* Dimitrovgrad
Carlisle 88 C4 *anc.* Caer Luel, Luguvallium, Luguvallum. NW England, United Kingdom
Carlow 89 B6 *Ir.* Ceatharlach. SE Ireland
Carlsbad 48 D3 New Mexico, SW USA
Carlsbad *see* Karlovy Vary
Carlsberg Ridge 140 B4 *undersea ridge* S Arabian Sea
Carlsruhe *see* Karlsruhe
Carmana/Carmania *see* Kermān
Carmarthen 89 C6 SW Wales, United Kingdom
Carmaux 91 C6 Tarn, S France
Carmel 40 C4 Indiana, N USA
Carmelita 52 B1 Petén, N Guatemala
Carmen 51 G4 *var.* Ciudad del Carmen. Campeche, SE Mexico
Carmona 92 C4 Andalucía, S Spain
Carmona *see* Uíge
Carnaro *see* Kvarner
Carnarvon 147 A5 Western Australia
Carnegie, Lake 147 B5 *salt lake* Western Australia
Car Nicobar 133 F3 *island* Nicobar Islands, India, NE Indian Ocean
Caroaço, Ilha 76 E1 *island* N Sao Tome and Principe, Africa, E Atlantic Ocean
Carolina 63 F2 Maranhão, E Brazil
Caroline Island *see* Millennium Island
Caroline Islands 144 B2 *island group* C Micronesia
Carolopois *see* Châlons-en-Champagne
Caroní, Río 59 E3 *river* E Venezuela
Caronium *see* A Coruña
Carora 58 C1 Lara, N Venezuela
Carpathian Mountains 81 E4 *var.* Carpathians, *Cz./Pol.* Karpaty, *Ger.* Karpaten. *mountain range* E Europe
Carpathians *see* Carpathian Mountains
Carpathos/Carpathus *see* Kárpathos
Carpaţii Sudici *see* Carpaţii Meridionalii
Carpentaria, Gulf of 148 B2 *gulf* N Australia
Carpi 96 C2 Emilia-Romagna, N Italy
Carrara 96 B3 Toscana, C Italy
Carson City 47 C5 *state capital* Nevada, W USA
Carson Sink 47 C5 *salt flat* Nevada, W USA
Carstensz, Puntjak *see* Jaya, Puncak
Cartagena 58 B1 *var.* Cartagena de los Indes. Bolívar, NW Colombia
Cartagena 93 F4 *anc.* Carthago Nova. Murcia, SE Spain
Cartagena de los Indes *see* Cartagena
Cartago 53 E4 Cartago, C Costa Rica
Carthage 45 F5 Missouri, C USA
Carthago Nova *see* Cartagena
Cartwright 39 F2 Newfoundland and Labrador, E Canada
Carúpano 59 E1 Sucre, NE Venezuela
Carusbur *see* Cherbourg
Caruthersville 45 H5 Missouri, C USA
Cary 43 F1 North Carolina, SE USA
Casablanca 70 C2 *Ar.* Dar-el-Beida. NW Morocco
Casa Grande 48 B2 Arizona, SW USA
Cascade Range 46 B3 *mountain range* Oregon/Washington, NW USA
Cascadia Basin 34 A4 *undersea basin* NE Pacific Ocean
Cascais 92 B4 Lisboa, C Portugal
Caserta 97 D5 Campania, S Italy
Casey 154 D4 *Australian research station* Antarctica
Čáslav 99 B5 *Ger.* Tschaslau. Střední Čechy, C Czech Republic (Czechia)
Casper 44 C3 Wyoming, C USA
Caspian Depression 111 B7 *Kaz.* Kaspiy Mangy Oypaty, *Rus.* Prikaspiyskaya Nizmennost'. *depression* Kazakhstan/Russia
Caspian Sea 114 A4 *Az.* Xäzär Dänizi, *Kaz.* Kaspiy Tengizi, *Per.* Baḥr-e Khazar, Daryā-ye Khazar, *Rus.* Kaspiyskoye More. *inland sea* Asia/Europe
Cassai *see* Kasai
Cassel *see* Kassel
Castamoni *see* Kastamonu
Casteggio 96 B2 Lombardia, N Italy
Castelló de la Plana *see* Castellón de la Plana
Castellón *see* Castellón de la Plana

Castellón de la Plana 93 F3 *var.* Castellón, *Cat.* Castelló de la Plana. Valenciana, E Spain
Castelnaudary 91 C6 Aude, S France
Castelo Branco 92 C3 Castelo Branco, C Portugal
Castelsarrasin 91 B6 Tarn-et-Garonne, S France
Castelvetrano 97 C7 Sicilia, Italy, C Mediterranean Sea
Castilla-La Mancha 93 E3 *autonomous community* NE Spain
Castilla y León 92 C2 *var.* Castillia Leon. *autonomous community* NW Spain
Castillia Leon *see* Castilla y León
Castlebar 89 A5 *Ir.* Caisleán an Bharraigh. W Ireland
Castleford 89 D5 N England, United Kingdom
Castle Harbour 42 B5 *inlet* Bermuda, NW Atlantic Ocean
Castra Regina *see* Regensburg
Castricum 86 C3 Noord-Holland, W Netherlands
Castries 55 F1 *country capital* (Saint Lucia) N Saint Lucia
Castro 65 B6 Los Lagos, W Chile
Castrovillari 97 D6 Calabria, SW Italy
Castuera 92 D4 Extremadura, W Spain
Caswell Sound 151 A7 *sound* South Island, New Zealand
Catacamas 52 D2 Olancho, C Honduras
Catacaos 60 B3 Piura, NW Peru
Catalan Bay 93 H4 *bay* E Gibraltar, Mediterranean Sea
Cataluña 93 G2 N Spain
Catamarca *see* San Fernando del Valle de Catamarca
Catania 97 D7 Sicilia, Italy, C Mediterranean Sea
Catanzaro 97 D6 Calabria, SW Italy
Catarroja 93 F3 Valenciana, E Spain
Cat Island 54 C1 *island* C The Bahamas
Catskill Mountains 41 F3 *mountain range* New York, NE USA
Cattaro *see* Kotor
Cauca, Río 58 B2 *river* N Colombia
Caucasia 58 B2 Antioquia, NW Colombia
Caucasus 81 G4 *Rus.* Kavkaz. *mountain range* Georgia/Russia
Caura, Río 59 E3 *river* C Venezuela
Cavaia *see* Kavajë
Cavalla 74 D5 *var.* Cavally, Cavally Fleuve. *river* Ivory Coast/Liberia
Cavally/Cavally Fleuve *see* Cavalla
Caviana de Fora, Ilha 63 E1 *var.* Ilha Caviana. *island* N Brazil
Caviana, Ilha *see* Caviana de Fora, Ilha
Cawnpore *see* Kānpur
Caxamarca *see* Cajamarca
Caxito 78 B1 Bengo, NW Angola
Cayenne 59 H3 *dependent territory/ arrondissement capital* (French Guiana) NE French Guiana
Cayes 54 D3 *var.* Les Cayes. SW Haiti
Cayman Brac 54 B3 *island* E Cayman Islands
Cayman Islands 54 B3 *UK Overseas Territory* W West Indies
Cayo *see* San Ignacio
Cay Sal 54 B2 *islet* SW The Bahamas
Cazin 100 B3 Federacija Bosne I Hercegovine, NW Bosnia and Herzegovina
Cazorla 93 E4 Andalucía, S Spain
Ceadâr-Lunga *see* Ciadir-Lunga
Ceará 63 F2 *off.* Estado do Ceará. *state/region* C Brazil
Ceará *see* Fortaleza
Ceará Abyssal Plain *see* Ceará Plain
Ceará, Estado do *see* Ceará
Ceará Plain 56 E3 *var.* Ceara Abyssal Plain. *abyssal plain* W Atlantic Ocean
Ceatharlach *see* Carlow
Cébaco, Isla 53 F5 *island* SW Panama
Cebu 139 E2 *off.* Cebu City. Cebu, C Philippines
Cebu City *see* Cebu
Čechy *see* Bohemia
Cecina 96 B3 Toscana, C Italy
Cedar City 44 A5 Utah, W USA
Cedar Falls 45 G3 Iowa, C USA
Cedar Lake 38 A2 *lake* Manitoba, C Canada
Cedar Rapids 45 G3 Iowa, C USA
Cedros, Isla 50 A2 *island* W Mexico

Ceduna 149 A6 South Australia
Cefalù 97 C7 *anc.* Cephaloedium. Sicilia, Italy, C Mediterranean Sea
Celebes 139 E4 *Eng.* Celebes. *island* C Indonesia
Celebes *see* Sulawesi
Celebes Sea 139 E3 *Ind.* Laut Sulawesi. *sea* Indonesia/Philippines
Celje 95 E7 *Ger.* Cilli. C Slovenia
Celldömölk 99 C6 Vas, W Hungary
Celle 94 B3 *var.* Zelle. Niedersachsen, N Germany
Celovec *see* Klagenfurt
Celtic Sea 89 B7 *Ir.* An Mhuir Cheilteach. *sea* SW British Isles
Celtic Shelf 80 B3 *continental shelf* E Atlantic Ocean
Cenderawasih, Teluk 139 G4 *var.* Teluk Irian, Teluk Sarera. *bay* W Pacific Ocean
Cenon 91 B5 Gironde, SW France
Centennial State *see* Colorado
Centrafrica, République *see* Central African Republic
Central African Republic 76 C4 *var.* République Centrafricaine, *abbrev.* CAR; *prev.* Ubangi-Shari, Oubangui-Chari, Territoire de l'Oubangui-Chari. *country* C Africa
Central, Cordillera 58 B3 *mountain range* W Colombia
Cordillera Central 55 E3 *mountain range* C Dominican Republic
Cordillera Central 53 F5 *mountain range* C Panama
Central, Cordillera 139 E1 *mountain range* Luzon, N Philippines
Central Group *see* Inner Islands
Centralia 46 B2 Washington, NW USA
Central Indian Ridge *see* Mid-Indian Ridge
Central Makran Range 134 A3 *mountain range* W Pakistan
Central Pacific Basin 142 D1 *undersea basin* C Pacific Ocean
Central Provinces and Berar *see* Madhya Pradesh
Central Range 144 B3 *mountain range* NW Papua New Guinea
Central Russian Upland 109 G1 *Eng.* Central Russian Upland. *mountain range* W Russia
Central Russian Upland *see* Srednerusskaya Vozvyshennost'
Central Siberian Plateau 114 D3 *var.* Central Siberian Uplands, *Eng.* Central Siberian Plateau. *mountain range* N Russia
Central Siberian Plateau/Central Siberian Uplands *see* Srednesibirskoye Ploskogor'ye
Central, Sistema 92 D3 *mountain range* C Spain
Central Valley 47 B6 *valley* California, W USA
Centum Cellae *see* Civitavecchia
Ceos *see* Tziá
Cephaloedium *see* Cefalù
Ceos *see* Seram, Pulau
Ceram Sea *see* Laut Seram
Cerasus *see* Giresun
Cereté 58 B2 Córdoba, NW Colombia
Cergy-Pontoise *see* Pontoise
Cerignola 97 D5 Puglia, SE Italy
Çerkeş 116 C2 Çankiri, N Turkey
Černăuţi *see* Chernivtsi
Cernay 90 E4 Haut-Rhin, NE France
Cerro de Pasco 60 C3 Pasco, C Peru
Cervera 93 F2 Cataluña, NE Spain
Cervino, Monte *see* Matterhorn
Cesena 96 C3 *anc.* Caesena. Emilia-Romagna, N Italy
Cēsis 106 D3 *Ger.* Wenden. C Latvia
Cetatea Dâmboviţei *see* Bucureşti
Cetinje 101 C5 *It.* Cettigne. S Montenegro
Cette *see* Sète
Cettigne *see* Cetinje
Ceuta 70 C2 *enclave affiliated to Spain* N Africa

Cévennes 91 C6 *mountain range* S France
Ceyhan 116 D4 Adana, S Turkey
Ceylanpinar 117 E4 Şanliurfa, SE Turkey
Ceylon *see* Sri Lanka
Ceylon Plain 124 B4 *abyssal plain* N Indian Ocean
Ceyre to the Caribs *see* Marie-Galante
Chachapoyas 60 B2 Amazonas, NW Peru
Chachevichy 107 D6 *Rus.* Chechevichi. Mahilyowskaya Voblasts', E Belarus
Chaco *see* Gran Chaco
Chad 76 C3 *off.* Republic of Chad, *Fr.* Tchad. *country* C Africa
Chad, Lake 76 B3 *Fr.* Lac Tchad. *lake* C Africa
Chad, Republic of *see* Chad
Chadron 44 D3 Nebraska, C USA
Chadyr-Lunga *see* Ciadir-Lunga
Chagai Hills 134 A2 *var.* Chāh Gay. *mountain range* Afghanistan/Pakistan
Chaghasarāy *see* Asadābād
Chagos-Laccadive Plateau 124 B4 *undersea plateau* N Indian Ocean
Chagos Trench 141 C5 *trench* N Indian Ocean
Chāh Gay *see* Chāgai Hills
Chaillu, Massif du 77 B6 *mountain range* C Gabon
Chain Ridge 140 B4 *undersea ridge* W Indian Ocean
Chajul 52 B2 Quiché, W Guatemala
Chakhānsūr 122 D5 Nīmrōz, SW Afghanistan
Chala 60 D4 Arequipa, SW Peru
Chalatenango 52 C3 Chalatenango, N El Salvador
Chalcidice *see* Chalkidikí
Chalcis *see* Chalkída
Chalki 105 E7 *island* Dodekánisa, Greece, Aegean Sea
Chalkída 105 C5 *var.* Halkída, *prev.* Khalkís; *anc.* Chalcis. Évvoia, E Greece
Chalkidikí 104 C4 *var.* Khalkidhikí; *anc.* Chalcidice. *peninsula* NE Greece
Challans 90 B4 Vendée, NW France
Challapata 61 F4 Oruro, SW Bolivia
Challenger Deep 152 B3 *trench* W Pacific Ocean
Challenger Deep *see* Mariana Trench
Challenger Fracture Zone 153 F4 *tectonic feature* SE Pacific Ocean
Châlons-en-Champagne 90 D3 *prev.* Châlons-sur-Marne, *hist.* Arcae Remorum; *anc.* Carolopois. Marne, NE France
Châlons-sur-Marne *see* Châlons-en-Champagne
Chalon-sur-Saône 90 D4 *anc.* Cabillonum. Saône-et-Loire, C France
Cha Mai *see* Thung Song
Chaman 134 B2 Baluchistan, SW Pakistan
Chambéry 91 D5 *anc.* Camberia. Savoie, E France
Champagne 90 D3 *cultural region* N France
Champaign 40 B4 Illinois, N USA
Champasak 137 D5 Champasak, S Laos
Champlain, Lake 41 F2 *lake* Canada/ USA
Champotón 51 G4 Campeche, SE Mexico
Chanak *see* Çanakkale
Chañaral 64 B3 Atacama, N Chile
Chan-chiang/Chanchiang *see* Zhanjiang
Chandeleur Islands 42 C3 *island group* Louisiana, S USA
Chandigarh 134 D2 *state capital* Punjab, N India
Chandrapur 135 E5 Mahārāshtra, C India
Changan *see* Xi'an, Shaanxi, C China
Changane 79 E3 *river* S Mozambique
Changchun 128 D3 *var.* Ch'angch'un, Ch'ang-ch'un; *prev.* Hsinking. *province capital* Jilin, NE China
Ch'angch'un/Ch'ang-ch'un *see* Changchun
Chang Jiang 128 A5 *Eng.* Yangtze; *var.* Yangtze Kiang. *river* C China
Changkiakow *see* Zhangjiakou
Chang, Ko 137 C6 *island* S Thailand
Changsha 128 C5 *var.* Ch'angsha, Ch'ang-sha. *province capital* Hunan, S China
Ch'angsha/Ch'ang-sha *see* Changsha

Changzhi 128 C4 Shanxi, C China
Chaniá 105 C7 var. Hania, Khaniá, Eng.
 Canea; anc. Cydonia. Kríti, Greece,
 E Mediterranean Sea
Chañi, Nevado de 64 B2 mountain
 NW Argentina
Chankiri see Çankırı
Channel Islands 89 C8 Fr. Iles
 Normandes. island group S English
 Channel
Channel Islands 47 B8 island group
 California, W USA
Channel-Port aux Basques 39 G4
 Newfoundland and Labrador,
 SE Canada
Channel, The see English Channel
Channel Tunnel 90 C2 tunnel France/
 United Kingdom
Chantabun/Chantaburi see Chanthaburi
Chantada 92 C1 Galicia, NW Spain
Chanthaburi 137 C6 var. Chantabun,
 Chantaburi. Chantaburi, S Thailand
Chanute 45 F5 Kansas, C USA
Chaouën see Chefchaouen
Chaoyang 128 D3 Liaoning, NE China
Chapala, Lago de 50 D4 lake C Mexico
Chapan, Gora 122 B3 mountain
 C Turkmenistan
Chapayevsk 111 C6 Samarskaya Oblast',
 W Russia
Chaplynka 109 F4 Khersons'ka Oblast',
 S Ukraine
Chapra see Chhapra
Charcot Seamounts 80 B3 seamount
 range E Atlantic Ocean
Chardzhev see Türkmenabat
Chardzhou/Chardzhui see Türkmenabat
Charente 91 B5 cultural region
 W France
Charente 91 B5 river W France
Chari 76 B3 var. Shari. river Central
 African Republic/Chad
Chārīkār 123 E4 Parwān,
 NE Afghanistan
Charity 59 F2 NW Guyana
Charjew see Türkmenabat
Charkhlik/Charkhliq see Ruoqiang
Charleroi 87 C7 Hainaut, S Belgium
Charlesbourg 39 E4 Québec, SE Canada
Charles de Gaulle 90 E1 (Paris)
 Seine-et-Marne, N France
Charles Island 38 D1 island Nunavut,
 NE Canada
Charles Island see Santa María, Isla
Charleston 43 F2 South Carolina,
 SE USA
Charleston 40 D5 state capital West
 Virginia, NE USA
Charleville 149 D5 Queensland,
 E Australia
Charleville-Mézières 90 D3 Ardennes,
 N France
Charlie-Gibbs Fracture Zone 66 C2
 tectonic feature N Atlantic Ocean
Charlotte 43 E1 North Carolina,
 SE USA
Charlotte Amalie 55 F3 prev. Saint
 Thomas. dependent territory capital
 (Virgin Islands (US)) Saint Thomas,
 N Virgin Islands (US)
Charlotte Harbor 43 E5 inlet Florida,
 SE USA
Charlottenhof see Aegviidu
Charlottesville 41 E5 Virginia, NE USA
Charlottetown 39 F4 province capital
 Prince Edward Island, Prince Edward
 Island, SE Canada
Charlotte Town see Roseau, Dominica
Charsk see Shar
Charters Towers 148 D3 Queensland,
 NE Australia
Chartres 90 C3 anc. Autricum, Civitas
 Carnutum. Eure-et-Loir, C France
Chashniki 107 D5 Vitsyebskaya
 Voblasts', N Belarus
Châteaubriant 90 B4 Loire-Atlantique,
 NW France
Châteaudun 90 C3 Eure-et-Loir,
 C France
Châteauroux 90 C4 prev. Indreville.
 Indre, C France
Château-Thierry 90 C3 Aisne, N France
Châtelet 87 C7 Hainaut, S Belgium
Châtelherault see Châtellerault
Châtellerault 90 B4 var. Châtelherault.
 Vienne, W France
Chatham Island see San Cristóbal, Isla
Chatham Island Rise see Chatham Rise
Chatham Islands 143 E5 island group
 New Zealand, SW Pacific Ocean

Chatham Rise 142 D5 var. Chatham
 Island Rise. undersea rise S Pacific
 Ocean
Chatkal Range 123 F2 Rus. Chatkal'skiy
 Khrebet. mountain range Kyrgyzstan/
 Uzbekistan
Chatkal'skiy Khrebet see Chatkal Range
Chattagām see Chittagong
Chattahoochee River 42 D3 river
 SE USA
Chattanooga 42 D1 Tennessee, S USA
Chatyr-Tash 123 G2 Narynskaya Oblast',
 C Kyrgyzstan
Châu Độc 137 D6 var. Chauphu, Chau
 Phu. An Giang, S Vietnam
Chauk 136 A3 Magway, W Myanmar
 (Burma)
Chaumont 90 D4 prev. Chaumont-en-
 Bassigny. Haute-Marne, N France
Chaumont-en-Bassigny see Chaumont
Chau Phu see Châu Độc
Chausy see Chavusy
Chaves 92 C2 anc. Aquae Flaviae. Vila
 Real, N Portugal
Chávez, Isla see Santa Cruz, Isla
Chavusy 107 E6 Rus. Chausy.
 Mahilyowskaya Voblasts', E Belarus
Chaykovskiy 111 D5 Permskiy Kray,
 NW Russia
Cheb 99 A5 Ger. Eger. Karlovarský Kraj,
 W Czech Republic (Czechia)
Cheboksary 111 C5 Chuvashskaya
 Respublika, W Russia
Cheboygan 40 C2 Michigan, N USA
Chechaouèn see Chefchaouen
Chech, Erg 74 D1 desert Algeria/Mali
Chechevichy see Chachevichy
Che-chiang see Zhejiang
Cheduba Island 136 A4 island
 W Myanmar (Burma)
Chefchaouen 70 C2 var. Chaouèn,
 Chechaouèn, Sp. Xauen. N Morocco
Chefoo see Yantai
Cheju-do see Jeju-do
Cheju Strait see Jeju Strait
Chekiang see Zhejiang
Cheken see Shalqar
Chelkar see Shalqar
Chełm 98 E4 Rus. Kholm. Lubelskie,
 SE Poland
Chełmno 98 C3 Ger. Culm, Kulm.
 Kujawsko-pomorskie, C Poland
Chełmża 98 C3 Ger. Culmsee, Kulmsee.
 Kujawsko-pomorskie, C Poland
Cheltenham 89 D6 C England, United
 Kingdom
Chelyabinsk 114 C3 Chelyabinskaya
 Oblast', C Russia
Chemnitz 94 D4 prev. Karl-Marx-Stadt.
 Sachsen, E Germany
Chemulpo see Incheon
Chenab 134 C2 river India/Pakistan
Chengchiatun see Liaoyuan
Chengde 128 D1 var. Jehol. Hebei,
 E China
Chengdu 128 B5 var. Chengtu,
 Ch'eng-tu. province capital Sichuan,
 C China
Chenghsien see Zhengzhou
Chengtu/Ch'eng-tu see Chengdu
Chennai 132 D2 prev. Madras. state
 capital Tamil Nādu, S India
Chenstokhov see Częstochowa
Chen Xian/Chenxian/Chen Xiang see
 Chenzhou
Chenzhou 128 C6 var. Chenxian, Chen
 Xian, Chen Xiang. Hunan, S China
Chepelare 104 C3 Smolyan, S Bulgaria
Chepén 60 B3 La Libertad, C Peru
Cher 90 C4 river C France
Cherbourg 90 B3 anc. Carusbur.
 Manche, N France
Cherepovets 110 B4 Vologodskaya
 Oblast', NW Russia
Chergui, Chott ech 70 D2 salt lake
 NW Algeria
Cherikov see Cherykaw
Cherkasy see Cherkasy
Cherkasy 109 E2 Rus. Cherkassy.
 Cherkas'ka Oblast', C Ukraine
Cherkessk 111 B7 Karachayevo-
 Cherkesskaya Respublika, SW Russia
Chernigov see Chernihiv
Chernihiv 109 E1 Rus. Chernigov.
 Chernihivs'ka Oblast', NE Ukraine
Chernivtsi 108 C3 Ger. Czernowitz,
 Rom. Cernăuţi, Rus. Chernovtsy.
 Chernivets'ka Oblast', W Ukraine
Cherno More see Black Sea

Chernomorskoye see Chornomors'ke
Chernovtsy see Chernivtsi
Chernoye More see Black Sea
Chernyakhovsk 106 A4 Ger. Insterburg.
 Kaliningradskaya Oblast', W Russia
Cherry Hill 41 F4 New Jersey, NE USA
Cherski Range see Cherskogo, Khrebet
Cherskiy 115 G2 Respublika Sakha
 (Yakutiya), NE Russia
Cherskogo, Khrebet 115 F2 var. Cherski
 Range. mountain range NE Russia
Cherso see Cres
Cherven' see Chervyen'
Chervonograd see Chervonohrad
Chervonohrad 108 C2 Rus.
 Chervonograd. L'vivs'ka Oblast',
 NW Ukraine
Chervyen' 107 D6 Rus. Cherven'.
 Minskaya Voblasts', C Belarus
Cherykaw 107 E7 Rus. Cherikov.
 Mahilyowskaya Voblasts', E Belarus
Chesapeake Bay 41 F5 inlet NE USA
Chesha Bay see Chëshskaya Guba
Chëshskaya Guba 155 D5 var.
 Archangel Bay, Chesha Bay, Dvina
 Bay. bay NW Russia
Chester 89 C6 Wel. Caerleon, hist.
 Legaceaster, Lat. Deva, Devana Castra.
 C England, United Kingdom
Chetumal 51 H4 var. Payo Obispo.
 Quintana Roo, SE Mexico
Cheviot Hills 88 D4 hill range England/
 Scotland, United Kingdom
Cheyenne 44 D4 state capital Wyoming,
 C USA
Cheyenne River 44 D3 river South
 Dakota/Wyoming, N USA
Chezdi-Oșorheiu see Târgu Secuiesc
Chhapra 135 F3 prev. Chapra. Bihār,
 N India
Chhattīsgarh 135 E4 cultural region
 E India
Chia-i see Chiayi
Chiai see Chiayi
Chiang-hsi see Jiangxi
Chiang Mai 136 B4 var. Chiangmai,
 Chiengmai, Kiangmai. Chiang Mai,
 NW Thailand
Chiangmai see Chiang Mai
Chiang Rai 136 C3 var. Chianpai,
 Chienrai, Muang Chiang Rai. Chiang
 Rai, NW Thailand
Chiang-su see Jiangsu
Chianning/Chian-ning see Nanjing
Chianpai see Chiang Rai
Chianti 96 C3 cultural region C Italy
Chiapa see Chiapa de Corzo
Chiapa de Corzo 51 G5 var. Chiapa.
 Chiapas, SE Mexico
Chiayi 129 D6 var. Chiai, Chia-i, Kiayi,
 Jiayi, Jap. Kagi. C Taiwan
Chiba 130 B1 var. Tiba. Chiba, Honshū,
 S Japan
Chibougamau 38 D3 Québec, SE Canada
Chicago 40 B3 Illinois, N USA
Ch'i-ch'i-ha-erh see Qiqihar
Chickasha 49 G2 Oklahoma, C USA
Chiclayo 60 B3 Lambayeque, NW Peru
Chico 47 B5 California, W USA
Chico, Río 65 B7 river SE Argentina
Chico, Río 65 B6 river S Argentina
Chicoutimi 39 E4 Québec, SE Canada
Chiengmai see Chiang Mai
Chienrai see Chiang Rai
Chiesanuova 96 D2 SW San Marino
Chieti 96 D4 var. Teate. Abruzzo,
 C Italy
Chifeng 127 G2 var. Ulanhad. Nei
 Mongol Zizhiqu, N China
Chigirin see Chyhyryn
Chih-fu see Yantai
Chihli see Hebei
Chihli, Gulf of see Bo Hai
Chihuahua 50 C2 Chihuahua,
 NW Mexico
Childress 49 F2 Texas, SW USA
Chile 64 B3 off. Republic of Chile.
 country SW South America
Chile Basin 57 A5 undersea basin
 E Pacific Ocean
Chile Chico 65 B6 Aisén, W Chile
Chile, Republic of see Chile
Chile Rise 57 A7 undersea rise SE Pacific
 Ocean
Chilia-Nouă see Kiliya
Chililabombwe 78 D2 Copperbelt,
 C Zambia
Chi-lin see Jilin
Chillán 65 B5 Bío Bío, C Chile
Chillicothe 40 D4 Ohio, N USA

Chill Mhantáin, Sléibhte see Wicklow
 Mountains
Chiloé, Isla de 65 A6 var. Isla Grande de
 Chiloé. island W Chile
Chilpancingo 51 E5 var. Chilpancingo
 de los Bravos. Guerrero, S Mexico
Chilpancingo de los Bravos see
 Chilpancingo
Chilung see Keelung
Chimán 53 G5 Panamá, E Panama
Chimbay see Chimboy
Chimborazo 60 A1 volcano C Ecuador
Chimbote 60 C3 Ancash, W Peru
Chimboy 122 D1 Rus. Chimbay.
 Qoraqalpog'iston Respublikasi,
 NW Uzbekistan
Chimkent see Shymkent
Chimoio 79 E3 Manica, C Mozambique
China 124 C2 off. People's Republic of
 China, Chin. Chung-hua Jen-min
 Kung-ho-kuo, Zhonghua Renmin
 Gongheguo; prev. Chinese Empire.
 country E Asia
Chi-nan/Chinan see Jinan
Chinandega 52 C3 Chinandega,
 NW Nicaragua
China, People's Republic of see China
China, Republic of see Taiwan
Chincha Alta 60 D4 Ica, SW Peru
Chin-chiang see Quanzhou
Chin-chou/Chinchow see Jinzhou
Chindwin 136 B2 var. Chindwin. river
 N Myanmar (Burma)
Chinese Empire see China
Chinghai see Qinghai
Ch'ing Hai see Qinghai Hu, China
Chingola 78 D2 Copperbelt, C Zambia
Ching-Tao/Ch'ing-tao see Qingdao
Chinguetti 74 C2 var. Chinguetti. Adrar,
 C Mauritania
Chin Hills 136 A3 mountain range
 W Myanmar (Burma)
Chinhsien see Jinzhou
Chinnereth see Tiberias, Lake
Chinook Trough 113 H4 trough
 N Pacific Ocean
Chioggia 96 C2 anc. Fossa Claudia.
 Veneto, NE Italy
Chios 105 D5 var. Hios, Khíos, It. Scio,
 Turk. Sakiz-Adasi. Chíos, E Greece
Chios 105 D5 var. Khíos. island
 E Greece
Chipata 78 D2 prev. Fort Jameson.
 Eastern, E Zambia
Chiquián 60 C3 Ancash, W Peru
Chiquimula 52 B2 Chiquimula,
 SE Guatemala
Chirāla 132 D1 Andhra Pradesh, E India
Chirchik see Chirchiq
Chirchiq 123 E2 Rus. Chirchik.
 Toshkent Viloyati, E Uzbekistan
Chiriquí Gulf see Chiriquí, Golfo de
Chiriquí, Golfo de 53 E5 lagoon
 NW Panama
Chiriquí Gulf see Chiriquí, Golfo de
 gulf SW Panama
Chiriquí, Laguna de 53 E5 lagoon
 NW Panama
Chiriquí, Volcán de see Barú, Volcán
Chirripó, Cerro see Chirripó Grande,
 Cerro
Chirripó Grande, Cerro 53 E4 var.
 Cerro Chirripó. mountain
 SE Costa Rica
Chisec 52 B2 Alta Verapaz, C Guatemala
Chisholm 45 F1 Minnesota, N USA
Chisimaio/Chisimayu see Kismaayo
Chişinău 108 D3 Rus. Kishinev. country
 capital (Moldova) C Moldova
Chita 115 F4 Zabaykal'skiy Kray,
 S Russia
Chitangwiza see Chitungwiza
Chitato 78 C1 Lunda Norte, NE Angola
Chitina 36 D3 Alaska, USA
Chitose 130 D2 var. Titose. Hokkaidō,
 NE Japan
Chitré 53 F5 Herrera, S Panama
Chittagong 135 G4 Ben. Chāttagām.
 Chittagong, SE Bangladesh
Chitungwiza 78 D3 prev. Chitangwiza.
 Mashonaland East, NE Zimbabwe
Chkalov see Orenburg
Chlef 70 D2 var. Ech Cheliff, Ech Chleff;
 prev. Al-Asnam, El Asnam,
 Orléansville. NW Algeria
Chocolate Mountains 47 D8 mountain
 range California, W USA
Chodorów see Khodoriv
Chodzież 98 C3 Wielkopolskie,
 C Poland
Choele Choel 65 C5 Río Negro,
 C Argentina

Choiseul 144 C3 var. Lauru. *island* NW Solomon Islands
Chojnice 98 C2 Ger. Konitz. Pomorskie, N Poland
Ch'ok'ē 72 C4 var. Choke Mountains. *mountain range* NW Ethiopia
Choke Mountains *see* Ch'ok'ē
Cholet 90 B4 Maine-et-Loire, NW France
Choluteca 52 C3 Choluteca, S Honduras
Choluteca, Río 52 C3 *river* SW Honduras
Choma 78 D2 Southern, S Zambia
Chomutov 98 A4 Ger. Komotau. Ústecký Kraj, NW Czech Republic (Czechia)
Chona 113 E2 *river* C Russia
Chon Buri 137 C5 *prev.* Bang Pla Soi. Chon Buri, S Thailand
Chone 60 A1 Manabí, W Ecuador
Ch'ŏngjin 129 E3 NE North Korea
Chongqing 129 B5 *var.* Ch'ung-ching, Ch'ung-ch'ing, Chungking, Pahsien, Tchongking, Yuzhou. Chongqing, C China
Chongqing 129 B5 *province* C China
Chonnacht *see* Connaught
Chonos, Archipiélago de los 65 A6 *island group* S Chile
Chóra 105 D7 Kykládes, Greece, Aegean Sea
Chóra Sfakíon 105 C8 *var.* Sfákia. Kríti, Greece, E Mediterranean Sea
Chorne More *see* Black Sea
Chornomors'k 109 E4 Rus. Illichivs'k. Odes'ka Oblast', SW Ukraine
Chornomors'ke 109 E4 Rus. Chernomorskoye. Avtonomna Respublika Krym, S Ukraine
Chorokh/Chorokhi *see* Çoruh Nehri
Chortkiv 108 C2 Rus. Chortkov. Ternopil's'ka Oblast', W Ukraine
Chortkov *see* Chortkiv
Chorzów 99 C5 Ger. Königshütte; *prev.* Królewska Huta. Śląskie, S Poland
Chośebuz *see* Cottbus
Chŏsen-kaikyō *see* Korea Strait
Chōshi 131 D5 *var.* Tyōsi. Chiba, Honshū, S Japan
Chosŏn-minjujuŭi-inmin-kanghwaguk *see* North Korea
Choszczno 98 B3 Ger. Arnswalde. Zachodnio-pomorskie, NW Poland
Chota Nagpur 135 E4 *plateau* N India
Choûm 74 C2 Adrar, C Mauritania
Choybalsan 127 F2 *prev.* Byan Tumen. Dornod, E Mongolia
Christchurch 151 C6 Canterbury, South Island, New Zealand
Christiana 54 B5 C Jamaica
Christiania *see* Oslo
Christiansand *see* Kristiansand
Christianshåb *see* Qasigiannguit
Christiansund *see* Kristiansund
Christmas Island 141 D5 *Australian external territory* E Indian Ocean
Christmas Island *see* Kiritimati
Christmas Ridge 143 E1 *undersea ridge* C Pacific Ocean
Chuan *see* Sichuan
Ch'uan-chou *see* Quanzhou
Chubek *see* Moskva
Chubut, Río 65 B6 *river* SE Argentina
Ch'u-chiang *see* Shaoguan
Chudskoye Ozero *see* Peipus, Lake
Chugoku-sanchi 131 B6 *mountain range* Honshū, SW Japan
Chuí *see* Chuy
Chukai *see* Cukai
Chukchi Plain 155 B2 *abyssal plain* Arctic Ocean
Chukchi Plateau 34 C2 *undersea plateau* Arctic Ocean
Chukchi Sea 34 B2 Rus. Chukotskoye More. *sea* Arctic Ocean
Chukotskoye More *see* Chukchi Sea
Chula Vista 47 C8 California, W USA
Chulucanas 60 B2 Piura, NW Peru
Chulym 114 D4 *river* C Russia
Chumphon 137 C6 *var.* Jumporn. Chumphon, SW Thailand
Chuncheon 129 E4 *prev.* Ch'unch'ŏn, *Jap.* Shunsen. N South Korea
Ch'unch'ŏn *see* Chuncheon
Ch'ung-ch'ing/Ch'ung-ching *see* Chongqing
Chung-hua Jen-min Kung-ho-kuo *see* China
Chungking *see* Chongqing
Chunya 115 E3 *river* C Russia

Chuquicamata 64 B2 Antofagasta, N Chile
Chuquisaca *see* Sucre
Chur 95 B7 Fr. Coire, It. Coira, Rmsch. Cuera, Quera; *anc.* Curia Rhaetorum. Graubünden, E Switzerland
Churchill 37 G4 Manitoba, C Canada
Churchill 38 B2 *river* Manitoba/ Saskatchewan, C Canada
Churchill 39 F2 *river* Newfoundland and Labrador, E Canada
Chuska Mountains 48 C1 *mountain range* Arizona/New Mexico, SW USA
Chusovoy 111 D5 Permskiy Kray, NW Russia
Chust *see* Khust
Chuuk Islands 144 B2 *var.* Hogoley Islands; *prev.* Truk Islands. *island group* Caroline Islands, C Micronesia
Chuy 64 E4 *var.* Chuí. Rocha, E Uruguay
Chyhyryn 109 E2 Rus. Chigirin. Cherkas'ka Oblast', N Ukraine
Chystyakove 87 H3 Rus. Torez. Donets'ka Oblast', SE Ukraine
Ciadîr-Lunga 108 D4 *var.* Ceadâr-Lunga, *Rus.* Chadyr-Lunga. S Moldova
Cide 116 C2 Kastamonu, N Turkey
Ciechanów 98 D3 *prev.* Zichenau. Mazowieckie, C Poland
Ciego de Ávila 54 C2 Ciego de Ávila, C Cuba
Ciénaga 58 B1 Magdalena, N Colombia
Cienfuegos 54 B2 Cienfuegos, C Cuba
Cieza 93 E4 Murcia, SE Spain
Cihanbeyli 116 C3 Konya, C Turkey
Cikobia 145 E4 *prev.* Thikombia. *island* N Fiji
Cilacap 138 C5 *prev.* Tjilatjap. Jawa, C Indonesia
Cill Airne *see* Killarney
Cill Chainnigh *see* Kilkenny
Cilli *see* Celje
Cill Mhantáin *see* Wicklow
Cimpina *see* Câmpina
Cîmpulung *see* Câmpulung
Cina Selatan, Laut *see* South China Sea
Cincinnati 40 C4 Ohio, N USA
Ciney 87 C7 Namur, SE Belgium
Cinto, Monte 91 E7 *mountain* Corse, France, C Mediterranean Sea
Cintra *see* Sintra
Cipolletti 65 B5 Río Negro, C Argentina
Cirebon 138 C4 *prev.* Tjirebon. Jawa, S Indonesia
Cirkvenica *see* Crikvenica
Cirò Marina 97 E6 Calabria, S Italy
Cirquenizza *see* Crikvenica
Cisnădie 108 B4 Ger. Heltau, Hung. Nagydisznód. Sibiu, SW Romania
Citharista *see* la Ciotat
Citlaltépetl *see* Orizaba, Volcán Pico de
Citrus Heights 47 B5 California, W USA
Ciudad Acuña *see* Villa Acuña
Ciudad Bolívar 59 E2 *prev.* Angostura. Bolívar, E Venezuela
Ciudad Camargo 50 D2 Chihuahua, N Mexico
Ciudad Cortés *see* Cortés
Ciudad Darío 52 D3 *var.* Dario. Matagalpa, W Nicaragua
Ciudad de Dolores Hidalgo *see* Dolores Hidalgo
Ciudad de Guatemala 52 B2 Eng. Guatemala City; *prev.* Santiago de los Caballeros. *country capital* (Guatemala) Guatemala, C Guatemala
Ciudad del Carmen *see* Carmen
Ciudad del Este 64 E3 *prev.* Ciudad Presidente Stroessner, Presidente Stroessner, Puerto Presidente Stroessner. Alto Paraná, SE Paraguay
Ciudad Delicias *see* Delicias
Ciudad de México *see* México
Ciudad de Panama *see* Panamá
Ciudad Guayana 59 E2 *prev.* San Tomé de Guayana, Santo Tomé de Guayana. Bolívar, NE Venezuela
Ciudad Guzmán 50 D4 Jalisco, SW Mexico
Ciudad Hidalgo 51 G5 Chiapas, SE Mexico
Ciudad Juárez 50 C1 Chihuahua, N Mexico
Ciudad Lerdo 50 D3 Durango, C Mexico
Ciudad Madero 51 E3 *var.* Villa Cecilia. Tamaulipas, C Mexico
Ciudad Mante 51 E3 Tamaulipas, C Mexico

Ciudad Miguel Alemán 51 E2 Tamaulipas, C Mexico
Ciudad Obregón 50 B2 Sonora, NW Mexico
Ciudad Ojeda 58 C1 Zulia, NW Venezuela
Ciudad Porfirio Díaz *see* Piedras Negras
Ciudad Presidente Stroessner *see* Ciudad del Este
Ciudad Quesada *see* Quesada
Ciudad Real 92 D3 Castilla-La Mancha, C Spain
Ciudad-Rodrigo 92 C3 Castilla y León, N Spain
Ciudad Trujillo *see* Santo Domingo
Ciudad Valles 51 E3 San Luis Potosí, C Mexico
Ciudad Victoria 51 E3 Tamaulipas, C Mexico
Ciutadella 93 H3 *var.* Ciutadella de Menorca, Ciutadella, Spain, W Mediterranean Sea
Ciutadella Ciutadella de Menorca *see* Ciutadella
Civitanova Marche 96 D3 Marche, C Italy
Civitas Altae Ripae *see* Brzeg
Civitas Carnutum *see* Chartres
Civitas Eburovicum *see* Évreux
Civitavecchia 96 C4 *anc.* Centum Cellae, Trajani Portus. Lazio, C Italy
Claremore 49 G1 Oklahoma, C USA
Clarence 151 C5 Canterbury, South Island, New Zealand
Clarence 151 C5 *river* South Island, New Zealand
Clarence Town 54 D2 Long Island, C The Bahamas
Clarinda 45 F4 Iowa, C USA
Clarion Fracture Zone 153 E2 *tectonic feature* NE Pacific Ocean
Clarión, Isla 50 A5 *island* W Mexico
Clark Fork 44 A1 *river* Idaho/Montana, NW USA
Clark Hill Lake 43 E2 *var.* J.Storm Thurmond Reservoir. *reservoir* Georgia/South Carolina, SE USA
Clarksburg 40 D4 West Virginia, NE USA
Clarksdale 42 B2 Mississippi, S USA
Clarksville 42 C1 Tennessee, S USA
Clausentum *see* Southampton
Clayton 49 E1 New Mexico, SW USA
Clearwater 43 E4 Florida, SE USA
Clearwater Mountains 46 D2 *mountain range* Idaho, NW USA
Cleburne 49 G3 Texas, SW USA
Clermont 148 D4 Queensland, E Australia
Clermont-Ferrand 91 C5 Puy-de-Dôme, C France
Cleveland 40 D3 Ohio, N USA
Cleveland 42 D1 Tennessee, S USA
Clifton 48 C2 Arizona, SW USA
Clinton 42 B2 Mississippi, S USA
Clinton 49 F1 Oklahoma, C USA
Clipperton Fracture Zone 153 E3 *tectonic feature* E Pacific Ocean
Clipperton Island 35 A7 *French dependency of French Polynesia* E Pacific Ocean
Cloncurry 148 B3 Queensland, C Australia
Clonmel 89 D6 Ir. Cluain Meala. S Ireland
Cloppenburg 94 B3 Niedersachsen, NW Germany
Cloquet 45 G2 Minnesota, N USA
Cloud Peak 44 C3 *mountain* Wyoming, C USA
Clovis 49 E2 New Mexico, SW USA
Cluain Meala *see* Clonmel
Cluj *see* Cluj-Napoca
Cluj-Napoca 108 B3 Ger. Klausenburg, Hung. Kolozsvár; *prev.* Cluj. Cluj, NW Romania
Clutha 151 B7 *river* South Island, New Zealand
Clyde 88 C4 *river* W Scotland, United Kingdom
Coari 62 D2 Amazonas, N Brazil
Coast Mountains 36 D4 Fr. Chaîne Côtière. *mountain range* Canada/USA
Coast Ranges 46 A4 *mountain range* W USA
Coats Island 37 G3 *island* Nunavut, NE Canada
Coats Land 154 B2 *physical region* Antarctica

Coatzacoalcos 51 G4 *var.* Quetzalcoalco; *prev.* Puerto México. Veracruz-Llave, E Mexico
Cobán 52 B2 Alta Verapaz, C Guatemala
Cobar 149 C6 New South Wales, SE Australia
Cobija 61 E3 Pando, NW Bolivia
Coblence/Coblenz *see* Koblenz
Coburg 95 C5 Bayern, SE Germany
Coca *see* Puerto Francisco de Orellana
Cocanada *see* Kākināda
Cochabamba 61 F4 *hist.* Oropeza. Cochabamba, C Bolivia
Cochin *see* Kochi
Cochrane 38 C4 Ontario, S Canada
Cochrane 65 B7 Aisén, S Chile
Cocibolca *see* Nicaragua, Lago de
Cockade State *see* Maryland
Cockburn Town 55 E2 San Salvador, E The Bahamas
Cockpit Country, The 54 A4 *physical region* W Jamaica
Cocobeach 77 A5 Estuaire, NW Gabon
Coconino Plateau 48 B1 *plain* Arizona, SW USA
Coco, Río 53 E2 *var.* Río Wanki, Segoviao Wangkí. *river* Honduras/ Nicaragua
Cocos Basin 124 C5 *undersea basin* E Indian Ocean
Cocos Island Ridge *see* Cocos Ridge
Cocos Islands 141 D5 *island group* E Indian Ocean
Cocos Ridge 35 C8 *var.* Cocos Island Ridge. *undersea ridge* E Pacific Ocean
Cod, Cape 41 G3 *headland* Massachusetts, NE USA
Codfish Island 151 A8 *island* SW New Zealand
Codlea 108 C4 Ger. Zeiden, Hung. Feketehalom. Braşov, C Romania
Cody 44 C2 Wyoming, C USA
Coeur d'Alene 46 C2 Idaho, NW USA
Coevorden 86 E2 Drenthe, NE Netherlands
Coffs Harbour 149 E6 New South Wales, SE Australia
Cognac 91 B5 *anc.* Compniacum. Charente, W France
Cohalm *see* Rupea
Coiba, Isla de 53 E5 *island* SW Panama
Coihaique 65 B6 *var.* Coyhaique. Aisén, S Chile
Coimbatore 132 C3 Tamil Nādu, S India
Coimbra 92 B3 *anc.* Conímbria, Conimbriga. Coimbra, W Portugal
Coín 92 D5 Andalucía, S Spain
Coira/Coire *see* Chur
Coirib, Loch *see* Corrib, Lough
Colby 45 E4 Kansas, C USA
Colchester 89 E6 Connecticut, NE USA
Coleman 49 F3 Texas, SW USA
Coleraine 88 B4 Ir. Cúil Raithin. N Northern Ireland, United Kingdom
Colesberg 78 C5 Northern Cape, C South Africa
Colima 50 D4 Colima, S Mexico
Coll 88 B3 *island* W Scotland, United Kingdom
College Station 49 G3 Texas, SW USA
Collie 147 A7 Western Australia
Collipo *see* Leiria
Colmar 90 E4 Ger. Kolmar. Haut-Rhin, NE France
Cöln *see* Köln
Cologne *see* Köln
Colomb-Béchar *see* Béchar
Colombia 58 B3 *off.* Republic of Colombia. *country* N South America
Colombian Basin 34 A1 *undersea basin* SW Caribbean Sea
Colombia, Republic of *see* Colombia
Colombie-Britannique *see* British Columbia
Colombo 132 C4 *country capital* (Sri Lanka) Western Province, W Sri Lanka
Colón 53 G4 *prev.* Aspinwall. Colón, C Panama
Colón, Archipiélago de *see* Galápagos Islands
Colonia Agrippina *see* Köln
Colón Ridge 35 B8 *undersea ridge* E Pacific Ocean
Colorado 44 C4 *off.* State of Colorado, *also known as* Centennial State, Silver State. *state* C USA
Colorado City 49 F3 Texas, SW USA
Colorado Plateau 48 B1 *plateau* W USA

Colorado, Río 65 C5 *river* E Argentina
Colorado, Río *see* Colorado River
Colorado River 35 B5 *var.* Río Colorado. *river* Mexico/USA
Colorado River 49 G4 *river* Texas, SW USA
Colorado Springs 44 D5 Colorado, C USA
Columbia 41 E4 Maryland, NE USA
Columbia 45 G4 Missouri, C USA
Columbia 43 E2 *state capital* South Carolina, SE USA
Columbia 42 C1 Tennessee, S USA
Columbia River 46 B3 *river* Canada/USA
Columbia Plateau 46 C3 *plateau* Idaho/Oregon, NW USA
Columbus 42 D2 Georgia, SE USA
Columbus 40 C4 Indiana, N USA
Columbus 40 C2 Mississippi, S USA
Columbus 45 F4 Nebraska, C USA
Columbus 40 D4 *state capital* Ohio, N USA
Colville Channel 150 D2 *channel* North Island, New Zealand
Colville River 36 C2 *river* Alaska, USA
Comacchio 96 C3 *var.* Commachio; *anc.* Comactium. Emilia-Romagna, N Italy
Comactium *see* Comacchio
Comalcalco 51 G4 Tabasco, SE Mexico
Coma Pedrosa, Pic de 91 A7 *mountain* NW Andorra
Comarapa 61 F4 Santa Cruz, C Bolivia
Comayagua 52 C2 Comayagua, W Honduras
Comer See *see* Como, Lago di
Comilla 135 G4 *Ben.* Kumillā. Chittagong, E Bangladesh
Comino *see* Kemmuna
Comitán 51 G5 *var.* Comitán de Domínguez. Chiapas, SE Mexico
Comitán de Domínguez *see* Comitán
Commachio *see* Comacchio
Commissioner's Point 42 A5 *headland* W Bermuda
Communism Peak 123 F3 *prev.* Qullai Kommunizm. *mountain* E Tajikistan
Como 96 B2 *anc.* Comum. Lombardia, N Italy
Comodoro Rivadavia 65 B6 Chubut, SE Argentina
Como, Lake 96 B2 *var.* Lario, *Eng.* Lake Como, *Ger.* Comer See. *lake* N Italy
Como, Lake *see* Como, Lago di
Comores, République Fédérale Islamique des *see* Comoros
Comoros 79 F2 *off.* Federal Islamic Republic of the Comoros, *Fr.* République Fédérale Islamique des Comores. *country* W Indian Ocean
Comoros, Federal Islamic Republic of the *see* Comoros
Compiègne 90 C3 Oise, N France
Complutum *see* Alcalá de Henares
Compniacum *see* Cognac
Compostella *see* Santiago de Compostela
Comrat 108 D4 *Rus.* Komrat. S Moldova
Comum *see* Como
Conakry 74 C4 *country capital* (Guinea) SW Guinea
Conca *see* Cuenca
Concarneau 90 A3 Finistère, NW France
Concepción 61 G3 Santa Cruz, E Bolivia
Concepción 65 B5 Bío Bío, C Chile
Concepción 64 D2 *var.* Villa Concepción. Concepción, C Paraguay
Concepción *see* La Concepción
Concepción de la Vega *see* La Vega
Conchos, Río 48 D4 *river* NW Mexico
Conchos, Río 50 D2 *river* C Mexico
Concord 41 G3 *state capital* New Hampshire, NE USA
Concordia 64 D4 Entre Ríos, E Argentina
Concordia 45 E4 Kansas, C USA
Concordia 154 C4 *French/Italian research station* Antarctica
Côn Dao Sơn 137 E7 *var.* Con Son. *island* S Vietnam
Condate *see* Rennes, Ille-et-Vilaine, France
Condate *see* St-Claude, Jura, France
Condega 52 D3 Estelí, NW Nicaragua
Condivincum *see* Nantes
Confluentes *see* Koblenz
Công Hoa Xa Hôi Chu Nghia Viêt Nam *see* Vietnam
Congo 77 D5 *off.* Republic of the Congo, *Fr.* Moyen-Congo; *prev.* Middle Congo. *country* C Africa

Congo, Dem. Rep. 77 C6 *off.* Democratic Republic of Congo; *prev.* Zaïre, Belgian Congo, Congo (Kinshasa). *country* C Africa
Congo 77 C6 *var.* Kongo, *Fr.* Zaire. *river* C Africa
Congo Basin 77 C6 *drainage basin* W Dem. Rep. Congo
Congo/Congo (Kinshasa) *see* Congo (Democratic Republic of)
Coni *see* Cuneo
Conimbria/Conimbriga *see* Coimbra
Conjeeveram *see* Kānchipuram
Connacht *see* Connaught
Connaught 89 A5 *var.* Connacht, *Ir.* Chonnacht, Cúige. *province* W Ireland
Connecticut 41 F3 *off.* State of Connecticut, *also known as* Blue Law State, Constitution State, Land of Steady Habits, Nutmeg State. *state* NE USA
Connecticut 41 G3 *river* Canada/USA
Conroe 49 G3 Texas, SW USA
Consentia *see* Cosenza
Consolación del Sur 54 A2 Pinar del Río, W Cuba
Con Son *see* Côn Dao Sơn
Constance *see* Konstanz
Constance, Lake 95 B7 *Ger.* Bodensee. *lake* C Europe
Constanţa 108 D5 *var.* Küstendje, *Eng.* Constanza, *Ger.* Konstanza, *Turk.* Küstence. Constanţa, SE Romania
Constantia *see* Coutances
Constantia *see* Konstanz
Constantine 71 E2 *var.* Qacentina, *Ar.* Qoussantina. NE Algeria
Constantinople *see* İstanbul
Constantiola *see* Oltenița
Constanz *see* Konstanz
Constanza *see* Constanţa
Constitution State *see* Connecticut
Coo *see* Kos
Coober Pedy 149 A5 South Australia
Cookeville 42 D1 Tennessee, S USA
Cook Islands 145 F4 *self-governing territory in free association with New Zealand* S Pacific Ocean
Cook, Mount *see* Aoraki
Cook Strait 151 D5 *var.* Raukawa. *strait* New Zealand
Cooktown 148 D2 Queensland, NE Australia
Coolgardie 147 B6 Western Australia
Cooma 149 D7 New South Wales, SE Australia
Coomassie *see* Kumasi
Coon Rapids 45 F2 Minnesota, N USA
Cooper Creek 148 C4 *var.* Barcoo, Cooper's Creek. *seasonal river* Queensland/South Australia
Cooper's Creek *see* Cooper Creek
Coos Bay 46 A3 Oregon, NW USA
Cootamundra 149 D6 New South Wales, SE Australia
Copacabana 61 E4 La Paz, W Bolivia
Copenhagen *see* København
Copiapó 64 B3 Atacama, N Chile
Copperas Cove 49 G3 Texas, SW USA
Coppermine *see* Kugluktuk
Copper State *see* Arizona
Coquilhatville *see* Mbandaka
Coquimbo 64 B3 Coquimbo, N Chile
Corabia 108 B5 Olt, S Romania
Coral Harbour 37 G4 *var.* Salliq. Southampton Island, Nunavut, NE Canada
Coral Sea 142 B3 *sea* W Pacific Ocean
Coral Sea Islands 144 B4 *Australian external territory* SW Pacific Ocean
Corantijn Rivier *see* Courantyne River
Corcovado, Golfo 65 B6 *gulf* S Chile
Corcyra Nigra *see* Korčula
Cordele 42 D3 Georgia, SE USA
Córdoba 64 C3 Córdoba, C Argentina
Córdoba 51 F4 Veracruz-Llave, E Mexico
Córdoba 92 D4 *var.* Cordoba, *Eng.* Cordova; *anc.* Corduba. Andalucía, SW Spain
Cordova 36 C3 Alaska, USA
Cordova/Cordoba *see* Córdoba
Corduba *see* Córdoba
Corentyne River *see* Courantyne River
Corfu 104 A4 *var.* Kérkira, *Eng.* Corfu. *island* Iónia Nisiá, Greece, C Mediterranean Sea
Corfu *see* Kérkyra
Coria 92 C3 Extremadura, W Spain
Corinth 42 C1 Mississippi, S USA

Corinth *see* Kórinthos
Corinth, Gulf of 105 B5 *Eng.* Gulf of Corinth; *anc.* Corinthiacus Sinus. *gulf* C Greece
Corinth, Gulf of/Corinthiacus Sinus *see* Korinthiakós Kólpos
Corinthus *see* Kórinthos
Corinto 52 C3 Chinandega, NW Nicaragua
Cork 89 A6 *Ir.* Corcaigh. S Ireland
Çorlu 116 A2 Tekirdağ, NW Turkey
Corner Brook 39 G3 Newfoundland, Newfoundland and Labrador, E Canada
Cornhusker State *see* Nebraska
Corn Islands 53 E3 *var.* Corn Islands. *island group* SE Nicaragua
Corn Islands *see* Maíz, Islas del
Cornwallis Island 37 F2 *Island* Nunavut, N Canada
Coro 58 C1 *prev.* Santa Ana de Coro. Falcón, NW Venezuela
Corocoro 61 F4 La Paz, W Bolivia
Coromandel 150 D2 Waikato, North Island, New Zealand
Coromandel Coast 132 D2 *coast* E India
Coromandel Peninsula 150 D2 *peninsula* North Island, New Zealand
Coronado, Bahía de 52 D5 *bay* S Costa Rica
Coronel Dorrego 65 C5 Buenos Aires, E Argentina
Coronel Oviedo 64 D2 Caaguazú, SE Paraguay
Corozal 52 C1 Corozal, N Belize
Corpus Christi 49 G4 Texas, SW USA
Corrales 48 D2 New Mexico, SW USA
Corrib, Lough 89 A5 *Ir.* Loch Coirib. *lake* W Ireland
Corrientes 64 D3 Corrientes, NE Argentina
Corriza *see* Korçë
Corsica 91 E7 *Eng.* Corsica. *island* France, C Mediterranean Sea
Corsica *see* Corse
Corsicana 49 G3 Texas, SW USA
Cortegana 92 C4 Andalucía, S Spain
Cortés 53 E5 *var.* Ciudad Cortés. Puntarenas, SE Costa Rica
Cortez, Sea of *see* California, Golfo de
Cortina d'Ampezzo 96 C1 Veneto, NE Italy
Coruche 92 B3 Santarém, C Portugal
Çoruh Nehri 117 E3 *Geor.* Chorokh, *Rus.* Chorokhi. *river* Georgia/Turkey
Çorum 116 D3 *var.* Chorum. Çorum, N Turkey
Corunna *see* A Coruña
Corvallis 46 B3 Oregon, NW USA
Corvo 92 A5 *var.* Ilha do Corvo. *island* Azores, Portugal, NE Atlantic Ocean
Corvo, Ilha do *see* Corvo
Cos *see* Kos
Cosenza 97 D6 *anc.* Consentia. Calabria, SW Italy
Cosne-Cours-sur-Loire 90 C4 Nièvre, Bourgogne, C France Europe
Costa Mesa 47 C8 California, W USA North America
Costa Rica 52 C4 *off.* Republic of Costa Rica. *country* Central America
Costa Rica, Republic of *see* Costa Rica
Costermansville *see* Bukavu
Cotagaita 61 F5 Potosí, S Bolivia
Côte d'Ivoire *see* Ivory Coast
Côte d'Ivoire, République de la *see* Ivory Coast
Côte d'Or 90 D4 *cultural region* C France
Côte Française des Somalis *see* Djibouti
Côtière, Chaine *see* Coast Mountains
Cotonou 75 F5 *var.* Kotonu. *country capital* (Benin - seat of government) S Benin
Cotrone *see* Crotone
Cotswold Hills 89 D6 *var.* Cotswolds. *hill range* S England, United Kingdom
Cotswolds *see* Cotswold Hills
Cottbus 94 D4 *Lus.* Chośebuz; *prev.* Kottbus. Brandenburg, E Germany
Cotton State, The *see* Alabama
Cotyora *see* Ordu
Council Bluffs 45 F4 Iowa, C USA
Countrey *see* Coventry
Courantyne River 59 G4 *var.* Corantijn Rivier, Corentyne River. *river* Guyana/Suriname
Courland Lagoon 106 A4 *Ger.* Kurisches Haff, *Rus.* Kurskiy Zaliv. *lagoon* Lithuania/Russia
Courtrai *see* Kortrijk
Coutances 90 B3 *anc.* Constantia. Manche, N France

Couvin 87 C7 Namur, S Belgium
Coventry 89 D6 *anc.* Couentrey. C England, United Kingdom
Covilhã 92 C3 Castelo Branco, E Portugal
Cowan, Lake 147 B6 *lake* Western Australia
Coxen Hole *see* Roatán
Coxin Hole *see* Roatán
Coyhaique *see* Coihaique
Coyote State, The *see* South Dakota
Cozhê 126 C5 Xizang Zizhiqu, W China
Cozumel, Isla 51 H3 *island* SE Mexico
Cracovia/Cracow *see* Kraków
Cradock 78 C5 Eastern Cape, S South Africa
Craig 44 C4 Colorado, C USA
Craiova 108 B5 Dolj, SW Romania
Cranbrook 37 E5 British Columbia, SW Canada
Crane *see* The Crane
Cranz *see* Zelenogradsk
Crawley 89 E7 SE England, United Kingdom
Cremona 96 B2 Lombardia, N Italy
Creole State *see* Louisiana
Cres 100 A3 *It.* Cherso; *anc.* Crexa. *island* W Croatia
Crescent City 46 A4 California, W USA
Crescent Group 128 C2 *island group* C Paracel Islands
Creston 45 F4 Iowa, C USA
Crestview 42 D3 Florida, SE USA
Crete 105 C7 *Eng.* Crete. *island* Greece, Aegean Sea
Crete 45 F4 Nebraska, C USA
Crête 90 E2 Val-de-Marne, N France
Sea of Crete 105 D7 *var.* Kretikon Delagos, *Eng.* Sea of Crete; *anc.* Mare Creticum. *sea* Greece, Aegean Sea
Crete, Sea of/Creticum, Mare *see* Kritikó Pélagos
Creuse 90 B4 *river* C France
Crewe 89 D6 C England, United Kingdom
Crexa *see* Cres
Crikvenica 100 A3 *It.* Cirquenizza; *prev.* Cirkvenica, Crikvenica. Primorje-Gorski Kotar, NW Croatia
Crimea *see* Kryms'kyy Pivostriv
Cristóbal 53 G4 Colón, C Panama
Cristóbal Colón, Pico 58 B1 *mountain* N Colombia
Cristur/Cristuru Săcuiesc *see* Cristuru Secuiesc
Cristuru Secuiesc 108 C4 *prev.* Cristur, Cristuru Săcuiesc, Sitás Cristuru, *Ger.* Kreutz, *Hung.* Székelykeresztúr, Szitás-Keresztúr. Harghita, C Romania
Crjkvenica *see* Crikvenica
Crna Gora *see* Montenegro
Crna Reka 101 D6 *river* S Macedonia
Crni Drim *see* Black Drin
Croatia 100 B3 *off.* Republic of Croatia, *Ger.* Kroatien, *SCr.* Hrvatska. *country* SE Europe
Croatia, Republic of *see* Croatia
Crocodile *see* Limpopo
Croia *see* Krujë
Croker Island 146 E2 *island* Northern Territory, N Australia
Cromwell 151 B7 Otago, South Island, New Zealand
Crooked Island 54 D2 *island* SE The Bahamas
Crooked Island Passage 54 D2 *channel* SE The Bahamas
Crookston 45 F1 Minnesota, N USA
Crossen *see* Krosno Odrzańskie
Croton/Crotona *see* Crotone
Crotone 97 D6 *var.* Cotrone; *anc.* Croton, Crotona. Calabria, SW Italy
Croydon 89 A8 SE England, United Kingdom
Crozet Basin 141 B6 *undersea basin* S Indian Ocean
Crozet Islands 141 B7 *island group* French Southern and Antarctic Lands
Crozet Plateau 141 B7 *var.* Crozet Plateaus. *undersea plateau* SW Indian Ocean
Crozet Plateaus *see* Crozet Plateau
Crystal Brook 149 B6 South Australia
Csakathurn/Csáktornya *see* Čakovec
Csíkszereda *see* Miercurea-Ciuc
Csorna 99 C6 Győr-Moson-Sopron, NW Hungary
Csurgó 99 C7 Somogy, SW Hungary
Cuando 78 C2 *var.* Kwando. *river* S Africa

Cuango *78 B1 var.* Kwango. *river* Angola/Dem. Rep. Congo
Cuango *see* Kwango
Cuanza *78 B1 var.* Kwanza. *river* C Angola
Cuauhtémoc *50 C2* Chihuahua, N Mexico
Cuautla *51 E4* Morelos, S Mexico
Cuba *54 B2 off.* Republic of Cuba. *country* W West Indies
Cubal *78 B2* Benguela, W Angola
Cubango *78 B2 var.* Kuvango, *Port.* Vila Artur de Paiva, Vila da Ponte. Huíla, SW Angola
Cubango *78 B2 var.* Kavango, Kavengo, Kubango, Okavango, Okavanggo. *river* S Africa
Cuba, Republic of *see* Cuba
Cúcuta *58 C2 var.* San José de Cúcuta. Norte de Santander, N Colombia
Cuddapah *132 C2* Andhra Pradesh, S India
Cuenca *60 B2* Azuay, S Ecuador
Cuenca *93 E3 anc.* Conca. Castilla-La Mancha, C Spain
Cuera *see* Chur
Cuernavaca *51 E4* Morelos, S Mexico
Cuiabá *63 E3 prev.* Cuyabá. *state capital* Mato Grosso, SW Brazil
Cúige *see* Connaught
Cúige Laighean *see* Leinster
Cúige Mumhan *see* Munster
Cuijck *86 D4* Noord-Brabant, SE Netherlands
Cúil Raithin *see* Coleraine
Cuito *78 B2 var.* Kwito. *river* SE Angola
Cukai *138 B3 var.* Chukai, Kemaman. Terengganu, Peninsular Malaysia
Cularo *see* Grenoble
Culiacán *50 C3 var.* Culiacán Rosales, Culiacán-Rosales. Sinaloa, C Mexico
Culiacán-Rosales/Culiacán Rosales *see* Culiacán
Cullera *93 F3* Valenciana, E Spain
Cullman *42 C2* Alabama, S USA
Culm *see* Chełmno
Culmsee *see* Chełmża
Cumaná *59 E1* Sucre, NE Venezuela
Cumbal, Nevado de *58 A4 elevation* S Colombia
Cumberland *41 E4* Maryland, NE USA
Cumberland Plateau *42 D1 plateau* E USA
Cumberland Sound *37 H3 inlet* Baffin Island, Nunavut, NE Canada
Cumpas *50 B2* Sonora, NW Mexico
Cuneo *96 A2 Fr.* Coni. Piemonte, NW Italy
Cunnamulla *149 C5* Queensland, E Australia
Ćuprija *100 E4* Serbia, E Serbia
Curaçao *55 E5 Self-governing country of the Netherlands* S West Indies
Curaçao *55 E5 island* Lesser Antilles
Curia Rhaetorum *see* Chur
Curicó *64 B4* Maule, C Chile
Curieta *see* Krk
Curitiba *63 E4 prev.* Curytiba. *state capital* Paraná, S Brazil
Curtbunar *see* Tervel
Curtea de Argeş *108 C4 var.* Curtea-de-Arges. Argeş, S Romania
Curtea-de-Arges *see* Curtea de Argeş
Curtici *108 A4 Ger.* Kurtitsch, *Hung.* Kürtös. Arad, W Romania
Curtis Island *148 E4 island* Queensland, SE Australia
Curytiba *see* Curitiba
Curzola *see* Korčula
Cusco *61 E4 var.* Cuzco. Cusco, C Peru
Cusset *91 C5* Allier, C France
Cutch, Gulf of *see* Kachchh, Gulf of
Cuttack *135 F4* Odisha, E India
Cuvier Plateau *141 E6 undersea plateau* E Indian Ocean
Cuxhaven *94 B2* Niedersachsen, NW Germany
Cuyabá *see* Cuiabá
Cuyuni, Río *see* Cuyuni River
Cuyuni River *59 F3 var.* Río Cuyuni. *river* Guyana/Venezuela
Cuzco *see* Cusco
Cyclades *105 D6 var.* Kikládhes, *Eng.* Cyclades. *island group* SE Greece
Cyclades *see* Kykládes
Cydonia *see* Chaniá
Cymru *see* Wales

Cyprus *102 C4 off.* Republic of Cyprus, *Gk.* Kypros, *Turk.* Kıbrıs, Kıbrıs Cumhuriyeti. *country* E Mediterranean Sea
Cyprus, Republic of *see* Cyprus
Cythnos *see* Kýthnos
Czechia *see* Czech Republic
Czech Republic *99 A5 var.* Czechia, Cz. Česká Republika. *country* C Europe
Czenstochau *see* Częstochowa
Czernowitz *see* Chernivtsi
Częstochowa *98 C4 Ger.* Czenstochau, Tschenstochau, *Rus.* Chenstokhov. Śląskie, S Poland
Człuchów *98 C3 Ger.* Schlochau. Pomorskie, NW Poland

D

Dabajuro *58 C1* Falcón, NW Venezuela
Dabeiba *58 B2* Antioquia, NW Colombia
Dąbrowa Tarnowska *99 D5* Małopolskie, S Poland
Dabryn' *107 C8 Rus.* Dobryn'. Homyel'skaya Voblasts', SE Belarus
Dacca *see* Dhaka
Daegu *107 E4 off.* Daegu Gwang-yeoksi, *prev.* Taegu, *Jap.* Taikyū. SE South Korea
Daegu Gwang-yeoksi *see* Daegu
Daejeon *107 E4 off.* Daejeon Gwang-yeoksi, *prev.* Taejŏn, *Jap.* Taiden. C South Korea
Daejeon Gwang-yeoksi *see* Daejeon
Dagana *74 B3* N Senegal
Dagda *106 D4* SE Latvia
Dagden *see* Hiiumaa
Dagenham *89 B8* United Kingdom
Dağlıq Quarabağ *see* Nagornyy-Karabakh
Dagö *see* Hiiumaa
Dagupan *139 E1 off.* Dagupan City. Luzon, N Philippines
Dagupan City *see* Dagupan
Dahm, Ramlat *121 B6 desert* NW Yemen
Dahomey *see* Benin
Daihoku *see* Taipei
Daimiel *92 D3* Castilla-La Mancha, C Spain
Daimóniá *105 B7* Pelopónnisos, S Greece
Dainan *see* Tainan
Daingin, Bá an *see* Dingle Bay
Dairen *see* Dalian
Dakar *74 B3 country capital* (Senegal) W Senegal
Dakhla *see* Ad Dakhla
Dakoro *75 G3* Maradi, S Niger
Đakovica *see* Gjakovë
Đakovo *100 C3 var.* Djakovo, *Hung.* Diakovár. Osijek-Baranja, E Croatia
Dakshin *see* Deccan
Dalain Hob *126 D3 var.* Ejin Qi. Nei Mongol Zizhiqu, N China
Dalai Nor *see* Hulun Nur
Dalaman *116 A4* Muğla, SW Turkey
Dalandzadgad *127 E3* Ömnögovi, S Mongolia
Đa Lat *137 E6* Lâm Đông, S Vietnam
Dalby *149 D5* Queensland, E Australia
Dale City *41 E4* Virginia, NE USA
Dalhart *49 E1* Texas, SW USA
Dali *128 A6 var.* Xiaguan. Yunnan, SW China
Dalian *128 D4 var.* Dairen, Dalien, Jap. Dairen, Lüda, Ta-lien, *Rus.* Dalny. Liaoning, NE China
Dalien *see* Dalian
Dallas *49 G2* Texas, SW USA
Dalmacija *100 B4 Eng.* Dalmatia, *Ger.* Dalmatien, *It.* Dalmazia. *cultural region* S Croatia
Dalmatia/Dalmatien/Dalmazia *see* Dalmacija
Dalny *see* Dalian
Dalton *42 D1* Georgia, SE USA
Dálvvadis *see* Jokkmokk
Daly Waters *148 A2* Northern Territory, N Australia
Damachava *see* Damachova
Damachova *107 A6 var.* Damachova, *Pol.* Domaczewo, *Rus.* Damachevo. Brestskaya Voblasts', SW Belarus
Damān *134 C4* Damān and Diu, W India
Damara *76 C4* Ombella-Mpoko, S Central African Republic
Damas *see* Dimashq
Damasco *see* Dimashq
Damascus *see* Dimashq

Qolleh-ye Damavand *120 D3 mountain* N Iran
Damietta *see* Dumyāţ
Dammām *see* Ad Dammām
Damoûr *119 A5 var.* Ad Dāmūr. W Lebanon
Dampier *146 A4* Western Australia
Dampier, Selat *139 F4 strait* Papua, E Indonesia
Damqawt *121 D6 var.* Damqut. E Yemen
Damqut *see* Damqawt
Damxung *126 C5 var.* Gongtang. Xizang Zizhiqu, W China
Danakil Desert *72 D4 var.* Afar Depression, Danakil Plain. *desert* E Africa
Danakil Plain *see* Danakil Desert
Danané *74 D5* W Ivory Coast
Đa Nāng *137 E5 prev.* Tourane. Quang Nam-Đa Nāng, C Vietnam
Danborg *see* Daneborg
Dandong *128 D3 var.* Tan-tung; *prev.* An-tung. Liaoning, NE China
Daneborg *83 E3 var.* Danborg. Tunu, N Greenland
Dänew *see* Galkynyş
Dangara *see* Danghara
Dangerous Archipelago *see* Tuamotu, Îles
Danghara *123 E3 Rus.* Dangara. SW Tajikistan
Danghe Nanshan *126 D3 mountain range* W China
Dang Raek, Phanom/Dangrek, Chaine des *see* Dângrêk, Chuŏr Phnum
Chuŏr Phnum Dângrêk *137 D5 var.* Phanom Dang Raek, Phanom Dong Rak, *Fr.* Chaine des Dangrek. *mountain range* Cambodia/Thailand
Dangriga *52 C1 prev.* Stann Creek. Stann Creek, E Belize
Danish West Indies *see* Virgin Islands (US)
Danlí *52 D2* El Paraíso, S Honduras
Danmark *see* Denmark
Danmarksstraedet *see* Denmark Strait
Dannenberg *94 C3* Niedersachsen, N Germany
Dannevirke *150 D4* Manawatu-Wanganui, North Island, New Zealand
Dantzig *see* Gdańsk
Danube *81 E4 Bul.* Dunav, *Cz.* Dunaj, *Ger.* Donau, *Hung.* Duna, *Rom.* Dunărea. *river* C Europe
Danubian Plain *104 C2 Eng.* Danubian Plain. *lowlands* N Bulgaria
Danubian Plain *see* Dunavska Ravnina
Danum *see* Doncaster
Danville *41 E5* Virginia, NE USA
Danxian/Dan Xian *see* Danzhou
Danzhou *128 C7 prev.* Danxian, Dan Xian, Nada. Hainan, S China
Danzig *see* Gdańsk
Danziger Bucht *see* Gdańsk, Gulf of
Danzig, Gulf of *see* Gdańsk, Gulf of
Daqm *see* Duqm
Dar'ā *119 B5 var.* Der'a, *Fr.* Déraa. Dar'ā, SW Syria
Darabani *108 C3* Botoşani, NW Romania
Daraut-Kurgan *see* Daroot-Korgon
Dardanelles *116 A2 Eng.* Dardanelles. *strait* NW Turkey
Dardanelles *see* Çanakkale Boğazı
Dardanelli *see* Çanakkale
Dar-el-Beida *see* Casablanca
Dar es Salaam *73 C7* Dar es Salaam, E Tanzania
Darfield *151 C6* Canterbury, South Island, New Zealand
Darfur *72 A4 var.* Darfur Massif. *cultural region* W Sudan
Darfur Massif *see* Darfur
Darhan *127 E2* Darhan Uul, N Mongolia
Darién, Golfo del *see* Darién, Gulf of
Darién, Gulf of *58 A2 Sp.* Golfo del Darién. *gulf* S Caribbean Sea
Darien, Isthmus of *see* Panama, Istmo de
Darién, Serranía del *53 H5 mountain range* Colombia/Panama
Dario *see* Ciudad Darío
Dariorigum *see* Vannes
Darjeeling *see* Dārjiling
Dārjiling *135 F3 prev.* Darjeeling. West Bengal, NE India
Darling River *149 C6 river* New South Wales, SE Australia
Darlington *89 D5* N England, United Kingdom

Darmstadt *95 B5* Hessen, SW Germany
Darnah *71 G2 var.* Dérna. NE Libya
Darnley, Cape *154 D2 cape* Antarctica
Daroca *93 E2* Aragón, NE Spain
Daroot-Korgon *123 F3 var.* Daraut-Kurgan. Oshskaya Oblast', SW Kyrgyzstan
Dartford *89 B8* SE England, United Kingdom
Dartmoor *89 C7 moorland* SW England, United Kingdom
Dartmouth *39 F4* Nova Scotia, SE Canada
Darvaza *see* Derweze, Turkmenistan
Darwin *146 D2 prev.* Palmerston, Port Darwin. *territory capital* Northern Territory, N Australia
Darwin, Isla *60 A4 island* Galápagos Islands, W Ecuador
Dashhowuz *see* Daşoguz
Dashkawka *107 D6 Rus.* Dashkovka. Mahilyowskaya Voblasts', E Belarus
Dashkovka *see* Dashkawka
Daşoguz *122 C2 Rus.* Dashkhovuz, *Turkm.* Dashhowuz; *prev.* Tashauz. Daşoguz Welaýaty, N Turkmenistan
Đa, Sông *see* Black River
Datong *128 C3 var.* Tatung, Ta-t'ung. Shanxi, C China
Daugava *see* Western Dvina
Daugavpils *106 D4 Ger.* Dünaburg; *prev. Rus.* Dvinsk. SE Latvia
Daung Kyun *137 B6 island* S Myanmar (Burma)
Dauphiné *91 D5 cultural region* E France
Dävangere *132 C2* Karnātaka, W India
Davao *139 F3 off.* Davao City. Mindanao, S Philippines
Davao City *see* Davao
Davao Gulf *139 F3 gulf* Mindanao, S Philippines
Davenport *45 G3* Iowa, C USA
David *53 E5* Chiriquí, W Panama
Davie Ridge *141 A5 undersea ridge* W Indian Ocean
Davis *154 D3 Australian research station* Antarctica
Davis Sea *154 D3 sea* Antarctica
Davis Strait *82 B3 strait* Baffin Bay/ Labrador Sea
Dawei *137 B5 var.* Tavoy, Htawei. Tanintharyi, S Myanmar (Burma)
Dawlat Qatar *see* Qatar
Dax *91 B6 var.* Ax; *anc.* Aquae Augustae, Aquae Tarbelicae. Landes, SW France
Dayr az Zawr *118 D3 var.* Deir ez Zor. Dayr az Zawr, E Syria
Dayton *40 C4* Ohio, N USA
Daytona Beach *43 E4* Florida, SE USA
De Aar *78 C5* Northern Cape, C South Africa
Dead Sea *119 B6 var.* Bahret Lut, Lacus Asphaltites, Ar. Al Bahr al Mayyit, Baḥrat Lūt, *Heb.* Yam HaMelaḥ. *salt lake* Israel/Jordan
Deán Funes *64 C3* Córdoba, C Argentina
Death Valley *47 C7 valley* California, W USA
Deatnu *84 D2 Fin.* Tenojoki, *Nor.* Tana. *river* Finland/Norway
Debar *101 D6 Ger.* Dibra, *Turk.* Debre. W Macedonia
De Behagle *see* Laï
Dębica *99 D5* Podkarpackie, SE Poland
De Bilt *see* De Bilt
De Bilt *86 C3 var.* De Bildt. Utrecht, C Netherlands
Dębno *98 B3* Zachodnio-pomorskie, NW Poland
Debrecen *99 D6 var.* Debreczin, *prev.* Debrezin; *prev.* Debreczen. Hajdú-Bihar, E Hungary
Debreczen/Debrezcin *see* Debrecen
Debrețin *see* Debrecen
Decatur *42 C1* Alabama, S USA
Decatur *40 B4* Illinois, N USA
Deccan *134 D5 Hind.* Dakshin. *plateau* C India
Děčín *98 B4 Ger.* Tetschen. Ústecký Kraj, NW Czech Republic (Czechia)
Dedeagaç/Dedeagach *see* Alexandroúpoli
Dedemsvaart *86 E3* Overijssel, E Netherlands
Dee *88 C3 river* NE Scotland, United Kingdom
Deering *36 C2* Alaska, USA
Deés *see* Dej
Deggendorf *95 D6* Bayern, SE Germany

INDEX – GAZETTEER: **Değirmenlik – Dolisie**

Değirmenlik *102 C5 Gk.* Kythréa. N Cyprus
Deh Bīd *see* Şafāshahr
Dehli *see* Delhi
Deh Shū *see* Dīshū
Deinze *87 B5* Oost-Vlaanderen, NW Belgium
Deir ez Zor *see* Dayr az Zawr
Deirgeirt, Loch *see* Derg, Lough
Dej *108 B3 Hung.* Dés; *prev.* Deés. Cluj, NW Romania
De Jouwer *see* Joure
Dekéleia *see* Dhekélia
Dékoa *76 C4* Kémo, C Central African Republic
De Land *43 E4* Florida, SE USA
Delano *47 C7* California, W USA
Delārām *see* Dilārām
Delaware *40 D4* Ohio, N USA
Delaware *41 F4 off.* State of Delaware, *also known as* Blue Hen State, Diamond State, First State. *state* NE USA
Delft *86 B4* Zuid-Holland, W Netherlands
Delfzijl *86 E1* Groningen, NE Netherlands
Delgo *72 B3* Northern, N Sudan
Delhi *134 D3 var.* Dehli, *Hind.* Dilli, *hist.* Shahjahanabad. *union territory capital* Delhi, N India
Delicias *50 D2 var.* Ciudad Delicias. Chihuahua, N Mexico
Déli-Kárpátok *see* Carpaţii Meridionalii
Delmenhorst *94 B3* Niedersachsen, NW Germany
Del Rio *49 F4* Texas, SW USA
Deltona *43 E4* Florida, SE USA
Demba *77 D6* Kasai-Occidental, C Dem. Rep. Congo
Dembia *76 D4* Mbomou, SE Central African Republic
Demchok *see* Dêmqog
Demerara Plain *56 C2 abyssal plain* W Atlantic Ocean
Deming *48 C3* New Mexico, SW USA
Demmin *94 C2* Mecklenburg-Vorpommern, NE Germany
Demopolis *42 C2* Alabama, S USA
Dêmqog *126 A5 var.* Demchok. *disputed region* China/India
Denali *36 C3 var.* Mount McKinley. *mountain* Alaska, USA
Denau *see* Denov
Dender *87 B6 Fr.* Dendre. *river* W Belgium
Dendre *see* Dender
Denekamp *86 E3* Overijssel, E Netherlands
Den Haag *see* 's-Gravenhage
Denham *147 A5* Western Australia
Den Ham *86 E3* Overijssel, E Netherlands
Den Helder *86 C2* Noord-Holland, NW Netherlands
Dénia *93 F4* Valenciana, E Spain
Deniliquin *149 C7* New South Wales, SE Australia
Denison *45 F3* Iowa, C USA
Denison *49 G2* Texas, SW USA
Denizli *116 B4* Denizli, SW Turkey
Denmark *85 A7 off.* Kingdom of Denmark, *Dan.* Danmark; *anc.* Hafnia. *country* N Europe
Denmark, Kingdom of *see* Denmark
Denmark Strait *82 D4 var.* Danmarksstraedet. *strait* Greenland/Iceland
Dennery *55 F1* E Saint Lucia
Denov *123 E3 Rus.* Denau. Surkhondaryo Viloyati, S Uzbekistan
Denpasar *138 D5 prev.* Paloe. Bali, C Indonesia
Denton *49 G2* Texas, SW USA
D'Entrecasteaux Islands *144 B3 island group* SE Papua New Guinea
Denver *44 D4 state capital* Colorado, C USA
Der'a/Derá/Déraa *see* Dar'ā
Dera Ghazi Khan *134 C2 var.* Dera Ghazikhan. Punjab, C Pakistan
Dera Ghazikhan *see* Dera Ghazi Khan
Đeravica *see* Gjeravicë
Derbent *111 B8* Respublika Dagestan, SW Russia
Derby *89 D6* C England, United Kingdom
Derelí *see* Gónnoi
Dergachi *see* Derhachi
Derg, Lough *89 A6 Ir.* Loch Deirgeirt. *lake* W Ireland
Derhachi *109 G2 Rus.* Dergachi. Kharkivs'ka Oblast', E Ukraine
De Ridder *42 A3* Louisiana, S USA
Dérna *see* Darnah
Derry *see* Londonderry
Dertosa *see* Tortosa
Derventa *100 B3* Republika Srpska, N Bosnia and Herzegovina
Derweze *122 C2 Rus.* Darvaza. Ahal Welaýaty, C Turkmenistan
Dés *see* Dej
Deschutes River *46 B3 river* Oregon, NW USA
Desē *72 C4 var.* Desse, *It.* Dessie. Āmara, N Ethiopia
Deseado, Río *65 B7 river* S Argentina
Desertas, Ilhas *70 A2 island group* Madeira, Portugal, NE Atlantic Ocean
Deshu *see* Dīshū
Des Moines *45 F3 state capital* Iowa, C USA
Desna *109 E2 river* Russia/Ukraine
Dessau *94 C4* Sachsen-Anhalt, E Germany
Desse *see* Desē
Dessie *see* Desē
Destêrro *see* Florianópolis
Detroit *40 D3* Michigan, N USA
Detroit Lakes *45 F2* Minnesota, N USA
Deurne *87 D5* Noord-Brabant, SE Netherlands
Deutschendorf *see* Poprad
Deutsch-Eylau *see* Iława
Deutsch Krone *see* Wałcz
Deutschland/Deutschland, Bundesrepublik *see* Germany
Deutsch-Südwestafrika *see* Namibia
Deva *108 B4 Ger.* Diemrich, *Hung.* Déva. Hunedoara, W Romania
Déva *see* Deva
Deva *see* Chester
Devana *see* Aberdeen
Devana Castra *see* Chester
Đevđelija *see* Gevgelija
Deventer *86 D3* Overijssel, E Netherlands
Devils Lake *45 E1* North Dakota, N USA
Devoll *see* Devollit, Lumi i
Devollit, Lumi i *101 D6 var.* Devoll. *river* SE Albania
Devon Island *37 F2 prev.* North Devon Island. *island* Parry Islands, Nunavut, NE Canada
Devonport *149 C8* Tasmania, SE Australia
Devrek *116 C2* Zonguldak, N Turkey
Dexter *45 H5* Missouri, C USA
Deynau *see* Galkynyş
Dezfūl *120 C3 var.* Dizful. Khūzestān, SW Iran
Dezhou *128 D4* Shandong, E China
Dhaka *135 G4 prev.* Dacca. *country capital* (Bangladesh) Dhaka, C Bangladesh
Dhanbād *135 F4* Jhārkhand, NE India
Dhekélia *102 C5 Gk.* Dekéleia. *UK air base* SE Cyprus
Dhidhimótikhon *see* Didymóteicho
Dhíkti Ori *see* Díkti
Dhodhekánisos *see* Dodekánisa
Dhomokós *see* Domokós
Dhráma *see* Dráma
Dhrepanon, Akrotírio *see* Drépano, Akrotírio
Dhún na nGall, Bá *see* Donegal Bay
Dhuusa Marreeb *73 E5 var.* Dusa Marreb, *It.* Dusa Mareb. Galguduud, C Somalia
Diakovár *see* Đakovo
Diamantina, Chapada *63 F3 mountain range* E Brazil
Diamantina Fracture Zone *141 E6 tectonic feature* E Indian Ocean
Diamond State *see* Delaware
Diarbekr *see* Diyarbakır
Dibio *see* Dijon
Dibra *see* Debar
Dibrugarh *135 H3* Assam, NE India
Dickinson *44 D2* North Dakota, N USA
Dicle *see* Tigris
Didimotiho *see* Didymóteicho
Didymóteicho *104 D3 var.* Dhidhimótikhon, Didimotiho. Anatolikí Makedonía kai Thráki, NE Greece
Diedenhofen *see* Thionville
Diekirch *87 D7* Diekirch, C Luxembourg
Diemrich *see* Deva
Điên Biên *see* Điên Biên Phu
Điên Biên Phu *136 D3 var.* Bien Bien, Điên Biên. Lai Châu, N Vietnam
Diepenbeek *87 D6* Limburg, NE Belgium
Diepholz *94 B3* Niedersachsen, NW Germany
Dieppe *90 C2* Seine-Maritime, N France
Dieren *86 D4* Gelderland, E Netherlands
Differdange *87 D8* Luxembourg, SW Luxembourg
Digne *91 D6 var.* Digne-les-Bains. Alpes-de-Haute-Provence, SE France
Digne-les-Bains *see* Digne
Digoel *see* Digul, Sungai
Digoin *90 C4* Saône-et-Loire, C France
Digul, Sungai *139 H5 prev.* Digoel. *river* Papua, E Indonesia
Dihang *see* Brahmaputra
Dijlah *see* Tigris
Dijon *90 D4 anc.* Dibio. Côte d'Or, C France
Dikhil *72 D4* SW Djibouti
Dikson *114 D2* Krasnoyarskiy Kray, N Russia
Dikti *105 D8 var.* Dhíkti Ori. *mountain range* Kríti, Greece, E Mediterranean Sea
Dilārām *122 D5 prev.* Delārām. Nīmrūz, SW Afghanistan
Dili *139 F5 var.* Dilli, Dilly. *country capital* (East Timor) N East Timor
Dilia *75 G3 var.* Dillia. *river* SE Niger
Di Linh *137 E6* Lâm Đông, S Vietnam
Dilli *see* Dili, East Timor
Dilli *see* Delhi, India
Dillia *see* Dilia
Dilling *72 B4 var.* Ad Dalanj. Southern Kordofan, C Sudan
Dillon *44 B2* Montana, NW USA
Dilly *see* Dili
Dilolo *77 D7* Katanga, S Dem. Rep. Congo
Dimashq *119 B5 var.* Ash Shām, Esh Sham, *Eng.* Damascus, *Fr.* Damas, *It.* Damasco. *country capital* (Syria) Rīf Dimashq, SW Syria
Dimitrovgrad *104 D3* Khaskovo, S Bulgaria
Dimitrovgrad *111 C6 prev.* Caribrod. Serbia, SE Serbia
Dimitrovo *see* Pernik
Dimovo *104 B1* Vidin, NW Bulgaria
Dinajpur *135 F3* Rajshahi, NW Bangladesh
Dinan *90 B3* Côtes d'Armor, NW France
Dinant *87 C7* Namur, S Belgium
Dinar *116 B4* Afyon, SW Turkey
Dinara *see* Dinaric Alps
Dinaric Alps *100 C4 var.* Dinara. *mountain range* Bosnia and Herzegovina/Croatia
Dindigul *132 C3* Tamil Nādu, SE India
Dingle Bay *89 A6 Ir.* Bá an Daingin. *bay* SW Ireland
Dinguiraye *74 C4* N Guinea
Diourbel *74 B3* W Senegal
Dirē Dawa *73 D5* Dirē Dawa, E Ethiopia
Dirk Hartog Island *147 A5 island* Western Australia
Dirschau *see* Tczew
Disappointment, Lake *146 C4 salt lake* Western Australia
Discovery Bay *54 B4* Middlesex, Jamaica, Greater Antilles, C Jamaica Caribbean Sea
Dīshū *122 D5 prev.* Deh Shū, *var.* Deshu. Helmand, S Afghanistan
Disko Bugt *see* Qeqertarsuup Tunua
Dispur *135 G3 state capital* Assam, NE India
Divinópolis *63 F4* Minas Gerais, SE Brazil
Divo *74 D5* S Ivory Coast
Divodurum Mediomatricum *see* Metz
Diyarbakır *117 E4 var.* Diarbekr; *anc.* Amida. Diyarbakır, SE Turkey
Dizful *see* Dezfūl
Djailolo *see* Halmahera, Pulau
Djajapura *see* Jayapura
Djakarta *see* Jakarta
Djakovo *see* Đakovo
Djambala *77 B6* Plateaux, C Congo
Djambi *see* Hari, Batang
Djambi *see* Jambi
Djanet *71 E4 prev.* Fort Charlet. SE Algeria
Djéblé *see* Jablah
Djelfa *70 D2 var.* El Djelfa. N Algeria
Djéma *76 D4* Haut-Mbomou, E Central African Republic
Djember *see* Jember
Djérablous *see* Jarābulus
Djerba, Île *71 F2 var.* Djerba, Jazīrat Jarbah. *island* E Tunisia
Djerba *see* Djerba, Île
Djérem *76 B4 river* C Cameroon
Djevdjelija *see* Gevgelija
Djibouti *72 D4 var.* Jibuti. *country capital* (Djibouti) E Djibouti
Djibouti *72 D4 off.* Republic of Djibouti, *var.* Jibuti; *prev.* French Somaliland, French Territory of the Afars and Issas, *Fr.* Côte Française des Somalis, Territoire Français des Afars et des Issas. *country* E Africa
Djibouti, Republic of *see* Djibouti
Djokjakarta *see* Yogyakarta
Djourab, Erg du *76 C2 desert* N Chad
Djúpivogur *83 E5* Austurland, SE Iceland
Dmitriyevsk *see* Makiyivka
Dnepr *see* Dnieper
Dneprodzerzhinsk *see* Romaniv
Dneprodzerzhinskoye Vodokhranilishche *see* Dniprodzerzhyns'ke Vodoskhovyshche
Dnepropetrovsk *see* Dnipropetrovs'k
Dneprorudnoye *see* Dniprorudne
Dnestr *see* Dniester
Dnieper *81 F4 Bel.* Dnyapro, *Rus.* Dnepr, *Ukr.* Dnipro. *river* E Europe
Dnieper Lowland *109 E2 Bel.* Prydnyaprowskaya Nizina, *Ukr.* Prydniprovs'ka Nyzovyna. *lowlands* Belarus/Ukraine
Dniester *81 E4 Rom.* Nistru, *Rus.* Dnestr, *Ukr.* Dnister; *anc.* Tyras. *river* Moldova/Ukraine
Dnipro *see* Dnieper
Dniprodzerzhyns'k *see* Kam''yans'ke
Dniprodzerzhyns'ke Vodoskhovyshche *109 F3 Rus.* Dneprodzerzhinskoye Vodokhranilishche. *reservoir* C Ukraine
Dnipro *109 F3 Rus.* Dnipropetrovs'k; *prev.* Yekaterinoslav. Dnipropetrovs'ka Oblast', E Ukraine
Dnipropetrovs'k *see* Dnipro
Dniprorudne *109 F3 Rus.* Dneprorudnoye. Zaporiz'ka Oblast', SE Ukraine
Dnister *see* Dniester
Dnyapro *see* Dnieper
Doba *76 C4* Logone-Oriental, S Chad
Döbeln *94 D4* Sachsen, E Germany
Doberai Peninsula *139 G4 Dut.* Vogelkop. *peninsula* Papua, E Indonesia
Doboj *100 C3* Republiks Srpska, N Bosnia and Herzegovina
Dobre Miasto *98 D2 Ger.* Guttstadt. Warmińsko-mazurskie, NE Poland
Dobrich *104 E1 Rom.* Bazargic; *prev.* Tolbukhin. Dobrich, NE Bulgaria
Dobrush *107 D7* Homyel'skaya Voblasts', SE Belarus
Dobryn' *see* Dabryn'
Dodecanese *105 D6 var.* Nóties Sporádes, *Eng.* Dodecanese; *prev.* Dhodhekánisos, Dodekanisos. *island group* SE Greece
Dodecanese *see* Dodekánisa
Dodekanisos *see* Dodekánisa
Dodge City *45 E5* Kansas, C USA
Dodoma *69 D5 country capital* (Tanzania) Dodoma, C Tanzania
Dogana *96 E1* NE San Marino Europe
Dogo *131 B6 island* Oki-shotō, SW Japan
Dogondoutchi *75 F3* Dosso, SW Niger
Dogrular *see* Pravda
Doğubayazıt *117 F3* Ağrı, E Turkey
Doğu Karadeniz Dağları *117 E3 var.* Anadolu Dağları. *mountain range* NE Turkey
Doha *see* Ad Dawḩah
Doire *see* Londonderry
Dokdo *see* Liancourt Rocks
Dokkum *86 D1* Fryslân, N Netherlands
Dokuchayevs'k *109 G3 var.* Dokuchayevsk. Donets'ka Oblast', SE Ukraine
Dokuchayevsk *see* Dokuchayevs'k
Doldrums Fracture Zone *66 C4 fracture zone* W Atlantic Ocean
Dôle *90 D4* Jura, E France
Dolina *see* Dolyna
Dolinskaya *see* Dolyns'ka
Dolisie *77 B6 prev.* Loubomo. Niari, S Congo

Dolna Oryakhovitsa 104 D2 *prev.*
Polikrayshte. Veliko Tŭrnovo,
N Bulgaria
Dolni Chiflik 104 E2 *prev.* Rudnik.
Varna, E Bulgaria
Dolomites 96 C1 *var.* Dolomiti, *Eng.*
Dolomites.
Dolomites/Dolomiti *see* Dolomitiche,
Alpi
Dolores 64 D4 Buenos Aires, E Argentina
Dolores 52 B1 Petén, N Guatemala
Dolores 64 D4 Soriano, SW Uruguay
Dolores Hidalgo 51 E4 *var.* Ciudad de
Dolores Hidalgo. Guanajuato,
C Mexico
Dolyna 108 B2 *Rus.* Dolina.
Ivano-Frankivs'ka Oblast', W Ukraine
Dolyns'ka 109 F3 *Rus.* Dolinskaya.
Kirovohrads'ka Oblast', S Ukraine
Domachëvo/Domaczewo *see* Damachava
Dombås 85 B5 Oppland, S Norway
Domel Island *see* Letsôk-aw Kyun
Domesnes, Cape *see* Kolkasrags
Domeyko 64 B3 Atacama, N Chile
Dominica 55 H4 *off.* Commonwealth of
Dominica. *country* E West Indies
Dominica Channel *see* Martinique
Passage
Dominica, Commonwealth of *see*
Dominica
Dominican Republic 55 E2 *country*
C West Indies
Domokós 105 B5 *var.* Dhomokós. Stereá
Elláda, C Greece
Don 111 B6 *var.* Duna, Tanais. *river*
SW Russia
Donau *see* Danube
Donauwörth 95 C6 Bayern, S Germany
Don Benito 92 C3 Extremadura,
W Spain
Doncaster 89 D5 *anc.* Danum.
N England, United Kingdom
Dondo 78 B1 Cuanza Norte, NW Angola
Donegal 89 B5 *Ir.* Dún na nGall.
Donegal, NW Ireland
Donegal Bay 89 A5 *Ir.* Bá Dhún na nGall.
bay NW Ireland
Donets 109 G2 *river* Russia/Ukraine
Donets'k 109 G3 *Rus.* Donetsk; *prev.*
Stalino. Donets'ka Oblast', E Ukraine
Dongfang 128 B7 *var.* Basuo. Hainan,
S China
Dongguan 128 C6 Guangdong, S China
Đông Ha 136 E4 Quang Tri, C Vietnam
Dong Hai *see* East China Sea
Đông Hơi 136 D4 Quang Binh,
C Vietnam
Dongliao *see* Liaoyuan
Dongola 72 B3 *var.* Donqola, Dunqulah.
Northern, N Sudan
Dongou 77 C5 Likouala, NE Congo
Dong Rak, Phanom *see* Dângrêk, Chuŏr
Phnum
Dongting Hu 128 C5 *var.* Tung-t'ing
Hu. *lake* S China
Donostia 93 E1 País Vasco, N Spain *see
also* San Sebastián
Donqola *see* Dongola
Doolow 73 D5 Sumalē, E Ethiopia
Doornik *see* Tournai
Door Peninsula 40 C2 *peninsula*
Wisconsin, N USA
Dooxo Nugaaleed 73 E5 *var.* Nogal
Valley. *valley* E Somalia
Dordogne 91 B5 *cultural region*
SW France
Dordogne 91 B5 *river* W France
Dordrecht 86 C4 *var.* Dordt, Dort.
Zuid-Holland, SW Netherlands
Dordt *see* Dordrecht
Dorohoi 108 C3 Botoșani, NE Romania
Dorotea 84 C4 Västerbotten, N Sweden
Dorpat *see* Tartu
Dorre Island 147 A5 *island* Western
Australia
Dort *see* Dordrecht
Dortmund 94 A4 Nordrhein-Westfalen,
W Germany
Dos Hermanas 92 C4 Andalucía, S Spain
Dospad Dagh *see* Rhodope Mountains
Dospat 104 C3 Smolyan, S Bulgaria
Dothan 42 D3 Alabama, S USA
Dotnuva 106 B4 Kaunas, C Lithuania
Douai 90 C2 *prev.* Douay; *anc.* Duacum.
Nord, N France
Douala 77 A5 *var.* Duala. Littoral,
W Cameroon
Douay *see* Douai
Douglas 89 C5 *dependent territory
capital* (Isle of Man) E Isle of Man

Douglas 48 C3 Arizona, SW USA
Douglas 44 D3 Wyoming, C USA
Douma *see* Dūmā
Douro *see* Duero
Douvres *see* Dover
Dover 89 E7 *Fr.* Douvres, *Lat.* Dubris
Portus. SE England, United Kingdom
Dover 41 F4 *state capital* Delaware,
NE USA
Dover, Strait of 90 C2 *var.* Straits of
Dover, *Fr.* Pas de Calais. *strait* England,
United Kingdom/France
Dover, Straits of *see* Dover, Strait of
Dovrefjell 85 B5 *plateau* S Norway
Downpatrick 89 B5 *Ir.* Dún Pádraig.
SE Northern Ireland,
United Kingdom
Dozen 131 B6 *island* Oki-shotō,
SW Japan
Drâa, Hammada du *see* Dra, Hamada du
Drač/Draç *see* Durrës
Drachten 86 D2 Fryslân, N Netherlands
Drăgăşani 108 B5 Vâlcea, SW Romania
Dragoman 104 B2 Sofiya, W Bulgaria
Dra, Hamada du 70 C3 *var.* Hamada
du Drâa, Haut Plateau du Dra. *plateau*
W Algeria
Dra, Haut Plateau du *see* Dra,
Hamada du
Drahichyn 107 B6 *Pol.* Drohiczyn
Poleski, *Rus.* Drogichin. Brestskaya
Voblasts', SW Belarus
Drakensberg 78 D5 *mountain range*
Lesotho/South Africa
Drake Passage 57 B8 *passage* Atlantic
Ocean/Pacific Ocean
Dralfa 104 D2 Tŭrgovishte, N Bulgaria
Dráma 104 C3 *var.* Dhráma. Anatolikí
Makedonía kai Thráki, NE Greece
Dramburg *see* Drawsko Pomorskie
Drammen 85 B6 Buskerud, S Norway
Drau *see* Drava
Drava 100 C3 *var.* Drau, *Eng.* Drave,
Hung. Dráva. *river* C Europe
Dráva/Drave *see* Drau/Drava
Drawsko Pomorskie 98 B3 *Ger.*
Dramburg. Zachodnio-pomorskie,
NW Poland
Drépano, Akrotírio 104 C4 *var.*
Akrotírio Dhrepanon. *headland*
N Greece
Drepanum *see* Trapani
Dresden 94 D4 Sachsen, E Germany
Drin *see* Drinit, Lumi i
Drina 100 C3 *river* Bosnia and
Herzegovina/Serbia
Drinit, Lumi i 101 D5 *var.* Drin. *river*
NW Albania
Drinit të Zi, Lumi i *see* Black Drin
Drissa *see* Drysa
Drobeta-Turnu Severin 108 B5 *prev.*
Turnu Severin. Mehedinți,
SW Romania
Drogheda 89 B5 *Ir.* Droichead Átha.
NE Ireland
Drogichin *see* Drahichyn
Drogobych *see* Drohobych
Drohiczyn Poleski *see* Drahichyn
Drohobych 108 B2 *Pol.* Drohobycz, *Rus.*
Drogobych. L'vivs'ka Oblast',
NW Ukraine
Drohobycz *see* Drohobych
Droichead Átha *see* Drogheda
Drôme 91 D5 *cultural region* E France
Dronning Maud Land 154 B2 *physical
region* Antarctica
Drontheim *see* Trondheim
Drug *see* Durg
Druk-yul *see* Bhutan
Drummondville 39 E4 Québec,
SE Canada
Druskienniki *see* Druskininkai
Druskininkai 107 B5 *Pol.* Druskienniki.
Alytus, S Lithuania
Druzhnaya4 154 D3 *Russian research
station* Antarctica
Dryden 38 B3 Ontario, C Canada
Drysa 107 D5 *Rus.* Drissa. *river*
N Belarus
Duacum *see* Douai
Duala *see* Douala
Dubai *see* Dubayy
Dubăsari 108 D3 *Rus.* Dubossary.
NE Moldova
Dubawnt 37 F4 *river* Nunavut,
NW Canada
Dubayy 120 D4 *Eng.* Dubai. Dubayy,
NE United Arab Emirates
Dubbo 149 D6 New South Wales,
SE Australia

Dublin 89 B5 *Ir.* Baile Átha Cliath; *anc.*
Eblana. *country capital* (Ireland)
Dublin, E Ireland
Dublin 43 E2 Georgia, SE USA
Dubno 108 C2 Rivnens'ka Oblast',
NW Ukraine
Dubossary *see* Dubăsari
Dubris Portus *see* Dover
Dubrovnik 101 B5 *It.* Ragusa.
Dubrovnik-Neretva, SE Croatia
Dubuque 45 G3 Iowa, C USA
Dudelange 87 D8 *var.* Forge du Sud, *Ger.*
Dudelingen. Luxembourg,
S Luxembourg
Dudelingen *see* Dudelange
Duero 92 D2 *Port.* Douro. *river*
Portugal/Spain
Duesseldorf *see* Düsseldorf
Duffel 87 C5 Antwerpen, C Belgium
Dugi Otok 100 A4 *var.* Isola Grossa, *It.*
Isola Lunga. *island* W Croatia
Duisburg 94 A4 *prev.* Duisburg-
Hamborn. Nordrhein-Westfalen,
W Germany
Duisburg-Hamborn *see* Duisburg
Duiven 86 D4 Gelderland,
E Netherlands
Duk Faiwil 73 B5 Jonglei, E South Sudan
Dulan 126 D4 *var.* Qagan Us. Qinghai,
C China
Dulce, Golfo 53 E5 *gulf* S Costa Rica
Dulce, Golfo *see* Izabal, Lago de
Dülmen 94 A4 Nordrhein-Westfalen,
W Germany
Dulovo 104 E1 Silistra, NE Bulgaria
Duluth 45 G2 Minnesota, N USA
Dūmā 119 B5 *Fr.* Douma. Rif Dimashq,
SW Syria
Dumas 49 E1 Texas, SW USA
Dumfries 88 C4 S Scotland, United
Kingdom
Dumont d'Urville 154 C4 *French
research station* Antarctica
Dumyāt 72 B1 *Eng.* Damietta. N Egypt
Duna *see* Danube, C Europe
Düna *see* Western Dvina
Duna *see* Don
Dünaburg *see* Daugavpils
Dunaj *see* Wien, Austria
Dunaj *see* Danube, C Europe
Dunapentele *see* Dunaújváros
Dunărea *see* Danube
Dunaújváros 99 C7 *prev.* Dunapentele,
Sztálinváros. Fejér, C Hungary
Dunav *see* Danube
Duncan 49 G2 Oklahoma, C USA
Dundalk 89 B5 *Ir.* Dún Dealgan. Louth,
NE Ireland
Dún Dealgan *see* Dundalk
Dundee 78 D4 KwaZulu/Natal, E South
Africa
Dundee 88 C4 E Scotland, United
Kingdom
Dunedin 151 B7 Otago, South Island,
New Zealand
Dunfermline 88 C4 C Scotland, United
Kingdom
Dungu 77 E5 Orientale, NE Dem. Rep.
Congo
Dungun 138 B3 *var.* Kuala Dungun.
Terengganu, Peninsular Malaysia
Dunholme *see* Durham
Dunkerque 90 C2 *Eng.* Dunkirk, *Flem.*
Duinekerke; *prev.* Dunquerque. Nord,
N France
Dunkirk *see* Dunkerque
Dún Laoghaire 89 B6 *Eng.* Dunleary;
prev. Kingstown. E Ireland
Dunleary *see* Dún Laoghaire
Dún Pádraig *see* Downpatrick
Dunqulah *see* Dongola
Dupnitsa 104 C2 *prev.* Marek, Stanke
Dimitrov. Kyustendil, W Bulgaria
Duqm 121 E5 *var.* Daqm. E Oman
Durance 91 D6 *river* SE France
Durango 50 D3 *var.* Victoria de
Durango. Durango, W Mexico
Durango 44 C5 Colorado, C USA
Durankulak 104 E1 *Rom.* Răcari; *prev.*
Blatnitsa, Duranulac. Dobrich,
NE Bulgaria
Durant 49 G2 Oklahoma, C USA
Duranulac *see* Durankulak
Durazzo *see* Durrës
Durban 78 D4 *var.* Port Natal. KwaZulu/
Natal, E South Africa
Durbe 106 B3 *Ger.* Durben. W Latvia
Durben *see* Durbe

Durg 135 E4 *prev.* Drug. Chhattisgarh,
C India
Durham 89 D5 *hist.* Dunholme.
N England, United Kingdom
Durham 43 F1 North Carolina,
SE USA
Durocortovum *see* Reims
Durostorum *see* Silistra
Durovernum *see* Canterbury
Durrës 101 C6 *var.* Durrësi, Dursi, *It.*
Durazzo, *SCr.* Drač, *Turk.* Draç.
Durrës, W Albania
Durrësi *see* Durrës
Dursi *see* Durrës
Durūz, Jabal ad 119 C5 *mountain*
SW Syria
D'Urville Island 150 C4 *island*
C New Zealand
Dusa Mareb/Dusa Marreb *see* Dhuusa
Marreeb
Dushanbe 123 E3 *var.* Dyushambe;
prev. Stalinabad, *Taj.* Stalinobod.
country capital (Tajikistan)
W Tajikistan
Düsseldorf 94 A4 *var.* Duesseldorf.
Nordrhein-Westfalen, W Germany
Düsti 123 E3 *Rus.* Dusti. SW Tajikistan
Dutch East Indies *see* Indonesia
Dutch Guiana *see* Suriname
Dutch Harbor 36 B3 Unalaska Island,
Alaska, USA
Dutch New Guinea *see* Papua
Duzdab *see* Zāhedān
Dvina Bay *see* Chëshskaya Guba
Dvinsk *see* Daugavpils
Dyanev *see* Galkynyş
Dyersburg 42 C1 Tennessee,
S USA
Dyushambe *see* Dushanbe
Dza Chu *see* Mekong
Dzaudzhikau *see* Vladikavkaz
Dzerzhinsk 111 C5 Nizhegorodskaya
Oblast', W Russia
Dzerzhinskiy *see* Nar'yan-Mar
Dzhalal-Abad 123 F2 *Kir.* Jalal-Abad.
Dzhalal-Abadskaya Oblast',
W Kyrgyzstan
Dzhambul *see* Taraz
Dzhankoy 109 F4 Avtonomna
Respublika Krym, S Ukraine
Dzharkurgan *see* Jarqo'rg'on
Dzhelandy 123 F3 SE Tajikistan
Dzhergalan 123 G2 *Kir.* Jyrgalan.
Issyk-Kul'skaya Oblast', NE Kyrgyzstan
Dzhezkazgan *see* Zhezkazgan
Dzhizak *see* Jizzax
Dzhugdzhur, Khrebet 115 G3 *mountain
range* E Russia
Dzhusaly *see* Zhosaly
Działdowo 98 D3 Warmińsko-
Mazurskie, C Poland
Dzuunmod 127 E2 Töv, C Mongolia
Dzüün Soyonï Nuruu *see* Vostochnyy
Sayan
Dzvina *see* Western Dvina

E

Eagle Pass 49 F4 Texas, SW USA
East Açores Fracture Zone *see* East
Azores Fracture Zone
East Antarctica 154 C3 *prev.* Greater
Antarctica. *physical region* Antarctica
East Australian Basin *see* Tasman Basin
East Azores Fracture Zone 66 C3 *var.*
East Açores Fracture Zone. *tectonic
feature* E Atlantic Ocean
Eastbourne 89 E7 SE England, United
Kingdom
East Cape 150 E3 *headland* North Island,
New Zealand
East China Sea 125 E2 *Chin.* Dong Hai.
sea W Pacific Ocean
Easter Fracture Zone 153 G4 *tectonic
feature* E Pacific Ocean
Easter Island 153 F4 *var.* Rapa Nui.
Chile. *island* E Pacific Ocean
Easter Island *see* Pascua, Isla de
Eastern Desert *see* Şaḥrā' ash Sharqīyah
Eastern Ghats 124 B3 *mountain range*
SE India
Eastern Sayans *see* Vostochnyy Sayan
Eastern Sierra Madre *see* Madre Oriental,
Sierra
East Falkland 65 D8 *var.* Isla Soledad.
island E Falkland Islands
East Frisian Islands *see* Ostfriesische
Inseln

East Grand Forks 45 E1 Minnesota, N USA
East Indiaman Ridge 141 D6 undersea ridge E Indian Ocean
East Indies 152 A3 island group SE Asia
East Kilbride 88 C4 S Scotland, United Kingdom
East Korea Bay 129 E3 bay E North Korea
Eastleigh 89 D7 S England, United Kingdom
East London 78 D5 Afr. Oos-Londen; prev. Emonti, Port Rex. Eastern Cape, S South Africa
Eastmain 38 D3 river Québec, C Canada
East Mariana Basin 142 B1 undersea basin W Pacific Ocean
East Novaya Zemlya Trough 112 C1 var. Novaya Zemlya Trough. trough W Kara Sea
East Pacific Rise 153 F4 undersea rise E Pacific Ocean
East Pakistan see Bangladesh
East Saint Louis 40 B4 Illinois, N USA
East Scotia Basin 67 C7 undersea basin SE Scotia Sea
East Sea 130 A4 var. Sea of Japan, Rus. Yapanskoye More. Sea NW Pacific Ocean
East Siberian Sea 115 F1 Eng. East Siberian Sea. sea Arctic Ocean
East Siberian Sea see Vostochno-Sibirskoye More
East Timor 139 F5 var. Loro Sae; prev. Portuguese Timor, Timor Timur. country S Indonesia
Eau Claire 40 A2 Wisconsin, N USA
Eau Claire, Lac à L' see St. Clair, Lake
Eauripik Rise 142 B2 undersea rise W Pacific Ocean
Ebensee 95 D6 Oberösterreich, N Austria
Eberswalde-Finow 94 D3 Brandenburg, E Germany
Ebetsu 130 D2 var. Ebetu. Hokkaidō, NE Japan
Ebetu see Ebetsu
Eblana see Dublin
Ebolowa 77 A5 Sud, S Cameroon
Ebon Atoll 144 D2 var. Epoon. atoll Ralik Chain, S Marshall Islands
Ebora see Évora
Eboracum see York
Ebro 93 E2 river NE Spain
Eburacum see York
Ebusus see Eivissa
Ecbatana see Hamadān
Ech Cheliff/Ech Chleff see Chlef
Echo Bay 37 E3 Northwest Territories, NW Canada
Echt 87 D5 Limburg, SE Netherlands
Écija 92 D4 anc. Astigi. Andalucía, SW Spain
Eckengraf see Viesīte
Ecuador 60 B1 off. Republic of Ecuador. country NW South America
Ecuador, Republic of see Ecuador
Ed Da'ein 72 A4 Southern Darfur, W Sudan
Ed Damazin 72 C4 var. Ad Damazin. Blue Nile, E Sudan
Ed Damer 72 C3 var. Ad Dāmir, Ad Damar. River Nile, NE Sudan
Ed Debba 72 B3 Northern, N Sudan
Ede 86 D4 Gelderland, C Netherlands
Ede 75 F5 Osun, SW Nigeria
Edéa 77 A5 Littoral, SW Cameroon
Edessa see Şanlıurfa
Edfu see Idfū
Edgeoya 83 G2 island S Svalbard
Edgware 89 A7 Harrow, SE England, United Kingdom
Edinburg 49 G5 Texas, SW USA
Edinburgh 88 C4 national capital S Scotland, United Kingdom
Edingen see Enghien
Edirne 116 A2 Eng. Adrianople; anc. Adrianopolis, Hadrianopolis. Edirne, NW Turkey
Edmonds 46 B2 Washington, NW USA
Edmonton 37 E5 province capital Alberta, SW Canada
Edmundston 39 E4 New Brunswick, SE Canada
Edna 49 G4 Texas, SW USA
Edolo 96 B1 Lombardia, N Italy
Edremit 116 A3 Balıkesir, NW Turkey

Edward, Lake 77 E5 var. Albert Edward Nyanza, Edward Nyanza, Lac Idi Amin, Lake Rutanzige. lake Uganda/ Dem. Rep. Congo
Edward Nyanza see Edward, Lake
Edwards Plateau 49 F3 plain Texas, SW USA
Edzo 53 E4 prev. Rae-Edzo. Northwest Territories, NW Canada
Eeklo 87 B5 var. Eekloo. Oost-Vlaanderen, NW Belgium
Eekloo see Eeklo
Eems see Ems
Eersel 87 C5 Noord-Brabant, S Netherlands
Eesti Vabariik see Estonia
Efate 144 D4 var. Efate, Fr. Vaté; prev. Sandwich Island. island C Vanuatu
Efate see Efate
Effingham 40 B4 Illinois, N USA
Eforie-Sud 108 D5 Constanţa, E Romania
Egadi Is. 97 B7 island group S Italy
Ege Denizi see Aegean Sea
Eger 99 D6 Ger. Erlau. Heves, NE Hungary
Eger see Cheb, Czech Republic (Czechia)
Egeria Fracture Zone 141 C5 tectonic feature W Indian Ocean
Éghezée 87 C6 Namur, C Belgium
Egina see Aígina
Egio see Aígio
Egmont see Taranaki, Mount
Egmont, Cape 150 C4 headland North Island, New Zealand
Egoli see Johannesburg
Egypt 72 B2 off. Arab Republic of Egypt, Ar. Jumhūrīyah Miṣr al 'Arabīyah, prev. United Arab Republic; anc. Aegyptus. country NE Africa
Eibar 93 E1 País Vasco, N Spain
Eibergen 86 E3 Gelderland, E Netherlands
Eidfjord 85 A5 Hordaland, S Norway
Eier-Berg see Suur Munamägi
Eifel 95 A5 plateau W Germany
Eiger 95 B7 mountain C Switzerland
Eigg 88 B3 island W Scotland, United Kingdom
Eight Degree Channel 132 B3 channel India/Maldives
Eighty Mile Beach 146 B4 beach Western Australia
Eijsden 87 D6 Limburg, SE Netherlands
Eilat see Elat
Eindhoven 87 D5 Noord-Brabant, S Netherlands
Eipel see Ipel'
Éire see Ireland
Éireann, Muir see Irish Sea
Eisenhüttenstadt 94 D4 Brandenburg, E Germany
Eisenmarkt see Hunedoara
Eisenstadt 95 E6 Burgenland, E Austria
Eisleben 94 C4 Sachsen-Anhalt, C Germany
Eivissa 93 G3 var. Iviza, Cast. Ibiza; anc. Ebusus. Ibiza, Spain, W Mediterranean Sea
Eivissa 93 G3 var. Iviza, Cast. Ibiza; anc. Ebusus. Ibiza, Spain, W Mediterranean Sea
Eivissa 93 G3 var. Iviza, Cast. Ibiza; anc. Ebusus. Ibiza, Spain, W Mediterranean Sea
Ejea de los Caballeros 93 E2 Aragón, NE Spain
Ejin Qi see Dalain Hob
Ekapa see Cape Town
Ekaterinodar see Krasnodar
Ekiatapskiy Khrebet see Ekvyvatapskiy Khrebet
Ekvyvatapskiy Khrebet 115 G1 prev. Ekiatapskiy Khrebet. mountain range NE Russia
El 'Alamein see Al 'Alamayn
El Asnam see Chlef
Elat 119 B8 var. Eilat, Elath. Southern, S Israel
Elat, Gulf of see Aqaba, Gulf of
Elath see Elat, Israel
Elath see Al 'Aqabah, Jordan
El'Atrun 72 B3 Northern Darfur, NW Sudan
Elâzığ 117 E3 var. Elâzig, Elâziz. Elâzığ, E Turkey
Elba 96 B4 island Archipelago Toscano, C Italy
Elbasan 101 D6 var. Elbasani. Elbasan, C Albania

Elbasani see Elbasan
Elbe 80 D3 Cz. Labe. river Czech Republic (Czechia)/Germany
Elbert, Mount 44 C4 mountain Colorado, C USA
Elbing see Elbląg
Elbląg 98 C2 var. Elbląg, Ger. Elbing. Warmińsko-Mazurskie, NE Poland
El Boulaïda/El Boulaïda see Blida
El'brus 111 A8 var. Gora El'brus. mountain SW Russia
El'brus, Gora see El'brus
El Burgo de Osma 93 E2 Castilla y León, C Spain
El Cajon 47 C8 California, W USA
El Calafate 65 B7 var. Calafate. Santa Cruz, S Argentina
El Callao 59 E2 Bolívar, E Venezuela
El Campo 49 G4 Texas, SW USA
El Carmen de Bolívar 58 B2 Bolívar, NW Colombia
El Cayo see San Ignacio
El Centro 47 D8 California, W USA
Elche 93 F4 Cat. Elx; anc. Ilici, Lat. Illicis. Valenciana, E Spain
Elda 93 F4 Valenciana, E Spain
El Djazaïr see Alger
El Djelfa see Djelfa
Eldorado 64 E3 Misiones, NE Argentina
El Dorado 42 B2 Arkansas, C USA
El Dorado 45 F5 Kansas, C USA
El Dorado 59 F2 Bolívar, E Venezuela
El Dorado see California
Eldoret 73 C6 Rift Valley, W Kenya
Elektrostal' 111 B5 Moskovskaya Oblast', W Russia
Elemi Triangle see Ilemi Triangle
Elephant Butte Reservoir 48 C2 reservoir New Mexico, SW USA
Élesd see Aleşd
Eleuthera Island 54 C1 island N The Bahamas
El Fasher 72 A4 var. Al Fāshir. Northern Darfur, W Sudan
El Ferrol/El Ferrol del Caudillo see Ferrol
El Gedaref see Gedaref
El Geneina 72 A4 var. Ajjinena, Al-Genain, Al Junaynah. Western Darfur, W Sudan
Elgin 88 C3 NE Scotland, United Kingdom
Elgin 40 B3 Illinois, N USA
El Giza see Giza
El Goléa 70 D3 var. Al Golea. C Algeria
El Hank 74 D1 cliff N Mauritania
El Haseke see Al Ḥasakah
Elimberrum see Auch
Eliocroca see Lorca
Élisabethville see Lubumbashi
Elista 111 B7 Respublika Kalmykiya, SW Russia
Elizabeth 149 B6 South Australia
Elizabeth City 43 G1 North Carolina, SE USA
Elizabethtown 40 C5 Kentucky, S USA
El-Jadida 70 C2 prev. Mazagan. W Morocco
Elk 98 E2 Ger. Lyck. Warmińsko-mazurskie, NE Poland
Elk City 49 F1 Oklahoma, C USA
El Khalil see Hebron
El Khârga see Al Khārijah
Elkhart 40 C3 Indiana, N USA
El Khartûm see Khartoum
Elk River 45 F2 Minnesota, N USA
El Kuneitra see Al Qunayţirah
Ellás see Greece
Ellef Ringnes Island 37 E1 island Nunavut, N Canada
Ellen, Mount 44 B5 mountain Utah, W USA
Ellensburg 46 B2 Washington, NW USA
Ellesmere Island 37 F1 island Queen Elizabeth Islands, Nunavut, N Canada
Ellesmere, Lake 151 C6 lake South Island, New Zealand
Ellice Islands see Tuvalu
Elliston 149 A6 South Australia
Ellsworth Land 154 A3 physical region Antarctica
El Mahbas 70 B3 var. Mahbés. SW Western Sahara
El Mina 118 B4 var. Al Mīnā'. N Lebanon

El Minya see Al Minyā
Elmira 41 E3 New York, NE USA
El Mreyyé 74 D2 desert E Mauritania
Elmshorn 94 B3 Schleswig-Holstein, N Germany
El Muglad 72 B4 Southern Kordofan, C Sudan
El Obeid 72 B4 var. Al Obayyid, Al Ubayyiḍ. Northern Kordofan, C Sudan
El Ouâdi see El Oued
El Oued 71 E2 var. Al Oued, El Ouâdi, El Wad. NE Algeria
Eloy 48 B2 Arizona, SW USA
El Paso 48 D3 Texas, SW USA
El Porvenir 53 G4 Kuna Yala, N Panama
El Progreso 52 C2 Yoro, NW Honduras
El Puerto de Santa María 92 C5 Andalucía, S Spain
El Qâhira see Cairo
El Quneitra see Al Qunayţirah
El Quseir see Al Quşayr
El Quweira see Al Quwayrah
El Rama 53 E3 Región Autónoma Atlántico Sur, SE Nicaragua
El Real 53 H5 var. El Real de Santa María. Darién, SE Panama
El Real de Santa María see El Real
El Reno 49 F1 Oklahoma, C USA
El Salvador 52 B3 off. Republica de El Salvador. country Central America
El Salvador, Republica de see El Salvador
Elsass see Alsace
El Sáuz 50 C2 Chihuahua, N Mexico
El Serrat 91 A7 N Andorra Europe
Elst 86 D4 Gelderland, E Netherlands
El Sueco 50 C2 Chihuahua, N Mexico
El Suweida see As Suwaydā'
El Suweis see Suez
Eltanin Fracture Zone 153 E5 tectonic feature SE Pacific Ocean
El Tigre 59 E2 Anzoátegui, NE Venezuela
Elvas 92 C4 Portalegre, C Portugal
El Vendrell 93 G2 Cataluña, NE Spain
El Vigía 58 C2 Mérida, NW Venezuela
El Wad see El Oued
Elwell, Lake 44 B1 reservoir Montana, NW USA
Elx see Elche
Ely 47 D5 Nevada, W USA
El Yopal see Yopal
Emajõgi 106 D3 Ger. Embach. river SE Estonia
Emämrüd see Shährüd
Emämshahr see Shährüd
Emba 114 B4 Kaz. Embi. Aktyubinsk, W Kazakhstan
Embach see Emajõgi
Embi see Emba
Emden 94 A3 Niedersachsen, NW Germany
Emerald 148 D4 Queensland, E Australia
Emerald Isle see Montserrat
Emesa see Ḥimş
Emmaste 106 C2 Hiiumaa, W Estonia
Emmeloord 86 D2 Flevoland, N Netherlands
Emmen 86 E2 Drenthe, NE Netherlands
Emmendingen 95 A6 Baden-Württemberg, SW Germany
Emona see Ljubljana
Emonti see East London
Emory Peak 49 E4 mountain Texas, SW USA
Empalme 50 B2 Sonora, NW Mexico
Emperor Seamounts 113 G3 seamount range NW Pacific Ocean
Empire State of the South see Georgia
Emporia 45 F5 Kansas, C USA
Empty Quarter see Ar Rub' al Khālī
Ems 94 A3 Dut. Eems. river NW Germany
Enareträsk see Inarijärvi
Encamp 91 A8 Encamp, C Andorra Europe
Encarnación 64 D3 Itapúa, S Paraguay
Encinitas 47 C8 California, W USA
Encs 99 D6 Borsod-Abaúj-Zemplén, NE Hungary
Endeavour Strait 148 C1 strait Queensland, NE Australia
Enderbury Island 145 F3 atoll Phoenix Islands, C Kiribati
Enderby Land 154 C2 physical region Antarctica
Enderby Plain 154 D2 abyssal plain S Indian Ocean
Endersdorf see Jędrzejów

Enewetak Atoll 144 C1 *var.* Ānewetak,
   Eniwetok. *atoll* Ralik Chain,
   W Marshall Islands
Enfield 89 A7 United Kingdom
Engeten *see* Aiud
Enghien 87 B6 *Dut.* Edingen. Hainaut,
   SW Belgium
England 89 D5 *Lat.* Anglia. *cultural
   region* England, United Kingdom
Englewood 44 D4 Colorado, C USA
English Channel 89 D8 *var.* The
   Channel, *Fr.* la Manche. *channel*
   NW Europe
Engure 106 C3 W Latvia
Engures Ezers 106 B3 *lake* NW Latvia
Enguri 117 F1 *Rus.* Inguri. *river*
   NW Georgia
Enid 49 F1 Oklahoma, C USA
Enikale Strait *see* Kerch Strait
Eniwetok *see* Enewetak Atoll
En Nâqoûra 119 A5 *var.* An Nāqūrah.
   SW Lebanon
En Nazira *see* Natzrat
Ennedi 76 D2 *plateau* E Chad
Ennis 89 A6 *Ir.* Inis. Clare, W Ireland
Ennis 49 G3 Texas, SW USA
Enniskillen 89 B5 *var.* Inniskilling, *Ir.*
   Inis Ceithleann. SW Northern Ireland,
   United Kingdom
Enns 95 D6 *river* C Austria
Enschede 86 E3 Overijssel, E Netherlands
Ensenada 50 A1 Baja California Norte,
   NW Mexico
Entebbe 73 B6 S Uganda
Entroncamento 92 B3 Santarém,
   C Portugal
Enugu 75 G5 Enugu, S Nigeria
Epanomí 104 B4 Kentrikí Makedonía,
   N Greece
Epéna 77 B5 Likouala, NE Congo
Eperies/Eperjes *see* Prešov
Epi 144 D4 *var.* Épi. *island* C Vanuatu
Épi *see* Epi
Épinal 90 D4 Vosges, NE France
Epiphania *see* Ḥamāh
Epoon *see* Ebon Atoll
Epsom 89 A8 United Kingdom
Equality State *see* Wyoming
Equatorial Guinea 77 A5 *off.* Equatorial
   Guinea, Republic of. *country* C Africa
Equatorial Guinea, Republic of *see*
   Equatorial Guinea
Erautini *see* Johannesburg
Erbil *see* Arbīl
Erciş 117 F3 Van, E Turkey
Erdély *see* Transylvania
Erdélyi-Havasok *see* Carpaţii
   Meridionalii
Erdenet 127 E2 Orhon, N Mongolia
Erdi 76 C2 *plateau* NE Chad
Erdi Ma 76 D2 *desert* NE Chad
Erebus, Mount 154 B4 *volcano* Ross
   Island, Antarctica
Ereğli 116 C4 Konya, S Turkey
Erenhot 127 F2 *var.* Erlian. Nei Mongol
   Zizhiqu, NE China
Erfurt 94 C4 Thüringen, C Germany
Ergene Çayı *see* Ergene Irmağı
Ergene Irmağı 116 A2 *var.* Ergene Çayı.
   river NW Turkey
Ergun 127 F1 *var.* Labudalin;
   prev. Ergun Youqi.
   Nei Mongol Zizhiqu, N China
Ergun He *see* Argun
Ergun Youqi *see* Ergun
Erie 40 D3 Pennsylvania, NE USA
Érié, Lac *see* Erie, Lake
Erie, Lake 40 D3 *Fr.* Lac Érié. *lake*
   Canada/USA
Eritrea 72 C4 *off.* State of Eritrea, Ērtra.
   country E Africa
Eritrea, State of *see* Eritrea
Erivan *see* Yerevan
Erlangen 95 C5 Bayern, S Germany
Erlau *see* Eger
Erlian *see* Erenhot
Ermelo 86 D3 Gelderland,
   C Netherlands
Ermióni 105 C6 Pelopónnisos, S Greece
Ermoúpoli 105 D6 *var.* Hermoupolis;
   prev. Ermoúpolis. Sýýros, Kykládes,
   Greece, Aegean Sea
Ermoúpolis *see* Ermoúpoli
Ernākulam 132 C3 Kerala, SW India
Erode 132 C2 Tamil Nādu, SE India
Erquelinnes 87 B7 Hainaut, S Belgium
Er-Rachidia 70 C2 *var.* Ksar al Soule.
   E Morocco
Er Rahad 72 B4 *var.* Ar Rahad. Northern
   Kordofan, C Sudan

Erromango 144 D4 *island* S Vanuatu
Ertis *see* Irtysh, C Asia
Ērtra *see* Eritrea
Erzerum *see* Erzurum
Erzgebirge 95 D5 *Cz.* Krušné Hory, *Eng.*
   Ore Mountains. *mountain range* Czech
   Republic (Czechia)/Germany
Erzincan 117 E3 *var.* Erzinjan. Erzincan,
   E Turkey
Erzinjan *see* Erzincan
Erzurum 117 F3 *prev.* Erzerum.
   Erzurum, NE Turkey
Esbjerg 85 A7 Syddtjylland, W Denmark
Esbo *see* Espoo
Escaldes 91 A8 Escaldes Engordany,
   C Andorra Europe
Escanaba 40 C2 Michigan, N USA
Escaut *see* Scheldt
Esch-sur-Alzette 87 D8 Luxembourg,
   S Luxembourg
Esclaves, Grand Lac des *see* Great Slave
   Lake
Escondido 47 C8 California, W USA
Escuinapa 50 D3 *var.* Escuinapa de
   Hidalgo. Sinaloa, C Mexico
Escuinapa de Hidalgo *see* Escuinapa
Escuintla 52 B2 Escuintla, S Guatemala
Escuintla 51 G5 Chiapas, SE Mexico
Esenguly 122 B3 *Rus.* Gasan-Kuli.
   Balkan Welaýaty, W Turkmenistan
Eşfahān 120 C3 *Eng.* Isfahan; *anc.*
   Aspadana. Eşfahān, C Iran
Esh Sharā *see* Ash Sharāh
Esil *see* Ishim, Kazakhstan/Russia
Eskimo Point *see* Arviat
Eskişehir 116 B3 *var.* Eskishehr.
   Eskişehir, W Turkey
Eskishehr *see* Eskişehir
Eslāmābād *see* Eslāmābād-e Gharb
Eslāmābād-e Gharb 120 C3 *var.*
   Eslāmābād; *prev.* Harunabad,
   Shāhābād. Kermānshāhān, W Iran
Esmeraldas 60 A1 Esmeraldas,
   N Ecuador
Esna *see* Isnā
España *see* Spain
Espanola 48 D1 New Mexico, SW USA
Esperance 147 B7 Western Australia
Esperanza 50 B2 Sonora, NW Mexico
Esperanza 154 A2 Argentinian research
   station Antarctica
Espinal 58 B3 Tolima, C Colombia
Espinhaço, Serra do 56 D4 *mountain
   range* SE Brazil
Espírito Santo 63 G3 *off.* Estado do
   Espírito Santo. *state* E Brazil
Espírito Santo 63 F4 *off.* Estado do
   Espírito Santo. *region* E Brazil
Espírito Santo, Estado do *see* Espírito
   Santo
Espiritu Santo 144 C4 *var.* Santo. *island*
   W Vanuatu
Espoo 85 D6 *Swe.* Esbo. Uusimaa,
   S Finland
Esquel 65 B6 Chubut, SW Argentina
Essaouira 70 B2 *prev.* Mogador.
   W Morocco
Esseg *see* Osijek
Es Semara *see* Smara
Essen 87 C5 Antwerpen, N Belgium
Essen 94 A4 *var.* Essen an der Ruhr.
   Nordrhein-Westfalen, W Germany
Essen an der Ruhr *see* Essen
Essequibo River 59 F3 *river* C Guyana
Es Suweida *see* As Suwaydā'
Estacado, Llano 49 E2 *plain* New
   Mexico/Texas, SW USA
Estados, Isla de los 65 C8 *prev. Eng.*
   Staten Island. *island* S Argentina
Estância 63 G3 Sergipe, E Brazil
Estelí 52 D3 Estelí, NW Nicaragua
Estella 93 E1 *Bas.* Lizarra. Navarra,
   N Spain
Estepona 92 D5 Andalucía, S Spain
Estevan 37 F5 Saskatchewan, S Canada
Estland *see* Estonia
Estonia 106 D2 *off.* Republic of Estonia,
   Est. Eesti Vabariik, *Ger.* Estland, *Latv.*
   Igaunija; *prev.* Estonian SSR, *Rus.*
   Estonskaya SSR. *country* NE Europe
Estonian SSR *see* Estonia
Estonia, Republic of *see* Estonia
Estonskaya SSR *see* Estonia
Estrela, Serra da 92 C3 *mountain range*
   C Portugal
Estremadura *see* Extremadura
Estremoz 92 C4 Évora, S Portugal
Eswatini 78 D4 *off.* Kingdom of Eswatini;
   prev. Swaziland. *country* S Africa
Eswatini, Kingdom of *see* Eswatini

Eszék *see* Osijek
Esztergom 99 C6 *Ger.* Gran; *anc.*
   Strigonium. Komárom-Esztergom,
   N Hungary
Étalle 87 D8 Luxembourg, SE Belgium
Etāwah 134 D3 Uttar Pradesh, N India
Ethiopia 73 C5 *off.* Federal Democratic
   Republic of Ethiopia; *prev.* Abyssinia,
   People's Democratic Republic of
   Ethiopia. *country* E Africa
**Ethiopia, Federal Democratic Republic
   of** *see* Ethiopia
Ethiopian Highlands 73 C5
   var. Ethiopian Plateau. *plateau*
   N Ethiopia
Ethiopian Plateau *see* Ethiopian
   Highlands
**Ethiopia, People's Democratic Republic
   of** *see* Ethiopia
Mount Etna 97 C7 *Eng.* Mount Etna.
   volcano Sicilia, Italy,
   C Mediterranean Sea
Etna, Mount *see* Etna, Monte
Etosha Pan 78 B3 *salt lake* N Namibia
Etoumbi 77 B5 Cuvette Ouest,
   NW Congo
Etsch *see* Adige
Et Tafila *see* Aṭ Ṭafilah
Ettelbrück 87 D8 Diekirch,
   C Luxembourg
'Eua 145 E5 *prev.* Middleburg Island.
   island Tongatapu Group, SE Tonga
Euboea 105 C5 *Lat.* Euboea. *island*
   C Greece
Euboea *see* Évvoia
Eucla 147 D6 Western Australia
Euclid 40 D3 Ohio, N USA
Eufaula Lake 49 G1 *var.* Eufaula
   Reservoir. *reservoir* Oklahoma,
   C USA
Eufaula Reservoir *see* Eufaula Lake
Eugene 46 B3 Oregon, NW USA
Eumolpias *see* Plovdiv
Eupen 87 D6 Liège, E Belgium
Euphrates 112 B4 *Ar.* Al-Furāt, *Turk.*
   Firat Nehri. *river* SW Asia
Eureka 47 A5 California, W USA
Eureka 44 A1 Montana, NW USA
Europa Point 93 H5 *headland*
   S Gibraltar
Europe 80 *continent*
Eutin 94 C2 Schleswig-Holstein,
   N Germany
Euxine Sea *see* Black Sea
Evansdale 45 G3 Iowa, C USA
Evanston 40 B3 Illinois, N USA
Evanston 44 B4 Wyoming, C USA
Evansville 40 B5 Indiana, N USA
Eveleth 45 G1 Minnesota, N USA
Everard, Lake 149 A6 *salt lake* South
   Australia
Everest, Mount 126 B5 *Chin.*
   Qomolangma Feng, *Nep.* Sagarmāthā.
   mountain China/Nepal
Everett 46 B2 Washington, NW USA
Everglades, The 43 F5 *wetland* Florida,
   SE USA
Evje 85 A6 Aust-Agder, S Norway
Evmolpia *see* Plovdiv
Évora 92 B4 *anc.* Ebora, *Lat.* Liberalitas
   Julia. Évora, C Portugal
Évreux 90 C3 *anc.* Civitas Eburovicum.
   Eure, N France
Évros *see* Maritsa
Évry 90 E2 Essonne, N France
Ewarton 54 B5 C Jamaica
Excelsior Springs 45 F4 Missouri,
   C USA
Exe 89 C7 *river* SW England, United
   Kingdom
Exeter 89 C7 *anc.* Isca Damnoniorum.
   SW England, United Kingdom
Exmoor 89 C7 *moorland* SW England,
   United Kingdom
Exmouth 146 A4 Western Australia
Exmouth 89 C7 SW England, United
   Kingdom
Exmouth Gulf 146 A4 *gulf* Western
   Australia
Exmouth Plateau 141 E5 *undersea
   plateau* E Indian Ocean
Extremadura 92 C3 *var.* Estremadura.
   autonomous community W Spain
Exuma Cays 54 C1 *islets* C The Bahamas
Exuma Sound 54 C1 *sound* C The
   Bahamas
Eyre Mountains 151 A7 *mountain range*
   South Island, New Zealand
Eyre North, Lake 149 A5 *salt lake* South
   Australia

Eyre Peninsula 149 A6 *peninsula* South
   Australia
Eyre South, Lake 149 A5 *salt lake* South
   Australia
Ezo *see* Hokkaidō

F

Faadhippolhu Atoll 132 B4 *var.*
   Fadiffolu, Lhaviyani Atoll. *atoll*
   N Maldives
Fabens 48 D3 Texas, SW USA
Fada 76 C2 Borkou-Ennedi-Tibesti,
   E Chad
Fada-Ngourma 75 E4 E Burkina Faso
Fadiffolu *see* Faadhippolhu Atoll
Faenza 96 C3 *anc.* Faventia.
   Emilia-Romagna, N Italy
Faeroe Islands *see* Faroe Islands
Færøerne *see* Faroe Islands
Faetano 96 E2 E San Marino
Făgăraş 108 C4 *Ger.* Fogarasch, *Hung.*
   Fogaras. Braşov, C Romania
Fagibina, Lake *see* Faguibine, Lac
Fagne 87 C7 *hill range* S Belgium
Faguibine, Lac 75 E3 *var.* Lake Fagibina.
   lake NW Mali
Fahlun *see* Falun
Fahraj 120 E4 Kermān, SE Iran
Faial 92 A5 *var.* Ilha do Faial. *island*
   Azores, Portugal, NE Atlantic Ocean
Faial, Ilha do *see* Faial
Faifo *see* Hôi An
Fairbanks 36 D3 Alaska, USA
Fairfield 47 B6 California, W USA
Fair Isle 88 D2 *island* NE Scotland,
   United Kingdom
Fairlie 151 B6 Canterbury, South Island,
   New Zealand
Fairmont 45 F3 Minnesota, N USA
Faisalabad 134 C2 *prev.* Lyallpur.
   Punjab, NE Pakistan
Faizābād 135 E3 Uttar Pradesh, N India
Faizābād 123 F3 *var.* Feīzābād,
   Feyzābād, Fyzabad; *prev.* Feyẓābād.
   Badakhshān, NE Afghanistan
Fakaofo Atoll 145 F3 *island* SE Tokelau
Falam 136 A3 Chin State, W Myanmar
   (Burma)
Falconara Marittima 96 C3 Marche,
   C Italy
Falkenau an der Eger *see* Sokolov
Falkland Islands 65 D7 *var.* Falklands,
   Islas Malvinas. *UK Overseas Territory*
   SW Atlantic Ocean
Falkland Plateau 57 D7 *var.* Argentine
   Rise. *undersea feature* SW Atlantic
   Ocean
Falklands *see* Falkland Islands
Falknov nad Ohří *see* Sokolov
Fallbrook 47 C8 California, W USA
Falmouth 54 A4 W Jamaica
Falmouth 89 C7 SW England, United
   Kingdom
Falster 85 B8 *island* SE Denmark
Fălticeni 108 C3 *Hung.* Falticsén.
   Suceava, NE Romania
Falticsén *see* Fălticeni
Falun 85 C6 *var.* Fahlun. Kopparberg,
   C Sweden
Famagusta *see* Gazimağusa
Famagusta Bay 102 C5 *var.* Famagusta
   Bay, *Gk.* Kólpos Ammóchostos. *bay*
   E Cyprus
Famagusta Bay *see* Gazimağusa Körfezi
Famenne 87 C7 *physical region*
   SE Belgium
Fang 136 C3 Chiang Mai, NW Thailand
Fanning Island *see* Tabuaeran
Fanø 96 C3 *island* W Denmark
Farafangana 79 G4 Fianarantsoa,
   SE Madagascar
Farāh 122 D4 *var.* Farah, Fararud.
   Farāh, W Afghanistan
Farah Rud 122 D4 *river* W Afghanistan
Faranah 74 C4 Haute-Guinée, S Guinea
Fararud *see* Farāh
Farasan, Jaza'ir 121 A6 *island group*
   SW Saudi Arabia
Farewell, Cape 150 C4 *headland* South
   Island, New Zealand
Farewell, Cape *see* Nunap Isua
Fargo 45 F2 North Dakota,
   N USA
Far'gona 123 F2 *Rus.* Fergana; *prev.*
   Novyy Margilan. Far'gona Viloyati,
   E Uzbekistan
Faribault 45 F2 Minnesota, N USA
Farīdābād 134 D3 Haryāna, N India

Farkhor 123 E3 *Rus.* Parkhar.
SW Tajikistan
Farmington 45 G5 Missouri, C USA
Farmington 48 C1 New Mexico,
SW USA
Faro 92 B5 Faro, S Portugal
Faroe-Iceland Ridge 80 C1 *undersea ridge* NW Norwegian Sea
Faroe Islands 83 E5 *var.* Faeroe Islands,
Dan. Færøerne, *Faer.* Føroyar.
Self-governing territory of Denmark
N Atlantic Ocean
Faroe-Shetland Trough 80 C2 *trough*
NE Atlantic Ocean
Farquhar Group 79 G2 *island group*
S Seychelles
Fars, Khalīj-e *see* Persian Gulf
Farvel, Kap *see* Nunap Isua
Fastiv 109 E2 *Rus.* Fastov. Kyyivs'ka
Oblast', NW Ukraine
Fastov *see* Fastiv
Fauske 84 C3 Nordland, C Norway
Faventia *see* Faenza
Faxa Bay *see* Faxaflói
Faxaflói 82 D5 *Eng.* Faxa Bay. *bay*
W Iceland
Faya 76 C2 *prev.* Faya-Largeau, Largeau.
Borkou-Ennedi-Tibesti, N Chad
Faya-Largeau *see* Faya
Fayetteville 42 A1 Arkansas, C USA
Fayetteville 43 F1 North Carolina,
SE USA
Fdérick *see* Fdérik
Fdérik 74 C2 *var.* Fdérick, *Fr.* Fort
Gouraud. Tiris Zemmour,
NW Mauritania
Fear, Cape 43 F2 *headland* Bald Head
Island, North Carolina, SE USA
Fécamp 90 B3 Seine-Maritime, N France
Fédala *see* Mohammedia
Federal Capital Territory *see* Australian
Capital Territory
Fehérgyarmat 99 E6 Szabolcs-Szatmár-
Bereg, E Hungary
Fehértemplom *see* Bela Crkva
Fehmarn 94 C2 *island* N Germany
Fehmarn Belt 94 C2 *Dan.* Femern Bælt,
Ger. Fehmarnbelt. *strait* Denmark /
Germany
Fehmarnbelt Fehmarn Belt/Femer Bælt
Feijó 62 C2 Acre, W Brazil
Feilding 150 D4 Manawatu-Wanganui,
North Island, New Zealand
Feira *see* Feira de Santana
Feira de Santana 63 G3 *var.* Feira.
Bahía, E Brazil
Feizābād *see* Faizābād
Feketehalom *see* Codlea
Felanitx 93 G3 Mallorca, Spain,
W Mediterranean Sea
Felicitas Julia *see* Lisboa
Felidhu Atoll 132 B4 *atoll* C Maldives
Felipe Carrillo Puerto 51 H4 Quintana
Roo, SE Mexico
Felixstowe 89 E6 E England, United
Kingdom
Fellin *see* Viljandi
Felsőbánya *see* Baia Sprie
Felsőmuzslya *see* Mužlja
Femunden 85 B5 *lake* S Norway
Fénérive *see* Fenoarivo Atsinanana
Fengcheng 128 D3 *var.* Feng-cheng,
Fenghwangcheng. Liaoning,
NE China
Feng-cheng *see* Fengcheng
Fenghwangcheng *see* Fengcheng
Fengtien *see* Liaoning, China
Fengtien *see* Shenyang, China
Fenoarivo Atsinanana 79 G3 *prev./Fr.*
Fénérive. Toamasina, E Madagascar
Fens, The 89 E6 *wetland* E England,
United Kingdom
Feodosiya 109 F5 *var.* Kefe, *It.* Kaffa;
anc. Theodosia. Avtonomna
Respublika Krym, S Ukraine
Ferdinand *see* Montana, Bulgaria
Ferdinandsberg *see* Oțelu Roșu
Féres 104 D3 Anatolikí Makedonía kai
Thráki, NE Greece
Fergana *see* Far'gona
Fergus Falls 45 F2 Minnesota, N USA
Ferizaj 101 D5 *Serb.* Uroševac. C Kosovo
Ferkessédougou 74 D4 N Ivory Coast
Fermo 96 C4 *anc.* Firmum Picenum.
Marche, C Italy
Fernandina, Isla 60 A5 *var.* Narborough
Island. *island* Galápagos Islands,
Ecuador, E Pacific Ocean
Fernando de Noronha 63 H2 *island*
E Brazil

Fernando Po/Fernando Póo *see* Bioco,
Isla de
Ferrara 96 C2 *anc.* Forum Alieni.
Emilia-Romagna, N Italy
Ferreñafe 60 B3 Lambayeque,
W Peru
Ferro *see* Hierro
Ferrol 92 B1 *var.* El Ferrol; *prev.* El Ferrol
del Caudillo. Galicia, NW Spain
Fertő *see* Neusiedler See
Ferwerd *see* Ferwert
Ferwert 86 D1 *Dutch.* Ferwerd.
Friesland, N Netherlands
Fès 70 C2 *Eng.* Fez. N Morocco
Feteşti 108 D5 Ialomița, SE Romania
Fethiye 116 B4 Muğla, SW Turkey
Fetlar 88 D1 *island* NE Scotland,
United Kingdom
Feuilles, Rivière aux 16 D2 *river*
Québec, E Canada
Feyzābād *see* Feizābād
Feyzābād *see* Feizābād
Fez *see* Fès
Fianarantsoa 79 F3 Fianarantsoa,
C Madagascar
Fianga 76 B4 Mayo-Kébbi, SW Chad
Fier 101 C6 *var.* Fieri. Fier,
SW Albania
Fieri *see* Fier
Figeac 91 C5 Lot, S France
Figig *see* Figuig
Figueira da Foz 92 B3 Coimbra,
W Portugal
Figueres 93 G2 Cataluña, E Spain
Figuig 70 D2 *var.* Figig. E Morocco
Fiji 145 E5 *off.* Sovereign Democratic
Republic of Fiji, *Fij.* Viti. *country*
SW Pacific Ocean
Fiji, Sovereign Democratic Republic of
see Fiji
Filadelfia 52 D4 Guanacaste,
W Costa Rica
Filiaşi 108 B5 Dolj, SW Romania
Filipstad 85 B6 Värmland, C Sweden
Finale Ligure 96 A3 Liguria, NW Italy
Finchley 89 A7 United Kingdom
Findlay 40 C4 Ohio, N USA
Finike 116 B4 Antalya, SW Turkey
Finland 84 D4 *off.* Republic of Finland,
Fin. Suomen Tasavalta, Suomi. *country*
N Europe
Finland, Gulf of 85 D6 *Est.* Soome Laht,
Fin. Suomenlahti, *Ger.* Finnischer
Meerbusen, *Rus.* Finskiy Zaliv, *Swe.*
Finska Viken. *gulf* E Baltic Sea
Finland, Republic of *see* Finland
Finnischer Meerbusen *see* Finland, Gulf
of
Finnmarksvidda 84 D2 *physical region*
N Norway
Finska Viken/Finskiy Zaliv *see* Finland,
Gulf of
Finsterwalde 94 D4 Brandenburg,
E Germany
Fiordland 151 A7 *physical region* South
Island, New Zealand
Fiorina 96 E1 NE San Marino
Firat Nehri *see* Euphrates
Firenze 96 C3 *Eng.* Florence; *anc.*
Florentia. Toscana, C Italy
Firmum Picenum *see* Fermo
First State *see* Delaware
Fischbacher Alpen 95 E7 *mountain
range* E Austria
Fischhausen *see* Primorsk
Fish 78 B4 *var.* Vis. *river* S Namibia
Fishguard 89 C6 *Wel.* Abergwaun.
SW Wales, United Kingdom
Fisterra, Cabo 92 B1 *headland*
NW Spain
Fitzroy Crossing 146 C3 Western
Australia
Fitzroy River 146 C3 *river* Western
Australia
Fiume *see* Rijeka
Flagstaff 48 B2 Arizona, SW USA
Flanders *see* Vlaanderen
Flandre *see* Vlaanderen
Flathead Lake 44 B1 *lake* Montana,
NW USA
Flat Island 128 C8 *island* NE Spratly
Islands
Flatts Village 42 B5 *var.* The Flatts
Village. C Bermuda
Flensburg 94 B2 Schleswig-Holstein,
N Germany
Flessingue *see* Vlissingen
Flickertail State *see* North Dakota
Flinders Island 149 C8 *island* Furneaux
Group, Tasmania, SE Australia

Flinders Ranges 149 B6 *mountain range*
South Australia
Flinders River 148 C3 *river* Queensland,
NE Australia
Flin Flon 37 F5 Manitoba, C Canada
Flint 40 C3 Michigan, N USA
Flint Island 145 G4 *island* Line Islands,
E Kiribati
Floreana, Isla *see* Santa María, Isla
Florence 42 C1 Alabama, S USA
Florence 43 F2 South Carolina, SE USA
Florence *see* Firenze
Florencia 58 B4 Caquetá, S Colombia
Florentia *see* Firenze
Flores 52 B1 Petén, N Guatemala
Flores 139 E5 *island* Nusa Tenggara,
C Indonesia
Flores 92 A5 *island* Azores, Portugal,
NE Atlantic Ocean
Flores, Laut *see* Flores Sea
Flores Sea 138 D5 *Ind.* Laut Flores. *sea*
C Indonesia
Floriano 63 F2 Piauí, E Brazil
Florianópolis 63 F5 *prev.* Destêrro. *state
capital* Santa Catarina, S Brazil
Florida 64 D4 Florida, S Uruguay
Florida 43 E4 *off.* State of Florida, *also
known as* Peninsular State, Sunshine
State. *state* SE USA
Florida Bay 43 E5 *bay* Florida, SE USA
Florida Keys 43 E5 *island group* Florida,
SE USA
Florida, Straits of 54 B1 *strait* Atlantic
Ocean/Gulf of Mexico
Flórina 104 B4 *var.* Phlórina. Dytikí
Makedonía, N Greece
Florissant 45 G4 Missouri, C USA
Floúda, Akrotírio 105 D7 *headland*
Astypálaia, Kykládes, Greece, Aegean
Sea
Flushing *see* Vlissingen
Flylân *see* Vlieland
Foča 100 C4 *var.* Srbinje. SE Bosnia and
Herzegovina
Focşani 108 C4 Vrancea, E Romania
Fogaras/Fogarasch *see* Făgăraş
Foggia 97 D5 Puglia, SE Italy
Fogo 74 A3 *island* Ilhas de Sotavento,
SW Cape Verde
Foix 91 B6 Ariège, S France
Folégandros 105 C7 *island* Kykládes,
Greece, Aegean Sea
Foleyet 38 C4 Ontario, S Canada
Foligno 96 C4 Umbria, C Italy
Folkestone 89 E7 SE England, United
Kingdom
Fond du Lac 40 B2 Wisconsin,
N USA
Fonseca, Golfo de *see* Fonseca, Gulf of
Fonseca, Gulf of 52 C3 *Sp.* Golfo de
Fonseca. *gulf* C Central America
Fontainebleau 90 C3 Seine-et-Marne,
N France
Fontenay-le-Comte 90 B4 Vendée,
NW France
Fontvieille 91 B8 SW Monaco Europe
Fonyód 99 C7 Somogy, W Hungary
Foochow *see* Fuzhou
Foochow *see* Fuzhou
Forchheim 95 C5 Bayern,
SE Germany
Forel, Mont 82 D4 *mountain*
SE Greenland
Forfar 88 C3 E Scotland, United
Kingdom
Forge du Sud *see* Dudelange
Forlì 96 C3 *anc.* Forum Livii.
Emilia-Romagna, N Italy
Formentera 93 G4 *anc.* Ophiusa, *Lat.*
Frumentum. *island* Islas Baleares,
Spain, W Mediterranean Sea
Formosa 64 D2 Formosa, NE Argentina
Formosa/Formo'sa *see* Taiwan
Formosa, Serra 63 E3 *mountain range*
C Brazil
Formosa Strait *see* Taiwan Strait
Føroyar *see* Faroe Islands
Forrest City 42 B1 Arkansas, C USA
Fort Albany 38 C3 Ontario, C Canada
Fortaleza 61 F2 Pando, N Bolivia
Fortaleza 63 G2 *prev.* Ceará. *state capital*
Ceará, NE Brazil
Fort-Archambault *see* Sarh
Fort-Bayard *see* Zhanjiang
Fort-Cappolani *see* Tidjikja
Fort Charlet *see* Djanet
Fort-Chimo *see* Kuujjuaq
Fort Collins 44 D4 Colorado, C USA
Fort-Crampel *see* Kaga Bandoro
Fort Davis 49 E3 Texas, SW USA

Fort-de-France 55 H4 *prev.* Fort-Royal.
dependent territory capital (Martinique)
W Martinique
Fort Dodge 45 F3 Iowa, C USA
Fortescue River 146 A4 *river* Western
Australia
Fort-Foureau *see* Kousséri
Fort Frances 38 B4 Ontario, S Canada
Fort Good Hope 37 E3 *var.* Rádeyilikóé.
Northwest Territories, NW Canada
Fort Gouraud *see* Fdérik
Forth 88 C4 *river* C Scotland, United
Kingdom
Forth, Firth of 88 C4 *estuary* E Scotland,
United Kingdom
Fortín General Eugenio Garay *see*
General Eugenio A. Garay
Fort Jameson *see* Chipata
Fort-Lamy *see* N'Djaména
Fort Lauderdale 43 F5 Florida, SE USA
Fort Liard 37 E4 *var.* Liard. Northwest
Territories, W Canada
Fort Madison 45 G4 Iowa, C USA
Fort McMurray 37 E4 Alberta, C Canada
Fort McPherson 36 D3 *var.* McPherson.
Northwest Territories, NW Canada
Fort Morgan 44 D4 Colorado, C USA
Fort Myers 43 E5 Florida, SE USA
Fort Nelson 37 E4 British Columbia,
W Canada
Fort Peck Lake 44 C1 *reservoir* Montana,
NW USA
Fort Pierce 43 F4 Florida, SE USA
Fort Providence 37 E4 *var.* Providence.
Northwest Territories, W Canada
Fort-Repoux *see* Akjoujt
Fort Rosebery *see* Mansa
Fort Rousset *see* Owando
Fort-Royal *see* Fort-de-France
Fort St. John 37 E4 British Columbia,
W Canada
Fort Scott 45 F5 Kansas, C USA
Fort Severn 38 C2 Ontario, C Canada
Fort-Shevchenko 114 A4 Mangistau,
W Kazakhstan
Fort-Sibut *see* Sibut
Fort Simpson 37 E4 *var.* Simpson.
Northwest Territories, W Canada
Fort Smith 37 E4 Northwest Territories,
W Canada
Fort Smith 42 B1 Arkansas, C USA
Fort Stockton 49 E3 Texas, SW USA
Fort-Trinquet *see* Bîr Mogreïn
Fort Vermilion 37 E4 Alberta,
W Canada
Fort Victoria *see* Masvingo
Fort Walton Beach 42 C3 Florida,
SE USA
Fort Wayne 40 C4 Indiana, N USA
Fort William 88 C3 N Scotland, United
Kingdom
Fort Worth 49 G2 Texas, SW USA
Fort Yukon 36 D3 Alaska, USA
Forum Alieni *see* Ferrara
Forum Livii *see* Forlì
Fossa Claudia *see* Chioggia
Fougamou 77 A6 Ngounié, C Gabon
Fougères 90 B3 Ille-et-Vilaine,
NW France
Fou-hsin *see* Fuxin
Foulwind, Cape 151 B5 *headland* South
Island, New Zealand
Foumban 76 A4 Ouest,
NW Cameroon
Fou-shan *see* Fushun
Foveaux Strait 151 A8 *strait* S New
Zealand
Foxe Basin 37 G3 *sea* Nunavut,
N Canada
Fox Glacier 151 B6 West Coast, South
Island, New Zealand
Fraga 93 F2 Aragón, NE Spain
Fram Basin *see* Amundsen Basin
France 90 B4 *off.* French Republic, *It./Sp.*
Francia; *prev.* Gaul, Gaule, *Lat.* Gallia.
country W Europe
Franceville 77 B6 *var.* Massoukou,
Masuku. Haut-Ogooué, E Gabon
Francfort *see* Frankfurt am Main
Franche-Comté 90 D4 *cultural region*
E France
Francia *see* France
Francis Case, Lake 45 E3 *reservoir*
South Dakota, N USA
Francisco Escárcega 51 G4 Campeche,
SE Mexico
Francistown 78 D3 North East,
NE Botswana
Franconian Jura *see* Fränkische Alb

Frankenalb see Fränkische Alb
Frankenstein/Frankenstein in Schlesien see Ząbkowice Śląskie
Frankfort 40 C5 state capital Kentucky, S USA
Frankfort on the Main see Frankfurt am Main
Frankfurt see Frankfurt am Main, Germany
Frankfurt see Słubice, Poland
Frankfurt am Main 95 B5 var. Frankfurt, Fr. Francfort; prev. Eng. Frankfort on the Main. Hessen, SW Germany
Frankfurt an der Oder 94 D3 Brandenburg, E Germany
Fränkische Alb 95 C6 var. Frankenalb, Eng. Franconian Jura. mountain range S Germany
Franklin 42 C1 Tennessee, S USA
Franklin D. Roosevelt Lake 46 C1 reservoir Washington, NW USA
Franz Josef Land 114 D1 Eng. Franz Josef Land. island group N Russia
Franz Josef Land see Frantsa-Iosifa, Zemlya
Fraserburgh 88 D3 NE Scotland, United Kingdom
Fraser Island 148 E4 var. Great Sandy Island. island Queensland, E Australia
Frauenbach see Baia Mare
Frauenburg see Saldus, Latvia
Fredericksburg 41 E5 Virginia, NE USA
Fredericton 39 F4 province capital New Brunswick, SE Canada
Frederikshåb see Paamiut
Frederikshald see Halden
Fredrikstad 85 B6 Østfold, S Norway
Freeport 54 C1 Grand Bahama Island, N The Bahamas
Freeport 49 H4 Texas, SW USA
Free State see Maryland
Freetown 74 C4 country capital (Sierra Leone) W Sierra Leone
Freiburg see Freiburg im Breisgau, Germany
Freiburg im Breisgau 95 A6 var. Freiburg, Fr. Fribourg-en-Brisgau. Baden-Württemberg, SW Germany
Freiburg in Schlesien see Świebodzice
Fremantle 147 A6 Western Australia
Fremont 45 F4 Nebraska, C USA
French Guiana 59 H3 var. Guiana, Guyane. French overseas department N South America
French Guinea see Guinea
French Polynesia 143 F4 French overseas territory S Pacific Ocean
French Republic see France
French Somaliland see Djibouti
French Southern and Antarctic Lands 141 B7 Fr. Terres Australes et Antarctiques Françaises. French overseas territory S Indian Ocean
French Sudan see Mali
French Territory of the Afars and Issas see Djibouti
French Togoland see Togo
Fresnillo 50 D3 var. Fresnillo de González Echeverría. Zacatecas, C Mexico
Fresnillo de González Echeverría see Fresnillo
Fresno 47 C6 California, W USA
Frías 64 C3 Catamarca, N Argentina
Fribourg-en-Brisgau see Freiburg im Breisgau
Friedek-Mistek see Frýdek-Místek
Friedrichshafen 95 B7 Baden-Württemberg, S Germany
Friendly Islands see Tonga
Frisches Haff see Vistula Lagoon
Frobisher Bay 82 B3 inlet Baffin Island, Nunavut, NE Canada
Frobisher Bay see Iqaluit
Frohavet 84 B4 sound C Norway
Frome, Lake 149 B6 salt lake South Australia
Frontera 51 G4 Tabasco, SE Mexico
Frontignan 91 C6 Hérault, S France
Frostviken se Kvarnbergsvattnet
Frøya 84 A4 island W Norway
Frumentum see Formentera
Frunze see Bishkek
Frýdek-Místek 99 C5 Ger. Friedek-Mistek. Moravskoslezský Kraj, E Czech Republic (Czechia)

Fu-chien see Fujian
Fu-chou see Fuzhou
Fuengirola 92 D5 Andalucía, S Spain
Fuerte Olimpo 64 D2 var. Olimpo. Alto Paraguay, NE Paraguay
Fuerte, Río 48 C5 river C Mexico
Fuerteventura 70 B3 island Islas Canarias, Spain, NE Atlantic Ocean
Fuhkien see Fujian
Fu-hsin see Fuxin
Fuji 131 D6 var. Huzi. Shizuoka, Honshū, S Japan
Fujian 128 D6 var. Fu-chien, Fuhkien, Fukien, Min, Fujian Sheng. province SE China
Fujian Sheng see Fujian
Mount Fuji 131 C6 var. Fujiyama, Eng. Mount Fuji. mountain Honshū, SE Japan
Fuji, Mount/Fujiyama see Fuji-san
Fukang 126 C2 Xinjiang Uygur Zizhiqu, W China
Fukien see Fujian
Fukui 131 C6 var. Hukui. Fukui, Honshū, SW Japan
Fukuoka 131 A7 var. Hukuoka, hist. Najima. Fukuoka, Kyūshū, SW Japan
Fukushima 130 D4 var. Hukusima. Fukushima, Honshū, C Japan
Fulda 95 B5 Hessen, C Germany
Funafuti Atoll 145 E3 atoll and capital (Tuvalu) C Tuvalu
Funchal 70 A2 Madeira, Portugal, NE Atlantic Ocean
Fünen see Fyn
Fünfkirchen see Pécs
Furnes see Veurne
Fürth 95 C5 Bayern, S Germany
Furukawa 130 D4 var. Hurukawa, Ōsaki. Miyagi, Honshū, C Japan
Fusan see Busan
Fushë Kosovë 101 D5 Serb. Kosovo Polje. C Kosovo
Fushun 128 D3 var. Fou-shan, Fu-shun. Liaoning, NE China
Fu-shun see Fushun
Fusin see Fuxin
Füssen 95 C7 Bayern, S Germany
Futog 100 D3 Vojvodina, NW Serbia
Futuna, Île 145 E4 island S Wallis and Futuna
Fuxin 128 D3 var. Fou-hsin, Fu-hsin, Fusin. Liaoning, NE China
Fuzhou 128 D5 var. Foochow, Fu-chou. province capital Fujian, SE China
Fuzhou 128 D6 var. Foochow, Fu-chou. province capital Fujian, SE China
Fyn 85 B8 Ger. Fünen. C Denmark
FYR Macedonia/FYROM see Macedonia
Fyzabad see Feizābād

G

Gaafu Alifu Atoll see North Huvadhu Atoll
Gaalkacyo 73 E5 var. Galka'yo, It. Galcaio. Mudug, C Somalia
Gabela 78 B2 Cuanza Sul, W Angola
Gaberones see Gaborone
Gabès 71 E2 var. Qābis. E Tunisia
Gabès, Golfe de 71 F2 Ar. Khalīj Qābis. gulf E Tunisia
Gabon 77 B6 off. Gabonese Republic. country C Africa
Gabonese Republic see Gabon
Gaborone 78 C4 prev. Gaberones. country capital (Botswana) South East, SE Botswana
Gabrovo 104 D2 Gabrovo, N Bulgaria
Gadag 132 C1 Karnātaka, W India
Gades/Gadier/Gadir/Gadire see Cádiz
Gadsden 42 D2 Alabama, S USA
Gaeta 97 C5 Lazio, C Italy
Gaeta, Gulf of 97 C5 var. Gulf of Gaeta. gulf C Italy
Gaeta, Gulf of see Gaeta, Golfo di
Gäfle see Gävle
Gafsa 71 E2 var. Qafşah. W Tunisia
Gagnoa 74 D5 C Ivory Coast
Gagra 117 E1 NW Georgia
Gaillac 91 C6 var. Gaillac-sur-Tarn. Tarn, S France
Gaillac-sur-Tarn see Gaillac
Gaillimh see Galway
Gaillimhe, Cuan na see Galway Bay
Gainesville 43 E3 Florida, SE USA
Gainesville 42 D2 Georgia, SE USA

Gainesville 49 G2 Texas, SW USA
Lake Gairdner 149 A6 salt lake South Australia
Gaizina Kalns see Gaiziņkalns
Gaiziņkalns 106 C3 var. Gaizina Kalns. mountain E Latvia
Gakkel Ridge 155 B3 var. Arctic Mid Oceanic Ridge, Nansen Cordillera. seamount range Arctic Ocean
Galán, Cerro 64 B3 mountain NW Argentina
Galanta 99 C6 Hung. Galánta. Trnavský Kraj, W Slovakia
Galapagos Fracture Zone 153 E3 tectonic feature E Pacific Ocean
Galápagos Islands 153 F3 var. Islas de los Galápagos, Sp. Archipiélago de Colón, Eng. Galapagos Islands, Tortoise Islands. island group Ecuador, E Pacific Ocean
Galapagos Islands see Galápagos Islands
Galápagos, Islas de los see Galápagos Islands
Galapagos Rise 153 F3 undersea rise E Pacific Ocean
Galashiels 88 C4 SE Scotland, United Kingdom
Galați 108 D4 Ger. Galatz. Galați, E Romania
Galatz see Galați
Galcaio see Gaalkacyo
Galesburg 40 B3 Illinois, N USA
Galicia 92 B1 anc. Gallaecia. autonomous community NW Spain
Galicia Bank 80 B4 undersea bank E Atlantic Ocean
Galilee, Sea of see Tiberias, Lake
Galka'yo see Gaalkacyo
Galkynyş 122 D3 prev. Rus. Deynau, Dyanev, Turkm. Dänew. Lebap Welaýaty, NE Turkmenistan
Gallaecia see Galicia
Galle 132 D4 prev. Point de Galle. Southern Province, SW Sri Lanka
Gallego Rise 153 F3 undersea rise E Pacific Ocean
Gallegos see Río Gallegos
Gallia see France
Gallipoli 97 E6 Puglia, SE Italy
Gällivare 84 C3 Lapp. Váhtjer. Norrbotten, N Sweden
Gallup 48 C1 New Mexico, SW USA
Galtat-Zemmour 70 B3 C Western Sahara
Galveston 49 H4 Texas, SW USA
Galway 89 A5 Ir. Gaillimh. W Ireland
Galway Bay 89 A6 Ir. Cuan na Gaillimhe. bay W Ireland
Gámas see Kaamanen
Gambell 36 C2 Saint Lawrence Island, Alaska, USA
Gambia, The 74 B3 off. Republic of The Gambia. country W Africa
Gambia 74 C3 Fr. Gambie. river W Africa
Gambia, Republic of The see Gambia, The
Gambie see Gambia
Gambier, Îles 143 G4 island group E French Polynesia
Gamboma 77 B6 Plateaux, E Congo
Gamlakarleby see Kokkola
Gan 132 B5 Addu Atoll, C Maldives
Gan see Gansu, China
Gan see Jiangxi, China
Ganaane see Juba
Gäncä 117 G2 Rus. Gyandzha; prev. Kirovabad, Yelisavetpol. W Azerbaijan
Gandajika 77 D7 Kasai-Oriental, S Dem. Rep. Congo
Gander 39 G3 Newfoundland and Labrador, SE Canada
Gändhīdhäm 134 C4 Gujarāt, W India
Gandia 93 F3 prev. Gandía. País Valenciana, E Spain
Gandía see Gandia
Ganges 135 F3 Ben. Padma. river Bangladesh/India
Ganges Cone see Ganges Fan
Ganges Fan 140 D3 var. Ganges Cone. undersea fan N Bay of Bengal
Ganges, Mouths of the 135 G4 delta Bangladesh/India
Gangra see Çankırı
Gangtok 135 F3 state capital Sikkim, N India
Gansos, Lago dos see Goose Lake
Gansu 128 B4 var. Gan, Gansu Sheng, Kansu. province N China

Gansu Sheng see Gansu
Gantsevichi see Hantsavichy
Ganzhou 128 D6 Jiangxi, S China
Gao 75 E3 Gao, E Mali
Gaocheng see Litang
Gaoual 74 C4 N Guinea
Gaoxiong see Kaohsiung
Gap 91 D5 anc. Vapincum. Hautes-Alpes, SE France
Gaplañgyr Platosy 122 C2 Rus. Plato Kaplangky. ridge Turkmenistan/Uzbekistan
Gar see Gar Xincun
Garabil Belentligi 122 D3 Rus. Vozvyshennost' Karabil'. mountain range S Turkmenistan
Garabogaz Aylagy 122 B2 Rus. Zaliv Kara-Bogaz-Gol. bay NW Turkmenistan
Garachiné 53 G5 Darién, SE Panama
Garagum 122 D3 var. Garagumy, Qara Qum, Eng. Black Sand Desert, Kara Kum; prev. Peski Karakumy. desert C Turkmenistan
Garagum Canal 122 D3 var. Kara Kum Canal, Rus. Karagumskiy Kanal, Karakumskiy Kanal. canal C Turkmenistan
Garagumy see Garagum
Gara Khitrino 104 D2 Shumen, NE Bulgaria
Gárasavvon see Kaaresuvanto
Garda, Lake 96 C2 var. Benaco, Eng. Lake Garda, Ger. Gardasee. lake NE Italy
Garda, Lake see Garda, Lago di
Gardasee see Garda, Lake
Garden City 45 E5 Kansas, C USA
Garden State, The see New Jersey
Gardēz 123 E4 prev. Gardiz. E Afghanistan
Gardiz see Gardēz
Gardner Island see Nikumaroro
Garegegasnjárga see Karigasniemi
Gargždai 106 B3 Klaipėda, W Lithuania
Garissa 73 D6 Coast, E Kenya
Garland 49 G2 Texas, SW USA
Garoe see Garoowe
Garonne 91 B5 anc. Garumna. river S France
Garoowe 73 E5 var. Garoe. Nugaal, N Somalia
Garoua 76 B4 var. Garua. Nord, N Cameroon
Garrygala see Magtymguly
Garry Lake 37 F3 lake Nunavut, C Canada
Garsen 73 D6 Coast, S Kenya
Garua see Garoua
Garumna see Garonne
Garwolin 98 D4 Mazowieckie, E Poland
Gar Xincun 126 A4 prev. Gar. Xizang Zizhiqu, W China
Gary 40 B3 Indiana, N USA
Garzón 58 B4 Huila, S Colombia
Gasan-Kuli see Esenguly
Gascogne 91 B6 Eng. Gascony. cultural region S France
Gascony see Gascogne
Gascoyne River 147 A5 river Western Australia
Gaspé 39 F3 Québec, SE Canada
Gaspé, Péninsule de 39 E4 var. Péninsule de la Gaspésie. peninsula Québec, SE Canada
Gaspésie, Péninsule de la see Gaspé, Péninsule de
Gastonia 43 E1 North Carolina, SE USA
Gastoúni 105 B6 Dytikí Elláda, S Greece
Gatchina 110 B4 Leningradskaya Oblast', NW Russia
Gatineau 38 D4 Québec, SE Canada
Gatooma see Kadoma
Gatún, Lake 53 F4 reservoir C Panama
Gauhāti see Guwāhāti
Gauja 106 D3 Ger. Aa. river Estonia/Latvia
Gaul/Gaule see France
Gauteng see Johannesburg, South Africa
Gävbandi 120 D4 Hormozgān, S Iran
Gávdos 105 C8 island SE Greece
Gavere 87 B6 Oost-Vlaanderen, NW Belgium
Gävle 85 C6 var. Gäfle; prev. Gefle. Gävleborg, C Sweden
Gawler 149 B6 South Australia
Gaya 135 F3 Bihār, N India
Gaya see Kyjov
Gayndah 149 E5 Queensland, E Australia

Gaysin see Haysyn
Gaza 119 A6 Ar. Ghazzah, Heb. 'Azza.
   NE Gaza Strip
Gaz-Achak see Gazojak
Gazandzhyk/Gazanjyk see Bereket
Gaza Strip 119 A7 Ar. Qita Ghazzah.
   disputed region SW Asia
Gaziantep 116 D4 var. Gazi Antep; prev.
   Aintab, Antep. Gaziantep, S Turkey
Gazi Antep see Gaziantep
Gazimağusa 102 D5 var. Famagusta, Gk.
   Ammóchostos. E Cyprus
Gazli 122 D2 Buxoro Viloyati,
   C Uzbekistan
Gazojak 122 D2 Rus. Gaz-Achak. Lebap
   Welaýaty, NE Turkmenistan
Gbanga 74 D5 var. Gbarnga. N Liberia
Gbarnga see Gbanga
Gdańsk 98 C2 Fr. Dantzig, Ger. Danzig.
   Pomorskie, N Poland
Gdańsk, Gulf of 98 C2 var. Gulf of
   Danzig, Ger. Danziger Bucht, Pol.
   Zakota Gdańska, Rus. Gdan'skaya
   Bukhta. gulf N Poland
Gdan'skaya Bukhta see Gdańsk, Gulf of
Gdańska, Zakota see Gdańsk, Gulf of
Gdingen see Gdynia
Gdynia 98 C2 Ger. Gdingen. Pomorskie,
   N Poland
Gedaref 72 C4 var. Al Qaḍārif, El
   Gedaref. Gedaref, E Sudan
Gediz 116 B3 Kütahya, W Turkey
Gediz Nehri 116 A3 river W Turkey
Geel 87 C5 var. Gheel. Antwerpen,
   N Belgium
Geelong 149 C7 Victoria, SE Australia
Ge'e'mu see Golmud
Gefle see Gävle
Geilo 85 A5 Buskerud, S Norway
Gejiu 128 B6 var. Kochiu. Yunnan,
   S China
Gëkdepe see Gökdepe
Gela 97 C7 prev. Terranova di Sicilia.
   Sicilia, Italy, C Mediterranean Sea
Geldermalsen 86 C4 Gelderland,
   C Netherlands
Geleen 87 D6 Limburg, SE Netherlands
Gelib see Jilib
Gellinsor 73 E5 Galguduud, C Somalia
Gembloux 87 C6 Namur, Belgium
Gemena 77 C5 Equateur, NW Dem. Rep.
   Congo
Gem of the Mountains see Idaho
Gemona del Friuli 96 D2 Friuli-Venezia
   Giulia, NE Italy
Gem State see Idaho
Genalē Wenz see Juba
Genck see Genk
General Alvear 64 B4 Mendoza,
   W Argentina
General Carrera, Lago see Buenos Aires,
   Lago
General Eugenio A. Garay 64 C1 var.
   Fortín General Eugenio Garay; prev.
   Yrendagüé. Nueva Asunción,
   NW Paraguay
General José F.Uriburu see Zárate
General Machado see Camacupa
General Santos 139 F3 off. General
   Santos City. Mindanao, S Philippines
General Santos City see General Santos
Gênes see Genova
Geneva see Genève
Geneva, Lake 95 A7 Fr. Lac de Genève,
   Lac Léman, le Léman, Ger. Genfer See.
   lake France/Switzerland
Genève 95 A7 Eng. Geneva, Ger. Genf, It.
   Ginevra. Genève, SW Switzerland
Genève, Lac de see Geneva, Lake
Genf see Genève
Genfer See see Geneva, Lake
Genichesk see Heniches'k
Genk 87 D6 var. Genck. Limburg,
   NE Belgium
Gennep 86 D4 Limburg, SE Netherlands
Genoa see Genova
Genoa, Gulf of 96 A3 Eng. Gulf of
   Genoa. gulf NW Italy
Genoa, Gulf of see Genova, Golfo di
Genova 102 D1 Eng. Genoa; anc. Genua,
   Fr. Gênes. Liguria, NW Italy
Genovesa, Isla 60 B5 var. Tower Island.
   island Galápagos Islands, Ecuador,
   E Pacific Ocean
Gent 87 B5 Eng. Ghent, Fr. Gand.
   Oost-Vlaanderen, NW Belgium
Genua see Genova
Geok-Tepe see Gökdepe
George 78 C5 Western Cape, S South
   Africa
George 82 A4 river Newfoundland and
   Labrador/Québec, E Canada
George, Lake 43 E3 lake Florida,
   SE USA
Georgenburg see Jurbarkas
Georges Bank 35 D5 undersea bank
   W Atlantic Ocean
George Sound 151 A7 sound South
   Island, New Zealand
Georges River 148 D2 river New South
   Wales, E Australia
Georgetown 59 F2 country capital
   (Guyana) (Guyana) N Guyana
George Town 54 C2 Great Exuma Island,
   C The Bahamas
George Town 54 B3 var. Georgetown.
   dependent territory capital (Cayman
   Islands) Grand Cayman, SW Cayman
   Islands
George Town 138 B3 var. Penang,
   Pinang. Pinang, Peninsular Malaysia
Georgetown 43 F2 South Carolina,
   SE USA
Georgetown see George Town
George V Land 154 C4 physical region
   Antarctica
Georgia 117 F2 off. Republic of Georgia,
   Geor. Sak'art'velo, Rus. Gruzinskaya
   SSR, Gruziya. country SW Asia
Georgia 42 D2 off. State of Georgia, also
   known as Empire State of the South,
   Peach State. state SE USA
Georgian Bay 40 D2 lake bay Ontario,
   S Canada
Georgia, Republic of see Georgia
Georgia, Strait of 46 A1 strait British
   Columbia, W Canada
Georgi Dimitrov see Kostenets
Georgiu-Dezh see Liski
Georg von Neumayer 154 A2 German
   research station Antarctica
Gera 94 C4 Thüringen, E Germany
Geráki 105 B6 Pelopónnisos, S Greece
Geraldine 151 B6 Canterbury, South
   Island, New Zealand
Geraldton 147 A6 Western Australia
Geral, Serra 57 D5 mountain range
   S Brazil
Gerede 116 C2 Bolu, N Turkey
Gereshk 122 D5 Helmand,
   SW Afghanistan
Gering 44 D3 Nebraska, C USA
German East Africa see Tanzania
Germanicopolis see Çankırı
Germanicum, Mare/German Ocean see
   North Sea
German Southwest Africa see Namibia
Germany 94 B4 off. Federal Republic of
   Germany, Bundesrepublik
   Deutschland, Ger. Deutschland.
   country N Europe
Germany, Federal Republic of
   see Germany
Geroliménas 105 B7 Pelopónnisos,
   S Greece
Gerona see Girona
Gerpinnes 87 C7 Hainaut, S Belgium
Gerunda see Girona
Gerze 116 D2 Sinop, N Turkey
Gesoriacum see Boulogne-sur-Mer
Gessoriacum see Boulogne-sur-Mer
Getafe 92 D3 Madrid, C Spain
Gevaş 117 F3 Van, SE Turkey
Gevgeli see Gevgelija
Gevgelija 101 E6 var. Đevđelija,
   Djevdjelija, Turk. Gevgeli.
   SE Macedonia
Ghaba see Al Ghābah
Ghana 75 E5 off. Republic of Ghana.
   country W Africa
Ghanzi 78 C3 var. Khanzi. Ghanzi,
   W Botswana
Gharandal 119 B7 Al'Aqabah,
   SW Jordan
Gharbt, Jabal al see Liban, Jebel
Ghardaïa 70 D2 N Algeria
Gharvān see Gharyān
Gharyān 71 F2 var. Gharvān.
   NW Libya
Ghawdex see Gozo
Ghaznī 123 E4 var. Ghazni. Ghaznī,
   E Afghanistan
Ghazzah see Gaza
Gheel see Geel
Ghent see Gent
Gheorgheni 108 C4 prev. Gheorghieni,
   Sin-Miclăuş, Ger. Niklasmarkt, Hung.
   Gyergyószentmiklós. Harghita,
   C Romania
Gheorghieni see Gheorgheni
Ghōriān 122 D4 prev. Ghūriān. Herāt,
   W Afghanistan
Ghūdara 123 F3 var. Gudara, Rus.
   Kudara. SE Tajikistan
Ghurdaqah see Al Ghardaqah
Ghūriān see Ghōriān
Giamame see Jamaame
Giannitsá 104 B4 var. Yiannitsá.
   Kentrikí Makedonía, N Greece
Gibraltar 93 G4 UK Overseas Territory
   SW Europe
Gibraltar, Bay of 93 G5 bay Gibraltar/
   SpainMediterranean Sea Atlantic Ocean
**Gibraltar, Détroit de/Gibraltar,
   Estrecho de** see Gibraltar, Strait of
Gibraltar, Strait of 92 C5 Fr. Détroit de
   Gibraltar, Sp. Estrecho de Gibraltar.
   strait Atlantic Ocean/Mediterranean Sea
Gibson Desert 147 B5 desert
   Western Australia
Giebnegáisi see Kebnekaise
Giedraičiai 107 C5 Utena, E Lithuania
Giessen 95 B5 Hessen, W Germany
Gifu 131 C6 var. Gihu. Gifu, Honshū,
   SW Japan
Giganta, Sierra de la 50 B3 mountain
   range NW Mexico
Gihu see Gifu
G'ijduvon 122 D2 Rus. Gizhduvon.
   Buxoro Viloyati, C Uzbekistan
Gijón 92 D1 var. Xixón. Asturias,
   NW Spain
Gila River 48 A2 river Arizona,
   SW USA
Gilbert Islands see Tungaru
Gilbert River 148 C3 river Queensland,
   NE Australia
Gilf Kebir Plateau see Ḥaḍabat al Jilf al
   Kabīr
Gillette 44 D3 Wyoming, C USA
Gilolo see Halmahera, Pulau
Gilroy 47 B6 California, W USA
Gimie, Mount 55 F1 mountain
   C Saint Lucia
Gimma see Jīma
Ginevra see Genève
Gingin 147 A6 Western Australia
Giohar see Jawhar
Gipeswic see Ipswich
Girardot 58 B3 Cundinamarca,
   C Colombia
Giresun 117 E2 var. Kerasunt; anc.
   Cerasus, Pharnacia. Giresun,
   NE Turkey
Girgenti see Agrigento
Girin see Jilin
Girne 102 C5 Gk. Kerýneia, Kyrenia.
   N Cyprus
Giron see Kiruna
Girona 93 G2 var. Gerona; anc. Gerunda.
   Cataluña, NE Spain
Gisborne 150 E3 Gisborne, North Island,
   New Zealand
Gissar Range 123 E3 Rus. Gissarskiy
   Khrebet. mountain range Tajikistan/
   Uzbekistan
Gissarskiy Khrebet see Gissar Range
Githio see Gýtheio
Giulianova 96 D4 Abruzzi, C Italy
Giumri see Gyumri
Giurgiu 108 C5 Giurgiu, S Romania
Giza 72 B1 var. Al Jīzah, El Gîza, Gizeh.
   N Egypt
Gizhduvon see G'ijduvon
Giżycko 98 D2 Ger. Lötzen.
   Warmińsko-Mazurskie, NE Poland
Gjakovë 101 D5 Serb. Đakovica.
   W Kosovo
Gjaravicë 101 D5 Serb. Đeravica.
   mountain S Serbia
Gjilan 101 D5 Serb. Gnjilane. E Kosovo
Gjinokastër see Gjirokastër
Gjirokastër 101 D7 var. Gjirokastra;
   prev. Gjinokastër, Gk. Argyrokastron,
   It. Argirocastro. Gjirokastër, S Albania
Gjirokastra see Gjirokastër
Gjoa Haven 37 F3 var. Uqsuqtuuq. King
   William Island, Nunavut, NW Canada
Gjøvik 85 B5 Oppland, S Norway
Glace Bay 39 G4 Cape Breton Island,
   Nova Scotia, SE Canada
Gladstone 148 E4 Queensland,
   E Australia
Gláma 85 B5 var. Glommen. river
   S Norway
Glavinitsa 104 D1 prev. Pravda,
   Dogrular. Silistra, NE Bulgaria
Glasgow 88 C4 S Scotland,
   United Kingdom
Glavn'a Morava see Velika Morava
Glazov 111 D5 Udmurtskaya Respublika,
   NW Russia
Gleiwitz see Gliwice
Glendale 48 B2 Arizona, SW USA
Glendive 44 D2 Montana, NW USA
Glens Falls 41 F3 New York,
   NE USA
Glevum see Gloucester
Glina 100 B3 var. Banijska Palanka.
   Sisak-Moslavina, NE Croatia
Glittertind 85 A5 mountain S Norway
Gliwice 99 C5 Ger. Gleiwitz. Śląskie,
   S Poland
Globe 48 B2 Arizona, SW USA
Globino see Hlobyne
Glogau see Głogów
Głogów 98 B4 Ger. Glogau, Glogow.
   Dolnośląskie, SW Poland
Glogow see Głogów
Glomma see Glåma
Glommen see Glåma
Gloucester 89 D6 hist. Caer Glou, Lat.
   Glevum. C England, United Kingdom
Głowno 98 D4 Łódź, C Poland
Glubokoye see Hlybokaye
Glukhov see Hlukhiv
Gnesen see Gniezno
Gniezno 98 C3 Ger. Gnesen.
   Weilkopolskie, C Poland
Gnjilane see Gjilan
Gobabis 78 B3 Omaheke, E Namibia
Gobi 126 D3 desert China/Mongolia
Gobō 131 C6 Wakayama, Honshū,
   SW Japan
Godavari 124 B3 var. Godavari. river
   C India
Godavari see Godāvari
Godhavn see Qeqertarsuaq
Godhra 134 C4 Gujarāt, W India
Göding see Hodonín
Godoy Cruz 64 B4 Mendoza,
   W Argentina
Godthaab/Godthåb see Nuuk
Godwin Austen, Mount see K2
Goede Hoop, Kaap de see Good Hope,
   Cape of
Goeie Hoop, Kaap die see Good Hope,
   Cape of
Goeree 86 B4 island SW Netherlands
Goes 87 B5 Zeeland, SW Netherlands
Goettingen see Göttingen
Gogebic Range 40 B1 hill range
   Michigan/Wisconsin, N USA
Goiânia 63 F3 prev. Goyania. state
   capital Goiás, C Brazil
Goiás 63 E3 off. Estado de Goiás; prev.
   Goiaz, Goyaz. region C Brazil
Goiás 63 E3 off. Estado de Goiás; prev.
   Goiaz, Goyaz. state C Brazil
Goiás, Estado de see Goiás
Goiaz see Goiás
Goidhoo Atoll see Horsburgh Atoll
Gojōme 130 D4 Akita, Honshū,
   NW Japan
Gökçeada 101 D4 var. Imroz Adası, Gk.
   Imbros. island NW Turkey
Gökdepe 122 C3 Rus. Gëkdepe,
   Geok-Tepe. Ahal Welaýaty,
   C Turkmenistan
Göksun 116 D4 Kahramanmaraş,
   C Turkey
Gol 85 A5 Buskerud, S Norway
Golan Heights 119 B5 Ar. Al Jawlān,
   Heb. HaGolan. mountain range
   SW Syria
Golaya Pristan see Hola Prystan'
Gołdap 98 E2 Ger. Goldap.
   Warmińsko-Mazurskie, NE Poland
Gold Coast 149 E5 cultural region
   Queensland, E Australia
Golden Bay 150 C4 bay South Island,
   New Zealand
Golden State, The see California
Goldingen see Kuldīga
Goldsboro 43 F1 North Carolina,
   SE USA
Goleniów 98 B3 Ger. Gollnow.
   Zachodnio-pomorskie, NW Poland
Gollnow see Goleniów
Golmo see Golmud
Golmud 126 D4 var. Ge'e'mu, Golmo,
   Chin. Ko-erh-mu. Qinghai, C China
Golovanevsk see Holovanivs'k
Golub-Dobrzyń 98 C3 Kujawski-
   pomorskie, C Poland
Goma 77 E6 Nord-Kivu, NE Dem.
   Rep. Congo
Gombi 75 H4 Adamawa, E Nigeria
Gombroon see Bandar-e 'Abbās
Gomel' see Homyel'

Gomera 70 A3 *island* Islas Canarias, Spain, NE Atlantic Ocean
Gómez Palacio 50 D3 Durango, C Mexico
Gonaïves 54 D3 *var.* Les Gonaïves. N Haiti
Gonâve, Île de la 54 D3 *island* C Haiti
Gondar *see* Gonder
Gonder 72 C4 *var.* Gondar. Āmara, NW Ethiopia
Gondia 135 E4 Mahārāshtra, C India
Gonggar 126 C5 *var.* Gyixong. Xizang Zizhiqu, W China
Gongola 75 G4 *river* E Nigeria
Gongtang *see* Damxung
Gonni/Gónnos *see* Gónnoi
Gónnoi 104 B4 *var.* Gonni, Gónnos; *prev.* Derelí. Thessalía, C Greece
Good Hope, Cape of 78 B5 *Afr.* Kaap de Goede Hoop, Kaap die Goeie Hoop. *headland* SW South Africa
Goodland 44 D4 Kansas, C USA
Goondiwindi 149 D5 Queensland, E Australia
Goor 86 E3 Overijssel, E Netherlands
Goose Green 65 D7 *var.* Prado del Ganso. East Falkland, Falkland Islands
Goose Lake 46 B4 *var.* Lago dos Gansos. *lake* California/Oregon, W USA
Gopher State *see* Minnesota
Göppingen 95 B6 Baden-Württemberg, SW Germany
Góra Kalwaria 114 D4 Mazowieckie, C Poland
Gorakhpur 135 E3 Uttar Pradesh, N India
Gorany *see* Harany
Goražde 100 C4 Federacija Bosne I Hercegovine, SE Bosnia and Herzegovina
Gorbovichi *see* Harbavichy
Goré 76 C4 Logone-Oriental, S Chad
Gorē 73 C5 Oromīya, C Ethiopia
Gore 151 B7 Southland, South Island, New Zealand
Gorgān 120 D2 *var.* Astarabad, Astrabad, Gurgan, *prev.* Asteräbäd; *anc.* Hyrcania. Golestán, N Iran
Gori 117 F2 C Georgia
Gorinchem 86 C4 *var.* Gorkum. Zuid-Holland, C Netherlands
Goris 117 G3 SE Armenia
Gorki *see* Horki
Gor'kiy *see* Nizhniy Novgorod
Gorkum *see* Gorinchem
Görlitz 94 D4 Sachsen, E Germany
Görlitz *see* Zgorzelec
Gorlovka *see* Horlivka
Gorna Dzhumaya *see* Blagoevgrad
Gornja Mužlja *see* Mužlja
Gornji Milanovac 100 C4 Serbia, C Serbia
Gorodets *see* Haradzyets
Gorodishche *see* Horodyshche
Gorodnya *see* Horodnya
Gorodok *see* Haradok
Gorodok/Gorodok Yagellonski *see* Horodok
Gorontalo 139 E4 Sulawesi, C Indonesia
Gorontalo, Teluk *see* Tomini, Teluk
Gorssel 86 D3 Gelderland, E Netherlands
Goryn *see* Horyn'
Gorzów Wielkopolski 98 B3 *Ger.* Landsberg, Landsberg an der Warthe. Lubuskie, W Poland
Gosford 149 D6 New South Wales, SE Australia
Goshogawara 130 D3 *var.* Gosyogawara. Aomori, Honshū, C Japan
Gospić 100 A3 Lika-Senj, C Croatia
Gostivar 101 D6 W Macedonia
Gosyogawara *see* Goshogawara
Göteborg 85 B7 *Eng.* Gothenburg. Västra Götaland, S Sweden
Gotel Mountains 75 G5 *mountain range* E Nigeria
Gotha 94 C4 Thüringen, C Germany
Gothenburg *see* Göteborg
Gotland 85 C7 *island* SE Sweden
Goto-retto 131 A7 *island group* SW Japan
Gotska Sandön 106 B1 *island* SE Sweden
Götsu 131 B6 *var.* Gōtu. Shimane, Honshū, SW Japan
Gotthard Base Tunnel 95 B7 *railway tunnel* C Switzerland
Göttingen 94 B4 *var.* Goettingen. Niedersachsen, C Germany
Gottschee *see* Kočevje

Gottwaldov *see* Zlín
Gōtu *see* Götsu
Gouda 86 C4 Zuid-Holland, C Netherlands
Gough Fracture Zone 67 C6 *tectonic feature* S Atlantic Ocean
Gough Island 69 B8 *island* Tristan da Cunha, S Atlantic Ocean
Gouin, Réservoir 38 D4 *reservoir* Québec, SE Canada
Goulburn 149 D6 New South Wales, SE Australia
Goundam 75 E3 Tombouctou, NW Mali
Gouré 75 G3 Zinder, SE Niger
Goverla, Gora *see* Hoverla, Hora
Governador Valadares 63 F4 Minas Gerais, SE Brazil
Govi Altayn Nuruu 127 E3 *mountain range* S Mongolia
Goya 64 D3 Corrientes, NE Argentina
Goyania *see* Goiânia
Goyaz *see* Goiás
Goz Beïda 76 C3 Ouaddaï, SE Chad
Gozo 97 C8 *var.* Ghawdex. *island* N Malta
Graciosa 92 A5 *var.* Ilha Graciosa. *island* Azores, Portugal, NE Atlantic Ocean
Graciosa, Ilha *see* Graciosa
Gradačac 100 C3 Federacija Bosne I Hercegovine, N Bosnia and Herzegovina
Gradiška *see* Bosanska Gradiška
Grafton 149 E5 New South Wales, SE Australia
Grafton 45 E1 North Dakota, N USA
Graham Land 154 A2 *physical region* Antarctica
Grajewo 98 E3 Podlaskie, NE Poland
Grampian Mountains 88 C3 *mountain range* C Scotland, United Kingdom
Gran *see* Esztergom, Hungary
Granada 52 D3 Granada, SW Nicaragua
Granada 70 D5 Andalucía, S Spain
Gran Canaria 70 A3 *var.* Grand Canary. *island* Islas Canarias, Spain, NE Atlantic Ocean
Gran Chaco 64 D2 *var.* Chaco. *lowland plain* South America
Grand Bahama Island 54 B1 *island* N The Bahamas
Grand Banks of Newfoundland 34 E4 *undersea basin* NW Atlantic Ocean
Grand Bassa *see* Buchanan
Grand Canary *see* Gran Canaria
Grand Canyon 48 A1 *canyon* Arizona, SW USA
Grand Canyon State *see* Arizona
Grand Cayman 54 B3 *island* SW Cayman Islands
Grand Duchy of Luxembourg *see* Luxembourg
Grande, Bahía 65 B7 *bay* S Argentina
Grande Comore *see* Ngazidja
Grande de Chiloé, Isla *see* Chiloé, Isla de
Grande Prairie 37 E4 Alberta, W Canada
Grand Erg Occidental 70 D3 *desert* W Algeria
Grand Erg Oriental 71 E3 *desert* Algeria/Tunisia
Rio Grande 50 C2 *var.* Río Bravo, *Sp.* Río Bravo del Norte, Bravo del Norte. *river* Mexico/USA
Grande Terre 55 G3 *island* E West Indies
Grand Falls 39 G3 Newfoundland, Newfoundland and Labrador, SE Canada
Grand Forks 45 E1 North Dakota, N USA
Grand Island 45 E4 Nebraska, C USA
Grand Junction 44 C4 Colorado, C USA
Grand Paradis *see* Gran Paradiso
Grand Rapids 40 C3 Michigan, N USA
Grand Rapids 45 F1 Minnesota, N USA
Grand-Saint-Bernard, Col du *see* Great Saint Bernard Pass
Grand-Santi 59 G3 W French Guiana
Granite State *see* New Hampshire
Gran Lago *see* Nicaragua, Lago de
Gran Malvina *see* West Falkland
Gran Paradiso 96 A2 *Fr.* Grand Paradis. *mountain* NW Italy
Gran San Bernardo, Passo di *see* Great Saint Bernard Pass
Gran Santiago *see* Santiago
Grants 48 C2 New Mexico, SW USA

Grants Pass 46 B4 Oregon, NW USA
Granville 90 B3 Manche, N France
Gratianopolis *see* Grenoble
Gratz *see* Graz
Graudenz *see* Grudziądz
Graulhet 91 C6 Tarn, S France
Grave 86 D4 Noord-Brabant, SE Netherlands
Grayling 36 C2 Alaska, USA
Graz 95 E7 *prev.* Gratz. Steiermark, SE Austria
Great Abaco 54 C1 *var.* Abaco Island. *island* N The Bahamas
Great Alfold *see* Great Hungarian Plain
Great Ararat *see* Büyükağrı Dağı
Great Australian Bight 147 D7 *bight* S Australia
Great Barrier Island 150 D2 *island* N New Zealand
Great Barrier Reef 148 D2 *reef* Queensland, NE Australia
Great Basin 47 C5 *basin* W USA
Great Bear Lake 37 E3 *Fr.* Grand Lac de l'Ours. *lake* Northwest Territories, NW Canada
Great Belt 85 B8 *var.* Store Bælt, *Eng.* Great Belt, Storebelt. *channel* Baltic Sea/Kattegat
Great Belt *see* Storebælt
Great Bend 45 E5 Kansas, C USA
Great Britain *see* Britain
Great Dividing Range 148 D4 *mountain range* NE Australia
Greater Antarctica *see* East Antarctica
Greater Antilles 54 D3 *island group* West Indies
Greater Caucasus 117 G2 *mountain range* Azerbaijan/Georgia/Russia Asia/Europe
Greater Sunda Islands 124 D5 *var.* Sunda Islands. *island group* Indonesia
Great Exhibition Bay 150 C1 *inlet* North Island, New Zealand
Great Exuma Island 54 C2 *island* C The Bahamas
Great Falls 44 B1 Montana, NW USA
Great Grimsby *see* Grimsby
Great Hungarian Plain 99 C7 *var.* Great Alfold, Plain of Hungary, *Hung.* Alföld. *plain* SE Europe
Great Inagua 54 D2 *var.* Inagua Islands. *island* S The Bahamas
Great Indian Desert *see* Thar Desert
Great Khingan Range 127 G1 *Eng.* Great Khingan Range. *mountain range* NE China
Great Khingan Range *see* Da Hinggan Ling
Great Lake *see* Tônlé Sap
Great Lakes 35 C5 *lakes* Ontario, Canada/USA
Great Lakes State *see* Michigan
Great Meteor Seamount *see* Great Meteor Tablemount
Great Meteor Tablemount 66 B3 *var.* Great Meteor Seamount. *seamount* E Atlantic Ocean
Great Nicobar 133 G3 *island* Nicobar Islands, India, NE Indian Ocean
Great Plain of China 125 E2 *plain* E China
Great Plains 35 E3 *var.* High Plains. *plains* Canada/USA
Great Rift Valley 73 C5 *var.* Rift Valley. *depression* Asia/Africa
Great Ruaha 73 C7 *river* S Tanzania
Great Saint Bernard Pass 96 A1 *Fr.* Col du Grand-Saint-Bernard, *It.* Passo del Gran San Bernardo. *pass* Italy/Switzerland
Great Salt Desert *see* Kavīr, Dasht-e
Great Salt Lake 44 A3 *salt lake* Utah, W USA
Great Salt Lake Desert 44 A4 *plain* Utah, W USA
Great Sand Sea 71 H3 *desert* Egypt/Libya
Great Sandy Desert 146 C4 *desert* Western Australia
Great Sandy Desert *see* Ar Rub' al Khālī
Great Sandy Island *see* Fraser Island
Great Slave Lake 37 E4 *Fr.* Grand Lac des Esclaves. *lake* Northwest Territories, NW Canada
Great Socialist People's Libyan Arab Jamahiriya *see* Libya
Great Sound 42 A5 *sound* Bermuda, NW Atlantic Ocean
Great Victoria Desert 147 C5 *desert* South Australia/Western Australia

Great Wall of China 128 C4 *ancient monument* N China Asia
Great Yarmouth 89 E6 *var.* Yarmouth. E England, United Kingdom
Grebenka *see* Hrebinka
Gredos, Sierra de 92 D3 *mountain range* W Spain
Greece 105 A5 *off.* Hellenic Republic, *Gk.* Ellás; *anc.* Hellas. *country* SE Europe
Greeley 44 D4 Colorado, C USA
Green Bay 40 B2 Wisconsin, N USA
Green Bay 40 B2 *lake bay* Michigan/Wisconsin, N USA
Greeneville 43 E1 Tennessee, S USA
Greenland 82 D3 *Dan.* Grønland, *Inuit* Kalaallit Nunaat. *Danish self-governing territory* NE North America
Greenland Sea 83 F2 *sea* Arctic Ocean
Green Mountains 41 G2 *mountain range* Vermont, NE USA
Green Mountain State *see* Vermont
Greenock 88 C4 W Scotland, United Kingdom
Green River 44 B3 Wyoming, C USA
Green River 40 C5 *river* Kentucky, C USA
Green River 44 B4 *river* Utah, W USA
Greensboro 43 F1 North Carolina, SE USA
Greenville 42 B2 Mississippi, S USA
Greenville 43 F1 North Carolina, SE USA
Greenville 43 E1 South Carolina, SE USA
Greenville 49 G2 Texas, SW USA
Greenwich 89 B8 United Kingdom
Greenwood 42 B2 Mississippi, S USA
Greenwood 43 E2 South Carolina, SE USA
Gregory Range 148 C3 *mountain range* Queensland, E Australia
Greifenberg/Greifenberg in Pommern *see* Gryfice
Greifswald 94 D2 Mecklenburg-Vorpommern, NE Germany
Grenada 42 C2 Mississippi, S USA
Grenada 55 G5 *country* SE West Indies
Grenadines, The 55 H4 *island group* Grenada/St Vincent and the Grenadines
Grenoble 91 D5 *anc.* Cularo, Gratianopolis. Isère, E France
Gresham 46 B3 Oregon, NW USA
Grevená 104 B4 Dytikí Makedonía, N Greece
Grevenmacher 87 E8 Grevenmacher, E Luxembourg
Greymouth 151 B5 West Coast, South Island, New Zealand
Grey Range 149 C5 *mountain range* New South Wales/Queensland, E Australia
Greytown *see* San Juan del Norte
Griffin 42 D2 Georgia, SE USA
Grimari 76 C4 Ouaka, C Central African Republic
Grimsby 89 E5 *prev.* Great Grimsby. E England, United Kingdom
Grobin *see* Grobiņa
Grobiņa 106 B3 *Ger.* Grobin. W Latvia
Gródek Jagielloński *see* Horodok
Grodno *see* Hrodna
Grodzisk Wielkopolski 98 B3 Wielkopolskie, C Poland
Groesbeek 86 D4 Gelderland, SE Netherlands
Grójec 98 D4 Mazowieckie, C Poland
Groningen 86 E1 Groningen, NE Netherlands
Grønland *see* Greenland
Groote Eylandt 148 B2 *island* Northern Territory, N Australia
Grootfontein 78 B3 Otjozondjupa, N Namibia
Groot Karasberge 78 B4 *mountain range* S Namibia
Gros Islet 55 F1 N Saint Lucia
Grossa, Isola *see* Dugi Otok
Grossbetschkerek *see* Zrenjanin
Grosse Morava *see* Velika Morava
Grosser Sund *see* Suur Väin
Grosseto 96 B4 Toscana, C Italy
Grossglockner 95 C7 *mountain* W Austria
Grosskanizsa *see* Nagykanizsa
Gross-Karol *see* Carei
Grosskikinda *see* Kikinda
Grossmichel *see* Michalovce
Gross-Schlatten *see* Abrud
Grosswardein *see* Oradea
Groznyy 111 B8 Chechenskaya Respublika, SW Russia
Grudovo *see* Sredets

Grudziądz *98 C3* Ger. Graudenz.
  Kujawsko-pomorskie, C Poland
Grums *85 B6* Värmland, C Sweden
Grünberg/Grünberg in Schlesien *see*
  Zielona Góra
Grüneberg *see* Zielona Góra
Gruzinskaya SSR/Gruziya *see* Georgia
Gryazi *111 B6* Lipetskaya Oblast',
  W Russia
Gryfice *98 B2* Ger. Greifenberg,
  Greifenberg in Pommern.
  Zachodnio-pomorskie, NW Poland
Guabito *53 E4* Bocas del Toro,
  NW Panama
Guadalajara *50 D4* Jalisco, C Mexico
Guadalajara *93 E3* Ar. Wad Al-Hajarah;
  anc. Arriaca. Castilla-La Mancha,
  C Spain
Guadalcanal *144 C3 island* C Solomon
  Islands
Guadalquivir *92 D4 river* W Spain
Guadalupe *50 D3* Zacatecas, C Mexico
Guadalupe Peak *48 D3 mountain* Texas,
  SW USA
Guadalupe River *49 G4 river* SW USA
Guadarrama, Sierra de *93 E2 mountain
  range* C Spain
Guadeloupe *55 H3 French overseas
  department* E West Indies
Guadiana *92 C4 river* Portugal/Spain
Guadix *93 E4* Andalucía, S Spain
Guaimaca *52 C2* Francisco Morazán,
  C Honduras
Guajira, Península de la *58 B1
  peninsula* N Colombia
Gualaco *52 D2* Olancho, C Honduras
Gualán *52 B2* Zacapa, C Guatemala
Gualdicciolo *96 D1* NW San Marino
Gualeguaychú *64 D4* Entre Ríos,
  E Argentina
Guam *144 B1* US unincorporated
  territory W Pacific Ocean
Guamúchil *50 C3* Sinaloa, C Mexico
Guanabacoa *54 B2* La Habana, W Cuba
Guanajuato *51 E4* Guanajuato,
  C Mexico
Guanare *58 C2* Portuguesa, N Venezuela
Guanare, Río *58 D2 river* W Venezuela
Guangdong *128 C7 var.* Guangdong
  Sheng, Kuang-tung, Kwangtung, Yue.
  province S China
Guangdong Sheng *see* Guangdong
Guangju *see* Gwangju
Guangxi *see* Guangxi Zhuangzu Zizhiqu
Guangxi Zhuangzu Zizhiqu *128 C6
  var.* Guangxi, Gui, Kuang-hsi,
  Kwangsi, *Eng.* Kwangsi Chuang
  Autonomous Region. *autonomous
  region* S China
Guangyuan *128 B5 var.* Kuang-yuan,
  Kwangyuan. Sichuan, C China
Guangzhou *128 C6 var.* Kuang-chou,
  Kwangchow, *Eng.* Canton. *province
  capital* Guangdong, S China
Guantánamo *54 D3* Guantánamo,
  SE Cuba
Guantánamo, Bahia de *54 D3 Eng.*
  Guantanamo Bay. *US military base*
  SE Cuba
Guantanamo Bay *see* Guantánamo, Bahia
  de
Guaporé, Río *62 D3 var.* Río Iténez.
  river Bolivia/Brazil
Guarda *92 C3* Guarda, N Portugal
Guarumal *53 F5* Veraguas, S Panama
Guasave *50 C3* Sinaloa, C Mexico
Guatemala *52 A2 off.* Republic of
  Guatemala. *country* Central America
Guatemala Basin *35 B7 undersea basin*
  E Pacific Ocean
Guatemala City *see* Ciudad de Guatemala
Guatemala, Republic of *see* Guatemala
Guaviare *56 B2 off.* Comisaría Guaviare.
  province S Colombia
Guaviare, Comisaría *see* Guaviare
Guaviare, Río *58 D3 river* E Colombia
Guayanas, Macizo de las *see* Guiana
  Highlands
Guayaquil *60 A2 var.* Santiago de
  Guayaquil. Guayas, SW Ecuador
Guayaquil, Gulf of *60 A2 var.* Gulf of
  Guayaquil. *gulf* SW Ecuador
Guayaquil, Gulf of *see* Guayaquil, Gulf
  de
Guaymas *50 B2* Sonora, NW Mexico
Gubadag *122 C2 Turkm.* Tel'man; *prev.*
  Tel'mansk. Daşoguz Welaýaty,
  N Turkmenistan
Guben *94 D4 var.* Wilhelm-Pieck-Stadt.
  Brandenburg, E Germany

Gudara *see* Ghūdara
Gudauta *117 E1 prev.* Gudaut'a.
  NW Georgia
Gudaut'a *see* Gudauta
Guéret *90 C4* Creuse, C France
Guernsey *89 D8 British Crown
  Dependency* Channel Islands,
  NW Europe
Guerrero Negro *50 A2* Baja California
  Sur, NW Mexico
Gui *see* Guangxi Zhuangzu Zizhiqu
Guiana *see* French Guiana
Guiana Highlands *62 D1 var.* Macizo de
  las Guayanas. *mountain range* N South
  America
Guiba *see* Juba
Guidder *see* Guider
Guider *76 B4 var.* Guidder. Nord,
  N Cameroon
Guidimouni *75 G3* Zinder, S Niger
Guildford *89 D7* SE England, United
  Kingdom
Guilin *128 C6 var.* Kuei-lin, Kweilin.
  Guangxi Zhuangzu Zizhiqu, S China
Guimarães *92 B2 var.* Guimaráes. Braga,
  N Portugal
Guimaráes *see* Guimarães
Guinea *74 C4 off.* Republic of Guinea,
  var. Guinée; *prev.* French Guinea,
  People's Revolutionary Republic of
  Guinea. *country* W Africa
Guinea Basin *69 A5 undersea basin*
  E Atlantic Ocean
Guinea-Bissau *74 B4 off.* Republic of
  Guinea-Bissau, *Fr.* Guinée-Bissau, *Port.*
  Guiné-Bissau; *prev.* Portuguese Guinea.
  country W Africa
Guinea-Bissau, Republic of *see*
  Guinea-Bissau
Guinea, Gulf of *68 B4 Fr.* Golfe de
  Guinée. *gulf* E Atlantic Ocean
**Guinea, People's Revolutionary
  Republic of** *see* Guinea
Guinea, Republic of *see* Guinea
Guiné-Bissau *see* Guinea-Bissau
Guinée *see* Guinea
Guinée-Bissau *see* Guinea-Bissau
Guinée, Golfe de *see* Guinea, Gulf of
Güiria *59 E1* Sucre, NE Venezuela
Guiyang *128 B6 var.* Kuei-Yang,
  Kuei-yang, Kueyang, Kweiyang; *prev.*
  Kweichu. *province capital* Guizhou,
  S China
Guizhou *128 B6* Guangdong, SE China
Gujarāt *134 C4 var.* Gujerat. *cultural
  region* W India
Gujerat *see* Gujarāt
Gujranwala *134 D2* Punjab, NE Pakistan
Gujrat *134 D2* Punjab, E Pakistan
Gulbarga *see* Kalaburagi
Gulbene *106 D3 Ger.* Alt-Schwanenburg.
  NE Latvia
Gulf of Liaotung *see* Liaodong Wan
Gulfport *42 C3* Mississippi, S USA
Gulf, The *see* Persian Gulf
Gulistan *see* Guliston
Guliston *123 E2 Rus.* Gulistan. Sirdaryo
  Viloyati, E Uzbekistan
Gulja *see* Yining
Gulkana *36 D3* Alaska, USA
Gulu *73 B6* N Uganda
Gulyantsi *104 C1* Pleven, N Bulgaria
Guma *see* Pishan
Gumbinnen *see* Gusev
Gumpolds *see* Humpolec
Gümülcine/Gümüljina *see* Komotiní
Gümüşane *see* Gümüşhane
Gümüşhane *117 E3 var.* Gümüşane,
  Gumushkhane. Gümüşhane,
  NE Turkey
Gumushkhane *see* Gümüşhane
Güney Doğu Toroslar *117 E4 mountain
  range* SE Turkey
Gunnbjørn Fjeld *82 D4 var.* Gunnbjörns
  Bjerge. *mountain* C Greenland
Gunnbjörns Bjerge *see* Gunnbjørn Fjeld
Gunnedah *149 D6* New South Wales,
  SE Australia
Gunnison *44 C5* Colorado, C USA
Gurbansoltan Eje *122 C2 prev.* Ýylanly,
  Rus. Il'yaly. Daşoguz Welaýaty,
  N Turkmenistan
Gurbantünggüt Shamo *126 B2 desert*
  W China
Gurgan *see* Gorgān
Guri, Embalse de *59 E2 reservoir*
  E Venezuela
Gurkfeld *see* Krško
Gurktaler Alpen *95 D7 mountain range*
  S Austria

Gürün *116 D3* Sivas, C Turkey
Gur'yev/Gur'yevskaya Oblast' *see*
  Atyrau
Gusau *75 G4* Zamfara, NW Nigeria
Gusev *106 B4 Ger.* Gumbinnen.
  Kaliningradskaya Oblast', W Russia
Gustavus *36 D4* Alaska, USA
Güstrow *94 C3* Mecklenburg-
  Vorpommern, NE Germany
Guta/Gúta *see* Kolárovo
Gütersloh *94 B4* Nordrhein-Westfalen,
  W Germany
Gutta *see* Kolárovo
Guttstadt *see* Dobre Miasto
Guwāhāti *135 G3 prev.* Gauhāti. Assam,
  NE India
Guyana *59 F3 off.* Co-operative Republic
  of Guyana; *prev.* British Guiana.
  country N South America
Guyana, Co-operative Republic of *see*
  Guyana
Guyane *see* French Guiana
Guymon *49 E1* Oklahoma, C USA
Güzelyurt Körfezi *102 C5 Gk.* Kólpos
  Mórfu, Morphou. W Cyprus
Gvardeysk *106 A4 Ger.* Tapaiu.
  Kaliningradskaya Oblast', W Russia
Gwadar *134 A3 var.* Gwadur.
  Baluchistan, SW Pakistan
Gwadur *see* Gwadar
Gwalior *134 D3* Madhya Pradesh,
  C India
Gwanda *78 D3* Matabeleland South,
  SW Zimbabwe
Gwangju *129 E4 off.* Gwangju
  Gwang-yeoksi, *prev.* Kwangju, *var.*
  Guangju, Kwangchu, *Jap.* Kōshū.
  SW South Korea
Gwangju Gwang-yeoksi *see* Gwangju
Gwy *see* Wye
Gyandzha *see* Gäncä
Gyangzê *126 C5* Xizang Zizhiqu,
  W China
Gyaring Co *126 C5 lake* W China
Gyêgu *see* Yushu
Gyergyószentmiklós *see* Gheorgheni
Gyixong *see* Gonggar
Gympie *149 E5* Queensland, E Australia
Gyomaendrőd *99 D7* Békés,
  SE Hungary
Gyöngyös *99 D6* Heves, NE Hungary
Győr *99 C6 Ger.* Raab, *Lat.* Arrabona.
  Győr-Moson-Sopron, NW Hungary
Gytheio *105 B6 var.* Githio; *prev.*
  Ýithion. Pelopónnisos, S Greece
Gyulafehérvár *see* Alba Iulia
Gyumri *117 F2 var.* Giumri, *Rus.*
  Kumayri; *prev.* Aleksandropol',
  Leninakan. W Armenia
Gyzylarbat *see* Serdar

H

Haabai *see* Ha'apai Group
Haacht *87 C6* Vlaams Brabant,
  C Belgium
Haaksbergen *86 E3* Overijssel,
  E Netherlands
Ha'apai Group *145 F4 var.* Haabai.
  island group C Tonga
Haapsalu *106 D2 Ger.* Hapsal.
  Läänemaa, W Estonia
Ha'Arava *see* 'Arabah, Wādī al
Haarlem *86 C3 prev.* Harlem.
  Noord-Holland, W Netherlands
Haast *151 B6* West Coast, South Island,
  New Zealand
Hachijō-jima *131 D6 island* Izu-shotō,
  SE Japan
Hachinohe *130 D3* Aomori, Honshū,
  C Japan
Hacıqabal *117 H3 prev.* Qazimämmäd.
  SE Azerbaijan
Hadabat al Jilf al Kabīr *72 A2 var.* Gilf
  Kebir Plateau. *plateau* SW Egypt
Hadama *see* Nazrēt
Hadejia *75 G4* Jigawa, N Nigeria
Hadejia *75 G3 river* N Nigeria
Hadera *119 A6 var.* Khadera; *prev.*
  Ḥadera. Haifa, N Israel
Ḥadera *see* Hadera
Hadhdhunmathi Atoll *132 A5 atoll*
  S Maldives
Ha Đông *136 D3 var.* Hadong. Ha Tây,
  N Vietnam
Hadong *see* Ha Đông
Hadramaut *121 C6 Eng.* Hadramaut.
  mountain range S Yemen
Hadramaut *see* Ḥaḍramawt

Hadrianopolis *see* Edirne
Haerbin/Haerhpin/Ha-erh-pin *see*
  Harbin
Hafnia *see* Denmark
Hafnia *see* København
Hafren *see* Severn
Hafun, Ras *see* Xaafuun, Raas
Hagåtña *144 B1* , *var.* Agaña. *dependent
  territory capital* (Guam) NW Guam
Hagerstown *41 E4* Maryland, NE USA
Ha Giang *136 D3* Ha Giang, N Vietnam
Hagios Evstrátios *see* Ágios Efstrátios
HaGolan *see* Golan Heights
Hagondange *90 D3* Moselle, NE France
Haguenau *90 E3* Bas-Rhin, NE France
Haibowan *see* Wuhai
Haicheng *128 D3* Liaoning, NE China
Haidarabad *see* Hyderabad
Haifa *see* Hefa
Haifa, Bay of *see* Mifrats Hefa
Haifong *see* Hai Phong
Haikou *128 C7 var.* Hai-k'ou, Hoihow,
  Fr. Hoï-Hao. *province capital* Hainan,
  S China
Hai-k'ou *see* Haikou
Ḥā'il *120 B4* Ḥā'il, NW Saudi Arabia
Hailuoto *84 D4 Swe.* Karlö. *island*
  W Finland
Hainan *128 B7 var.* Hainan Sheng,
  Qiong. *province* S China
Hainan Dao *128 C7 island* S China
Hainan Sheng *see* Hainan
Hainasch *see* Ainaži
Haines *36 D4* Alaska, USA
Hainichen *94 D4* Sachsen, E Germany
Hai Phong *136 D3 var.* Haifong,
  Haiphong. N Vietnam
Haiphong *see* Hai Phong
Haiti *54 D3 off.* Republic of Haiti.
  country C West Indies
Haiti, Republic of *see* Haiti
Haiya *72 C3* Red Sea, NE Sudan
Hajdúhadház *99 D6* Hajdú-Bihar,
  E Hungary
Hajine *see* Abū Ḥardān
Hajnówka *98 E3 Ger.* Hermhausen.
  Podlaskie, NE Poland
Hakodate *130 D3* Hokkaidō, NE Japan
Hal *see* Halle
Ḥalab *118 B2 Eng.* Aleppo, *Fr.* Alep; *anc.*
  Beroea. Ḥalab, NW Syria
Hala'ib Triangle *72 C3 region*
  Egypt/Sudan
Ḥalāniyāt, Juzur al *121 D6 var.* Jazā'ir
  Bin Ghalfān, *Eng.* Kuria Muria Islands.
  island group S Oman
Halberstadt *94 C4* Sachsen-Anhalt,
  C Germany
Halden *85 B6 prev.* Fredrikshald.
  Østfold, S Norway
Halfmoon Bay *151 A8 var.* Oban.
  Stewart Island, Southland, New Zealand
Haliacmon *see* Aliákmonas
Halifax *39 F4 province capital* Nova
  Scotia, SE Canada
Halkida *see* Chalkida
Halle *87 B6 Fr.* Hal. Vlaams Brabant,
  C Belgium
Halle *94 C4 var.* Halle an der Saale.
  Sachsen-Anhalt, C Germany
Halle an der Saale *see* Halle
Halle-Neustadt *94 C4* Sachsen-Anhalt,
  C Germany
Halley *154 B2 UK research station*
  Antarctica
Hall Islands *142 B2 island group*
  C Micronesia
Halls Creek *146 C3* Western Australia
Halmahera, Laut *139 F4 Eng.*
  Halmahera Sea. *sea* E Indonesia
Halmahera, Pulau *139 F3 prev.* Djailolo,
  Gilolo, Jailolo. *island* E Indonesia
Halmahera Sea *see* Halmahera, Laut
Halmstad *85 B7* Halland, S Sweden
Ha Long *136 E3 var.* Hong Gai, *var.*
  Hon Gai, Hongay. Quang Ninh,
  N Vietnam
Hälsingborg *see* Helsingborg
Hamada *131 B6* Shimane, Honshū,
  SW Japan
Hamadān *120 C3 anc.* Ecbatana.
  Hamadān, W Iran
Ḥamāh *118 B3 var.* Hama; *anc.*
  Epiphania, *Bibl.* Hamath. Ḥamāh,
  W Syria
Hamamatsu *131 D6 var.* Hamamatu.
  Shizuoka, Honshū, S Japan
Hamamatu *see* Hamamatsu
Hamar *85 B5 prev.* Storhammer.
  Hedmark, S Norway

Hamath see Ḥamāh
Hamburg 94 B3 Hamburg, N Germany
Hamd, Wadi al 120 A4 dry watercourse
W Saudi Arabia
Hämeenlinna 85 D5 Swe. Tavastehus.
Kanta-Häme, S Finland
HaMela h, Yam see Dead Sea
Hamersley Range 146 A4 mountain
range Western Australia
Hamhŭng 129 E3 C North Korea
Hami 126 C3 var. Ha-mi, Uigh. Kumul,
Qomul. Xinjiang Uygur Zizhiqu,
NW China
Ha-mi see Hami
Hamilton 42 A5 dependent territory
capital (Bermuda) C Bermuda
Hamilton 38 D5 Ontario, S Canada
Hamilton 150 D3 Waikato, North Island,
New Zealand
Hamilton 88 C4 S Scotland, United
Kingdom
Hamilton 42 C2 Alabama, S USA
Hamim, Wadi al 71 G2 river NE Libya
Hamis Musait see Khamīs Mushayṭ
Hamm 94 B4 var. Hamm in Westfalen.
Nordrhein-Westfalen, W Germany
Ḥammāmāt, Khalīj al see Hammamet,
Golfe de
Hammamet, Golfe de 102 D3 Ar. Khalīj
al Ḥammāmāt. gulf NE Tunisia
Ḥammēr, Hawr al 120 C3 lake SE Iraq
Hamm in Westfalen see Hamm
Hampden 151 B7 Otago, South Island,
New Zealand
Hampstead 89 A7 Maryland, USA
Ḥamrun 102 B5 C Malta
Hāmūn, Daryācheh-ye see Ṣāberī,
Hāmūn-e/Sīstān, Daryācheh-ye
Hamwih see Southampton
Hânceşti see Hînceşti
Hancewicze see Hantsavichy
Handan 128 C4 var. Han-tan. Hebei,
E China
Haneda 130 A2 (Tōkyō) Tōkyō, Honshū,
S Japan
Hanford 47 C6 California, W USA
Hangayn Nuruu 126 D2 mountain
range C Mongolia
Hang-chou/Hangchow see Hangzhou
Hangö see Hanko
Hangzhou 128 D5 var. Hang-chou,
Hangchow. province capital Zhejiang,
SE China
Hania see Chaniá
Hanka, lake see Khanka, Lake
Hanko 85 D6 Swe. Hangö. Uusimaa,
SW Finland
Han-kou/Han-k'ou/Hankow see Wuhan
Hanmer Springs 151 C5 Canterbury,
South Island, New Zealand
Hannibal 45 G4 Missouri, C USA
Hannover 94 B3 Eng. Hanover.
Niedersachsen, NW Germany
Hanöbukten 85 B7 bay S Sweden
Ha Nôi 136 D3 Eng. Hanoi, Fr. Hanoï.
country capital (Vietnam) N Vietnam
Hanover see Hannover
Han Shui 127 E4 river C China
Han-tan see Handan
Hantsavichy 107 B6 Pol. Hancewicze,
Rus. Gantsevichi. Brestskaya Voblasts',
SW Belarus
Hanyang see Wuhan
Hanzhong 128 B5 Shaanxi, C China
Hāora 135 F4 prev. Howrah. West
Bengal, NE India
Haparanda 84 D4 Norrbotten,
N Sweden
Hapsal see Haapsalu
Haradok 107 E5 Rus. Gorodok.
Vitsyebskaya Voblasts', N Belarus
Haradzyets 107 B6 Rus. Gorodets.
Brestskaya Voblasts', SW Belarus
Haramachi 130 D4 Fukushima, Honshū,
E Japan
Harany 107 D5 Rus. Gorany.
Vitsyebskaya Voblasts', N Belarus
Harare 78 D3 prev. Salisbury. country
capital (Zimbabwe) Mashonaland East,
NE Zimbabwe
Harbavichy 107 E6 Rus. Gorbovichi.
Mahilyowskaya Voblasts', E Belarus
Harbel 74 C5 W Liberia
Harbin 129 E2 var. Haerbin,
Ha-erh-pin, Kharbin; prev. Haerhpin,
Pingkiang, Pinkiang. province capital
Heilongjiang, NE China
Hardangerfjorden 85 A6 fjord S Norway
Hardangervidda 85 A6 plateau
S Norway

Hardenberg 86 E3 Overijssel,
E Netherlands
Harelbeke 87 A6 var. Harlebeke.
West-Vlaanderen, W Belgium
Harem see Ḥārim
Haren 86 E2 Groningen, NE Netherlands
Härer 73 D5 E Ethiopia
Hargeisa see Hargeysa
Hargeysa 73 D5 var. Hargeisa. Woqooyi
Galbeed, NW Somalia
Hariana see Haryāna
Hari, Batang 138 B4 prev. Djambi. river
Sumatera, W Indonesia
Ḥārim 118 B2 var. Harem. Idlib, W Syria
Harima-nada 131 B6 sea S Japan
Harirud 123 E4 var. Tedzhen, Turkm.
Tejen. river Afghanistan/Iran
Harlan 45 F3 Iowa, C USA
Harlebeke see Harelbeke
Harlem see Haarlem
Harlingen 86 D2 Fris. Harns. Fryslân,
N Netherlands
Harlingen 49 G5 Texas, SW USA
Harlow 89 E6 E England, United
Kingdom
Harney Basin 46 B4 basin Oregon,
NW USA
Härnösand 85 C5 var. Hernösand.
Västernorrland, C Sweden
Harns see Harlingen
Harper 74 D5 var. Cape Palmas.
NE Liberia
Harricana 38 D3 river Québec,
SE Canada
Harris 88 B3 physical region
NW Scotland, United Kingdom
Harrisburg 41 E4 state capital
Pennsylvania, NE USA
Harrisonburg 41 E4 Virginia, NE USA
Harrison, Cape 39 F2 headland
Newfoundland and Labrador, E Canada
Harris Ridge see Lomonosov Ridge
Harrogate 89 D5 N England, United
Kingdom
Hârşova 108 D5 prev. Hîrşova.
Constanţa, SE Romania
Harstad 84 C2 Troms, N Norway
Hartford 41 G3 state capital Connecticut,
NE USA
Hartlepool 89 D5 N England, United
Kingdom
Harunabad see Eslāmābād-e Gharb
Har Us Gol 126 C2 lake Hovd,
W Mongolia
Har Us Nuur 126 C2 lake
NW Mongolia
Harwich 89 E6 E England, United
Kingdom
Haryāna 134 D2 var. Hariana. cultural
region N India
Hashemite Kingdom of Jordan see
Jordan
Hasselt 87 C6 Limburg, NE Belgium
Hassetché see Al Ḥasakah
Hasta Colonia/Hasta Pompeia see Asti
Hastings 150 E4 Hawke's Bay, North
Island, New Zealand
Hastings 89 E7 SE England, United
Kingdom
Hastings 45 E4 Nebraska, C USA
Haţeg 108 B4 Ger. Wallenthal, Hung.
Hátszeg; prev. Hatzeg, Hötzing.
Hunedoara, SW Romania
Hátszeg see Haţeg
Hattem 86 D3 Gelderland, E Netherlands
Hatteras, Cape 43 G1 headland North
Carolina, SE USA
Hatteras Plain 35 D6 abyssal plain
W Atlantic Ocean
Hattiesburg 42 C3 Mississippi, S USA
Hatton Bank see Hatton Ridge
Hatton Ridge 80 B2 var. Hatton Bank.
undersea ridge N Atlantic Ocean
Hat Yai 137 C7 var. Ban Hat Yai.
Songkhla, SW Thailand
Hatzeg see Haţeg
Hatzfeld see Jimbolia
Haugesund 85 A6 Rogaland, S Norway
Haukeligrend 85 A6 Telemark,
S Norway
Haukivesi 85 E5 lake SE Finland
Hauraki Gulf 150 D2 gulf North Island,
N New Zealand
Hauroko, Lake 151 A7 lake South
Island, New Zealand
Hautes Fagnes 87 D6 Ger. Hohes Venn.
mountain range E Belgium
Hauts Plateaux 70 D2 plateau Algeria/
Morocco
Hauzenberg 95 D6 Bayern, SE Germany

Havana 35 D6 Illinois, N USA
Havana see La Habana
Havant 89 D7 S England, United
Kingdom
Havelock 43 F1 North Carolina, SE USA
Havelock North 150 E4 Hawke's Bay,
North Island, New Zealand
Haverfordwest 89 C6 SW Wales, United
Kingdom
Havířov 99 C5 Moravskoslezský Kraj,
E Czech Republic (Czechia)
Havre 44 C1 Montana, NW USA
Havre see le Havre
Havre-St-Pierre 39 F3 Québec,
E Canada
Hawaii 47 A8 off. State of Hawaii, also
known as Aloha State, Paradise of the
Pacific, var. Hawai'i. state USA,
C Pacific Ocean
Hawai'i 47 B8 var. Hawaii. island
Hawaiian Islands, USA, C Pacific Ocean
Hawaiian Islands 152 D2 prev.
Sandwich Islands. island group Hawaii,
USA
Hawaiian Ridge 152 H4 undersea ridge
N Pacific Ocean
Hawea, Lake 151 B6 lake South Island,
New Zealand
Hawera 150 D4 Taranaki, North Island,
New Zealand
Hawick 88 C4 SE Scotland, United
Kingdom
Hawke Bay 150 E4 bay North Island,
New Zealand
Hawkeye State see Iowa
Hawthorne 47 C6 Nevada, W USA
Hay 149 C6 New South Wales,
SE Australia
HaYarden see Jordan
Hayastani Hanrapetut'yun
see Armenia
Hayes 38 B2 river Manitoba, C Canada
Hay River 37 E4 Northwest Territories,
W Canada
Hays 45 E5 Kansas, C USA
Haysyn 108 D3 Rus. Gaysin. Vinnyts'ka
Oblast', C Ukraine
Hazar 122 B2 prev. Rus. Cheleken.
Balkan Welaýaty, W Turkmenistan
Heard and McDonald Islands 141 B7
Australian external territory
S Indian Ocean
Hearst 38 C4 Ontario, S Canada
Heart of Dixie see Alabama
Heathrow 89 A8 (London) SE England,
United Kingdom
Hebei 128 C4 var. Hebei Sheng, Hopeh,
Hopei, Ji; prev. Chihli. province
E China
Hebei Sheng see Hebei
Hebron 119 A6 var. Al Khalīl, El Khalīl,
Heb. Hevron; anc. Kiriath-Arba.
S West Bank
Heemskerk 86 C3 Noord-Holland,
W Netherlands
Heerde 86 D3 Gelderland, E Netherlands
Heerenveen 86 D2 Fris. It Hearrenfean.
Fryslân, N Netherlands
Heerhugowaard 86 C2 Noord-Holland,
NW Netherlands
Heerlen 87 D6 Limburg, SE Netherlands
Heerwegen see Polkowice
Hefa 119 A5 var. Haifa, hist. Caiffa,
Caiphas; anc. Sycaminum. Haifa,
N Israel
Hefa, Mifraz see Mifrats Hefa
Hefei 128 D5 var. Hofei, hist. Luchow.
province capital Anhui, E China
Hegang 129 E2 Heilongjiang, NE China
Hei see Heilongjiang
Heide 94 B2 Schleswig-Holstein,
N Germany
Heidelberg 95 B5 Baden-Württemberg,
SW Germany
Heidenheim see Heidenheim an der
Brenz
Heidenheim an der Brenz 95 B6 var.
Heidenheim. Baden-Württemberg,
S Germany
Hei-ho see Nagqu
Heilbronn 95 B6 Baden-Württemberg,
SW Germany
Heiligenbeil see Mamonovo
Heilongjiang 128 D2 var. Hei,
Heilongjiang Sheng, Hei-lung-chiang,
Heilungkiang. province NE China
Heilong Jiang see Amur
Heilongjiang Sheng see Heilongjiang
Heiloo 86 C3 Noord-Holland,
NW Netherlands

Heilsberg see Lidzbark Warmiński
Hei-lung-chiang/Heilungkiang see
Heilongjiang
Heimdal 85 B5 Sør-Trøndelag, S Norway
Heinaste see Ainaži
Hekimhan 116 D3 Malatya, C Turkey
Helena 44 B2 state capital Montana,
NW USA
Helensville 150 D2 Auckland, North
Island, New Zealand
Helgoland Bay see Helgoländer Bucht
Helgoländer Bucht 94 A2 var.
Helgoland Bay, Heligoland Bight. bay
NW Germany
Heligoland Bight see Helgoländer Bucht
Heliopolis see Baalbek
Hellas see Greece
Hellenic Republic see Greece
Hellevoetsluis 86 B4 Zuid-Holland,
SW Netherlands
Hellín 93 E4 Castilla-La Mancha,
C Spain
Darya-ye Helmand 122 D5 var. Rūd-e
Hīrmand. river Afghanistan/Iran
Helmantica see Salamanca
Helmond 87 D5 Noord-Brabant,
S Netherlands
Helsingborg 85 B7 prev. Hälsingborg.
Skåne, S Sweden
Helsingfors see Helsinki
Helsinki 85 D6 Swe. Helsingfors.
country capital (Finland) Etelä-Suomi,
S Finland
Heltau see Cisnădie
Helvetia see Switzerland
Henan 128 C5 var. Henan Sheng,
Honan, Yu. province C China
Henderson 40 B5 Kentucky, S USA
Henderson 47 D7 Nevada, W USA
Henderson 49 H3 Texas, SW USA
Hendū Kosh see Hindu Kush
Hengchow see Hengyang
Hengduan Shan 128 A5 mountain range
SW China
Hengelo 86 E3 Overijssel, E Netherlands
Hengnan see Hengyang
Hengyang 128 C5 var. Hengnan,
Heng-yang; prev. Hengchow. Hunan,
S China
Heng-yang see Hengyang
Heniches'k 109 F4 Rus. Genichesk.
Khersons'ka Oblast', S Ukraine
Hennebont 90 A3 Morbihan, NW France
Henrique de Carvalho see Saurimo
Henzada see Hinthada
Herakleion see Irákleio
Herāt 122 D4 var. Herat; anc. Aria.
Herāt, W Afghanistan
Heredia 53 E4 Heredia, C Costa Rica
Hereford 89 D6 W England, United
Kingdom
Herford 94 B4 Nordrhein-Westfalen,
NW Germany
Héristal see Herstal
Herk-de-Stad 87 C6 Limburg,
NE Belgium
Herlen Gol/Herlen He see Kerulen
Hermannstadt see Sibiu
Hermansverk 85 A5 Sogn Og Fjordane,
S Norway
Hermhausen see Hajnówka
Hermiston 46 C2 Oregon, NW USA
Hermon, Mount 119 B5 Ar. Jabal ash
Shaykh. mountain S Syria
Hermosillo 50 B2 Sonora, NW Mexico
Hermoupolis see Ermoúpoli
Hernösand see Härnösand
Herrera del Duque 92 D3 Extremadura,
W Spain
Herselt 87 C5 Antwerpen, C Belgium
Herstal 87 D6 Fr. Héristal. Liège,
E Belgium
Herzogenbusch see 's-Hertogenbosch
Hesse see Hessen
Hessen 95 B5 Eng./Fr. Hesse. state
C Germany
Hevron see Hebron
Hewlêr see Arbīl
Heydebrech see Kędzierzyn-Kozle
Heydekrug see Šilutė
Heywood Islands 146 C3 island group
Western Australia
Hibbing 45 F1 Minnesota, N USA
Hibernia see Ireland
Hidalgo del Parral 50 C2 var. Parral.
Chihuahua, N Mexico
Hida-sanmyaku 131 C5 mountain range
Honshū, S Japan
Hierosolyma see Jerusalem
Hierro 70 A3 var. Ferro. island Islas
Canarias, Spain, NE Atlantic Ocean

High Atlas 70 C2 Eng. High Atlas.
mountain range C Morocco
High Atlas see Haut Atlas
High Plains see Great Plains
High Point 43 E1 North Carolina,
SE USA
Hiiumaa 106 C2 Ger. Dagden, Swe.
Dagö. island W Estonia
Hikurangi 150 D2 Northland, North
Island, New Zealand
Hildesheim 94 B4 Niedersachsen,
N Germany
Hilla see Al Ḥillah
Hillaby, Mount 55 G1 mountain
N Barbados
Hill Bank 52 C1 Orange Walk, N Belize
Hillegom 86 C3 Zuid-Holland,
W Netherlands
Hilo 47 B8 Hawaii, USA, C Pacific Ocean
Hilton Head Island 43 E2 South
Carolina, SE USA
Hilversum 86 C3 Noord-Holland,
C Netherlands
Himalaya/Himalaya Shan see Himalayas
Himalayas 135 E2 var. Himalaya, Chin.
Himalaya Shan. mountain range S Asia
Himeji 131 C6 var. Himezi. Hyōgo,
Honshū, SW Japan
Himezi see Himeji
Ḥimṣ 118 B4 var. Homs; anc. Emesa.
Ḥimṣ, C Syria
Hînceşti 108 D4 var. Hânceşti; prev.
Kotovsk. C Moldova
Hinchinbrook Island 148 D3 island
Queensland, NE Australia
Hinds 151 C6 Canterbury, South Island,
New Zealand
Hindu Kush 123 F4 Per. Hendū Kosh.
mountain range Afghanistan/Pakistan
Hinesville 43 E3 Georgia, SE USA
Hinnoya 84 C3 Lapp. Iinnasuolu. island
C Norway
Hinson Bay 42 A5 bay W Bermuda
W Atlantic Ocean
Hinthada 136 B4 var. Henzada.
Ayeyarwady, SW Myanmar (Burma)
Hios see Chíos
Hîrfanlı Barajı 116 C3 reservoir
C Turkey
Hīrmand, Rūd-e see Helmand, Daryā-ye
Hirosaki 130 D3 Aomori, Honshū,
C Japan
Hiroshima 131 B6 var. Hirosima.
Hiroshima, Honshū, SW Japan
**Hirschberg/Hirschberg im
Riesengebirge/Hirschberg in
Schlesien** see Jelenia Góra
Hirson 90 D3 Aisne, N France
Hîrşova see Hârşova
Hispalis see Sevilla
Hispana/Hispania see Spain
Hispaniola 56 B1 island Dominion
Republic/Haiti
Hitachi 131 D5 var. Hitati. Ibaraki,
Honshū, S Japan
Hitati see Hitachi
Hitra 84 A4 prev. Hitteren. island
S Norway
Hitteren see Hitra
Hjälmaren 85 C6 Eng. Lake Hjalmar.
lake C Sweden
Hjalmar, Lake see Hjälmaren
Hjørring 85 B7 Nordjylland,
N Denmark
Hkakabo Razi 136 B1 mountain
Myanmar (Burma)/China
Hlobyne 109 F2 Rus. Globino.
Poltavs'ka Oblast', NE Ukraine
Hlukhiv 109 F1 Rus. Glukhov. Sums'ka
Oblast', NE Ukraine
Hlybokaye 107 D5 Rus. Glubokoye.
Vitsyebskaya Voblasts', N Belarus
Hoa Bình 136 D3 Hoa Bình, N Vietnam
Hoang Lien Son 136 D3 mountain range
N Vietnam
Hobart 149 C8 prev. Hobarton, Hobart
Town. state capital Tasmania,
SE Australia
Hobarton/Hobart Town see Hobart
Hobbs 49 E3 New Mexico, SW USA
Hobro 85 A7 Nordjylland, N Denmark
Hồ Chí Minh 137 E6 var. Ho Chi Minh
City; prev. Saigon. S Vietnam
Ho Chi Minh City see Hồ Chí Minh
Hodeida see Al Ḥudaydah
Hódmezővásárhely 99 D7 Csongrád,
SE Hungary
Hodna, Chott El 102 C4 var. Chott
el-Hodna, Ar. Shatt al-Hodna. salt lake
N Algeria

Hodna, Chott el-/Hodna, Shatt al- see
Hodna, Chott El
Hodonín 99 C5 Ger. Göding.
Jihomoravský Kraj, SE Czech Republic
(Czechia)
Hoei see Huy
Hoey see Huy
Hof 95 C5 Bayern, SE Germany
Hofei see Hefei
Hōfu 131 B7 Yamaguchi, Honshū,
SW Japan
Hofuf see Al Hufūf
Hogoley Islands see Chuuk Islands
Hohensalza see Inowrocław
Hohenstadt see Zábřeh
Hohes Venn see Hautes Fagnes
Hohe Tauern 95 C7 mountain range
W Austria
Hohhot 127 F3 var. Huhehot,
Huhohaote, Mong. Kukukhoto; prev.
Kweisui, Kwesui. Nei Mongol Zizhiqu,
N China
Hôi An 137 E5 prev. Faifo. Quang
Nam-Đa Nẵng, C Vietnam
Hoï-Hao/Hoihow see Haikou
Hokianga Harbour 150 C2 inlet
SE Tasman Sea
Hokitika 151 B5 West Coast, South
Island, New Zealand
Hokkaido 130 C2 prev. Ezo, Yeso, Yezo.
island NE Japan
Hola Prystan' 109 E4 Rus. Golaya
Pristan. Khersons'ka Oblast', S Ukraine
Holbrook 48 B2 Arizona, SW USA
Holetown 55 G1 prev. Jamestown.
W Barbados
Holguín 54 C2 Holguín, SE Cuba
Holin Gol 127 G2 prev. Hulingol. Nei
Mongol Zizhiqu, N China
Hollabrunn 95 E6 Niederösterreich,
NE Austria
Holland see Netherlands
Hollandia see Jayapura
Holly Springs 42 C1 Mississippi, S USA
Holman 37 E3 Victoria Island, Northwest
Territories, N Canada
Holmsund 84 D4 Västerbotten,
N Sweden
Holon 119 A6 var. Kholon; prev. Ḥolon.
Tel Aviv, C Israel
Holon see Holon
Holovanivs'k 109 E3 Rus. Golovanevsk.
Kirovohrads'ka Oblast', C Ukraine
Holstebro 85 A7 Midtjylland,
W Denmark
**Holsteinborg/Holsteinsborg/
Holstenborg/Holstensborg** see
Sisimiut
Holyhead 89 C5 Wel. Caer Gybi.
NW Wales, United Kingdom
Hombori 75 E3 Mopti, S Mali
Homs see Al Khums, Libya
Homs see Ḥimṣ
Homyel' 107 D7 Rus. Gomel'.
Homyel'skaya Voblasts', SE Belarus
Honan see Henan, China
Honan see Luoyang, China
Hondo 49 F4 Texas, SW USA
Hondo see Honshū
Honduras 52 C2 off. Republic of
Honduras. country Central America
Honduras, Golfo de see Honduras, Gulf
of
Honduras, Gulf of 52 C2 Sp. Golfo de
Honduras. gulf W Caribbean Sea
Honduras, Republic of see Honduras
Honefoss 85 B6 Buskerud, S Norway
Honey Lake 47 B5 lake California,
W USA
Hon Gai see Ha Long
Hongay see Ha Long
Hông Gai see Ha Long
Hông Hà, Sông see Red River
Hong Kong 128 A1 Special
Administrative Region Hong Kong,
S China
Hong Kong Island 128 B2 island
S China Asia
Honiara 144 C3 country capital
(Solomon Islands) Guadalcanal,
C Solomon Islands
Honjō 130 D4 var. Honzyô, Yurihonjô.
Akita, Honshū, C Japan
Honolulu 47 A8 state capital O'ahu,
Hawaii, USA, C Pacific Ocean
Honshu 131 E5 var. Hondo, Honsyû.
island SW Japan
Honsyû see Honshū
Honte see Westerschelde
Honzyô see Honjō

Hoogeveen 86 E2 Drenthe,
NE Netherlands
Hoogezand-Sappemeer 86 E2
Groningen, NE Netherlands
Hoorn 86 C2 Noord-Holland,
NW Netherlands
Hoosier State see Indiana
Hopa 117 E2 Artvin, NE Turkey
Hope 36 C3 British Columbia,
SW Canada
Hopedale 39 F2 Newfoundland and
Labrador, NE Canada
Hopeh/Hopei see Hebei
Hopkinsville 40 B5 Kentucky,
S USA
Horasan 117 F3 Erzurum, NE Turkey
Horizon Deep 152 D4 trench W Pacific
Ocean
Horki 107 E6 Rus. Gorki.
Mahilyowskaya Voblasts', E Belarus
Horlivka 109 G3 Rom. Adâncata, Rus.
Gorlovka. Donets'ka Oblast', E Ukraine
Hormoz, Tangeh-ye see Hormuz, Strait
of
Hormuz, Strait of 120 D4 var. Strait of
Ormuz, Per. Tangeh-ye Hormoz. strait
Iran/Oman
Cape Horn 65 C8 Eng. Cape Horn.
headland S Chile
Horn, Cape see Hornos, Cabo de
Hornsby 148 E1 New South Wales,
SE Australia
Horodnya 109 E1 Rus. Gorodnya.
Chernihivs'ka Oblast', NE Ukraine
Horodok 108 B2 Pol. Gródek
Jagielloński, Rus. Gorodok, Gorodok
Yagellonski. L'vivs'ka Oblast',
NW Ukraine
Horodyshche 109 E2 Rus. Gorodishche.
Cherkas'ka Oblast', C Ukraine
Horoshiri-dake 130 D2 var. Horosiri
Dake. mountain Hokkaidō, N Japan
Horosiri Dake see Horoshiri-dake
Horsburgh Atoll 132 A4 var. Goidhoo
Atoll. atoll N Maldives
Horseshoe Bay 42 A5 bay W Bermuda
W Atlantic Ocean
Horseshoe Seamounts 80 A4 seamount
range E Atlantic Ocean
Horsham 149 B7 Victoria,
SE Australia
Horst 87 D5 Limburg, SE Netherlands
Horten 85 B6 Vestfold, S Norway
Horyn' 107 B7 Rus. Goryn. river
NW Ukraine
Hosingen 87 D7 Diekirch,
NE Luxembourg
Hospitalet see L'Hospitalet de Llobregat
Hotan 126 B4 var. Khotan, Chin.
Ho-t'ien. Xinjiang Uygur Zizhiqu,
NW China
Ho-t'ien see Hotan
Hoting 84 C4 Jämtland, C Sweden
Hot Springs 42 B1 Arkansas, C USA
Hötzing see Hateg
Houayxay 136 C3 var. Ban Houayxay.
Bokèo, N Laos
Houghton 40 B1 Michigan, N USA
Houilles 90 B5 Yvelines, Île-de-France,
N France Europe
Houlton 41 H1 Maine, NE USA
Houma 42 B3 Louisiana, S USA
Houston 49 H4 Texas, SW USA
Hovd 126 C2 var. Khovd, Kobdo; prev.
Jirgalanta. Hovd, W Mongolia
Hove 89 E7 SE England,
United Kingdom
Hoverla, Hora 108 C3 Rus. Gora
Goverla. mountain W Ukraine
Hovsgol, Lake see Hövsgöl Nuur
Hövsgöl Nuur 126 D1 var. Lake
Hovsgol. lake N Mongolia
Howa, Ouadi see Howar, Wâdi
Howar, Wadi 72 A3 var. Ouadi Howa.
river Chad/Sudan
Howland Island 145 E2 US
unincorporated territory W Polynesia
Howrah see Hãora
Hoy 88 C2 island N Scotland, United
Kingdom
Hoyerswerda 94 D4 Lus. Wojerecy.
Sachsen, E Germany
Hpa-an 136 B4 var. Pa-an. Kayin State,
S Myanmar (Burma)
Hpyu see Phyu
Hradec Králové 99 B5 Ger. Königgrätz.
Královéhradecký Kraj, N Czech
Republic (Czechia)
Hradzichy 107 B5 Rus. Grandichi.
Hrodzyenskaya Voblasts', W Belarus

Hranice 99 C5 Ger. Mährisch-
Weisskirchen. Olomoucký Kraj,
E Czech Republic (Czechia)
Hrebinka 109 E2 Rus. Grebenka.
Poltavs'ka Oblast', NE Ukraine
Hrodna 107 B5 Pol. Grodno.
Hrodzyenskaya Voblasts', W Belarus
Hrvatska see Croatia
Hsia-men see Xiamen
Hsiang-t'an see Xiangtan
Hsi Chiang see Xi Jiang
Hsing-K'ai Hu see Khanka, Lake
Hsi-ning/Hsining see Xining
Hsinking see Changchun
Hsin-yang see Xinyang
Hsu-chou see Xuzhou
Htawei see Dawei
Huacho 60 C4 Lima, W Peru
Hua Hin see Ban Hua Hin
Huaihua 128 C6 Hunan, S China
Huailai 128 C3 var. Shacheng. Hebei,
E China
Huainan 128 D5 var. Huai-nan,
Hwainan. Anhui, E China
Huai-nan see Huainan
Huajuapan 51 F5 var. Huajuapan de
León. Oaxaca, SE Mexico
Huajuapan de León see Huajuapan
Hualapai Peak 48 A2 mountain Arizona,
SW USA
Huallaga, Río 60 C3 river N Peru
Huambo 78 B2 Port. Nova Lisboa.
Huambo, C Angola
Huancavelica 60 D4 Huancavelica,
SW Peru
Huancayo 60 C3 Junín, C Peru
Huang Hai see Yellow Sea
Huangshi 128 C5 var. Huang-shih,
Hwangshih. Hubei, C China
Huang-shih see Huangshi
Huanta 60 D4 Ayacucho, C Peru
Huánuco 60 C3 Huánuco, C Peru
Huanuni 61 F4 Oruro, W Bolivia
Huaral 60 C4 Lima, W Peru
Huarás see Huaraz
Huaraz 60 C3 var. Huarás. Ancash,
W Peru
Huarmey 60 C3 Ancash, W Peru
Huatabampo 50 C2 Sonora,
NW Mexico
Hubballi 132 B2 prev. Hubli. Karnātaka,
SW India
Hubli see Hubballi
Huddersfield 89 D5 N England, United
Kingdom
Hudiksvall 85 C5 Gävleborg, C Sweden
Hudson Bay 37 G4 bay NE Canada
Hudson, Détroit d' see Hudson Strait
Hudson Strait 37 H3 Fr. Détroit
d'Hudson. strait Northwest Territories/
Québec, NE Canada
Hudur see Xuddur
Huê 136 E4 Th,a Thiên-Huê,
C Vietnam
Huehuetenango 52 A2 Huehuetenango,
W Guatemala
Huelva 92 C4 anc. Onuba. Andalucía,
SW Spain
Huesca 93 F2 anc. Osca. Aragón,
NE Spain
Huéscar 93 E4 Andalucía, S Spain
Hughenden 148 C3 Queensland,
NE Australia
Hugo 49 G2 Oklahoma, C USA
Huhehot/Huhohaote see Hohhot
Huila Plateau 78 B2 plateau S Angola
Huixtla 51 G5 Chiapas, SE Mexico
Hulingol see Holin Gol
Hull 38 D4 Québec, SE Canada
Hull see Kingston upon Hull
Hull Island see Orona
Hulst 87 B5 Zeeland, SW Netherlands
Hulun see Hulun Buir
Hulun Buir 127 F1 var. Hailar; prev.
Hulun. Nei Mongol Zizhiqu, N China
Hu-lun Ch'ih see Hulun Nur
Hulun Nur 127 F1 var. Hu-lun Ch'ih;
prev. Dalai Nor. lake NE China
Humaitá 62 D2 Amazonas, N Brazil
Humboldt River 47 C5 river Nevada,
W USA
Humphreys Peak 48 B1 mountain
Arizona, SW USA
Humpolec 99 B5 Ger. Gumpolds,
Humpoletz. Vysočina, C Czech
Republic (Czechia)
Humpoletz see Humpolec
Hunan 128 C6 var. Hunan Sheng,
Xiang. province S China
Hunan Sheng see Hunan

Hunedoara 108 B4 Ger. Eisenmarkt,
Hung. Vajdahunyad. Hunedoara,
SW Romania
Hünfeld 95 B5 Hessen, C Germany
Hungarian People's Republic see
Hungary
Hungary 99 C6 off. Hungary, Ger.
Ungarn, Hung. Magyarország, Rom.
Ungaria, SCr. Madarska, Ukr.
Uhorshchyna; prev. Hungarian People's
Republic. country C Europe
Hungary, Plain of see Great Hungarian
Plain
Hunjiang see Baishan
Hunter Island 149 B8 island Tasmania,
SE Australia
Huntington 40 D4 West Virginia,
NE USA
Huntington Beach 47 B8 California,
W USA
Huntly 150 D3 Waikato, North Island,
New Zealand
Huntsville 42 D1 Alabama, S USA
Huntsville 49 G3 Texas, SW USA
Hurghada see Al Ghardaqah
Huron 45 E3 South Dakota, N USA
Huron, Lake 40 D2 lake Canada/USA
Hurukawa see Furukawa
Hurunui 151 C5 river South Island,
New Zealand
Húsavík 83 E4 Nordhurland Eystra,
NE Iceland
Husté see Khust
Husum 94 B2 Schleswig-Holstein,
N Germany
Huszt see Khust
Hutchinson 45 E5 Kansas,
C USA
Hutchinson Island 43 F4 island Florida,
SE USA
Huy 87 C6 Dut. Hoei, Hoey. Liège,
E Belgium
Huzi see Fuji
Hvannadalshnúkur 83 E5 volcano
S Iceland
Hvar 100 B4 It. Lesina; anc. Pharus.
island S Croatia
Hwainan see Huainan
Hwange 78 D3 prev. Wankie.
Matabeleland North, W Zimbabwe
Hwang-Hae see Yellow Sea
Hwangshih see Huangshi
Hyargas Nuur 126 C2 lake
NW Mongolia
Hyderābād 134 D5 var. Haidarabad.
state capital Telangana, C India
Hyderabad 134 B3 var. Haidarabad.
Sind, SE Pakistan
Hyères 91 D6 Var, SE France
Hyères, Îles d' 91 D6 island group
S France
Hypanis see Kuban'
Hyrcania see Gorğan
Hyvinge see Hyvinkää
Hyvinkää 85 D5 Swe. Hyvinge. Uusimaa,
S Finland

I

Iader see Zadar
Ialomița 108 C5 river SE Romania
Iaşi 108 D3 Ger. Jassy. Iaşi, NE Romania
Ibadan 75 F5 Oyo, SW Nigeria
Ibagué 58 B3 Tolima, C Colombia
Ibar see Ibër
Ibarra 60 B1 var. San Miguel de Ibarra.
Imbabura, N Ecuador
Ibër 100 D4 Serb. Ibar. river C Serbia
Iberia see Spain
Iberian Mountains see Ibérico, Sistema
Iberian Peninsula 80 B4 physical region
Portugal/Spain
Iberian Plain 80 B4 abyssal plain
E Atlantic Ocean
Ibérica, Cordillera see Ibérico, Sistema
Ibérico, Sistema 93 E2 var. Cordillera
Ibérica, Eng. Iberian Mountains.
mountain range NE Spain
Ibiza see Eivissa
Ibo see Sassandra
Ica 60 D4 Ica, SW Peru
Icaria see Ikaría
Içá, Rio 62 C2 var. Río Putumayo. river
NW South America
Içá, Rio see Putumayo, Río
İçel see Mersin
Iceland 83 E4 off. Republic of Iceland,
Dan. Island, Icel. Ísland. country
N Atlantic Ocean

Iceland Basin 80 B1 undersea basin
N Atlantic Ocean
Icelandic Plateau see Iceland Plateau
Iceland Plateau 155 B6 var. Icelandic
Plateau. undersea plateau S Greenland
Sea
Iceland, Republic of see Iceland
Iconium see Konya
Iculisma see Angoulême
Idabel 49 H2 Oklahoma, C USA
Idaho 46 D3 off. State of Idaho, also
known as Gem of the Mountains, Gem
State. state NW USA
Idaho Falls 46 E3 Idaho, NW USA
Idensalmi see Iisalmi
Idfu 72 B2 var. Edfu. SE Egypt
Idi Amin, Lac see Edward, Lake
Idini 74 B2 Trarza, W Mauritania
Idlib 118 B3 Idlib, NW Syria
Idre 85 B5 Dalarna, C Sweden
Iecava 106 C3 S Latvia
Ieper 87 A6 Fr. Ypres. West-Vlaanderen,
W Belgium
Ierápetra 105 D8 Kríti, Greece,
E Mediterranean Sea
Ierisós see Ierissós
Ierissós 104 C4 var. Ierisós. Kentrikí
Makedonía, N Greece
Iferouâne 75 G2 Agadez, N Niger
Ifôghas, Adrar des 75 E2 var. Adrar des
Iforas. mountain range NE Mali
Iforas, Adrar des see Ifôghas, Adrar des
Igarka 114 D3 Krasnoyarskiy Kray,
N Russia
Igaunija see Estonia
Iglau/Iglawa/Iglawa see Jihlava
Iglesias 97 A5 Sardegna, Italy,
C Mediterranean Sea
Igloolik 37 G2 Nunavut, N Canada
Igoumenitsa 104 A4 Ípeiros, W Greece
Iguaçu, Rio 63 E4 Sp. Río Iguazú. river
Argentina/Brazil
Iguaçu, Saltos do 63 E4 Sp. Cataratas del
Iguazú; prev. Victoria Falls. waterfall
Argentina/Brazil
Iguala 51 E4 var. Iguala de la
Independencia. Guerrero, S Mexico
Iguala de la Independencia see Iguala
Iguazú, Cataratas del see Iguaçu, Saltos
do
Iguazú, Río see Iguaçu, Rio
Iguid, Erg see Iguidi, 'Erg
Iguidi, 'Erg 70 C3 var. Erg Iguid. desert
Algeria/Mauritania
Ihavandhippolhu Atoll 132 A3 var.
Ihavandiffulu Atoll. atoll N Maldives
Ihavandiffulu Atoll see Ihavandhippolhu
Atoll
Ihosy 79 F4 Fianarantsoa,
S Madagascar
Iinnasuolu see Hinnøya
Iisalmi 84 E4 var. Idensalmi.
Pohjois-Savo, C Finland
IJmuiden 86 C3 Noord-Holland,
W Netherlands
IJssel 86 D3 var. Yssel. river Netherlands
IJsselmeer 86 C2 prev. Zuider Zee. lake
N Netherlands
IJsselmuiden 86 D3 Overijssel,
E Netherlands
Ijzer 87 A6 river W Belgium
Ikaahuk see Sachs Harbour
Ikaluktutiak see Cambridge Bay
Ikaría 105 D6 var. Kariot, Nicaria,
Nikaria; anc. Icaria. island Dodekánisa,
Greece, Aegean Sea
Ikela 77 D6 Équateur, C Dem. Rep.
Congo
Iki 131 A7 island SW Japan
Ilagan 139 E1 Luzon, N Philippines
Ilave 61 E4 Puno, S Peru
Iława 98 D3 Ger. Deutsch-Eylau.
Warmińsko-Mazurskie, NE Poland
Ilebo 77 C6 prev. Port-Francqui.
Kasai-Occidental, W Dem. Rep. Congo
Île-de-France 90 C3 cultural region
N France
Ilemi Triangle 73 B5 var. Elemi Triangle.
disputed region Kenya/Sudan
Ilerda see Lleida
Ilfracombe 89 C7 SW England, United
Kingdom
Ílhavo 92 B2 Aveiro, N Portugal
Iliamna Lake 36 C3 lake Alaska, USA
Il'ichevsk see Illichivs'k, Ukraine
Ilici see Elche
Iligan 139 E2 off. Iligan City. Mindanao,
S Philippines
Iligan City see Iligan
Illapel 64 B4 Coquimbo, C Chile

Illichivs'k see Chornomors'k
Illicis see Elche
Illinois 40 A4 off. State of Illinois, also
known as Prairie State, Sucker State.
state C USA
Illinois River 40 B4 river Illinois, N USA
Illurco see Lorca
Illuro see Mataró
Ilo 61 E4 Moquegua, SW Peru
Iloilo 139 E2 off. Iloilo City. Panay
Island, C Philippines
Iloilo City see Iloilo
Ilorin 75 F4 Kwara, W Nigeria
Ilovlya 111 B6 Volgogradskaya Oblast',
SW Russia
Iluh see Batman
Il'yaly see Gurbansoltan Eje
Imatra 85 E5 Etelä-Kariala, SE Finland
Imbros see Gökçeada
Imishli see İmişli
İmişli 117 H3 Rus. Imishli.
C Azerbaijan
Imola 96 C3 Emilia-Romagna, N Italy
Imperatriz 63 F2 Maranhão,
NE Brazil
Imperia 96 A3 Liguria, NW Italy
Impfondo 77 C5 Likouala, NE Congo
Imphal 135 H3 state capital Manipur,
NE India
Imroz Adası see Gökçeada
Inagua Islands see Little Inagua
Inagua Islands see Great Inagua
Inarijärvi 84 D2 Lapp. Aanaarjärvi, Swe.
Enareträsk. lake N Finland
Inău see Ineu
Inawashiro-ko 131 D5 var. Inawasiro
Ko. lake Honshū, C Japan
Inawasiro Ko see Inawashiro-ko
İncesu 116 D3 Kayseri, Turkey Asia
Incheon 129 E4 off. Incheon
Gwang-yeoksi, prev.Inch'ŏn, Jap.
Jinsen; prev. Chemulpo. NW South
Korea
Incheon-Gwang-yeoksi see Incheon
Inch'ŏn see Incheon
Incudine, Monte 91 E7 mountain Corse,
France, C Mediterranean Sea
Indefatigable Island see Santa Cruz, Isla
Independence 45 F4 Missouri, C USA
Independence Fjord 83 E1 fjord
N Greenland
Independence Island see Malden Island
Independence Mountains 46 C4
mountain range Nevada, W USA
India 124 B3 off. Republic of India, var.
Indian Union, Union of India, Hind.
Bhārat. country S Asia
India see India
Indiana 40 B4 off. State of Indiana, also
known as Hoosier State. state N USA
Indianapolis 40 C4 state capital Indiana,
N USA
Indian Church 52 C1 Orange Walk,
N Belize
Indian Desert see Thar Desert
Indianola 45 F4 Iowa, C USA
Indian Union see India
India, Republic of see India
Indigirka 115 F2 river NE Russia
Indija 100 D3 Hung. India; prev. Indjija.
Vojvodina, N Serbia
Indija see Indija
Indomed Fracture Zone 141 B6 tectonic
feature SW Indian Ocean
Indonesia 138 B4 off. Republic of
Indonesia, Ind. Republik Indonesia;
prev. Dutch East Indies, Netherlands
East Indies, United States of Indonesia.
country SE Asia
Indonesian Borneo see Kalimantan
Indonesia, Republic of see Indonesia
Indonesia, Republik see Indonesia
Indonesia, United States of see
Indonesia
Indore 134 D4 Madhya Pradesh,
C India
Indre see Châteauroux
Indravāti see Châteauroux
Indus 134 C2 Chin. Yindu He; prev.
Yin-tu Ho. river C Asia
Indus Cone see Indus Fan
Indus Fan 112 C5 var. Indus Cone.
undersea fan N Arabian Sea
Indus, Mouths of the 134 B4 delta
S Pakistan
İnebolu 116 C2 Kastamonu,
N Turkey

Ineu 108 A4 Hung. Borosjenő; prev. Inău.
Arad, W Romania
Infiernillo, Presa del 51 E4 reservoir
S Mexico
Inglewood 46 D2 California,
W USA
Ingolstadt 95 C6 Bayern, S Germany
Ingulets see Inhulets'
Inguri see Enguri
Inhambane 79 E4 Inhambane,
SE Mozambique
Inhulets' 109 F3 Rus. Ingulets.
Dnipropetrovs'ka Oblast', E Ukraine
I-ning see Yining
Inis see Ennis
Inis Ceithleann see Enniskillen
Inn 95 C6 river C Europe
Innaanganeq 82 C1 var. Kap York.
headland NW Greenland
Inner Hebrides 88 B4 island group
W Scotland, United Kingdom
Inner Islands 79 H1 var. Central Group.
island group N Seychelles
Innisfail 148 D3 Queensland,
NE Australia
Inniskilling see Enniskillen
Innsbruck see Innsbruck
Innsbruck 95 C7 var. Innsbruch. Tirol,
W Austria
Inoucdjouac see Inukjuak
Inowrazlaw see Inowrocław
Inowrocław 98 C3 Ger. Hohensalza;
prev. Inowrazlaw. Kujawski-
pomorskie, C Poland
I-n-Sakane, 'Erg 75 E2 desert N Mali
I-n-Salah 70 D3 var. In Salah. C Algeria
Insterburg see Chernyakhovsk
Insula see Lille
Inta 110 E3 Respublika Komi, NW Russia
Interamna see Terni
Interamna Nahars see Terni
International Falls 45 F1 Minnesota,
N USA
Inukjuak 38 D2 var. Inoucdjouac; prev.
Port Harrison. Québec, NE Canada
Inuvik 36 D3 var. Inuvik
Inuvik 36 D3 var. Inuuvik. Northwest
Territories, NW Canada
Invercargill 151 A7 Southland, South
Island, New Zealand
Inverness 88 C3 N Scotland,
United Kingdom
Investigator Ridge 141 D5 undersea
ridge E Indian Ocean
Investigator Strait 149 B7 strait
South Australia
Inyangani 78 D3 mountain
NE Zimbabwe
Ioánnina 104 A4 var. Janina, Yannina.
Ípeiros, W Greece
Iola 45 F5 Kansas, C USA
Ionia Basin see Ionian Basin
Ionian Basin 80 D5 var. Ionia Basin.
undersea basin Ionian Sea,
C Mediterranean Sea
Ionian Islands see Iónia Nisiá
Ionian Sea 103 E3 Gk. Iónio Pélagos, It.
Mar Ionio. sea C Mediterranean Sea
Iónioi Nísoi 105 A5 Eng. Ionian Islands.
region W Greece
Ionio, Mar/Iónio Pélagos see Ionian Sea
Ios 105 D6 var. Nio. island Kykládes,
Greece, Aegean Sea
Ioulida 105 C6 prev. Ioulís, Kykládes,
Greece, Aegean Sea
Iowa 45 F3 off. State of Iowa, also known
as Hawkeye State. state C USA
Iowa City 45 G3 Iowa, C USA
Iowa Falls 45 G3 Iowa, C USA
Ipel' 99 C6 var. Ipoly, Ger. Eipel. river
Hungary/Slovakia
Ipiales 58 A4 Nariño, SW Colombia
Ipoh 138 B3 Perak, Peninsular Malaysia
Ipoly see Ipel'
Ippy 76 C4 Ouaka, C Central African
Republic
Ipswich 149 E5 Queensland, E Australia
Ipswich 89 E6 hist. Gipeswic. E England,
United Kingdom
Iqaluit 37 H3 prev. Frobisher Bay.
province capital Baffin Island, Nunavut,
NE Canada
Iquique 64 B1 Tarapacá, N Chile
Iquitos 60 C1 Loreto, N Peru
Irákleio 105 D7 var. Herakleion, Eng.
Candia; prev. Iráklion. Kríti, Greece,
E Mediterranean Sea
Iráklion see Irákleio
Iran 120 C3 off. Islamic Republic of Iran;
prev. Persia. country SW Asia

Iranian Plateau 120 D3 var. Plateau of Iran. *plateau* N Iran
Iran, Islamic Republic of *see* Iran
Iran, Plateau of *see* Iranian Plateau
Irapuato 51 E4 Guanajuato, C Mexico
Iraq 120 B3 *off.* Republic of Iraq, *Ar.* 'Irāq. *country* SW Asia
'Irāq *see* Iraq
Iraq, Republic of *see* Iraq
Irbid 119 B5 Irbid, N Jordan
Irbil *see* Arbil
Ireland 89 A5 *off.* Republic of Ireland, *Ir.* Éire. *country* NW Europe
Ireland 80 C3 *Lat.* Hibernia. *island* Ireland/United Kingdom
Ireland, Republic of *see* Ireland
Irian *see* New Guinea
Irian Barat *see* Papua
Irian Jaya *see* Papua
Irian, Teluk *see* Cenderawasih, Teluk
Iringa 73 C7 Iringa, C Tanzania
Iriomote-jima 130 A4 *island* Sakishima-shotō, SW Japan
Iriona 52 D2 Colón, NE Honduras
Irish Sea 115 E4 Irkutskaya Oblast', C British Isles
Irkutsk 115 E4 Irkutskaya Oblast', S Russia
Irminger Basin *see* Reykjanes Basin
Iroise 90 A3 *sea* NW France
Iron Mountain 40 B2 Michigan, N USA
Ironwood 40 B1 Michigan, N USA
Irrawaddy 136 B2 *var.* Ayeyarwady. *river* W Myanmar (Burma)
Irrawaddy, Mouths of the 137 A5 *delta* SW Myanmar (Burma)
Irtish *see* Yertis
Irtysh *see* Yertis
Irun 93 E1 *Cast.* Irún. País Vasco, N Spain
Irún *see* Irun
Iruña *see* Pamplona
Isabela, Isla 60 A5 *var.* Albemarle Island. *island* Galápagos Islands, Ecuador, E Pacific Ocean
Isaccea 108 D4 Tulcea, E Romania
Isachsen 37 F1 Ellef Ringnes Island, Nunavut, N Canada
Ísafjörður 83 E4 Vestfirðhir, NW Iceland
Isbarta *see* Isparta
Isca Damnoniorum *see* Exeter
Ise 131 C6 Mie, Honshū, SW Japan
Iseghem *see* Izegem
Isère 91 D5 *river* E France
Isernia 97 D5 *var.* Æsernia. Molise, C Italy
Ise-wan 131 C6 *bay* S Japan
Isfahan *see* Esfahān
Isha Baydhabo *see* Baydhabo
Ishigaki-jima 130 A4 *island* Sakishima-shotō, SW Japan
Ishikari-wan 130 C2 *bay* Hokkaidō, NE Japan
Ishim 114 C4 Tyumenskaya Oblast', C Russia
Ishinomaki 130 D4 *var.* Isinomaki. Miyagi, Honshū, C Japan
Ishkāshim 123 F3 *var.* Ishkoshim. NE Afghanistan
Ishkoshim *see* Ishkāshim
Isinomaki *see* Ishinomaki
Isiro 77 E5 Orientale, NE Dem. Rep. Congo
Iskăr *see* Iskŭr
İskenderun 116 D4 *Eng.* Alexandretta. Hatay, S Turkey
İskenderun Körfezi 118 A2 *Eng.* Gulf of Alexandretta. *gulf* S Turkey
Iskur 104 C2 *var.* Iskăr. *river* NW Bulgaria
Yazovir Iskur 104 B2 *prev.* Yazovir Stalin. *reservoir* W Bulgaria
Isla Cristina 92 C4 Andalucía, S Spain
Isla de León *see* San Fernando
Islamabad 134 C1 *country capital* (Pakistan) Federal Capital Territory Islamabad, NE Pakistan
Island/Ísland *see* Iceland
Islay 88 B4 *island* SW Scotland, United Kingdom
Isle 91 B5 *river* W France
Isle of Man 89 B5 *British Crown Dependency* NW Europe
Isles of Scilly 89 B8 *island group* SW England, United Kingdom
Ismailia *see* Al Ismāʻīlīya
Ismâ'iliya *see* Al Ismāʻīlīya
Ismid *see* İzmit
Isnā 72 B2 *var.* Esna. SE Egypt
Isoka 78 D1 Northern, NE Zambia

Isparta 116 B4 *var.* Isbarta. Isparta, SW Turkey
İspir 117 E3 Erzurum, NE Turkey
Israel 119 A7 *off.* State of Israel, *var.* Medinat Israel, *Heb.* Yisrael, Yisra'el. *country* SW Asia
Israel, State of *see* Israel
Issa *see* Vis
Issiq Köl *see* Issyk-Kul', Ozero
Issoire 91 C5 Puy-de-Dôme, C France
Issyk-Kul' *see* Balykchy
Issyk-Kul', Ozero 123 G2 *var.* Issiq Köl, *Kir.* Ysyk-Köl. *lake* E Kyrgyzstan
İstanbul 116 B2 *Bul.* Tsarigrad, *Eng.* Istanbul, *prev.* Constantinople; *anc.* Byzantium. Istanbul, NW Turkey
İstanbul Boğazı 116 B2 *var.* Bosporus Thracius, *Eng.* Bosphorus, Bosporus, *Turk.* Karadeniz Boğazi. *strait* NW Turkey
Istarska Županija *see* Istra
Istra 100 A3 *off.* Istarska Županija. *province* NW Croatia
Istra 100 A3 *Eng.* Istria, *Ger.* Istrien. *cultural region* NW Croatia
Istria/Istrien *see* Istra
Itabuna 63 G3 Bahia, E Brazil
Itagüí 58 B3 Antioquia, W Colombia
Itaipú, Represa de 63 E4 *reservoir* Brazil/Paraguay
Itaituba 63 E2 Pará, NE Brazil
Italia/Italiana, Repubblica/Italian Republic, The *see* Italy
Italian Somaliland *see* Somalia
Italy 96 C3 *off.* The Italian Republic, *It.* Italia, Repubblica Italiana. *country* S Europe
Iténez, Río *see* Guaporé, Rio
Ithaca 41 E3 New York, NE USA
It Hearrenfean *see* Heerenveen
Itoigawa 131 C5 Niigata, Honshū, C Japan
Itseqqortoormiit *see* Ittoqqortoormiit
Ittoqqortoormiit 83 E3 *var.* Itseqqortoormiit, *Dan.* Scoresbysund, *Eng.* Scoresby Sound. Tunu, C Greenland
Iturup, Ostrov 130 E1 *island* Kuril'skiye Ostrova, SE Russia
Itzehoe 94 B2 Schleswig-Holstein, N Germany
Ivalo 84 D2 Lappi. Avveel, Avvil. Lappi, N Finland
Ivanava 107 B7 *Pol.* Janów, Janów Poleski, *Rus.* Ivanovo. Brestskaya Voblasts', SW Belarus
Ivangrad *see* Berane
Ivanhoe 149 C6 New South Wales, SE Australia
Ivano-Frankivs'k 108 C2 *Ger.* Stanislau, *Pol.* Stanisławów, *Rus.* Ivano-Frankovsk; *prev.* Stanislav. Ivano-Frankivs'ka Oblast', W Ukraine
Ivano-Frankovsk *see* Ivano-Frankivs'k
Ivanovo 111 B5 Ivanovskaya Oblast', W Russia
Ivanovo *see* Ivanava
Ivantsevichi/Ivatsevichi *see* Ivatsevichy
Ivatsevichy 107 B6 *Pol.* Iwacewicze, *Rus.* Ivantsevichi, Ivatsevichi. Brestskaya Voblasts', SW Belarus
Ivigtut *see* Ivittuut
Ivittuut 82 B4 *var.* Ivigtut. Kitaa, S Greenland
Iviza *see* Eivissa\Ibiza
Ivory Coast 74 D4 *off.* Republic of Côte d'Ivoire; *var.* Republic of the Ivory Coast; *Fr.* République de la Côte d'Ivoire. *country* W Africa
Ivory Coast, Republic of the *see* Ivory Coast
Ivujivik 38 D1 Québec, NE Canada
Iwacewicze *see* Ivatsevichy
Iwaki 131 D5 Fukushima, Honshū, N Japan
Iwakuni 131 B7 Yamaguchi, Honshū, SW Japan
Iwanai 130 C2 Hokkaidō, NE Japan
Iwate 130 D3 Iwate, Honshū, N Japan
Ixtapa 51 E5 Guerrero, S Mexico
Ixtepec 51 F5 Oaxaca, SE Mexico
Iyo-nada 131 B7 *sea* S Japan
Izabal, Lago de 52 B2 *prev.* Golfo Dulce. *lake* E Guatemala
Izad Khvāst 120 D3 Fārs, C Iran
Izegem 87 A6 *prev.* Iseghem. West-Vlaanderen, W Belgium
Izhevsk 111 D5 *prev.* Ustinov. Udmurtskaya Respublika, NW Russia

Izmail *see* Izmayïl
Izmayïl 108 D4 *Rus.* Izmail. Odes'ka Oblast', SW Ukraine
İzmir 116 A3 *prev.* Smyrna. İzmir, W Turkey
İzmit 116 B2 *var.* Ismid; *anc.* Astacus. Kocaeli, NW Turkey
İznik Gölü 116 B3 *lake* NW Turkey
Izu-hanto 131 D6 *peninsula* Honshū, S Japan
Izu Shichito *see* Izu-shotō
Izu-shoto 131 D6 *var.* Izu Shichito. *island group* S Japan
Izvor 104 B2 Pernik, W Bulgaria
Izyaslav 108 C2 Khmel'nyts'ka Oblast', W Ukraine
Izyum 109 G2 Kharkiv's'ka Oblast', E Ukraine

J

Jabal ash Shifa 120 A4 *desert* NW Saudi Arabia
Jabalpur 135 E4 *prev.* Jubbulpore. Madhya Pradesh, C India
Jabbūl, Sabkhat al 118 B2 *sabkha* NW Syria
Jablah 118 A3 *var.* Jeble, *Fr.* Djéblé. Al Lādhiqīyah, W Syria
Jaca 93 F1 Aragón, NE Spain
Jacaltenango 52 A2 Huehuetenango, W Guatemala
Jackson 42 B2 *state capital* Mississippi, S USA
Jackson 45 H5 Missouri, C USA
Jackson 42 C1 Tennessee, S USA
Jackson Head 151 A6 *headland* South Island, New Zealand
Jacksonville 43 E3 Florida, SE USA
Jacksonville 40 B4 Illinois, N USA
Jacksonville 43 F1 North Carolina, SE USA
Jacksonville 49 G3 Texas, SW USA
Jacmel 54 D3 *var.* Jaquemel. S Haiti
Jacob *see* Nkayi
Jacobabad 134 B3 Sind, SE Pakistan
Jadotville *see* Likasi
Jadransko More/Jadransko Morje *see* Adriatic Sea
Jaén 60 B2 Cajamarca, N Peru
Jaén 92 D4 Andalucía, SW Spain
Jaffna 132 D3 Northern Province, N Sri Lanka
Jagannath *see* Puri
Jagdalpur 135 E5 Chhattīsgarh, C India
Jagdaqi 127 G1 Nei Mongol Zizhiqu, N China
Jagodina 100 D4 *prev.* Svetozarevo. Serbia, C Serbia
Jahra *see* Al Jahrā'
Jailolo *see* Halmahera, Pulau
Jaipur 134 D3 *prev.* Jeypore. *state capital* Rājasthān, N India
Jaisalmer 134 C3 Rājasthān, NW India
Jajce 100 B3 Federacija Bosne I Hercegovine, W Bosnia and Herzegovina
Jakarta 138 C5 *prev.* Djakarta, *Dut.* Batavia. *country capital* (Indonesia) Jawa, C Indonesia
Jakobstad 84 D4 *Fin.* Pietarsaari. Österbotten, W Finland
Jakobstadt *see* Jēkabpils
Jalālābād 123 F4 *var.* Jalalabad, Jelalabad. Nangarhār, E Afghanistan
Jalal-Abad *see* Dzhalal-Abad, Dzhalal-Abadskaya Oblast', Kyrgyzstan
Jalandhar 134 D2 *prev.* Jullundur. Punjab, N India
Jalapa 52 D3 Nueva Segovia, NW Nicaragua
Jalpa 50 D4 Zacatecas, C Mexico
Jālū 71 G3 *var.* Jūlā. NE Libya
Jaluit Atoll 144 D2 *var.* Jālwōj. *atoll* Ralik Chain, S Marshall Islands
Jālwōj *see* Jaluit Atoll
Jamaame 73 D6 *It.* Giamame; *prev.* Margherita. Jubbada Hoose, S Somalia
Jamaica 54 A4 *country* W West Indies
Jamaica 56 A1 *island* W West Indies
Jamaica Channel 54 D3 *channel* Haiti/Jamaica
Jamālpur 135 F3 Bihār, NE India
Jambi 138 B4 *var.* Telanaipura; *prev.* Djambi. Sumatera, W Indonesia
Jamdena *see* Yamdena, Pulau

James River 45 E2 *river* North Dakota/South Dakota, N USA
James River 41 E5 *river* Virginia, NE USA
Jamestown 41 E3 New York, NE USA
Jamestown 45 E2 North Dakota, N USA
Jamestown *see* Holetown
Jammu 134 D2 *prev.* Jummoo. *state capital* Jammu and Kashmir, NW India
Jammu and Kashmir 134 D1 *disputed region* India/Pakistan
Jāmnagar 134 C4 *prev.* Navanagar. Gujarāt, W India
Jamshedpur 135 F4 Jhārkhand, NE India
Jamuna *see* Brahmaputra
Janaúba 63 F3 Minas Gerais, SE Brazil
Janesville 40 B3 Wisconsin, N USA
Janina *see* Ioánnina
Janischken *see* Joniškis
Jankovac *see* Jánoshalma
Jan Mayen 83 F2 *var.* constituent part of Norway. *island* N Atlantic Ocean
Jánoshalma 99 C7 *SCr.* Jankovac. Bács-Kiskun, S Hungary
Janów *see* Ivanava, Belarus
Janów/Janów *see* Jonava, Lithuania
Janów Poleski *see* Ivanava
Japan 130 C4 *var.* Nippon, *Jap.* Nihon. *country* E Asia
Japan, Sea of 130 A4 *var.* East Sea, *Rus.* Yapanskoye More. *sea* NW Pacific Ocean
Japan Trench 125 F1 *trench* NW Pacific Ocean
Japen *see* Yapen, Pulau
Japiim 62 C2 *var.* Máncio Lima. Acre, W Brazil
Japurá, Rio 62 C2 *var.* Río Caquetá, Yapurá. *river* Brazil/Colombia
Japurá, Rio *see* Caquetá, Río
Jaque 53 G5 Darién, SE Panama
Jaquemel *see* Jacmel
Jarablos *see* Jarābulus
Jarābulus 118 C2 *var.* Jarablos, Jerablus, *Fr.* Djérablous. Ḥalab, N Syria
Jarbah, Jazīrat *see* Djerba, Île
Jardines de la Reina, Archipiélago de los 54 B2 *island group* C Cuba
Jarid, Shaṭṭ al *see* Jerid, Chott el
Jarocin 98 C4 Wielkopolskie, C Poland
Jaroslau *see* Jarosław
Jarosław 99 E5 *Ger.* Jaroslau, *Rus.* Yaroslav. Podkarpackie, SE Poland
Jarqo'rg'on 123 E3 *Rus.* Dzharkurgan. Surkhondaryo Viloyati, S Uzbekistan
Jarvis Island 145 G2 *US unincorporated territory* C Pacific Ocean
Jasło 99 D5 Podkarpackie, SE Poland
Jastrzębie-Zdrój 99 C5 Śląskie, S Poland
Jataí 63 E3 Goiás, C Brazil
Jativa *see* Xàtiva
Jauf *see* Al Jawf
Jaunpiebalga 106 D3 NE Latvia
Jaunpur 135 E3 Uttar Pradesh, N India
Java 152 A3 South Dakota, N USA
Javalambre 93 E3 *mountain* S Spain
Java Sea 138 D4 *Ind.* Laut Jawa. *sea* W Indonesia
Java Trench 124 D5 *var.* Sunda Trench. *trench* E Indian Ocean
Jawa, Laut *see* Java Sea
Jawhar 73 D6 *var.* Jowhar, *It.* Giohar. Shabeellaha Dhexe, S Somalia
Jaworów *see* Yavoriv
Jaya, Puncak 139 G4 *prev.* Puntjak Carstensz, Puntjak Sukarno. *mountain* Papua, E Indonesia
Jayapura 139 H4 *var.* Djajapura, *Dut.* Hollandia; *prev.* Kotabaru, Sukarnapura. Papua, E Indonesia
Jay Dairen *see* Dalian
Jayhawker State *see* Kansas
Jāzān 121 B6 *var.* Qīzān, Jīzān. SW Saudi Arabia
Jaz Murian, Hamun-e 120 E4 *lake* SE Iran
Jebba 75 F4 Kwara, W Nigeria
Jebel, Bahr el *see* White Nile
Jeble *see* Jablah
Jedda *see* Jiddah
Jędrzejów 98 D4 *Ger.* Endersdorf. Świętokrzyskie, C Poland
Jefferson City 45 G5 *state capital* Missouri, C USA
Jega 75 F4 Kebbi, NW Nigeria
Jehol *see* Chengde
Jeju-do 129 E4 *Jap.* Saishū; *prev.* Cheju-do, Quelpart. *island* S South Korea

Jeju Strait 129 E4 var. Jeju-haehyŏp;
  prev. Cheju-Strait. strait S South Korea
Jeju-haehyŏp see Jeju Strait
Jēkabpils 106 D4 Ger. Jakobstadt.
  S Latvia
Jelalabad see Jalālābād
Jelenia Góra 98 B4 Ger. Hirschberg,
  Hirschberg im Riesengebirge,
  Hirschberg in Riesengebirge,
  Hirschberg in Schlesien. Dolnośląskie,
  SW Poland
Jelgava 106 C3 Ger. Mitau. C Latvia
Jemappes 87 B6 Hainaut, S Belgium
Jember 138 D5 prev. Djember. Jawa,
  C Indonesia
Jena 94 C4 Thüringen, C Germany
Jengish Chokusu see Tömür Feng
Jenin 119 A6 N West Bank
Jerablus see Jarābulus
Jerada 70 D2 NE Morocco
Jérémie 54 D3 SW Haiti
Jerez see Jeréz de la Frontera, Spain
Jerez de la Frontera 92 C5 var. Jerez;
  prev. Xeres. Andalucía, SW Spain
Jerez de los Caballeros 92 C4
  Extremadura, W Spain
Jericho 119 B7 Ar. Arīḥā, Heb. Yeriḥo.
  E West Bank
Jerid, Chott el 71 E2 var. Shaṭṭ al Jarīd.
  salt lake SW Tunisia
Jersey 89 D8 British Crown Dependency
  Channel Islands, NW Europe
Jerusalem 103 H4 Ar. Al Quds, Al Quds
  ash Sharīf, Heb. Yerushalayim; anc.
  Hierosolyma. country capital (Israel
  - not internationally recognized)
  Jerusalem, NE Israel
Jesenice 95 D7 Ger. Assling.
  NW Slovenia
Jesselton see Kota Kinabalu
Jessore 135 G4 Khulna, W Bangladesh
Jesús María 64 C3 Córdoba,
  C Argentina
Jeypore see Jaipur, Rājasthān, India
Jhānsi 134 D3 Uttar Pradesh, N India
Jhārkhand 135 F4 cultural region
  NE India
Jhelum 134 C2 Punjab, NE Pakistan
Ji see Hebei, China
Ji see Jilin, China
Jiangmen 128 C6 Guangdong, S China
Jiangsu 128 D4 var. Chiang-su, Jiangsu
  Sheng, Kiangsu, Su. province E China
Jiangsu see Nanjing
Jiangsu Sheng see Jiangsu
Jiangxi 128 C6 var. Chiang-hsi, Gan,
  Jiangxi Sheng, Kiangsi. province
  S China
Jiangxi Sheng see Jiangxi
Jiaxing 128 D5 Zhejiang, SE China
Jiayi see Chiayi
Jibuti see Djibouti
Jiddah 121 A5 Eng. Jedda. Makkah,
  W Saudi Arabia
Jih-k'a-tse see Xigazê
Jihlava 99 B5 Ger. Iglau, Pol. Igława.
  Vysočina, S Czech Republic (Czechia)
Jilib 73 D6 It. Gelib. Jubbada Dhexe,
  S Somalia
Jilin 128 E3 var. Chi-lin, Girin, Kirin;
  prev. Yunki, Yunki. Jilin, NE China
Jilin 128 E3 var. Chi-lin, Girin, Ji, Jilin
  Sheng, Kirin. province NE China
Jilin Sheng see Jilin
Jilong see Keelung
Jima 73 C5 var. Jimma, It. Gimma.
  Oromīya, C Ethiopia
Jimbolia 108 A4 Ger. Hatzfeld, Hung.
  Zsombolya. Timiş, W Romania
Jimma see Jima
Jiménez 50 D2 Chihuahua, N Mexico
Jimsar 126 C3 Xinjiang Uygur Zizhiqu,
  NW China
Jin see Shanxi
Jin see Tianjin Shi
Jinan 128 C4 var. Chinan, Chi-nan,
  Tsinan. province capital Shandong,
  E China
Jingdezhen 128 C5 Jiangxi, S China
Jinghong 128 A6 var. Yunjinghong.
  Yunnan, SW China
Jinhua 128 D5 Zhejiang, SE China
Jining 127 F3 Shandong, E China
Jinja 73 C6 S Uganda
Jinotega 52 D3 Jinotega,
  NW Nicaragua
Jinotepe 52 D3 Carazo, SW Nicaragua
Jinsen see Incheon
Jinzhong 128 C4 var. Yuci. Shanxi,
  C China

Jinzhou 128 D3 var. Chin-chou,
  Chinchow; prev. Chinhsien. Liaoning,
  NE China
Jirgalanta see Hovd
Jisr ash Shadadi see Ash Shadādah
Jiu 108 B5 Ger. Schil, Schyl, Hung. Zsil,
  Zsily. river S Romania
Jiujiang 128 C5 Jiangxi, S China
Jixi 129 E2 Heilongjiang, NE China
Jīzān see Jāzān
Jizzax 123 E2 Rus. Dzhizak. Jizzax
  Viloyati, C Uzbekistan
João Belo see Xai-Xai
João Pessoa 63 G2 prev. Paraíba. state
  capital Paraíba, E Brazil
Joazeiro see Juazeiro
Job'urg see Johannesburg
Jo-ch'iang see Ruoqiang
Jodhpur 134 C3 Rājasthān, NW India
Joensuu 85 E5 Pohjois-Karjala,
  SE Finland
Jõetsu 131 C5 var. Zyôetu. Niigata,
  Honshū, C Japan
Jogjakarta see Yogyakarta
Johannesburg 78 D4 var. Egoli,
  Erautini, Gauteng, abbrev. Job'urg.
  Gauteng, NE South Africa
Johannisburg see Pisz
John Day River 46 C3 river Oregon,
  NW USA
John o'Groats 88 C2 N Scotland, United
  Kingdom
Johnston Atoll 143 E1 US
  unincorporated territory C Pacific
  Ocean
Johor Baharu see Johor Bahru
Johor Bahru 138 B3 var. Johor Baharu,
  Johore Bahru. Johor, Peninsular
  Malaysia
Johore Bahru see Johor Bahru
Johore Strait 138 A1 strait Johor,
  Peninsular Malaysia, Malaysia/
  Singapore Asia Andaman Sea/South
  China Sea
Joinvile see Joinville
Joinville 63 E4 var. Joinvile. Santa
  Catarina, S Brazil
Jokkmokk 84 C3 Lapp. Dálvvadis.
  Norrbotten, N Sweden
Jokyakarta see Yogyakarta
Joliet 40 B3 Illinois, N USA
Jonava 106 B4 Ger. Janow, Pol. Janów.
  Kaunas, C Lithuania
Jonesboro 42 B1 Arkansas, C USA
Joniškis 106 C3 Ger. Janischken. Šiauliai,
  N Lithuania
Jönköping 85 B7 Jönköping,
  S Sweden
Jonquière 39 E4 Québec, SE Canada
Joplin 45 F5 Missouri, C USA
Jordan 119 B6 off. Hashemite Kingdom
  of Jordan, Ar. Al Mamlaka al Urduniya
  al Hashemīyah, Al Urdunn; prev.
  Transjordan. country SW Asia
Jordan 119 B5 Ar. Urdunn, Heb.
  HaYarden. river SW Asia
Jorhat 135 H3 Assam, NE India
Jos 75 G4 Plateau, C Nigeria
Joseph Bonaparte Gulf 146 D2 gulf
  N Australia
Jos Plateau 75 G4 plateau C Nigeria
Jotunheimen 85 A5 mountain range
  S Norway
Joûnié 118 A4 var. Junīyah. W Lebanon
Joure 86 D2 Fris. De Jouwer. Fryslân,
  N Netherlands
Joutseno 85 E5 Etelä-Kariala, SE Finland
Jowhar see Jawhar
J.Storm Thurmond Reservoir see Clark
  Hill Lake
Juan Aldama 50 D3 Zacatecas, C Mexico
Juan de Fuca, Strait of 46 A1 strait
  Canada/USA
Juan Fernández, Islas 57 A6 Eng. Juan
  Fernandez Islands. island group
  W Chile
Juan Fernandez Islands see Juan
  Fernández, Islas
Juazeiro 63 G2 prev. Joazeiro. Bahia,
  E Brazil
Juazeiro do Norte 63 G2 Ceará, E Brazil
Juba 73 B5 var. Jūbā. country capital
  (South Sudan) Central Equatoria,
  S South Sudan
Juba 73 D6 Amh. Genalē Wenz, It. Guiba,
  Som. Ganaane, Webi Jubba. river
  Ethiopia/Somalia
Jubba, Webi see Juba
Jubbulpore see Jabalpur
Júcar 93 E3 var. Jucar. river C Spain

Juchitán 51 F5 var. Juchitán de Zaragosa.
  Oaxaca, SE Mexico
Juchitán de Zaragosa see Juchitán
Judayyidat Hāmir 120 B3 Al Anbār,
  S Iraq
Judenburg 95 D7 Steiermark, C Austria
Jugoslavija see Serbia
Juigalpa 52 D3 Chontales, S Nicaragua
Juiz de Fora 63 F4 Minas Gerais,
  SE Brazil
Jujuy see San Salvador de Jujuy
Jūla see Jālū, Libya
Julia Beterrae see Béziers
Juliaca 61 E4 Puno, SE Peru
Juliana Top 59 G3 mountain
  C Suriname
Julianehåb see Qaqortoq
Julio Briga see Bragança
Juliobriga see Logroño
Juliomagus see Angers
Jullundur see Jalandhar
Jumilla 93 E4 Murcia, SE Spain
Jummoo see Jammu
Jumna see Yamuna
Jumporn see Chumphon
Junction City 45 F4 Kansas, C USA
Juneau 36 D4 state capital Alaska, USA
Junín 64 C4 Buenos Aires, E Argentina
Junīyah see Joûnié
Junkseylon see Phuket
Jur 73 B5 river W South Sudan
Jura 90 D4 cultural region E France
Jura 95 A7 var. Jura Mountains.
  mountain range France/Switzerland
Jura 88 B4 island SW Scotland, United
  Kingdom
Jura Mountains see Jura
Jurbarkas 106 B4 Ger. Georgenburg,
  Jurburg. Tauragė, W Lithuania
Jurburg see Jurbarkas
Jūrmala 106 C3 C Latvia
Juruá, Rio 62 C2 var. Río Yuruá. river
  Brazil/Peru
Juruena, Rio 62 D3 river
  W Brazil
Jutiapa 52 B2 Jutiapa, S Guatemala
Juticalpa 52 D2 Olancho, C Honduras
Jutland 63 A7 Den. Jylland. peninsula
  W Denmark
Juvavum see Salzburg
Južna Morava 101 E5 Ger. Südliche
  Morava. river SE Serbia
Juzur Qarqannah see Kerkennah, Îles
Jwaneng 78 C4 Southern, S Botswana
Jylland see Jutland
Jyrgalan see Dzhergalan
Jyväskylä 85 D5 Keski-Suomi, C Finland

K

K2 126 A4 Chin. Qogir Feng, Eng. Mount
  Godwin Austen. mountain China/
  Pakistan
Kaafu Atoll see Male' Atoll
Kaaimanston 59 G3 Sipaliwini,
  N Suriname
Kaakhka see Kaka
Kaala see Caála
Kaamanen 84 D2 Lapp. Gámas. Lappi,
  N Finland
Kaapstad see Cape Town
Kaaresuvanto 84 C3 Lapp. Gárassavon.
  Lappi, N Finland
Kabale 73 B6 SW Uganda
Kabinda 77 D7 Kasai-Oriental, SE Dem.
  Rep. Congo
Kabinda see Cabinda
Kābol see Kabul
Kabompo 78 C2 river W Zambia
Kābul 123 E4 prev. Kābol. country
  capital (Afghanistan) Kābul, E
  Afghanistan
Kabul 123 E4 var. Daryā-ye Kābul. river
  Afghanistan/Pakistan
Kābul, Daryā-ye see Kabul
Kabwe 78 D2 Central, C Zambia
Kachchh, Gulf of 134 B4 var. Gulf of
  Cutch, Gulf of Kutch. gulf W India
Kachchh, Rann of 134 B4 var. Rann of
  Kachh, Rann of Kutch. salt marsh
  India/Pakistan
Kadan Kyun 137 B5 prev. King Island.
  island Myeik Archipelago, S Myanmar
  (Burma)
Kadavu 145 E4 prev. Kandavu. island
  S Fiji
Kadiyivka 109 H3 Rus. Stakhanov.
  Luhans'ka Oblast', E Ukraine

Kadoma 78 D3 prev. Gatooma.
  Mashonaland West, C Zimbabwe
Kadugli 72 B4 Southern Kordofan,
  S Sudan
Kaduna 75 G4 Kaduna, C Nigeria
Kadzhi-Say see Bokonbayevo
Kaédi 74 C3 Gorgol, S Mauritania
Kaffa see Feodosiya
Kafue 78 D2 Lusaka, SE Zambia
Kafue 78 C2 river C Zambia
Kaga Bandoro 76 C4 prev.
  Fort-Crampel. Nana-Grébizi, C Central
  African Republic
Kagan see Kogon
Kāghet 74 D1 var. Karet. physical region
  N Mauritania
Kagi see Chiayi
Kagoshima 131 B8 var. Kagosima.
  Kagoshima, Kyūshū, SW Japan
Kagoshima-wan 131 A8 bay SW Japan
Kagosima see Kagoshima
Kagul see Cahul
Darya-ye Kahmard 123 E4 prev.
  Darya-i-surkhab. river NE Afghanistan
Kahramanmaraş 116 D4 var. Kahraman
  Maraş, Maraş, Marash.
  Kahramanmaraş, S Turkey
Kaiapoi 151 C6 Canterbury, South
  Island, New Zealand
Kaifeng 128 C4 Henan, C China
Kai, Kepulauan 139 F4 prev. Kei Islands.
  island group Maluku, SE Indonesia
Kaikohe 150 C2 Northland, North
  Island, New Zealand
Kaikoura 151 C5 Canterbury, South
  Island, New Zealand
Kaikoura Peninsula 151 C5 peninsula
  South Island, New Zealand
Kainji Lake see Kainji Reservoir
Kainji Reservoir 75 F4 var. Kainji Lake.
  reservoir W Nigeria
Kaipara Harbour 150 C2 harbour North
  Island, New Zealand
Kairouan 71 E2 var. Al Qayrawān.
  E Tunisia
Kaisaria see Kayseri
Kaiserslautern 95 A5 Rheinland-Pfalz,
  SW Germany
Kaišiadorys 107 B5 Kaunas, S Lithuania
Kaitaia 150 C2 Northland, North Island,
  New Zealand
Kajaani 84 E4 Swe. Kajana. Oulu,
  C Finland
Kajan see Kayan, Sungai
Kajana see Kajaani
Kajisay see Bokonbayevo
Kaka 122 C2 Rus. Kaakhka. Ahal
  Welaýaty, S Turkmenistan
Kake 36 D4 Kupreanof Island, Alaska,
  USA
Kakhovka 109 F4 Khersons'ka Oblast',
  S Ukraine
Kakhovs'ke Vodoskhovyshche 109 F4
  Rus. Kakhovskoye Vodokhranilishche.
  reservoir SE Ukraine
Kakhovskoye Vodokhranilishche see
  Kakhovs'ke Vodoskhovyshche
Kākināda 132 D1 prev. Cocanada.
  Andhra Pradesh, E India
Kakshaal-Too, Khrebet see
  Kokshaal-Tau
Kaktovik 36 D2 Alaska, USA
Kalaallit Nunaat see Greenland
Kalaburagi 132 C1 prev. Gulbarga.
  Karnātaka, C India
Kalahari Desert 78 B4 desert Southern
  Africa
Kalaikhum see Qal'aikhum
Kalámai see Kalámata
Kalamariá 104 B4 Kentrikí Makedonía,
  N Greece
Kalamás 104 A4 var. Thiamis; prev.
  Thýamis. river W Greece
Kalámata 105 B6 prev. Kalámai.
  Pelopónnisos, S Greece
Kalamazoo 40 C3 Michigan, N USA
Kalambaka see Kalampáka
Kálamos 105 C5 Attikí, C Greece
Kalampáka 104 A4 var. Kalambaka.
  Thessalía, C Greece
Kalanchak 109 F4 Khersons'ka Oblast',
  S Ukraine
Kalarash see Călăraşi
Kalasin 136 D4 var. Muang Kalasin.
  Kalasin, E Thailand
Kalat 134 B2 var. Kelat, Khelat.
  Baluchistan, SW Pakistan
Kalāt see Qalāt
Kalbarri 147 A5 Western Australia
Kalecik 116 C3 Ankara, N Turkey

Kalemie 77 E6 prev. Albertville. Katanga, SE Dem. Rep. Congo
Kale Sultanie see Çanakkale
Kalgan see Zhangjiakou
Kalgoorlie 147 B6 Western Australia
Kalima 77 D6 Maniema, E Dem. Rep. Congo
Kalimantan 138 D4 Eng. Indonesian Borneo. geopolitical region Borneo, C Indonesia
Kalinin see Tver'
Kaliningrad 106 A4 Kaliningradskaya Oblast', W Russia
Kaliningrad see Kaliningradskaya Oblast'
Kaliningradskaya Oblast' 106 B4 var. Kaliningrad. province and enclave W Russia
Kalinkavichy 107 C7 Rus. Kalinkovichi. Homyel'skaya Voblasts', SE Belarus
Kalinkovichi see Kalinkavichy
Kalisch/Kalish see Kalisz
Kalispell 44 B1 Montana, NW USA
Kalisz 98 C4 Ger. Kalisch, Rus. Kalish; anc. Calisia. Wielkopolskie, C Poland
Kalix 84 D4 Norrbotten, N Sweden
Kalixälven 84 D3 river N Sweden
Kallaste 106 E3 Ger. Krasnogor. Tartumaa, SE Estonia
Kallavesi 85 E5 lake SE Finland
Kalloní 105 D5 Lésvos, E Greece
Kalmar 85 C7 var. Calmar. Kalmar, S Sweden
Kalmthout 87 C5 Antwerpen, N Belgium
Kalpáki 104 A4 Ípeiros, W Greece
Kalpeni Island 132 B3 island Lakshadweep, India, N Indian Ocean
Kaltdorf see Pruszków
Kaluga 111 B5 Kaluzhskaya Oblast', W Russia
Kalush 108 C2 Pol. Kałusz. Ivano-Frankivs'ka Oblast', W Ukraine
Kałusz see Kalush
Kalutara 132 C3 Western Province, SW Sri Lanka
Kalvarija 107 B5 Pol. Kalwaria. Marijampolė, S Lithuania
Kalwaria see Kalvarija
Kalyān 134 C5 Mahārāshtra, W India
Kálymnos 105 D6 var. Kálimnos. island Dodekánisa, Greece, Aegean Sea
Kama 110 D4 river NW Russia
Kamarang 59 F3 W Guyana
Kambryk see Cambrai
Kamchatka 115 G3 Eng. Kamchatka. peninsula E Russia
Kamchatka see Kamchatka, Poluostrov
Kamenets-Podol'skiy see Kam"yanets'-Podil's'kyy
Kamenka Dneprovskaya see Kam"yanka-Dniprovs'ka
Kamenskoye see Kam"yans'ke
Kamensk-Shakhtinskiy 111 B6 Rostovskaya Oblast', SW Russia
Kamina 77 D7 Katanga, S Dem. Rep. Congo
Kamishli see Al Qāmishlī
Kamloops 37 E5 British Columbia, SW Canada
Kammu Seamount 152 C2 guyot N Pacific Ocean
Kampala 73 B6 country capital (Uganda) S Uganda
Kampong Cham 137 D6 Khmer. Kâmpóng Cham. Kampong Cham, C Cambodia
Kâmpóng Cham see Kampong Cham
Kampong Chhang 137 D6 Khmer. Kâmpóng Chhnăng. Kampong Chhang, C Cambodia
Kâmpóng Chhnăng see Kampong Chhang
Kampong Speu 137 D6 Khmer. Kâmpóng Spœ. Kampong Speu, S Cambodia
Kâmpóng Spœ see Kampong Speu
Kampong Thom 137 D6 Khmer. Kâmpóng Thum, prev. Trâpeăng Vêng. Kampong Thom, C Cambodia
Kâmpóng Thum see Kampong Thom
Kâmpóng Trâbêk 137 D6 prev. Phumĭ Kâmpóng Trâbêk, Phum Kompong Trabek. Kampong Thom, C Cambodia
Kampot 137 D6 Khmer. Kâmpôt. Kampot, SW Cambodia
Kâmpôt see Kampot
Kampuchea see Cambodia
Kampuchea, Democratic see Cambodia
Kampuchea, People's Democratic Republic of see Cambodia

Kam"yanets'-Podil's'kyy 108 C3 Rus. Kamenets-Podol'skiy. Khmel'nyts'ka Oblast', W Ukraine
Kam"yanka-Dniprovs'ka 109 F3 Rus. Kamenka Dneprovskaya. Zaporiz'ka Oblast', SE Ukraine
Kam"yans'ke 109 F3 Rus. Dniprodzerzhyns'k, prev. Kamenskoye. Dnipropetrovs'ka Oblast', E Ukraine
Kamyshin 111 B6 Volgogradskaya Oblast', SW Russia
Kanaky see New Caledonia
Kananga 77 D6 prev. Luluabourg. Kasai-Occidental, S Dem. Rep. Congo
Kanara see Karnātaka
Kanash 111 C5 Chuvashskaya Respublika, W Russia
Kanazawa 131 C5 Ishikawa, Honshū, SW Japan
Kanbe 136 B4 Yangon, SW Myanmar (Burma)
Kānchipuram 132 C2 prev. Conjeeveram. Tamil Nādu, SE India
Kandahār 123 E5 Per. Qandahār. Kandahār, S Afghanistan
Kandalakša see Kandalaksha
Kandalaksha 110 D2 var. Kandalaksa, Fin. Kantalahti. Murmanskaya Oblast', NW Russia
Kandangan 138 D4 Borneo, C Indonesia
Kandau see Kandava
Kandava 106 C3 Ger. Kandau. W Latvia
Kandavu see Kadavu
Kandi 75 F4 N Benin
Kandy 132 D3 Central Province, C Sri Lanka
Kane Fracture Zone 66 B4 fracture zone NW Atlantic Ocean
Kāne'ohe 47 A8 var. Kaneohe. O'ahu, Hawaii, USA, C Pacific Ocean
Kanestron, Akrotírio see Palioúri, Akrotírio
Kanëv see Kaniv
Kanevskoye Vodokhranilishche see Kaniv's'ke Vodoskhovyshche
Kangān see Bandar-e Kangān
Kangaroo Island 149 A7 island South Australia
Kangertittivaq 83 E4 Dan. Scoresby Sund. fjord E Greenland
Kangikajik 83 E4 var. Kap Brewster. headland E Greenland
Kaniv 109 E2 Rus. Kanëv. Cherkas'ka Oblast', C Ukraine
Kaniv's'ke Vodoskhovyshche 109 E2 Rus. Kanevskoye Vodokhranilishche. reservoir C Ukraine
Kanjiža 100 D2 Ger. Altkanischa, Hung. Magyarkanizsa, Ókanizsa; prev. Stara Kanjiža. Vojvodina, N Serbia
Kankaanpää 85 D5 Satakunta, SW Finland
Kankakee 40 B3 Illinois, N USA
Kankan 74 D4 E Guinea
Kannur 132 B2 var. Cannanore. Kerala, SW India
Kano 75 G4 Kano, N Nigeria
Kānpur 135 E3 Eng. Cawnpore. Uttar Pradesh, N India
Kansas 45 F5 off. State of Kansas, also known as Jayhawker State, Sunflower State. state C USA
Kansas City 45 F4 Kansas, C USA
Kansas City 45 F4 Missouri, C USA
Kansk 115 E4 Krasnoyarskiy Kray, S Russia
Kansu see Gansu
Kantalahti see Kandalaksha
Kántanos 105 C7 Kríti, Greece, E Mediterranean Sea
Kantemirovka 111 B6 Voronezhskaya Oblast', W Russia
Kantipur see Kathmandu
Kanton 145 F3 var. Abariringa, Canton Island; prev. Mary Island. atoll Phoenix Islands, C Kiribati
Kanye 78 C4 Southern, SE Botswana
Kaohsiung 129 D6 var. Gaoxiong, Jap. Takao, Takow. S Taiwan
Kaolack 74 B3 var. Kaolak. W Senegal
Kaolak see Kaolack
Kaolan see Lanzhou
Kaoma 78 C2 Western, W Zambia
Kapelle 87 B5 Zeeland, SW Netherlands
Kapellen 87 C5 Antwerpen, N Belgium
Kapka, Massif du 76 C2 mountain range E Chad
Kaplangky, Plato see Gaplaňgyr Platosy
Kapoeas see Kapuas, Sungai

Kapoeta 73 C5 Eastern Equatoria, SE South Sudan
Kaposvár 99 C7 Somogy, SW Hungary
Kappeln 94 B2 Schleswig-Holstein, N Germany
Kapronca see Koprivnica
Kapstad see Cape Town
Kapsukas see Marijampolė
Kaptsevichy 107 C7 Rus. Koptsevichi. Homyel'skaya Voblasts', SE Belarus
Kapuas, Sungai 138 C4 prev. Kapoeas. river Borneo, C Indonesia
Kapuskasing 38 C4 Ontario, S Canada
Kapyl' 107 C6 Rus. Kopyl'. Minskaya Voblasts', C Belarus
Kara-Balta 123 F2 Chuyskaya Oblast', N Kyrgyzstan
Karabil', Vozvyshennost' see Garabil Belentligi
Kara-Bogaz-Gol, Zaliv see Garabogaz Aylagy
Karabük 116 C2 Karabük, NW Turkey
Karachi 134 B3 Sind, SE Pakistan
Karácsonkő see Piatra-Neamţ
Karadeniz see Black Sea
Karadeniz Boğazı see İstanbul Boğazı
Karaferiye see Véroia
Karaganda see Karagandy
Karagandy 114 C4 prev. Karaganda, Kaz. Qaraghandy. Karagandy, C Kazakhstan
Karaginskiy, Ostrov 115 H2 island E Russia
Karagumskiy Kanal see Garagum Kanaly
Karak see Al Karak
Kara-Kala see Magtymguly
Karakax see Moyu
Karakılısse see Ağrı
Karakol 123 G2 var. Karakolka. Issyk-Kul'skaya Oblast', NE Kyrgyzstan
Karakol 123 G2 prev. Przheval'sk. Issyk-Kul'skaya Oblast', NE Kyrgyzstan
Karakolka see Karakol
Karakoram Range 134 D1 mountain range C Asia
Karaköse see Ağrı
Karakul' see Qarokŭl, Tajikistan
Kara Kum see Garagum
Kara Kum Canal/Karakumskiy Kanal see Garagum Kanaly
Karakumy, Peski see Garagum
Karamai see Karamay
Karaman 116 C4 Karaman, S Turkey
Karamay 126 B2 var. Karamai, Kelamayi; prev. Chin. K'o-la-ma-i. Xinjiang Uygur Zizhiqu, NW China
Karamea Bight 151 B5 gulf South Island, New Zealand
Karapelit 104 E1 Rom. Stejarul. Dobrich, NE Bulgaria
Kara-Say 123 G2 Issyk-Kul'skaya Oblast', NE Kyrgyzstan
Karasburg 78 B4 Karas, S Namibia
Kara Sea 114 D2 Eng. Kara Sea. sea Arctic Ocean
Kara Sea see Karskoye More
Kara Strait 110 E2 Eng. Kara Strait. strait N Russia
Kara Strait see Karskiye Vorota, Proliv
Karatau 114 C5 Kaz. Qarataū. Zhambyl, S Kazakhstan
Karavás 105 B7 Kýthira, S Greece
Karbalā' 120 B3 var. Kerbala, Kerbela. Karbalā', S Iraq
Kardeljevo see Ploče
Kardhítsa see Kardítsa
Karditsa 105 B5 var. Kardhítsa. Thessalía, C Greece
Kärdla 106 C2 Ger. Kertel. Hiiumaa, W Estonia
Karet see Kāghet
Kargı 116 C2 Çorum, N Turkey
Kargilik see Yecheng
Kariba 78 D2 Mashonaland West, N Zimbabwe
Kariba, Lake 78 D3 reservoir Zambia/Zimbabwe
Karibib 78 B3 Erongo, C Namibia
Karies see Karyés
Karigasniemi 84 D2 Lapp. Garegegasnjárga. Lappi, N Finland
Karimata, Selat 138 C4 strait W Indonesia
Karimnagar 134 D5 Telangana, C India
Karin 72 D4 Woqooyi Galbeed, N Somalia
Kariot see Ikaría
Káristos see Kárystos
Karkinits'ka Zatoka 109 E4 Rus. Karkinitskiy Zaliv. gulf S Ukraine

Karkinitskiy Zaliv see Karkinits'ka Zatoka
Karkük see Kirkük
Karleby see Kokkola
Karl-Marx-Stadt see Chemnitz
Karlö see Hailuoto
Karlovac 100 B3 Ger. Karlstadt, Hung. Károlyváros. Karlovac, C Croatia
Karlovy Vary 99 A5 Ger. Karlsbad; prev. Eng. Carlsbad. Karlovarský Kraj, W Czech Republic (Czechia)
Karlsbad see Karlovy Vary
Karlsburg see Alba Iulia
Karlskrona 85 C7 Blekinge, S Sweden
Karlsruhe 95 B6 var. Carlsruhe. Baden-Württemberg, SW Germany
Karlstad 85 B6 Värmland, C Sweden
Karlstadt see Karlovac
Karnāl 134 D2 Haryāna, N India
Karnātaka 132 C1 var. Kanara; prev. Maisur, Mysore. cultural region W India
Karnobat 104 D2 Burgas, E Bulgaria
Karnul see Kurnool
Karol see Carei
Károly-Fehérvár see Alba Iulia
Károlyváros see Karlovac
Karpaten see Carpathian Mountains
Kárpathos 105 E7 Kárpathos, SE Greece
Kárpathos 105 E7 It. Scarpanto; anc. Carpathos, Carpathus. island SE Greece
Karpaty see Carpathian Mountains
Karpenísi 105 B5 prev. Karpenísion. Stereá Elláda, C Greece
Karpenísion see Karpenísi
Karpilovka see Aktsyabrski
Kars 117 F2 var. Qars. Kars, NE Turkey
Karsau see Kārsava
Kārsava 106 D4 Ger. Karsau; prev. Rus. Korsovka. E Latvia
Karshi see Qarshi, Uzbekistan
Karyés 104 C4 var. Karies. Ágion Óros, N Greece
Kárystos 105 C6 var. Káristos. Évvoia, C Greece
Kasai 77 C6 var. Cassai, Kassai. river Angola/Dem. Rep. Congo
Kasaji 77 D7 Katanga, S Dem. Rep. Congo
Kasama 78 D1 Northern, N Zambia
Kasan see Koson
Kāsaragod 132 B2 Kerala, SW India
Kaschau see Košice
Kāshān 120 C3 Eşfahān, C Iran
Kashgar see Kashi
Kashi 126 A3 Chin. Kaxgar, K'o-shih, Uigh. Kashgar. Xinjiang Uygur Zizhiqu, NW China
Kasi see Vārānasi
Kasongo 77 D6 Maniema, E Dem. Rep. Congo
Kasongo-Lunda 77 C7 Bandundu, SW Dem. Rep. Congo
Kásos 105 D7 island S Greece
Kaspiy Mangy Oypaty see Caspian Depression
Kaspiysk 111 B8 Respublika Dagestan, SW Russia
Kaspiyskoye More/Kaspiy Tengizi see Caspian Sea
Kassa see Košice
Kassai see Kasai
Kassala 72 C4 Kassala, E Sudan
Kassel 94 B4 prev. Cassel. Hessen, C Germany
Kasserine 71 E2 var. Al Qaşrayn, W Tunisia
Kastamoni 116 C2 var. Castamoni, Kastamuni. Kastamonu, N Turkey
Kastamuni see Kastamoni
Kastaneá see Kastaniá
Kastaniá 104 B4 prev. Kastaneá. Kentrikí Makedonía, N Greece
Kastélli see Kíssamos
Kastoría 104 B4 Dytikí Makedonía, N Greece
Kástro 105 C6 Sífnos, Kykládes, Greece, Aegean Sea
Kastsyukovichy 107 E7 Rus. Kostyukovichi. Mahilyowskaya Voblasts', E Belarus
Kastsyukowka 107 D7 Rus. Kostyukovka. Homyel'skaya Voblasts', SE Belarus
Kasulu 73 B7 Kigoma, W Tanzania
Kasumiga-ura 131 D5 lake Honshū, S Japan

Katahdin, Mount *41 G1 mountain* Maine, NE USA

Katalla *36 C3* Alaska, USA

Katana *see* Qaṭanā

Katanning *147 B7* Western Australia

Katawaz *see* Zarghūn Shahr

Katchall Island *133 F3 island* Nicobar Islands, India, NE Indian Ocean

Kateríni *104 B4* Kentrikí Makedonía, N Greece

Katha *136 B2* Sagaing, N Myanmar (Burma)

Katherine *148 A2* Northern Territory, N Australia

Kathmandu *124 C3 prev.* Kantipur. *country capital* (Nepal) Central, C Nepal

Katikati *150 D3* Bay of Plenty, North Island, New Zealand

Katima Mulilo *78 C3* Caprivi, NE Namibia

Katiola *74 D4* C Ivory Coast

Káto Achaḯa *105 B5 var.* Kato Ahaia, Káto Akhaía. Dytikí Elláda, S Greece

Kato Ahaia/Káto Akhaía *see* Káto Achaḯa

Katoúna *105 A5* Dytikí Elláda, C Greece

Katowice *99 C5 Ger.* Kattowitz. Śląskie, S Poland

Katsina *75 G3* Katsina, N Nigeria

Kattakurgan *see* Kattaqo'rg'on

Kattaqo'rg'on *123 E2 Rus.* Kattakurgan. Samarqand Viloyati, C Uzbekistan

Kattavía *105 E7* Ródos, Dodekánisa, Greece, Aegean Sea

Kattegat *85 B7 Dan.* Kattegatt. *strait* N Europe

Kattegatt *see* Kattegat

Kattowitz *see* Katowice

Kaua'i *47 A1 var.* Kauai. *island* Hawaiian Islands, Hawaii, USA, C Pacific Ocean

Kauai *see* Kaua'i

Kauen *see* Kaunas

Kaufbeuren *95 C6* Bayern, S Germany

Kaunas *106 B4 Ger.* Kauen, *Pol.* Kowno; *prev. Rus.* Kovno. Kaunas, C Lithuania

Kavadar *see* Kavadarci

Kavadarci *101 E6 Turk.* Kavadar. C Macedonia

Kavaja *see* Kavajë

Kavajë *101 C6 It.* Cavaia, Kavaja. Tiranë, W Albania

Kavakli *see* Topolovgrad

Kavála *104 C3 prev.* Kaválla. Anatolikí Makedonía kai Thráki, NE Greece

Kávali *132 D2* Andhra Pradesh, E India

Kaválla *see* Kavála

Kavango *see* Cubango/Okavango

Kavaratti Island *132 A3 island* Lakshadweep, Lakshadweep, SW India Asia N Indian Ocean

Kavarna *104 E2* Dobrich, NE Bulgaria

Kavengo *see* Cubango/Okavango

Kavir, Dasht-e *120 D3 var.* Great Salt Desert. *salt pan* N Iran

Kavkaz *see* Caucasus

Kawagoe *131 D5* Saitama, Honshū, S Japan

Kawasaki *130 A2* Kanagawa, Honshū, S Japan

Kawerau *150 E3* Bay of Plenty, North Island, New Zealand

Kaxgar *see* Kashi

Kaya *75 E3* C Burkina Faso

Kayan *136 B4* Yangon, SW Myanmar (Burma)

Kayan, Sungai *138 D3 prev.* Kajan. *river* Borneo, C Indonesia

Kayes *74 C3* Kayes, W Mali

Kayseri *116 C3 var.* Kaisaria; *anc.* Caesarea Mazaca, Mazaca. Kayseri, C Turkey

Kazach'ye *115 F2* Respublika Sakha (Yakutiya), NE Russia

Kazakhskaya SSR/Kazakh Soviet Socialist Republic *see* Kazakhstan

Kazakhstan *114 B4 off.* Republic of Kazakhstan, *var.* Kazakhstan, *Kaz.* Qazaqstan, Qazaqstan Respublikasy; *prev.* Kazakh Soviet Socialist Republic, *Rus.* Kazakhskaya SSR. *country* C Asia

Kazakhstan, Republic of *see* Kazakhstan

Kazakh Uplands *114 C4 Eng.* Kazakh Uplands, Kirghiz Steppe. *uplands* C Kazakhstan

Kazakh Uplands *see* Saryarka

Kazakstan *see* Kazakhstan

Kazan' *111 C5* Respublika Tatarstan, W Russia

Kazandzhik *see* Bereket

Kazanlik *see* Kazanlŭk

Kazanlŭk *104 D2 prev.* Kazanlik. Stara Zagora, C Bulgaria

Kazatin *see* Kozyatyn

Kazbegi *see* Kazbek

Kazbek *117 F1 var.* Kazbegi, *Geor.* Mqinvartsveri. *mountain* N Georgia

Käzerün *120 D4* Färs, S Iran

Kazvin *see* Qazvin

Kéa *105 C6 var.* Tziá, Kéos; *anc.* Ceos. *island* Kykládes, Greece, Aegean Sea

Kea, Mauna *47 B8 mountain* Hawaii, USA

Kéamu *see* Aneityum

Kearney *45 E4* Nebraska, C USA

Keban Baraji *117 E3 reservoir* C Turkey

Kebkabiya *72 A4* Northern Darfur, W Sudan

Kebnekaise *84 C3 Lapp.* Giebnegáisi. *mountain* N Sweden

Kecskemét *99 D7* Bács-Kiskun, C Hungary

Kediri *138 D5* Jawa, C Indonesia

Kędzierzyn-Kozle *99 C5 Ger.* Heydebrech. Opolskie, S Poland

Keelung *129 D6 var.* Chilung, Jilong; *Jap.* Kirun, Kirun'; *prev. Sp.* Santissima Trinidad. N Taiwan

Keetmanshoop *78 B4* Karas, S Namibia

Kefallinía *see* Kefalloniá

Kefalloniá *105 A5 var.* Kefallinía. *island* Iónia Nisiá, Greece, C Mediterranean Sea

Kefe *see* Feodosiya

Kegel *see* Keila

Kehl *95 A6* Baden-Württemberg, SW Germany

Kei Islands *see* Kai, Kepulauan

Keijō *see* Seoul

Keila *106 D2 Ger.* Kegel. Harjumaa, NW Estonia

Keïta *75 F3* Tahoua, C Niger

Keith *149 B7* South Australia

Kĕk-Art *123 G2 prev.* Alaykel', Alay-Kuu. Oshskaya Oblast', SW Kyrgyzstan

Kékes *99 C6 mountain* N Hungary

Kelamayi *see* Karamay

Kelang *see* Klang

Kelat *see* Kalat

Kelifskiy Uzboy *see* Kelif Uzboýy

Kelif Uzboýy *122 D3 Rus.* Kelifskiy Uzboy. *salt marsh* E Turkmenistan

Kelkit Çayı *117 E3 river* N Turkey

Kelmė *106 B4* Lithuania, NW Lithuania

Kélo *76 B4* Tandjilé, SW Chad

Kelowna *37 E5* British Columbia, SW Canada

Kelso *46 B2* Washington, NW USA

Keltsy *see* Kielce

Keluang *138 B3 var.* Kluang. Johor, Peninsular Malaysia

Kem' *110 B3* Respublika Kareliya, NW Russia

Kemah *117 E3* Erzincan, E Turkey

Kemaman *see* Cukai

Kemerovo *114 D4 prev.* Shcheglovsk. Kemerovskaya Oblast', C Russia

Kemi *84 D4* Lappi, NW Finland

Kemijärvi *84 D3 Swe.* Kemiträsk. Lappi, N Finland

Kemijoki *84 D3 river* NW Finland

Kemin *123 G2 prev.* Bystrovka. Chuyskaya Oblast', N Kyrgyzstan

Kemins Island *see* Nikumaroro

Kemiträsk *see* Kemijärvi

Kemmuna *102 A5 var.* Comino. *island* C Malta

Kempele *84 D4* Pohjois-Pohjanmaa, C Finland

Kempten *95 B7* Bayern, S Germany

Kendal *89 D5* NW England, United Kingdom

Kendari *139 E4* Sulawesi, C Indonesia

Kenedy *49 G4* Texas, SW USA

Kenema *74 C4* SE Sierra Leone

Këneurgench *see* Köneürgenç

Kenge *77 C6* Bandundu, SW Dem. Rep. Congo

Kengtung *136 C3 pev.* Keng Tung. Shan State, E Myanmar (Burma)

Keng Tung *see* Kengtung

Kénitra *70 C2 prev.* Port-Lyautey. NW Morocco

Kennett *45 H5* Missouri, C USA

Kennewick *46 C2* Washington, NW USA

Kenora *38 A3* Ontario, S Canada

Kenosha *40 B3* Wisconsin, N USA

Kentau *114 B5* Yuzhnyy Kazakhstan, S Kazakhstan

Kentucky *40 C5 off.* Commonwealth of Kentucky, *also known as* Bluegrass State. *state* C USA

Kentucky Lake *40 B5 reservoir* Kentucky/Tennessee, S USA

Kenya *73 C6 off.* Republic of Kenya. *country* E Africa

Kenya, Mount *see* Kirinyaga

Kenya, Republic of *see* Kenya

Keokuk *45 G4* Iowa, C USA

Kéos *see* Kéa

Kępno *98 C4* Wielkopolskie, C Poland

Keppel Island *see* Niuatoputapu

Kerak *see* Al Karak

Kerala *132 C2 cultural region* S India

Kerasunt *see* Giresun

Keratéa *105 C6 var.* Keratea. Attikí, C Greece

Keratea *see* Keratéa

Kerbala/Kerbela *see* Karbala'

Kerch *109 G5 Rus.* Kerch'. Avtonomna Respublika Krym, SE Ukraine

Kerch' *see* Kerch

Kerchens'ka Protska/Kerchenskiy Proliv *see* Kerch Strait

Kerch Strait *109 G4 var.* Bosporus Cimmerius, Enikale Strait, *Rus.* Kerchenskiy Proliv, *Ukr.* Kerchens'ka Protska. *strait* Black Sea/Sea of Azov

Keremitlik *see* Lyulyakovo

Kerguelen *141 C7 island* C French Southern and Antarctic Lands

Kerguelen Plateau *141 E7 undersea plateau* S Indian Ocean

Keri *105 A6* Zákynthos, Iónia Nisiá, Greece, C Mediterranean Sea

Kerikeri *150 D2* Northland, North Island, New Zealand

Kerkennah, Îles *102 D4 var.* Kerkenna Islands, *Ar.* Juzur Qarqannah. *island group* E Tunisia

Kerkenna Islands *see* Kerkennah, Îles

Kerki *see* Atamyrat

Kérkira *see* Kérkyra

Kerkrade *87 D6* Limburg, SE Netherlands

Kerkuk *see* Kirkūk

Kérkyra *104 A4 var.* Kérkira, *Eng.* Corfu. Kérkyra, Iónia Nisiá, Greece, C Mediterranean Sea

Kermadec Islands *152 C4 island group* New Zealand, SW Pacific Ocean

Kermadec Trench *143 E4 trench* SW Pacific Ocean

Kermān *120 D3 var.* Kirman; *anc.* Carmana. Kermān, C Iran

Kermānshāh *120 C3 var.* Qahremānshahr; *prev.* Bākhtarān. Kermānshāhān, W Iran

Kerrville *49 F4* Texas, SW USA

Kertel *see* Kärdla

Kerulen *127 E2 Chin.* Herlen He, *Mong.* Herlen Gol. *river* China/Mongolia

Kerýneia *see* Kyrenia

Kesennuma *130 D4* Miyagi, Honshū, C Japan

Keszthely *99 C7* Zala, SW Hungary

Ketchikan *36 D4* Revillagigedo Island, Alaska, USA

Kętrzyn *98 D2 Ger.* Rastenburg. Warmińsko-Mazurskie, NE Poland

Kettering *89 D6* C England, United Kingdom

Kettering *40 C4* Ohio, N USA

Keupriya *see* Primorsko

Keuruu *85 D5* Keski-Suomi, C Finland

Keweenaw Peninsula *40 B1 peninsula* Michigan, N USA

Key Largo *43 F5* Key Largo, Florida, SE USA

Keystone State *see* Pennsylvania

Key West *43 E5* Florida Keys, Florida, SE USA

Kezdivásárhely *see* Târgu Secuiesc

Khabarovsk *115 G4* Khabarovskiy Kray, SE Russia

Khachmas *see* Xaçmaz

Khadera *see* Hadera

Khairpur *134 B3* Sind, SE Pakistan

Khalij as Suways *72 B2 var.* Suez, Gulf of. *gulf* NE Egypt

Khalkidhikí *see* Chalkidikí

Khalkís *see* Chalkída

Gulf of Khambhat *134 C4 Eng.* Gulf of Cambay. *gulf* W India

Khamis Mushayt *121 B6 var.* Hamīs Musait. 'Asīr, SW Saudi Arabia

Khānābād *123 E3* Kunduz, NE Afghanistan

Khān al Baghdādī *see* Al Baghdādī

Khandwa *134 D4* Madhya Pradesh, C India

Khanh Hung *see* Soc Trăng

Khaniá *see* Chaniá

Khanka, Lake *129 E2 var.* Hsing-K'ai Hu, Lake Hanka, *Chin.* Xingkai Hu, *Rus.* Ozero Khanka. *lake* China/Russia

Khanka, Ozero *see* Khanka, Lake

Khankendi *see* Xankändi

Khanthabouli *see* Savannakhét

Khanty-Mansiysk *114 C3 prev.* Ostyako-Voguls'k. Khanty-Mansiyskiy Avtonomnyy Okrug-Yugra, C Russia

Khān Yūnis *119 A7 var.* Khān Yūnus. S Gaza Strip

Khān Yūnus *see* Khān Yūnis

Khanzi *see* Ghanzi

Kharagpur *135 F4* West Bengal, NE India

Kharbin *see* Harbin

Kharga *see* Al Khārijah

Khar'kiv *109 G2 Rus.* Khar'kov. Kharkivs'ka Oblast', NE Ukraine

Khar'kov *see* Kharkiv

Kharmanli *104 D3* Khaskovo, S Bulgaria

Khartoum *72 B4 var.* El Khartûm, Khartum. *country capital* (Sudan) Khartoum, C Sudan

Khartum *see* Khartoum

Khasavyurt *111 B8* Respublika Dagestan, SW Russia

Khash, Dasht-e *122 D5 Eng.* Khash Desert. *desert* SW Afghanistan

Khash Desert *see* Khāsh, Dasht-e

Khashim Al Qirba/Khashm al Qirbah *see* Khashm el Girba

Khashm el Girba *72 C4 var.* Khashim Al Qirba, Khashm al Qirbah. Kassala, E Sudan

Khaskovo *104 D3* Khaskovo, S Bulgaria

Khaybar, Kowtal-e *see* Khyber Pass

Khaydarkan *123 F2 var.* Khaydarken. Batkenskaya Oblast', SW Kyrgyzstan

Khaydarken *see* Khaydarkan

Khazar, Bahr-e/Khazar, Daryā-ye *see* Caspian Sea

Khelat *see* Kalat

Kherson *109 E4* Khersons'ka Oblast', S Ukraine

Kheta *115 E2 river* N Russia

Khíos *see* Chíos

Khirbet el 'Aujâ et Taḥtâ *119 E7* E West Bank USA

Khiva/Khiwa *see* Xiva

Khmel'nitskiy *see* Khmel 'nyts'kyy

Khmel 'nyts'kyy *108 C2 Rus.* Khmel'nitskiy; *prev.* Proskurov. Khmel'nyts'ka Oblast', W Ukraine

Khodasy *107 E6 Rus.* Khodosy. Mahilyowskaya Voblasts', E Belarus

Khodoriv *108 C2 Pol.* Chodorów, *Rus.* Khodorov. L'vivs'ka Oblast', NW Ukraine

Khodorov *see* Khodoriv

Khodosy *see* Khodasy

Khodzhent *see* Khujand

Khoi *see* Khvoy

Khojend *see* Khujand

Khokand *see* Qo'qon

Kholm *see* Khulm

Kholm *see* Chełm

Kholon *see* Holon

Khoms *see* Al Khums

Khong Sedone *see* Muang Khôngxédôn

Khon Kaen *136 D4 var.* Muang Khon Kaen. Khon Kaen, E Thailand

Khor *115 G4* Khabarovskiy Kray, SE Russia

Khorat *see* Nakhon Ratchasima

Khorog *see* Khorugh

Khorugh *123 F3 Rus.* Khorog. S Tajikistan

Khotan *see* Hotan

Khouribga *70 B2* C Morocco

Khovd *see* Hovd

Khowst *see* Khōst

Khoy *see* Khvoy

Khoyniki *107 D8* Homyel'skaya Voblasts', SE Belarus

Khrustal'nyy *109 H3 Rus.* Krasnyy Luch. *prev.* Krindachevka. Luhans'ka Oblast', E Ukraine

Khudzhand *see* Khujand

Khujand *123 E2 var.* Khodzhent, Khojend, *Rus.* Khudzhand; *prev.* Leninabad, *Taj.* Leninobod. N Tajikistan

Khulm 123 E3 var. Kholm, Tashqurghan. Balkh, N Afghanistan
Khulna 135 G4 Khulna, SW Bangladesh
Khums see Al Khums
Khust 108 B3 var. Husté, Cz. Chust, Hung. Huszt. Zakarpats'ka Oblast', W Ukraine
Khvoy 120 C2 var. Khoi, Khoy. Āžarbāyjān-e Bākhtari, NW Iran
Khyber Pass 134 C1 var. Kowtal-e Khaybar. pass Afghanistan/Pakistan
Kiangmai see Chiang Mai
Kiang-ning see Nanjing
Kiangsi see Jiangxi
Kiangsu see Jiangsu
Kiáto 105 B6 prev. Kiáton. Pelopónnisos, S Greece
Kiáton see Kiáto
Kiayi see Chiayi
Kibangou 77 B6 Niari, SW Congo
Kibombo 77 D6 Maniema, E Dem. Rep. Congo
Kıbrıs/Kıbrıs Cumhuriyeti see Cyprus
Kičevo 101 D6 W Macedonia
Kidderminster 89 D6 C England, United Kingdom
Kiel 94 B2 Schleswig-Holstein, N Germany
Kielce 98 D4 Rus. Keltsy. Świętokrzyskie, C Poland
Kieler Bucht 94 B2 bay N Germany
Kiev see Kyiv
Kiev Reservoir 109 E1 Eng. Kiev Reservoir, Rus. Kiyevskoye Vodokhranilishche. reservoir N Ukraine
Kiev Reservoir see Kyyivs'ke Vodoskhovyshche
Kiffa 74 C3 Assaba, S Mauritania
Kigali 73 B6 country capital (Rwanda) C Rwanda
Kigoma 73 B7 Kigoma, W Tanzania
Kihnu 106 C2 var. Kihnu Saar, Ger. Kühno. island SW Estonia
Kihnu Saar see Kihnu
Kii-suidō 131 C7 strait S Japan
Kikinda 100 D3 Ger. Grosskikinda, Hung. Nagykikinda; prev. Velika Kikinda. Vojvodina, N Serbia
Kikládhes see Kykládes
Kikwit 77 C6 Bandundu, W Dem. Rep. Congo
Kilien Mountains see Qilian Shan
Kilimane see Quelimane
Kilimanjaro 69 E5 region E Tanzania
Kilimanjaro 73 C7 var. Uhuru Peak. volcano NE Tanzania
Kilingi-Nōmme 106 D3 Ger. Kurkund. Pärnumaa, SW Estonia
Kilis 116 D4 Kilis, S Turkey
Kiliya 108 D4 Rom. Chilia-Nouă. Odes'ka Oblast', SW Ukraine
Kilkenny 89 B6 Ir. Cill Chainnigh. Kilkenny, S Ireland
Kilkís 104 B3 Kentrikí Makedonía, N Greece
Killarney 89 A6 Ir. Cill Airne. Kerry, SW Ireland
Killeen 49 G3 Texas, SW USA
Kilmain see Quelimane
Kilmarnock 88 C4 W Scotland, United Kingdom
Kilwa see Kilwa Kivinje
Kilwa Kivinje 73 C7 var. Kilwa. Lindi, SE Tanzania
Kimberley 78 C4 Northern Cape, C South Africa
Kimberley Plateau 146 C3 plateau Western Australia
Kimch'aek 129 E3 prev. Sŏngjin. E North Korea
Kími see Kými
Kinabalu, Gunung 138 D3 mountain East Malaysia
Kindersley 37 F5 Saskatchewan, S Canada
Kindia 74 C4 Guinée-Maritime, SW Guinea
Kindley Field 42 A4 air base E Bermuda
Kindu 77 D6 prev. Kindu-Port-Empain. Maniema, C Dem. Rep. Congo
Kindu-Port-Empain see Kindu
Kineshma 111 C5 Ivanovskaya Oblast', W Russia
King Abdullah Economic City 121 A5 Makkah, W Saudi Arabia
King Charles Islands see Kong Karls Land
King Christian IX Land see Kong Christian IX Land

King Frederik VI Coast see Kong Frederik VI Kyst
King Frederik VIII Land see Kong Frederik VIII Land
King Island 149 B8 island Tasmania, SE Australia
King Island see Kadan Kyun
Kingisepp see Kuressaare
Kingman 48 A1 Arizona, SW USA
Kingman Reef 145 E2 US territory C Pacific Ocean
Kingsford Smith 148 E2 (Sydney) New South Wales, SE Australia
King's Lynn 89 E6 var. Bishop's Lynn, Kings Lynn, Lynn, Lynn Regis. E England, United Kingdom
Kings Lynn see King's Lynn
King Sound 146 B3 sound Western Australia
Kingsport 43 E1 Tennessee, S USA
Kingston 38 D5 Ontario, SE Canada
Kingston 54 B5 country capital (Jamaica) E Jamaica
Kingston 41 F3 New York, NE USA
Kingston upon Hull 89 D5 var. Hull. E England, United Kingdom
Kingston upon Thames 89 A8 SE England, United Kingdom
Kingstown 55 H4 country capital (Saint Vincent and the Grenadines) Saint Vincent, Saint Vincent and the Grenadines
Kingstown see Dún Laoghaire
Kingsville 49 G5 Texas, SW USA
King William Island 37 F3 island Nunavut, N Canada
Kinneret, Yam see Tiberias, Lake
Kinrooi 87 D5 Limburg, NE Belgium
Kinshasa 77 B6 prev. Léopoldville. country capital (Dem. Rep. Congo) Kinshasa, W Dem. Rep. Congo
Kintyre 88 B4 peninsula W Scotland, United Kingdom
Kinyeti 73 B5 mountain S South Sudan
Kiparissía see Kyparissía
Kipili 73 B7 Rukwa, W Tanzania
Kipushi 77 D8 Katanga, SE Dem. Rep. Congo
Kirdzhali see Kŭrdzhali
Kirghizia see Kyrgyzstan
Kirghiz Range 123 F2 Rus. Kirgizskiy Khrebet; prev. Alexander Range. mountain range Kazakhstan/Kyrgyzstan
Kirghiz SSR see Kyrgyzstan
Kirghiz Steppe see Saryarka
Kirgizskaya SSR see Kyrgyzstan
Kirgizskiy Khrebet see Kirghiz Range
Kiriath-Arba see Hebron
Kiribati 145 F2 off. Republic of Kiribati. country C Pacific Ocean
Kiribati, Republic of see Kiribati
Kırıkhan 116 D4 Hatay, S Turkey
Kırıkkale 116 C3 province C Turkey
Kirin see Jilin
Kirinyaga 73 C6 prev. Mount Kenya. volcano C Kenya
Kirishi 110 B4 var. Kirisi. Leningradskaya Oblast', NW Russia
Kirisi see Kirishi
Kiritimati 145 G2 prev. Christmas Island. atoll Line Islands, E Kiribati
Kirkenes 84 E2 Fin. Kirkkoniemi. Finnmark, N Norway
Kirk-Kilissa see Kırklareli
Kirkkoniemi see Kirkenes
Kirkland Lake 38 D4 Ontario, S Canada
Kırklareli 116 A2 prev. Kirk-Kilissa. Kırklareli, NW Turkey
Kirkpatrick, Mount 154 B3 mountain Antarctica
Kirksville 45 G4 Missouri, C USA
Kirkūk 120 B3 var. Karkūk, Kerkuk. At Ta'mīm, N Iraq
Kirkwall 88 C2 NE Scotland, United Kingdom
Kirkwood 45 G4 Missouri, C USA
Kir Moab/Kir of Moab see Al Karak
Kirov 111 C5 prev. Vyatka. Kirovskaya Oblast', NW Russia
Kirovabad see Gäncä
Kirovakan see Vanadzor
Kirovo-Chepetsk 111 D5 Kirovskaya Oblast', NW Russia
Kirovohrad see Kropyvnyts'kyy
Kirovo see Kropyvnyts'kyy
Kirthar Range 134 B3 mountain range S Pakistan
Kiruna 84 C3 Lapp. Giron. Norrbotten, N Sweden

Kirun/Kirun' see Keelung
Kisalföld see Little Alföld
Kisangani 77 D5 prev. Stanleyville. Orientale, NE Dem. Rep. Congo
Kishinev see Chişinău
Kislovodsk 111 B7 Stavropol'skiy Kray, SW Russia
Kismaayo 73 D6 var. Chisimayu, Kismayu, It. Chisimaio. Jubbada Hoose, S Somalia
Kismayu see Kismaayo
Kíssamos 105 C7 prev. Kastélli. Kríti, Greece, E Mediterranean Sea
Kissidougou 74 C4 Guinée-Forestière, S Guinea
Kissimmee, Lake 43 E4 lake Florida, SE USA
Kistna see Krishna
Kisumu 73 C6 prev. Port Florence. Nyanza, W Kenya
Kisvárda 99 E6 Ger. Kleinwardein. Szabolcs-Szatmár-Bereg, E Hungary
Kita 74 D3 Kayes, W Mali
Kitab see Kitob
Kitakyūshū 131 A7 var. Kitakyūsyū. Fukuoka, Kyūshū, SW Japan
Kitakyūsyū see Kitakyūshū
Kitami 130 D2 Hokkaidō, NE Japan
Kitchener 38 C5 Ontario, S Canada
Kíthnos see Kýthnos
Kitimat 36 D4 British Columbia, SW Canada
Kitinen 84 D3 river N Finland
Kitob 123 E3 Rus. Kitab. Qashqadaryo Viloyati, S Uzbekistan
Kitwe 78 D2 var. Kitwe-Nkana. Copperbelt, C Zambia
Kitwe-Nkana see Kitwe
Kitzbüheler Alpen 95 C7 mountain range W Austria
Kivalina 36 C2 Alaska, USA
Kivalo 84 D3 ridge C Finland
Kivertsi 108 C1 Pol. Kiwerce, Rus. Kivertsy. Volyns'ka Oblast', NW Ukraine
Kivertsy see Kivertsi
Kivu, Lac see Kivu, Lake
Kivu, Lake 77 E6 Fr. Lac Kivu. lake Rwanda/Dem. Rep. Congo
Kiwerce see Kivertsi
Kiyev see Kyiv
Kiyevskoye Vodokhranilishche see Kyyivs'ke Vodoskhovyshche
Kızıl Irmak 116 C3 river C Turkey
Kizil Kum see Kyzyl Kum
Kizyl-Arvat see Serdar
Kjølen see Kölen
Kladno 99 A5 Středočeský, NW Czech Republic (Czechia)
Klagenfurt 95 D7 Slvn. Celovec. Kärnten, S Austria
Klaipėda 106 B3 Ger. Memel. Klaipeda, NW Lithuania
Klamath Falls 46 B4 Oregon, NW USA
Klamath Mountains 46 A4 mountain range California/Oregon, W USA
Klang 138 B3 var. Kelang; prev. Port Swettenham. Selangor, Peninsular Malaysia
Klarälven 85 B6 river Norway/Sweden
Klatovy 99 A5 Ger. Klattau. Plzeňský Kraj, W Czech Republic (Czechia)
Klattau see Klatovy
Klausenburg see Cluj-Napoca
Klazienaveen 86 E2 Drenthe, NE Netherlands
Klein Karas 78 B4 Karas, S Namibia
Kleinwardein see Kisvárda
Kleisoúra 105 A5 Ípeiros, W Greece
Klerksdorp 78 D4 North-West, N South Africa
Klimavichy 107 E7 Rus. Klimovichi. Mahilyowskaya Voblasts', E Belarus
Klimovichi see Klimavichy
Klintsy 111 A5 Bryanskaya Oblast', W Russia
Klisura 104 C2 Plovdiv, C Bulgaria
Ključ 100 B3 Federacija Bosne I Hercegovine, NW Bosnia and Herzegovina
Kłobuck 98 C4 Śląskie, S Poland
Klosters 95 B7 Graubünden, SE Switzerland
Kluang see Keluang
Kluczbork 98 C4 Ger. Kreuzburg, Kreuzburg in Oberschlesien. Opolskie, S Poland

Klyuchevskaya Sopka, Vulkan 115 H3 volcano E Russia
Knin 100 B4 Šibenik-Knin, S Croatia
Knjaževac 100 E4 Serbia, E Serbia
Knokke-Heist 87 A5 West-Vlaanderen, NW Belgium
Knoxville 42 D1 Tennessee, S USA
Knud Rasmussen Land 82 D1 physical region N Greenland
Kobdo see Hovd
Kōbe 131 C6 Hyōgo, Honshū, SW Japan
København 85 B7 Eng. Copenhagen; anc. Hafnia. country capital (Denmark) Sjælland, København, E Denmark
Kobenni 74 D3 Hodh el Gharbi, S Mauritania
Koblenz 95 A5 prev. Coblenz, Fr. Coblence; anc. Confluentes. Rheinland-Pfalz, W Germany
Kobrin see Kobryn
Kobryn 107 A6 Rus. Kobrin. Brestskaya Voblasts', SW Belarus
Kobuleti 117 F2 prev. K'obulet'i. W Georgia
K'obulet'i see Kobuleti
Kočani 101 E6 NE Macedonia
Kočevje 95 D8 Ger. Gottschee. S Slovenia
Koch Bihār 135 G3 West Bengal, NE India
Kochchi see Kochi
Kochi 132 C3 var. Cochin, Kochchi. Kerela SW India
Kōchi 131 B7 var. Kôti. Kōchi, Shikoku, SW Japan
Kochiu see Gejiu
Kodiak 36 C3 Kodiak Island, Alaska, USA
Kodiak Island 36 C3 island Alaska, USA
Koedoes see Kudus
Koeln see Köln
Koepang see Kupang
Ko-erh-mu see Golmud
Koetai see Mahakam, Sungai
Koetaradja see Banda Aceh
Kōfu 131 D5 var. Kōhu. Yamanashi, Honshū, S Japan
Kogarah 148 E2 New South Wales, E Australia
Kogon 122 D2 Rus. Kagan. Buxoro Viloyati, C Uzbekistan
Kohalom see Rupea
Kohīma 135 H3 state capital Nāgāland, E India
Koh I Noh see Büyükağrı Dağı
Kohtla-Järve 106 E2 Ida-Virumaa, NE Estonia
Kōhu see Kōfu
Kokand see Qo'qon
Kokchetav see Kokshetau
Kokkola 84 D4 Swe. Karleby; prev. Swe. Gamlakarleby. Österbotten, W Finland
Koko 75 F4 Kebbi, W Nigeria
Kokomo 40 C4 Indiana, N USA
Koko Nor see Qinghai, China
Koko Nor see Qinghai Hu, China
Kokrines 36 C2 Alaska, USA
Kokshaal-Tau 123 G2 Rus. Khrebet Kakshaal-Too. mountain range China/Kyrgyzstan
Kokshetau 114 C4 Kaz. Kökshetaū; prev. Kokchetav. Akmola, N Kazakhstan
Kökshetaū see Kokshetau
Koksijde 87 A5 West-Vlaanderen, W Belgium
Koksoak 38 D2 river Québec, E Canada
Kokstad 78 D5 KwaZulu/Natal, E South Africa
Kolaka 139 E4 Sulawesi, C Indonesia
K'o-la-ma-i see Karamay
Kola Peninsula 72 C2 Eng. Kola Peninsula. peninsula NW Russia
Kola Peninsula see Kol'skiy Poluostrov
Kolari 84 D3 Lappi, NW Finland
Kolárovo 99 C6 Ger. Gutta; prev. Guta, Hung. Guta. Nitriansky Kraj, SW Slovakia
Kolberg see Kołobrzeg
Kolda 74 C3 S Senegal
Kolding 85 A7 Syddanmark, C Denmark
Kölen 81 E1 Nor. Kjølen. mountain range Norway/Sweden
Kolguyev, Ostrov 110 C2 island NW Russia
Kolhāpur 132 B1 Mahārāshtra, SW India
Kolhumadulu 132 A5 var. Thaa Atoll. atoll S Maldives
Kolín 99 B5 Ger. Kolin. Střední Čechy, C Czech Republic (Czechia)

Kolka 106 C2 NW Latvia
Kolkasrags 106 C2 prev. Eng. Cape
Domesnes. headland NW Latvia
Kolkata 135 G4 prev. Calcutta. West
Bengal, N India
Kollam 132 C3 var. Quilon. Kerala,
SW India
Kolmar see Colmar
Köln 94 A4 var. Koeln, Eng./Fr. Cologne,
prev. Cöln; anc. Colonia Agrippina,
Oppidum Ubiorum. Nordrhein-
Westfalen, W Germany
Kolo 98 C3 Wielkopolskie, C Poland
Kołobrzeg 98 B2 Ger. Kolberg.
Zachodnio-pomorskie, NW Poland
Kolokani 74 D3 Koulikoro, W Mali
Kolomea see Kolomyya
Kolomna 111 B5 Moskovskaya Oblast',
W Russia
Kolomyya 108 C3 Ger. Kolomea.
Ivano-Frankivs'ka Oblast',
W Ukraine
Kolosjoki see Nikel'
Kolozsvár see Cluj-Napoca
Kolpa 100 A2 Ger. Kulpa, SCr. Kupa.
river Croatia/Slovenia
Kolpino 110 B4 Leningradskaya Oblast',
NW Russia
Kólpos Mórfu see Güzelyurt Körfezi
Kolwezi 77 D7 Katanga, S Dem. Rep.
Congo
Kolyma 115 G2 river NE Russia
Komatsu 131 C5 var. Komatu. Ishikawa,
Honshū, SW Japan
Komatu see Komatsu
Kommunizm, Qullai see Ismoili Somoní,
Qullai
Komoé 75 E4 var. Komoé Fleuve. river
E Ivory Coast
Komoé Fleuve see Komoé
Komotau see Chomutov
Komotiní 104 D3 var. Gümüljina, Turk.
Gümülcine. Anatolikí Makedonía kai
Thráki, NE Greece
Kompong Som see Sihanoukville
Komrat see Comrat
Komsomolets, Ostrov 115 E1 island
Severnaya Zemlya, N Russia
Komsomol'sk-na-Amure 115 G4
Khabarovskiy Kray, SE Russia
Kondolovo 104 E3 Burgas, E Bulgaria
Kondopoga 110 B3 Respublika Kareliya,
NW Russia
Kondoz see Kunduz
Köneürgenç 122 C2 var. Köneürgench,
Rus. Këneurgench; prev.
Kunya-Urgench. Daşoguz Welaýaty,
N Turkmenistan
Kong Christian IX Land 82 D4 Eng.
King Christian IX Land. physical region
SE Greenland
Kong Frederik IX Land 82 C3 physical
region SW Greenland
Kong Frederik VIII Land 83 E2 Eng.
King Frederik VIII Land. physical
region NE Greenland
Kong Frederik VI Kyst 82 C4 Eng. King
Frederik VI Coast. physical region
SE Greenland
Kong Karls Land 83 G2 Eng. King
Charles Islands. island group
SE Svalbard
Kongo see Congo (river)
Kongolo 77 D6 Katanga, E Dem. Rep.
Congo
Kongor 73 B5 Jonglei, E South Sudan
Kong Oscar Fjord 83 E3 fjord
E Greenland
Kongsberg 85 B6 Buskerud, S Norway
Kông, Tônlé 137 E2 var. Xê Kong. river
Cambodia/Laos
Kong, Xê see Kông, Tônlé
Königgrätz see Hradec Králové
Königshütte see Chorzów
Konin 98 C3 Ger. Kuhnau.
Weilkopolskie, C Poland
Koninkrijk der Nederlanden see
Netherlands
Konispol 101 C7 var. Konispoli. Vlorë,
S Albania
Konispoli see Konispol
Kónitsa 104 A4 Ípeiros, W Greece
Konitz see Chojnice
Konjic 100 C4 Federacija Bosne I
Hercegovine, S Bosnia and
Herzegovina
Konosha 110 C4 Arkhangel'skaya
Oblast', NW Russia
Konotop 109 F1 Sums'ka Oblast',
NE Ukraine

Konstantinovka see Kostyantynivka
Konstanz 95 B7 var. Constanz, Eng.
Constance, hist. Kostnitz; anc.
Constantia. Baden-Württemberg,
S Germany
Konstanza see Constanţa
Konya 116 C4 var. Konieh, prev. Konia;
anc. Iconium. Konya, C Turkey
Kopaonik 101 D5 mountain range
S Serbia
Kopar see Koper
Koper 95 D8 It. Capodistria; prev. Kopar.
SW Slovenia
Köpetdag Gershi 122 C3 mountain
range Iran/Turkmenistan
Köpetdag Gershi/Kopetdag, Khrebet
see Koppeh Dägh
Koppeh Dagh 120 D2 Rus. Khrebet
Kopetdag, Turkm. Köpetdag Gershi.
mountain range Iran/Turkmenistan
Kopreinitz see Koprivnica
Koprivnica 100 B2 Ger. Kopreinitz,
Hung. Kaproncza. Koprivnica-
Križevci, N Croatia
Köprülü see Veles
Koptsevichi see Kaptsevichy
Kopyl' see Kapyl'
Korat see Nakhon Ratchasima
Korat Plateau 136 D4 plateau
E Thailand
Korba 135 E4 Chhattīsgarh, C India
Korça see Korçë
Korçë 101 D6 var. Korça, Gk. Korytsa, It.
Corriza; prev. Koritsa. Korçë,
SE Albania
Korčula 100 B4 It. Curzola; anc. Corcyra
Nigra. island Croatia
Korea Bay 127 G3 bay China/North
Korea
**Korea, Democratic People's Republic
of** see North Korea
Korea, Republic of see South Korea
Korea Strait 131 A7 Jap. Chōsen-kaikyō,
Kor. Taehan-haehyŏp. channel Japan/
South Korea
Korhogo 74 D4 N Ivory Coast
Kórinthos 105 B6 anc. Corinthus Eng.
Corinth. Pelopónnisos, S Greece
Koritsa see Korçë
Kōriyama 131 D5 Fukushima, Honshū,
C Japan
Korla 126 C3 Chin. K'u-erh-lo. Xinjiang
Uygur Zizhiqu, NW China
Körmend 99 B7 Vas, W Hungary
Koróni 105 B6 Pelopónnisos,
S Greece
Koror 144 A2 (Palau) Oreor, N Palau
Körös see Križevci
Korosten' 108 D1 Zhytomyrs'ka Oblast',
NW Ukraine
Koro Toro 76 C2 Borkou-Ennedi-
Tibesti, N Chad
Korsovka see Kārsava
Kortrijk 87 A6 Fr. Courtrai.
West-Vlaanderen, W Belgium
Koryak Range 115 H2 var. Koryakskiy
Khrebet, Eng. Koryak Range. mountain
range NE Russia
Koryak Range see Koryakskoy
e Nagor'ye
Koryakskiy Khrebet see Koryakskoye
Nagor'ye
Koryazhma 110 C4 Arkhangel'skaya
Oblast', NW Russia
Korytsa see Korçë
Kos 105 E6 Kos, Dodekánisa, Greece,
Aegean Sea
Kos 105 E6 It. Coo; anc. Cos. island
Dodekánisa, Greece, Aegean Sea
Ko-saki 131 A7 headland Nagasaki,
Tsushima, SW Japan
Kościan 98 B4 Ger. Kosten.
Wielkopolskie, C Poland
Kościerzyna 98 C2 Pomorskie,
NW Poland
Kosciusko, Mount see Kosciuszko,
Mount
Kosciuszko, Mount 149 C7 prev. Mount
Kosciusko. mountain New South
Wales, SE Australia
K'o-shih see Kashi
Koshikijima-rettō 131 A8 var.
Kosikizima Rettō. island group
SW Japan
Kōshū see Gwangju
Košice 99 D6 Ger. Kaschau, Hung. Kassa.
Košický Kraj, E Slovakia
Kosikizima-rettō see
Koshikijima-rettō
Köslin see Koszalin

Koson 123 E3 Rus. Kasan. Qashqadaryo
Viloyati, S Uzbekistan
Kosovo 101 D5 prev. Autonomous
Province of Kosovo and Metohija.
country (not fully recognised) SE Europe
**Kosovo and Metohija, Autonomous
Province of** see Kosovo
Kosovo Polje see Fushë Kosovë
Kosovska Mitrovica see Mitrovicë
Kosrae 144 C2 prev. Kusaie. island
Caroline Islands, E Micronesia
Kossou, Lac de 74 D5 lake
C Ivory Coast
Kostanay 114 C4 var. Kustanay, Kaz.
Qostanay. Kostanay, N Kazakhstan
Kosten see Kościan
Kostenets 104 C2 prev. Georgi Dimitrov.
Sofiya, W Bulgaria
Kostnitz see Konstanz
Kostroma 111 B4 Kostromskaya Oblast',
NW Russia
Kostyantynivka 109 G3 Rus.
Konstantinovka. Donets'ka Oblast',
SE Ukraine
Kostyukovichi see Kastsyukovichy
Kostyukova see Kastsyukowka
Koszalin 98 B2 Ger. Köslin.
Zachodnio-pomorskie, NW Poland
Kota 134 D3 prev. Kotah. Rājasthān,
N India
Kota Baharu see Kota Bharu
Kota Baru see Kota Bharu
Kotabaru see Jayapura
Kota Bharu 138 B3 var. Kota Baharu,
Kota Bahru. Kelantan, Peninsular
Malaysia
Kotaboemi see Kotabumi
Kotabumi 138 B4 prev. Kotaboemi.
Sumatera, W Indonesia
Kotah see Kota
Kota Kinabalu 138 D3 prev. Jesselton.
Sabah, East Malaysia
Kotel'nyy, Ostrov 115 E2 island
Novosibirskiye Ostrova, N Russia
Kotka 85 E5 Kymenlaakso, S Finland
Kotlas 110 C4 Arkhangel'skaya Oblast',
NW Russia
Kotonu see Cotonou
Kotor 101 C5 It. Cattaro.
SW Montenegro
Kotovs'k see Podil's'k
Kotovsk see Hînceşti
Kottbus see Cottbus
Kotto 76 D4 river Central African
Republic/Dem. Rep. Congo
Kotuy 115 E2 river N Russia
Koudougou 75 E4 C Burkina Faso
Koulamoutou 77 B6 Ogooué-Lolo,
C Gabon
Koulikoro 74 D3 Koulikoro, SW Mali
Koumra 76 C4 Moyen-Chari, S Chad
Kourou 59 H3 N French Guiana
Kousséri see Al Qusayr
Kousséri 76 B3 prev. Fort-Foureau.
Extrême-Nord, NE Cameroon
Koutiala 74 D4 Sikasso, S Mali
Kouvola 85 E5 Kymenlaakso, S Finland
Kovel' 108 C1 Pol. Kowel. Volyns'ka
Oblast', NW Ukraine
Kovno see Kaunas
Koweit see Kuwait
Kowel see Kovel'
Kowloon 128 A2 Hong Kong, S China
Kowno see Kaunas
Kozáni 104 B4 Dytikí Makedonía,
N Greece
Kozara 100 B3 mountain range
NW Bosnia and Herzegovina
Kozarska Dubica see Bosanska Dubica
Kozhikode 132 C2 var. Calicut. Kerala,
SW India
Kozu-shima 131 D6 island E Japan
Kozyatyn 108 D2 Rus. Kazatin.
Vinnyts'ka Oblast', C Ukraine
Kpalimé 75 E5 var. Palimé. SW Togo
Kráchéh see Krâchéh
Kragujevac 100 D4 Serbia, C Serbia
Kra, Isthmus of 137 B6 isthmus
Malaysia/Thailand
Krakau see Kraków
Kraków 99 D5 Eng. Cracow, Ger.
Krakau; anc. Cracovia. Małopolskie,
S Poland
Kralánh 137 D5 Siêmréab,
NW Cambodia
Kralendijk 55 F5 dependent territory
capital (Bonaire) Bonaire, E Caribbean
Kraljevo 100 D4 prev. Rankovićevo.
Serbia, C Serbia

Kramators'k 109 G3 Rus. Kramatorsk.
Donets'ka Oblast', SE Ukraine
Kramatorsk see Kramators'k
Kramfors 85 C5 Västernorrland,
C Sweden
Kranéa see Kraniá
Kraniá 104 B4 var. Kranéa. Dytikí
Makedonía, N Greece
Kranj 95 D7 Ger. Krainburg.
N Slovenia
Kranz see Zelenogradsk
Kräslava 106 D4 SE Latvia
Krasnaye 107 C5 Rus. Krasnoye.
Minskaya Voblasts', C Belarus
Krasnoarmeysk 111 C6 Saratovskaya
Oblast', W Russia
Krasnodar 111 A7 prev. Ekaterinodar,
Yekaterinodar. Krasnodarskiy Kray,
SW Russia
Krasnodon see Sorokyne
Krasnogor see Kallaste
Krasnogvardeyskoye see
Krasnohvardiys'ke
Krasnohvardiys'ke 109 F4 Rus.
Krasnogvardeyskoye. Avtonomna
Respublika Krym, S Ukraine
Krasnokamensk 115 F4 Zabaykal'skiy
Kray, S Russia
Krasnokamsk 111 D5 Permskiy Kray,
W Russia
Krasnoperekops'k see Yany Kapu
Krasnostav see Krasnystaw
Krasnovodsk see Türkmenbaşy
Krasnovodskiy Zaliv see Türkmenbasy
Aylagy
Krasnovodsk Aylagy see Türkmenbasy
Aylagy
Krasnoyarsk 114 D4 Krasnoyarskiy
Kray, S Russia
Krasnoye see Krasnaye
Krasnystaw 98 E4 Rus. Krasnostav.
Lubelskie, SE Poland
Krasnyy Kut 111 C6 Saratovskaya
Oblast', W Russia
Krasnyy Luch see Khrustal'nyy
Kratie 137 D6 Khmer. Krâchéh. Kratie,
E Cambodia
Krávanh, Chuôr Phnum 137 C6 Eng.
Cardamom Mountains, Fr. Chaine des
Cardamomes. mountain range
W Cambodia
Krefeld 94 A4 Nordrhein-Westfalen,
W Germany
Kreisstadt see Krosno Odrzańskie
Kremenchug see Kremenchuk
**Kremenchugskoye Vodokhranilishche/
Kremenchuk Reservoir** see
Kremenchuts'ke Vodoskhovyshche
Kremenchuk 109 F2 Rus. Kremenchug.
Poltavs'ka Oblast', NE Ukraine
Kremenchuk Reservoir 109 F2 Eng.
Kremenchuk Reservoir, Rus.
Kremenchugskoye Vodokhranilishche.
reservoir C Ukraine
Kremenets' 108 C2 Pol. Krzemieniec,
Rus. Kremenets. Ternopil's'ka Oblast',
W Ukraine
Kreminna 109 G2 Rus. Kremennaya.
Luhans'ka Oblast', E Ukraine
Kresena see Kresna
Kresna 104 C3 var. Kresena.
Blagoevgrad, SW Bulgaria
Kretikon Pelagos see Kritikó Pélagos
Kretinga 106 B3 Ger. Krottingen.
Klaipėda, NW Lithuania
Kreuz see Cristuru Secuiesc
Kreuz see Križevci, Croatia
Kreuz see Risti, Estonia
**Kreuzburg/Kreuzburg in
Oberschlesien** see Kluczbork
Krichëv see Krychaw
Krievija see Russia
Krindachevka see Krasnyy Luch
Krishna 132 C2 prev. Kistna. river
C India
Krishnagiri 132 C2 Tamil Nādu,
SE India
Kristiania see Oslo
Kristiansand 85 A6 var. Christiansand.
Vest-Agder, S Norway
Kristianstad 85 B7 Skåne, S Sweden
Kristiansund 84 A4 var. Christiansund.
Møre og Romsdal, S Norway
Krivoy Rog see Kryvyy Rih
Križevci 100 B2 Ger. Kreuz, Hung.
Körös. Varaždin, NE Croatia
Krk 100 A3 It. Veglia; anc. Curieta.
island NW Croatia
Kroatien see Croatia

Krolevets' 109 F1 Rus. Krolevets.
Sums'ka Oblast', NE Ukraine
Krolevets see Krolevets'
Królewska Huta see Chorzów
Kronach 95 C5 Bayern, E Germany
Kronstadt see Braşov
Kroonstad 78 D4 Free State, C South
Africa
Kropotkin 111 A7 Krasnodarskiy Kray,
SW Russia
Kropyvnyts'kyy 109 E3 Rus.
Kirovohrad; prev. Kirovo,
Yelizavetgrad, Zinov'yevsk.
Kirovohrads'ka Oblast', C Ukraine
Krosno 99 D5 Ger. Krossen.
Podkarpackie, SE Poland
Krosno Odrzańskie 98 B3
Ger. Crossen, Kreisstadt. Lubuskie,
W Poland
Krossen see Krosno
Krottingen see Kretinga
Krško 95 E8 Ger. Gurkfeld;
prev. Videm-Krško. E Slovenia
Krugloye see Kruhlaye
Kruhlaye 107 D6 Rus. Krugloye.
Mahilyowskaya Voblasts', E Belarus
Kruja see Krujë
Krujë 101 C6 var. Kruja, It. Croia.
Durrës, C Albania
Krummau see Český Krumlov
Krung Thep, Ao 137 C5 var. Bight of
Bangkok. bay S Thailand
Krung Thep Mahanakhon see Ao Krung
Thep
Krupki 107 D6 Minskaya Voblasts',
C Belarus
Krušné Hory see Erzgebirge
Krychaw 107 E7 Rus. Krichëv.
Mahilyowskaya Voblasts', E Belarus
Kryms'ki Hory 109 F5 mountain range
S Ukraine
Kryms'kyy Pivostriv 109 F5 Eng.
Crimea. peninsula (Ukrainian territory
annexed by Russia since 2014).
S Ukraine
Krynica 99 D5 Ger. Tannenhof.
Małopolskie, S Poland
Kryve Ozero 109 E3 Odes'ka Oblast',
SW Ukraine
Kryvyy Rih 109 F3 Rus. Krivoy Rog.
Dnipropetrovs'ka Oblast', SE Ukraine
Krzemieniec see Kremenets'
Ksar al Kabir see Ksar-el-Kebir
Ksar al Soule see Er-Rachidia
Ksar-el-Kebir 70 C2 var. Alcázar, Ksar
al-Kebir, Ksar-el-Kébir, Ar. Al-Kasr
al-Kebir, Al-Qsar al-Kbir, Sp.
Alcazarquivir. NW Morocco
Ksar-el-Kébir see Ksar-el-Kebir
Kuala Dungun see Dungun
Kuala Lumpur 138 B3 country capital
(Malaysia) Kuala Lumpur, Peninsular
Malaysia
Kuala Terengganu 138 B3 var. Kuala
Trengganu. Terengganu, Peninsular
Malaysia
Kualatungkal 138 B4 Sumatera,
W Indonesia
Kuang-chou see Guangzhou
Kuang-hsi see Guangxi Zhuangzu Zizhiqu
Kuang-tung see Guangdong
Kuang-yuan see Guangyuan
Kuantan 138 B3 Pahang, Peninsular
Malaysia
Kuba see Quba
Kuban' 109 G5 var. Hypanis. river
SW Russia
Kubango see Cubango/Okavango
Kuching 138 C3 prev. Sarawak. Sarawak,
East Malaysia
Kučnay Darwāshān 122 D5 prev.
Kūchnay Darweyshān. Helmand,
S Afghanistan
Kūchnay Darweyshān see Kūchnay
Darwāshān
Kuçova see Kuçovë
Kuçovë 101 C6 var. Kuçova; prev. Qyteti
Stalin. Berat, C Albania
Kudara see Ghūdara
Kudus 138 C5 prev. Koedoes. Jawa,
C Indonesia
Kuei-lin see Guilin
Kuei-Yang/Kuei-yang see Guiyang
K'u-erh-lo see Korla
Kueyang see Guiyang
Kugaaruk 37 G3 prev. Pelly Bay.
Nunavut, N Canada
Kugluktuk 53 E3 var. Qurlurtuuq; prev.
Coppermine. Nunavut, NW Canada
Kuhmo 84 E4 Kainuu, E Finland

Kuhnau see Konin
Kühnö see Kihnu
Kuibyshev see Kuybyshevskoye
Vodokhranilishche
Kuito 78 B2 Port. Silva Porto. Bié,
C Angola
Kuji 130 D3 var. Kuzi. Iwate, Honshū,
C Japan
Kukës 101 D5 var. Kukësi. Kukës,
NE Albania
Kukësi see Kukës
Kukong see Shaoguan
Kukukhoto see Hohhot
Kula Kangri 135 G3 var. Kulhakangri.
mountain Bhutan/China
Kuldiga 106 B3 Ger. Goldingen.
W Latvia
Kuldja see Yining
Kulhakangri see Kula Kangri
Kullorsuaq 82 D2 var. Kuvdlorssuak.
Kitaa, C Greenland
Kulm see Chełmno
Kulmsee see Chełmża
Kŭlob 123 F3 Rus. Kulyab. SW Tajikistan
Kulpa see Kolpa
Kulu 116 C3 Konya, W Turkey
Kulunda Steppe see Ravnina Kulyndy
Kulundinskaya Ravnina see Ravnina
Kulyndy
Kulyab see Kŭlob
Kum see Qom
Kuma 111 B7 river SW Russia
Kumamoto 131 A7 Kumamoto, Kyūshū,
SW Japan
Kumanova see Kumanovo
Kumanovo 101 E5 Turk. Kumanova.
N Macedonia
Kumasi 75 E5 prev. Coomassie.
C Ghana
Kumayri see Gyumri
Kumba 77 A5 Sud-Ouest,
W Cameroon
Kumertau 111 D6 Respublika
Bashkortostan, W Russia
Kumillä see Comilla
Kumo 75 G4 Gombe, E Nigeria
Kumon Range 136 B2 mountain range
N Myanmar (Burma)
Kumul see Hami
Kunashiri see Kunashir, Ostrov
Kunashir, Ostrov 130 E1 var. Kunashiri.
island Kuril'skiye Ostrova, SE Russia
Kunda 106 E2 Lääne-Virumaa,
NE Estonia
Kunduz 123 E3 prev. Kondoz. province
NE Afghanistan
Kunene 60 C4 var. Kunene. river
Angola/Namibia
Kunene see Cunene
Kungsbacka 85 B7 Halland, S Sweden
Kungur 111 D5 Permskiy Kray,
NW Russia
Kunlun Mountains see Kunlun Shan
Kunlun Shan 126 B4 Eng. Kunlun
Mountains. mountain range
NW China
Kunming 128 B6 var. K'un-ming; prev.
Yunnan. province capital Yunnan,
SW China
K'un-ming see Kunming
Kununurra 146 D3 Western Australia
Kunya-Urgench see Köneürgenç
Kuopio 85 E5 Pohjois-Savo,
C Finland
Kupa see Kolpa
Kupang 139 E5 prev. Koepang. Timor,
C Indonesia
Kup"yans'k 109 G2 Rus. Kupyansk.
Kharkivs'ka Oblast', E Ukraine
Kupyansk see Kup"yans'k
Kür see Kura
Kura 117 H3 Az. Kür, Geor. Mtkvari,
Turk. Kura Nehri. river SW Asia
Kura Nehri see Kura
Kurashiki 131 B6 var. Kurasiki.
Okayama, Honshū, SW Japan
Kurasiki see Kurashiki
Kurdistan 117 F4 cultural region
SW Asia
Kürdzhali 104 D3 var. Kirdzhali.
Kürdzhali, S Bulgaria
Kure 131 B7 Hiroshima, Honshū,
SW Japan
Küre Dağları 116 C2 mountain range
N Turkey
Kuressaare 106 C2 Ger. Arensburg;
prev. Kingissepp. Saaremaa,
W Estonia
Kureyka 112 D2 river N Russia
Kurgan-Tyube see Qŭrghonteppa

Kuria Muria Islands see Ḥalāniyāt,
Juzur al
Kuril'skiye Ostrova 115 H4
Eng. Kuril Islands. island group
SE Russia
Kuril Islands see Kuril'skiye Ostrova
Kuril-Kamchatka Depression see
Kuril-Kamchatka Trench
Kuril-Kamchatka Trench 113 F3 var.
Kuril-Kamchatka Depression. trench
NW Pacific Ocean
Kuril'sk 130 E1 Jap. Shana. Kuril'skiye
Ostrova, Sakhalinskaya Oblast',
SE Russia
Kurishes Haff see Courland Lagoon
Kurkund see Kilingi-Nõmme
Kurnool 132 C1 var. Karnul. Andhra
Pradesh, S India
Kursk 111 A6 Kurskaya Oblast',
W Russia
Kurskiy Zaliv see Courland Lagoon
Kuršumlija 101 D5 Serbia, S Serbia
Kurtbunar see Tervel
Kurtitsch/Kürtös see Curtici
Kuruktag 126 C3 mountain range
NW China
Kurume 131 A7 Fukuoka, Kyūshū,
SW Japan
Kurupukari 59 F3 C Guyana
Kusaie see Kosrae
Kushiro 130 D2 var. Kusiro. Hokkaidō,
NE Japan
Kushka see Serhetabat
Kusiro see Kushiro
Kuskokwim Mountains 36 C3
mountain range Alaska, USA
Kustanay see Kostanay
Küstence/Küstendje see Constanţa
Kütahya 116 B3 prev. Kutaia. Kütahya,
W Turkey
Kutai see Mahakam, Sungai
Kutaisi 117 F2 prev. K'ut'aisi 95 F2
W Georgia W Georgia
K'ut'aisi see Kutaisi
Kūt al 'Amārah see Al Kūt
Kut al Imara see Al Kūt
Kutaradja/Kutaraja see Banda Aceh
Kutch, Gulf of see Kachchh, Gulf of
Kutch, Rann of see Kachchh, Rann of
Kutina 100 B3 Sisak-Moslavina,
NE Croatia
Kutno 98 C3 Łódzkie, C Poland
Kuujjuaq 39 E2 prev. Fort-Chimo.
Québec, E Canada
Kuusamo 84 E3 Pohjois-Pohjanmaa,
E Finland
Kuvango see Cubango
Kuvdlorssuak see Kullorsuaq
Kuwait 120 C4 off. State of Kuwait, var.
Dawlat al Kuwait, Koweit, Kuwait.
country SW Asia
Kuwait see Al Kuwayt
Kuwait City see Al Kuwayt
Kuwait, Dawlat al see Kuwait
Kuwait, State of see Kuwait
Kuwajleen see Kwajalein Atoll
Kuwayt 120 C3 Maysān, E Iraq
Kuweit see Kuwait
Kuybyshev see Samara
Kuybyshev Reservoir 111 C5 var.
Kuibyshev, Eng. Kuybyshev Reservoir.
reservoir W Russia
Kuybyshev Reservoir see
Kuybyshevskoye Vodokhranilishche
Kuytun 126 B2 Xinjiang Uygur Zizhiqu,
NW China
Kuzi see Kuji
Kuznetsk 111 B6 Penzenskaya Oblast',
W Russia
Kvaløya 84 C2 island N Norway
Kvarnbergsvattnet 84 B4 var.
Frostviken. lake N Sweden
Kvarner 100 A3 var. Carnaro, It.
Quarnero. gulf W Croatia
Kvitøya 83 G1 island NE Svalbard
Kwajalein Atoll 144 C1 var. Kuwajleen.
atoll Ralik Chain, C Marshall Islands
Kwando see Cuando
Kwangchow see Guangzhou
Kwangchu see Gwangju
Kwangju see Gwangju
Kwango 77 C7 Port. Cuango. river
Angola/Dem. Rep. Congo
**Kwangsi/Kwangsi Chuang
Autonomous Region** see Guangxi
Zhuangzu Zizhiqu

Kwangtung see Guangdong
Kwangyuan see Guangyuan
Kwanza see Cuanza
Kweichu see Guiyang
Kweilin see Guilin
Kweisui see Hohhot
Kweiyang see Guiyang
Kwekwe 78 D3 prev. Que Que. Midlands,
C Zimbabwe
Kwesui see Hohhot
Kwidzyń 98 C2 Ger. Marienwerder.
Pomorskie, N Poland
Kwigillingok 36 C2 Alaska,
USA
Kwilu 77 C6 river W Dem. Rep. Congo
Kwito see Cuito
Kyabé 76 C4 Moyen-Chari, S Chad
Kyaikkami 137 B5 prev. Amherst. Mon
State, S Myanmar (Burma)
Kyaiklat 136 B3 Ayeyarwady,
SW Myanmar (Burma)
Kyaikto 136 B4 Mon State, S Myanmar
(Burma)
Kyakhta 115 E5 Respublika Buryatiya,
S Russia
Kyaukse 136 B3 Mandalay, C Myanmar
(Burma)
Kyiv 109 E2 var. Kyyiv, Eng. Kiev, Rus.
Kiyev. country capital (Ukraine)
Kyyiv's'ka Oblast', N Ukraine
Kyjov 99 C5 Ger. Gaya. Jihomoravský
Kraj, SE Czech Republic (Czechia)
Kými 105 C5 prev. Kími. Évvoia,
C Greece
Kyŏngsŏng see Seoul
Kyōto 131 C6 Kyōto, Honshū,
SW Japan
Kyparissía 105 B6 var. Kiparissía.
Pelopónnisos, S Greece
Kypros see Cyprus
Kyrá Panagía 105 C5 island Vóreies
Sporádes, Greece, Aegean Sea
Kyrenia see Girne
Kyrgyz Republic see Kyrgyzstan
Kyrgyzstan 123 F2 off. Kyrgyz Republic,
var. Kirghizia; prev. Kirgizskaya SSR,
Kirghiz SSR, Republic of Kyrgyzstan.
country C Asia
Kyrgyzstan, Republic of see Kyrgyzstan
Kythira 105 C7 var. Kíthira, It. Cerigo,
Lat. Cythera. island S Greece
Kýthnos 105 C6 Kýnthos, Kykládes,
Greece, Aegean Sea
Kythnos 105 C6 var. Kíthnos, Thermiá,
It. Termia; anc. Cythnos. island
Kykládes, Greece, Aegean Sea
Kythréa see Değirmenlik
Kyushu 131 B7 var. Kyūsyû. island
SW Japan
Kyushu-Palau Ridge 125 F3 var.
Kyusyu-Palau Ridge. undersea ridge
W Pacific Ocean
Kyustendil 104 B2 anc. Pautalia.
Kyustendil, W Bulgaria
Kyūsyû see Kyūshū
Kyusyu-Palau Ridge see Kyushu-Palau
Ridge
Kyyiv see Kyiv
Kyzyl 114 D4 Respublika Tyva, C Russia
Kyzyl Kum 122 D2 var. Kizil Kum, Qizil
Qum, Uzb. Qizilqum. desert
Kazakhstan/Uzbekistan
Kyzylorda 114 B5 var. Kzyl-Orda, Qizil
Orda, Qyzylorda; prev. Kzylorda,
Perovsk. Kyzylorda, S Kazakhstan
Kyzyl-Suu 123 G2 prev. Pokrovka.
Issyk-Kul'skaya Oblast', NE Kyrgyzstan
Kzyl-Orda see Kyzylorda
Kzylorda see Kyzylorda

L

Laaland see Lolland
La Algaba 92 C4 Andalucía, S Spain
Laarne 87 B5 Oost-Vlaanderen,
NW Belgium
La Asunción 59 E1 Nueva Esparta,
NE Venezuela
Laatokka see Ladozhskoye, Ozero
Laâyoune 70 B3 var. Aaiún. country
capital (Western Sahara)
NW Western Sahara
La Banda Oriental see Uruguay
la Baule-Escoublac 90 A4
Loire-Atlantique, NW France
Labé 74 C4 NW Guinea
Labe see Elbe
Laborca see Laborec

Laborec *99 E5 Hung.* Laborca. *river*
E Slovakia
Labrador *39 F2 cultural region*
Newfoundland and Labrador,
SW Canada
Labrador Basin *34 E3 var.* Labrador Sea
Basin. *undersea basin* Labrador Sea
Labrador Sea *82 A4 sea* NW Atlantic
Ocean
Labrador Sea Basin *see* Labrador Basin
Labudalin *see* Ergun
Labutta *137 A5* Ayeyarwady,
SW Myanmar (Burma)
Laç *101 C6 var.* Laci. Lezhë, C Albania
La Calera *64 B4* Valparaíso, C Chile
La Carolina *92 D4* Andalucía, S Spain
Laccadive Islands *132 A3 Eng.* Laccadive
Islands. *island group* India, N Indian
Ocean
**Laccadive Islands/Laccadive Minicoy
and Amindivi Islands, the** *see*
Lakshadweep
La Ceiba *52 D2* Atlántida, N Honduras
Lachanás *104 B3* Kentrikí Makedonía,
N Greece
La Chaux-de-Fonds *95 A7* Neuchâtel,
W Switzerland
Lachlan River *149 C6 river* New South
Wales, SE Australia
Laci *see* Laç
la Ciotat *91 D6 anc.* Citharista.
Bouches-du-Rhône, SE France
Lacobriga *see* Lagos
La Concepción *53 E5 var.* Concepción.
Chiriquí, W Panama
La Concepción *58 C1* Zulia,
NW Venezuela
La Condamine *91 C8* W Monaco
Laconia *41 G2* New Hampshire,
NE USA
La Crosse *40 A2* Wisconsin, N USA
La Cruz *52 D4* Guanacaste, NW Costa
Rica
Lake Ladoga *110 B3 Eng.* Lake Ladoga,
Fin. Laatokka. *lake* NW Russia
Ladoga, Lake *see* Ladozhskoye, Ozero
Ladysmith *40 B2* Wisconsin, N USA
Lae *144 B3* Morobe, W Papua New
Guinea
La Esperanza *52 C2* Intibucá,
SW Honduras
Lafayette *40 C4* Indiana, N USA
Lafayette *42 B3* Louisiana, S USA
La Fé *54 A2* Pinar del Río, W Cuba
Lafia *75 G4* Nassarawa, C Nigeria
la Flèche *90 B4* Sarthe, NW France
Lagdo, Lac de *76 B4 lake* N Cameroon
Laghouat *70 D2* N Algeria
Lagos *75 F5* Lagos, SW Nigeria
Lagos *92 B5 anc.* Lacobriga. Faro,
S Portugal
Lagos de Moreno *51 E4* Jalisco,
SW Mexico
Lagouira *70 A4* SW Western Sahara
La Grande *46 C3* Oregon, NW USA
La Guaira *66 B4* Distrito Federal,
N Venezuela
Lagunas *64 B1* Tarapacá, N Chile
Lagunillas *61 G4* Santa Cruz, SE Bolivia
La Habana *54 B2 var.* Havana. *country
capital* (Cuba) Ciudad de La Habana,
W Cuba
Lahat *138 B4* Sumatera, W Indonesia
La Haye *see* 's-Gravenhage
Laholm *85 B7* Halland, S Sweden
Lahore *134 D2* Punjab, NE Pakistan
Lahr *95 A6* Baden-Württemberg,
S Germany
Lahti *85 D5 Swe.* Lahtis. Päijät-Häme,
S Finland
Lahtis *see* Lahti
Lai *76 B4 prev.* Behagle, De Behagle.
Tandjilé, S Chad
Lai Châu *136 D3* Lai Châu, N Vietnam
Laila *see* Laylā
La Junta *44 D5* Colorado, C USA
Lake Charles *42 A3* Louisiana, S USA
Lake City *43 E4* Florida, SE USA
Lake District *89 C5 physical region*
NW England, United Kingdom
Lake Havasu City *48 A2* Arizona,
SW USA
Lake Jackson *49 H4* Texas, SW USA
Lakeland *43 E4* Florida, SE USA
Lakeside *47 C8* California, W USA
Lake State *see* Michigan
Lakewood *44 C4* Colorado, C USA
Lakhnau *see* Lucknow
Lakonikós Kólpos *105 B7 gulf* S Greece

Lakselv *84 D2 Lapp.* Leavdnja.
Finnmark, N Norway
la Laon *see* Laon
Lalibela *72 C4* Āmara, Ethiopia
La Libertad *52 B1* Petén, N Guatemala
La Ligua *64 B4* Valparaíso, C Chile
Lalín *92 C1* Galicia, NW Spain
Lalitpur *135 F3* Central, C Nepal
La Louvière *87 B6* Hainaut, S Belgium
la Maddalena *96 A4* Sardegna, Italy,
C Mediterranean Sea
la Manche *see* English Channel
Lamar *44 D5* Colorado, C USA
La Marmora, Punta *97 A5 mountain*
Sardegna, Italy, C Mediterranean Sea
La Massana *91 A8* La Massana,
W Andorra Europe
Lambaréné *77 A6* Moyen-Ogooué,
W Gabon
Lamego *92 C2* Viseu, N Portugal
Lamesa *49 E3* Texas, SW USA
Lamezia Terme *97 D6* Calabria, SE Italy
Lamía *105 B5* Stereá Elláda, C Greece
Lamoni *45 F4* Iowa, C USA
Lampang *136 C4 var.* Muang Lampang,
Lampang, NW Thailand
Lámpeia *105 B6* Dytikí Elláda, S Greece
Lanbi Kyun *137 B6 prev.* Sullivan Island.
island Myeik Archipelago, S Myanmar
(Burma)
Lancang Jiang *see* Mekong
Lancaster *89 D5* NW England, United
Kingdom
Lancaster *47 C7* California, W USA
Lancaster *41 F4* Pennsylvania, NE USA
Lancaster Sound *37 F2 sound* Nunavut,
N Canada
Lan-chou/Lan-chow/Lanchow *see*
Lanzhou
Landao *see* Lantau Island
Landen *87 C6* Vlaams Brabant,
C Belgium
Lander *44 C3* Wyoming, C USA
Landerneau *90 A3* Finistère, NW France
Landes *91 B5 cultural region* SW France
Land of Enchantment *see* New Mexico
The Land of Opportunity *see* Arkansas
Land of Steady Habits *see* Connecticut
Land of the Midnight Sun *see* Alaska
Landsberg *see* Gorzów Wielkopolski,
Lubuskie, Poland
Landsberg an der Warthe *see* Gorzów
Wielkopolski
Land's End *89 B8 headland* SW England,
United Kingdom
Landshut *95 C6* Bayern, SE Germany
Langar *123 E2 Rus.* Lyangar. Navoiy
Viloyati, C Uzbekistan
Langfang *128 D4* Hebei, E China
Langkawi, Pulau *137 B7 island*
Peninsular Malaysia
Langres *90 D4* Haute-Marne, N France
Langsa *138 A3* Sumatera, W Indonesia
Lang Shan *127 E3 mountain range*
N China
Lang Son *136 D3 var.* Langson. Lang
Sơn, N Vietnam
Langson *see* Lang Son
Lang Suan *137 B6* Chumphon,
SW Thailand
Languedoc *91 C6 cultural region*
S France
Länkäran *117 H3 Rus.* Lenkoran'.
S Azerbaijan
Lansing *40 C3 state capital* Michigan,
N USA
Lanta, Ko *137 B7 island* S Thailand
Lantau Island *128 A2 Cant.* Tai Yue
Shan, *Chin.* Landao. *island* Hong
Kong, S China
Lantung, Gulf of *see* Liaodong Wan
Lanzarote *70 B3 island* Islas Canarias,
Spain, NE Atlantic Ocean
Lanzhou *128 B4 var.* Lan-chou,
Lanchow, Lan-chow; *prev.* Kaolan.
province capital Gansu, C China
Lao Cai *136 D3* Lao Cai, N Vietnam
Laodicea/Laodicea ad Mare *see* Al
Lādhiqīyah
Laoet *see* Laut, Pulau
Laon *90 D3 var.* la Laon; *anc.* Laudunum.
Aisne, N France
Lao People's Democratic Republic *see*
Laos
La Orchila, Isla *58 D1 island*
N Venezuela
La Oroya *60 C3* Junín, C Peru
Laos *136 D4 off.* Lao People's Democratic
Republic. *country* SE Asia

La Palma *53 G5* Darién, SE Panama
La Palma *70 A3 island* Islas Canarias,
Spain, NE Atlantic Ocean
La Paz *61 F4 var.* La Paz de Ayacucho.
country capital (Bolivia-seat of
government) La Paz, W Bolivia
La Paz *50 B3* Baja California Sur,
NW Mexico
La Paz, Bahía de *50 B3 bay* NW Mexico
La Paz de Ayacucho *see* La Paz
La Pérouse Strait *130 D1 Jap.*
Sōya-kaikyō, *Rus.* Proliv Laperuza.
strait Japan/Russia
Laperuza, Proliv *see* La Pérouse Strait
Lápithos *see* Lapta
Lapland *84 D3 Fin.* Lappi, *Swe.*
Lappland. *cultural region* N Europe
La Plata *64 D4* Buenos Aires,
E Argentina
La Plata *see* Sucre
La Pola *92 D1 var.* Pola de Lena.
Asturias, N Spain
Lappeenranta *85 E5 Swe.* Villmanstrand.
Etelä-Karjala, SE Finland
Lappi/Lappland *see* Lapland
Lappo *see* Lapua
Lapta *102 C5 Gk.* Lápithos. NW Cyprus
Laptev Sea *115 E2 Eng.* Laptev Sea. *sea*
Arctic Ocean
Laptev Sea *see* Laptevykh, More
Lapua *85 D5 Swe.* Lappo.
Etelä-Pohjanmaa, W Finland
Lapurdum *see* Bayonne
Łapy *98 E3* Podlaskie, NE Poland
La Quiaca *64 C2* Jujuy, N Argentina
L'Aquila *96 C4 var.* Aquila, Aquila degli
Abruzzi. Abruzzo, C Italy
Laracha *92 B1* Galicia, NW Spain
Laramie *44 C4* Wyoming, C USA
Laramie Mountains *44 C3 mountain
range* Wyoming, C USA
Laredo *93 E1* Cantabria, N Spain
Laredo *49 F5* Texas, SW USA
La Réunion *see* Réunion
Largeau *see* Faya
Largo *43 E4* Florida, SE USA
Largo, Cayo *54 B2 island* W Cuba
Lario *see* Como, Lago di
La Rioja *64 B3* La Rioja, NW Argentina
La Rioja *93 E2 autonomous community*
N Spain
Lárisa *104 B4 var.* Larissa. Thessalía,
C Greece
Larissa *see* Lárisa
Larkana *134 B3 var.* Larkhana. Sind,
SE Pakistan
Larkhana *see* Larkana
Larnaca *see* Lárnaka
Lárnaka *102 C5 var.* Larnaca, Larnax.
SE Cyprus
Larnax *see* Lárnaka
la Rochelle *90 B4 anc.* Rupella.
Charente-Maritime, W France
La Roche-sur-Yon *90 B4 prev.* Bourbon
Vendée, Napoléon-Vendée. Vendée,
NW France
La Roda *93 E3* Castilla-La Mancha,
C Spain
La Romana *55 E3* E Dominican Republic
Larvotto *91 C8* N Monaco Europe
La-sa *see* Lhasa
Las Cabezas de San Juan *92 C5*
Andalucía, S Spain
Las Cruces *48 D3* New Mexico, SW USA
La See d'Urgel *see* La Seu d'Urgell
La Serena *64 B3* Coquimbo, C Chile
La Seu d'Urgell *93 G1 prev.* La See
d'Urgel, Seo de Urgel. Cataluña,
NE Spain
La Seu d'Urgell *see* La Seu d'Urgell
Le Seyne-sur-Mer *91 D6* Var, SE France
Lashio *136 B3* Shan State, E Myanmar
(Burma)
Lashkar Gāh *122 D5 var.* Lash-Kar-Gar'.
Helmand, S Afghanistan
Lash-Kar-Gar' *see* Lashkar Gāh
La Sila *97 D6 mountain range* SW Italy
La Sirena *53 D2* Región Autónoma
Atlántico Sur, E Nicaragua
Lask *98 C4* Łódzkie, C Poland
Las Lomitas *64 D2* Formosa,
N Argentina
La Solana *93 E4* Castilla-La Mancha,
C Spain
Las Palmas *70 A3 var.* Las Palmas de
Gran Canaria. Gran Canaria, Islas
Canarias, Spain, NE Atlantic Ocean
Las Palmas de Gran Canaria *see* Las
Palmas
La Spezia *96 B3* Liguria, NW Italy

Lassa *see* Lhasa
Las Tablas *53 F5* Los Santos, S Panama
Last Frontier, The *see* Alaska
Las Tunas *54 C2 var.* Victoria de las
Tunas. Las Tunas, E Cuba
La Suisse *see* Switzerland
Las Vegas *47 D7* Nevada, W USA
Latacunga *60 B1* Cotopaxi, C Ecuador
Latakia *see* Al Lādhiqīyah
la Teste *91 B5* Gironde, SW France
Latina *97 C5 prev.* Littoria. Lazio, C Italy
La Tortuga, Isla *59 E1 var.* Isla Tortuga.
island N Venezuela
La Tuque *39 E4* Québec, SE Canada
Latvia *106 C3 off.* Republic of Latvia, *Ger.*
Lettland, *Latv.* Latvija, Latvijas
Republika; *prev.* Latvian SSR, *Rus.*
Latviyskaya SSR. *country* NE Europe
**Latvian SSR/Latvija/Latvijas
Republika/Latviyskaya SSR** *see* Latvia
Latvia, Republic of *see* Latvia
Laudunum *see* Laon
Laudus *see* St-Lô
Lauenburg/Lauenburg in Pommern *see*
Lębork
Lau Group *145 E4 island group* E Fiji
Lauis *see* Lugano
Launceston *149 C8* Tasmania,
SE Australia
La Unión *52 C3* Olancho, C Honduras
La Unión *93 F4* Murcia, SE Spain
Laurel *43 C5* Mississippi, S USA
Laurel *44 C2* Montana, NW USA
Laurentian Highlands *see* Laurentian
Mountains
Laurentian Mountains *39 E3 var.*
Laurentian Highlands, *Fr.* Les
Laurentides. *plateau* Newfoundland
and Labrador/Québec, Canada
Laurentides, Les *see* Laurentian
Mountains
Lauria *97 D6* Basilicata, S Italy
Laurinburg *43 F1* North Carolina,
SE USA
Lauru *see* Choiseul
Lausanne *95 A7 It.* Losanna. Vaud,
SW Switzerland
Laut, Pulau *138 D4 prev.* Laoet. *island*
Borneo, C Indonesia
Laval *38 D4* Québec, SE Canada
Laval *90 B3* Mayenne, NW France
La Vall d'Uixó *93 F3 var.* Vall d'Uxó.
Valenciana, E Spain
La Vega *55 E3 var.* Concepción de la
Vega. C Dominican Republic
La Vila Joiosa *see* Villajoyosa
Lávrio *105 C6 prev.* Lávrion. Attikí,
C Greece
Lávrion *see* Lávrio
Lawrence *41 G3* Massachusetts, NE USA
Lawrenceburg *42 C1* Tennessee, S USA
Lawton *49 F2* Oklahoma, C USA
La Yarada *61 E4* Tacna, SW Peru
Laylā *121 C5 var.* Laila. Ar Riyāḍ,
C Saudi Arabia
Lazarev Sea *154 B2 sea* Antarctica
Lázaro Cárdenas *51 E5* Michoacán,
SW Mexico
Leal *see* Lihula
Leamhcán *see* Lucan
Leamington *38 C5* Ontario, S Canada
Leavdnja *see* Lakselv
Lebak *139 E3* Mindanao, S Philippines
Lebanese Republic *see* Lebanon
Lebanon *45 G5* Missouri, C USA
Lebanon *41 G2* New Hampshire,
NE USA
Lebanon *46 B3* Oregon, NW USA
Lebanon *118 A4 off.* Lebanese Republic,
Ar. Al Lubnān, *Fr.* Liban. *country*
SW Asia
Lebanon, Mount *see* Liban, Jebel
Lebap *122 D2* Lebapskiy Velayat,
NE Turkmenistan
Lebedin *see* Lebedyn
Lebedyn *109 F2 Rus.* Lebedin. Sums'ka
Oblast', NE Ukraine
Lębork *98 C2 var.* Lębórk, *Ger.*
Lauenburg, Lauenburg in Pommern.
Pomorskie, N Poland
Lebrija *92 C5* Andalucía, S Spain
Lebu *65 A5* Bío Bío, C Chile
le Cannet *91 D6* Alpes-Maritimes,
SE France
Le Cap *see* Cap-Haïtien
Lecce *97 E6* Puglia, SE Italy
Lechainá *105 B6 var.* Lehena, Lekhainá.
Dytikí Elláda, S Greece
Ledo Salinarius *see* Lons-le-Saunier
Leduc *37 E5* Alberta, SW Canada

Leech Lake 45 F2 *lake* Minnesota, N USA
Leeds 89 D5 N England, United Kingdom
Leek 86 E2 Groningen, NE Netherlands
Leer 94 A3 Niedersachsen, NW Germany
Leeuwarden 86 D1 *Fris.* Ljouwert.
    Fryslân, N Netherlands
Leeuwin, Cape 142 A5 *headland*
    Western Australia
Leeward Islands 55 G3 *island group*
    E West Indies
Leeward Islands *see* Sotavento, Ilhas de
Lefkáda 105 A5 *prev.* Levkás. Lefkáda,
    Iónia Nisiá, Greece,
    C Mediterranean Sea
Lefkáda 105 A5 *It.* Santa Maura, *prev.*
    Levkás; *anc.* Leucas. *island* Iónia Nisiá,
    Greece, C Mediterranean Sea
Lefká Óri 105 C7 *mountain range* Kríti,
    Greece, E Mediterranean Sea
Lefkímmi 105 A5 *var.* Levkímmi.
    Kérkyra, Iónia Nisiá, Greece,
    C Mediterranean Sea
Lefkosía/Lefkoşa *see* Nicosia
Legaceaster *see* Chester
Legaspi *see* Legazpi City
Legazpi City 139 E2 *var.* Legaspi.
    C Philippines
Leghorn *see* Livorno
Legnica 98 B4 *Ger.* Liegnitz.
    Dolnośląskie, SW Poland
le Havre 90 B3 *Eng.* Havre; *prev.* le
    Havre-de-Grâce. Seine-Maritime,
    N France
le Havre-de-Grâce *see* le Havre
Lehena *see* Lechainá
Leicester 89 D6 *Lat.* Batae Coritanorum.
    C England, United Kingdom
Leiden 86 B3 *prev.* Leyden; *anc.*
    Lugdunum Batavorum. Zuid-Holland,
    W Netherlands
Leie 90 D2 *Fr.* Lys. *river* Belgium/France
Leinster 89 B6 *Ir.* Cúige Laighean.
    cultural region E Ireland
Leipsic *see* Leipzig
Leipsoí 105 E6 *island* Dodekánisa,
    Greece, Aegean Sea
Leipzig 94 C4 *Pol.* Lipsk, *hist.* Leipsic;
    anc. Lipsia. Sachsen, E Germany
Leiria 92 B3 *anc.* Collipo. Leiria,
    C Portugal
Leirvik 85 A6 Hordaland, S Norway
Lek 86 C4 *river* SW Netherlands
Lekhainá *see* Lechainá
Lekhchevo *see* Boychinovtsi
Leksand 85 C5 Dalarna, C Sweden
Lel'chitsy *see* Lyel'chytsy
le Léman *see* Geneva, Lake
Lelystad 86 D3 Flevoland, C Netherlands
Léman, Lac *see* Geneva, Lake
le Mans 90 B3 Sarthe, NW France
Lemberg *see* L'viv
Lemesós 102 C5 *var.* Limassol.
    SW Cyprus
Lemhi Range 46 D3 *mountain range*
    Idaho, C USA North America
Lemnos *see* Límnos
Lemovices *see* Limoges
Lena 115 F3 *river* NE Russia
Lena Tablemount 141 B7 *seamount*
    S Indian Ocean
Len Dao 128 C8 *island* N Spratly Islands
Leninabad *see* Khujand
Leninakan *see* Gyumri
Lenine 109 G5 *Rus.* Lenino. Avtonomna
    Respublika Krym, S Ukraine
Leningor *see* Leninogorsk
Leningrad *see* Sankt-Peterburg
Leningradskaya 154 B4 *Russian research
    station* Antarctica
Lenino *see* Lenine, Ukraine
Leninobod *see* Khujand
Leninogorsk *see* Ridder
Leninpol' 123 F2 Talasskaya Oblast',
    NW Kyrgyzstan
Lenin-Turkmenski *see* Türkmenabat
Lenkoran' *see* Länkäran
Lenti 99 B7 Zala, SW Hungary
Lentia *see* Linz
Leoben 95 E7 Steiermark, C Austria
León 51 E4 *var.* León de los Aldamas.
    Guanajuato, C Mexico
León 52 C3 León, NW Nicaragua
León 92 C3 Castilla y León, NW Spain
León de los Aldamas *see* León
Leonídi *see* Leonídio
Leonídio 105 B6 *var.* Leonídi.
    Pelopónnisos, S Greece
Léopold II, Lac *see* Mai-Ndombe, Lac
Léopoldville *see* Kinshasa
Lepe 92 C4 Andalucía, S Spain

Lepel' *see* Lyepyel'
le Portel 90 C2 Pas-de-Calais, N France
Le Puglie *see* Puglia
le Puy 91 C5 *prev.* le Puy-en-Velay, *hist.*
    Anicium, Podium Anicensis.
    Haute-Loire, C France
le Puy-en-Velay *see* le Puy
Léré 76 B4 Mayo-Kébbi, SW Chad
Lérida *see* Lleida
Lerma 92 D2 Castilla y León, N Spain
Leros 105 D6 *island* Dodekánisa, Greece,
    Aegean Sea
Lerrnayin Gharabakh *see*
    Nagornyy-Karabakh
Lerwick 88 D1 NE Scotland, United
    Kingdom
Lesbos 116 A3 *anc.* Lesbos. *island*
    E Greece
Lesbos *see* Lésvos
Les Cayes *see* Cayes
Les Gonaïves *see* Gonaïves
Leshan 128 B5 Sichuan, C China
les Herbiers 90 B4 Vendée, NW France
Lesh/Leshi *see* Lezhë
Lesina *see* Hvar
Leskovac 101 E5 Serbia, SE Serbia
Lesnoy 114 C3 Sverdlovskaya Oblast',
    C Russia
Lesotho 78 D4 *off.* Kingdom of Lesotho;
    prev. Basutoland. *country* S Africa
Lesotho, Kingdom of *see* Lesotho
les Sables-d'Olonne 90 B4 Vendée,
    NW France
Lesser Antarctica *see* West Antarctica
Lesser Antilles 55 G4 *island group*
    E West Indies
Lesser Caucasus 117 F2 *Rus.* Malyy
    Kavkaz. *mountain range* SW Asia
Lesser Khingan Range *see* Xiao Hinggan
    Ling
Lesser Sunda Islands 139 E5 *Eng.* Lesser
    Sunda Islands. *island group*
    C Indonesia
Lesser Sunda Islands *see* Nusa Tenggara
Leszno 98 B4 *Ger.* Lissa. Wielkopolskie,
    C Poland
Lethbridge 37 E5 Alberta, SW Canada
Lethem 59 F3 S Guyana
Leti, Kepulauan 139 F5 *island group*
    E Indonesia
Letpadan 136 B4 Bago, SW Myanmar
    (Burma)
Letsôk-aw Kyun 137 B6 *var.* Letsutan
    Island; *prev.* Domel Island. *island*
    Myeik Archipelago, S Myanmar
    (Burma)
Letsutan Island *see* Letsôk-aw Kyun
Lettland *see* Latvia
Lëtzebuerg *see* Luxembourg
Leucas *see* Lefkáda
Leuven 87 C6 *Fr.* Louvain, *Ger.* Löwen.
    Vlaams Brabant, C Belgium
Leuze *see* Leuze-en-Hainaut
Leuze-en-Hainaut 87 B6 *var.* Leuze.
    Hainaut, SW Belgium
Léva *see* Levice
Levanger 84 B4 Nord-Trøndelag,
    C Norway
Levelland 49 E2 Texas, SW USA
Leverkusen 94 A4 Nordrhein-Westfalen,
    W Germany
Levice 99 C6 *Ger.* Lewentz, *Hung.* Léva,
    Lewenz. Nitriansky Kraj, SW Slovakia
Levin 150 D4 Manawatu-Wanganui,
    North Island, New Zealand
Levkás *see* Lefkáda
Levkímmi *see* Lefkímmi
Lewentz/Lewenz *see* Levice
Lewis, Isle of 88 B2 *island* NW Scotland,
    United Kingdom
Lewis Range 44 B1 *mountain range*
    Montana, NW USA
Lewiston 46 C2 Idaho, NW USA
Lewiston 41 G2 Maine, NE USA
Lewistown 44 C1 Montana,
    NW USA
Lexington 40 C5 Kentucky, S USA
Lexington 45 E4 Nebraska, C USA
Leyden *see* Leiden
Leyte 139 F2 *island* C Philippines
Leżajsk 99 E5 Podkarpackie,
    SE Poland
Lezha *see* Lezhë
Lezhë 101 C6 *var.* Lezha; *prev.* Lesh,
    Leshi. Lezhë, NW Albania
Lhasa 126 C5 *var.* La-sa, Lassa. Xizang
    Zizhiqu, W China
Lhaviyani Atoll *see* Faadhippolhu Atoll
Lhazê 126 C5 *var.* Quxar. Xizang
    Zizhiqu, China E Asia

L'Hospitalet de Llobregat 93 G2 *var.*
    Hospitalet. Cataluña, NE Spain
Liancourt Rocks 131 A5 *Jap.* Takeshima,
    Kor. Dokdo. *island group*
    Japan/South Korea
Lianyungang 128 D4 *var.* Xinpu.
    Jiangsu, E China
Liao *see* Liaoning
Liaodong Wan 127 G3 *Eng.* Gulf of
    Lantung, Gulf of Liantung. *gulf*
    NE China
Liao He 125 E1 *river* NE China
Liaoning 128 D3 *var.* Liao, Liaoning
    Sheng, Shengking, *hist.* Fengtien,
    Shenking. *province* NE China
Liaoning Sheng *see* Liaoning
Liaoyuan 129 E3 *var.* Dongliao,
    Shuang-liao, *Jap.* Chengchiatun. Jilin,
    NE China
Liard *see* Fort Liard
Liban *see* Lebanon
Liban, Jebel 118 B4 *Ar.* Jabal al Gharbt,
    Jabal Lubnān, *Eng.* Mount Lebanon.
    mountain range C Lebanon
Libau *see* Liepāja
Libby 44 A1 Montana, NW USA
Liberal 45 E5 Kansas, C USA
Liberalitas Julia *see* Évora
Liberec 98 B4 *Ger.* Reichenberg.
    Liberecký Kraj, N Czech Republic
    (Czechia)
Liberia 52 D4 Guanacaste, NW Costa
    Rica
Liberia 74 C5 *off.* Republic of Liberia.
    country W Africa
Liberia, Republic of *see* Liberia
Libian Desert *see* Libyan Desert
Libīyah, Aş Şahrā' al *see* Libyan Desert
Libourne 91 B5 Gironde, SW France
Libreville 77 A5 *country capital* (Gabon)
    Estuaire, NW Gabon
Libya 71 F3 *off.* Libya, *Ar.* Al Jamāhīrīyah
    al 'Arabīyah al Lībīyah ash Sha'bīyah al
    Ishtirākīy; *prev.* Libyan Arab Republic,
    Great Socialist People's Libyan Arab
    Jamahiriya. *country* N Africa
Libyan Arab Republic *see* Libya
Libyan Desert 71 H4 *var.* Libian Desert,
    Ar. Aş Şahrā' al Lībīyah. *desert*
    N Africa
Libyan Plateau 103 F4 *var.* Aḍ Diffah.
    plateau Egypt/Libya
Lichtenfels 95 C5 Bayern, SE Germany
Lichtenvoorde 86 E4 Gelderland,
    E Netherlands
Lichuan 128 C5 Hubei, C China
Lida 107 B5 Hrodzyenskaya Voblasts',
    W Belarus
Lidhoríkion *see* Lidoríki
Lidköping 85 B6 Västra Götaland,
    S Sweden
Lidokhorikion *see* Lidoríki
Lidoríki 105 B5 *prev.* Lidhoríkion,
    Lidokhorikion. Stereá Elláda,
    C Greece
Lidzbark Warmiński 98 D2 *Ger.*
    Heilsberg. Olsztyn, N Poland
Liechtenstein 94 D1 *off.* Principality of
    Liechtenstein. *country* C Europe
Liechtenstein, Principality of *see*
    Liechtenstein
Liège 87 D6 *Dut.* Luik, *Ger.* Lüttich.
    Liège, E Belgium
Liegnitz *see* Legnica
Lienz 95 D7 Tirol, W Austria
Liepāja 106 B3 *Ger.* Libau. W Latvia
Lietuva *see* Lithuania
Lievenhof *see* Līvāni
Liezen 95 D7 Steiermark, C Austria
Liffey 89 B5 *river* Ireland
Lifou 150 D5 *island* Îles Loyauté,
    E New Caledonia
Liger *see* Loire
Ligure, Appennino 96 A2 *Eng.* Ligurian
    Mountains. *mountain range* NW Italy
Ligure, Mar *see* Ligurian Sea
Ligurian Mountains *see* Ligure,
    Appennino
Ligurian Sea 96 A3 *Fr.* Mer Ligurienne,
    It. Mar Ligure. *sea* N Mediterranean Sea
Ligurienne, Mer *see* Ligurian Sea
Lihu'e 47 A7 *var.* Lihue. Kaua'i, Hawaii,
    USA
Lihue *see* Lihu'e
Lihula 106 D2 *Ger.* Leal. Läänemaa,
    W Estonia
Liivi Laht *see* Riga, Gulf of
Likasi 77 D7 *prev.* Jadotville. Shaba,
    SE Dem. Rep. Congo
Liknes 85 A6 Vest-Agder, S Norway

Lille 90 C2 *var.* l'Isle, *Dut.* Rijssel, *Flem.*
    Ryssel, *prev.* Lisle; *anc.* Insula. Nord,
    N France
Lillehammer 85 B5 Oppland, S Norway
Lillestrøm 85 B6 Akershus, S Norway
Lilongwe 79 E2 *country capital* (Malawi)
    Central , W Malawi
Lilybaeum *see* Marsala
Lima 60 C4 *country capital* (Peru) Lima,
    W Peru
Limanowa 99 D5 Małopolskie, S Poland
Limassol *see* Lemesós
Limerick 89 A6 *Ir.* Luimneach. Limerick,
    SW Ireland
Limín Vathéos *see* Sámos
Límnos 103 F3 *anc.* Lemnos. *island*
    E Greece
Limoges 91 C5 *anc.* Augustoritum
    Lemovicensium, Lemovices.
    Haute-Vienne, C France
Limón 53 E4 *var.* Puerto Limón. Limón,
    E Costa Rica
Limón 52 D2 Colón, NE Honduras
Limonum *see* Poitiers
Limousin 91 C5 *cultural region* C France
Limoux 91 C6 Aude, S France
Limpopo 78 D3 *var.* Crocodile. *river*
    S Africa
Linares 64 B4 Maule, C Chile
Linares 51 E3 Nuevo León, NE Mexico
Linares 92 D4 Andalucía, S Spain
Lincoln 89 D5 *anc.* Lindum, Lindum
    Colonia. E England, United Kingdom
Lincoln 41 H2 Maine, NE USA
Lincoln 45 F4 *state capital* Nebraska,
    C USA
Lincoln Sea 34 D2 *sea* Arctic Ocean
Linden 59 F3 E Guyana
Lindhos *see* Líndos
Lindi 73 D8 Lindi, SE Tanzania
Líndos 105 E7 *var.* Líndhos. Ródos,
    Dodekánisa, Greece, Aegean Sea
Lindum/Lindum Colonia *see* Lincoln
Line Islands 145 G3 *island group*
    E Kiribati
Lingeh *see* Bandar-e Lengeh
Lingen 94 A3 *var.* Lingen an der Ems.
    Niedersachsen, NW Germany
Lingen an der Ems *see* Lingen
Lingga, Kepulauan 138 B4 *island group*
    W Indonesia
Lingling 129 C6 *prev.* Yongzhou,
    Zhishan. Hunan, S China
Linköping 85 C6 Östergötland,
    S Sweden
Linz 95 D6 *anc.* Lentia. Oberösterreich,
    N Austria
Lion, Gulf of 91 C7 *Eng.* Gulf of Lion,
    Gulf of Lions; *anc.* Sinus Gallicus. *gulf*
    S France
Lion, Gulf of/Lions, Gulf of *see* Lion,
    Golfe du
Liozno *see* Lyozna
Lipari 97 D6 *island* Isole Eolie, S Italy
Lipari Islands/Lipari, Isole *see* Eolie,
    Isole
Lipetsk 111 B5 Lipetskaya Oblast',
    W Russia
Lipno 98 C3 Kujawsko-pomorskie,
    C Poland
Lipova 108 A4 *Hung.* Lippa. Arad,
    W Romania
Lipovets *see* Lypovets'
Lippa *see* Lipova
Lipsia/Lipsk *see* Leipzig
Lira 73 B6 N Uganda
Lisala 77 C5 Equateur, N Dem. Rep.
    Congo
Lisboa 92 B4 *Eng.* Lisbon; *anc.* Felicitas
    Julia, Olisipo. *country capital*
    (Portugal) Lisboa, W Portugal
Lisbon *see* Lisboa
Lisichansk *see* Lysychans'k
Lisieux 90 B3 *anc.* Noviomagus.
    Calvados, N France
Liski 111 B6 *prev.* Georgiu-Dezh.
    Voronezhskaya Oblast', W Russia
Lisle/l'Isle *see* Lille
Lismore 149 E5 New South Wales,
    SE Australia
Lissa *see* Vis, Croatia
Lissa *see* Leszno, Poland
Lisse 86 C3 Zuid-Holland,
    W Netherlands
Litang 128 A5 *var.* Gaocheng. Sichuan,
    C China
Litani, Nahr el 119 B5 *var.* Nahr el
    Litant. *river* C Lebanon
Litant, Nahr el *see* Litani, Nahr el
Litauen *see* Lithuania

Lithgow *149 D6* New South Wales, SE Australia
Lithuania *106 B4 off.* Republic of Lithuania, *Ger.* Litauen, *Lith.* Lietuva, *Pol.* Litwa, *Rus.* Litva; *prev.* Lithuanian SSR, *Rus.* Litovskaya SSR. *country* NE Europe
Lithuanian SSR *see* Lithuania
Lithuania, Republic of *see* Lithuania
Litóchoro *104 B4 var.* Litohoro, Litókhoron. Kentrikí Makedonía, N Greece
Litohoro/Litókhoron *see* Litóchoro
Litovskaya SSR *see* Lithuania
Little Alföld *99 C6 Ger.* Kleines Ungarisches Tiefland, *Hung.* Kisalföld, *Slvk.* Podunajská Rovina. *plain* Hungary/Slovakia
Little Andaman *133 F2 island* Andaman Islands, India, NE Indian Ocean
Little Barrier Island *150 D2 island* N New Zealand
Little Bay *93 H5 bay* Alboran Sea, Mediterranean Sea
Little Cayman *54 B3 island* E Cayman Islands
Little Falls *45 F2* Minnesota, N USA
Littlefield *49 E2* Texas, SW USA
Little Inagua *54 D2 var.* Inagua Islands. *island* S The Bahamas
Little Minch, The *88 B3 strait* NW Scotland, United Kingdom
Little Missouri River *44 D2 river* NW USA
Little Nicobar *133 G3 island* Nicobar Islands, India, NE Indian Ocean
Little Rhody *see* Rhode Island
Little Rock *42 B1 state capital* Arkansas, C USA
Little St Bernard Pass *91 D5 Fr.* Col du Petit St-Bernard, *It.* Colle del Piccolo San Bernardo. *pass* France/Italy
Little Sound *42 A5 bay* Bermuda, NW Atlantic Ocean
Littleton *44 D4* Colorado, C USA
Littoria *see* Latina
Litva/Litwa *see* Lithuania
Liu-chou/Liuchow *see* Liuzhou
Liuzhou *128 C6 var.* Liu-chou, Liuchow. Guangxi Zhuangzu Zizhiqu, S China
Livanátai *see* Livanátes
Livanátes *105 B5 prev.* Livanátai. Stereá Elláda, C Greece
Lïväni *106 D4 Ger.* Lievenhof. SE Latvia
Liverpool *39 F5* Nova Scotia, SE Canada
Liverpool *89 C5* NW England, United Kingdom
Livingston *44 B2* Montana, NW USA
Livingston *49 H3* Texas, SW USA
Livingstone *49 H3 var.* Maramba. Southern, S Zambia
Livingstone *78 C3 var.* Maramba. Southern, S Zambia
Livingstone Mountains *151 A7 mountain range* South Island, New Zealand
Livno *100 B4* Federacija Bosne I Hercegovine, SW Bosnia and Herzegovina
Livojoki *84 D4 river* C Finland
Livonia *40 D3* Michigan, N USA
Livorno *96 B3 Eng.* Leghorn. Toscana, C Italy
Lixian Jiang *see* Black River
Lixoúri *105 A5 prev.* Lixoúrion. Kefallinía, Iónia Nisiá, Greece, C Mediterranean Sea
Lixoúrion *see* Lixoúri
Lizarra *see* Estella
Ljouwert *see* Leeuwarden
Ljubelj *see* Loibl Pass
Ljubljana *95 D7 Ger.* Laibach, *It.* Lubiana; *anc.* Aemona, Emona. *country capital* (Slovenia) C Slovenia
Ljungby *85 B7* Kronoberg, S Sweden
Ljusdal *85 C5* Gävleborg, C Sweden
Ljusnan *85 C5 river* C Sweden
Llanelli *89 C6 prev.* Llanelly. SW Wales, United Kingdom
Llanelly *see* Llanelli
Llanes *92 D1* Asturias, N Spain
Llanos *58 D2 physical region* Colombia/ Venezuela
Lleida *93 F2 Cast.* Lérida; *anc.* Ilerda. Cataluña, NE Spain
Llucmajor *93 G3* Mallorca, Spain, W Mediterranean Sea
Loaita Island *128 C8 island* W Spratly Islands
Loanda *see* Luanda

Lobamba *78 D4 country capital* (Eswatini - royal and legislative) NW Eswatini (Swaziland)
Lobatse *78 C4 var.* Lobatsi. Kgatleng, SE Botswana
Lobatsi *see* Lobatse
Löbau *94 D4* Sachsen, E Germany
Lobito *78 B2* Benguela, W Angola
Lob Nor *see* Lop Nur
Lobositz *see* Lovosice
Loburi *see* Lop Buri
Locarno *95 B8 Ger.* Luggarus. Ticino, S Switzerland
Lochem *86 E3* Gelderland, E Netherlands
Lockport *41 E3* New York, NE USA
Lodja *77 D6* Kasai-Oriental, C Dem. Rep. Congo
Lodwar *73 C6* Rift Valley, NW Kenya
Łódź *98 D4 Rus.* Lodz. Łódź, C Poland
Loei *136 C4 var.* Loey, Muang Loei. Loei, C Thailand
Loey *see* Loei
Lofoten *84 B3 var.* Lofoten Islands. *island group* C Norway
Lofoten Islands *see* Lofoten
Logan *44 B3* Utah, W USA
Logan, Mount *36 D3 mountain* Yukon, W Canada
Logroño *93 E1 anc.* Vareia, *Lat.* Juliobriga. La Rioja, N Spain
Loibl Pass *95 D7 Ger.* Loiblpass, *Slvn.* Ljubelj. *pass* Austria/Slovenia
Loiblpass *see* Loibl Pass
Loikaw *136 B4* Kayah State, C Myanmar (Burma)
Loire *90 B4 var.* Liger. *river* C France
Loja *60 B2* Loja, S Ecuador
Loja *92 D5* Andalucía, S Spain
Lokitaung *73 C5* Rift Valley, NW Kenya
Lokoja *75 G4* Kogi, C Nigeria
Loksa *106 E2 Ger.* Loxa. Harjumaa, NW Estonia
Lolland *85 B8 prev.* Laaland. *island* S Denmark
Lom *104 C1 prev.* Lom-Palanka. Montana, NW Bulgaria
Lomami *77 D6 river* C Dem. Rep. Congo
Lomas *60 D4* Arequipa, SW Peru
Lomas de Zamora *64 D4* Buenos Aires, E Argentina
Lombardia *96 B2 Eng.* Lombardy. *region* N Italy
Lombardy *see* Lombardia
Lombok, Pulau *138 D5 island* Nusa Tenggara, C Indonesia
Lomé *75 F5 country capital* (Togo) S Togo
Lomela *77 D6* Kasai-Oriental, C Dem. Rep. Congo
Lommel *87 C5* Limburg, N Belgium
Lomond, Loch *88 B4 lake* C Scotland, United Kingdom
Lomonosov Ridge *155 B3 var.* Harris Ridge, *Rus.* Khrebet Homonsova. *undersea ridge* Arctic Ocean
Lomonsova, Khrebet *see* Lomonosov Ridge
Lom-Palanka *see* Lom
Lompoc *47 B7* California, W USA
Lom Sak *136 C4 var.* Muang Lom Sak. Phetchabun, C Thailand
Lomza *see* Łomża
Łomża *98 D3 Rus.* Lomzha. Podlaskie, NE Poland
Lomzha *see* Łomża
Loncoche *65 B5* Araucanía, C Chile
Londinium *see* London
London *89 A7 anc.* Augusta, *Lat.* Londinium. *country capital* (United Kingdom) SE England, United Kingdom
London *38 C5* Ontario, S Canada
London *40 C5* Kentucky, S USA
Londonderry *88 B4 var.* Derry, *Ir.* Doire. NW Northern Ireland, United Kingdom
Londonderry, Cape *146 C2 cape* Western Australia
Londrina *63 E4* Paraná, S Brazil
Lone Star State *see* Texas
Long Bay *43 F2 bay* W Jamaica
Long Beach *47 C7* California, W USA
Longford *89 B5 Ir.* An Longfort. Longford, C Ireland
Long Island *54 D2 island* C The Bahamas
Long Island *41 G4 island* New York, NE USA
Longlac *38 C3* Ontario, S Canada
Longmont *44 D4* Colorado, C USA
Longreach *148 C4* Queensland, E Australia

Long Strait *115 G1 Eng.* Long Strait. *strait* NE Russia
Long Strait *see* Longa, Proliv
Longview *49 H3* Texas, SW USA
Longview *46 B2* Washington, NW USA
Long Xuyên *137 D6 var.* Longxuyen. An Giang, S Vietnam
Longxuyen *see* Long Xuyên
Longyan *128 D6* Fujian, SE China
Longyearbyen *83 G2 dependent territory capital* (Svalbard) Spitsbergen, W Svalbard
Lons-le-Saunier *90 D4 anc.* Ledo Salinarius. Jura, E France
Lop Buri *137 C5 var.* Loburi. Lop Buri, C Thailand
Lop Nor *see* Lop Nur
Lop Nur *126 C3 var.* Lob Nor, Lop Nor, Lo-pu Po. *seasonal lake* NW China
Lo-pu Po *see* Lop Nur
Loppersum *86 E1* Groningen, NE Netherlands
Lorca *93 E4 Ar.* Lurka; *anc.* Eliocroca, *Lat.* Illurco. Murcia, S Spain
Lord Howe Island *142 C4 island* E Australia
Lord Howe Rise *142 C4 undersea rise* SW Pacific Ocean
Loreto *50 B3* Baja California Sur, NW Mexico
Lorient *90 A3 prev.* l'Orient. Morbihan, NW France
l'Orient *see* Lorient
Lorn, Firth of *88 B4 inlet* W Scotland, United Kingdom
Loro Sae *see* East Timor
Lörrach *95 A7* Baden-Württemberg, S Germany
Lorraine *90 D3 cultural region* NE France
Los Alamos *48 C1* New Mexico, SW USA
Los Amates *52 B2* Izabal, E Guatemala
Los Ángeles *65 B5* Bío Bío, C Chile
Los Angeles *47 C7* California, W USA
Losanna *see* Lausanne
Lošinj *100 A3 Ger.* Lussin, *It.* Lussino. *island* W Croatia
Loslau *see* Wodzisław Śląski
Los Mochis *50 C3* Sinaloa, C Mexico
Losonc/Losontz *see* Lučenec
Los Roques, Islas *58 D1 island group* N Venezuela
Lot *91 B5 cultural region* S France
Lot *91 B5 river* S France
Lotagipi Swamp *73 C5 wetland* Kenya/ Sudan
Lötzen *see* Giżycko
Loualaba *see* Lualaba
Louangnamtha *136 C3 var.* Luong Nam Tha. Louang Namtha, N Laos
Louangphabang *124 D3 var.* Louangphrabang, Luang Prabang. Louangphabang, N Laos
Louangphrabang *see* Louangphabang
Loubomo *see* Dolisie
Loudéac *90 A3 Côtes d'Armor, NW France
Loudi *128 C5* Hunan, S China
Louga *74 B3* NW Senegal
Louisiade Archipelago *144 B4 island group* SE Papua New Guinea
Louisiana *42 A2 off.* State of Louisiana, *also known as* Creole State, Pelican State. *state* S USA
Louisville *40 C5* Kentucky, S USA
Louisville Ridge *143 E4 undersea ridge* S Pacific Ocean
Loup River *45 E4 river* Nebraska, C USA
Lourdes *91 B6* Hautes-Pyrénées, S France
Lourenço Marques *see* Maputo
Louth *89 E5* E England, United Kingdom
Loutrá *104 C4* Kentrikí Makedonía, N Greece
Louvain *see* Leuven
Louvain-la-Neuve *87 C6* Walloon Brabant, C Belgium
Louviers *90 C3* Eure, N France
Lovech *104 C2* Lovech, N Bulgaria
Loveland *44 D4* Colorado, C USA
Lovosice *98 A4 Ger.* Lobositz. Ustecký Kraj, NW Czech Republic (Czechia)
Lóvua *78 D1* Moxico, E Angola
Lowell *41 G3* Massachusetts, NE USA
Löwen *see* Leuven
Lower California *48 A4 Eng.* Lower California. *peninsula* NW Mexico
Lower California *see* Baja California
Lower Hutt *151 D5* Wellington, North Island, New Zealand

Long Strait *115 G1 Eng.* Long Strait. *strait* NE Russia
Lower Lough Erne *89 A5 lake* SW Northern Ireland, United Kingdom
Lower Red Lake *45 F1 lake* Minnesota, N USA
Lower Rhine *see* Neder Rijn
Lower Tunguska *115 E3 Eng.* Lower Tunguska. *river* N Russia
Lower Tunguska *see* Nizhnyaya Tunguska
Lowestoft *89 E6* E England, United Kingdom
Loxa *see* Loksa
Lo-yang *see* Luoyang
Loyauté, Îles *144 D5 island group* S New Caledonia
Loyev *see* Loyew
Loyew *107 D8 Rus.* Loyev. Homyel'skaya Voblasts', SE Belarus
Loznica *100 C3* Serbia, W Serbia
Lu *see* Shandong, China
Lualaba *77 D6 Fr.* Loualaba. *river* SE Dem. Rep. Congo
Luanda *78 A1 var.* Loanda, *Port.* São Paulo de Loanda. *country capital* (Angola) Luanda, NW Angola
Luang Prabang *see* Louangphabang
Luang, Thale *137 C7 lagoon* S Thailand
Luangua, Rio *see* Luangwa
Luangwa *73 B8 var.* Aruângua, Rio Luangua. *river* Mozambique/Zambia
Luanshya *78 D2* Copperbelt, C Zambia
Luarca *92 C1* Asturias, N Spain
Lubaczów *99 E5 var.* Lúbaczów. Podkarpackie, SE Poland
L'uban' *98 B4* Leningradskaya Oblast', Russia
Lubānas Ezers *see* Lubāns
Lubango *78 B2 Port.* Sá da Bandeira. Huíla, SW Angola
Lubāns *106 D4 var.* Lubānas Ezers. *lake* E Latvia
Lubao *77 D6* Kasai-Oriental, C Dem. Rep. Congo
Lübben *94 D4* Brandenburg, E Germany
Lübbenau *94 D4* Brandenburg, E Germany
Lubbock *49 E2* Texas, SW USA
Lübeck *94 C2* Schleswig-Holstein, N Germany
Lubelska, Wyżyna *98 E4 plateau* SE Poland
Lüben *see* Lubin
Lubiana *see* Ljubljana
Lubin *98 B4 Ger.* Lüben. Dolnośląskie, SW Poland
Lublin *98 E4 Rus.* Lyublin. Lubelskie, E Poland
Lubliniec *98 C4* Śląskie, S Poland
Lubnān, Jabal *see* Liban, Jebel
Lubny *109 F2* Poltavs'ka Oblast', NE Ukraine
Lubsko *98 B4 Ger.* Sommerfeld. Lubuskie, W Poland
Lubumbashi *77 E8 prev.* Élisabethville. Shaba, SE Dem. Rep. Congo
Lubutu *77 D6* Maniema, E Dem. Rep. Congo
Luca *see* Lucca
Lucan *89 B5 Ir.* Leamhcán. Dublin, E Ireland
Lucanian Mountains *see* Lucano, Appennino
Lucano, Appennino *97 D5 Eng.* Lucanian Mountains. *mountain range* S Italy
Lucapa *78 C1 var.* Lukapa. Lunda Norte, NE Angola
Lucca *96 B3 anc.* Luca. Toscana, C Italy
Lucea *54 A4* W Jamaica
Lucena *139 E1 off.* Lucena City. Luzon, N Philippines
Lucena *92 D4* Andalucía, S Spain
Lucena City *see* Lucena
Lučenec *99 D6 Ger.* Losontz, *Hung.* Losonc. Banskobystrický Kraj, C Slovakia
Lucentum *see* Alicante
Luchow/Lucerne *see* Luzern
Luchow *see* Hefei
Łuck *see* Luts'k
Lucknow *134 D3 var.* Lakhnau. *state capital* Uttar Pradesh, N India
Lüda *see* Dalian
Luda Kamchiya *104 D2 river* E Bulgaria
Lüderitz *78 B4 prev.* Angra Pequena. Karas, SW Namibia
Ludhiāna *134 D2* Punjab, N India
Ludington *40 C2* Michigan, N USA

Ludsan see Ludza
Luduş 108 B4 Ger. Ludasch, Hung.
Marosludas.
Ludvika 85 C6 Dalarna, C Sweden
Ludwigsburg 95 B6 Baden-
Württemberg, SW Germany
Ludwigsfelde 94 D3 Brandenburg,
NE Germany
Ludwigshafen 95 B5 var. Ludwigshafen
am Rhein. Rheinland-Pfalz,
W Germany
Ludwigshafen am Rhein see
Ludwigshafen
Ludwigslust 94 C3 Mecklenburg-
Vorpommern, N Germany
Ludza 106 D4 Ger. Ludsan. E Latvia
Luebo 77 C6 Kasai-Occidental,
SW Dem. Rep. Congo
Luena 78 C2 var. Lwena, Port. Luso.
Moxico, E Angola
Lufira 77 E7 river SE Dem. Rep. Congo
Lufkin 49 H3 Texas, SW USA
Luga 110 A4 Leningradskaya Oblast',
NW Russia
Lugano 95 B8 Ger. Lauis. Ticino,
S Switzerland
Lugansk see Luhans'k
Lugdunum see Lyon
Lugdunum Batavorum see Leiden
Lugenda, Rio 79 E2 river N Mozambique
Luggarus see Locarno
Lugh Ganana see Luuq
Lugo 92 C1 anc. Lugus Augusti. Galicia,
NW Spain
Lugoj 108 A4 Ger. Lugosch, Hung.
Lugos. Timiş, W Romania
Lugos/Lugosch see Lugoj
Lugus Augusti see Lugo
Luguvallium/Luguvallum see Carlisle
Luhans'k 109 H3 Rus. Lugansk; prev.
Voroshilovgrad. Luhans'ka Oblast',
E Ukraine
Luimneach see Limerick
Lukapa see Lucapa
Lukenie 77 C6 river C Dem. Rep. Congo
Lukovit 104 C2 Lovech, N Bulgaria
Łuków 98 E4 Ger. Bogendorf. Lubelskie,
E Poland
Lukuga 77 D7 river SE Dem. Rep. Congo
Luleå 84 D4 Norrbotten, N Sweden
Luleälven 84 C3 river N Sweden
Lulonga 77 C5 river NW Dem. Rep.
Congo
Lulua 77 D7 river S Dem. Rep. Congo
Luluabourg see Kananga
Lumber State see Maine
Lumbo 79 F2 Nampula,
NE Mozambique
Lumsden 151 A7 Southland, South
Island, New Zealand
Lund 85 B7 Skåne, S Sweden
Lüneburg 94 C3 Niedersachsen,
N Germany
Lunga, Isola see Dugi Otok
Lungkiang see Qiqihar
Lungué-Bungo 72 C2 var.
Lungwebungu. river Angola/Zambia
Lungwebungu see Lungué-Bungo
Luninets see Luninyets
Łuniniec see Luninyets
Luninyets 107 B7 Pol. Łuniniec, Rus.
Luninets. Brestskaya Voblasts',
SW Belarus
Lunteren 86 D4 Gelderland,
C Netherlands
Luong Nam Tha see Louangnamtha
Luoyang 128 C4 var. Honan, Lo-yang.
Henan, C China
Lupatia see Altamura
Lúrio 79 F2 Nampula, NE Mozambique
Lúrio, Rio 79 E2 river NE Mozambique
Lurka see Lorca
Lusaka 78 D2 country capital (Zambia)
Lusaka, SE Zambia
Lushnja see Lushnjë
Lushnjë 101 C6 var. Lushnja. Fier,
C Albania
Luso see Luena
Lussin/Lussino see Lošinj
Lüt, Baḥrat/Lut, Bahret see Dead Sea
Lut, Dasht-e 120 D3 var. Kavīr-e Lūt.
desert E Iran
Lutetia/Lutetia Parisiorum see Paris
Lūt, Kavīr-e see Lūt, Dasht-e
Luton 89 D6 E England, United Kingdom
Łutselk'e 37 F4 prev. Snowdrift.
Northwest Territories, W Canada
Luts'k 108 C1 Pol. Łuck, Rus. Lutsk.
Volyns'ka Oblast', NW Ukraine
Lutsk see Luts'k

Lüttich see Liège
Lutzow-Holm Bay 154 C2 var.
Lutzow-Holm Bay. bay Antarctica
Lützow-Holm Bay see Lützow
Holmbukta
Luuq 73 D6 It. Lugh Ganana. Gedo,
SW Somalia
Luvua 77 D7 river SE Dem. Rep. Congo
Luwego 73 C8 river S Tanzania
Luxembourg 87 D8 country capital
(Luxembourg) Luxembourg,
S Luxembourg
Luxembourg 87 D8 off. Grand Duchy of
Luxembourg, var. Lëtzebuerg,
Luxemburg. country NW Europe
Luxemburg see Luxembourg
Luxor 72 B2 Ar. Al Uqsur. E Egypt
Luza 110 C4 Kirovskaya Oblast',
NW Russia
Luz, Costa de la 92 C5 coastal region
SW Spain
Luzern 95 B7 Fr. Lucerne, It. Lucerna.
Luzern, C Switzerland
Luzon 139 E1 island N Philippines
Luzon Strait 125 E3 strait Philippines/
Taiwan
L'viv 108 B2 Ger. Lemberg, Pol. Lwów,
Rus. L'vov. L'vivs'ka Oblast',
W Ukraine
L'vov see L'viv
Lwena see Luena
Lwów see L'viv
Lyakhavichy 107 B6 Rus. Lyakhovichi.
Brestskaya Voblasts', SW Belarus
Lyakhovichi see Lyakhavichy
Lyallpur see Faisalabad
Lyangar see Langar
Lyck see Ełk
Lycksele 84 C4 Västerbotten, N Sweden
Lycopolis see Asyūṭ
Lyel'chytsy 107 C7 Rus. Lel'chitsy.
Homyel'skaya Voblasts', SE Belarus
Lyepyel' 107 D5 Rus. Lepel'.
Vitsyebskaya Voblasts', N Belarus
Lyme Bay 89 C7 bay S England, United
Kingdom
Lynchburg 41 E5 Virginia, NE USA
Lynn see King's Lynn
Lynn Lake 37 F4 Manitoba, C Canada
Lynn Regis see King's Lynn
Lyon 91 D5 Eng. Lyons; anc. Lugdunum.
Rhône, E France
Lyons see Lyon
Lyozna 107 E6 Rus. Liozno.
Vitsyebskaya Voblasts', NE Belarus
Lypovets' 108 D2 Rus. Lipovets.
Vinnyts'ka Oblast', C Ukraine
Lys see Leie
Lysychans'k 109 H3 Rus. Lisichansk.
Luhans'ka Oblast', E Ukraine
Lyttelton 151 C6 South Island, New
Zealand
Lyublin see Lublin
Lyubotin see Lyubotyn
Lyubotyn 109 G2 Rus. Lyubotin.
Kharkivs'ka Oblast', E Ukraine
Lyulyakovo 104 E2 prev. Keremitlik.
Burgas, E Bulgaria
Lyusina see Lyusino
Lyusino 107 B6 Rus. Lyusino. Brestskaya
Voblasts', SW Belarus
Lyusino see Lyusina

M

Maale 132 B4 var. Male.
country capital (Maldives) Male' Atoll,
C Maldives
Ma'ān 119 B7 Ma'ān, SW Jordan
Maardu 106 D2 Ger. Maart. Harjumaa,
NW Estonia
Ma'aret-en-Nu'man see Ma'arrat an
Nu'mān
Ma'arrat an Nu'mān 118 B3 var.
Ma'aret-en-Nu'man, Fr. Maarret enn
Naamâne. Idlib, NW Syria
Maarret enn Naamâne see Ma'arrat an
Nu'mān
Maart see Maardu
Maas see Meuse
Maaseik 87 D5 prev. Maeseyck.
Limburg, NE Belgium
Maastricht 87 D6 var. Maestricht; anc.
Traiectum ad Mosam, Traiectum
Tungrorum. Limburg, SE Netherlands
Macao 129 C6 Port. Macau. Special
Administrative Region Guangdong,
SE China
Macapá 63 E1 state capital Amapá,
N Brazil

Macarsca see Makarska
Macassar see Makassar
Macău see Makó, Hungary
Macau see Macao
MacCluer Gulf see Berau, Teluk
Macdonnell Ranges 146 D4 mountain
range Northern Territory, C Australia
Macedonia 79 D6 off. Republic of
Macedonia, var. the former Yugoslav
Republic of Macedonia (used by UN),
Mac. Makedonija, abbrev. FYR
Macedonia, FYROM. country
SE Europe
Macedonia, FYR see Macedonia
Macedonia, Republic of see Macedonia
**Macedonia, the former Yugoslav
Republic of** see Macedonia
Maceió 63 G3 state capital Alagoas,
E Brazil
Machachi 60 B1 Pichincha, C Ecuador
Machala 60 B2 El Oro, SW Ecuador
Machanga 79 E3 Sofala, E Mozambique
Machilipatnam 132 D1 var. Bandar
Masulipatnam. Andhra Pradesh,
E India
Machiques 58 C2 Zulia, NW Venezuela
Macías Nguema Biyogo see Bioco, Isla de
Măcin 108 D5 Tulcea, SE Romania
Mackay 148 D4 Queensland,
NE Australia
Mackay, Lake 146 C4 salt lake Northern
Territory/Western Australia
Mackenzie 37 E3 river Northwest
Territories, NW Canada
Mackenzie Bay 154 D3 bay Antarctica
Mackenzie Mountains 36 D3 mountain
range Northwest Territories,
NW Canada
Macleod, Lake 146 A4 lake Western
Australia
Macomb 40 A4 Illinois, N USA
Macomer 97 A5 Sardegna, Italy,
C Mediterranean Sea
Mâcon 91 D5 anc. Matisco, Matisco
Ædurum. Saône-et-Loire, C France
Macon 42 D2 Georgia, SE USA
Macon 45 G4 Missouri, C USA
Macquarie Ridge 154 C5 undersea ridge
SW Pacific Ocean
Macuspana 51 G4 Tabasco, SE Mexico
Ma'dabā 119 B6 var. Mādabā, Madeba;
anc. Medeba. Ma'dabā, NW Jordan
Mādabā see Ma'dabā
Madagascar 79 F3 off. Democratic
Republic of Madagascar, Malg.
Madagasikara; prev. Malagasy Republic.
country W Indian Ocean
Madagascar 79 F3 island W Indian
Ocean
Madagascar Basin 69 E7 undersea basin
W Indian Ocean
Madagascar, Democratic Republic of
see Madagascar
Madagascar Plateau 69 E7 var.
Madagascar Ridge, Madagascar Rise,
Rus. Madagaskarskiy Khrebet.
undersea plateau W Indian Ocean
Madagascar Rise/Madagascar Ridge see
Madagascar Plateau
Madagasikara see Madagascar
Madagaskarskiy Khrebet see
Madagascar Plateau
Madang 144 B3 Madang, N Papua New
Guinea
Madaniyīn see Médenine
Madarska see Hungary
Made 86 C4 Noord-Brabant,
S Netherlands
Madeba see Ma'dabā
Madeira 70 A2 var. Ilha de Madeira.
island Madeira, Portugal, NE Atlantic
Ocean
Madeira, Ilha de see Madeira
Madeira Plain 66 C3 abyssal plain
E Atlantic Ocean
Madeira, Rio 62 D2 var. Río Madera.
river Bolivia/Brazil
Madeleine, Îles de la 39 F4 Eng.
Magdalen Islands. island group
Québec, E Canada
Madera 47 B6 California, W USA
Madera, Río see Madeira, Rio
Madhya Pradesh 135 E4 prev. Central
Provinces and Berar. cultural region
C India
Madinat ath Thawrah 118 C2 var. Ath
Thawrah. Ar Raqqah, N Syria
Madioen see Madiun
Madison 45 F3 South Dakota,
N USA

Madison 40 B3 state capital Wisconsin,
N USA
Madiun 138 D5 prev. Madioen. Jawa,
C Indonesia
Madoera see Madura, Pulau
Madona 106 D4 Ger. Modohn. E Latvia
Madras see Tamil Nādu
Madras see Chennai
Madre de Dios, Río 61 E3 river Bolivia/
Peru
Madre del Sur, Sierra 51 E5 mountain
range S Mexico
Madre, Laguna 51 F3 lagoon NE Mexico
Madre, Laguna 49 G5 lagoon Texas,
SW USA
Madre Occidental, Sierra 50 C3 var.
Western Sierra Madre. mountain range
C Mexico
Madre Oriental, Sierra 51 E3 var.
Eastern Sierra Madre. mountain range
C Mexico
Madre, Sierra 52 B2 var. Sierra de
Soconusco. mountain range
Guatemala/Mexico
Madrid 92 D3 country capital (Spain)
Madrid, C Spain
Madura see Madurai
Madurai 132 C3 prev. Madura,
Mathurai. Tamil Nādu, S India
Madura, Pulau 138 D5 prev. Madoera.
island C Indonesia
Maebashi 131 D5 var. Maebasi,
Mayebashi. Gunma, Honshū, S Japan
Maebasi see Maebashi
Mae Nam Khong see Mekong
Mae Nam Nan 136 C4 river
NW Thailand
Mae Nam Yom 136 C4 river W Thailand
Maeseyck see Maaseik
Maestricht see Maastricht
Maéwo 144 D4 prev. Aurora. island
C Vanuatu
Mafia 73 D7 island E Tanzania
Mafraq/Muḥāfaẓat al Mafraq see Al
Mafraq
Magadan 115 G3 Magadanskaya Oblast',
E Russia
Magallanes see Punta Arenas
Magallanes, Estrecho de see Magellan,
Strait of
Magangué 58 B2 Bolívar, N Colombia
Magdalena 61 F3 El Beni, N Bolivia
Magdalena 50 B1 Sonora, NW Mexico
Magdalena, Isla 50 B3 island
NW Mexico
Magdalena, Río 58 B2 river C Colombia
Magdalen Islands see Madeleine, Îles de
la
Magdeburg 94 C4 Sachsen-Anhalt,
C Germany
Magelang 138 C5 Jawa, C Indonesia
Magellan, Strait of 65 B8 Sp. Estrecho de
Magallanes. strait Argentina/Chile
Magerøy 84 D1 var. Magerøy, Lapp.
Máhkarávju. island N Norway
Maggiore, Lago see Maggiore, Lake
Maggiore, Lake 96 B1 It. Lago Maggiore.
lake Italy/Switzerland
Maglaj 100 C3 Federacija Bosne I
Hercegovine, N Bosnia and
Herzegovina
Maglie 97 E6 Puglia, SE Italy
Magna 44 B4 Utah, W USA
Magnesia see Manisa
Magnitogorsk 114 B4 Chelyabinskaya
Oblast', C Russia
Magnolia State see Mississippi
Magta' Lahjar 74 C3 var. Magta Lahjar,
Magta' Lahjar, Magtá Lahjar. Brakna,
SW Mauritania
Magtymguly 122 C3 prev. Garrygala;
Rus. Kara-gala. W Turkmenistan
Magway 136 A3 var. Magwe. Magway,
W Myanmar (Burma)
Magyar-Becse see Bečej
Magyarkanizsa see Kanjiža
Magyarország see Hungary
Mahajanga 79 F2 var. Majunga.
Mahajanga, NW Madagascar
Mahakam, Sungai 138 D4 var. Koetai,
Kutai. river Borneo, C Indonesia
Mahalapye 78 D3 var. Mahalatswe.
Central, SE Botswana
Mahalatswe see Mahalapye
Mahān 120 D3 Kermān, E Iran
Mahanādi 135 F4 river E India
Mahārāshtra 134 D5 cultural region
W India
Mahbés see El Mahbas

Mahbūbnagar *134 D5* Telangana, C India

Mahdia *71 F2* var. Al Mahdīyah, Mehdia. NE Tunisia

Mahé *79 H1* island Inner Islands, NE Seychelles

Mahia Peninsula *150 E4* peninsula North Island, New Zealand

Mahilyow *107 D6* Rus. Mogilëv. Mahilyowskaya Voblasts', E Belarus

Máhkarávju *see* Magerøya

Mahmūd-e 'Erāqī *see* Maḥmūd-e Rāqī

Maḥmūd-e Rāqī *123 E4* var. Maḥmūd-e 'Erāqī. Kāpīsā, NE Afghanistan

Māhren *see* Moravia

Mährisch-Weisskirchen *see* Hranice

Maicao *58 C1* La Guajira, N Colombia

Mai Ceu/Mai Chio *see* Maych'ew

Maidān Shahr *123 E4* prev. Meydān Shahr. Vardak, E Afghanistan

Maidstone *89 E7* SE England, United Kingdom

Maiduguri *75 H4* Borno, NE Nigeria

Mailand *see* Milano

Maimāna *see* Maimanah

Maimanah *122 D3* var. Meymaneh, Maymana. Fāryāb, NW Afghanistan

Main *95 B5* river C Germany

Mai-Ndombe, Lac *77 C6* prev. Lac Léopold II. lake W Dem. Rep. Congo

Maine *41 G2* off. State of Maine, also known as Lumber State, Pine Tree State. state NE USA

Maine *90 B3* cultural region NW France

Maine, Gulf of *41 H2* gulf NE USA

Mainland *88 C2* island N Scotland, United Kingdom

Mainland *88 D1* island NE Scotland, United Kingdom

Mainz *95 B5* Fr. Mayence. Rheinland-Pfalz, SW Germany

Maio *74 A3* var. Mayo. island Ilhas de Sotavento, SE Cape Verde

Maisur *see* Mysūru

Maisur *see* Karnātaka

Maitri *132 C2* Indian research station Antarctica

Maizhokunggar *126 C5* Xizang Zizhiqu, W China

Majorca *93 G3* Eng. Majorca; anc. Baleares Major. island Islas Baleares, Spain, W Mediterranean Sea

Majorca *see* Mallorca

Mājro *see* Majuro Atoll

Majunga *see* Mahajanga

Majuro Atoll *144 D2* var. Mājro. atoll and capital (Marshall Islands) Ratak Chain, SE Marshall Islands

Makale *see* Mek'elē

Makarov Basin *155 B3* undersea basin Arctic Ocean

Makarska *100 B4* It. Macarsca. Split-Dalmacija, SE Croatia

Makasar *see* Makassar

Makasar, Selat *see* Makassar Straits

Makassar *139 E4* var. Macassar, Makasar; prev. Ujungpandang. Sulawesi, C Indonesia

Makassar Straits *138 D4* Ind. Makasar Selat. strait C Indonesia

Makay *79 F3* var. Massif du Makay. mountain range SW Madagascar

Makay, Massif du *see* Makay

Makedonija *see* Macedonia

Makeni *74 C4* C Sierra Leone

Makeyevka *see* Makiyivka

Makhachkala *114 A4* prev. Petrovsk-Port. Respublika Dagestan, SW Russia

Makin *144 D2* prev. Pitt Island. atoll Tungaru, W Kiribati

Makira *see* San Cristobal

Makiyivka *109 G3* Rus. Makeyevka; prev. Dmitriyevsk. Donets'ka Oblast', E Ukraine

Makkah *121 A5* Eng. Mecca. Makkah, W Saudi Arabia

Makkovik *39 F2* Newfoundland and Labrador, NE Canada

Makó *99 D7* Rom. Macău. Csongrád, SE Hungary

Makoua *77 B5* Cuvette, C Congo

Makran Coast *120 E4* coastal region SE Iran

Makrany *107 A6* Rus. Mokrany. Brestskaya Voblasts', SW Belarus

Mākū *120 B2* Āżarbāyjān-e Gharbī, NW Iran

Makurdi *75 G4* Benue, C Nigeria

Mala *see* Malaita, Solomon Islands

Malabār Coast *132 B3* coast SW India

Malabo *77 A5* prev. Santa Isabel. country capital (Equatorial Guinea) Isla de Bioco, NW Equatorial Guinea

Malaca *see* Málaga

Malacca, Strait of *138 B3* Ind. Selat Malaka. strait Indonesia/Malaysia

Malacka *see* Malacky

Malacky *99 C6* Hung. Malacka. Bratislavský Kraj, W Slovakia

Maladzyechna *107 C5* Pol. Molodeczno, Rus. Molodechno. Minskaya Voblasts', C Belarus

Málaga *92 D5* anc. Malaca. Andalucía, S Spain

Malagarasi River *73 B7* river W Tanzania Africa

Malagasy Republic *see* Madagascar

Malaita *144 C3* var. Mala. island N Solomon Islands

Malakal *73 B5* Upper Nile, NE South Sudan

Malakula *see* Malekula

Malang *138 D5* Jawa, C Indonesia

Malange *see* Malanje

Malanje *78 B1* var. Malange. Malanje, NW Angola

Mälaren *85 C6* lake C Sweden

Malatya *117 E4* anc. Melitene. Malatya, SE Turkey

Mala Vyska *109 E3* Rus. Malaya Viska. Kirovohrads'ka Oblast', S Ukraine

Malawi *79 E1* off. Republic of Malaŵi; prev. Nyasaland, Nyasaland Protectorate. country S Africa

Malawi, Lake *see* Nyasa, Lake

Malaŵi, Republic of *see* Malawi

Malaya Viska *see* Mala Vyska

Malay Peninsula *124 C6* peninsula Malaysia/Thailand

Malaysia *138 B3* off. Malaysia, var. Federation of Malaysia; prev. the separate territories of Federation of Malaya, Sarawak and Sabah (North Borneo) and Singapore. country SE Asia

Malaysia, Federation of *see* Malaysia

Malbork *98 C2* Ger. Marienburg, Marienburg in Westpreussen. Pomorskie, N Poland

Malchin *94 C3* Mecklenburg-Vorpommern, N Germany

Malden *45 H5* Missouri, C USA

Malden Island *145 G3* prev. Independence Island. atoll E Kiribati

Maldives *132 A4* off. Maldivian Divehi, Republic of Maldives. country N Indian Ocean

Maldives, Republic of *see* Maldives

Maldivian Divehi *see* Maldives

Male *see* Maale

Male' Atoll *132 B4* var. Kaafu Atoll. atoll C Maldives

Malekula *144 D4* var. Malakula; prev. Mallicolo. island W Vanuatu

Malesína *105 C5* Stereá Elláda, E Greece

Malheur Lake *46 C3* lake Oregon, NW USA

Mali *75 E3* off. Republic of Mali, Fr. République du Mali; prev. French Sudan, Sudanese Republic. country W Africa

Malik, Wadi al *see* Milk, Wadi el

Mali Kyun *137 B5* var. Tavoy Island. island Myeik Archipelago, S Myanmar (Burma)

Malin *see* Malyn

Malindi *73 D7* Coast, SE Kenya

Malines *see* Mechelen

Mali, Republic of *see* Mali

Mali, République du *see* Mali

Malkiye *see* Al Mālikīyah

Malko Tŭrnovo *104 E3* Burgas, E Bulgaria

Mallaig *88 B3* N Scotland, United Kingdom

Mallawī *72 B2* var. Mallawi. C Egypt

Mallawi *see* Mallawī

Mallicolo *see* Malekula

Malmberget *84 C3* Lapp. Malmivaara. Norrbotten, N Sweden

Malmédy *87 D6* Liège, E Belgium

Malmivaara *see* Malmberget

Malmö *85 B7* Skåne, S Sweden

Maloelap *see* Maloelap Atoll

Maloelap Atoll *144 D1* var. Maloeļap. atoll E Marshall Islands

Małopolska, Wyżyna *98 D4* plateau S Poland

Malozemel'skaya Tundra *110 D3* physical region NW Russia

Malta *106 D4* SE Latvia

Malta *97 C8* off. Republic of Malta. country C Mediterranean Sea

Malta *97 C8* island Malta, C Mediterranean Sea

Malta, Canale di *see* Malta Channel

Malta Channel *97 C8* It. Canale di Malta. strait Italy/Malta

Malta, Republic of *see* Malta

Maluku, Laut *see* Molucca Sea

Malung *85 B6* Dalarna, C Sweden

Malventum *see* Benevento

Malvina, Isla Gran *see* West Falkland

Malvinas, Islas *see* Falkland Islands

Malyn *108 D2* Rus. Malin. Zhytomyrs'ka Oblast', N Ukraine

Malyy Kavkaz *see* Lesser Caucasus

Mamberamo, Sungai *139 H4* river Papua, E Indonesia

Mambij *see* Manbij

Mamonovo *106 A4* Ger. Heiligenbeil. Kaliningradskaya Oblast', W Russia

Mamoré, Rio *61 F3* river Bolivia/Brazil

Mamou *74 C4* W Guinea

Mamoudzou *79 F2* dependent territory capital (Mayotte) C Mayotte

Mamuno *78 C3* Ghanzi, W Botswana

Manacor *93 G3* Mallorca, Spain, W Mediterranean Sea

Manado *139 F3* prev. Menado. Sulawesi, C Indonesia

Managua *52 D3* country capital (Nicaragua) Managua, W Nicaragua

Managua, Lake *52 C3* var. Xolotlán. lake W Nicaragua

Manakara *79 G4* Fianarantsoa, SE Madagascar

Manama *see* Al Manāmah

Mananjary *79 G3* Fianarantsoa, SE Madagascar

Manáos *see* Manaus

Manapouri, Lake *151 A7* lake South Island, New Zealand

Manar *see* Mannar

Manas, Gora *123 E2* mountain Kyrgyzstan/Uzbekistan

Manaus *62 D2* prev. Manáos. state capital Amazonas, NW Brazil

Manavgat *116 B4* Antalya, SW Turkey

Manbij *118 C2* var. Mambij, Fr. Membidj. Ḩalab, N Syria

Manchester *89 D5* Lat. Mancunium. NW England, United Kingdom

Manchester *41 G3* New Hampshire, NE USA

Man-chou-li *see* Manzhouli

Manchurian Plain *125 E3* plain NE China

Mandalay *136 B3* Mandalay, C Myanmar (Burma)

Mandan *45 E2* North Dakota, N USA

Mandeville *54 B5* C Jamaica

Mándra *105 C6* Attikí, C Greece

Rud-e Mand *120 D4* var. Mand. river S Iran

Mandurah *147 A6* Western Australia

Manduria *97 E5* Puglia, SE Italy

Mandya *132 C2* Karnātaka, C India

Manfredonia *97 D5* Puglia, SE Italy

Mangai *77 C6* Bandundu, W Dem. Rep. Congo

Mangaia *145 G5* island group S Cook Islands

Mangalia *108 D5* anc. Callatis. Constanţa, SE Romania

Mangalmé *76 C3* Guéra, SE Chad

Mangalore *see* Mangalūru

Mangalūru *132 B2* prev. Mangalore. Karnātaka, W India

Mangaung *see* Bloemfontein

Mango *see* Sansanné-Mango, Togo

Mangoky *79 F3* river W Madagascar

Manhattan *45 F4* Kansas, C USA

Manicouagan, Réservoir *38 D3* lake Québec, E Canada

Manihiki *145 G4* atoll N Cook Islands

Manihiki Plateau *143 E3* undersea plateau C Pacific Ocean

Maniitsoq *82 C3* var. Manîtsoq, Dan. Sukkertoppen. Kitaa, S Greenland

Manila *139 E1* off. City of Manila. country capital (Philippines) Luzon, N Philippines

Manila, City of *see* Manila

Manisa *116 A3* var. Manissa, prev. Saruhan; anc. Magnesia. Manisa, W Turkey

Manissa *see* Manisa

Manitoba *37 F5* province S Canada

Manitoba, Lake *37 F5* lake Manitoba, S Canada

Manitoulin Island *38 C4* island Ontario, S Canada

Manitsoq *see* Maniitsoq

Manizales *58 B3* Caldas, W Colombia

Manjimup *147 A7* Western Australia

Mankato *45 F3* Minnesota, N USA

Manlleu *93 G2* Cataluña, NE Spain

Manly *148 E1* Iowa, C USA

Manmād *134 C5* Mahārāshtra, W India

Mannar *132 C3* var. Manar. Northern Province, NW Sri Lanka

Mannar, Gulf of *132 C3* gulf India/Sri Lanka

Mannheim *95 B5* Baden-Württemberg, SW Germany

Manokwari *139 G4* New Guinea, E Indonesia

Manono *77 E7* Shaba, SE Dem. Rep. Congo

Manosque *91 D6* Alpes-de-Haute-Provence, SE France

Manra *145 F3* prev. Sydney Island. atoll Phoenix Islands, C Kiribati

Mansa *78 D2* prev. Fort Rosebery. Luapula, N Zambia

Mansel Island *37 G3* island Nunavut, NE Canada

Mansfield *40 D4* Ohio, N USA

Manta *60 A2* Manabí, W Ecuador

Manteca *47 B6* California, W USA

Mantoue *see* Mantova

Mantova *96 B2* Eng. Mantua, Fr. Mantoue. Lombardia, NW Italy

Mantua *see* Mantova

Manuae *145 G4* island S Cook Islands

Manukau *see* Manurewa

Manurewa *150 D3* var. Manukau. Auckland, North Island, New Zealand

Manzanares *93 E3* Castilla-La Mancha, C Spain

Manzanillo *54 C3* Granma, E Cuba

Manzanillo *50 D4* Colima, SW Mexico

Manzhouli *127 F1* var. Man-chou-li. Nei Mongol Zizhiqu, N China

Mao *76 B3* Kanem, W Chad

Maó-Mahón *93 H3* Eng. Port Mahon; anc. Portus Magonis. Menorca, Spain, W Mediterranean Sea

Maoke, Pegunungan *139 H4* Dut. Sneeuw-gebergte, Eng. Snow Mountains. mountain range Papua, E Indonesia

Maoming *128 C6* Guangdong, S China

Mapmaker Seamounts *125 H2* seamount range N Pacific Ocean

Maputo *78 D4* prev. Lourenço Marques. country capital (Mozambique) Maputo, S Mozambique

Marabá *63 F2* Pará, NE Brazil

Maracaibo *58 C1* Zulia, NW Venezuela

Maracaibo, Gulf of *see* Venezuela, Golfo de

Maracaibo, Lake *58 C2* var. Lake Maracaibo. inlet NW Venezuela

Maracaibo, Lake *see* Maracaibo, Lago de

Maracay *58 D2* Aragua, N Venezuela

Marada *see* Marādah

Marādah *71 G3* var. Marada. N Libya

Maradi *75 G3* Maradi, S Niger

Maragha *see* Marāgheh

Marāgheh *120 C2* var. Maragha. Āżarbāyjān-e Khāvari, NW Iran

Marajó, Baía de *63 F1* bay N Brazil

Marajó, Ilha de *63 E1* island N Brazil

Marakesh *see* Marrakech

Maramba *see* Livingstone

Maramba *see* Livingstone

Maranhão *63 F2* off. Estado do Maranhão. state/region E Brazil

Maranhão, Estado do *see* Maranhão

Marañón, Río *60 B2* river N Peru

Marathon *38 C4* Ontario, S Canada

Marathón *105 C5* prev. Marathon. Attikí, C Greece

Marbella *92 D5* Andalucía, S Spain

Marble Bar *146 B4* Western Australia

Marburg *see* Marburg an der Lahn, Germany

Marburg see Maribor, Slovenia
Marburg an der Lahn 94 B4 hist.
 Marburg. Hessen, W Germany
March see Morava
Marche 96 C3 Eng. Marches. region
 C Italy
Marche 91 C5 cultural region C France
Marche-en-Famenne 87 C7
 Luxembourg, SE Belgium
Marchena, Isla 60 B5 var. Bindloe
 Island. island Galápagos Islands,
 Ecuador, E Pacific Ocean
Marches see Marche
Mar Chiquita, Laguna 64 C3 lake
 C Argentina
Marcounda see Markounda
Mardan 134 C1 Khyber Pakhtunkhwa,
 N Pakistan
Mar del Plata 65 D5 Buenos Aires,
 E Argentina
Mardin 117 E4 Mardin, SE Turkey
Maré 144 D5 island Îles Loyauté, E New
 Caledonia
Marea Neagră see Black Sea
Mareeba 148 D3 Queensland,
 NE Australia
Marek see Dupnitsa
Marganets see Marhanets'
Margarita, Isla de 51 E1 island
 N Venezuela
Margate 89 E7 prev. Mergate.
 SE England, United Kingdom
Margherita see Jamaame
Margherita, Lake 73 C5 Eng. Lake
 Margherita, It. Abbaia. lake
 SW Ethiopia
Margherita, Lake see Ābaya Hāyk'
Marghita 108 B3 Hung. Margitta. Bihor,
 NW Romania
Margitta see Marghita
Märgo, Dasht-e 123 D5 desert SW
 Afghanistan
Marhanets' 109 F3 Rus. Marganets.
 Dnipropetrovs'ka Oblast', E Ukraine
María Cleofas, Isla 50 C4 island
 C Mexico
Maria Island 149 C8 island Tasmania,
 SE Australia
María Madre, Isla 50 C4 island
 C Mexico
María Magdalena, Isla 50 C4 island
 C Mexico
Mariana Trench 125 G4 var. Challenger
 Deep. trench W Pacific Ocean
Mariánské Lázně 99 A5 Ger. Marienbad.
 Karlovarský Kraj, W Czech Republic
 (Czechia)
Marías, Islas 50 C4 island group
 C Mexico
Maria-Theresiopel see Subotica
Maribor 95 E7 Ger. Marburg.
 NE Slovenia
Marica see Maritsa
Maridi 73 B5 Western Equatoria,
 SW South Sudan
Marie Byrd Land 154 A3 physical region
 Antarctica
Marie-Galante 55 G4 var. Ceyre to the
 Caribs. island SE Guadeloupe
Marienbad see Mariánské Lázně
Marienburg see Alüksne, Latvia
Marienburg see Malbork, Poland
Marienburg in Westpreussen see
 Malbork
Marienhausen see Viļaka
Mariental 78 B4 Hardap, SW Namibia
Marienwerder see Kwidzyń
Mariestad 85 B6 Västra Götaland,
 S Sweden
Marietta 42 D2 Georgia, SE USA
Marijampolė 106 B4 prev. Kapsukas.
 Marijampolė, S Lithuania
Marília 63 E4 São Paulo, S Brazil
Marin 92 B1 Galicia, NW Spain
Mar'ina Gorka see Mar'ina Horka
Mar"ina Horka 107 C6 Rus. Mar'ina
 Gorka. Minskaya Voblasts', C Belarus
Maringá 63 E4 Paraná, S Brazil
Marion 40 D4 Ohio, N USA
Marion, Lake 43 E2 reservoir South
 Carolina, SE USA
Mario Zucchelli 132 C4 Italian research
 station Antarctica
Mariscal Estigarribia 64 D2 Boquerón,
 NW Paraguay
Maritsa 104 D3 var. Marica, Gk. Évros,
 Turk. Meriç; anc. Hebrus. river
 SW Europe
Maritzburg see Pietermaritzburg

Mariupol' 109 G4 prev. Zhdanov.
 Donets'ka Oblast', SE Ukraine
Marka 73 B6 var. Merca. Shabeellaha
 Hoose, S Somalia
Markham, Mount 154 B4 mountain
 Antarctica
Markounda 76 C4 var. Marcounda.
 Ouham, NW Central African Republic
Marktredwitz 95 C5 Bayern,
 E Germany
Marlborough 148 D4 Queensland,
 E Australia
Marmande see Marmande
Marmande 91 B5 anc. Marmanda.
 Lot-et-Garonne, SW France
Sea of Marmara 116 A2 Eng. Sea of
 Marmara. sea NW Turkey
Marmara, Sea of see Marmara Denizi
Marmaris 116 A4 Muğla, SW Turkey
Marne 90 C3 cultural region N France
Marne 90 D3 river N France
Maro 76 C4 Moyen-Chari, S Chad
Maroantsetra 79 G2 Toamasina,
 NE Madagascar
Maromokotro 79 G2 mountain
 N Madagascar
Maroni 59 G3 Dut. Marowijne. river
 French Guiana/Suriname
Marosheviz see Topliţa
Marosludas see Luduş
Marosvásárhely see Târgu Mureş
Marotiri 143 F4 var. Îlots de Bass,
 Morotiri. island group Îles Australes,
 SW French Polynesia
Maroua 79 B3 Extrême-Nord,
 N Cameroon
Marowijne see Maroni
Marquesas Fracture Zone 153 E3
 fracture zone E Pacific Ocean
Marquette 40 B1 Michigan, N USA
Marrakech 70 C2 var. Marakesh, Eng.
 Marrakesh; prev. Morocco. W Morocco
Marrakesh see Marrakech
Marrawah 149 C8 Tasmania,
 SE Australia
Marree 149 B5 South Australia
Marsá al Burayqah 71 G3 var. Al
 Burayqah. N Libya
Marsabit 73 C6 Eastern, N Kenya
Marsala 97 B7 anc. Lilybaeum. Sicilia,
 Italy, C Mediterranean Sea
Marsberg 94 B4 Nordrhein-Westfalen,
 W Germany
Marseille 91 D6 Eng. Marseilles; anc.
 Massilia. Bouches-du-Rhône,
 SE France
Marseilles see Marseille
Marshall 45 F2 Minnesota, N USA
Marshall 49 H2 Texas, SW USA
Marshall Islands 144 C1
 off. Republic of the Marshall Islands.
 country W Pacific Ocean
Marshall Islands, Republic of the see
 Marshall Islands
Marshall Seamounts 125 H3 seamount
 range SW Pacific Ocean
Marsh Harbour 54 C1 Great Abaco,
 W The Bahamas
Martaban see Mottama
Martha's Vineyard 41 G3 island
 Massachusetts, NE USA
Martigues 91 D6 Bouches-du-Rhône,
 SE France
Martin 99 C5 Ger. Sankt Martin, Hung.
 Turócszentmárton; prev. Turčianský
 Svätý Martin. Žilinský Kraj,
 N Slovakia
Martinique 55 G4 French overseas
 department E West Indies
Martinique Channel see Martinique
 Passage
Martinique Passage 55 G4 var.
 Dominica Channel, Martinique
 Channel. channel Dominica/
 Martinique
Marton 150 D4 Manawatu-Wanganui,
 North Island, New Zealand
Martos 92 D4 Andalucía, S Spain
Marungu 77 E7 mountain range SE Dem.
 Rep. Congo
Mary 122 D3 prev. Merv. Mary
 Welaýaty, S Turkmenistan
Maryborough 149 D4 Queensland,
 E Australia
Maryborough see Port Laoise
Mary Island see Kanton
Maryland 41 E5 off. State of Maryland,
 also known as America in Miniature,
 Cockade State, Free State, Old Line
 State. state NE USA

Maryland, State of see Maryland
Maryville 45 F4 Missouri, C USA
Maryville 42 D1 Tennessee, S USA
Masai Steppe 73 C7 grassland
 NW Tanzania
Masaka 73 B6 SW Uganda
Masallı 117 H3 Rus. Masally.
 S Azerbaijan
Masally see Masallı
Masasi 73 C8 Mtwara, SE Tanzania
Masawa/Massawa see Mits'iwa
Masaya 52 D3 Masaya, W Nicaragua
Mascarene Basin 141 B5 undersea basin
 W Indian Ocean
Mascarene Islands 79 H4 island group
 W Indian Ocean
Mascarene Plain 141 B5 abyssal plain
 W Indian Ocean
Mascarene Plateau 141 B5 undersea
 plateau W Indian Ocean
Maseru 78 D4 country capital (Lesotho)
 W Lesotho
Mas-ha 119 D7 W West Bank Asia
Mashhad 120 E2 var. Meshed.
 Khorāsān-Razavī, NE Iran
Masindi 73 B6 W Uganda
Masira see Maşīrah
Masira, Gulf of 121 E5 var. Gulf of
 Masira. bay E Oman
Masira, Gulf of see Maşīrah, Khalīj
Maşīrah, Jazīrat 121 E5 var. Masira.
 island E Oman
Masis see Büyükağrı Dağı
Maskat see Masqaţ
Mason City 45 F3 Iowa, C USA
Masqaţ 121 E5 var. Maskat, Eng. Muscat.
 country capital (Oman) NE Oman
Massa 96 B3 Toscana, C Italy
Massachusetts 41 G3 off.
 Commonwealth of Massachusetts, also
 known as Bay State, Old Bay State, Old
 Colony State. state NE USA
Massenya 76 B3 Chari-Baguirmi,
 SW Chad
Massif Central 91 C5 plateau
 C France
Massilia see Marseille
Massoukou see Franceville
Mastanli see Momchilgrad
Masterton 151 D5 Wellington, North
 Island, New Zealand
Masty 107 B5 Rus. Mosty.
 Hrodzyenskaya Voblasts', W Belarus
Masuda 131 B6 Shimane, Honshū,
 SW Japan
Masuku see Franceville
Masvingo 78 D3 prev. Fort Victoria,
 Nyanda, Victoria. Masvingo,
 SE Zimbabwe
Maşyāf 118 B3 Fr. Misiaf. Ḥamāh,
 C Syria
Matadi 77 B6 Bas-Congo, W Dem. Rep.
 Congo
Matagalpa 52 D3 Matagalpa,
 C Nicaragua
Matale 132 D3 Central Province,
 C Sri Lanka
Matam 74 C3 NE Senegal
Matamata 150 D3 Waikato, North
 Island, New Zealand
Matamoros 50 C3 Coahuila, NE Mexico
Matamoros 51 E2 Tamaulipas, C Mexico
Matane 39 E4 Québec, SE Canada
Matanzas 54 B2 Matanzas, NW Cuba
Matara 132 D4 Southern Province,
 S Sri Lanka
Mataram 138 D5 Pulau Lombok,
 C Indonesia
Mataró 93 G2 anc. Illuro. Cataluña,
 E Spain
Mataura 151 B7 Southland, South Island,
 New Zealand
Mataura 151 B7 river South Island, New
 Zealand
Mata Uta see Matā'utu
Matā'utu 145 E4 var. Mata Uta.
 dependent territory capital (Wallis and
 Futuna) Île Uvea, Wallis and Futuna
Matera 97 E5 Basilicata, S Italy
Mathura see Madurai
Matianus see Orūmīyeh, Daryācheh-ye
Matías Romero 51 F5 Oaxaca,
 SE Mexico
Matisco/Matisco Ædourum see Mâcon
Mato Grosso 63 E3 off. Estado de Mato
 Grosso; prev. Matto Grosso. state/
 region W Brazil
Mato Grosso do Sul 63 E4 off. Estado de
 Mato Grosso do Sul. state/region
 S Brazil

Mato Grosso do Sul, Estado de see Mato
 Grosso do Sul
Mato Grosso, Estado de see Mato Grosso
Mato Grosso, Planalto de 56 C4 plateau
 C Brazil
Matosinhos 92 B2 prev. Matozinhos.
 Porto, NW Portugal
Matozinhos see Matosinhos
Matsue 131 B6 var. Matsuye, Matue.
 Shimane, Honshū, SW Japan
Matsumoto 131 C5 var. Matumoto.
 Nagano, Honshū, S Japan
Matsuyama 131 B7 var. Matuyama.
 Ehime, Shikoku, SW Japan
Matsuye see Matsue
Matterhorn 95 A8 It. Monte Cervino.
 mountain Italy/Switzerland
Matthews Ridge 59 F2 N Guyana
Matthew Town 54 D2 Great Inagua,
 S The Bahamas
Matto Grosso see Mato Grosso
Matucana 60 C4 Lima, W Peru
Matue see Matsue
Matumoto see Matsumoto
Maturín 59 E2 Monagas, NE Venezuela
Matuyama see Matsuyama
Mau 135 E3 var. Maunāth Bhanjan.
 Uttar Pradesh, N India
Maui 47 B8 island Hawaii, USA,
 C Pacific Ocean
Maun 78 C3 North-West, C Botswana
Maunāth Bhanjan see Mau
Mauren 94 E1 NE Liechtenstein Europe
Maurice see Mauritius
Mauritania 75 C2 off. Islamic Republic of
 Mauritania, Ar. Mūrītānīyah. country
 W Africa
Mauritania, Islamic Republic of see
 Mauritania
Mauritius 79 H3 off. Republic of
 Mauritius, Fr. Maurice. country
 W Indian Ocean
Mauritius 141 B5 island
 W Indian Ocean
Mauritius, Republic of see Mauritius
Mawlamyaing see Mawlamyine
Mawlamyine 136 B4 var. Mawlamyaing,
 Moulmein. Mon State, S Myanmar
 (Burma)
Mawson 154 D2 Australian research
 station Antarctica
Mayadin see Al Mayādīn
Mayaguana 54 D2 island SE The
 Bahamas
Mayaguana Passage 54 D2 passage
 SE The Bahamas
Mayagüez 55 F3 W Puerto Rico
Mayamey 120 D2 Semnān, N Iran
Maya Mountains 52 B2 Sp. Montañas
 Mayas. mountain range Belize/
 Guatemala
Mayas, Montañas see Maya Mountains
Maych'ew 72 C4 var. Mai Chio, It. Mai
 Ceu. Tigray, N Ethiopia
Mayebashi see Maebashi
Mayence see Mainz
Mayfield 151 B6 Canterbury, South
 Island, New Zealand
Maykop 111 A7 Respublika Adygeya,
 SW Russia
Maymana see Maimanah
Maymyo see Pyin-Oo-Lwin
Mayo see Maio
Mayor Island 150 D3 island NE New
 Zealand
Mayor Pablo Lagerenza see Capitán
 Pablo Lagerenza
Mayotte 79 F2 French overseas
 department E Africa
May Pen 54 B5 C Jamaica
Mayyit, Al Baḩr al see Dead Sea
Mazabuka 78 D2 Southern, S Zambia
Mazaca see Kayseri
Mazagan see El-Jadida
Mazār-e Sharīf 123 E3 var. Mazār-i
 Sharif. Balkh, N Afghanistan
Mazār-i Sharīf see Mazār-e Sharīf
Mazatlán 50 C3 Sinaloa, C Mexico
Mažeikiai 106 B3 Telšiai, NW Lithuania
Mazirbe 106 C2 NW Latvia
Mazra'a see Al Mazra'a
Mazury 98 D3 physical region NE Poland
Mazyr 107 C7 Rus. Mozyr'.
 Homyel'skaya Voblasts', SE Belarus
Mbabane 78 D4 country capital
 (Eswatini - administrative capital)
 NW Eswatini (Swaziland)
Mbacké see Mbaké
Mbaïki 77 C5 var. M'Baïki. Lobaye,
 SW Central African Republic

M'Baiki see Mbaïki
Mbaké 74 B3 var. Mbacké. W Senegal
Mbala 78 D1 prev. Abercorn. Northern, NE Zambia
Mbale 73 C6 E Uganda
Mbandaka 77 C5 prev. Coquilhatville. Equateur, NW Dem. Rep. Congo
M'Banza Congo 78 B1 var. Mbanza Congo; prev. São Salvador, São Salvador do Congo. Dem. Rep. Congo, NW Angola
Mbanza-Ngungu 77 B6 Bas-Congo, W Dem. Rep. Congo
Mbarara 73 B6 SW Uganda
Mbé 76 B4 Nord, N Cameroon
Mbeya 73 C7 Mbeya, SW Tanzania
Mbomou/Mbomu/Mbomu see Bomu
Mbour 74 B3 W Senegal
Mbuji-Mayi 77 D7 prev. Bakwanga. Kasai-Oriental, S Dem. Rep. Congo
McAlester 49 G2 Oklahoma, C USA
McAllen 49 G5 Texas, SW USA
McCamey 49 E3 Texas, SW USA
McComb 42 B3 Mississippi, S USA
McCook 45 E4 Nebraska, C USA
McKean Island 145 E3 island Phoenix Islands, C Kiribati
McKinley, Mount see Denali
McKinley Park 36 C3 Alaska, USA
M'Clintock Channel 37 F2 channel Nunavut, N Canada
McMinnville 46 B3 Oregon, NW USA
McMurdo 154 B4 US research station Antarctica
McPherson 45 E5 Kansas, C USA
McPherson see Fort McPherson
Mdantsane 78 D5 Eastern Cape, SE South Africa
Mead, Lake 47 D6 reservoir Arizona/Nevada, W USA
Mecca see Makkah
Mechelen 87 C5 Eng. Mechlin, Fr. Malines. Antwerpen, C Belgium
Mechlin see Mechelen
Mecklenburger Bucht 94 C2 bay N Germany
Mecsek 99 C7 mountain range SW Hungary
Medan 138 B3 Sumatera, E Indonesia
Medeba see Ma'dabā
Medellín 58 B3 Antioquia, NW Colombia
Médenine 71 F2 var. Madanīyīn. SE Tunisia
Medeshamstede see Peterborough
Medford 46 B4 Oregon, NW USA
Medgidia 108 D5 Constanța, SE Romania
Medgyes see Mediaş
Mediaş 108 B4 Ger. Mediasch, Hung. Medgyes. Sibiu, C Romania
Mediasch see Mediaş
Medicine Hat 37 F5 Alberta, SW Canada
Medina see al Madīnah
Medinaceli 93 E2 Castilla y León, N Spain
Medina del Campo 92 D2 Castilla y León, N Spain
Medinat Israel see Israel
Mediolanum see Saintes, France
Mediolanum see Milano, Italy
Mediomatrica see Metz
Mediterranean Sea 102 D3 Fr. Mer Méditerranée, see Africa/Asia/Europe
Méditerranée, Mer see Mediterranean Sea
Médoc 91 B5 cultural region SW France
Medvezh'yegorsk 110 B3 Respublika Kareliya, NW Russia
Meekatharra 147 B5 Western Australia
Meemu Atoll see Mulakatholhu
Meerssen 87 D6 var. Mersen. Limburg, SE Netherlands
Meerut 134 D2 Uttar Pradesh, N India
Megáli Préspa, Límni see Prespa, Lake
Meghālaya 113 G3 cultural region NE India
Mehdia see Mahdia
Meheso see Mī'ēso
Me Hka see Nmai Hka
Mehrīz 120 D3 Yazd, C Iran
Mehtar Lām 123 F4 var. Mehtarläm, Meterlam, Methariam, Metharlam. Laghmän, E Afghanistan
Mehtarlām see Mehtar Lām
Meiktila 136 B3 Mandalay, C Myanmar (Burma)
Méjico see Mexico
Mejillones 64 B2 Antofagasta, N Chile

Mek'elē 72 C4 var. Makale. Tigray, N Ethiopia
Mékhé 74 B3 NW Senegal
Mekong 124 D3 var. Lan-ts'ang Chiang, Cam. Mékôngk, Chin. Lancang Jiang, Lao. Mènam Khong, Nam Khong, Th. Mae Nam Khong, Tib. Dza Chu, Vtn. Sông Tiên Giang. river SE Asia
Mékôngk see Mekong
Mekong, Mouths of the 137 E6 delta S Vietnam
Melaka 138 B3 var. Malacca. Melaka, Peninsular Malaysia
Melaka, Selat see Malacca, Strait of
Melanesia 144 D3 island group W Pacific Ocean
Melanesian Basin 142 C2 undersea basin W Pacific Ocean
Melbourne 149 C7 state capital Victoria, SE Australia
Melbourne 43 E4 Florida, SE USA
Meleda see Mljet
Melghir, Chott 71 E2 var. Chott Melrhir. salt lake E Algeria
Melilla 70 D2 anc. Rusaddir, Russadir. enclave affiliated to Spain N Africa
Melita 37 F5 Manitoba, S Canada
Melita see Mljet
Melitene see Malatya
Melitopol' 109 F4 Zaporiz'ka Oblast', SE Ukraine
Melle 87 B5 Oost-Vlaanderen, NW Belgium
Mellerud 85 B6 Västra Götaland, S Sweden
Mellieħa 102 B5 E Malta
Mellizo Sur, Cerro 65 A7 mountain S Chile
Melo 64 E4 Cerro Largo, NE Uruguay
Melodunum see Melun
Melrhir, Chott see Melghir, Chott
Melsungen 94 B4 Hessen, C Germany
Melun 90 C3 anc. Melodunum. Seine-et-Marne, N France
Melville Bay/Melville Bugt see Qimusseriarsuaq
Melville Island 146 D2 island Northern Territory, N Australia
Melville Island 37 E2 island Parry Islands, Northwest Territories, NW Canada
Melville, Lake 39 F2 lake Newfoundland and Labrador, E Canada
Melville Peninsula 37 G3 peninsula Nunavut, NE Canada
Melville Sound see Viscount Melville Sound
Membidj see Manbij
Memel see Neman, NE Europe
Memel see Klaipeda, Lithuania
Memmingen 95 B6 Bayern, S Germany
Memphis 42 C1 Tennessee, S USA
Menaam see Menaldum
Menado see Manado
Ménaka 75 F3 Goa, E Mali
Menaldum 86 D1 Fris. Menaam. Fryslân, N Netherlands
Mènam Khong see Mekong
Mendaña Fracture Zone 153 F4 fracture zone E Pacific Ocean
Mende 91 C5 anc. Mimatum. Lozère, S France
Mendeleyev Ridge 155 B2 undersea ridge Arctic Ocean
Mendocino Fracture Zone 152 D2 fracture zone NE Pacific Ocean
Mendoza 64 B4 Mendoza, W Argentina
Menemen 116 A3 İzmir, W Turkey
Menengiyn Tal 127 F2 plain E Mongolia
Menongue 78 B2 var. Vila Serpa Pinto, Port. Serpa Pinto. Cuando Cubango, C Angola
Mentawai, Kepulauan 138 A4 island group W Indonesia
Meppel 86 D2 Drenthe, NE Netherlands
Meran see Merano
Merano 96 C1 Ger. Meran. Trentino-Alto Adige, N Italy
Merca see Marka
Mercedes 64 D3 Corrientes, NE Argentina
Mercedes 64 D4 Soriano, SW Uruguay
Meredith, Lake 49 E1 reservoir Texas, SW USA
Merefa 109 G2 Kharkivs'ka Oblast', E Ukraine
Mergate see Margate
Mergui see Myeik

Mergui Archipelago see Myeik Archipelago
Mérida 51 H3 Yucatán, SW Mexico
Mérida 92 C4 anc. Augusta Emerita. Extremadura, W Spain
Mérida 58 C2 Mérida, W Venezuela
Meridian 42 C2 Mississippi, S USA
Mérignac 91 B5 Gironde, SW France
Merín, Laguna see Mirim Lagoon
Merkulovichi see Myerkulavichy
Merowe 72 B3 Northern, N Sudan
Merredin 147 B6 Western Australia
Mersen see Meerssen
Mersey 89 D5 river NW England, United Kingdom
Mersin 116 C4 var. İçel. İçel, S Turkey
Mērsrags 106 C3 NW Latvia
Meru 73 C6 Eastern, C Kenya
Merv see Mary
Merzifon 116 D2 Amasya, N Turkey
Merzig 95 A5 Saarland, SW Germany
Mesa 48 B2 Arizona, SW USA
Meseritz see Międzyrzecz
Meshed see Mashhad
Mesopotamia 57 C5 var. Mesopotamia Argentina. physical region NE Argentina
Mesopotamia Argentina see Mesopotamia
Messalo, Rio 79 E2 var. Mualo. river NE Mozambique
Messana/Messene see Messina
Messina 97 D7 var. Messana, Messene; anc. Zancle. Sicilia, Italy, C Mediterranean Sea
Messina see Musina
Messina, Strait of 97 D7 Eng. Strait of Messina. strait SW Italy
Messina, Strait of see Messina, Stretto di
Messíni 105 B6 Pelopónnisos, S Greece
Mesta see Néstos
Mestghanem see Mostaganem
Mest'ia 117 F1 prev. Mestia, var. Mestiya. N Georgia
Mestia see Mest'ia
Mestiya see Mest'ia
Mestre 96 C2 Veneto, NE Italy
Metairie 42 B3 Louisiana, S USA
Metán 64 C2 Salta, N Argentina
Metapán 52 B2 Santa Ana, NW El Salvador
Meta, Río 58 D3 river Colombia/Venezuela
Meterlam see Mehtar Lām
Methariam/Metharlam see Mehtar Lām
Metis see Metz
Metković 100 B4 Dubrovnik-Neretva, SE Croatia
Métsovo 104 B4 prev. Métsovon. Ípeiros, C Greece
Métsovon see Métsovo
Metz 90 D3 anc. Divodurum Mediomatricum, Mediomatrica, Metis. Moselle, NE France
Meulaboh 138 A3 Sumatera, W Indonesia
Meuse 87 C6 Dut. Maas. river W Europe
Mexcala, Río see Balsas, Río
Mexicali 50 A1 Baja California Norte, NW Mexico
Mexicanos, Estados Unidos see Mexico
México 51 E4 var. Ciudad de México, Eng. Mexico City. country capital (Mexico) México, C Mexico
México 50 C5 off. United Mexican States, var. Méjico, México, Sp. Estados Unidos Mexicanos. country N Central America
México see Mexico
Mexico City see México
México, Golfo de see Mexico, Gulf of
Mexico, Gulf of 51 F2 Sp. Golfo de México. gulf W Atlantic Ocean
Meyadine see Al Mayādīn
Meydân Shahr see Maīdân Shahr
Meymaneh see Maīmanah
Mezen' 110 D3 river NW Russia
Mezőtúr 99 D7 Jász-Nagykun-Szolnok, E Hungary
Mgarr 102 A5 Gozo, N Malta
Miadzioł Nowy see Myadzyel
Miahuatlán 51 F5 var. Miahuatlán de Porfirio Díaz. Oaxaca, SE Mexico
Miahuatlán de Porfirio Díaz see Miahuatlán
Miami 43 F5 Florida, SE USA
Miami 49 G1 Oklahoma, C USA
Miami Beach 43 F5 Florida, SE USA

Miäneh 120 C2 var. Miyäneh. Āzarbäyjän-e Sharqī, NW Iran
Mianyang 128 B5 Sichuan, C China
Miastko 98 C2 Ger. Rummelsburg in Pommern. Pomorskie, N Poland
Mi Chai see Nong Khai
Michalovce 99 E5 Ger. Grossmichel, Hung. Nagymihály. Košický Kraj, E Slovakia
Michigan 40 C1 off. State of Michigan, also known as Great Lakes State, Lake State, Wolverine State. state N USA
Michigan, Lake 40 C2 lake N USA
Michurin see Tsarevo
Michurinsk 111 B5 Tambovskaya Oblast', W Russia
Micoud 55 F2 SE Saint Lucia
Micronesia 144 B1 off. Federated States of Micronesia. country W Pacific Ocean
Micronesia 144 C1 island group W Pacific Ocean
Micronesia, Federated States of see Micronesia
Mid-Atlantic Cordillera see Mid-Atlantic Ridge
Mid-Atlantic Ridge 66 C3 var. Mid-Atlantic Cordillera, Mid-Atlantic Rise, Mid-Atlantic Swell. undersea ridge Atlantic Ocean
Mid-Atlantic Rise/Mid-Atlantic Swell see Mid-Atlantic Ridge
Middelburg 87 B5 Zeeland, SW Netherlands
Middelharnis 86 B4 Zuid-Holland, SW Netherlands
Middelkerke 87 A5 West-Vlaanderen, W Belgium
Middle America Trench 35 B7 trench E Pacific Ocean
Middle Andaman 133 F2 island Andaman Islands, India, NE Indian Ocean
Middle Atlas 70 C2 Eng. Middle Atlas. mountain range N Morocco
Middle Atlas see Moyen Atlas
Middle Congo see Congo (Republic of)
Middlesboro 40 C5 Kentucky, S USA
Middlesbrough 89 D5 N England, United Kingdom
Middletown 41 F4 New Jersey, NE USA
Middletown 41 F3 New York, NE USA
Mid-Indian Basin 141 C5 undersea basin N Indian Ocean
Mid-Indian Ridge 141 C5 var. Central Indian Ridge. undersea ridge C Indian Ocean
Midland 38 D5 Ontario, S Canada
Midland 40 C3 Michigan, N USA
Midland 49 E3 Texas, SW USA
Mid-Pacific Mountains 152 C2 var. Mid-Pacific Seamounts. seamount range NW Pacific Ocean
Mid-Pacific Seamounts see Mid-Pacific Mountains
Midway Islands 152 D2 US unincorporated territory C Pacific Ocean
Miechów 99 D5 Małopolskie, S Poland
Międzyrzec Podlaski 98 E3 Lubelskie, E Poland
Międzyrzecz 98 B3 Ger. Meseritz. Lubuskie, W Poland
Mielec 99 D5 Podkarpackie, SE Poland
Miercurea-Ciuc 108 C4 Ger. Szeklerburg, Hung. Csíkszereda. Harghita, C Romania
Mieres del Camín 92 D1 var. Mieres del Camino. Asturias, NW Spain
Mieres del Camino see Mieres del Camín
Mī'ēso 73 D5 var. Meheso, Miesso. Oromīya, C Ethiopia
Miesso see Mī'ēso
Mifrats Hefa 119 A5 Eng. Bay of Haifa; prev. Mifraẓ Ḥefa. bay N Israel
Miguel Asua 50 D3 var. Miguel Auza. Zacatecas, C Mexico
Miguel Auza see Miguel Asua
Mijdrecht 86 C3 Utrecht, C Netherlands
Mikashevichi see Mikashevichy
Mikashevichy 107 C7 Pol. Mikaszewicze, Rus. Mikashevichi. Brestskaya Voblasts', SW Belarus
Mikaszewicze see Mikashevichy
Mikhaylovgrad see Montana
Mikhaylovka 111 B6 Volgogradskaya Oblast', SW Russia
Mikonos see Mýkonos
Mikre 104 C2 Lovech, N Bulgaria

Mikun' *110 D4* Respublika Komi,
NW Russia
Mikuni-sanmyaku *131 D5 mountain
range* Honshū, N Japan Asia
Mikura-jima *131 D6 island* E Japan
Milagro *60 B2* Guayas, SW Ecuador
Milan *see* Milano
Milange *79 E2* Zambézia,
NE Mozambique
Milano *96 B2 Eng.* Milan, *Ger.* Mailand;
anc. Mediolanum. Lombardia, N Italy
Milas *116 A4* Muğla, SW Turkey
Milashavichy *107 C2 Rus.* Milashevichi.
Homyel'skaya Voblasts', SE Belarus
Milashevichi *see* Milashavichy
Mildura *149 C6* Victoria, SE Australia
Mile *see* Mili Atoll
Miles *149 D5* Queensland, E Australia
Miles City *44 C2* Montana,
NW USA
Milford *see* Milford Haven
Milford Haven *89 C6 prev.* Milford.
SW Wales, United Kingdom
Milford Sound *151 A6* Southland, South
Island, New Zealand
Milford Sound *151 A6 inlet* South
Island, New Zealand
Milḩ, Baḥr al *see* Razāzah, Buḩayrat ar
Mili Atoll *144 D2 var.* Mile. *atoll* Ratak
Chain, SE Marshall Islands
Mil'kovo *115 H3* Kamchatskiy Kray,
E Russia
Milk River *37 E5* Alberta, SW Canada
Milk River *44 C1 river* Montana,
NW USA
Milk, Wadi el *88 B4 var.* Wadi al Malik.
river C Sudan
Milledgeville *43 E2* Georgia, SE USA
Mille Lacs Lake *45 F2 lake* Minnesota,
N USA
Millennium Island *143 F3 prev.*
Caroline Island, Thornton Island. *atoll*
Line Islands, E Kiribati
Millerovo *111 B6* Rostovskaya Oblast',
SW Russia
Mílos *105 C6 island* Kykládes, Greece,
Aegean Sea
Milton *151 B7* Otago, South Island, New
Zealand
Milton Keynes *89 D6* SE England,
United Kingdom
Milwaukee *40 B3* Wisconsin, N USA
Mimatum *see* Mende
Min *see* Fujian
Minā' Qābūs *120 B3* NE Oman
Minas Gerais *63 F3 off.* Estado de Minas
Gerais. *state/region* E Brazil
Minas Gerais, Estado de *see* Minas
Gerais
Minatitlán *51 F4* Veracruz-Llave,
E Mexico
Minbu *136 A3* Magway, W Myanmar
(Burma)
Minch, The *88 B3 var.* North Minch.
strait NW Scotland, United Kingdom
Mindanao *139 F2 island* S Philippines
Mindanao Sea *see* Bohol Sea
Mindelheim *95 C6* Bayern, S Germany
Mindello *see* Mindelo
Mindelo *74 A2 var.* Mindello;
prev. Porto Grande. São Vicente,
N Cape Verde
Minden *94 B4 anc.* Minthun.
Nordrhein-Westfalen, NW Germany
Mindoro *139 E2 island* N Philippines
Mindoro Strait *139 E2 strait*
W Philippines
Mineral Wells *49 F2* Texas,
SW USA
Mingäçevir *117 G2 Rus.* Mingechaur,
Mingechevir. C Azerbaijan
Mingãora *see* Saïdu
Mingechaur/Mingechevir *see*
Mingäçevir
Mingora *see* Saïdu
Minho, Rio *see* Miño
Minho *92 B2 Sp.* Miño. *river* Portugal/
Spain
Minho, Rio *see* Miño
Minicoy Island *132 B3 island* SW India
Minius *see* Miño
Minna *75 G4* Niger, C Nigeria
Minneapolis *45 F2* Minnesota, N USA
Minnesota *45 F2 off.* State of Minnesota,
also known as Gopher State,
New England of the West,
North Star State. *state* N USA
Miño *92 B2 var.* Mino, Minius, *Port.* Rio
Minho. *river* Portugal/Spain
Miño *see* Minho, Rio

Minorca *93 H3 Eng.* Minorca; *anc.*
Balearis Minor. *island* Islas Baleares,
Spain, W Mediterranean Sea
Minorca *see* Menorca
Minot *45 E1* North Dakota, N USA
Minsk *107 C6 country capital* (Belarus)
Minskaya Voblasts', C Belarus
Minskaya Wzvyshsha *107 C6 mountain
range* C Belarus
Mińsk Mazowiecki *98 D3 var.*
Nowo-Minsk. Mazowieckie, C Poland
Minthun *see* Minden
Minto, Lac *38 D2 lake* Québec, C Canada
Minya *see* Al Minyā
Miraflores *50 C3* Baja California Sur,
NW Mexico
Miranda de Ebro *93 E1* La Rioja,
N Spain
Mirgorod *see* Myrhorod
Miri *138 D3* Sarawak, East Malaysia
Mirim Lagoon *63 E5 var.* Lake Mirim,
Sp. Laguna Merín. *lagoon* Brazil/
Uruguay
Mirim, Lake *see* Mirim Lagoon
Mirina *see* Mýrina
Mirjāveh *120 E4* Sīstān va Balūchestān,
SE Iran
Mirny *154 C3 Russian research station*
Antarctica
Mirnyy *115 F3* Respublika Sakha
(Yakutiya), NE Russia
Mirpur Khas *134 B3* Sind, SE Pakistan
Mirtóo Pélagos *105 C6 Eng.* Mirtoan
Sea; *anc.* Myrtoum Mare. *sea* S Greece
Misiaf *see* Maşyāf
Miskito Coast *see* La Mosquitia
Miskitos, Cayos *53 E2 island group*
NE Nicaragua
Miskolc *99 D6* Borsod-Abaúj-Zemplén,
NE Hungary
Misool, Pulau *139 F4 island* Maluku,
E Indonesia
Mişrātah *71 F2 var.* Misurata.
NW Libya
Mission *49 G5* Texas, SW USA
Mississippi *42 B2 off.* State of
Mississippi, *also known as* Bayou State,
Magnolia State. *state* SE USA
Mississippi Delta *42 B4 delta* Louisiana,
S USA
Mississippi River *35 C6 river* C USA
Missoula *44 B1* Montana, NW USA
Missouri *45 F5 off.* State of Missouri,
also known as Bullion State, Show Me
State. *state* C USA
Missouri River *45 E3 river* C USA
Mistassini, Lac *38 D3 lake* Québec,
SE Canada
Mistelbach an der Zaya *95 E6*
Niederösterreich, NE Austria
Misti, Volcán *61 E4 volcano* S Peru
Misurata *see* Mişrātah
Mitau *see* Jelgava
Mitchell *149 D5* Queensland,
E Australia
Mitchell *45 E3* South Dakota, N USA
Mitchell, Mount *43 E1 mountain* North
Carolina, SE USA
Mitchell River *148 C2 river* Queensland,
NE Australia
Mi Tho *see* My Tho
Mitilíni *see* Mytilíni
Mito *131 D5* Ibaraki, Honshū, S Japan
Mitrovica *see* Mitrovicë
Mitrovica/Mitrowitz *see* Sremska
Mitrovica, Serbia
Mitrovicë *101 D5 Serb.* Mitrovica, *prev.*
Kosovska Mitrovica, Titova Mitrovica.
N Kosovo
Mits'iwa *72 C4 var.* Masawa, Massawa.
E Eritrea
Mitspe Ramon *119 A7 prev.* Mizpe
Ramon. Southern, S Israel
Mittelstadt *see* Baia Sprie
Mitú *58 C4* Vaupés, SE Colombia
Mitumba, Chaîne des/Mitumba Range
see Mitumba, Monts
Mitumba Range *77 E7 var.* Chaîne des
Mitumba, Mitumba Range. *mountain
range* E Dem. Rep. Congo
Miueru Wantipa, Lake *77 E7 lake*
N Zambia
Miyake-jima *131 D6 island*
Sakishima-shotō, SW Japan
Miyako *130 D4* Iwate, Honshū, C Japan
Miyakonojō *131 B8 var.* Miyakonozyô.
Miyazaki, Kyūshū, SW Japan
Miyakonozyô *see* Miyakonojō
Miyāneh *see* Mīāneh
Miyazaki *131 B8* Miyazaki, Kyūshū,
SW Japan

Mizil *108 C5* Prahova, SE Romania
Miziya *104 C1* Vratsa, NW Bulgaria
Mizpe Ramon *see* Mitspe Ramon
Mjøsa *85 B6 var.* Mjøsen. *lake*
S Norway
Mjøsen *see* Mjøsa
Mladenovac *100 D4* Serbia
Mława *98 D3* Mazowieckie, C Poland
Mljet *101 B5 It.* Meleda; *anc.* Melita.
island S Croatia
Mmabatho *78 C4* North-West,
N South Africa
Moab *44 B5* Utah, W USA
Moa Island *148 C1 island* Queensland,
NE Australia
Moanda *77 B6 var.* Mouanda.
Haut-Ogooué, SE Gabon
Moba *77 E7* Katanga,
E Dem. Rep. Congo
Mobay *see* Montego Bay
Mobaye *77 C5* Basse-Kotto, S Central
African Republic
Moberly *45 G4* Missouri, C USA
Mobile *42 C3* Alabama, S USA
Mobutu Sese Seko, Lac *see* Albert, Lake
Moçâmedes *see* Namibe
Mochudi *78 C4* Kgatleng,
SE Botswana
Mocímboa da Praia *79 F2 var.* Vila de
Mocímboa da Praia. Cabo Delgado,
N Mozambique
Môco *78 B2 var.* Morro de Môco.
mountain W Angola
Mocoa *58 A4* Putumayo, SW Colombia
Môco, Morro de *see* Môco
Mocuba *79 E3* Zambézia,
NE Mozambique
Modena *96 B3 anc.* Mutina.
Emilia-Romagna, N Italy
Modesto *47 B6* California, W USA
Modica *97 C7 anc.* Motyca. Sicilia, Italy,
C Mediterranean Sea
Modimolle *78 D4 prev.* Nylstroom.
Limpopo, NE South Africa
Modohn *see* Madona
Modriča *100 C3* Republika Srpska,
N Bosnia and Herzegovina
Moe *149 C7* Victoria, SE Australia
Møen *see* Møn, Denmark
Moero, Lac *see* Mweru, Lake
Moeskroen *see* Mouscron
Mogadischu/Mogadishu *see* Muqdisho
Mogador *see* Essaouira
Mogilëv *see* Mahilyow
Mogilev-Podol'skiy *see*
Mohyliv-Podil's'kyy
Mogilno *98 C3* Kujawsko-pomorskie,
C Poland
Moḩammadābād-e Rīgān *120 E4*
Kermān, SE Iran
Mohammedia *70 C2 prev.* Fédala.
NW Morocco
Mohave, Lake *47 D7 reservoir* Arizona/
Nevada, W USA
Mohawk River *41 F3 river* New York,
NE USA
Mohéli *see* Mwali
Mohns Ridge *83 F3 undersea ridge*
Greenland Sea/Norwegian Sea
Moho *61 E4* Puno, S Peru
Mohoro *73 C7* Pwani, E Tanzania
Mohyliv-Podil's'kyy *108 D3 Rus.*
Mogilev-Podol'skiy. Vinnyts'ka
Oblast', C Ukraine
Moi *85 A6* Rogaland, S Norway
Moili *see* Mwali
Mo i Rana *84 C3* Nordland,
C Norway
Môisaküla *106 D3 Ger.* Moiseküll.
Viljandimaa, S Estonia
Moiseküll *see* Môisaküla
Moissac *91 B6* Tarn-et-Garonne,
S France
Mojácar *93 E5* Andalucía, S Spain
Mojave Desert *47 D7 plain* California,
W USA
Mokrany *see* Makrany
Moktama *see* Mottama
Mol *87 C5 prev.* Moll. Antwerpen,
N Belgium
Molai *see* Moláoi
Moldavian SSR/Moldavskaya SSR
see Moldova
Molde *85 A5* Møre og Romsdal,
S Norway
Moldotau, Khrebet *see* Moldo-Too,
Khrebet
Moldo-Too, Khrebet *123 G2 prev.*
Khrebet Moldotau. *mountain range*
C Kyrgyzstan

Moldova *108 D3 off.* Republic of
Moldova, *var.* Moldavia; *prev.*
Moldavian SSR, *Rus.* Moldavskaya SSR.
country SE Europe
Moldova Nouă *108 A4 Ger.*
Neumoldowa, *Hung.* Újmoldova.
Caraş-Severin, SW Romania
Moldova, Republic of *see* Moldova
Moldoveanul *see* Vârful Moldoveanu
Molfetta *97 E5* Puglia, SE Italy
Moll *see* Mol
Mollendo *61 E4* Arequipa, SW Peru
Mölndal *85 B7* Västra Götaland,
S Sweden
Molochans'k *109 G4 Rus.* Molochansk.
Zaporiz'ka Oblast', SE Ukraine
Molodechno/Molodeczno *see*
Maladzyechna
Moloka'i *47 B8 var.* Molokai. *island*
Hawaiian Islands, Hawaii, USA
Molokai Fracture Zone *153 E2 tectonic
feature* NE Pacific Ocean
Molopo *78 C4 seasonal river* Botswana/
South Africa
Mólos *105 B5* Stereá Elláda,
C Greece
Molotov *see* Severodvinsk,
Arkhangel'skaya Oblast', Russia
Molotov *see* Perm', Permskaya Oblast',
Russia
Moluccas *139 F4 Dut.* Molukken, *Eng.*
Moluccas; *prev.* Spice Islands. *island
group* E Indonesia
Moluccas *see* Maluku
Molucca Sea *139 F4 Ind.* Laut Maluku,
sea E Indonesia
Molukken *see* Maluku
Mombasa *73 D7* Coast, SE Kenya
Mombetsu *see* Monbetsu
Momchilgrad *104 D3 prev.* Mastanli.
Kŭrdzhali, S Bulgaria
Møn *85 B8 prev.* Møen. *island*
SE Denmark
Mona, Canal de la *see* Mona Passage
Monaco *91 C7 var.* Monaco-Ville; *anc.*
Monoecus. *country capital* (Monaco)
S Monaco
Monaco *91 E6 off.* Principality of
Monaco. *country* W Europe
Monaco *see* Monochos
Monaco, Port de *91 C8 bay* S Monaco
W Mediterranean Sea
Monaco, Principality of *see* Monaco
Monaco-Ville *see* Monaco
Monahans *49 E3* Texas,
SW USA
Mona, Isla *55 E3 island* W Puerto Rico
Mona Passage *55 E3 Sp.* Canal de la
Mona. *channel* Dominican Republic/
Puerto Rico
Monastir *see* Bitola
Monbetsu *130 D2 var.* Mombetsu,
Monbetu. Hokkaidō, NE Japan
Monbetu *see* Monbetsu
Moncalieri *96 A2* Piemonte, NW Italy
Monchegorsk *110 C2* Murmanskaya
Oblast', NW Russia
Monclova *50 D2* Coahuila, NE Mexico
Moncton *39 G4* New Brunswick,
SE Canada
Mondovì *96 A2* Piemonte, NW Italy
Monfalcone *96 D2* Friuli-Venezia Giulia,
NE Italy
Monforte de Lemos *92 C1* Galicia,
NW Spain
Mongo *76 C3* Guéra, C Chad
Mongolia *126 C2 Mong.* Mongol Uls.
country E Asia
Mongolia, Plateau of *124 D1 plateau*
E Asia
Mongol Uls *see* Mongolia
Mongora *see* Saïdu
Mongos, Chaîne des *see* Bongo, Massif
des
Mongu *78 C2* Western, W Zambia
Monkchester *see* Newcastle upon Tyne
Monkey Bay *79 E2* Southern, SE Malawi
Monkey River *see* Monkey River Town
Monkey River Town *52 C2 var.* Monkey
River. Toledo, SE Belize
Monoecus *see* Monaco
Mono Lake *47 C6* lake California,
W USA
Monostor *see* Beli Manastir
Monóvar *93 F4 Cat.* Monòver.
Valenciana, E Spain
Monòver *see* Monóvar
Monroe *42 B2* Louisiana, S USA
Monrovia *74 C5 country capital* (Liberia)
W Liberia

Mons 87 B6 Dut. Bergen. Hainaut, S Belgium
Monselice 96 C2 Veneto, NE Italy
Montana 104 C2 prev. Ferdinand, Mikhaylovgrad. Montana, NW Bulgaria
Montana 44 B1 off. State of Montana, also known as Mountain State, Treasure State. state NW USA
Montargis 90 C4 Loiret, C France
Montauban 91 B6 Tarn-et-Garonne, S France
Montbéliard 90 D4 Doubs, E France
Mont Cenis, Col du 91 D5 pass E France
Mont-de-Marsan 91 B6 Landes, SW France
Monteagudo 61 G4 Chuquisaca, S Bolivia
Montecarlo 91 C8 Misiones, NE Argentina
Monte Caseros 64 D3 Corrientes, NE Argentina
Monte Cristi 54 D3 var. San Fernando de Monte Cristi. NW Dominican Republic
Monte Croce Carnico, Passo di see Plöcken Pass
Montegiardino 96 E2 SE San Marino
Montego Bay 54 A4 var. Mobay. W Jamaica
Montélimar 91 D5 anc. Acunum Acusio, Montilium Adhemari. Drôme, E France
Montemorelos 51 E3 Nuevo León, NE Mexico
Montenegro 101 C5 Serb. Crna Gora. country SW Europe
Monte Patria 64 B3 Coquimbo, N Chile
Monterey 47 B6 California, W USA
Monterey see Monterrey
Monterey Bay 47 A6 bay California, W USA
Montería 58 B2 Córdoba, NW Colombia
Montero 61 G4 Santa Cruz, C Bolivia
Monterrey 51 E3 var. Monterey. Nuevo León, NE Mexico
Montes Claros 63 F3 Minas Gerais, SE Brazil
Montevideo 64 D4 country capital (Uruguay) Montevideo, S Uruguay
Montevideo 45 F2 Minnesota, N USA
Montgenèvre, Col de 91 D5 pass France/Italy
Montgomery 42 D2 state capital Alabama, S USA
Montgomery see Sahiwal
Monthey 95 A7 Valais, SW Switzerland
Montilium Adhemari see Montélimar
Montluçon 90 C4 Allier, C France
Montoro 92 D4 Andalucía, S Spain
Montpelier 41 G2 state capital Vermont, NE USA
Montpellier 91 C6 Hérault, S France
Montréal 39 E4 Eng. Montreal. Québec, SE Canada
Montrose 88 D3 E Scotland, United Kingdom
Montrose 44 C5 Colorado, C USA
Montserrat 55 G3 var. Emerald Isle. UK Overseas Territory E West Indies
Monywa 136 B3 Sagaing, C Myanmar (Burma)
Monza 96 B2 Lombardia, N Italy
Monze 78 D2 Southern, S Zambia
Monzón 93 F2 Aragón, NE Spain
Moonie 149 D5 Queensland, E Australia
Moon-Sund see Väinameri
Moora 147 A6 Western Australia
Moore 9 G1 Oklahoma, C USA
Moore, Lake 147 B6 lake Western Australia
Moorhead 45 F2 Minnesota, N USA
Moose 38 C3 river Ontario, S Canada
Moosehead Lake 41 G1 lake Maine, NE USA
Moosonee 38 C3 Ontario, SE Canada
Mopti 75 E3 Mopti, C Mali
Moquegua 61 E4 Moquegua, SE Peru
Mora 85 C5 Dalarna, C Sweden
Morales 52 C2 Izabal, E Guatemala
Morant Bay 54 B5 E Jamaica
Moratalla 93 E4 Murcia, SE Spain
Morava 99 C5 var. March. river C Europe
Morava see Moravia, Czech Republic (Czechia)
Morava see Velika Morava, Serbia
Moravia 99 B5 Cz. Morava, Ger. Mähren. cultural region E Czech Republic (Czechia)

Moray Firth 88 C3 inlet N Scotland, United Kingdom
Morea see Pelopónnisos
Moreau River 44 D2 river South Dakota, N USA
Moree 149 D5 New South Wales, SE Australia
Morelia 51 E4 Michoacán, S Mexico
Morena, Sierra 92 C4 mountain range S Spain
Moreni 108 C5 Dâmbovița, S Romania
Morgan City 42 B3 Louisiana, S USA
Murghāb, Daryā-ye see Murgap
Morioka 130 D4 Iwate, Honshū, C Japan
Morlaix 90 A3 Finistère, NW France
Mormon State see Utah
Mornington Abyssal Plain 67 A7 abyssal plain SE Pacific Ocean
Mornington Island 148 B2 island Wellesley Islands, Queensland, N Australia
Morocco 70 B3 off. Kingdom of Morocco, Ar. Al Mamlakah. country N Africa
Morocco see Marrakech
Morocco, Kingdom of see Morocco
Morogoro 73 C7 Morogoro, E Tanzania
Moro Gulf 139 E3 gulf S Philippines
Morón 54 C2 Ciego de Ávila, C Cuba
Mörön 126 D2 Hövsgöl, N Mongolia
Morondava 79 F3 Toliara, W Madagascar
Moroni 79 F2 country capital (Comoros) Grande Comore, NW Comoros
Morotai, Pulau 139 F3 island Maluku, E Indonesia
Morotiri see Marotiri
Morphou see Güzelyurt
Morrinsville 150 D3 Waikato, North Island, New Zealand
Morris 45 F2 Minnesota, N USA
Morris Jesup, Kap 83 E1 headland N Greenland
Morvan 90 D4 physical region C France
Moscow 47 C2 Idaho, NW USA
Moscow see Moskva
Mosel 95 A5 Fr. Moselle. river W Europe
Mosel see Moselle
Moselle 87 E8 Ger. Mosel. river W Europe
Moselle see Mosel
Mosgiel 151 B7 Otago, South Island, New Zealand
Moshi 73 C7 Kilimanjaro, NE Tanzania
Mosjøen 84 B4 Nordland, C Norway
Moskovskiy see Moskva
Moskva 111 B5 Eng. Moscow. country capital (Russia) Gorod Moskva, W Russia
Moskva 123 E3 Rus. Moskovskiy; prev. Chubek. SW Tajikistan
Moson and Magyaróvár see Mosonmagyaróvár
Mosonmagyaróvár 99 C6 Ger. Wieselburg-Ungarisch-Altenburg; prev. Moson and Magyaróvár, Cz. Wieselburg and Ungarisch-Altenburg. Győr-Moson-Sopron, NW Hungary
Mosquito Coast 53 E3 var. Miskito Coast, Eng. Mosquito Coast. coastal region E Nicaragua
Mosquito Coast see La Mosquitia
Mosquito Gulf 53 F4 Eng. Mosquito Gulf. gulf N Panama
Mosquito Gulf see Mosquitos, Golfo de los
Moss 85 B6 Østfold, S Norway
Mossâmedes see Namibe
Mosselbaai 78 C5 var. Mosselbai, Eng. Mossel Bay. Western Cape, SW South Africa
Mosselbai/Mossel Bay see Mosselbaai
Mossendjo 77 B6 Niari, SW Congo
Mossoró 63 G2 Rio Grande do Norte, NE Brazil
Most 98 A4 Ger. Brüx. Ústecký Kraj, NW Czech Republic (Czechia)
Mosta 102 B5 var. Musta. C Malta
Mostaganem 70 D2 var. Mestghanem. NW Algeria
Mostar 100 C4 Federacija Bosne I Hercegovina, S Bosnia and Herzegovina
Mosty see Masty
Mosul see Al Mawşil
Mota del Cuervo 93 E3 Castilla-La Mancha, C Spain
Motagua, Río 52 B2 river Guatemala/Honduras

Mother of Presidents/Mother of States see Virginia
Motril 92 D5 Andalucía, S Spain
Motru 108 B4 Gorj, SW Romania
Mottama 136 B4 prev. Martaban; var. Moktama. Mon State, S Myanmar (Burma)
Motueka 151 C5 Tasman, South Island, New Zealand
Motul 51 H3 var. Motul de Felipe Carrillo Puerto. Yucatán, SE Mexico
Motul de Felipe Carrillo Puerto see Motul
Motyca see Modica
Mouanda see Moanda
Mouhoun see Black Volta
Mouila 77 A6 Ngounié, C Gabon
Moukden see Shenyang
Mould Bay 37 E2 Prince Patrick Island, Northwest Territories, N Canada
Moulins 90 C4 Allier, C France
Moulmein see Mawlamyine
Moundou 76 B4 Logone-Occidental, SW Chad
Moung Roessei 137 D5 Battambang, W Cambodia
Moun Hou see Black Volta
Mountain Home 42 B1 Arkansas, C USA
Mountain State see Montana
Mountain State see West Virginia
Mount Cook 151 B6 Canterbury, South Island, New Zealand
Mount Desert Island 41 H2 island Maine, NE USA
Mount Gambier 149 B7 South Australia
Mount Isa 148 B3 Queensland, C Australia
Mount Magnet 147 B5 Western Australia
Mount Pleasant 45 G4 Iowa, C USA
Mount Pleasant 40 C3 Michigan, N USA
Mount Vernon 45 B5 Illinois, N USA
Mount Vernon 46 B1 Washington, NW USA
Mourdi, Dépression du 76 C2 desert lowland Chad/Sudan
Mouscron 87 A6 Dut. Moeskroen. Hainaut, W Belgium
Mouse River see Souris River
Moussoro 76 B3 Kanem, W Chad
Moyen-Congo see Congo (Republic of)
Mo'ynoq 122 C1 Rus. Muynak. Qoraqalpog'iston Respublikasi, NW Uzbekistan
Moyobamba 60 B2 San Martín, NW Peru
Moyu 126 B3 var. Karakax. Xinjiang Uygur Zizhiqu, NW China
Moynnkum, Peski 123 F1 Kaz. Moyynqum. desert S Kazakhstan
Moyynqum see Moynnkum, Peski
Mozambika, Lakandranon' i see Mozambique Channel
Mozambique 79 E3 off. Republic of Mozambique; prev. People's Republic of Mozambique, Portuguese East Africa. country S Africa
Mozambique Basin see Natal Basin
Mozambique, Canal de see Mozambique Channel
Mozambique Channel 79 E3 Fr. Canal de Mozambique, Mal. Lakandranon' i Mozambika. strait W Indian Ocean
Mozambique, People's Republic of see Mozambique
Mozambique Plateau 69 D7 var. Mozambique Rise. undersea plateau SW Indian Ocean
Mozambique, Republic of see Mozambique
Mozambique Rise see Mozambique Plateau
Mozyr' see Mazyr
Mpama 77 B6 river C Congo
Mpika 78 D2 Northern, NE Zambia
Mqinvartsveri see Kazbek
Mragowo 98 D2 Ger. Sensburg. Warmińsko-Mazurskie, NE Poland
Mthatha 78 D5 prev. Umtata. Eastern Cape, SE South Africa
Mtkvari see Kura
Mtwara 73 D8 Mtwara, SE Tanzania
Mualo see Messalo, Rio
Muang Chiang Rai see Chiang Rai
Muang Kalasin see Kalasin
Muang Khammouan see Thakhèk
Muang Khôngxédôn 137 D5 var. Khong Sedone. Salavan, S Laos
Muang Khon Kaen see Khon Kaen

Muang Lampang see Lampang
Muang Loei see Loei
Muang Lom Sak see Lom Sak
Muang Nakhon Sawan see Nakhon Sawan
Muang Namo 136 C3 Oudômxai, N Laos
Muang Nan see Nan
Muang Phalan 136 D4 var. Muang Phalane. Savannakhét, S Laos
Muang Phalane see Muang Phalan
Muang Phayao see Phayao
Muang Phitsanulok see Phitsanulok
Muang Phrae see Phrae
Muang Roi Et see Roi Et
Muang Sakon Nakhon see Sakon Nakhon
Muang Samut Prakan see Samut Prakan
Muang Sing 136 C3 Louang Namtha, N Laos
Muang Ubon see Ubon Ratchathani
Muang Xaignabouri see Xaignabouli
Muar 138 B3 var. Bandar Maharani. Johor, Peninsular Malaysia
Mucojo 79 F2 Cabo Delgado, N Mozambique
Mudanjiang 129 E3 var. Mu-tan-chiang. Heilongjiang, NE China
Mudon 137 B5 Mon State, S Myanmar (Burma)
Muenchen see München
Muenster see Münster
Mufulira 78 D2 Copperbelt, C Zambia
Mughla see Muğla
Muğla 116 A4 var. Mughla. Muğla, SW Turkey
Mûḥ, Sabkhat al 118 C3 lake C Syria
Muhu Väin see Väinameri
Muisne 60 A1 Esmeraldas, NW Ecuador
Mukachevo 108 B3 Hung. Munkács, Rus. Mukachevo. Zakarpats'ka Oblast', W Ukraine
Mukachevo see Mukacheve
Mukalla see Al Mukallā
Mukden see Shenyang
Mula 93 E4 Murcia, SE Spain
Mulakatholhu 132 B4 var. Meemu Atoll, Mulaku Atoll. atoll C Maldives
Mulaku Atoll see Mulakatholhu
Muleshoe 49 E2 Texas, SW USA
Mulhacén 93 E5 var. Cerro de Mulhacén. mountain S Spain
Mulhacén, Cerro de see Mulhacén
Mülhausen see Mulhouse
Mülheim 95 A6 var. Mulheim an der Ruhr. Nordrhein-Westfalen, W Germany
Mulheim an der Ruhr see Mülheim
Mulhouse 90 E4 Ger. Mülhausen. Haut-Rhin, NE France
Müller-gerbergte see Muller, Pegunungan
Muller, Pegunungan 138 D4 Dut. Müller-gerbergte. mountain range Borneo, C Indonesia
Mull, Isle of 88 B4 island W Scotland, United Kingdom
Mulongo 77 D7 Katanga, SE Dem. Rep. Congo
Multan 134 C2 Punjab, E Pakistan
Mumbai 134 C5 prev. Bombay. state capital Mahārāshtra, W India
Munamägi see Suur Munamägi
Münchberg 95 C5 Bayern, E Germany
München 95 C6 var. Muenchen, Eng. Munich, It. Monaco. Bayern, SE Germany
Muncie 40 C4 Indiana, N USA
Mungbere 77 E5 Orientale, NE Dem. Rep. Congo
Mu Nggava see Rennell
Munich see München
Munkács see Mukacheve
Münster 94 A4 var. Muenster, Münster in Westfalen. Nordrhein-Westfalen, W Germany
Münster in Westfalen see Münster
Muonio 89 D3 Lappi, N Finland
Muonioälv/Muoniojoki see Muonionjoki
Muonionjoki 84 D3 var. Muoniojoki, Swe. Muonioälv. river Finland/Sweden
Muqät 119 E3 Al Mafraq, E Jordan
Muqdisho 73 D6 Eng. Mogadishu, It. Mogadiscio. country capital (Somalia) Banaadir, S Somalia

Mur 95 E7 *SCr.* Mura. *river* C Europe
Mura *see* Mur
Muradiye 117 F3 Van, E Turkey
Murapara *see* Murupara
Murata 96 E2 S San Marino
Murchison River 147 A5 *river* Western Australia
Murcia 93 F4 Murcia, SE Spain
Murcia 93 E4 *autonomous community* SE Spain
Mureş 108 A4 *river* Hungary/Romania
Murfreesboro 42 D1 Tennessee, S USA
Murgab *see* Murghob
Murgap 122 D3 Mary Welaýaty, S Turkmenistan
Murgap 122 D3 *var.* Deryasu Murgap, Murghab, *Pash.* Daryā-ye Murghāb, *Rus.* Murgab. *river* Afghanistan/ Turkmenistan
Murghob 123 F3 *Rus.* Murgab. SE Tajikistan
Murgon 149 E5 Queensland, E Australia
Müritäniyah *see* Mauritania
Müritz 94 C3 *var.* Müritzee. *lake* NE Germany
Müritzee *see* Müritz
Murmansk 110 C2 Murmanskaya Oblast', NW Russia
Murmashi 110 C2 Murmanskaya Oblast', NW Russia
Murom 111 B5 Vladimirskaya Oblast', W Russia
Muroran 130 D3 Hokkaidō, NE Japan
Muros 92 B1 Galicia, NW Spain
Murray Fracture Zone 153 E2 *fracture zone* NE Pacific Ocean
Murray Range *see* Murray Ridge
Murray Ridge 112 C5 *var.* Murray Range. *undersea ridge* N Arabian Sea
Murray River 149 B6 *river* SE Australia
Murrumbidgee River 149 C6 *river* New South Wales, SE Australia
Murska Sobota 95 E7 Ger. Olsnitz. NE Slovenia
Murupara 150 E3 *var.* Murapara. Bay of Plenty, North Island, New Zealand
Murviedro *see* Sagunto
Murwāra 135 E4 Madhya Pradesh, N India
Murwillumbah 149 E5 New South Wales, SE Australia
Murzuq, Edeyin *see* Murzuq, Idhān
Murzuq, Idhan 71 F4 *var.* Edeyin Murzuq. *desert* SW Libya
Mürzzuschlag 95 E7 Steiermark, E Austria
Muş 117 F3 *var.* Mush. Muş, E Turkey
Musa, Gebel 72 C2 *var.* Gebel Mûsa. *mountain* NE Egypt
Mûsa, Gebel *see* Mûsā, Jabal
Musala 104 B3 *mountain* W Bulgaria
Muscat *see* Masqaţ
Muscat and Oman *see* Oman
Muscatine 45 G3 Iowa, C USA
Musgrave Ranges 147 D5 *mountain range* South Australia
Musina 78 D3 *prev.* Messina. Limpopo, NE South Africa
Muskegon 40 C3 Michigan, N USA
Muskogean *see* Tallahassee
Muskogee 49 G1 Oklahoma, C USA
Musoma 73 C6 Mara, N Tanzania
Musta *see* Mosta
Mustafa-Pasha *see* Svilengrad
Musters, Lago 65 B6 *lake* S Argentina
Muswellbrook 149 D6 New South Wales, SE Australia
Mut 116 C4 İçel, S Turkey
Mu-tan-chiang *see* Mudanjiang
Mutare 78 D3 *var.* Mutari; *prev.* Umtali. Manicaland, E Zimbabwe
Mutari *see* Mutare
Mutina *see* Modena
Mutsu-wan 130 D3 *bay* N Japan
Muttonbird Islands 151 A8 *island group* SW New Zealand
Mu Us Shadi 127 E3 *var.* Ordos Desert; *prev.* Mu Us Shamo. *desert* N China
Mu Us Shamo *see* Mu Us Shadi
Muy Muy 52 D3 Matagalpa, C Nicaragua
Muynak *see* Mo'ynoq
Mužlja 100 D3 Hung. Felsőmuzslya; *prev.* Gornja Mužlja. Vojvodina, N Serbia
Mwali 79 F2 *var.* Moili, *Fr.* Mohéli. *island* S Comoros
Mwanza 73 B6 Mwanza, NW Tanzania
Mweka 77 C6 Kasai-Occidental, C Dem. Rep. Congo

Mwene-Ditu 77 D7 Kasai-Oriental, S Dem. Rep. Congo
Mweru, Lake 77 D7 *var.* Lac Moero. *lake* Dem. Rep. Congo/Zambia
Myadel' *see* Myadzyel
Myadzyel 107 C5 *Pol.* Miadzioł Nowy, *Rus.* Myadel'. Minskaya Voblasts', N Belarus
Myanaung 136 B4 Ayeyarwady, SW Myanmar (Burma)
Myanmar 136 A3 *off.* Union of Myanmar. *country* SE Asia. *See also* Burma
Myaungmya 136 A4 Ayeyarwady, SW Myanmar (Burma)
Myaydo *see* Aunglan
Myeik 137 B6 *var.* Mergui. Tanintharyi, S Myanmar (Burma)
Myeik Archipelago 137 B6 *prev.* Mergui Archipelago. *island group* S Myanmar (Burma)
Myerkulavichy 107 D7 *Rus.* Merkulovichi. Homyel'skaya Voblasts', SE Belarus
Myingyan 136 B3 Mandalay, C Myanmar (Burma)
Myitkyina 136 B2 Kachin State, N Myanmar (Burma)
Mykolayiv 109 E4 *Rus.* Nikolayev. Mykolayivs'ka Oblast', S Ukraine
Mykonos 105 D6 *var.* Míkonos. *island* Kykládes, Greece, Aegean Sea
Myrhorod 109 F2 *Rus.* Mirgorod. Poltavs'ka Oblast', NE Ukraine
Mýrina 104 D4 *var.* Mírina. Límnos, SE Greece
Myrtle Beach 43 F2 South Carolina, SE USA
Myrtoan Sea *see* Mirtóo Pélagos
Mýrtos 105 D8 Kríti, Greece, E Mediterranean Sea
Myrtoum Mare *see* Mirtóo Pélagos
Myślibórz 98 B3 Zachodnio-pomorskie, NW Poland
Mysore *see* Mysūru
Mysore *see* Karnātaka
Mysūru 132 C2 *prev.* Mysore, *var.* Maisur. Karnātaka, W India
My Tho 137 E6 *var.* Mi Tho. Tiên Giang, S Vietnam
Mytilene *see* Mytilíni
Mytilíni 105 D5 *var.* Mitilíni; *anc.* Mytilene. Lésvos, E Greece
Mzuzu 79 E2 Northern, N Malawi

N

Naberezhnyye Chelny 111 D5 *prev.* Brezhnev. Respublika Tatarstan, W Russia
Nablus 119 A6 *var.* Nābulus, *Heb.* Shekhem; *anc.* Neapolis, *Bibl.* Shechem. N West Bank
Nābulus *see* Nablus
Nacala 79 F2 Nampula, NE Mozambique
Na-Ch'ii *see* Nagqu
Nada *see* Danzhou
Nadi 145 E4 *prev.* Nandi. Viti Levu, W Fiji
Nadur 102 A5 Gozo, N Malta
Nadvirna 108 C3 *Pol.* Nadwórna, *Rus.* Nadvornaya. Ivano-Frankivs'ka Oblast', W Ukraine
Nadvoitsy 110 B3 Respublika Kareliya, NW Russia
Nadvornaya/Nadwórna *see* Nadvirna
Nadym 114 D3 Yamalo-Nenetskiy Avtonomnyy Okrug, N Russia
Náfpaktos 105 B5 *var.* Návpaktos. Dytikí Ellás, C Greece
Náfplio 105 B6 *prev.* Návplion. Pelopónnisos, S Greece
Naga 139 E2 *off.* Naga City; *prev.* Nueva Caceres. Luzon, N Philippines
Naga City *see* Naga
Nagano 131 C5 Nagano, Honshū, S Japan
Nagaoka 131 D5 Niigata, Honshū, C Japan
Nagara Pathom *see* Nakhon Pathom
Nagara Sridharmaraj *see* Nakhon Si Thammarat
Nagara Svarga *see* Nakhon Sawan
Nagasaki 131 A7 Nagasaki, Kyūshū, SW Japan
Nagato 131 A7 Yamaguchi, Honshū, SW Japan
Nāgercoil 132 C3 Tamil Nādu, SE India
Nagorno-Karabakh *see* Nagornyy-Karabakh

Nagorno-Karabakhskaya Avtonomnaya Oblast *see* Nagornyy-Karabakh
Nagornyy Karabakh 117 G3 *var.* Nagorno-Karabakh, Nagorno-Karabakhskaya Avtonomnaya Oblast, *Arm.* Lernnayin Gharabakh, *Az.* Quarabağ. *former autonomous region* SW Azerbaijan
Nagoya 131 C6 Aichi, Honshū, SW Japan
Nāgpur 134 D4 Mahārāshtra, C India
Nagqu 126 C5 Chin. Na-Ch'ii; *prev.* Hei-ho. Xizang Zizhiqu, W China
Nagybánya *see* Baia Mare
Nagybecskerek *see* Zrenjanin
Nagydisznód *see* Cisnădie
Nagyenyed *see* Aiud
Nagykálló 99 E6 Szabolcs-Szatmár-Bereg, E Hungary
Nagykanizsa 99 C7 Ger. Grosskanizsa. Zala, SW Hungary
Nagykároly *see* Carei
Nagykikinda *see* Kikinda
Nagykőrös 99 D7 Pest, C Hungary
Nagymihály *see* Michalovce
Nagysurány *see* Šurany
Nagyszalonta *see* Salonta
Nagyszeben *see* Sibiu
Nagyszentmiklós *see* Sânnicolau Mare
Nagyszőllős *see* Vynohradiv
Nagyszombat *see* Trnava
Nagytapolcsány *see* Topoľčany
Nagyvárad *see* Oradea
Naha 130 A3 Okinawa, Okinawa, SW Japan
Nahariya 119 A5 *prev.* Nahariyya. Northern, N Israel
Nahariyya *see* Nahariya
Nahuel Huapí, Lago 65 B5 *lake* W Argentina
Nain 39 F2 Newfoundland and Labrador, NE Canada
Nā'īn 120 D3 Eşfahān, C Iran
Nairobi 69 E5 *country capital* (Kenya) Nairobi Area, S Kenya
Nairobi 73 C6 Nairobi Area, S Kenya
Naissus *see* Niš
Najaf *see* An Najaf
Najima *see* Fukuoka
Najrān 121 B6 *var.* Abā as Su'ūd. Najrān, S Saudi Arabia
Nakambé *see* White Volta
Nakamura 131 B7 *var.* Shimanto. Kōchi, Shikoku, SW Japan
Nakatsugawa 131 C6 *var.* Nakatugawa. Gifu, Honshū, SW Japan
Nakatugawa *see* Nakatsugawa
Nakhichevan' *see* Naxçıvan
Nakhodka 115 G5 Primorskiy Kray, SE Russia
Nakhon Pathom 137 C5 *var.* Nagara Pathom, Nakorn Pathom. Nakhon Pathom, W Thailand
Nakhon Ratchasima 137 C5 *var.* Khorat, Korat. Nakhon Ratchasima, E Thailand
Nakhon Sawan 137 C5 *var.* Muang Nakhon Sawan, Nagara Svarga. Nakhon Sawan, W Thailand
Nakhon Si Thammarat 137 C7 *var.* Nagara Sridharmaraj, Nakhon Sithammarat, Nakhon Si Thammarat, SW Thailand
Nakhon Sithamnaraj *see* Nakhon Si Thammarat
Nakorn Pathom *see* Nakhon Pathom
Nakuru 73 C6 Rift Valley, SW Kenya
Nal'chik 111 B8 Kabardino-Balkarskaya Respublika, SW Russia
Nālūt 71 F2 NW Libya
Namakan Lake 40 A1 *lake* Canada/USA
Namangan 123 F2 Namangan Viloyati, E Uzbekistan
Nambala 78 D2 Central, C Zambia
Nam Co 126 C5 *lake* W China
Nam Đinh 136 D3 Nam Ha, N Vietnam
Namib Desert 78 B3 *desert* W Namibia
Namibe 78 A2 Port. Moçâmedes, Mossâmedes. Namibe, SW Angola
Namibia 78 B3 *off.* Republic of Namibia, *var.* South West Africa, *Afr.* Suidwes-Afrika, *Ger.* Deutsch-Südwestafrika; *prev.* German Southwest Africa, South-West Africa. *country* S Africa
Namibia, Republic of *see* Namibia
Nam Khong *see* Mekong
Namnetes *see* Nantes
Namo *see* Namu Atoll
Nam Ou 136 C3 *river* N Laos

Nampa 46 D3 Idaho, NW USA
Nampula 79 E2 Nampula, NE Mozambique
Namsos 84 B4 Nord-Trøndelag, C Norway
Nam Tha 136 C4 *river* N Laos
Namu Atoll 144 D2 *var.* Namo. *atoll* Ralik Chain, C Marshall Islands
Namur 87 C6 Dut. Namen. Namur, SE Belgium
Namyit Island 128 C8 *island* S Spratly Islands
Nan 136 C4 *var.* Muang Nan. Nan, NW Thailand
Nanaimo 36 D5 Vancouver Island, British Columbia, SW Canada
Nanchang 128 C5 *var.* Nan-ch'ang, Nanch'ang-hsien. *province capital* Jiangxi, S China
Nan-ch'ang *see* Nanchang
Nanch'ang-hsien *see* Nanchang
Nan-ching *see* Nanjing
Nancy 90 D3 Meurthe-et-Moselle, NE France
Nandaime 52 D3 Granada, SW Nicaragua
Nānded 134 D5 Mahārāshtra, C India
Nandi *see* Nadi
Nándorhegy *see* Oţelu Roşu
Nandyāl 132 C1 Andhra Pradesh, E India
Nan Hai *see* South China Sea
Naniwa *see* Ōsaka
Nanjing 128 D5 *var.* Nan-ching, Nanking; *prev.* Chianning, Chian-ning, Kiang-ning, Jiangsu. *province capital* Jiangsu, E China
Nanking *see* Nanjing
Nanning 128 B6 *var.* Nan-ning; *prev.* Yung-ning. Guangxi Zhuangzu Zizhiqu, S China
Nan-ning *see* Nanning
Nanortalik 82 C5 Kitaa, S Greenland
Nanpan Jiang 136 D2 *river* S China
Nanping 128 D6 *var.* Nan-p'ing; *prev.* Yenping. Fujian, SE China
Nan-p'ing *see* Nanping
Nansei Shotō Trench *see* Ryukyu Trench
Nansei Shotō 130 A2 Eng. Ryukyu Islands. *island group* SW Japan
Nansen Basin 155 C4 *undersea basin* Arctic Ocean
Nansen Cordillera *see* Gakkel Ridge
Nansha Qundao *see* Spratly Islands
Nanterre 90 D1 Hauts-de-Seine, N France
Nantes 90 B4 Bret. Naoned; *anc.* Condivincum, Namnetes. Loire-Atlantique, NW France
Nantucket Island 41 G3 *island* Massachusetts, NE USA
Nanumaga 145 E3 *var.* Nanumaga. *atoll* NW Tuvalu
Nanumaga *see* Nanumaga
Nanumea Atoll 145 E3 *atoll* NW Tuvalu
Nanyang 128 C5 *var.* Nan-yang. Henan, C China
Nan-yang *see* Nanyang
Naoned *see* Nantes
Napa 47 B6 California, W USA
Napier 150 E4 Hawke's Bay, North Island, New Zealand
Naples 43 E5 Florida, SE USA
Naples *see* Napoli
Napo 56 B3 *river* NE Ecuador/Peru
Napoléon-Vendée *see* la Roche-sur-Yon
Napoli 97 C5 Eng. Naples, Ger. Neapel; *anc.* Neapolis. Campania, S Italy
Napo, Río 60 C1 *river* Ecuador/Peru
Naracoorte 149 B7 South Australia
Naradhivas *see* Narathiwat
Narathiwat 137 C7 *var.* Naradhivas. Narathiwat, SW Thailand
Narbada *see* Narmada
Narbo Martius *see* Narbonne
Narbonne 91 C6 *anc.* Narbo Martius. Aude, S France
Narborough Island *see* Fernandina, Isla
Nares Abyssal Plain *see* Nares Plain
Nares Plain 35 E6 *var.* Nares Abyssal Plain. *abyssal plain* NW Atlantic Ocean
Nares Strait *see* Nares Strait
Nares Strait 82 D1 Dan. Nares Stræde. *strait* Canada/Greenland
Narew 98 E3 *river* E Poland
Narmada 124 B3 *var.* Narbada. *river* C India
Narova *see* Narva
Narovlya *see* Narowlya

Narowlya 107 C8 Rus. Narovlya. Homyel'skaya Voblasts', SE Belarus
Närpes 85 D5 Fin. Närpiö. Österbotten, W Finland
Närpiö see Närpes
Narrabri 149 D6 New South Wales, SE Australia
Narrogin 147 B6 Western Australia
Narva 106 E2 Ida-Virumaa, NE Estonia
Narva 106 E2 prev. Narova. river Estonia/Russia
Narva Bay 106 E2 Est. Narva Laht, Ger. Narwa-Bucht, Rus. Narvskiy Zaliv. bay Estonia/Russia
Narva Laht see Narva Bay
Narva Reservoir 106 E2 Est. Narva Veehoidla, Rus. Narvskoye Vodokhranilishche. reservoir Estonia/Russia
Narva Veehoidla see Narva Reservoir
Narvik 84 C3 Nordland, C Norway
Narvskiy Zaliv see Narva Bay
Narvskoye Vodokhranilishche see Narva Reservoir
Narwa-Bucht see Narva Bay
Nar'yan-Mar 110 D3 prev. Beloshchel'ye, Dzerzhinskiy. Nenetskiy Avtonomnyy Okrug, NW Russia
Naryn 123 G2 Narynskaya Oblast', C Kyrgyzstan
Nassau 54 C1 country capital (The Bahamas) New Providence, N The Bahamas
Năsăud 108 B3 Ger. Nussdorf, Hung. Naszód. Bistriţa-Năsăud, N Romania
Nase see Naze
Nāshik 134 C5 prev. Nāsik. Mahārāshtra, W India
Nashua 41 G3 New Hampshire, NE USA
Nashville 42 C1 state capital Tennessee, S USA
Näsijärvi 85 D5 lake SW Finland
Nāsik see Nāshik
Nasir, Buhayrat/ Nâşir, Buhayrat/ Nâşir,Buheiret see Nasser, Lake
Nāsiri see Ahvāz
Nasiriya see An Nāşirīyah
Nasser, Lake 72 B3 var. Buhayrat Nasir, Buḩayrat Nâşir, Buḩeiret Nâşir. lake Egypt/Sudan
Naszód see Năsăud
Nata 78 C3 Central, NE Botswana
Natal 63 G2 state capital Rio Grande do Norte, E Brazil
Natal Basin 141 A6 var. Mozambique Basin. undersea basin N Indian Ocean
Natanya see Netanya
Natchez 42 B3 Mississippi, S USA
Natchitoches 42 A2 Louisiana, S USA
Nathanya see Netanya
Natitingou 75 F4 NW Benin
Natsrat see Natzrat
Natuna Islands see Natuna, Kepulauan
Natuna, Kepulauan 124 D4 var. Natuna Islands. island group W Indonesia
Naturaliste Plateau 141 E6 undersea plateau E Indian Ocean
Natzrat 119 A5 var. Natsrat, Ar. En Nazira, Eng. Nazareth; prev. Nazerat. Northern, N Israel
Naugard see Nowogard
Naujamiestis 106 C4 Panevėžys, C Lithuania
Nauru 144 D2 off. Republic of Nauru; prev. Pleasant Island. country W Pacific Ocean
Nauru, Republic of see Nauru
Nauta 60 C2 Loreto, N Peru
Navahrudak 107 C6 Pol. Nowogródek, Rus. Novogrudok. Hrodzyenskaya Voblasts', W Belarus
Navanagar see Jāmnagar
Navapolatsk 107 D5 Rus. Novopolotsk. Vitsyebskaya Voblasts', N Belarus
Navarra 93 E2 Eng./Fr. Navarre. autonomous community N Spain
Navarre see Navarra
Navassa Island 54 C3 US unincorporated territory C West Indies
Navoi see Navoiy
Navoiy 123 E2 Rus. Navoi. Navoiy Viloyati, C Uzbekistan
Navojoa 50 C2 Sonora, NW Mexico
Navolat see Navolato
Navolato 50 C3 var. Navolat. Sinaloa, C Mexico
Návpaktos see Náfpaktos
Návplion see Náfplio
Nawabashah see Nawabshah

Nawabshah 134 B3 var. Nawabashah. Sind, S Pakistan
Naxçıvan 117 G3 Rus. Nakhichevan'. SW Azerbaijan
Náxos 105 D6 var. Naxos. Náxos, Kykládes, Greece, Aegean Sea
Náxos 105 D6 island Kykládes, Greece, Aegean Sea
Nayoro 130 D2 Hokkaidō, NE Japan
Nay Pyi Taw 136 B4 country capital (Myanmar (Burma)) Mandalay, C Myanmar (Burma)
Nazareth see Natzrat
Nazca 60 D4 Ica, S Peru
Nazca Ridge 57 A5 undersea ridge E Pacific Ocean
Naze 130 B3 var. Nase. Kagoshima, Amami-ōshima, SW Japan
Nazerat see Natzrat
Nazilli 116 A4 Aydın, SW Turkey
Nazrēt 73 C5 var. Adama, Hadama. Oromīya, C Ethiopia
N'Dalatando 78 B1 Port. Salazar, Vila Salazar. Cuanza Norte, NW Angola
Ndélé 76 C4 Bamingui-Bangoran, N Central African Republic
Ndendé 77 B6 Nyanga, S Gabon
Ndindi 77 A6 Nyanga, S Gabon
N'Djaména 76 B3 var. Ndjamena; prev. Fort-Lamy. country capital (Chad) Chari-Baguirmi, W Chad
N see N'Djaména
Ndjolé 77 A5 Moyen-Ogooué, W Gabon
Ndola 78 D2 Copperbelt, C Zambia
Ndzouani see Nzwani
Neagh, Lough 89 B5 lake E Northern Ireland, United Kingdom
Néa Moudanía 104 C4 var. Néa Moudhaniá. Kentrikí Makedonía, N Greece
Néa Moudhaniá see Néa Moudanía
Neapel see Napoli
Neápoli 104 B4 prev. Neápolis. Dytikí Makedonía, N Greece
Neápoli 105 D8 Kríti, Greece, E Mediterranean Sea
Neápoli 105 C7 Pelopónnisos, S Greece
Neápolis see Neápoli, Greece
Neapolis see Napoli, Italy
Neapolis see Nablus, West Bank
Near Islands 36 A2 island group Aleutian Islands, Alaska, USA
Néa Zíkhni 104 C3 var. Néa Zíkhni; prev. Néa Zíkhna. Kentrikí Makedonía, NE Greece
Néa Zíkhna/Néa Zíkhni see Néa Zíchni
Nebaj 52 B2 Quiché, W Guatemala
Nebitdag see Balkanabat
Neblina, Pico da 62 C1 mountain NW Brazil
Nebraska 44 D4 off. State of Nebraska, also known as Blackwater State, Cornhusker State, Tree Planters State. state C USA
Nebraska City 45 F4 Nebraska, C USA
Neches River 49 H3 river Texas, SW USA
Neckar 95 B6 river SW Germany
Necochea 65 D5 Buenos Aires, E Argentina
Nederland see Netherlands
Neder Rijn 86 D4 Eng. Lower Rhine. river C Netherlands
Nederweert 87 D5 Limburg, SE Netherlands
Neede 86 E3 Gelderland, E Netherlands
Neerpelt 87 D5 Limburg, NE Belgium
Neftekamsk 111 D5 Respublika Bashkortostan, W Russia
Neftezavodsk see Seýdi
Negara Brunei Darussalam see Brunei
Negēlē 73 D5 var. Negelli, It. Neghelli. Oromīya, C Ethiopia
Negelli see Negēlē
Negev 119 A7 Eng. Negev. desert S Israel
Negev see HaNegev
Neghelli see Negēlē
Negomane 79 E2 var. Negomano. Cabo Delgado, N Mozambique
Negomano see Negomane
Negombo 132 C3 Western Province, SW Sri Lanka
Negotin 100 E4 Serbia, E Serbia
Negra, Punto 60 A3 headland NW Peru
Negreşti see Negreşti-Oaş
Negreşti-Oaş 108 B3 Hung. Avasfelsőfalu; prev. Negreşti. Satu Mare, NE Romania
Negro, Río 65 C5 river E Argentina
Negro, Rio 62 D1 river N South America
Negro, Río 64 D4 river Brazil/Uruguay

Negros 139 E2 island C Philippines
Nehbandān 120 E3 Khorāsān, E Iran
Neijiang 128 B5 Sichuan, C China
Neiva 58 B3 Huila, S Colombia
Nellore 132 D2 Andhra Pradesh, E India
Nelson 151 C5 Nelson, South Island, New Zealand
Nelson 37 G4 river Manitoba, C Canada
Néma 74 D3 Hodh ech Chargui, SE Mauritania
Neman 106 B4 Bel. Nyoman, Ger. Memel, Lith. Nemunas, Pol. Niemen. river NE Europe
Nemausus see Nîmes
Neméa 105 B6 Pelopónnisos, S Greece
Nemetocenna see Arras
Nemours 90 C3 Seine-et-Marne, N France
Nemunas see Neman
Nemuro 130 E2 Hokkaidō, NE Japan
Neochóri 105 B5 Dytikí Elláda, C Greece
Nepal 135 E3 off. Nepal. country S Asia
Nereta 106 C4 S Latvia
Neretva 100 C4 river Bosnia and Herzegovina/Croatia
Neris 107 C5 Bel. Viliya, Pol. Wilia; prev. Pol. Wiliya. river Belarus/Lithuania
Neris see Viliya
Nerva 92 C4 Andalucía, S Spain
Neryungri 115 F4 Respublika Sakha (Yakutiya), NE Russia
Neskaupstaður 83 E5 Austurland, E Iceland
Ness, Loch 88 C3 lake N Scotland, United Kingdom
Nesterov see Zhovkva
Néstos 104 C3 Bul. Mesta, Turk. Kara Su. river Bulgaria/Greece
Nesvizh see Nyasvizh
Netanya 119 A6 var. Natanya, Nathanya. Central, C Israel
Netherlands 86 C3 off. Kingdom of the Netherlands, var. Holland, Dut. Koninkrijk der Nederlanden, Nederland. country NW Europe
Netherlands East Indies see Indonesia
Netherlands Guiana see Suriname
Netherlands, Kingdom of the see Netherlands
Netherlands New Guinea see Papua
Nettiling Lake 37 G3 lake Baffin Island, Nunavut, N Canada
Netze see Noteć
Neu Amerika see Puławy
Neubrandenburg 94 D3 Mecklenburg-Vorpommern, NE Germany
Neuchâtel 95 A7 Ger. Neuenburg. Neuchâtel, W Switzerland
Neuchâtel, Lac de 95 A7 Ger. Neuenburger See. lake W Switzerland
Neuenburg see Neuchâtel
Neuenburger See see Neuchâtel, Lac de
Neufchâteau 87 D8 Luxembourg, SE Belgium
Neugradisk see Nova Gradiška
Neuhof see Zgierz
Neukuhren see Pionerskiy
Neumarkt see Târgu Secuiesc, Covasna, Romania
Neumarkt see Târgu Mureş
Neumoldowa see Moldova Nouă
Neumünster 94 B2 Schleswig-Holstein, N Germany
Neunkirchen 95 A5 Saarland, SW Germany
Neuquén 65 B5 Neuquén, SE Argentina
Neuruppin 94 C3 Brandenburg, NE Germany
Neusalz an der Oder see Nowa Sól
Neu Sandec see Nowy Sącz
Neusatz see Novi Sad
Neusiedler See 95 E6 Hung. Fertő. lake Austria/Hungary
Neusohl see Banská Bystrica
Neustadt see Baia Mare, Maramureş, Romania
Neustadt an der Haardt see Neustadt an der Weinstrasse
Neustadt an der Weinstrasse 95 B5 prev. Neustadt an der Haardt, hist. Niewenstat; anc. Nova Civitas. Rheinland-Pfalz, SW Germany
Neustadt see Novo mesto
Neustettin see Szczecinek
Neustrelitz 94 D3 Mecklenburg-Vorpommern, NE Germany
Neutra see Nitra
Neu-Ulm 95 B6 Bayern, S Germany

Neuwied 95 A5 Rheinland-Pfalz, W Germany
Neuzen see Terneuzen
Nevada 47 C5 off. State of Nevada, also known as Battle Born State, Sagebrush State, Silver State. state W USA
Nevada Sierra 92 D5 mountain range S Spain
Nevada, Sierra 47 C6 mountain range W USA
Nevers 90 C4 anc. Noviodunum. Nièvre, C France
Neves 76 E2 São Tomé, S Sao Tome and Principe, Africa
Nevinnomyssk 111 B7 Stavropol'skiy Kray, SW Russia
Nevşehir 116 C3 var. Nevsehir. Nevşehir, C Turkey
Newala 73 C8 Mtwara, SE Tanzania
New Albany 40 C5 Indiana, N USA
New Amsterdam 59 G3 E Guyana
Newark 41 F4 New Jersey, NE USA
New Bedford 41 G3 Massachusetts, NE USA
Newberg 46 B3 Oregon, NW USA
New Bern 43 F1 North Carolina, SE USA
New Braunfels 49 G4 Texas, SW USA
Newbridge 89 B6 Ir. An Droichead Nua. Kildare, C Ireland
New Britain 144 B3 island E Papua New Guinea
New Brunswick 39 E4 Fr. Nouveau-Brunswick. province SE Canada
New Caledonia 144 D4 var. Kanaky, Fr. Nouvelle-Calédonie. French self-governing territory of special status SW Pacific Ocean
New Caledonia 144 C5 island SW Pacific Ocean
New Caledonia Basin 142 C4 undersea basin W Pacific Ocean
Newcastle 149 D6 New South Wales, SE Australia
Newcastle see Newcastle upon Tyne
Newcastle upon Tyne 88 D4 var. Newcastle, hist. Monkchester, Lat. Pons Aelii. NE England, United Kingdom
New Delhi 134 D3 country capital (India) Delhi, N India
New England of the West see Minnesota
Newfoundland 39 G3 Fr. Terre-Neuve. island Newfoundland and Labrador, SE Canada
Newfoundland and Labrador 39 F2 Fr. Terre Neuve. province E Canada
Newfoundland Basin 66 B3 undersea feature NW Atlantic Ocean
New Georgia Islands 144 C3 island group NW Solomon Islands
New Glasgow 39 F4 Nova Scotia, SE Canada
New Goa see Panaji
New Guinea 144 A3 Dut. Nieuw Guinea, Ind. Irian. island Indonesia/Papua New Guinea
New Hampshire 41 F2 off. State of New Hampshire, also known as Granite State. state NE USA
New Haven 41 G3 Connecticut, NE USA
New Hebrides see Vanuatu
New Iberia 42 B3 Louisiana, S USA
New Ireland 144 C3 island NE Papua New Guinea
New Jersey 41 F4 off. State of New Jersey, also known as The Garden State. state NE USA
Newman 146 B4 Western Australia
Newmarket 89 E6 E England, United Kingdom
New Mexico 48 C2 off. State of New Mexico, also known as Land of Enchantment, Sunshine State. state SW USA
New Orleans 42 B3 Louisiana, S USA
New Plymouth 150 C4 Taranaki, North Island, New Zealand
Newport 89 D7 S England, United Kingdom
Newport 89 C7 SE Wales, United Kingdom
Newport 40 C4 Kentucky, S USA
Newport 41 G3 Rhode Island, NE USA
Newport News 41 F5 Virginia, NE USA
New Providence 54 C1 island The Bahamas
Newquay 89 C7 SW England, United Kingdom

Newry 89 B5 Ir. An tIúr. SE Northern
Ireland, United Kingdom
New Sarum see Salisbury
New Siberian Islands 115 F1 Eng. New
Siberian Islands. island group N Russia
New Siberian Islands see Novosibirskiye
Ostrova
New South Wales 149 C6 state
SE Australia
Newton 45 G3 Iowa, C USA
Newton 45 F5 Kansas, C USA
Newtownabbey 89 B5 Ir. Baile na
Mainistreach. E Northern Ireland,
United Kingdom
New Ulm 45 F2 Minnesota, N USA
New York 41 F4 New York, NE USA
New York 41 F3 state NE USA
New Zealand 150 A4 country
SW Pacific Ocean
Neyveli 132 C2 Tamil Nādu, SE India
Nezhin see Nizhyn
Ngangze Co 126 B5 lake W China
Ngaoundéré 76 B4 var. N'Gaoundéré.
Adamaoua, N Cameroon
N'Gaoundéré see Ngaoundéré
Ngazidja 79 F2 Fr. Grande Comore, var.
Njazidja. island NW Comoros
Ngerulmud 144 A2 country capital
(Palau) NW Pacific Ocean
N'Giva 78 B3 var. Ondjiva, Port. Vila
Pereira de Eça. Cunene, S Angola
Ngo 77 B6 Plateaux, SE Congo
Ngoko 77 B5 river Cameroon/Congo
Ngourti 75 H3 Diffa, E Niger
Nguigmi 75 H3 var. N'Guigmi. Diffa,
SE Niger
N'Guigmi see Nguigmi
N'Gunza see Sumbe
Nguru 75 G3 Yobe, NE Nigeria
Nha Trang 137 E6 Khanh Hoa,
S Vietnam
Niagara Falls 38 D5 Ontario, S Canada
Niagara Falls 41 E3 New York, NE USA
Niagara Falls 40 D3 waterfall Canada/
USA
Niamey 75 F3 country capital (Niger)
Niamey, SW Niger
Niangay, Lac 75 E3 lake E Mali
Nia-Nia 77 E5 Orientale, NE Dem. Rep.
Congo
Nias, Pulau 138 A3 island W Indonesia
Nicaea see Nice
Nicaragua 52 D3 off. Republic of
Nicaragua. country Central America
Lake Nicaragua 52 D4 var. Cocibolca,
Gran Lago, Eng. Lake Nicaragua. lake
S Nicaragua
Nicaragua, Lake see Nicaragua, Lago de
Nicaragua, Republic of see Nicaragua
Nicaria see Ikaría
Nice 91 D6 It. Nizza; anc. Nicaea.
Alpes-Maritimes, SE France
Nicephorium see Ar Raqqah
Nicholas II Land see Severnaya Zemlya
Nicholls Town 54 C1 Andros Island,
NW The Bahamas
Nicobar Islands 124 B4 island group
India, E Indian Ocean
Nicosia 102 C5 Gk. Lefkosía, Turk.
Lefkoşa. country capital (Cyprus)
C Cyprus
Nicoya 52 D4 Guanacaste, W Costa Rica
Nicoya, Golfo de 52 D5 gulf W Costa
Rica
Nicoya, Península de 52 D4 peninsula
NW Costa Rica
Nida 106 A3 Ger. Nidden. Klaipėda,
SW Lithuania
Nidaros see Trondheim
Nidden see Nida
Nidzica 98 D3 Ger. Niedenburg.
Warmińsko-Mazurskie, NE Poland
Niedenburg see Nidzica
Niedere Tauern 99 A6 mountain range
C Austria
Niemen see Neman
Nieśwież see Nyasvizh
Nieuw Amsterdam 59 G3 Commewijne,
NE Suriname
Nieuw-Bergen 86 D4 Limburg,
SE Netherlands
Nieuwegein 86 C4 Utrecht,
C Netherlands
Nieuw Guinea see New Guinea
Nieuw Nickerie 59 G3 Nickerie,
NW Suriname
Niewenstat see Neustadt an der
Weinstrasse

Niğde 116 C4 Niğde, C Turkey
Niger 75 F3 off. Republic of Niger.
country W Africa
Niger 75 F4 river W Africa
Nigeria 75 F4 off. Federal Republic of
Nigeria. country W Africa
Nigeria, Federal Republic of see Nigeria
Niger, Mouths of the 75 F5 delta
S Nigeria
Niger, Republic of see Niger
Nihon see Japan
Niigata 131 D5 Niigata, Honshū,
C Japan
Niihama 131 B7 Ehime, Shikoku,
SW Japan
Ni'ihau 47 A7 var. Niihau. island
Hawaii, USA, C Pacific Ocean
Nii-jima 131 D6 island E Japan
Nijkerk 86 D3 Gelderland,
C Netherlands
Nijlen 87 C5 Antwerpen, N Belgium
Nijmegen 86 D4 Ger. Nimwegen; anc.
Noviomagus. Gelderland,
SE Netherlands
Nikaria see Ikaría
Nikel' 110 C2 Finn. Kolosjoki.
Murmanskaya Oblast', NW Russia
Nikiniki 139 E5 Timor, S Indonesia
Niklasmarkt see Gheorgheni
Nikolainkaupunki see Vaasa
Nikolayev see Mykolaiv
Nikol'sk see Ussuriysk
Nikol'sk-Ussuriyskiy see Ussuriysk
Nikopol' 109 F3 Dnipropetrovs'ka
Oblast', SE Ukraine
Nikšić 101 C5 C Montenegro
Nikumaroro 145 E3 prev. Gardner
Island. atoll Phoenix Islands, C Kiribati
Nikunau 145 E3 var. Nukunau; prev.
Byron Island. atoll Tungaru, W Kiribati
Nile 72 B2 former province NW Uganda
Nile 68 D3 Ar. Nahr an Nil. river
N Africa
Nile Delta 72 B1 delta N Egypt
Nil, Nahr an see Nile
Nîmes 91 C6 anc. Nemausus, Nismes.
Gard, S France
Nimwegen see Nijmegen
Nine Degree Channel 132 B3 channel
India/Maldives
Ninetyeast Ridge 141 D5 undersea
feature E Indian Ocean
Ninety Mile Beach 150 C1 beach North
Island, New Zealand
Ningbo 128 D5 var. Ning-po, Yin-hsien;
prev. Ninghsien. Zhejiang, SE China
Ning-hsia see Ningxia
Ninghsien see Ningbo
Ning-po see Ningbo
**Ningsia/Ningsia Hui/Ningsia Hui
Autonomous Region** see Ningxia
Ningxia 128 B4 off. Ningxia Huizu
Zizhiqu, var. Ning-hsia, Ningsia, Eng.
Ningsia Hui, Ningsia Hui Autonomous
Region. autonomous region N China
Ningxia Huizu Zizhiqu see Ningxia
Nio see Ios
Niobrara River 45 E3 river Nebraska/
Wyoming, C USA
Nioro 74 D3 var. Nioro du Sahel. Kayes,
W Mali
Nioro du Sahel see Nioro
Niort 90 B4 Deux-Sèvres, W France
Nipigon 38 B4 Ontario, S Canada
Nipigon, Lake 38 B3 lake Ontario,
S Canada
Nippon see Japan
Niš 101 E5 Eng. Nish, Ger. Nisch; anc.
Naissus. Serbia, SE Serbia
Nişab 120 B4 Al Ḥudūd ash Shamālīyah,
N Saudi Arabia
Nisch/Nish see Niš
Nisibin see Nusaybin
Nísiros see Nísyros
Nisko 98 E4 Podkarpackie,
SE Poland
Nismes see Nîmes
Nistru see Dniester
Nísyros 105 E7 var. Nísiros. island
Dodekánisa, Greece, Aegean Sea
Nitra 99 C6 Ger. Neutra, Hung. Nyitra.
Nitriansky Kraj, SW Slovakia
Nitra 99 C6 Ger. Neutra, Hung. Nyitra.
river W Slovakia
Niuatobutabu see Niuatoputapu
Niuatoputapu 145 E4 var.
Niuatobutabu; prev. Keppel Island.
island N Tonga

Niue 145 F4 self-governing territory in
free association with New Zealand
S Pacific Ocean
Niulakita 145 E3 var. Nurakita. atoll
S Tuvalu
Niutao 145 E3 atoll NW Tuvalu
Nivernais 90 C4 cultural region
C France
Nizāmābād 134 D5 Telangana, C India
Nizhnegorskiy see Nyzhn'ohirs'kyy
Nizhnekamsk 111 C5 Respublika
Tatarstan, W Russia
Nizhnevartovsk 114 D3
Khanty-Mansiyskiy Avtonomnyy
Okrug-Yugra, C Russia
Nizhniy Novgorod 111 C5 prev. Gor'kiy.
Nizhegorodskaya Oblast', W Russia
Nizhniy Odes 110 D4 Respublika Komi,
NW Russia
Nizhyn 109 E1 Rus. Nezhin.
Chernihivs'ka Oblast', NE Ukraine
Nizza see Nice
Njazidja see Ngazidja
Njombe 73 C8 Iringa, S Tanzania
Nkayi 77 B6 prev. Jacob. Bouenza,
S Congo
Nkongsamba 76 A4 var. N'Kongsamba.
Littoral, W Cameroon
N'Kongsamba see Nkongsamba
Nmai Hka 136 B2 var. Me Hka. river
N Myanmar (Burma)
Nobeoka 131 B7 Miyazaki, Kyūshū,
SW Japan
Noboribetsu 130 D3 var. Noboribetu.
Hokkaidō, NE Japan
Noboribetu see Noboribetsu
Nogales 50 B1 Sonora, NW Mexico
Nogales 48 B3 Arizona, SW USA
Nogal Valley see Dooxo Nugaaleed
Noire, Rivi`ere see Black River
Nokia 85 D5 Pirkanmaa,
W Finland
Nokou 76 B3 Kanem, W Chad
Nola 77 B5 Sangha-Mbaéré, SW Central
African Republic
Nolinsk 111 C5 Kirovskaya Oblast',
NW Russia
Nongkaya see Nong Khai
Nong Khai 136 C4 var. Mi Chai,
Nongkaya. Nong Khai, E Thailand
Nonouti 144 D2 prev. Sydenham Island.
atoll Tungaru, W Kiribati
Noord-Beveland 86 B4 island SW
Beveland. island SW Netherlands
Noordwijk aan Zee 86 C3 Zuid-Holland,
W Netherlands
Noordzee see North Sea
Nora 85 C6 Örebro, C Sweden
Norak 123 E3 Rus. Nurek. W Tajikistan
Nordaustlandet 83 G1 island
NE Svalbard
Norden 94 A3 Niedersachsen,
NW Germany
Norderstedt 94 B3 Schleswig-Holstein,
N Germany
Nordfriesische Inseln see North Frisian
Islands
Nordhausen 94 C4 Thüringen,
C Germany
Nordhorn 94 A3 Niedersachsen,
NW Germany
Nord, Mer du see North Sea
Nord-Ouest, Territoires du see
Northwest Territories
Nordsee/Nordsjøen/Nordsøen see
North Sea
Norfolk 45 E3 Nebraska, C USA
Norfolk 41 F5 Virginia, NE USA
Norfolk Island 142 D4 Australian
self-governing territory
SW Pacific Ocean
Norfolk Ridge 142 D4 undersea feature
W Pacific Ocean
Norge see Norway
Norias 49 G5 Texas, SW USA
Noril'sk 114 D3 Krasnoyarskiy Kray,
N Russia
Norman 49 G1 Oklahoma, C USA
Normandes, Îles see Channel Islands
Normandie 90 B3 Eng. Normandy.
cultural region N France
Normandy see Normandie
Normanton 148 C2 Queensland,
NE Australia
Norrköping 85 C6 Östergötland,
S Sweden
Norrtälje 85 C6 Stockholm, C Sweden
Norseman 147 B6 Western Australia
Norske Havet see Norwegian Sea

North Albanian Alps 101 C5 Alb.
Bjeshkët e Namuna, SCr. Prokletije.
mountain range SE Europe
Northallerton 89 D5 N England,
United Kingdom
Northam 147 A6 Western Australia
North America 34 continent
Northampton 89 D6 C England,
United Kingdom
North Andaman 133 F2 island
Andaman Islands, India,
NE Indian Ocean
North Australian Basin 141 E5 Fr.
Bassin Nord de l' Australie. undersea
feature E Indian Ocean
North Bay 38 D4 Ontario, S Canada
North Beveland see Noord-Beveland
North Borneo see Sabah
North Cape 150 C1 headland North
Island, New Zealand
North Cape 84 D1 Eng. North Cape.
headland N Norway
North Cape see Nordkapp
North Carolina 43 E1 off. State of North
Carolina, also known as Old North
State, Tar Heel State, Turpentine State.
state SE USA
North Channel 40 D2 lake channel
Canada/USA
North Charleston 43 F2 South Carolina,
SE USA
North Dakota 44 D2 off. State of North
Dakota, also known as Flickertail State,
Peace Garden State, Sioux State. state
N USA
North Devon Island see Devon Island
**North East Frontier Agency/North East
Frontier Agency of Assam** see
Arunáchal Pradesh
Northeast Providence Channel 54 C1
channel N The Bahamas
Northeim 94 B4 Niedersachsen,
C Germany
Northern Cook Islands 145 F4 island
group N Cook Islands
Northern Dvina 110 C4 var. Northern
Dvina. river NW Russia
Northern Dvina see Severnaya Dvina
Northern Ireland 88 B4 var. The Six
Counties. cultural region Northern
Ireland, United Kingdom
Northern Mariana Islands 142 B1 US
commonwealth territory
W Pacific Ocean
Northern Rhodesia see Zambia
Northern Sporades 105 C5 var. Vóreioi
Sporádes, Vóreioi Sporádhes, Eng.
Northern Sporades. island group
E Greece
Northern Sporades see Vóreies Sporádes
Northern Territory 144 A5 territory
N Australia
North European Plain 81 E3 plain
N Europe
Northfield 45 F2 Minnesota, N USA
North Fiji Basin 142 D3 undersea
feature N Coral Sea
North Frisian Islands 94 B2 var.
Nordfriesische Inseln. island group
N Germany
North Huvadhu Atoll 132 B5 var. Gaafu
Alifu Atoll. atoll S Maldives
North Island 150 B2 island N New
Zealand
North Korea 129 E3 off. Democratic
People's Republic of Korea, Kor.
Chosón-minjujuŭi-inmin-kanghwaguk.
country E Asia
North Little Rock 42 B1 Arkansas,
C USA
North Minch see Minch, The
North Mole 93 G4 harbour wall
NW Gibraltar Europe
North Platte 45 E4 Nebraska, C USA
North Platte River 44 D4 river C USA
North Pole 155 B3 pole Arctic Ocean
North Saskatchewan 37 F5 river
Alberta/Saskatchewan, S Canada
North Sea 80 D3 Dan. Nordsøen, Dut.
Noordzee, Fr. Mer du Nord, Ger.
Nordsee, Nor. Nordsjøen; prev. German
Ocean, Lat. Mare Germanicum. sea
NW Europe
North Siberian Lowland 115 E2 var.
North Siberian Plain, Eng. North
Siberian Lowland. lowlands N Russia
**North Siberian Lowland/North
Siberian Plain** see Severo-Sibirskaya
Nizmennost'
North Star State see Minnesota

North Taranaki Bight *150 C3 gulf* North Island, New Zealand
North Uist *88 B3 island* NW Scotland, United Kingdom
Northwest Atlantic Mid-Ocean Canyon *34 E4 undersea feature* N Atlantic Ocean
North West Highlands *88 C3 mountain range* N Scotland, United Kingdom
Northwest Pacific Basin *113 G4 undersea feature* NW Pacific Ocean
Northwest Territories *37 E3 Fr.* Territoires du Nord-Ouest. *territory* NW Canada
Northwind Plain *155 B2 undersea feature* Arctic Ocean
Norton Sound *36 C2 inlet* Alaska, USA
Norway *85 A5 off.* Kingdom of Norway, *Nor.* Norge. *country* N Europe
Norway, Kingdom of *see* Norway
Norwegian Basin *83 F4 undersea feature* NW Norwegian Sea
Norwegian Sea *83 F4 var.* Norske Havet. *sea* NE Atlantic Ocean
Norwich *89 E6* E England, United Kingdom
Nösen *see* Bistrița
Noshiro *130 D4 var.* Nosiro; *prev.* Noshirominato. Akita, Honshū, C Japan
Noshirominato/Nosiro *see* Noshiro
Nosivka *109 E1 Rus.* Nosovka. Chernihivs'ka Oblast', NE Ukraine
Nosop *78 C4 var.* Nossob. *river* E Namibia
Nosovka *see* Nosivka
Noṣratābād *120 E3* Sīstān va Balūchestān, E Iran
Noteć *98 C3 Ger.* Netze. *river* NW Poland
Nóties Sporádes *see* Dodekánisa
Nottingham *89 D6* C England, United Kingdom
Nouâdhibou *74 B2 prev.* Port-Étienne. Dakhlet Nouâdhibou, W Mauritania
Nouakchott *74 B2 country capital* (Mauritania) Nouakchott District, SW Mauritania
Nouméa *144 C5 dependent territory capital* (New Caledonia) Province Sud, S New Caledonia
Nouveau-Brunswick *see* New Brunswick
Nouvelle-Calédonie *see* New Caledonia
Nouvelle Écosse *see* Nova Scotia
Nova Civitas *see* Neustadt an der Weinstrasse
Nova Gorica *95 D8* W Slovenia
Nova Gradiška *100 C3 Ger.* Neugradisk, *Hung.* Újgradiska. Brod-Posavina, NE Croatia
Nova Iguaçu *63 F4* Rio de Janeiro, SE Brazil
Nova Lisboa *see* Huambo
Novara *96 B2 anc.* Novaria. Piemonte, NW Italy
Novaria *see* Novara
Nova Scotia *33 F4 Fr.* Nouvelle Écosse. *province* SE Canada
Nova Scotia *35 E5 physical region* SE Canada
Novaya Sibir', Ostrov *111 F1 island* Novosibirskiye Ostrova, NE Russia
Novaya Zemlya *110 D1 island group* N Russia
Novaya Zemlya Trough *see* East Novaya Zemlya Trough
Novgorod *see* Velikiy Novgorod
Novi Grad *see* Bosanski Novi
Novi Iskŭr *104 C2* Sofiya-Grad, W Bulgaria
Noviodunum *see* Nevers, Nièvre, France
Noviomagus *see* Lisieux, Calvados, France
Noviomagus *see* Nijmegen, Netherlands
Novi Pazar *101 D5 Turk.* Yenipazar. Serbia, S Serbia
Novi Sad *100 D3 Ger.* Neusatz, *Hung.* Újvidék. Vojvodina, N Serbia
Novoazovs'k *109 G4 Rus.* Novoazovsk. Donets'ka Oblast', E Ukraine
Novocheboksarsk *111 C5* Chuvashskaya Respublika, W Russia
Novocherkassk *111 B7* Rostovskaya Oblast', SW Russia
Novodvinsk *110 C3* Arkhangel'skaya Oblast', NW Russia
Novograd-Volynskiy *see* Novohrad-Volyns'kyy
Novogrudok *see* Navahrudak

Novohrad-Volyns'kyy *108 D2 Rus.* Novograd-Volynskiy. Zhytomyrs'ka Oblast', N Ukraine
Novokazalinsk *see* Ayteke Bi
Novokuznetsk *114 D4 prev.* Stalinsk. Kemerovskaya Oblast', S Russia
Novolazarevskaya *154 C2 Russian research station* Antarctica
Novo Mesto *95 E8 Ger.* Rudolfswert; *prev.* Ger. Neustadtl. SE Slovenia
Novomoskovsk *111 B5* Tul'skaya Oblast', W Russia
Novomoskovs'k *109 F3 Rus.* Novomoskovsk. Dnipropetrovs'ka Oblast', E Ukraine
Novopolotsk *see* Navapolatsk
Novoradomsk *see* Radomsko
Novo Redondo *see* Sumbe
Novorossiysk *111 A7* Krasnodarskiy Kray, SW Russia
Novoshakhtinsk *111 B6* Rostovskaya Oblast', SW Russia
Novosibirsk *114 D4* Novosibirskaya Oblast', C Russia
Novotroitsk *111 D6* Orenburgskaya Oblast', W Russia
Novotroitskoye *see* Novotroyits'ke, Ukraine
Novotroyits'ke *109 F4 Rus.* Novotroitskoye. Khersons'ka Oblast', S Ukraine
Novo-Urgench *see* Urganch
Novovolyns'k *108 C1 Rus.* Novovolynsk. Volyns'ka Oblast', NW Ukraine
Novy Dvor *107 B6 Rus.* Novyy Dvor. Hrodzyenskaya Voblasts', W Belarus
Novyy Bug *see* Novyy Buh
Novyy Buh *109 E3 Rus.* Novyy Bug. Mykolayivs'ka Oblast', S Ukraine
Novyy Dvor *see* Novy Dvor
Novyy Margilan *see* Far'gona
Novyy Uzen' *see* Zhanaozen
Nowa Sól *98 B4 var.* Nowasól. Neusalz an der Oder. Lubuskie, W Poland
Nowasól *see* Nowa Sól
Nowogard *98 B2 var.* Nowógard, *Ger.* Naugard. Zachodnio-pomorskie, NW Poland
Nowogródek *see* Navahrudak
Nowo-Minsk *see* Mińsk Mazowiecki
Nowy Dwór Mazowiecki *98 D3* Mazowieckie, C Poland
Nowy Sącz *99 D5 Ger.* Neu Sandec. Małopolskie, S Poland
Nowy Tomyśl *98 B3 var.* Nowy Tomysl. Wielkopolskie, C Poland
Nowy Tomysl *see* Nowy Tomyśl
Noyon *90 D3* Oise, N France
Nsanje *79 E3* Southern, S Malawi
Nsawam *75 E5* SE Ghana
Ntomba, Lac *77 C6 var.* Lac Tumba. *lake* NW Dem. Rep. Congo
Nubian Desert *72 B3 desert* NE Sudan
Nu Chiang *see* Salween
Nu'eima *119 E7* E West Bank Asia
Nueva Caceres *see* Naga
Nueva Gerona *54 B2* Isla de la Juventud, S Cuba
Nueva Rosita *50 D2* Coahuila, NE Mexico
Nuevitas *54 C2* Camagüey, E Cuba
Nuevo, Bajo *53 G1 island* NW Colombia South America
Nuevo Casas Grandes *50 C1* Chihuahua, N Mexico
Nuevo, Golfo *65 C6 gulf* S Argentina
Nuevo Laredo *51 E2* Tamaulipas, NE Mexico
Nui Atoll *145 E3 atoll* W Tuvalu
Nu Jiang *see* Salween
Nûk *see* Nuuk
Nukha *see* Şäki
Nuku'alofa *145 E5 country capital* (Tonga) Tongatapu, S Tonga
Nukufetau Atoll *145 E3 atoll* C Tuvalu
Nukulaelae Atoll *145 E3 var.* Nukulailai. *atoll* E Tuvalu
Nukulailai *see* Nukulaelae Atoll
Nukunau *see* Nikunau
Nukunonu Atoll *145 E3 island* C Tokelau
Nukus *122 C2* Qoraqalpog'iston Respublikasi, W Uzbekistan
Nullarbor Plain *147 C6 plateau* South Australia/Western Australia
Nunap Isua *82 C5 var.* Uummannarsuaq, *Dan.* Kap Farvel, *Eng.* Cape Farewell. *cape* S Greenland

Nunavut *37 F3 territory* N Canada
Nuneaton *89 D6* C England, United Kingdom
Nunivak Island *36 B2 island* Alaska, USA
Nunspeet *86 D3* Gelderland, E Netherlands
Nuoro *97 A5* Sardegna, Italy, C Mediterranean Sea
Nuquí *58 A3* Chocó, W Colombia
Nurakita *see* Niulakita
Nurata *see* Nurota
Nurek *see* Norak
Nuremberg *see* Nürnberg
Nurmes *84 E4* Pohjois-Karjala, E Finland
Nürnberg *95 C5 Eng.* Nuremberg. Bayern, S Germany
Nurota *123 E2 Rus.* Nurata. Navoiy Viloyati, C Uzbekistan
Nusaybin *117 F4 var.* Nisibin. Manisa, SE Turkey
Nussdorf *see* Năsăud
Nutmeg State *see* Connecticut
Nuuk *82 C4 var.* Nûk, *Dan.* Godthaab, Godthåb. *dependent territory capital* (Greenland) Kitaa, SW Greenland
Nyagan' *114 C3* Khanty-Mansiyskiy Avtonomnyy Okrug-Yugra, N Russia
Nyainqentanglha Shan *126 C5 mountain range* W China
Nyala *72 A4* Southern Darfur, W Sudan
Nyamapanda *78 D3* Mashonaland East, NE Zimbabwe
Nyamtumbo *73 C8* Ruvuma, S Tanzania
Nyanda *see* Masvingo
Nyandoma *110 C4* Arkhangel'skaya Oblast', NW Russia
Nyantakara *73 B7* Kagera, NW Tanzania
Nyasa, Lake *79 E2 var.* Lake Malawi; *prev.* Lago Nyassa. *lake* E Africa
Nyasaland/Nyasaland Protectorate *see* Malawi
Nyassa, Lago *see* Nyasa, Lake
Nyasvizh *107 C6 Pol.* Nieśwież, *Rus.* Nesvizh. Minskaya Voblasts', C Belarus
Nyaunglebin *136 B4* Bago, SW Myanmar (Burma)
Nyeri *73 C6* Central, C Kenya
Nyíregyháza *99 D6* Szabolcs-Szatmár-Bereg, NE Hungary
Nyitra *see* Nitra
Nykøbing *85 B8* Sjælland, SE Denmark
Nyköping *85 C6* Södermanland, S Sweden
Nylstroom *see* Modimolle
Nyngan *149 D6* New South Wales, SE Australia
Nyoman *see* Neman
Nyurba *115 F3* Respublika Sakha (Yakutiya), NE Russia
Nyzhn'ohirs'kyy *109 F4 Rus.* Nizhnegorskiy. Avtonomna Respublika Krym, S Ukraine
NZ *see* New Zealand
Nzega *73 C7* Tabora, C Tanzania
Nzérékoré *74 D4* SE Guinea
Nzwani *79 F2 Fr.* Anjouan, *var.* Ndzouani. *see* Comoros

O

Oa'hu *47 A7 var.* Oahu. *island* Hawaiian Islands, Hawaii, USA
Oak Harbor *46 B1* Washington, NW USA
Oakland *47 B6* California, W USA
Oamaru *151 B7* Otago, South Island, New Zealand
Oaxaca *51 F5 var.* Oaxaca de Juárez; *prev.* Antequera. Oaxaca, SE Mexico
Oaxaca de Juárez *see* Oaxaca
Ob' *112 C2 river* C Russia
Obal' *107 D5 Rus.* Obol'. Vitsyebskaya Voblasts', N Belarus
Oban *88 C4* W Scotland, United Kingdom
Oban *see* Halfmoon Bay
Obando *see* Puerto Inírida
Obdorsk *see* Salekhard
Óbecse *see* Bečej
Obeliai *106 C4* Panevėžys, NE Lithuania
Oberhollabrunn *see* Tulln
Ob', Gulf of *114 D3 Eng.* Gulf of Ob. *gulf* N Russia
Ob', Gulf of *see* Obskaya Guba
Obidovichi *see* Abidavichy
Obihiro *130 D2* Hokkaidō, NE Japan
Obo *76 D4* Haut-Mbomou, E Central African Republic

Obock *72 D4* E Djibouti
Obol' *see* Obal'
Oborniki *98 C3* Wielkopolskie, W Poland
Obrovo *see* Abrova
Ob' Tablemount *141 B7 undersea feature* S Indian Ocean
Ocala *43 E4* Florida, SE USA
Ocaña *58 B2* Norte de Santander, N Colombia
Ocaña *92 D3* Castilla-La Mancha, C Spain
O Carballiño *92 C1 Cast.* Carballiño. Galicia, NW Spain
Occidental, Cordillera *58 B2 mountain range* W South America
Occidental, Cordillera *61 E4 mountain range* Bolivia/Chile
Ocean Falls *36 D5* British Columbia, SW Canada
Ocean Island *see* Banaba
Oceanside *47 C8* California, W USA
Ocean State *see* Rhode Island
Ochakiv *109 E4 Rus.* Ochakov. Mykolayivs'ka Oblast', S Ukraine
Ochakov *see* Ochakiv
Ochamchira *see* Ochamchire
Ochamchire *117 E2 prev.* Och'amch'ire. W Georgia
Och'amch'ire *see* Ochamchire
Ocho Rios *54 B4* C Jamaica
Ochrida *see* Ohrid
Ochrida, Lake *see* Ohrid, Lake
Ocotal *52 D3* Nueva Segovia, NW Nicaragua
Ocozocuautla *51 G5* Chiapas, SE Mexico
October Revolution Island *115 E2 Eng.* October Revolution Island. *island* Severnaya Zemlya, N Russia
October Revolution Island *see* Oktyabr'skoy Revolyutsii, Ostrov
Ocú *53 F5* Herrera, S Panama
Ōdate *130 D3* Akita, Honshū, C Japan
Oddur *see* Xuddur
Ödemiş *116 A4* İzmir, SW Turkey
Ödenburg *see* Sopron
Odenpäh *see* Otepää
Odense *85 B7* Sydtjylland, C Denmark
Oder *98 B3 Cz./Pol.* Odra. *river* C Europe
Oderhaff *see* Szczeciński, Zalew
Odesa *109 E4 Eng.* Odessa. Odes'ka Oblast', SW Ukraine
Odessa *49 E3* Texas, SW USA
Odessa *see* Odesa
Odessus *see* Varna
Odienné *74 D4* NW Ivory Coast
Odisha *135 F4 prev.* Orissa. *cultural region* NE India
Ôđôngk *137 D6* Kampong Speu, S Cambodia
Odoorn *86 E2* Drenthe, NE Netherlands
Odra *see* Oder
Oesel *see* Saaremaa
Of *117 E2* Trabzon, NE Turkey
Ofanto *97 D5 river* S Italy
Offenbach *95 B5 var.* Offenbach am Main. Hessen, W Germany
Offenbach am Main *see* Offenbach
Offenburg *95 B6* Baden-Württemberg, SW Germany
Ogaadeen *see* Ogaden
Ogaden *73 D5 Som.* Ogaadeen. *plateau* Ethiopia/Somalia
Ōgaki *131 C6* Gifu, Honshū, SW Japan
Ogallala *44 D4* Nebraska, C USA
Ogbomoso *75 F4 var.* Ogmoboso. Oyo, W Nigeria
Ogden *44 B4* Utah, W USA
Ogdensburg *41 F2* New York, NE USA
Ogmoboso *see* Ogbomosho
Ogulin *100 A3* Karlovac, NW Croatia
Ohio *40 C4 off.* State of Ohio, *also known as* Buckeye State. *state* N USA
Ohio River *40 C4 river* N USA
Ohlau *see* Oława
Ohri *see* Ohrid
Ohrid *101 D6 Turk.* Ochrida, Ohri. SW Macedonia
Ohrid, Lake *101 D6 var.* Lake Ochrida, *Alb.* Liqeni i Ohrit, *Mac.* Ohridsko Ezero. *lake* Albania/Macedonia
Ohridsko Ezero/Ohrit, Liqeni i *see* Ohrid, Lake
Ohura *150 D3* Manawatu-Wanganui, North Island, New Zealand
Oirschot *87 C5* Noord-Brabant, S Netherlands
Oise *90 C3 river* N France

Oistins 55 G2 S Barbados
Ōita 131 B7 Ōita, Kyūshū, SW Japan
Ojinaga 50 D2 Chihuahua, N Mexico
Ojos del Salado, Cerro 64 B3 mountain W Argentina
Okaihau 150 C2 Northland, North Island, New Zealand
Okanizsa see Kanjiža
Okara 134 C2 Punjab, E Pakistan
Okavanggo see Cubango/Okavango
Okavango see Cubango
Okavango Delta 78 C3 wetland N Botswana
Okayama 131 B6 Okayama, Honshū, SW Japan
Okazaki 131 C6 Aichi, Honshū, C Japan
Okeechobee, Lake 43 E4 lake Florida, SE USA
Okefenokee Swamp 43 E3 wetland Georgia, SE USA
Okhotsk 115 G3 Khabarovskiy Kray, E Russia
Okhotsk, Sea of 113 F3 sea NW Pacific Ocean
Okhtyrka 109 F2 Rus. Akhtyrka. Sums'ka Oblast', NE Ukraine
Oki-guntō see Oki-shotō
Okinawa 130 A3 island SW Japan
Okinawa-shoto 130 A4 island group Nansei-shotō, SW Japan Asia
Oki-shoto 131 B6 var. Oki-guntō. island group SW Japan
Oklahoma 49 F2 off. State of Oklahoma, also known as The Sooner State. state C USA
Oklahoma City 49 G1 state capital Oklahoma, C USA
Okmulgee 49 G1 Oklahoma, C USA
Oko, Wadi 72 C3 river NE Sudan
Oktyabr'skiy 111 D6 Volgogradskaya Oblast', SW Russia
Oktyabr'skiy see Aktsyabrski
Okulovka 110 B4 var. Okulovka. Novgorodskaya Oblast', W Russia
Okulovka see Okulovka
Okushiri-to 130 C3 var. Okusiri Tô. island NE Japan
Okusiri Tô see Okushiri-tô
Oláh-Toplicza see Topliţa
Olavarría 65 D5 Buenos Aires, E Argentina
Oława 98 C4 Ger. Ohlau. Dolnośląskie, SW Poland
Olbia 97 A5 prev. Terranova Pausania. Sardegna, Italy, C Mediterranean Sea
Old Bay State/Old Colony State see Massachusetts
Old Dominion see Virginia
Oldebroek 86 D3 Gelderland, E Netherlands
Oldenburg 94 B3 Niedersachsen, NW Germany
Oldenburg 94 C2 var. Oldenburg in Holstein. Schleswig-Holstein, N Germany
Oldenburg in Holstein see Oldenburg
Oldenzaal 86 E3 Overijssel, E Netherlands
Old Harbour 54 B5 C Jamaica
Old Line State see Maryland
Old North State see North Carolina
Olëkma 115 F4 river C Russia
Olëkminsk 115 F3 Respublika Sakha (Yakutiya), NE Russia
Oleksandrivka 109 E3 Rus. Aleksandrovka. Kirovohrads'ka Oblast', C Ukraine
Oleksandriya 109 F3 Rus. Aleksandriya. Kirovohrads'ka Oblast', C Ukraine
Olenegorsk 110 C2 Murmanskaya Oblast', NW Russia
Olenëk 115 E3 Respublika Sakha (Yakutiya), NE Russia
Olenëk 115 E3 river NE Russia
Oléron, Île d' 91 A5 island W France
Oleshk 109 F4 Rus. Tsyurupyns'k. Khersons'ka Oblast', S Ukraine
Olevs'k 108 D1 Rus. Olevsk. Zhytomyrs'ka Oblast', N Ukraine
Olevsk see Olevs'k
Ölgiy 126 C2 Bayan-Ölgiy, W Mongolia
Olhão 92 B5 Faro, S Portugal
Olifa 78 B3 Kunene, NW Namibia
Ólimbos see Ólympos
Olimpo see Fuerte Olimpo
Olisipo see Lisboa
Olita see Alytus
Oliva 93 F4 Valenciana, E Spain
Olivet 90 C4 Loiret, C France

Olmaliq 123 E2 Rus. Almalyk. Toshkent Viloyati, E Uzbekistan
Olmütz see Olomouc
Olomouc 99 C5 Ger. Olmütz, Pol. Ołomuniec. Olomoucký Kraj, E Czech Republic (Czechia)
Ołomuniec see Olomouc
Olonets 110 B3 Respublika Kareliya, NW Russia
Olovyannaya 115 F4 Zabaykal'skiy Kray, S Russia
Olpe 94 B4 Nordrhein-Westfalen, W Germany
Olshanka see Vil'shanka
Olsnitz see Murska Sobota
Olsztyn 98 D2 Ger. Allenstein. Warmińsko-Mazurskie, N Poland
Olt 108 B5 var. Oltul, Ger. Alt. river S Romania
Olteniţa 108 C5 prev. Eng. Oltenitsa; anc. Constantiola. Călăraşi, SE Romania
Oltenitsa see Olteniţa
Oltul see Olt
Olvera 92 D5 Andalucía, S Spain
Ol'viopol' see Pervomays'k
Olympia 46 B2 state capital Washington, NW USA
Olympic Mountains 46 A2 mountain range Washington, NW USA
Olympus, Mount 104 B4 var. Ólimbos, Eng. Mount Olympus. mountain N Greece
Omagh 89 B5 Ir. An Ómaigh. W Northern Ireland, United Kingdom
Omaha 45 F4 Nebraska, C USA
Oman 121 D6 off. Sultanate of Oman, Ar. Salṭanat 'Umān; prev. Muscat and Oman. country SW Asia
Oman, Gulf of 120 E4 Ar. Khalīj 'Umān. gulf N Arabian Sea
Oman, Sultanate of see Oman
Omboué 77 A6 Ogooué-Maritime, W Gabon
Omdurman 72 B4 var. Umm Durmān. Khartoum, C Sudan
Ometepe, Isla de 52 D4 island S Nicaragua
Ommen 86 E3 Overijssel, E Netherlands
Omsk 114 C4 Omskaya Oblast', C Russia
Ōmuta 131 A7 Fukuoka, Kyūshū, SW Japan
Onda 93 F3 Valenciana, E Spain
Ondjiva see N'Giva
Öndörhaan 127 E2 var. Undur Khan; prev. Tsetsen Khan. Hentiy, E Mongolia
Onega 110 C3 Arkhangel'skaya Oblast', NW Russia
Onega, Lake 110 B4 Eng. Lake Onega. lake NW Russia
Onega, Lake see Onezhskoye Ozero
Onex 95 A7 Genève, SW Switzerland
Ongole 132 D1 Andhra Pradesh, E India
Onitsha 75 G5 Anambra, S Nigeria
Onon Gol 127 E2 river N Mongolia
Onslow 146 A4 Western Australia
Onslow Bay 43 F1 bay North Carolina, E USA
Ontario 38 B3 province S Canada
Ontario, Lake 41 E3 lake Canada/USA
Onteniente see Ontinyent
Ontinyent 93 F4 var. Onteniente. Valenciana, E Spain
Ontong Java Rise 125 H4 undersea feature W Pacific Ocean
Onuba see Huelva
Oodeypore see Udaipur
Oos-Londen see East London
Oostakker 87 B5 Oost-Vlaanderen, NW Belgium
Oostburg 87 B5 Zeeland, SW Netherlands
Oostende 87 A5 Eng. Ostend, Fr. Ostende. West-Vlaanderen, NW Belgium
Oosterbeek 86 D4 Gelderland, SE Netherlands
Oosterhout 86 C4 Noord-Brabant, S Netherlands
Opatija 100 A2 It. Abbazia. Primorje-Gorski Kotar, NW Croatia
Opava 99 C5 Ger. Troppau. Moravskoslezský Kraj, E Czech Republic (Czechia)
Ópazova see Stara Pazova
Opelika 42 D2 Alabama, S USA
Opelousas 42 B3 Louisiana, S USA
Ophiusa see Formentera
Opmeer 86 C2 Noord-Holland, NW Netherlands

Opochka 110 A4 Pskovskaya Oblast', W Russia
Opole 98 C4 Ger. Oppeln. Opolskie, S Poland
Oporto see Porto
Opotiki 150 E3 Bay of Plenty, North Island, New Zealand
Oppeln see Opole
Oppidum Ubiorum see Köln
Oqtosh 123 E2 Rus. Aktash. Samarqand Viloyati, C Uzbekistan
Oradea 108 B3 prev. Oradea Mare, Ger. Grosswardein, Hung. Nagyvárad. Bihor, NW Romania
Oradea Mare see Oradea
Orahovac see Rahovec
Oral see Ural'sk
Oran 70 D2 var. Ouahran, Wahran. NW Algeria
Orange 149 D6 New South Wales, SE Australia
Orange 91 D6 anc. Arausio. Vaucluse, SE France
Orangeburg 43 E2 South Carolina, SE USA
Orange Cone see Orange Fan
Orange Fan 69 C7 var. Orange Cone. undersea feature SW Indian Ocean
Orange Mouth/Orangemund see Oranjemund
Orange River 78 B4 Afr. Oranjerivier. river S Africa
Orange Walk 52 C1 Orange Walk, N Belize
Oranienburg 94 D3 Brandenburg, NE Germany
Oranjemund 78 B4 var. Orangemund; prev. Orange Mouth. Karas, SW Namibia
Oranjerivier see Orange River
Oranjestad 55 E5 dependent territory capital (Aruba) Lesser Antilles, S Caribbean Sea
Orany see Varéna
Oraşul Stalin see Braşov
Oravicabánya see Oraviţa
Oraviţa 108 A4 Ger. Orawitza, Hung. Oravicabánya. Caraş-Severin, SW Romania
Orawitza see Oraviţa
Orbetello 96 B4 Toscana, C Italy
Orcadas 154 A1 Argentinian research station South Orkney Islands, Antarctica
Orchard Homes 44 B1 Montana, NW USA
Ordino 91 A8 Ordino, NW Andorra Europe
Ordos Desert see Mu Us Shadi
Ordu 116 D2 anc. Cotyora. Ordu, N Turkey
Ordzhonikidze see Pokrov, Ukraine
Ordzhonikidze see Vladikavkaz, Russia
Ordzhonikidze see Yenakiyeve, Ukraine
Orealla 59 G3 E Guyana
Oregon 46 B3 off. State of Oregon, also known as Beaver State, Sunset State, Valentine State, Webfoot State. state NW USA
Oregon City 46 B3 Oregon, NW USA
Oregon, State of see Oregon
Orekhov see Orikhiv
Orël 111 B5 Orlovskaya Oblast', W Russia
Orem 44 B4 Utah, W USA
Ore Mountains see Erzgebirge
Orenburg 111 D6 prev. Chkalov. Orenburgskaya Oblast', W Russia
Orense see Ourense
Orestiáda 104 D3 prev. Orestiás. Anatolikí Makedonía kai Thráki, NE Greece
Orestiás see Orestiáda
Organ Peak 48 D3 mountain New Mexico, SW USA
Orgeyev see Orhei
Orhei 108 D3 var. Orheiu, Rus. Orgeyev. N Moldova
Orheiu see Orhei
Oriental, Cordillera 60 D3 mountain range Bolivia/Peru
Oriental, Cordillera 58 B3 mountain range C Colombia
Orihuela 93 F4 Valenciana, E Spain
Orikhiv 109 G3 Rus. Orekhov. Zaporiz'ka Oblast', SE Ukraine
Orinoco, Río 59 E2 river Colombia/Venezuela
Orinoquía 58 C3 region NE Colombia

Orissa see Odisha
Orissaar see Orissaare
Orissaare 106 C2 Ger. Orissaar. Saaremaa, W Estonia
Oristano 97 A5 Sardegna, Italy, C Mediterranean Sea
Orito 58 A4 Putumayo, SW Colombia
Orizaba, Volcán Pico de 35 C7 var. Citlaltépetl. mountain S Mexico
Orkney see Orkney Islands
Orkney Islands 88 C2 var. Orkney, Orkneys. island group N Scotland, United Kingdom
Orkneys see Orkney Islands
Orlando 43 E4 Florida, SE USA
Orléanais 90 C4 cultural region C France
Orléans 90 C4 anc. Aurelianum. Loiret, C France
Orléansville see Chlef
Orly 90 E2 (Paris) Essonne, N France
Orlya 107 B6 Hrodzyenskaya Voblasts', W Belarus
Ormsö see Vormsi
Ormuz, Strait of see Hormuz, Strait of
Örnsköldsvik 85 C5 Västernorrland, C Sweden
Orolaunum see Arlon
Orol Dengizi see Aral Sea
Oromocto 39 F4 New Brunswick, SE Canada
Orona 145 F3 prev. Hull Island. atoll Phoenix Islands, C Kiribati
Oropeza see Cochabamba
Orosirá Rodhópis see Rhodope Mountains
Orpington 89 B8 United Kingdom
Orschowa see Orşova
Orsha 107 E6 Vitsyebskaya Voblasts', NE Belarus
Orsk 114 B4 Orenburgskaya Oblast', W Russia
Orşova 108 A4 Ger. Orschowa, Hung. Orsova. Mehedinţi, SW Romania
Ortelsburg see Szczytno
Orthez 91 B6 Pyrénées-Atlantiques, SW France
Ortona 96 D4 Abruzzo, C Italy
Oruba see Aruba
Oruro 61 F4 Oruro, W Bolivia
Oryokko see Yalu
Oss 86 D4 Noord-Brabant, S Netherlands
Ōsaka 131 C6 hist. Naniwa. Ōsaka, Honshū, SW Japan
Ōsaki see Furukawa
Osa, Península de 53 E5 peninsula S Costa Rica
Osborn Plateau 141 D5 undersea feature E Indian Ocean
Osca see Huesca
Ösel see Saaremaa
Osh 123 F2 Oshkskaya Oblast', SW Kyrgyzstan
Oshawa 38 D5 Ontario, SE Canada
Oshikango 78 B3 Ohangwena, N Namibia
O-shima 131 D6 island S Japan
Oshkosh 40 B2 Wisconsin, N USA
Oshmyany see Ashmyany
Osijek 100 C3 prev. Osiek, Osijek, Ger. Esseg, Hung. Eszék. Osijek-Baranja, E Croatia
Osijek see Osijek
Osipenko see Berdyans'k
Osipovichi see Asipovichy
Osjek see Osijek
Oskaloosa 45 G4 Iowa, C USA
Oskarshamn 85 C7 Kalmar, S Sweden
Öskemen see Ust'-Kamenogorsk
Oskil see Oskol
Oskol 109 G2 Rus. Oskil. river Russia/Ukraine
Oslo 85 B6 prev. Christiania, Kristiania. country capital (Norway) Oslo, S Norway
Osmaniye 116 D4 Osmaniye, S Turkey
Osnabrück 94 A3 Niedersachsen, NW Germany
Osogov Mountains 104 B3 var. Osogovske Planine, Osogovski Planina, Mac. Osogovski Planini. mountain range Bulgaria/Macedonia
Osogovske Planine/Osogovski Planina/Osogovski Planini see Osogov Mountains
Osorhei see Târgu Mureş
Osorno 65 B5 Los Lagos, C Chile
Ossa, Serra d' 92 C4 mountain range SE Portugal

Ossora 115 H2 Krasnoyarskiy Kray,
E Russia
Ostee see Baltic Sea
Ostend/Ostende see Oostende
Oster 109 E1 Chernihivs'ka Oblast',
N Ukraine
Östermyra see Seinäjoki
Osterode/Osterode in Ostpreussen see
Ostróda
Österreich see Austria
Östersund 85 C5 Jämtland, C Sweden
Ostfriesische Inseln 94 A3 Eng. East
Frisian Islands. island group
NW Germany
Ostia Aterni see Pescara
Ostiglia 96 C2 Lombardia, N Italy
Ostrava 99 C5 Moravskoslezský Kraj,
E Czech Republic (Czechia)
Ostróda 98 D3 Ger. Osterode, Osterode
in Ostpreussen. Warmińsko-
Mazurskie, NE Poland
Ostrołęka 98 D3 Ger. Wiesenhof, Rus.
Ostrolenka.
Ostrolenka see Ostrołęka
Ostrov 110 A4 Latv. Austrava.
Pskovskaya Oblast', W Russia
Ostrovets see Ostrowiec Świętokrzyski
Ostrovnoy 110 C2 Murmanskaya
Oblast', NW Russia
Ostrów see Ostrów Wielkopolski
Ostrowiec see Ostrowiec Świętokrzyski
Ostrowiec Świętokrzyski 98 D4 var.
Ostrowiec, Rus. Ostrovets.
Świętokrzyskie, C Poland
Ostrów Mazowiecka 98 D3 var. Ostrów
Mazowiecki. Mazowieckie, NE Poland
Ostrów Mazowiecki see Ostrów
Mazowiecka
Ostrowo see Ostrów Wielkopolski
Ostrów Wielkopolski 98 C4 var.
Ostrów, Ger. Ostrowo. Wielkopolskie,
C Poland
Ostyako-Voguls'k see Khanty-Mansiysk
Osum see Osumit, Lumi i
Osumi-shoto 131 A8 island group
Kagoshima, Nansei-shotō, SW Japan
Asia East China Sea Pacific Ocean
Osumit, Lumi i 101 D7 var. Osum.
river SE Albania
Osuna 92 D4 Andalucía, S Spain
Oswego 41 F2 New York,
NE USA
Otago Peninsula 151 B7 peninsula
South Island, New Zealand
Otaki 150 D4 Wellington, North Island,
New Zealand
Otaru 130 C2 Hokkaidō, NE Japan
Otavalo 60 B1 Imbabura, N Ecuador
Otavi 78 B3 Otjozondjupa, N Namibia
Oţelu Roşu 108 B4 Ger. Ferdinandsberg,
Hung. Nándorhgy. Caras-Severin,
SW Romania
Otepää 106 D3 Ger. Odenpäh.
Valgamaa, SE Estonia
Oti 75 E4 river N Togo
Otira 151 C6 West Coast, South Island,
New Zealand
Otjiwarongo 78 B3 Otjozondjupa,
N Namibia
Otorohanga 150 D3 Waikato, North
Island, New Zealand
Otranto, Canale d' see Otranto, Strait of
Otranto, Strait of 101 C6 It. Canale
d'Otranto. strait Albania/Italy
Otrokovice 99 C5 Ger. Otrokowitz.
Zlínský Kraj, E Czech Republic (Czechia)
Otrokowitz see Otrokovice
Ōtsu 131 C6 var. Ōtu. Shiga, Honshū,
SW Japan
Ottawa 38 D5 country capital (Canada)
Ontario, SE Canada
Ottawa 40 B3 Illinois, N USA
Ottawa 45 F5 Kansas, C USA
Ottawa 41 E2 Fr. Outaouais. river
Ontario/Québec, SE Canada
Ottawa Islands 38 C1 island group
Nunavut, C Canada
Ottignies 87 C6 Wallon Brabant,
C Belgium
Ottumwa 45 G4 Iowa, C USA
Ōtu see Ōtsu
Ouachita Mountains 42 A1 mountain
range Arkansas/Oklahoma,
C USA
Ouachita River 42 B2 river Arkansas/
Louisiana, C USA
Ouagadougou 75 E4 var. Wagadugu.
country capital (Burkina Faso)
C Burkina Faso
Ouahigouya 75 E3 NW Burkina Faso
Ouahran see Oran

Oualâta 74 D3 var. Oualata. Hodh ech
Chargui, SE Mauritania
Ouanary 59 H3 E French Guiana
Ouanda Djallé 76 D4 Vakaga,
NE Central African Republic
Ouaráne 74 D2 desert C Mauritania
Ouargla 71 E2 var. Wargla. NE Algeria
Ouarzazate 70 C3 S Morocco
Oubangui 77 C5 Fr. Oubangui. river
C Africa
Oubangui see Ubangi
Oubangui-Chari see Central African
Republic
Oubangui-Chari, Territoire de l' see
Central African Republic
Oudjda see Oujda
Ouessant, Île d' 90 A3 Eng. Ushant.
island NW France
Ouésso 77 B5 Sangha, NW Congo
Oujda 70 D2 Ar. Oudjda, Ujda.
NE Morocco
Oujeft 74 C2 Adrar, C Mauritania
Oulu 84 D4 Swe. Uleåborg.
Pohjois-Pohjanmaa, Finland
Oulujärvi 84 D4 Swe. Uleträsk. lake
C Finland
Oulujoki 84 D4 Swe. Uleälv. river
C Finland
Ounasjoki 84 D3 river N Finland
Ounianga Kébir 76 C2 Borkou-Ennedi-
Tibesti, N Chad
Oup see Auob
Oupeye 87 D6 Liège, E Belgium
Our 87 D6 river NW Europe
Ourense 92 C1 Cast. Orense, Lat.
Aurium. Galicia, NW Spain
Ourique 92 B4 Beja, S Portugal
Ours, Grand Lac de l' see Great Bear Lake
Ourthe 87 D7 river E Belgium
Ouse 89 D5 river N England,
United Kingdom
Outaouais see Ottawa
Outer Hebrides 88 B3 var. Western
Isles. island group NW Scotland,
United Kingdom
Outer Islands 79 G1 island group
SW Seychelles Africa W Indian Ocean
Ouvéa 144 D5 island Îles Loyauté,
NE New Caledonia
Ouyen 149 C6 Victoria, SE Australia
Ovalle 64 B3 Coquimbo, N Chile
Ovar 92 B2 Aveiro, N Portugal
Overflakkee 86 B4 island
SW Netherlands
Overijse 87 C6 Vlaams Brabant,
C Belgium
Oviedo 92 C1 anc. Asturias. Asturias,
NW Spain
Ovruch 108 D1 Zhytomyrs'ka Oblast',
N Ukraine
Owando 77 B5 prev. Fort Rousset.
Cuvette, C Congo
Owase 131 C6 Mie, Honshū, SW Japan
Owatonna 45 F3 Minnesota, N USA
Owen Fracture Zone 140 B4 tectonic
feature W Arabian Sea
Owen, Mount 151 C5 mountain South
Island, New Zealand
Owensboro 40 B5 Kentucky, S USA
Owen Stanley Range 144 B3 mountain
range S Papua New Guinea
Owerri 75 G5 Imo, S Nigeria
Owo 75 F5 Ondo, SW Nigeria
Owyhee River 46 C4 river Idaho/Oregon,
NW USA
Oxford 151 C6 Canterbury, South Island,
New Zealand
Oxford 89 D6 Lat. Oxonia. S England,
United Kingdom
Oxkutzcab 51 H4 Yucatán, SE Mexico
Oxnard 47 B7 California, W USA
Oxonia see Oxford
Oxus see Amu Darya
Oyama 131 D5 Tochigi, Honshū,
SW Japan
Oyem 77 B5 Woleu-Ntem, N Gabon
Oyo 77 B6 Cuvette, C Congo
Oyo 75 F4 Oyo, W Nigeria
Ozark 42 D3 Alabama,
S USA
Ozark Plateau 45 G5 plain Arkansas/
Missouri, C USA
Ozarks, Lake of the 45 F5 reservoir
Missouri, C USA
Ozbourn Seamount 152 D4 undersea
feature W Pacific Ocean
Ózd 99 D6 Borsod-Abaúj-Zemplén,
NE Hungary
Ozieri 97 A5 Sardegna, Italy,
C Mediterranean Sea

P

Paamiut 82 B4 var. Pámiut, Dan.
Frederikshåb. S Greenland
Pa-an see Hpa-an
Pabianice 98 C4 Łódzski, Poland
Pabna 135 G4 Rajshahi, W Bangladesh
Pacaraima, Sierra/Pacaraim, Serra see
Pakaraima Mountains
Pachuca 51 E4 var. Pachuca de Soto.
Hidalgo, C Mexico
Pachuca de Soto see Pachuca
Pacific-Antarctic Ridge 154 B5
undersea feature S Pacific Ocean
Pacific Ocean 152 D3 ocean
Padalung see Phatthalung
Padang 138 B4 Sumatera, W Indonesia
Paderborn 94 B4 Nordrhein-Westfalen,
NW Germany
Padma see Brahmaputra
Padma see Ganges
Padova 96 C2 Eng. Padua; anc. Patavium.
Veneto, NE Italy
Padre Island 49 G5 island Texas,
SW USA
Padua see Padova
Paducah 40 B5 Kentucky, S USA
Paeroa 150 D3 Waikato, North Island,
New Zealand
Páfos 102 C5 var. Paphos. W Cyprus
Pag 100 A3 It. Pago. island Zadar,
C Croatia
Page 48 B1 Arizona, SW USA
Pago see Pag
Pago Pago 145 F4 dependent territory
capital (American Samoa) Tutuila,
W American Samoa
Pahiatua 150 D4 Manawatu-Wanganui,
North Island, New Zealand
Pahsien see Chongqing
Paide 106 D2 Ger. Weissenstein.
Järvamaa, N Estonia
Paihia 150 D2 Northland, North Island,
New Zealand
Päijänne 85 D5 lake S Finland
Paine, Cerro 65 A7 mountain S Chile
Painted Desert 48 B1 desert Arizona,
SW USA
Paisance see Piacenza
Paisley 88 C4 W Scotland, United
Kingdom
País Vasco 93 E1 cultural region N Spain
País Valenciano 93 F3 cultural region
E Spain
Paita 60 B3 Piura, NW Peru
Pakanbaru see Pekanbaru
Pakaraima Mountains 59 E3 var. Serra
Pacaraim, Sierra Pacaraima.
mountain range N South America
Pakistan 134 A2 Islamic Republic of
Pakistan, var. Islami Jamhuriya e
Pakistan. country S Asia
Pakistan, Islamic Republic of see
Pakistan
Pakistan, Islami Jamhuriya e see
Pakistan
Paknam see Samut Prakan
Pakokku 136 A3 Magway, C Myanmar
(Burma)
Pak Phanang 137 C7 var. Ban Pak
Phanang. Nakhon Si Thammarat,
SW Thailand
Pakruojis 106 C4 Šiauliai, N Lithuania
Paks 99 C7 Tolna, S Hungary
Paksé see Pakxé
Pakxé 137 D5 var. Paksé. Champasak,
S Laos
Palafrugell 93 G2 Cataluña,
NE Spain
Palagruža 101 B5 It. Pelagosa. island
SW Croatia
Palaiá Epídavros 105 C6 Pelopónnisos,
S Greece
Palaiseau 90 D2 Essonne, N France
Palamós 93 G2 Cataluña, NE Spain
Palamuse 106 D2 Ger. Sankt-
Bartholomäi. Jõgevamaa, E Estonia
Palanka see Bačka Palanka
Pālanpur 134 C4 Gujarāt, W India
Palantia see Palencia
Palapye 78 D3 Central, SE Botswana
Palau 147 A2 var. Belau. country
W Pacific Ocean
Palawan 139 E2 island W Philippines
Palawan Passage 138 D2 passage
W Philippines
Paldiski 106 D2 prev. Baltiski, Eng. Baltic
Port, Ger. Baltischport. Harjumaa,
NW Estonia

Palembang 138 B4 Sumatera,
W Indonesia
Palencia 92 D2 anc. Palantia, Pallantia.
Castilla y León, NW Spain
Palerme see Palermo
Palestine, State of see West Bank;
Gaza Strip
Palermo 97 C7 Fr. Palerme; anc.
Panhormus, Panormus. Sicilia, Italy,
C Mediterranean Sea
Pāli 134 C3 Rājasthān, N India
Palikir 144 C2 country capital
(Micronesia) Pohnpei, E Micronesia
Palimé see Kpalimé
Palioúri, Akrotírio 104 C4 var.
Akrotírio Kanestron. headland
N Greece
Palk Strait 132 C3 strait India/Sri Lanka
Pallantia see Palencia
Palliser, Cape 151 D5 headland North
Island, New Zealand
Palma 93 G3 var. Palma de Mallorca.
Mallorca, Spain, W Mediterranean Sea
Palma del Río 92 D4 Andalucía,
S Spain
Palma de Mallorca see Palma
Palmar Sur 53 E5 Puntarenas,
SE Costa Rica
Palma Soriano 54 C3 Santiago de Cuba,
E Cuba
Palm Beach 148 E1 New South Wales,
E Australia
Palmer 154 A2 US research station
Antarctica
Palmer Land 154 A3 physical region
Antarctica
Palmerston 145 F4 island S Cook Islands
Palmerston see Darwin
Palmerston North 150 D4
Manawatu-Wanganui, North Island,
New Zealand
The Palmetto State see South Carolina
Palmi 97 D7 Calabria, SW Italy
Palmira 58 B3 Valle del Cauca,
W Colombia
Palm Springs 47 D7 California,
W USA
Palmyra see Tudmur
Palmyra Atoll 145 G2 US privately
owned unincorporated territory
C Pacific Ocean
Palo Alto 47 B6 California, W USA
Paloe see Denpasar, Bali, C Indonesia
Paloe see Palu
Palu 139 E4 prev. Paloe. Sulawesi,
C Indonesia
Pamiers 91 B6 Ariège, S France
Pamir 123 F3 var. Daryā-ye Pāmīr, Taj.
Dar"yoi Pomir. river Afghanistan/
Tajikistan
Pāmir, Daryā-ye see Pamir
Pamirs 123 F3 Pash. Daryā-ye Pāmīr,
Rus. Pamir. mountain range C Asia
Pāmiut see Paamiut
Pamlico Sound 43 G1 sound North
Carolina, SE USA
Pampa 49 F1 Texas, SW USA
Pampa Aullagas, Lago see Poopó, Lago
Pampas 64 C4 plain C Argentina
Pampeluna see Pamplona
Pamplona 58 C2 Norte de Santander,
N Colombia
Pamplona 93 E1 Basq. Iruña, prev.
Pampeluna; anc. Pompaelo. Navarra,
N Spain
Panaji 132 B1 var. Pangim, Panjim, New
Goa. state capital Goa, W India
Panamá 53 G4 var. Ciudad de Panama,
Eng. Panama City. country capital
(Panama) Panamá, C Panama
Panama 53 G5 off. Republic of Panama.
country Central America
Panama Basin 35 C8 undersea feature
E Pacific Ocean
Panama Canal 53 F4 canal E Panama
Panama City 42 D3 Florida, SE USA
Panama City see Panamá
Gulf of Panama 53 G5 var. Gulf of
Panama. gulf S Panama
Panama, Gulf of see Panamá, Golfo de
Isthmus of Panama 53 G4 Eng. Isthmus
of Panama; prev. Isthmus of Darien.
isthmus E Panama
Panama, Isthmus of see Panama, Istmo de
Panamá, Istmo de see Panama, Isthmus of
Panay Island 139 E2 island C Philippines
Pančevo 100 D3 Ger. Pantschowa, Hung.
Pancsova. Vojvodina, N Serbia
Pancsova see Pančevo
Paneas see Bāniyās

Panevėžys 106 C4 Panevėžys, C Lithuania
Pangim see Panaji
Pangkalpinang 138 C4 Pulau Bangka, W Indonesia
Pang-Nga see Phang-Nga
Panhormus see Palermo
Panjim see Panaji
Panopolis see Akhmim
Pánormos 105 C7 Kríti, Greece, E Mediterranean Sea
Panormus see Palermo
Pantanal 63 E3 var. Pantanalmato-Grossense. swamp SW Brazil
Pantelleria, Isola di 97 B7 island SW Italy
Pantschowa see Pančevo
Pánuco 51 E3 Veracruz-Llave, E Mexico
Pao-chi/Paoki see Baoji
Paola 102 B5 E Malta
Pao-shan see Baoshan
Pao-t'ou/Paotow see Baotou
Papagayo, Golfo de 52 C4 gulf NW Costa Rica
Papakura 150 D3 Auckland, North Island, New Zealand
Papantla 51 F4 var. Papantla de Olarte. Veracruz-Llave, E Mexico
Papantla de Olarte see Papantla
Papeete 145 H4 dependent territory capital (French Polynesia) Tahiti, W French Polynesia
Paphos see Páfos
Papile 106 B3 Šiauliai, NW Lithuania
Papillion 45 F4 Nebraska, C USA
Papua 139 H4 var. Irian Barat, West Irian, West New Guinea, West Papua; prev. Dutch New Guinea, Irian Jaya, Netherlands New Guinea. province E Indonesia
Papua and New Guinea, Territory of see Papua New Guinea
Papua, Gulf of 144 B3 gulf S Papua New Guinea
Papua New Guinea 144 B3 off. Independent State of Papua New Guinea; prev. Territory of Papua and New Guinea. country NW Melanesia
Papua New Guinea, Independent State of see Papua New Guinea
Papuk 100 C2 mountain range NE Croatia
Pará 63 E2 off. Estado do Pará. state/region NE Brazil
Pará see Belém
Paracel Islands 125 E3 disputed territory SE Asia
Paraćin 100 D4 Serbia, C Serbia
Paradise of the Pacific see Hawaii
Pará, Estado do see Pará
Paragua, Río 59 E3 river SE Venezuela
Paraguay 64 C2 country C South America
Paraguay 64 D2 var. Río Paraguay. river C South America
Paraguay, Río see Paraguay
Parahiba/Parahyba see Paraíba
Paraíba 63 G2 off. Estado da Paraíba; prev. Parahiba, Parahyba. state/region E Brazil
Paraíba see João Pessoa
Paraíba, Estado da see Paraíba
Parakou 75 F4 C Benin
Paramaribo 59 G3 country capital (Suriname) Paramaribo, N Suriname
Paramushir, Ostrov 115 H3 island SE Russia
Paraná 63 E4 Entre Ríos, E Argentina
Paraná 63 E5 off. Estado do Paraná. state/region S Brazil
Paraná 57 C5 var. Alto Paraná. river C South America
Paraná, Estado do see Paraná
Paranésti 104 C3 var. Paranéstio. Anatolikí Makedonía kai Thráki, NE Greece
Paranéstio see Paranésti
Paraparaumu 151 D5 Wellington, North Island, New Zealand
Parchim 94 C3 Mecklenburg-Vorpommern, N Germany
Parczew 98 E4 Lubelskie, E Poland
Pardubice 99 B5 Ger. Pardubitz. Pardubický Kraj, C Czech Rep. (Czechia)
Pardubitz see Pardubice
Parechcha 107 B5 Pol. Porzecze, Rus. Porech'ye. Hrodzyenskaya Voblasts', W Belarus
Parecis, Chapada dos 62 D3 var. Serra dos Parecis. mountain range W Brazil

Parecis, Serra dos see Parecis, Chapada dos
Parenzo see Poreč
Parepare 139 E4 Sulawesi, C Indonesia
Párga 105 A5 Ípeiros, W Greece
Paria, Golfo de see Paria, Gulf of
Paria, Gulf of 59 E1 var. Golfo de Paria. gulf Trinidad and Tobago/Venezuela
Paříka 59 F2 NE Guyana
Parikiá 105 D6 Kykládes, Greece, Aegean Sea
Paris 90 D1 anc. Lutetia, Lutetia Parisiorum, Parisii. country capital (France) Paris, N France
Paris 49 G2 Texas, SW USA
Parisii see Paris
Parkersburg 40 D4 West Virginia, NE USA
Parkes 149 D6 New South Wales, SE Australia
Parkhar see Farkhor
Parma 96 B2 Emilia-Romagna, N Italy
Parnahyba see Parnaíba
Parnaíba 63 F2 var. Parnahyba. Piauí, E Brazil
Pärnu 106 D2 Ger. Pernau, Latv. Pērnava; prev. Rus. Pernov. Pärnumaa, SW Estonia
Pärnu 106 D2 var. Parnu Jõgi, Ger. Pernau. river SW Estonia
Pärnu-Jaagupi 106 D2 Ger. Sankt-Jakobi. Pärnumaa, SW Estonia
Parnu Jõgi see Pärnu
Pärnu Laht 106 D2 Ger. Pernauer Bucht. bay SW Estonia
Paroikiá see Páros
Paropamisus Range see Sefīd Kūh, Selseleh-ye
Páros 105 D6 var. Paroikiá, Greece
Páros 105 C6 island Kykládes, Greece, Aegean Sea
Parral 64 B4 Maule, C Chile
Parral see Hidalgo del Parral
Parramatta 148 D1 New South Wales, SE Australia
Parras 50 D3 var. Parras de la Fuente. Coahuila, NE Mexico
Parras de la Fuente see Parras
Parsons 45 F5 Kansas, C USA
Pasadena 47 C7 California, W USA
Pasadena 49 H4 Texas, SW USA
Pașcani 108 C3 Hung. Páskán. Iași, NE Romania
Pasco 46 C2 Washington, NW USA
Pasewalk 94 D3 Mecklenburg-Vorpommern, NE Germany
Pashkeni see Bolyarovo
Pasinler 117 F3 Erzurum, NE Turkey
Páskán see Pașcani
Pasłęk 98 D2 Ger. Preußisch Holland. Warmińsko-Mazurskie, NE Poland
Pasni 134 A3 Baluchistan, SW Pakistan
Paso de Indios 65 B6 Chubut, S Argentina
Passarowitz see Požarevac
Passau 95 D6 Bayern, SE Germany
Passo Fundo 63 E5 Rio Grande do Sul, S Brazil
Pastavy 107 C5 Pol. Postawy, Rus. Postovy. Vitsyebskaya Voblasts', NW Belarus
Pastaza, Río 60 B2 river Ecuador/Peru
Pasto 58 A4 Nariño, SW Colombia
Pasvalys 106 C4 Panevėžys, N Lithuania
Patagonia 57 B7 physical region Argentina/Chile
Patalung see Phatthalung
Patani see Pattani
Patavium see Padova
Patea 150 D4 Taranaki, North Island, New Zealand
Paterson 41 F3 New Jersey, NE USA
Pathein 136 A4 var. Bassein. Ayeyarwady, SW Myanmar (Burma)
Pátmos 105 D6 island Dodekánisa, Greece, Aegean Sea
Patna 135 F3 var. Azimabad. state capital Bihār, N India
Patnos 117 F3 Ağrı, E Turkey
Patos, Lagoa dos 63 E5 lagoon S Brazil
Pátra 105 B5 Eng. Patras; prev. Pátrai. Dytikí Elláda, S Greece
Pátrai/Patras see Pátra
Pattani 137 C7 var. Patani. Pattani, SW Thailand
Pattaya 137 C5 Chon Buri, S Thailand
Patuca, Río 52 D2 river E Honduras
Pau 91 B7 Pyrénées-Atlantiques, SW France
Paulatuk 37 E3 Northwest Territories, NW Canada

Paungde 136 B4 Bago, C Myanmar (Burma)
Pautalia see Kyustendil
Pavia 96 B2 anc. Ticinum. Lombardia, N Italy
Pāvilosta 106 B3 W Latvia
Pavlikeni 104 D2 Veliko Tŭrnovo, N Bulgaria
Pavlodar 114 C4 Pavlodar, NE Kazakhstan
Pavlograd see Pavlohrad
Pavlohrad 109 G3 Rus. Pavlograd. Dnipropetrovs'ka Oblast', E Ukraine
Pawai, Pulau 138 A2 island SW Singapore Asia
Pawn, Nam 136 B3 river C Myanmar (Burma)
Pax Augusta see Badajoz
Pax Julia see Beja
Paxoí 105 A5 island Iónia Nisiá, Greece, C Mediterranean Sea
Payo Obispo see Chetumal
Paysandú 64 D4 Paysandú, W Uruguay
Pazar 117 E2 Rize, NE Turkey
Pazardzhik 104 C3 prev. Tatar Pazardzhik. Pazardzhik, SW Bulgaria
Peace Garden State see North Dakota
Peach State see Georgia
Pearl Islands 53 G5 Eng. Pearl Islands. island group SE Panama
Pearl Islands see Perlas, Archipiélago de las
Pearl Lagoon 53 E3 Eng. Pearl Lagoon. lagoon E Nicaragua
Pearl Lagoon see Perlas, Laguna de
Pearl River 42 B3 river Louisiana/Mississippi, S USA
Pearsall 49 F4 Texas, SW USA
Peawanuk 38 C2 Ontario, S Canada
Peć see Pejë
Pechora 110 D3 Respublika Komi, NW Russia
Pechora 110 D3 river NW Russia
Pechora Sea 110 D2 Eng. Pechora Sea. sea NW Russia
Pechora Sea see Pechorskoye More
Pecos 49 E3 Texas, SW USA
Pecos River 49 E3 river New Mexico/Texas, SW USA
Pécs 99 C7 Ger. Fünfkirchen, Lat. Sopianae. Baranya, SW Hungary
Pedra Lume 74 A3 Sal, NE Cape Verde
Pedro Cays 54 C3 island group Greater Antilles, S Jamaica North America
Pedro Juan Caballero 64 D2 Amambay, E Paraguay
Peer 87 D5 Limburg, NE Belgium
Pegasus Bay 151 C6 bay South Island, New Zealand
Pegu see Bago
Pehuajó 64 C4 Buenos Aires, E Argentina
Pei-ching see Beijing/Beijing Shi
Peine 94 B3 Niedersachsen, C Germany
Pei-p'ing see Beijing/Beijing Shi
Peipsi Järv/Peipus-See see Peipus, Lake
Peipus, Lake 106 E3 Est. Peipsi Järv, Ger. Peipus-See, Rus. Chudskoye Ozero. lake Estonia/Russia
Peiraiás 105 C6 prev. Piraiévs, Eng. Piraeus. Attikí, C Greece
Pejë 101 D5 Serb. Peć. W Kosovo
Pëk see Phônsavan
Pekalongan 138 C5 Jawa, C Indonesia
Pekanbaru 138 B3 var. Pakanbaru. Sumatera, W Indonesia
Pekin 40 B4 Illinois, N USA
Peking see Beijing/Beijing Shi
Pelagie 97 B8 island group SW Italy
Pelagosa see Palagruža
Pelican State see Louisiana
Pelly Bay see Kugaaruk
Pélmonostor see Beli Manastir
Peloponnese 105 B6 var. Morea, Eng. Peloponnese; anc. Peloponnesus. peninsula S Greece
Peloponnese/Peloponnesus see Pelopónnisos
Pematangsiantar 138 B3 Sumatera, W Indonesia
Pemba 79 E2 prev. Port Amelia, Porto Amélia. Cabo Delgado, NE Mozambique
Pemba 73 D7 island E Tanzania
Pembroke 38 D4 Ontario, SE Canada
Penang see Pinang, Pulau, Peninsular Malaysia
Penang see George Town
Penas, Golfo de 65 A7 gulf S Chile
Penderma see Bandırma

Pendleton 46 C3 Oregon, NW USA
Pend Oreille, Lake 46 D2 lake Idaho, NW USA
Peneius see Pineiós
Peng-pu see Bengbu
Penibético, Sistema see Béticos, Sistemas
Peniche 92 B3 Leiria, W Portugal
Peninsular State see Florida
Penninae, Alpes/Pennine, Alpi see Pennine Alps
Pennine Alps 95 A8 Fr. Alpes Pennines, It. Alpi Pennine, Lat. Alpes Penninae. mountain range Italy/Switzerland
Pennine Chain see Pennines
Pennines 89 D5 var. Pennine Chain. mountain range N England, United Kingdom
Pennines, Alpes see Pennine Alps
Pennsylvania 41 E4 off. Commonwealth of Pennsylvania, also known as Keystone State. state NE USA
Penobscot River 41 G2 river Maine, NE USA
Penong 149 A6 South Australia
Penonomé 53 F5 Coclé, C Panama
Penrhyn 145 E3 atoll N Cook Islands
Penrhyn Basin 143 F3 undersea feature C Pacific Ocean
Penrith 148 D1 New South Wales, SE Australia
Penrith 89 D5 NW England, United Kingdom
Pensacola 42 C3 Florida, SE USA
Pentecost 144 D4 Fr. Pentecôte. island C Vanuatu
Pentecôte see Pentecost
Penza 111 C6 Penzenskaya Oblast', W Russia
Penzance 89 C7 SW England, United Kingdom
Peoria 40 B4 Illinois, N USA
Perchtoldsdorf 95 E6 Niederösterreich, NE Austria
Percival Lakes 146 C4 lakes Western Australia
Perdido, Monte 93 F1 mountain NE Spain
Perece Vela Basin see West Mariana Basin
Pereira 58 B3 Risaralda, W Colombia
Peremyshl see Przemyśl
Pergamino 64 C4 Buenos Aires, E Argentina
Périgueux 91 C5 anc. Vesuna. Dordogne, SW France
Perito Moreno 65 B6 Santa Cruz, S Argentina
Perleberg 94 C3 Brandenburg, N Germany
Perlepe see Prilep
Perm' 114 C3 prev. Molotov. Permskiy Kray, NW Russia
Pernambuco 63 G2 off. Estado de Pernambuco. state/region E Brazil
Pernambuco see Recife
Pernambuco Abyssal Plain see Pernambuco Plain
Pernambuco, Estado de see Pernambuco
Pernambuco Plain 67 C5 var. Pernambuco Abyssal Plain. undersea feature E Atlantic Ocean
Pernau see Pärnu
Pernauer Bucht see Pärnu Laht
Pērnava see Pärnu
Pernik 104 B2 prev. Dimitrovo. Pernik, W Bulgaria
Pernov see Pärnu
Perote 51 F4 Veracruz-Llave, E Mexico
Pérouse see Perugia
Perovsk see Kyzylorda
Perpignan 91 C6 Pyrénées-Orientales, S France
Perryton 49 F1 Texas, SW USA
Perryville 45 H5 Missouri, C USA
Persia see Iran
Persian Gulf 120 C4 var. Gulf, The, Ar. Khalij al 'Arabī, Per. Khalij-e Fars. gulf SW Asia
Perth 147 A6 state capital Western Australia
Perth 88 C4 C Scotland, United Kingdom
Perth Basin 141 E6 undersea feature SE Indian Ocean
Peru 60 C3 off. Republic of Peru. country W South America
Peru see Beru
Peru Basin 67 A5 undersea feature E Pacific Ocean
Peru-Chile Trench 56 A4 undersea feature E Pacific Ocean

Perugia 96 C4 Fr. Pérouse; anc. Perusia.
Umbria, C Italy
Perugia, Lake of see Trasimeno, Lago
Peru, Republic of see Peru
Perusia see Perugia
Péruwelz 87 B6 Hainaut, SW Belgium
Pervomaysk 109 E3 prev. Ol'viopol'.
Mykolayivs'ka Oblast', S Ukraine
Pervyy Kuril'skiy Proliv 115 H3 strait
E Russia
Pesaro 96 C3 anc. Pisaurum. Marche,
C Italy
Pescara 96 D4 anc. Aternum, Ostia
Aterni. Abruzzo, C Italy
Peshawar 134 C1 Khyber Pakhtunkhwa,
N Pakistan
Peshkopi 101 C6 var. Peshkopia,
Peshkopija. Dibër, NE Albania
Peshkopia/Peshkopija see Peshkopi
Pessac 91 B5 Gironde, SW France
Petach-Tikva see Petah Tikva
Petah Tikva 119 A6 var. Petach-Tikva,
Petah Tiqva, Petah Tikva; prev. Petah
Tiqwa. Tel Aviv, C Israel
Petah Tiqwa see Petah Tikva
Petakh Tikva/Petah Tiqva see Petah
Tikva
Pétange 87 D8 Luxembourg,
SW Luxembourg
Petchaburi see Phetchaburi
Peterborough 149 B6 South Australia
Peterborough 38 D5 Ontario, SE Canada
Peterborough 89 E6 prev.
Medeshamstede. E England,
United Kingdom
Peterhead 88 D3 NE Scotland,
United Kingdom
Peter I Øy 154 A3 Norwegian
dependency Antarctica
Petermann Bjerg 83 E3 mountain
C Greenland
Petersburg 41 E5 Virginia, NE USA
Peters Mine 59 F3 var. Peter's Mine.
N Guyana
Petit St-Bernard, Col du see Little Saint
Bernard Pass
Peto 51 H4 Yucatán, SE Mexico
Petoskey 40 C2 Michigan, N USA
Petra see Wādī Mūsá
Petrich 104 C3 Blagoevgrad, SW Bulgaria
Petrikau see Piotrków Trybunalski
Petrikov see Pyetrykaw
Petrinja 100 B3 Sisak-Moslavina,
C Croatia
Petroaleksandrovsk see To'rtkok'l
Petrodvorets 110 A4 Fin. Pietarhovi.
Leningradskaya Oblast', NW Russia
Petrograd see Sankt-Peterburg
Petrokov see Piotrków Trybunalski
Petropavl see Petropavlovsk
Petropavlovsk 114 C4 Kaz. Petropavl.
Severnyy Kazakhstan, N Kazakhstan
Petropavlovsk-Kamchatskiy 115 H3
Kamchatskiy Kray, E Russia
Petroşani 108 B4 var. Petroseni, Ger.
Petroschen, Hung. Petrozsény.
Hunedoara, W Romania
Petroschen/Petroşeni see Petroşani
Petroskoi see Petrozavodsk
Petrovgrad see Zrenjanin
Petrovsk-Port see Makhachkala
Petrozavodsk 114 B2 Fin. Petroskoi.
Respublika Kareliya, NW Russia
Petrozsény see Petroşani
Pettau see Ptuj
Pevek 115 G1 Chukotskiy Avtonomnyy
Okrug, NE Russia
Pezinok 99 C6 Ger. Bösing, Hung. Bazin.
Bratislavský Kraj, W Slovakia
Pforzheim 95 B6 Baden-Württemberg,
SW Germany
Pfungstadt 95 B5 Hessen, W Germany
Phangan, Ko 137 C6 island SW Thailand
Phang-Nga 137 B7 var. Pang-Nga,
Phangnga. Phangnga, SW Thailand
Phangnga see Phang-Nga
Phan Rang/Phanrang see Phan
Rang-Thap Cham
Phan Rang-Thap Cham 137 E6 var.
Phanrang, Phan Rang, Phan Rang
Thap Cham. Ninh Thuân, S Vietnam
Phan Thiêt 137 E6 Binh Thuân,
S Vietnam
Pharnacia see Giresun
Pharus see Hvar
Phatthalung 137 C7 var. Padalung,
Patalung. Phatthalung, SW Thailand
Phayao 136 C4 var. Muang Phayao.
Phayao, NW Thailand
Phenix City 42 D2 Alabama, S USA

Phet Buri see Phetchaburi
Phetchaburi 137 C5 var. Bejraburi,
Petchaburi, Phet Buri. Phetchaburi,
SW Thailand
Philadelphia 41 F4 Pennsylvania,
NE USA
Philadelphia see 'Amman
Philippine Basin 125 F3 undersea
feature W Pacific Ocean
Philippine Islands 139 E1 island group
W Pacific Ocean
Philippines 139 E1 off. Republic of the
Philippines. country SE Asia
Philippine Sea 125 F3 sea
W Pacific Ocean
Philippines, Republic of the see
Philippines
Philippine Trench 142 A1 undersea
feature W Philippine Sea
Philippopolis see Plovdiv
Phitsanulok 136 C4 var. Bisnulok,
Muang Phitsanulok, Pitsanulok.
Phitsanulok, C Thailand
Phlórina see Flórina
Phnom Penh 137 D6 Khmer. Phnum
Pénh. country capital (Cambodia)
Phnom Penh, S Cambodia
Phnum Pénh see Phnom Penh
Phoenix 48 B2 state capital Arizona,
SW USA
Phoenix Islands 145 E3 island group
C Kiribati
Phôngsali 136 C3 var. Phong Saly.
Phôngsali, N Laos
Phong Saly see Phôngsali
Phônsaven 136 D4 var. Xieng Khouang;
prev. Pèk, Xiangkhoang. Xiangkhoang,
N Laos
Phou Louang see Annamite Mountains
Phrae 136 C4 var. Muang Phrae, Prae.
Phrae, NW Thailand
Phra Nakhon Si Ayutthaya see
Ayutthaya
Phra Thong, Ko 137 B6 island
SW Thailand
Phuket 137 B7 var. Bhuket, Puket, Mal.
Ujung Salang; prev. Junkseylon, Salang.
Phuket, SW Thailand
Phuket, Ko 137 B7 island SW Thailand
Phumĭ Kâmpóng Trâbêk see Kâmpóng
Trâbêk
Phumĭ Sâmraông see Sâmraông
Phum Kompong Trabek see Kâmpóng
Trâbêk
Phum Samrong see Sâmraông
Phu Vinh see Tra Vinh
Phyu 136 B4 var. Hpyu, Pyu. Bago,
C Myanmar (Burma)
Piacenza 96 B2 Fr. Paisance; anc.
Placentia. Emilia-Romagna, N Italy
Piatra-Neamţ 108 C4 Hung.
Karácsonkő. Neamţ, NE Romania
Piauhy see Piauí
Piauí 63 F2 off. Estado do Piauí; prev.
Piauhy. state/region E Brazil
Piauí, Estado do see Piauí
Picardie 90 C3 Eng. Picardy. cultural
region N France
Picardy see Picardie
Piccolo San Bernardo, Colle di see Little
Saint Bernard Pass
Pichilemu 64 B4 Libertador, C Chile
Pico 92 A5 var. Ilha do Pico. island
Azores, Portugal, NE Atlantic Ocean
Pico, Ilha do see Pico
Picos 63 F2 Piauí, E Brazil
Picton 151 C5 Marlborough, South
Island, New Zealand
Piedmont see Piemonte
Piedras Negras 51 E2 var. Ciudad
Porfirio Díaz. Coahuila, NE Mexico
Pielavesi 84 D4 lake C Finland
Pielinen 84 E4 var. Pielisjärvi. lake
E Finland
Pielisjärvi see Pielinen
Piemonte 96 A2 Eng. Piedmont. region
NW Italy
Pierre 45 E3 state capital South Dakota,
N USA
Piešt'any 99 C6 Ger. Pistyan, Hung.
Pöstyén. Trnavský Kraj, W Slovakia
Pietarhovi see Petrodvorets
Pietari see Sankt-Peterburg
Pietarsaari see Jakobstad
Pietermaritzburg 78 C3 var.
Maritzburg. KwaZulu/Natal,
E South Africa
Pietersburg see Polokwane

Pigs, Bay of see Cochinos, Bahía de
Pihkva Järv see Pskov, Lake
Pijijiapán 51 G5 Chiapas, SE Mexico
Pikes Peak 44 C5 mountain Colorado,
C USA
Pikeville 40 D5 Kentucky, S USA
Pikinni see Bikini Atoll
Piła 98 B3 Ger. Schneidemühl.
Wielkopolskie, C Poland
Pilar 64 D3 var. Villa del Pilar.
Ñeembucú, S Paraguay
Pilcomayo, Río 57 C5 river
C South America
Pílos see Pýlos
Pilsen see Plzeň
Pilzno see Plzeň
Pinang see Pinang, Pulau, Peninsular
Malaysia
Pinang see George Town
Pinang, Pulau 138 B3 var. Penang,
Pinang; prev. Prince of Wales Island.
island Peninsular Malaysia
Pinar del Río 54 A2 Pinar del Río,
W Cuba
Píndhos/Píndhos Óros see Píndos
Pindos 104 A4 var. Píndhos Óros, Eng.
Pindus Mountains; prev. Píndhos.
mountain range C Greece
Pindus Mountains see Píndos
Pine Bluff 42 B2 Arkansas, C USA
Pine Creek 146 D2 Northern Territory,
N Australia
Pinega 110 C3 river NW Russia
Pineiós 104 B4 var. Piniós; anc. Peneius.
river C Greece
Pineland 49 H3 Texas, SW USA
Pines, Akrotírio 104 C4 var. Akrotírio
Pínnes. headland N Greece
Pines, The Isle of the see Juventud, Isla de la
Pine Tree State see Maine
Pingdingshan 128 C4 Henan, C China
Pingkiang see Harbin
Ping, Mae Nam 136 B4 river W Thailand
Piniós see Pineiós
Pinkiang see Harbin
Pínnes, Akrotírio see Pínes, Akrotírio
Pinos, Isla de see Juventud, Isla de la
Pinotepa Nacional 51 F5 var. Santiago
Pinotepa Nacional. Oaxaca, SE Mexico
Pinsk 107 B7 Pol. Pińsk. Brestskaya
Voblasts', SW Belarus
Pinta, Isla 60 A5 var. Abingdon. island
Galápagos Islands, Ecuador, E Pacific
Ocean
Piombino 96 B3 Toscana, C Italy
Pioneer Mountains 46 D3 mountain
range Montana, N USA North America
Pionerskiy 106 A4 Ger. Neukuhren.
Kaliningradskaya Oblast', W Russia
Piotrków Trybunalski 98 D4 Ger.
Petrikau, Rus. Petrokov. Łodzkie,
C Poland
Piraeus/Piraiévs see Peiraiás
Pírgos see Pýrgos
Pirineos see Pyrenees
Piripiri 63 F2 Piauí, E Brazil
Pirna 94 D4 Sachsen, E Germany
Pirot 101 E5 Serbia, SE Serbia
Piryatin see Pyryatyn
Pisa 96 B3 var. Pise. Toscana, C Italy
Pisae see Pisa
Pisaurum see Pesaro
Pisco 60 D4 Ica, SW Peru
Písek 99 A5 Budějovický Kraj, S Czech
Republic (Czechia)
Pishan 126 A3 var. Guma. Xinjiang
Uygur Zizhiqu, NW China
Pishpek see Bishkek
Pistoia 96 B3 anc. Pistoria, Pistoriæ.
Toscana, C Italy
Pistoria/Pistoriæ see Pistoia
Pistyan see Piešt'any
Pisz 98 D3 Ger. Johannisburg.
Warmińsko-Mazurskie, NE Poland
Pita 74 C4 NW Guinea
Pitalito 58 B4 Huila, S Colombia
Pitcairn Group of Islands see Pitcairn,
Henderson, Ducie & Oeno Islands
Pitcairn Island 143 G4 island S Pitcairn
Group of Islands
**Pitcairn, Henderson, Ducie & Oeno
Islands** 143 G4 var. Pitcairn Group of
Islands. UK dependent territory
C Pacific Ocean
Piteå 84 D4 Norrbotten, N Sweden
Piteşti 108 B5 Argeş, S Romania
Pitsanulok see Phitsanulok
Pitt Island see Makin
Pittsburg 45 F5 Kansas, C USA
Pittsburgh 41 E4 Pennsylvania, NE USA

Pittsfield 41 F3 Massachusetts, NE USA
Piura 60 B2 Piura, NW Peru
Pivdennyy Buh 109 E3 Rus. Yuzhnyy
Bug. river S Ukraine
Placentia see Piacenza
Placetas 54 B2 Villa Clara, C Cuba
Plainview 49 E2 Texas, SW USA
Pláka 105 C7 Kykládes, Greece,
Aegean Sea
Planeta Rica 58 B2 Córdoba,
NW Colombia
Planken 94 E1 C Liechtenstein Europe
Plano 49 G2 Texas, SW USA
Plasencia 92 C3 Extremadura, W Spain
Plate, River 64 D4 var. River Plate.
estuary Argentina/Uruguay
Plate, River see Plata, Río de la
Platinum 36 C3 Alaska, USA
Plattensee see Balaton
Platte River 45 E4 river Nebraska, C USA
Plattsburgh 41 F2 New York, NE USA
Plauen 95 C6 var. Plauen im Vogtland.
Sachsen, E Germany
Plauen im Vogtland see Plauen
Plavinas 106 D4 Ger. Stockmannshof.
S Latvia
Plây Cu see Plei Ku
Pleasant Island see Nauru
Plei Ku 137 E5 prev. Plây Cu. Gia Lai,
C Vietnam
Plenty, Bay of 150 E3 bay North Island,
New Zealand
Plérin 90 A3 Côtes d'Armor, NW France
Plesetsk 110 C3 Arkhangel'skaya Oblast',
NW Russia
Pleshchenitsy see Plyeshchanitsy
Pleskau see Pskov
Pleskauer See see Pskov, Lake
Pleskava see Pskov
Pleszew 98 C4 Wielkopolskie, C Poland
Pleven 104 C2 prev. Plevna. Pleven,
N Bulgaria
Plevlja/Plevlje see Pljevlja
Plevna see Pleven
Pljevlja 104 C4 prev. Plevlja, Plevlje.
N Montenegro
Plocce see Ploče
Ploče 100 B4 It. Plocce; prev. Kardeljevo.
Dubrovnik-Neretva, SE Croatia
Płock 98 D3 Ger. Plozk. Mazowieckie,
C Poland
Plöcken Pass 95 C7 Ger. Plöckenpass, It.
Passo di Monte Croce Carnico. pass
SW Austria
Plöckenpass see Plöcken Pass
Ploeşti see Ploieşti
Ploieşti 108 C5 prev. Ploeşti. Prahova,
SE Romania
Plomári 105 D5 prev. Plomárion.
Lésvos, E Greece
Plomárion see Plomári
Płońsk 98 D3 Mazowieckie, C Poland
Plovdiv 104 C3 prev. Eumolpias; anc.
Evmolpia, Philippopolis, Lat.
Trimontium. Plovdiv, C Bulgaria
Plozk see Płock
Plunge 106 B3 Telšiai, W Lithuania
Plymouth 89 C7 SW England, United
Kingdom
Plzeň 99 A5 Ger. Pilsen, Pol. Pilzno.
Plzeňský Kraj, W Czech Republic
(Czechia)
Po 80 D4 river N Italy
Pobedy, Pik see Tömür Feng
Po, Bocche del see Po, Foci del
Pocahontas 42 B1 Arkansas, C USA
Pocatello 46 E4 Idaho, NW USA
Pochinok 111 A5 Smolenskaya Oblast',
W Russia
Pocking 95 D6 Bayern, SE Germany
Poděbrady 99 B5 Ger. Podiebrad.
Středočeský Kraj, C Czech Republic
(Czechia)
Podgorica 101 C5 prev. Titograd.
country capital (Montenegro)
S Montenegro
Podiebrad see Poděbrady
Podil's'k 109 E3 Rus. Kotovs'k. Odes'ka
Oblast', SW Ukraine
Podil's'ka Vysochina 108 D3 plateau
W Ukraine
Podium Anicensis see le Puy
Podol'sk 111 B5 Moskovskaya Oblast',
W Russia
Podravska Slatina see Slatina
Podujevë 101 D5 Serb. Podujevo.
N Kosovo

Podujevo see Podujevë
Podunajská Rovina see Little Alföld
Poetovio see Ptuj
Pogradec 101 D6 var. Pogradeci. Korçë, SE Albania
Pogradeci see Pogradec
Pohjanlahti see Bothnia, Gulf of
Pohnpei 144 C2 prev. Ponape Ascension Island. island E Micronesia
Poictiers see Poitiers
Poinsett, Cape 154 D4 headland Antarctica
Point de Galle see Galle
Pointe-à-Pitre 55 G3 Grande Terre, C Guadeloupe
Pointe-Noire 77 B6 Kouilou, S Congo
Point Lay 36 C2 Alaska, USA
Poitiers 90 B4 prev. Poictiers; anc. Limonum. Vienne, W France
Poitou 90 B4 cultural region W France
Pokharā 135 E3 Western, C Nepal
Pokrov 109 F3 Rus. Ordzhonikidze. Dnipropetrovs'ka Oblast', E Ukraine
Pokrovka see Kyzyl-Suu
Pokrovs'ke 109 G3 Rus. Pokrovskoye. Dnipropetrovs'ka Oblast', E Ukraine
Pokrovskoye see Pokrovs'ke
Pola see Pula
Pola de Lena see La Pola
Poland 98 B4 off. Republic of Poland, var. Polish Republic, Pol. Polska, Rzeczpospolita Polska; prev. Pol. Polish People's Republic. country C Europe
Poland, Republic of see Poland
Polath 116 C3 Ankara, C Turkey
Polatsk 107 D5 Rus. Polotsk. Vitsyebskaya Voblasts', N Belarus
Pol-e Khomri see Pul-e Khumri
Poli see Pólis
Polikastro/Polikástron see Polýkastro
Polikrayshte see Dolna Oryakhovitsa
Pólis 102 C5 var. Poli. W Cyprus
Polish People's Republic, The see Poland
Polish Republic see Poland
Polkowice 98 B4 Ger. Heerwegen. Dolnośląskie, W Poland
Pollença 93 G3 Mallorca, Spain, W Mediterranean Sea
Pologi see Polohy
Polohy 109 G3 Rus. Pologi. Zaporiz'ka Oblast', SE Ukraine
Polokwane 78 D4 prev. Pietersburg. Limpopo, NE South Africa
Polonne 108 D2 Rus. Polonnoye. Khmel'nyts'ka Oblast', NW Ukraine
Polonnoye see Polonne
Polotsk see Polatsk
Polska/Polska, Rzeczpospolita/Polska Rzeczpospolita Ludowa see Poland
Polski Trümbesh 104 D2 prev. Polsko Kosovo. Ruse, N Bulgaria
Polsko Kosovo see Polski Trümbesh
Poltava 109 F2 Poltavs'ka Oblast', NE Ukraine
Poltoratsk see Aşgabat
Pôlva 106 E3 Ger. Pölwe. Pôlvamaa, SE Estonia
Pölwe see Pôlva
Polyarnyy 110 C2 Murmanskaya Oblast', NW Russia
Polýkastro 104 B3 var. Polikastro; prev. Polikastron. Kentrikí Makedonía, N Greece
Polynesia 143 F4 island group C Pacific Ocean
Pomeranian Bay 94 D2 Ger. Pommersche Bucht, Pol. Zatoka Pomorska. bay Germany/Poland
Pomir, Dar''yoi see Pamir/Pāmir, Daryā-ye
Pommersche Bucht see Pomeranian Bay
Pomorska, Zatoka see Pomeranian Bay
Pomorskiy Proliv 110 D2 strait NW Russia
Po, Mouth of the 96 C2 var. Bocche del Po. river NE Italy
Pompaelo see Pamplona
Pompano Beach 43 F5 Florida, SE USA
Ponape Ascension Island see Pohnpei
Ponca City 49 G1 Oklahoma, C USA
Ponce 55 F3 C Puerto Rico
Pondicherry see Puducherry
Pondichéry see Puducherry
Ponferrada 92 C1 Castilla y León, NW Spain
Poniatowa 98 E4 Lubelskie, E Poland
Pons Aelii see Newcastle upon Tyne
Pons Vetus see Pontevedra

Ponta Delgada 92 B5 São Miguel, Azores, Portugal, NE Atlantic Ocean
Ponta Grossa 63 E4 Paraná, S Brazil
Pontarlier 90 D4 Doubs, E France
Ponteareas 92 B2 Galicia, NW Spain
Ponte da Barca 92 B2 Viana do Castelo, N Portugal
Pontevedra 92 B1 anc. Pons Vetus. Galicia, NW Spain
Pontiac 40 D3 Michigan, N USA
Pontianak 138 C4 Borneo, C Indonesia
Pontisarae see Pontoise
Pontivy 90 A3 Morbihan, NW France
Pontoise 90 C3 anc. Briva Isarae, Cergy-Pontoise, Pontisarae. Val-d'Oise, N France
Ponziane Island 97 C5 island C Italy
Poole 89 D7 S England, United Kingdom
Poona see Pune
Poopó, Lago 61 F4 var. Lago Pampa Aullagas. lake W Bolivia
Popayán 58 B4 Cauca, SW Colombia
Poperinge 87 A6 West-Vlaanderen, W Belgium
Poplar Bluff 45 G5 Missouri, C USA
Popocatépetl 51 E4 volcano S Mexico
Popper see Poprad
Poprad 99 D5 Ger. Deutschendorf, Hung. Poprád. Prešovský Kraj, E Slovakia
Poprád 99 D5 Ger. Popper, Hung. Poprád. river Poland/Slovakia
Porbandar 134 B4 Gujarāt, W India
Porcupine Plain 80 B3 undersea feature E Atlantic Ocean
Pordenone 96 C2 anc. Portenau. Friuli-Venezia Giulia, NE Italy
Poreč 100 A2 It. Parenzo. Istra, NW Croatia
Porech'ye see Parechcha
Pori 85 D5 Swe. Björneborg. Satakunta, SW Finland
Porirua 151 D5 Wellington, North Island, New Zealand
Porkhov 110 A4 Pskovskaya Oblast', W Russia
Porlamar 59 E1 Nueva Esparta, NE Venezuela
Póros 105 C6 Póros, S Greece
Póros 105 A5 Kefallinía, Iónia Nisiá, Greece, C Mediterranean Sea
Porsangenfjorden 84 D2 Lapp. Porsángguvuotna. fjord N Norway
Porsángguvuotna see Porsangenfjorden
Porsgrunn 85 B6 Telemark, S Norway
Portachuelo 61 G4 Santa Cruz, C Bolivia
Portadown 89 B5 Ir. Port An Dúnáin. S Northern Ireland, United Kingdom
Portalegre 92 C3 anc. Ammaia, Amoea. Portalegre, E Portugal
Port Alexander 36 D4 Baranof Island, Alaska, USA
Port Alfred 78 D5 Eastern Cape, S South Africa
Port Amelia see Pemba
Port An Dúnáin see Portadown
Port Angeles 46 B1 Washington, NW USA
Port Antonio 54 B5 NE Jamaica
Port Arthur 49 H4 Texas, SW USA
Port Augusta 149 B6 South Australia
Port-au-Prince 54 D3 country capital (Haiti) C Haiti
Port Blair 133 F2 Andaman and Nicobar Islands, SE India
Port Charlotte 43 E4 Florida, SE USA
Port Darwin see Darwin
Port d'Envalira 91 B8 E Andorra Europe
Port Douglas 148 D3 Queensland, NE Australia
Port Elizabeth 78 C5 Eastern Cape, S South Africa
Portenau see Pordenone
Porterville 47 C7 California, W USA
Port-Étienne see Nouâdhibou
Port Florence see Kisumu
Port-Francqui see Ilebo
Port-Gentil 77 A6 Ogooué-Maritime, W Gabon
Port Harcourt 75 G5 Rivers, S Nigeria
Port Hardy 36 D5 Vancouver Island, British Columbia, SW Canada
Port Harrison see Inukjuak
Port Hedland 146 B4 Western Australia
Port Huron 40 D3 Michigan, N USA
Portimão 92 B4 var. Vila Nova de Portimão. Faro, S Portugal
Port Jackson 148 E1 harbour New South Wales, E Australia
Portland 149 B7 Victoria, SE Australia

Portland 41 G2 Maine, NE USA
Portland 46 B3 Oregon, NW USA
Portland 49 G4 Texas, SW USA
Portland Bight 54 B5 bay S Jamaica
Portlaoighise see Port Laoise
Port Laoise 89 B6 var. Portlaoise, Ir. Portlaoighise; prev. Maryborough. C Ireland
Portlaoise see Port Laoise
Port Lavaca 49 G4 Texas, SW USA
Port Lincoln 149 A6 South Australia
Port Louis 79 H3 country capital (Mauritius) NW Mauritius
Port-Lyautey see Kénitra
Port Macquarie 149 E6 New South Wales, SE Australia
Port Mahon see Maó-Mahón
Portmore 54 B5 C Jamaica
Port Moresby 144 B3 country capital (Papua New Guinea) Central/National Capital District, SW Papua New Guinea
Port Natal see Durban
Porto 92 B2 Eng. Oporto; anc. Portus Cale. Porto, NW Portugal
Porto Alegre 63 E5 var. Pôrto Alegre. state capital Rio Grande do Sul, S Brazil
Porto Alegre 76 E2 São Tomé, S Sao Tome and Principe, Africa
Porto Alegre 76 E2 São Tomé, S Sao Tome and Principe, Africa
Porto Alexandre see Tombua
Porto Amélia see Pemba
Portobelo 53 G4 var. Porto Bello, Puerto Bello. Colón, N Panama
Port O'Connor 49 G4 Texas, SW USA
Porto Edda see Sarandë
Portoferraio 96 B4 Toscana, C Italy
Port of Spain 55 H5 country capital (Trinidad and Tobago) Trinidad, Trinidad and Tobago
Porto Grande see Mindelo
Portogruaro 96 C2 Veneto, NE Italy
Porto-Novo 75 F5 country capital (Benin - official) S Benin
Porto Rico see Puerto Rico
Porto Santo 70 A2 var. Ilha de Porto Santo. island Madeira, Portugal, NE Atlantic Ocean
Porto Santo, Ilha do see Porto Santo
Porto Torres 97 A5 Sardegna, Italy, C Mediterranean Sea
Porto Velho 62 D3 var. Velho. state capital Rondônia, W Brazil
Portoviejo 60 A2 var. Puertoviejo. Manabí, W Ecuador
Port Pirie 149 B6 South Australia
Port Rex see East London
Port Said see Būr Sa'īd
Portsmouth 89 D7 S England, United Kingdom
Portsmouth 41 G3 New Hampshire, NE USA
Portsmouth 40 D4 Ohio, N USA
Portsmouth 41 F5 Virginia, NE USA
Port Stanley see Stanley
Port Sudan 72 C3 Red Sea, NE Sudan
Port Swettenham see Klang/Pelabuhan Klang
Port Talbot 89 C7 S Wales, United Kingdom
Portugal 92 B3 off. Portuguese Republic. country SW Europe
Portuguese East Africa see Mozambique
Portuguese Guinea see Guinea-Bissau
Portuguese Republic see Portugal
Portuguese Timor see East Timor
Portuguese West Africa see Angola
Portus Cale see Porto
Portus Magnus see Almería
Portus Magonis see Maó-Mahón
Port-Vila 144 D4 var. Vila. country capital (Vanuatu) Éfaté, C Vanuatu
Porvenir 61 E3 Pando, NW Bolivia
Porvenir 65 B8 Magallanes, S Chile
Porvoo 85 E6 Swe. Borgå. Uusimaa, S Finland
Porzecze see Parechcha
Posadas 64 D3 Misiones, NE Argentina
Poschega see Požega
Posen see Poznań
Posnania see Poznań
Posterholt 87 D5 Limburg, SE Netherlands
Postojna 95 D8 Ger. Adelsberg, It. Postumia. SW Slovenia
Postovy/Postawy see Pastavy
Postumia see Postojna

Pöstyén see Piešt'any
Potamós 105 C7 Antikýthira, S Greece
Potentia see Potenza
Potenza 97 D5 anc. Potentia. Basilicata, S Italy
Poti 117 F2 prev. P'ot'i. W Georgia
P'ot'i see Poti
Potiskum 75 G4 Yobe, NE Nigeria
Potomac River 41 E5 river NE USA
Potosí 61 F4 Potosí, S Bolivia
Potsdam 94 D3 Brandenburg, NE Germany
Potwar Plateau 134 C2 plateau NE Pakistan
Poŭthisăt see Pursat
Po, Valle del see Po Valley
Po Valley 96 C2 It. Valle del Po. valley N Italy
Považská Bystrica 99 C5 Ger. Waagbistritz, Hung. Vágbeszterce. Trenčiansky Kraj, W Slovakia
Poverty Bay 150 E4 inlet North Island, New Zealand
Póvoa de Varzim 92 B2 Porto, NW Portugal
Powder River 44 D2 river Montana/ Wyoming, NW USA
Powell 44 C2 Wyoming, C USA
Powell, Lake 44 B5 lake Utah, W USA
Požarevac 100 D4 Ger. Passarowitz. Serbia, NE Serbia
Poza Rica 51 F4 var. Poza Rica de Hidalgo. Veracruz-Llave, E Mexico
Poza Rica de Hidalgo see Poza Rica
Požega 100 D4 prev. Slavonska Požega, Ger. Poschega, Hung. Pozsega. Požega-Slavonija, NE Croatia
Požega 100 D4 Serbia
Poznań 98 C3 Ger. Posen, Posnania. Wielkolpolska, C Poland
Pozoblanco 92 D4 Andalucía, S Spain
Pozsega see Požega
Pozsony see Bratislava
Pozzallo 97 C8 Sicilia, Italy, C Mediterranean Sea
Prachatice 99 A5 Ger. Prachatitz. Jihočeský Kraj, S Czech Republic (Czechia)
Prachatitz see Prachatice
Prado del Ganso see Goose Green
Prae see Phrae
Prag/Praga/Prague see Praha
Praha 99 A5 Eng. Prague, Ger. Prag, Pol. Praga. country capital (Czech Republic (Czechia)) Středočeský Kraj, NW Czech Republic (Czechia)
Praia 74 A3 country capital (Cape Verde) Santiago, S Cape Verde
Prairie State see Illinois
Prathet Thai see Thailand
Prato 96 B3 Toscana, C Italy
Pratt 45 E5 Kansas, C USA
Prattville 42 D2 Alabama, S USA
Pravda see Glavinitsa
Pravia 92 C1 Asturias, N Spain
Preăh Seihánŭ see Sihanoukville
Preny see Prienai
Prenzlau 94 D3 Brandenburg, NE Germany
Prerau see Přerov
Přerov 99 C5 Ger. Prerau. Olomoucký Kraj, E Czech Republic (Czechia)
Preschau see Prešov
Prescott 48 B2 Arizona, SW USA
Prešov 101 D5 Serbia, SE Serbia
Presidente Epitácio 63 E4 São Paulo, S Brazil
Presidente Stroessner see Ciudad del Este
Prešov 99 D5 var. Preschau, Ger. Eperies, Hung. Eperjes. Prešovský Kraj, E Slovakia
Prespa, Lake 101 D6 Alb. Liqen i Prespës, Gk. Límni Megáli Préspa, Límni Prespa, Mac. Prespansko Ezero, Serb. Prespansko Jezero. lake SE Europe
Prespa, Limni/Prespansko Ezero/Prespansko Jezero/Prespës, Liqen i see Prespa, Lake
Presque Isle 41 H1 Maine, NE USA
Pressburg see Bratislava
Preston 89 D5 NW England, United Kingdom
Prestwick 88 C4 W Scotland, United Kingdom
Pretoria 78 D4 country capital (South Africa) (admin. capital) NE South Africa
Preussisch Eylau see Bagrationovsk

Preußisch Holland see Pasłęk
Preussisch-Stargard see Starogard Gdański
Préveza 105 A5 Ípeiros, W Greece
Pribilof Islands 36 A3 island group Alaska, USA
Priboj 100 C4 Serbia, W Serbia
Price 44 B4 Utah, W USA
Prichard 42 C3 Alabama, S USA
Priekulė 106 B3 Ger. Prökuls. Klaipėda, W Lithuania
Prienai 107 B5 Pol. Preny. Kaunas, S Lithuania
Prieska 78 C4 Northern Cape, C South Africa
Prijedor 100 B3 Republika Srpska, NW Bosnia and Herzegovina
Prijepolje 100 D4 Serbia, W Serbia
Prikaspiyskaya Nizmennost' see Caspian Depression
Prilep 101 D6 Turk. Perlepe. S Macedonia
Priluki see Pryluky
Primorsk 106 A4 Ger. Fischhausen. Kaliningradskaya Oblast', W Russia
Primorsko 104 E2 prev. Keupria. Burgas, E Bulgaria
Primorsk/Primorskoye see Prymors'k
Prince Albert 37 F5 Saskatchewan, S Canada
Prince Edward Island 39 F4 Fr. Île-du Prince-Édouard. province SE Canada
Prince Edward Islands 69 E8 island group S South Africa
Prince George 37 E5 British Columbia, SW Canada
Prince of Wales Island 148 B1 island Queensland, E Australia
Prince of Wales Island 37 F2 island Queen Elizabeth Islands, Nunavut, NW Canada
Prince of Wales Island see Pinang, Pulau
Prince Patrick Island 37 E2 island Parry Islands, Northwest Territories, NW Canada
Prince Rupert 36 D4 British Columbia, SW Canada
Prince's Island see Príncipe
Princess Charlotte Bay 148 C2 bay Queensland, NE Australia
Princess Elizabeth Land 154 C3 physical region Antarctica
Príncipe 77 A5 var. Príncipe Island, Eng. Prince's Island. island N Sao Tome and Principe
Principe Island see Príncipe
Prinzapolka 53 E3 Región Autónoma Atlántico Norte, NE Nicaragua
Pripet 107 C7 Bel. Prypyats', Ukr. Pryp"yat'. river Belarus/Ukraine
Pripet Marshes 107 B7 wetland Belarus/Ukraine
Prishtinë 101 D5 var. Pristina, Serb. Priština. C Kosovo
Priština/Pristina see Prishtinë
Privas 91 D5 Ardèche, E France
Prizren 101 D5 S Kosovo
Probolinggo 138 D5 Jawa, C Indonesia
Probstberg see Wyszków
Progreso 51 H3 Yucatán, SE Mexico
Prokhladnyy 111 B8 Kabardino-Balkarskaya Respublika, SW Russia
Prokletije see North Albanian Alps
Prökuls see Priekulė
Prokuplje 101 D5 Serbia, SE Serbia
Prome see Pyay
Promyshlennyy 110 E3 Respublika Komi, NW Russia
Prościejów see Prostějov
Proskurov see Khmel 'nyts'kyy
Prossnitz see Prostějov
Prostějov 99 C5 Ger. Prossnitz, Pol. Prościejów. Olomoucký Kraj, E Czech Republic (Czechia)
Provence 91 D6 cultural region SE France
Providence 41 G3 state capital Rhode Island, NE USA
Providence see Fort Providence
Providencia, Isla de 53 F3 island NW Colombia, Caribbean Sea
Providenya 155 B1 Chukotskiy Avtonomnyy Okrug, NE Russia
Provo 44 B4 Utah, W USA
Prudhoe Bay 36 D2 Alaska, USA
Prusa see Bursa
Pruszków 98 D3 C Poland
Prut 108 D4 Ger. Pruth. river E Europe
Pruth see Prut
Pružana see Pruzhany

Pruzhany 107 B6 Pol. Pružana. Brestskaya Voblasts', SW Belarus
Prychornomor'ska Nyzovyna see Black Sea Lowland
Prydniprovs'ka Nyzovyna/ Prydnyaprowskaya Nizina see Dnieper Lowland
Prydz Bay 154 D3 bay Antarctica
Pryluky 109 E2 Rus. Priluki. Chernihivs'ka Oblast', NE Ukraine
Prymors'k 109 G4 Rus. Primorsk; prev. Primorskoye. Zaporiz'ka Oblast', SE Ukraine
Pryp"yat'/Prypyats' see Pripet
Przemyśl 99 E5 Rus. Peremyshl. Podkarpackie, C Poland
Przheval'sk see Karakol
Psará 105 D5 island E Greece
Psel 109 F2 Rus. Psël. river Russia/Ukraine
Psël see Psel
Pskov 114 B2 Ger. Pleskau, Latv. Pleskava. Pskovskaya Oblast', W Russia
Pskov, Lake 106 E3 Est. Pihkva Järv, Ger. Pleskauer See, Rus. Pskovskoye Ozero. lake Estonia/Russia
Pskovskoye Ozero see Pskov, Lake
Ptich' see Ptsich
Ptsich 107 C7 Rus. 'Ptich'. Homyel'skaya Voblasts', SE Belarus
Ptsich 107 C7 Rus. Ptich'. river SE Belarus
Ptuj 95 E7 Ger. Pettau; anc. Poetovio. NE Slovenia
Pucallpa 60 C3 Ucayali, C Peru
Puck 98 C2 Pomorskie, N Poland
Pudasjärvi 84 D4 Pohjois-Pohjanmaa, C Finland
Puduchcheri see Puducherry
Puducherry 132 C2 prev. Pondicherry. var. Puducheheri, Fr. Pondichéry. Pondicherry, SE India
Puebla 51 F4 var. Puebla de Zaragoza. Puebla, S Mexico
Puebla de Zaragoza see Puebla
Pueblo 44 D5 Colorado, C USA
Puerto Acosta 61 E4 La Paz, W Bolivia
Puerto Aisén 65 B6 Aisén, S Chile
Puerto Ángel 51 F5 Oaxaca, SE Mexico
Puerto Argentino see Stanley
Puerto Ayacucho 58 D3 Amazonas, SW Venezuela
Puerto Baquerizo Moreno 60 B5 var. Baquerizo Moreno. Galápagos Islands, Ecuador, E Pacific Ocean
Puerto Barrios 52 C2 Izabal, E Guatemala
Puerto Bello see Portobelo
Puerto Berrío 58 B2 Antioquia, C Colombia
Puerto Cabello 58 D1 Carabobo, N Venezuela
Puerto Cabezas 53 F2 var. Bilwi. Región Autónoma Atlántico Norte, NE Nicaragua
Puerto Carreño 58 D3 Vichada, E Colombia
Puerto Cortés 52 C2 Cortés, NW Honduras
Puerto Cumarebo 58 C1 Falcón, N Venezuela
Puerto Deseado 65 C7 Santa Cruz, SE Argentina
Puerto Escondido 51 F5 Oaxaca, SE Mexico
Puerto Francisco de Orellana 60 B1 var. Coca. NE Ecuador
Puerto Gallegos see Río Gallegos
Puerto Inírida 58 D3 var. Obando. Guainía, E Colombia
Puerto La Cruz 59 E1 Anzoátegui, NE Venezuela
Puerto Lempira 53 E2 Gracias a Dios, E Honduras
Puerto Limón see Limón
Puertollano 92 D4 Castilla-La Mancha, C Spain
Puerto López 58 C1 La Guajira, N Colombia
Puerto Maldonado 61 E3 Madre de Dios, E Peru
Puerto México see Coatzacoalcos
Puerto Montt 65 B5 Los Lagos, C Chile
Puerto Natales 65 B7 Magallanes, S Chile
Puerto Obaldía 53 H5 Kuna Yala, NE Panama
Puerto Plata 55 E3 var. San Felipe de Puerto Plata. N Dominican Republic
Puerto Presidente Stroessner see Ciudad del Este

Puerto Princesa 139 E2 off. Puerto Princesa City. Palawan, W Philippines
Puerto Princesa City see Puerto Princesa
Puerto Príncipe see Camagüey
Puerto Rico 55 F3 off. Commonwealth of Puerto Rico; prev. Porto Rico. US C West Indies
Puerto Rico 56 B1 island C West Indies
Puerto Rico, Commonwealth of see Puerto Rico
Puerto Rico Trench 56 B1 trench NE Caribbean Sea
Puerto San José see San José
Puerto San Julián 65 B7 var. San Julián. Santa Cruz, SE Argentina
Puerto Suárez 61 H4 Santa Cruz, E Bolivia
Puerto Vallarta 50 D4 Jalisco, SW Mexico
Puerto Varas 65 B5 Los Lagos, C Chile
Puerto Viejo 53 E4 Heredia, NE Costa Rica
Puertoviejo see Portoviejo
Puget Sound 46 B1 sound Washington, NW USA
Puglia 97 E5 var. Le Puglie, Eng. Apulia. region SE Italy
Pukaki, Lake 151 B6 lake South Island, New Zealand
Pukekohe 150 D3 Auckland, North Island, New Zealand
Puket see Phuket
Pukhavichy 107 C6 Rus. Pukhovichi. Minskaya Voblasts', C Belarus
Pukhovichi see Pukhavichy
Pula 100 A3 It. Pola; prev. Pulj. Istra, NW Croatia
Pulaski 40 D5 Virginia, NE USA
Puławy 98 D4 Ger. Neu Amerika. Lubelskie, E Poland
Pul-e Khumrī 123 E4 prev. Pol-e Khomrī, var. Pul-i-Khumri. Baghlān, NE Afghanistan
Pul-i-Khumri see Pul-e Khumrī
Pulj see Pula
Pullman 46 C2 Washington, NW USA
Pułtusk 98 D3 Mazowieckie, C Poland
Puná, Isla 60 A2 island SW Ecuador
Pune 134 C5 prev. Poona. Mahārāshtra, W India
Punjab 134 C2 prev. West Punjab, Western Punjab. province E Pakistan
Puno 61 E4 Puno, SE Peru
Punta Alta 65 C5 Buenos Aires, E Argentina
Punta Arenas 65 B8 prev. Magallanes. Magallanes, S Chile
Punta Gorda 52 C2 Toledo, SE Belize
Punta Gorda 53 E4 Región Autónoma Atlántico Sur, SE Nicaragua
Puntarenas 52 D4 Puntarenas, W Costa Rica
Punto Fijo 58 C1 Falcón, N Venezuela
Pupuya, Nevado 61 E4 mountain W Bolivia
Puri 135 F5 var. Jagannath. Odisha, E India
Puriramya see Buriram
Purmerend 86 C3 Noord-Holland, C Netherlands
Pursat 137 D6 Khmer. Poŭthĭsăt. Pursat, W Cambodia
Purus, Rio 62 C2 var. Río Purús. river Brazil/Peru
Pusan see Busan
Pushkino see Bilāsuvar
Püspökladány 99 D6 Hajdú-Bihar, E Hungary
Putorana, Gory/Putorana Mountains see Putorana, Plato
Putorana Mountains 115 E3 var. Gory Putorana, Eng. Putorana Mountains. mountain range N Russia
Putrajaya 138 B3 administrative capital (Malaysia) Kuala Lumpur, Peninsular Malaysia
Puttalam 132 C3 North Western Province, W Sri Lanka
Puttgarden 94 C2 Schleswig-Holstein, N Germany
Putumayo, Río 58 B5 var. Içá, Rio. river NW South America
Putumayo, Río see Içá, Rio

Pyatigorsk 111 B7 Stavropol'skiy Kray, SW Russia
Pyatikhatki see P''yatykhatky
P''yatykhatky 109 F3 Rus. Pyatikhatki. Dnipropetrovs'ka Oblast', E Ukraine
Pyay 136 B4 var. Prome, Pye. Bago, C Myanmar (Burma)
Pye see Pyay
Pyetrykaw 107 C7 Rus. Petrikov. Homyel'skaya Voblasts', SE Belarus
Pyin-Oo-Lwin 136 B3 var. Maymyo. Mandalay, C Myanmar (Burma)
Pylos 105 B6 var. Pílos. Pelopónnisos, S Greece
P'yŏngyang 129 E3 var. P'yŏngyang-si, Eng. Pyongyang. country capital (North Korea) SW North Korea
P'yŏngyang-si see P'yŏngyang
Pyramid Lake 47 C5 lake Nevada, W USA
Pyrenaei Montes see Pyrenees
Pyrenees 102 B2 Fr. Pyrénées, Sp. Pirineos; anc. Pyrenaei Montes. mountain range SW Europe
Pýrgos 105 B6 var. Pírgos. Dytikí Elláda, S Greece
Pyritz see Pyrzyce
Pyryatyn 109 E2 Rus. Piryatin. Poltavs'ka Oblast', NE Ukraine
Pyrzyce 98 B3 Ger. Pyritz. Zachodnio-pomorskie, NW Poland
Pyu see Phyu
Pyuntaza 136 B4 Bago, SW Myanmar (Burma)

Q

Qāʻ al Jafr 119 C7 lake S Jordan
Qaanaaq 82 D1 var. Qânâq, Dan. Thule. Avannaarsua, N Greenland
Qabātiya 119 E6 N West Bank Asia
Qābis see Gabès
Qābis, Khalīj see Gabès, Golfe de
Qacentina see Constantine
Qafṣah see Gafsa
Qagan Us see Dulan
Qahremānshahr see Kermānshāh
Qaidam Pendi 126 C4 basin C China
Qal'aikhum 123 F3 Rus. Kalaikhum. S Tajikistan
Qalāt 123 E5 Per. Kalāt. Zābul, S Afghanistan
Qal'at Bīshah 121 B5 'Asīr, SW Saudi Arabia
Qalqīlya see Qalqīlya
Qalqīlya 119 D6 var. Qalqilīya. Central, W West Bank Asia
Qamanittuaq see Baker Lake
Qamdo 126 D5 Xizang Zizhiqu, W China
Qamishly see Al Qāmishlī
Qânâq see Qaanaaq
Qaqortoq 82 C4 Dan. Julianehåb. Kitaa, S Greenland
Qaraghandy/Qaraghandy Oblysy see Karagandy
Qara Qum see Garagum
Qarataū see Karatau, Zhambyl, Kazakhstan
Qarkilik see Ruoqiang
Qarokūl 123 F3 Rus. Karakul'. E Tajikistan
Qarqannah, Juzur see Kerkenah, Îles de
Qars see Kars
Qarshi 123 E3 Rus. Karshi; prev. Bek-Budi. Qashqadaryo Viloyati, S Uzbekistan
Qasigiannguit see Qasigiannguit
Qasigiannguit 82 C3 var. Qasigiannguit, Dan. Christianshåb. Kitaa, C Greenland
Qasr al Farāfirah 72 B2 var. Qasr Farâfra. N Egypt
Qasr Farâfra see Qasr al Farāfirah
Qaṭanā 119 B5 var. Katana. Rif Dimashq, S Syria
Qatar 120 C4 off. State of Qatar, Ar. Dawlat Qatar. country SW Asia
Qatar, State of see Qatar
Qattara Depression 72 A1 var. Munkhafad al Qattârah var. Monkhafad el Qaṭṭâra, Eng. Qattara Depression. desert NW Egypt
Qaṭṭârah, Munkhafad al see Qattara Depression
Qaṭṭâra, Monkhafad el see Qattara Depression

Qausuittuq see Resolute
Qazaqstan/Qazaqstan Respublikasy see Kazakhstan
Qazimämmäd see Hacıqabal
Qazris see Cáceres
Qazvīn *120 C2 var.* Kazvin. Qazvīn, N Iran
Qena see Qinā
Qeqertarssuaq see Qeqertarsuaq
Qeqertarsuaq *82 C3 var.* Qeqertarssuaq, Dan. Godhavn. Kitaa, S Greenland
Qeqertarsuaq *82 C3 island* W Greenland
Qeqertarsuup Tunua *82 C3 Dan.* Disko Bugt. *inlet* W Greenland
Qerveh see Qorveh
Qeshm *120 D4 var.* Jazīreh-ye Qeshm, Qeshm Island. *island* S Iran
Qeshm Island/Qeshm, Jazīreh-ye see Qeshm
Qilian Shan *126 D3 var.* Kilien Mountains. *mountain range* N China
Qimusseriarsuaq *82 C2 Dan.* Melville Bugt, *Eng.* Melville Bay. *bay* NW Greenland
Qinā *72 B2 var.* Qena; *anc.* Caene, Caenepolis. E Egypt
Qing see Qinghai
Qingdao *128 D4 var.* Ching-Tao, Ch'ing-tao, Tsingtao, Tsintao, *Ger.* Tsingtau. Shandong, E China
Qinghai *126 C4 var.* Chinghai, Koko Nor, Qing, Qinghai Sheng, Tsinghai. *province* C China
Qinghai Hu *126 D4 var.* Ch'ing Hai, Tsing Hai, *Mong.* Koko Nor. *lake* C China
Qinghai Sheng see Qinghai
Qinhuangdao *128 D3* Hebei, E China
Qinzhou *128 B6* Guangxi Zhuangzu Zizhiqu, S China
Qiong see Hainan
Qiqihar *128 D2 var.* Ch'i-ch'i-ha-erh, Tsitsihar; *prev.* Lungkiang. Heilongjiang, NE China
Qira *126 B4* Xinjiang Uygur Zizhiqu, NW China
Qita Ghazzah see Gaza Strip
Qitai *126 C3* Xinjiang Uygur Zizhiqu, NW China
Qīzān see Jāzān
Qizil Orda see Kyzylorda
Qizil Qum/Qizilqum see Kyzyl Kum
Qizilrabot *123 G3 Rus.* Kyzylrabot. SE Tajikistan
Qobustan *117 H2 prev.* Märäzä. E Azerbaijan
Qogir Feng see K2
Qom *120 C3 var.* Kum, Qum. Qom, N Iran
Qomolangma Feng see Everest, Mount
Qomul see Hami
Qo'qon *123 F2 var.* Khokand, *Rus.* Kokand. Farg'ona Viloyati, E Uzbekistan
Qorveh *120 C3 var.* Qerveh, Qurveh. Kordestān, W Iran
Qostanay/Qostanay Oblysy see Kostanay
Qoubaïyât *118 B4 var.* Al Qubayyāt. N Lebanon
Qoussantína see Constantine
Quang Ngai *137 E5 var.* Quangngai, Quang Nghia. Quang Ngai, C Vietnam
Quangngai see Quang Ngai
Quang Nghia see Quang Ngai
Quan Long see Ca Mau
Quanzhou *128 D6 var.* Ch'uan-chou, Tsinkiang; *prev.* Chin-chiang. Fujian, SE China
Quanzhou *128 C6* Guangxi Zhuangzu Zizhiqu, S China
Qu'Appelle *37 F5 river* Saskatchewan, S Canada
Quarles, Pegunungan *139 E4 mountain range* Sulawesi, C Indonesia
Quarnero see Kvarner
Quartu Sant' Elena *97 A6* Sardegna, Italy, C Mediterranean Sea
Quba *117 H2 Rus.* Kuba. N Azerbaijan
Qubba see Ba'qūbah
Québec *39 E4 var.* Quebec. *province capital* Québec, SE Canada
Québec *38 D3 var.* Quebec. *province* SE Canada
Queen Charlotte Islands *36 C5 Fr.* Îles de la Reine-Charlotte. *island group* British Columbia, SW Canada
Queen Charlotte Sound *36 C5 sea area* British Columbia, W Canada

Queen Elizabeth Islands *37 E1 Fr.* Îles de la Reine-Élisabeth. *island group* Nunavut, N Canada
Queensland *148 B4 state* N Australia
Queenstown *151 B7* Otago, South Island, New Zealand
Queenstown *78 D5* Eastern Cape, S South Africa
Quelimane *79 E3 var.* Kilimane, Kilmain, Quilimane. Zambézia, NE Mozambique
Quelpart see Jeju-do
Quepos *53 E4* Puntarenas, S Costa Rica
Que Que see Kwekwe
Quera see Chur
Querétaro *51 E4* Querétaro de Arteaga, C Mexico
Quesada *53 E4 var.* Ciudad Quesada, San Carlos. Alajuela, N Costa Rica
Quetta *134 B2* Baluchistan, SW Pakistan
Quetzalcoalco see Coatzacoalcos
Quezaltenango *52 A2 var.* Quetzaltenango. Quezaltenango, W Guatemala
Quibdó *58 A3* Chocó, W Colombia
Quilimane see Quelimane
Quillabamba *60 D3* Cusco, C Peru
Quilon see Kollam
Quimper *90 A3 anc.* Quimper Corentin. Finistère, NW France
Quimper Corentin see Quimper
Quimperlé *90 A3* Finistère, NW France
Quincy *40 A4* Illinois, N USA
Qui Nhon/Quinhon see Quy Nhơn
Quissico *79 E4* Inhambane, S Mozambique
Quito *60 B1* country capital (Ecuador) Pichincha, N Ecuador
Qulyndy Zhazyghy see Ravnina Kulyndy
Qum see Qom
Qurein see Al Kuwayt
Qŭrghonteppa *123 E3 Rus.* Kurgan-Tyube. SW Tajikistan
Qurlurtuuq see Kugluktuk
Qurveh see Qorveh
Quşayr see Al Quşayr
Quxar see Lhazê
Quy Nhơn *137 E5 var.* Quinhon, Qui Nhon. Bình Đinh, C Vietnam
Qyteti Stalin see Kuçovë
Qyzylorda see Kyzylorda

R

Raab *100 B1 Hung.* Rába. *river* Austria/ Hungary
Raab see Rába
Raab see Győr
Raahe *84 D4 Swe.* Brahestad. Pohjois-Pohjanmaa, W Finland
Raalte *86 D3* Overijssel, E Netherlands
Raamsdonksveer *86 C4* Noord-Brabant, S Netherlands
Raasiku *106 D2 Ger.* Rasik. Harjumaa, NW Estonia
Rába *99 B7 Ger.* Raab. *river* Austria/ Hungary
Rába see Raab
Rabat *70 C2 var.* al Dar al Baida. *country capital* (Morocco) NW Morocco
Rabat *102 B5* W Malta
Rabat see Victoria
Rabbah Ammon/Rabbath Ammon see 'Amman
Rabinal *52 B2* Baja Verapaz, C Guatemala
Rabka *99 D5* Małopolskie, S Poland
Râbniţa see Rîbniţa
Rabyanah Ramlat *71 G4 var.* Rebiana Sand Sea, Ṣaḥrāʾ Rabyānah. *desert* SE Libya
Rabyānah, Ṣaḥrāʾ see Rabyānah, Ramlat
Răcari see Durankulak
Race, Cape *39 H3 headland* Newfoundland, Newfoundland and Labrador, E Canada
Rach Gia *137 D6* Kiên Giang, S Vietnam
Rach Gia, Vinh *137 D6 bay* S Vietnam
Racine *40 B3* Wisconsin, N USA
Rácz-Becse see Bečej
Rădăuţi *108 C3 Ger.* Radautz, *Hung.* Rádóc. Suceava, N Romania
Radautz see Rădăuţi
Rădeyilikóé see Fort Good Hope
Rádóc see Rădăuţi
Radom *98 D4* Mazowieckie, C Poland

Radomsko *98 D4 Rus.* Novoradomsk. Łódzkie, C Poland
Radomyshl' *108 D2* Zhytomyrs'ka Oblast', N Ukraine
Radoviš *101 E6 prev.* Radovište. E Macedonia
Radovište see Radoviš
Radviliškis *106 B4* Šiauliai, N Lithuania
Radzyń Podlaski *98 E4* Lubelskie, E Poland
Rae-Edzo see Edzo
Raetihi *150 D4* Manawatu-Wanganui, North Island, New Zealand
Rafa see Rafah
Rafaela *64 C3* Santa Fe, E Argentina
Rafah *119 A7 var.* Rafa, Rafaḥ, *Heb.* Rafiaḥ, Raphiah. *var.* Gaza Strip
Rafḥah *120 B4* Al Ḥudūd ash Shamāliyah, N Saudi Arabia
Rafiaḥ see Rafah
Raga *73 A5* Western Bahr el Ghazal, W South Sudan
Ragged Island Range *54 C2 island group* S The Bahamas
Ragnit see Neman
Ragusa *97 C7* Sicilia, Italy, C Mediterranean Sea
Ragusa see Dubrovnik
Rahachow *107 D7 Rus.* Rogachëv. Homyel'skaya Voblasts', SE Belarus
Rahaeng see Tak
Raḥaṭ, Ḥarrat *121 B5 lava flow* W Saudi Arabia
Rahimyar Khan *134 C3* Punjab, SE Pakistan
Rahovec *101 D5 Serb.* Orahovac. W Kosovo
Raiatea *145 G4 island* Îles Sous le Vent, W French Polynesia
Rāichūr *132 C1* Karnātaka, C India
Raidestos see Tekirdağ
Rainier, Mount *34 A4 volcano* Washington, NW USA
Rainy Lake *38 A4 lake* Canada/USA
Raipur *135 E4* Chhattisgarh, C India
Rājahmundry *135 E5* Andhra Pradesh, E India
Rajang see Rajang, Batang
Rajang, Batang *138 D3 var.* Rajang. *river* East Malaysia
Rājapālaiyam *132 C3* Tamil Nādu, SE India
Rājasthān *134 C3 cultural region* NW India
Rajin *129 E3* NE North Korea
Rājkot *134 C4* Gujarāt, W India
Rāj Nāndgaon *135 E4* Chhattisgarh, C India
Rajshahi *135 G3 prev.* Rampur Boalia. Rajshahi, W Bangladesh
Rakahanga *145 F3 atoll* N Cook Islands
Rakaia *151 B6 river* South Island, New Zealand
Rakka see Ar Raqqah
Rakke *106 E2* Lääne-Virumaa, NE Estonia
Rakvere *106 E2 Ger.* Wesenberg. Lääne-Virumaa, N Estonia
Ralik Chain *144 D1 island group* Ralik Chain, W Marshall Islands
Ramadi see Ar Ramādī
Râmnicul-Sārat see Râmnicu Sărat
Râmnicu Sărat *108 C4 prev.* Râmnicul-Sărat, Rîmnicu-Sărat. Buzău, E Romania
Râmnicu Vâlcea *108 B4 prev.* Rîmnicu Vîlcea. Vîlcea, C Romania
Rampur Boalia see Rajshahi
Ramree Island *136 A4 island* W Myanmar (Burma)
Ramtha see Ar Ramthā
Rancagua *64 B4* Libertador, C Chile
Rānchī *135 F4* Jhārkhand, N India
Randers *85 B7* Midtjylland, C Denmark
Rānēs see Ringvassøya
Rangiora *151 C6* Canterbury, South Island, New Zealand
Rangitikei *150 D4 river* North Island, New Zealand
Rangoon see Yangon
Rangpur *135 G3* Rajshahi, N Bangladesh
Rankin Inlet *37 G3* Nunavut, C Canada
Rankovićevo see Kraljevo
Ranong *137 B6* Ranong, SW Thailand
Rapa Nui see Pascua, Isla de
Raphiah see Rafah
Rapid City *44 D3* South Dakota, N USA

Räpina *106 E3 Ger.* Rappin. Põlvamaa, SE Estonia
Rapla *106 D2 Ger.* Rappel. Raplamaa, NW Estonia
Rappel see Rapla
Rappin see Räpina
Raqqa see Ar Raqqah
Rarotonga *145 G5 island* S Cook Islands, C Pacific Ocean
Ras al'Ain see Ra's al 'Ayn
Ra's al 'Ayn *118 D1 var.* Ras al'Ain. Al Ḥasakah, N Syria
Ra's an Naqb *119 B7* Ma'ān, S Jordan
Raseiniai *106 B4* Kaunas, C Lithuania
Rasht *120 C2 var.* Resht. Gilān, NW Iran
Rasik see Raasiku
Râşnov *108 C4 prev.* Rîşno, Rozsnyó, *Hung.* Barcarozsnyó. Braşov, C Romania
Rastenburg see Kętrzyn
Ratak Chain *144 D1 island group* Ratak Chain, E Marshall Islands
Ratän *85 C5* Jämtland, C Sweden
Rat Buri see Ratchaburi
Ratchaburi *137 C5 var.* Rat Buri. Ratchaburi, W Thailand
Ratisbon/Ratisbona/Ratisbonne see Regensburg
Rat Islands *36 A2 island group* Aleutian Islands, Alaska, USA
Ratlām *134 D4 prev.* Rutlam. Madhya Pradesh, C India
Ratnapura *132 D4* Sabaragamuwa Province, S Sri Lanka
Raton *48 D1* New Mexico, SW USA
Rättvik *85 C5* Dalarna, C Sweden
Raudhatain see Ar Rawḍatayn
Raufarhöfn *83 E4* Nordhurland Eystra, NE Iceland
Raukawa see Cook Strait
Raukumara Range *150 E3 mountain range* North Island, New Zealand
Rauma *85 D5 Swe.* Raumo. Satakunta, SW Finland
Raumo see Rauma
Räurkela *135 F4 var.* Rāulakela, Rourkela. Odisha, E India
Ravenna *96 C3* Emilia-Romagna, N Italy
Ravi *134 C2 river* India/Pakistan
Ravnina Kulyndy *114 C4 prev.* Kulunda Steppe, *Rus.* Qulyndy Zhazyghy. *grassland* Kazakhstan/Russia
Rawalpindi *134 C1* Punjab, NE Pakistan
Rawa Mazowiecka *98 D4* Łódzkie, C Poland
Rawicz *98 C4 Ger.* Rawitsch. Wielkopolskie, C Poland
Rawitsch see Rawicz
Rawlins *44 C3* Wyoming, C USA
Rawson *65 C6* Chubut, SE Argentina
Rayak *118 B4 var.* Rayaq, Riyāq. E Lebanon
Rayaq see Rayak
Rayong *137 C5* Rayong, S Thailand
Razazah, Buhayrat ar *120 B3 var.* Baḥr al Milḥ. *lake* C Iraq
Razdolnoye see Rozdol'ne
Razelm, Lacul see Razim, Lacul
Razgrad *104 D2* Razgrad, N Bulgaria
Razim, Lacul *108 D5 prev.* Lacul Razelm. *lagoon* NW Black Sea
Reading *89 D7* S England, United Kingdom
Reading *41 F4* Pennsylvania, NE USA
Realicó *64 C4* La Pampa, C Argentina
Reăng Kesei *137 D5* Battambang, W Cambodia
Rebecca, Lake *147 C6 lake* Western Australia
Rebiana Sand Sea see Rabyānah, Ramlat
Rebun-to *130 C2 island* NE Japan
Rechitsa see Rechytsa
Rechytsa *107 D7 Rus.* Rechitsa. Brestskaya Voblasts', SW Belarus
Recife *63 G2 prev.* Pernambuco. *state capital* Pernambuco, E Brazil
Recklinghausen *94 A4* Nordrhein-Westfalen, W Germany
Recogne *87 C7* Luxembourg, SE Belgium
Reconquista *64 D3* Santa Fe, C Argentina
Red Deer *37 E5* Alberta, SW Canada
Redding *47 B5* California, W USA
Redon *90 B4* Ille-et-Vilaine, NW France
Red River *45 E1 river* Canada/USA

Red River 136 C2 var. Yuan, Chin. Yuan Jiang, Vtn. Sông Hồng Hà. river China/ Vietnam

Red River 35 C6 river S USA

Red River 42 B3 river Louisiana, S USA

Red Sea 72 C3 var. Sinus Arabicus. sea Africa/Asia

Red Wing 45 G2 Minnesota, N USA

Reefton 151 C5 West Coast, South Island, New Zealand

Reese River 47 C5 river Nevada, W USA

Refahiye 117 E3 Erzincan, C Turkey

Regensburg 95 C6 Eng. Ratisbon, Fr. Ratisbonne, hist. Ratisbona; anc. Castra Regina, Reginum. Bayern, SE Germany

Regenstauf 95 C6 Bayern, SE Germany

Rêgêstän 122 D5 prev. Rīgestän, var. Registan. desert region S Afghanistan

Reggane 70 D3 C Algeria

Reggio see Reggio nell'Emilia

Reggio Calabria see Reggio di Calabria

Reggio di Calabria 97 D7 var. Reggio Calabria, Gk. Rhegion; anc. Regium, Rhegium. Calabria, SW Italy

Reggio Emilia see Reggio nell'Emilia

Reggio nell'Emilia 96 B2 var. Reggio Emilia, abbrev. Reggio; anc. Regium Lepidum. Emilia-Romagna, N Italy

Reghin 108 C4 Ger. Sächsisch-Reen, Hung. Szászrégen; prev. Reghinul Săsesc, Ger. Sächsisch-Regen. Mureş, C Romania

Reghinul Săsesc see Reghin

Regina 37 F5 province capital Saskatchewan, S Canada

Reginum see Regensburg

Registan see Rêgêstän

Regium see Reggio di Calabria

Regium Lepidum see Reggio nell'Emilia

Rehoboth 78 B3 Hardap, C Namibia

Rehovot 119 A6 ; prev. Reḥovot. Central, C Israel

Reḥovot see Rehovot

Reichenau see Bogatynia, Poland

Reichenberg see Liberec

Reid 147 D6 Western Australia

Reikjavík see Reykjavík

Ré, Île de 90 A4 island W France

Reims 90 D3 Eng. Rheims; anc. Durocortorum, Remi. Marne, N France

Reindeer Lake 37 F4 lake Manitoba/ Saskatchewan, C Canada

Reine-Charlotte, Îles de la see Queen Charlotte Islands

Reine-Élisabeth, Îles de la see Queen Elizabeth Islands

Reinga, Cape 150 C1 headland North Island, New Zealand

Reinosa 92 D1 Cantabria, N Spain

Reka see Rijeka

Rekhovot see Rehovot

Reliance 37 F4 Northwest Territories, C Canada

Remi see Reims

Rendina see Rentína

Rendsburg 94 B2 Schleswig-Holstein, N Germany

Rengat 138 B4 Sumatera, W Indonesia

Reni 108 D4 Odes'ka Oblast', SW Ukraine

Rennell 144 C4 var. Mu Nggava. island S Solomon Islands

Rennes 90 B3 Bret. Roazon; anc. Condate. Ille-et-Vilaine, NW France

Reno 47 C5 Nevada, W USA

Renqiu 128 C4 Hebei, E China

Rentína 105 B5 var. Rendina. Thessalía, C Greece

Reps see Rupea

Repulse Bay 37 G3 Northwest Terretories, N Canada

Reschitza see Reşiţa

Resht see Rasht

Resicabánya see Reşiţa

Resistencia 64 D3 Chaco, NE Argentina

Reşiţa 108 A4 Ger. Reschitza, Hung. Resicabánya. Caraş-Severin, W Romania

Resolute 37 F2 Inuit Qausuittuq. Cornwallis Island, N Canada

Resolution Island 39 E1 island Nunavut, NE Canada

Resolution Island 151 A7 island SW New Zealand

Réunion 79 H4 off. La Réunion. French overseas department W Indian Ocean

Réunion 141 B5 island W Indian Ocean

Reus 93 F2 Cataluña, E Spain

Reutlingen 95 B6 Baden-Württemberg, S Germany

Reuver 87 D5 Limburg, SE Netherlands

Reval/Revel see Tallinn

Revillagigedo Island 50 B5 island Alexander Archipelago, Alaska, USA

Rexburg 46 E3 Idaho, NW USA

Reyes 61 F3 El Beni, NW Bolivia

Rey, Isla del 53 G5 island Archipiélago de las Perlas, SE Panama

Reykjanes Basin 82 C5 var. Irminger Basin. undersea basin N Atlantic Ocean

Reykjanes Ridge 80 A1 undersea ridge N Atlantic Ocean

Reykjavík 83 E5 var. Reikjavik. country capital (Iceland) Höfudhborgarsvaedhí, W Iceland

Reynosa 51 E2 Tamaulipas, C Mexico

Rezā'īyeh, Daryācheh-ye see Orūmīyeh, Daryācheh-ye

Rezé 90 A4 Loire-Atlantique, NW France

Rēzekne 106 D4 Ger. Rositten; prev. Rus. Rezhitsa. SE Latvia

Rezhitsa see Rēzekne

Rezovo 104 E3 Turk. Rezve. Burgas, E Bulgaria

Rezve see Rezovo

Rhaedestus see Tekirdağ

Rhegion/Rhegium see Reggio di Calabria

Rheims see Reims

Rhein see Rhine

Rheine 94 A3 var. Rheine in Westfalen. Nordrhein-Westfalen, NW Germany

Rheine in Westfalen see Rheine

Rheinisches Schiefergebirge 95 A5 var. Rhine State Uplands, Eng. Rhenish Slate Mountains. mountain range W Germany

Rhenish Slate Mountains see Rheinisches Schiefergebirge

Rhin see Rhine

Rhine 80 D4 Dut. Rijn, Fr. Rhin, Ger. Rhein. river W Europe

Rhinelander 40 B2 Wisconsin, N USA

Rhine State Uplands see Rheinisches Schiefergebirge

Rho 96 B2 Lombardia, N Italy

Rhode Island 41 G3 off. State of Rhode Island and Providence Plantations, also known as Little Rhody, Ocean State. state NE USA

Rhodes 105 E7 var. Ródhos, It. Rodi, anc. Rhodes, It. Rodi; anc. Rhodos. island Dodekánisa, Greece, Aegean Sea

Rhodes see Ródos

Rhodesia see Zimbabwe

Rhodope Mountains 104 C3 var. Rodhópi Óri, Bul. Rhodope Planina, Rodopi, Gk. Orosirá Rodhópis, Turk. Dospad Dagh. mountain range Bulgaria/Greece

Rhodope Planina see Rhodope Mountains

Rhône 80 C4 river France/Switzerland

Rhum 88 B3 var. Rum. island W Scotland, United Kingdom

Ribble 89 D5 river NW England, United Kingdom

Ribeira see Sanata Uxía de Ribeira

Ribeirão Preto 63 F4 São Paulo, S Brazil

Riberalta 61 F2 El Beni, N Bolivia

Râbniţa 108 D4 var. Râbniţa, Rus. Rybnitsa. NE Moldova

Rice Lake 40 A2 Wisconsin, N USA

Richard Toll 74 B3 N Senegal

Richfield 44 B4 Utah, W USA

Richland 46 C2 Washington, NW USA

Richmond 151 C5 Tasman, South Island, New Zealand

Richmond 40 D5 Kentucky, S USA

Richmond 41 E5 state capital Virginia, NE USA

Richmond Range 151 C5 mountain range South Island, New Zealand

Ricobayo, Embalse de 92 C2 reservoir NW Spain

Ricomagus see Riom

Ridder 114 D4 Kaz. Leninqor, prev. Leninogorsk. Vostochnyy Kazakhstan, E Kazakhstan

Ridgecrest 47 C7 California, W USA

Ried see Ried im Innkreis

Ried im Innkreis 95 D6 var. Ried. Oberösterreich, NW Austria

Riemst 87 D6 Limburg, NE Belgium

Riesa 94 D4 Sachsen, E Germany

Rift Valley see Great Rift Valley

Riga 106 C3 Eng. Riga. country capital (Latvia) C Latvia

Rigaer Bucht see Riga, Gulf of

Riga, Gulf of 106 C3 Est. Liivi Laht, Ger. Rigaer Bucht, Latv. Rīgas Jūras Līcis, Rus. Rizhskiy Zaliv; prev. Est. Riia Laht. gulf Estonia/Latvia

Rīgas Jūras Līcis see Riga, Gulf of

Rigestän see Rêgêstän

Riia Laht see Riga, Gulf of

Riihimäki 85 D5 Kanta-Häme, S Finland

Rijeka 100 A2 Ger. Sankt Veit am Flaum, It. Fiume, Slvn. Reka; anc. Tarsatica. Primorje-Gorski Kotar, NW Croatia

Rijn see Rhine

Rijssel see Lille

Rijssen 86 E3 Overijssel, E Netherlands

Rīmah, Wadi ar 120 B4 var. Wādī ar Rummah. dry watercourse C Saudi Arabia

Rimini 96 C3 anc. Ariminum. Emilia-Romagna, N Italy

Râmnicu-Sărat see Râmnicu Sărat

Râmnicu Vâlcea see Râmnicu Vâlcea

Rimouski 39 E4 Québec, SE Canada

Ringebu 85 B5 Oppland, S Norway

Ringen see Rõngu

Ringkøbing Fjord 85 A7 fjord W Denmark

Ringvassøya 84 C2 Lapp. Ráneš. island N Norway

Rio see Rio de Janeiro

Riobamba 60 B1 Chimborazo, C Ecuador

Rio Branco 56 B3 state capital Acre, W Brazil

Rio Branco, Território de see Roraima

Río Bravo 51 E2 Tamaulipas, C Mexico

Río Cuarto 64 C4 Córdoba, C Argentina

Rio de Janeiro 63 F4 var. Rio. state capital Rio de Janeiro, SE Brazil

Río Gallegos 65 B7 var. Gallegos, Puerto Gallegos. Santa Cruz, S Argentina

Rio Grande 63 E5 var. São Pedro do Rio Grande do Sul. Rio Grande do Sul, S Brazil

Río Grande 50 D3 Zacatecas, C Mexico

Rio Grande do Norte 63 G2 off. Estado do Rio Grande do Norte. state/region E Brazil

Rio Grande do Norte, Estado do see Rio Grande do Norte

Rio Grande do Sul 63 E5 off. Estado do Rio Grande do Sul. state/region S Brazil

Rio Grande do Sul, Estado do see Rio Grande do Sul

Rio Grande Rise 57 E6 var. Rio Grande Plateau. undersea plateau SW Atlantic Ocean

Riohacha 58 B1 La Guajira, N Colombia

Río Lagartos 51 H3 Yucatán, SE Mexico

Riom 91 C5 anc. Ricomagus. Puy-de-Dôme, C France

Río Verde 51 E4 var. Rioverde. San Luis Potosí, C Mexico

Rioverde see Río Verde

Ripoll 93 G2 Cataluña, NE Spain

Rishiri-to 130 C2 var. Risiri Tô. island NE Japan

Risiri Tô see Rishiri-tô

Risti 106 D2 Ger. Kreuz. Läänemaa, W Estonia

Rivas 52 D4 Rivas, SW Nicaragua

Rivera 64 D3 Rivera, NE Uruguay

River Falls 40 A2 Wisconsin, N USA

Riverside 47 C7 California, W USA

Riverton 151 A7 Southland, South Island, New Zealand

Riverton 44 C3 Wyoming, C USA

Rivière-du-Loup 39 E4 Québec, SE Canada

Rivne 108 C2 Pol. Równe, Rus. Rovno. Rivnens'ka Oblast', NW Ukraine

Rivoli 96 A2 Piemonte, NW Italy

Riyadh/Riyāḍ, Minţaqat ar see Ar Riyāḍ

Riyāq see Rayak

Rize 117 E2 Rize, NE Turkey

Rizhao 128 D4 Shandong, E China

Rizhskiy Zaliv see Riga, Gulf of

Rkîz 74 C3 Trarza, W Mauritania

Road Town 55 F3 dependent territory capital (British Virgin Islands) Tortola, C British Virgin Islands

Roanne 91 C5 anc. Rodunna. Loire, E France

Roanoke 41 E5 Virginia, NE USA

Roanoke River 43 F1 river North Carolina/Virginia, SE USA

Roatán 52 C2 var. Coxen Hole, Coxin Hole. Islas de la Bahía, N Honduras

Roat Kampuchea see Cambodia

Roazon see Rennes

Robbie Ridge 143 E3 undersea ridge W Pacific Ocean

Robert Williams see Caála

Robinson Range 147 B5 mountain range Western Australia

Robson, Mount 37 E5 mountain British Columbia, SW Canada

Robstown 49 G4 Texas, SW USA

Roca Partida, Isla 50 B5 island W Mexico

Rocas, Atol das 63 G2 island E Brazil

Rochefort 87 C7 Namur, SE Belgium

Rochefort 90 B4 var. Rochefort sur Mer. Charente-Maritime, W France

Rochefort sur Mer see Rochefort

Rochester 45 G3 Minnesota, N USA

Rochester 41 G2 New Hampshire, NE USA

Rocheuses, Montagnes/Rockies see Rocky Mountains

Rockall Bank 82 B2 undersea bank N Atlantic Ocean

Rockall Trough 80 B2 trough N Atlantic Ocean

Rockdale 148 E2 Texas, SW USA

Rockford 40 B3 Illinois, N USA

Rockhampton 148 D4 Queensland, E Australia

Rock Hill 43 E1 South Carolina, SE USA

Rockingham 147 A6 Western Australia

Rock Island 40 B3 Illinois, N USA

Rock Sound 54 C1 Eleuthera Island, C The Bahamas

Rock Springs 44 C3 Wyoming, C USA

Rockstone 59 F3 C Guyana

Rocky Mount 43 F1 North Carolina, SE USA

Rocky Mountains 34 B4 var. Rockies, Fr. Montagnes Rocheuses. mountain range Canada/USA

Roden 86 E2 Drenthe, NE Netherlands

Rodez 91 C5 anc. Segodunum. Aveyron, S France

Rodhópi Óri see Rhodope Mountains

Ródhos/Rodi see Ródos

Rodopi see Rhodope Mountains

Rodosto see Tekirdağ

Rodunna see Roanne

Roermond 87 D5 Limburg, SE Netherlands

Roeselare 87 A6 Fr. Roulers; prev. Rousselaere. West-Vlaanderen, W Belgium

Rogachëv see Rahachow

Rogatica 100 C4 Republika Srpska, SE Bosnia and Herzegovina

Rogers 42 A1 Arkansas, C USA

Roger Simpson Island see Abemama

Roi Ed see Roi Et

Roi Et 137 D5 var. Muang Roi Et, Roi Ed. Roi Et, E Thailand

Roja 106 C2 NW Latvia

Rokiškis 106 C4 Panevėžys, NE Lithuania

Rokycany see Rokycany

Rôlas, Ilha das 76 E2 island S Sao Tome and Principe, Africa, E Atlantic Ocean

Rolla 45 G5 Missouri, C USA

Röm see Rømø

Roma 96 C4 Eng. Rome. country capital (Italy) Lazio, C Italy

Roma 149 D5 Queensland, E Australia

Roman 104 C2 Vratsa, NW Bulgaria

Roman 108 C4 Hung. Románvásár. Neamţ, NE Romania

Romania 108 B4 Bul. Rumüniya, Ger. Rumänien, Hung. Románia, Rom. Rumänia; prev. Republica Socialistă România, Roumania, Rumania, Socialist Republic of Romania, prev. Rom. Romínia. country SE Europe

România, Republica Socialistă see Romania

Romania, Socialist Republic of see Romania

Románvásár see Roman

Rome 42 D2 Georgia, SE USA

Rome see Roma

Rominia see Romania

Romny 109 F2 Sums'ka Oblast', NE Ukraine

Rømø *85 A7 Ger.* Röm. *island* SW Denmark
Roncador, Serra do *56 D4 mountain range* C Brazil
Ronda *92 D5* Andalucía, S Spain
Rondônia *62 D3 off.* Estado de Rondônia; *prev.* Território de Rondônia. *state/region* W Brazil
Rondônia, Estado de *see* Rondônia
Rondônia, Território de *see* Rondônia
Rondonópolis *63 E3* Mato Grosso, W Brazil
Rongelap Atoll *144 D1 var.* Rönlap. *atoll* Ralik Chain, NW Marshall Islands
Rôngu *106 D3 Ger.* Ringen. Tartumaa, SE Estonia
Rönlap *see* Rongelap Atoll
Rønne *85 B8* Bornholm, E Denmark
Ronne Ice Shelf *154 A3 ice shelf* Antarctica
Roosendaal *87 C5* Noord-Brabant, S Netherlands
Roosevelt Island *154 B4 island* Antarctica
Roraima *62 D1 off.* Estado de Roraima; *prev.* Território de Rio Branco, Território de Roraima. *state/region* N Brazil
Roraima, Estado de *see* Roraima
Roraima, Mount *59 E3 mountain* N South America
Roraima, Território de *see* Roraima
Røros *85 B5* Sør-Trøndelag, S Norway
Ross *151 B6* West Coast, South Island, New Zealand
Rosa, Lake *54 D2 lake* Great Inagua, S The Bahamas
Rosario *64 D4* Santa Fe, C Argentina
Rosario *64 D2* San Pedro, C Paraguay
Rosario *see* Rosarito
Rosarito *50 A1 var.* Rosario. Baja California Norte, NW Mexico
Roscianum *see* Rossano
Roscommon *40 C2* Michigan, N USA
Roseau *55 G4 prev.* Charlotte Town. *country capital* (Dominica) SW Dominica
Roseburg *46 B4* Oregon, NW USA
Rosenau *see* Rožňava
Rosenberg *49 G4* Texas, SW USA
Rosenberg *see* Ružomberok, Slovakia
Rosengarten *94 B3* Niedersachsen, N Germany
Rosenheim *95 C6* Bayern, S Germany
Rosia *93 H5* W Gibraltar Europe
Rosia Bay *93 H5 bay* SW Gibraltar Europe W Mediterranean Sea Atlantic Ocean
Roşiori de Vede *108 B5* Teleorman, S Romania
Rositten *see* Rēzekne
Roslavl' *111 A5* Smolenskaya Oblast', W Russia
Rosmalen *86 C4* Noord-Brabant, S Netherlands
Rossano *97 E6 anc.* Roscianum. Calabria, SW Italy
Ross Ice Shelf *154 B4 ice shelf* Antarctica
Rossiyskaya Federatsiya *see* Russia
Rosso *74 B3* Trarza, SW Mauritania
Rossosh' *111 B6* Voronezhskaya Oblast', W Russia
Ross Sea *154 B4 sea* Antarctica
Rostak *see* Ar Rustāq
Rostock *94 C2* Mecklenburg-Vorpommern, NE Germany
Rostov *see* Rostov-na-Donu
Rostov-na-Donu *111 B7 var.* Rostov, *Eng.* Rostov-on-Don. Rostovskaya Oblast', SW Russia
Rostov-on-Don *see* Rostov-na-Donu
Roswell *48 D2* New Mexico, SW USA
Rota *144 B1 island* S Northern Mariana Islands
Rotcher Island *see* Tamana
Rothera *154 A2 UK research station* Antarctica
Rotomagus *see* Rouen
Rotorua *150 D3* Bay of Plenty, North Island, New Zealand
Rotorua, Lake *150 D3 lake* North Island, New Zealand
Rotterdam *86 C4* Zuid-Holland, SW Netherlands
Rottweil *95 B6* Baden-Württemberg, S Germany
Rotuma *145 E4 island* NW Fiji Oceania S Pacific Ocean

Roubaix *90 C2* Nord, N France
Rouen *90 C3 anc.* Rotomagus. Seine-Maritime, N France
Roulers *see* Roeselare
Roumania *see* Romania
Round Rock *49 G3* Texas, SW USA
Rourkela *see* Räurkela
Rousselaere *see* Roeselare
Roussillon *91 C6 cultural region* S France
Rouyn-Noranda *38 D4* Québec, SE Canada
Rovaniemi *84 D3* Lappi, N Finland
Rovigno *see* Rovinj
Rovigo *96 C2* Veneto, NE Italy
Rovinj *100 A3 It.* Rovigno. Istra, NW Croatia
Rovno *see* Rivne
Rovuma, Rio *79 F2 var.* Ruvuma. *river* Mozambique/Tanzania
Rovuma, Rio *see* Ruvuma
Równe *see* Rivne
Roxas City *139 E2* Panay Island, C Philippines
Royale, Isle *40 B1 island* Michigan, N USA
Royan *91 B5* Charente-Maritime, W France
Rozdol'ne *109 F4 Rus.* Razdolnoye. Avtonomna Respublika Krym, S Ukraine
Rožňava *99 D6 Ger.* Rosenau, *Hung.* Rozsnyó. Košický Kraj, E Slovakia
Rózsahegy *see* Ružomberok
Rozsnyó *see* Râşnov, Romania
Rozsnyó *see* Rožňava, Slovakia
Ruanda *see* Rwanda
Ruapehu, Mount *150 D4 volcano* North Island, New Zealand
Ruapuke Island *151 B8 island* SW New Zealand
Ruatoria *150 E3* Gisborne, North Island, New Zealand
Ruawai *150 D2* Northland, North Island, New Zealand
Rubezhnoye *see* Rubizhne
Rubizhne *109 H3 Rus.* Rubezhnoye. Luhans'ka Oblast', E Ukraine
Ruby Mountains *47 D5 mountain range* Nevada, W USA
Rucava *106 B3* SW Latvia
Rudensk *see* Rudzyensk
Rūdišķēs *107 B5* Vilnius, S Lithuania
Rudnik *see* Dolni Chiflik
Rudny *see* Rudnyy
Rudnyy *114 C4 var.* Rudny. Kostanay, N Kazakhstan
Rudolf, Lake *see* Turkana, Lake
Rudolfswert *see* Novo mesto
Rudzyensk *107 C6 Rus.* Rudensk. Minskaya Voblasts', C Belarus
Rufiji *73 C7 river* E Tanzania
Rufino *64 C4* Santa Fe, C Argentina
Rugāji *106 D4* E Latvia
Rügen *94 D2 headland* NE Germany
Ruggell *94 E1* N Liechtenstein Europe
Ruhja *see* Rūjiena
Ruhnu *106 C2 var.* Ruhnu Saar, *Swe.* Runö. *island* SW Estonia
Ruhnu Saar *see* Ruhnu
Rujen *see* Rūjiena
Rūjiena *106 D3 Est.* Ruhja, *Ger.* Rujen. N Latvia
Rukwa, Lake *73 B7 lake* SE Tanzania
Rum *see* Rhum
Ruma *100 D3* Vojvodina, N Serbia
Rumadiya *see* Ar Ramādī
Rumania/Rumänien *see* Romania
Rumbek *73 B5* El Buhayrat, C South Sudan
Rum Cay *54 D2 island* C The Bahamas
Rumia *98 C2* Pomorskie, N Poland
Rummah, Wādi ar *see* Rimah, Wādi ar
Rummelsburg in Pommern *see* Miastko
Rumuniya/Rumûniya/Rumunjska *see* Romania
Runanga *151 B5* West Coast, South Island, New Zealand
Rundu *78 C3 var.* Runtu. Okavango, NE Namibia
Runö *see* Ruhnu
Runtu *see* Rundu
Ruoqiang *126 C3 var.* Jo-ch'iang, *Uigh.* Charkhlik, Charkhliq, Qarkilik. Xinjiang Uygur Zizhiqu, NW China
Rupea *108 C4 Ger.* Reps, *Hung.* Kőhalom; *prev.* Cohalm. Braşov, C Romania
Rupel *87 B5 river* N Belgium

Rupella *see* la Rochelle
Rupert, Rivière de *38 D3 river* Québec, C Canada
Rusaddir *see* Melilla
Ruschuk/Rusçuk *see* Ruse
Ruse *104 D1 var.* Ruschuk, Rustchuk, *Turk.* Rusçuk. Ruse, N Bulgaria
Russadir *see* Melilla
Russellville *42 A1* Arkansas, C USA
Russia *112 D2 off.* Russian Federation, *var.* Russia, *Latv.* Krievija, *Rus.* Rossiyskaya Federatsiya. *country* Asia/Europe
Russian America *see* Alaska
Russian Federation *see* Russia
Rustaq *see* Ar Rustāq
Rustavi *117 G2 prev.* Rust'avi. SE Georgia
Rust'avi *see* Rustavi
Rustchuk *see* Ruse
Ruston *42 B2* Louisiana, S USA
Rutanzige, Lake *see* Edward, Lake
Rutba *see* Ar Ruţbah
Rutlam *see* Ratlām
Rutland *41 F2* Vermont, NE USA
Rutog *126 A4 var.* Rutög, Rutok. Xizang Zizhiqu, W China
Rutok *see* Rutog
Ruvuma *69 C5 var.* Rio Rovuma. *river* Mozambique/Tanzania
Ruvuma, Rio *see* Rovuma, Rio
Ruwenzori *77 E5 mountain range* Dem. Rep. Congo/Uganda
Ruzhany *107 B6* Brestskaya Voblasts', SW Belarus
Ružomberok *99 C5 Ger.* Rosenberg, *Hung.* Rózsahegy. Zilinský Kraj, N Slovakia
Rwanda *73 B6 off.* Rwandese Republic; *prev.* Ruanda. *country* C Africa
Rwandese Republic *see* Rwanda
Ryazan' *111 B5* Ryazanskaya Oblast', W Russia
Rybach'ye *see* Balykchy
Rybinsk *110 B4 prev.* Andropov. Yaroslavskaya Oblast', W Russia
Rybnik *99 C5* Śląskie, S Poland
Rybnitsa *see* Rîbniţa
Ryde *148 E1* United Kingdom
Ryki *98 D4* Lubelskie, E Poland
Rykovo *see* Yenakiyeve
Rypin *98 D3* Kujawsko-pomorskie, C Poland
Ryssel *see* Lille
Rysy *99 C5 mountain* S Poland
Ryukyu Islands *see* Nansei-shotō
Ryukyu Trench *125 F3 var.* Nansei Shotō Trench. *trench* S East China Sea
Rzeszów *99 E5* Podkarpackie, SE Poland
Rzhev *110 B4* Tverskaya Oblast', W Russia

S

Saale *94 C4 river* C Germany
Saalfeld *95 C5 var.* Saalfeld an der Saale. Thüringen, C Germany
Saalfeld an der Saale *see* Saalfeld
Saarbrücken *95 A6 Fr.* Sarrebruck. Saarland, SW Germany
Sääre *106 C2 var.* Sjar. Saaremaa, W Estonia
Saare *see* Saaremaa
Saaremaa *106 C2 Ger.* Oesel, Ösel; *prev.* Saare. *island* W Estonia
Saariselkä *84 D2 Lapp.* Suoločielgi. Lappi, N Finland
Sab' Ābār *118 C4 var.* Sab'a Biyar, Sa'b Bi'ār. Ḥimş, C Syria
Sab'a Biyar *see* Sab' Ābār
Šabac *100 D3* Serbia, W Serbia
Sabadell *93 G2* Cataluña, E Spain
Sabah *138 D3 prev.* British North Borneo, North Borneo. *state* East Malaysia
Sabanalarga *58 B1* Atlántico, N Colombia
Sabaneta *58 C1* Falcón, N Venezuela
Sabaria *see* Szombathely
Sab'atayn, Ramlat as *121 C6 desert* C Yemen
Sabaya *61 F4* Oruro, S Bolivia
Sa'b Bi'ār *see* Sab' Ābār
Saberi, Hamun-e *122 C5 var.* Daryācheh-ye Hāmūn, Daryācheh-ye Sīstān. *lake* Afghanistan/Iran
Sabḥā *71 F3* C Libya
Sabi *see* Save

Sabinas *51 E2* Coahuila, NE Mexico
Sabinas Hidalgo *51 E2* Nuevo León, NE Mexico
Sabine River *49 H3 river* Louisiana/Texas, SW USA
Sabkha *see* As Sabkhah
Sable, Cape *43 E5 headland* Florida, SE USA
Sable Island *39 G4 island* Nova Scotia, SE Canada
Şabyā *121 B6* Jīzān, SW Saudi Arabia
Sabzawar *see* Sabzevār
Sabzevār *120 D2 var.* Sabzawar. Khorāsān-Razavī, NE Iran
Sachsen *94 D4 Eng.* Saxony, *Fr.* Saxe. *state* E Germany
Sachs Harbour *37 E2 var.* Ikaahuk. Banks Island, Northwest Territories, N Canada
Sächsisch-Reen/Sächsisch-Regen *see* Reghin
Sacramento *47 B5 state capital* California, W USA
Sacramento Mountains *48 D2 mountain range* New Mexico, SW USA
Sacramento River *47 B5 river* California, W USA
Sacramento Valley *47 B5 valley* California, W USA
Sá da Bandeira *see* Lubango
Şa'dah *121 B6* NW Yemen
Sado *see* Sadoga-shima
Sadoga-shima *131 C5 var.* Sado. *island* C Japan
Saena Julia *see* Siena
Safad *see* Tsefat
Şafāqis *see* Sfax
Şafāshahr *120 D3 var.* Deh Bīd. Fārs, C Iran
Safed *see* Tsefat
Säffle *85 B6* Värmland, C Sweden
Safford *48 C3* Arizona, SW USA
Safi *70 B2* W Morocco
Sagaing *136 B3* Sagaing, C Myanmar (Burma)
Sagami-nada *131 D6 inlet* SW Japan
Sagan *see* Żagań
Sāgar *134 D4 prev.* Saugor. Madhya Pradesh, C India
Sagarmāthā *see* Everest, Mount
Sagebrush State *see* Nevada
Saghez *see* Saqqez
Saginaw *40 C3* Michigan, N USA
Saginaw Bay *40 C2 lake bay* Michigan, N USA
Sagua la Grande *54 B2* Villa Clara, C Cuba
Sagunto *93 F3 Cat.* Sagunt, *Ar.* Murviedro; *anc.* Saguntum. Valenciana, E Spain
Sagunt/Saguntum *see* Sagunto
Sahara *68 B3 desert* Libya/Algeria
Şaharā al Gharbīya *72 B2 Eng.* Western Desert, *desert* Egypt
Şahrā' ash Sharqīyah *103 H5 Eng.* Arabian Desert, Eastern Desert. *desert* E Egypt
Saharan Atlas *70 D2 var.* Saharan Atlas. *mountain range* Algeria/Morocco
Saharan Atlas *see* Atlas Saharien
Sahel *74 D3 physical region* C Africa
Sāḥilīyah, Jibāl as *118 B3 mountain range* NW Syria
Sahiwal *134 C2 prev.* Montgomery. Punjab, E Pakistan
Saïda *119 A5 var.* Şaydā, Sayida; *anc.* Sidon. W Lebanon
Saidpur *135 G3 var.* Syedpur. Rajshahi, NW Bangladesh
Saidu *134 C1 var.* Mingora, Mingaori; *prev.* Mingåora. Khyber Pakhtunkhwa, N Pakistan
Saigon *see* Hồ Chi Minh
Saimaa *85 E5 lake* SE Finland
St Albans *89 E6 anc.* Verulamium. E England, United Kingdom
Saint Albans *40 D5* West Virginia, NE USA
St Andrews *88 C4* E Scotland, United Kingdom
Saint Anna Trough *see* Svyataya Anna Trough
St. Ann's Bay *54 B4* C Jamaica
St. Anthony *39 G3* Newfoundland and Labrador, SE Canada
Saint Augustine *43 E3* Florida, SE USA
St Austell *89 C7* SW England, United Kingdom
St.Botolph's Town *see* Boston

St-Brieuc *90 A3* Côtes d'Armor, NW France
St. Catharines *38 D5* Ontario, S Canada
St-Chamond *91 D5* Loire, E France
Saint Christopher and Nevis, Federation of *see* Saint Kitts and Nevis
Saint Christopher-Nevis *see* Saint Kitts and Nevis
St Clair, Lake *40 D3* var. Lac à L'Eau Claire. *lake* Canada/USA
St-Claude *91 D5* anc. Condate. Jura, E France
Saint Cloud *45 F2* Minnesota, N USA
Saint Croix *55 F3* island S Virgin Islands (US)
Saint Croix River *40 A2* river Minnesota/Wisconsin, N USA
St David's Island *42 B5* island E Bermuda
St-Denis *79 G4* dependent territory capital (Réunion) NW Réunion
St-Dié *90 E4* Vosges, NE France
St-Egrève *91 D5* Isère, E France
Sainte Marie, Cap *see* Vohimena, Tanjona
Saintes *91 B5* anc. Mediolanum. Charente-Maritime, W France
St-Étienne *91 D5* Loire, E France
St-Flour *91 C5* Cantal, C France
St-Gall/Saint Gall/St. Gallen *see* Sankt Gallen
St-Gaudens *91 B6* Haute-Garonne, S France
Saint George *149 D5* Queensland, E Australia
Saint George *42 B4* N Bermuda
Saint George *44 A5* Utah, W USA
St. George's *55 G5* country capital (Grenada) SW Grenada
St-Georges *39 E4* Québec, SE Canada
St-Georges *59 H3* E French Guiana
Saint George's Channel *89 B6* channel Ireland/Wales, United Kingdom
St George's Island *42 B4* E Bermuda
St Helena *see* St Helena, Ascension and Tristan da Cunha
St Helena, Ascension and Tristan da Cunha *69 A6* UK overseas territory C Atlantic Ocean
St Helier *89 D8* British Crown Dependency capital (Jersey) S Jersey, Channel Islands
St.Iago de la Vega *see* Spanish Town
Saint Ignace *40 C2* Michigan, N USA
St-Jean, Lac *39 F4* lake Québec, SE Canada
Saint Joe River *46 D2* river Idaho, NW USA North America
St. John *39 F4* New Brunswick, SE Canada
Saint-John *see* Saint John
Saint John *41 H1* Fr. Saint-John. river Canada/USA
St John's *55 G3* country capital (Antigua and Barbuda) Antigua, Antigua and Barbuda
St. John's *39 H3* province capital Newfoundland and Labrador, E Canada
Saint Joseph *45 F4* Missouri, C USA
St Julian's *see* San Giljan
St Kilda *88 A3* island NW Scotland, United Kingdom
Saint Kitts and Nevis *55 F3* off. Federation of Saint Christopher and Nevis, var. Saint Christopher-Nevis. country E West Indies
St-Laurent *see* St-Laurent-du-Maroni
St-Laurent-du-Maroni *59 H3* var. St-Laurent. NW French Guiana
St-Laurent, Fleuve *see* St. Lawrence
St. Lawrence *39 E4* Fr. Fleuve St-Laurent. river Canada/USA
St. Lawrence, Gulf of *39 F3* gulf NW Atlantic Ocean
Saint Lawrence Island *36 B2* island Alaska, USA
St-Lô *90 B3* anc. Briovera, Laudus. Manche, N France
Saint-Louis *90 E4* Haut-Rhin, NE France
Saint Louis *74 B3* NW Senegal
Saint Louis *45 G4* Missouri, C USA
Saint Lucia *55 E1* country SE West Indies
Saint Lucia Channel *55 H4* channel Martinique/Saint Lucia
St-Malo *90 B3* Ille-et-Vilaine, NW France
St-Malo, Golfe de *90 A3* gulf NW France
Saint Martin *see* Sint Maarten
St.Matthew's Island *see* Zadetkyi Kyun

St.Matthias Group *144 B3* island group NE Papua New Guinea
St. Moritz *95 B7* Ger. Sankt Moritz, Rmsch. San Murezzan. Graubünden, SE Switzerland
St-Nazaire *90 A4* Loire-Atlantique, NW France
Saint Nicholas *see* São Nicolau
Saint-Nicolas *see* Sint-Niklaas
St-Omer *90 C2* Pas-de-Calais, N France
Saint Paul *45 F2* state capital Minnesota, N USA
St-Paul, Île *141 C6* var. St.Paul Island. island Île St-Paul, NE French Southern and Antarctic Lands, Antarctica, Indian Ocean
St.Paul Island *see* St-Paul, Île
St Peter Port *89 D8* British Crown Dependency capital (Guernsey) C Guernsey, Channel Islands
Saint Petersburg *43 E4* Florida, SE USA
Saint Petersburg *see* Sankt-Peterburg
St-Pierre and Miquelon *39 G4* Fr. Îles St-Pierre et Miquelon. French overseas collectivity NE North America
St-Quentin *90 C3* Aisne, N France
Saint Thomas *see* São Tomé, Sao Tome and Príncipe
Saint Thomas *see* Charlotte Amalie, Virgin Islands (US)
Saint Ubes *see* Setúbal
Saint Vincent *55 G4* island N Saint Vincent and the Grenadines
Saint Vincent *see* São Vicente
Saint Vincent and the Grenadines *55 H4* country SE West Indies
Saint Vincent, Cape *see* São Vicente, Cabo de
Saint Vincent Passage *55 H4* passage Saint Lucia/Saint Vincent and the Grenadines
Saint Yves *see* Setúbal
Saipan *142 B1* island/country capital (Northern Mariana Islands) S Northern Mariana Islands
Saishū tō *see* Jeju-do
Sajama, Nevado *61 F4* mountain W Bolivia
Sajószentpéter *99 D6* Borsod-Abaúj-Zemplén, NE Hungary
Sakākah *120 B4* Al Jawf, NW Saudi Arabia
Sakakawea, Lake *44 D1* reservoir North Dakota, N USA
Sakata *130 D4* Yamagata, Honshū, C Japan
Sakhalin *115 G4* var. Sakhalin. island SE Russia
Sakhalin *see* Sakhalin, Ostrov
Sakhon Nakhon *see* Sakon Nakhon
Şaki *117 G2* Rus. Sheki; prev. Nukha. NW Azerbaijan
Saki *see* Saky
Sakishima-shoto *130 A3* var. Sakisima Syotō. island group SW Japan
Sakisima Syotō *see* Sakishima-shotō
Sakiz *see* Saqqez
Sakiz-Adasi *see* Chíos
Sakon Nakhon *136 D4* var. Muang Sakon Nakhon, Sakhon Nakhon. NE Thailand
Saky *109 F5* Rus. Saki. Avtonomna Respublika Krym, S Ukraine
Sal *74 A3* island Ilhas de Barlavento, NE Cape Verde
Sala *85 C6* Västmanland, C Sweden
Salacgrīva *106 C3* Est. Salatsi. N Latvia
Sala Consilina *97 D5* Campania, S Italy
Salado, Río *60 D3* river E Argentina
Salado, Río *64 C3* river C Argentina
Şalālah *121 D6* SW Oman
Salamá *52 B2* Baja Verapaz, C Guatemala
Salamanca *64 B4* Coquimbo, C Chile
Salamanca *92 D2* anc. Helmantica, Salmantica. Castilla y León, NW Spain
Salamīyah *118 B3* var. As Salamiyah. Ḥamāh, W Syria
Salang *see* Phuket
Salantai *106 B3* Klaipėda, NW Lithuania
Salatsi *see* Salacgrīva
Salavan *137 D5* var. Saravan, Saravane. Salavan, S Laos
Salavat *111 D6* Respublika Bashkortostan, W Russia
Sala y Gomez *153 F4* island Chile, E Pacific Ocean

Sala y Gomez Fracture Zone *see* Sala y Gomez Ridge
Sala y Gomez Ridge *153 G4* var. Sala y Gomez Fracture Zone. fracture zone SE Pacific Ocean
Salazar *see* N'Dalatando
Šalčininkai *107 C5* Vilnius, SE Lithuania
Salduba *see* Zaragoza
Saldus *106 B3* Ger. Frauenburg. W Latvia
Sale *149 C7* Victoria, SE Australia
Salé *70 C2* NW Morocco
Salekhard *114 D3* prev. Obdorsk. Yamalo-Nenetskiy Avtonomnyy Okrug, N Russia
Salem *132 C2* Tamil Nādu, SE India
Salem *46 B3* state capital Oregon, NW USA
Salerno *97 D5* anc. Salernum. Campania, S Italy
Salerno, Gulf of *97 C5* Eng. Gulf of Salerno. gulf S Italy
Salerno, Gulf of *see* Salerno, Golfo di
Salernum *see* Salerno
Salihorsk *107 C7* Rus. Soligorsk. Minskaya Voblasts', S Belarus
Salima *79 E2* Central, C Malawi
Salina *45 E5* Kansas, C USA
Salina Cruz *51 F5* Oaxaca, SE Mexico
Salinas *60 A2* Guayas, W Ecuador
Salinas *47 B6* California, W USA
Salisbury *89 D7* var. New Sarum. S England, United Kingdom
Salisbury *see* Harare
Sállan *see* Sørøya
Salliq *see* Coral Harbour
Sallyana *see* Şalyān
Salmantica *see* Salamanca
Salmon River *46 D3* river Idaho, NW USA
Salmon River Mountains *46 D3* mountain range Idaho, NW USA
Salo *85 D6* Länsi-Suomi, SW Finland
Salon-de-Provence *91 D6* Bouches-du-Rhône, SE France
Salonica/Salonika *see* Thessaloníki
Salonta *108 A3* Hung. Nagyszalonta. Bihor, W Romania
Sal'sk *111 B7* Rostovskaya Oblast', SW Russia
Salt *see* As Salt
Salta *64 C2* Salta, NW Argentina
Saltash *89 C7* SW England, United Kingdom
Saltillo *51 E3* Coahuila, NE Mexico
Salt Lake City *44 B4* state capital Utah, W USA
Salto *64 D4* Salto, N Uruguay
Salton Sea *47 D8* lake California, W USA
Salvador *63 G3* prev. São Salvador. state capital Bahia, E Brazil
Salween *124 C2* Bur. Thanlwin, Chin. Nu Chiang, Nu Jiang. river SE Asia
Salzburg *95 D6* anc. Juvavum. Salzburg, N Austria
Salzgitter *94 C4* prev. Watenstedt-Salzgitter. Niedersachsen, C Germany
Salzwedel *94 C3* Sachsen-Anhalt, N Germany
Samac *see* Bosanski Šamac
Samakhixai *see* Attapu
Samalayuca *50 C1* Chihuahua, N Mexico
Samales *139 F2* island C Philippines
Samar *114 B3* prev. Kuybyshev. Samarskaya Oblast', W Russia
Samarang *see* Semarang
Samarinda *138 D4* Borneo, C Indonesia
Samarkand *see* Samarqand
Samarkandski/Samarkandskoye *see* Temirtau
Samarobriva *see* Amiens
Samarqand *123 E2* Rus. Samarkand. Samarqand Viloyati, C Uzbekistan
Samawa *see* As Samāwah
Samawah *117 H2* E Azerbaijan
Sambalpur *135 F4* Odisha, E India
Sambava *79 G2* Antsiranana, NE Madagascar
Sambir *108 B2* Rus. Sambor. L'vivs'ka Oblast', NW Ukraine
Sambor *see* Sambir
Sambre *79 E2* river Belgium/France
Samfya *78 D2* Luapula, N Zambia
Saminatal *94 E2* valley Austria/Liechtenstein Europe
Samnān *see* Semnān
Sam Neua *see* Xam Nua

Samoa *145 E4* off. Independent State of Samoa, var. Sāmoa; prev. Western Samoa. country W Polynesia
Sāmoa *see* Samoa
Samoa Basin *143 E3* undersea basin W Pacific Ocean
Samoa, Independent State of *see* Samoa
Samobor *100 A2* Zagreb, N Croatia
Sámos *105 E6* prev. Limín Vathéos. Sámos, Dodekánisa, Greece, Aegean Sea
Sámos *105 D6* island Dodekánisa, Greece, Aegean Sea
Samothrace *see* Samothráki
Samothráki *104 D4* var. Samothráki, NE Greece
Samothraki *104 C4* anc. Samothrace. island NE Greece
Sampit *138 C4* Borneo, C Indonesia
Sâmraông *137 D5* prev. Phumĭ Sâmraông, Phum Samrong. Siĕmréab, NW Cambodia
Samsun *116 D2* anc. Amisus. Samsun, N Turkey
Samt'redia *117 F2* prev. Samtredia. W Georgia
Samtredia *see* Samt'redia
Samui, Ko *137 C6* island SW Thailand
Samut Prakan *137 C5* var. Muang Samut Prakan, Paknam. Samut Prakan, C Thailand
San *74 D3* Ségou, C Mali
San *99 E5* river SE Poland
Şan'a' *121 B6* Eng. Sanaa. country capital (Yemen) W Yemen
Sana *100 B3* river NW Bosnia and Herzegovina
Sanaa *see* Şan'a'
Sanae *154 B2* South African research station Antarctica
Sanaga *77 B5* river C Cameroon
San Ambrosio, Isla *57 A5* Eng. San Ambrosio Island. island W Chile
San Ambrosio Island *see* San Ambrosio, Isla
Sanandaj *120 C3* prev. Sinneh. Kordestān, W Iran
San Andrés, Isla de *53 F3* island NW Colombia, Caribbean Sea
San Andrés Tuxtla *51 F4* var. Tuxtla. Veracruz-Llave, E Mexico
San Angelo *49 F3* Texas, SW USA
San Antonio *52 B2* Toledo, S Belize
San Antonio *64 B4* Valparaíso, C Chile
San Antonio *49 F4* Texas, SW USA
San Antonio Oeste *65 C5* Río Negro, E Argentina
San Antonio River *49 G4* river Texas, SW USA
Sanata Uxía de Ribeira *92 B1* var. Ribeira. Galicia, NW Spain
Sanāw *121 C6* var. Sanaw. NE Yemen
San Benedicto, Isla *50 B4* island W Mexico
San Benito *52 B1* Petén, N Guatemala
San Benito *49 G5* Texas, SW USA
San Bernardino *47 C7* California, W USA
San Blas *50 C3* Sinaloa, C Mexico
San Blas, Cape *42 D3* headland Florida, SE USA
San Blas, Cordillera de *53 G4* mountain range NE Panama
San Carlos *52 D4* Río San Juan, S Nicaragua
San Carlos *48 B2* Arizona, SW USA
San Carlos *see* Quesada, Costa Rica
San Carlos de Ancud *see* Ancud
San Carlos de Bariloche *65 B5* Río Negro, SW Argentina
San Carlos del Zulia *58 C2* Zulia, W Venezuela
San Clemente Island *47 B8* island California, USA
San Cristóbal *58 C2* Táchira, W Venezuela
San Cristóbal *144 C4* var. Makira. island SE Solomon Islands
San Cristóbal *see* San Cristóbal de Las Casas
San Cristóbal de Las Casas *51 G5* var. San Cristóbal. Chiapas, SE Mexico
San Cristóbal, Isla *60 B5* var. Chatham Island. island Galápagos Islands, Ecuador, E Pacific Ocean
Sancti Spíritus *54 B2* Sancti Spíritus, C Cuba
Sandakan *138 D3* Sabah, East Malaysia
Sandaland Island *see* Sumba, Pulau
Sandanski *104 C3* prev. Sveti Vrach. Blagoevgrad, SW Bulgaria

Sanday *88 D2 island* NE Scotland, United Kingdom
Sanders *48 C2* Arizona, SW USA
Sand Hills *44 D3 mountain range* Nebraska, C USA
San Diego *47 C8* California, W USA
Sandnes *85 A6* Rogaland, S Norway
Sandomierz *98 D4 Rus.* Sandomir. Świętokrzyskie, C Poland
Sandomir *see* Sandomierz
Sandoway *see* Thandwe
Sandpoint *46 C1* Idaho, NW USA
Sand Springs *49 G1* Oklahoma, C USA
Sandusky *40 D3* Ohio, N USA
Sandvika *85 A6* Akershus, S Norway
Sandviken *85 C6* Gävleborg, C Sweden
Sandwich Island *see* Efate
Sandwich Islands *see* Hawaiian Islands
Sandy Bay *93 H5* Saskatchewan, C Canada
Sandy City *44 B4* Utah, W USA
Sandy Lake *38 B3 lake* Ontario, C Canada
San Esteban *52 D2* Olancho, C Honduras
San Eugenio/San Eugenio del Cuareim *see* Artigas
San Felipe *58 D1* Yaracuy, NW Venezuela
San Felipe de Puerto Plata *see* Puerto Plata
San Félix, Isla *57 A5 Eng.* San Felix Island. *island* W Chile
San Felix Island *see* San Félix, Isla
San Fernando *92 C5 prev.* Isla de León. Andalucía, S Spain
San Fernando *55 H5* Trinidad, Trinidad and Tobago
San Fernando *46 D1* California, W USA
San Fernando *58 D2 var.* San Fernando de Apure. Apure, C Venezuela
San Fernando de Apure *see* San Fernando
San Fernando del Valle de Catamarca *64 C3 var.* Catamarca. Catamarca, NW Argentina
San Fernando de Monte Cristi *see* Monte Cristi
San Francisco *47 B6* California, W USA
San Francisco del Oro *50 C2* Chihuahua, N Mexico
San Francisco de Macorís *55 E3* C Dominican Republic
San Fructuoso *see* Tacuarembó
San Gabriel *60 A1* Carchi, N Ecuador
San Gabriel Mountains *46 E1 mountain range* California, USA
Sangihe, Kepulauan *see* Sangir, Kepulauan
San Giljan *102 B5 var.* St Julian's. N Malta
Sangir, Kepulauan *139 F3 var.* Kepulauan Sangihe. *island group* N Indonesia
Sāngli *132 B1* Mahārāshtra, W India
Sangmélima *77 B5* Sud, S Cameroon
Sangre de Cristo Mountains *48 D1 mountain range* Colorado/New Mexico, C USA
San Ignacio *52 B1 prev.* Cayo, El Cayo. Cayo, W Belize
San Ignacio *61 F3* El Beni, N Bolivia
San Ignacio *50 B2* Baja California Sur, NW Mexico
San Joaquin Valley *47 B7 valley* California, W USA
San Jorge, Gulf of *65 C6 var.* Gulf of San Jorge. *gulf* S Argentina
San Jorge, Gulf of *see* San Jorge, Golfo
San José *53 E4 country capital* (Costa Rica) San José, C Costa Rica
San José *61 G3 var.* San José de Chiquitos. Santa Cruz, E Bolivia
San José *52 B3 var.* Puerto San José. Escuintla, S Guatemala
San Jose *47 B6* California, W USA
San José *see* San José del Guaviare, Colombia
San José de Chiquitos *see* San José
San José de Cúcuta *see* Cúcuta
San José del Guaviare *58 C4 var.* San José. Guaviare, S Colombia
San Juan *64 B4* San Juan, W Argentina
San Juan *55 F3 dependent territory capital* (Puerto Rico) NE Puerto Rico
San Juan *see* San Juan de los Morros
San Juan Bautista *64 D3* Misiones, S Paraguay
San Juan Bautista *see* Villahermosa
San Juan Bautista Tuxtepec *see* Tuxtepec

San Juan de Alicante *see* Sant Joan d'Alacant
San Juan del Norte *53 E4 var.* Greytown. Río San Juan, SE Nicaragua
San Juan de los Morros *58 D2 var.* San Juan. Guárico, N Venezuela
Juanito, Isla *50 C4 island* C Mexico
San Juan Mountains *48 D1 mountain range* Colorado, C USA
San Juan, Río *53 E4 river* Costa Rica/Nicaragua
San Juan River *48 C1 river* Colorado/Utah, W USA
San Julián *see* Puerto San Julián
Sankt-Bartholomäi *see* Palamuse
Sankt Gallen *95 B7 var.* St. Gallen, *Eng.* Saint Gall, *Fr.* St-Gall. Sankt Gallen, NE Switzerland
Sankt-Georgen *see* Sfântu Gheorghe
Sankt-Jakobi *see* Pärnu-Jaagupi, Pärnumaa, Estonia
Sankt Martin *see* Martin
Sankt Moritz *see* St. Moritz
Sankt-Peterburg *110 B4 prev.* Leningrad, Petrograd, *Eng.* Saint Petersburg, *Fin.* Pietari. Leningradskaya Oblast', NW Russia
Sankt Pölten *95 E6* Niederösterreich, N Austria
Sankt Veit am Flaum *see* Rijeka
Sankuru *77 D6 river* C Dem. Rep. Congo
Şanlıurfa *117 E4 prev.* Sanli Urfa, Urfa; *anc.* Edessa. şanlıurfa, S Turkey
Sanli Urfa *see* Şanlıurfa
San Lorenzo *61 G5* Tarija, S Bolivia
San Lorenzo *60 A1* Esmeraldas, N Ecuador
San Lorenzo, Isla *60 C4 island* W Peru
Sanlúcar de Barrameda *92 C5* Andalucía, S Spain
San Luis *64 C4* San Luis, C Argentina
San Luis *52 B2* Petén, NE Guatemala
San Luis *see* San Luis Río Colorado
San Luis Obispo *47 B7* California, W USA
San Luis Potosí *51 E3* San Luis Potosí, C Mexico
San Luis Río Colorado *50 A1 var.* San Luis Río Colorado. Sonora, NW Mexico
San Luis Río Colorado *see* San Luis Río Colorado
San Marcos *52 A2* San Marcos, W Guatemala
San Marcos *49 G4* Texas, SW USA
San Marcos de Arica *see* Arica
San Marino *96 E1 country capital* (San Marino) C San Marino
San Marino *96 D1 off.* Republic of San Marino. *country* S Europe
San Marino, Republic of *see* San Marino
San Martín *154 A2 Argentinian research station* Antarctica
San Mateo *59 E2* Anzoátegui, NE Venezuela
San Matías *61 H3* Santa Cruz, E Bolivia
San Matías, Gulf of *65 C5 var.* Gulf of San Matías. *gulf* E Argentina
San Matías, Gulf of *see* San Matías, Golfo
Sanmenxia *128 C4 var.* Shan Xian. Henan, C China
Sânmiclăuş Mare *see* Sânnicolau Mare
San Miguel *52 C3* San Miguel, SE El Salvador
San Miguel *50 D2* Coahuila, N Mexico
San Miguel de Ibarra *see* Ibarra
San Miguel de Tucumán *64 C3 var.* Tucumán. Tucumán, N Argentina
San Miguelito *53 G4* Panamá, C Panama
San Miguel, Río *61 G3 river* E Bolivia
San Murezzan *see* St. Moritz
Sannär *see* Sennar
Sânnicolaul-Mare *see* Sânnicolau Mare
Sânnicolau Mare *108 A4 var.* Sânnicolaul-Mare, *Hung.* Nagyszentmiklós; *prev.* Sânmiclăuş Mare, Sinnicolau Mare. Timiş, W Romania
Sanok *99 E5* Podkarpackie, SE Poland
San Pablo *61 F5* Potosí, S Bolivia
San-Pédro *74 D5* S Ivory Coast
San Pedro *50 D3 var.* San Pedro de las Colonias. Coahuila, NE Mexico
San Pedro de la Cueva *50 C2* Sonora, NW Mexico
San Pedro de las Colonias *see* San Pedro
San Pedro de Lloc *60 B3* La Libertad, NW Peru

San Pedro Mártir, Sierra *50 A1 mountain range* NW Mexico
San Pedro Sula *52 C2* Cortés, NW Honduras
San Rafael *64 B4* Mendoza, W Argentina
San Rafael Mountains *47 C7 mountain range* California, W USA
San Ramón de la Nueva Orán *64 C2* Salta, N Argentina
San Remo *96 A3* Liguria, NW Italy
San Salvador *52 B3 country capital* (El Salvador) San Salvador, SW El Salvador
San Salvador *54 D2 prev.* Watlings Island. *island* E The Bahamas
San Salvador de Jujuy *64 C2 var.* Jujuy. Jujuy, N Argentina
San Salvador, Isla *60 A4 island* Ecuador
Sansanné-Mango *75 E4 var.* Mango. N Togo
San Sebastián *93 E1* País Vasco, N Spain *see also* Donostia
Sansepolcro *96 C3* Toscana, C Italy
San Severo *97 D5* Puglia, SE Italy
Santa Ana *61 F3* El Beni, N Bolivia
Santa Ana *52 B3* Santa Ana, NW El Salvador
Santa Ana *46 D2* California, W USA
Santa Ana de Coro *see* Coro
Santa Ana Mountains *46 E2 mountain range* California, W USA
Santa Barbara *50 C2* Chihuahua, N Mexico
Santa Barbara *47 C7* California, W USA
Santa Catalina de Armada *92 B1 var.* Santa Comba. Galicia, NW Spain
Santa Catalina Island *47 B8 island* Channel Islands, California, W USA
Santa Catarina *63 E5 off.* Estado de Santa Catarina. *state/region* S Brazil
Santa Catarina, Estado de *see* Santa Catarina
Santa Clara *54 B2* Villa Clara, C Cuba
Santa Clarita *46 D1* California, USA
Santa Comba *see* Santa Catalina de Armada
Santa Cruz *76 E2* São Tomé, S Sao Tome and Principe, Africa
Santa Cruz *47 B6* California, W USA
Santa Cruz *61 G4 department* E Bolivia
Santa Cruz Barillas *see* Barillas
Santa Cruz del Quiché *52 B2* Quiché, W Guatemala
Santa Cruz de Tenerife *70 A3* Tenerife, Islas Canarias, Spain, NE Atlantic Ocean
Santa Cruz, Isla *60 B1 var.* Indefatigable Island, Isla Chávez. *island* Galápagos Islands, Ecuador, E Pacific Ocean
Santa Cruz Islands *144 D3 island group* E Solomon Islands
Santa Cruz, Río *65 B7 river* S Argentina
Santa Elena *52 B1* Cayo, W Belize
Santa Fe *64 C4* Santa Fe, C Argentina
Santa Fe *48 D1 state capital* New Mexico, SW USA
Santa Fe *see* Bogotá
Santa Fe de Bogotá *see* Bogotá
Santa Genoveva *50 B3 mountain* NW Mexico
Santa Isabel *144 C3 var.* Bughotu. *island* N Solomon Islands
Santa Isabel *see* Malabo
Santa Lucia Range *47 B7 mountain range* California, W USA
Santa Margarita, Isla *50 B3 island* NW Mexico
Santa Maria *63 E5* Rio Grande do Sul, S Brazil
Santa Maria *47 B7* California, USA
Santa Maria *92 A5 island* Azores, Portugal, NE Atlantic Ocean
Santa Maria del Buen Aire *see* Buenos Aires
Santa María, Isla *60 A4 var.* Isla Floreana, Charles Island. *island* Galápagos Islands, Ecuador, E Pacific Ocean
Santa Marta *58 B1* Magdalena, N Colombia
Santa Maura *see* Lefkáda
Santa Monica *46 D1* California, W USA
Santana *76 E2* São Tomé, S Sao Tome and Principe, Africa
Santander *92 D1* Cantabria, N Spain
Santarém *63 E2* Pará, N Brazil
Santarém *92 B3 anc.* Scalabis. Santarém, W Portugal
Santa Rosa *64 C4* La Pampa, C Argentina

Santa Rosa *see* Santa Rosa de Copán
Santa Rosa de Copán *52 C2 var.* Santa Rosa. Copán, W Honduras
Santa Rosa Island *47 B8 island* California, W USA
Santa Uxía de Ribeira *92 B1 var.* Ribeira. NW Spain
Sant Carles de la Ràpida *see* Sant Carles de la Ràpita
Sant Carles de la Ràpita *93 F3 var.* Sant Carles de la Rápida. Cataluña, NE Spain
Santiago *64 B4 var.* Gran Santiago. *country capital* (Chile) Santiago, C Chile
Santiago *55 E3 var.* Santiago de los Caballeros. N Dominican Republic
Santiago *53 F5* Veraguas, S Panama
Santiago *74 A3 var.* São Tiago. *island* Ilhas de Sotavento, S Cape Verde
Santiago *see* Santiago de Compostela
Santiago *see* Santiago de Cuba, Cuba
Santiago de Compostela *92 B1 var.* Santiago; *Eng.* Compostella; *anc.* Campus Stellae. Galicia, NW Spain
Santiago de Cuba *54 C3 var.* Santiago. Santiago de Cuba, E Cuba
Santiago de Guayaquil *see* Guayaquil
Santiago del Estero *64 C3* Santiago del Estero, C Argentina
Santiago de los Caballeros *see* Santiago, Dominican Republic
Santiago de los Caballeros *see* Ciudad de Guatemala, Guatemala
Santiago Pinotepa Nacional *see* Pinotepa Nacional
Santiago, Río *60 B2 river* N Peru
Santi Quaranta *see* Sarandë
Santíssima Trinidad *see* Keeling
Sant Joan d'Alacant *93 F4 Cast.* San Juan de Alicante. País Valenciana, E Spain
Sant Julià de Lòria *91 A8 var.* Sant Julià de Lòria, SW Andorra Europe
Santo *see* Espíritu Santo
Santo Antão *74 A2 island* Ilhas de Barlavento, N Cape Verde
Santo António *76 E1* Príncipe, N Sao Tome and Principe, Africa
Santo Domingo *55 D3 prev.* Ciudad Trujillo. *country capital* (Dominican Republic) SE Dominican Republic
Santo Domingo de los Colorados *60 B1* Pichincha, NW Ecuador
Santo Domingo Tehuantepec *see* Tehuantepec
Santoríni *see* Thíra
Santoríni *105 D7 var.* Thíra. *island* Kykládes, Greece, Aegean Sea
San Tomé de Guayana *see* Ciudad Guayana
Santos *63 F4* São Paulo, S Brazil
Santos Plateau *57 D5 undersea plateau* SW Atlantic Ocean
Santo Tomé *64 D3* Corrientes, NE Argentina
Santo Tomé de Guayana *see* Ciudad Guayana
San Valentín, Cerro *65 A6 mountain* S Chile
San Vicente *52 C3* San Vicente, C El Salvador
São Francisco, Rio *63 F3 river* E Brazil
Sao Hill *73 C7* Iringa, S Tanzania
São João da Madeira *92 B2* Aveiro, N Portugal
São Jorge *92 A5 island* Azores, Portugal, NE Atlantic Ocean
São Luís *63 F2 state capital* Maranhão, NE Brazil
São Mandol *see* São Manuel, Rio
São Manuel, Rio *63 E3 var.* São Mandol, Teles Pirés. *river* C Brazil
São Marcos, Baía de *63 F1 bay* NE Brazil
São Miguel *92 A5 island* Azores, Portugal, NE Atlantic Ocean
Saona, Isla *55 E3 island* SE Dominican Republic
Saône *91 D5 river* E France
São Nicolau *74 A3 Eng.* Saint Nicholas. *island* Ilhas de Barlavento, N Cape Verde
São Paulo *63 E4 state capital* São Paulo, S Brazil
São Paulo *63 E4 off.* Estado de São Paulo. *state/region* S Brazil
São Paulo de Loanda *see* Luanda

São Paulo, Estado de *see* São Paulo
São Pedro do Rio Grande do Sul *see* Rio Grande
São Roque, Cabo de *63 G2 headland* E Brazil
São Salvador *see* Salvador, Brazil
São Salvador/São Salvador do Congo *see* M'Banza Congo, Angola
São Tiago *see* Santiago
São Tomé *77 A5 country capital* (Sao Tome and Principe) São Tomé, S Sao Tome and Principe
São Tomé *76 E2 Eng. Saint Thomas. island* S Sao Tome and Principe
Sao Tome and Principe *76 D1 off.* Democratic Republic of Sao Tome and Principe. *country* E Atlantic Ocean
Sao Tome and Principe, Democratic Republic of *see* Sao Tome and Principe
São Tomé, Pico de *76 D2 mountain* São Tomé, C Sao Tome and Principe, Africa
São Vicente *74 A3 Eng. Saint Vincent. island* Ilhas de Barlavento, N Cape Verde
São Vicente, Cabo de *92 B5 Eng. Cape Saint Vincent, Port. Cabode São Vicente. cape* S Portugal
São Vicente, Cabo de *see* São Vicente, Cabo de
Sápai *see* Sápes
Sapele *75 F5* Delta, S Nigeria
Sápes *104 D3 var.* Sápai. Anatolikí Makedonía kai Thráki, NE Greece
Sapir *119 B7 prev.* Sappir. Southern, S Israel
Sa Pobla *93 G3* Mallorca, Spain, W Mediterranean Sea
Sappir *see* Sapir
Sapporo *130 D2* Hokkaidō, NE Japan
Sapri *97 D6* Campania, S Italy
Sapulpa *49 G1* Oklahoma, C USA
Saqqez *120 C2 var.* Saghez, Sakiz, Saqqiz. Kordestān, NW Iran
Saqqiz *see* Saqqez
Sara Buri *137 C5 var.* Saraburi. Saraburi, C Thailand
Saragossa *see* Zaragoza
Saragt *see* Sarahs
Saraguro *60 B2* Loja, S Ecuador
Sarahs *122 D3 var.* Saragt, *Rus.* Serakhs. Ahal Welaýaty, S Turkmenistan
Sarajevo *100 C4 country capital* (Bosnia and Herzegovina) Federacija Bosne I Hercegovine, SE Bosnia and Herzegovina
Sarakhs *120 E2* Khorāsān-Razavī, E Iran
Saraktash *111 D6* Orenburgskaya Oblast', W Russia
Saran' *114 C4 Kaz.* Saran. Karagandy, C Kazakhstan
Saranda *see* Sarandë
Sarandë *101 C7 var.* Saranda, *It.* Porto Edda; *prev.* Santi Quaranta. Vlorë, S Albania
Saransk *111 C5* Respublika Mordoviya, W Russia
Sarasota *43 E4* Florida, SE USA
Saratov *114 B3* Saratovskaya Oblast', W Russia
Saravan/Saravane *see* Salavan
Sarawak *138 D3 state* East Malaysia
Sarawak *see* Kuching
Sarcelles *90 D1* Val-d'Oise, Île-de-France, N France Europe
Sardinia *97 A5 Eng.* Sardinia. *island* Italy, C Mediterranean Sea
Sardinia *see* Sardegna
Sarera, Teluk *see* Cenderawasih, Teluk
Sargasso Sea *66 B4 sea* W Atlantic Ocean
Sargodha *134 C2* Punjab, NE Pakistan
Sarh *76 C4 prev.* Fort-Archambault. Moyen-Chari, S Chad
Sāri *120 D2 var.* Sari, Sāri. Māzandarān, N Iran
Saría *105 E7 island* SE Greece
Sarıkamış *117 F3* Kars, NE Turkey
Sarikol Range *123 G3 Rus.* Sarykol'skiy Khrebet. *mountain range* China/Tajikistan
Sark *89 D8 Fr.* Sercq. *island* Channel Islands
Şarkışla *116 D3* Sivas, C Turkey
Sarmiento *65 B6* Chubut, S Argentina
Sarnia *38 C5* Ontario, S Canada
Sarny *108 C1* Rivnens'ka Oblast', NW Ukraine
Sarochyna *107 D5 Rus.* Sorochino. Vitsyebskaya Voblasts', N Belarus

Sarov *111 C5 prev.* Sarova. Respublika Mordoviya, SW Russia
Sarova *see* Sarov
Sarpsborg *85 B6* Østfold, S Norway
Sarrebruck *see* Saarbrücken
Sartène *91 E7* Corse, France, C Mediterranean Sea
Sarthe *90 B4 river* N France
Sárti *104 C4* Kentrikí Makedonía, N Greece
Saruhan *see* Manisa
Sarykol'skiy Khrebet *see* Sarikol Range
Sary-Tash *123 F2* Oshskaya Oblast', SW Kyrgyzstan
Saryyesik-Atyrau, Peski *123 G1 desert* E Kazakhstan
Sasebo *131 A7* Nagasaki, Kyūshū, SW Japan
Saskatchewan *37 F5 province* SW Canada
Saskatchewan *37 F5 river* Manitoba/ Saskatchewan, C Canada
Saskatoon *37 F5* Saskatchewan, S Canada
Sasovo *111 B5* Ryazanskaya Oblast', W Russia
Sassandra *74 D5* S Ivory Coast
Sassandra *74 D5 var.* Ibo, Sassandra Fleuve. *river* S Ivory Coast
Sassandra Fleuve *see* Sassandra
Sassari *97 A5* Sardegna, Italy, C Mediterranean Sea
Sassenheim *86 C3* Zuid-Holland, W Netherlands
Sassnitz *94 D2* Mecklenburg-Vorpommern, NE Germany
Sathmar *see* Satu Mare
Sátoraljaújhely *99 D6* Borsod-Abaúj-Zemplén, NE Hungary
Satpura Range *134 D4 mountain range* C India
Satsuma-Sendai *131 A8* Kagoshima, Kyūshū, SW Japan
Satsunan-shoto *130 A3 island group* Nansei-shotō, SW Japan Asia
Sattanen *84 D3* Lappi, NE Finland
Satu Mare *108 B3 Ger.* Sathmar, *Hung.* Szatmárrnémeti. Satu Mare, NW Romania
Sau *see* Sava
Saudi Arabia *121 B5 off.* Kingdom of Saudi Arabia, Al 'Arabīyah as Su'ūdīyah, *Ar.* Al Mamlakah al 'Arabīyah as Su'ūdīyah. *country* SW Asia
Saudi Arabia, Kingdom of *see* Saudi Arabia
Sauer *see* Sûre
Saugor *see* Sagar
Saulkrasti *106 C3* C Latvia
Sault Sainte Marie *38 C4* Michigan, N USA
Sault Sainte Marie *40 C1* Michigan, N USA
Sault Ste. Marie *38 C4* Ontario, S Canada
Saumur *90 B4* Maine-et-Loire, NW France
Saurimo *78 C1 Port.* Henrique de Carvalho, Vila Henrique de Carvalho. Lunda Sul, NE Angola
Sava *107 E6* Mahilyowskaya Voblasts', E Belarus
Savá *52 D2* Colón, N Honduras
Savai'i *145 E4 island* NW Samoa
Savannah *43 E2* Georgia, SE USA
Savannah River *43 E2 river* Georgia/ South Carolina, SE USA
Savannakhét *136 D4 var.* Khanthabouli. Savannakhét, S Laos
Savanna-La-Mar *54 A5* W Jamaica
Savaria *see* Szombathely
Save *100 B3 Eng.* Save, *Ger.* Sau, *Hung.* Száva. *river* SE Europe
Save *see* Sava
Save, Rio *79 E3 var.* Sabi. *river* Mozambique/Zimbabwe
Saverne *90 E3 var.* Zabern; *anc.* Tres Tabernae. Bas-Rhin, NE France
Savigliano *96 A2* Piemonte, NW Italy
Savigsivik *see* Savissivik
Savinski *see* Savinskiy
Savinskiy *110 C3 var.* Savinski. Arkhangel'skaya Oblast', NW Russia
Savissivik *82 D1 var.* Savigsivik. Avannaarsua, N Greenland
Savoie *91 D5 cultural region* E France
Savona *96 A2* Liguria, NW Italy
Savu Sea *139 E5 Ind.* Laut Sawu. *sea* S Indonesia

Sawakin *see* Suakin
Sawdirī *see* Sodiri
Sawhāj *see* Suhāj
Şawqirah *121 D6 var.* Suqrah. S Oman
Sawu, Laut *see* Savu Sea
Saxe *see* Sachsen
Saxony *see* Sachsen
Sayaboury *see* Xaignabouli
Sayanskiy Khrebet *112 D3 mountain range* S Russia
Sa'yat *122 D3 Rus.* Sayat. Lebap Welaýaty, E Turkmenistan
Sayaxché *52 B2* Petén, N Guatemala
Şaydā/Sayida *see* Saïda
Sayhūt *121 D6* E Yemen
Saynshand *127 E2* Dornogovĭ, SE Mongolia
Sayre *41 E3* Pennsylvania, NE USA
Say'ūn *121 C6 var.* Saywūn. C Yemen
Scalabis *see* Santarém
Scandinavia *68 D2 geophysical region* NW Europe
Scarborough *89 D5* N England, United Kingdom
Scarpanto *see* Kárpathos
Scebeli *see* Shebeli
Schaan *94 E1* W Liechtenstein Europe
Schaerbeek *87 C6* Brussels, C Belgium
Schaffhausen *95 B7 Fr.* Schaffhouse. Schaffhausen, N Switzerland
Schaffhouse *see* Schaffhausen
Schagen *86 C2* Noord-Holland, NW Netherlands
Schaulen *see* Šiauliai
Schebschi Mountains *see* Shebshi Mountains
Scheessel *94 B3* Niedersachsen, NW Germany
Schefferville *39 E2* Québec, E Canada
Schelde *see* Scheldt
Scheldt *87 B5 Dut.* Schelde, *Fr.* Escaut. *river* W Europe
Schell Creek Range *47 D5 mountain range* Nevada, W USA
Schenectady *41 F3* New York, NE USA
Schertz *49 G4* Texas, SW USA
Schiermonnikoog *86 D1 Fris.* Skiermûntseach. *island* Waddeneilanden, N Netherlands
Schijndel *86 D4* Noord-Brabant, S Netherlands
Schil *see* Jiu
Schiltigheim *90 E3* Bas-Rhin, NE France
Schivelbein *see* Świdwin
Schleswig *94 B2* Schleswig-Holstein, N Germany
Schleswig-Holstein *94 B2 state* N Germany
Schlettstadt *see* Sélestat
Schlochau *see* Człuchów
Schneekoppe *see* Sněžka
Schneidemühl *see* Piła
Schoden *see* Skuodas
Schönebeck *94 C4* Sachsen-Anhalt, C Germany
Schönlanke *see* Trzcianka
Schooten *see* Schoten
Schoten *87 C5 var.* Schooten. Antwerpen, N Belgium
Schouwen *86 B4 island* SW Netherlands
Schwabenalb *see* Schwäbische Alb
Schwäbische Alb *95 B6 var.* Schwabenalb, *Eng.* Swabian Jura. *mountain range* S Germany
Schwandorf *95 C5* Bayern, SE Germany
Schwaz *95 C7* Tirol, W Austria
Schweidnitz *see* Świdnica
Schweinfurt *95 B5* Bayern, SE Germany
Schweiz *see* Switzerland
Schwerin *94 C3* Mecklenburg-Vorpommern, N Germany
Schwertberg *see* Świecie
Schwiebus *see* Świebodzin
Schwyz *95 B7 var.* Schwiz. Schwyz, C Switzerland
Schyl *see* Jiu
Scio *see* Chíos
Scoresby Sound/Scoresbysund *see* Ittoqqortoormiit
Scoresby Sund *see* Ittoqqortoormiit
Scotia Sea *57 C8 sea* SW Atlantic Ocean
Scotland *88 C3 cultural region* Scotland, U K
Scott Base *154 B4 NZ research station* Antarctica
Scott Island *154 B5 island* Antarctica
Scottsbluff *44 D3* Nebraska, C USA
Scottsboro *42 D1* Alabama, S USA
Scottsdale *48 B2* Arizona, SW USA

Scranton *41 F3* Pennsylvania, NE USA
Scrobesbyrig' *see* Shrewsbury
Scupi *see* Skopje
Scutari *see* Shkodër
Scutari, Lake *101 C5 Alb.* Liqeni i Shkodrës, *SCr.* Skadarsko Jezero. *lake* Albania/Montenegro
Scyros *see* Skýros
Searcy *42 B1* Arkansas, C USA
Seattle *46 B2* Washington, NW USA
Sébaco *52 D3* Matagalpa, W Nicaragua
Sebaste/Sebastia *see* Sivas
Sebastián Vizcaíno, Bahía *50 A2 bay* NW Mexico
Sebastopol *see* Sevastopol'
Sebenico *see* Šibenik
Sechura, Bahía de *60 A3 bay* NW Peru
Secunderābād *134 D5 var.* Sikandarabad. Telangana, C India
Sedan *90 D3* Ardennes, N France
Seddon *151 D5* Marlborough, South Island, New Zealand
Seddonville *151 C5* West Coast, South Island, New Zealand
Sédhiou *74 B3* SW Senegal
Sedlez *see* Siedlce
Sedona *48 B2* Arizona, SW USA
Sedunum *see* Sion
Seeland *see* Sjælland
Seenu Atoll *see* Addu Atoll
Seesen *94 B4* Niedersachsen, C Germany
Segestica *see* Sisak
Segezha *110 B3* Respublika Kareliya, NW Russia
Seghedin *see* Szeged
Segna *see* Senj
Segodunum *see* Rodez
Ségou *74 D3 var.* Segu. Ségou, C Mali
Segovia *92 D2* Castilla y León, C Spain
Segoviao Wangki *see* Coco, Río
Segu *see* Ségou
Séguédine *75 H2* Agadez, NE Niger
Seguin *49 G4* Texas, SW USA
Segura *93 E4 river* S Spain
Seinäjoki *85 D5 Swe.* Östermyra. Etelä-Pohjanmaa, W Finland
Seine *90 B1 river* N France
Seine, Baie de la *90 B3 bay* N France
Sejong City *128 E4 administrative capital* (South Korea) C South Korea
Sekondi *see* Sekondi-Takoradi
Sekondi-Takoradi *75 E5 var.* Sekondi. S Ghana
Selânik *see* Thessaloníki
Selenga *127 E1 Mong.* Selenge Mörön. *river* Mongolia/Russia
Selenge Mörön *see* Selenga
Sélestat *90 E4 Ger.* Schlettstadt. Bas-Rhin, NE France
Seleucia *see* Silifke
Selfoss *83 E5* Suðhurland, SW Iceland
Sélibabi *74 C3 var.* Sélibaby. Guidimaka, S Mauritania
Sélibaby *see* Sélibabi
Selma *47 C6* California, W USA
Selseleh-ye Sefīd Kūh *122 D4 Eng.* Paropamisus Range. *mountain range* W Afghanistan
Selway River *46 D2 river* Idaho, NW USA North America
Selwyn Range *148 B3 mountain range* Queensland, C Australia
Selzaete *see* Zelzate
Semarang *138 C5 var.* Samarang. Jawa, C Indonesia
Sembé *77 B5* Sangha, NW Congo
Semendria *see* Smederevo
Semey *114 D4 prev.* Semipalatinsk. Vostochnyy Kazakhstan, E Kazakhstan
Semichevo *see* Syemyezhava
Seminole *49 E3* Texas, SW USA
Seminole, Lake *42 D3 reservoir* Florida/ Georgia, SE USA
Semipalatinsk *see* Semey
Semnān *120 D3 var.* Samnān. Semnān, N Iran
Semois *87 C8 river* SE Belgium
Sendai *130 D4* Miyagi, Honshū, C Japan
Sendai-wan *130 D4 bay* E Japan
Senec *99 C6 Ger.* Wartberg, *Hung.* Szenc; *prev.* Szempcz. Bratislavský Kraj, W Slovakia
Senegal *74 B3 off.* Republic of Senegal, *Fr.* Sénégal. *country* W Africa
Senegal *72 B4 Fr.* Sénégal. *river* W Africa
Senegal, Republic of *see* Senegal
Senftenberg *94 D4* Brandenburg, E Germany

Senia *see* Senj
Senica 99 C6 Ger. Senitz, Hung. Szenice.
 Trnavský Kraj, W Slovakia
Seniça *see* Sjenica
Senitz *see* Senica
Senj 100 A3 Ger. Zengg, It. Segna; *anc.*
 Senia. Lika-Senj, NW Croatia
Senja 84 C2 *prev.* Senjen. *island*
 N Norway
Senjen *see* Senja
Sejong City 128 E4 *country capital*
 (South Korea) (administrative)
 C South Korea
Senkaku-shoto 130 A3 *island group*
 SW Japan
Senlis 90 C3 Oise, N France
Sennar 72 C4 *var.* Sannâr. Sinnar,
 C Sudan
Senones *see* Sens
Sens 90 C3 *anc.* Agendicum, Senones.
 Yonne, C France
Sensburg *see* Mragowo
Sên, Stœng 137 D5 *river* C Cambodia
Senta 100 D3 Hung. Zenta. Vojvodina,
 N Serbia
Seo de Urgel *see* La Seu d'Urgell
Seoul 129 E4 *off.* Seoul Teukbyeolsi,
 prev. Sôul, Jap. Keijö; *prev.* Kyöngsông.
 country capital (South Korea)
 NW South Korea
Seoul Teukbyeolsi *see* Seoul
Şepşi-Sângeorz/Sepsiszentgyörgy *see*
 Sfântu Gheorghe
Sept-Îles 39 E3 Québec,
 SE Canada
Seraing 87 D6 Liège, E Belgium
Serakhs *see* Sarahs
Seram, Laut 139 F4 Eng. Ceram Sea. *sea*
 E Indonesia
Pulau Seram 139 F4 *var.* Serang,
 Eng. Ceram. *island* Maluku,
 E Indonesia
Serang 138 C5 Jawa, C Indonesia
Serang *see* Seram, Pulau
Serasan, Selat 138 C3 *strait* Indonesia/
 Malaysia
Serbia 100 C4 *off.* Federal Republic of
 Serbia; *prev.* Yugoslavia, *SCr.*
 Jugoslavija. *country* SE Europe
Serbia, Federal Republic of *see* Serbia
Sercq *see* Sark
Serdar 122 C2 *prev.* Rus. Gyzyrlabat,
 Kizyl-Arvat. Balkan Welaýaty,
 W Turkmenistan
Serdica *see* Sofiya
Serdobol' *see* Sortavala
Serenje 78 D2 Central, E Zambia
Seres *see* Sérres
Seret/Sereth *see* Siret
Serhetabat 122 D4 *prev.* Rus. Gushgy,
 Kushka. Mary Welaýaty,
 S Turkmenistan
Sérifos 105 C6 *anc.* Seriphos. *island*
 Kykládes, Greece, Aegean Sea
Seriphos *see* Sérifos
Serov 114 C3 Sverdlovskaya Oblast',
 C Russia
Serowe 78 D3 Central, SE Botswana
Serpa Pinto *see* Menongue
Serpent's Mouth, The 59 F2 *Sp.* Boca de
 la Serpiente. *strait* Trinidad and
 Tobago/Venezuela
Serpiente, Boca de la *see* Serpent's
 Mouth, The
Serpukhov 111 B5 Moskovskaya Oblast',
 W Russia
Sérrai *see* Sérres
Serrana, Cayo de 53 F2 *island group*
 NW Colombia South America
Serranilla, Cayo de 53 F2 *island group*
 NW Colombia South America
 Caribbean Sea
Serravalle 96 E1 N San Marino
Sérres 104 C3 *var.* Seres; *prev.* Sérrai.
 Kentrikí Makedonía, NE Greece
Sesdlets *see* Siedlce
Sesto San Giovanni 96 B2 Lombardia,
 N Italy
Sesvete 100 B2 Zagreb, N Croatia
Setabis *see* Xàtiva
Sète 91 C6 *prev.* Cette. Hérault, S France
Setesdal 85 A6 *valley* S Norway
Sétif 71 E2 *var.* Stif. N Algeria
Setté Cama 77 A6 Ogooué-Maritime,
 SW Gabon
Setúbal 92 B4 Eng. Saint Ubes, Saint
 Yves. Setúbal, W Portugal
Setúbal, Baía de 92 B4 *bay* W Portugal
Seul, Lac 38 B3 *lake* Ontario, S Canada
Sevan 117 G2 C Armenia

Sevan, Lake 117 G3 Eng. Lake Sevan,
 Rus. Ozero Sevan. *lake* E Armenia
Sevan, Lake/Sevan, Ozero
 see Sevana Lich
Sevastopol' 109 F5 Eng. Sebastopol.
 Avtonomna Respublika Krym, Ukraine
Severn 38 B2 *river* Ontario, S Canada
Severn 89 D6 Wel. Hafren. *river*
 England/Wales, United Kingdom
Severnaya Zemlya 115 E2 *var.* Nicholas
 II Land. *island group* N Russia
Severnyy 110 E3 Respublika Komi,
 NW Russia
Severodonetsk *see* Syeverodonets'k
Severodvinsk 110 C3 *prev.* Molotov,
 Sudostroy. Arkhangel'skaya Oblast',
 NW Russia
Severomorsk 110 C2 Murmanskaya
 Oblast', NW Russia
Seversk 114 D4 Tomskaya Oblast',
 C Russia
Sevier Lake 44 A4 *lake* Utah, W USA
Sevilla 92 C4 Eng. Seville; *anc.* Hispalis.
 Andalucía, SW Spain
Seville *see* Sevilla
Sevlievo 104 D2 Gabrovo, N Bulgaria
Sevluš/Sevlyush *see* Vynohradiv
Seward's Folly *see* Alaska
Seychelles 79 G1 *off.* Republic of
 Seychelles. *country* W Indian Ocean
Seychelles, Republic of *see* Seychelles
Seyðisfjörður 83 E5 Austurland,
 E Iceland
Seydi 122 D2 Rus. Seydi; *prev.*
 Neftezavodsk. Lebap Welaýaty,
 E Turkmenistan
Seyhan *see* Adana
Sfákia *see* Chóra Sfakíon
Sfântu Gheorghe 108 C4 Ger.
 Sankt-Georgen, Hung.
 Sepsiszentgyörgy; *prev.* Şepşi-Sângeorz,
 Sfîntu Gheorghe. Covasna, C Romania
Sfax 71 F2 Ar. Şafāqis. E Tunisia
Sfîntu Gheorghe *see* Sfântu Gheorghe
's-Gravenhage 86 B4 *var.* Den Haag,
 Eng. The Hague, Fr. La Haye.
 country capital (Netherlands)
 (seat of government)
 Zuid-Holland, W Netherlands
's-Gravenzande 86 B4 Zuid-Holland,
 W Netherlands
Shaan/Shaanxi Sheng *see* Shaanxi
Shaanxi 128 B5 *var.* Shaan, Shaanxi
 Sheng, Shan-hsi, Shenshi, Shensi.
 province C China
Shabani *see* Zvishavane
Shabeelle, Webi *see* Shebeli
Shache 126 A3 *var.* Yarkant. Xinjiang
 Uygur Zizhiqu, NW China
Shacheng *see* Huailai
Shackleton Ice Shelf 154 D3 *ice shelf*
 Antarctica
Shaddādī *see* Ash Shadādah
Shahābād *see* Eslāmābād-e Gharb
Sha Hi *see* Orūmīyeh, Daryācheh-ye
Shahjahanabad *see* Delhi
Shahr-e Kord 120 C3 *var.* Shahr Kord.
 Chahār MaHāl va Bakhtiārī, C Iran
Shahr Kord *see* Shahr-e Kord
Shāhrūd 120 D2 *prev.* Emāmrūd,
 Emāmshahr. Semnān, N Iran
Shakhar 114 B4 *var.* Chelkar.
 Aktyubinsk, W Kazakhstan
Shām, Bādiyat ash *see* Syrian Desert
Shana *see* Kuril'sk
Shandī *see* Shendi
Shandong 128 C4 *var.* Lu, Shandong
 Sheng, Shantung. *province* E China
Shandong Sheng *see* Shandong
Shanghai 128 D5 *var.* Shang-hai.
 Shanghai Shi, E China
Shangrao 128 D5 Jiangxi, S China
Shan-hsi *see* Shaanxi, China
Shan-hsi *see* Shanxi, China
Shannon 89 A6 Ir. An tSionainn. *river*
 W Ireland
Shan Plateau 136 B3 *plateau* E Myanmar
 (Burma)
Shansi *see* Shanxi
Shantar Islands *see* Shantarskiye Ostrova
Shantarskiye Ostrova 115 G3 Eng.
 Shantar Islands. *island group* E Russia
Shantou 128 D6 *var.* Shan-t'ou, Swatow.
 Guangdong, S China
Shan-t'ou *see* Shantou
Shantung *see* Shandong
Shanxi 128 C4 *var.* Jin, Shan-hsi,
 Shansi, Shanxi Sheng. *province*
 C China
Shan Xian *see* Sanmenxia

Shanxi Sheng *see* Shanxi
Shaoguan 128 C6 *var.* Shao-kuan, Cant.
 Kukong; *prev.* Ch'u-chiang.
 Guangdong, S China
Shao-kuan *see* Shaoguan
Shaqrā' 120 B4 Ar Riyāḍ,
 C Saudi Arabia
Shaqrā *see* Shuqrah
Shar 114 D5 *var.* Charsk. Vostochnyy
 Kazakhstan, E Kazakhstan
Shari 130 D2 Hokkaidō, NE Japan
Shari *see* Chari
Sharjah *see* Ash Shāriqah
Shark Bay 147 A5 *bay*
 Western Australia
Sharqī, Al Jabal ash/Sharqi, Jebel esh
 see Anti-Lebanon
Shashe 78 D3 *var.* Shashi. *river*
 Botswana/Zimbabwe
Shashi *see* Shashe
Shatskiy Rise 125 G1 *undersea rise*
 N Pacific Ocean
Shawnee 49 G1 Oklahoma,
 C USA
Shaykh, Jabal ash *see* Hermon, Mount
Shchadryn 107 D7 Rus. Shchedrin.
 Homyel'skaya Voblasts', SE Belarus
Shchedrin *see* Shchadryn
Shcheglovsk *see* Kemerovo
Shchëkino 111 B5 Tul'skaya Oblast',
 W Russia
Shchors *see* Snovs'k
Shchuchin *see* Shchuchyn
Shchuchinsk 114 C4 *prev.* Shchuchye.
 Akmola, N Kazakhstan
Shchuchye *see* Shchuchinsk
Shchuchyn 107 B5 Pol. Szczuczyn
 Nowogródzki, Rus. Shchuchin.
 Hrodzyenskaya Voblasts', W Belarus
Shebekino 111 A6 Belgorodskaya
 Oblast', W Russia
Shebelē Wenz, Wabē *see* Shebeli
Shebeli 73 D5 Amh. Wabē Shebelē Wenz,
 It. Scebeli, Som. Webi Shabeelle. *river*
 Ethiopia/Somalia
Sheberghān *see* Shiberghān
Sheboygan 40 B2 Wisconsin, N USA
Shebshi Mountains 76 A4 *var.*
 Schebschi Mountains. *mountain range*
 E Nigeria
Shechem *see* Nablus
Shedadi *see* Ash Shadādah
Sheffield 89 D5 N England, United
 Kingdom
Shekhem *see* Nablus
Sheki *see* Şäki
Shelby 44 B1 Montana, NW USA
Sheldon 45 F3 Iowa, C USA
Shelekhov Gulf 115 G2 Eng. Shelekhov
 Gulf. *gulf* E Russia
Shelekhov Gulf *see* Shelikhova, Zaliv
Shendi 72 C4 *var.* Shandī. River Nile,
 NE Sudan
Shengking *see* Liaoning
Shenking *see* Liaoning
Shenshi/Shensi *see* Shaanxi
Shenyang 128 D3 Chin. Shen-yang, Eng.
 Moukden, Mukden; *prev.* Fengtien.
 province capital Liaoning, NE China
Shen-yang *see* Shenyang
Shepetivka 108 D2 Rus. Shepetovka.
 Khmel'nyts'ka Oblast', NW Ukraine
Shepetovka *see* Shepetivka
Shepparton 149 C7 Victoria,
 SE Australia
Sherbrooke 39 E4 Québec, SE Canada
Shereïk 72 C3 River Nile, N Sudan
Sheridan 44 C2 Wyoming, C USA
Sherman 49 G2 Texas, SW USA
's-Hertogenbosch 86 C4 Fr.
 Bois-le-Duc, Ger. Herzogenbusch.
 Noord-Brabant, S Netherlands
Shetland Islands 88 D1 *island group*
 NE Scotland, United Kingdom
Shevchenko *see* Aktau
Shibarghan *see* Shiberghān
Shiberghan/Shiberghān *see* Shibirghān
Shibirghān 123 E3 *var.* Shiberghān,
 Shiberghan, Sheberghān. Jowzjān,
 N Afghanistan
Shibetsu 130 D2 *var.* Sibetu. Hokkaidō,
 NE Japan
Shibh Jazirat Sīnā' *see* Sinai
Shibirghān 123 E3 *var.* Shiberghān,
 Shiberghan, Sheberghān; *prev.*
 Sheberghān, Shibarghān. N Afghanistan
Shigatse *see* Xigazê
Shih-chia-chuang/Shihmen *see*
 Shijiazhuang

Shanxi Sheng *see* Shanxi
Shihezi 126 C2 Xinjiang Uygur Zizhiqu,
 NW China
Shiichi *see* Shyichy
Shijiazhuang 128 C4 *var.*
 Shih-chia-chuang; *prev.* Shihmen.
 province capital Hebei, E China
Shikarpur 134 B3 Sind, S Pakistan
Shikoku 131 C7 *var.* Sikoku. *island*
 SW Japan
Shikoku Basin 125 F2 *var.* Sikoku Basin.
 undersea basin N Philippine Sea
Shikotan, Ostrov 130 E2 Jap.
 Shikotan-tō. *island* NE Russia
Shikotan-tō *see* Shikotan, Ostrov
Shilabo 73 D5 Sumalē, E Ethiopia
Shiliguri 135 F3 *prev.* Siliguri. West
 Bengal, NE India
Shilka 115 F4 *river* S Russia
Shillong 135 G3 *state capital* Meghālaya,
 NE India
Shimanto *see* Nakamura
Shimbir Berris *see* Shimbiris
Shimbiris 72 E4 *var.* Shimbir Berris.
 mountain N Somalia
Shimoga *see* Shivamogga
Shimonoseki 131 A7 *var.* Simonoseki,
 hist. Akamagaseki. Bakan. Yamaguchi,
 Honshū, SW Japan
Shinano-gawa 131 C5 *var.* Sinano Gawa.
 river Honshū, C Japan
Shīndand 122 D4 *prev.* Shīndand. Herāt,
 W Afghanistan
Shīndand *see* Shīndand
Shingū 131 C6 *var.* Singū. Wakayama,
 Honshū, SW Japan
Shinjo 130 D4 *var.* Sinzyō. Yamagata,
 Honshū, C Japan
Shinyanga 73 C7 Shinyanga,
 NW Tanzania
Shiprock 48 C1 New Mexico, SW USA
Shīrāz 120 D4 *var.* Shīrāz. Fārs, S Iran
Shishchitsy *see* Shyshchytsy
Shivamogga 110 C2 *prev.* Shimoga.
 Karnātaka, W India
Shivpuri 134 D3 Madhya Pradesh,
 C India
Shizugawa 130 D4 Miyagi, Honshū,
 NE Japan
Shizuoka 131 D6 *var.* Sizuoka. Shizuoka,
 Honshū, S Japan
Shklov *see* Shklow
Shklow 107 D6 Rus. Shklov.
 Mahilyowskaya Voblasts', E Belarus
Shkodër 101 C5 *var.* Shkodra, It. Scutari,
 SCr. Skadar. Shkodër, NW Albania
Shkodra *see* Shkodër
Shkodrës, Liqeni i *see* Scutari, Lake
Shkumbini, Lumi i 101 C6 *var.*
 Shkumbi, Shkumin. *river* C Albania
Shkumbi/Shkumbin *see* Shkumbinit,
 Lumi i
Sholāpur *see* Solāpur
Shostka 109 F1 Sums'ka Oblast',
 NE Ukraine
Show Low 48 B2 Arizona, SW USA
Show Me State *see* Missouri
Shpola 109 E3 Cherkas'ka Oblast',
 N Ukraine
Shqipëria/Shqipërisë, Republika e *see*
 Albania
Shreveport 42 A2 Louisiana, S USA
Shrewsbury 89 D6 *hist.* Scrobesbyrig'.
 W England, United Kingdom
Shu 114 C5 Kaz. Shū. Zhambyl,
 SE Kazakhstan
Shuang-liao *see* Liaoyuan
Shū, Kazakhstan *see* Shu
Shumagin Islands 36 B3 *island group*
 Alaska, USA
Shumen 104 D2 Shumen, NE Bulgaria
Shumilina 107 E5 Rus. Shumilino.
 Vitsyebskaya Voblasts', NE Belarus
Shumilino *see* Shumilina
Shunsen *see* Chuncheon
Shuqrah 121 B7 *var.* Shaqrā. SW Yemen
Shwebo 136 B3 Sagaing, C Myanmar
 (Burma)
Shyichy 107 C7 Rus. Shiichi.
 Homyel'skaya Voblasts', SE Belarus
Shymkent 114 B5 *prev.* Chimkent.
 Yuzhnyy Kazakhstan, S Kazakhstan
Shyshchytsy 107 C6 Rus. Shishchitsy.
 Minskaya Voblasts', C Belarus
Siam *see* Thailand
Siam, Gulf of *see* Thailand, Gulf of
Siang *see* Brahmaputra
Siangtan *see* Xiangtan
Šiauliai 106 B4 Ger. Schaulen. Šiauliai,
 N Lithuania

Siazan' *see* Siyäzän
Sibay *111 D6* Respublika Bashkortostan, W Russia
Šibenik *100 B4* It. Sebenico.
 Šibenik-Knin, S Croatia
Sîberia *115 E3 var.* Siberia. *physical region* NE Russia
Siberia *see* Sibir'
Siberoet *see* Siberut, Pulau
Siberut, Pulau *138 A4 prev.* Siberoet.
 island Kepulauan Mentawai, W Indonesia
Sibi *134 B2* Baluchistan, SW Pakistan
Sibir' *115 E3 var.* Siberia. *physical region* NE Russia
Sibiti *77 B6* Lékoumou, S Congo
Sibiu *108 B4 Ger.* Hermannstadt, *Hung.* Nagyszeben. Sibiu, C Romania
Sibolga *138 B3* Sumatera, W Indonesia
Sibu *138 D3* Sarawak, East Malaysia
Sibut *76 C4 prev.* Fort-Sibut. Kémo, S Central African Republic
Sibuyan Sea *139 E2 sea* W Pacific Ocean
Sichon *137 C6 var.* Ban Sichon, Si Chon. Nakhon Si Thammarat, SW Thailand
Si Chon *see* Sichon
Sichuan *128 B5 var.* Chuan, Sichuan Sheng, Ssu-ch'uan, Szechuan, Szechwan. *province* C China
Sichuan Pendi *128 B5 basin* C China
Sichuan Sheng *see* Sichuan
Sicilian Channel *see* Sicily, Strait of
Sicily *97 C7 Eng.* Sicily; *anc.* Trinacria. *island* Italy, C Mediterranean Sea
Sicily, Strait of *97 B7 var.* Sicilian Channel. *strait* C Mediterranean Sea
Sicuani *61 E4* Cusco, S Peru
Sidári *104 A4* Kérkyra, Iónia Nisiá, Greece, C Mediterranean Sea
Sidas *138 C4* Borneo, C Indonesia
Siderno *97 D7* Calabria, SW Italy
Sidhirókastron *see* Sidirókastro
Sîdi Barrânî *72 A1* NW Egypt
Sidi Bel Abbès *70 D2 var.* Sidi bel Abbès, Sidi-Bel-Abbès. NW Algeria
Sidirókastro *104 C3 prev.*
 Sidhirókastron. Kentrikí Makedonía, NE Greece
Sidley, Mount *154 B4 mountain* Antarctica
Sidney *44 D1* Montana, NW USA
Sidney *44 D4* Nebraska, C USA
Sidney *40 C4* Ohio, N USA
Sidon *see* Saïda
Sidra *see* Surt
Sidra/Sidra, Gulf of *see* Surt, Khalij, N Libya
Siebenbürgen *see* Transylvania
Siedlce *98 E3 Ger.* Sedlez, *Rus.* Sesdlets. Mazowieckie, C Poland
Siegen *94 B4* Nordrhein-Westfalen, W Germany
Siemiatycze *98 E3* Podlaskie, NE Poland
Siena *96 B3 Fr.* Sienne; *anc.* Saena Julia. Toscana, C Italy
Sienne *see* Siena
Sieradz *98 C4* Sieradz, C Poland
Sierpc *98 D3* Mazowieckie, C Poland
Sierra Leone *74 C4 off.* Republic of Sierra Leone. *country* W Africa
Sierra Leone Basin *66 C4 undersea basin* E Atlantic Ocean
Sierra Leone, Republic of *see* Sierra Leone
Sierra Leone Ridge *see* Sierra Leone Rise
Sierra Leone Rise *66 C4 var.* Sierra Leone Ridge, Sierra Leone Schwelle. *undersea rise* E Atlantic Ocean
Sierra Leone Schwelle *see* Sierra Leone Rise
Sierra Vista *48 B3* Arizona, SW USA
Sífnos *105 C6 anc.* Siphnos. *island* Kykládes, Greece, Aegean Sea
Sigli *138 A3* Sumatera, W Indonesia
Siglufjörður *83 E4* Nordhurland Vestra, N Iceland
Signal Peak *48 A2 mountain* Arizona, SW USA
Signan *see* Xi'an
Signy *154 A2 UK research station* South Orkney Islands, Antarctica
Siguatepeque *52 C2* Comayagua, W Honduras
Siguiri *74 D4* NE Guinea
Sihanoukville *137 D6 Khmer.* Preăh Seihânŭ; *prev.* Kompong Som. Sihanoukville, SW Cambodia
Siilinjärvi *84 E4* Itä-Suomi, C Finland

Siirt *117 F4 var.* Sert; *anc.* Tigranocerta. Siirt, SE Turkey
Sikandarabad *see* Secunderābād
Sikasso *74 D4* Sikasso, S Mali
Sikeston *45 H5* Missouri, C USA
Sikhote-Alin', Khrebet *115 G4 mountain range* SE Russia
Siking *see* Xi'an
Siklós *99 C7* Baranya, SW Hungary
Sikoku *see* Shikoku
Sikoku Basin *see* Shikoku Basin
Šilalé *106 B4* Tauragė, W Lithuania
Silchar *135 G3* Assam, NE India
Silesia *98 B4 physical region* SW Poland
Silifke *116 C4 anc.* Seleucia. Içel, S Turkey
Siliguri *see* Shiliguri
Siling Co *126 C5 lake* W China
Silinhot *see* Xilinhot
Silistra *104 E1 var.* Silistria; *anc.* Durostorum. Silistra, NE Bulgaria
Silistria *see* Silistra
Sillamäe *106 E2 Ger.* Sillamäggi. Ida-Virumaa, NE Estonia
Sillamäggi *see* Sillamäe
Sillein *see* Žilina
Šilutė *106 B4 Ger.* Heydekrug. Klaipėda, W Lithuania
Silvan *117 E4* Diyarbakır, SE Turkey
Silva Porto *see* Kuito
Silver State *see* Colorado
Silver State *see* Nevada
Simanichy *107 C7 Rus.* Simonichi. Homyel'skaya Voblasts', SE Belarus
Simav *116 B3* Kütahya, W Turkey
Simav Çayı *116 A3 river* NW Turkey
Simbirsk *see* Ul'yanovsk
Simeto *97 C7 river* Sicilia, Italy, C Mediterranean Sea
Simeulue, Pulau *138 A3 island* NW Indonesia
Simferopol' *109 F5* Avtonomna Respublika Krym, S Ukraine
Simitía *104 C3* Blagoevgrad, SW Bulgaria
Şimlāul Silvaniei/Şimleul Silvaniei *see* Şimleu Silvaniei
Şimleu Silvaniei *108 B3 Hung.* Szilágysomlyó; *prev.* Şimlăul Silvaniei, Şimleul Silvaniei. Sălaj, NW Romania
Simonichi *see* Simanichy
Simonoseki *see* Shimonoseki
Simpelveld *87 D6* Limburg, SE Netherlands
Simplon Pass *95 B8 pass* S Switzerland
Simpson *see* Fort Simpson
Simpson Desert *148 B4 desert* Northern Territory/South Australia
Sinai *72 C2 var.* Sinai Peninsula, *Ar.* Shibh Jazīrat Sīnā', Sīnā. *physical region* NE Egypt
Sinaia *108 C4* Prahova, SE Romania
Sinano Gawa *see* Shinano-gawa
Sīnā/Sinai Peninsula *see* Sinai
Sincelejo *58 B2* Sucre, NW Colombia
Sind *see* Sindh
Sindelfingen *95 B6* Baden-Württemberg, SW Germany
Sindh *134 B3 prev.* Sind. *province* SE Pakistan
Sindi *106 D2 Ger.* Zintenhof. Pärnumaa, SW Estonia
Sines *92 B4* Setúbal, S Portugal
Singan *see* Xi'an
Singapore *138 B3 country capital* (Singapore) (Singapore) S Singapore
Singapore *138 A1 off.* Republic of Singapore. *country* SE Asia
Singapore, Republic of *see* Singapore
Singen *95 B6* Baden-Württemberg, S Germany
Singida *73 C7* Singida, C Tanzania
Singkang *139 E4* Sulawesi, C Indonesia
Singkawang *138 C3* Borneo, C Indonesia
Singora *see* Songkhla
Singū *see* Shingū
Sining *see* Xining
Siniscola *97 A5* Sardegna, Italy, C Mediterranean Sea
Sinj *100 B4* Split-Dalmacija, SE Croatia
Sinkiang/Sinkiang Uighur Autonomous Region *see* Xinjiang Uygur Zizhiqu
Sinneh *see* Sanandaj
Sînnicolau Mare *see* Sânnicolau Mare
Sinoe, Lacul *see* Sinoie, Lacul
Sinoie, Lacul *108 D5 prev.* Lacul Sinoe. *lagoon* SE Romania

Sinop *116 D2 anc.* Sinope. Sinop, Turkey
Sinope *see* Sinop
Sinsheim *95 B6* Baden-Württemberg, SW Germany
Sint Maarten *55 G3 Eng.* Saint Martin. *Constituent country of the Netherlands* Lesser Antilles
Sint-Michielsgestel *86 C4* Noord-Brabant, S Netherlands
Sin-Miclăuş *see* Gheorgheni
Sint-Niklaas *87 B5 Fr.* Saint-Nicolas. Oost-Vlaanderen, N Belgium
Sint-Pieters-Leeuw *87 B6* Vlaams Brabant, C Belgium
Sintra *92 B3 prev.* Cintra. Lisboa, W Portugal
Sinŭiju *73 E5* Nugaal, NE Somalia
Sinus Aelaniticus *see* Aqaba, Gulf of
Sinus Gallicus *see* Lion, Golfe du
Sinyang *see* Xinyang
Sinzyô *see* Shinjô
Sion *95 A7 Ger.* Sitten; *anc.* Sedunum. Valais, SW Switzerland
Sioux City *45 F3* Iowa, C USA
Sioux Falls *45 F3* South Dakota, N USA
Sioux State *see* North Dakota
Siphnos *see* Sífnos
Siping *128 D3 var.* Ssu-p'ing, Szeping; *prev.* Ssu-p'ing-chieh. Jilin, NE China
Siple, Mount *154 A4 mountain* Siple Island, Antarctica
Siquirres *53 E4* Limón, E Costa Rica
Siracusa *97 D7 Eng.* Syracuse. Sicilia, Italy, C Mediterranean Sea
Sir Edward Pellew Group *148 B2 island group* Northern Territory, NE Australia
Siret *108 C3 var.* Siretul, *Ger.* Sereth, *Rus.* Seret. *river* Romania/Ukraine
Siretul *see* Siret
Siria *see* Syria
Sirikit Reservoir *136 C4 lake* N Thailand
Sīrjān *120 D4 prev.* Sa'īdābād. Kermān, S Iran
Sirna *see* Sýrna
Şırnak *117 F4* Şırnak, SE Turkey
Síros *see* Sýros
Sirte *see* Surt
Sirte, Gulf of *71 F2 Eng.* Gulf of Sidra, Gulf of Sirti, Sidra, *Ar.* Khalij Surt. *gulf* N Libya
Sirti, Gulf of *see* Surt, Khalij
Sirvan *117 H3 prev.* Äli-Bayramlı. SE Azerbaijan
Sisak *100 B3 var.* Siscia, *Ger.* Sissek, *Hung.* Sziszek; *anc.* Segestica. Sisak-Moslavina, C Croatia
Siscia *see* Sisak
Sisimiut *82 C3 var.* Holsteinborg, Holsteinsborg, Holstenborg, Holstensborg. Kitaa, S Greenland
Sissek *see* Sisak
Sīstān, Daryācheh-ye *see* Şāberī, Hāmūn-e
Sitas Cristuru *see* Cristuru Secuiesc
Sitéia *105 D8 var.* Sitía. Kríti, Greece, E Mediterranean Sea
Sitges *93 G2* Cataluña, NE Spain
Sitía *see* Sitéia
Sittang *see* Sittoung
Sittard *87 D5* Limburg, SE Netherlands
Sitten *see* Sion
Sittoung *136 B4 var.* Sittang. *river* S Myanmar (Burma)
Sittwe *136 A3 var.* Akyab. Rakhine State, W Myanmar (Burma)
Siuna *52 D3* Región Autónoma Atlántico Norte, NE Nicaragua
Siut *see* Asyût
Sivas *116 D3 anc.* Sebastia, Sebaste. Sivas, C Turkey
Siverek *117 E4* Şanlıurfa, S Turkey
Siwa *see* Sîwah
Sîwah *72 A2 var.* Siwa. NW Egypt
Six Counties, The *see* Northern Ireland
Six-Fours-les-Plages *91 D6 Var,* SE France
Siyäzän *117 H2 Rus.* Siazan'. NE Azerbaijan
Sjar *see* Sääre
Sjenica *101 D5 Turk.* Seniça. Serbia, SW Serbia
Skadar *see* Shkodër
Skadarsko Jezero *see* Scutari, Lake
Skagerak *see* Skagerrak
Skagerrak *85 A6 var.* Skagerak. *channel* N Europe
Skagit River *46 B1 river* Washington, NW USA
Skalka *84 C3 Lapp.* Skallkká. *lake* N Sweden

Skalkká *see* Skalka
Skarżysko-Kamienna *98 D4* Świętokrzyskie, C Poland
Skaudvilė *106 B4* Tauragė, SW Lithuania
Skegness *89 E6* E England, United Kingdom
Skellefteå *84 D4* Västerbotten, N Sweden
Skellefteälven *84 C4* river N Sweden
Ski *85 B6* Akershus, S Norway
Skíathos *105 C5* Skíathos, Vóreies Sporádes, Greece, Aegean Sea
Skidal' *107 B5 Rus.* Skidel'. Hrodzyenskaya Voblasts', W Belarus
Skidel' *see* Skidal'
Skierniewice *98 D3* Łódzkie, C Poland
Skiftet *106 C1 strait* Finland Atlantic Ocean Baltic Sea Gulf of Bothnia/Gulf of Finland
Skíros *see* Skýros
Skópelos *105 C5* Skópelos, Vóreies Sporádes, Greece, Aegean Sea
Skopje *101 D6 var.* Üsküb, *Turk.* Üsküp; *prev.* Skoplje; *anc.* Scupi. *country capital* (Macedonia) N Macedonia
Skoplje *see* Skopje
Skovorodino *115 F4* Amurskaya Oblast', SE Russia
Skudnesfjorden *85 A6 fjord* S Norway
Skuodas *106 B3 Ger.* Schoden, *Pol.* Szkudy. Klaipėda, NW Lithuania
Skye, Isle of *88 B3 island* NW Scotland, United Kingdom
Skylge *see* Terschelling
Skýros *105 C5 var.* Skíros. Skýros, Vóreies Sporádes, Greece, Aegean Sea
Skýros *105 C5 var.* Skíros; *anc.* Scyros. *island* Vóreies Sporádes, Greece, Aegean Sea
Slagelse *85 B7* Sjælland, E Denmark
Slatina *100 C3* Hung. Szlatina; *prev.* Podravska Slatina. Virovitica-Podravina, NE Croatia
Slatina *108 B5* Olt, S Romania
Slavgorod *see* Slawharad
Slavonski Brod *100 C3 Ger.* Brod, *Hung.* Bród; *prev.* Brod, Brod na Savi. Brod-Posavina, NE Croatia
Slavuta *108 C2* Khmel'nyts'ka Oblast', NW Ukraine
Slavyansk *see* Slov"yans'k
Slawharad *107 E7 Rus.* Slavgorod. Mahilyowskaya Voblasts', E Belarus
Sławno *98 C2* Zachodnio-pomorskie, NW Poland
Slēmani *see* As Sulaymānīyah
Sliema *102 B5* N Malta
Sligo *89 A5 Ir.* Sligeach. Sligo, NW Ireland
Sliven *104 D2 var.* Slivno. Sliven, C Bulgaria
Slivnitsa *104 B2* Sofiya, W Bulgaria
Slivno *see* Sliven
Slobozia *108 C5* Ialomiţa, SE Romania
Slonim *107 B6 Pol.* Słonim. Hrodzyenskaya Voblasts', W Belarus
Słonim *see* Slonim
Slovakia *99 C6 off.* Slovenská Republika, *Ger.* Slowakei, *Hung.* Szlovákia, *Slvk.* Slovensko. *country* C Europe
Slovak Ore Mountains *see* Slovenské rudohorie
Slovenia *95 D8 off.* Republic of Slovenia, *Ger.* Slowenien, *Slvn.* Slovenija. *country* SE Europe
Slovenia, Republic of *see* Slovenia
Slovenija *see* Slovenia
Slovenská Republika *see* Slovakia
Slovenské rudohorie *99 D6 Eng.* Slovak Ore Mountains, *Ger.* Slowakisches Erzgebirge, Ungarisches Erzgebirge. *mountain range* C Slovakia
Slovensko *see* Slovakia
Slov"yans'k *109 G3 Rus.* Slavyansk. Donets'ka Oblast', E Ukraine
Slowakei *see* Slovakia
Slowakisches Erzgebirge *see* Slovenské rudohorie
Slowenien *see* Slovenia
Słubice *98 B3 Ger.* Frankfurt. Lubuskie, W Poland
Sluch *108 D1 river* NW Ukraine
Słupsk *98 C2 Ger.* Stolp. Pomorskie, N Poland
Slutsk *107 C6* Minskaya Voblasts', S Belarus
Smallwood Reservoir *39 F2 lake* Newfoundland and Labrador, S Canada

Smara 70 B3 var. Es Semara. N Western Sahara

Smarhon' 107 C5 Pol. Smorgonie, Rus. Smorgon'. Hrodzyenskaya Voblasts', W Belarus

Smederevo 100 D4 Ger. Semendria. Serbia, N Serbia

Smederevska Palanka 100 D4 Serbia, C Serbia

Smela see Smila

Smila 109 E2 Rus. Smela. Cherkas'ka Oblast', C Ukraine

Smilten see Smiltene

Smiltene 106 D3 Ger. Smilten. N Latvia

Smola 84 A4 island W Norway

Smolensk 111 A5 Smolenskaya Oblast', W Russia

Smorgon'/Smorgonie see Smarhon'

Smyrna see Izmir

Snake 34 B4 river Yukon, NW Canada

Snake River 46 C3 river NW USA

Snake River Plain 46 D4 plain Idaho, NW USA

Sneek 86 D2 Fris. Snits. Fryslân, N Netherlands

Sneeuw-gebergte see Maoke, Pegunungan

Sněžka 98 B4 Ger. Schneekoppe, Pol. Śnieżka. mountain N Czech Republic (Czechia)/Poland

Śniardwy, Jezioro 98 D2 Ger. Spirdingsee. lake NE Poland

Sniečkus see Visaginas

Śnieżka see Sněžka

Snina 99 E5 Hung. Szinna. Prešovský Kraj, E Slovakia

Snits see Sneek

Snovs'k 109 E1 Rus. Shchors. Chernihivs'ka Oblast', N Ukraine

Snowdonia 89 C6 mountain range NW Wales, United Kingdom

Snowdrift see Łutselk'e

Snow Mountains see Maoke, Pegunungan

Snyder 49 F3 Texas, SW USA

Sobradinho, Barragem de see Sobradinho, Represa de

Sobradinho, Represa de 63 F2 var. Barragem de Sobradinho. reservoir E Brazil

Sochi 111 A7 Krasnodarskiy Kray, SW Russia

Société, Îles de la/Society Islands see Société, Archipel de la

Society Islands 145 G4 var. Archipel de Tahiti, Îles de la Société, Eng. Society Islands. island group W French Polynesia

Soconusco, Sierra de see Madre, Sierra

Socorro 48 D2 New Mexico, SW USA

Socorro, Isla 50 B5 island W Mexico

Socotra 121 C7 var. Sokotra, Eng. Socotra. island SE Yemen

Socotra see Suquţrā

Soc Trăng 137 D6 var. Khanh Hung. Soc Trăng, S Vietnam

Socuéllamos 93 E3 Castilla-La Mancha, C Spain

Sodankylä 84 D3 Lappi, N Finland

Sodari see Sodiri

Söderhamn 85 C5 Gävleborg, C Sweden

Södertälje 85 C6 Stockholm, C Sweden

Sodiri 72 B4 var. Sawdīrī, Sodari. Northern Kordofan, C Sudan

Soekaboemi see Sukabumi

Soemba see Sumba, Pulau

Soengaipenoeh see Sungaipenuh

Soerabaja see Surabaya

Soerakarta see Surakarta

Sofia see Sofiya

Sofiya 104 C2 var. Sophia, Eng. Sofia, Lat. Serdica. country capital (Bulgaria) Sofiya-Grad, W Bulgaria

Sogamoso 58 B3 Boyacá, C Colombia

Sognefjorden 85 A5 fjord NE North Sea

Sohag see Suhāj

Sohar see Şuḩār

Sohm Plain 66 B3 abyssal plain NW Atlantic Ocean

Sohrau see Żory

Sokal' 108 C2 Rus. Sokal. L'vivs'ka Oblast', NW Ukraine

Söke 116 A4 Aydın, SW Turkey

Sokhumi 117 E1 Rus. Sukhumi. NW Georgia

Sokodé 75 F4 C Togo

Sokol 110 C4 Vologodskaya Oblast', NW Russia

Sokółka 98 E3 Podlaskie, NE Poland

Sokolov 99 A5 Ger. Falkenau an der Eger; prev. Falknov nad Ohří. Karlovarský Kraj, W Czech Republic (Czechia)

Sokone 74 B3 W Senegal

Sokoto 75 F3 Sokoto, NW Nigeria

Sokoto 75 F4 river NW Nigeria

Sokotra see Suquţrā

Solāpur 124 B3 var. Sholāpur. Mahārāshtra, W India

Solca 108 C3 Ger. Solka. Suceava, N Romania

Sol, Costa del 92 D5 coastal region S Spain

Soldeu 91 B7 NE Andorra Europe

Solec Kujawski 98 C3 Kujawsko-pomorskie, C Poland

Soledad 58 B1 Atlántico, N Colombia

Isla Soledad see East Falkland

Soligorsk see Salihorsk

Solikamsk 114 C3 Permskiy Kray, NW Russia

Sol'-Iletsk 111 D6 Orenburgskaya Oblast', W Russia

Solingen 94 A4 Nordrhein-Westfalen, W Germany

Solka see Solca

Sollentuna 85 C6 Stockholm, C Sweden

Solo see Surakarta

Solok 138 B4 Sumatera, W Indonesia

Solomon Islands 144 C3 prev. British Solomon Islands Protectorate. country W Solomon Islands N Melanesia W Pacific Ocean

Solomon Islands 144 C3 island group Papua New Guinea/Solomon Islands

Solomon Sea 144 B3 sea W Pacific Ocean

Soltau 94 B3 Niedersachsen, NW Germany

Sol'tsy 110 A4 Novgorodskaya Oblast', W Russia

Solun see Thessaloníki

Solwezi 78 D2 North Western, NW Zambia

Sōma 130 D4 Fukushima, Honshū, C Japan

Somalia 73 D5 off. Somali Democratic Republic, Som. Jamuuriyada Demuqraadiga Soomaaliyeed, Soomaaliya; prev. Italian Somaliland, Somaliland Protectorate. country E Africa

Somali Basin 69 E5 undersea basin W Indian Ocean

Somali Democratic Republic see Somalia

Somaliland 73 D5 disputed territory N Somalia

Somaliland Protectorate see Somalia

Sombor 100 C3 Hung. Zombor. Vojvodina, NW Serbia

Someren 87 D5 Noord-Brabant, SE Netherlands

Somerset 42 A5 var. Somerset Village. W Bermuda

Somerset 40 C5 Kentucky, S USA

Somerset Island 42 A5 island W Bermuda

Somerset Island 37 F2 island Queen Elizabeth Islands, Nunavut, NW Canada

Somerset Village see Somerset

Somers Islands see Bermuda

Somerton 48 A2 Arizona, SW USA

Someş 108 B3 river Hungary/Romania Europe

Somme 90 C2 river N France

Sommerfeld see Lubsko

Somotillo 52 C3 Chinandega, NW Nicaragua

Somoto 52 D3 Madriz, NW Nicaragua

Songea 73 C8 Ruvuma, S Tanzania

Sŏngjin see Kimch'aek

Songkhla 137 C7 var. Songkla, Mal. Singora. Songkhla, SW Thailand

Songkla see Songkhla

Sonoran Desert 48 A3 var. Desierto de Altar. desert Mexico/USA

Sonsonate 52 B3 Sonsonate, W El Salvador

Soochow see Suzhou

Soomaaliya/Soomaaliyeed, Jamuuriyada Demuqraadiga see Somalia

Soome Laht see Finland, Gulf of

Sop Hao 136 D3 Houaphan, N Laos

Sophia see Sofiya

Sopianae see Pécs

Sopot 98 C2 Ger. Zoppot. Pomorskie, N Poland

Sopron 99 B6 Ger. Ödenburg. Győr-Moson-Sopron, NW Hungary

Sorau/Sorau in der Niederlausitz see Żary

Sorgues 91 D6 Vaucluse, SE France

Sorgun 116 D3 Yozgat, C Turkey

Soria 93 E2 Castilla y León, N Spain

Soroca 108 D3 Rus. Soroki. N Moldova

Soroki see Soroca

Sorokyne 190 H3 Rus. Krasnodon. Luhans'ka Oblast', E Ukraine

Sorong 139 F4 Papua, E Indonesia

Sørøy see Sørøya

Sørøya 84 C2 var. Sørøy, Lapp. Sállan. island N Norway

Sortavala 83 B5 prev. Serdobol'. Respublika Kareliya, NW Russia

Sotavento, Ilhas de 74 A3 var. Leeward Islands. island group E Cape Verde

Sotkamo 84 E4 Kainuu, C Finland

Souanké 77 B5 Sangha, NW Congo

Soueida see As Suwaydā'

Souflí 104 D3 prev. Souflíon. Anatolikí Makedonía kai Thráki, NE Greece

Souflíon see Souflí

Soufrière 55 F2 W Saint Lucia

Soukhné see As Sukhnah

Sŏul see Seoul

Soûr 119 A5 var. Şūr; anc. Tyre. SW Lebanon

Souris River 45 E1 var. Mouse River. river Canada/USA

Soúrpi 105 B5 Thessalía, C Greece

Sousse 71 F2 var. Sūsah. NE Tunisia

South Africa 78 C4 off. Republic of South Africa, Afr. Suid-Afrika. country S Africa

South Africa, Republic of see South Africa

South America 56 continent

Southampton 89 D7 hist. Hamwih, Lat. Clausentum. S England, United Kingdom

Southampton Island 37 G3 island Nunavut, NE Canada

South Andaman 133 F2 island Andaman Islands, India, NE Indian Ocean

South Australia 149 A5 state S Australia

South Australian Basin 142 B5 undersea basin SW Indian Ocean

South Bend 40 C3 Indiana, N USA

South Beveland see Zuid-Beveland

South Bruny Island 149 C8 island Tasmania, SE Australia

South Carolina 43 E2 off. State of South Carolina, also known as The Palmetto State. state SE USA

South Carpathians see Carpaţii Meridionalii

South China Basin 125 E4 undersea basin SE South China Sea

South China Sea 125 E4 Chin. Nan Hai, Ind. Laut Cina Selatan, Vtn. Biên Đông. sea SE Asia

South Dakota 44 D2 off. State of South Dakota, also known as The Coyote State, Sunshine State. state N USA

Southeast Indian Ridge 141 D7 undersea ridge Indian Ocean/Pacific Ocean

Southeast Pacific Basin 153 E5 var. Belling Hausen Mulde. undersea basin SE Pacific Ocean

South East Point 149 C7 headland Victoria, SE Australia

Southend-on-Sea 89 E6 E England, United Kingdom

Southern Alps 151 B6 mountain range South Island, New Zealand

Southern Cook Islands 145 F4 island group S Cook Islands

Southern Cross 147 B6 Western Australia

Southern Indian Lake 37 F4 lake Manitoba, C Canada

Southern Ocean 67 B7 ocean Atlantic Ocean/Indian Ocean/Pacific Ocean

Southern Uplands 88 C4 mountain range S Scotland, United Kingdom

South Fiji Basin 142 D4 undersea basin S Pacific Ocean

South Geomagnetic Pole 154 B3 pole Antarctica

South Georgia 57 D8 island South Georgia and the South Sandwich Islands, SW Atlantic Ocean

South Goulburn Island 146 E2 island Northern Territory, N Australia

South Huvadhu Atoll 132 A5 atoll S Maldives

South Indian Basin 141 D7 undersea basin Indian Ocean/Pacific Ocean

South Island 151 C6 island S New Zealand

South Korea 129 E4 off. Republic of Korea, Kor. Taehan Min'guk. country E Asia

South Lake Tahoe 47 C5 California, W USA

South Orkney Islands 154 A2 island group Antarctica

South Ossetia 117 F2 former autonomous region SW Georgia

South Pacific Basin see Southwest Pacific Basin

South Platte River 44 D4 river Colorado/Nebraska, C USA

South Pole 154 B3 pole Antarctica

South Sandwich Islands 57 D8 island group SW Atlantic Ocean

South Sandwich Trench 57 E8 trench SW Atlantic Ocean

South Shetland Islands 154 A2 island group Antarctica

South Shields 88 D4 NE England, United Kingdom

South Sioux City 45 F3 Nebraska, C USA

South Sudan 73 B5 off. Republic of South Sudan. country E Africa

South Taranaki Bight 150 C4 bight SE Tasman Sea

South Tasmania Plateau see Tasman Plateau

South Uist 88 B3 island NW Scotland, United Kingdom

South-West Africa/South West Africa see Namibia

South West Cape 151 A8 headland Stewart Island, New Zealand

Southwest Indian Ocean Ridge see Southwest Indian Ridge

Southwest Indian Ridge 141 B6 var. Southwest Indian Ocean Ridge. undersea ridge SW Indian Ocean

Southwest Pacific Basin 143 E4 var. South Pacific Basin. undersea basin SE Pacific Ocean

Sovereign Base Area 102 C5 uk military installation S Cyprus

Soweto 78 D4 Gauteng, NE South Africa

Sōya-kaikyō see La Pérouse Strait

Spain 92 D3 off. Kingdom of Spain, Sp. España; anc. Hispania, Iberia, Lat. Hispana. country SW Europe

Spain, Kingdom of see Spain

Spalato see Split

Spanish Town 54 B5 hist. St.Iago de la Vega. C Jamaica

Sparks 47 C5 Nevada, W USA

Sparta see Spárti

Spartanburg 43 E1 South Carolina, SE USA

Spárti 105 B6 Eng. Sparta. Pelopónnisos, S Greece

Spearfish 44 D2 South Dakota, N USA

Speightstown 55 G1 NW Barbados

Spencer 45 F3 Iowa, C USA

Spencer Gulf 149 B6 gulf South Australia

Spey 88 C3 river NE Scotland, United Kingdom

Spice Islands see Maluku

Spiess Seamount 67 C7 seamount S Atlantic Ocean

Spijkenisse 86 B4 Zuid-Holland, SW Netherlands

Spíli 105 C8 Kríti, Greece, E Mediterranean Sea

Spin Böldak 123 E5 prev. Spīn Būldak. Kandahār, S Afghanistan

Spīn Būldak see Spin Böldak

Spirdingsee see Śniardwy, Jezioro

Spitsbergen 83 F2 island NW Svalbard

Split 100 B4 It. Spalato. Split-Dalmacija, S Croatia

Špogi 106 D4 SE Latvia

Spokane 46 C2 Washington, NW USA

Spratly Islands 138 D2 Chin. Nansha Qundao. disputed territory SE Asia

Spree 94 D4 river E Germany

Springbok 78 B5 NE South Africa

Springfield 40 B4 state capital Illinois, N USA

Springfield 41 G3 Massachusetts, NE USA

Springfield 45 G5 Missouri, C USA

Springfield *40 C4* Ohio, N USA
Springfield *46 B3* Oregon, NW USA
Spring Garden *59 F2* NE Guyana
Spring Hill *43 E4* Florida, SE USA
Springs Junction *151 C5* West Coast,
  South Island, New Zealand
Springsure *148 D4* Queensland,
  E Australia
Sprottau *see* Szprotawa
Spruce Knob *41 E4 mountain* West
  Virginia, NE USA
Srbinje *see* Foča
Srbobran *100 D3 var.* Bácsszenttamás,
  Hung. Szenttamás. Vojvodina,
  N Serbia
Srebrenica *100 C4* Republika Srpska,
  E Bosnia and Herzegovina
Sredets *104 D2 prev.* Syulemeshlii. Stara
  Zagora, C Bulgaria
Sredets *104 E2 prev.* Grudovo. Burgas,
  E Bulgaria
Sremska Mitrovica *100 C3 prev.*
  Mitrovica, *Ger.* Mitrowitz. Vojvodina,
  NW Serbia
Srepok, Sông *see* Srêpôk, Tônle
Srêpôk, Tônle *137 E5 var.* Sông Srepok.
  river Cambodia/Vietnam
Sri Aman *138 C3* Sarawak, East Malaysia
Sri Jayewardanapura Kotte *132 D3*
  administrative capital (Sri Lanka) *var.*
  Sri Jayawardanapura. Western
  Province, W Sri Lanka
Srikakulam *135 F5* Andhra Pradesh,
  E India
Sri Lanka *132 D3 off.* Democratic
  Socialist Republic of Sri Lanka; *prev.*
  Ceylon. *country* S Asia
Sri Lanka, Democratic Socialist
  Republic of *see* Sri Lanka
Srinagarind Reservoir *137 C5 lake*
  W Thailand
Srpska, Republika *100 D3 republic*
  Bosnia and Herzegovina
Ssu-ch'uan *see* Sichuan
Ssu-p'ing/Ssu-p'ing-chieh *see* Siping
Stabroek *87 B5* Antwerpen,
  N Belgium
Stade *94 B3* Niedersachsen,
  NW Germany
Stadskanaal *86 E2* Groningen,
  NE Netherlands
Stafford *89 D6* C England, United
  Kingdom
Staicele *106 D3* N Latvia
Ştaierdorf-Anina *see* Anina
Stäjerlakanina *see* Anina
Stakhanov *see* Kadiyivka
Stalin *see* Varna
Stalinabad *see* Dushanbe
Stalingrad *see* Volgograd
Stalino *see* Donets'k
Stalinobod *see* Dushanbe
Stalinsk *see* Novokuznetsk
Stalinski Zaliv *see* Varnenski Zaliv
Stalin, Yazovir *see* Iskŭr, Yazovir
Stalowa Wola *98 E4* Podkarpackie,
  SE Poland
Stamford *41 F3* Connecticut, NE USA
Stampalia *see* Astypálaia
Stanislau *see* Ivano-Frankivs'k
Stanislav *see* Ivano-Frankivs'k
Stanisławów *see* Ivano-Frankivs'k
Stanke Dimitrov *see* Dupnitsa
Stanley *65 D7 var.* Port Stanley, Puerto
  Argentino. *dependent territory capital*
  (Falkland Islands) East Falkland,
  Falkland Islands
Stanleyville *see* Kisangani
Stann Creek *see* Dangriga
Stanovoy Khrebet *113 E3 mountain*
  range SE Russia
Stanthorpe *149 D5* Queensland,
  E Australia
Staphorst *86 D2* Overijssel,
  E Netherlands
Starachowice *98 D4* Świętokrzyskie,
  C Poland
Stara Kanjiža *see* Kanjiža
Stara Pazova *100 D3 Ger.* Altpasua,
  Hung. Ópazova. Vojvodina, N Serbia
Stara Planina *see* Balkan Mountains
Stara Zagora *104 D2 Lat.* Augusta
  Trajana. Stara Zagora, C Bulgaria
Starbuck Island *145 G3 prev.* Volunteer
  Island. *island* E Kiribati
Stargard in Pommern *see* Stargard
  Szczeciński
Stargard Szczeciński *98 B3 Ger.*
  Stargard in Pommern.
  Zachodnio-pomorskie, NW Poland

Stari Bečej *see* Bečej
Starobel'sk *see* Starobil's'k
Starobil's'k *109 H2 Rus.* Starobel'sk.
  Luhans'ka Oblast', E Ukraine
Starobin *107 C7 var.* Starobyn.
  Minskaya Voblasts', S Belarus
Starobyn *see* Starobin
Starogard Gdański *98 C2 Ger.*
  Preussisch-Stargard. Pomorskie,
  N Poland
Starokonstantinov *see* Starokostyantyniv
Starokostyantyniv *108 D2 Rus.*
  Starokonstantinov. Khmel'nyts'ka
  Oblast', NW Ukraine
**Sta
rominskaya** *111 A7* Krasnodarskiy
  Kray, SW Russia
Staryya Darohi *107 C6 Rus.* Staryye
  Dorogi. Minskaya Voblasts', S Belarus
Staryye Dorogi *see* Staryya Darohi
Staryy Oskol *111 B6* Belgorodskaya
  Oblast', W Russia
State College *41 E4* Pennsylvania,
  NE USA
Staten Island *see* Estados, Isla de los
Statesboro *43 E2* Georgia, SE USA
States, The *see* United States of America
Staunton *41 E5* Virginia, NE USA
Stavanger *85 A6* Rogaland, S Norway
Stavers Island *see* Vostok Island
Stavropol' *111 B7 prev.* Voroshilovsk.
  Stavropol'skiy Kray, SW Russia
Stavropol' *see* Tol'yatti
Steamboat Springs *44 C4* Colorado,
  C USA
Steenwijk *86 D2* Overijssel,
  N Netherlands
Steier *see* Steyr
Steierdorf/Steierdorf-Anina *see* Anina
Steinamanger *see* Szombathely
Steinkjer *84 B4* Nord-Trøndelag,
  C Norway
Stejarul *see* Karapelit
Stendal *94 C3* Sachsen-Anhalt,
  C Germany
Stepanakert *see* Xankändi
Stephenville *49 F3* Texas, SW USA
Sterling *44 D4* Colorado, C USA
Sterling *40 B3* Illinois, N USA
Sterlitamak *111 B3* Respublika
  Bashkortostan, W Russia
Stettin *see* Szczecin
Stettiner Haff *see* Szczeciński, Zalew
Stevenage *89 E6* E England, United
  Kingdom
Stevens Point *40 B2* Wisconsin, N USA
Stewart Island *151 A8 island* S New
  Zealand
Steyerlak-Anina *see* Anina
Steyr *95 D6 var.* Steier. Oberösterreich,
  N Austria
St. Helena Bay *78 B5 bay* SW South
  Africa
Stif *see* Sétif
Stillwater *49 G1* Oklahoma, C USA
Štip *101 E6* E Macedonia
Stirling *88 C4* C Scotland, United
  Kingdom
Stjørdalshalsen *84 B4* Nord-Trøndelag,
  C Norway
St-Maur-des-Fossés *90 E2*
  Val-de-Marne, Île-de-France, N France
  Europe
Stockach *95 B6* Baden-Württemberg,
  S Germany
Stockholm *85 C6 country capital*
  (Sweden) Stockholm, C Sweden
Stockmannshof *see* Pļaviņas
Stockton *47 B6* California, W USA
Stockton Plateau *49 E4 plain* Texas,
  SW USA
Stœng Trêng *see* Stung Treng
Stoke *see* Stoke-on-Trent
Stoke-on-Trent *89 D6 var.* Stoke.
  C England, United Kingdom
Stolbce *see* Stowbtsy
Stolbtsy *see* Stowbtsy
Stolp *see* Słupsk
Stolpmünde *see* Ustka
Stómio *104 B4* Thessalía, C Greece
Store Bælt *see* Storebælt
Storebælt *see* Storebælt
Støren *85 B5* Sør-Trøndelag, S Norway
Storfjorden *83 G2 fjord* S Norway
Storhammer *see* Hamar
Stornoway *88 B2* NW Scotland, United
  Kingdom
Storsjön *85 B5 lake* C Sweden
Storuman *84 C4* Västerbotten,
  N Sweden
Storuman *84 C4 lake* N Sweden

Stowbtsy *107 C6 Pol.* Stolbce, *Rus.*
  Stolbtsy. Minskaya Voblasts', C Belarus
Strabane *89 B5 Ir.* An Srath Bán.
  W Northern Ireland, United Kingdom
Strakonice *99 A5 Ger.* Strakonitz.
  Jihočeský Kraj, S Czech Republic
  (Czechia)
Strakonitz *see* Strakonice
Stralsund *94 D2* Mecklenburg-
  Vorpommern, NE Germany
Stranraer *89 C5* S Scotland, United
  Kingdom
Strasbourg *90 E3 Ger.* Strassburg; *anc.*
  Argentoratum. Bas-Rhin, NE France
Strasburg *see* Aiud, Romania
Strassburg *see* Strasbourg, France
Strassburg *see* Aiud, Romania
Stratford *150 D4* Taranaki, North Island,
  New Zealand
Strathfield *148 E2* New South Wales,
  E Australia
Straubing *95 C6* Bayern, SE Germany
Strehaia *108 B5* Mehedinţi,
  SW Romania
Strelka *114 D4* Krasnoyarskiy Kray,
  C Russia
Strigonium *see* Esztergom
Strofilia *see* Strofyliá
Strofyliá *105 C5 var.* Strofilia. Évvoia,
  C Greece
Stromboli *97 D6 island* Isole Eolie,
  S Italy
Stromeferry *88 C3* N Scotland, United
  Kingdom
Strömstad *85 B6* Västra Götaland,
  S Sweden
Strömsund *84 C4* Jämtland, C Sweden
Struga *101 D6* SW Macedonia
Struma *see* Strymónas
Strumica *101 E6* E Macedonia
Strumyani *104 C3* Blagoevgrad,
  SW Bulgaria
Strymónas *104 C3 Bul.* Struma. *river*
  Bulgaria/Greece
Stryy *108 B2* L'vivs'ka Oblast',
  NW Ukraine
Studholme *151 B6* Canterbury, South
  Island, New Zealand
Stuhlweissenberg *see* Székesfehérvár
Stung Treng *137 D5 Khmer.* Stœng
  Trêng. Stung Treng, NE Cambodia
Sturgis *44 D3* South Dakota, N USA
Stuttgart *95 B6* Baden-Württemberg,
  SW Germany
Stykkishólmur *83 E4* Vesturland,
  W Iceland
Styr *108 C1 Rus.* Styr'. *river* Belarus/
  Ukraine
Su *see* Jiangsu
Suakin *72 C3 var.* Sawakin. Red Sea,
  NE Sudan
Subačius *106 C4* Panevėžys,
  NE Lithuania
Subaykhan *118 E3* Dayr az Zawr, E Syria
Subotica *100 D2 Ger.* Maria-Theresiopel,
  Hung. Szabadka. Vojvodina, N Serbia
Suceava *108 C3 Ger.* Suczawa, *Hung.*
  Szucsava. Suceava, NE Romania
Su-chou *see* Suzhou
Suchow *see* Xuzhou, Jiangsu, China
Suchow *see* Suzhou, Jiangsu, China
Sucker State *see* Illinois
Sucre *61 F4 hist.* Chuquisaca, La Plata.
  country capital (Bolivia-legal capital)
  Chuquisaca, S Bolivia
Suczawa *see* Suceava
Sudan *72 A4 off.* Republic of Sudan,
  Ar. Jumhuriyat as-Sudan; *prev.*
  Anglo-Egyptian Sudan. *country*
  N Africa
Sudanese Republic *see* Mali
Sudan, Jumhuriyat as- *see* Sudan
Sudan, Republic of *see* Sudan
Sudbury *38 C4* Ontario, S Canada
Sudd *73 B5 swamp region*
  C South Sudan
Sudeten *98 B4 var.* Sudetes, Sudetic
  Mountains, *Cz./Pol.* Sudety. *mountain*
  range Czech Republic (Czechia)/Poland
Sudetes/Sudetic Mountains/Sudety *see*
  Sudeten
Südkarpaten *see* Carpaţii Meridionali
Südliche Morava *see* Južna Morava
Sudong, Pulau *138 A2 island*
  SW Singapore Asia
Sudostroy *see* Severodvinsk
Sue *73 B5 river* W South Sudan
Sueca *93 F3* Valenciana, E Spain

Sue Wood Bay *42 B5 bay* W Bermuda
  North America W Atlantic Ocean
Suez *72 B1 Ar.* As Suways, El Suweis.
  NE Egypt
Suez Canal *72 B1 Ar.* Qanât as Suways.
  canal NE Egypt
Suez, Gulf of *see* Khalij as Suways
Suğla Gölü *116 C4 lake* SW Turkey
Şuḩār *121 D5 var.* Sohar. N Oman
Suḩāj *72 B2 var.* Sawhāj, Sohag, Suliag.
  C Egypt
Sühbaatar *127 E1* Selenge,
  N Mongolia
Suhl *95 C5* Thüringen, C Germany
Suicheng *see* Suixi
Suid-Afrika *see* South Africa
Suidwes-Afrika *see* Namibia
Suixi *128 C6 var.* Suicheng. Guangdong,
  S China
Sujawal *134 B3* Sind, SE Pakistan
Sukabumi *138 C5 prev.* Soekaboemi.
  Jawa, C Indonesia
Sukagawa *131 D5* Fukushima, Honshū,
  C Japan
Sukarnapura *see* Jayapura
Sukarno, Puntjak *see* Jaya, Puncak
Sukhne *see* As Sukhnah
Sukhona *110 C4 var.* Tot'ma. *river*
  NW Russia
Sukhumi *see* Sokhumi
Sukkertoppen *see* Maniitsoq
Sukkur *134 B3* Sind, SE Pakistan
Sukumo *131 B7* Kōchi, Shikoku,
  SW Japan
Sulaimaniya *see* As Sulaymānīyah
Sulaiman Range *134 C2 mountain range*
  C Pakistan
Sula, Kepulauan *139 E4 island group*
  C Indonesia
Sulawesi, Laut *see* Celebes Sea
Sulechów *98 B3 Ger.* Züllichau.
  Lubuskie, W Poland
Suliag *see* Suḩāj
Sullana *60 B2* Piura, NW Peru
Sullivan Island *see* Lanbi Kyun
Sulphur Springs *49 G2* Texas,
  SW USA
Sultānābād *see* Arāk
Sulu Archipelago *139 E3 island group*
  SW Philippines
Sülüktü *see* Sulyukta
Sulu, Laut *see* Sulu Sea
Sulu Sea *139 E2 var.* Laut Sulu. *sea*
  SW Philippines
Sulyukta *123 E2 Kir.* Sülüktü.
  SW Kyrgyzstan
Sumatra *137 B8 Eng.* Sumatra. *island*
  W Indonesia
Sumatra *see* Sumatera
Šumava *see* Bohemian Forest
Sumba, Pulau *139 E5 Eng.* Sandalwood
  Island; *prev.* Soemba. *island* Nusa
  Tenggara, C Indonesia
Sumba, Selat *139 E5 strait* Nusa
  Tenggara, S Indonesia
Sumbawanga *73 B7* Rukwa, W Tanzania
Sumbe *78 B2 var.* N'Gunza, *Port.* Novo
  Redondo. Cuanza Sul, W Angola
Sumeih *73 B5* Southern Darfur,
  S Sudan
Sumgait *see* Sumqayıt, Azerbaijan
Summer Lake *46 B4 lake* Oregon,
  NW USA
Summit *93 H5* Alaska, USA
Sumqayıt *117 H2 Rus.* Sumgait.
  E Azerbaijan
Sumy *109 F2* Sums'ka Oblast',
  NE Ukraine
Sunbury *149 C7* Victoria,
  SE Australia
Sunda Islands *see* Greater Sunda Islands
Sunda, Selat *see* Sunda Strait
Sunda Strait *138 B5 var.* Selat Sunda
  strait Jawa/Sumatera, SW Indonesia
Sunda Trench *see* Java Trench
Sunderland *88 D4 var.* Wearmouth.
  NE England, United Kingdom
Sundsvall *85 C5* Västernorrland,
  C Sweden
Sunflower State *see* Kansas
Sungaipenuh *138 B4 prev.*
  Soengaipenoeh. Sumatera,
  W Indonesia
Sunnyvale *47 A6* California, W USA
Sunset State *see* Oregon
Sunshine State *see* Florida
Sunshine State *see* New Mexico
Sunshine State *see* South Dakota
Suntar *115 F3* Respublika Sakha
  (Yakutiya), NE Russia

Sunyani 75 E5 W Ghana
Suoločielgi see Saariselkä
Suomenlahti see Finland, Gulf of
Suomen Tasavalta/Suomi see Finland
Suomussalmi 84 E4 Kainuu, E Finland
Suông 137 D6 Kampong Cham, C Cambodia
Suoyarvi 110 B3 Respublika Kareliya, NW Russia
Supe 60 C3 Lima, W Peru
Supérieur, Lac see Superior, Lake
Superior 40 A1 Wisconsin, N USA
Superior, Lake 40 B1 Fr. Lac Supérieur. lake Canada/USA
Suqrah see Şawqirah
Şūr 121 E5 NE Oman
Şūr see Soûr
Surabaia see Surabaya
Surabaya 138 D5 prev. Surabaja, Soerabaja. Jawa, C Indonesia
Surakarta 138 C5 Eng. Solo; prev. Soerakarta. Jawa, S Indonesia
Šurany 99 C6 Hung. Nagysurány. Nitriansky Kraj, SW Slovakia
Sūrat 134 C4 Gujarāt, W India
Suratdhani see Surat Thani
Surat Thani 137 C6 var. Suratdhani. Surat Thani, SW Thailand
Surazh 107 E5 Vitsyebskaya Voblasts', NE Belarus
Surdulica 101 E5 Serbia, SE Serbia
Sûre 87 D7 var. Sauer. river W Europe
Surendranagar 134 C4 Gujarāt, W India
Surfers Paradise 149 E5 Queensland, E Australia
Surgut 114 D3 Khanty-Mansiyskiy Avtonomnyy Okrug-Yugra, C Russia
Surin 137 D5 Surin, E Thailand
Surinam see Suriname
Suriname 59 G3 off. Republic of Suriname, var. Surinam; prev. Dutch Guiana, Netherlands Guiana. country N South America
Suriname, Republic of see Suriname
Sūriya/Sūriyah, Al-Jumhūrīyah al-'Arabīyah as- see Syria
Surkhab, Darya-i- see Kahmard, Daryā-ye
Surkhob 123 F3 river C Tajikistan
Surt 71 G2 var. Sidra, Sirte. N Libya
Surtsey 83 E5 island S Iceland
Suruga-wan 131 D6 bay SE Japan
Susa 96 A2 Piemonte, NE Italy
Sūsah see Sousse
Susanville 47 B5 California, W USA
Susitna 36 C3 Alaska, USA
Susteren 87 D5 Limburg, SE Netherlands
Susuman 115 G3 Magadanskaya Oblast', E Russia
Sutlej 134 C2 river India/Pakistan
Suur Munamägi 106 D3 var. Munamägi, Ger. Eier-Berg. mountain SE Estonia
Suur Väin 106 C2 Ger. Grosser Sund. strait W Estonia
Suva 145 E4 country capital (Fiji) Viti Levu, W Fiji
Suvalkai/Suvalki see Suwałki
Suvorovo 104 E2 prev. Vetrino. Varna, E Bulgaria
Suwałki 98 E2 Lith. Suvalkai, Rus. Suvalki. Podlaskie, NE Poland
Şuwār see Aş Şuwār
Suways, Qanāt as see Suez Canal
Suweida see As Suwaydā'
Suzhou 128 D5 var. Soochow, Su-chou, Suchow; prev. Wuhsien. Jiangsu, E China
Svalbard 83 E1 constituent part of Norway. island group Arctic Ocean
Svartisen 84 C3 glacier C Norway
Svay Rieng 137 D6 Khmer. Svay Riĕng. Svay Rieng, S Cambodia
Svay Riĕng see Svay Rieng
Sveg 85 B5 Jämtland, C Sweden
Svenstavik 85 C5 Jämtland, C Sweden
Sverdlovsk see Yekaterinburg
Sverige see Sweden
Sveti Vrach see Sandanski
Svetlogorsk see Svietlahorsk
Svetlograd 111 B7 Stavropol'skiy Kray, SW Russia
Svetlovodsk see Svitlovods'k
Svetozarevo see Jagodina
Svietlahorsk 107 D7 Rus. Svetlogorsk. Homyel'skaya Voblasts', SE Belarus
Svilengrad 104 D3 prev. Mustafa-Pasha. Khaskovo, S Bulgaria
Svitlovods'k 109 F3 Rus. Svetlovodsk. Kirovohrads'ka Oblast', C Ukraine
Svizzera see Switzerland

Svobodnyy 115 G4 Amurskaya Oblast', SE Russia
Svyataya Anna Trough 155 C4 var. Saint Anna Trough. trough N Kara Sea
Swabian Jura see Schwäbische Alb
Swakopmund 78 B3 Erongo, W Namibia
Swan Islands 53 E1 island group NE Honduras North America
Swansea 89 C7 Wel. Abertawe. S Wales, United Kingdom
Swarzędz 98 C3 Poznań, W Poland
Swatow see Shantou
Swaziland see Eswatini
Sweden 84 B4 off. Kingdom of Sweden, Swe. Sverige. country N Europe
Sweden, Kingdom of see Sweden
Sweetwater 49 F3 Texas, SW USA
Świdnica 98 B4 Ger. Schweidnitz. Wałbrzych, SW Poland
Świdwin 98 B2 Ger. Schivelbein. Zachodnio-pomorskie, NW Poland
Świebodzice 98 B4 Ger. Freiburg in Schlesien, Swiebodzice. Wałbrzych, SW Poland
Świebodzin 98 B3 Ger. Schwiebus. Lubuskie, W Poland
Świecie 98 C3 Ger. Schwertberg. Kujawsko-pomorskie, C Poland
Swindon 89 D7 S England, United Kingdom
Swinemünde see Świnoujście
Świnoujście 98 B2 Ger. Swinemünde. Zachodnio-pomorskie, NW Poland
Swiss Confederation see Switzerland
Switzerland 95 A7 off. Swiss Confederation, Fr. La Suisse, Ger. Schweiz, It. Svizzera; anc. Helvetia. country C Europe
Sycaminum see Hefa
Sydenham Island see Nonouti
Sydney 148 D1 state capital New South Wales, SE Australia
Sydney 39 G4 Cape Breton Island, Nova Scotia, SE Canada
Sydney Island see Manra
Syedpur see Saidpur
Syemyezhava 107 C6 Rus. Semechevo. Minskaya Voblasts', C Belarus
Syene see Aswan
Syeverodonets'k 109 H3 Rus. Severodonetsk. Luhans'ka Oblast', E Ukraine
Syktyvkar 110 D4 prev. Ust'-Sysol'sk. Respublika Komi, NW Russia
Sylhet 135 G3 Sylhet, NE Bangladesh
Synel'nykove 109 G3 Dnipropetrovs'ka Oblast', E Ukraine
Syowa 154 C2 Japanese research station Antarctica
Syracuse 41 E3 New York, NE USA
Syracuse see Siracusa
Syrdar'ya 114 B4 Sirdaryo Viloyati, E Uzbekistan
Syria 118 B3 off. Syrian Arab Republic, var. Siria, Syrie, Ar. Al-Jumhūrīyah al-'Arabīyah as-Sūrīyah, Sūrīya. country SW Asia
Syrian Arab Republic see Syria
Syrian Desert 119 D5 Ar. Al Hamad, Bādiyat ash Shām. desert SW Asia
Syrie see Syria
Sýrna 105 E7 var. Sirna. island Kykládes, Greece, Aegean Sea
Sýros 105 C6 var. Síros. island Kykládes, Greece, Aegean Sea
Syulemeshlii see Sredets
Syvash, Zaliv see Syvash, Zatoka
Syvash, Zatoka 109 F4 Rus. Zaliv Syvash. inlet S Ukraine
Syzran' 111 C6 Samarskaya Oblast', W Russia
Szabadka see Subotica
Szamotuły 98 B3 Poznań, W Poland
Szászrégen see Reghin
Szatmárrnémeti see Satu Mare
Száva see Sava
Szczecin 98 B3 Eng./Ger. Stettin. Zachodnio-pomorskie, NW Poland
Szczecinek 98 B2 Ger. Neustettin. Zachodnio-pomorskie, NW Poland
Szczeciński, Zalew 90 A2 var. Stettiner Haff, Ger. Oderhaff. bay Germany/Poland
Szczuczyn Nowogródzki see Shchuchyn
Szczytno 98 D3 Ger. Ortelsburg. Warmińsko-Mazurskie, NE Poland
Szechuan/Szechwan see Sichuan

Szeged 99 D7 Ger. Szegedin, Rom. Seghedin. Csongrád, SE Hungary
Szegedin see Szeged
Székelykeresztúr see Cristuru Secuiesc
Székesfehérvár 99 C6 Ger. Stuhlweissenberg; anc. Alba Regia. Fejér, W Hungary
Szeklerburg see Miercurea-Ciuc
Szekler Neumarkt see Târgu Secuiesc
Szekszárd 99 C7 Tolna, S Hungary
Szempcz/Szenc see Senec
Szenice see Senica
Szenttamás see Srbobran
Szeping see Siping
Szilágysomlyó see Şimleu Silvaniei
Szinna see Snina
Sziszek see Sisak
Szitás-Keresztúr see Cristuru Secuiesc
Szkudy see Skuodas
Szlatina see Slatina
Szlovákia see Slovakia
Szolnok 99 D6 Jász-Nagykun-Szolnok, C Hungary
Szombathely 99 B6 Ger. Steinamanger; anc. Sabaria, Savaria. Vas, W Hungary
Szprotawa 98 B4 Ger. Sprottau. Lubuskie, W Poland
Sztálinváros see Dunaújváros
Szucsava see Suceava

T

Tabariya, Bahrat see Tiberias, Lake
Table Rock Lake 49 G1 reservoir Arkansas/Missouri, C USA
Tábor 99 B5 Jihočeský Kraj, S Czech Republic (Czechia)
Tabora 73 B7 Tabora, W Tanzania
Tabriz 120 C2 var. Tebriz; anc. Tauris. Āžarbāyjān-e Sharqī, NW Iran
Tabuaeran 145 G2 prev. Fanning Island. atoll Line Islands, E Kiribati
Tabūk 120 A4 Tabūk, NW Saudi Arabia
Täby 85 C6 Stockholm, C Sweden
Tachau see Tachov
Tachov 99 A5 Ger. Tachau. Plzeňský Kraj, W Czech Republic (Czechia)
Tacloban 139 F2 off. Tacloban City. Leyte, C Philippines
Tacloban City see Tacloban
Tacna 61 E4 Tacna, SE Peru
Tacoma 46 B2 Washington, NW USA
Tacuarembó 64 D4 prev. San Fructuoso. Tacuarembó, C Uruguay
Tademaït, Plateau du 70 D3 plateau C Algeria
Tadmor/Tadmur see Tudmur
Tādpatri 132 C2 Andhra Pradesh, E India
Tadzhikistan see Tajikistan
Taegu see Daegu
Taehan-haehyŏp see Korea Strait
Taehan Min'guk see South Korea
Taejŏn see Daejeon
Tafassâsset, Ténéré du 75 G2 desert N Niger
Tafila/Ţafīlah, Muḩāfaẓat aţ see Aţ Ţafīlah
Taganrog 111 A7 Rostovskaya Oblast', SW Russia
Taganrog, Gulf of 109 G4 Rus. Taganrogskiy Zaliv, Ukr. Tahanroz'ka Zatoka. gulf Russia/Ukraine
Taganrogskiy Zaliv see Taganrog, Gulf of
Taguatinga 63 F3 Tocantins, C Brazil
Tagus 92 C3 Port. Rio Tejo, Sp. Río Tajo. river Portugal/Spain
Tagus Plain 80 A4 abyssal plain E Atlantic Ocean
Tahanroz'ka Zatoka see Taganrog, Gulf of
Tahat 71 E4 mountain SE Algeria
Tahiti 145 H4 island Îles du Vent, W French Polynesia
Tahiti, Archipel de see Société, Archipel de la
Tahlequah 49 G1 Oklahoma, C USA
Tahoe, Lake 47 B5 lake California/Nevada, W USA
Tahoua 75 F3 Tahoua, W Niger
Taibei see Taipei
Taichū see Taichung
Taichung 128 D6 Jap. Taichū; var. Taizhong, Taiwan. C Taiwan
Taiden see Daejeon

Taieri 151 B7 river South Island, New Zealand
Taihape 150 D4 Manawatu-Wanganui, North Island, New Zealand
Taihoku see Taibei
Taikyū see Daegu
Tailem Bend 149 B7 South Australia
T'ainan see Tainan
Tainan 128 D6 prev. Dainan, T'ainan. S Taiwan
Taipei 128 D6 var. Taibei, T'aipei; Jap. Taihoku; prev. Daihoku. country capital (Taiwan) N Taiwan
Taiping 138 B3 Perak, Peninsular Malaysia
Taiwan 128 D6 off. Republic of China, var. Formosa, Formo'sa. country E Asia
T'aiwan Haihsia/Taiwan Haixia see Taiwan Strait
Taiwan Strait 128 D6 var. Formosa Strait, Chin. T'aiwan Haihsia, Taiwan Haixia. strait China/Taiwan
Taiyuan 128 C4 var. T'ai-yuan, T'ai-yüan; prev. Yangku. province capital Shanxi, C China
T'ai-yuan/T'ai-yüan see Taiyuan
Taizhong see Taichung
Ta'izz 121 B7 SW Yemen
Tajikistan 123 E3 off. Republic of Tajikistan, Rus. Tadzhikistan, Taj. Jumhurii Tojikiston; prev. Tajik S.S.R. country C Asia
Tajikistan, Republic of see Tajikistan
Tajik S.S.R see Tajikistan
Tajo, Río see Tagus
Tak 136 C4 var. Rahaeng. Tak, W Thailand
Takao see Kaohsiung
Takaoka 131 C5 Toyama, Honshū, SW Japan
Takapuna 150 D2 Auckland, North Island, New Zealand
Takeshima see Liancourt Rocks
Takhiatash see Taxiatosh
Takhtakupyr see Taxtako'pir
Takikawa 130 D2 Hokkaidō, NE Japan
Takla Makan Desert 126 B3 Eng. Takla Makan Desert. desert NW China
Takla Makan Desert see Taklimakan Shamo
Takow see Kaohsiung
Takutea 145 G4 island S Cook Islands
Talabriga see Aveiro, Portugal
Talabriga see Talavera de la Reina, Spain
Talachyn 107 D6 Rus. Tolochin. Vitsyebskaya Voblasts', NE Belarus
Talamanca, Cordillera de 53 E5 mountain range S Costa Rica
Talara 60 B2 Piura, NW Peru
Talas 123 F2 Talasskaya Oblast', NW Kyrgyzstan
Talaud, Kepulauan 139 F3 island group E Indonesia
Talavera de la Reina 92 D3 anc. Caesarobriga, Talabriga. Castilla-La Mancha, C Spain
Talca 64 B4 Maule, C Chile
Talcahuano 65 B5 Bío Bío, C Chile
Taldykorgan 114 C5 Kaz. Taldyqorghan; prev. Taldy-Kurgan. Taldykorgan, SE Kazakhstan
Taldy-Kurgan/Taldyqorghan see Taldykorgan
Ta-lien see Dalian
Taliq-an see Tāloqān
Tal'ka 107 C6 Minskaya Voblasts', C Belarus
Talkhof see Puurmani
Tallahassee 42 D3 prev. Muskogean. state capital Florida, SE USA
Tall al Abyaḑ see At Tall al Abyaḑ
Tallin see Tallinn
Tall Kalakh 118 B4 var. Tell Kalakh. Ḩimş, C Syria
Tallulah 42 B2 Louisiana, S USA
Talnakh 114 D3 Krasnoyarskiy Kray, N Russia
Tal'ne 109 E3 Rus. Tal'noye. Cherkas'ka Oblast', C Ukraine
Tal'noye see Tal'ne
Taloga 49 F1 Oklahoma, C USA
Tāloqān 123 E3 var. Taliq-an. Takhār, NE Afghanistan
Talsen see Talsi

Talsi 106 C3 Ger. Talsen.
NW Latvia
Taltal 64 B2 Antofagasta, N Chile
Talvik 84 D2 Finnmark, N Norway
Tamabo, Banjaran 138 D3 *mountain range* East Malaysia
Tamale 75 E4 C Ghana
Tamana 145 E3 *prev.* Rotcher Island. *atoll* Tungaru, W Kiribati
Tamanrasset 71 E4 *var.* Tamenghest.
S Algeria
Tamar 89 C7 *river* SW England, United Kingdom
Tamar *see* Tudmur
Tamatave *see* Toamasina
Tamazunchale 51 E4 San Luis Potosí, C Mexico
Tambacounda 74 C3 SE Senegal
Tambov 111 B6 Tambovskaya Oblast', W Russia
Tambura 73 B5 Western Equatoria, SW South Sudan
Tamchaket *see* Tâmchekket
Tâmchekket 74 C3 *var.* Tamchaket.
Hodh el Gharbi, S Mauritania
Tamenghest *see* Tamanrasset
Tamil Nādu 132 C3 *prev.* Madras.
cultural region SE India
Tam Ky 137 E5 Quang Nam-ſa Năng, C Vietnam
Tammerfors *see* Tampere
Tampa 43 E4 Florida, SE USA
Tampa Bay 43 E4 *bay* Florida, SE USA
Tampere 85 D5 Swe. Tammerfors.
Pirkanmaa, W Finland
Tampico 51 E3 Tamaulipas, C Mexico
Tamworth 149 D6 New South Wales, SE Australia
Tanabe 131 C7 Wakayama, Honshū, SW Japan
Tana Bru 84 D2 Finnmark, N Norway
Tanais *see* Don
Lake Tana 72 C4 *var.* Lake Tana. *lake* NW Ethiopia
Tana, Lake *see* T'ana Hāyk'
Tanami Desert 146 D3 *desert* Northern Territory, N Australia
Tananarive *see* Antananarivo
Ţăndărei 108 D3 Ialomiţa, SE Romania
Tandil 65 D5 Buenos Aires, E Argentina
Tandjoengkarang *see* Bandar Lampung
Tanega-shima 131 B8 *island* Nansei-shotō, SW Japan
Tanen Taunggyi *see* Tane Range
Tane Range 136 B4 Bur. Tanen Taunggyi. *mountain range* W Thailand
Tanezrouft 70 D4 *desert* Algeria/Mali
Ţanf, Jabal aṭ 118 D4 *mountain* SE Syria
Tanga 73 C7 Tanga, E Tanzania
Tanganyika and Zanzibar *see* Tanzania
Tanganyika, Lake 73 B7 *lake* E Africa
Tanger 70 C2 *var.* Tangiers, Tangier, *Fr./Ger.* Tangerk, *Sp.* Tánger; *anc.* Tingis.
NW Morocco
Tangerk *see* Tanger
Tanggula Shan 126 C4 *mountain* W China
Tangier *see* Tanger
Tangiers *see* Tanger
Tangra Yumco 126 B5 *var.* Tangro Tso. *lake* W China
Tangro Tso *see* Tangra Yumco
Tangshan 128 D3 *var.* T'ang-shan.
Hebei, E China
T'ang-shan *see* Tangshan
Tanimbar, Kepulauan 139 F5 *island group* Maluku, E Indonesia
Tanintharyi 137 B6 *prev.* Tenasserim.
S Myanmar (Burma)
Tanjungbalai/Tanjungkarang-Telukbetung *see* Bandar Lampung
Tanna 144 D4 *island* S Vanuatu
Tannenhof *see* Krynica
Tan-Tan 70 B3 SW Morocco
Tan-tung *see* Dandong
Tanzania 73 C7 *off.* United Republic of Tanzania, *Swa.* Jamhuri ya Muungano wa Tanzania; *prev.* German East Africa, Tanganyika and Zanzibar. *country* E Africa
Tanzania, Jamhuri ya Muungano wa *see* Tanzania
Tanzania, United Republic of *see* Tanzania
Taoudenit *see* Taoudenni
Taoudenni *see* Tombouctou

Tapa 106 E2 Ger. Taps. Lääne-Virumaa, NE Estonia
Tapachula 51 G5 Chiapas, SE Mexico
Tapaiu *see* Gvardeysk
Tapajós, Rio 63 E2 *var.* Tapajóz. *river* NW Brazil
Tapajóz *see* Tapajós, Rio
Taps *see* Tapa
Ţarābulus 71 F2 *var.* Ţarābulus al Gharb, *Eng.* Tripoli. *country capital* (Libya) NW Libya
Ţarābulus al Gharb *see* Ţarābulus
Ţarābulus/Ţarābulus ash Shām *see* Tripoli
Taraclia 108 D4 Rus. Tarakilya.
S Moldova
Tarakilya *see* Taraclia
Mount Taranaki 150 C4 *var.* Egmont.
volcano North Island, New Zealand
Tarancón 93 E3 Castilla-La Mancha, C Spain
Taranto 97 E5 *var.* Tarentum. Puglia, SE Italy
Taranto, Gulf of 97 E6 *Eng.* Gulf of Taranto. *gulf* S Italy
Taranto, Gulf of *see* Taranto, Golfo di
Tarapoto 60 C2 San Martín, N Peru
Tarare 91 D5 Rhône, E France
Tarascon 91 D6 Bouches-du-Rhône, SE France
Tarawa 144 D2 *atoll and capital* (Kiribati) Tungaru, W Kiribati
Taraz 114 C5 *prev.* Aulie Ata, Auliye-Ata, Dzhambul, Zhambyl.
Zhambyl, S Kazakhstan
Tarazona 93 E2 Aragón, NE Spain
Tarbes 91 B6 *anc.* Bigorra.
Hautes-Pyrénées, S France
Tarcoola 149 A6 South Australia
Taree 149 D6 New South Wales, SE Australia
Tarentum *see* Taranto
Târgovişte 108 C5 *prev.* Tîrgovişte.
Dâmboviţa, S Romania
Targu Jiu 108 B4 *prev.* Tîrgu Jiu. Gorj, W Romania
Târgul-Neamţ *see* Târgu-Neamţ
Târgul-Săcuiesc *see* Târgu Secuiesc
Târgu Mureş 108 B4 *prev.* Oşorhei, Tîrgu Mures, *Ger.* Neumarkt, *Hung.* Marosvásárhely. Mureş, C Romania
Târgu-Neamţ 108 C3 *var.* Târgul-Neamţ; *prev.* Tîrgu-Neamţ.
Neamţ, NE Romania
Târgu Ocna 108 C4 Hung. Aknavásár; *prev.* Tîrgu Ocna. Bacău, E Romania
Târgu Secuiesc 108 C4 Ger. Neumarkt, Szekler Neumarkt, Hung. Kezdivásárhely; *prev.* Chezdi-Oşorheiu, Târgul-Săcuiesc, Tîrgu Secuiesc. Covasna, E Romania
Tar Heel State *see* North Carolina
Tarija 61 G5 Tarija, S Bolivia
Tarim 121 C6 C Yemen
Tarim Basin 124 C2 *Eng.* Tarim Basin. *basin* NW China
Tarim Basin *see* Tarim Pendi
Tarim He 126 B3 *river* NW China
Tarma 60 C3 Junín, C Peru
Tarn 126 *cultural region* S France
Tarn 91 C6 *river* S France
Tarnobrzeg 98 D3 Podkarpackie, SE Poland
Tarnopol *see* Ternopil'
Tarnów 99 D5 Małopolskie, S Poland
Tarraco *see* Tarragona
Tarragona 93 G2 *anc.* Tarraco.
Cataluña, E Spain
Tarrasa *see* Terrassa
Tàrrega 93 F2 *var.* Tarrega. Cataluña, NE Spain
Tarsatica *see* Rijeka
Tarsus 116 C4 İçel, S Turkey
Tartous/Tartouss *see* Ţarţūs
Tartu 106 D3 Ger. Dorpat; *prev.* Rus. Yurev, Yury'ev. Tartumaa, SE Estonia
Ţarţūs 118 A3 *off.* Muḥāfaẓat Ţarţūs, *var.* Tartous, Tartus. *governorate* W Syria
Ţarţūs, Muḥāfaẓat *see* Ţarţūs
Ta Ru Tao, Ko 137 B7 *island* S Thailand Asia
Tarvisio 96 D2 Friuli-Venezia Giulia, NE Italy
Tarvisium *see* Treviso
Tashauz *see* Daşoguz
Tashi Chho Dzong *see* Thimphu

Tashkent *see* Toshkent
Tash-Kömür *see* Tash-Kumyr
Tash-Kumyr 123 F2 Kir. Tash-Kömür.
Dzhalal-Abadskaya Oblast', W Kyrgyzstan
Tashqurghan *see* Khulm
Tasikmalaja *see* Tasikmalaya
Tasikmalaya 138 C5 *prev.* Tasikmalaja.
Jawa, C Indonesia
Tasman Basin 142 C5 *var.* East Australian Basin. *undersea basin* S Tasman Sea
Tasman Bay 151 C5 *inlet* South Island, New Zealand
Tasmania 149 B8 *prev.* Van Diemen's Land. *state* SE Australia
Tasmania 152 B4 *island* SE Australia
Tasman Plateau 142 C5 *var.* South Tasmania Plateau. *undersea plateau* SW Tasman Sea
Tasman Sea 142 C5 *sea* SW Pacific Ocean
Tassili-n-Ajjer 71 E4 *plateau* E Algeria
Tatabánya 99 C6 Komárom-Esztergom, NW Hungary
Tatar Pazardzhik *see* Pazardzhik
Tathlith 121 B5 'Asīr, S Saudi Arabia
Tatra Mountains 99 D5 Ger. Tatra, Hung. Tátra, Pol./Slvk. Tatry.
mountain range Poland/Slovakia
Tatra/Tátra *see* Tatra Mountains
Tatry *see* Tatra Mountains
Ta-t'ung/Tatung *see* Datong
Tatvan 117 F3 Bitlis, SE Turkey
Ta'ū 145 F4 *var.* Tau. *island* Manua Islands, E American Samoa
Taukum, Peski 123 G1 *desert* SE Kazakhstan
Taumarunui 150 D4 Manawatu-Wanganui, North Island, New Zealand
Taungdwingyi 136 B3 Magway, C Myanmar (Burma)
Taunggyi 136 B3 Shan State, C Myanmar (Burma)
Taungoo 136 B4 Bago, C Myanmar (Burma)
Taunton 89 C7 SW England, United Kingdom
Taupo 150 D3 Waikato, North Island, New Zealand
Taupo, Lake 150 D3 *lake* North Island, New Zealand
Tauragė 106 B4 Ger. Tauroggen.
Tauragė, SW Lithuania
Tauranga 150 D3 Bay of Plenty, North Island, New Zealand
Tauris *see* Tabrīz
Tauroggen *see* Tauragė
Taurus Mountains 116 C4 *Eng.* Taurus Mountains. *mountain range* S Turkey
Taurus Mountains *see* Toros Dağları
Tavas 116 B4 Denizli, SW Turkey
Tavastehus *see* Hämeenlinna
Tavira 92 C5 Faro, S Portugal
Tavoy *see* Dawei
Tavoy Island *see* Mali Kyun
Ta Waewae Bay 151 A7 *bay* South Island, New Zealand
Tawakoni, Lake 49 G2 *reservoir* Texas, SW USA
Tawau 138 D3 Sabah, East Malaysia
Tawkar *see* Tokar
Tawzar *see* Tozeur
Taxco 51 E4 *var.* Taxco de Alarcón.
Guerrero, S Mexico
Taxco de Alarcón *see* Taxco
Taxiatosh 122 C2 *var.* Takhiatash.
Qoraqalpogʻiston Respublikasi, W Uzbekistan
Taxtako'pir 122 D1 Rus. Takhtakupyr.
Qoraqalpogʻiston Respublikasi, NW Uzbekistan
Tay 88 C3 *river* C Scotland, United Kingdom
Taylor 49 G3 Texas, SW USA
Taymā' 120 A4 Tabūk, NW Saudi Arabia
Taymyr, Ozero 115 E2 *lake* N Russia
Taymyr, Poluostrov 115 E2 *peninsula* N Russia
Taz 114 D3 *river* N Russia
Tbilisi 117 G2 *var.* T'bilisi, *Eng.* Tiflis.
country capital (Georgia) SE Georgia
T'bilisi *see* Tbilisi
Tchad *see* Chad
Tchad, Lac *see* Chad, Lake
Tchien *see* Zwedru
Tchongking *see* Chongqing
Tczew 98 C2 Ger. Dirschau. Pomorskie, N Poland

Te Anau 151 A7 Southland, South Island, New Zealand
Te Anau, Lake 151 A7 *lake* South Island, New Zealand
Teapa 51 G4 Tabasco, SE Mexico
Teate *see* Chieti
Tebingtinggi 138 B3 Sumatera, N Indonesia
Tebriz *see* Tabrīz
Techirghiol 108 D5 Constanţa, SE Romania
Tecomán 50 D4 Colima, SW Mexico
Tecpan 51 E5 *var.* Tecpan de Galeana.
Guerrero, S Mexico
Tecpan de Galeana *see* Tecpan
Tecuci 108 C4 Galaţi, E Romania
Tedzhen *see* Harīrūd/Tejen
Tees 89 D5 *river* N England, United Kingdom
Tefé 62 D2 Amazonas, N Brazil
Tegal 138 C4 Jawa, C Indonesia
Tegelen 87 D5 Limburg, SE Netherlands
Tegucigalpa 52 C3 *country capital* (Honduras) Francisco Morazán, SW Honduras
Teheran *see* Tehrān
Tehrān 120 C3 *var.* Teheran. *country capital* (Iran) Tehrān, N Iran
Tehuacán 51 F4 Puebla, S Mexico
Tehuantepec 51 F5 *var.* Santo Domingo Tehuantepec. Oaxaca, SE Mexico
Gulf of Tehuantepec 51 F5 *var.* Gulf of Tehuantepec. *gulf* S Mexico
Tehuantepec, Gulf of *see* Tehuantepec, Golfo de
Isthmus of Tehuantepec 51 F5 *var.* Isthmus of Tehuantepec. *isthmus* SE Mexico
Tehuantepec, Isthmus of *see* Tehuantepec, Istmo de
Tejen 122 C3 Rus. Tedzhen. Ahal Welaýaty, S Turkmenistan
Tejen *see* Harīrūd
Tejo, Rio *see* Tagus
Te Kao 150 C1 Northland, North Island, New Zealand
Tekax 51 H4 *var.* Tekax de Álvaro Obregón. Yucatán, SE Mexico
Tekax de Álvaro Obregón *see* Tekax
Tekeli 114 C5 Almaty, SE Kazakhstan
Tekirdağ 116 A2 It. Rodosto; *anc.* Bisanthe, Raidestos, Rhaedestus.
Tekirdağ, NW Turkey
Te Kuiti 150 D3 Waikato, North Island, New Zealand
Tela 52 C2 Atlántida, NW Honduras
Telanaipura *see* Jambi
Telangana 134 D5 *cultural region* SE India
Tel Aviv-Jaffa *see* Tel Aviv-Yafo
Tel Aviv-Yafo 119 A6 *var.* Tel Aviv-Jaffa.
Tel Aviv, C Israel
Teles Pirés *see* São Manuel, Rio
Telish 104 C2 *prev.* Azizie. Pleven, N Bulgaria
Tell Abiad/Tell Abyad *see* At Tall al Abyaḑ
Tell Kalakh *see* Tall Kalakh
Tell Shedadi *see* Ash Shadādah
Tel'man/Tel'mansk *see* Gubadag
Teloekbetoeng *see* Bandar Lampung
Telo Martius *see* Toulon
Telschen *see* Telšiai
Telšiai 106 B3 Ger. Telschen. Telšiai, NW Lithuania
Telukbetung *see* Bandar Lampung
Temerin 100 D3 Vojvodina, N Serbia
Temeschburg/Temeschwar *see* Timişoara
Temesvár/Temeswar *see* Timişoara
Temirtau 114 C4 *prev.* Samarkandski, Samarkandskoye. Karagandy, C Kazakhstan
Tempio Pausania 97 A5 Sardegna, Italy, C Mediterranean Sea
Temple 49 G3 Texas, SW USA
Temuco 65 B5 Araucanía, C Chile
Temuka 151 B6 Canterbury, South Island, New Zealand
Tenali 132 D1 Andhra Pradesh, E India
Ténenkou 74 D3 Mopti, C Mali
Ténéré 75 G3 *physical region* C Niger
Tenerife 70 A3 *island* Islas Canarias, Spain, NE Atlantic Ocean
Tengger Shamo 127 E3 *desert* N China

Tengréla 74 D4 var. Tingréla.
N Ivory Coast
Tenkodogo 75 E4 S Burkina Faso
Tennant Creek 148 A3 Northern
Territory, C Australia
Tennessee 42 C1 off. State of Tennessee,
also known as The Volunteer State.
state SE USA
Tennessee River 42 C1 river S USA
Tenos see Tínos
Tepelena see Tepelenë
Tepelenë 101 C7 var. Tepelena, It.
Tepeleni. Gjirokastër, S Albania
Tepeleni see Tepelenë
Tepic 50 D4 Nayarit, C Mexico
Teplice 98 A4 Ger. Teplitz; prev.
Teplice-Šanov, Teplitz-Schönau.
Ústecký Kraj, NW Czech Republic
(Czechia)
Teplice-Šanov/Teplitz/Teplitz-Schönau
see Teplice
Tequila 50 D4 Jalisco, SW Mexico
Teraina 145 G2 prev. Washington Island.
atoll Line Islands, E Kiribati
Teramo 96 C4 anc. Interamna. Abruzzi,
C Italy
Tercan 117 E3 Erzincan, NE Turkey
Terceira 92 A5 var. Ilha Terceira. island
Azores, Portugal, NE Atlantic Ocean
Terceira, Ilha see Terceira
Terekhovka see Tsyerakhowka
Teresina 63 F2 var. Therezina. state
capital Piauí, NE Brazil
Termez see Termiz
Termia see Kýthnos
Términos, Laguna de 51 G4 lagoon
SE Mexico
Termiz 123 E3 Rus. Termez.
Surkhondaryo Viloyati, S Uzbekistan
Termoli 96 D4 Molise, C Italy
Terneuzen 87 B5 var. Neuzen. Zeeland,
SW Netherlands
Terni 96 C4 anc. Interamna Nahars.
Umbria, C Italy
Ternopil' 108 C2 Pol. Tarnopol, Rus.
Ternopol'. Ternopil's'ka Oblast',
W Ukraine
Ternopol' see Ternopil'
Terracina 97 C5 Lazio, C Italy
Terranova di Sicilia see Gela
Terranova Pausania see Olbia
Terrassa 93 G2 Cast. Tarrasa. Cataluña,
E Spain
Terre Adélie 154 C4 physical region
Antarctica
Terre Haute 40 B4 Indiana, N USA
Terre Neuve see Newfoundland and
Labrador
Terschelling 86 C1 Fris. Skylge. island
Waddeneilanden, N Netherlands
Teruel 93 F3 anc. Turba. Aragón,
E Spain
Tervel 104 E1 prev. Kurtbunar, Rom.
Curtbunar. Dobrich, NE Bulgaria
Tervueren see Tervuren
Tervuren 87 C6 var. Tervueren. Vlaams
Brabant, C Belgium
Teseney 72 C4 var. Tessenei. W Eritrea
Tessalit 75 E2 Kidal, NE Mali
Tessaoua 75 G3 Maradi, S Niger
Tessenderlo 87 C5 Limburg,
NE Belgium
Tessenei see Teseney
Testigos, Islas los 59 E1 island group
N Venezuela
Tete 79 E2 Tete, NW Mozambique
Teterow 94 C3 Mecklenburg-
Vorpommern, NE Germany
Tétouan 70 C2 var. Tetouan, Tetuán.
N Morocco
Tetovo 101 D5 Razgrad, N Bulgaria
Tetschen see Děčín
Tetuán see Tétouan
Teverya see Tverya
Te Waewae Bay 151 A7 bay South
Island, New Zealand
Texarkana 42 A2 Arkansas, C USA
Texarkana 49 H2 Texas, SW USA
Texas 49 F3 off. State of Texas, also
known as Lone Star State. state
S USA
Texas City 49 H4 Texas, SW USA
Texel 86 C2 island Waddeneilanden,
NW Netherlands
Texoma, Lake 49 G2 reservoir
Oklahoma/Texas, C USA
Teziutlán 51 F4 Puebla, S Mexico
Thaa Atoll see Kolhumadulu
Thai, Ao see Thailand, Gulf of
Thai Binh 136 D3 Thai Binh, N Vietnam

Thailand 137 C5 off. Kingdom of
Thailand, Th. Prathet Thai; prev. Siam.
country SE Asia
Thailand, Gulf of 137 C6 var. Gulf of
Siam, Th. Ao Thai, Vtn. Vinh Thai Lan.
gulf SE Asia
Thailand, Kingdom of see Thailand
Thai Lan, Vinh see Thailand, Gulf of
Thai Nguyên 136 D3 Bắc Thai,
N Vietnam
Thakhèk 136 D4 var. Muang
Khammouan. Khammouan, C Laos
Thamarid see Thamarīt
Thamarīt 121 D6 var. Thamarid,
Thumrayt. SW Oman
Thames 150 D3 Waikato, North Island,
New Zealand
Thames 89 B8 river S England, United
Kingdom
Thandwe 136 A4 var. Sandoway.
Rakhine State, W Myanmar (Burma)
Thanh Hoa 136 D3 Thanh Hoa,
N Vietnam
Thanintari Taungdan see Bilauktaung
Range
Thanlwin see Salween
Thar Desert 134 C3 var. Great Indian
Desert, Indian Desert. desert India/
Pakistan
Tharthar, Buhayrat ath 120 B3 lake
C Iraq
Thásos 104 C4 Thásos, E Greece
Thásos 104 C4 island E Greece
Thaton 136 B4 Mon State, S Myanmar
(Burma)
Thayetmyo 136 A4 Magway, C Myanmar
(Burma)
The Crane 55 H2 var. Crane.
S Barbados
The Dalles 46 B3 Oregon, NW USA
The Flatts Village see Flatts Village
The Hague see 's-Gravenhage
Theodosia see Feodosiya
The Pas 37 F5 Manitoba, C Canada
Therezina see Teresina
Thérma 105 D6 Ikaría, Dodekánisa,
Greece, Aegean Sea
Thermaic Gulf 104 B4 Eng. Thermaic
Gulf; anc. Thermaicus Sinus. gulf
N Greece
Thermaic Gulf/Thermaicus Sinus see
Thermaïkós Kólpos
Thermaïkós Kólpos see
Thermaic Gulf
Thermiá see Kýthnos
Thérmo 105 B5 Dytikí Elláda,
C Greece
The Rock 93 H4 New South Wales,
SE Australia
The Sooner State see Oklahoma
Thessaloníki 104 C3 Eng. Salonica,
Salonika, SCr. Solun, Turk. Selânik.
Kentrikí Makedonía, N Greece
The Valley 55 G3 dependent territory
capital (Anguilla) E Anguilla
The Village 49 G1 Oklahoma,
C USA
The Volunteer State see Tennessee
Thiamis see Kalamás
Thian Shan see Tien Shan
Thibet see Xizang Zizhiqu
Thief River Falls 45 F1 Minnesota,
N USA
Thienen see Tienen
Thiers 91 C5 Puy-de-Dôme, C France
Thiès 74 B3 W Senegal
Thikombia see Cikobia
Thimbu see Thimphu
Thimphu 135 G3 var. Thimbu; prev.
Tashi Chho Dzong. country capital
(Bhutan) W Bhutan
Thionville 90 D3 Ger. Diedenhofen.
Moselle, NE France
Thíra see Santoríni
Thíra 105 D7 var. Santoríni. S Greece
Thíra 105 D7 island Kykládes, Greece,
Aegean Sea
Thiruvananthapuram 132 C3 var.
Trivandrum, Tiruvantapuram. state
capital Kerala, SW India
Thitu Island 128 C8 island NW Spratly
Islands
Tholen 86 B4 island SW Netherlands
Thomasville 42 D3 Georgia,
SE USA
Thompson 37 F4 Manitoba, C Canada
Thonon-les-Bains 91 D5 Haute-Savoie,
E France
Thorenburg see Turda
Thorlákshöfn 83 E5 Sudhurland,
SW Iceland
Thorn see Toruń
Thornton Island see Millennium Island
Thorshavn see Tórshavn

Thospitis see Van Gölü
Thouars 90 B4 Deux-Sèvres,
W France
Thoune see Thun
Thracian Sea 104 D4 Gk. Thrakikó
Pélagos; anc. Thracium Mare. sea
Greece/Turkey
Thracium Mare/Thrakikó Pélagos see
Thracian Sea
Three Gorges Reservoir 129 C5
reservoir C China
Three Kings Islands 150 C1 island
group N New Zealand
Thrissur 132 C3 var. Trichūr. Kerala,
SW India
Thuin 87 B7 Hainaut, S Belgium
Thule see Qaanaaq
Thumrayt see Thamarīt
Thun 95 A7 Fr. Thoune. Bern,
W Switzerland
Thunder Bay 38 B4 Ontario, S Canada
Thuner See 95 A7 lake C Switzerland
Thung Song 137 C7 var. Cha Mai.
Nakhon Si Thammarat, SW Thailand
Thurso 88 C2 N Scotland, United
Kingdom
Thýamis see Kalamás
Tianjin 128 D4 var. Tientsin. Tianjin
Shi, E China
Tianjin see Tianjin Shi
Tianjin Shi 128 D4 var. Jin, Tianjin,
T'ien-ching, Tientsin. municipality
E China
Tian Shan see Tien Shan
Tianshui 128 B4 Gansu, C China
Tiba see Chiba
Tiber 96 C4 Eng. Tiber. river C Italy
Tiber see Tevere, Italy
Tiber see Tivoli, Italy
Tiberias see Teverya
Tiberias, Lake 119 B5 var. Chinnereth,
Sea of Bahr Tabariya, Sea of Galilee, Ar.
Bahrat Tabariya, Heb. Yam Kinneret.
lake N Israel
Tibesti 76 C2 var. Tibesti Massif, Ar.
Tibistī. mountain range N Africa
Tibesti Massif see Tibesti
Tibet see Xizang Zizhiqu
Tibetan Autonomous Region see Xizang
Zizhiqu
Tibet, Plateau of 126 B4 var. Xizang
Gaoyuan, Eng. Plateau of Tibet. plateau
W China
Tibet, Plateau of see Qingzang Gaoyuan
Tibistī see Tibesti
Tibni see al Tibnī
Tiburón, Isla 50 B2 var. Isla del Tiburón.
island NW Mexico
Tiburón, Isla del see Tiburón, Isla
Tichau see Tychy
Tichitt 74 D2 var. Tichitt. Tagant,
C Mauritania
Tichitt see Tîchît
Ticinum see Pavia
Ticul 51 H3 Yucatán, SE Mexico
Tidjikdja see Tidjikja
Tidjikja 74 C2 var. Tidjikdja; prev.
Fort-Cappolani. Tagant, C Mauritania
Tienen 87 C6 var. Thienen, Fr.
Tirlemont. Vlaams Brabant,
C Belgium
Tiên Giang, Sông see Mekong
Tien Shan 126 B3 Chin. Thian Shan,
Tian Shan, T'ien Shan, Rus.
Tyan'-Shan'. mountain range C Asia
Tientsin see Tianjin
Tierp 85 C6 Uppsala, C Sweden
Tierra del Fuego 65 B8 island Argentina/
Chile
Tiflis see Tbilisi
Tifton 42 D3 Georgia, SE USA
Tifu 139 F4 Pulau Buru, E Indonesia
Tighina 108 D4 Rus. Bendor; prev.
Bender. E Moldova
Tigranocerta see Siirt
Tigris 120 B2 Ar. Dijlah, Turk. Dicle.
river Iraq/Turkey
Tiguentourine 71 E3 E Algeria
Ti-hua/Tihwa see Ürümqi
Tijuana 50 A1 Baja California Norte,
NW Mexico
Tikhoretsk 111 A7 Krasnodarskiy Kray,
SW Russia
Tikhvin 110 B4 Leningradskaya Oblast',
NW Russia
Tikiarjuaq see Whale Cove
Tiki Basin 143 G3 undersea basin
S Pacific Ocean
Tikinsso 52 C4 river C Guinea

Tikirarjuaq see Whale Cove
Tiksi 115 F2 Respublika Sakha
(Yakutiya), NE Russia
Tilburg 86 C4 Noord-Brabant,
S Netherlands
Tilimsen see Tlemcen
Tilio Martius see Toulon
Tillabéri 75 F3 var. Tillabéry. Tillabéri,
W Niger
Tillabéry see Tillabéri
Tílos 105 E7 island Dodekánisa, Greece,
Aegean Sea
Timan Ridge 110 D3 Eng. Timan Ridge.
ridge NW Russia
Timan Ridge see Timanskiy Kryazh
Timaru 151 B6 Canterbury, South Island,
New Zealand
Timbaki/Timbákion see Tympáki
Timbedgha 74 D3 var. Timbédra. Hodh
ech Chargui, SE Mauritania
Timbédra see Timbedgha
Timbuktu see Tombouctou
Timiş 108 A4 county SW Romania
Timişoara 108 A4 Ger. Temeschwar,
Temeswar, Hung. Temesvár;
prev. Temeschburg. Timiş,
W Romania
Timmins 38 C4 Ontario, S Canada
Timor 125 F5 island Nusa Tenggara,
C Indonesia
Timor Sea 125 F5 sea E Indian Ocean
Timor Timur see East Timor
Timor Trench see Timor Trough
Timor Trough 125 F4 var. Timor
Trench. trough NE Timor Sea
Timrå 85 C5 Västernorrland,
C Sweden
Tindouf 70 C3 W Algeria
Tineo 92 C1 Asturias, N Spain
Tingis see Tanger
Tingo María 60 C3 Huánuco, C Peru
Tingréla see Tengréla
Tinhosa Grande 76 E2 island
N Sao Tome and Principe, Africa,
E Atlantic Ocean
Tinhosa Pequena 76 E1 island
N Sao Tome and Principe, Africa,
E Atlantic Ocean
Tinian 144 B1 island S Northern
Mariana Islands
Tínos 105 D6 Tínos, Kykládes, Greece,
Aegean Sea
Tínos 105 D6 anc. Tenos. island
Kykládes, Greece, Aegean Sea
Tip 101 E6 Papua, E Indonesia
Tipitapa 52 D3 Managua, W Nicaragua
Tip Top Mountain 38 C4 mountain
Ontario, S Canada
Tirana see Tiranë
Tiranë 101 C6 var. Tirana. country
capital (Albania) Tiranë, C Albania
Tiraspol 108 D4 Rus. Tiraspol'.
E Moldova
Tiraspol' see Tiraspol
Tiree 88 B3 island W Scotland,
United Kingdom
Tîrgovişte see Târgovişte
Tîrgu Jiu see Targu Jiu
Tîrgu Mures see Târgu Mureş
Tîrgu-Neamţ see Târgu-Neamţ
Tîrgu Ocna see Târgu Ocna
Tîrgu Secuiesc see Târgu Secuiesc
Tirlemont see Tienen
Tírnavos see Týrnavos
Tîrnovo see Veliko Tŭrnovo
Tirol 95 C7 off. Land Tirol, var. Tyrol, It.
Tirolo. state W Austria
Tirol, Land see Tirol
Tirolo see Tirol
Tirreno, Mare see Tyrrhenian Sea
Tiruchchirāppalli 132 C3 prev.
Trichinopoly. Tamil Nādu,
SE India
Tiruppattūr 132 C2 Tamil Nādu,
SE India
Tiruvantapuram see
Thiruvananthapuram
Tisa 103 F1 Ger. Theiss, Rom./Slvn./SCr.
Tisa, Rus. Tissa, Ukr. Tysa. river
SE Europe
Tisa see Tisza
Tiszakécske 99 D7 Bács-Kiskun,
C Hungary
Titano, Monte 96 E1 mountain
C San Marino
Titicaca, Lake 61 E4 lake Bolivia/
Peru
Titograd see Podgorica
Titose see Chitose
Titova Mitrovica see Mitrovicë

Titovo Užice see Užice
Titu 108 C5 Dâmboviţa,
    S Romania
Titule 77 D5 Orientale, N Dem. Rep.
    Congo
Tiverton 89 C7 SW England, United
    Kingdom
Tivoli 96 C4 anc. Tiber. Lazio, C Italy
Tizimín 51 H3 Yucatán, SE Mexico
Tizi Ouzou 71 E1 var. Tizi-Ouzou.
    N Algeria
Tizi-Ouzou see Tizi Ouzou
Tiznit 70 B3 SW Morocco
Tjilatjap see Cilacap
Tjirebon see Cirebon
Tlaquepaque 50 D4 Jalisco, C Mexico
Tlascala see Tlaxcala
Tlaxcala 51 F4 var. Tlascala, Tlaxcala de
    Xicohténcatl. Tlaxcala, C Mexico
Tlaxcala de Xicohténcatl see Tlaxcala
Tlemcen 70 D2 var. Tilimsen, Tlemsen.
    NW Algeria
Tlemsen see Tlemcen
Toamasina 79 G3 prev./Fr. Tamatave.
    Toamasina, E Madagascar
Toba, Danau 138 B3 lake Sumatera,
    W Indonesia
Tobago 55 H5 island NE Trinidad and
    Tobago
Toba Kakar Range 134 B2 mountain
    range NW Pakistan
Tobol see Tobyl
Tobol'sk 114 C3 Tyumenskaya Oblast',
    C Russia
Tobruch/Tobruk see Ţubruq
Tobyl 114 C4 prev. Tobol. river
    Kazakhstan/Russia
Tocantins 63 E3 off. Estado do
    Tocantins. state/region C Brazil
Tocantins, Estado do see Tocantins
Tocantins, Rio 63 F2 river N Brazil
Tocoa 52 D2 Colón, N Honduras
Tocopilla 64 B2 Antofagasta, N Chile
Todi 96 C4 Umbria, C Italy
Todos os Santos, Baía de 63 G3 bay
    E Brazil
Toetoes Bay 151 B8 bay South Island,
    New Zealand
Tofua 145 E4 island Ha'apai Group,
    C Tonga
Togo 75 E4 off. Togolese Republic; prev.
    French Togoland. country W Africa
Togolese Republic see Togo
Tojikiston, Jumhurii see Tajikistan
Tokanui 151 B7 Southland, South Island,
    New Zealand
Tokar 72 C3 var. Ţawkar. Red Sea,
    NE Sudan
Tokat 116 D3 Tokat, N Turkey
Tokelau 145 E3 NZ overseas territory
    W Polynesia
Tőketerebes see Trebišov
Tokio see Tōkyō
Tokmak 109 G4 var. Velykyy Tokmak.
    Zaporiz'ka Oblast', SE Ukraine
Tokmak see Tomok
Tokoroa 150 D3 Waikato, North Island,
    New Zealand
Tokounou 74 C4 C Guinea
Tokushima 131 C6 var. Tokusima.
    Tokushima, Shikoku, SW Japan
Tōkyō 130 A1 var. Tokio. country
    capital (Japan) Tōkyō, Honshū,
    S Japan
Tōkyō-wan 130 A2 bay S Japan
Tolbukhin see Dobrich
Toledo 92 D3 anc. Toletum. Castilla-La
    Mancha, C Spain
Toledo 40 D3 Ohio, N USA
Toledo Bend Reservoir 49 G3 reservoir
    Louisiana/Texas, SW USA
Toletum see Toledo
Toliara 79 F4 var. Toliary; prev. Tuléar.
    Toliara, SW Madagascar
Toliary see Toliara
Tolmein see Tolmin
Tolmin 95 D7 Ger. Tolmein, It. Tolmino.
    W Slovenia
Tolmino see Tolmin
Tolna 99 C7 Ger. Tolnau. Tolna,
    S Hungary
Tolnau see Tolna
Tolochin see Talachyn
Tolosa 93 E1 País Vasco, N Spain
Tolosa see Toulouse
Toluca 51 E4 var. Toluca de Lerdo.
    México, S Mexico
Toluca de Lerdo see Toluca
Tol'yatti 111 C6 prev. Stavropol'.
    Samarskaya Oblast', W Russia

Tomah 40 B2 Wisconsin, N USA
Tomakomai 130 D2 Hokkaidō,
    NE Japan
Tomar 92 B3 Santarém, W Portugal
Tomaschow see Tomaszów Mazowiecki
Tomaschow see Tomaszów Lubelski
Tomaszów see Tomaszów Mazowiecki
Tomaszów Lubelski 98 E4 Ger.
    Tomaschow. Lubelskie,
    E Poland
Tomaszów Mazowiecka see Tomaszów
    Mazowiecki
Tomaszów Mazowiecki 98 D4 var.
    Tomaszów Mazowiecka; prev.
    Tomaszów, Ger. Tomaschow. Łódzkie,
    C Poland
Tombigbee River 42 C3 river Alabama/
    Mississippi, S USA
Tombouctou 75 E3 Eng. Timbuktu; var.
    Taoudenni. Tombouctou, N Mali
Tombua 78 A2 Port. Porto Alexandre.
    Namibe, SW Angola
Tomelloso 93 E3 Castilla-La Mancha,
    C Spain
Tomini, Gulf of see Teluk Tomini
Tomini, Teluk 139 E4 Eng. Gulf of
    Tomini; prev. Teluk Gorontalo. bay
    Sulawesi, C Indonesia
Tomok 123 G2 prev. Tokmak.
    Chuyskaya Oblast', N Kyrgyzstan
Tomsk 114 D4 Tomskaya Oblast',
    C Russia
Tomür Feng 126 B3 pre. Pik Pobedy;
    Kyrg. Jengish Chokusu. mountain
    China/Kyrgyzstan
Toncontín 52 C3 prev. Tegucigalpa.
    country capital (Honduras) Francisco
    Morazán, SW Honduras
Tonezh see Tonyezh
Tonga 145 E4 off. Kingdom of Tonga,
    var. Friendly Islands. country
    SW Pacific Ocean
Tongatapu 145 E5 island Tongatapu
    Group, S Tonga
Tongatapu Group 145 E5 island group
    S Tonga
Tonga Trench 143 E3 trench S Pacific
    Ocean
Tongchuan 128 C4 Shaanxi, C China
Tongeren 87 D6 Fr. Tongres. Limburg,
    NE Belgium
Tongking, Gulf of see Tonkin, Gulf of
Tongliao 127 G2 Nei Mongol Zizhiqu,
    N China
Tongres see Tongeren
Tongshan see Xuzhou, Jiangsu, China
Tongtian He 126 C4 var. Zhi Qu. river
    C China
Tonj 73 B5 Warap, W South Sudan
Tonkin, Gulf of 128 B7 var. Tongking,
    Gulf of, Chin. Beibu Wan, Vtn. Vinh
    Bắc Bộ. gulf China/Vietnam
Tônlé Sap 137 D5 Eng. Great Lake. lake
    W Cambodia
Tonopah 47 C6 Nevada, W USA
Tonyezh 107 C7 Rus. Tonezh.
    Homyel'skaya Voblasts', SE Belarus
Tooele 44 B4 Utah, W USA
Toowoomba 149 E5 Queensland,
    E Australia
Topeka 45 F4 state capital Kansas,
    C USA
Toplica see Topliţa
Topliţa 108 C3 Ger. Töplitz, Hung.
    Maroshévíz; prev. Topliţa Română,
    Hung. Oláh-Toplicza, Toplicza.
    Harghita, C Romania
Topliţa Română/Töplitz see Topliţa
Topol'čany 99 C6 Hung. Nagytapolcsány.
    Nitriansky Kraj, W Slovakia
Topolovgrad 104 D3 prev. Kavaklí.
    Khaskovo, S Bulgaria
Topolya see Bačka Topola
Top Springs Roadhouse 146 E3
    Northern Territory, N Australia
Tor 154 C2 Norwegian research station
    Antarctica
Torda see Turda
Torez see Chystyakove
Torgau 94 D4 Sachsen, E Germany
Torhout 87 A5 West-Vlaanderen,
    W Belgium
Torino 96 A2 Eng. Turin. Piemonte,
    NW Italy
Tornacum see Tournai
Torneà see Tornio
Torneträsk 84 C3 lake N Sweden
Tornio 84 D4 Swe. Torneà. Lappi,
    NW Finland

Tornionjoki 84 D3 river Finland/Sweden
Tornionjoki 84 D3 river Finland/
    Sweden
Toro 92 D2 Castilla y León, N Spain
Toronto 38 D5 province capital Ontario,
    S Canada
Torquay 89 C7 SW England, United
    Kingdom
Torrance 46 D2 California, W USA
Torre, ilcha da 92 B3 mountain
    C Portugal
Torre del Greco 97 D5 Campania,
    S Italy
Torrejón de Ardoz 93 E3 Madrid,
    C Spain
Torrelavega 92 D1 Cantabria,
    N Spain
Torrens, Lake 149 A6 salt lake South
    Australia
Torrent 93 F3 Cas. Torrente, var.
    Torrent de l'Horta. Valenciana,
    E Spain
Torrent de l'Horta/Torrente see
    Torrent
Torreón 50 D3 Coahuila, NE Mexico
Torres Strait 148 C1 strait Australia/
    Papua New Guinea
Torres Vedras 92 B3 Lisboa,
    C Portugal
Torrington 44 D3 Wyoming,
    C USA
Tórshavn 83 F5 Dan. Thorshavn.
    Dependent territory capital Faroe
    Islands
To'rtkok'l 122 D2 var. Türtkül, Rus.
    Turtkul'; prev. Petroaleksandrovsk.
    Qoraqalpog'iston Respublikasi,
    W Uzbekistan
Tortoise Islands see Galápagos Islands
Tortosa 93 F2 anc. Dertosa. Cataluña,
    E Spain
Tortue, Montagne 59 H3 mountain
    range C French Guiana
Tortuga, Isla see La Tortuga, Isla
Toruń 98 C3 Ger. Thorn. Toruń,
    Kujawsko-pomorskie, C Poland
Tõrva 106 D3 Ger. Tõrwa. Valgamaa,
    S Estonia
Tõrwa see Tõrva
Torzhok 110 B4 Tverskaya Oblast',
    W Russia
Tosa-wan 131 B7 bay SW Japan
Toscana 96 B3 Eng. Tuscany. region
    C Italy
Toscano, Archipelago 96 B4 Eng.
    Tuscan Archipelago. island group
    C Italy
Toshkent 123 E2 Eng./Rus. Tashkent.
    country capital (Uzbekistan) Toshkent
    Viloyati, E Uzbekistan
Totana 93 E4 Murcia, SE Spain
Tot'ma see Sukhona
Totness 59 G3 Coronie, N Suriname
Tottori 131 B6 Tottori, Honshū,
    SW Japan
Touâjîl 74 C2 Tiris Zemmour,
    N Mauritania
Touggourt 71 E2 NE Algeria
Toukoto 74 C3 Kayes, W Mali
Toul 90 D3 Meurthe-et-Moselle,
    NE France
Toulon 91 D6 anc. Telo Martius, Tilio
    Martius. Var, SE France
Toulouse 91 B6 anc. Tolosa.
    Haute-Garonne, S France
Toungoo see Taungoo
Touraine 90 B4 cultural region C France
Tourane see Đa Nẵng
Tourcoing 90 C2 Nord, N France
Tournai 87 A6 var. Tournay, Dut.
    Doornik; anc. Tornacum. Hainaut,
    SW Belgium
Tournay see Tournai
Tours 90 B4 anc. Caesarodunum,
    Turoni. Indre-et-Loire, C France
Tovarkovsky 111 B5 Tul'skaya Oblast',
    W Russia
Tower Island see Genovesa, Isla
Townsville 148 D3 Queensland,
    NE Australia
Towoeti Meer see Towuti, Danau
Towraghoudi 122 D4 Herät,
    NW Afghanistan
Towson 41 F4 Maryland, NE USA
Towuti, Danau 139 E4 Dut. Towoeti
    Meer. lake Sulawesi, C Indonesia
Toyama 131 C5 Toyama, Honshū,
    SW Japan
Toyama-wan 131 B5 bay W Japan
Toyohara see Yuzhno-Sakhalinsk

Toyota 131 C6 Aichi, Honshū,
    SW Japan
Tozeur 71 E2 var. Tawzar. W Tunisia
Tráblous see Tripoli
Trabzon 117 E2 Eng. Trebizond; anc.
    Trapezus. Trabzon, NE Turkey
**Traiectum ad Mosam/Traiectum
    Tungorum** see Maastricht
Traiskirchen 95 E6 Niederösterreich,
    NE Austria
Trajani Portus see Civitavecchia
Trajectum ad Rhenum see Utrecht
Trakai 107 C5 Ger. Traken, Pol. Troki.
    Vilnius, SE Lithuania
Traken see Trakai
Tralee 89 A6 Ir. Trá Lí. SW Ireland
Trá Lí see Tralee
Tralles Aydin see Aydın
Trang 137 C7 Trang, S Thailand
Transantarctic Mountains 154 B3
    mountain range Antarctica
Transilvania see Transylvania
Transilvaniei, Alpi see Carpaţii
    Meridionali
Transjordan see Jordan
Transnistria 108 D3 cultural region
    NE Moldova
**Transsylvanische Alpen/
    Transylvanian Alps** see Carpaţii
    Meridionali
Transylvania 108 B4 Eng. Ardeal,
    Transilvania, Ger. Siebenbürgen, Hung.
    Erdély. cultural region NW Romania
Transylvanian Alps 108 B4 var. Alpi
    Transilvaniei, Carpaţii Sudici, Eng.
    South Carpathians, Transylvanian
    Alps, Ger. Südkarpaten,
    Transsylvanische Alpen, Hung.
    Déli-Kárpátok, Erdélyi-Havasok.
    mountain range C Romania
Trapani 97 B7 anc. Drepanum. Sicilia,
    Italy, C Mediterranean Sea
Trâpeăng Vêng see Kampong Thom
Trapezus see Trabzon
Traralgon 149 C7 Victoria, SE Australia
Trasimenischersee see Trasimeno, Lago
Trasimeno, Lago 96 C4 Eng. Lake of
    Perugia, Ger. Trasimenischersee. lake
    C Italy
Traù see Trogir
Traverse City 40 C2 Michigan, N USA
Tra Vinh 137 D6 var. Phu Vinh. Tra
    Vinh, S Vietnam
Travis, Lake 49 F3 reservoir Texas,
    SW USA
Travnik 100 C4 Federacija Bosne I
    Hercegovine, C Bosnia and Herzegovina
Trbovlje 95 E7 Ger. Trifail.
    C Slovenia
Treasure State see Montana
Třebíč 99 B5 Ger. Trebitsch. Vysočina,
    C Czech Republic (Czechia)
Trebinje 101 C5 Republika Srpska,
    S Bosnia and Herzegovina
Trebišov 99 D6 Hung. Tőketerebes.
    Košický Kraj, E Slovakia
Trebitsch see Třebíč
Trebnitz see Trzebnica
Tree Planters State see Nebraska
Trélazé 90 B4 Maine-et-Loire,
    NW France
Trelew 65 C6 Chubut, SE Argentina
Tremelo 87 C5 Vlaams Brabant,
    C Belgium
Trenčín 99 C5 Ger. Trentschin, Hung.
    Trencsén. Trenčiansky Kraj,
    W Slovakia
Trencsén see Trenčín
Trengganu, Kuala see
    Kuala Terengganu
Trenque Lauquen 64 C4 Buenos Aires,
    E Argentina
Trent see Trento
Trento 96 C2 Eng. Trent, Ger. Trient;
    anc. Tridentum. Trentino-Alto Adige,
    N Italy
Trenton 41 F4 state capital New Jersey,
    NE USA
Trentschin see Trenčín
Tres Arroyos 65 D5 Buenos Aires,
    E Argentina
Treskavica 100 C4 mountain range
    SE Bosnia and Herzegovina
Tres Tabernae see Saverne
Treves/Trèves see Trier
Treviso 96 C2 anc. Tarvisium. Veneto,
    NE Italy
Trichinopoly see Tiruchchirāppalli
Trichûr see Thrissur
Tridentum/Trient see Trento

Trier 95 A5 *Eng.* Treves, *Fr.* Trèves; *anc.*
   Augusta Treverorum. Rheinland-Pfalz,
   SW Germany
Triesen 94 E2 SW Liechtenstein Europe
Triesenberg 94 E2 SW Liechtenstein
Trieste 96 D2 *Slvn.* Trst. Friuli-Venezia
   Giulia, NE Italy
Trifail *see* Trbovlje
Tríkala 104 B4 *prev.* Trikkala. Thessalía,
   C Greece
Trikkala *see* Tríkala
Trimontium *see* Plovdiv
Trinacria *see* Sicilia
Trincomalee 132 D3 *var.* Trinkomali.
   Eastern Province, NE Sri Lanka
Trindade, Ilha da 67 C5 *island* Brazil,
   W Atlantic Ocean
Trinidad 61 F3 El Beni, N Bolivia
Trinidad 64 D4 Flores, S Uruguay
Trinidad 44 D5 Colorado, C USA
Trinidad 55 H5 *island* C Trinidad and
   Tobago
Trinidad and Tobago 55 H5 *off.*
   Republic of Trinidad and Tobago.
   country SE West Indies
Trinidad and Tobago, Republic of *see*
   Trinidad and Tobago
Trinité, Montagnes de la 59 H3
   mountain range C French Guiana
Trinity River 49 G3 *river* Texas, SW USA
Trinkomali *see* Trincomalee
Trípoli 105 B6 *prev.* Trípolis.
   Pelopónnisos, S Greece
Tripoli 118 B4 *var.* Ţarābulus, Ţarābulus
   ash Shām, Trâblous; *anc.* Tripolis.
   N Lebanon
Tripoli *see* Ţarābulus
Trípolis *see* Trípoli, Greece
Tripolis *see* Tripoli, Lebanon
Tristan da Cunha *see* St Helena,
   Ascension and Tristan da Cunha
Triton Island 128 B7 *island* S Paracel
   Islands
Trivandrum *see* Thiruvananthapuram
Trnava 99 C6 *Ger.* Tyrnau, *Hung.*
   Nagyszombat. Trnavský Kraj,
   W Slovakia
Trnovo *see* Veliko Tŭrnovo
Trogir 100 B4 *It.* Traù. Split-Dalmacija,
   S Croatia
Troglav 100 B4 *mountain* Bosnia and
   Herzegovina/Croatia
Trois-Rivières 39 E4 Québec, SE Canada
Troki *see* Trakai
Troll 154 C2 *Norwegian research station*
   Antarctica
Trollhättan 85 B6 Västra Götaland,
   S Sweden
Tromsø 84 C2 *Fin.* Tromssa. Troms,
   N Norway
Tromssa *see* Tromsø
Trondheim 84 B4 *Ger.* Drontheim; *prev.*
   Nidaros, Trondhjem. Sør-Trøndelag,
   S Norway
Trondheimsfjorden 84 B4 *fjord*
   S Norway
Trondhjem *see* Trondheim
Troódos 102 C5 *var.* Troodos
   Mountains. *mountain range*
   C Cyprus
Troodos Mountains *see* Troódos
Troppau *see* Opava
Troy 42 D3 Alabama, S USA
Troy 41 F3 New York, NE USA
Troyan 104 C2 Lovech, N Bulgaria
Troyes 90 D3 *anc.* Augustobona
   Tricassium. Aube, N France
Trst *see* Trieste
Trstenik 100 E4 Serbia, C Serbia
Trucial States *see* United Arab Emirates
Trujillo 52 D2 Colón, NE Honduras
Trujillo 60 B3 La Libertad, NW Peru
Trujillo 92 C3 Extremadura, W Spain
Truk Islands *see* Chuuk Islands
Trŭn 104 B2 Pernik, W Bulgaria
Truro 39 F4 Nova Scotia, SE Canada
Truro 89 C7 SW England, United
   Kingdom
Trzcianka 98 B3 *Ger.* Schönlanke. Piła,
   Wielkopolskie, C Poland
Trzebnica 98 C4 *Ger.* Trebnitz.
   Dolnośląskie, SW Poland
Ts'alk'a 117 F2 *var.* Tsalka.
   S Georgia Asia
Tsalka *see* Ts'alk'a
Tsamkong *see* Zhanjiang
Tsangpo *see* Brahmaputra
Tsarevo 104 E2 *prev.* Michurin. Burgas,
   E Bulgaria
Tsarigrad *see* İstanbul

Tsaritsyn *see* Volgograd
Tschakathurn *see* Čakovec
Tschaslau *see* Čáslav
Tschenstochau *see* Częstochowa
Tsefat 119 B5 *var.* Safed, *Ar.* Safad; *prev.*
   Żefat. Northern, N Israel
Tselinograd *see* Astana
Tsetsen Khan *see* Öndörhaan
Tsetserleg 126 D2 Arhangay,
   C Mongolia
Tshela 77 B6 Bas-Congo, W Dem. Rep.
   Congo
Tshikapa 77 C7 Kasai-Occidental,
   SW Dem. Rep. Congo
Tshuapa 77 D6 *river* C Dem. Rep.
   Congo
Tsinan *see* Jinan
Tsing Hai *see* Qinghai Hu, China
Tsinghai *see* Qinghai, China
Tsingtao/Tsingtau *see* Qingdao
Tsinkiang *see* Quanzhou
Tsintao *see* Qingdao
Tsitsihar *see* Qiqihar
Tsu 131 C6 *var.* Tu. Mie, Honshū,
   SW Japan
Tsugaru-kaikyo 130 C3 *strait*
   N Japan
Tsumeb 78 B3 Oshikoto, N Namibia
Tsuruga 131 C6 *var.* Turuga. Fukui,
   Honshū, SW Japan
Tsuruoka 130 D4 *var.* Turuoka.
   Yamagata, Honshū, C Japan
Tsushima 131 A7 *var.* Tsushima-tō,
   Tusima. *island group* SW Japan
Tsushima-tō *see* Tsushima
Tsyerakhowka 107 D8 *Rus.* Terekhovka.
   Homyel'skaya Voblasts', SE Belarus
Tsyurupyns'k *see* Oleshk
Tu *see* Tsu
Tuamotu, Archipel des *see* Tuamotu, Îles
Tuamotu Fracture Zone 143 H3
   fracture zone E Pacific Ocean
Tuamotu Islands 145 H4 *var.* Archipel
   des Tuamotu, Dangerous Archipelago,
   Tuamotu Islands. *island group*
   N French Polynesia
Tuamotu Islands *see* Tuamotu, Îles
Tuapi 53 E2 Región Autónoma Atlántico
   Norte, NE Nicaragua
Tuapse 111 A7 Krasnodarskiy Kray,
   SW Russia
Tuba City 48 B1 Arizona, SW USA
Tubbergen 86 E3 Overijssel,
   E Netherlands
Tubeke *see* Tubize
Tubize 87 B6 *Dut.* Tubeke. Walloon
   Brabant, C Belgium
Tubmanburg 74 C5 NW Liberia
Ţubruq 71 H2 *Eng.* Tobruk, *It.* Tobruch.
   NE Libya
Tubuai, Îles/Tubuai Islands *see*
   Australes, Îles
Tucker's Town 42 B5 E Bermuda
Tuckum *see* Tukums
Tucson 48 B3 Arizona,
   SW USA
Tucumán *see* San Miguel de Tucumán
Tucumcari 49 E2 New Mexico,
   SW USA
Tucupita 59 E2 Delta Amacuro,
   NE Venezuela
Tucuruí, Represa de 63 F2 *reservoir*
   NE Brazil
Tudela 93 E2 *Basq.* Tutera; *anc.* Tutela.
   Navarra, N Spain
Tudmur 118 C3 *var.* Tadmur, Tamar,
   Gk. Palmyra, *Bibl.* Tadmor. Ḥimş,
   C Syria
Tuguegarao 139 E1 Luzon,
   N Philippines
Tuktoyaktuk 37 E3 Northwest
   Territories, NW Canada
Tukums 106 C3 *Ger.* Tuckum.
   W Latvia
Tula 111 B5 Tul'skaya Oblast',
   W Russia
Tulancingo 51 E4 Hidalgo, C Mexico
Tulare Lake Bed 47 C7 *salt flat*
   California, W USA
Tulcán 60 B1 Carchi, N Ecuador
Tulcea 108 D5 Tulcea, E Romania
Tul'chin *see* Tul'chyn
Tul'chyn 108 D3 *Rus.* Tul'chin.
   Vinnyts'ka Oblast', C Ukraine
Tuléar *see* Toliara
Tulia 49 E2 Texas, SW USA
Tülkarm 119 D7 West Bank, Israel

Tulle 91 C5 *anc.* Tutela. Corrèze,
   C France
Tulln 95 F6 *var.* Oberhollabrunn.
   Niederösterreich, NE Austria
Tully 148 D3 Queensland, NE Australia
Tulsa 49 G1 Oklahoma, C USA
Tuluá 58 B3 Valle del Cauca,
   W Colombia
Tulun 121 E4 Irkutskaya Oblast',
   S Russia
Tumaco 58 A4 Nariño, SW Colombia
Tumakūru 132 C2 *prev.* Tumkūr.
   Karnātaka, W India
Tumba, Lac *see* Ntomba, Lac
Tumbes 60 A2 Tumbes, NW Peru
Tumkür *see* Tumakūru
Tumuc-Humac Mountains 63 E1 *var.*
   Serra Tumucumaque. *mountain range*
   N South America
Tumucumaque, Serra *see*
   Tumuc-Humac Mountains
Tunca Nehri *see* Tundzha
Tunduru 73 C8 Ruvuma, S Tanzania
Tundzha 104 D3 *Turk.* Tunca Nehri.
   river Bulgaria/Turkey
Tungabhadra Reservoir 132 C2 *lake*
   S India
Tungaru 145 E2 *prev.* Gilbert Islands.
   island group W Kiribati
T'ung-shan *see* Xuzhou
Tungsten 36 D4 Northwest Territories,
   W Canada
Tung-t'ing Hu *see* Dongting Hu
Tunis 71 E1 *var.* Tūnis. *country capital*
   (Tunisia) NE Tunisia
Tunis, Golfe de 102 D3 *Ar.* Khalīj Tūnis.
   gulf NE Tunisia
Tunisia 71 F2 *off.* Republic of Tunisia,
   Ar. Al Jumhūrīyah at Tūnisīyah, *Fr.*
   République Tunisienne. *country*
   N Africa
Tunisia, Republic of *see* Tunisia
Tunisienne, République *see* Tunisia
Tūnisiyah, Al Jumhūrīyah at *see*
   Tunisia
Tūnis, Khalīj *see* Tunis, Golfe de
Tunja 58 B3 Boyacá, C Colombia
Tuong Buong *see* Tương Đương
Tương Đương 136 D4 *var.* Tuong
   Buong. Nghệ An, N Vietnam
Tüp *see* Tyup
Tupelo 42 C2 Mississippi,
   S USA
Tupiza 61 G5 Potosí, S Bolivia
Turabah 121 B5 Makkah, W Saudi
   Arabia
Turangi 150 D4 Waikato, North Island,
   New Zealand
Turan Lowland 122 C2 *var.* Turan Plain,
   Kaz. Turan Oypaty, *Rus.* Turanskaya
   Nizmennost', *Turk.* Turan Pesligi, *Uzb.*
   Turan Pasttekisligi. *plain* C Asia
**Turan Oypaty/Turan Pesligi/Turan
   Plain/Turanskaya Nizmennost'** *see*
   Turan Lowland
Turan Pasttekisligi *see* Turan Lowland
Ţurayf 120 A3 Al Ḥudūd ash
   Shamālīyah, NW Saudi Arabia
Turba *see* Teruel
Turbat 134 A3 Baluchistan,
   SW Pakistan
Turčiansky Svätý Martin *see* Martin
Turda 108 B4 *Ger.* Thorenburg, *Hung.*
   Torda. Cluj, NW Romania
Turek 98 C3 Wielkopolskie, C Poland
Turfan *see* Turpan
Turin *see* Torino
Turkana, Lake 73 C6 *var.* Lake Rudolf.
   lake N Kenya
Turkestan *see* Turkistan
Turkey 116 B3 *off.* Republic of Turkey,
   Turk. Türkiye Cumhuriyeti. *country*
   SW Asia
Turkey, Republic of *see* Turkey
Turkish Republic of Northern Cyprus
   102 D5 *disputed territory administered
   by* Turkey Cyprus
Turkistan 114 B5 *prev.* Turkestan.
   Yuzhnyy Kazakhstan, S Kazakhstan
Türkiye Cumhuriyeti *see* Turkey
Türkmenabat 122 D3 *prev.* Rus.
   Chardzhev, Chardzhou, Chardzhui,
   Lenin-Turkmenski, *Turkm.* Chärjew.
   Lebap Welaýaty, E Turkmenistan
Türkmen Aylagy 122 B2 *Rus.*
   Turkmenskiy Zaliv. *lake gulf*
   W Turkmenistan

Turkmenbashi *see* Türkmenbaşy
Türkmenbaşy 122 B2 *Rus.*
   Turkmenbashi; *prev.* Krasnovodsk.
   Balkan Welaýaty, W Turkmenistan
Türkmenbaşy Aylagy 122 A2 *prev. Rus.*
   Krasnovodskiy Zaliv, *Turkm.*
   Krasnovodsk Aylagy. *lake Gulf*
   W Turkmenistan
Turkmenistan 122 B2; *prev.*
   Turkmenskaya Soviet Socialist
   Republic. *country* C Asia
**Turkmenskaya Soviet Socialist
   Republic** *see* Turkmenistan
Turkmenskiy Zaliv *see* Türkmen
   Aylagy
Turks and Caicos Islands 55 E2 *UK
   Overseas Territory* N West Indies
Turku 85 D6 *Swe.* Åbo.
   Varsinais-Suomi, SW Finland
Turlock 47 B6 California, W USA
Turnagain, Cape 150 D4 *headland*
   North Island, New Zealand
Turnau *see* Turnov
Turnhout 87 C5 Antwerpen,
   N Belgium
Turnov 98 B4 *Ger.* Turnau. Liberecký
   Kraj, N Czech Republic (Czechia)
Tŭrnovo *see* Veliko Tŭrnovo
Turnu Măgurele 108 B5 *var.*
   Turnu-Măgurele. Teleorman,
   S Romania
Turnu Severin *see* Drobeta-Turnu
   Severin
Turócszentmárton *see* Martin
Turoni *see* Tours
Turpan 126 C3 *var.* Turfan. Xinjiang
   Uygur Zizhiqu, NW China
Turpan Depression *see* Turpan Pendi
Turpan Pendi 126 C3 *Eng.* Turpan
   Depression. *depression* NW China
Turpentine State *see* North Carolina
Türtkül/Turtkul' *see* To'rtko'l'
Turuga *see* Tsuruga
Turuoka *see* Tsuruoka
Tuscaloosa 42 C2 Alabama, S USA
Tuscan Archipelago *see* Toscano,
   Arcipelago
Tuscany *see* Toscana
Tusima *see* Tsushima
Tutela *see* Tulle, France
Tutela *see* Tudela, Spain
Tutera *see* Tudela
Tuticorin 132 C3 Tamil Nādu,
   SE India
Tutrakan 104 D1 Silistra, NE Bulgaria
Tutuila 145 F4 *island* W American
   Samoa
Tuvalu 145 E3 *prev.* Ellice Islands.
   country SW Pacific Ocean
Tuwayq, Jabal 121 C5 *mountain range*
   C Saudi Arabia
Tuxpan 50 D4 Jalisco, C Mexico
Tuxpan 50 D4 Nayarit, C Mexico
Tuxpán 51 F4 *var.* Tuxpán de Rodríguez
   Cano. Veracruz-Llave, E Mexico
Tuxpán de Rodríguez Cano *see* Tuxpán
Tuxtepec 51 F4 *var.* San Juan Bautista
   Tuxtepec. Oaxaca, S Mexico
Tuxtla 51 G5 *var.* Tuxtla Gutiérrez.
   Chiapas, SE Mexico
Tuxtla *see* San Andrés Tuxtla
Tuxtla Gutiérrez *see* Tuxtla
Tuy Hoa 137 E5 Phu Yên, S Vietnam
Tuz, Lake 116 C3 *lake* C Turkey
Tver' 110 B4 *prev.* Kalinin. Tverskaya
   Oblast', W Russia
Tverya 119 B5 *var.* Tiberias; *prev.*
   Teverya. Northern, N Israel
Twin Falls 46 D4 Idaho, NW USA
Tyan'-Shan' *see* Tien Shan
Tychy 99 D5 *Ger.* Tichau. Śląskie,
   S Poland
Tyler 49 G3 Texas, SW USA
Tylos *see* Bahrain
Tympáki 105 C8 *var.* Timbaki; *prev.*
   Timbákion. Kríti, Greece,
   E Mediterranean Sea
Tynda 115 F4 Amurskaya Oblast',
   SE Russia
Tyne 88 D4 *river* N England, United
   Kingdom
Tyōsi *see* Chōshi
Tyras *see* Dniester
Tyre *see* Soûr
Tyrnau *see* Trnava
Týrnavos 104 B4 *var.* Tírnavos.
   Thessalía, C Greece

Tyrol see Tirol
Tyros see Bahrain
Tyrrhenian Sea 97 B6 It. Mare Tirreno.
  sea N Mediterranean Sea
Tyumen' 114 C3 Tyumenskaya Oblast',
  C Russia
Tyup 123 G2 Kir. Tüp. Issyk-Kul'skaya
  Oblast', NE Kyrgyzstan
Tywyn 89 C6 W Wales, United
  Kingdom
Tzekung see Zigong
Tziá see Kéa

U

Uaco Cungo 78 B1 C Angola
UAE see United Arab Emirates
Uanle Uen see Wanlaweyn
Uaupés, Rio see Vaupés, Río
Ubangi-Shari see Central African
  Republic
Ube 131 B7 Yamaguchi, Honshū,
  SW Japan
Ubeda 93 E4 Andalucía, S Spain
Uberaba 63 F4 Minas Gerais,
  SE Brazil
Uberlândia 63 F4 Minas Gerais, S
  E Brazil
Ubol Rajadhani/Ubol Ratchathani see
  Ubon Ratchathani
Ubon Ratchathani 137 D5 var. Muang
  Ubon, Ubol Rajadhani, Ubol
  Ratchathani, Udon Ratchathani.
  Ubon Ratchathani, E Thailand
Ubrique 92 D5 Andalucía, S Spain
Ubsu-Nur, Ozero see Uvs Nuur
Ucayali, Río 60 D3 river C Peru
Uchiura-wan 130 D3 bay
  NW Pacific Ocean
Uchkuduk see Uchquduq
Uchquduq 122 D2 Rus. Uchkuduk.
  Navoiy Viloyati, N Uzbekistan
Uchtagan Gumy/Uchtagan, Peski see
  Uçtagan Gumy
Uçtagan Gumy 122 C2 var. Uchtagan
  Gumy, Rus. Peski Uchtagan. desert
  NW Turkmenistan
Udaipur 134 C3 prev. Oodeypore.
  Rājasthān, N India
Uddevalla 85 B6 Västra Götaland,
  S Sweden
Udine 96 D2 anc. Utina. Friuli-Venezia
  Giulia, NE Italy
Udintsev Fracture Zone 154 A5 tectonic
  feature S Pacific Ocean
Udipi see Udupi
Udon Ratchathani see
  Ubon Ratchathani
Udon Thani 136 C4 var. Ban Mak
  Khaeng, Udorndhani. Udon Thani,
  N Thailand
Udorndhani see Udon Thani
Udupi 132 B2 var. Udipi. Karnātaka,
  SW India
Uele 77 D5 var. Welle. river NE Dem.
  Rep. Congo
Uelzen 94 C3 Niedersachsen,
  N Germany
Ufa 111 D6 Respublika Bashkortostan,
  W Russia
Ugāle 106 C2 NW Latvia
Uganda 73 B6 off. Republic of Uganda.
  country E Africa
Uganda, Republic of see Uganda
Uhorshchyna see Hungary
Uhuru Peak see Kilimanjaro
Uíge 78 B1 Port. Carmona, Vila
  Marechal Carmona. Uíge, N
  NW Angola
Uinta Mountains 44 B4 mountain range
  Utah, W USA
Uitenhage 78 C5 Eastern Cape,
  S South Africa
Uithoorn 86 C3 Noord-Holland,
  C Netherlands
Ujda see Oujda
Ujelang Atoll 144 C1 var. Wujlān. atoll
  Ralik Chain, W Marshall Islands
Ujung Pandang see Makassar
Ujung Salang see Phuket
Ujvidék see Novi Sad
UK see United Kingdom
Ukhta 114 C3 Respublika Komi,
  NW Russia

Ukiah 47 B5 California, W USA
Ukmergė 106 C4 Pol. Wiłkomierz.
  Vilnius, C Lithuania
Ukraina see Ukraine
Ukraine 108 C2 off. Ukraine, Rus.
  Ukraina, Ukr. Ukrayina; prev.
  Ukrainian Soviet Socialist Republic,
  Ukrainskay S.S.R. country SE Europe
Ukraine see Ukraine
Ukrainian Soviet Socialist Republic see
  Ukraine
Ukrainskay S.S.R/Ukrayina see
  Ukraine
Ulaanbaatar 127 E2 Eng. Ulan Bator;
  prev. Urga. country capital (Mongolia)
  Töv, C Mongolia
Ulaangom 126 C2 Uvs, NW Mongolia
Ulan Bator see Ulaanbaatar
Ulanhad see Chifeng
Ulan-Ude 115 E4 prev. Verkhneudinsk.
  Respublika Buryatiya, S Russia
Uleälv see Oulujoki
Uleträsk see Oulujärvi
Ulft 86 E4 Gelderland, E Netherlands
Ullapool 88 C3 N Scotland, United
  Kingdom
Ulm 95 B6 Baden-Württemberg,
  S Germany
Ulsan 129 E4 Jap. Urusan. SE South
  Korea
Ulster 89 B5 province Northern Ireland,
  United Kingdom/Ireland
Ulungur Hu 126 B2 lake NW China
Uluru 147 D5 var. Ayers Rock. monolith
  Northern Territory, C Australia
Ul'yanovka see Blahovishchens'ke
Ul'yanovsk 111 C5 prev. Simbirsk.
  Ul'yanovskaya Oblast', W Russia
Umán 51 H3 Yucatán, SE Mexico
Uman' 109 E3 Rus. Uman. Cherkas'ka
  Oblast', C Ukraine
Uman see Uman'
Umanak/Umanaq see Uummannaq
'Umān, Khalīj see Oman, Gulf of
'Umān, Salţanat see Oman
Umbrian-Machigian Mountains see
  Umbro-Marchigiano, Appennino
Umbro-Marchigiano, Appennino 96
  C3 Eng. Umbrian-Machigian
  Mountains. mountain range C Italy
Umeå 84 C4 Västerbotten,
  N Sweden
Umeälven 84 C4 river N Sweden
Umiat 36 D2 Alaska, USA
Umm Buru 72 A4 Western Darfur,
  W Sudan
Umm Durmān see Omdurman
Umm Ruwaba 72 C4 var. Umm
  Ruwābah, Um Ruwāba. Northern
  Kordofan, C Sudan
Umm Ruwābah see Umm Ruwaba
Umnak Island 36 A3 island Aleutian
  Islands, Alaska, USA
Um Ruwāba see Umm Ruwaba
Umtali see Mutare
Umtata see Mthatha
Una 100 B3 river Bosnia and
  Herzegovina/Croatia
Unac 100 B3 river W Bosnia and
  Herzegovina
Unalaska Island 36 A3 island Aleutian
  Islands, Alaska, USA
'Unayzah 120 B4 var. Anaiza. Al Qaşīm,
  C Saudi Arabia
Unci see Almería
Uncía 61 F4 Potosí, C Bolivia
Uncompahgre Peak 44 B5 mountain
  Colorado, C USA
Undur Khan see Öndörhaan
Ungaria see Hungary
Ungarisches Erzgebirge see Slovenské
  rudohorie
Ungarn see Hungary
Ungava Bay 39 E1 bay Québec,
  E Canada
Ungava Peninsula see Ungava, Péninsule
  d'
Ungava, Péninsule d' 38 D1 Eng. Ungava
  Peninsula. peninsula Québec,
  SE Canada
Ungeny see Ungheni
Ungheni 108 D3 Rus. Ungeny.
  W Moldova
Unguja see Zanzibar
Üngüz Angyrsyndaky Garagum 122 C2
  Rus. Zaungaguzskiye Garagumy. desert
  N Turkmenistan
Ungvár see Uzhhorod
Unimak Island 36 B3 island Aleutian
  Islands, Alaska, USA

Union 43 E1 South Carolina,
  SE USA
Union City 42 C1 Tennessee, S USA
Union of Myanmar see Burma
United Arab Emirates 121 C5 Ar. Al
  Imārāt al 'Arabīyah al Muttaḥidah,
  abbrev. UAE; prev. Trucial States.
  country SW Asia
United Arab Republic see Egypt
United Kingdom 89 B5
  off. United Kingdom of Great Britain
  and Northern Ireland, abbrev. UK.
  country NW Europe
**United Kingdom of Great Britain and
  Northern Ireland** see
  United Kingdom
United Mexican States see Mexico
United Provinces see Uttar Pradesh
United States of America 35 B5
  off. United States of America,
  var. America, The States,
  abbrev. U.S., USA.
  country North America
United States of America see United
  States of America
Unst 88 D1 island NE Scotland, United
  Kingdom
Ünye 116 D2 Ordu, W Turkey
Upala 52 D4 Alajuela, NW Costa Rica
Upata 59 E2 Bolívar, E Venezuela
Upemba, Lac 77 D7 lake SE Dem. Rep.
  Congo
Upernavik 82 C2 var. Upernivik. Kitaa,
  C Greenland
Upernivik see Upernavik
Upington 78 C4 Northern Cape,
  W South Africa
'Upolu 145 F4 island SE Samoa
Upper Klamath Lake 46 A4 lake
  Oregon, NW USA
Upper Lough Erne 89 A5 lake
  SW Northern Ireland, United
  Kingdom
Upper Red Lake 45 F1 lake Minnesota,
  N USA
Upper Volta see Burkina Faso
Uppsala 85 C6 Uppsala, C Sweden
Uqsuqtuuq see Gjoa Haven
Ural 114 B4 Kaz. Zayyq. river
  Kazakhstan/Russia
Ural Mountains 114 C3 var. Ural'skiy
  Khrebet, Eng. Ural Mountains.
  mountain range Kazakhstan/Russia
Ural Mountains see Ural'skiye Gory
Ural'sk 114 B3 Kaz. Oral. Zapadnyy
  Kazakhstan, NW Kazakhstan
Ural'skiy Khrebet see Ural'skiye Gory
Uraricoera 62 D1 Roraima, N Brazil
Ura-Tyube see Üroteppa
Urbandale 45 F3 Iowa, C USA
Urdunn see Jordan
Uren' 111 C5 Nizhegorodskaya Oblast',
  W Russia
Urga see Ulaanbaatar
Urganch 122 D2 Rus. Urgench; prev.
  Novo-Urgench. Xorazm Viloyati,
  W Uzbekistan
Urgench see Urganch
Urgut 123 E3 Samarqand Viloyati,
  C Uzbekistan
Urmia, Lake 121 C2 var. Matianus, Sha
  Hi, Urumi Yeh, Eng. Lake Urmia; prev.
  Daryācheh-ye Rezā'īyeh. lake
  NW Iran
Urmia, Lake see Orūmīyeh, Daryācheh-ye
Uroševac see Ferizaj
Üroteppa 123 E2 Rus. Ura-Tyube.
  NW Tajikistan
Uruapan 51 E4 var. Uruapan del
  Progreso. Michoacán, SW Mexico
Uruapan del Progreso see Uruapan
Uruguai, Rio see Uruguay
Uruguay 64 D4 off. Oriental Republic of
  Uruguay; prev. La Banda Oriental.
  country E South America
Uruguay see Uruguay. Río Uruguai, Río
  Uruguay. river E South America
Uruguay, Oriental Republic of see
  Uruguay
Uruguay, Río see Uruguay
Urumchi see Ürümqi
Urumi Yeh see Orūmīyeh, Daryācheh-ye
Ürümqi 126 C3 var. Tihwa, Urumchi,
  Urumqi, Urumtsi, Wu-lu-k'o-mu-shi,
  Wu-lu-mu-ch'i; prev. Ti-hua. Xinjiang
  Uygur Zizhiqu, NW China
Urumtsi see Ürümqi
Urundi see Burundi
Urup, Ostrov 115 H4 island Kuril'skiye
  Ostrova, SE Russia

Urusan see Ulsan
Urziceni 108 C5 Ialomiţa, SE Romania
Usa 110 E3 river NW Russian
  Federation
Uşak 116 B3 prev. Ushak. Uşak,
  W Turkey
Ushak see Uşak
Ushant see Ouessant, Île d'
Ushuaia 65 B8 Tierra del Fuego,
  S Argentina
Usinsk 110 E3 Respublika Komi,
  NW Russia
Üsküb/Üsküp see Skopje
Usmas Ezers 106 B3 lake NW Latvia
Usol'ye-Sibirskoye 115 E4 Irkutskaya
  Oblast', C Russia
Ussel 91 C5 Corrèze, C France
Ussuriysk 115 G5 prev. Nikol'sk,
  Nikol'sk-Ussuriyskiy, Voroshilov.
  Primorskiy Kray, SE Russian
  Federation
Ustica 97 B6 island S Italy
Ust'-Ilimsk 115 E4 Irkutskaya Oblast',
  C Russia
Ustí nad Labem 98 A4 Ger. Aussig.
  Ústecký Kraj, NW Czech Republic
  (Czechia)
Ustinov see Izhevsk
Ustka 98 C2 Ger. Stolpmünde.
  Pomorskie, N Poland
Ust'-Kamchatsk 115 H2 Kamchatskiy
  Kray, E Russia
Ust'-Kamenogorsk 114 D5 Kaz.
  Öskemen. Vostochnyy Kazakhstan,
  E Kazakhstan
Ust'-Kut 115 E4 Irkutskaya Oblast',
  C Russia
Ust'-Olenëk 115 E3 Respublika Sakha
  (Yakutiya), NE Russia
Ustrzyki Dolne 99 E5 Podkarpackie,
  SE Poland
Ust'-Sysol'sk see Syktyvkar
Ust Urt see Ustyurt Plateau
Ustyurt Plateau 122 B1 var. Ust Urt,
  Uzb. Ustyurt Platosi. plateau
  Kazakhstan/Uzbekistan
Ustyurt Platosi see Ustyurt Plateau
Usulután 52 C3 Usulután,
  SE El Salvador
Usumacinta, Río 52 B1 river
  Guatemala/Mexico
Usumbura see Bujumbura
U.S./USA see United States of America
Utah 44 B4 off. State of Utah, also known
  as Beehive State, Mormon State. state
  W USA
Utah Lake 44 B4 lake Utah,
  W USA
Utena 106 C4 Utena, E Lithuania
Utica 41 F3 New York, NE USA
Utina see Udine
Utrecht 86 C4 Lat. Trajectum ad
  Rhenum. Utrecht, C Netherlands
Utsunomiya 131 D5 var. Utunomiya.
  Tochigi, Honshū, S Japan
Uttarakhand 135 E2 cultural region
  N India
Uttar Pradesh 135 E3 prev. United
  Provinces, United Provinces of Agra
  and Oudh. cultural region N India
Utunomiya see Utsunomiya
Uulu 106 D2 Pärnumaa, SW Estonia
Uummannaq 82 C3 var. Umanak,
  Umanaq. Kitaa, C Greenland
Uummannarsuaq see Nunap Isua
Uvalde 49 F4 Texas,
  SW USA
Uvarovichi 107 D7 Rus. Uvarovichi.
  Homyel'skaya Voblasts', SE Belarus
Uvarovichi see Uvarovichy
Uvea, Île 145 E4 island N Wallis and
  Futuna
Uvs Nuur 126 C1 var. Ozero Ubsu-Nur.
  lake Mongolia/Russia
'Uwaynāt, Jabal al 88 A3 var. Jebel
  Uweinat. mountain Libya/Sudan
Uweinat, Jebel see 'Uwaynāt, Jabal al
Uyo 75 G5 Akwa Ibom, S Nigeria
Uyuni 61 F5 Potosí, W Bolivia
Uzbekistan 122 D2 off. Republic of
  Uzbekistan. country C Asia
Uzbekistan, Republic of see Uzbekistan
Uzhgorod see Uzhhorod
Uzhhorod 108 B2 Rus. Uzhgorod; prev.
  Ungvár. Zakarpats'ka Oblast',
  W Ukraine
Užice 100 D4 prev. Titovo Užice. Serbia,
  W Serbia

V

Vaal 78 D4 *river* C South Africa
Vaals 87 D6 Limburg, SE Netherlands
Vaasa 85 D5 Swe. Vasa; *prev.*
Nikolainkaupunki. Österbotten,
W Finland
Vaassen 86 D3 Gelderland,
E Netherlands
Vác 99 C6 *Ger.* Waitzen. Pest,
N Hungary
Vadodara 134 C4 *prev.* Baroda.
Gujarāt, W India
Vaduz 94 E2 *country capital*
(Liechtenstein) W Liechtenstein
Vág *see* Váh
Vágbeszterce *see* Považská Bystrica
Váh 99 C5 *Ger.* Waag, *Hung.* Vág. *river*
W Slovakia
Váhtjer *see* Gällivare
Väinameri 106 C2 *prev.* Muhu Väin,
Ger. Moon-Sund. *sea* E Baltic Sea
Vajdahunyad *see* Hunedoara
Valachia *see* Wallachia
Valday 110 B4 Novgorodskaya Oblast',
W Russia
Valdecañas, Embalse de 92 D3 *reservoir*
W Spain
Valdepeñas 93 E4 Castilla-La Mancha,
C Spain
Valdez 36 C3 Alaska, USA
Valdia *see* Weldiya
Valdivia 65 B5 Los Ríos, C Chile
Val-d'Or 38 D4 Québec, SE Canada
Valdosta 43 E3 Georgia, SE USA
Valence 91 D5 *anc.* Valentia, Valentia
Julia, Ventia. Drôme, E France
Valencia 93 F3 Valenciana, E Spain
Valencia 46 D1 California, W USA
Valencia 58 D1 Carabobo, N Venezuela
Valencia, Gulf of 93 F3 *var.* Gulf of
Valencia. *gulf* E Spain
Valencia, Gulf of *see* Valencia, Golfo de
Valenciana 93 F3 *var.* Valencia, Cat.
València; *anc.* Valentia. *autonomous
community* NE Spain
Valencia/València *see* Valenciana
Valenciennes 90 D2 Nord, N France
Valentia *see* Valence, France
Valentia *see* Valenciana
Valentia Julia *see* Valence
Valentine State *see* Oregon
Valera 58 C2 Trujillo, NW Venezuela
Valetta *see* Valletta
Valga 106 D3 *Ger.* Walk, *Latv.* Valka.
Valgamaa, S Estonia
Valira 91 A8 *river* Andorra/Spain
Valjevo 100 C4 Serbia, W Serbia
Valjok *see* Válljohka
Valka 106 D3 *Ger.* Walk. N Latvia
Valka *see* Valga
Valkenswaard 87 D5 Noord-Brabant,
S Netherlands
Valladolid 51 H3 Yucatán, SE Mexico
Valladolid 92 D2 Castilla y León,
NW Spain
Vall d'Uxó *see* La Vall d'Uixó
Valle de La Pascua 58 D2 Guárico,
N Venezuela
Valledupar 58 B1 Cesar, N Colombia
Vallejo 47 B6 California, W USA
Vallenar 64 B3 Atacama, N Chile
Valletta 97 C8 *prev.* Valetta. *country
capital* (Malta) E Malta
Valley City 45 E2 North Dakota,
N USA
Válljohka 84 D2 *var.* Valjok. Finnmark,
N Norway
Valls 93 G2 Cataluña, NE Spain
Valmiera 106 D3 *Est.* Volmari, *Ger.*
Wolmar. N Latvia
Valona *see* Vlorë
Valozhyn 107 C5 *Pol.* Wołożyn, *Rus.*
Volozhin. Minskaya Voblasts',
C Belarus
Valparaíso 64 B4 Valparaíso, C Chile
Valparaiso 40 C3 Indiana, N USA
Valverde del Camino 92 C4 Andalucía,
S Spain
Van 117 F3 Van, E Turkey
Vanadzor 117 F2 *prev.* Kirovakan.
N Armenia
Vancouver 36 D5 British Columbia,
SW Canada
Vancouver 46 B3 Washington, NW USA
Vancouver Island 36 D5 *island* British
Columbia, SW Canada
Vanda *see* Vantaa

Van Diemen Gulf 146 D2 *gulf* Northern
Territory, N Australia
Van Diemen's Land *see* Tasmania
Vaner, Lake *see* Vänern
Vänern 85 B6 *Eng.* Lake Vaner; *prev.*
Lake Vener. *lake* S Sweden
Vangaindrano 79 G4 Fianarantsoa,
SE Madagascar
Van Horn 48 D3 Texas, SW USA
Lake Van 117 F3 *Eng.* Lake Van; *anc.*
Thospitis. *salt lake* E Turkey
Van, Lake *see* Van Gölü
Vannes 90 A3 *anc.* Dariorigum.
Morbihan, NW France
Vantaa 85 D6 *Swe.* Vanda. Uusimaa,
S Finland
Vanua Levu 145 E4 *island* N Fiji
Vanuatu 144 C4 *off.* Republic of
Vanuatu; *prev.* New Hebrides.
country SW Pacific Ocean
Vanuatu, Republic of *see* Vanuatu
Van Wert 40 C4 Ohio, N USA
Vapincum *see* Gap
Varakļāni 106 D4 C Latvia
Vārānasi 135 F3 *prev.* Banaras, Benares,
hist. Kasi. Uttar Pradesh, N India
Varangerfjorden 84 E2 Lapp.
Várjjatvuotna. *fjord* N Norway
Varangerhalvøya 84 D2 Lapp.
Várnjárga. *peninsula* N Norway
Varannó *see* Vranov nad Topl'ou
Varasd *see* Varaždin
Varaždin 100 B2 *Ger.* Warasdin, *Hung.*
Varasd. Varaždin, N Croatia
Varberg 85 B7 Halland, S Sweden
Vardar 101 E6 Alb. Axiós. *river*
Macedonia/Greece
Varde 85 A7 Syddtjylland,
W Denmark
Vareia *see* Logroño
Varēna 107 B5 Pol. Orany. Alytus,
S Lithuania
Varese 96 B2 Lombardia, N Italy
Vârful Moldoveanu 108 B4 *var.*
Moldoveanul; *prev.* Vîrful Moldoveanu.
mountain C Romania
Várjjatvuotna *see* Varangerfjorden
Varkaus 85 E5 Pohjois-Savo, C Finland
Varna 104 E2 *prev.* Stalin; *anc.* Odessus.
Varna, E Bulgaria
Varnenski Zaliv 104 E2 *prev.* Stalinski
Zaliv. *bay* E Bulgaria
Várnjárga *see* Varangerhalvøya
Varshava *see* Warszawa
Vasa *see* Vaasa
Vasilikí 105 A5 Lefkáda, Iónia Nisiá,
Greece, C Mediterranean Sea
Vasilishki 107 B5 Pol. Wasiliszki.
Hrodzyenskaya Voblasts', W Belarus
Vasil'kov *see* Vasyl'kiv
Vaslui 108 D4 Vaslui, C Romania
Västerås 85 C6 Västmanland,
C Sweden
Vasyl'kiv 109 E2 *var.* Vasil'kov.
Kyyivs'ka Oblast', N Ukraine
Vaté *see* Efate
Vatican City 97 A7 *off.* Vatican City.
country S Europe
Vatican City *see* Vatican City
Vatnajökull 83 E5 *glacier*
SE Iceland
Vatter, Lake *see* Vättern
Vättern 85 B6 *Eng.* Lake Vatter; *prev.*
Lake Vetter. *lake* S Sweden
Vaughn 48 D2 New Mexico,
SW USA
Vaupés, Río 58 C4 *var.* Rio Uaupés.
river Brazil/Colombia
Vava'u Group 145 E4 *island group*
N Tonga
Vavuniya 132 D3 Northern Province,
N Sri Lanka
Vawkavysk 107 B6 Pol. Wołkowysk,
Rus. Volkovysk. Hrodzyenskaya
Voblasts', W Belarus
Växjö 85 C7 *var.* Vexiö. Kronoberg,
S Sweden
Vaygach, Ostrov 110 E2 *island*
NW Russia
Veendam 86 E2 Groningen,
NE Netherlands
Veenendaal 86 D4 Utrecht,
C Netherlands
Vega 84 B4 *island* C Norway
Veglia *see* Krk
Veisiejai 107 B5 Alytus, S Lithuania
Vejer de la Frontera 92 C5 Andalucía,
S Spain
Veldhoven 87 D5 Noord-Brabant,
S Netherlands

Velebit 100 A3 *mountain range*
C Croatia
Velenje 95 E7 *Ger.* Wöllan.
N Slovenia
Veles 101 E6 *Turk.* Köprülü. C
Macedonia
Velho *see* Porto Velho
Velika Kikinda *see* Kikinda
Velika Morava 100 D4 *var.* Glavn'a
Morava, Morava, *Ger.* Grosse
Morava. *river* C Serbia
Velikaya 113 G2 *river* NE Russia
Veliki Bečkerek *see* Zrenjanin
Velikiye Luki 110 A4 Pskovskaya
Oblast', W Russia
Velikiy Novgorod 110 B4 *prev.*
Novgorod. Novgorodskaya Oblast',
W Russia
Veliko Tŭrnovo 104 D2 *prev.* Tirnovo,
Trnovo, Tŭrnovo. Veliko Tŭrnovo,
N Bulgaria
Velingrad 104 C3 Pazardzhik,
C Bulgaria
Vel'ký Krtíš 99 D6 Banskobystrický Kraj,
C Slovakia
Vellore 132 C2 Tamil Nādu, SE India
Velobriga *see* Viana do Castelo
Velsen *see* Velsen-Noord
Velsen-Noord 86 C3 *var.* Velsen.
Noord-Holland, W Netherlands
Vel'sk 110 C4 *var.* Velsk.
Arkhangel'skaya Oblast', NW Russia
Velvendós *see* Velvéntos
Velvéntos 104 B4 *var.* Velvendós. C
Greece
Velykyy Tokmak *see* Tokmak
Vendôme 90 C4 Loir-et-Cher,
C France
Venedig *see* Venezia
Vener, Lake *see* Vänern
Venetia *see* Venezia
Venezia 96 C2 *Eng.* Venice, *Fr.* Venise,
Ger. Venedig; *anc.* Venetia. Veneto,
NE Italy
Venezia, Golfo di *see* Venice, Gulf of
Venezuela 58 D2 *off.* Republic of
Venezuela; *prev.* Estados Unidos de
Venezuela, United States of Venezuela.
country N South America
Venezuela, Estados Unidos de *see*
Venezuela
Venezuela, Gulf of 58 C1 *Eng.* Gulf of
Maracaibo, Gulf of Venezuela. *gulf*
NW Venezuela
Venezuela, Gulf of *see* Venezuela, Golfo
de
Venezuelan Basin 56 B1 *undersea basin*
E Caribbean Sea
Venezuela, Republic of *see*
Venezuela
Venezuela, United States of *see*
Venezuela
Venice 42 C1 Louisiana, S USA
Venice *see* Venezia
Venice, Gulf of 96 C2 *It.* Golfo di
Venezia, *Svn.* Beneški Zaliv. *gulf*
N Adriatic Sea
Venise *see* Venezia
Venlo 87 D5 *prev.* Venloo. Limburg,
SE Netherlands
Venloo *see* Venlo
Venta 106 B3 *Ger.* Windau. *river* Latvia/
Lithuania
Venta Belgarum *see* Winchester
Ventia *see* Valence
Ventimiglia 96 A3 Liguria, NW Italy
Ventspils 106 B2 *Ger.* Windau.
NW Latvia
Vera 64 D3 Santa Fe, C Argentina
Veracruz 51 F4 *var.* Veracruz Llave.
Veracruz-Llave, E Mexico
Veracruz Llave *see* Veracruz
Vercellae *see* Vercelli
Vercelli 96 A2 *anc.* Vercellae. Piemonte,
NW Italy
Verdal *see* Verdalsøra
Verdalsøra 84 B4 *var.* Verdal.
Nord-Trøndelag, C Norway
Verde, Cabo *see* Cape Verde
Verde, Costa 92 D1 *coastal region*
N Spain
Verden 94 B3 Niedersachsen,
NW Germany
Veria *see* Véroia
Verkhnedvinsk *see* Vyerkhnyadzvinsk
Verkhneudinsk *see* Ulan-Ude
Verkhoyanskiy Khrebet 115 F3
mountain range NE Russia
Vermillion 45 F3 South Dakota,
N USA

Vermont 41 F2 *off.* State of Vermont,
also known as Green Mountain State.
state NE USA
Vernadsky 154 A2 *Ukrainian research
station* Antarctica
Vernal 44 B4 Utah, W USA
Vernon 49 F2 Texas, SW USA
Veröcze *see* Virovitica
Véroia 104 B4 *var.* Veria, Vérroia, *Turk.*
Karaferiye. Kentrikí Makedonía,
N Greece
Verona 96 C2 Veneto, NE Italy
Vérroia *see* Véroia
Versailles 90 D1 Yvelines, N France
Versecz *see* Vršac
Verulamium *see* St Albans
Verviers 87 D6 Liège, E Belgium
Vesdre 87 D6 *river* E Belgium
Veselinovo 104 D2 Shumen,
NE Bulgaria
Vesontio *see* Besançon
Vesoul 90 D4 *anc.* Vesulium, Vesulum.
Haute-Saône, E France
Vesterålen 84 B2 *island group*
N Norway
Vestfjorden 84 C3 *fjord* C Norway
Vestmannaeyjar 83 E5 Sudharland,
S Iceland
Vesulium/Vesulum *see* Vesoul
Vesuna *see* Périgueux
Vesuvio 97 D5 *Eng.* Vesuvius. *volcano*
S Italy
Vesuvius *see* Vesuvio
Veszprém 99 C7 *Ger.* Veszprim.
Veszprém, W Hungary
Veszprim *see* Veszprém
Vetrino *see* Suvorovo
Vetrino *see* Vyetryna
Vetter, Lake *see* Vättern
Veurne 87 A5 *var.* Furnes.
West-Vlaanderen, W Belgium
Vexiö *see* Växjö
Viacha 61 F4 La Paz, W Bolivia
Viana de Castelo *see* Viana do Castelo
Viana do Castelo 92 B2 *var.* Viana de
Castelo; *anc.* Velobriga. Viana do
Castelo, NW Portugal
Vianen 86 C4 Utrecht, C Netherlands
Viangchan 136 C4 *Eng./Fr.* Vientiane.
country capital (Laos) C Laos
Viangphoukha 136 C3 *var.* Vieng Pou
Kha. Louang Namtha, N Laos
Viareggio 96 B3 Toscana, C Italy
Viborg 85 A7 Midtjylland,
NW Denmark
Vic 93 G2 *var.* Vich; *anc.* Ausa, Vicus
Ausonensis. Cataluña, NE Spain
Vicentia *see* Vicenza
Vicenza 96 C2 *anc.* Vicentia. Veneto,
NE Italy
Vich *see* Vic
Vichy 90 C5 Allier, C France
Vicksburg 42 B2 Mississippi, S USA
Victoria 79 H1 *country capital*
(Seychelles) Mahé, SW Seychelles
Victoria 36 D5 *province capital*
Vancouver Island, British Columbia,
SW Canada
Victoria 102 A5 *var.* Rabat. Gozo,
NW Malta
Victoria 49 G4 Texas, SW USA
Victoria 149 C2 *state* SE Australia
Victoria *see* Masvingo, Zimbabwe
Victoria Bank *see* Vitória Seamount
Victoria de Durango *see* Durango
Victoria de Las Tunas *see* Las Tunas
Victoria Falls 78 C3 Matabeleland
North, W Zimbabwe
Victoria Falls 78 C2 *waterfall* Zambia/
Zimbabwe
Victoria Falls *see* Iguaçu, Saltos do
Victoria Island 37 F3 *island* Northwest
Territories/Nunavut, NW Canada
Victoria, Lake 73 B6 *var.* Victoria
Nyanza. *lake* E Africa
Victoria Land 154 C4 *physical region*
Antarctica
Victoria Nyanza *see* Victoria, Lake
Victoria River 146 D3 *river* Northern
Territory, N Australia
Victorville 47 C7 California, W USA
Vicus Ausonensis *see* Vic
Vidalia 43 E2 Georgia, SE USA
Videm-Krško *see* Krško
Videň *see* Wien
Vidin 104 B1 *anc.* Bononia. Vidin,
NW Bulgaria
Vidzy 107 C5 Vitsyebskaya Voblasts',
NW Belarus

Viedma 65 C5 Río Negro,
E Argentina
Vieja, Sierra 48 D3 *mountain range*
Texas, SW USA
Vieng Pou Kha *see* Viangphoukha
Vienna *see* Wien, Austria
Vienna *see* Vienne, France
Vienne 91 D5 *anc.* Vienna. Isère,
E France
Vienne 90 B4 *river* W France
Vientiane *see* Viangchan
Vientos, Paso de los *see* Windward
Passage
Vierzon 90 C4 Cher, C France
Viesite 106 C4 Ger. Eckengraf. S Latvia
Vietnam 136 D4 *off.* Socialist Republic of
Vietnam, *Vtn.* Công Hòa Xã Hôi Chu
Nghia Viêt Nam. *country* SE Asia
Vietnam, Socialist Republic of *see*
Vietnam
Vietri *see* Viêt Tri
Viêt Tri 136 D3 *var.* Vietri. Vinh Phu,
N Vietnam
Vieux Fort 55 F2 S Saint Lucia
Vigo 92 B2 Galicia, NW Spain
Viipuri *see* Vyborg
Vijayawäda 132 D1 *prev.* Bezwada.
Andhra Pradesh, SE India
Vila *see* Port-Vila
Vila Artur de Paiva *see* Cubango
Vila da Ponte *see* Cubango
Vila de João Belo *see* Xai-Xai
Vila de Mocímboa da Praia *see*
Mocímboa da Praia
Vila do Conde 92 B2 Porto,
NW Portugal
Vila do Zumbo 78 D2 *prev.* Vila do
Zumbu, Zumbo. Tete,
NW Mozambique
Vila do Zumbu *see* Vila do Zumbo
Vilafranca del Penedès 93 G2 *var.*
Villafranca del Panadés. Cataluña,
NE Spain
Vila General Machado *see* Camacupa
Vila Henrique de Carvalho *see*
Saurimo
Vilaka 106 D4 Ger. Marienhausen.
NE Latvia
Vilalba 92 C1 Galicia, NW Spain
Vila Marechal Carmona *see* Uíge
Vila Nova de Gaia 92 B2 Porto,
NW Portugal
Vila Nova de Portimão *see* Portimão
Vila Pereira de Eça *see* N'Giva
Vila Real 92 C2 *var.* Vila Rial. Vila Real,
N Portugal
Vila Rial *see* Vila Real
Vila Robert Williams *see* Caála
Vila Salazar *see* N'Dalatando
Vila Serpa Pinto *see* Menongue
Vileyka *see* Vilyeyka
Vilhelmina 84 C4 Västerbotten,
N Sweden
Vilhena 62 D3 Rondônia, W Brazil
Vília 105 C5 Attikí, C Greece
Viliya 107 C5 Lith. Neris. *river*
W Belarus
Viliya *see* Neris
Viljandi 106 D2 Ger. Fellin.
Viljandimaa, S Estonia
Vilkaviškis 106 B4 Pol. Wyłkowyszki.
Marijampolė, SW Lithuania
Villa Acuña 50 D2 *var.* Ciudad Acuña.
Coahuila, NE Mexico
Villa Bella 61 F4 El Beni, N Bolivia
Villacarrillo 93 E4 Andalucía,
S Spain
Villa Cecilia *see* Ciudad Madero
Villach 95 D7 Slvn. Beljak. Kärnten,
S Austria
Villacidro 97 A5 Sardegna, Italy,
C Mediterranean Sea
Villa Concepción *see* Concepción
Villa del Pilar *see* Pilar
Villafranca de los Barros 92 C4
Extremadura, W Spain
Villafranca del Panadés *see* Vilafranca
del Penedès
Villahermosa 51 G4 *prev.* San Juan
Bautista. Tabasco, SE Mexico
Villajoyosa 93 F4 Cat. La Vila Joíosa.
Valenciana, E Spain
Villa María 64 C4 Córdoba,
C Argentina
Villa Martín 61 F5 Potosí, SW Bolivia
Villa Mercedes 64 C4 San Juan,
Argentina
Villanueva 50 D3 Zacatecas, C Mexico
Villanueva de la Serena 92 C3
Extremadura, W Spain

Villanueva de los Infantes 93 E4
Castilla-La Mancha, C Spain
Villarrica 64 D2 Guairá, SE Paraguay
Villavicencio 58 B3 Meta, C Colombia
Villaviciosa 92 D1 Asturias,
N Spain
Villazón 61 G5 Potosí, S Bolivia
Villena 93 F4 Valenciana, E Spain
Villeurbanne 91 D5 Rhône,
E France
Villingen-Schwenningen 95 B6
Baden-Württemberg, S Germany
Villmanstrand *see* Lappeenranta
Vilna *see* Vilnius
Vilnius 107 C5 Pol. Wilno, Ger. Wilna;
prev. Rus. Vilna. *country capital*
(Lithuania) Vilnius, SE Lithuania
Vilvoorde 87 C6 Fr. Vilvorde. Vlaams
Brabant, C Belgium
Vilvorde *see* Vilvoorde
Vilyeyka 107 C5 Pol. Wilejka, Rus.
Vileika. Minskaya Voblasts',
NW Belarus
Vilyuy 115 F3 *river* NE Russia
Viña del Mar 64 B4 Valparaíso,
C Chile
Vinarós 93 F3 Valenciana, E Spain
Vincennes 40 B4 Indiana, N USA
Vindhya Mountains *see* Vindhya Range
Vindhya Range 134 D4 *var.* Vindhya
Mountains. *mountain range* N India
Vindobona *see* Wien
Vineland 41 F4 New Jersey, NE USA
Vinh 136 D4 Nghê An, N Vietnam
Vinh Loi *see* Bac Liêu
Vinishte 104 C2 Montana, NW Bulgaria
Vinita 49 G1 Oklahoma, C USA
Vinkovci 100 C3 Ger. Winkowitz, Hung.
Vinkovce. Vukovar-Srijem, E Croatia
Vinkovce *see* Vinkovci
Vinnitsa *see* Vinnytsya
Vinnytsya 108 D2 Rus. Vinnitsa.
Vinnyts'ka Oblast', C Ukraine
Vinogradov *see* Vynohradiv
Vinson Massif 154 A3 *mountain*
Antarctica
Viranşehir 117 E4 Şanlıurfa,
SE Turkey
Virful Moldoveanu *see* Vârful
Moldoveanu
Virginia 45 G1 Minnesota, N USA
Virginia 41 E5 *off.* Commonwealth of
Virginia, *also known as* Mother of
Presidents, Mother of States, Old
Dominion. *state* NE USA
Virginia Beach 41 F5 Virginia,
NE USA
Virgin Islands *see* British Virgin Islands
Virgin Islands (US) 55 F3 *var.* Virgin
Islands of the United States; *prev.*
Danish West Indies. *US unincorporated
territory* E West Indies
Virgin Islands of the United States *see*
Virgin Islands (US)
Viróchey 137 E5 Ratanakiri,
NE Cambodia
Virovitica 100 C2 Ger. Virovititz, Hung.
Verőcze; *prev. Ger.* Werowitz.
Virovitica-Podravina, NE Croatia
Virovititz *see* Virovitica
Virton 87 D8 Luxembourg,
SE Belgium
Virtsu 106 D2 Ger. Werder. Läänemaa,
W Estonia
Vis 100 B4 It. Lissa; *anc.* Issa. *island*
S Croatia
Vis *see* Fish
Visaginas 106 C4 *prev.* Sniečkus. Utena,
E Lithuania
Visākhapatnam *see* Vishakhapatnam
Vislinskiy Zaliv *see* Vistula Lagoon
Visoko 100 C4 Federacija Bosne I
Hercegovine, C Bosnia and
Herzegovina
Vistastjokka 84 D3 *river* N Sweden
Vistula 98 C2 Eng. Vistula, Ger.
Weichsel. *river* C Poland
Vistula *see* Wisła

Vistula Lagoon 98 C2 Ger. Frisches Haff,
Pol. Zalew Wiślany, Rus. Vislinskiy
Zaliv. *lagoon* Poland/Russia
Vitebsk *see* Vitsyebsk
Viterbo 96 C4 *anc.* Vicus Elbii. Lazio,
C Italy
Viti *see* Fiji
Viti Levu 145 E4 *island* W Fiji
Vitim 115 F4 *river* C Russia
Vitória 63 F4 *state capital* Espírito Santo,
SE Brazil
Vitoria *see* Vitoria-Gasteiz
Vitoria Bank *see* Vitória Seamount
Vitória da Conquista 63 F3 Bahia,
E Brazil
Vitoria-Gasteiz 93 E1 *var.* Vitoria, Eng.
Vittoria. País Vasco, N Spain
Vitória Seamount 67 B5 *var.* Victoria
Bank, Vitoria Bank. *seamount*
C Atlantic Ocean
Vitré 90 B3 Ille-et-Vilaine, NW France
Vitsyebsk 107 E5 Rus. Vitebsk.
Vitsyebskaya Voblasts', NE Belarus
Vittoria 97 C7 Sicilia, Italy,
C Mediterranean Sea
Vittoria *see* Vitoria-Gasteiz
Vizcaya, Golfo de *see* Biscay, Bay of
Vizianagaram 135 E5 *var.* Vizianagram.
Andhra Pradesh, E India
Vizianagram *see* Vizianagaram
Vjosës, Lumi i 101 C7 *var.* Vijosa,
Vijosë, Gk. Aóos.
river Albania/Greece
Vlaanderen 87 A6 Eng. Flanders, Fr.
Flandre. *cultural region* Belgium/
France
Vlaardingen 86 B4 Zuid-Holland,
SW Netherlands
Vladikavkaz 111 B8 *prev.* Dzaudzhikau,
Ordzhonikidze. Respublika Severnaya
Osetiya, SW Russia
Vladimir 111 B5 Vladimirskaya Oblast',
W Russia
Vladimirovka *see* Yuzhno-Sakhalinsk
Vladimir-Volynskiy *see*
Volodymyr-Volyns'kyy
Vladivostok 115 G5 Primorskiy Kray,
SE Russia
Vlagtwedde 86 E2 Groningen,
NE Netherlands
Vlasotince 101 E5 Serbia, SE Serbia
Vlieland 86 C1 Fris. Flylân. *island*
Waddeneilanden, N Netherlands
Vlijmen 86 C4 Noord-Brabant,
S Netherlands
Vlissingen 87 B5 Eng. Flushing, Fr.
Flessingue. Zeeland, SW Netherlands
Vlodava *see* Włodawa
Vlonë/Vlora *see* Vlorë
Vlorë 101 C7 *prev.* Vlonë, It. Valona,
Vlora. Vlorë, SW Albania
Vlotslavsk *see* Włocławek
Vöcklabruch 95 D6 Oberösterreich,
NW Austria
Vogelkop *see* Doberai, Jazirah
Vohimena, Tanjona 79 F4 Fr. Cap
Sainte Marie. *headland*
S Madagascar
Voiron 91 D5 Isère, E France
Vojvodina 100 D3 Ger. Wojwodina.
Vojvodina, N Serbia
Volga 111 B7 *river* NW Russia
Volga Uplands 81 G3 *var.* Volga
Uplands. *mountain range* W Russia
Volga Uplands *see* Privolzhskaya
Vozvyshennost'
Volgodonsk 111 B7 Rostovskaya Oblast',
SW Russia
Volgograd 111 B7 *prev.* Stalingrad,
Tsaritsyn. Volgogradskaya Oblast',
SW Russia
Volkhov 110 B4 Leningradskaya Oblast',
NW Russia
Volkoysk *see* Vawkavysk
Volmari *see* Valmiera
Volnovakha 109 G3 Donets'ka Oblast',
SE Ukraine
Volodymyr-Volyns'kyy 108 C1 Pol.
Włodzimierz, Rus. Vladimir-Volynskiy.
Volyns'ka Oblast', NW Ukraine
Vologda 110 B4 Vologodskaya Oblast',
W Russia
Vólos 105 B5 Thessalía, C Greece
Volozhin *see* Valozhyn
Vol'sk 111 C6 Saratovskaya Oblast',
W Russia
Volta 75 E5 *river* SE Ghana
Volta Blanche *see* White Volta
Volta, Lake 75 E5 *reservoir* SE Ghana
Volta Noire *see* Black Volta

Volturno 97 D5 *river* S Italy
Volunteer Island *see* Starbuck Island
Volzhskiy 111 B6 Volgogradskaya
Oblast', SW Russia
Võnnu 106 E3 Ger. Wendau. Tartumaa,
SE Estonia
Voorst 86 D3 Gelderland, E Netherlands
Voranava 107 C5 Pol. Werenów, Rus.
Voronovo. Hrodzyenskaya Voblasts',
W Belarus
Vorderrhein 95 B7 *river* SE Switzerland
Vóreioi Sporádes *see* Vóreies Sporádes
Vóreies Sporádes 105 C5 *var.* Vórioi
Sporádhes, Northern Sporades, Eng.
Northern Sporades. *island group*
E Greece
Vórioi Sporádes *see* Vóreies Sporádes
Vorkuta 114 C2 Respublika Komi,
NW Russia
Vormsi 106 C2 *var.* Vormsi Saar, Ger.
Worms, Swed. Ormsö. *island*
W Estonia
Vormsi Saar *see* Vormsi
Voronezh 111 B6 Voronezhskaya
Oblast', W Russia
Voronovo *see* Voranava
Voroshilov *see* Ussuriysk
Voroshilovgrad *see* Luhans'k, Ukraine
Voroshilovsk *see* Stavropol', Russia
Võru 106 D3 Ger. Werro. Võrumaa,
SE Estonia
Vosges 90 E4 *mountain range*
NE France
Vostochnyy Sayan 115 E4 Mong. Dzüün
Soyonï Nuruu, Eng. Eastern Sayans.
mountain range Mongolia/Russia
Vostock Island *see* Vostok Island
Vostok 154 C3 Russian research station
Antarctica
Vostok Island 145 G3 *var.* Vostock
Island; *prev.* Stavers Island. *island* Line
Islands, SE Kiribati
Voznesens'k 109 E3 Rus. Voznesensk.
Mykolayivs'ka Oblast', S Ukraine
Vrangelya, Ostrov 115 F1 Eng. Wrangel
Island. *island* NE Russia
Vranje 101 E5 Serbia, SE Serbia
Vranov *see* Vranov nad Topl'ou
Vranov nad Topl'ou 99 D5 *var.* Vranov,
Hung. Varannó. Prešovský Kraj,
E Slovakia
Vratsa 104 C2 Vratsa, NW Bulgaria
Vrbas 100 C3 Vojvodina, NW Serbia
Vrbas 100 C3 *river* N Bosnia and
Herzegovina
Vršac 100 D3 Ger. Werschetz, Hung.
Versecz. Vojvodina, NE Serbia
Vsetín 99 C5 Ger. Wsetin. Zlínský Kraj,
E Czech Republic (Czechia)
Vučitrn *see* Vushtrri
Vukovar 100 D3 Hung. Vukovár.
Vukovar-Srijem, E Croatia
Vulcano, Isola 97 C7 *island* Isole Eolie,
S Italy
Vung Tau 132 E6 *prev. Fr.* Cape Saint
Jacques, Cap Saint-Jacques. Ba
Ria-Vung Tau, S Vietnam
Vusan *see* Busan
Vushtrri 101 D5 Serb. Vučitrn.
N Kosovo
Vyatka 111 C5 *river* NW Russia
Vyatka *see* Kirov
Vyborg 110 B3 Fin. Viipuri.
Leningradskaya Oblast', NW Russia
Vyerkhnyadzvinsk 107 D5 Rus.
Verkhnedvinsk. Vitsyebskaya
Voblasts', N Belarus
Vyetryna 107 D5 Rus. Vetrino.
Vitsyebskaya Voblasts', N Belarus
Vynohradiv 108 B3 Cz. Sevluš, Hung.
Nagyszöllős, Rus. Vinogradov; *prev.*
Sevlyush. Zakarpats'ka Oblast',
W Ukraine

W

Wa 75 E4 NW Ghana
Waag *see* Váh
Waagbistritz *see* Považská Bystrica
Waal 86 D4 *river* S Netherlands
Waagbistritz *see* Považská Bystrica
Wabash 40 C4 Indiana, N USA
Wabash River 40 B5 *river* N USA
Waco 49 G3 Texas, SW USA
Wad Al-Hajarah *see* Guadalajara
Waddān 71 F3 NW Libya
Waddenzee 86 C1 *var.* Wadden Zee.
sea NE North Sea
Wadden Zee *see* Waddenzee
Waddington, Mount 36 D5 *mountain*
British Columbia, SW Canada
Wādi as Sīr 119 B6 *var.* Wadi es Sir.
'Ammān, NW Jordan
Wadi es Sir *see* Wādi as Sīr

Wadi Halfa *72 B3 var.* Wādī Ḩalfā'.
Northern, N Sudan
Wādī Mūsā *119 B7 var.* Petra. Ma'ān,
S Jordan
Wad Madani *see* Wad Medani
Wad Medani *72 C4 var.* Wad Madanī.
Gezira, C Sudan
Waflia *139 F4* Pulau Buru, E Indonesia
Wagadugu *see* Ouagadougou
Wagga Wagga *149 C7* New South Wales,
SE Australia
Wagin *147 B7* Western Australia
Wah *134 C1* Punjab, NE Pakistan
Wahai *139 F4* Pulau Seram, E Indonesia
Wahaybah, Ramlat Al *see* Wahībah,
Ramlat Āl
Wahiawā *47 A8 var.* Wahiawa. O'ahu,
Hawaii, USA, C Pacific Ocean
Wahībah, Ramlat Ahl *see* Wahībah,
Ramlat Āl
Wahibah Sands *121 E5 var.* Ramlat Ahl
Wahībah, Ramlat Al Wahaybah, *Eng.*
Wahībah Sands. *desert* N Oman
Wahībah Sands *see* Wahībah, Ramlat Āl
Wahpeton *45 F2* North Dakota,
N USA
Wahran *see* Oran
Waiau *151 A7 river* South Island, New
Zealand
Waigeo, Pulau *139 G4 island* Maluku,
E Indonesia
Waikaremoana, Lake *150 E4 lake*
North Island, New Zealand
Wailuku *47 B8* Maui, Hawaii, USA,
C Pacific Ocean
Waimate *151 B6* Canterbury, South
Island, New Zealand
Waiouru *150 D4* Manawatu-Wanganui,
North Island, New Zealand
Waipara *151 C6* Canterbury, South
Island, New Zealand
Waipawa *150 E4* Hawke's Bay, North
Island, New Zealand
Waipukurau *150 D4* Hawke's Bay,
North Island, New Zealand
Wairau *151 C5 river* South Island,
New Zealand
Wairoa *150 E4* Hawke's Bay, North
Island, New Zealand
Wairoa *150 D2 river* North Island,
New Zealand
Waitaki *151 B6 river* South Island, New
Zealand
Waitara *150 D4* Taranaki, North Island,
New Zealand
Waitzen *see* Vác
Waiuku *150 D3* Auckland, North Island,
New Zealand
Wakasa-wan *131 C6 bay* C Japan
Wakatipu, Lake *151 A7 lake* South
Island, New Zealand
Wakayama *131 C6* Wakayama, Honshū,
SW Japan
Wake Island *122 C2 US unincorporated
territory* NW Pacific Ocean
Wake Island *142 D1 atoll*
NW Pacific Ocean
Wakkanai *130 C1* Hokkaidō, NE Japan
Walachei/Walachia *see* Wallachia
Wałbrzych *98 B4 Ger.* Waldenburg,
Waldenburg in Schlesien. Dolnośląskie,
SW Poland
Walcourt *87 C7* Namur, S Belgium
Wałcz *98 B3 Ger.* Deutsch Krone.
Zachodnio-pomorskie, NW Poland
Waldenburg/Waldenburg in Schlesien
see Wałbrzych
Waldia *see* Weldiya
Wales *36 C2* Alaska, USA
Wales *89 C6 Wel.* Cymru. *cultural region*
Wales, United Kingdom
Walgett *149 D5* New South Wales,
SE Australia
Walk *see* Valga, Estonia
Walk *see* Valka, Latvia
Walker Lake *47 C5 lake* Nevada,
W USA
Wallachia *108 B5 var.* Walachia, *Ger.*
Walachei, *Rom.* Valahia. *cultural
region* S Romania
Walla Walla *46 C2* Washington,
NW USA
Wallenthal *see* Hațeg
Wallis and Futuna *145 E4 Fr.* Territoire
de Wallis et Futuna. *French overseas
territory* C Pacific Ocean
Wallis et Futuna, Territoire de *see*
Wallis and Futuna
Walnut Ridge *42 B1* Arkansas,
C USA

Waltenberg *see* Zalău
Walthamstow *89 B7* Waltham Forest,
SE England, United Kingdom
Walvisbaai *see* Walvis Bay
Walvis Bay *78 A4 Afr.* Walvisbaai.
Erongo, NW Namibia
Walvish Ridge *see* Walvis Ridge
Walvis Ridge *69 B7 var.* Walvish Ridge.
undersea ridge E Atlantic Ocean
Wan *see* Anhui
Wanaka *151 B6* Otago, South Island,
New Zealand
Wanaka, Lake *151 A6 lake* South Island,
New Zealand
Wanchuan *see* Zhangjiakou
Wandel Sea *83 E1 sea* Arctic Ocean
Wandsworth *89 A8* Wandsworth,
SE England, United Kingdom
Wanganui *150 D4* Manawatu-
Wanganui, North Island,
New Zealand
Wangaratta *149 C7* Victoria,
SE Australia
Wankie *see* Hwange
Wanki, Río *see* Coco, Río
Wanlaweyn *73 D6 var.* Wanle Weyn, *It.*
Uanle Uen. Shabeellaha Hoose,
SW Somalia
Wanle Weyn *see* Wanlaweyn
Wanxian *see* Wanzhou
Wanzhou *128 B3 var.* Wanxian.
Chongqing, C China
Warangal *135 E5* Telangana, C India
Waraśdin *see* Varaždin
Warburg *94 B4* Nordrhein-Westfalen,
W Germany
Ware *37 E4* British Columbia,
W Canada
Waremme *87 C6* Liège, E Belgium
Waren *94 C3* Mecklenburg-
Vorpommern, NE Germany
Wargla *see* Ouargla
Warkworth *150 D2* Auckland, North
Island, New Zealand
Warnemünde *94 C2* Mecklenburg-
Vorpommern, NE Germany
Warner *49 G1* Oklahoma, C USA
Warnes *61 G4* Santa Cruz, C Bolivia
Warrego River *149 C5 seasonal river*
New South Wales/Queensland,
E Australia
Warren *40 D3* Michigan, N USA
Warren *40 D3* Ohio, N USA
Warren *41 F3* Pennsylvania,
NE USA
Warri *75 F5* Delta, S Nigeria
Warrnambool *149 B7* Victoria,
SE Australia
Warsaw/Warschau *see* Warszawa
Warszawa *98 D3 Eng.* Warsaw,
Ger. Warschau, *Rus.* Varshava.
country capital (Poland) Mazowieckie,
C Poland
Warta *98 B3 Ger.* Warthe. *river*
W Poland
Wartberg *see* Senec
Warthe *see* Warta
Warwick *149 E5* Queensland,
E Australia
Wasa *154 B2 Swedish research station*
Antarctica
Washington *44 A2* NE England, United
Kingdom
Washington D.C. *41 F4 country capital*
(USA) District of Columbia, NE USA
Washington Island *see* Teraina
Washington, Mount *41 G2 mountain*
New Hampshire, NE USA
Wash, The *89 E6 inlet* E England, United
Kingdom
Wasiliszki *see* Vasilishki
Waspam *53 E2 var.* Waspán. Región
Autónoma Atlántico Norte,
NE Nicaragua
Waspán *see* Waspam
Watampone *139 E4 var.* Bone. Sulawesi,
C Indonesia
Watenstedt-Salzgitter *see* Salzgitter
Waterbury *41 F3* Connecticut,
NE USA
Waterford *89 B6 Ir.* Port Láirge.
Waterford, S Ireland
Waterloo *45 G3* Iowa, C USA
Watertown *41 F2* New York, NE USA
Watertown *45 F2* South Dakota,
N USA
Waterville *41 G2* Maine, NE USA
Watford *89 A7* E England, United
Kingdom
Watlings Island *see* San Salvador

Watsa *77 E5* Orientale, NE Dem.
Rep. Congo
Watts Bar Lake *42 D1 reservoir*
Tennessee, S USA
Wau *73 B5 var.* Wāw. Western Bahr el
Ghazal, W South Sudan
Waukegan *40 B3* Illinois, N USA
Waukesha *40 B3* Wisconsin, N USA
Wausau *40 B2* Wisconsin, N USA
Waverly *45 G3* Iowa, C USA
Wavre *87 C6* Walloon Brabant,
C Belgium
Wāw *see* Wau
Wawa *38 C4* Ontario, S Canada
Waycross *43 E3* Georgia, SE USA
Wearmouth *see* Sunderland
Webfoot State *see* Oregon
Webster City *45 F3* Iowa, C USA
Weddell Plain *154 A2 abyssal plain*
SW Atlantic Ocean
Weddell Sea *154 A2
sea* SW Atlantic Ocean
Weener *94 A3* Niedersachsen,
NW Germany
Weert *87 D5* Limburg, SE Netherlands
Weesp *86 C3* Noord-Holland,
C Netherlands
Węgorzewo *98 D2 Ger.* Angerburg.
Warmińsko-Mazurskie, NE Poland
Weichsel *see* Wisła
Weimar *94 C4* Thüringen, C Germany
Weissenburg *see* Alba Iulia, Romania
Weissenburg in Bayern *95 C6* Bayern,
SE Germany
Weissenstein *see* Paide
Weisskirchen *see* Bela Crkva
Weiswampach *87 D7* Diekirch,
N Luxembourg
Wejherowo *98 C2* Pomorskie,
NW Poland
Welchman Hall *55 G1* C Barbados
Weldiya *72 C4 var.* Waldia, *It.* Valdia.
Āmara, N Ethiopia
Welkom *78 D4* Free State,
C South Africa
Welle *see* Uele
Wellesley Islands *148 B2 island group*
Queensland, N Australia
Wellington *151 D5 country capital*
(New Zealand) Wellington, North
Island, New Zealand
Wellington *45 F5* Kansas, C USA
Wellington *see* Wellington, Isla
Wellington, Isla *65 A7 var.* Wellington.
island S Chile
Wells *46 D4* Nevada, W USA
Wellsford *150 D2* Auckland, North
Island, New Zealand
Wells, Lake *147 C5 lake* Western
Australia
Wels *95 D6 anc.* Ovilava. Oberösterreich,
N Austria
Wembley *89 A8* Alberta, W Canada
Wemmel *87 B6* Vlaams Brabant,
C Belgium
Wenatchee *46 B2* Washington,
NW USA
Wenchi *75 E4* W Ghana
Wen-chou/Wenchow *see* Wenzhou
Wendau *see* Võnnu
Wenden *see* Cēsis
Wenzhou *128 D5 var.* Wen-chou,
Wenchow. Zhejiang, SE China
Werda *78 C4* Kgalagadi, S Botswana
Werder *see* Virtsu
Werenów *see* Voranava
Werkendam *86 C4* Noord-Brabant,
S Netherlands
Werowitz *see* Virovitica
Werro *see* Võru
Werschetz *see* Vršac
Wesenberg *see* Rakvere
Weser *94 B3 river* NW Germany
Wessel Islands *148 B1 island group*
Northern Territory, N Australia
West Antarctica *154 A3 prev.* Lesser
Antarctica. *physical region* Antarctica
West Australian Basin *see*
Wharton Basin
West Bank *119 A6 disputed region*
SW Asia
West Bend *40 B3* Wisconsin,
N USA
West Bengal *135 F4 cultural region*
NE India
West Cape *151 A7 headland* South
Island, New Zealand
West Des Moines *45 F3* Iowa, C USA
Westerland *94 B2* Schleswig-Holstein,
N Germany

Western Australia *146 B4 state*
W Australia
Western Bug *see* Bug
Western Carpathians *99 E7 mountain
range* W Romania Europe
Western Desert *72 B2 var.* Sahra' al
Gharbīya, *Eng.* Western Desert. *desert*
C Egypt
Western Desert *see* Sahrā' al Gharbīya
Western Dvina *85 E7 Bel.* Dzvina, *Ger.*
Düna, *Latv.* Daugava, *Rus.* Zapadnaya
Dvina. *river* W Europe
Western Ghats *134 C5 mountain range*
SW India
Western Isles *see* Outer Hebrides
Western Punjab *see* Punjab
Western Sahara *70 B3 disputed territory
administered by Morocco* N Africa
Western Samoa *see* Samoa
Western Sayans *114 D4 Eng.* Western
Sayans. *mountain range* S Russia
Western Sayans *see* Zapadnyy Sayan
Western Scheldt *87 B5 Eng.* Western
Scheldt; *prev.* Honte. *inlet* S
North Sea
Western Scheldt *see* Westerschelde
Western Sierra Madre *see* Madre
Occidental, Sierra
West Falkland *65 C7 var.* Gran Malvina,
Isla Gran Malvina. *island* W Falkland
Islands
West Fargo *45 F2* North Dakota,
N USA
West Frisian Islands *86 C1 Eng.* West
Frisian Islands. *island group*
N Netherlands
West Frisian Islands *see*
Waddeneilanden
West Irian *see* Papua
Westlice Morava *see* Zapadna Morava
West Mariana Basin *142 B1 var.* Perece
Vela Basin. *undersea feature*
W Pacific Ocean
West Memphis *42 B1* Arkansas, C USA
West New Guinea *see* Papua
Weston-super-Mare *89 D7* SW England,
United Kingdom
West Palm Beach *43 F4* Florida,
SE USA
West Papua *see* Papua
Westport *151 C5* West Coast, South
Island, New Zealand
West Punjab *see* Punjab
West River *see* Xi Jiang
West Siberian Plain *114 C3 Eng.* West
Siberian Plain. *plain* C Russia
West Siberian Plain *see*
Zapadno-Sibirskaya Ravnina
West Virginia *40 D4 off.* State of West
Virginia, *also known as* Mountain State.
state NE USA
Wetar, Pulau *139 F5 island* Kepulauan
Damar, E Indonesia
Wetzlar *95 B5* Hessen, W Germany
Wevok *36 C2 var.* Wewuk. Alaska,
USA
Wewuk *see* Wevok
Wexford *89 B6 Ir.* Loch Garman.
SE Ireland
Weyburn *37 F5* Saskatchewan, S Canada
Weymouth *89 D7* S England, United
Kingdom
Wezep *86 D3* Gelderland,
E Netherlands
Whakatane *150 E3* Bay of Plenty,
North Island, New Zealand
Whale Cove *37 G3 var.* Tikiarjuaq.
Nunavut, C Canada
Whangarei *150 D2* Northland, North
Island, New Zealand
Wharton Basin *141 D5 var.* West
Australian Basin. *undersea feature*
E Indian Ocean
Whataroa *151 B6* West Coast, South
Island, New Zealand
Wheatland *44 D3* Wyoming, C USA
Wheeler Peak *48 D1 mountain* New
Mexico, SW USA
Wheeling *40 D4* West Virginia,
NE USA
Whitby *89 D5* N England, United
Kingdom
Whitefish *44 B1* Montana, NW USA
Whitehaven *89 C5* NW England,
United Kingdom
Whitehorse *36 D4 territory capital*
Yukon, W Canada
White Nile *72 B4 Ar.* Al Baḥr al Abyaḍ,
An Nīl al Abyaḍ, Bahr el Jebel. *river*
NE South Sudan

White Nile 72 B4 var. Bahr el Jebel. river S Sudan
White River 44 D3 river South Dakota, N USA
White Sea see Beloye More
White Volta 75 E4 var. Nakambé, Fr. Volta Blanche. river Burkina Faso/ Ghana
Whitianga 150 D2 Waikato, North Island, New Zealand
Whitney, Mount 47 C6 mountain California, W USA
Whitsunday Group 148 D3 island group Queensland, E Australia
Whyalla 149 B6 South Australia
Wichita 45 F5 Kansas, C USA
Wichita Falls 49 F2 Texas, SW USA
Wichita River 49 F2 river Texas, SW USA
Wickenburg 48 B2 Arizona, SW USA
Wicklow 89 B6 Ir. Cill Mhantáin. county E Ireland
Wicklow Mountains 89 B6 Ir. Sléibhte Chill Mhantáin. mountain range E Ireland
Wieliczka 99 D5 Małopolskie, S Poland
Wieluń 98 C4 Sieradz, C Poland
Wien 95 E6 Eng. Vienna, Hung. Bécs, Slvk. Vídeň, Slvn. Dunaj; anc. Vindobona. country capital (Austria) Wien, NE Austria
Wiener Neustadt 95 E6 Niederösterreich, E Austria
Wierden 86 E3 Overijssel, E Netherlands
Wiesbaden 95 B5 Hessen, W Germany
Wieselburg and Ungarisch-Altenburg/ Wieselburg-Ungarisch-Altenburg see Mosonmagyaróvár
Wiesenhof see Ôstroŀęka
Wight, Isle of 89 D7 island United Kingdom
Wigorna Ceaster see Worcester
Wijchen 86 D4 Gelderland, SE Netherlands
Wijk bij Duurstede 86 D4 Utrecht, C Netherlands
Wilcannia 149 C6 New South Wales, SE Australia
Wileyka see Vilyeyka
Wilhelm, Mount 144 B3 mountain C Papua New Guinea
Wilhelm-Pieck-Stadt see Guben
Wilhelmshaven 94 B3 Niedersachsen, NW Germany
Wilia/Wilja see Neris
Wilkes Barre 41 F3 Pennsylvania, NE USA
Wilkes Land 154 C4 physical region Antarctica
Wiłkomierz see Ukmergė
Willard 48 D2 New Mexico, SW USA
Willcox 48 C3 Arizona, SW USA
Willebroek 87 B5 Antwerpen, C Belgium
Willemstad 55 E5 dependent territory capital (Curaçao) Lesser Antilles, S Caribbean Sea
Williston 44 D1 North Dakota, N USA
Wilmington 41 F4 Delaware, NE USA
Wilmington 43 F2 North Carolina, SE USA
Wilmington 40 C4 Ohio, N USA
Wilna/Wilno see Vilnius
Wilrijk 87 C5 Antwerpen, N Belgium
Winchester 89 D7 hist. Wintanceaster, Lat. Venta Belgarum. S England, United Kingdom
Winchester 41 E4 Virginia, NE USA
Windau see Ventspils, Latvia
Windau see Venta, Latvia/Lithuania
Windhoek 78 B3 Ger. Windhuk. country capital (Namibia) Khomas, C Namibia
Windhuk see Windhoek
Windorah 148 C4 Queensland, C Australia
Windsor 38 C5 Ontario, S Canada
Windsor 89 D7 S England, United Kingdom
Windsor 41 G3 Connecticut, NE USA
Windward Islands 55 I14 island group E West Indies

Windward Islands see Barlavento, Ilhas de, Cape Verde
Windward Passage 54 D3 Sp. Paso de los Vientos. channel Cuba/Haiti
Winisk 38 C2 river Ontario, C Canada
Winkowitz see Vinkovci
Winnebago, Lake 40 B2 lake Wisconsin, N USA
Winnemucca 47 C5 Nevada, W USA
Winnipeg 37 G5 province capital Manitoba, S Canada
Winnipeg, Lake 37 G5 lake Manitoba, C Canada
Winnipegosis, Lake 38 A3 lake Manitoba, C Canada
Winona 45 G2 Minnesota, N USA
Winschoten 86 E2 Groningen, NE Netherlands
Winsen 94 B3 Niedersachsen, N Germany
Winston Salem 43 E1 North Carolina, SE USA
Winsum 86 D1 Groningen, NE Netherlands
Wintanceaster see Winchester
Winterswijk 86 E4 Gelderland, E Netherlands
Winterthur 95 B7 Zürich, NE Switzerland
Winton 148 C4 Queensland, E Australia
Winton 151 A7 Southland, South Island, New Zealand
Wisby see Visby
Wisconsin 40 A2 off. State of Wisconsin, also known as Badger State. state N USA
Wisconsin Rapids 40 B2 Wisconsin, N USA
Wisconsin River 40 A3 river Wisconsin, N USA
Wiślany, Zalew see Vistula Lagoon
Wismar 94 C2 Mecklenburg-Vorpommern, N Germany
Wittenberge 94 C3 Brandenburg, N Germany
Wittlich 95 A5 Rheinland-Pfalz, SW Germany
Wittstock 94 C3 Brandenburg, NE Germany
W. J. van Blommesteinmeer 59 G3 reservoir E Suriname
Władysławowo 98 C2 Pomorskie, N Poland
Włocławek 98 C3 Ger./Rus. Vlotslavsk. Kujawsko-pomorskie, C Poland
Włodawa 98 E4 Rus. Vlodava. Lubelskie, SE Poland
Włodzimierz see Volodymyr-Volyns'kyy
Wlotzkasbaken 78 B3 Erongo, W Namibia
Wodonga 149 C7 Victoria, SE Australia
Wodzisław Śląski 99 C5 Ger. Loslau. Śląskie, S Poland
Wojerecy see Hoyerswerda
Wójjä see Wotje Atoll
Wojwodina see Vojvodina
Woking 89 D7 SE England, United Kingdom
Wolf, Isla 60 A4 island Galápagos Islands, W Ecuador, South America
Wolfsberg 95 D7 Kärnten, SE Austria
Wolfsburg 94 C3 Niedersachsen, N Germany
Wolgast 94 D2 Mecklenburg-Vorpommern, NE Germany
Wołkowysk see Vawkavysk
Wöllan see Velenje
Wollaston Lake 37 F4 Saskatchewan, C Canada
Wollongong 149 D6 New South Wales, SE Australia
Wolmar see Valmiera
Wołożyn see Valozhyn
Wolvega 86 D2 Fris. Wolvegea. Fryslân, N Netherlands
Wolvegea see Wolvega
Wolverhampton 89 D6 C England, United Kingdom
Wolverine State see Michigan
Wŏnsan 129 E3 SE North Korea
Woodburn 46 B3 Oregon, NW USA
Woodland 47 B5 California, W USA
Woodruff 40 B2 Wisconsin, N USA

Woods, Lake of the 38 A3 Fr. Lac des Bois. lake Canada/USA
Woodville 150 D4 Manawatu-Wanganui, North Island, New Zealand
Woodward 49 F1 Oklahoma, C USA
Worcester 78 C5 Western Cape, SW South Africa
Worcester 89 D6 hist. Wigorna Ceaster. W England, United Kingdom
Worcester 41 G3 Massachusetts, NE USA
Workington 89 C5 NW England, United Kingdom
Worland 44 C3 Wyoming, C USA
Wormatia see Worms
Worms 95 B5 anc. Augusta Vangionum, Borbetomagus, Wormatia. Rheinland-Pfalz, SW Germany
Worms see Vormsi
Worthington 45 F3 Minnesota, N USA
Wotje Atoll 144 D1 var. Wójjä. atoll Ratak Chain, E Marshall Islands
Woudrichem 86 C4 Noord-Brabant, S Netherlands
Wrangel Island see Vrangelya, Ostrov
Wrangel Plain 155 B2 undersea feature Arctic Ocean
Wrocław 98 C4 Eng./Ger. Breslau. Dolnośląskie, SW Poland
Września 98 C3 Wielkopolskie, C Poland
Wsetin see Vsetín
Wuchang see Wuhan
Wuday'ah 121 C6 spring/well S Saudi Arabia
Wuhai 127 E3 var. Haibowan. Nei Mongol Zizhiqu, N China
Wuhan 128 C5 var. Han-kou, Han-k'ou, Hanyang, Wuchang, Wu-han; prev. Hankow. province capital Hubei, C China
Wu-han see Wuhan
Wuhsien see Suzhou
Wuhsi/Wu-his see Wuxi
Wuhu 128 D5 var. Wu-na-mu. Anhui, E China
Wujlän see Ujelang Atoll
Wukari 75 G4 Taraba, E Nigeria
Wuliang Shan 128 A6 mountain range SW China
Wu-lu-k'o-mu-shi/Wu-lu-mu-ch'i see Ürümqi
Wu-na-mu see Wuhu
Wuppertal 94 A4 prev. Barmen-Elberfeld. Nordrhein-Westfalen, W Germany
Würzburg 95 B5 Bayern, SW Germany
Wusih see Wuxi
Wuxi 128 D5 var. Wuhsi, Wu-hsi, Wusih. Jiangsu, E China
Wuyi Shan 125 E3 mountain range SE China
Wye 89 C6 Wel. Gwy. river England/ Wales, United Kingdom
Wyłkowyszki see Vilkaviškis
Wyndham 146 D3 Western Australia
Wyoming 40 C3 Michigan, N USA
Wyoming 44 B3 off. State of Wyoming, also known as Equality State. state C USA
Wyszków 98 D3 Ger. Probstberg. Mazowieckie, NE Poland

X

Xaafuun, Raas 72 E4 var. Ras Hafun. cape NE Somalia
Xaçmaz 117 H2 Rus. Khachmas. N Azerbaijan
Xaignabouli 136 C4 prev. Muang Xaignabouri, Fr. Sayaboury. Xaignabouli, N Laos
Xai-Xai 79 E4 prev. João Belo, Vila de João Belo. Gaza, S Mozambique
Xalapa 51 F4 Veracruz-Llave, Mexico
Xam Nua 136 D3 var. Sam Neua. Houaphan, N Laos
Xankändi 117 G3 Rus. Khankendi; prev. Stepanakert. SW Azerbaijan
Xánthi 104 C3 Anatolikí Makedonía kai Thráki, NE Greece
Xàtiva 93 F3 Cas. Xátiva; anc. Setabis, var. Jativa. Valenciana, E Spain
Xauen see Chefchaouen
Xäzär Dänizi see Caspian Sea
Xeres see Jerez de la Frontera
Xiaguan see Dali
Xiamen 128 D6 var. Hsia-men; prev. Amoy. Fujian, SE China

Xi'an 128 C4 var. Changan, Sian, Signan, Siking, Singan, Xian. province capital Shaanxi, C China
Xiang see Hunan
Xiangkhoang see Phônsaven
Xiangtan 128 C5 var. Hsiang-t'an, Siangtan. Hunan, S China
Xiao Hinggan Ling 128 D2 Eng. Lesser Khingan Range. mountain range NE China
Xichang 128 B5 Sichuan, C China
Xieng Khouang see Phônsaven
Xieng Ngeun see Muong Xiang Ngeun
Xigazê 126 C5 var. Jih-k'a-tse, Shigatse, Xigaze. Xizang Zizhiqu, W China
Xi Jiang 124 D3 var. Hsi Chiang, Eng. West River. river S China
Xilinhot 127 F2 var. Silinhot. Nei Mongol Zizhiqu, N China
Xilokastro see Xylókastro
Xin see Xinjiang Uygur Zizhiqu
Xingkai Hu see Khanka, Lake
Xingu, Rio 63 E2 river C Brazil
Xingxingxia 126 D3 Xinjiang Uygur Zizhiqu, NW China
Xining 127 E4 var. Hsining, Hsi-ning, Sining. province capital Qinghai, C China
Xinjiang see Xinjiang Uygur Zizhiqu
Xinjiang Uygur Zizhiqu 126 B3 var. Sinkiang, Sinkiang Uighur Autonomous Region, Xin, Xinjiang. autonomous region NW China
Xinpu see Lianyungang
Xinxiang 128 C4 Henan, C China
Xinyang 128 C5 var. Hsin-yang, Sinyang. Henan, C China
Xiorda lima 92 C2 Galicia, NW Spain
Xiqing Shan 124 D2 mountain range C China
Xiva 122 D2 Rus. Khiva, Khiwa. Xorazm Viloyati, W Uzbekistan
Xixón see Gijón
Xizang see Xizang Zizhiqu
Xizang Gaoyuan see Qingzang Gaoyuan
Xizang Zizhiqu 126 B4 var. Thibet, Tibetan Autonomous Region, Xizang, Eng. Tibet. autonomous region W China
Xolotlán see Managua, Lago de
Xucheng see Xuwen
Xuddur 73 D5 var. Hudur, It. Oddur. Bakool, SW Somalia
Xuwen 128 C7 var. Xucheng. Guangdong, S China
Xuzhou 128 D4 var. Hsu-chou, Suchow, Tongshan; prev. T'ung-shan. Jiangsu, E China
Xylókastro 105 B5 var. Xilokastro. Pelopónnisos, S Greece

Y

Ya'an 128 B5 var. Yaan. Sichuan, C China
Yabēlo 73 C5 Oromīya, C Ethiopia
Yablis 53 E2 Región Autónoma Atlántico Norte, NE Nicaragua
Yablonovyy Khrebet 115 F4 mountain range S Russia
Yabrai Shan 127 E3 mountain range N China
Yafran 71 F2 NW Libya
Yaghan Basin 67 B7 undersea feature SE Pacific Ocean
Yagotin see Yahotyn
Yahotyn 109 E2 Rus. Yagotin. Kyyivs'ka Oblast', N Ukraine
Yahualica 50 D4 Jalisco, SW Mexico
Yakima 46 B2 Washington, NW USA
Yakima River 46 B2 river Washington, NW USA
Yakoruda 104 C3 Blagoevgrad, SW Bulgaria
Yaku-shima 131 B8 island Nansei-shotō, SW Japan
Yakutat 36 D4 Alaska, USA
Yakutsk 115 F3 Respublika Sakha (Yakutiya), NE Russia
Yala 137 C7 Yala, SW Thailand
Yalizava 107 D6 Rus. Yelizovo. Mahilyowskaya Voblasts', E Belarus
Yalong Jiang 128 A5 river C China
Yalova 116 B3 Yalova, NW Turkey
Yalpug, Ozero see Yalpuh, Ozero
Yalpuh, Ozero 108 D4 Rus. Ozero Yalpug. lake SW Ukraine
Yalta 109 F5 Avtonomna Respublika Krym, S Ukraine

Yalu 125 E2 Chin. Yalu Jiang, Jap. Oryokko, Kor. Amnok-kang. river China/North Korea
Yalu Jiang see Yalu
Yamaguchi 131 B7 var. Yamaguti. Yamaguchi, Honshū, SW Japan
Yamal, Poluostrov 114 D2 peninsula N Russia
Yamaniyah, Al Jumhūriyah al see Yemen
Yambio 73 B5 var. Yambiyo. Western Equatoria, S South Sudan
Yambiyo see Yambio
Yambol 104 D2 Turk. Yanboli. Yambol, E Bulgaria
Yamdena, Pulau 139 G5 prev. Jamdena. island Kepulauan Tanimbar, E Indonesia
Yamoussoukro 74 D5 country capital (Ivory Coast) C Ivory Coast
Yamuna 134 D3 prev. Jumna. river N India
Yana 115 F2 river NE Russian Federation
Yanboli see Yambol
Yanbu' al Bahr 121 A5 Al Madīnah, W Saudi Arabia
Yangambi 77 D5 Orientale, N Dem. Rep. Congo
Yangchow see Yangzhou
Yangiyo'l 123 E2 Rus. Yangiyul'. Toshkent Viloyati, E Uzbekistan
Yangiyul' see Yangiyo'l
Yangku see Taiyuan
Yangon 136 B4 Eng. Rangoon. Yangon, S Myan mar (Burma)
Yangtze 128 B5 var. Yangtze Kiang, Eng. Yangtze. river C China
Yangtze see Chang Jiang
Yangtze Kiang see Chang Jiang
Yangzhou 128 D5 var. Yangchow. Jiangsu, E China
Yankton 45 E3 South Dakota, N USA
Yany Kapu 109 F4 Rus. Krasnoperekops'k. Respublika Krym, S Ukraine
Yannina see Ioánnina
Yanskiy Zaliv 113 F2 bay N Russia
Yantai 128 D4 var. Yan-t'ai; prev. Chefoo, Chih-fu. Shandong, E China
Yaoundé 77 B5 var. Yaunde. country capital (Cameroon) Centre, S Cameroon
Yap 144 A1 island Caroline Islands, W Micronesia
Yapanskoye More East Sea/ Japan, Sea of
Yapen, Pulau 139 G4 prev. Japen. island E Indonesia
Yap Trench 142 B2 var. Yap Trough. undersea feature SE Philippine Sea
Yap Trough see Yap Trench
Yapurá see Caquetá, Río, Brazil/ Colombia
Yapurá see Japurá, Rio, Brazil/ Colombia
Yaqui, Río 50 C2 river NW Mexico
Yaransk 111 C5 Kirovskaya Oblast', NW Russia
Yarega 110 D4 Respublika Komi, NW Russia
Yaren District 144 D2 de facto country capital (Nauru) Nauru, SW Pacific
Yarkant see Shache
Yarlung Zangbo Jiang see Brahmaputra
Yarmouth 39 F5 Nova Scotia, SE Canada
Yarmouth see Great Yarmouth
Yaroslav see Jarosław
Yaroslavl' 110 B4 Yaroslavskaya Oblast', W Russia
Yarumal 58 B2 Antioquia, NW Colombia
Yasyel'da 107 B7 river Brestskaya Voblasts', SW Belarus Europe
Yatsushiro 131 A7 var. Yatusiro. Kumamoto, Kyūshū, SW Japan
Yatusiro see Yatsushiro
Yaunde see Yaoundé
Yavari, Rio see Javari, Rio
Rio Yavari 62 C2 var. Yavarí. river Brazil/Peru
Yaviza 53 H5 Darién, SE Panama
Yavoriv 108 B2 Pol. Jaworów, Rus. Yavorov. L'vivs'ka Oblast', NW Ukraine
Yavorov see Yavoriv

Yazd 120 D3 var. Yezd. Yazd, C Iran
Yazoo City 42 B2 Mississippi, S USA
Yding Skovhøj 85 A7 hill C Denmark
Ýdra 105 C6 var. Ídhra. island Ýdra, S Greece
Ye 137 B5 Mon State, S Myanmar (Burma)
Yecheng 126 A3 var. Kargilik. Xinjiang Uygur Zizhiqu, NW China
Yefremov 111 B5 Tul'skaya Oblast', W Russia
Yekaterinburg 114 C3 prev. Sverdlovsk. Sverdlovskaya Oblast', C Russia
Yekaterinodar see Krasnodar
Yekaterinoslav see Dnipro
Yelets 111 B5 Lipetskaya Oblast', W Russia
Yelisavetpol see Gäncä
Yelizavetgrad see Kropyvnyts'kyy
Yelizovo see Yalizava
Yell 88 D1 island NE Scotland, United Kingdom
Yellowhammer State see Alabama
Yellowknife 37 E4 territory capital Northwest Territories, W Canada
Yellow River 128 C4 var. Yellow River. river C China
Yellow River see Huang He
Yellow Sea 128 D4 Chin. Huang Hai, Kor. Hwang-Hae. sea E Asia
Yellowstone River 44 C2 river Montana/ Wyoming, NW USA
Yel'sk 107 C7 Homyel'skaya Voblasts', SE Belarus
Yelwa 75 F4 Kebbi, W Nigeria
Yemen 121 C7 off. Republic of Yemen, Ar. Al Jumhuriyah al Yamaniyah, Al Yaman. country SW Asia
Yemen, Republic of see Yemen
Yemva 110 D4 prev. Zheleznodorozhnyy. Respublika Komi, NW Russia
Yenakiyeve 109 G3 Rus. Yenakiyevo; prev. Ordzhonikidze, Rykovo. Donets'ka Oblast', E Ukraine
Yenakiyevo see Yenakiyeve
Yenangyaung 136 A3 Magway, W Myanmar (Burma)
Yendi 75 E4 NE Ghana
Yengisar 126 A3 Xinjiang Uygur Zizhiqu, NW China
Yenierenköy 102 C5 var. Yialousa, Gk. Agialoúsa. NE Cyprus
Yenipazar see Novi Pazar
Yenisey 114 D3 river Mongolia/Russia
Yenping see Nanping
Yeovil 89 D7 SW England, United Kingdom
Yeppoon 148 D4 Queensland, E Australia
Yerevan 117 F3 Eng. Erivan. country capital (Armenia) C Armenia
Yeriho see Jericho
Yertis 114 C4 var. Irtish, Kaz. Ertis; prev. Irtysh. river C Asia
Yerushalayim see Jerusalem
Yeso see Hokkaidō
Yeu, Île d' 90 A4 island NW France
Yevlakh see Yevlax
Yevlax 117 G2 Rus. Yevlakh. C Azerbaijan
Yevpatoriya 109 F5 Avtonomna Respublika Krym, S Ukraine
Yeya 109 H4 river SW Russia
Yezerishche see Yezyaryshcha
Yezo see Hokkaidō
Yezyaryshcha 107 E5 Rus. Yezerishche. Vitsyebskaya Voblasts', NE Belarus
Yialousa see Yenierenköy
Yiannitsá see Giannitsá
Yichang 128 C5 Hubei, C China
Yıldızeli 116 D3 Sivas, N Turkey
Yinchuan 128 B4 var. Yinch'uan, Yin-ch'uan, Yinchwan. province capital Ningxia, N China
Yinchwan see Yinchuan
Yindu He see Indus
Yin-hsien see Ningbo
Yining 126 B2 var. I-ning, Uigh. Gulja, Kuldja. Xinjiang Uygur Zizhiqu, NW China
Yin-tu Ho see Indus
Yisrael/Yisra'el see Israel
Ýithion see Gýtheio

Yogyakarta 138 C5 prev. Djokjakarta, Jogjakarta, Jokyakarta. Jawa, C Indonesia
Yokohama 131 D5 Aomori, Honshū, C Japan
Yokohama 130 A2 Kanagawa, Honshū, S Japan
Yokote 130 D4 Akita, Honshū, C Japan
Yola 75 H4 Adamawa, E Nigeria
Yonago 131 B6 Tottori, Honshū, SW Japan
Yong'an 128 D6 var. Yongan. Fujian, SE China
Yongzhou see Lingling
Yonkers 41 F3 New York, NE USA
Yonne 90 C4 river C France
Yopal 58 C2 var. El Yopal. Casanare, C Colombia
York 89 D5 anc. Eboracum, Eburacum. N England, United Kingdom
York 45 E4 Nebraska, C USA
York, Cape 148 C1 headland Queensland, NE Australia
York, Kap see Innaanganeq
Yorkton 37 F5 Saskatchewan, S Canada
Yoro 52 C2 Yoro, C Honduras
Yoshkar-Ola 111 C5 Respublika Mariy El, W Russia
Yösönbulag see Altay
Youngstown 40 D4 Ohio, N USA
Youth, Isle of 54 A2 var. Isla de Pinos, Eng. Isle of Youth; prev. The Isle of the Pines. island W Cuba
Youth, Isle of see Juventud, Isla de la
Ypres see Ieper
Yreka 46 B4 California, W USA
Yrendagüé see General Eugenio A. Garay
Yssel see IJssel
Ysyk-Köl see Issyk-Kul', Ozero
Ysyk-Köl see Balykchy
Yu see Henan
Yuan see Red River
Yuan Jiang see Red River
Yuba City 47 B5 California, W USA
Yucatán, Canal de see Yucatan Channel
Yucatan Channel 51 H3 Sp. Canal de Yucatán. channel Cuba/Mexico
Yucatan Peninsula 35 C7 Eng. Yucatan Peninsula. peninsula Guatemala/ Mexico
Yucatan Peninsula see Yucatán, Península de
Yuci see Jinzhong
Yue see Guangdong
Yue Shan, Tai see Lantau Island
Yueyang 128 C5 Hunan, S China
Yugoslavia see Serbia
Yukhavichy 107 D5 Rus. Yukhovichi. Vitsyebskaya Voblasts', N Belarus
Yukhovichi see Yukhavichy
Yukon 36 D3 prev. Yukon Territory, Fr. Territoire du Yukon. territory NW Canada
Yukon River 36 C2 river Canada/USA
Yukon, Territoire du see Yukon
Yukon Territory see Yukon
Yulin 128 C6 Guangxi Zhuangzu Zizhiqu, S China
Yuma 48 A2 Arizona, SW USA
Yumendong 128 A3 prev. Laojunmiao. Gansu, N China
Yun see Yunnan
Yungki see Jilin
Yung-ning see Nanning
Yunjinghong see Jinghong
Yunki see Jilin
Yunnan 128 A6 var. Yun, Yunnan Sheng, Yünnan, Yun-nan. province SW China
Yunnan see Kunming
Yunnan Sheng see Yunnan
Yünnan/Yun-nan see Yunnan
Yurev see Tartu
Yurihonjō see Honjō
Yuruá, Río see Juruá, Rio
Yury'ev see Tartu
Yushu 126 D4 var. Gyêgu. Qinghai, C China
Yuty 64 D3 Caazapá, S Paraguay
Yuzhno-Sakhalinsk 115 H4 Jap. Toyohara; prev. Vladimirovka. Ostrov Sakhalin, Sakhalinskaya Oblast', SE Russia

Yuzhnyy Bug see Pivdennyy Buh
Yuzhou see Chongqing
Ýylanly see Gurbansoltan Eje

Z

Zaandam see Zaanstad
Zaanstad 86 C3 prev. Zaandam. Noord-Holland, C Netherlands
Zabaykal'sk 115 F5 Zabaykal'skiy Kray, S Russia
Zabern see Saverne
Zabid 121 B7 W Yemen
Żabinka see Zhabinka
Ząbkowice see Ząbkowice Śląskie
Ząbkowice Śląskie 98 B4 var. Ząbkowice, Ger. Frankenstein, Frankenstein in Schlesien. Dolnośląskie, SW Poland
Zábřeh 99 C5 Ger. Hohenstadt. Olomoucký Kraj, E Czech Republic (Czechia)
Zacapa 52 B2 Zacapa, E Guatemala
Zacatecas 50 D3 Zacatecas, C Mexico
Zacatepec 51 E4 Morelos, S Mexico
Zacháro 105 B6 var. Zaharo, Zakháro. Dytikí Elláda, S Greece
Zadar 100 A3 It. Zara; anc. Iader. Zadar, SW Croatia
Zadetkyi Kyun 137 B6 var. St.Matthew's Island. island Myeik Archipelago, S Myanmar (Burma)
Zafra 92 C4 Extremadura, W Spain
Żagań 98 B4 var. Zagań, Żegań, Ger. Sagan. Lubuskie, W Poland
Zagazig see Az Zaqāziq
Zágráb see Zagreb
Zagreb 100 B2 Ger. Agram, Hung. Zágráb. country capital (Croatia) Zagreb, N Croatia
Zagros Mountains 120 C3 Eng. Zagros Mountains. mountain range W Iran
Zagros Mountains see Zagros, Kūhhā-ye
Zaharo see Zacháro
Zāhedān 120 E4 var. Zahidan; prev. Duzdab. Sīstān va Balūchestān, SE Iran
Zahidan see Zāhedān
Zahlah see Zahlé
Zahlé 118 B4 var. Zahlah. C Lebanon
Záhony 99 E6 Szabolcs-Szatmár-Bereg, NE Hungary
Zaire see Congo (river)
Zaire see Congo (Democratic Republic of)
Zaječar 100 E4 Serbia, E Serbia
Zakataly see Zaqatala
Zakháro see Zacháro
Zakhidnyy Buh/Zakhodni Buh see Bug
Zákhō see Zaxo
Zákhū see Zaxo
Zakopane 99 D5 Małopolskie, S Poland
Zákynthos 105 A6 var. Zákinthos, It. Zante. island Iónia Nísoi, Greece, C Mediterranean Sea
Zalaegerszeg 99 B7 Zala, W Hungary
Zalău 108 B3 Ger. Waltenberg, Hung. Zilah; prev. Ger. Zillenmarkt. Sălaj, NW Romania
Zalim 121 B5 Makkah, W Saudi Arabia
Zambesi/Zambeze see Zambezi
Zambezi 78 C2 North Western, W Zambia
Zambezi 78 D2 var. Zambesi, Port. Zambeze. river S Africa
Zambia 78 C2 off. Republic of Zambia; prev. Northern Rhodesia. country S Africa
Zambia, Republic of see Zambia
Zamboanga 139 E3 off. Zamboanga City. Mindanao, S Philippines
Zamboanga City see Zamboanga
Zambrów 98 E3 Łomża, E Poland
Zamora 92 D2 Castilla y León, NW Spain
Zamora de Hidalgo 50 D4 Michoacán, SW Mexico
Zamość 98 E4 Rus. Zamoste. Lubelskie, E Poland
Zamoste see Zamość
Zancle see Messina
Zanda 126 A4 Xizang Zizhiqu, W China
Zanesville 40 D4 Ohio, N USA
Zanjān 120 C2 var. Zenjan, Zinjan. Zanjān, NW Iran
Zante see Zákynthos
Zanthus 147 C6 Western Australia, S Australia Oceania
Zanzibar 73 D7 Zanzibar, E Tanzania

Zanzibar *73 C7 Swa.* Unguja. *island* E Tanzania
Zaozhuang *128 D4* Shandong, E China
Zapadna Morava *100 D4 Ger.* Westliche Morava. *river* C Serbia
Zapadnaya Dvina *110 A4* Tverskaya Oblast', W Russia
Zapadnaya Dvina *see* Western Dvina
Zapadnyy Bug *see* Bug
Zapala *65 B5* Neuquén, W Argentina
Zapiola Ridge *67 B6 undersea feature* SW Atlantic Ocean
Zapolyarnyy *110 C2* Murmanskaya Oblast', NW Russia
Zaporizhzhya *109 F3 Rus.* Zaporozh'ye; *prev.* Aleksandrovsk. Zaporiz'ka Oblast', SE Ukraine
Zaporozh'ye *see* Zaporizhzhya
Zapotiltic *50 D4* Jalisco, SW Mexico
Zaqatala *117 G2 Rus.* Zakataly. NW Azerbaijan
Zara *116 D3* Sivas, C Turkey
Zara *see* Zadar
Zarafshan *see* Zarafshon
Zarafshon *122 D2 Rus.* Zarafshan. Navoiy Viloyati, N Uzbekistan
Zarafshon *see* Zeravshan
Zaragoza *93 F2 Eng.* Saragossa; *anc.* Caesaraugusta, Salduba. Aragón, NE Spain
Zarand *120 D3* Kermān, C Iran
Zaranj *122 D5* Nīmrōz, SW Afghanistan
Zarasai *106 C4* Utena, E Lithuania
Zárate *64 D4 prev.* General José F. Uriburu. Buenos Aires, E Argentina
Zarautz *93 E1 var.* Zarauz. País Vasco, N Spain
Zarauz *see* Zarautz
Zaraza *59 E2* Guárico, N Venezuela
Zarghūn Shahr *123 E4 var.* Katawaz. Paktīkā, SE Afghanistan
Zaria *75 G4* Kaduna, C Nigeria
Zarós *105 D8* Kríti, Greece, E Mediterranean Sea
Zarqa *see* Az Zarqā'
Żary *98 B4 Ger.* Sorau, Sorau in der Niederlausitz. Lubuskie, W Poland
Zaunguzskiye Garagumy *see* Üngüz Angyrsyndaky Garagum
Zavertse *see* Zawiercie
Zavet *104 D1* Razgrad, NE Bulgaria
Zavidovići *100 C3* Federacija Bosne I Hercegovine, N Bosnia and Herzegovina
Zawia *see* Az Zāwiyah
Zawiercie *98 D4 Rus.* Zavertse. Śląskie, S Poland
Zawīlah *71 F3 var.* Zuwaylah, *It.* Zueila. C Libya
Zaxo *120 B2 Ar.* Zākhū,*var.* Zākhō. Dahūk, N Iraq
Zaysan Köl *see* Zaysan, Ozero
Zaysan, Ozero *114 D5 Kaz.* Zaysan Köl. *lake* E Kazakhstan
Zayyq *see* Zhayyk
Zbarazh *108 C2* Ternopil's'ka Oblast', W Ukraine
Zduńska Wola *98 C4* Sieradz, C Poland
Zealand *85 B8 Eng.* Zealand, *Ger.* Seeland. *island* E Denmark
Zealand *see* Sjælland
Zeebrugge *87 A5* West-Vlaanderen, NW Belgium
Zeewolde *86 D3* Flevoland, C Netherlands
Zefat *see* Tsefat
Żegań *see* Żagań
Zeiden *see* Codlea
Zeist *86 C4* Utrecht, C Netherlands
Zele *87 B5* Oost-Vlaanderen, NW Belgium

Zelenoborskiy *110 B2* Murmanskaya Oblast', NW Russia
Zelenograd *111 B5* Moskovskaya Oblast', W Russia
Zelenogradsk *106 A4 Ger.* Cranz, Kranz. Kaliningradskaya Oblast', W Russia
Zelle *see* Celle
Zel'va *107 B6 Pol.* Zelwa. Hrodzyenskaya Voblasts', W Belarus
Zelwa *see* Zel'va
Zelzate *87 B5 var.* Selzaete. Oost-Vlaanderen, NW Belgium
Žemaičių Aukštumas *106 B4 physical region* W Lithuania
Zemst *87 C5* Vlaams Brabant, C Belgium
Zemun *100 D3* Serbia, N Serbia
Zengg *see* Senj
Zenica *100 C4* Federacija Bosne I Hercegovine, C Bosnia and Herzegovina
Zenta *see* Senta
Zeravshan *123 E3 Taj./Uzb.* Zarafshon. *river* Tajikistan/Uzbekistan
Zevenaar *86 D4* Gelderland, SE Netherlands
Zevenbergen *86 C4* Noord-Brabant, S Netherlands
Zeya *113 E3 river* SE Russia
Zgerzh *see* Zgierz
Zgierz *98 C4 Ger.* Neuhof, *Rus.* Zgerzh. Łódź, C Poland
Zgorzelec *98 B4 Ger.* Görlitz. Dolnośląskie, SW Poland
Zhabinka *107 A6 Pol.* Zabinka. Brestskaya Voblasts', SW Belarus
Zhambyl *see* Taraz
Zhanaozen *114 A4 Kaz.* Zhangaözen; *prev.* Novyy Uzen'. Mangistau, W Kazakhstan
Zhangaözen *see* Zhanaozen
Zhangaqazaly *see* Ayteke Bi
Zhang-chia-k'ou *see* Zhangjiakou
Zhangdian *see* Zibo
Zhangjiakou *128 C3 var.* Changkiakow, Zhang-chia-k'ou, *Eng.* Kalgan; *prev.* Wanchuan. Hebei, E China
Zhangzhou *128 D6* Fujian, SE China
Zhanjiang *128 C7 var.* Chanchiang, Chan-chiang, *Cant.* Tsamkong, *Fr.* Fort-Bayard. Guangdong, S China
Zhaoqing *128 C6* Guangdong, S China
Zhayyk *see* Ural
Zhdanov *see* Mariupol'
Zhe *see* Zhejiang
Zhejiang *128 D5 var.* Che-chiang, Chekiang, Zhe, Zhejiang Sheng. *province* SE China
Zhejiang Sheng *see* Zhejiang
Zheleznodorozhnyy *106 A4* Kaliningradskaya Oblast', W Russia
Zheleznodorozhnyy *see* Yemva
Zheleznogorsk *111 A5* Kurskaya Oblast', W Russia
Zhëltyye Vody *see* Zhovti Vody
Zhengzhou *128 C4 var.* Ch'eng-chou, Chengchow; *prev.* Chenghsien. *province capital* Henan, C China
Zhezkazgan *see* Zhezkazgan
Zhidachov *see* Zhydachiv
Zhishan *see* Lingling
Zhitkovichi *see* Zhytkavichy
Zhitomir *see* Zhytomyr
Zhlobin *107 D7* Homyel'skaya Voblasts', SE Belarus
Zhmerinka *see* Zhmerynka

Zhmerynka *108 D2 Rus.* Zhmerinka. Vinnyts'ka Oblast', C Ukraine
Zhodino *see* Zhodzina
Zhodzina *107 D6 Rus.* Zhodino. Minskaya Voblasts', C Belarus
Zholkev/Zholkva *see* Zhovkva
Zhonghua Renmin Gongheguo *see* China
Zhosaly *114 B4 prev.* Dzhusaly. Kzylorda, SW Kazakhstan
Zhovkva *108 B2 Pol.* Żółkiew, *Rus.* Zholkev, Zholkva; *prev.* Nesterov. L'vivs'ka Oblast', NW Ukraine
Zhovti Vody *109 F3 Rus.* Zhëltyye Vody. Dnipropetrovs'ka Oblast', E Ukraine
Zhovtnevoe *109 E4 Rus.* Zhovtnevoye. Mykolayivs'ka Oblast', S Ukraine
Zhovtnevoye *see* Zhovtneve
Zhi Qu *see* Tongtian He
Zhydachiv *108 B2 Pol.* Żydaczów, *Rus.* Zhidachov. L'vivs'ka Oblast', NW Ukraine
Zhytkavichy *107 C7 Rus.* Zhitkovichi. Homyel'skaya Voblasts', SE Belarus
Zhytomyr *108 D2 Rus.* Zhitomir. Zhytomyrs'ka Oblast', NW Ukraine
Zibo *128 D4 var.* Zhangdian. Shandong, E China
Zichenau *see* Ciechanów
Zielona Góra *98 B4 Ger.* Grünberg, Grünberg in Schlesien, Grüneberg. Lubuskie, W Poland
Zierikzee *86 B4* Zeeland, SW Netherlands
Zigong *128 B5 var.* Tzekung. Sichuan, C China
Ziguinchor *74 B3* SW Senegal
Zilah *see* Zalău
Žilina *99 C5 Ger.* Sillein, *Hung.* Zsolna. Žilinský Kraj, N Slovakia
Zillenmarkt *see* Zalău
Zimbabwe *78 D3 off.* Republic of Zimbabwe; *prev.* Rhodesia. *country* S Africa
Zimbabwe, Republic of *see* Zimbabwe
Zimnicea *108 C5* Teleorman, S Romania
Zimovniki *111 B7* Rostovskaya Oblast', SW Russia
Zinder *75 G3* Zinder, S Niger
Zinov'yevsk *see* Kropyvnyts'kyy
Zintenhof *see* Sindi
Zipaquirá *58 B3* Cundinamarca, C Colombia
Zittau *94 D4* Sachsen, E Germany
Zlatni Pyasŭtsi *104 E2* Dobrich, NE Bulgaria
Zlín *99 C5 prev.* Gottwaldov. Zlínský Kraj, E Czech Republic (Czechia)
Złoczów *see* Zolochiv
Złotów *98 C3* Wielkopolskie, C Poland
Zlynka *see* Zolochiv
Zmiyev *see* Zmiyiv
Zmiyiv *109 G2 Rus.* Zmiyev. Kharkivs'ka Oblast', E Ukraine
Znam"yanka *see* Znam"yanka
Żnin *98 C3* Kujawsko-pomorskie, C Poland
Zoetermeer *86 C4* Zuid-Holland, W Netherlands
Zólkiew *see* Zhovkva
Zolochev *see* Zolochiv
Zolochiv *109 G2 Rus.* Zolochev. Kharkivs'ka Oblast', E Ukraine
Zolochiv *108 C2 Pol.* Złoczów, *var.* Zolochev. L'vivs'ka Oblast', W Ukraine
Zolote *109 H3 Rus.* Zolotoye. Luhans'ka Oblast', E Ukraine
Zolotonosha *109 E2* Cherkas'ka Oblast', C Ukraine
Zolotoye *see* Zolote
Zólyom *see* Zvolen
Zomba *79 E2* Southern, S Malawi

Zombor *see* Sombor
Zongo *77 C5* Equateur, N Dem. Rep. Congo
Zonguldak *116 C2* Zonguldak, NW Turkey
Zonhoven *87 D6* Limburg, NE Belgium
Zoppot *see* Sopot
Żory *99 C5 var.* Zory, *Ger.* Sohrau. Śląskie, S Poland
Zouar *76 C2* Borkou-Ennedi-Tibesti, N Chad
Zouérat *74 C2 var.* Zouérate, Zouïrât. Tiris Zemmour, N Mauritania
Zouérate *see* Zouérat
Zouïrât *see* Zouérat
Zrenjanin *100 D3 prev.* Petrovgrad, Veliki Bečkerek, *Ger.* Grossbetschkerek, *Hung.* Nagybecskerek. Vojvodina, N Serbia
Zsil/Zsily *see* Jiu
Zsolna *see* Žilina
Zsombolya *see* Jimbolia
Zsupanya *see* Županja
Zubov Seamount *67 D5 undersea feature* E Atlantic Ocean
Zueila *see* Zawīlah
Zug *95 B7 Fr.* Zoug. Zug, C Switzerland
Zugspitze *95 C7 mountain* S Germany
Zuid-Beveland *85 B5 var.* South Beveland. *island* SW Netherlands
Zuider Zee *see* IJsselmeer
Zuidhorn *86 E1* Groningen, NE Netherlands
Zuidlaren *86 E2* Drenthe, NE Netherlands
Zula *72 C4* E Eritrea
Zumbo *see* Vila do Zumbo
Zundert *87 C5* Noord-Brabant, S Netherlands
Zunyi *128 B5* Guizhou, S China
Županja *100 C3 Hung.* Zsupanya. Vukovar-Srijem, E Croatia
Zürich *95 B7 Eng./Fr.* Zurich, *It.* Zurigo. Zürich, N Switzerland
Zurich, Lake *95 B7 Eng.* Lake Zurich. *lake* NE Switzerland
Zurich, Lake *see* Zürichsee
Zurigo *see* Zürich
Zutphen *86 D3* Gelderland, E Netherlands
Zuwārah *71 F2* NW Libya
Zuwaylah *see* Zawīlah
Zuyevka *111 D5* Kirovskaya Oblast', NW Russia
Zvenigorodka *see* Zvenyhorodka
Zvenyhorodka *109 E2 Rus.* Zvenigorodka. Cherkas'ka Oblast', C Ukraine
Zvishavane *78 D3 prev.* Shabani. Matabeleland South, S Zimbabwe
Zvolen *99 C6 Ger.* Altsohl, *Hung.* Zólyom. Banskobystrický Kraj, C Slovakia
Zvornik *100 C4* E Bosnia and Herzegovina
Zwedru *74 D5 var.* Tchien. E Liberia
Zwettl *95 E6* Wien, NE Austria
Zwevegem *87 A6* West-Vlaanderen, W Belgium
Zwickau *95 C5* Sachsen, E Germany
Zwolle *86 D3* Overijssel, E Netherlands
Żydaczów *see* Zhydachiv
Zyôetu *see* Jōetsu
Żyrardów *98 D3* Mazowieckie, C Poland
Zyryanovsk *114 D5* Vostochnyy Kazakhstan, E Kazakhstan

Key to map pages

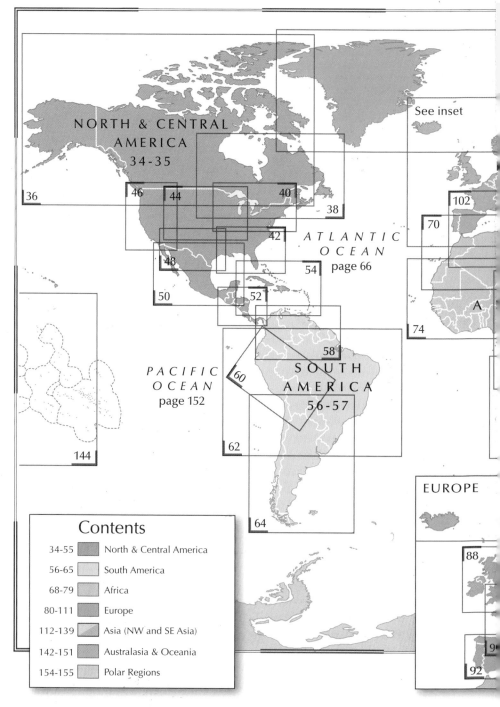

NORTH & CENTRAL AMERICA 34-35

36 · 46 · 44 · 40 · 38 · 42 · 48 · 54 · 50 · 52 · 58 · 60 · 62 · 64

ATLANTIC OCEAN page 66

PACIFIC OCEAN page 152

SOUTH AMERICA 56-57

See inset

102 · 70 · 74 · A

EUROPE

88 · 9 · 92

144